1 Euro = 100 Cent	SOS ☎ ⚠	🛣	🚗	road	🏘	TOLL	‰
...eich	(A)	1 Euro (EUR) = 100 Cent	133 / 144	130	100	100	50	🛣🚗	0,5 ‰
...éria	(AL)	1 Lek (ALL) = 100 Quindarka	129 / 126	120	100	80	40		0,0 ‰
.../Belgique	(B)	1 Euro (EUR) = 100 Cent	101 / 100	120	120	90	50		0,5 ‰
...ija	(BG)	1 Lew (BGN) = 100 Stótinki	166 / 150	130	90	90	50	🛣🚗	0,5 ‰
...i Hercegovina	(BIH)	Konvert. Marka (BAM) = 100 Fening	92 / 94	120	100	80	60		0,3 ‰
...iz/Suisse/Svizzera	(CH)	1 Franken (CHF) = 100 Rappen	117 / 144	120	100	80	50	🛣	0,5 ‰
...s/Kibris	(CY)	1 Euro (EUR) = 100 Cent	199	100	80	80	50		0,5 ‰
...Republika	(CZ)	1 Koruna (CZK) = 100 Haliru	112 / 155	130	130	90	50	🛣🚗	0,0 ‰
...chland	(D)	1 Euro (EUR) = 100 Cent	110 / 112	⊘	⊘	100	50		0,5 ‰
...ark	(DK)	1 Krone (DKK) = 100 Øre	112	130	80	80	50		0,5 ‰
...a	(E)	1 Euro (EUR) = 100 Cent	112	120	100	90	50	🛣	0,5 ‰
	(EST)	1 Euro (EUR) = 100 Cent	110 / 112	110	110	90	50		0,0 ‰
	(F)	1 Euro (EUR) = 100 Cent	112	130	110	90	50	🛣	0,5 ‰
.../Finland	(FIN)	1 Euro (EUR) = 100 Cent	112	120	100	100	50		0,5 ‰
...Kingdom	(GB)	1 Pound Sterling (GBP) = 100 Pence	999 / 112	70 mph (112)	70 mph (112)	60 mph (96)	30 mph (48)		0,8 ‰
...(Hellás)	(GR)	1 Euro (EUR) = 100 Cent	100 / 166	120	110	90	50	🛣🚗	0,5 ‰
...rország	(H)	1 Forint (HUF) = 100 Filler	112	130	110	90	50	🛣	0,0 ‰
...ska	(HR)	1 Kuna (HRK) = 100 Lipa	112 / 94	130	110	90	50	🛣	0,5 ‰
	(I)	1 Euro (EUR) = 100 Cent	112 / 118	130	110	90	50	🛣	0,5 ‰
...eland	(IRL)	1 Euro (EUR) = 100 Cent	999 / 112	120	100	60/100	50		0,5 ‰
	(IS)	1 Krona (ISK) = 100 Aurar	112			80/90	50		0,5 ‰
...bourg	(L)	1 Euro (EUR) = 100 Cent	113 / 112	130	90	80	50		0,5 ‰
	(LT)	1 Euro (EUR) = 100 Cent	02 / 03 / 112	110	90	90	50		0,4 ‰
	(LV)	1 Euro (EUR) = 100 Cent	02 / 03 / 112	110	90	90	50		0,5 ‰
...onija	(MK)	1 Denar (MKD) = 100 Deni	192 / 194	120	100	90	40/60	🛣🚗	0,5 ‰
	(N)	1 Krone (NOK) = 100 Øre	112 / 113	90	90	80	50	🛣🚗	0,2 ‰
...land	(NL)	1 Euro (EUR) = 100 Cent	112	120	100	80	50		0,5 ‰
...al	(P)	1 Euro (EUR) = 100 Cent	112	120	100	80	50		0,5 ‰
	(PL)	1 Zloty (PLN) = 100 Groszy	112 / 999	130/140	100/120	90	50	🛣	0,2 ‰
...o	(RKS)	1 Euro (EUR) = 100 Cent	112 / 92	130	110	80	50		0,5 ‰
...nia	(RO)	1 Leu (RON) = 100 Bani	112	130	100	90	50	🛣🚗	0,0 ‰
...a	(RUS)	1 Rubel (RUB) = 100 Kopeek	02 / 03	110	90	90	60		0,0 ‰
...e	(S)	1 Krona (SEK) = 100 Öre	112	110	110/90	70/90	50		0,2 ‰
...ská Republika	(SK)	1 Euro (EUR) = 100 Cent	112 / 155	130	90	90	60	🛣🚗	0,0 ‰
...nija	(SLO)	1 Euro (EUR) = 100 Cent	113 / 112	130	100	90	50	🛣	0,5 ‰
.../Crna Gora	(SRB) (MNE)	1 Dinar (CSM) = 100 Para ; Euro	92 / 94	120	100	80	60	🛣🚗	0,5 ‰
...e	(TR)	1 Lira (TRY) = 100 Kurus	155 / 112	120	90	90	50	🛣	0,5 ‰
...na	(UA)	1 Griwna (UAH) = 100 Kopijken	02 / 03	130	110	90	60		0,0 ‰

Europe
Europa

South Hun
146 P
Huntingt

© Kunth Verlag GmbH & Co. KG 2017
Königinstraße 11, D-80539 München,
phone +49-89-458020-0, fax +49-89-458020-21
e-mail: info@kunth-verlag.de
www.kunth-verlag.de

Printed in Slovakia

© AA Media Limited 2017
Fanum House, Basing View,
Basingstoke, Hampshire RG21 4EA, UK
ISBN: 978-0-7495-7870-1
        978-0-7495-7871-8
A05511

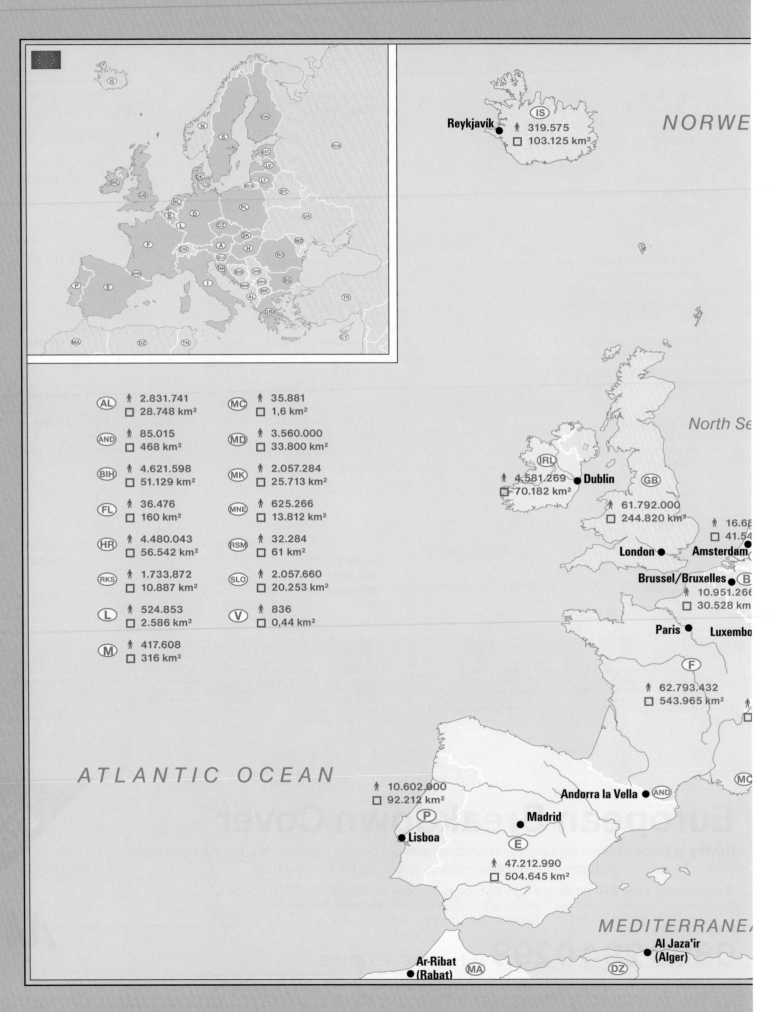

NORWE...

Reykjavik ♦ 319.575
          □ 103.125 km²

North Se...

(AL) ♦ 2.831.741   (MC) ♦ 35.881
     □ 28.748 km²   □ 1,6 km²

(AND) ♦ 85.015   (MD) ♦ 3.560.000
      □ 468 km²   □ 33.800 km²

(BIH) ♦ 4.621.598   (MK) ♦ 2.057.284
      □ 51.129 km²   □ 25.713 km²

(FL) ♦ 36.476   (MNE) ♦ 625.266
     □ 160 km²   □ 13.812 km²

(HR) ♦ 4.480.043   (RSM) ♦ 32.284
     □ 56.542 km²   □ 61 km²

(RKS) ♦ 1.733.872   (SLO) ♦ 2.057.660
      □ 10.887 km²   □ 20.253 km²

(L) ♦ 524.853   (V) ♦ 836
    □ 2.586 km²   □ 0,44 km²

(M) ♦ 417.608
    □ 316 km²

(IRL) ♦ 4.581.269 ● Dublin   (GB)
      □ 70.182 km²

♦ 61.792.000
□ 244.820 km²

♦ 16.68...
□ 41.54...

London ●   Amsterdam ●

Brussel/Bruxelles ● (B)
♦ 10.951.266
□ 30.528 km...

Paris ●   Luxembo...

(F)

♦ 62.793.432
□ 543.965 km²

♦ ...
□ ...

ATLANTIC OCEAN

♦ 10.602.000
□ 92.212 km²

Andorra la Vella ● (AND)

(P)   ● Madrid

● Lisboa   (E)

♦ 47.212.990
□ 504.645 km²

MEDITERRANE...

● Al Jaza'ir
  (Alger)

Ar-Ribat (MA)
● (Rabat)   (DZ)

IV

GIAN SEA

NORWEGIAN SEA

Baltic Sea

Black Sea

AN SEA

S

N

FIN

⚭ 5.404.956
▢ 338.432 km²

Helsinki

⚭ 4.985.900
▢ 385.199 km²

⚭ 9.514.406
▢ 450.295 km²

Oslo

Stockholm

Tallinn **EST**
⚭ 1.340.021
▢ 45.227 km²

⚭ 2.074.605
▢ 64.589 km²

Riga **LV**

⚭ 143.200.000
▢ 17.075.400 km²

Moskva

RUS

DK
⚭ 5.475.791
▢ 43.094 km²

København

⚭ 2.988.381
▢ 65.301 km²

LT

RUS Vilnius

Minsk **BY**

⚭ 9.457.000
▢ 207.595 km²

Berlin

PL Warszawa

⚭ 38.501.000
▢ 312.685 km²

Kyjiv

NL

⚭ 81.903.000
▢ 357.121 km²

L

D

CZ Praha
⚭ 10.526.685
▢ 78.866 km²

UA

⚭ 45.665.281
▢ 603.700 km²

0.000
8 km²

urg

⚭ 5.404.322
SK ▢ 49.034 km²

A Wien Bratislava

⚭ 8.460.390
▢ 83.878 km²

H Budapest
⚭ 10.005.000
▢ 93.036 km²

MD

Chişinău

RO

⚭ 19.042.936
▢ 238.391 km²

CH Bern **FL**
7.952.600 Vaduz
41.285 km²

Ljubljana **SLO**

Zagreb

Beograd

Bucureşti

⚭ 7.120.666
▢ 77.474 km²

HR

BIH

SRB

⚭ 7.364.570
▢ 110.994 km²

RSM

Monaco

San Marino

I

Sarajevo

Priština

Sofija **BG**

MNE

RKS

V Roma

Podgorica

Skopje

⚭ 60.626.442
▢ 301.338 km²

MK

Ankara

TR

Tiranë

AL

GR

⚭ 9.903.268
▢ 131.957 km²

⚭ 74.724.269
▢ 814.578 km²

AN SEA

Athína

Tunis

TN

⚭ 1.193.976
▢ 9.251 km² **CY**

	Ⓐ	Österreich
	ⒶL	Shqipëria
	AND	Andorra
	Ⓑ	België/Belgique
	BG	Bâlgarija
	BIH	Bosna i Hercegovina
	BY	Belarus'
	MNE	Crna Gora
	CH	Schweiz/Suisse/Svizzera
	CY	Kýpros
	CZ	Česká Republika
	Ⓓ	Deutschland
	DK	Danmark
	Ⓔ	España
	EST	Eesti
	Ⓕ	France
	FIN	Finland
	FL	Liechtenstein
	GB	United Kingdom
	GR	Elláda
	Ⓗ	Magyarország
	HR	Hrvatska
	Ⓘ	Italia
	IRL	Éire/Ireland
	IS	Ísland
	RKS	Kosovo
	Ⓛ	Luxembourg
	LT	Lietuva
	LV	Latvija
	Ⓜ	Malta
	MC	Monaco
	MD	Moldova
	MK	Makedonija
	Ⓝ	Norge
	NL	Nederland
	Ⓟ	Portugal
	PL	Polska
	RO	România
	RSM	San Marino
	RUS	Rossija
	Ⓢ	Sverige
	SK	Slovenská Republika
	SLO	Slovenija
	SRB	Srbija
	TR	Türkiye
	UA	Ukrajina
	Ⓥ	Città del Vaticano

(GB) (D) (F) (DK)

Legend **Zeichenerklärung** **Légende** **Tegnforklaring**

GB	D		F	DK
Motorway (under construction)	Autobahn (im Bau)		Autoroute (en construction)	Motorvej (under bygning)
Toll motorway	Gebührenpflichtige Autobahn		Autoroute à péage	Motorvej med betalingspligt
Tunnel motorway	Autobahn mit Tunnel		Autoroute avec tunnel	Motorvej met tunnel
Dual carriageway (under construction)	4-oder mehrspurige Autobahn (im Bau)		Double chaussée (en construction)	Vej med to vejbaner (under bygning)
Tunnel dual carriageway	Tunnel mehrspurige Straße		Tunnel double chaussée	Vej med to vejbaner met tunnel
Primary route (under construction)	Fernstraße (im Bau)		Route principale (en construction)	Fjerntrafikvej (under bygning)
Tunnel primary route	Fernstraßentunnel		Route principale avec tunnel	Fjerntrafikvej met tunnel
Important Main road (under construction)	Wichtige Hauptstraße (im Bau)		Route principale importante (en construction)	Vigtig hovedvej (under bygning)
Main road	Hauptstraße		Route départementale	Hovedvej
Secondary road	Nebenstraße		Route secondaire	Bivej
Touristic / historic route	Touristenstraße		Route touristique	Toeristische route
Railway	Eisenbahn		Chemin de fer	Jernbane
Distances in kilometres (within UK in miles)	Entfernung in Kilometern (in UK in Meilen)	25	Distances kilométriques (au sein du RU en miles)	Afstand i kilometer (UK i miles)
Steep gradient / Mountain pass height in metres	Steigung / Passhöhe in Metern	Col de la Schlucht 9 % (1361)	Indication de la pente / Col et sa cote d'altitude	Hældning / Pass højde i meter
Motorway number	Autobahnnummer	4 2 A22	Numéro autoroute	Nummer for motorvej
Number of main European road	Europastraßennummer	E54	Numéro des routes européennes	Nummer for europavejsrute
Other road numbers	Andere Straßennummern	34 28 N22 322	Autre numéro de routes	Andre vejnummer
Motorway junction number	Autobahnanschlussnummer	22	Numéros d'échangeurs	Tilslutning med nummer
Junction	Anschlussstelle		Échangeur	Tilslutning
Not suitable / closed for caravans	Für Wohnwagen nicht geeignet / gesperrt		Non recommandé aux caravans - interdite	Anbefales ikke for campingvogne-forbudt
Filling station	Autobahntankstelle		Station-service	Tankanlæg
Restaurant	Autobahnrasthaus		Restaurant	Rasteplads
Restaurant with motel	Autobahnrasthaus mit Motel		Hôtel	Rasteplads med overnatning
Major airport	Wichtiger Flughafen		Aéroport important	Vigtig Lufthavn
Airport	Flughafen		Aéroport	Lufthavn
Airfield	Flugplatz		Aérodrome	Flyveplads
Ferry	Autofähre		Ferry	Bilfærge
Border crossing	Grenzübergang		Passage frontalier - douane	Grænseovergang
Windmill	Windmühle		Moulin	Vejrmølle
Lighthouse	Leuchtturm		Phare	Fyrtårn
International boundary	Staatsgrenze		Frontière de l'État	Statsgrænsen
Administrative boundary	Provinzgrenze		Limite administrative	Provinsielle grænse
Restricted area	Sperrgebiet		Zone interdite	Afspærret område
National or nature park	National- und Naturpark		Parc national, parc naturel	Nationalpark, naturpark
Mountain summit with height in metres	Berggipfel mit Höhenangabe in Meter	Grand 1424 Ballon ▲	Sommet avec cote d'altitude	Bjergtoppe med højden i meter
Place of interest	Sehenswerter Ort	COLMAR	Ville très intéressante	Seværdighed

VI

GB · **D** · **F** · **DK** · **GB** · **D** · **F** · **DK**

Significant points of interest · Herausragende Sehenswürdigkeiten · Curiosités remarquables · Betydningsfulde seværdigheder

GB	D	F	DK
Major tourist route	Autoroute	Autoroute	Bilvej
Major tourist railway	Bahnstrecke	Ligne ferroviaire	Jernbane
Highspeed train	Hochgeschwindigkeitszug	Train à Grande Vitesse	Højhastighedstog
Shipping route	Schiffsroute	Itinéraire en bateau	Skibsruter
UNESCO World Natural Heritage	UNESCO-Weltnaturerbe	Patrimoine naturel de l'humanité de l'UNESCO	UNESCO Verdensarvsted (natur)
Mountain landscape	Gebirgslandschaft	Paysage de montagne	Bjerglandskab
Rock landscape	Felslandschaft	Paysage rocheux	Klippelandskab
Ravine/canyon	Schlucht/Canyon	Gorge/canyon	Kløfter/canyons
Glacier	Gletscher	Glacier	Gletsjer
Active volcano	Vulkan, aktiv	Volcan actif	Aktive vulkaner
Extinct volcano	Vulkan, erloschen	Volcan éteint	Udslukte vulkaner
Geyser	Geysir	Geyser	Gejser
Cave	Höhle	Grotte	Hule/grotte
River landscape	Flusslandschaft	Paysage fluvial	Flodlandskab
Waterfall/rapids	Wasserfall/Stromschnelle	Chute d'eau/rapide	Vandfald/strømhvirvler
Lake country	Seenlandschaft	Paysage de lacs	Søområder
Desert	Wüstenlandschaft	Désert	Ørken
Oasis	Oase	Oasis	Oase
Depression	Depression	Bassin	Sænkning
Fossil site	Fossilienfundstätte	Site fossile	Forekomster af fossiler
Nature park	Naturpark	Parc naturel	Naturpark
National park (landscape)	Nationalpark (Landschaft)	Parc national (paysage)	Nationalpark (landskab)
National park (flora)	Nationalpark (Flora)	Parc national (flore)	Nationalpark (flora)
National park (fauna)	Nationalpark (Fauna)	Parc national (faune)	Nationalpark (fauna)
National park (culture)	Nationalpark (Kultur)	Parc national (site culturel)	Nationalpark (kultur)
Botanic gardens	Botanischer Garten	Jardin botanique	Botanisk have
Biosphere reserve	Biosphärenreservat	Réserve de biosphère	Biosfæreområde
Wildlife reserve	Wildreservat	Réserve animale	Dyrereservat
Zoo/safari park	Zoo/Safaripark	Zoo/parc de safari	Zoologisk have/dyrepark
Coastal landscape	Küstenlandschaft	Paysage côtier	Kystlandskab
Beach	Strand	Plage	Strand
Island	Insel	Île	Ø
Underwater reserve	Unterwasserreservat	Réserve sous-marine	Undervandsreservat
Spring	Quelle	Source	Kilde
UNESCO World Cultural Heritage	UNESCO-Weltkulturerbe	Patrimoine culturel de l'humanité de l'UNESCO	UNESCO-Verdensarvsted (kultur)
Remarkable city	Außergewöhnliche Metropole	Métropole d'exception	Bemærkelsesværdig storby
Pre-and early history	Vor- und Frühgeschichte	Préhistoire et protohistoire	Forhistorisk sted
Prehistoric rockscape	Prähistorische Felsbilder/Naturvölker	Peintures rupestres préhistoriques	Forhistoriske klippebilleder
The Ancient Orient	Alter Orient	Ancien Orient	Oldtidens Orient
Minoan site	Minoische Kultur	Civilisation minoenne	Minoisk kultur
Phoenecian site	Phönikische Kultur	Civilisation phénicienne	Fønikisk kultur
Etruscan site	Etruskische Kultur	Civilisation étrusque	Etruskisk kultur
Greek antiquity	Griechische Antike	Antiquité grecque	Den gamle græske kultur
Roman antiquity	Römische Antike	Antiquité romaine	Den gamle romerske kultur
Vikings	Wikinger	Vikings	Vikinger
Places of Jewish cultural interest	Jüdische Kulturstätte	Site juif	Steder af jødisk kulturel interesse
Places of Islamic cultural interest	Islamische Kulturstätte	Site islamique	Steder af islamisk kulturel interesse
Places of Christian cultural interest	Christliche Kulturstätte	Site chrétien	Steder af kristen kulturel interesse
Roman church	Romanische Kirche	Église romane	Romersk kirke
Gothic church	Gotische Kirche	Église gothique	Gotisk kirke
Renaissance church	Renaissance-Kirche	Église renaissance	Renæssance kirke
Baroque church	Barock-Kirche	Église baroque	Barok kirke
Christian monastery	Christliches Kloster	Monastère chrétien	Kristent kloster
Cultural landscape	Kulturlandschaft	Paysage culturel	Kulturlandskab
Historical city scape	Historisches Stadtbild	Cité historique	Historiske byer
Impressive skyline	Imposante Skyline	Gratte-ciel	Flot silhuet
Castle/fortress/fort	Burg/Festung/Wehranlage	Château/forteresse/remparts	Slot/fæstning/borg
Castle ruin	Burgruine	Château ruine	Slotsruin
Tower of interest	Sehenswerter Turm	Tour intéressante	Seværdigt tårn
Windmill	Windmühle	Moulin	Vindmølle
Palace	Palast/Schloss	Palais	Palads
Technical/industrial monument	Techn./industrielles Monument	Monument technique/industriel	Teknisk/industrielt monument
Working mine	Bergwerk in Betrieb	Mine en activité	Mine i drift
Disused mine	Bergwerk geschlossen	Mine fermée	Lukket mine
Dam	Staumauer	Barrage	Dæmning
Impressive lighthouse	Sehenswerter Leuchtturm	Très beau phare	Seværdigt fyrtårn
Notable bridge	Herausragende Brücke	Pont remarquable	Seværdig bro
Remarkable building	Herausragendes Gebäude	Bâtiment remarquable	Seværdig bygning
Tomb/grave	Grabmal	Tombeau	Gravmæle
Monument	Denkmal	Monument	Monument
Memorial	Mahnmal	Mémorial	Mindesmærke
Theater of war/battlefield	Kriegsschauplatz/Schlachtfeld	Champs de bataille	Slagmark
Space mission launch site	Weltraumbahnhof	Base spatiale	Rumcenter
Space telescope	Weltraumteleskop	Télescope astronomique	Rumfartsteleskop
Market	Markt	Marché	Marked
Festivals	Feste und Festivals	Fêtes et festivals	Byfester og festivals
Museum	Museum	Musée	Muséer
State Historical Park	Freilichtmuseum	Musée de plein air	Frilandsmuseum
Theatre	Theater	Théâtre	Teater
World exhibition/World Fair	Weltausstellung	Exposition universelle	Verdensudstilling
Arena/stadium	Arena/Stdion	Arène/stade	Arena/stadion
Race track	Rennstrecke	Circuit automobile	Væddeløbsbane
Golf	Golf	Golf	Golf
Horse racing	Pferdesport	Équitation	Hestevæddeløb
Skiing	Skigebiet	Station de ski	Skiområde
Sailing	Segeln	Voile	Sejlads
Wind surfing	Windsurfen	Planche à voile	Vindsurfing
Surfing	Wellenreiten	Surf	Surfing
Diving	Tauchen	Plongée	Dykning
Canoeing/rafting	Kanu/Rafting	Canoë/rafting	Kanosejlads/rafting
Seaport	Seehafen	Port	Havn
Deep-sea fishing	Hochseeangeln	Pêche en mer	Fiskeri
Waterskiing	Wasserski	Ski nautique	Vandski
Beach resort	Badeort	Station balnéaire	Badested
Leisure bath	Freizeitbad	Piscine découverte	Svømmehal/vandland
Mineral/thermal spa	Mineralbad/Therme	Station hydrothermale	Mineralbad/termalbad
Leisure park	Freizeitpark	Parc de loisirs	Forlystelsespark
Casino	Spielcasino	Casino	Kasino
Hill resort	Hill Resort	Station de montagne	Bjerghoteller
Mountain refuge/alpine pasture	Berghütte/Alm	Refuge/pâturages	Bjerghytte/alpe
Rambling/rambling area	Wandern/Wandergebiet	Randonnées/zone de randonnées	Vandring/vandreområde
Viewpoint	Aussichtspunkt	Point de vue	Udsigtspunkt
Mountain railway	Bergbahn	Chemin de fer de montagne	Bjergbane
Shipwreck	Schiffswrack	Épave de navire	Skibsvrag

Road Distances

Road Distances	Amsterdam	Athína	Barcelona	Belfast	Beograd	Berlin	Bern	Birmingham	Bordeaux	Bratislava	Bruxelles/Brussel	București	Budapest	Calais	Dublin	Edinburgh	Frankfurt a.M.	Genova	Hamburg	Helsinki	Istanbul	København	Köln	Kyjiv	Le Havre	Lisboa	Ljubljana	London	Luxembourg	Lyon	Madrid	Málaga	Marseille	Milano	Minsk	Moskva	München	Oslo	Paris	Praha	Riga	Roma	Rotterdam	Sankt-Peterburg	Sarajevo	Skopje	Sofija	Stockholm	Strasbourg	Tallinn	Tiranë	Vilnius	Warszawa	Wien	Zagreb
Amsterdam		2827	1566	1286	1720	656	833	734	1082	1211	210	2267	1398	363	1125	1196	443	1216	466	1953	2693	788	263	1943	598	2241	1234	532	360	923	1770	2321	1235	1076	1768	2469	826	1268	502	883	1873	1662	76	2424	1743	2155	2113	1435	602	2183	2217	1665	1209	1148	1330
Athína	2827		2612	3758	1106	2338	2010	3206	2682	1662	2598	1168	1466	2844	3598	3668	2386	1780	2627	3227	1094	2767	2568	2307	2744	3768	1633	2952	2414	2115	3215	3619	2156	1691	2583	3283	2039	3440	2554	1991	2830	1267	2834	3381	1175	701	798	3415	2170	3140	713	2622	2343	1705	1493
Barcelona	1566	2612		2280	1988	1877	915	1728	637	1894	1376	2574	1926	1365	2120	2190	1336	857	1776	3263	2961	2099	1383	3048	1251	1259	1462	1526	1180	639	627	1031	508	978	2989	3690	1343	2578	1071	1715	3093	1366	1525	3645	2014	2422	2380	2746	1130	3450	2360	2886	2430	1829	1597
Belfast	1286	3758	2280		2800	1850	1745	594	1784	2349	1119	3415	2545	925	166	319	1521	2119	1676	3161	3773	1999	1331	3244	1191	2941	2316	776	1347	1672	2474	3009	1983	2057	2957	3660	1856	2478	1206	2025	3062	2651	1226	3601	2864	3241	3193	2647	1540	3373	3296	2864	2401	2227	2405
Beograd	1720	1106	1988	2800		1236	1334	2248	2031	560	1680	592	363	1877	2639	2709	1287	1159	1525	2125	979	1665	1469	1472	1971	3147	534	2046	1500	1464	2594	2998	1535	1036	1480	2181	940	2338	1771	889	1728	1296	1735	2279	305	439	398	2312	1314	2038	748	1520	1051	603	395
Berlin	656	2338	1877	1850	1236		956	1298	1632	683	774	1751	881	927	1689	1760	549	1177	289	1649	2320	434	576	1325	1148	2791	997	1096	743	1238	2320	2879	1549	1038	1150	1850	588	1031	1053	355	991	1518	693	1711	1418	1687	1714	1082	753	1486	1967	1026	590	686	1053
Bern	833	2010	915	1745	1334	956		1167	889	950	637	1920	1136	796	1564	1629	429	450	910	2397	2307	1232	583	2205	752	2044	809	965	453	305	1543	1947	573	318	1992	2693	433	1723	561	806	2183	903	802	2648	1271	1767	1726	1879	238	2320	1706	1943	1448	867	943
Birmingham	734	3206	1728	594	2248	1298	1167		1232	1797	566	2794	1924	373	385	472	968	1567	1124	2609	3221	1447	779	2582	432	2233	1764	191	795	1120	1768	2302	1431	1498	2405	3108	1317	1926	654	1460	2608	2099	674	2913	2278	2682	2641	2095	988	2615	2730	2312	1849	1675	1853
Bordeaux	1082	2682	637	1784	2031	1632	889	1232		1936	891	2616	1967	869	1470	1540	1167	997	1483	2970	3003	1806	1065	2998	686	1162	1503	1030	995	588	691	1242	648	1014	2744	3445	1276	2285	586	1549	2829	1506	1039	3249	2059	2463	2422	2453	964	2944	2389	2641	2185	1870	1639
Bratislava	1211	1662	1894	2349	560	683	950	1797	1936		1203	1071	201	1388	2151	2221	799	1063	968	1751	1640	1109	987	1256	1521	3052	447	1557	1031	1368	2498	2902	1439	940	1201	1902	490	1705	1350	333	1353	1200	1237	1904	723	1007	1034	1756	893	1664	1316	1146	684	65	442
Bruxelles/Brussel	210	2598	1376	1119	1680	774	637	566	891	1203		2227	1357	195	958	1028	402	1023	601	2088	2653	923	212	2163	406	2049	1156	364	230	732	1578	2129	1044	884	1884	2585	737	1403	311	902	1775	1469	151	2389	1702	2113	2072	1570	434	2094	2177	1781	1325	1107	1289
București	2267	1168	2574	3415	592	1751	1920	2794	2616	1071	2227		874	2426	3196	3256	1833	1746	2035	2183	625	2175	2015	947	2585	3735	1122	2592	2077	2052	3182	3586	2122	1624	1357	1790	1525	2713	2356	1399	1786	1884	2286	2366	915	690	383	2764	1906	2096	923	1756	1338	1113	982
Budapest	1398	1466	1926	2545	363	881	1136	1924	1967	201	1357	874		1577	2315	2386	963	1094	1165	1776	1350	1305	1152	1123	1685	3083	460	1722	1195	1399	2529	2933	1470	971	1132	1832	655	1901	1491	529	1356	1231	1411	1907	545	810	769	1952	1067	1666	1119	1148	687	273	344
Calais	363	2844	1365	925	1877	927	796	373	869	1388	195	2426	1577		764	777	600	1189	754	2241	2851	1077	410	2213	273	2025	1382	171	414	759	1554	2105	1070	1023	2038	2738	935	1556	288	1100	1929	1608	304	2543	1905	2311	2270	1724	617	2237	2332	1934	1478	1305	1487
Dublin	1125	3598	2120	166	2639	1689	1564	385	1470	2151	958	3196	2315	764		450	1326	1926	1480	2979	3578	1803	1136	2939	789	2616	2106	546	1145	1479	2146	2717	1792	1751	2770	3470	1677	2288	1019	1826	2874	2342	1030	3272	2618	3040	3033	2450	1343	2969	3101	2672	2204	2031	2213
Edinburgh	1196	3668	2190	319	2709	1760	1629	472	1540	2221	1028	3256	2386	777	450		1430	2021	1586	3071	3683	1909	1241	3043	894	2697	2183	650	1256	1582	2230	2764	1893	1959	2866	3569	1765	2387	1116	1922	2971	2553	893	3375	2682	3143	3102	2556	1450	3070	3206	2773	2310	2137	2315
Frankfurt a.M.	443	2386	1336	1521	1287	549	429	968	1167	799	402	1833	963	600	1326	1430		808	496	1968	2261	818	189	1841	772	2306	801	766	231	700	1835	2341	1012	668	1663	2364	393	1308	573	510	1768	1254	456	2319	1299	1721	1680	1465	223	1882	1785	1560	1104	715	897
Genova	1216	1780	857	2119	1159	1177	450	1567	997	1063	1023	1746	1094	1189	1926	2021	808		1244	2746	2123	1566	971	2210	1104	2013	623	1364	828	475	1459	1863	400	140	2196	2897	628	2057	914	1081	2348	522	1177	2899	1068	1583	1542	2213	613	2674	1482	2141	1679	991	759
Hamburg	466	2627	1776	1676	1525	289	910	1124	1483	968	601	2035	1165	754	1480	1586	496	1244		1502	2646	338	425	1603	997	2639	1184	922	623	1140	2169	2720	1452	1109	1428	2128	776	814	892	646	1280	1669	501	1893	1684	2104	2063	985	703	1588	2170	1324	868	976	1280
Helsinki	1953	3227	3263	3161	2125	1649	2397	2609	2970	1751	2088	2183	1776	2241	2979	3071	1968	2746	1502		3081	1173	1910	1546	2482	4125	2126	2407	2106	2625	3654	4205	2937	2424	882	1107	1974	1019	2387	1641	396	2879	1986	389	2334	2570	2476	517	2189	88	2879	689	1062	1754	2121
Istanbul	2693	1094	2961	3773	979	2320	2307	3221	3003	1640	2653	625	1350	2851	3578	3683	2261	2123	2646	3081		2642	2442	1475	2944	4121	1508	3019	2449	2438	3567	3971	2508	2009	2006	2524	1914	3314	2745	1866	2569	1743	2708	2948	1168	787	580	3289	2287	2879	1015	2361	1943	1580	1368
København	788	2767	2099	1999	1665	434	1232	1447	1806	1109	923	2175	1305	1077	1803	1909	818	1566	338	1173	2642		748	1744	1320	2962	1390	1245	944	1463	2492	3043	1775	1432	1104	1786	981	607	1215	785	912	1911	824	1473	1832	2117	2144	658	1026	1139	2360	919	1009	1116	1472
Köln	263	2568	1383	1331	1469	576	583	779	1065	987	212	2015	1152	410	1136	1241	189	971	425	1910	2442	748		1947	580	2223	984	575	207	746	1752	2303	1058	826	1683	2384	575	1224	485	692	1575	1411	257	2138	1493	1910	1862	1392	354	1883	1967	1580	1124	897	1079
Kyjiv	1943	2307	3048	3244	1472	1325	2205	2582	2998	1256	2163	947	1123	2213	2939	3043	1841	2210	1603	1546	1475	1744	1947		2532	4183	1560	2379	2048	2480	3629	4033	2570	2071	560	852	1749	2343	2336	1405	1045	2331	1977	1378	1652	1645	1320	1591	2003	1461	1859	751	767	1343	1444
Le Havre	598	2744	1251	1191	1971	1148	752	432	686	1521	406	2585	1685	273	789	894	772	1104	997	2482	2944	1320	580	2532		1845	1437	298	531	658	1374	1925	970	1044	2261	2962	1022	1802	197	1230	2153	1638	540	2715	2006	2404	2363	1970	688	2461	2432	2158	1702	1436	1580
Lisboa	2241	3768	1259	2941	3147	2791	2044	2233	1162	3052	2049	3735	3083	2025	2616	2697	2306	2013	2639	4125	4121	2962	2223	4183	1845		2616	2187	2128	1742	626	683	1662	2132	3901	4602	2430	3442	1743	2702	3793	2520	2196	4347	3175	3576	3535	3610	2118	4101	3474	3798	3342	2983	2751
Ljubljana	1234	1633	1462	2316	534	997	809	1764	1503	447	1156	1122	460	1382	2106	2183	801	623	1184	2126	1508	1390	984	1560	1437	2616		1538	942	939	2068	2472	1009	510	1588	2289	409	1999	1240	708	1741	770	1251	2245	554	965	924	2038	782	2051	949	1533	1072	383	140
London	532	2952	1526	776	2046	1096	965	191	1030	1557	364	2592	1722	171	546	650	766	1364	922	2407	3019	1245	575	2379	298	2187	1538		587	918	1720	2254	1229	1260	2202	2905	1120	1724	452	1270	2098	1897	472	2661	2067	2479	2438	1892	786	2098	2542	2109	1646	1473	1651
Luxembourg	360	2414	1180	1347	1500	743	453	795	995	1031	230	2077	1195	414	1145	1256	231	828	623	2106	2449	944	207	2048	531	2128	942	587		517	1634	2158	829	669	1878	2579	523	1427	372	732	1788	1254	355	2352	1494	1906	1864	1595	219	2096	1969	1774	1319	938	1081
Lyon	923	2115	639	1672	1464	1238	305	1120	588	1368	732	2052	1399	759	1479	1582	700	475	1140	2625	2438	1463	746	2480	658	1742	939	918	517		1242	1646	317	448	2354	3044	733	1943	468	1080	2265	983	849	2958	1473	1897	1856	2111	495	2573	1823	2251	1795	1304	1072
Madrid	1770	3215	627	2474	2594	2320	1543	1768	691	2498	1578	3182	2529	1554	2146	2230	1835	1459	2169	3654	3567	2492	1752	3629	1374	626	2068	1720	1634	1242		545	1105	1576	3434	4135	1941	2975	1275	2312	3538	1964	1728	3887	2605	3028	2987	3140	1733	3630	2923	3334	2871	2433	2200
Málaga	2321	3619	1031	3009	2998	2879	1947	2302	1242	2902	2129	3586	2933	2105	2717	2764	2341	1863	2720	4205	3971	3043	2303	4033	1925	683	2472	2254	2158	1646	545		1506	1977	3988	4689	2342	3577	1810	2713	4092	2365	2263	4596	2979	3420	3379	3677	2129	4206	3319	3884	3428	2828	2596
Marseille	1235	2156	508	1983	1535	1549	573	1431	648	1439	1044	2122	1470	1070	1792	1893	1012	400	1452	2937	2508	1775	1058	2570	970	1662	1009	1229	829	317	1105	1506		521	2577	3278	1010	2255	779	1382	2729	909	1160	3234	1544	1965	1924	2422	806	2884	1863	2522	2060	1372	1140
Milano	1076	1691	978	2057	1036	1038	318	1498	1014	940	884	1624	971	1023	1751	1959	668	140	1109	2424	2009	1432	826	2071	1044	2132	510	1260	669	448	1576	1977	521		2077	2778	493	1921	853	865	2229	584	1041	2732	1045	1465	1423	2078	477	2365	1400	2022	1512	872	540
Minsk	1768	2583	2989	2957	1480	1150	1992	2405	2744	1201	1884	1357	1132	2038	2770	2866	1663	2196	1428	882	2006	1104	1683	560	2261	3901	1588	2202	1878	2354	3434	3988	2577	2077		720	1627	1516	2159	1281	484	2338	1800	783	2447	1926	1744	1030	1791	794	2235	191	550	1213	1473
Moskva	2469	3283	3690	3660	2181	1850	2693	3108	3445	1902	2585	1790	1832	2738	3470	3569	2364	2897	2128	1107	2524	1786	2384	852	2962	4602	2289	2905	2579	3044	4135	4689	3278	2778	720		2362	1997	2863	1873	917	3041	2503	697	2382	2496	2265	1464	2570	1014	2938	908	1253	1916	2176
München	826	2039	1343	1856	940	588	433	1317	1276	490	737	1525	655	935	1677	1765	393	628	776	1974	1914	981	575	1749	1022	2430	409	1120	523	733	1941	2342	1010	493	1627	2362		1588	822	381	1608	928	824	2166	962	1374	1332	1627	364	1916	1435	1594	992	406	549
Oslo	1268	3440	2578	2478	2338	1031	1723	1926	2285	1705	1403	2713	1901	1556	2288	2387	1308	2057	814	1019	3314	607	1224	2343	1802	3442	1999	1724	1427	1943	2975	3577	2255	1921	1516	1997	1588		1703	1382	1069	2507	1302	1341	2430	2713	2741	523	1516	986	2956	1331	1605	1712	2068
Paris	502	2554	1071	1206	1771	1053	561	654	586	1350	311	2356	1491	288	1019	1116	573	914	892	2387	2745	1215	485	2336	197	1743	1240	452	372	468	1275	1810	779	853	2159	2863	822	1703		1030	2055	1445	458	2619	1805	2204	2163	1873	488	2363	2262	2061	1605	1237	1377
Praha	883	1991	1715	2025	889	355	806	1460	1549	333	902	1399	529	1100	1826	1922	510	1081	646	1641	1866	785	692	1405	1230	2702	708	1270	732	1080	2312	2713	1382	865	1281	1873	381	1382	1030		1282	1296	909	1777	1044	1334	1362	1427	606	1593	1542	1075	613	333	654
Riga	1873	2830	3093	3062	1728	991	2183	2608	2829	1353	1775	1786	1356	1929	2874	2971	1768	2348	1280	396	2569	912	1575	1045	2153	3793	1741	2098	1788	2265	3538	4092	2729	2229	484	917	1608	1069	2055	1282		2482	1905	561	1916	2173	2078	547	1752	310	2482	291	664	1356	1723
Roma	1662	1267	1366	2651	1296	1518	903	2099	1506	1200	1469	1884	1231	1608	2342	2553	1254	522	1669	2879	1743	1911	1411	2331	1638	2520	770	1897	1254	983	1964	2365	909	584	2338	3041	928	2507	1445	1296	2482		1626	2993	892	1190	1686	2556	1062	2803	975	2284	1823	1135	903
Rotterdam	76	2834	1525	1226	1735	693	802	674	1039	1237	151	2286	1411	304	1030	893	456	1177	501	1986	2708	824	257	1977	540	2196	1251	472	355	849	1728	2263	1160	1041	1800	2503	824	1302	458	909	1905	1626		2260	1757	2167	2126	1469	566	2002	2231	1699	1243	1161	1343
Sankt-Peterburg	2424	3381	3645	3601	2279	1711	2648	2913	3249	1904	2389	2366	1907	2543	3272	3375	2319	2899	1893	389	2948	1473	2138	1378	2715	4347	2245	2661	2352	2958	3887	4596	3234	2732	783	697	2166	1341	2619	1777	561	2993	2260		2447	2665	2571	899	2317	361	2975	714	1157	1849	2216
Sarajevo	1743	1175	2014	2864	305	1418	1271	2278	2059	723	1702	915	545	1905	2618	2682	1299	1068	1684	2334	1168	1832	1493	1652	2006	3175	554	2067	1494	1473	2605	2979	1544	1045	2447	2382	962	2430	1805	1044	1916	892	1757	2447		459	586	2482	1340	2249	498	1691	1250	759	414
Skopje	2155	701	2422	3241	439	1687	1767	2682	2463	1007	2113	690	810	2311	3040	3143	1721	1583	2104	2570	787	2117	1910	1645	2404	3576	965	2479	1906	1897	3028	3420	1965	1465	1926	2496	1374	2713	2204	1334	2173	1190	2167	2665	459		229	2750	1747	2475	311	1957	1488	1040	828
Sofija	2113	798	2380	3193	398	1714	1726	2641	2422	1034	2072	383	769	2270	3033	3102	1680	1542	2063	2476	580	2144	1862	1320	2363	3535	924	2438	1864	1856	2987	3379	1924	1423	1744	2265	1332	2741	2163	1362	2078	1686	2126	2571	586	229		2709	1706	2389	540	1916	1447	999	787
Stockholm	1435	3415	2746	2647	2312	1082	1879	2095	2453	1756	1570	2764	1952	1724	2450	2556	1465	2213	985	517	3289	658	1392	1591	1970	3610	2038	1892	1595	2111	3140	3677	2422	2078	1030	1464	1627	523	1873	1427	547	2556	1469	899	2482	2750	2709		1674	482	3008	838	1198	1764	2120
Strasbourg	602	2170	1130	1540	1314	753	238	988	964	893	434	1906	1067	617	1343	1450	223	613	703	2189	2287	1026	354	2003	688	2118	782	786	219	495	1733	2129	806	477	1791	2570	364	1516	488	606	1752	1062	566	2317	1340	1747	1706	1674		2090	1815	1767	1311	769	927
Tallinn	2183	3140	3450	3373	2038	1486	2320	2615	2944	1664	2094	2096	1666	2237	2969	3070	1882	2674	1588	88	2879	1139	1883	1461	2461	4101	2051	2098	2096	2573	3630	4206	2884	2365	794	1014	1916	986	2363	1593	310	2803	2002	361	2249	2475	2389	482	2090		2793	602	975	1667	2034
Tiranë	2217	713	2360	3296	748	1967	1706	2730	2389	1316	2177	923	1119	2332	3101	3206	1785	1482	2170	2879	1015	2360	1967	1859	2432	3474	949	2542	1969	1823	2923	3319	1863	1400	2235	2938	1435	2956	2262	1542	2482	975	2231	2975	498	311	540	3008	1815	2793		2268	1799	1264	910
Vilnius	1665	2622	2886	2864	1520	1026	1943	2312	2641	1146	1781	1756	1148	1934	2672	2773	1560	2141	1324	689	2361	919	1580	751	2158	3798	1533	2109	1774	2251	3334	3884	2522	2022	191	908	1594	1331	2061	1075	291	2284	1699	714	1691	1957	1916	838	1767	602	2268		466	1158	1525
Warszawa	1209	2343	2430	2401	1051	590	1448	1849	2185	684	1325	1338	687	1478	2204	2310	1104	1679	868	1062	1943	1009	1124	767	1702	3342	1072	1646	1319	1795	2871	3428	2060	1512	550	1253	992	1605	1605	613	664	1823	1243	1157	1250	1488	1447	1198	1311	975	1799	466		689	1056
Wien	1148	1705	1829	2227	603	686	867	1675	1870	65	1107	1113	243	1305	2031	2137	715	991	976	1754	1580	1116	897	1343	1436	2983	383	1473	938	1304	2433	2828	1372	872	1213	1916	406	1712	1237	333	1356	1135	1161	1849	759	1040	999	1764	769	1667	1264	1158	689		376
Zagreb	1330	1493	1597	2405	395	1053	943	1853	1639	442	1289	982	344	1487	2213	2315	897	759	1280	2121	1368	1472	1079	1444	1580	2751	140	1651	1081	1072	2200	2596	1140	640	1473	2176	549	2068	1377	654	1723	903	1343	2216	414	828	787	2120	927	2034	910	1525	1056	376	

All distances in this chart are in kilometres and include any part of the route taken by ferry.

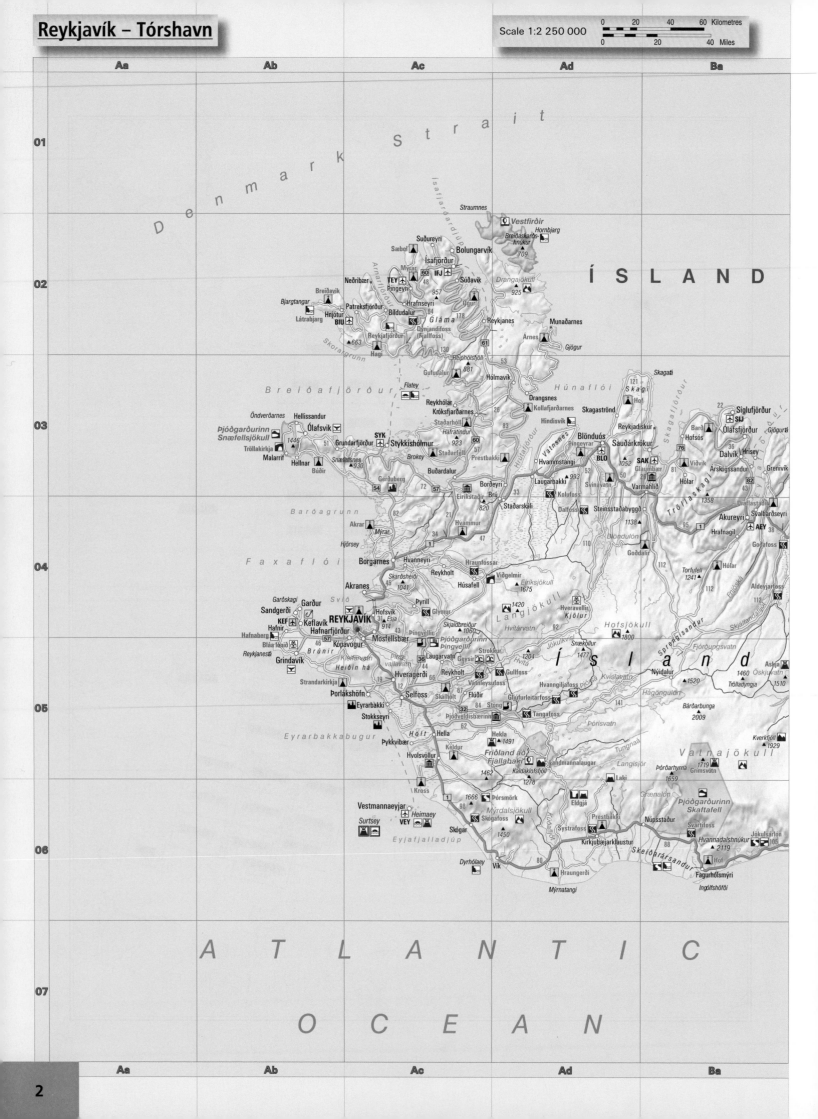

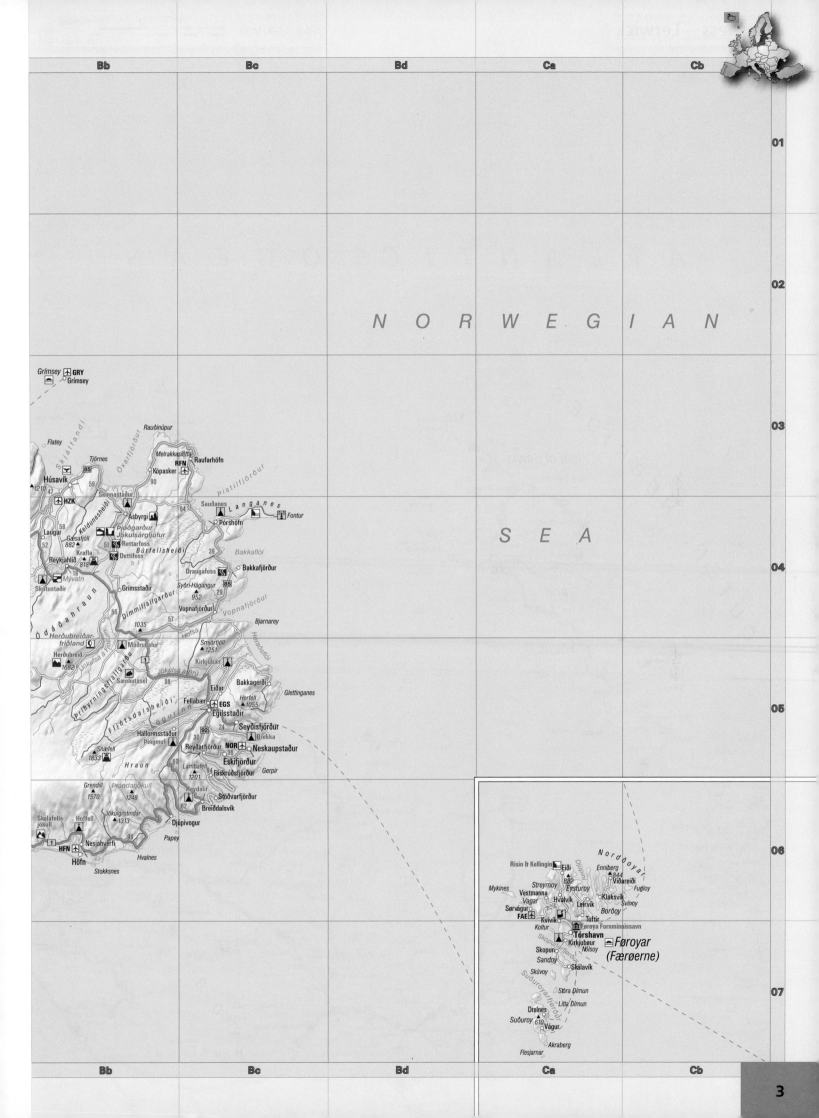

01

N O R W E G I A N

02

03

Grímsey ✈ **GRY**
🚢 Grímsey

Flatey
Skjálftandi
Tjörnes
Rauðinúpur
Öxarfjörður
Melrakkaslétta
Raufarhöfn
RFN
Kópasker
85
90
Húsavík
1210 47
59
Skinnastaðir
✈ **HZK**
Sauðanes
L a n g a n e s
Fontur
64
Keldunesheiði
Ásbyrgi
Þórshöfn
Laugar
58
Gæsafjöll
Þjóðgarður
Jökulsárgljúfur
52
882
51
Rettarfoss
39
Bakkaflói
Krafla
Búrfellsheiði
Reykjahlíð
818
Dettifoss
Bakkafjörður

04

Skútustaðir
Mývatn
Draugafoss
Bakkafjörður
Óðáðahraun
Grímsstaðir
Syðri-Hágangur
85
Dimmifjallgarður
952
29
Herðubreiðar-
friðland
1035
56
Vopnafjörður
Vopnafjörður
57
Hofsá
Bjarnarey
Herðubreið
1682
Jökulsá á Brú
Möðrudalur
Smjörfjöll
1251
Héraðsflói
Þrýhyrningsfjallgarður
Jökulsá á Brú
Kirkjubær
Sænautasel
88
Eiðar
Bakkagerði
Glettinganes

05

Fljótsdalsheiði
Lagurinn
Fellabær
✈ **EGS**
Herfell
1055
Hallormsstaður
92
Egilsstaðir
Þingmúli
30
24
Seyðisfjörður
Brekka
Snæfell
1833
Reyðarfjörður
NOR ✈
Neskaupstaður
36
Hraun
80
Lambafell
1201
Eskifjörður
Gerpir
Fáskrúðsfjörður
Grendill
1570
Þrándarjökull
1248
Heydalir
Stöðvarfjörður
Skálafells-
jökull
Hoffell
Jökulgilstindar
1313
62
Breiðdalsvík
1
HFN ✈
98
Djúpivogur
Papey
Nesjahverfi
Höfn
Hvalnes
Stokksnes

06

N o r ð o y a r
Risin & Kellingin
Eiði
Enniberg
844
Viðareiði
Fugloy
Mykines
Streymoy
882
Eysturoy
Klaksvík
Svínoy
Vestmanna
Hvalvík
Leirvík
Borðoy
Vágar
Sørvágur
FAE ✈
Kvívík
Toftir
Føroya Fornminnissavn
Koltur
Tórshavn
🚢 **Føroyar**
Skopun
Kirkjubøur
Nólsoy
(Færøerne)
Sandoy
Skálavík
Skúvoy

07

Stóra Dímun
Litla Dímun
Drelnes
Suðuroy
610
Vágur
Suðuroyarfjørður
Akraberg
Flesjarnar

S E A

Scale 1:900 000

| 0 | 10 | 20 | 30 | Kilometres |

| 0 | 10 | 20 | Miles |

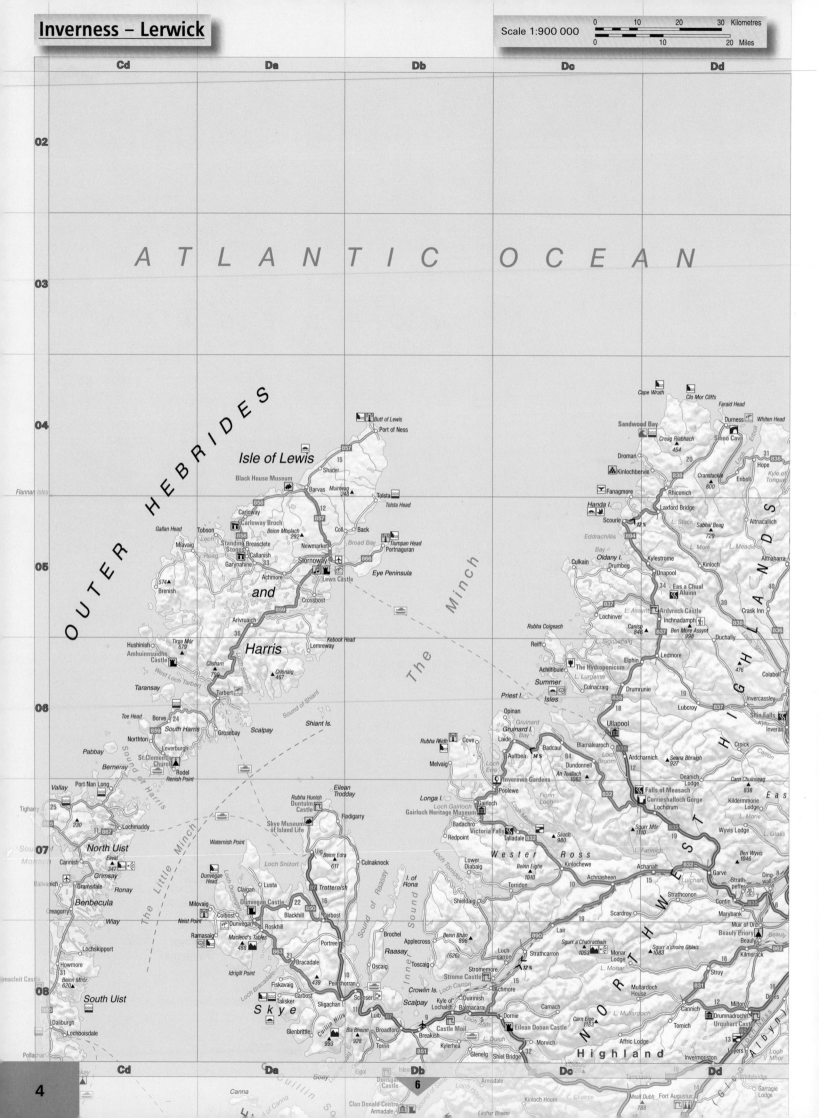

Cd   **Da**   **Db**   **Dc**   **Dd**

02

A T L A N T I C   O C E A N

03

O U T E R   H E B R I D E S

04

Cape Wrath
Clo Mor Cliffs
Faraid Head
Sandwood Bay
Durness
Whiten Head
Creag Riabhach 454
Sù’oo Cave
Droman
Hope
Kyle of Tongue
Kinlochbervie
Cranstackie 800
Eriboll
Fanagmore
Rhiconich
Handa I.
Laxford Bridge
Altnacallich
Scourie 12%
L. Stack
Sabhal Beag 729
Eddrachillis
894
L. More
L. Meadie
Culkein
Drumbeg
Oldany I.
Kylestrome
Altnaharra
Bay
Unapool
Kinloch
Eas a Chual Aluinn 34
40
Lochinver
Inchnadamph
L. Assynt
Ardvreck Castle
Crask Inn
Rubha Coigeach
Canisp 846
Ben More Assynt 998
Duchally
Reiff
Elphin
Ledmore
Colaboll
Achiltibuie
The Hydroponicum
L. Lurgainn
Drumrunie
476
Invercassley
Summer
Culnacraig
Lubcroy
Priest I.
Isles
835
18
19
Shin Falls
Ullapool
837
Inver
Opinan
Gruinard
Gruinard I.
Bay
Blarnaleroch
835
Croick
Rubha Reidh
Cove
Laide
Badcaul
Ardcharnich
Seana Bhraigh 927
Carn Chuinneag 838
Melvaig
Aultbea 14%
64
Dundonnell
Deanich Lodge
Inverewe Gardens
An Teallach 1062
Longa I.
Poolewe
L. Broom
Kildermorie Lodge
Gairloch
Fionn Loch
832
Sgurr Mór 1110
L. Morie
Gairloch Heritage Museum
Badachro
835
19
Wyvis Lodge
Redpoint
Victoria Falls
Talladale 832
Slioch 980
Falls of Measach
Corrieshalloch Gorge
L. Glass
Lochdrum
Lower Diabaig
Beinn Eighe 1010
Kinlochewe
Ben Wyvis 1046
Wester Ross
832
Garve
Torridon
Achnasheen
Ding-wall
Shieldaig
10
15
Achanalt
Luichart
Strath-peffer
Brochel
Applecross
Scardroy
Contin
I. of Rona
Lair
19
Maryburgh
Beinn Bhàn 896
Sgurr a'Chaorachain 1053
Sgurr a'choire Ghlais 1083
Muir of Ord
Oscaig
Raasay
Loch-carron
Strathcarron
Monar Lodge
Beauly Priory
Beauly
Toscaig
Stromemore 12%
L. Monar
Crowlin Is.
Strome Castle
Kilmorack
Scalpay
Achmore
Carn Eige 1183
Struy
Kyle of Lochalsh
Loch Carron
Kyleakin
Balmacara
Carnach
Mullardoch House
Cannich
Milton
831
Dornie
Eilean Donan Castle
L. Mullardoch
Drumnadrochit
Urquhart Castle
Kylerhea
L. Quoich
Morvich
Affric Lodge
Tomich
13
Glenelg
Shiel Bridge
32
Invermoriston
Highland
Ioyers

Isle of Lewis
Butt of Lewis
Port of Ness
857
Shader 15
Black House Museum
Barvas
Muirneag 248
Tolsta
858
Carloway
12
Tolsta Head
Carloway Broch
Beinn Mholach 292
857
Coll
Back
Gallan Head
Tobson
Standing Stones
Breasclete
Newmarket
Tiumpan Head
Miavaig
858
Portnaguran
Callanish 33
Stornoway
Broad Bay
866
Garynahine
574
Lews Castle
Eye Peninsula
Brenish
and
Achmore
859
Crossbost
Arivruaich
The Minch
Harris
Kebock Head
36
Lemreway
Hushinish
Tirga Mór 679
Clisham 799
Amhuinnsuidhe Castle
Crionaig 467
Taransay
Tarbert
West Loch Tarbert
Sound of Shiant
Borve 24
South Harris
Shiant Is.
Toe Head
859
Grosebay
Scalpay
Northton
Leverburgh
Pabbay
St. Clement's Church
Berneray
Rodel
Renish Point
Vallay
Port Nan Long
Sound of Harris
Eilean Trodday
Rubha Hunish
Duntulm Castle
Tighary 25
Flodigarry
230
Sound of
Lochmaddy
Skye Museum of Island Life
867
The Little Minch
Monach
North Uist
Waternish Point
Uig
Carinish
Eaval 347
Culnaknock
Beinn Edra 611
Grimsay
Loch Snizort
Trotternish
Gramsdale
Ronay
Dunvegan Head
Claigan
Lusta
Benbecula
Ballivanich
Milovaig
Dunvegan Castle
Wiay
22
850
16
Creagorry
Neist Point
Colbost
Dunvegan
Blackhill
Carbost
Ramasaig
Roskhill
I. of Raasay
Lochskipport
Macleod's Tables 488
Portree
863
21
Bracadale
Sound of Raasay
Idrigill Point
Fiskavaig
439
Peinchorran
Howmore 31
Raasay
Beinn Mhòr 620
Talisker
Carbost
Sligachan
Oscaig
South Uist
Skye
11
Luib
Macleit Castle
Cuillin Hills 993
Bla Bheinn 928
Broadford
Breakish
Daliburgh
Glenbrittle
Torrin
Castle Moil
Lochboisdale
851
Pollachar
Cuillin So

Cd   **Da**   **Db**   **Dc**   **Dd**

Canna
Arnisdale
Kinloch Hourn
Fort Augustus
Garragie Lodge
Clan Donald Centre
Armadale

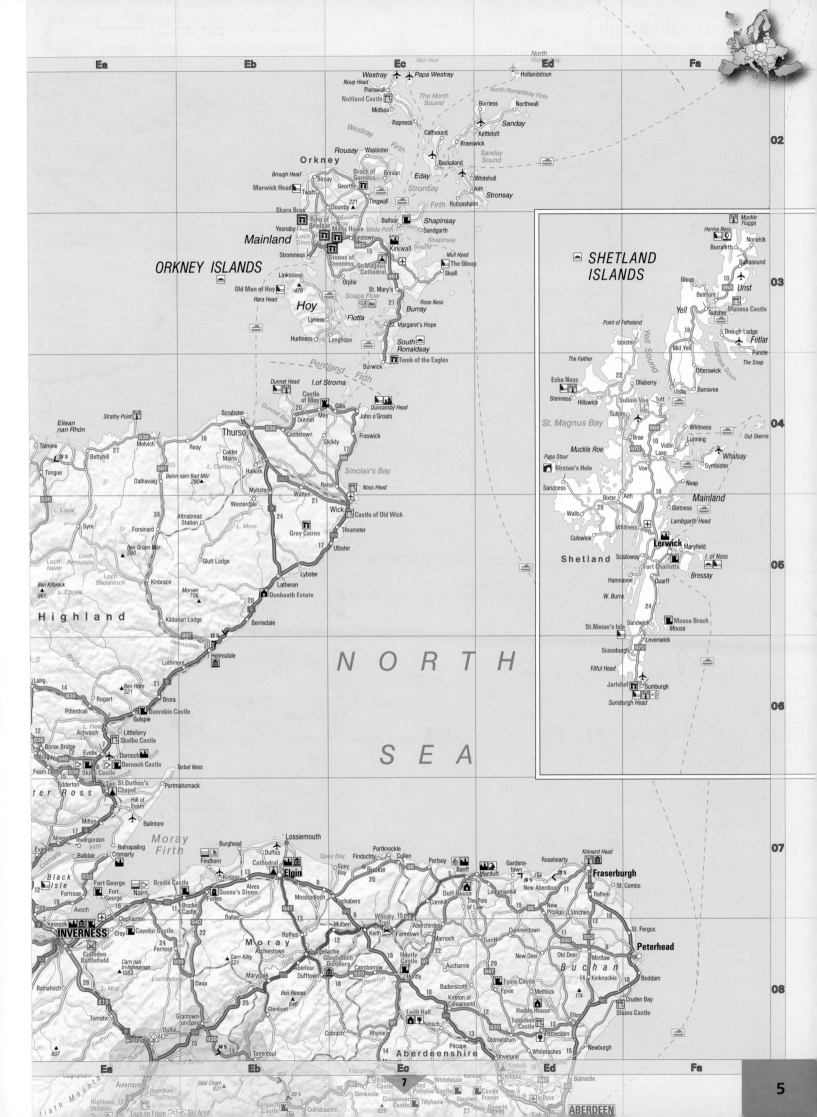

North Ronaldsay

Hollandstoun

Westray
Papa Westray
Noup Head
Pierowall
Noltland Castle
Midbea

The North Sound

Burness
Northwall

Sanday

Rapness
Calfsound
Kettletoft
Braeswick

Rousay
Wasbister

Sanday Sound

Backaland
Whitehall
Stronsay

Orkney

Brough Head
Birsay
Geowrth
Broch of Gurness
Brinian
Eday

Marwick Head
Twatt
221
Dounby
Tingwall
Firth
Rothiesholm

Aith
Stronsay

Skara Brae
Yesnaby
Ring of Brodgar
Hillray
Balfour
Shapinsay
Sandgarth

Mainland
Maes Howe
Wide Firth
Finstown
Shapinsay
Sound

Stromness
Loch
Stenness
965
15
Kirkwall
Mull Head

ORKNEY ISLANDS
Stones of Stenness
St.Magnus Cathedral
961
The Gloup
Skaill

Linksness
Órphir
St. Mary's

Old Man of Hoy
479
Scapa Flow
Rose Ness

Rora Head
21
Burray

Hoy
Lyness
Flotta
St. Margaret's Hope

Hurliness
Longhope
South
Ronaldsay

Burwick
Tomb of the Eagles

Pentland Firth

SHETLAND
ISLANDS

Muckle
Flugga
Herma Ness
Norwick
Burrafirth
Baltasound

Gloup
10
Unst
968

Belmont
Muness Castle

Point of Fethaland
18
Yell
Gutcher
Brough Lodge
Fetlar

The Faither
Isbister
Mid Yell
Funzie
The Snap

Esha Ness
22
Ollaberry
Otterswick
Burravoe

Stenness
Hillswick
Ulsta

St. Magnus Bay
Sullom Voe
Tott

Muckle Roe
Sullom
968
Whitness
Out Skerrie

Papa Stour
Brae
10
Vidlin
Lunning

Kirstan's Hole
Laxo
Whalsay

Sandness
Voe
Symbister

Bixter
Aith
Neap

Walls
29
Mainland

Culswick
Gletness
Lambgarth Head

Whitness

Shetland
Scalloway
Lerwick
Maryfield

Hamnavoe
Fort Charlotte
I. of Noss
Bressay

W. Burra
Quarff

24
Sandwick
Mousa Broch
Mousa

St.Ninian's Isle
Levenwick

Scousburgh
970

Fitful Head

Jarlshof
Sumburgh

Sumburgh Head

Eilean
nan Rhón
Strathy Point

Scrabster
Dunnet Head
I.of Stroma

Talmine
836
Melvich
Reay
Thurso
836
Castle
of May
Gills
Mey
Duncansby Head

Tongue
Bettyhill
27
Calder
Mains
Castletown
Dunnet
John o'Groats

15 %
Dalhavaig
897
Beinn nam Bad Mòr
290▲
Halkirk
882
Watten
Slickly
Freswick

Syre
Forsinard
Altnabreac
Station
Mybster
Reiss
17
99

L. Loyal
39
L. More
Westerdale
Watten
21
Wick
Sinclair's Bay

Ben Griam Mòr
590
Glutt Lodge
9
24
Castle of Old Wick
Noss Head

Loch
Rimsdale
Kinbrace
Grey Cairns
Thrumster
99

Loch
Badanloch
Morven
706
17
Ulbster

Ben Klibreck
961
L. Choire
20
Lybster

Highland
Kildonan Lodge
Dunbeath Estate

Berriedale
Latheron

897
13 %
Helmsdale

Kinbrace
Lothmore
Helmsdale

Lairg
14
Ben Horn
521
21
9

Rogart
Brora

839
Pittentrail

12
836
Dunrobin Castle
Golspie

Achvaich
Littleferry

Bonar Bridge
Skelbo Castle
Evelix
Dornoch

Ardgay
949
Fearn Lodge
Skibo Castle
Dornoch Castle
Tarbat Ness

St.Duthus's
Chapel
Portmahomack

Edderton
Tain

er Ross
Hill of
Fearn

Milton
Balintore

Alness
Invergordon
Balnapaling
Cromarty
**Moray
Firth**

Evanton
Balblair
Burghead
Lossiemouth

Black
Isle
832
Fort George
Duffus
Spey Bay
Findochty
Portknockie
Cullen

Fortrose
Fort
George
Nairn
Findhorn
Cathedral
Elgin
Spey
Bay
Buckie
Portsoy
Banff

Tore
19
Avoch
Brodie Castle
Sueno's Stone
8
20
Macduff

Kessock
INVERNESS
Croy
Cawdor Castle
Brodie
Castle
Alves
Mosstodloch
Fochabers
Cornhill
The Pole
of Law

Culloden Battlefield
24
Ferness
22
Dallas
941
Mulben
Keith
Aberchirder

Carn nan
tri-tighearnan
1093
939
Rothes
8
Farmtown
Marnoch

Balnafoich
Dava
Marypark
Aberlour
Glenfiddich
Distillery
Cairnborrow
Huntly
Castle

E15
Carn Kitty
521
95
Dufftown
920
Huntly

Tomatin
Ben Rinnes
840
18
Deveron

Grantown-
on-Spey
Glenlivet
Kirkton of
Culsalmond

14 %
25
Leith Hall
Insch

807
Dulnain
939
Aberdeenshire

Tomintoul

N O R T H

S E A

Kinnaird Head
Rosehearty
Fraserburgh

Gardens-
town
20 %
New Aberdour
St. Combs
Rathen

Longmanhill
11
New
Pitsligo
Strichen

Duff House
95
13
18

Whisky
Trail
95
St. Fergus
Cuminestown
950
952

Turriff
9
Peterhead

New Deer
Old Deer
Mintlaw

Aucharnie
29
947
Buchan

Badenscoth
14
Kinknockie
Boddam

Fyvie Castle
Fyvie
Methlick
174
Cruden Bay

Kirkton of
Culsalmond
Hadda House
12
Ellon
Slains Castle

Rhynie
Pitcaple
Tolquhon
Castle
Pitmedden

Cabrach
Oldmeldrum
Newburgh

Whiterashes
15

Kildrummy
Inverurie

Aviemore
Highland
Wildlife
Ski Area
Corgarff
Castle
Colnabaichin
629
Kintore
Castle Fraser
Dunecht
Dyce

807

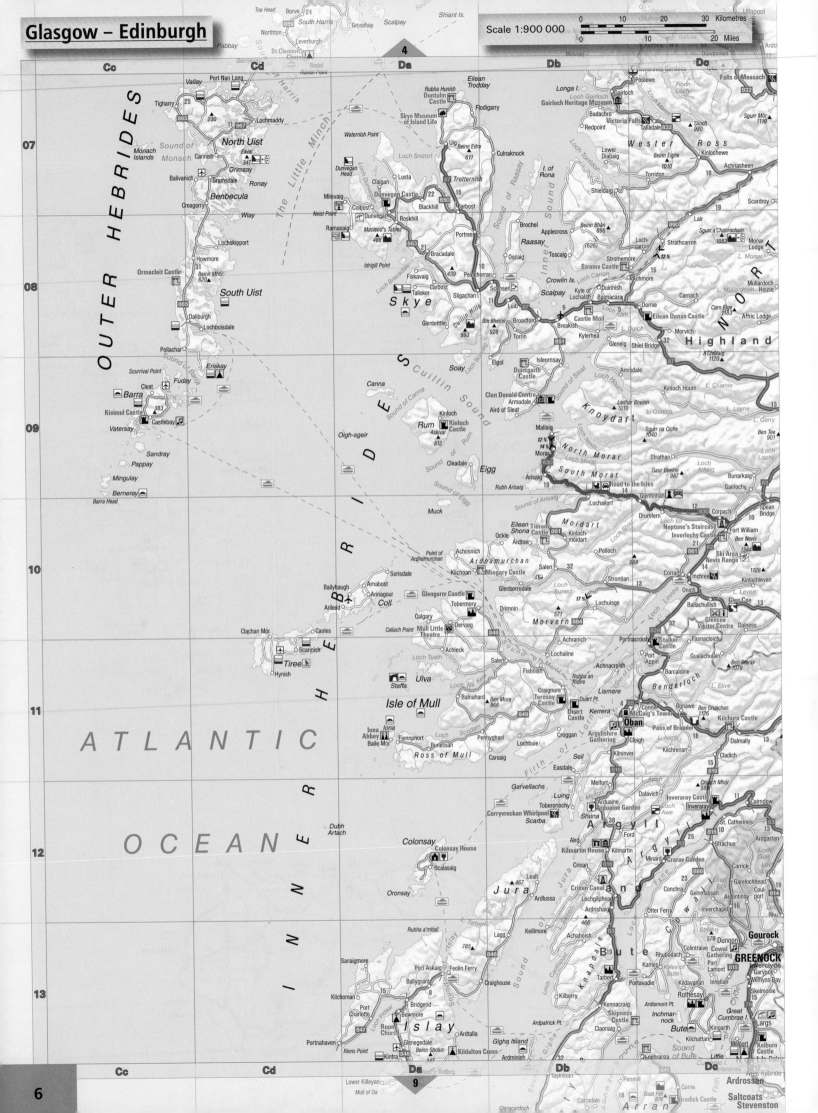

Scale 1:900 000

| 0 | 10 | 20 | 30 Kilometres |
| 0 | | 10 | 20 Miles |

OUTER HEBRIDES

Toe Head Borve 24
South Harris Grosebay Scalpay Shiant Is.
Northton Leverburgh
Pabbay St. Clement's Church Rodel
Berneray Renish Point

Vallay Port Nan Long
Tigharry 25
Lochmaddy
865 230 11 867
North Uist Eaval
Carinish 347
Balivanich Grimsay
Gramsdale Ronay
Creagorry Wiay
Benbecula
Lochskipport

Howmore 31
865 Ormacleit Castle Beinn Mhòr 620
Daliburgh South Uist
Lochboisdale

Pollachar
Scurrival Point Eriskay
Cleat Fuday
Barra 383
Kisimul Castle Castlebay
Vatersay
Sandray
Mingulay Pappay
Berneray
Barra Head

ATLANTIC

OCEAN

Eilean Trodday
Rubha Hunish Duntulm Castle
Longa I. Loch Gairloch
Flodigarry
Skye Museum of Island Life
Uig Beinn Edra 611
Waternish Point Trotternish Culnaknock
Loch Snizort I. of Rona
Dunvegan Head Claigan Lusta
Milovaig 87
Colbost Dunvegan Castle 22 16 Carbost Brochel
Neist Point Dunvegan Roskhill Blackhill
Ramasaig Macleod's Tables 488 Portree Raasay Applecross
863 21 Oscaig
Idrigill Point Bracadale Toscaig
Loch Bracadale 439 10
Fiskavaig Carbost Peinchorran Sconser Sound of Raasay
Talisker Glamaig
Skye Sligachan Luib Crowlin Is.
Glenbrittle Cuillin Hills 993 Bia Bheinn 928 Broadford
Soay Torrin Breakish
Elgol Kylerhea
Isleornsay
Dunscaith Castle
Canna Kinloch
Clan Donald Centre
Sound of Canna Rum Armadale Aird of Sleat
Askival 812
Oigh-sgeir Sound of Rum Cleadale Eigg
Rubh Arisaig
Sound of Eigg
Muck

Point of Ardnamurchan
Achosnich
Ockle Ardtoe
Kilchoan Mingary Castle Ardnamurchan
Sorisdale Glenborrodale
Bailyhaugh Arnabost Kilchoan Salen
Arinagour Arileod Coll Drimnin
Glengorm Castle Tobermory
Calgary Dervaig
Caliach Point Mull Little Theatre Morvern
Clachan Mòr Caoles Achleck Salen
Scarinish Achnacroish
Tiree Hynish Staffa Ulva Fishnish
Loch Tuath Lochaline
Isle of Mull
Balnahard Ben More 966
Iona Craignure Torosay Castle Duart Pt.
Iona Abbey Fionnphort Duart Castle
Baile Mòr Loch Scridain Pennyghael
Ross of Mull Carsaig Lochbuie Croggan

INNER HEBRIDES

Wester Ross
Falls of Measach
Poolewe Fionn Loch 832
Gairloch Badachro Victoria Falls
Gairloch Heritage Museum Redpoint Talladale 832
Sgurr Mòr 1110
Slioch 980
Beinn Eighe 1010
Lower Diabaig Kinlochewe
Shieldaig Achnasheen
Torridon 19 10
Beinn Bhàn 896 Scardroy
(626) Lair
Sgurr a'Chaorachain 1053
Strathcarron Monar Lodge
12% L. Monar
Stromeferry 15
Strome Castle Achmore
Kyle of Lochalsh Duirinish Carnach
Scalpay Balmacara Dornie Carn Eige 1183
Sconser Kyleakin Castle Moil 5 Eilean Donan Castle
Loch Alsh 9 Morvich Affric Lodge
Duich Shiel Bridge 32
Kylerhea Glenelg A'Chralaig 1120
851 Arnisdale Ladhar Bheinn 1010
Kinloch Hourn L. Cluanie
Knoydart L. Quoich
Loch Hourn Sgurr na Ciche 1040 L. Loyne
Mallaig Loch Nevis L. Garry 13
Morar North Morar Strathan Ben Tee 901
12% South Morar Gaor Bheinn 987 Loch Arkaig
14% Arisaig 19 Gairlochy
Road to the Isles Lochailort Glenfinnan Loch Lochy
Loch Shiel 12 Bunarkaig
Moidart Drumfern 830 Corpach Spean Bridge
Eilean Shona Kinloch-moidart Neptune's Staircase
Tioram Castle 861 Inverlochy Castle Fort William
Ardtoe Kinlochmoidart 21 Ben Nevis 1344
Acharacle Polloch Ski Area 14
Strontian 888 Nevis Range 1128
Salen 32 Loch Sunart Corran Inchree Kinlochleven
17% Lochuisge Onich Glen Coe
Morvern 384 571 Loch Leven Ballachulish Glencoe
Achranich Loch Linnhe Glencoe Visitor Centre Dalness
Portnacroish Stalker Castle Fasnacloich
Port Appin Gualachulain Ben Starav 1078
Lochaline Rubha an Ridire Barcaldine L. Etive
Lismore Benderloch Ben Cruachan 1126
Duart Pt. Connel Bonawe Kilchurn Castle
Kerrera McCaig's Tower Pass of Brander
Oban Argyllshire Gathering 18 Dalmally 13
Kilninver Cleigh Nant Kilchrenan Cladich
Seil 15 819
Easdale Loch Awe
Garvellachs Melfort Cruach Mhòr 586
Luing Arduaine Inveraray Castle 11 Cairndow
Toberonochy Arduaine Garden Inveraray St. Catherines
Corryvreckan Whirlpool Shuna Loch Awe Ardgartan
Scarba Aird Argyll 25 Strachur Loch Goil
Colonsay Kilmartin House Ford Minard Crarae Garden Carrick Loch Eck
Colonsay House Kilmartin Argyll 23 886 Garelochhead
Scalasaig Crinan 816 Coul port
Dubh Artach Lealt Crinan Canal Lochgilphead Glenmassan Argyntony 814
Oronsay 467 Ardlussa Ardrishaig Otter Ferry Inverchapel Rhu
Jura Knapdale 466 Loch Striven Dunoon
Rubha a'mhàil Tarbert Kames Cowal Gathering GREENOCK
Jura Lagg Achahoish Portavadie Inverclyde
785 846 Keillmore Colintraive Port Greenock
Sanaigmore Kilberry Skipness Castle Rhubodach Lamont Wemyss Bay
Port Askaig Feolin Ferry Kennacraig Ardlamont Pt. Kyles of Bute 15
Ballygrant Craighouse Kilberry Inchmarnock Bute Great Cumbrae I.
Kilchoman 15 8 Tarbert Portavadie Largs
Bridgend Kilberry Inchmarnock Kingarth Millport Kelburn Castle
Port Charlotte Bowmore Gigha Island Kildavanan Little North
Round Church Islay Kilberry Lochranza Cumbrae Ardrossan
847 Claonaig Sound of Bute
Beinn Sholum Ardtalla Ardpatrick Pt. Ardminish
Portnahaven Glenegedale 846 Kintra Kildalton Cross Arran
Rinns Point 347 Ardbeg Carradale Brodick Castle
Lower Killeyan Goat Fell 874 Saltcoats
Mull of Oa Glenacardoch Corrie Stevenston

07 08 09 10 11 12 13

Cc Cd Da Db Dc

4 9

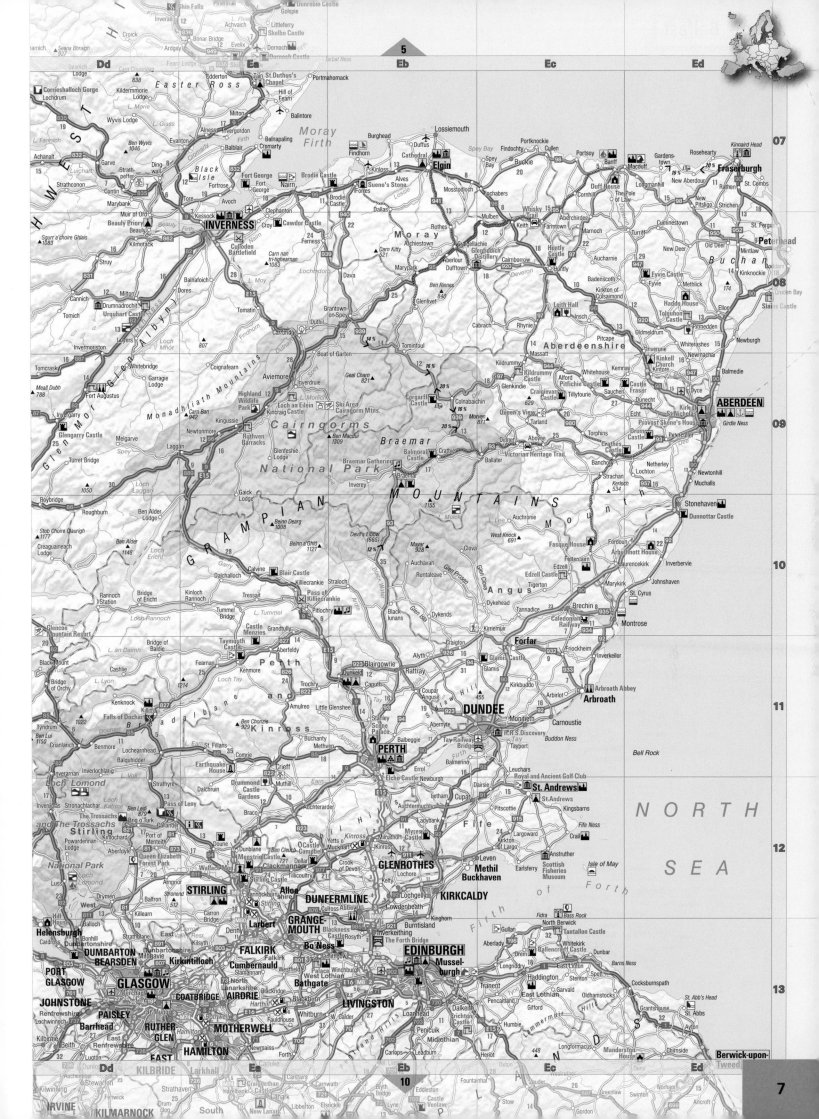

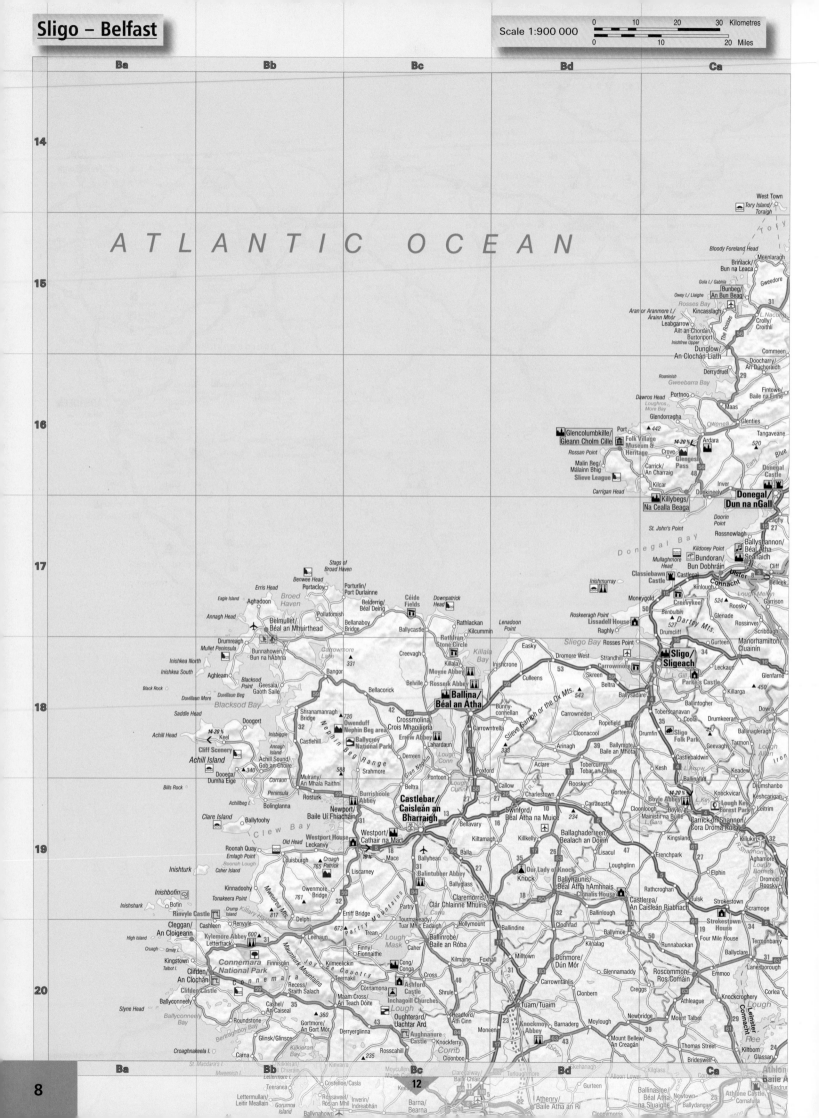

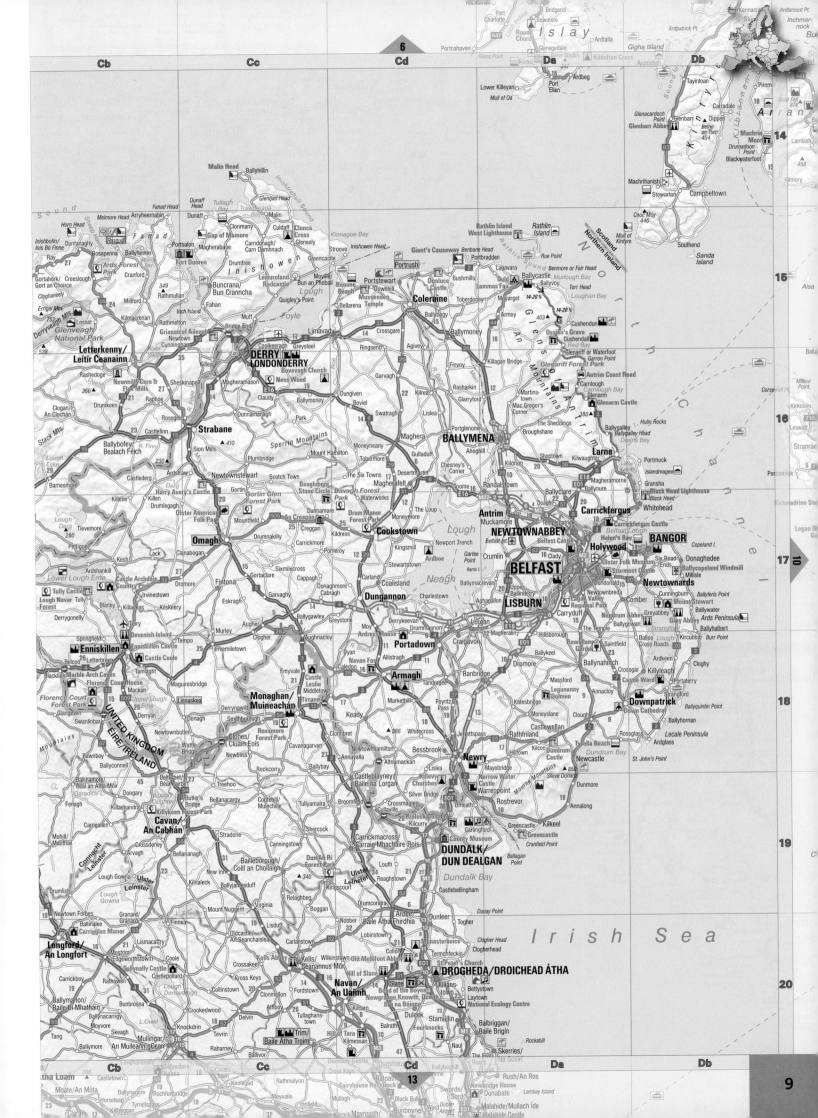

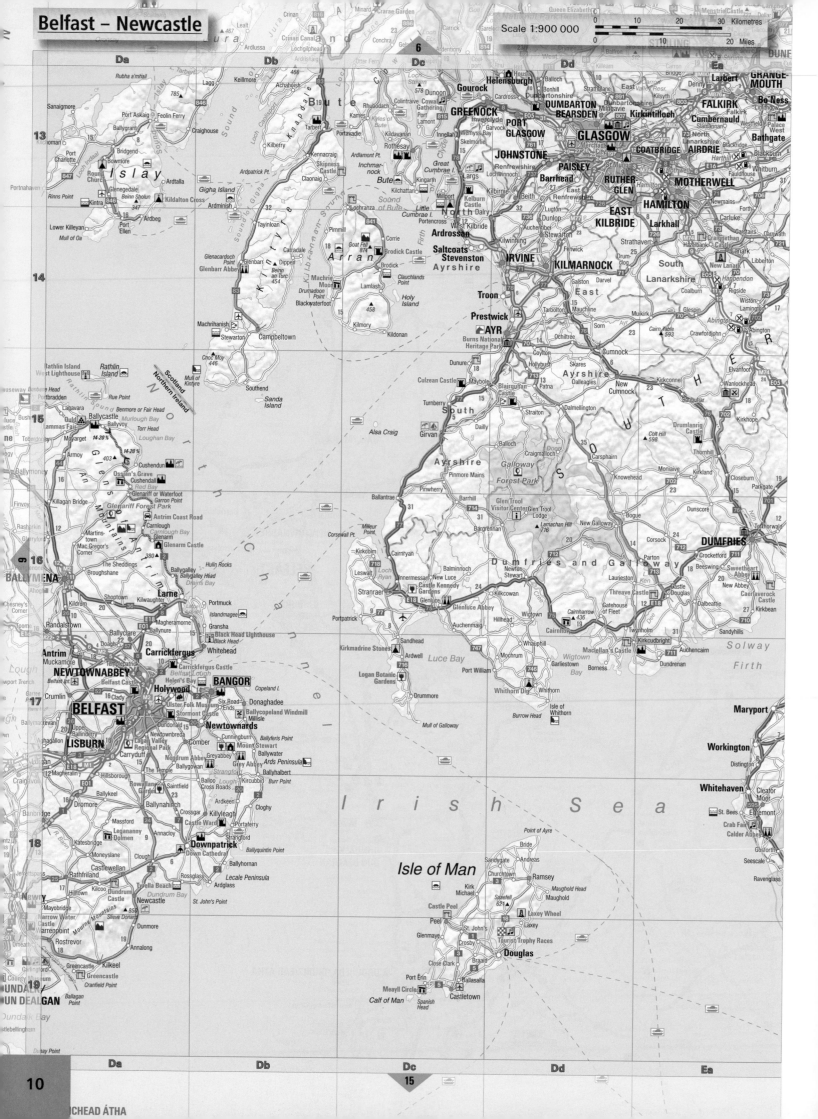

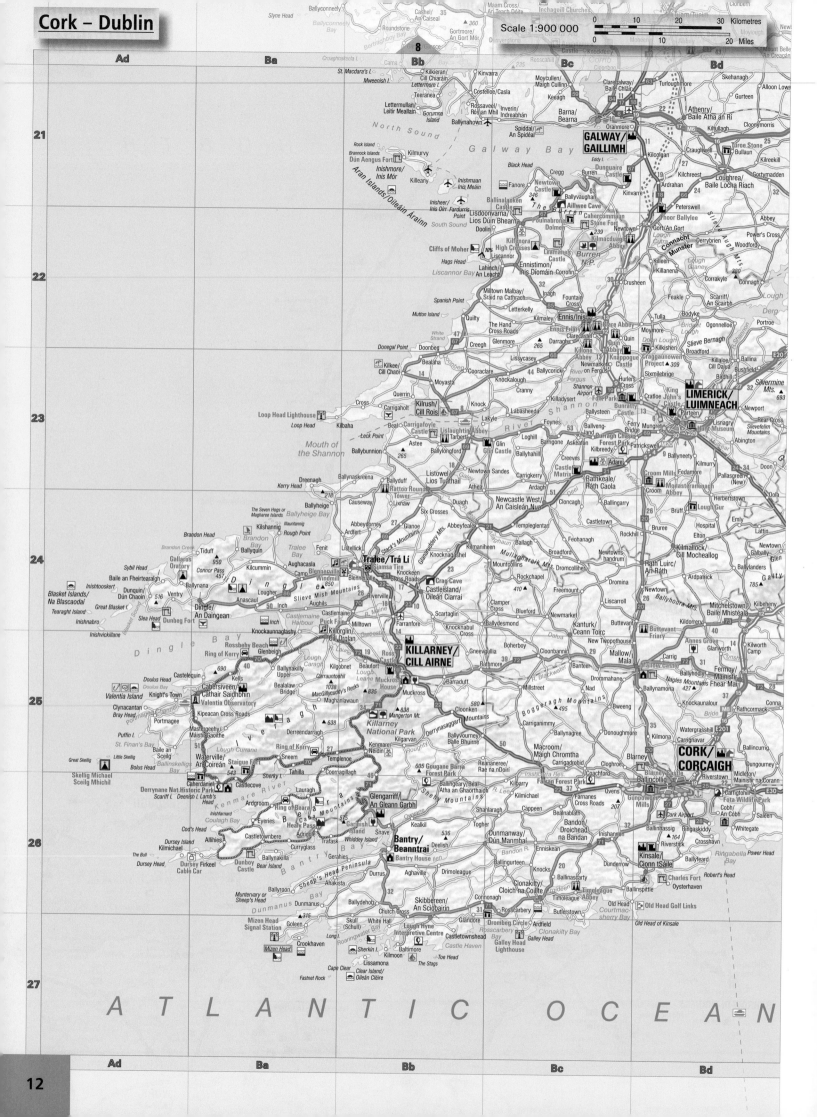

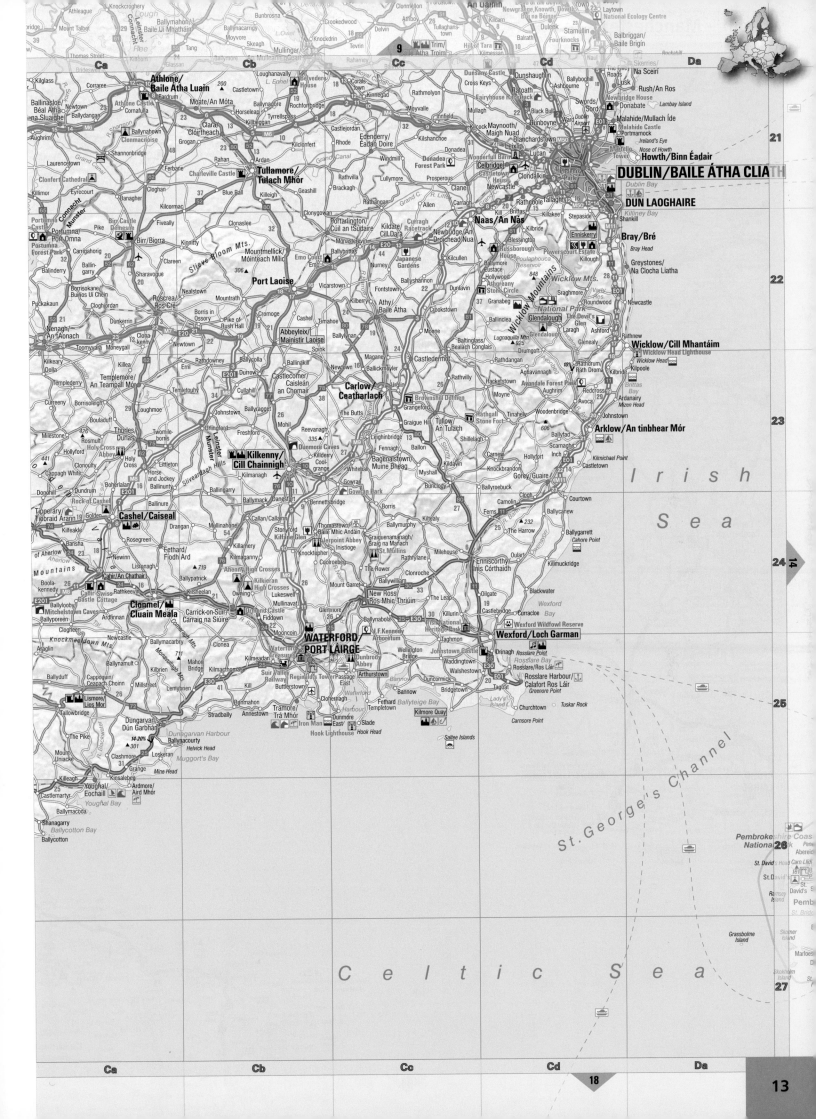

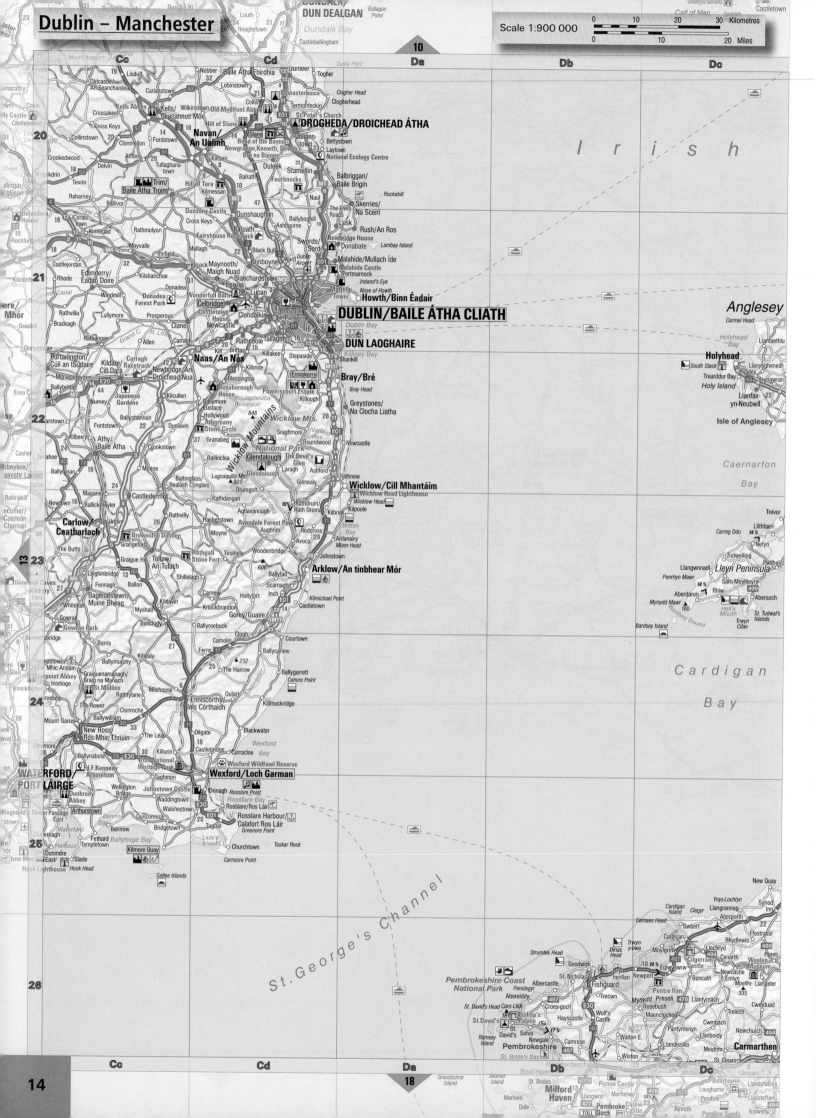

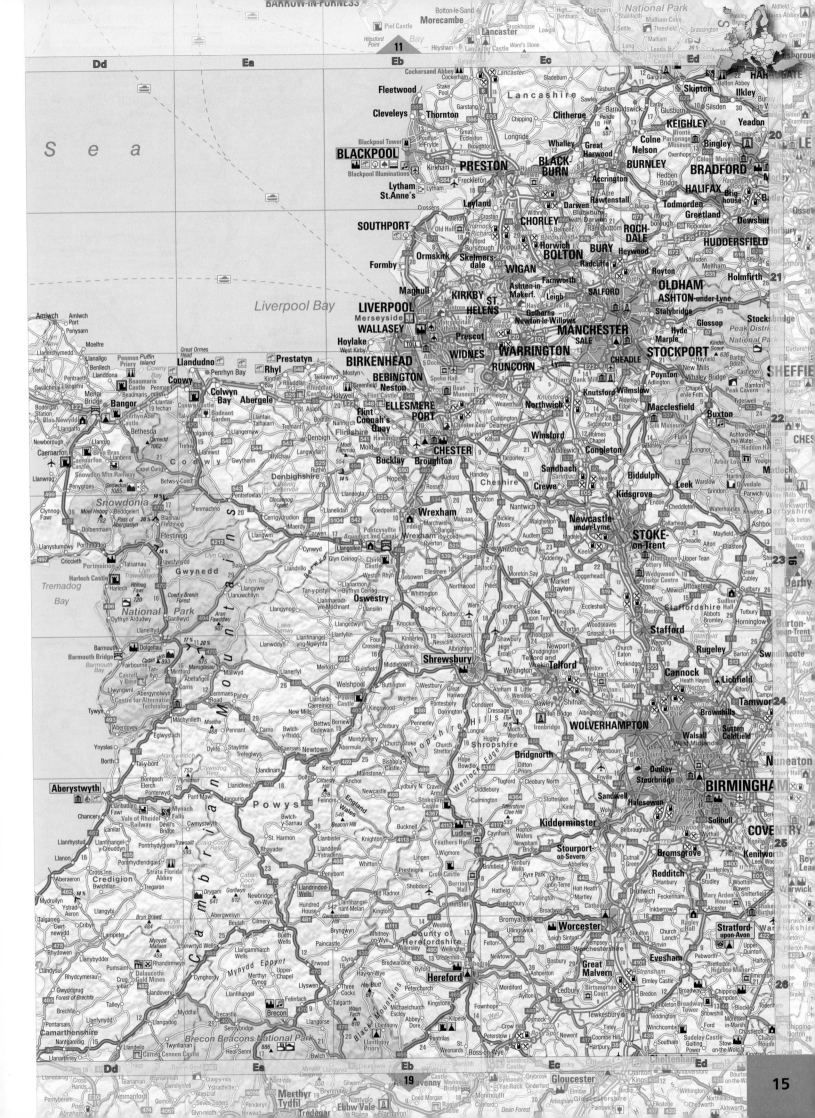

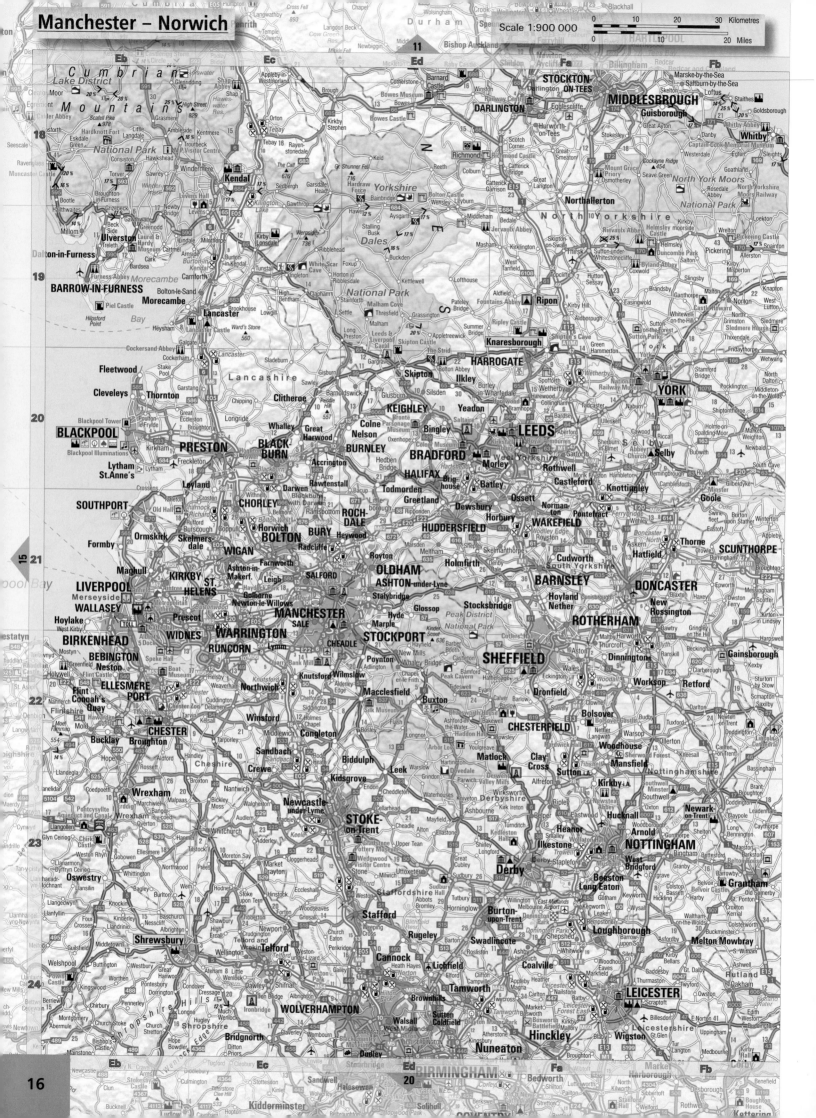

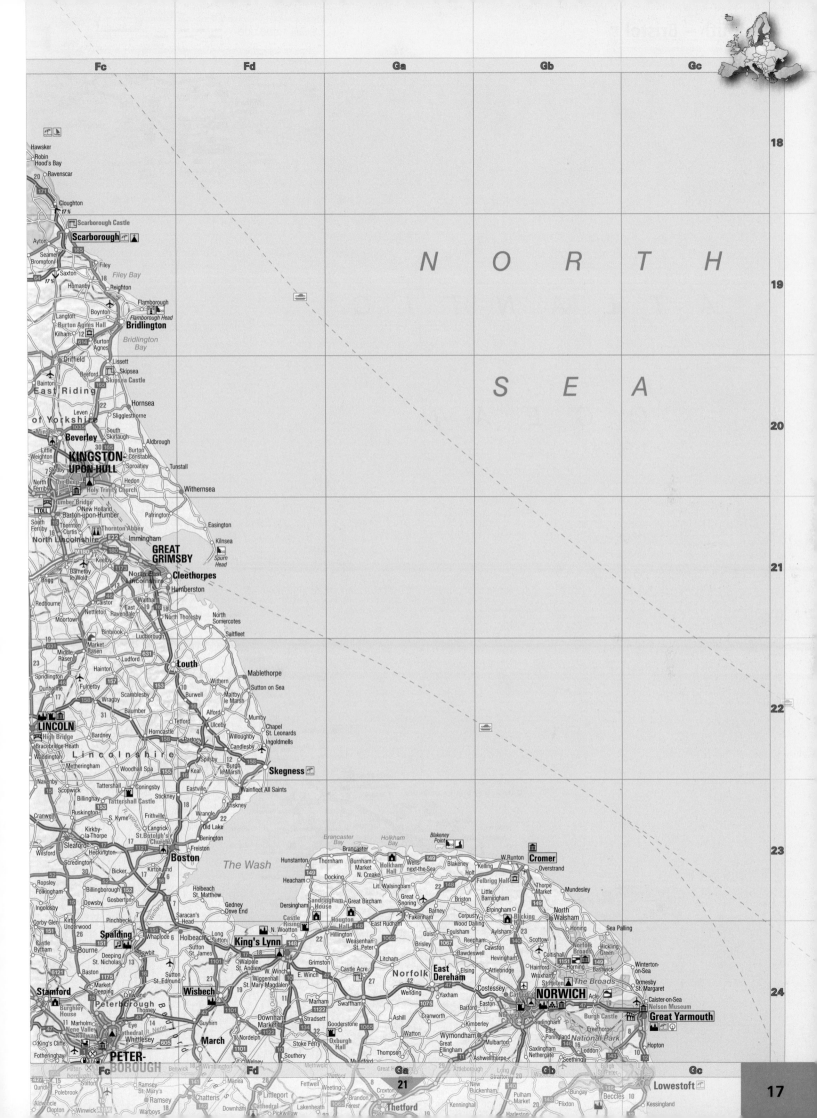

18

Hawsker
Robin
Hood's Bay
20 Ravenscar
171 17 %
Cloughton
Scarborough Castle
Scarborough
Ayton
Seamer
Brompton
165
Saxton
Filey
17 % Humanby
Reighton
Filey Bay
Langtoft
Burton Agnes Hall
Kilham 12
614 Burton
Agnes
Flamborough
Flamborough Head
Bridlington
Bridlington
Bay
Boynton

N O R T H

19

Driffield
Lissett
Beeford Skipsea
Bainton 165 Skipsea Castle
East Riding
Leven 22 Hornsea
of Yorkshire Sigglesthorne
Minster 1035
South
Skirlaugh
Beverley Aldbrough
Little 30 165 Burton
Weighton Constable
7 Skidby Sproatley Tunstall
KINGSTON-
UPON-HULL Hedon
North
Ferriby The Deep Withernsea
Holy Trinity Church
Humber Bridge
New Holland
TOLL Barton-upon-Humber
South Thornton Patrington
Ferriby Curtis Easington
Thornton Abbey Kilnsea
North Lincolnshire Immingham
E22 Spurn
5 M180 180 **GREAT** Head
Keelby **GRIMSBY**
Barnetby 173 North East **Cleethorpes**
le Wold Lincolnshire Humberston
Brigg

S E A

20

Redbourne Caistor
Nettleton East 19 16 18
Moortown Ravendale North Thoresby
North
Binbrook Somercotes
19 631 Ludborough Saltfleet
Middle Market
Rasen Rasen
23 631
Spridlington Ludford Louth
Dunholme Hainton
17 157 Withern Mablethorpe
Fulnetby 153 10 Sutton on Sea
158 Wragby Burwell
Scamblesby Maltby
Baumber le Marsh
31 Alford Mumby
Tetford Ulceby Chapel
Horncastle 4 Willoughby St. Leonards
LINCOLN Bardney Partney Ingoldmells
High Bridge Candlesby
Bracebridge Heath Spilsby 12
Waddington Woodhall Spa Burgh 158 **Skegness**
Navenby 155 Keal le Marsh
Scopwick Coningsby 16
Billinghay Eastville
Tattershall 52 Wainfleet All Saints
153 Stickney
Ruskington Tattershall Castle
Cranwell Frithville Friskney
S. Kyme Langrick 18 Wrangle
Kirkby- Old Lake
la-Thorpe Benington
Sleaford St.Botolph's Freiston
Heckington Church
Wilsford 1121 **Boston**
Scredington Kirton end
Bicker 17

21

Brancaster
Bay Holkham
Brancaster Bay Blakeney
Point
Hunstanton Thornham W.Runton **Cromer**
Heacham Burnham Wells Kelling Overstrand
Market next-the-Sea 149 Blakeney
149 Docking N. Creake Holt Felbrigg Hall
Lit. Walsingham Thorpe
Holbeach Dersingham Great Great Briston Market Mundesley
St. Matthew Bircham Snoring Barney North
Gedney Sandringham Houghton Fakenham Wood Dalling Blicking Walsham
Dove End House Hall Guist 149
Saracen's Castle Hillington East Rudham Reepham
Head Rising N. Wootton Weasenham Brisley Aylsham Honing
Long St. Peter 1065 Cawston Norfolk
Spalding Sutton **King's Lynn** 148 Foulsham Bawdeswell Broads
151 Holbeach Litcham Elsing Hickling
Bourne Whaplode 6 Walpole Grimston Hainford Green
Bowbit St. Andrew Castle Acre Scottow
Deeping Sutton Wiggenhall E. Winch **Norfolk** **East** 148 Winterton-
St. Nicholas St. James St. Mary Magdalen Dereham Coltishall on-Sea
13 Marham Wendling St. Margaret
Stamford Market **Wisbech** Swaffham Yaxham Costessey Ormesby
Deeping Downham **NORWICH** Caister-on-Sea
Burghley Crowland Market Stradsett Nelson Museum
House Thorney Nordelph 1101 Goodestone Wymondham **Great Yarmouth**
Peterborough Guyhirn Stoke Ferry Great Mulbarton Freethorpe
Eye Whittlesey Ellingham Loddon Hopton
Nene Valley **March** 605 Thompson
Railway Whittlesey Welney Southery Ashwellthorpe Seething
PETER-
Fotheringhay **BOROUGH**

22

23

24

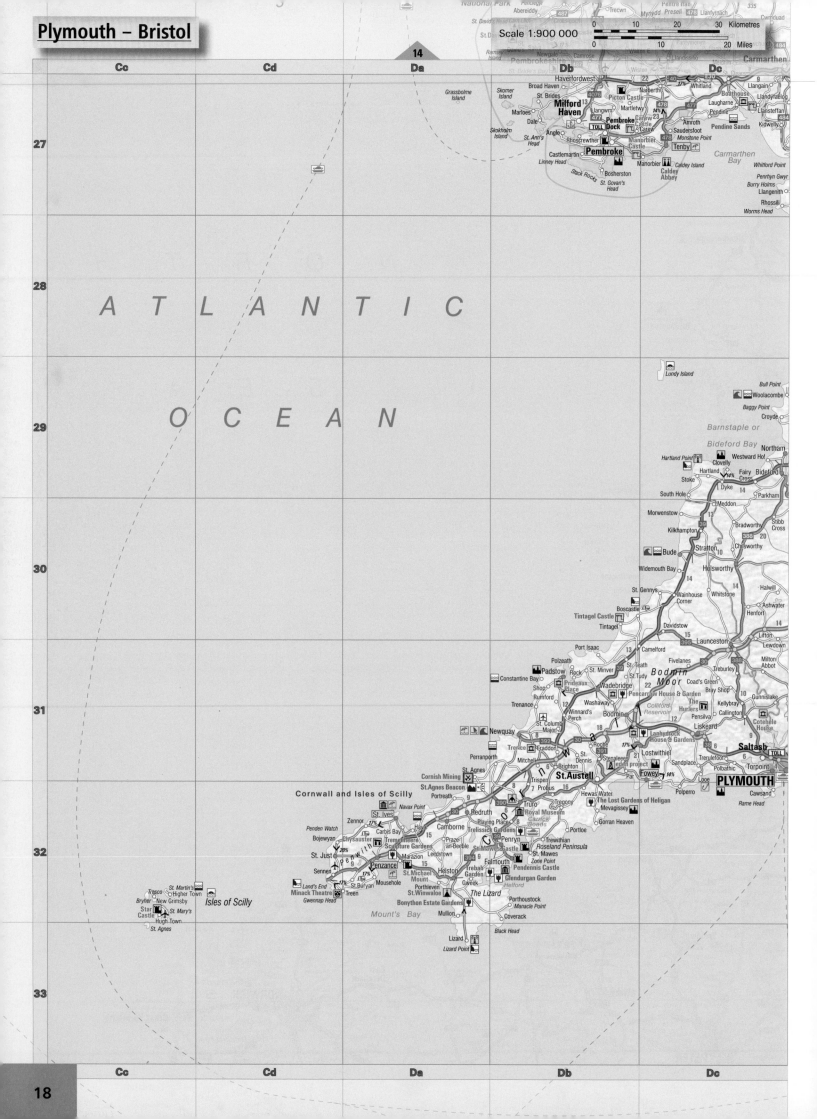

Scale 1:900 000

| | 0 | 10 | 20 | 30 | Kilometres |
| | 0 | | 10 | | 20 | Miles |

14

Cc   Cd   Da   Db   Dc

27

ATLANTIC

28

OCEAN

29

Carmarthen

Pembrokeshire

Grassholme Island

Broad Haven
St. Brides
Milford Haven
Llangwm
Martletwy
Whitland
Llandyfaelog
Llangain
Boathouse
Marloes
Dale
Skomer Island
Skokholm Island
St. Ann's Head
Angle
Rhoscrowther
Pembroke Dock
TOLL
Carew Castle
Carew
Saundersfoot
Amroth
Monstone Point
Pendine Sands
Kidwelly
Castlemartin
Pembroke
Manorbier Castle
Manorbier
Tenby
Caldey Island
Caldey Abbey
Carmarthen Bay
Whitford Point
Penrhyn Gwyr
Burry Holms
Llangenith
Rhossili
Worms Head
Limney Head
Stack Rocks
Bosherston
St. Govan's Head

Lundy Island
Bull Point
Woolacombe
Baggy Point
Croyde
Barnstaple or Bideford Bay
Northam
Hartland Point
Westward Ho!
Clovelly
Hartland
Fairy Cross
Bideford
Stoke
Dyke
Parkham
South Hole
Meddon
Morwenstow
Bradworthy
Stibb Cross
Kilkhampton
Chilsworthy
Bude
Stratton
Holsworthy
Widemouth Bay
St. Gennys
Wainhouse Corner
Whitstone
Halwill
Ashwater
Boscastle
Henford
Tintagel Castle
Tintagel
Davidstow
Lifton
Lewdown
Port Isaac
Camelford
Launceston
Milton Abbot
Polzeath
St. Teath
Fivelanes
Treburley
Rock
St. Minver
St. Tudy
Bodmin Moor
Coad's Green
Gunnislake
Padstow
Wadebridge
Pencarrow House & Garden
Bray Shop
Constantine Bay
Shop
Prideaux Place
The Hurlers
Kellybray
Callington
Rumford
Washaway
Bodmin
Pensilva
Cotehele House
Trenance
Winnard's Perch
Colliford Reservoir
Liskeard
St. Columb Major
Roche
Lanhydrock House & Gardens
Trerulefoot
Saltash
Newquay
Lostwithiel
Polbathic
Torpoint
Perranporth
Trenance
Fraddon
St. Dennis
Stenalees
eden project
Sandplace
PLYMOUTH
Mitchell
Brighton
Par
Fowey
Looe
Cawsand
St. Agnes
Trispen
St.Austell
Rame Head
Cornish Mining
St.Agnes Beacon
Probus
Hewas Water
Polperro
Portreath
Tregony
The Lost Gardens of Heligan
Mevagissey
Cornwall and Isles of Scilly
Truro
Royal Museum
Gorran Haven
St. Ives
Navax Point
Redruth
Playing Place
Carrick Roads
Portloe
Penden Watch
Zennor
Hayle
Camborne
Praze-an-Beeble
Trelissick Gardens
Bojewyan
Carbis Bay
Leedstown
Penryn
Trewithian
Roseland Peninsula
Chysauster
Tremenheere Sculpture Gardens
St.Mawes Castle
St. Mawes
St. Just
Marazion
St.Michael's Mount
Helston
Trebah Garden
Falmouth
Zone Point
Pendennis Castle
Sennen
Penzance
Gweek
Glendurgan Garden
Land's End
Mousehole
Porthleven
Helford
Minack Theatre
St.Wimwaloe
Bonython Estate Gardens
The Lizard
Porthoustock
Manacle Point
St. Buryan
Treen
Gwennap Head
Mount's Bay
Mullion
Coverack
St. Martin's
Higher Town
Tresco
New Grimsby
St. Mary's
Bryher
Star Castle
St. Agnes
Hugh Town
Isles of Scilly
Lizard
Lizard Point
Black Head

30

31

32

33

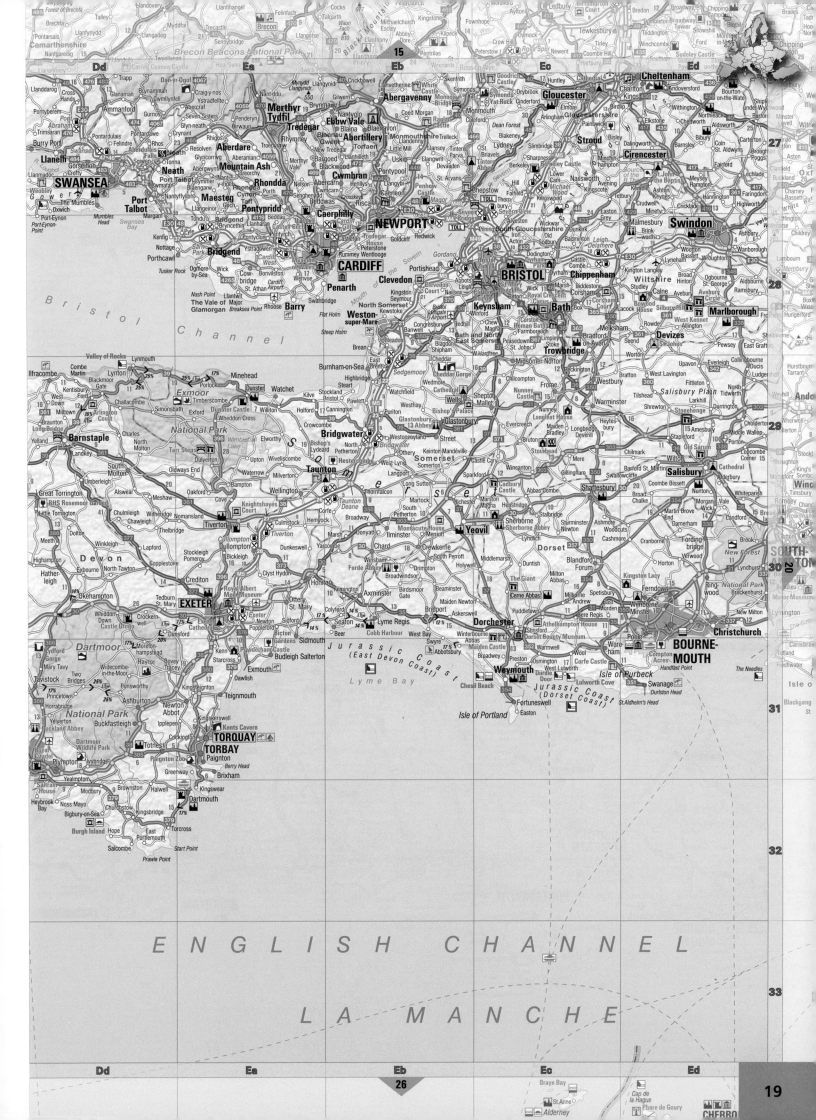

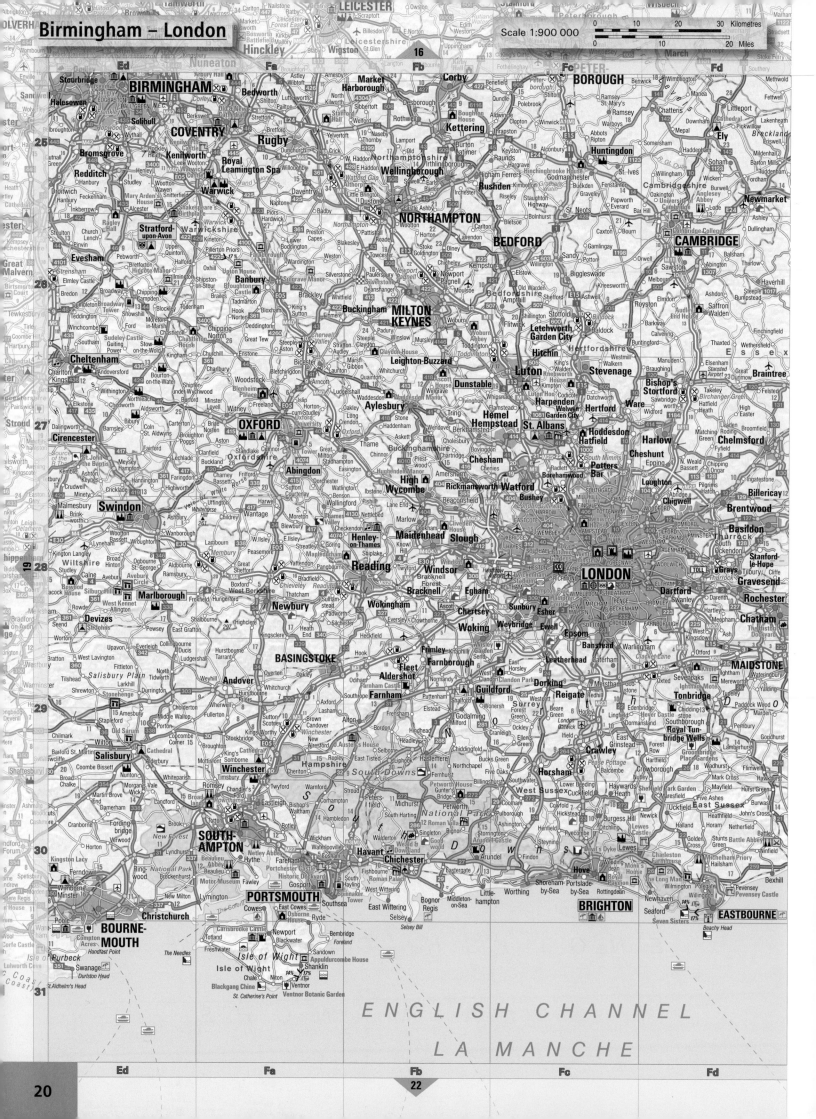

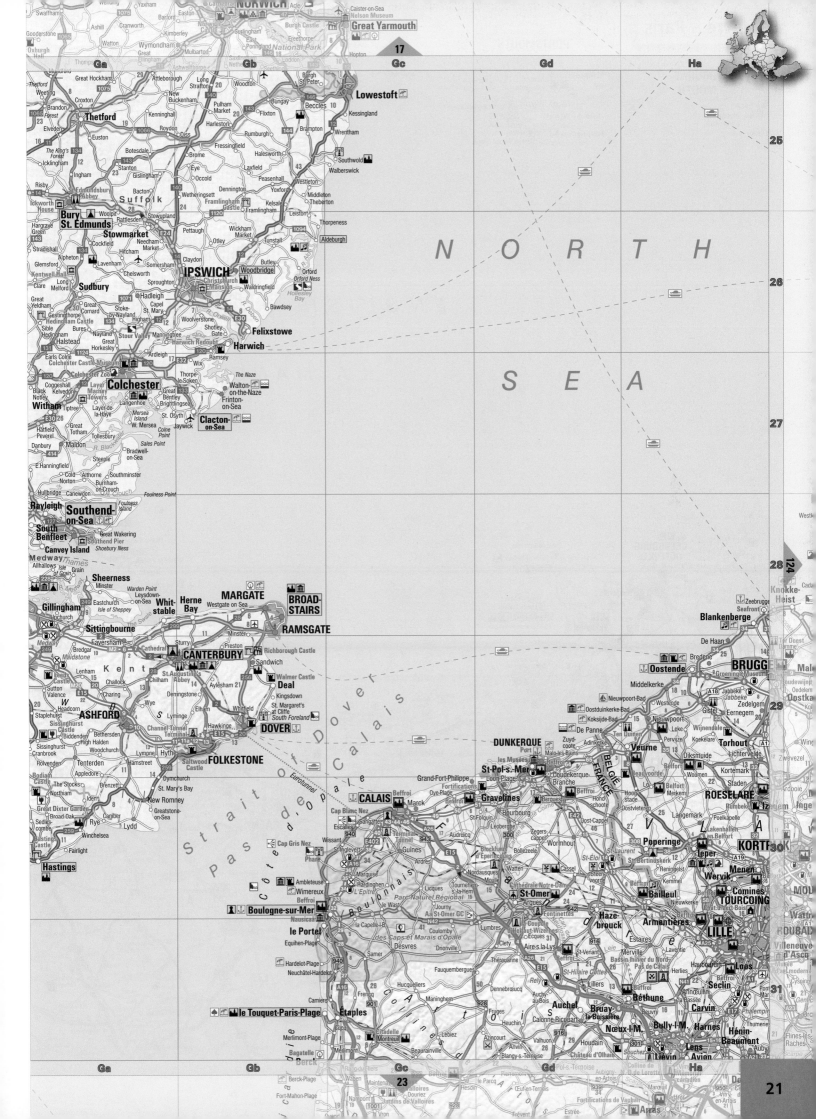

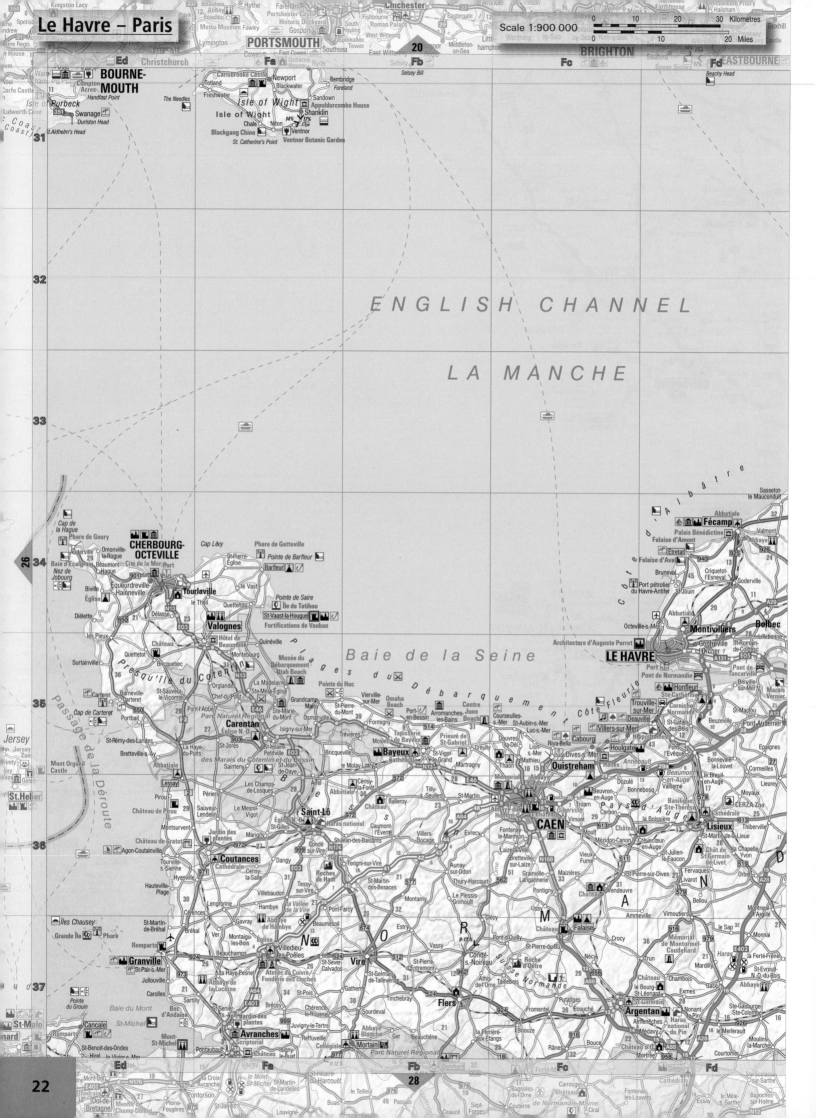

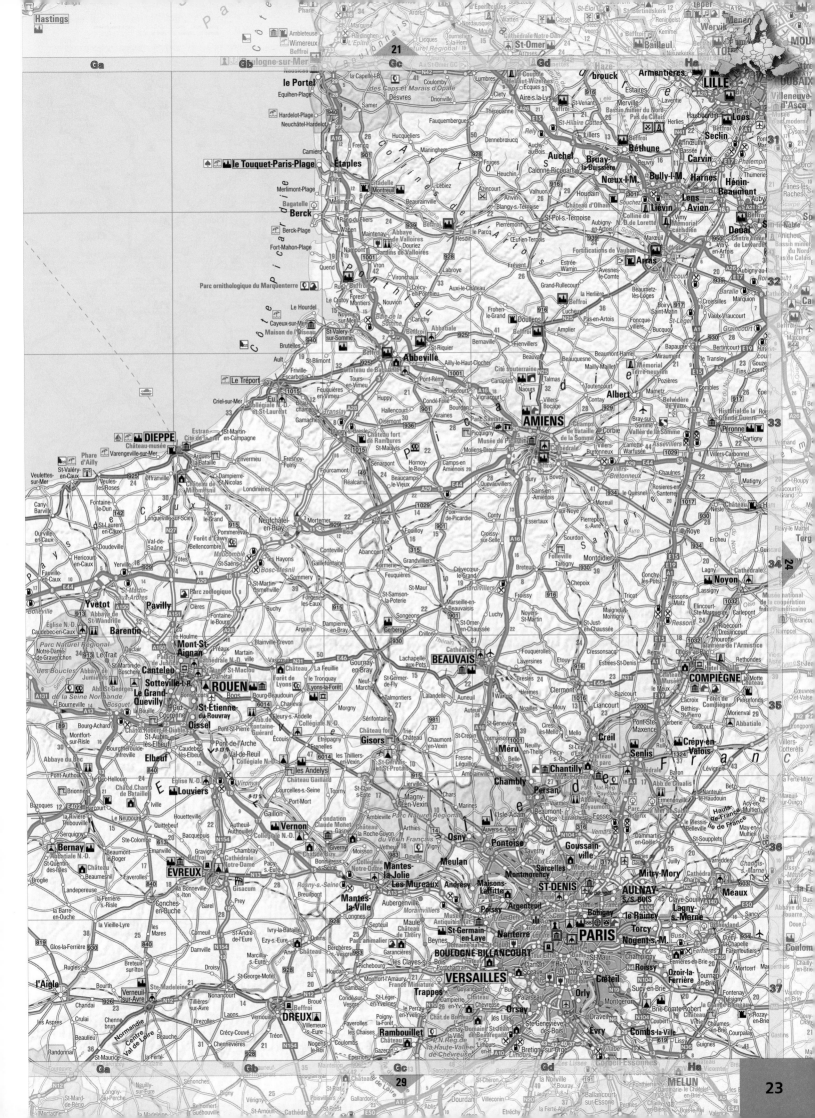

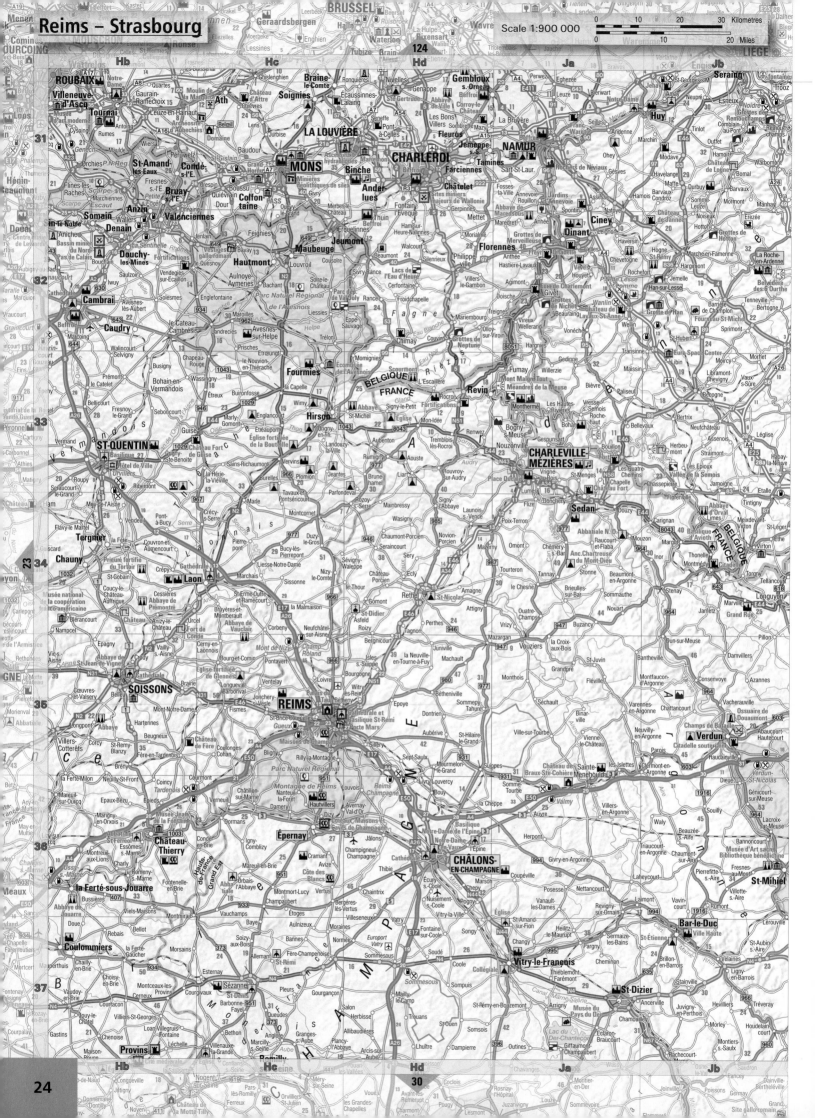

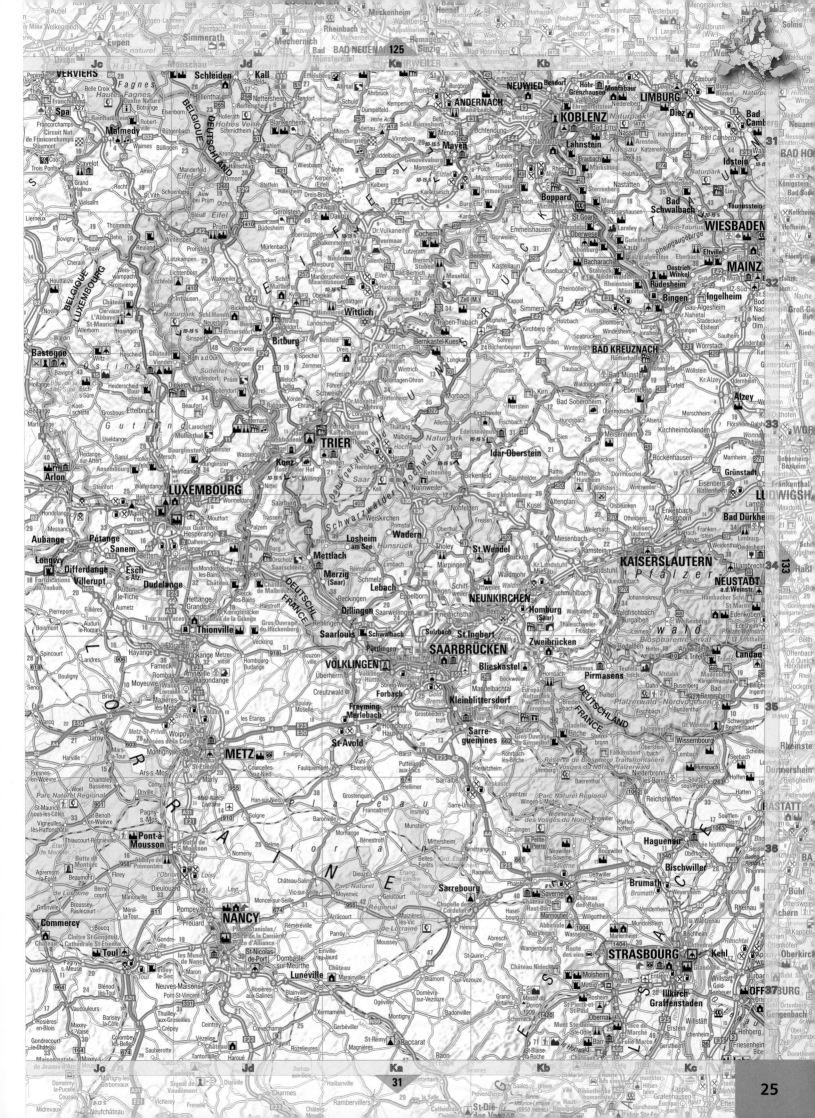

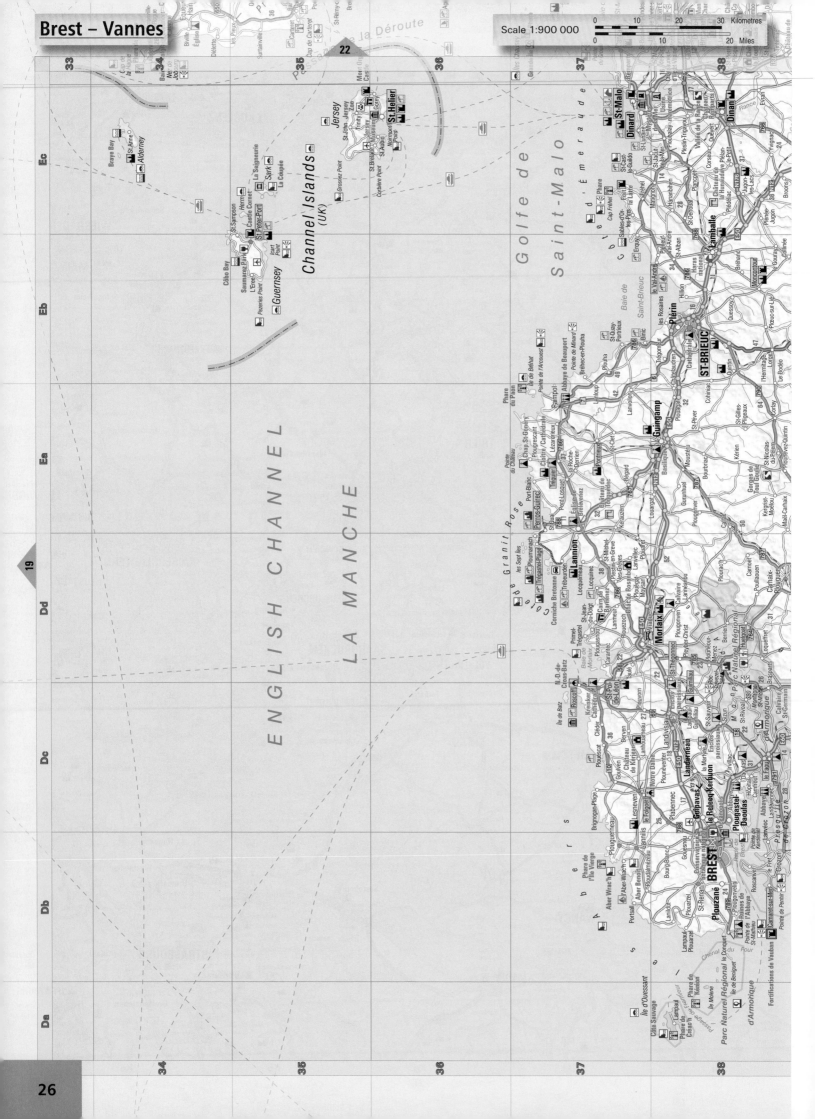

Scale 1:900 000

0   10   20   30 Kilometres
0   10   20 Miles

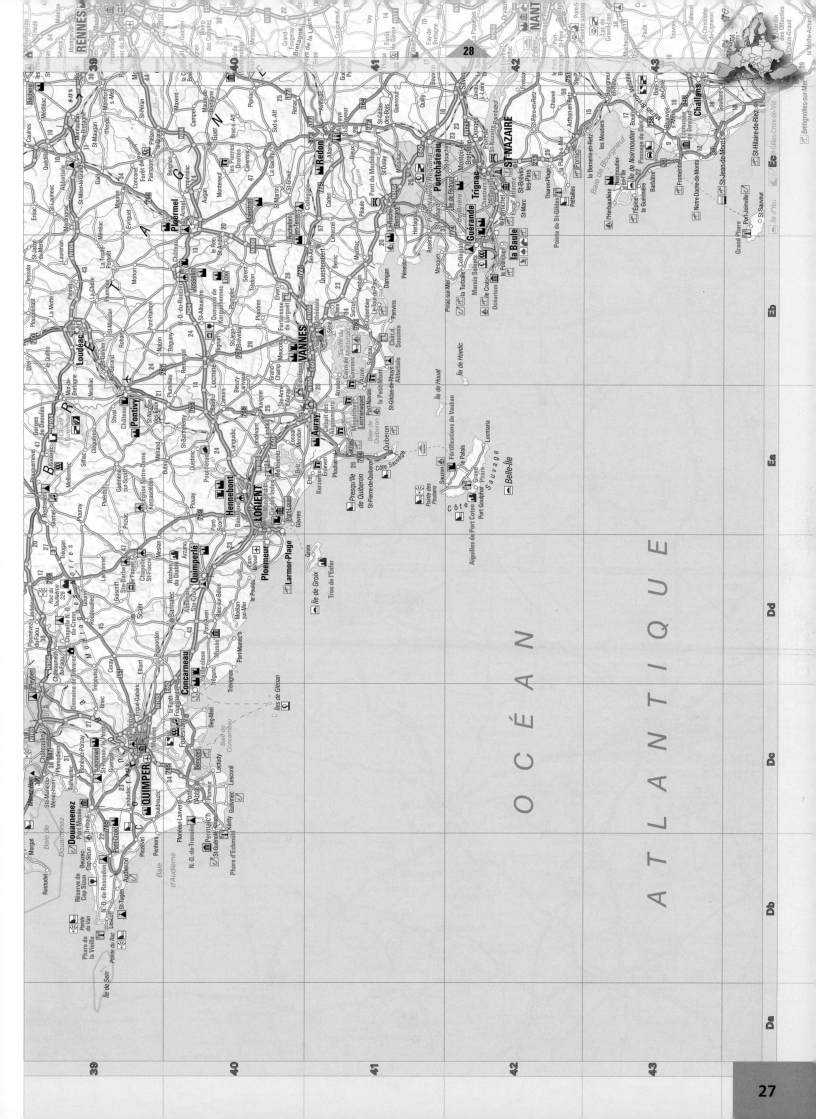

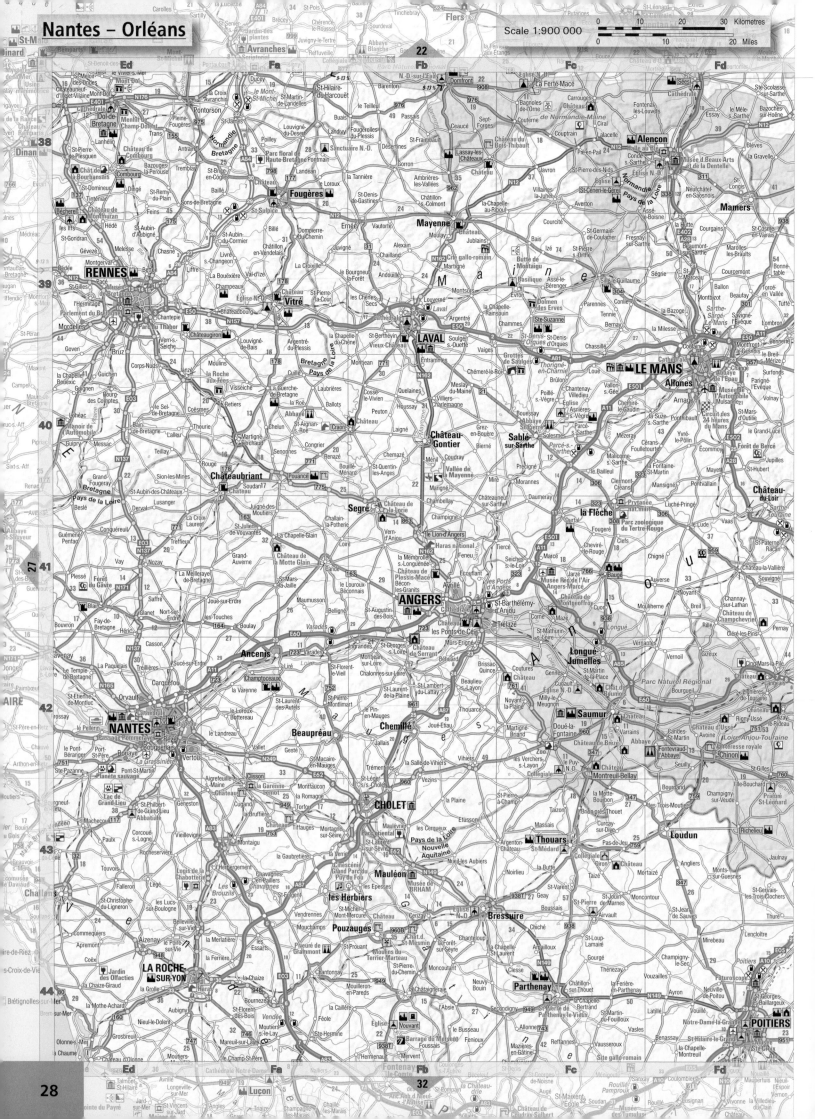

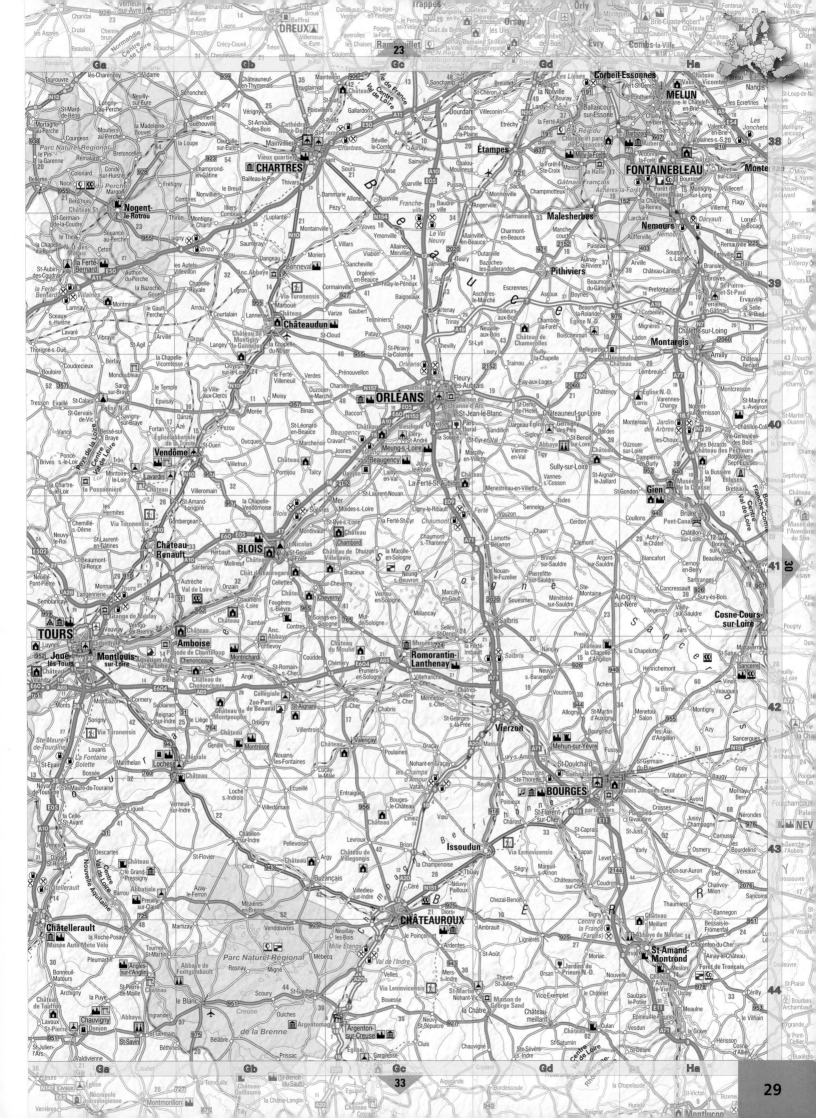

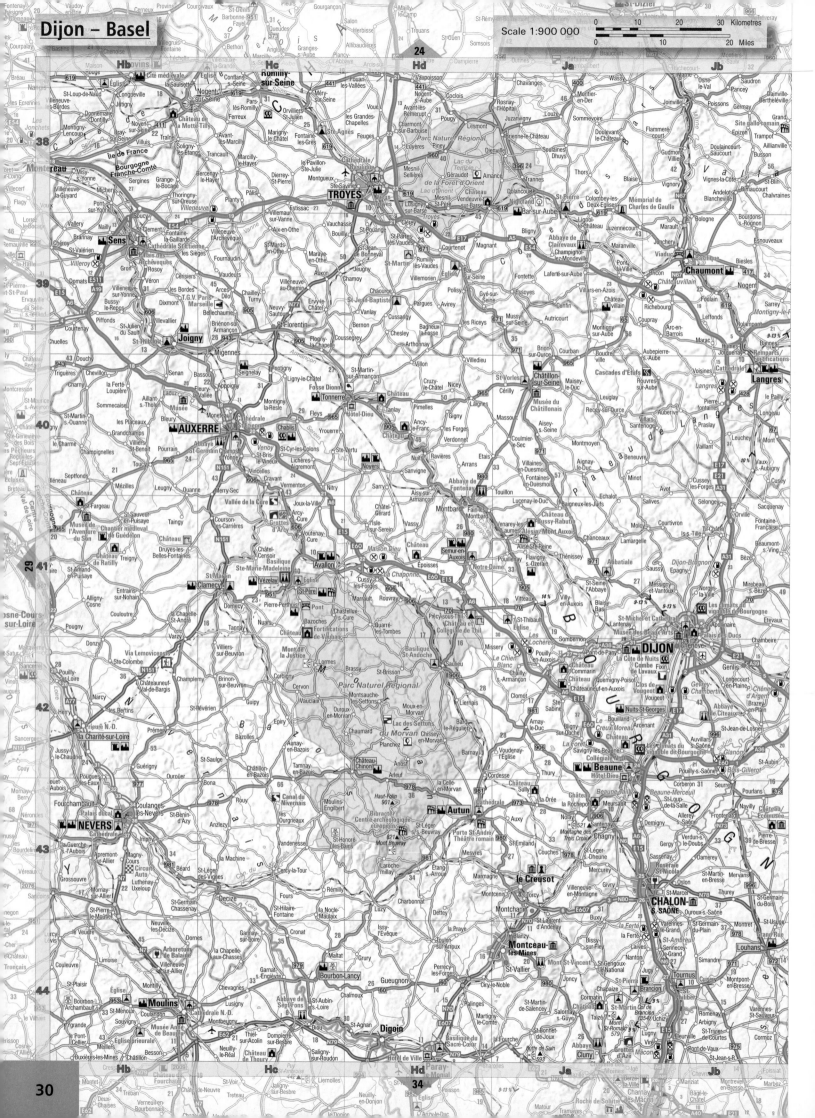

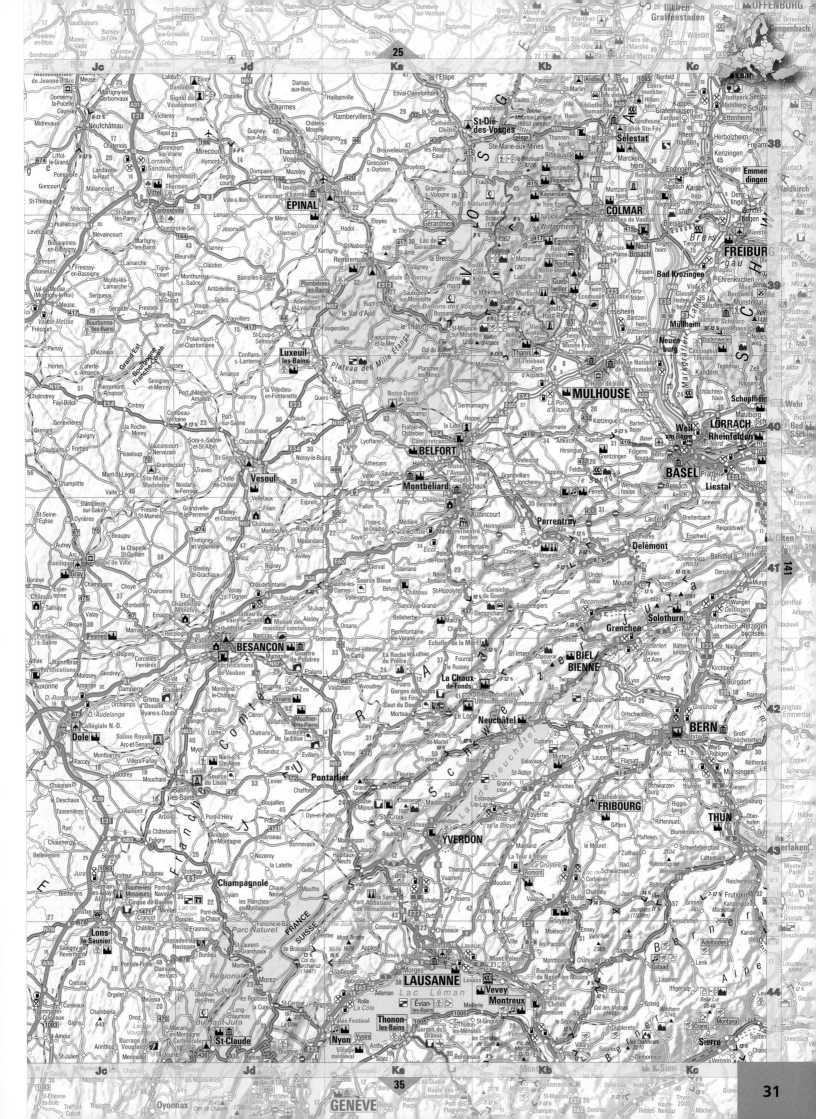

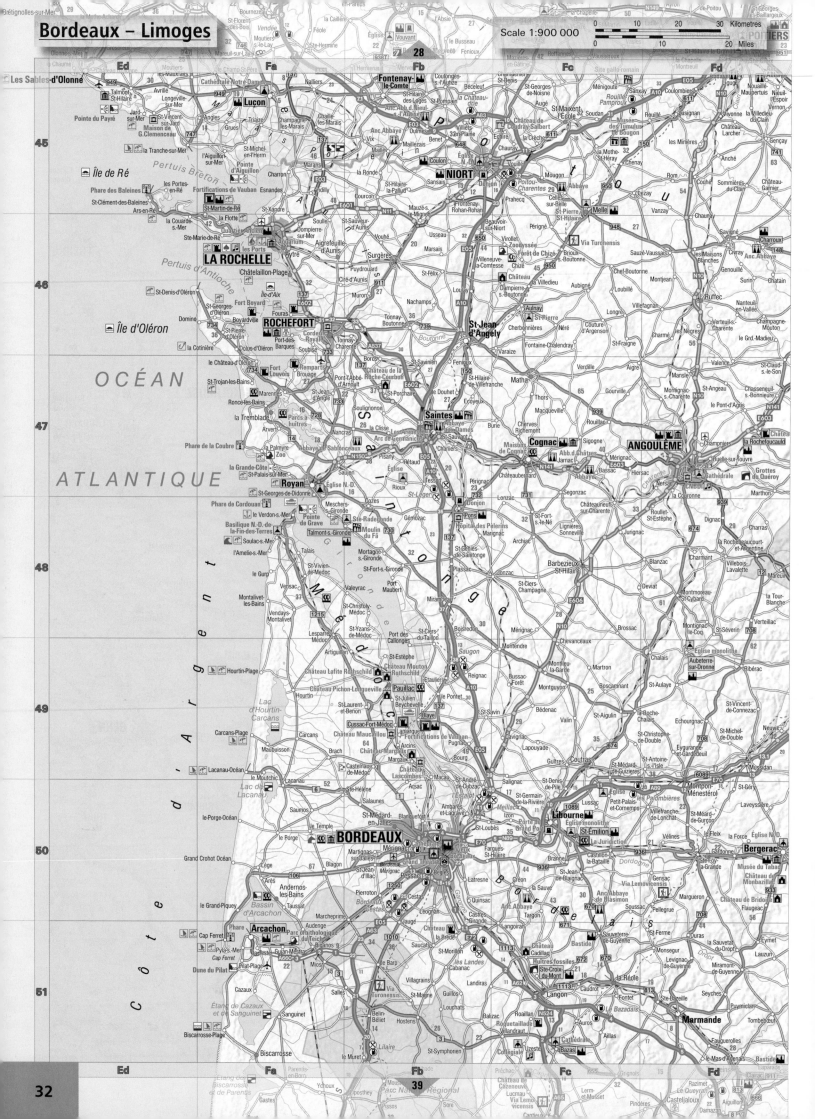

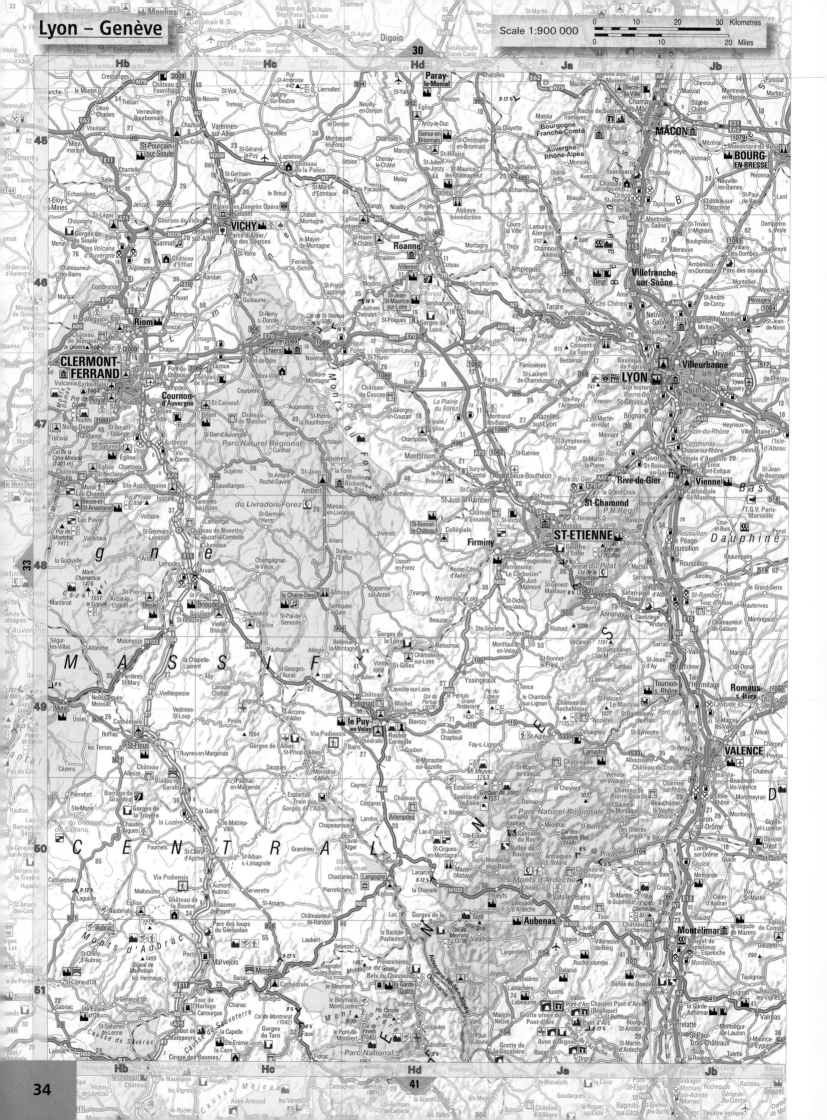

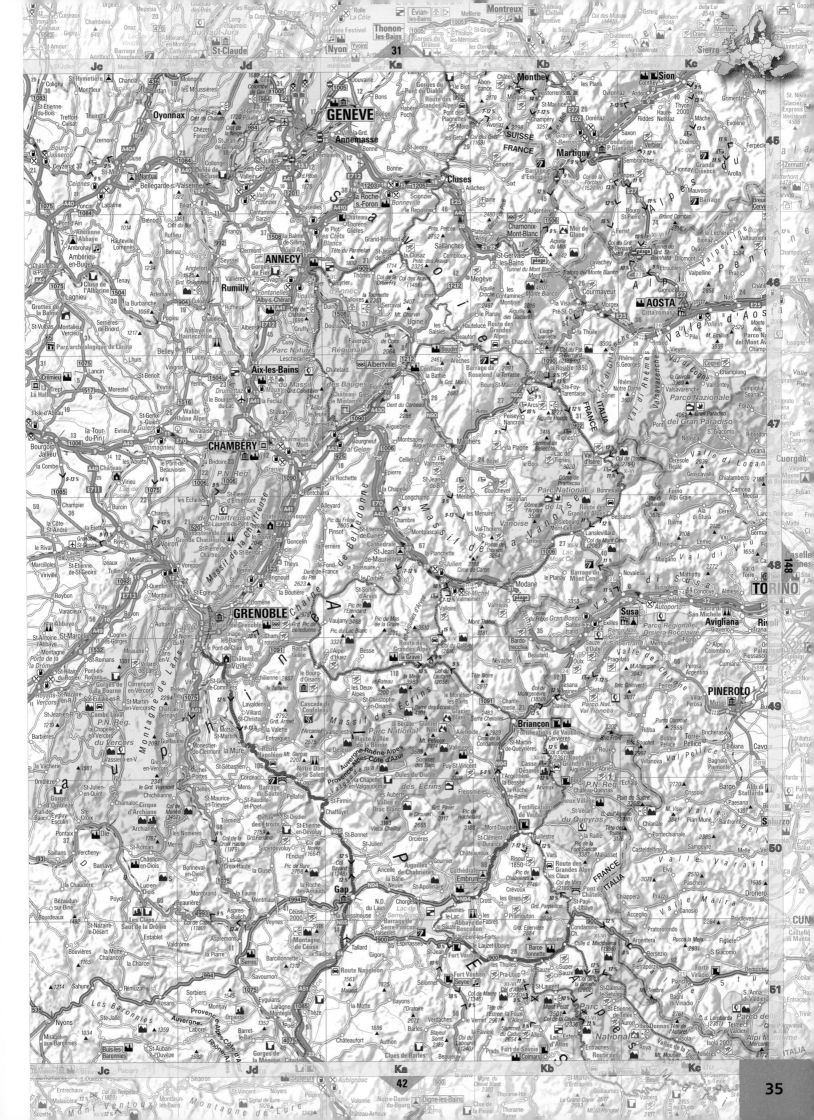

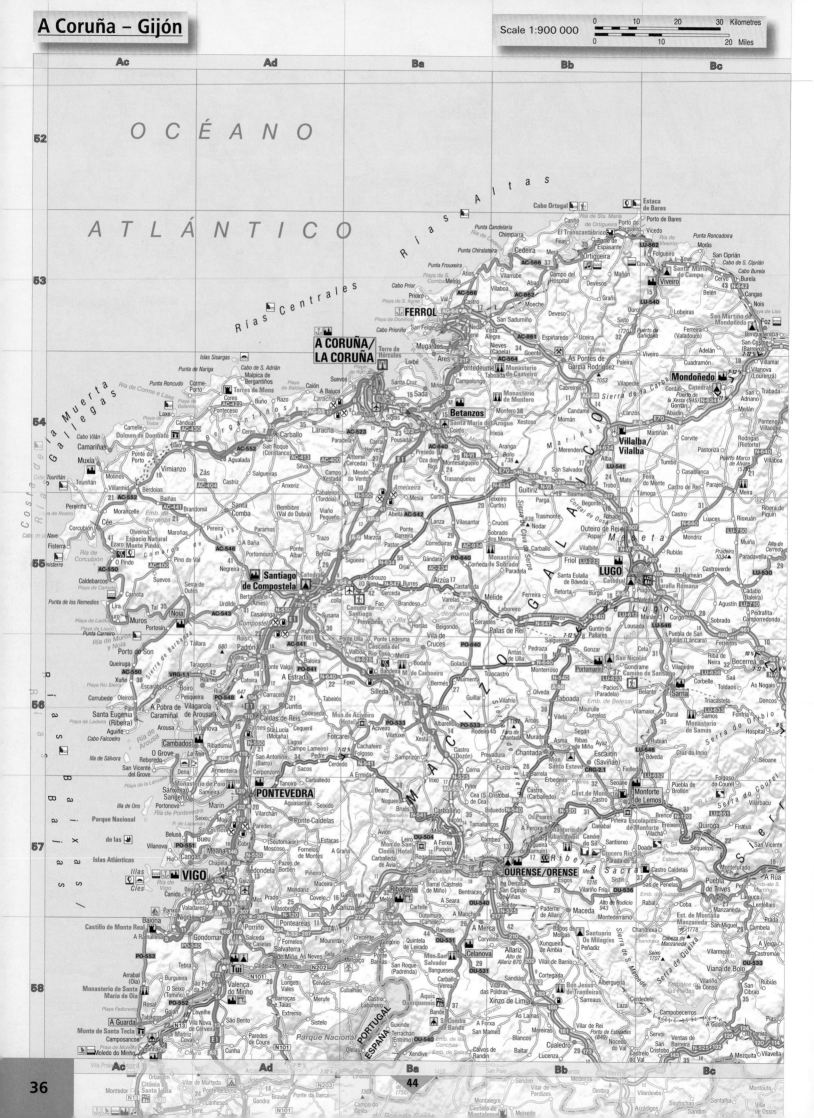

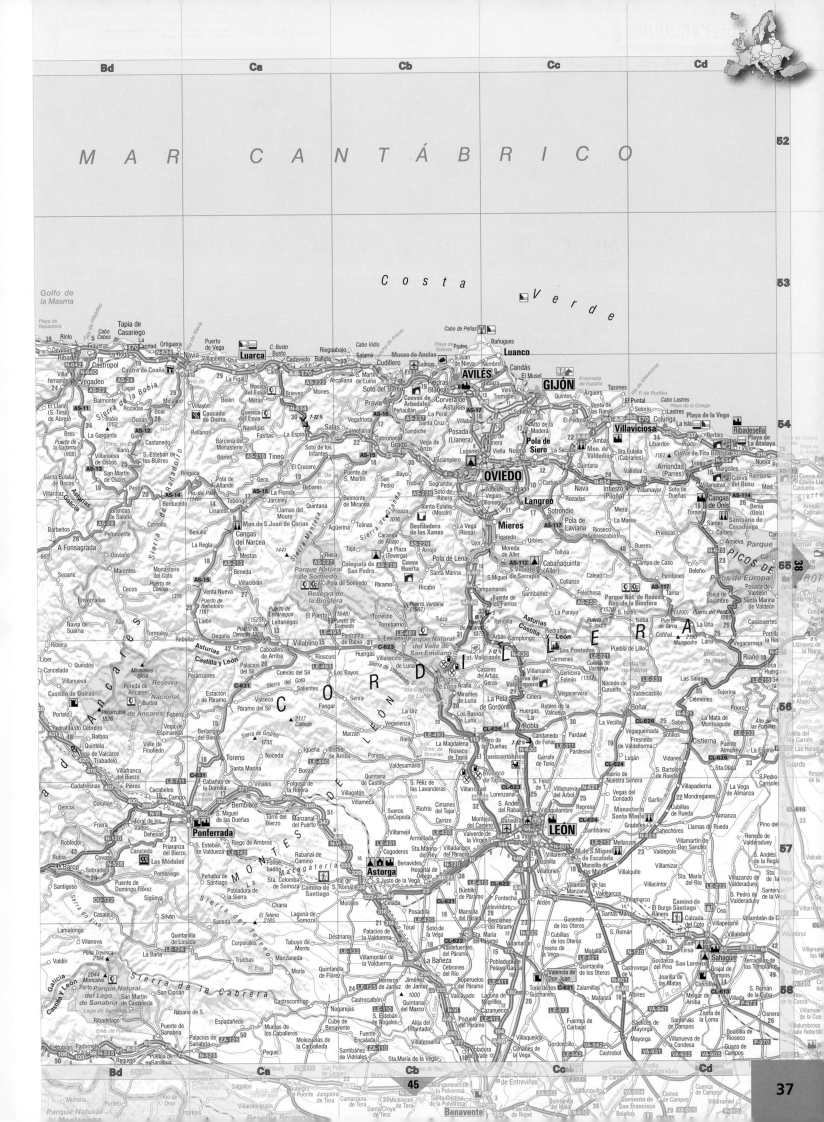

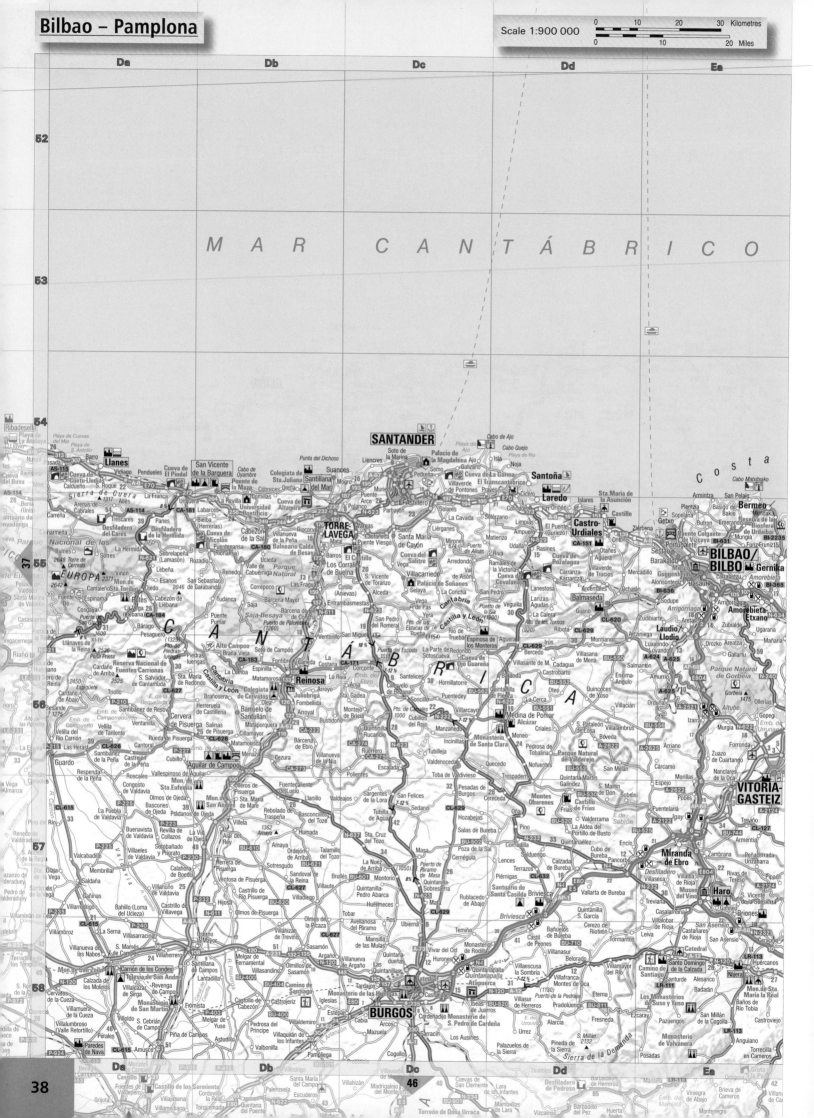

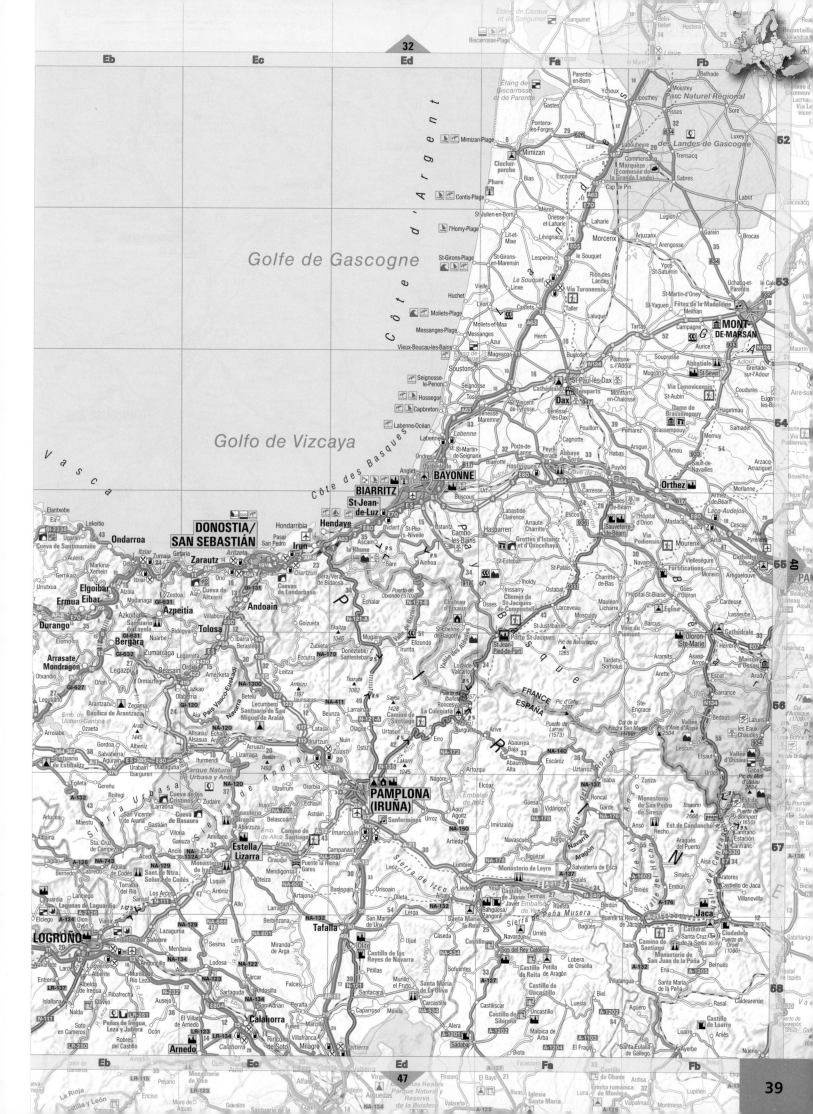

Golfe de Gascogne

Golfe de Vizcaya

Vasca

Côte d'Argent

Côte des Basques

Parc Naturel Régional
des Landes de Gascogne

**MONT-
DE-MARSAN**

Dax

BAYONNE

BIARRITZ

Orthez

**DONOSTIA/
SAN SEBASTIÁN**

**PAMPLONA
(IRUÑA)**

**Estella/
Lizarra**

Tafalla

LOGROÑO

Calahorra

Arnedo

Jaca

FRANCE
ESPAÑA

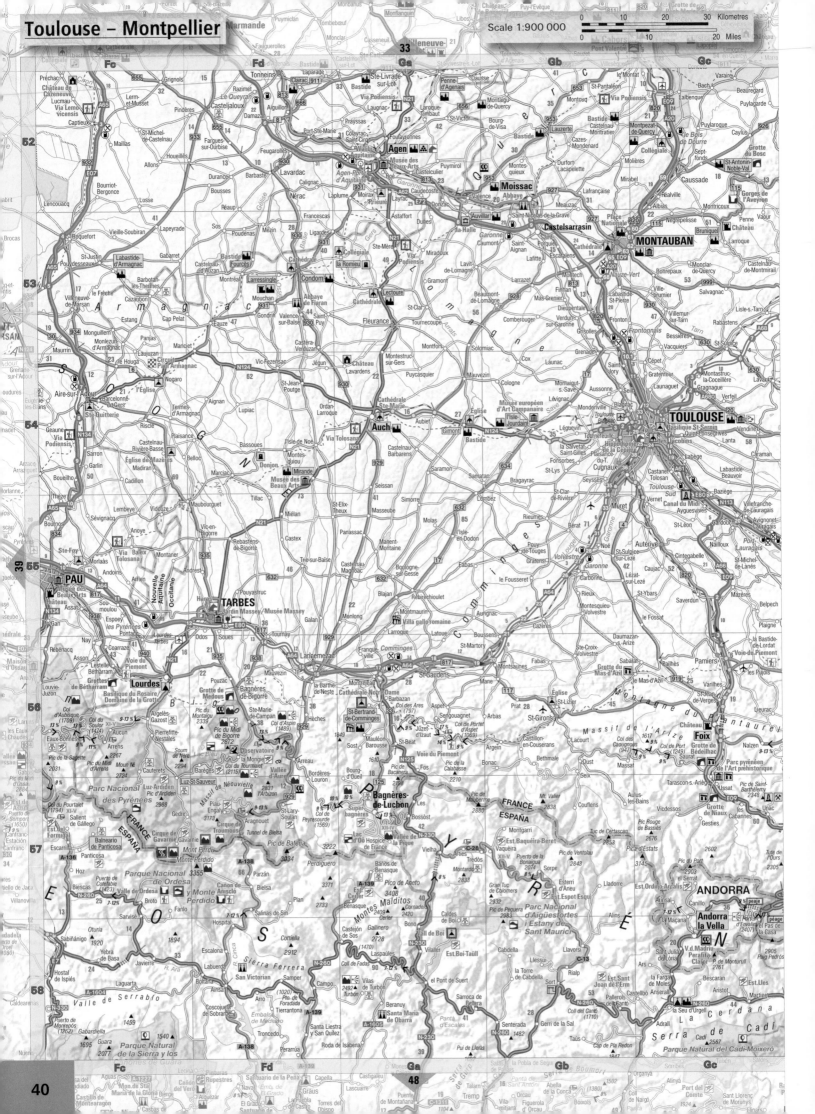

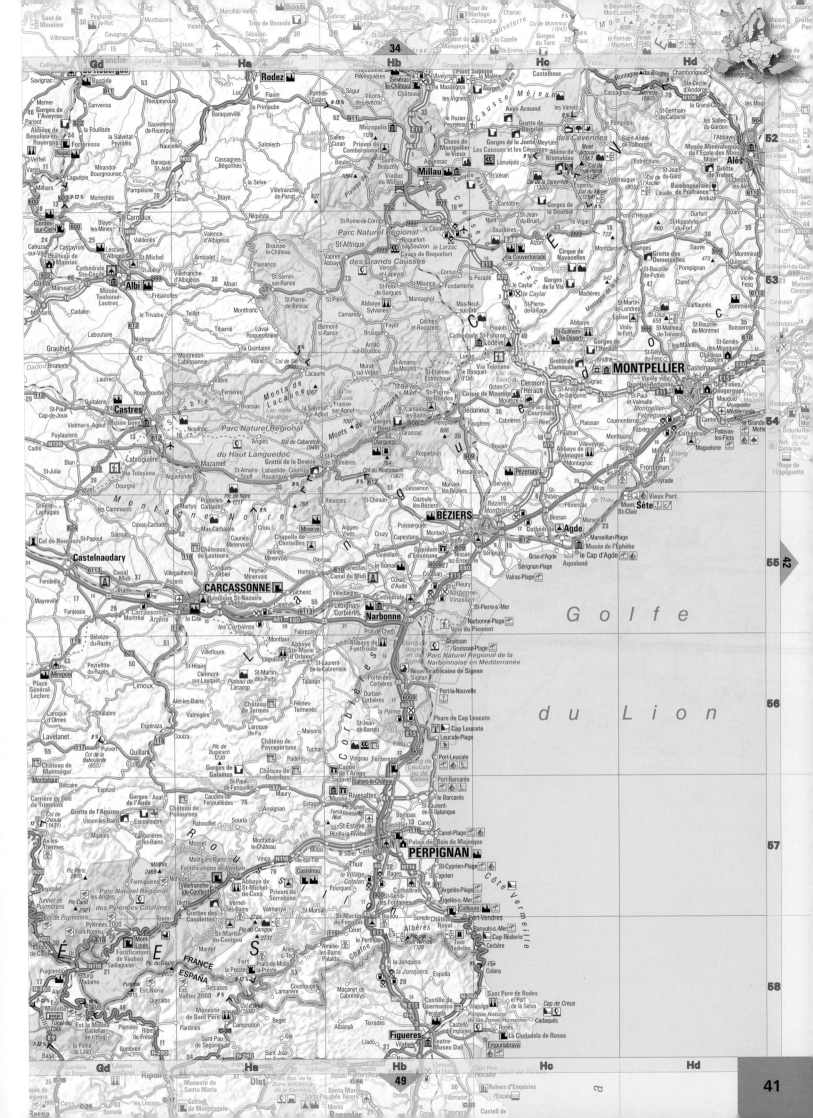

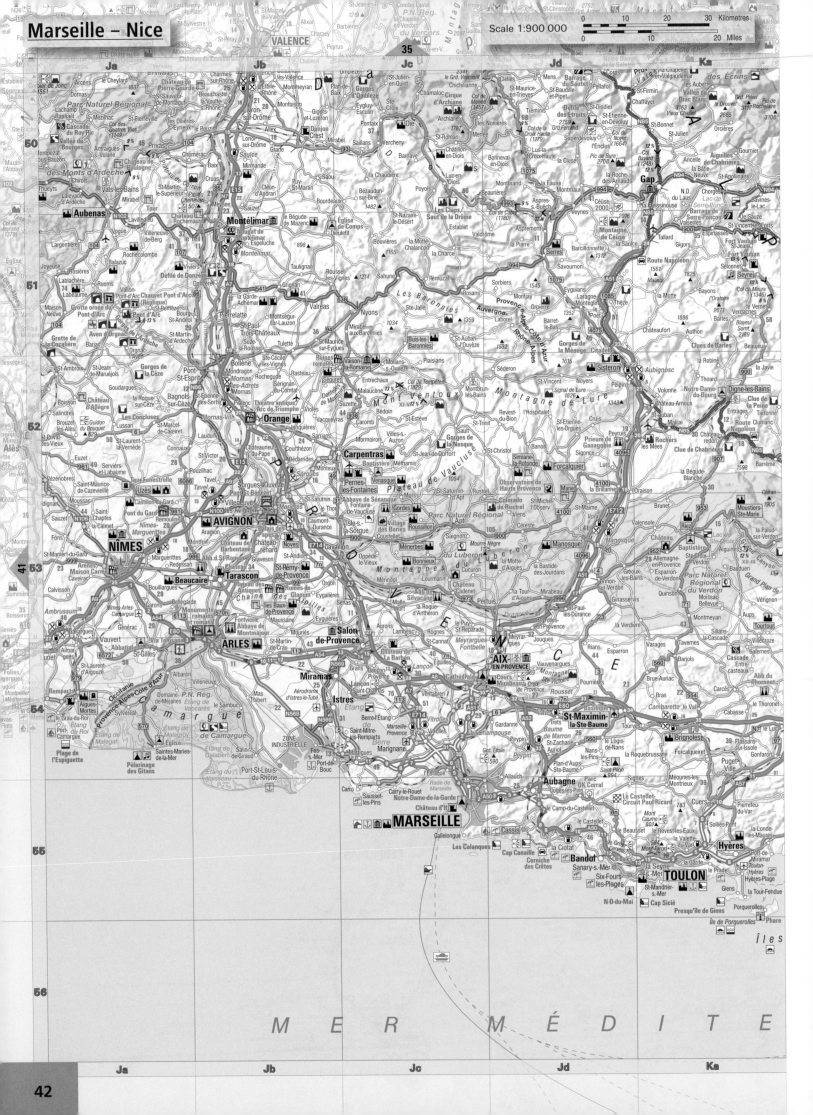

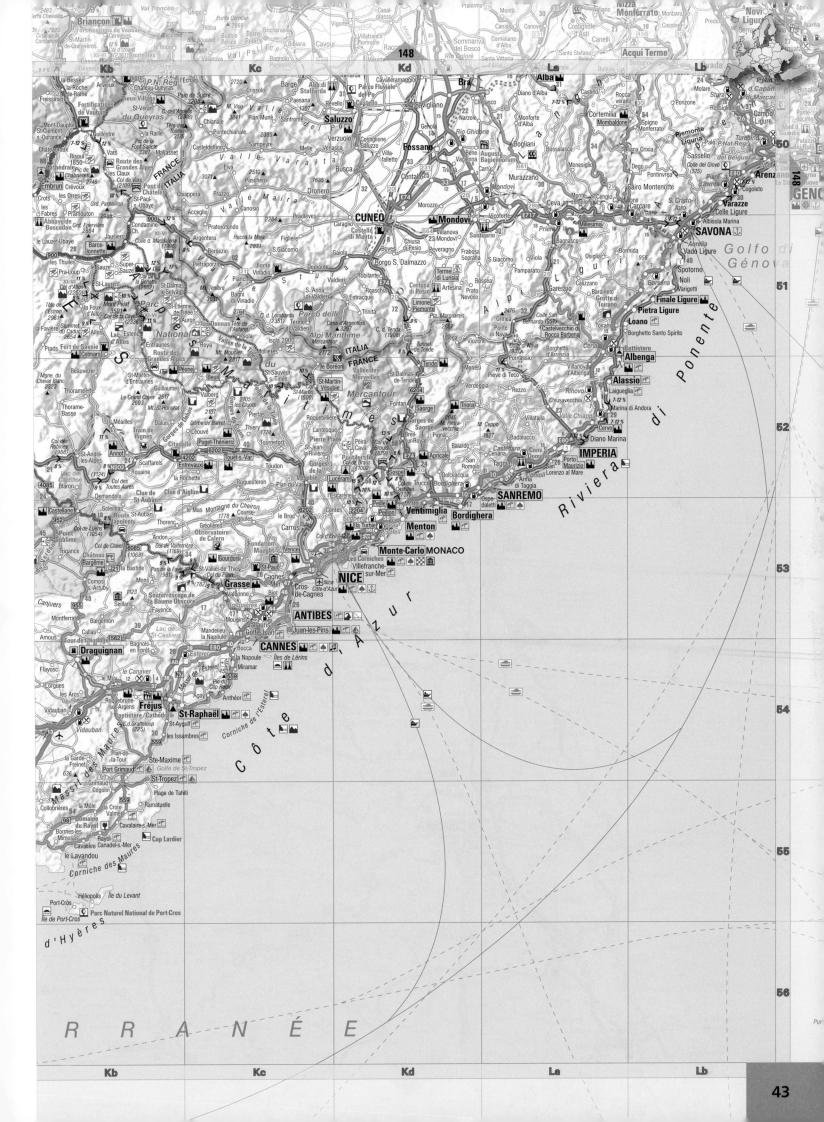

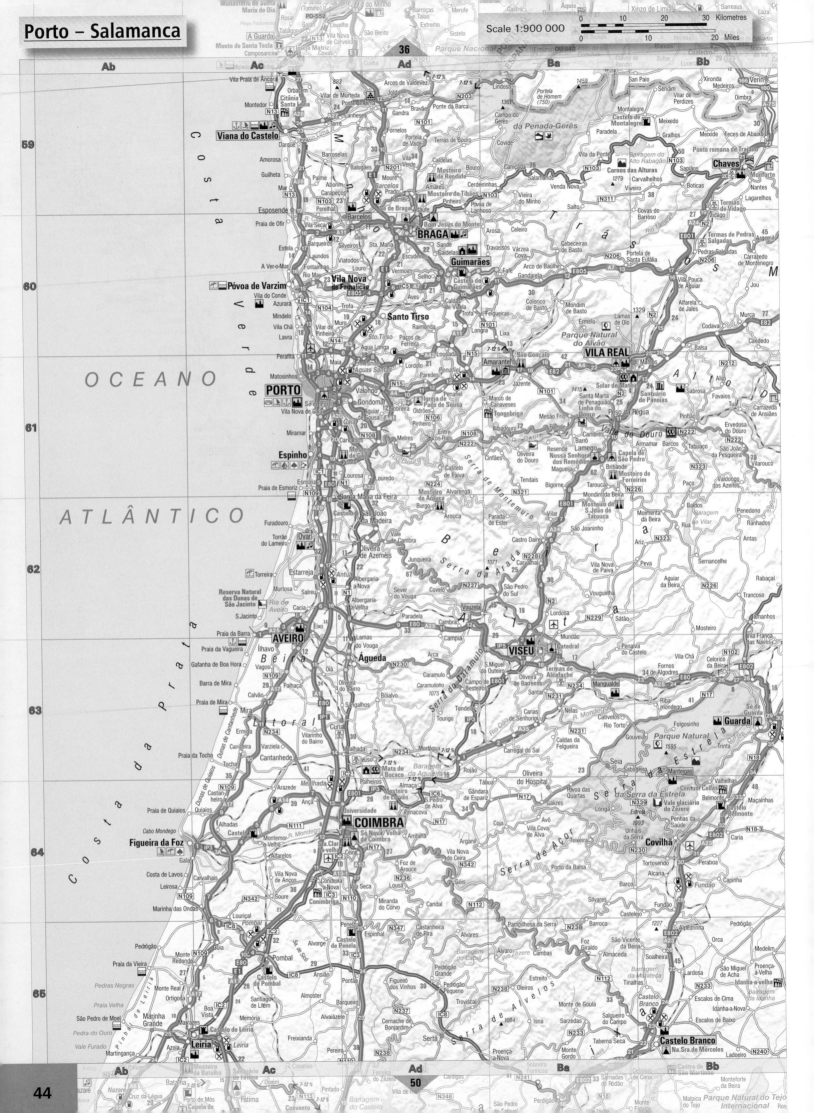

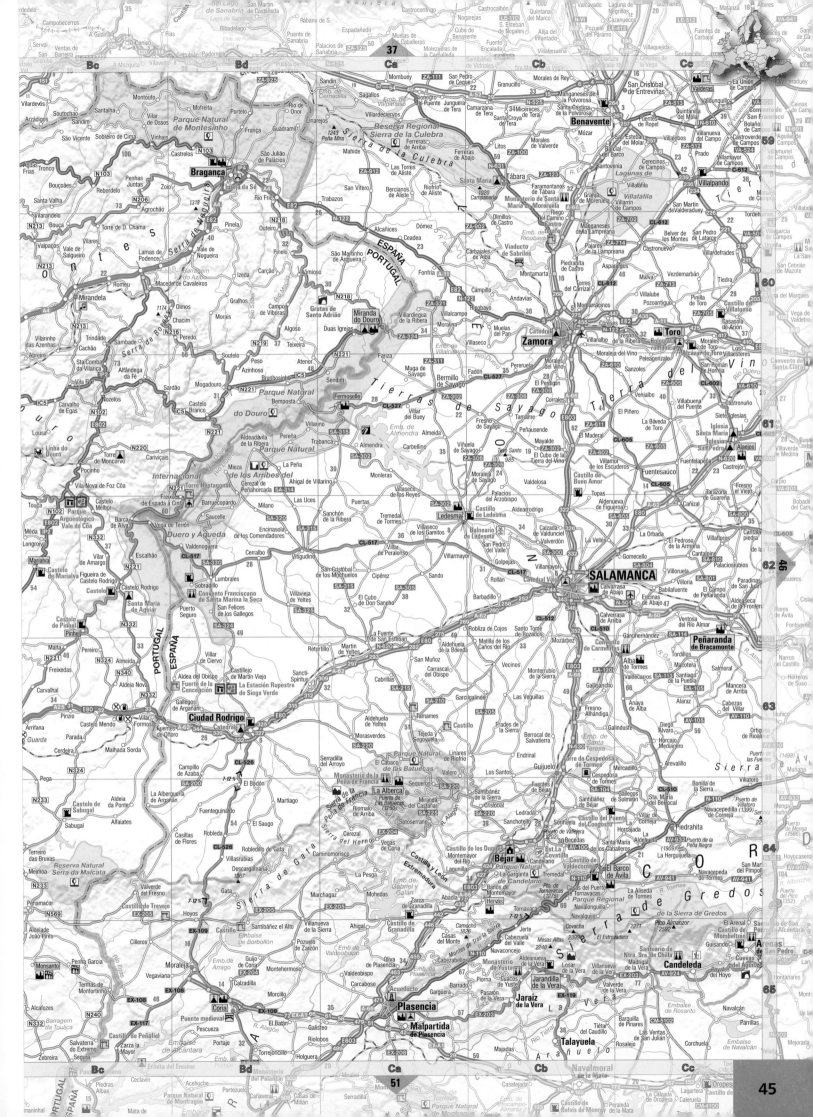

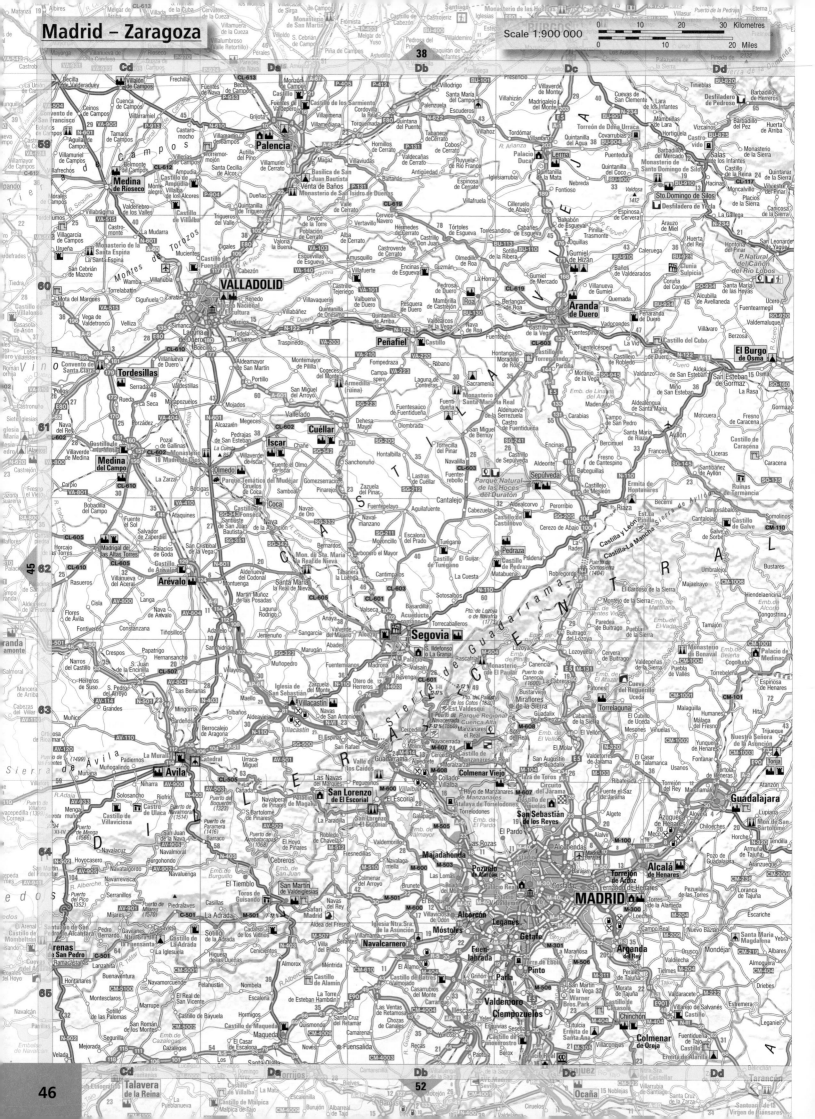

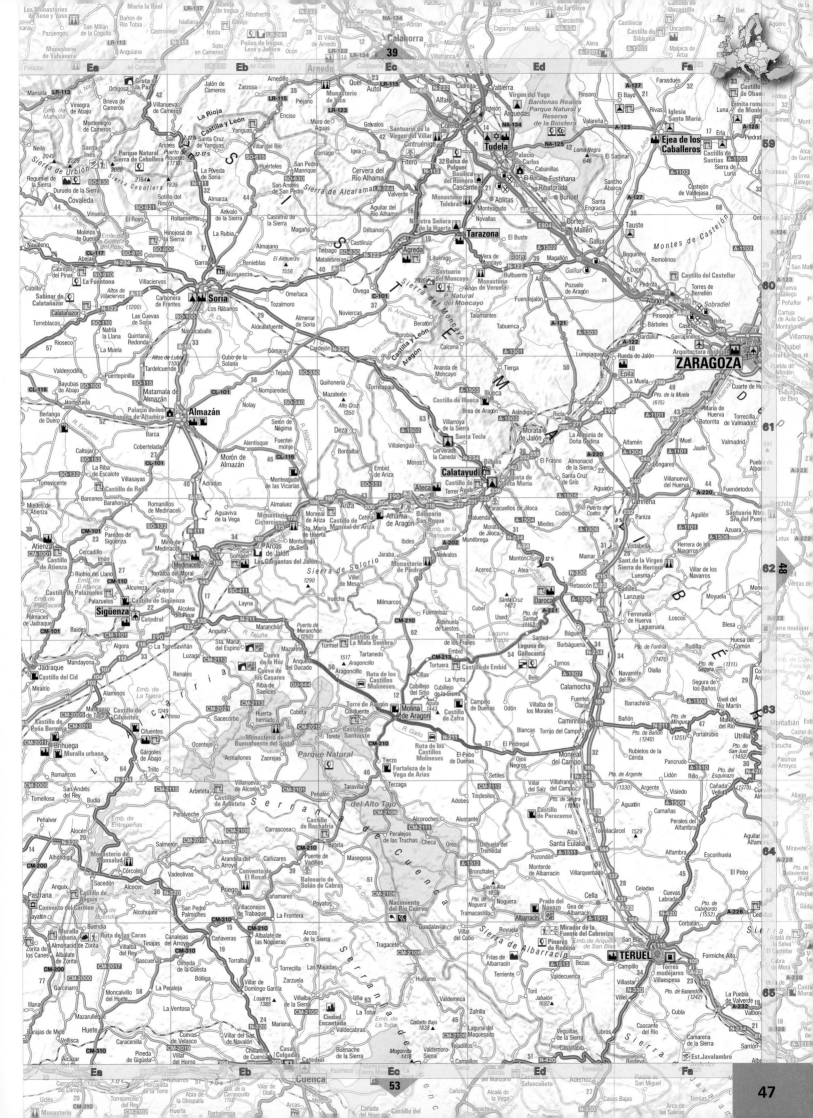

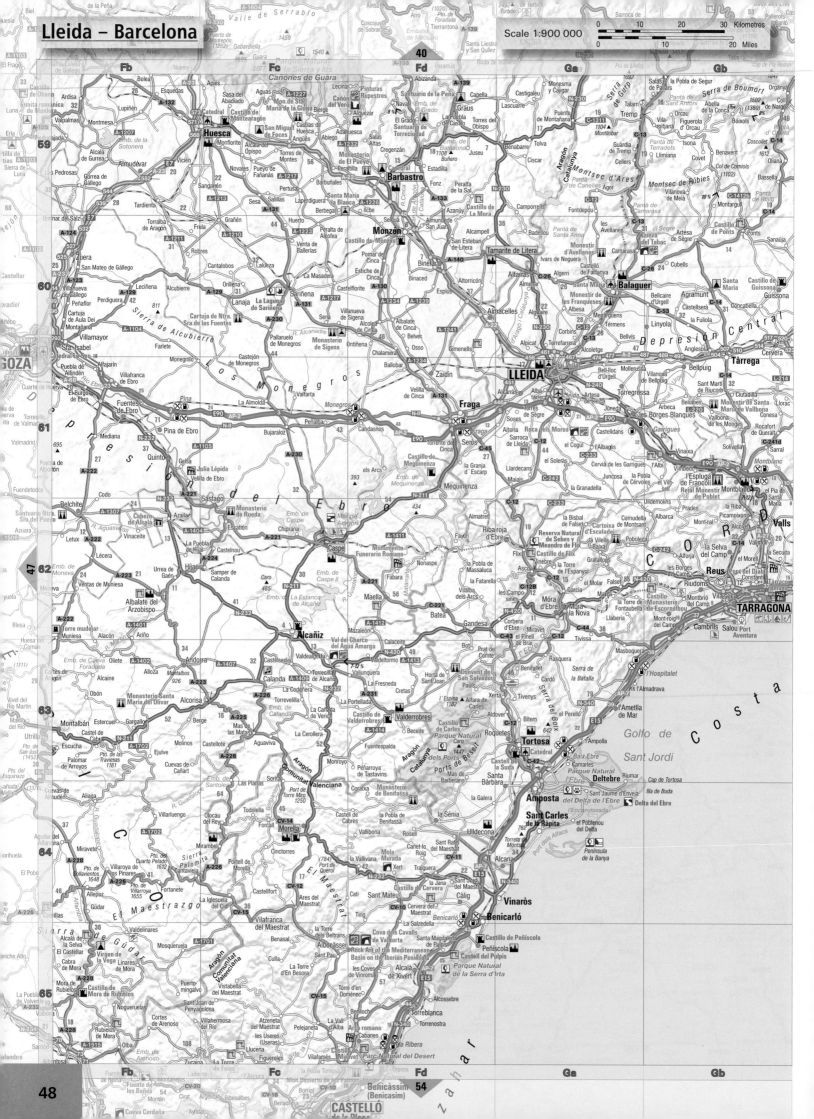

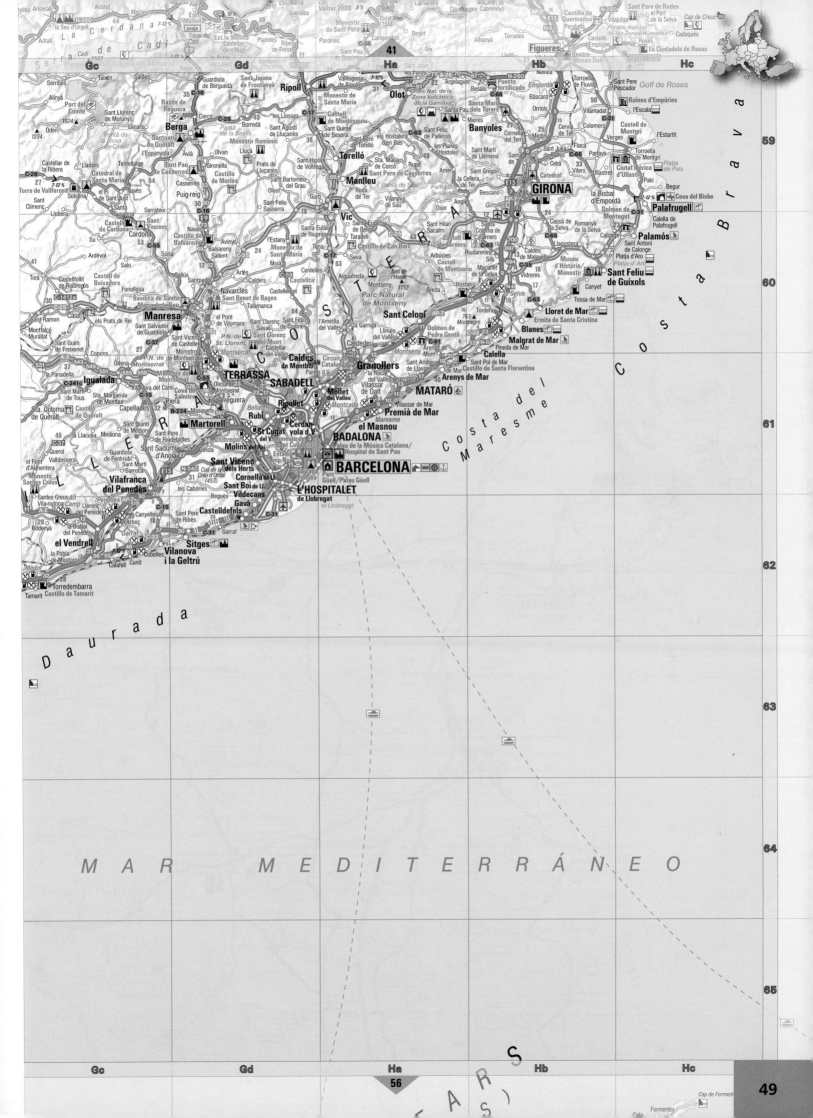

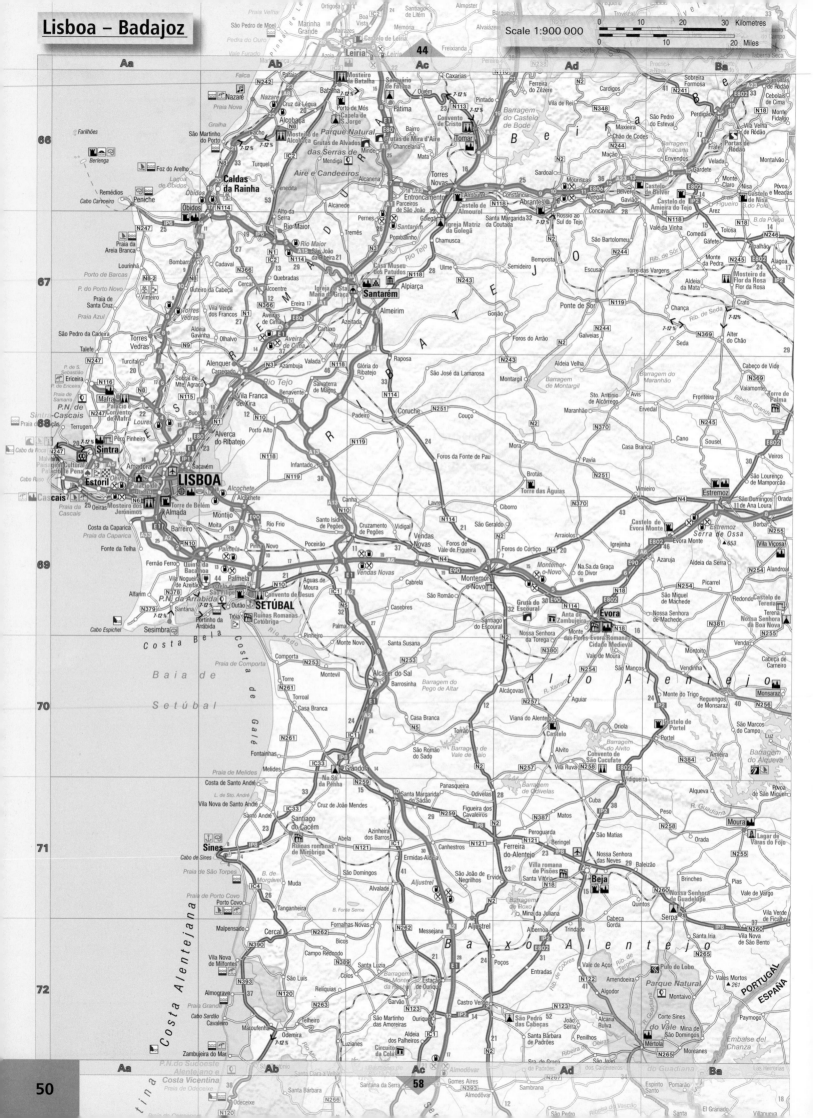

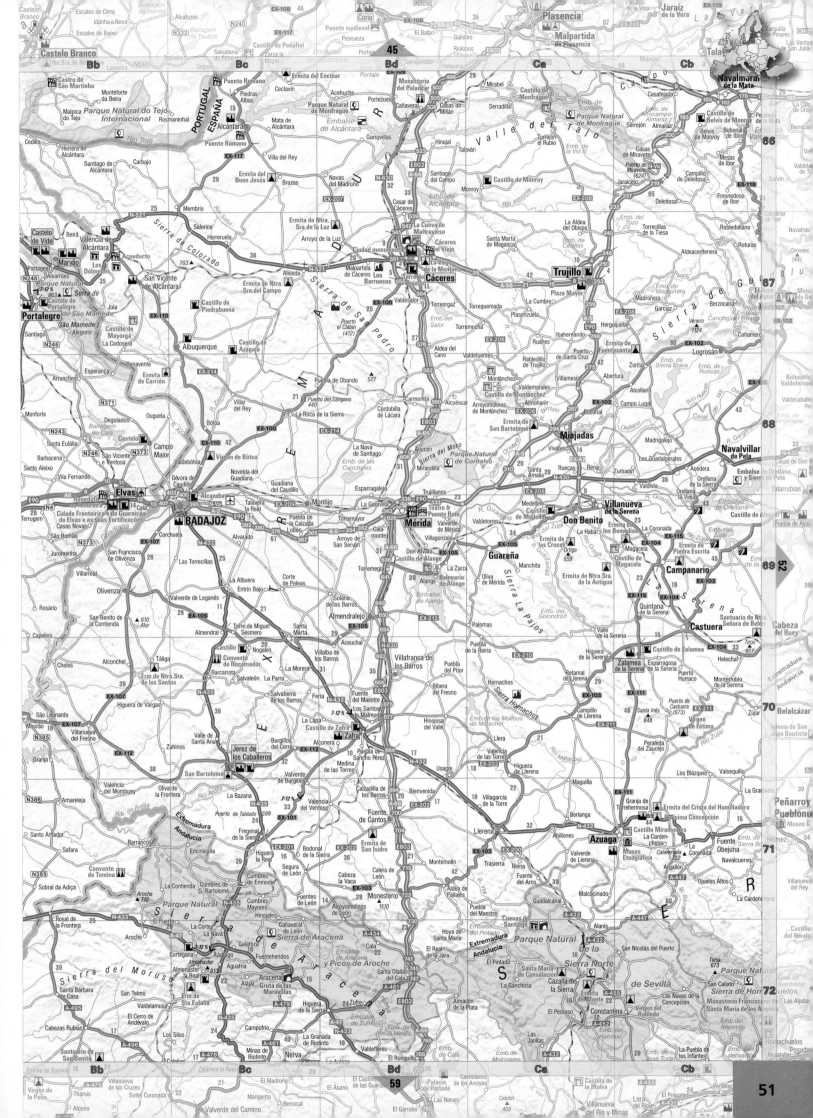

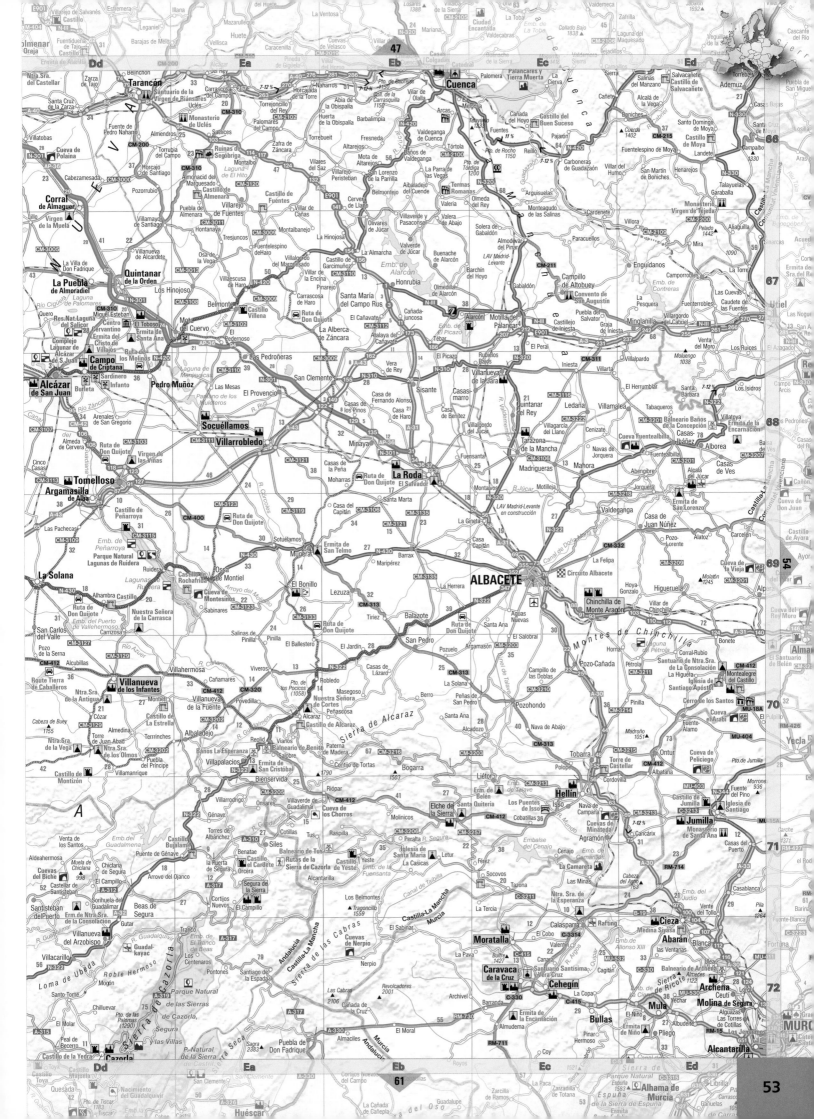

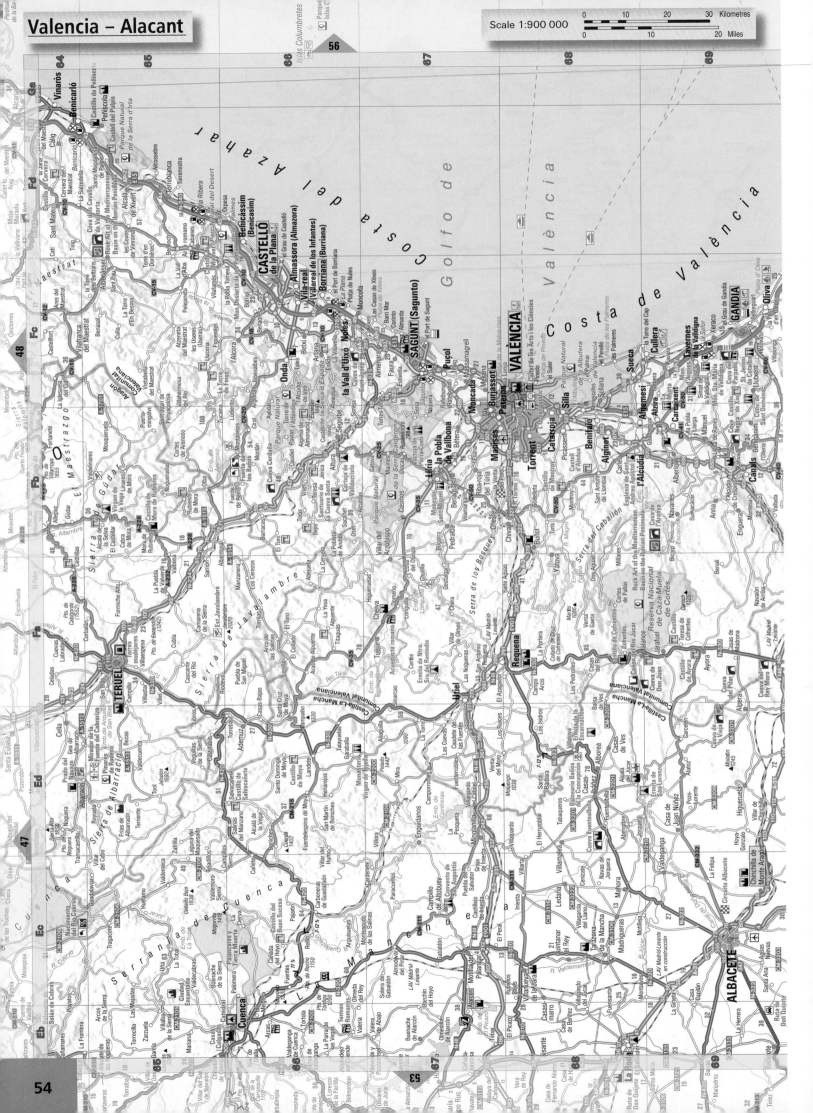

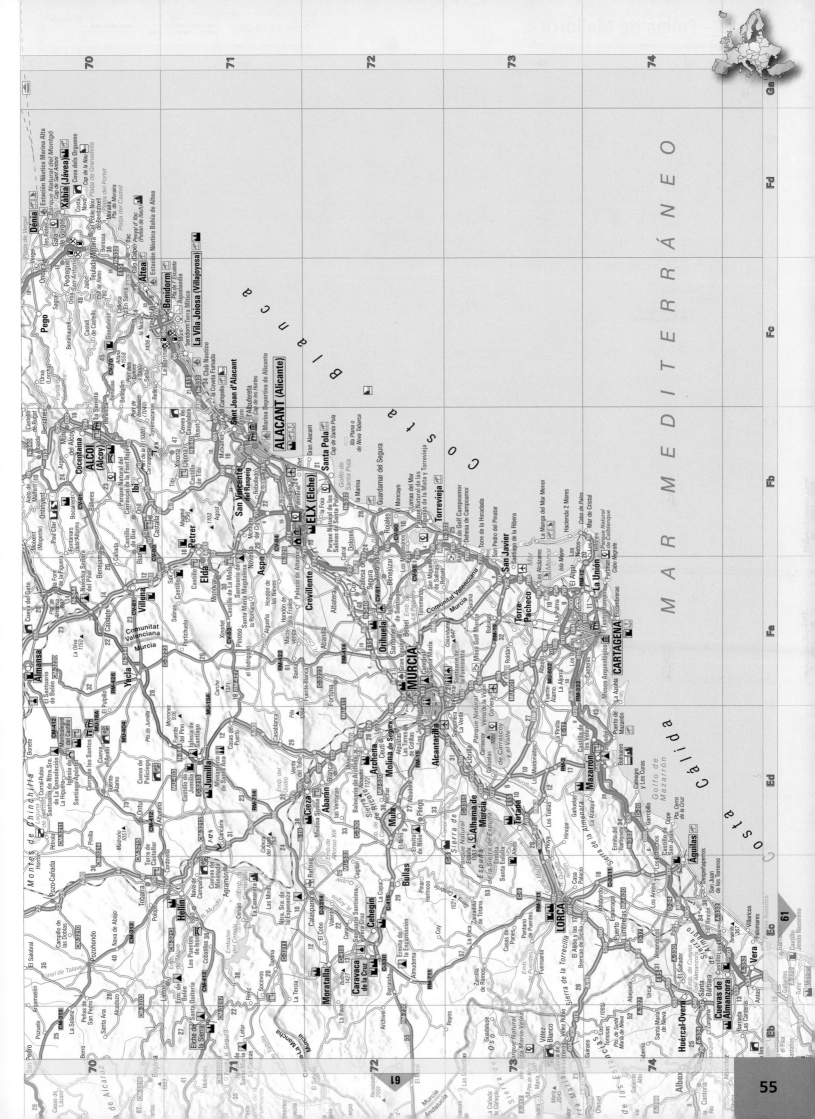

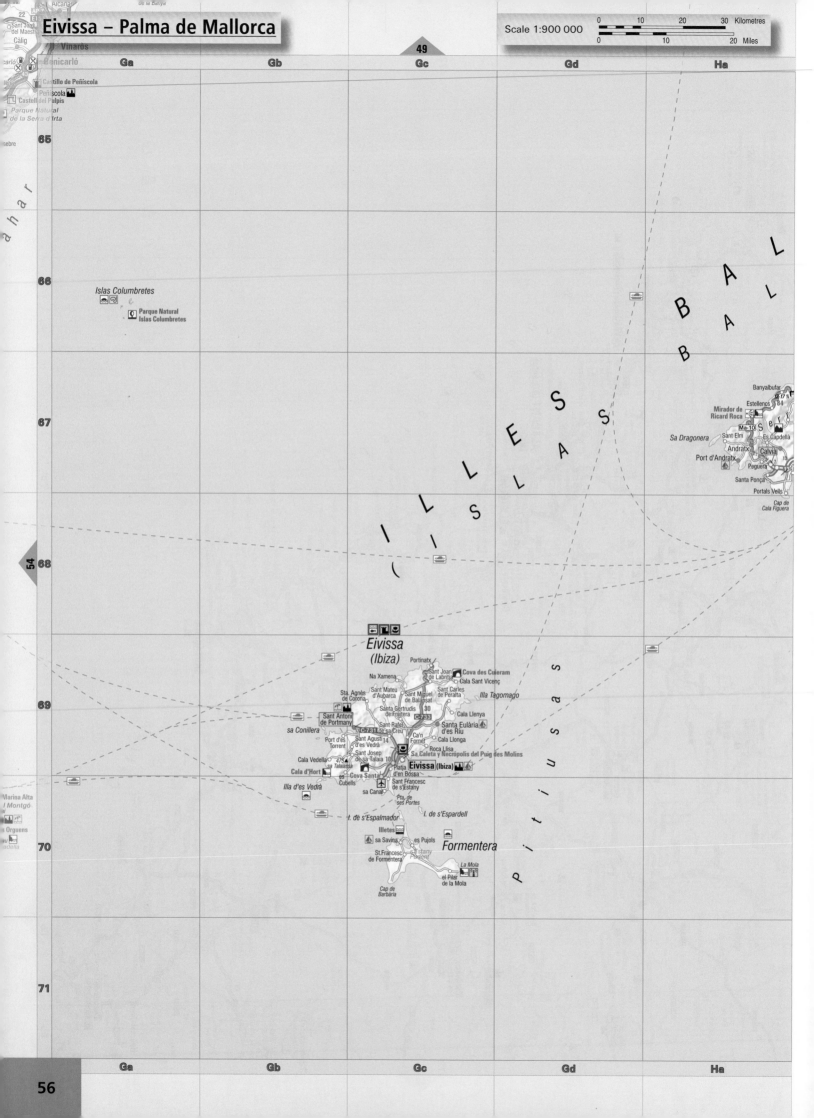

Scale 1:900 000

| 0 | 10 | 20 | 30 | Kilometres |
| 0 | | 10 | 20 | Miles |

22

Aicanar

de la Bahya

Sant Jordi
del Maestr
Càlig

Vinaròs

arló

Benicarló

Castillo de Peñíscola
Peñíscola
Castell del Pulpis
Parque Natural
de la Serra d'Irta

sebre

65

a h a r

66

Islas Columbretes

Parque Natural
Islas Columbretes

e

67

I L L E S

Banyalbufar
17%
Estellencs 84
Mirador de
Ricard Roca
Sa Dragonera Ma-10
Sant Elm Es Capdellà
Andratx Calvià
Port d'Andratx
Peguera
Santa Ponça
Portals Vells
Cap de
Cala Figuera

B A L
B A L

I S

54
68

(I)

Eivissa
(Ibiza)

69

Portinatx
Na Xamena Sant Joan Cova des Cuieram
de Labritja Cala Sant Vicenç
Sant Mateu Sant Carles
Sta. Agnès d'Aubarca Sant Miquel de Peralta
de Corona de Balansat Illa Tagomago
Santa Gertrudis 30
Sant Antoni de Fruitera C-733 Cala Llenya
de Portmany Sant Rafel de sa Creu
sa Conillera C-731 Santa Eulària
Ca'n d'es Riu
Port d'es Sant Agusti 14 Forner
Torrent d'es Vedrà Cala Llonga
Sant Josep 10 Roca Llisa
Cala Vedella de sa Talaia Sa Caleta y Necròpolis del Puig des Molins
475 sa Talaiassa
Cala d'Hort Eivissa (Ibiza)
es Cubells Cova Santa Platja
Illa d'es Vedrà d'en Bossa
sa Canal Sant Francesc
de s'Estany
Pta. de
ses Portes

I. de s'Espardell

P i t i u s a s

70

I. de s'Espalmador

Illetes
sa Savina es Pujols
St.Francesc Estany **Formentera**
de Formentera Pudent
La Mola
el Pilar
de la Mola
Cap de
Barbària

Marina Alta
I Montgó

s Orguens

adella

71

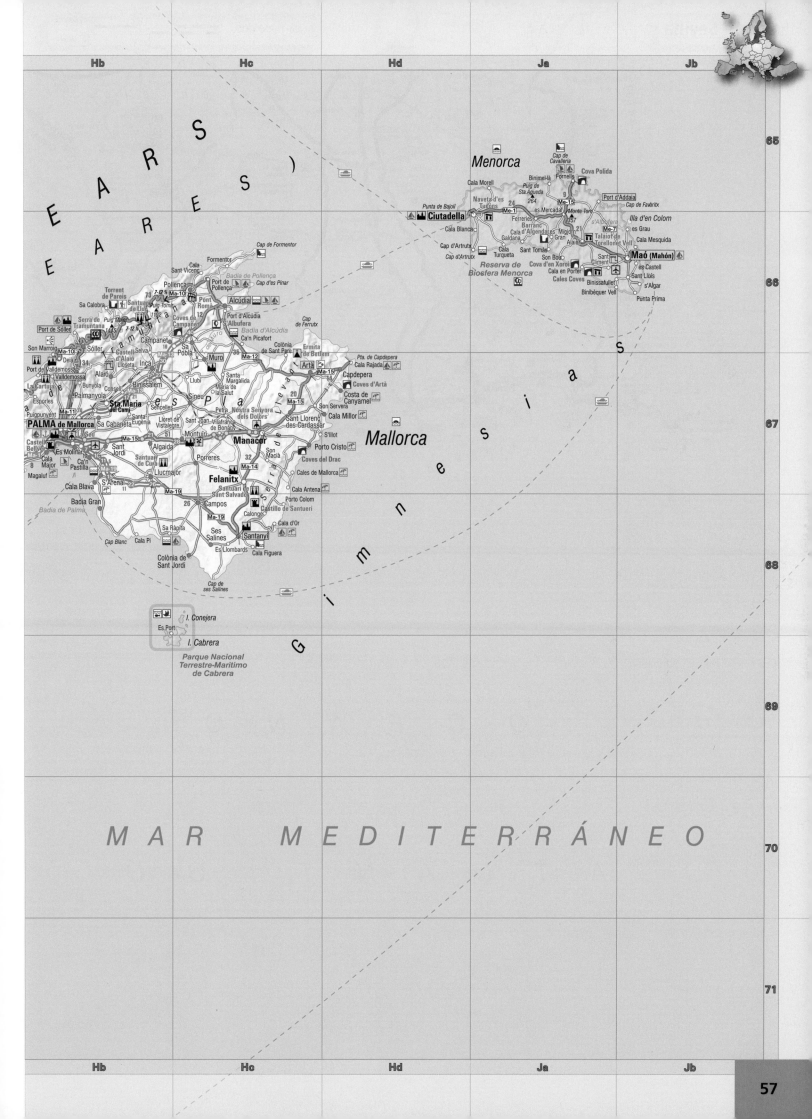

B E A R S)

E A R E S)
E A R E A
R S

Menorca

Cap de Cavalleria
Cova Polida
Fornells
Cala Morell
Binimel·là
Puig de Sta Agueda
264
9
Port d'Addaia
Cap de Favàritx
Punta de Bajoli
Naveta d'es Tudons
24
es Mercadal
Me-15
Me-1
Ciutadella
Ferreries
357
s'Albufera
Illa d'en Colom
Cala Blanca
Barranc
Cala d'Algendar
Migjorn
Gran
Me-7
Talaiot de
Torellonet Vell
es Grau
Cala Mesquida
Cap d'Artrutx
Galdana
Cala
Turqueta
Sant Tomàs
Alaior
21
Maó (Mahón)
Cap d'Artrutx
Son Bou
Cova d'en Xoroi
Sant
Climent
es Castell
Sant Lluís
Reserva de
Biosfera Menorca
Cala en Porter
Cales Coves
Binissafullet
s'Algar
Binibèquer Vell
Punta Prima

Cap de Formentor
Formentor
Cala
Sant Vicenç
Badia de Pollença
Port de
Pollença
Cap d'es Pinar
Torrent
de Pareis
73
7-12 %
Ma-10
Pollença
Pont
Romà
Alcúdia
Sa Calobra
Santuari
de Lluc
Puig Tomir
1102
Port d'Alcúdia
d'Albufera
Serra de
Tramuntana
Puig Major
1445
7-12 %
Coves de
Campanet
Cap
de Ferrutx
Badia d'Alcúdia
Port de Sóller
Son Marroig
Ma-10
Sóller
Campanet
Ca'n Picafort
Colònia
de Sant Pere
Ermita
de Betlem
Deià
34
Castell
d'Alaró
Selva
Inca
Sa
Pobla
Muro
Artà
Pta. de Capdepera
Port de Valldemossa
Valldemossa
Alaró
Lloseta
16
Santa
Margalida
Ma-12
Capdepera
Cala Rajada
La Cartuja
Bunyola
Consell
Llubí
Maria de
la Salut
Coves d'Artà
Esporles
Palmanyola
Binissalem
Sineu
20
Costa de
Canyamel
Puigpunyent
Ma-11
Sta.Maria
del Camí
Sa Cabaneta
Santa
Eugènia
Sencelles
Petra
Ma-15
Son Servera
PALMA de Mallorca
Seu
Lloret de
Vistalegre
Sant Joan
Nostra Senyora
dels Dolors
Vilafranca
de Bonany
Sant Llorenç
des-Cardassar
Cala Millor
Castell
Bellver
Algaida
Montuïri
51
Ma-15
Manacor
S'illot
Mallorca
Cala Major
Ca'n
Pastilla
Sant
Jordi
Porreres
32
Son
Macià
Porto Cristo
Magaluf
S'Arenal
Santuari
de Cura
Ma-14
Coves del Drac
Cala Blava
Llucmajor
Felanitx
Cales de Mallorca
Badia Gran
Ma-19
26
Santuari de
Sant Salvador
Cala Antena
Campos
Castillo de Santueri
Porto Colom
Badia de Palma
Ma-19
Calonge
Cap Blanc
Cala Pi
Sa Ràpita
Ses
Salines
Santanyí
Cala d'Or
Colònia de
Sant Jordi
Es Llombards
Cala Figuera
Cap de
ses Salines

G i m n e s i a s

G

I. Conejera
Es Port
I. Cabrera
Parque Nacional
Terrestre-Marítimo
de Cabrera

M A R   M E D I T E R R Á N E O

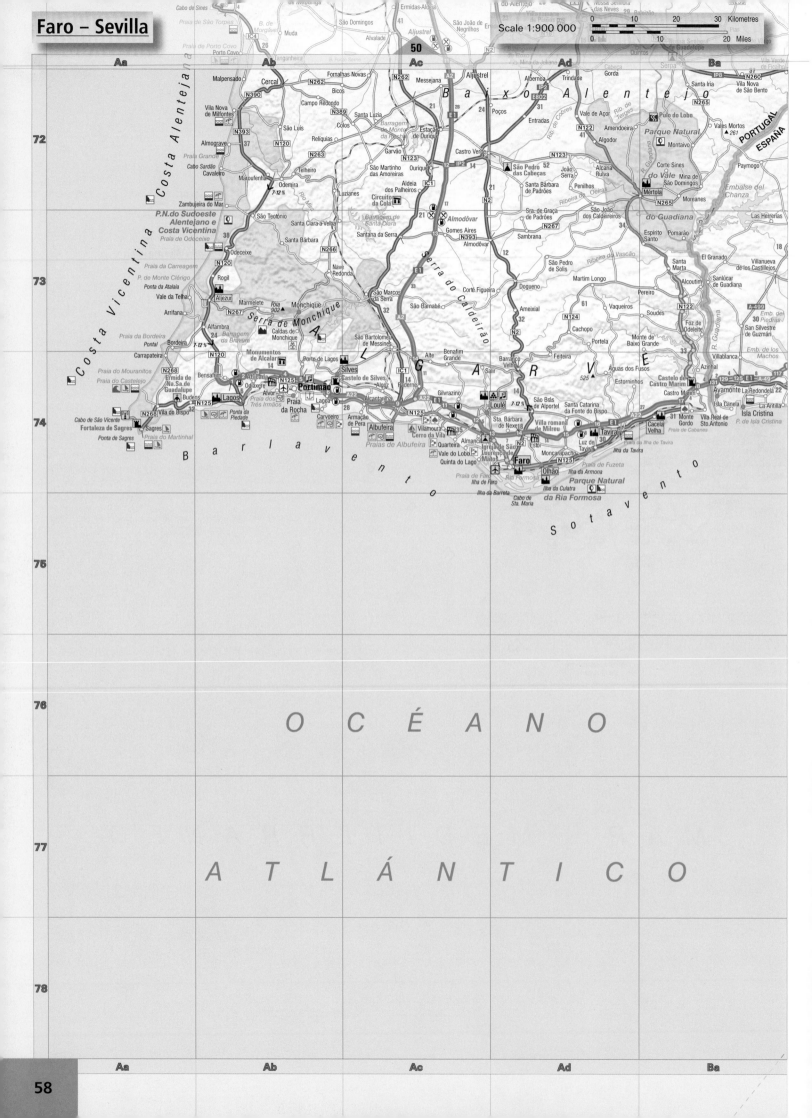

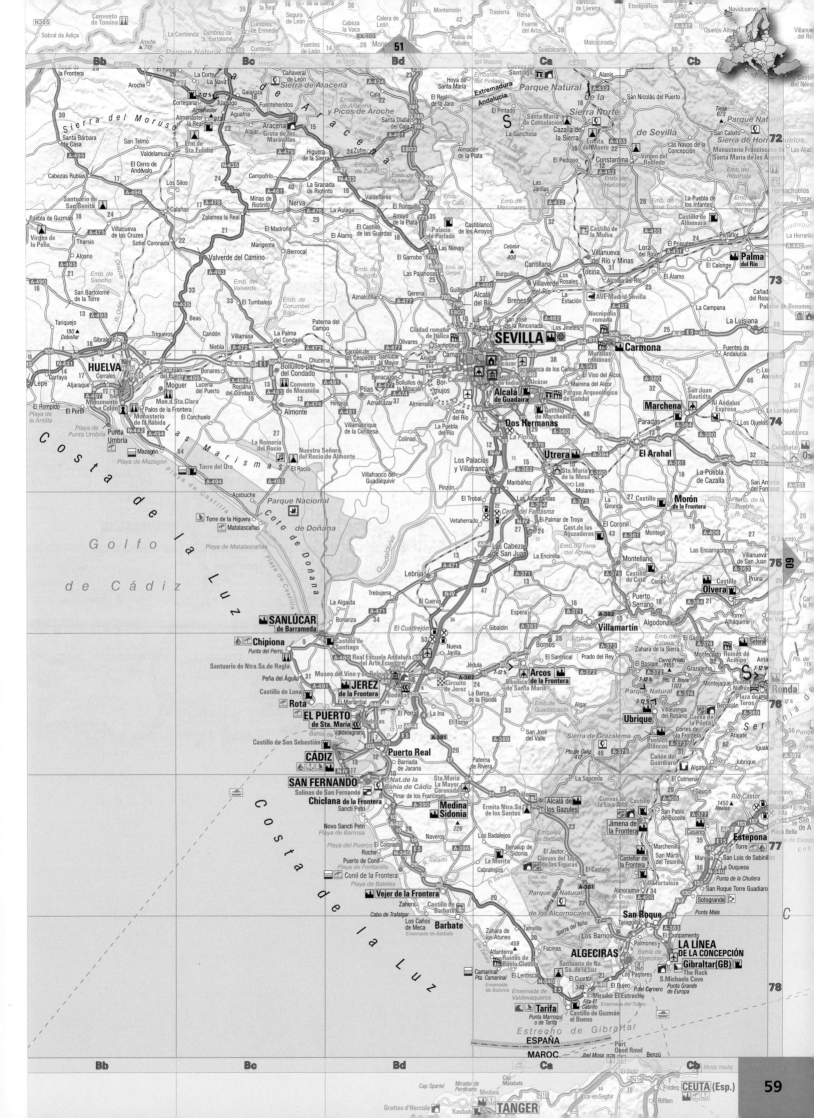

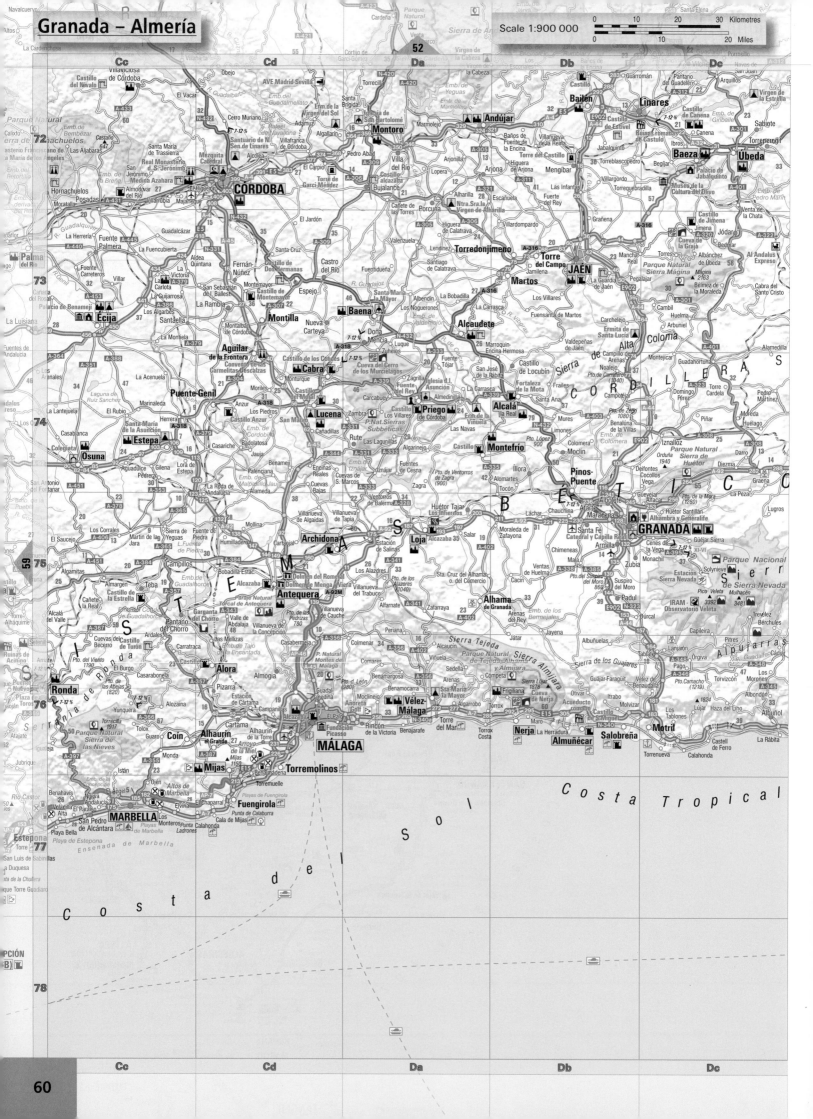

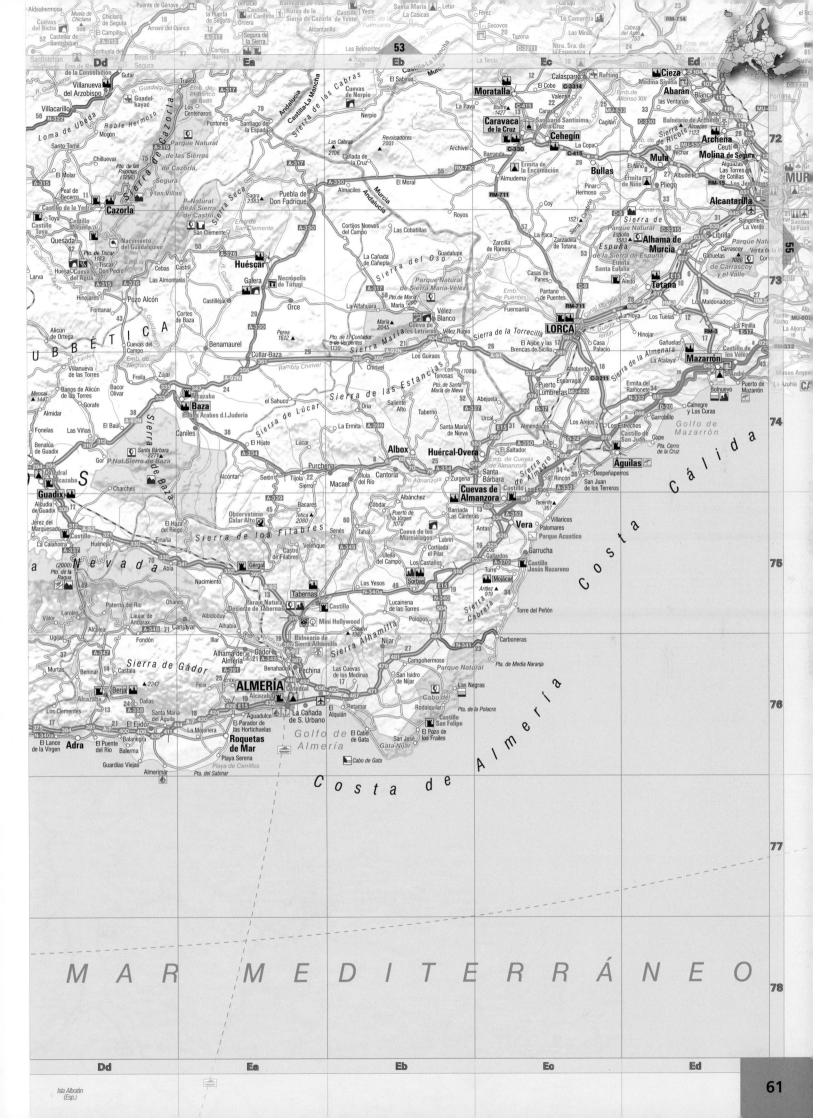

Scale 1:900 000

| 0 | 10 | 20 | 30 | Kilometres |
| 0 | 10 | | 20 | Miles |

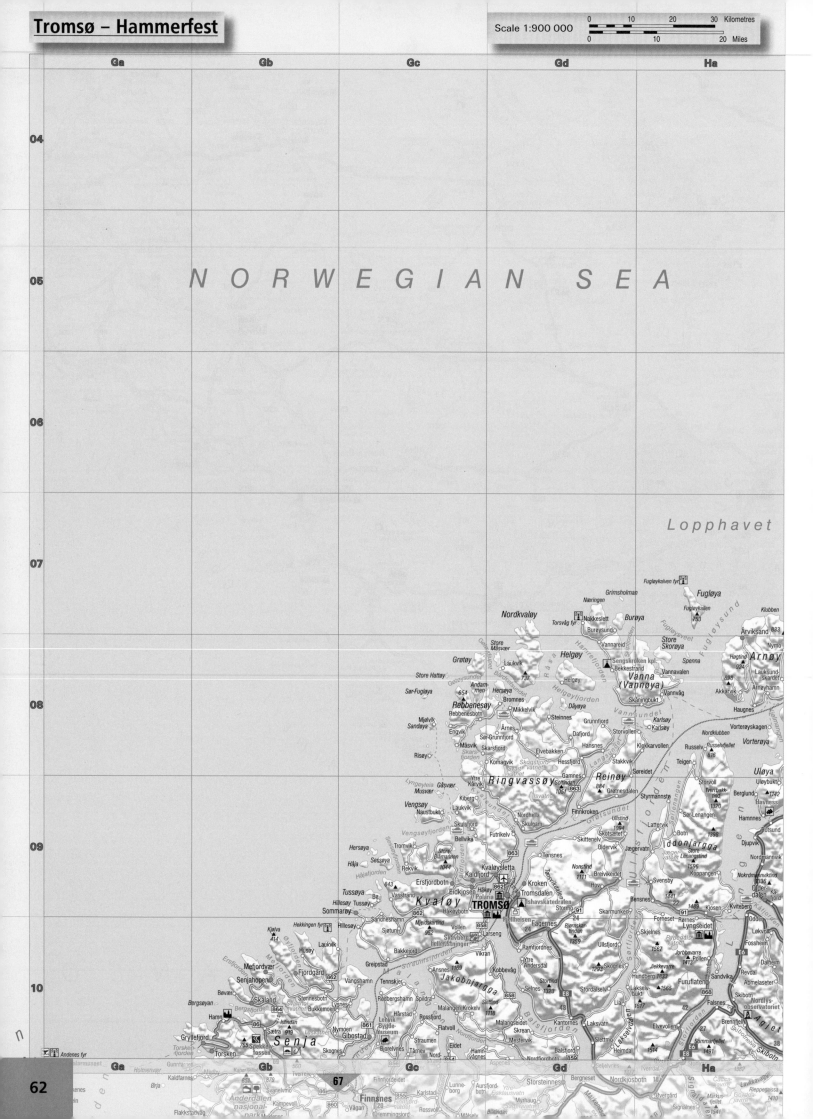

N O R W E G I A N   S E A

Lopphavet

Fugløykalven fyr

Grimsholman
Næringen   Fugløya

Nordkvaløy   Torsvåg fyr   Burøya   Fugløykalilen
                  Nakkeslett   753   Klubben

                  Store   Burøysund
                  Måsvær   Vannareid   Store   Årviksand 833
Grøtøy   Laukvik   Skorøya   Nymo

Store Hattøy   Helgøy   Sengskroken kpl.   Høgtind Arnøy
                  Andam-   Bekkestrand   Spenna   924
Sør-Fugløya   men   Hersøya   Helgøy   Vannavalen   898   Lauksund-
                  654   Bromnes   skardet
Rebbenesøy   Dåvøya   Skåningbukt Vannvåg Akkarvik Arnøyhamn
Rebbenesbotn   Mikkelvik   Haugnes

Mjelvik   Steinnes   Karlsøy   Grunnfjord   Vorterøyskagen
Sandøya   Årnes   Dafjord   Karlsøy   Nordklubben   Vorterøya
                  Sør-Grunnfjord   Storvollen   Russelvfjellet
Måsvik   Skarsfjord   Elvebakken   Hansnes   Klokkarvollen   816   Russelv
Risøy   Skars-   Komagvik   Hessfjord   Stakkvik   Teigen   Uløya
         fjorden   Skogsfjord   Gamnes   Søreidet   Uløybukt
         Lyngøyleia Gåsvær   Ytre   vatnet   Solfinnan 863   Storvoll Tverrbakk- 1142
         Musvær   Kårvik   1051   Grøtnesdalen Styrmannsto tind Berglund Havnnes
Hersøya   Kiberg   Nordhella Finnkroken   1320 Hamnnes
         Vengsøy   Laukvik   Skulgam   Ullstind   1398
         Naustbukt   Skulsfjord   Skotsætet 1094   Botn   Rotsund
Sessøya   Vengsøyfjorden Bellvika   Futrikelv   Oldervik Jægervatn   Djupvik
Håja   Tromvik   863   Skittenelv   Koppangen Nordmannvik
         Store   Tønsnes   Nonstind Svensby   Nokrdmannviktind
         Blåmannen   Kvaløysletta   1111 Breivikeidet   1336
         1044   Eidkjosen Kaldfjord Håkøy   Kroken   Hov   Older-
Tussøya   Vasstrand 862   Polaria   Tromsdalen   1441   1489   Kviteberg dalen
Hillesøy   Tussøy   Håkøybotn   Ishavskatedralen Stormo 91   Kjosen
Sommarøy   Kvaløy   TROMSØ   Fjellheisen Skarmunken 24   Forneset Rørnes Odden
         Sandneshamn   Mjeldkartind 858   Bjørnskar-   Lyngseidet   Lokvoll
Kjølva   Hekkingen fyr Sjøtun Vollen   952 Larsnes 24 tinden   Fossheim
414   Hillesøy   Skavberg Fagernes 1359 Ullsfjord   Rypedals-   Dalheim
         Husøy   Laukvik   helleristninger   Ramfjordnes   vatnet
Mefjordvær   Greipstad   Vikran   Ytre   1567 Jorbbavarre Sandvika
Senjahopen Fjordgård   Vangshamn Tennskjer   Kobbevåg Andersdal   Jiekkevarre Revdal Abmelaseter
Bøvær   862   Ansnes 1169   Stortind   1293 Skognes   1473 Furuflaten
         Stønnesbotn   Jakobnjargga Selnes 1323   Hundberg 1833
Skaland   Svartvatnet   Rødbergshamn Spildra   858   E8 Lakselv- 1565 Falsnes Nordlys-
Bergsøyan 864   Lysnes   Malangen Krokel Slettmo   bukt 1617   observatoriet
Hamn   Bukkemoen   1118   Malangseidet   42   Brennfjell
Gryllefjord   Sætra 919   Nymoen Lenvik Straumen Kantornes Lakvatn 48 E6   Sommarfjell
Torsken-   Spekkalv-   Gibostad Bygde-   Flatvoll Skrean Mesterv.   1514 1491 E8
fjorden   fossen   museet   Bjørnelvnes   Eidet   Hamn-   Skibotn
Andenes fyr   765   S e n j a   Tårnev   Nord-   vågnes Balsfjorden Heimdal   Skibotn
                                        Ga   **Gb**   **Gc**   **Gd**   **Ha**

67

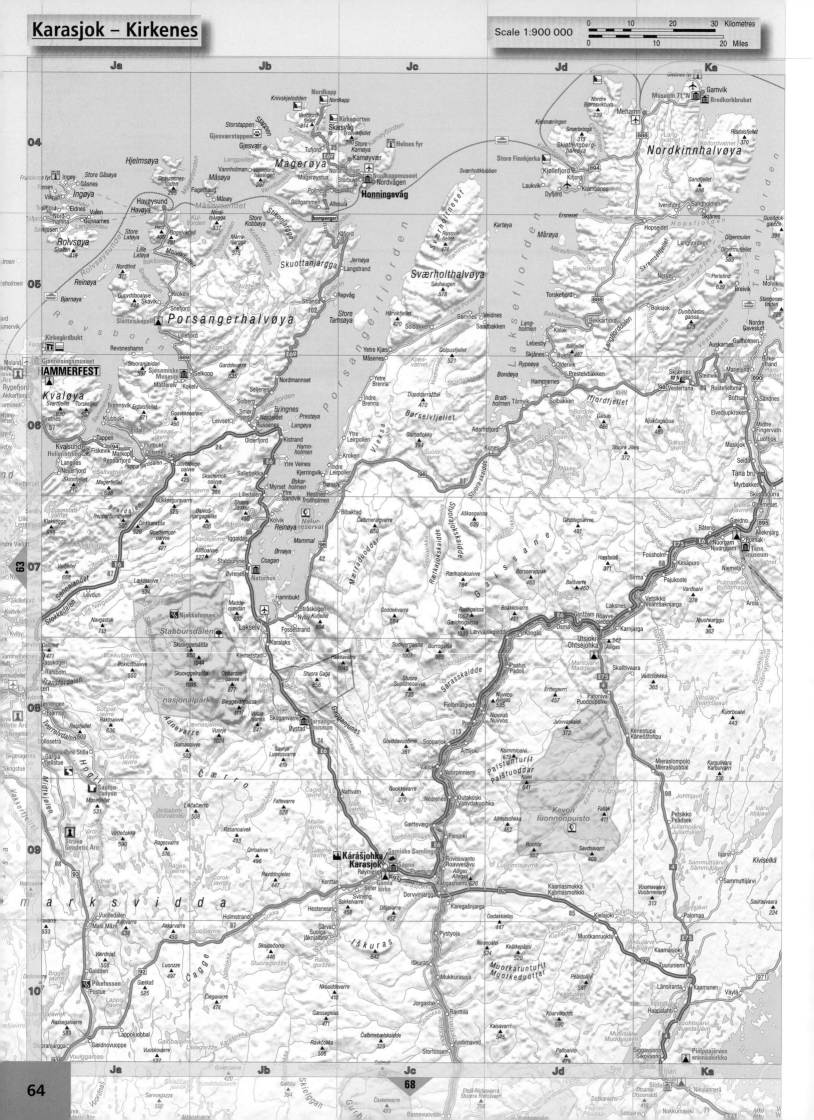

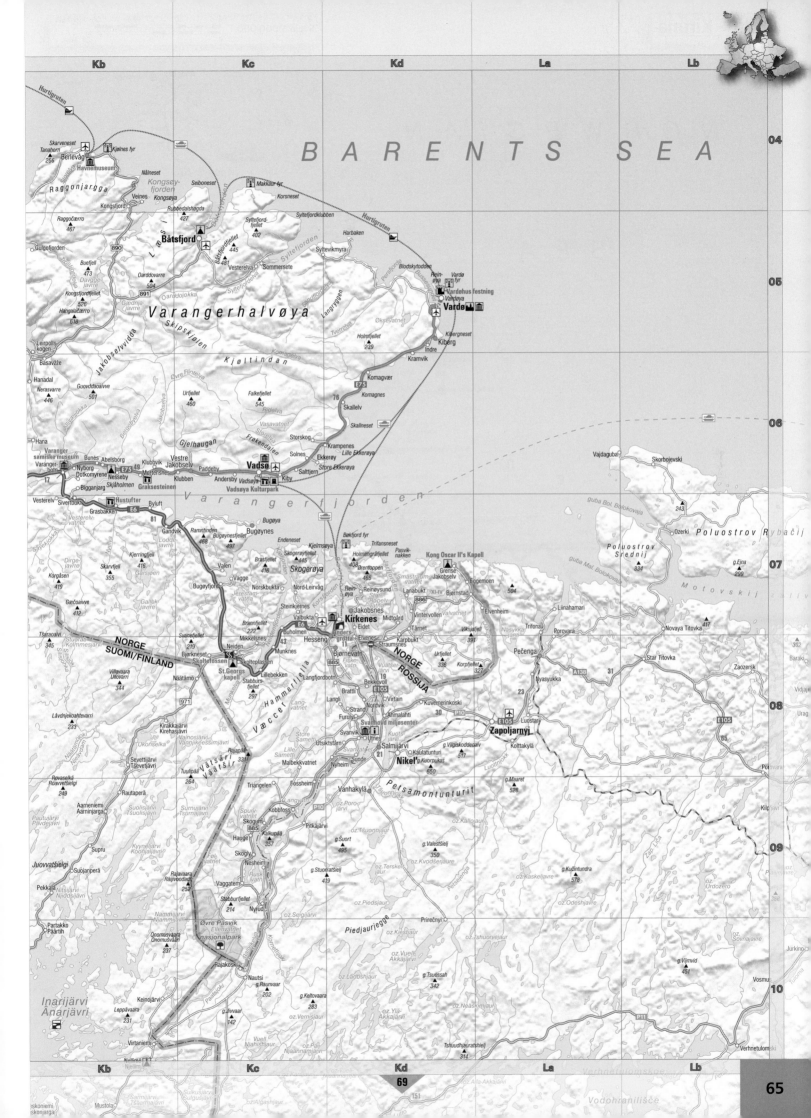

04

B A R E N T S   S E A

Hurtigruten

Skarveneset
Tanahorn
266
Berlevåg
Kjølnes fyr
Havnemuseum
Nålneset
Kongsøy-
fjorden
Seiboneset
Makkaur fyr
Korsneset
Raggonjargga
Kongsfjord
Veines
Kongsøya
Rubbedalshøgda
427
Raggočærro
467
Syltefjord-
fjellet
402
Syltefjordklubben
Harbaken
Hurtigruten
05
Gulgofjorden
890
Båtsfjord
Båtsfjordfjellet
445
Vesterelva
Sommerset
Syltevikmyra
Blodskytoddden
Rein-
øya
Vardø
Vardø fyr
Buefjell
473
Dåvggejavrre
Oarddovarre
504
Båtsfjordfjellet
481
Vardøhus festning
Vardø
Kongsfjordfjellet
526
891
Oaredojokka
Syltefjord-
Vardøya
Hangalačærro
516
Gæsdnjá-
javrre
Varangerhalvøya
Langryggen
Øksevatnet
Holmfjellet
239
Kibergneset
Kiberg
Leirpolls-
kogen
Skipskjølen
Kjøltindan
Komagelva
Indre
Kramvik
Basavžže
Hanadal
Øvre Flintelva
Tverrelva
06
Nerasvarre
446
Guovddaoaivve
501
Urfjellet
460
Falkefjellet
545
Ridelva
76
Komagvær
E75
Komagnes
Skallelv
Jakobselva
Gjelhaugan
Vasavatnet
Storelva
Frokendalen
Skallelv
Storskog
Skallneset
Hana
Varanger
samiske museum
Varanger-
botn
Bunes
Abelsborg
Vestre
Jakobselv
Krampenes
Solnes
Ekkerøy
Lille Ekkerøya
Store Ekkerøya
Nyborg
Dotkomyrene
E75 49
Klubbvik
Mortensnes
Nesseby
Paddeby
Vadsø
Kiby
Saltjern
17
81
Bigganjarg
Skjåholmen
Andersby
Vadsøya
Vadsøya Kulturpark
Graksesteinen
Vesterelv
Sivertbukta
Hustufter
Grasbakken
Byluft
V a r a n g e r f j o r d e n
Vesterelv-
vatnet
E6
Gandvik
Ramntinden
468
Bugøynesfjellet
497
Bugøynes
Endeneset
Bøkfjord fyr
07
Såyekjokka
Dirge-
javrre
Kjerringfjell
Skarvfjell
416
Garsjøen
Valen
Brasfjellet
416
Skogerøyfjellet
445
Skogerøya
Ørentoppen
465
Kjelmsøya
Holmengråfjellet
408
Pasvik-
nakken
Trifanseset
Kong Oscar II's Kapell
guba Mal. Bolokovaja
Korgåsen
419
Gæčoaivve
412
Gallok-
javrre
Bugøyfjord
Vagge
Norskbukta
Nord-Leirvåg
Jerestam-
vatra
Rein-
øya
Reinøysund
Småstraum-
vatnet
Store
Ropelv-
vatnet
Lanabukt
XI-IV
Grense
Jakobselv
Eggemoen
504
Bjørnstad
Liinahamari
Motovskij
Tsáraoaivi
345
Stuorrač
Kolmmesjavri
Svanefjellet
219
Brannfjellet
222
Mikkelsnes
Valbukta
Steinkjernes
886
Jakobsnes
Kirkenes
Eidet
Midtgård
Vintervollen
Valvatnet
Nasykka
javrre
Trifona
Porovara
Novaya Titovka
417
NORGE
SUOMI/FINLAND
Bjerkneset
Skoltefossen
43
Buholmen
Hesseng
Anders-
grotta
Elvenes
Straumsnes
Tårnet
Karpbukt
Viksjafjell
391
Urfjellet
336
Korpfjellet
327
Pečenga
Star Titovka
Zaozersk
Villavaara
Ulfovarri
344
Näätämö
St.Georgs
kapell
971
Stabburs-
fjellet
297
Munkelv
Langfjordbotn
885
Bjørnevatn
Fisker-
vatn
19
Bekkevoll
Svanvik
NORGE
ROSSIJA
A138
31
23
E105
Lávdnjekoahtevarri
233
Kirakájávri
Kirehasjávri
Vainosjávri
Vanjikeessimjávri
Skolteplassen
Lillebekken
Langfjordbotn
Brattli
Langli
E105
Virtain
Nordvik
Ahmalahti
Kuvernerinkoski
30
P10
Nyasyukka
Luostari
E105
65
Sevettijärvi
Tševetjävri
Rajapää
331
Tuulipää
264
Malbekkvatnet
Nyheim
Sunde
Kuots
jávri
Svanhovd miljøsenter
Utnes
Salmijärvi
21
Nikel'
Kuorpukas
650
Zapoljarnyj
Kolttakylä
Luttjokk
g.Vilgiskoddeoaiv
517
Kåulatunturi
g.Maaret
526
Petsamontunturit
Rovaselkä
Roavvetšielgi
249
Rautaperä
Triangelen
Fossheim
Vanhakylä
Langvatn
08
Juovvatšielgi
Aarneniemi
Aarninjarga
Suolisjärvi
Tšuolisjávri
Surnujärvi
Tšurnajávri
Spurv-
vatnet
Skogum
885
Kobbfoss
P10
oz.Poro-
järvi
Pitkäjärvi
g.Valestšielj
350
g.Kučintundra
578
Supru
Kyynejärvi
Koonjajävri
Kalkupää
357
Hauge
Skogly
Nesheim
g.Suort
495
oz.Ksuonnjaur
g.Stuorratšielj
419
oz.Terski-
jaur
oz.Kvodserjaure
oz.Käskeljavre
09
Pekkala
Nitsijärvi
Niidosjävri
Juovvatšielgi
Suojanperä
Rajavaara
Räijivoodaš
252
Vaggatem
Ruskil-
vatnj
Stabburfjellet
214
Nyfud
oz.Seijijärvi
g.Stuorratšielj
g.Tsuossah
342
g.Vijmvid
451
Partakko
Päärtih
Nammijärvi
Njammijävri
Onomusvaara
Onomusvaari
237
Øvre Pasvik
Ellenvatnet
nasjonalpark
oz.Piedsjaur
Piedjaurjegge
oz.Tshuorvejaur
oz.Vuell
Akkajávri
oz.Neáskimjaur
oz.Odeshjavre
oz.
Urdozero
Inarijärvi
Ånarjävri
Rajakoski
Nautsi
g.Raunvaar
202
Päätsjoki
g.Jivvaar
142
g.Keltovaara
283
oz.Ylä-
Akkajávri
g.Tsuossah
314
Vosmu
Partakko
Keinojärvi
Leppävaara
231
Nellim
P10
Virtaniemi
Vuell
Njahishjaur
oz.Pää
Njanamjávri
Tshuudhjauratshielj
Vodohranilišče

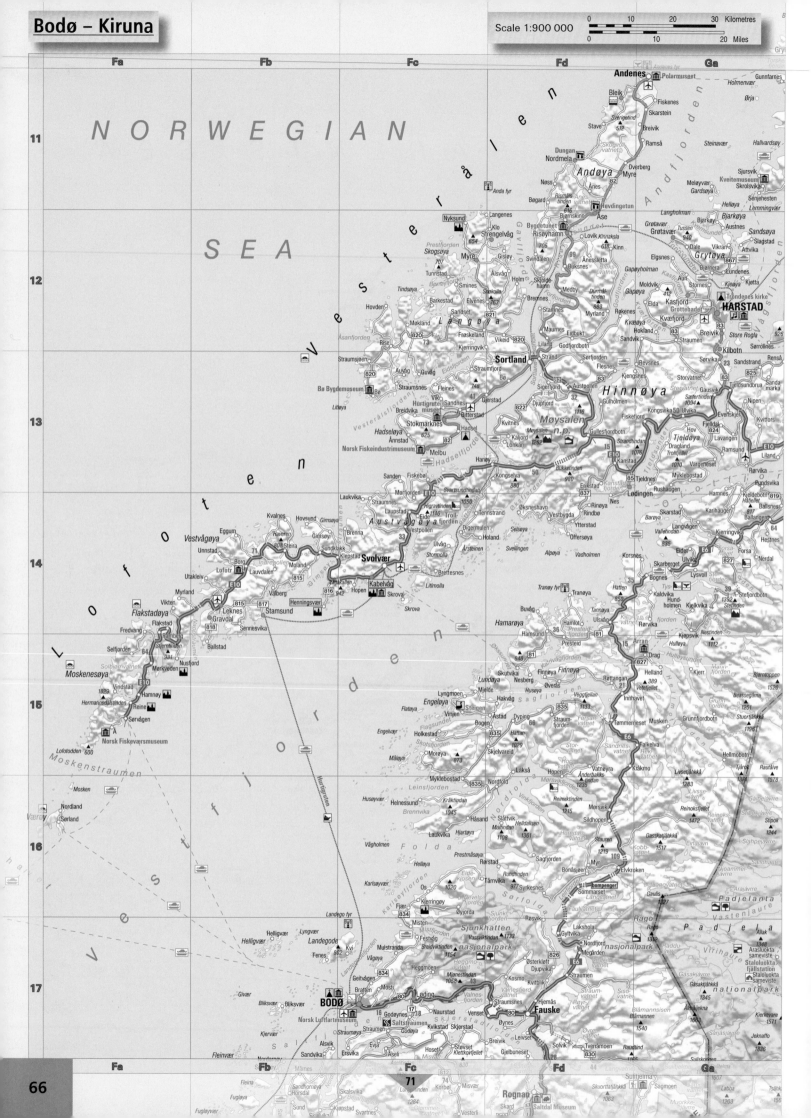

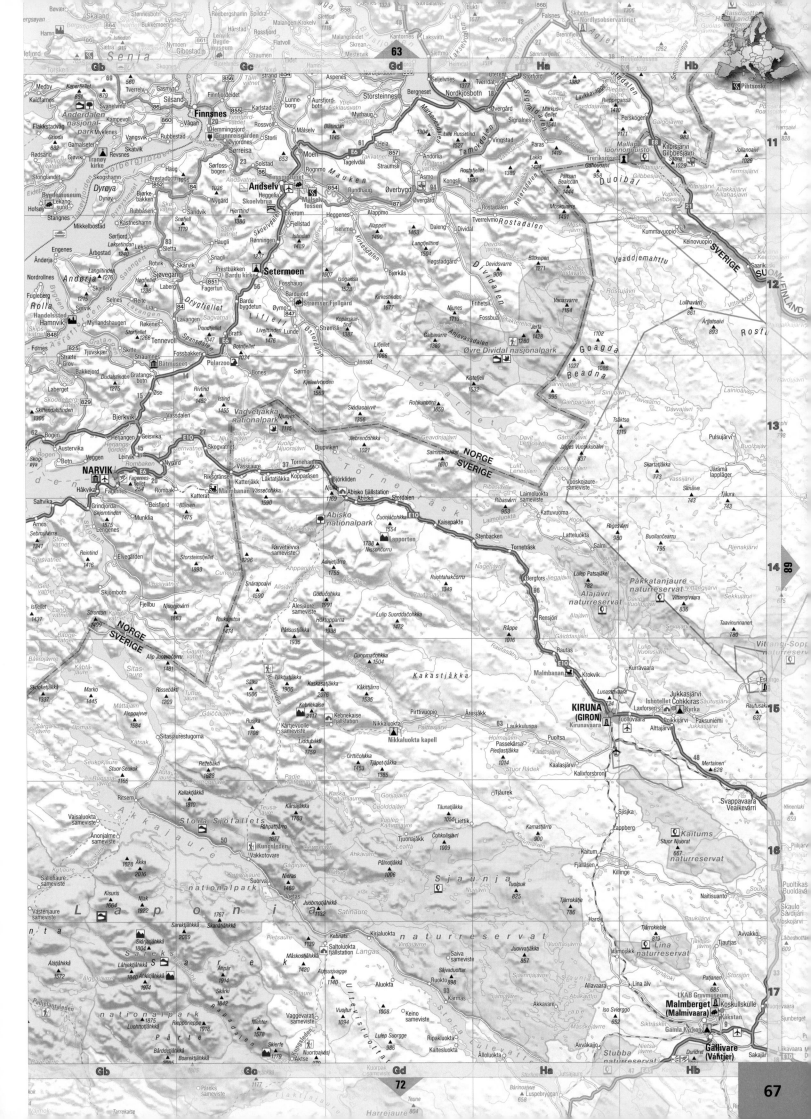

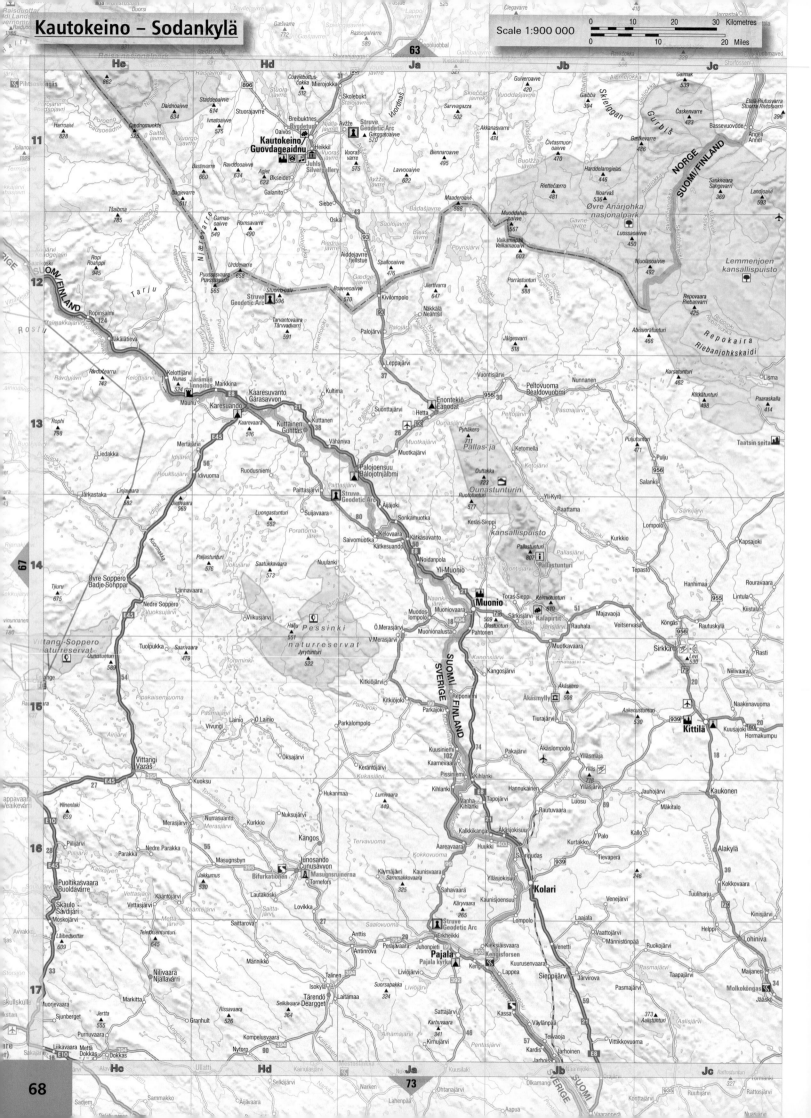

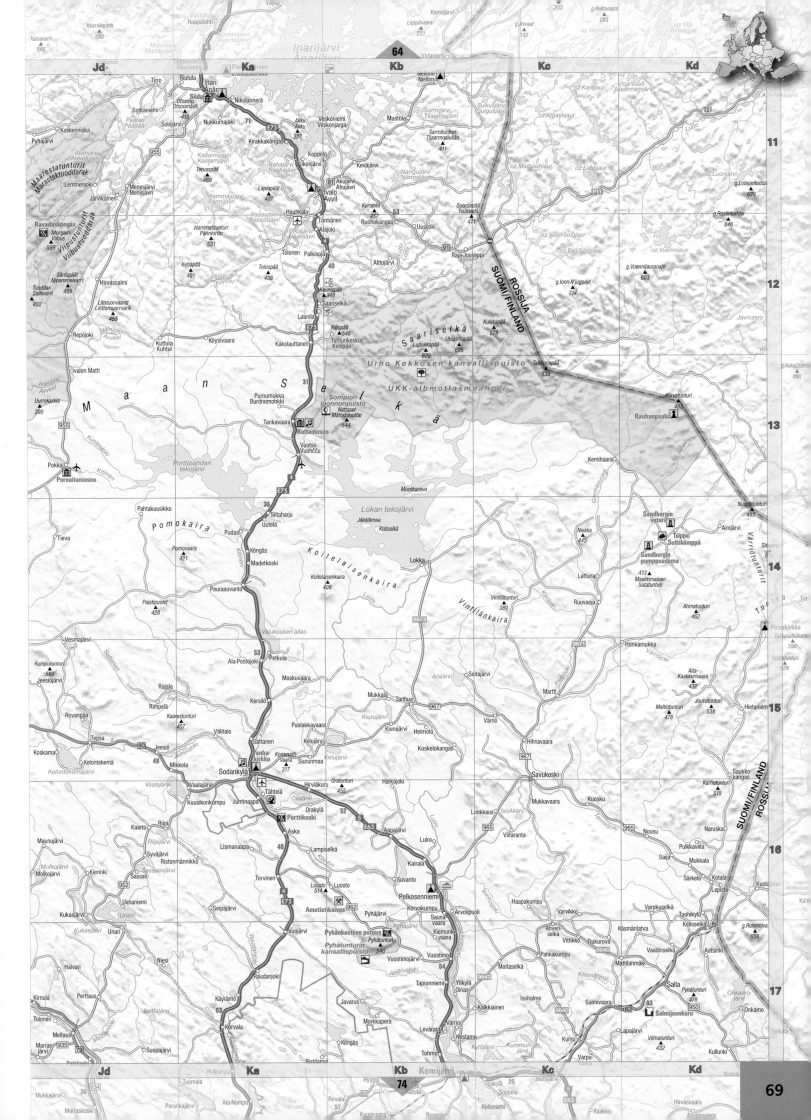

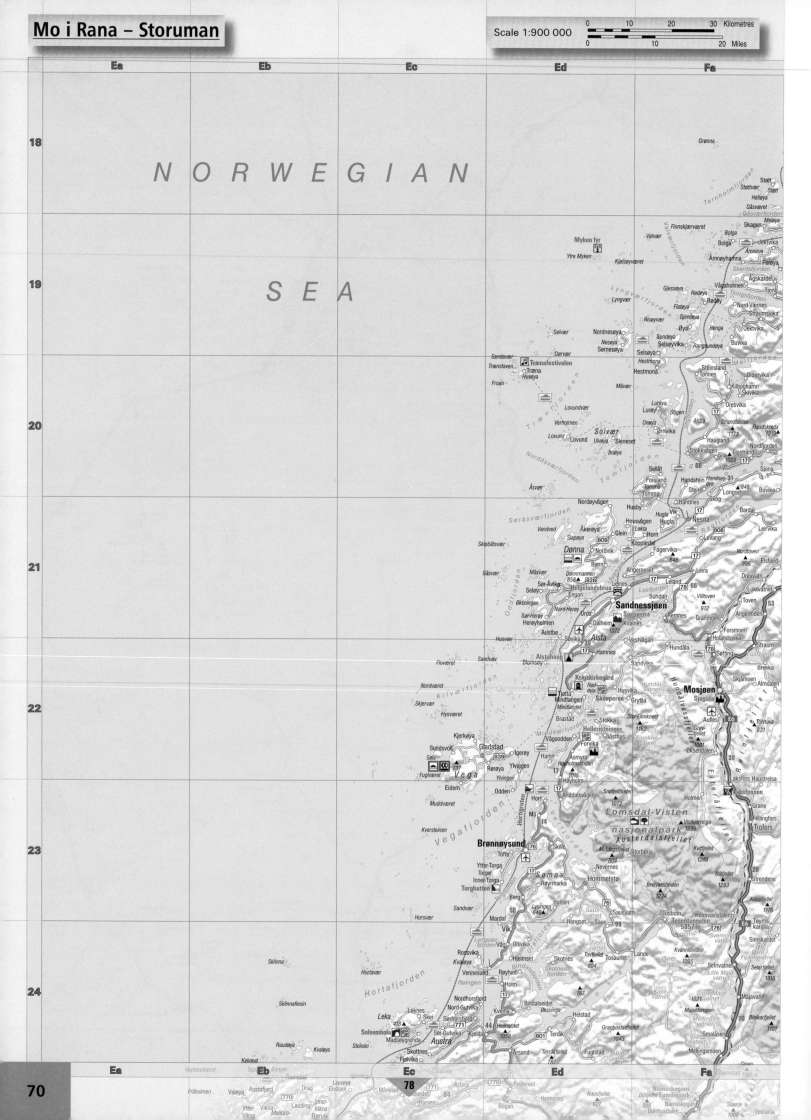

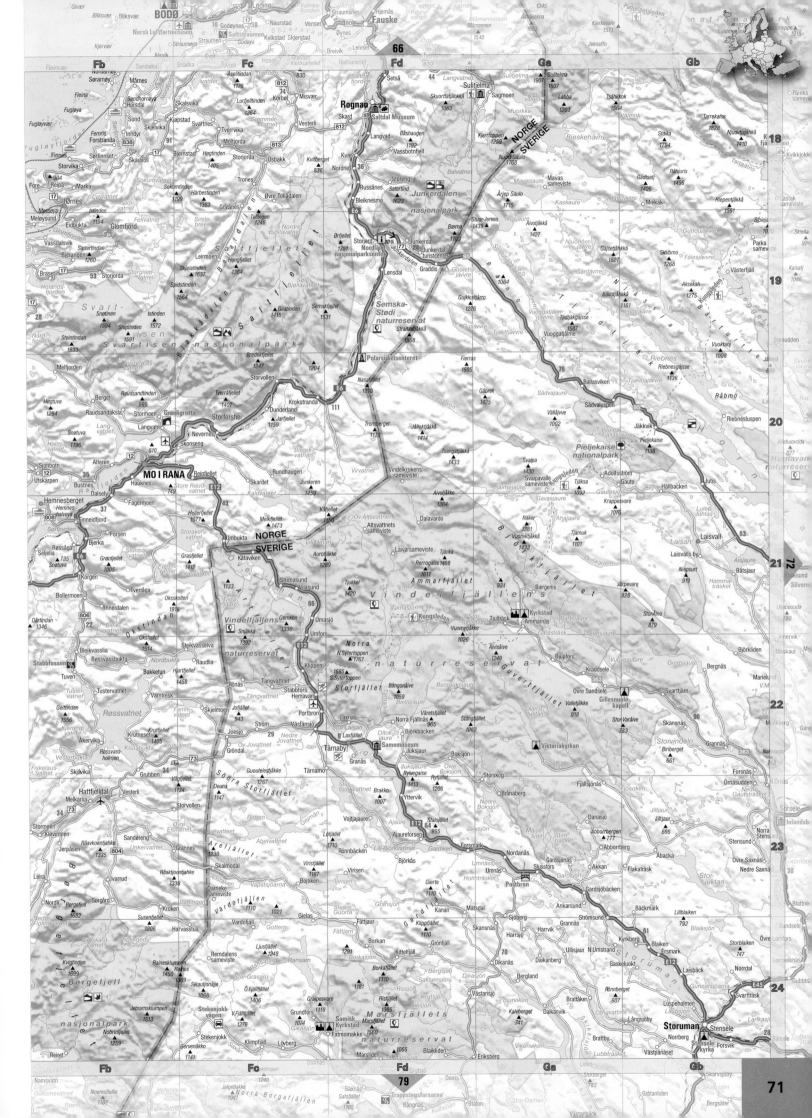

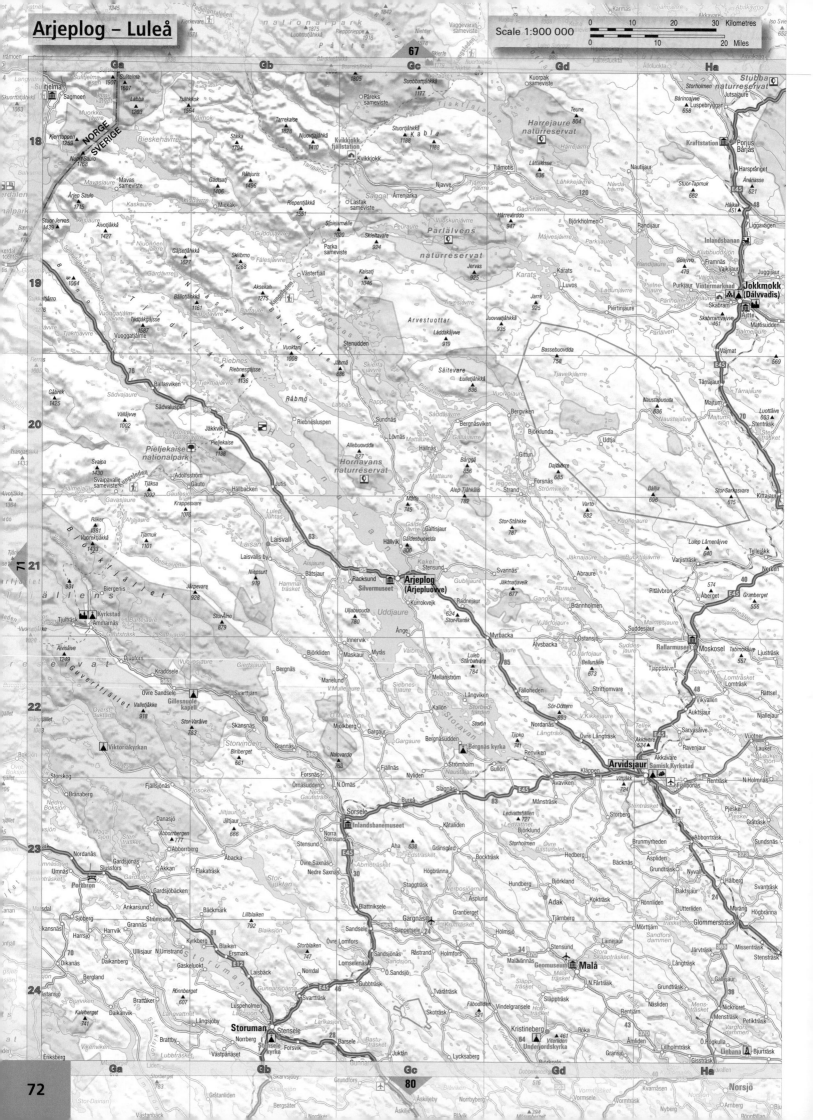

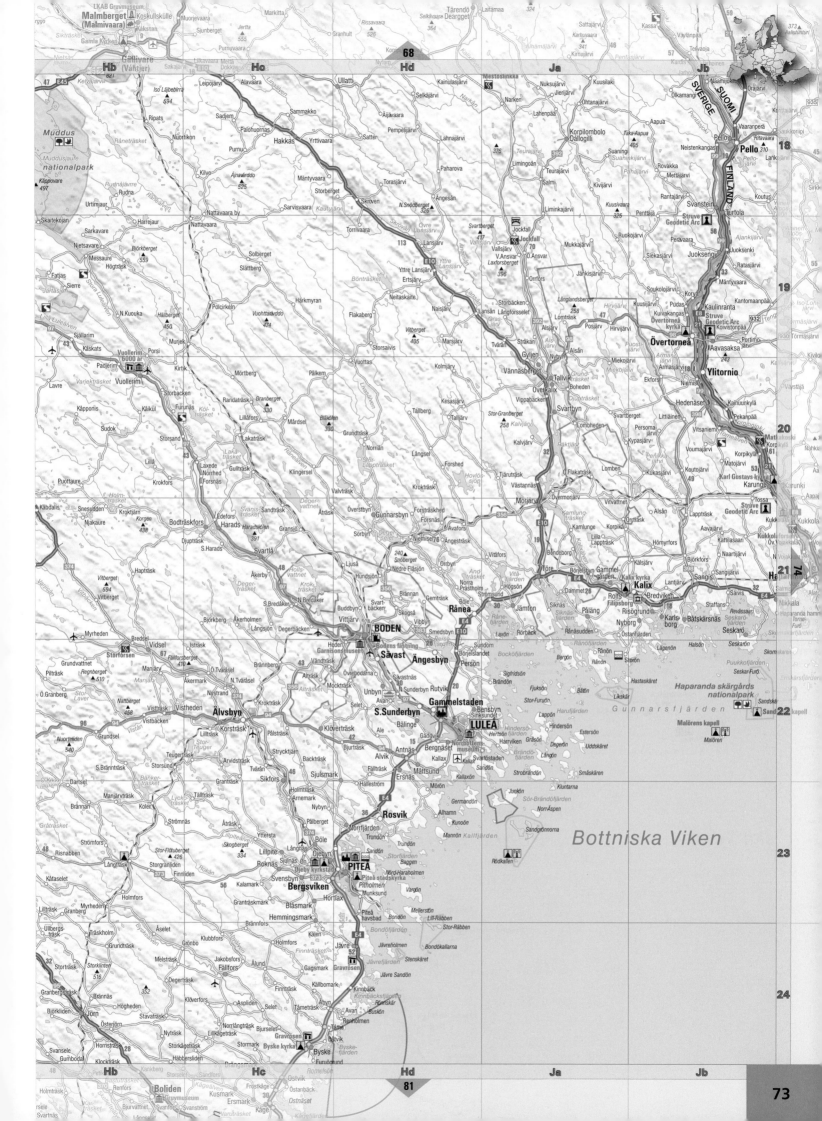

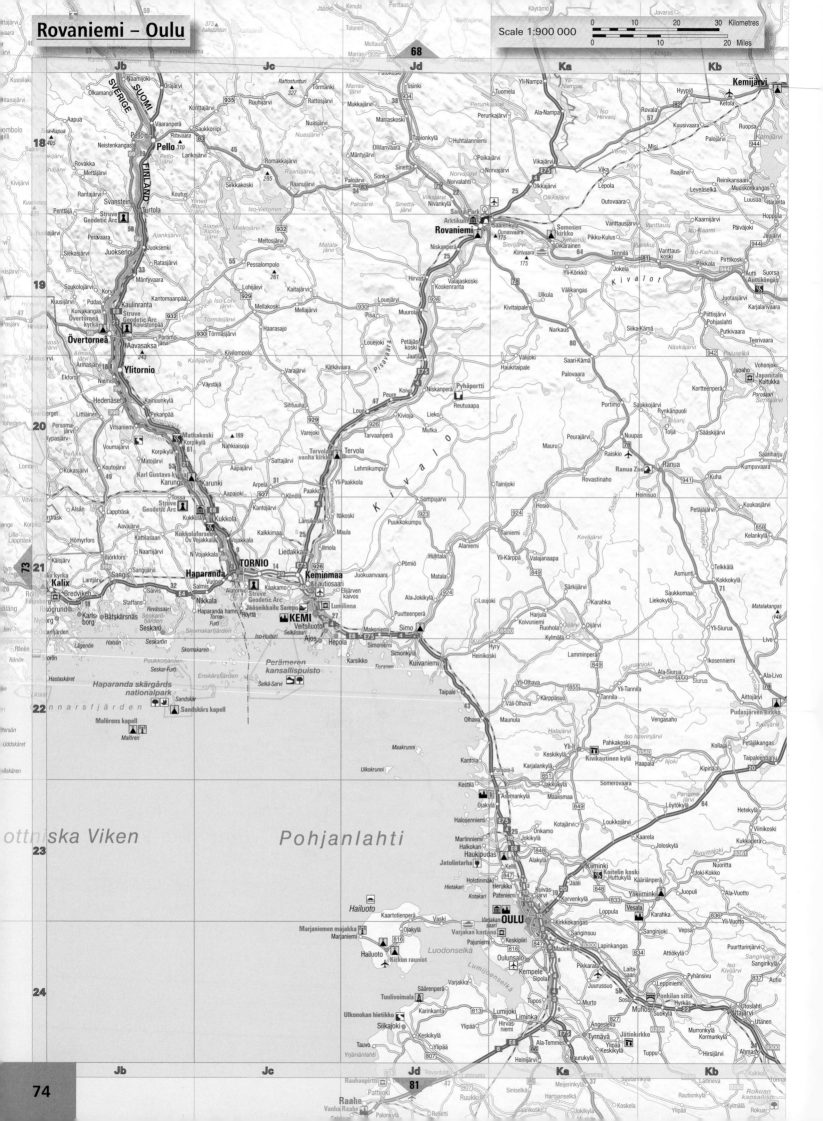

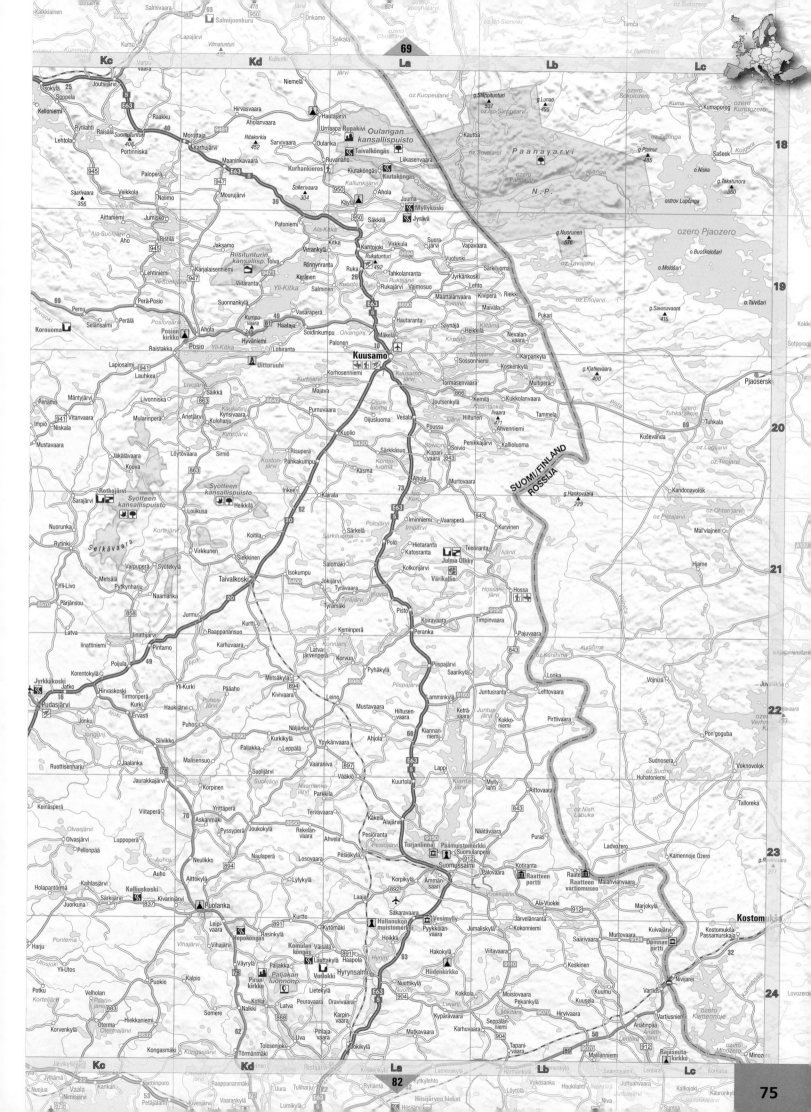

Scale 1:900 000

0 10 20 30 Kilometres
0   10   20 Miles

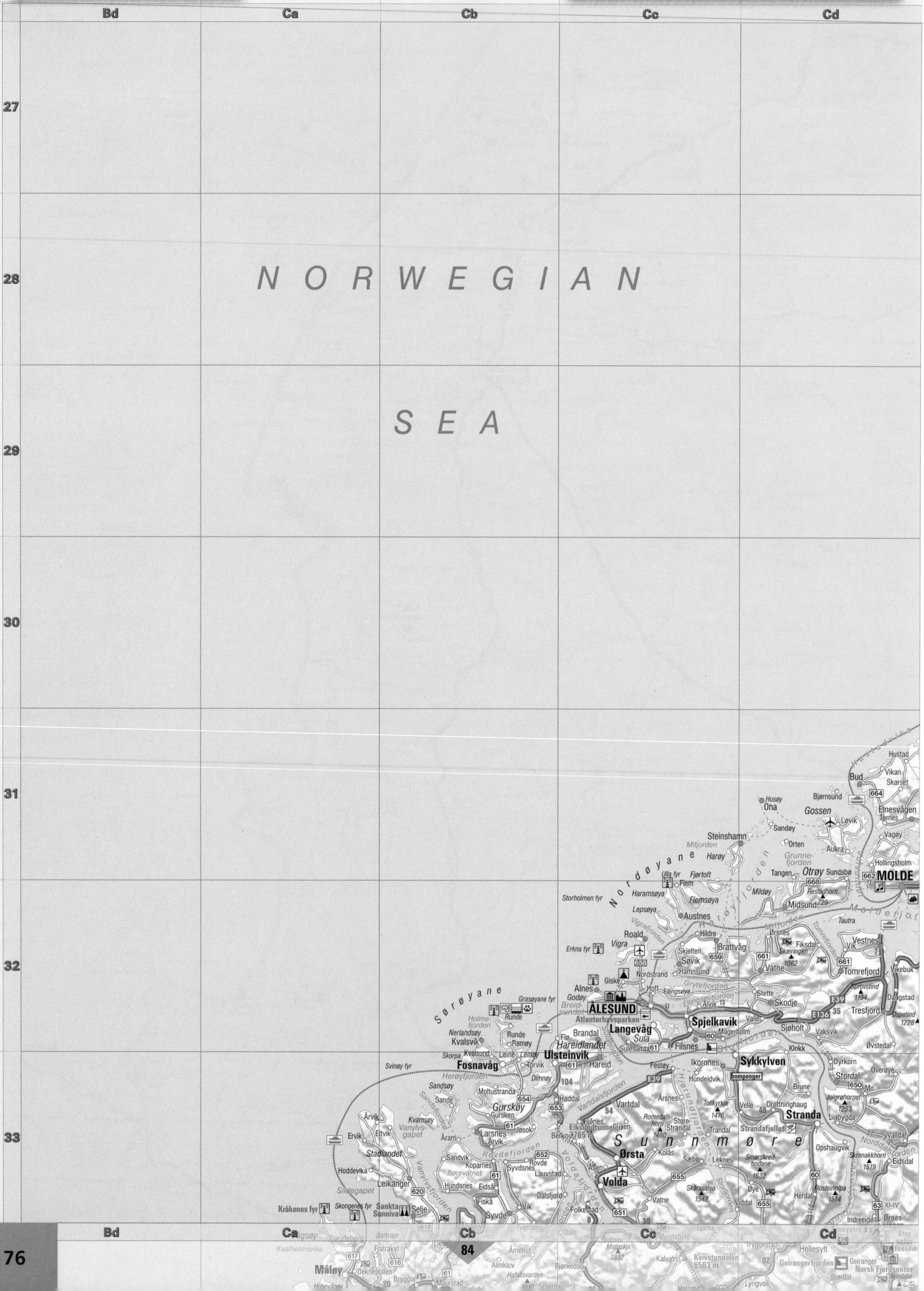

Bd   Ca   Cb   Cc   Cd

27

28

N O R W E G I A N

29

S E A

30

31

Hustad
Bud Vikan
Skarset

Husøy Bjørnsund 664
Ona Gossen Elnesvågen
Tornes
Steinshamn Sandøy Løvik Vågøy
Mitjorden Orten Aukra Hollingsholm
Grunne- MOLDE
Harøy fjorden Otrøy 668 Sundsbø 662
Ulla fyr Flem Mildøy Restadhorn
Storholmen fyr Haramsøya Flemsøya Midsund 729 Tautra
Lepsøya Austnes Ørnes Vestnes
Vigra Hildre Tomrefjord Vik
Roald Skjelten Brattvåg Fiksdal 661 Vikebukt
Erkna fyr Vigra Søvik 659 1062 661
659 Hamnsund Vatne Tomrefjord
Nordstrand Grytefjorden Stette Sprovstind Daugstad
Giske Hoff Ellingsøya Alvik Skodje 1794 E39 Tresfjord
Alnes Godøy 35 Øspetind
Runde Breid- ÅLESUND Valle E136 1228
sundet Atlanterhavsparken Spjelkavik Sjøholt
Holme- Langevåg Magerholm 60 Vaksvik Øvstedal
Nerlandsøy Brandal Sula Finnes Klokk
Kvalsvik Hareidlandet Sulesund 61 Ikornnes Dyrkorn
Skorpa Kvalsund Leine Leinøy Ulsteinvik Festøy Sykkylven Stordal Overøye
Fosnavåg Tørvik 61 Hareid E39 bompenger 650 Mo
Dimnøy 104 Hundeidvik Brune
Herøyfjord Vartdal Arsnes Velle Drottninghaug Jølgrøhorner
Sandsøy Moltustranda 654 Vartdal Tollkyrkja 1253
Gurskøy 653 Bjørnes Romedals- 1476 Stranda
Årvik Eltvik Kvamsøy Gursken Eiksundtunnelen horn Store Strandafjellet
Ervik Vanylvsgapet Aram Berkno 765 1480 Trandal Opshaugvik
Stadlandet Rovdefjorden 652 Åsebø Ørsta Smørskred- Skrenakkhorn Eidsdal
Hoddevika Sandvik Koparnes Rovde Trandal tindane 1519
Børevatnet Syvdsnes Øye Fjøsteinnipa
Sildegapet Leikanger Hundsnes Eidså Volda 655 Skårasalen Herdal 1514
620 Fiskå Dalstjord 1542 Viddal 655 63
Kråkenes fyr Skongenes fyr Sankta Selje Vik 651 Vatne Indreeide Ørnes
Sunniva Syvde 39

76

Bd   Ca   Cb   Cc   Cd

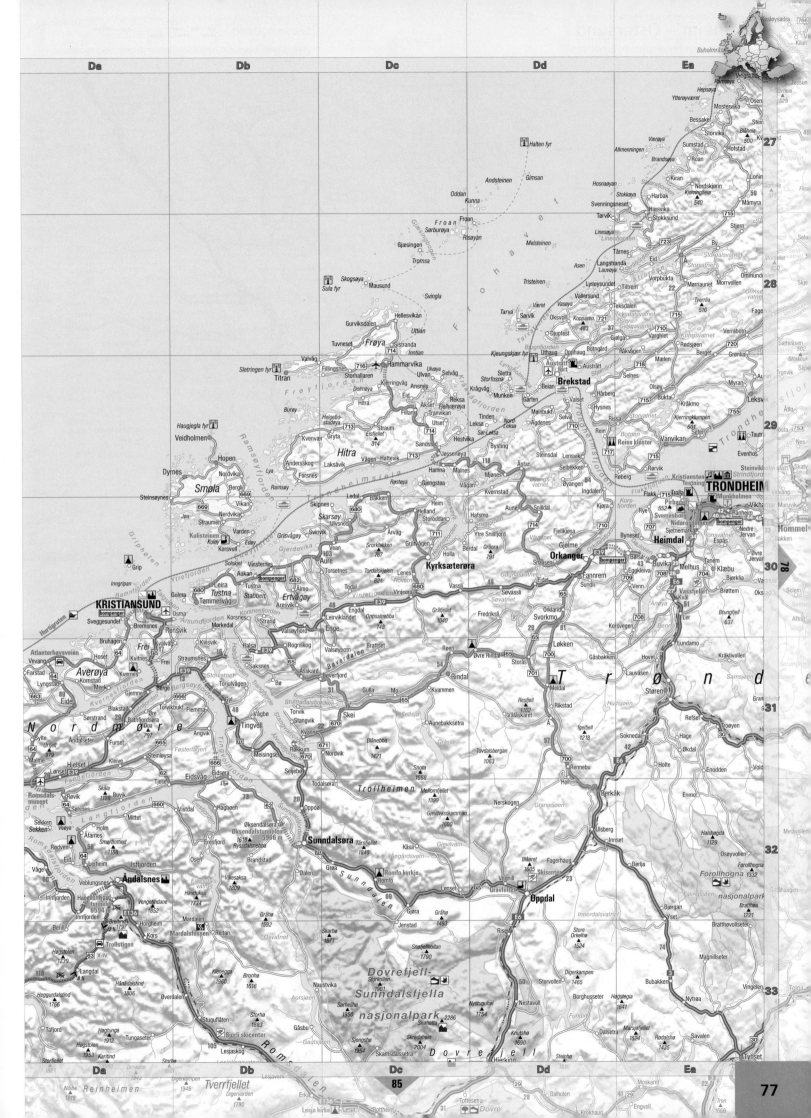

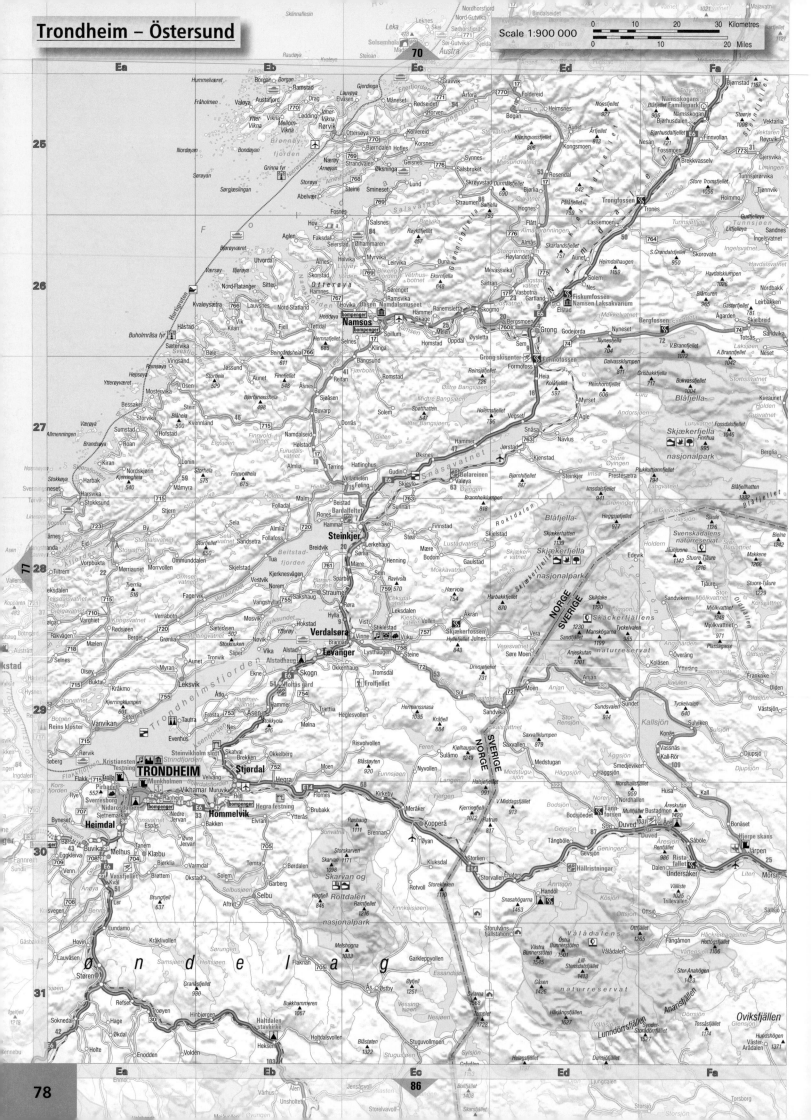

Scale 1:900 000

| 0 | 10 | 20 | 30 Kilometres |
| 0 | 10 | | 20 Miles |

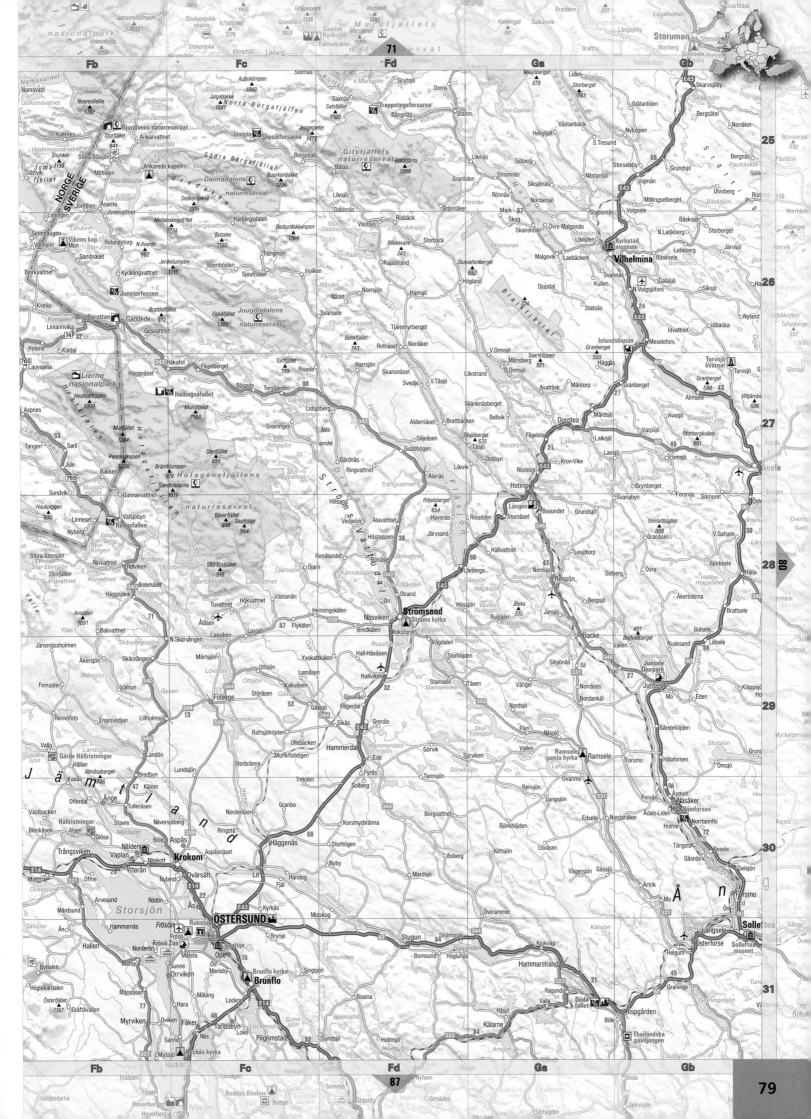

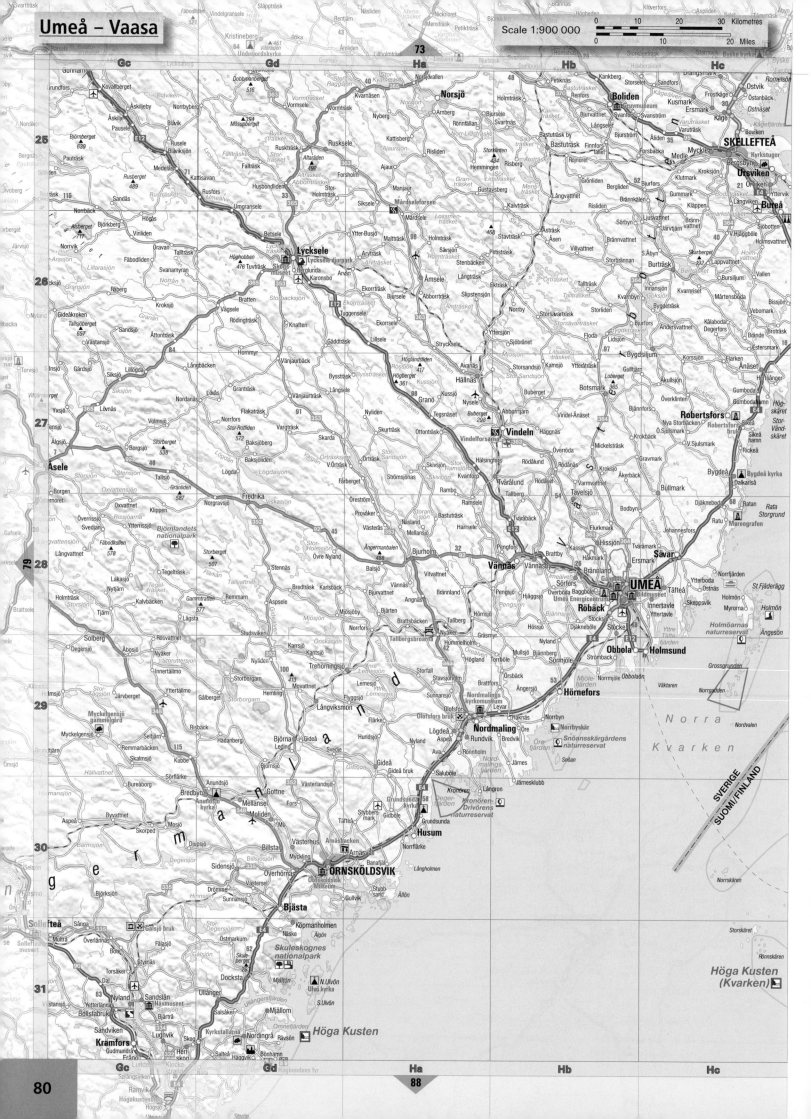

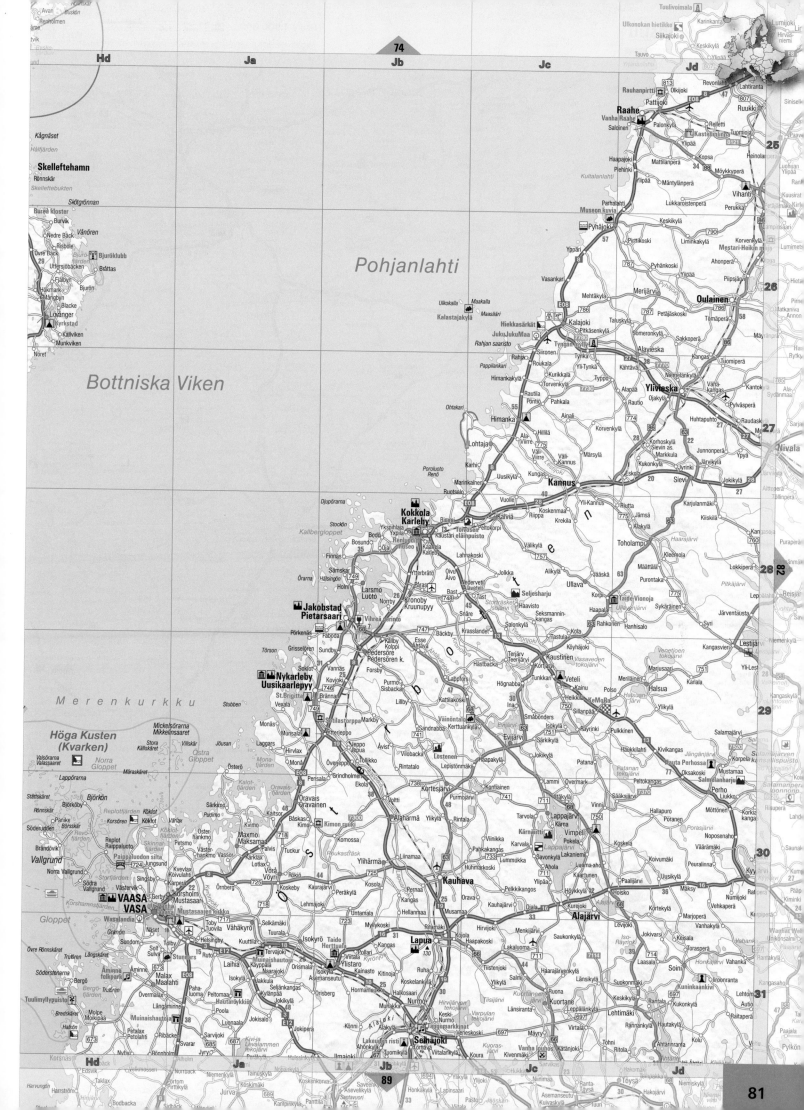

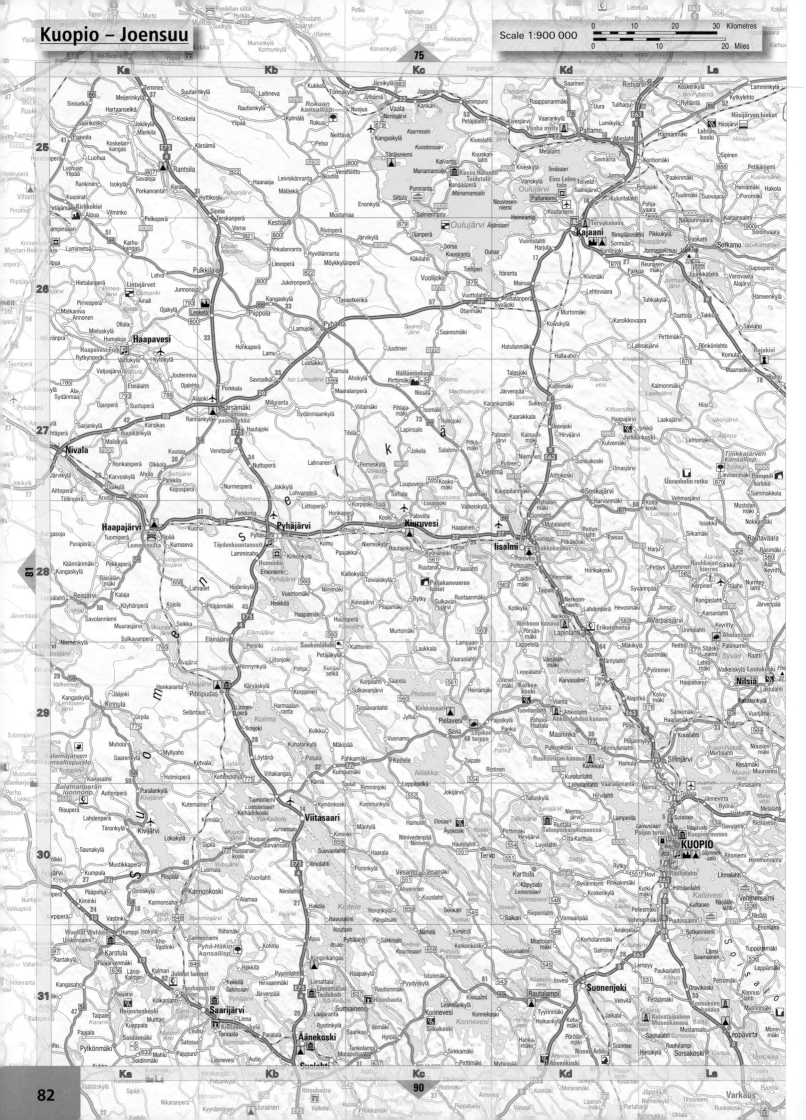

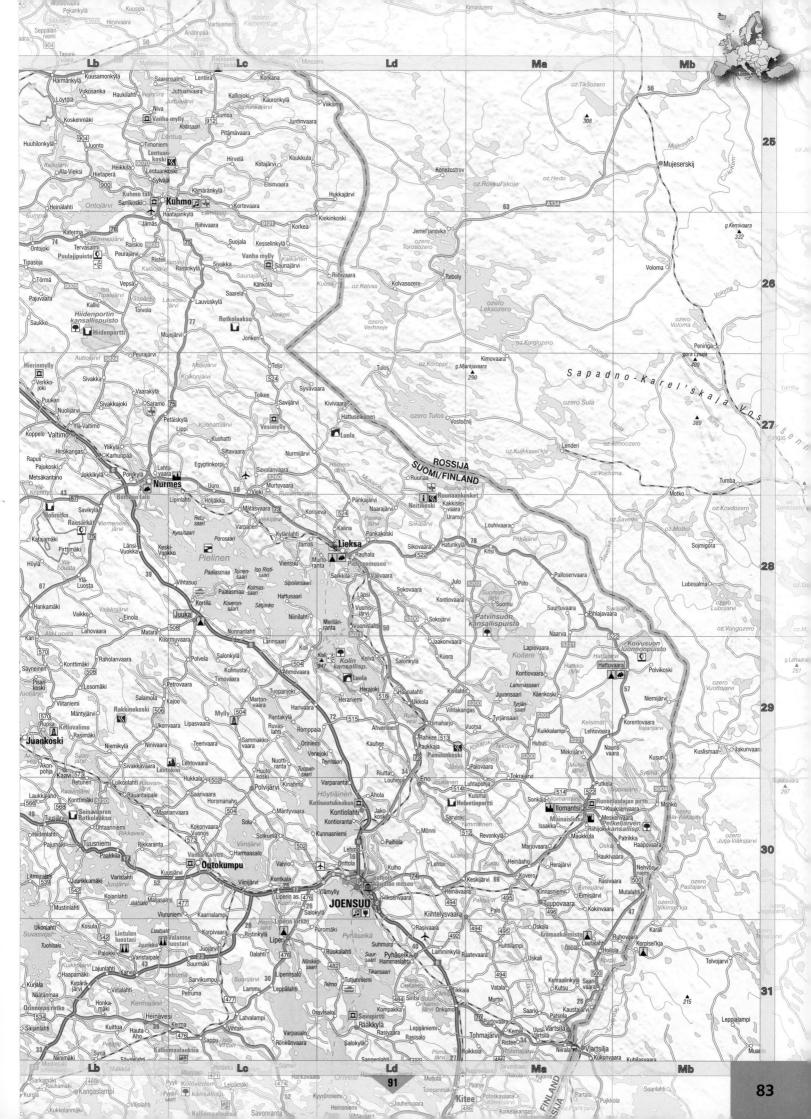

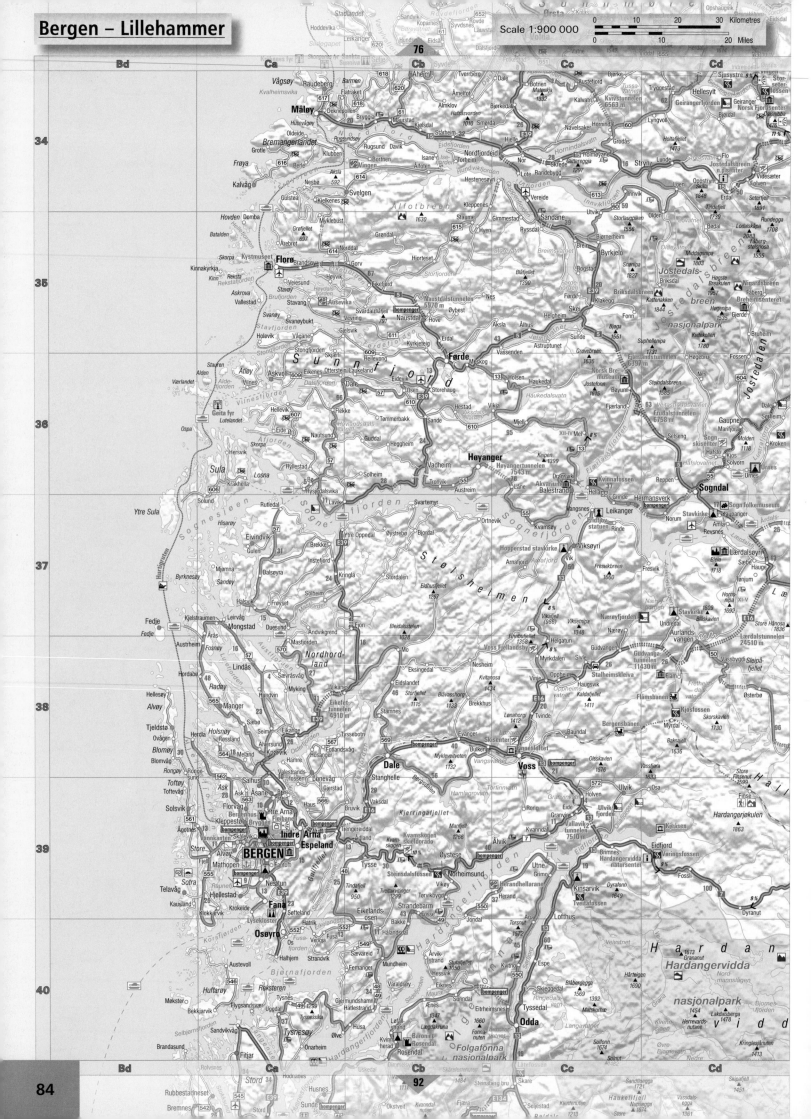

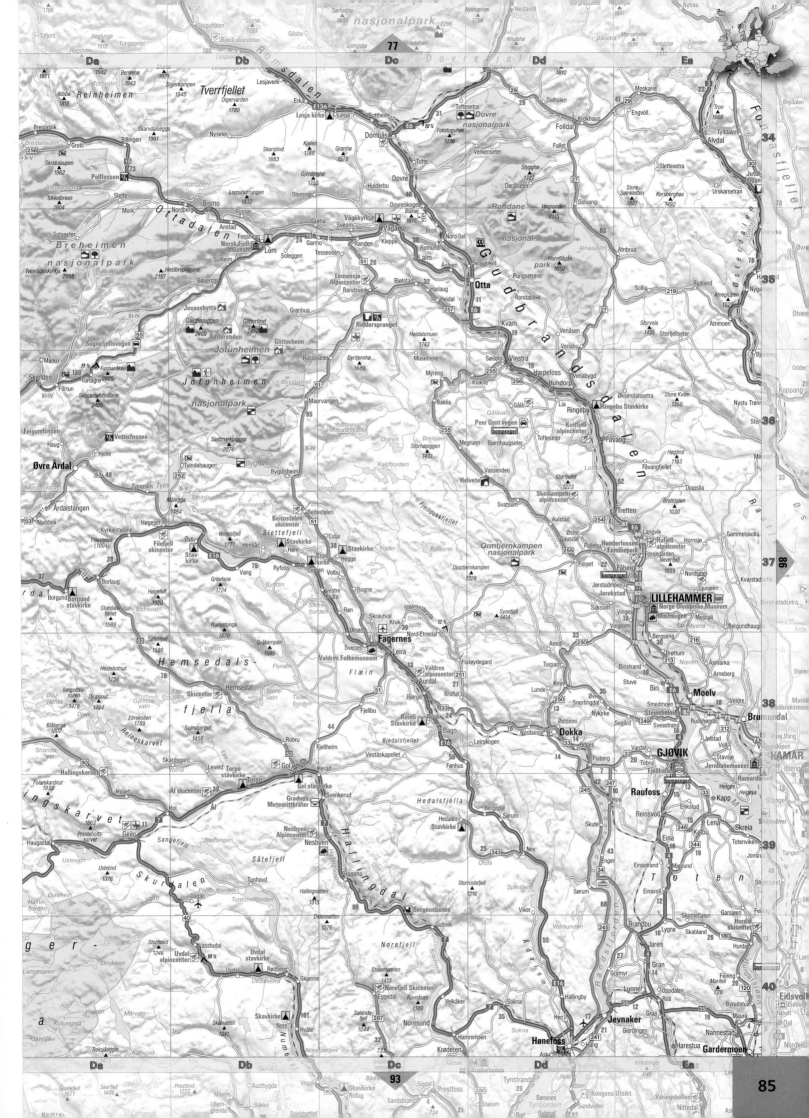

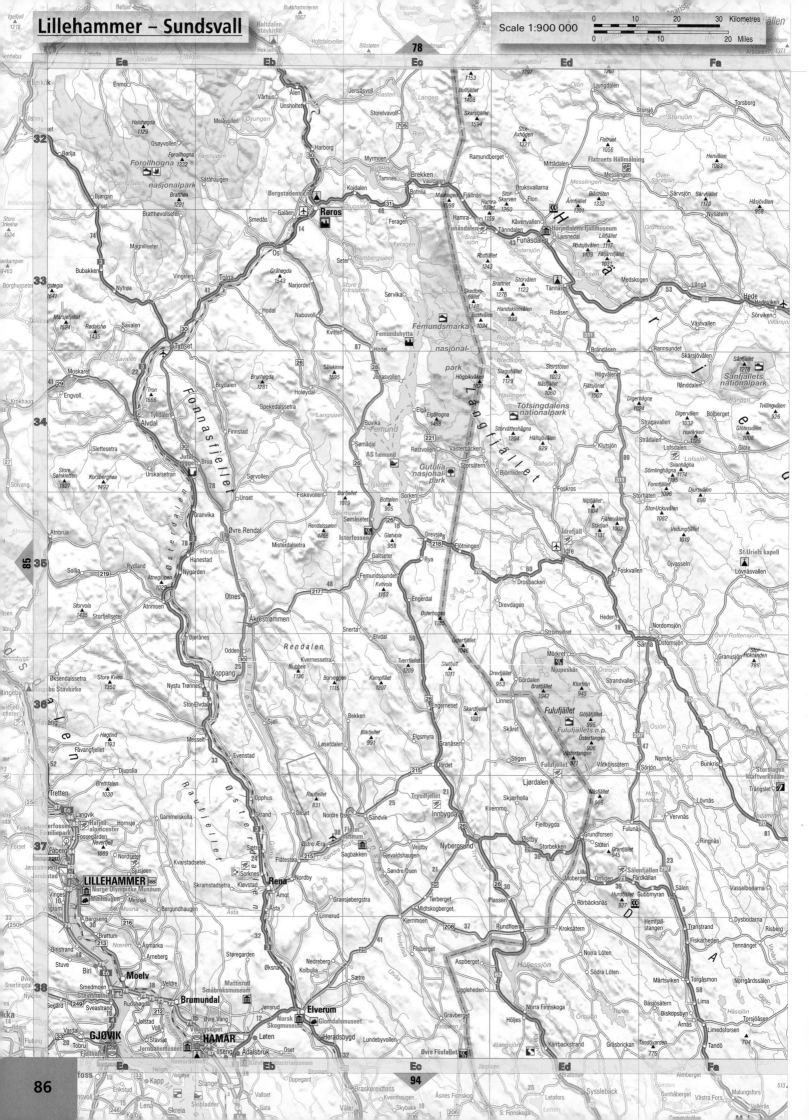

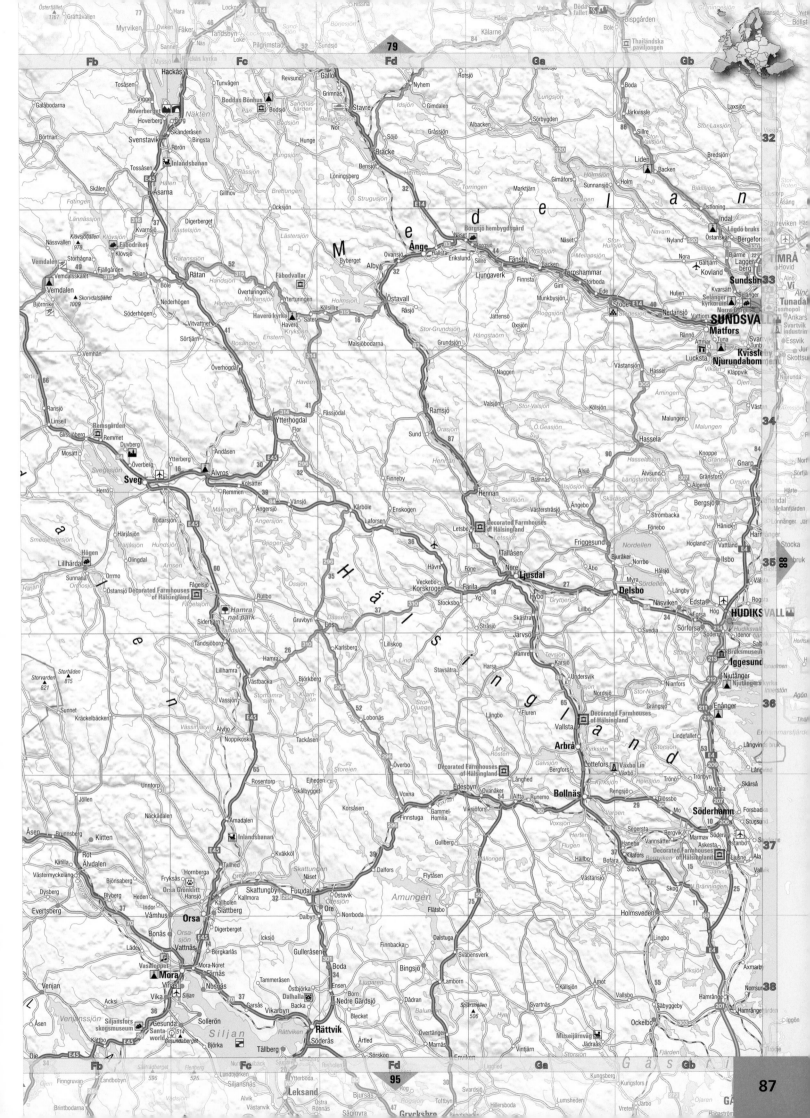

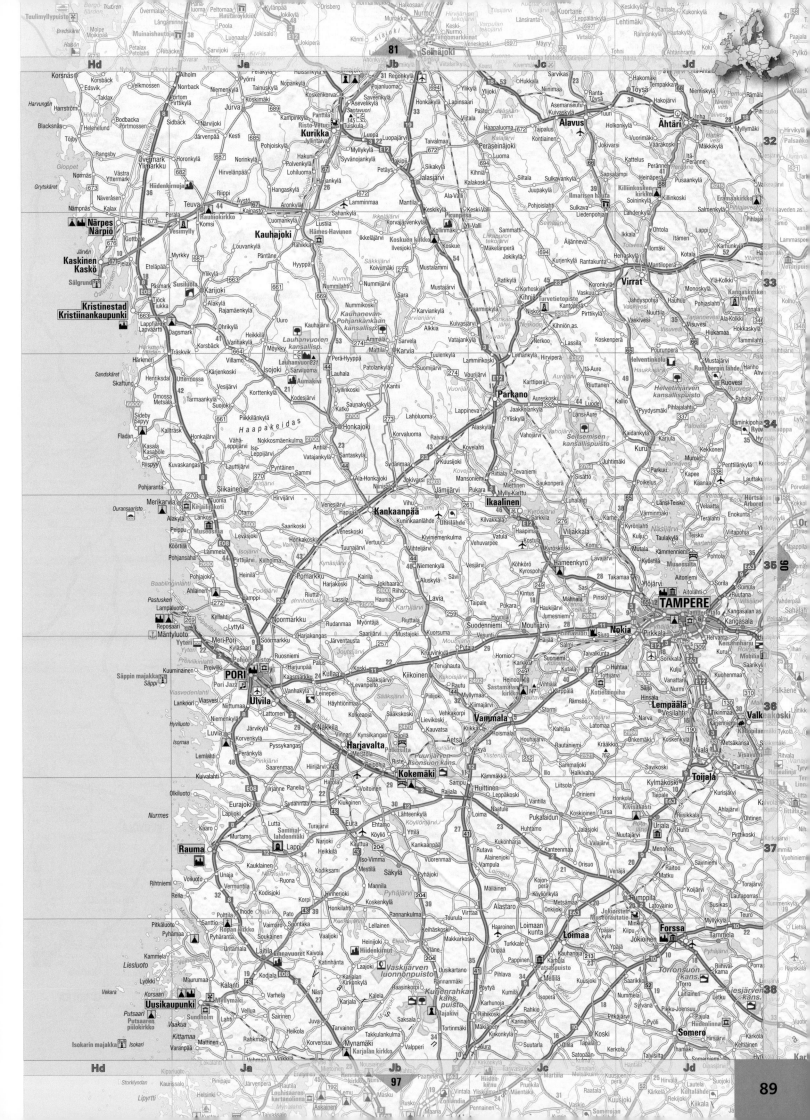

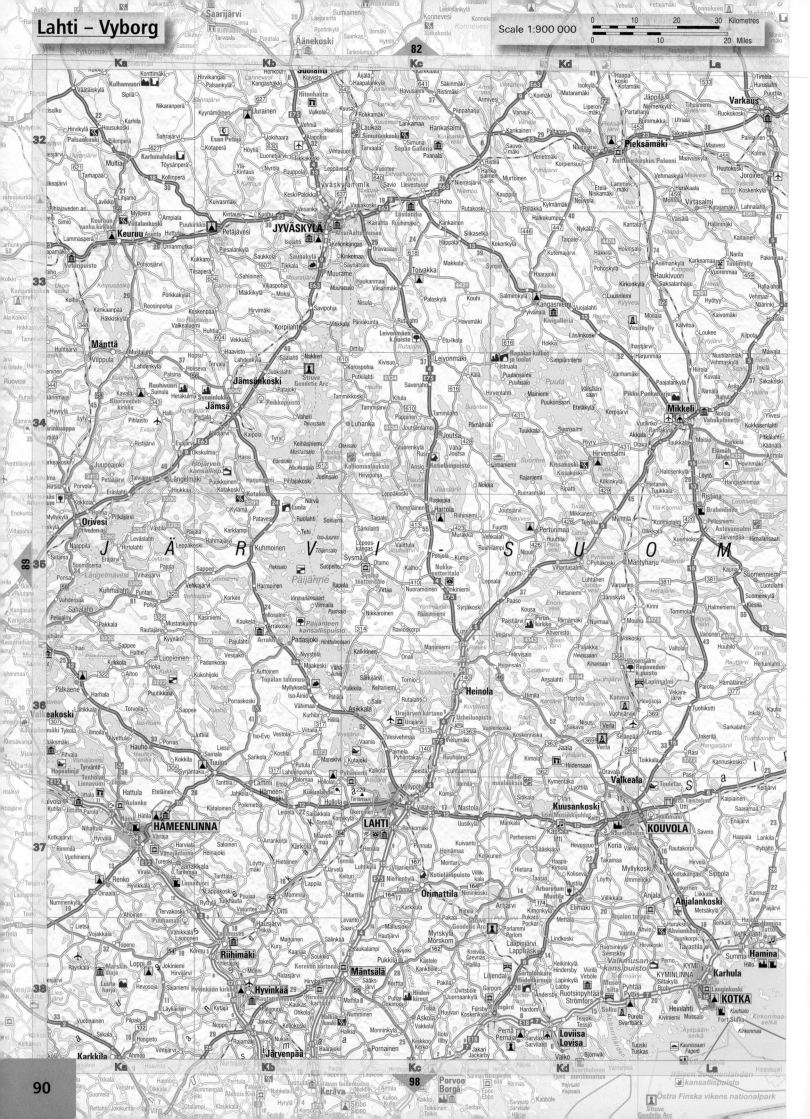

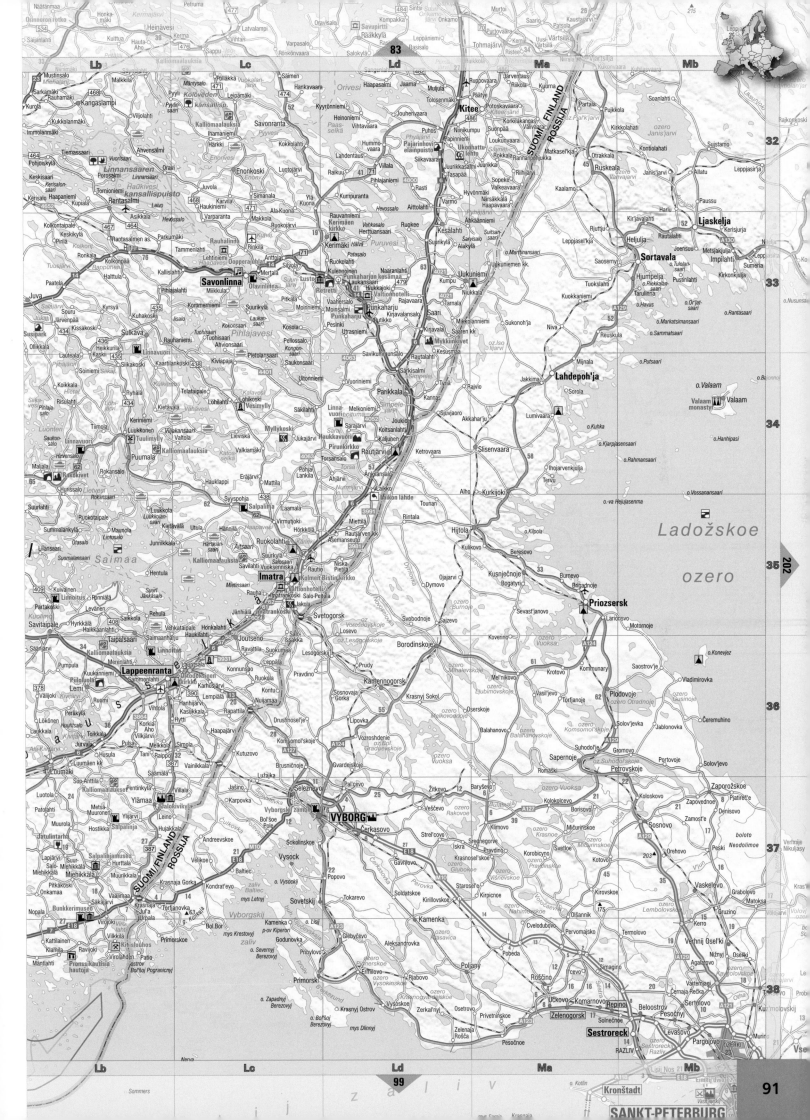

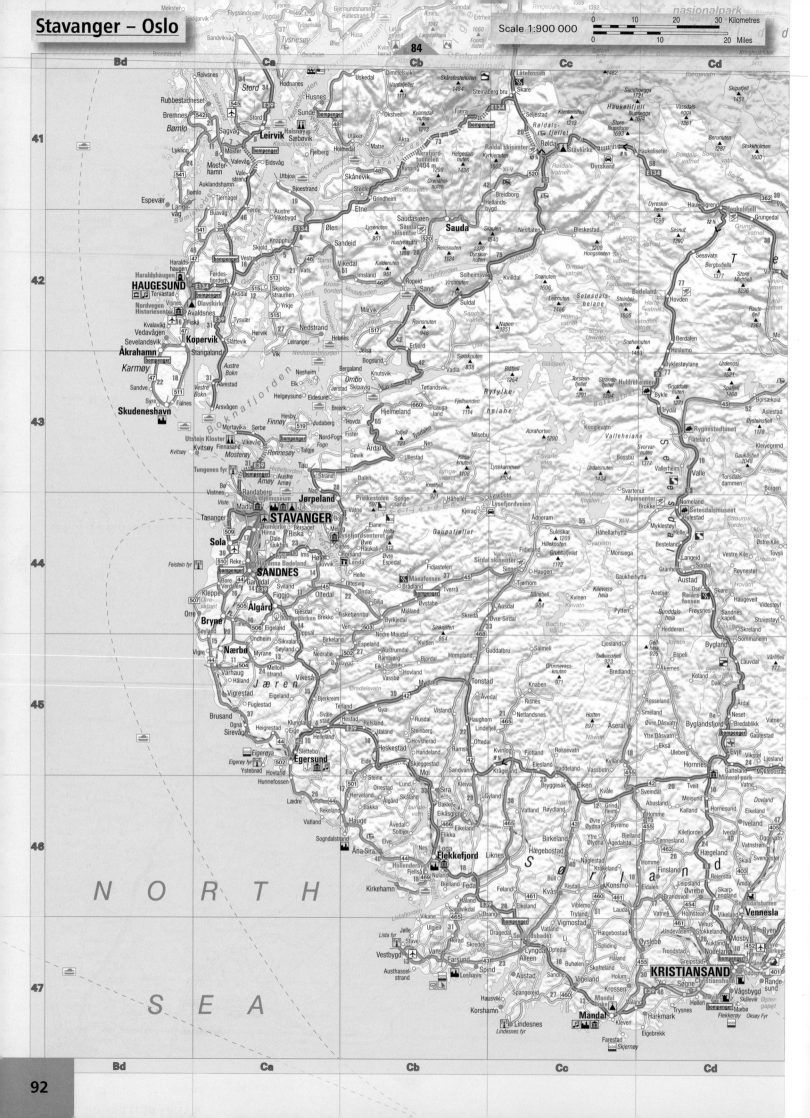

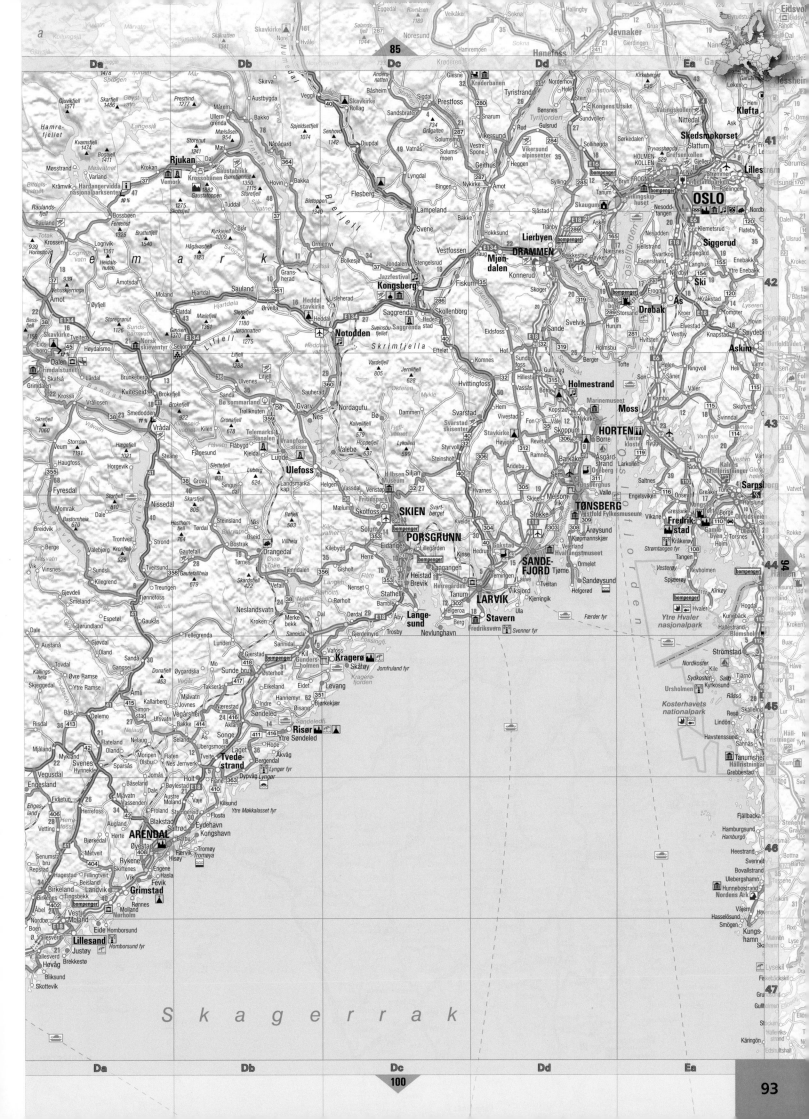

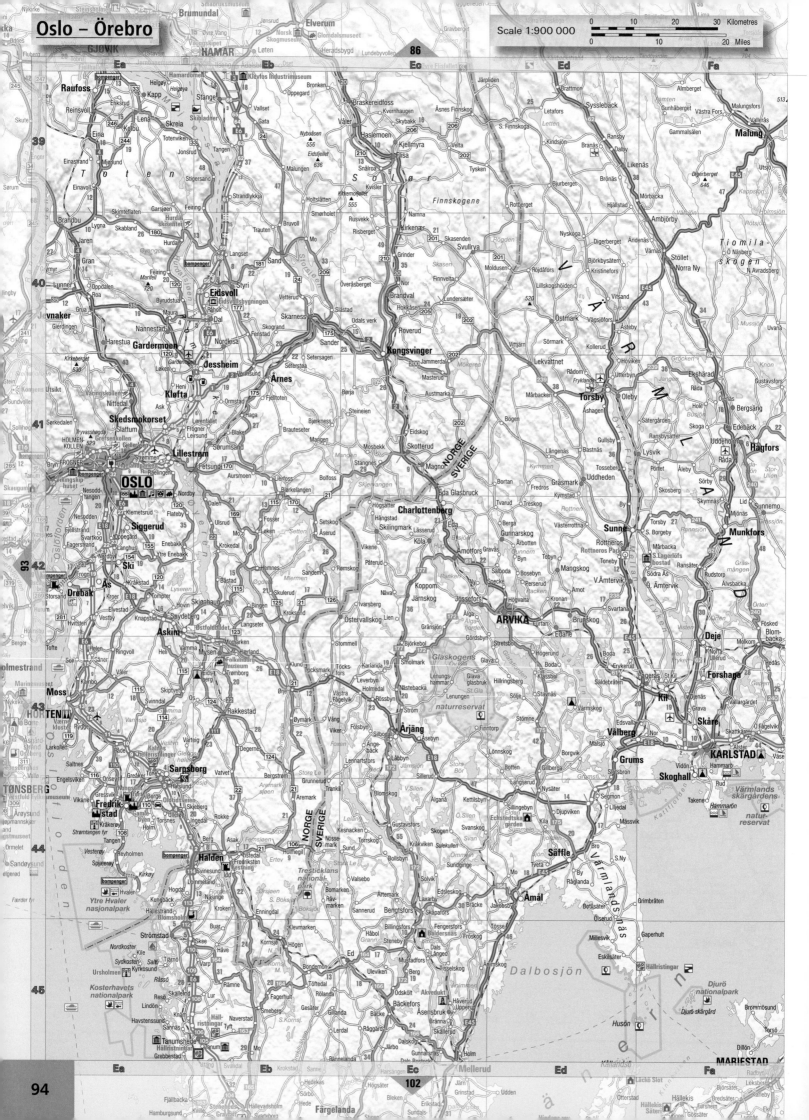

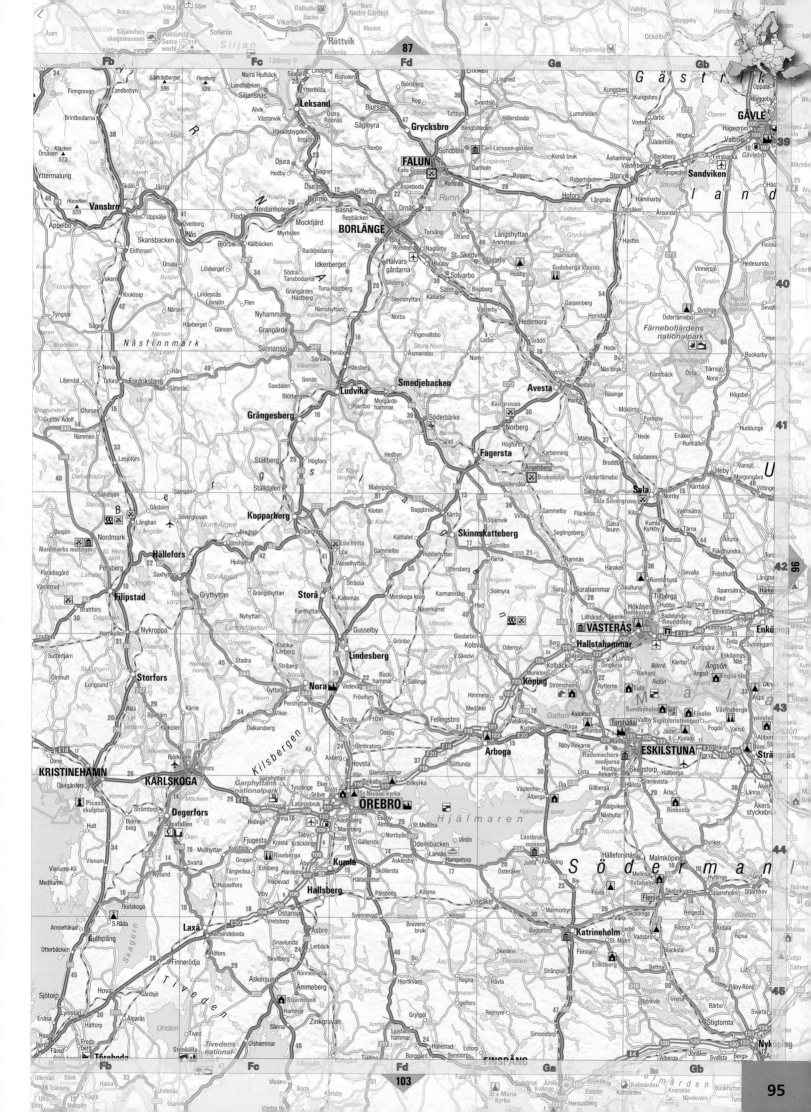

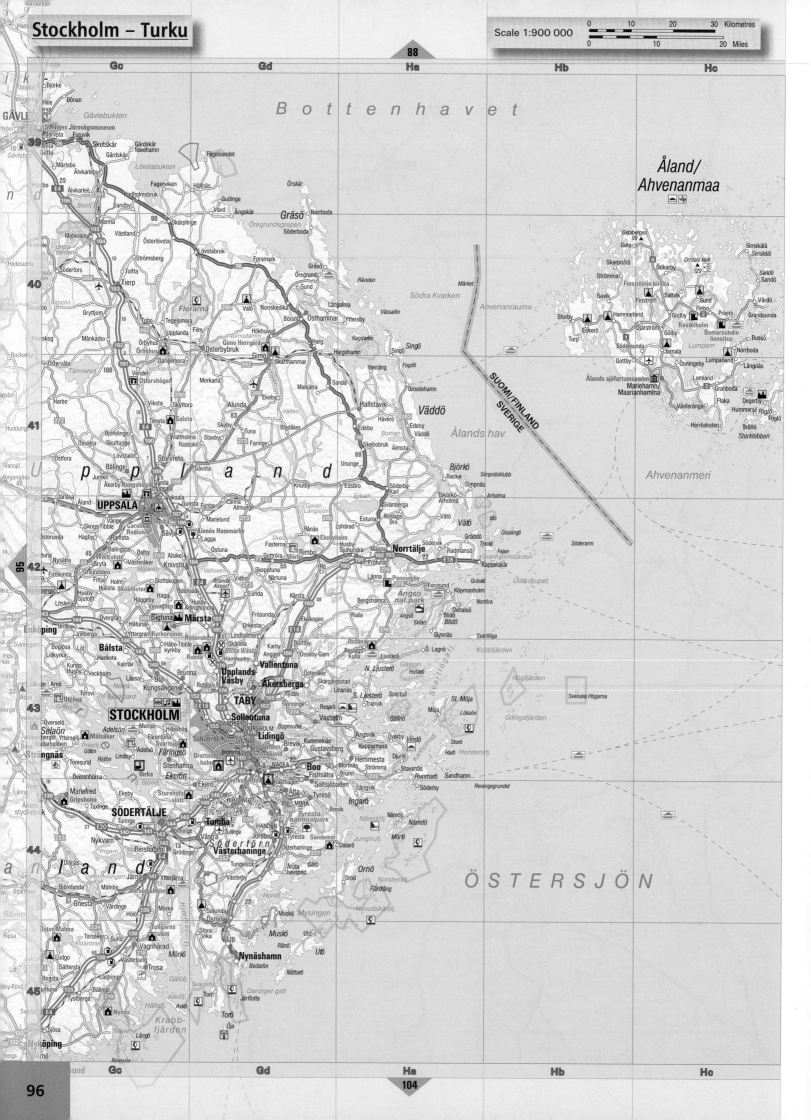

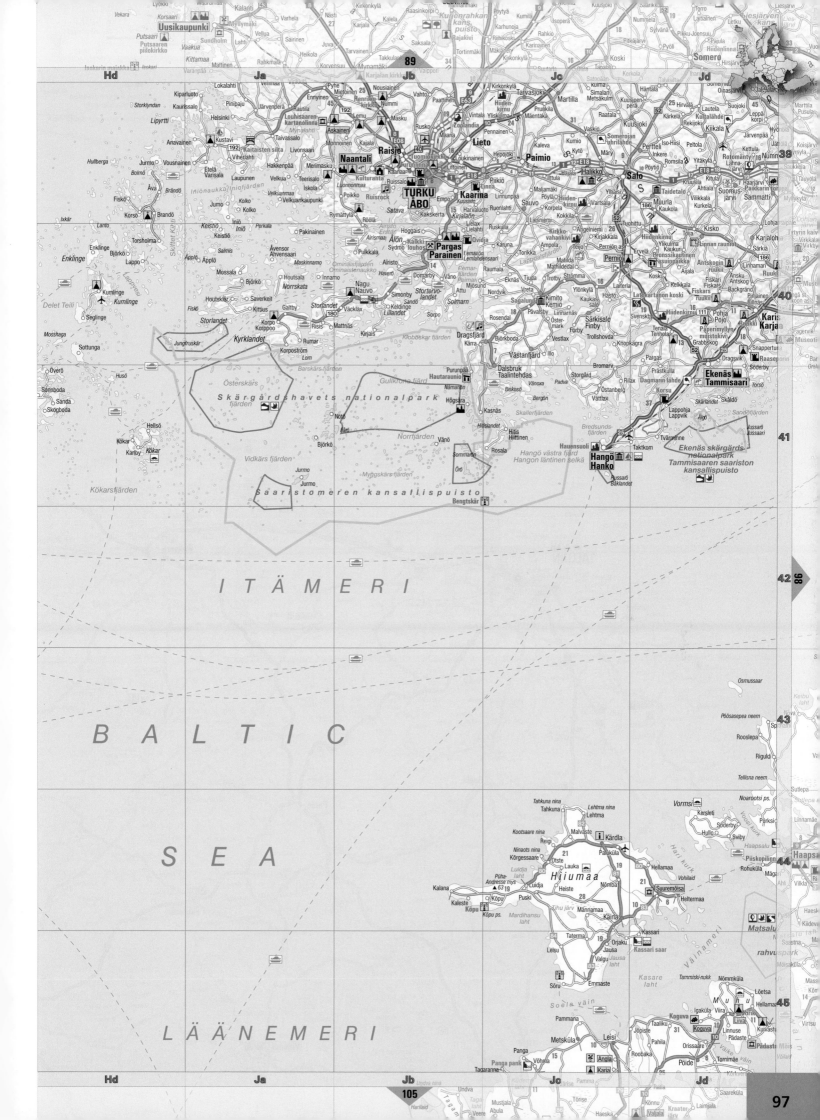

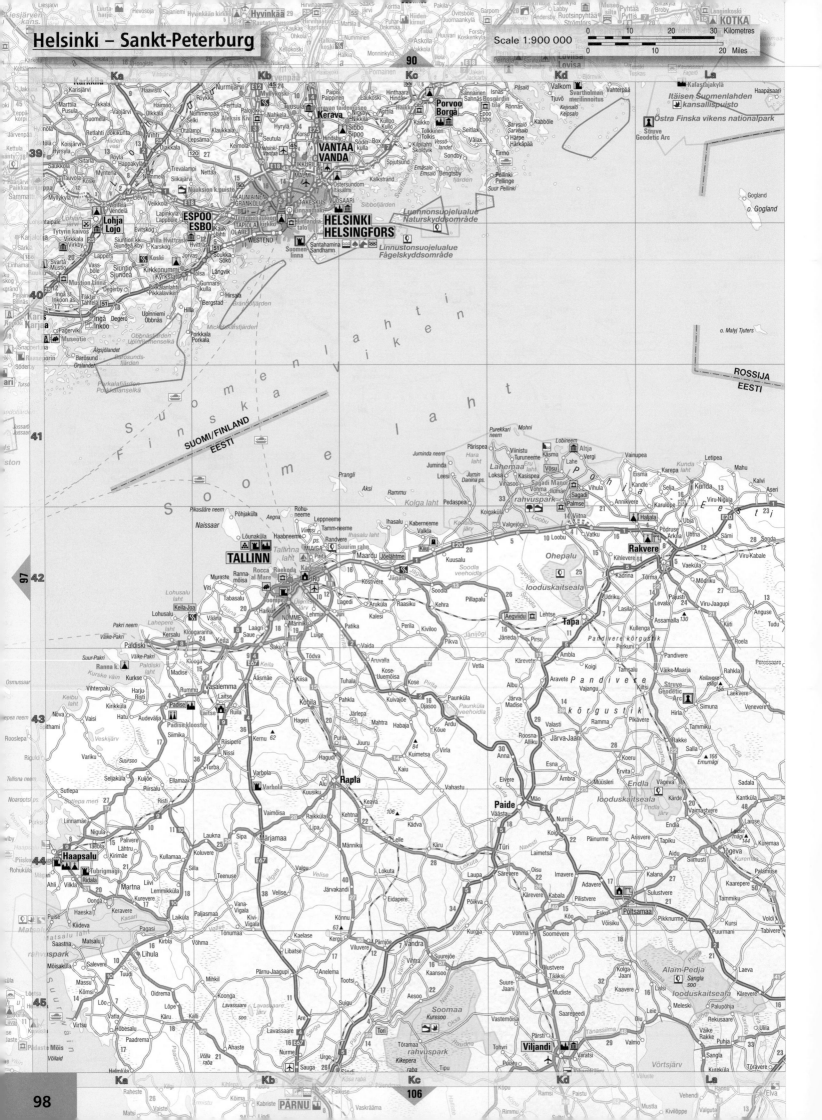

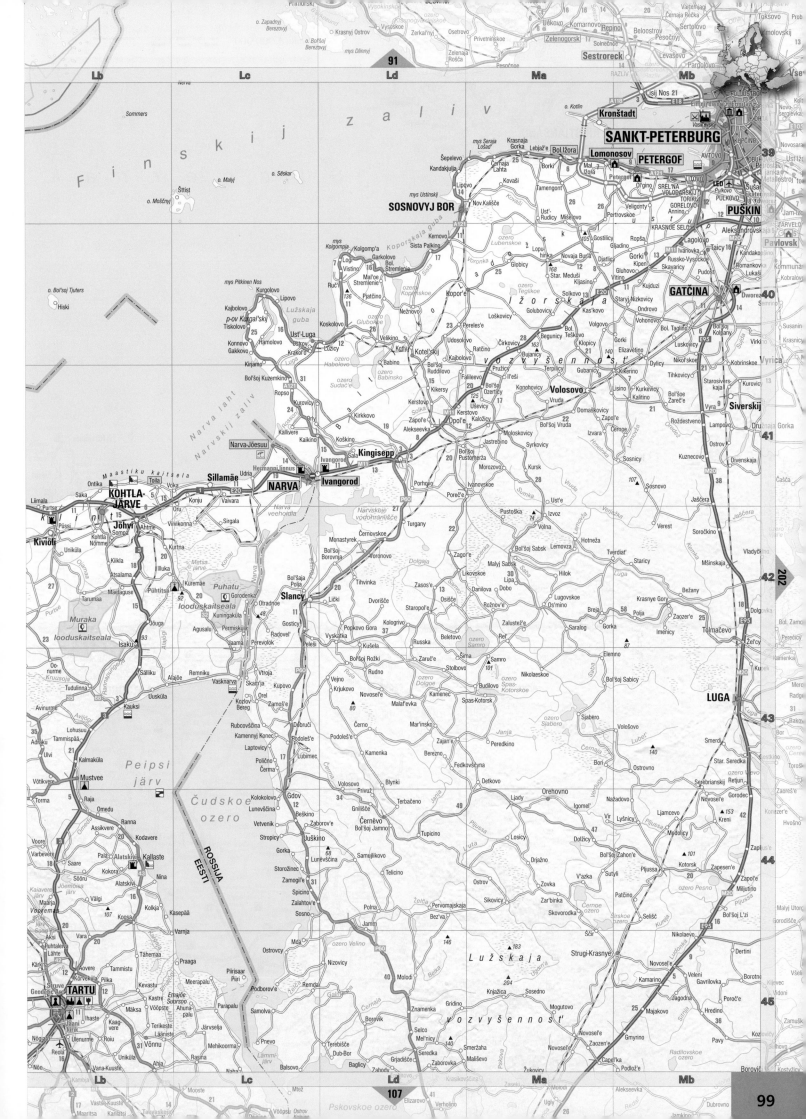

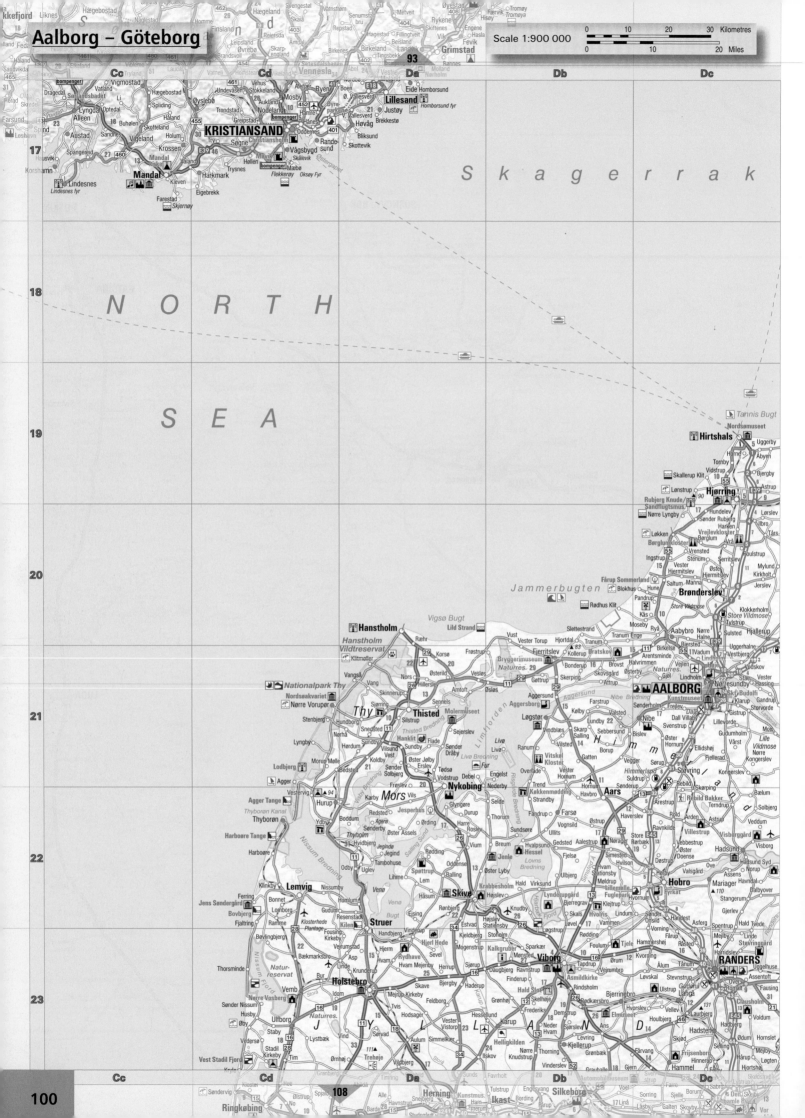

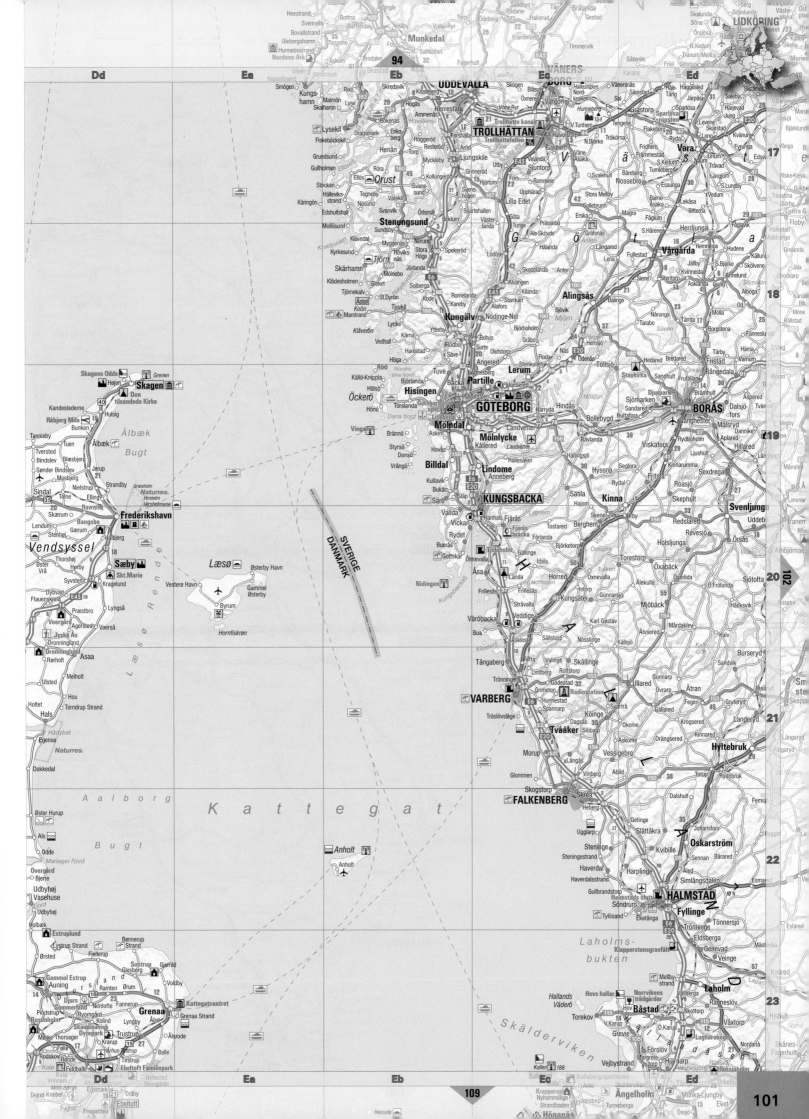

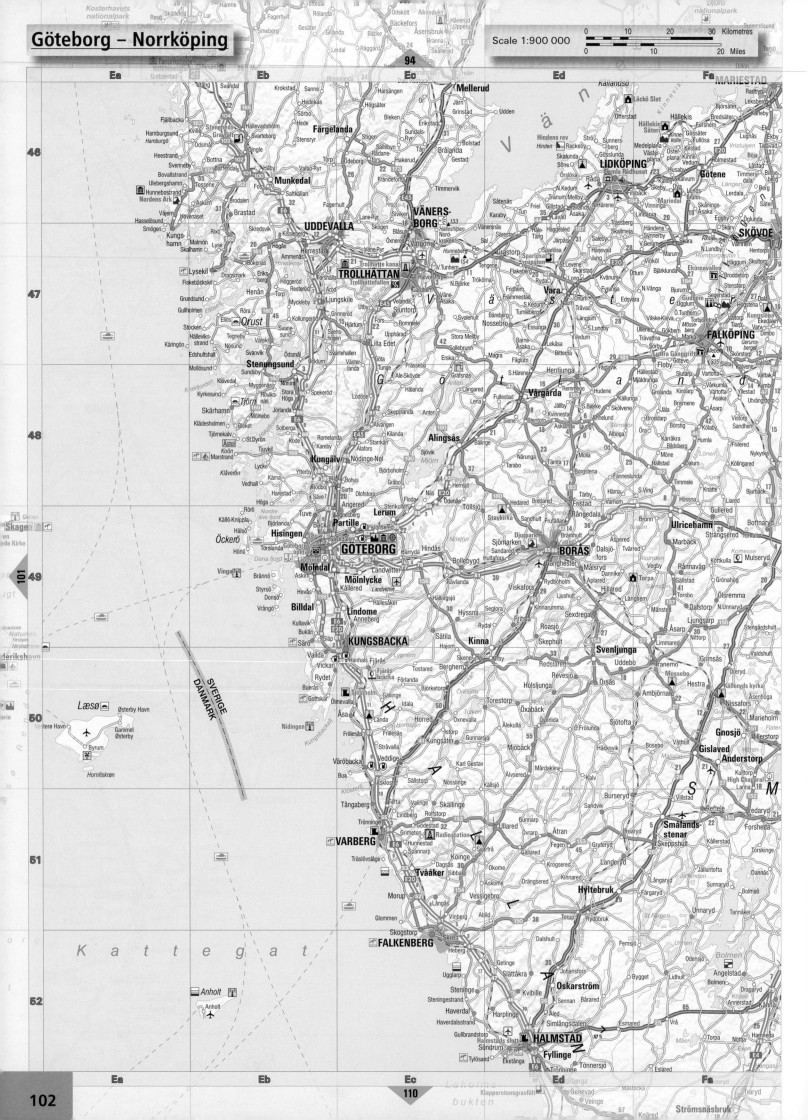

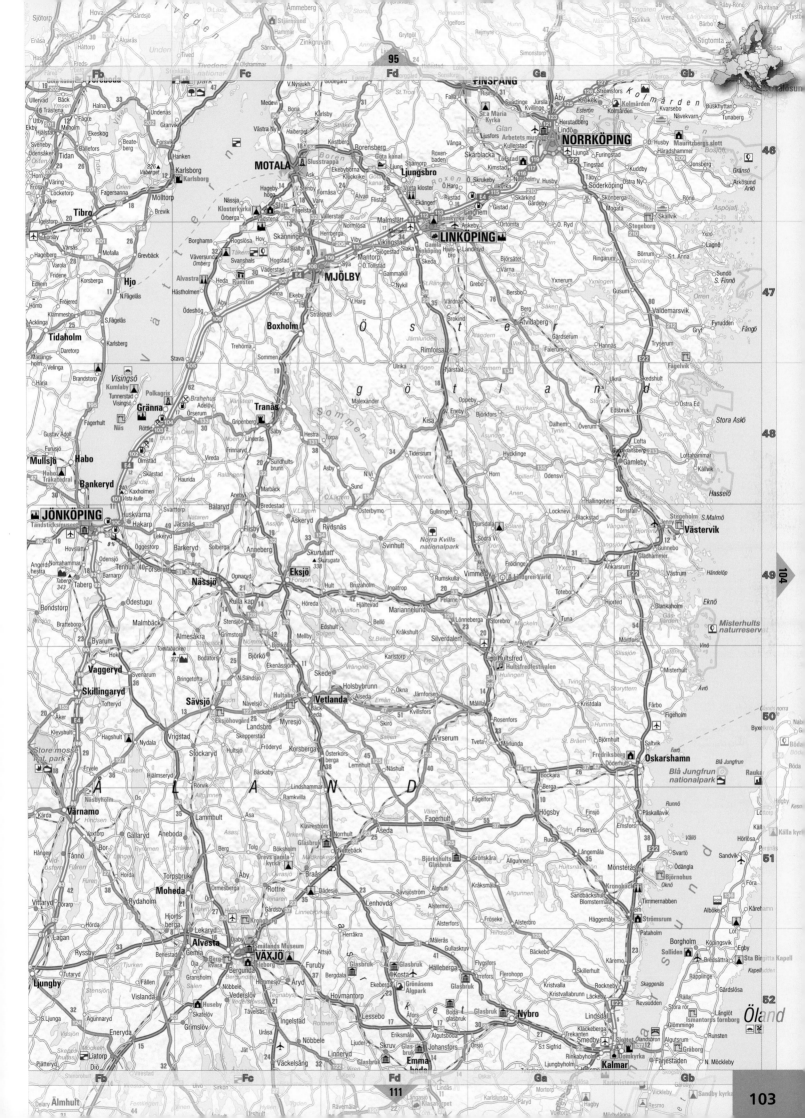

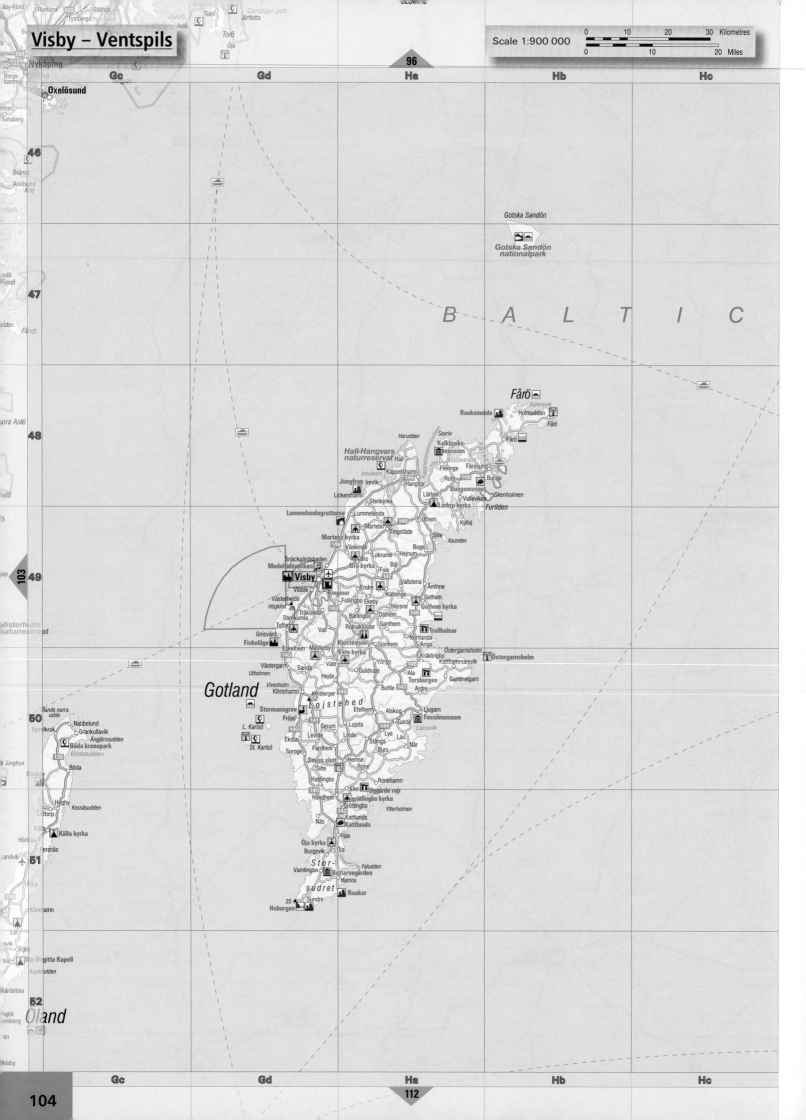

Scale 1:900 000

0   10   20   30   Kilometres

0   10   20   Miles

Nyköping

Oxelösund

46

Gränsö
Arkösund
Arkö

47

B   A   L   T   I   C

Gotska Sandön

Gotska Sandön
nationalpark

48

Fårö

Ajkesvik

Raukområde   Holmudden   Fårö

Harudden   Saxriv   Fårö

Hall-Hangvars
naturreservat   Hall   Kalkbruks
                              museum

Ireviken   Kappelshamn   Bästeträsk
                                   Fleringe   Fårösund

Jungfrun   Irevik   Hangvar   Rute   Bunge

Lickershamn   Lärbro   Bungemuseet

Stenkyrka   Valleviken   Skenholmen

Lummelundagrottorna   Lummelunda   Lärbro kyrka   *Furilden*

Martebo kyrka   Martebo   Tingstäde   Othem   Kyllaj

149   Väskinde   Lokrume   Hejnum   Boge   Slite   Asunden

Snäckgärdsbaden   Bro
Medeltidsveckan   Bro kyrka   Fole   Bäl

49   **Visby**   Vibble   Endre   Vallstena   Åminne

Ringmur   Follingbo Ekeby   Källunge   Gothem

Västerhejde   Barlingbo   Hörsne   Gothem kyrka

Högklint   Träkumla   Dalhem   146

Stenkumla   Romakloster   Ganthem   Norrlanda   Trullhalsar

Totta   Vall   Anga

Gnisvärd   Klosterruin   Sjonhem   Östergarnsholm

Fiskeläge   Mästerby   Väte kyrka   Kräklingbo   Östergarnsholm

140   Vate   Vänge   Katthammarsvik

Västergarn   Sanda   Guldrupe   Ala   Gammelgarn

Viveholm   Hejde   Buttle   Torsburgen   Ardre

Gotland   Klinteham   Klintberget   *Lojsthed*   Etelhem   Alskog   Ljugarn

Stormansgrav   Fröjel   Gerum   Lojsta   Garde   Fossilmuseum
                                                                              Lausvik

50   L. Karlsö   Levide   Linde   144   Lye   Lau
                                                                   Stånga   När

St. Karlsö   Eksta   Fardhem   Burs

Sproge   Hemse   Rone

Smiss slott   Silte   Ronehamn

Hablingbo

Eke   Uggårde rojr

Havdhem   Grötlingbo kyrka

Grötlingbo   Ytterholmen

Näs   Kattlunds
                    Kattlunds

Öja kyrka   Fide
Burgsvik   Öja

Stor-   Faludden
Vamlingbo   Bottarvegården
          Hamra

Sudret   Raukar

Sundre

Hoburgen

51

52

Öland

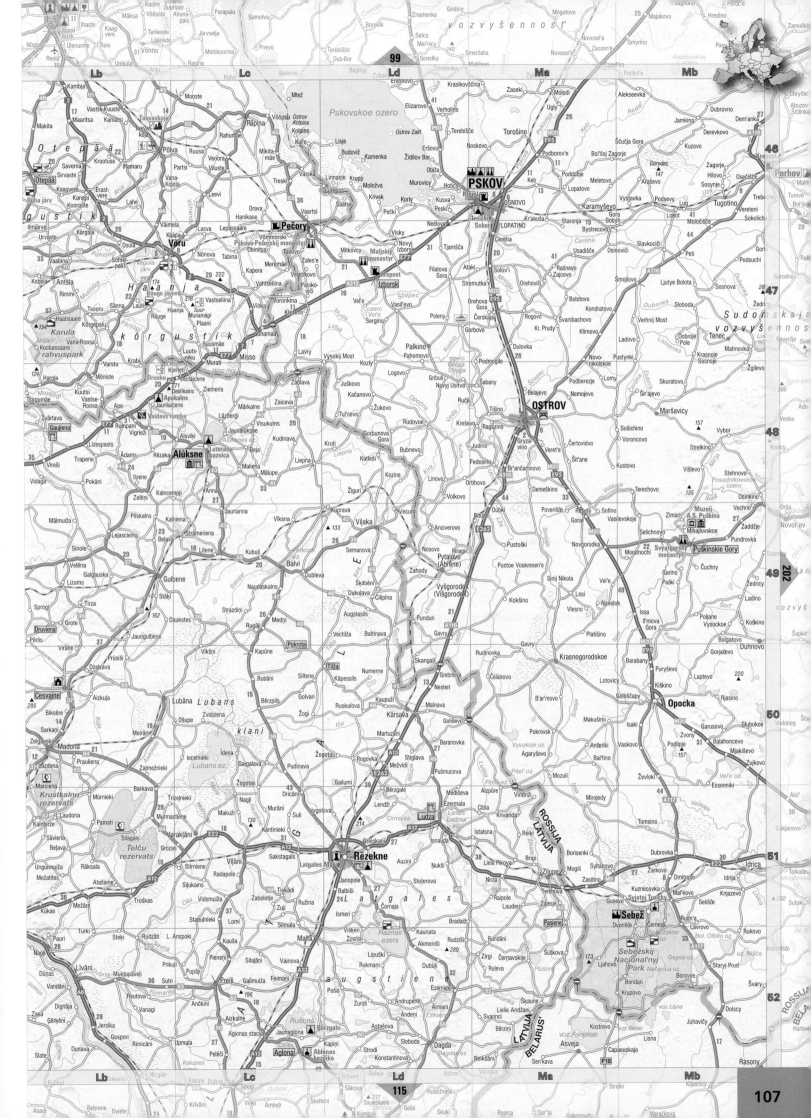

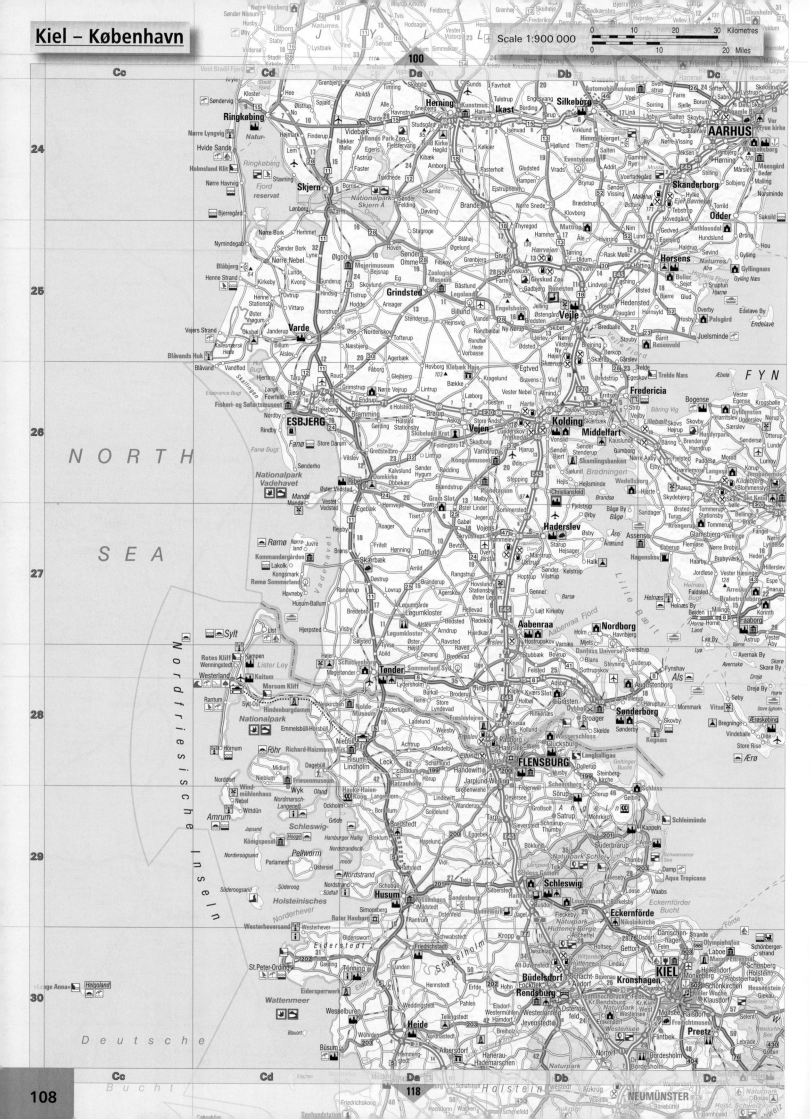

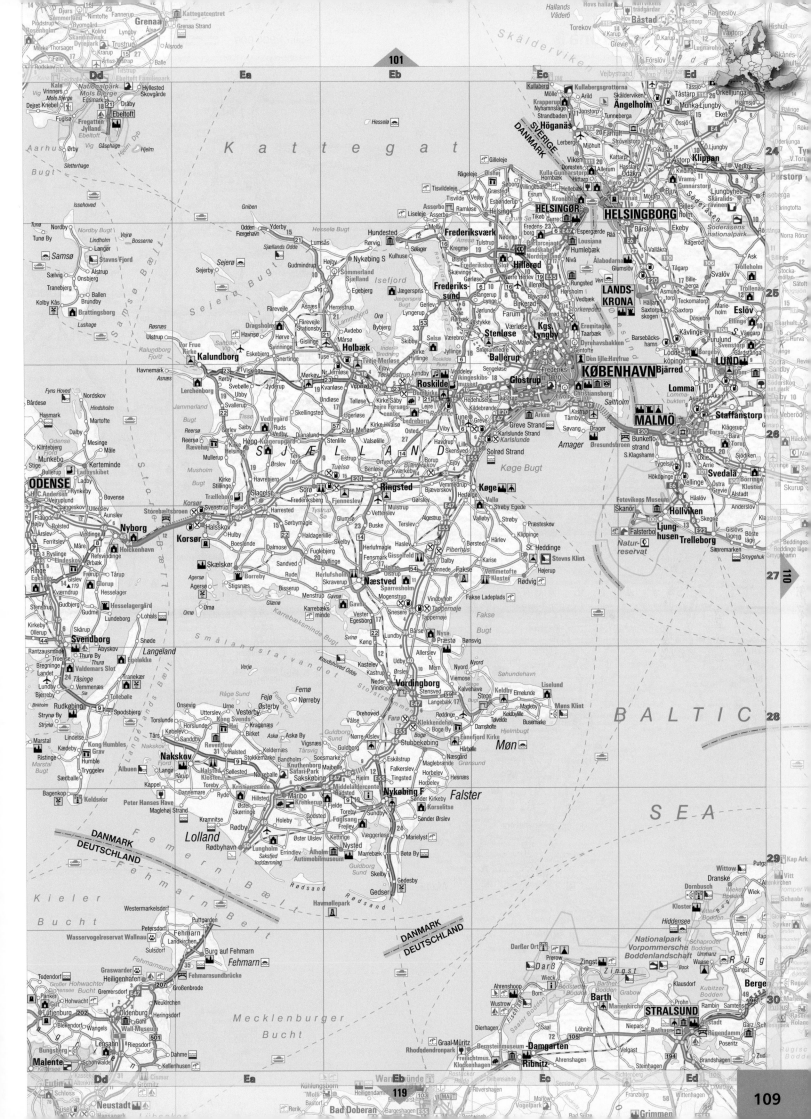

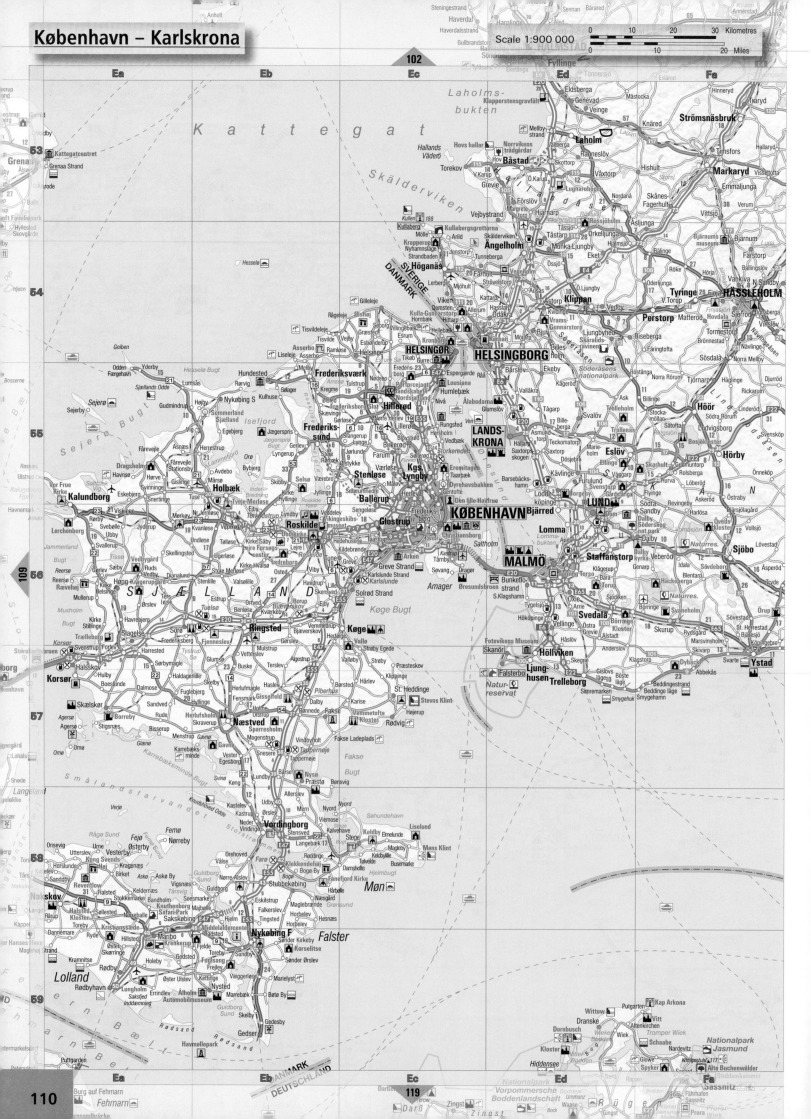

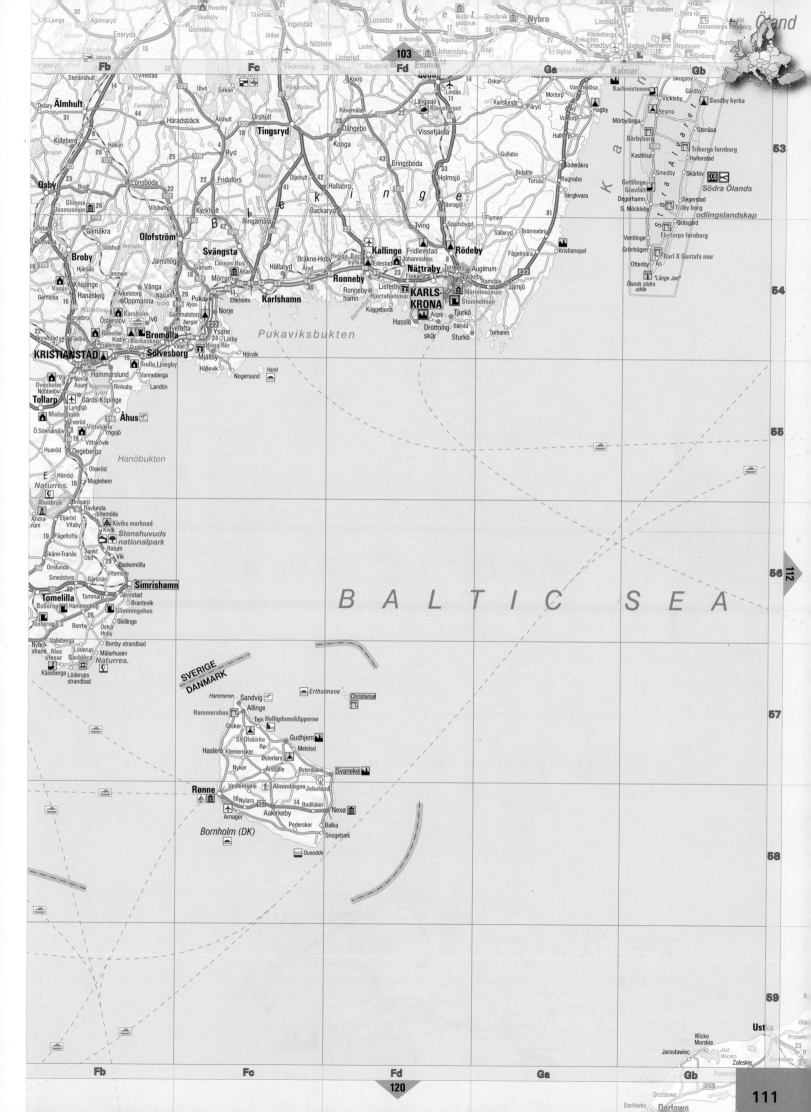

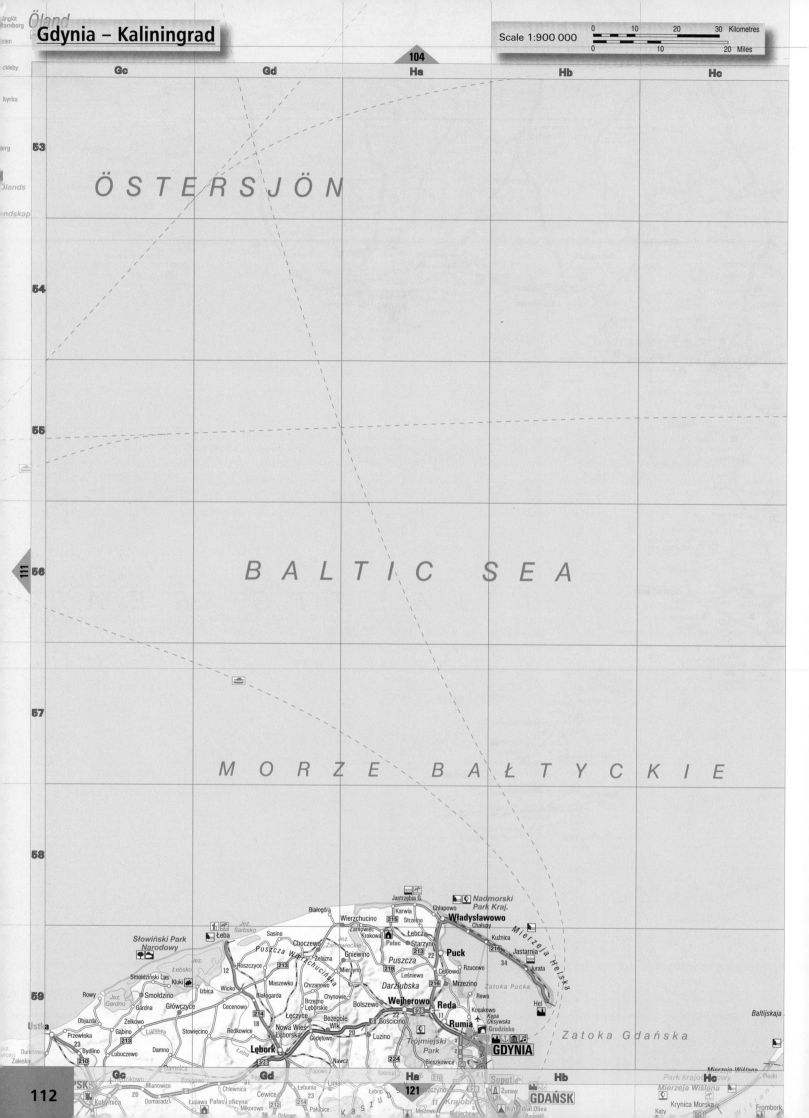

Scale 1:900 000

| 0 | 10 | 20 | 30 Kilometres |
| 0 | 10 | 20 Miles |

104
Ha

Gc · Gd · Ha · Hb · Hc

53

Ö S T E R S J Ö N

54

55

111 56

B A L T I C   S E A

57

M O R Z E   B A Ł T Y C K I E

58

59

Słowiński Park Narodowy

Białogóra · Jastrzębia G. · Karwia · Chłapowo · Nadmorski Park Kraj.

Wierzchucino · Strzelno · Władysławowo · Chałupy · Kuźnica · Mierzeja Helska · Jastarnia

Łeba · Jez. Sarbsko · Sasino · Choczewo · Żarnowiec · Krokowa · Pałac · Łebcz · Puck · Rzucewo · Jurata

Puszcza Wierzchucińska · Żelazna · Gniewino · Mierzyno · Puszcza Darżlubska · Leśniewo · Celbowo · Zatoka Pucka · Hel

Smołdziński Las · Kluki · Izbica · Wicko · Maszewko · Chrzanowo · Chynowie · Mrzezino · Rewa · Kępa Oksywska · Baltijskaja

Rowy · Jez. Gardno · Gardna · Smołdzino · Główczyce · Cecenowo · Białogarda · Bolszewo · Wejherowo · Reda · Kosakowo · Grodzisko · Zatoka Gdańska

Objazda · Zelkowo · Redkowice · Łęczyce · Bożepole Wik · Gościcino · Luzino · Rumia · Trójmiejski Park · GDYNIA

Przewłoka · Gąbino · Stowięcino · Nowa Wieś Lęborska · Gędetowo · Krajobr. · Mierzeja Wiślana

Bydlino · Lubuczewo · Damno · Łeba · Lębork · Nawcz · Bieszkowice · Sopot · Żuraw · GDAŃSK · Krynica Morska

Ustka · Duninowo · Zaleskie

Gc · Gd · Ha · **121** · Hb · Hc

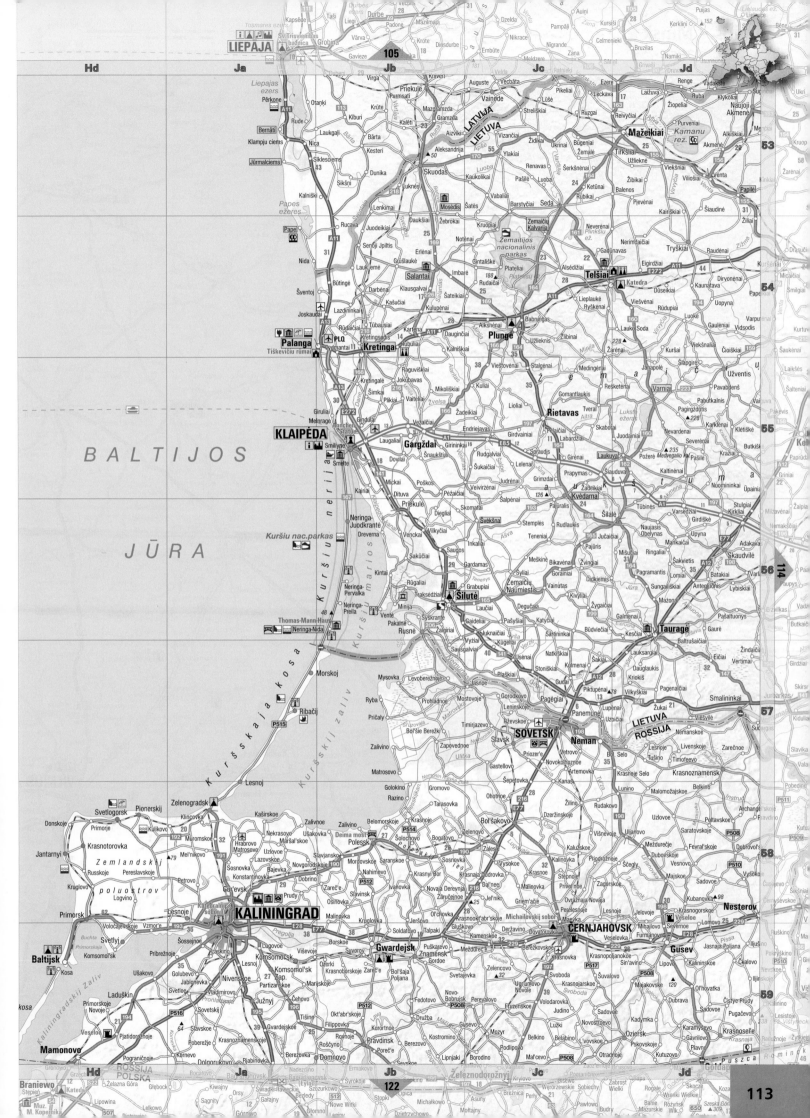

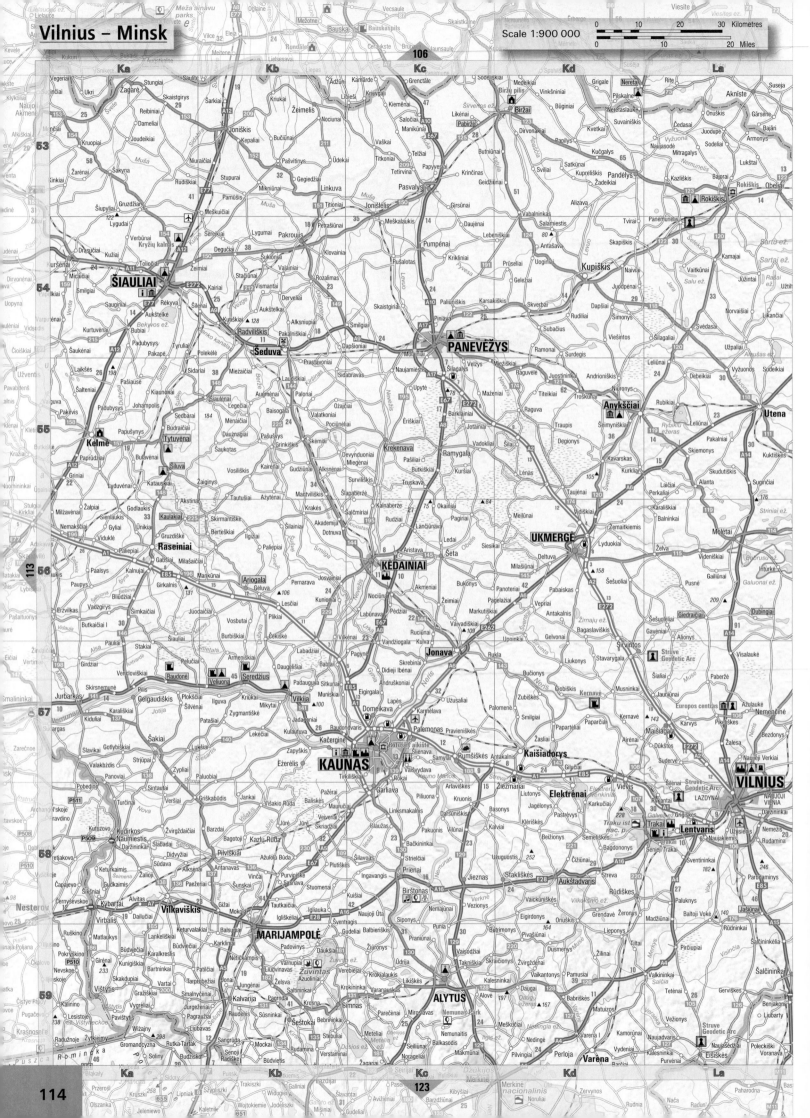

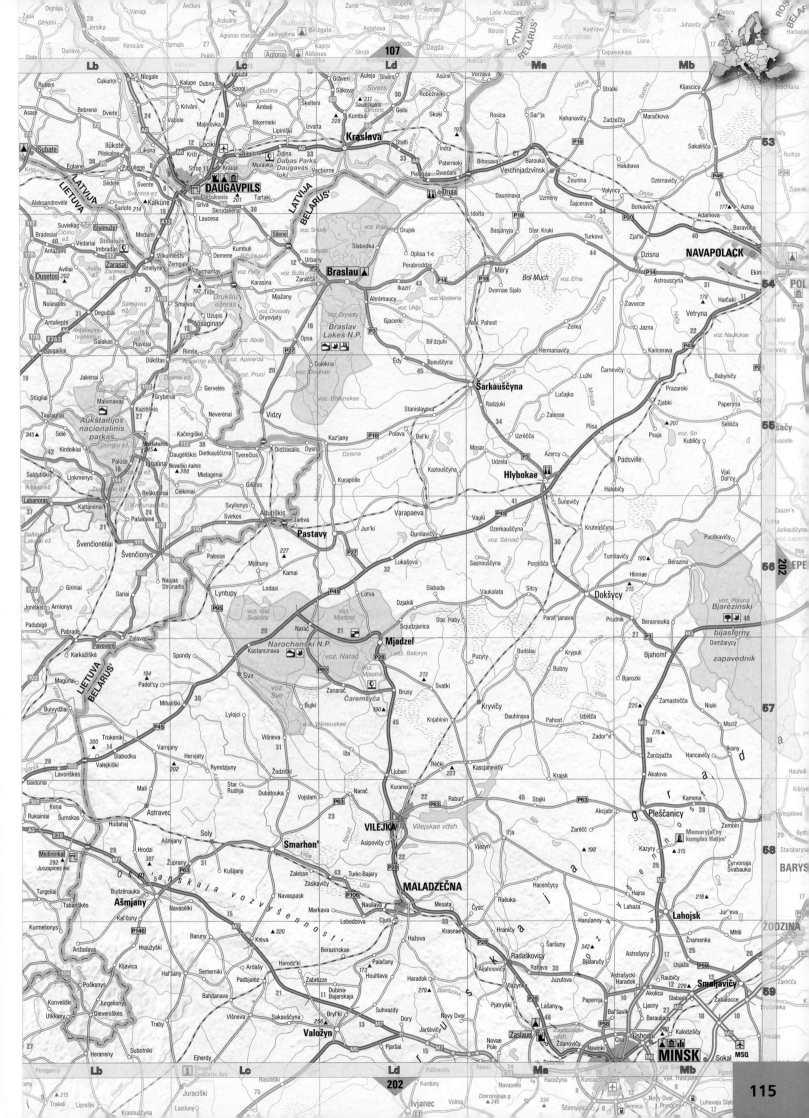

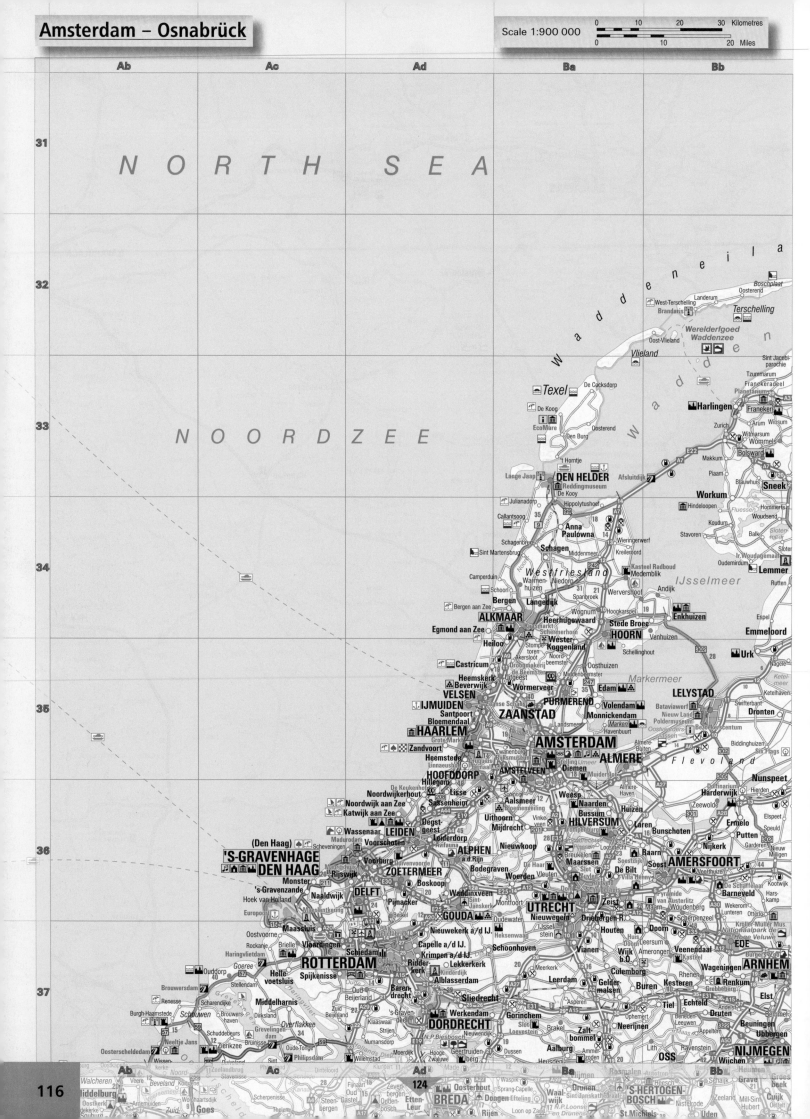

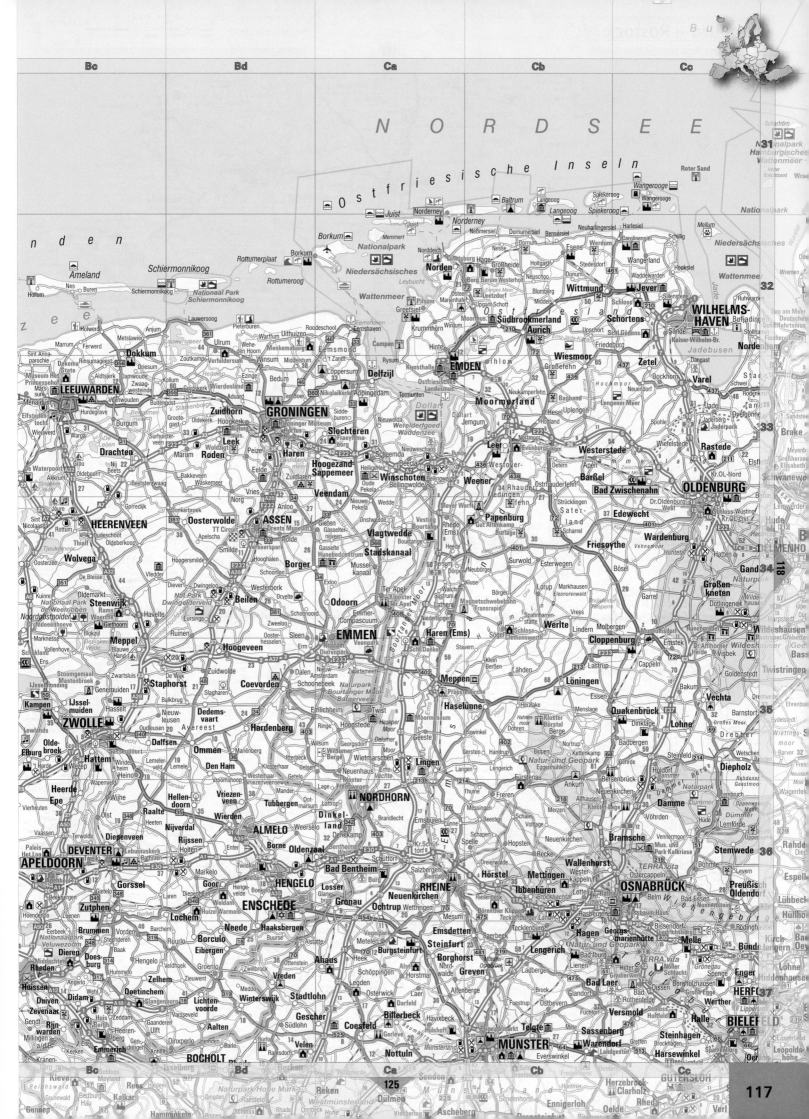

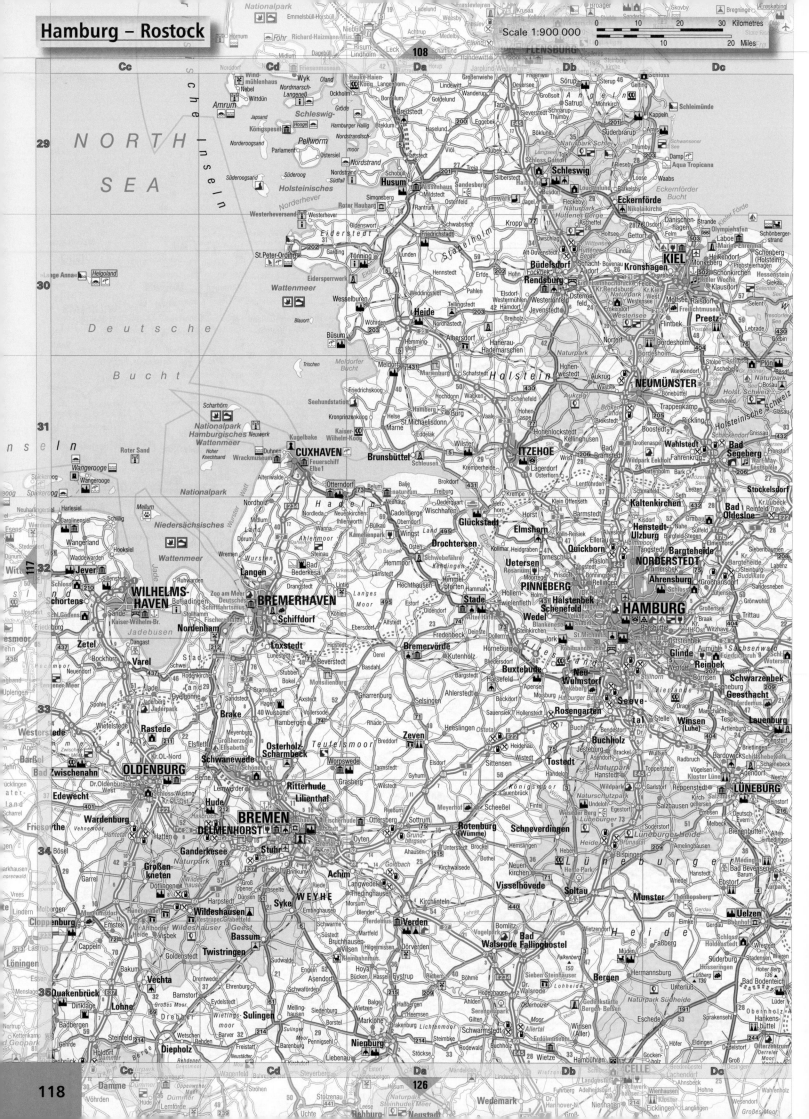

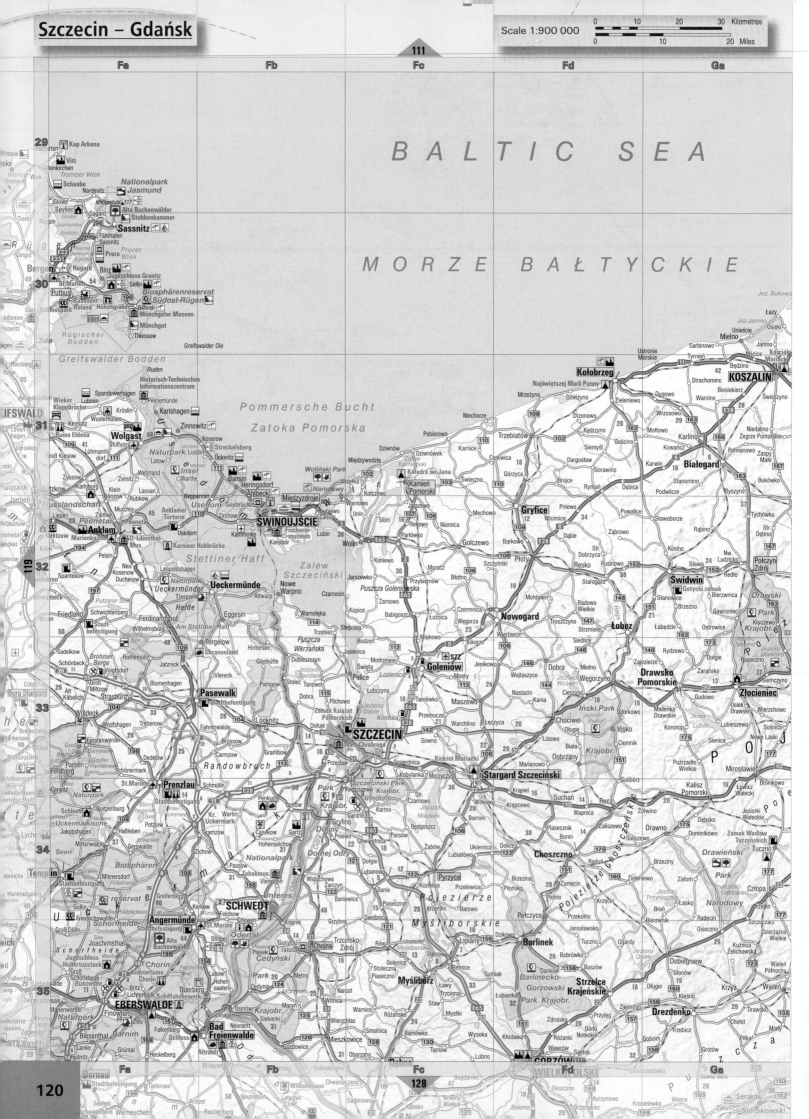

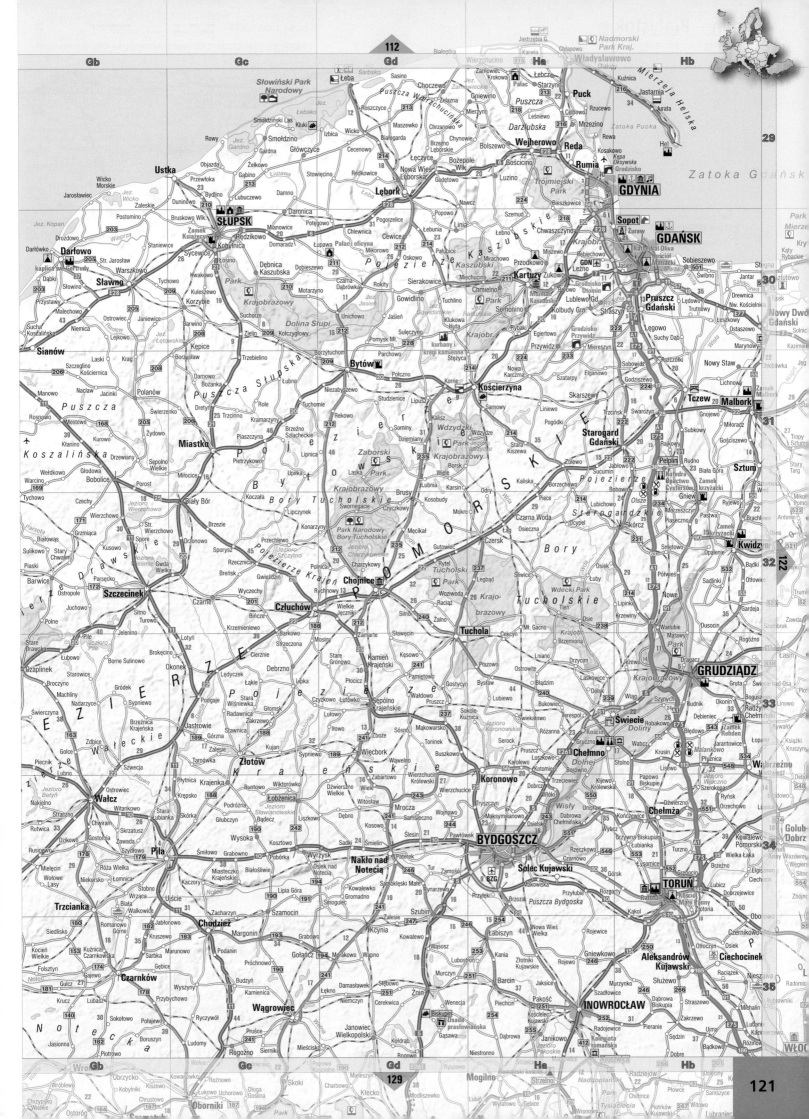

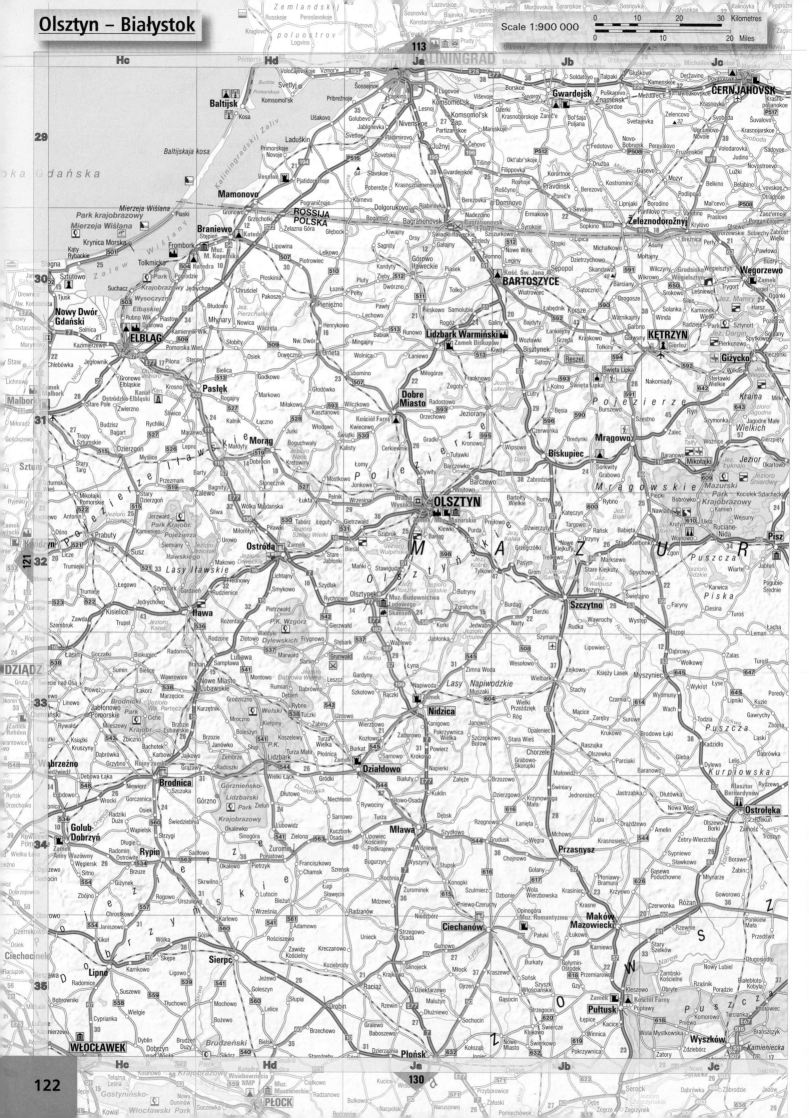

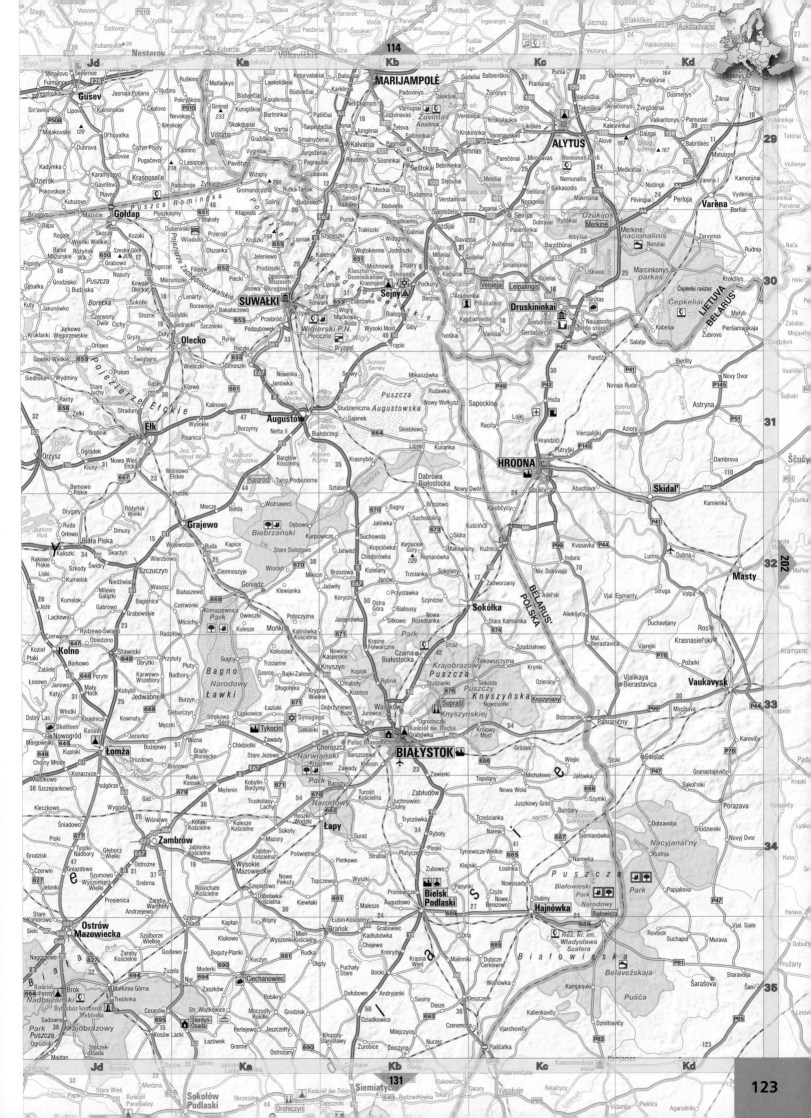

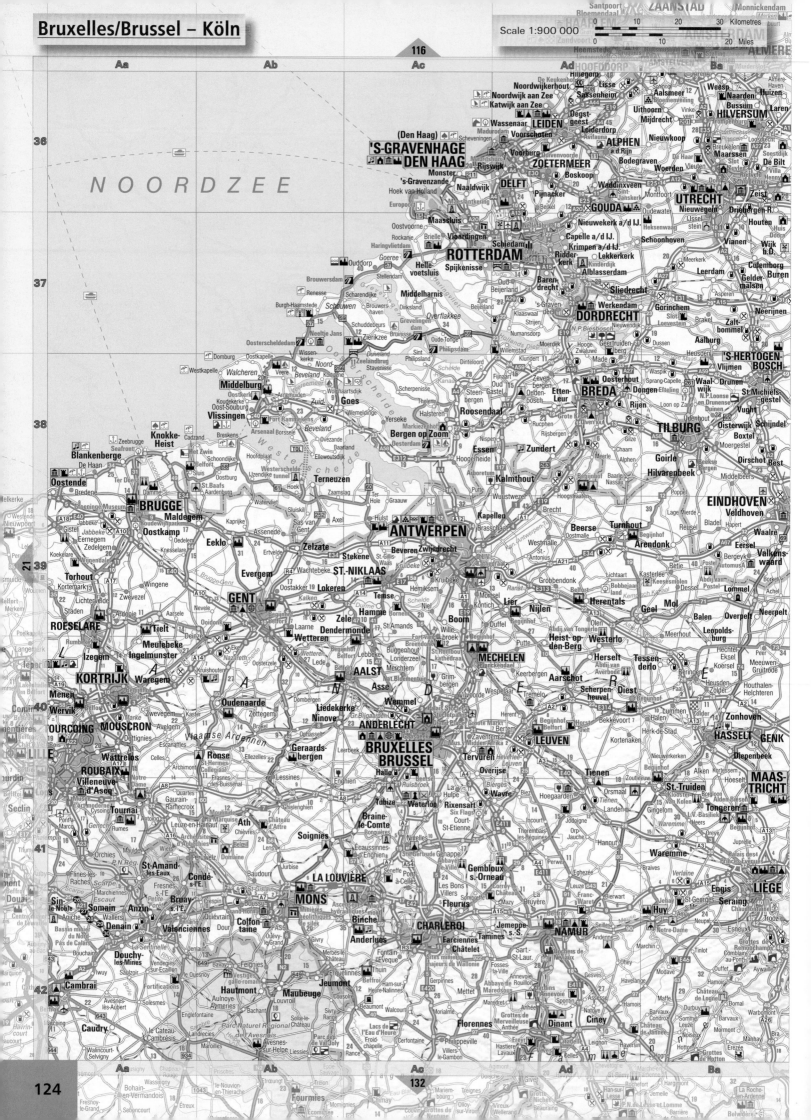

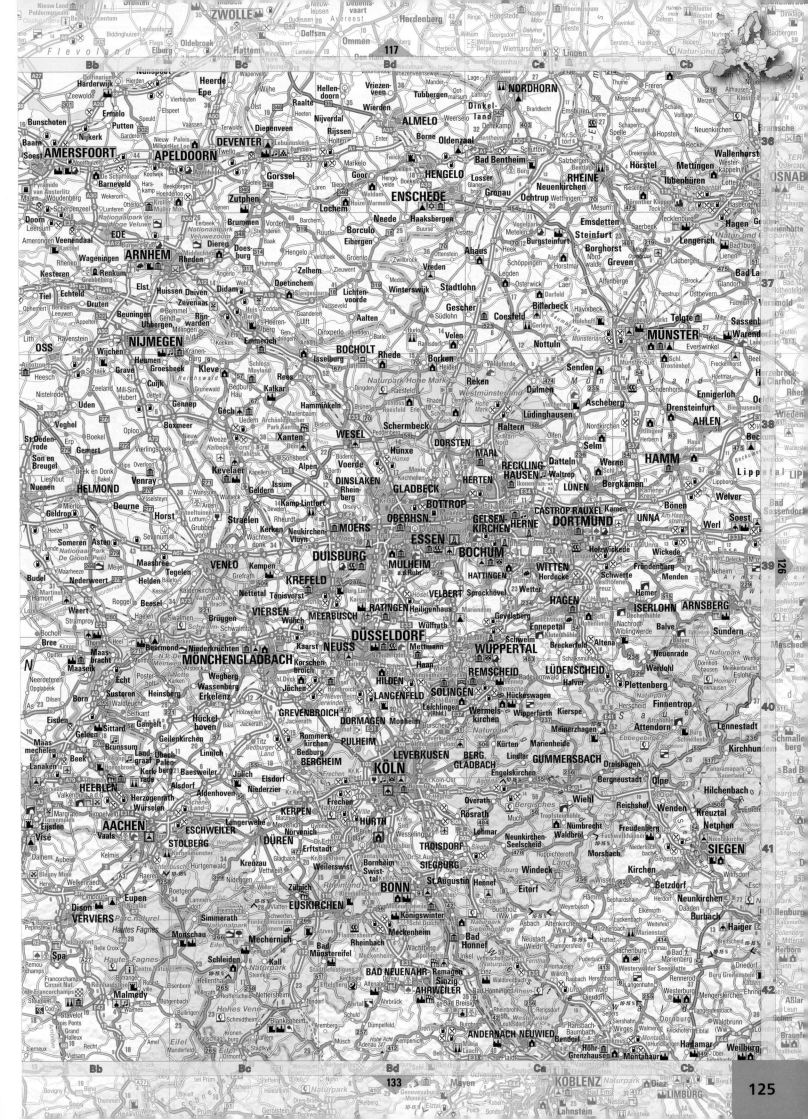

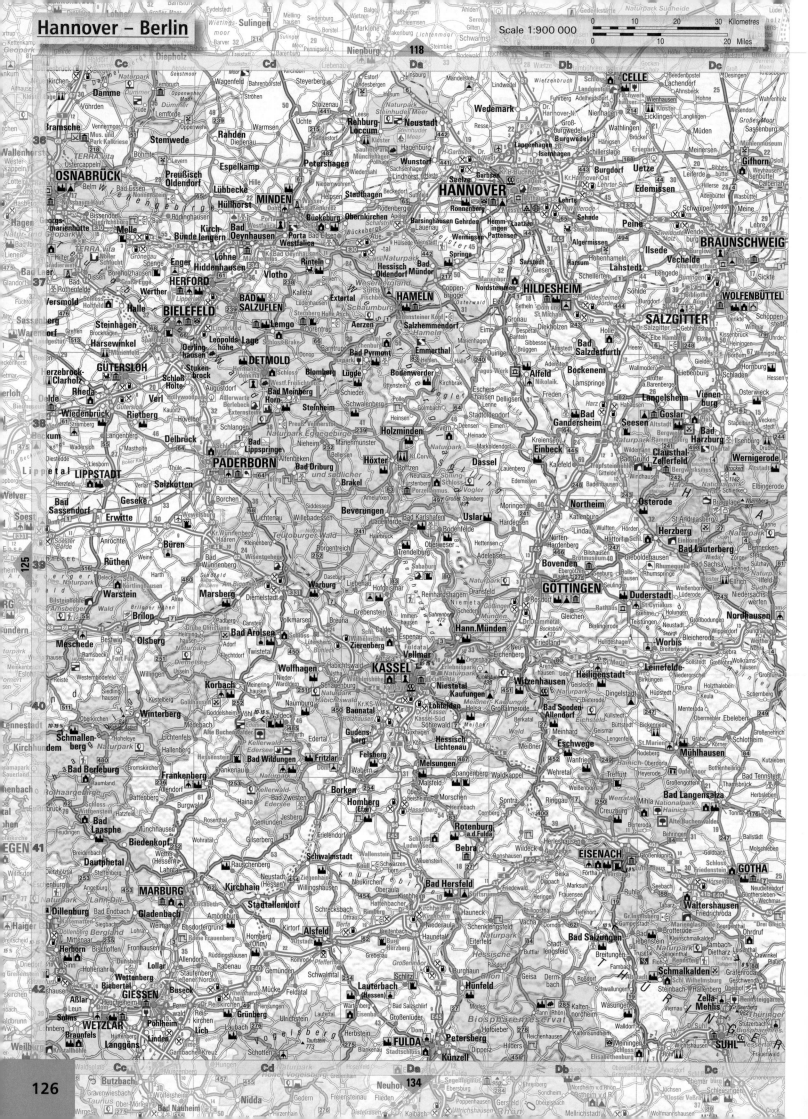

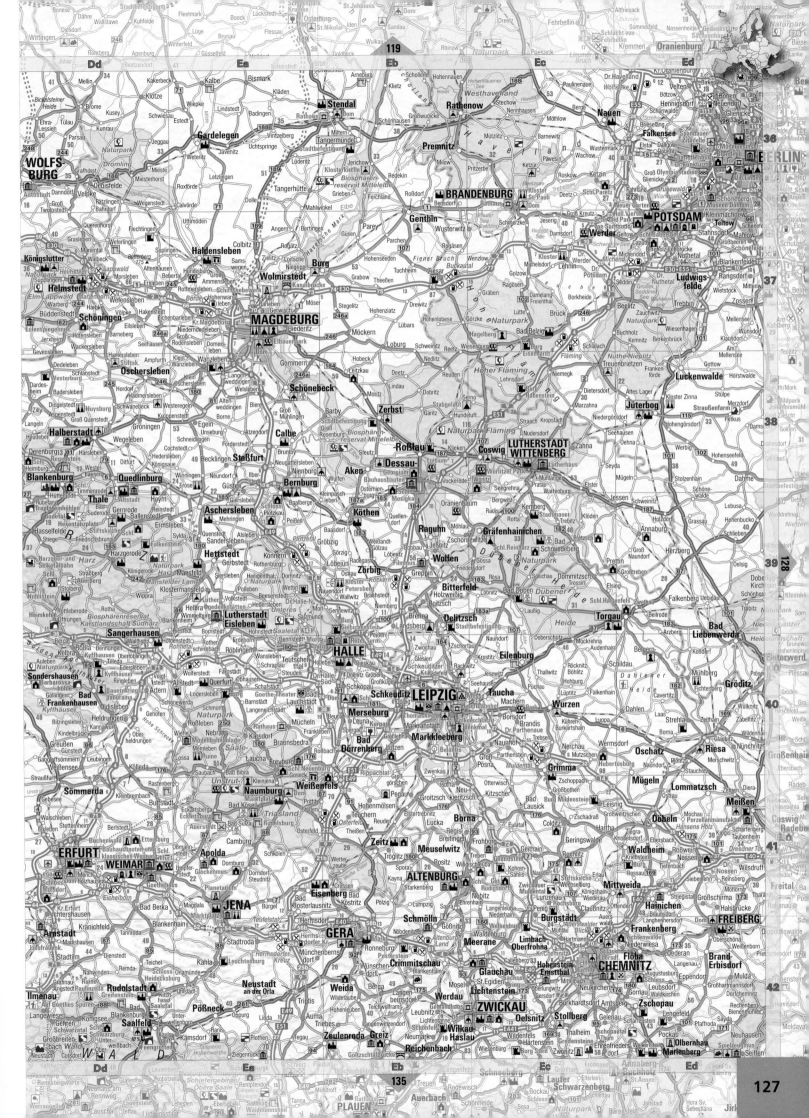

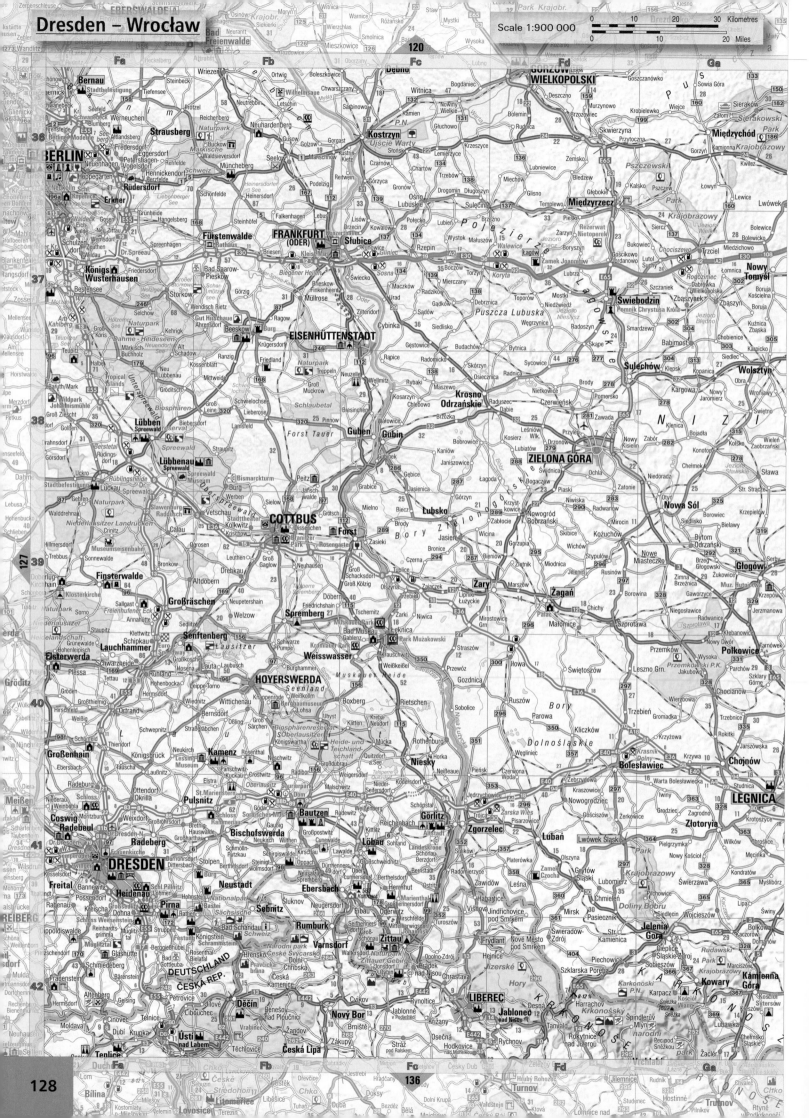

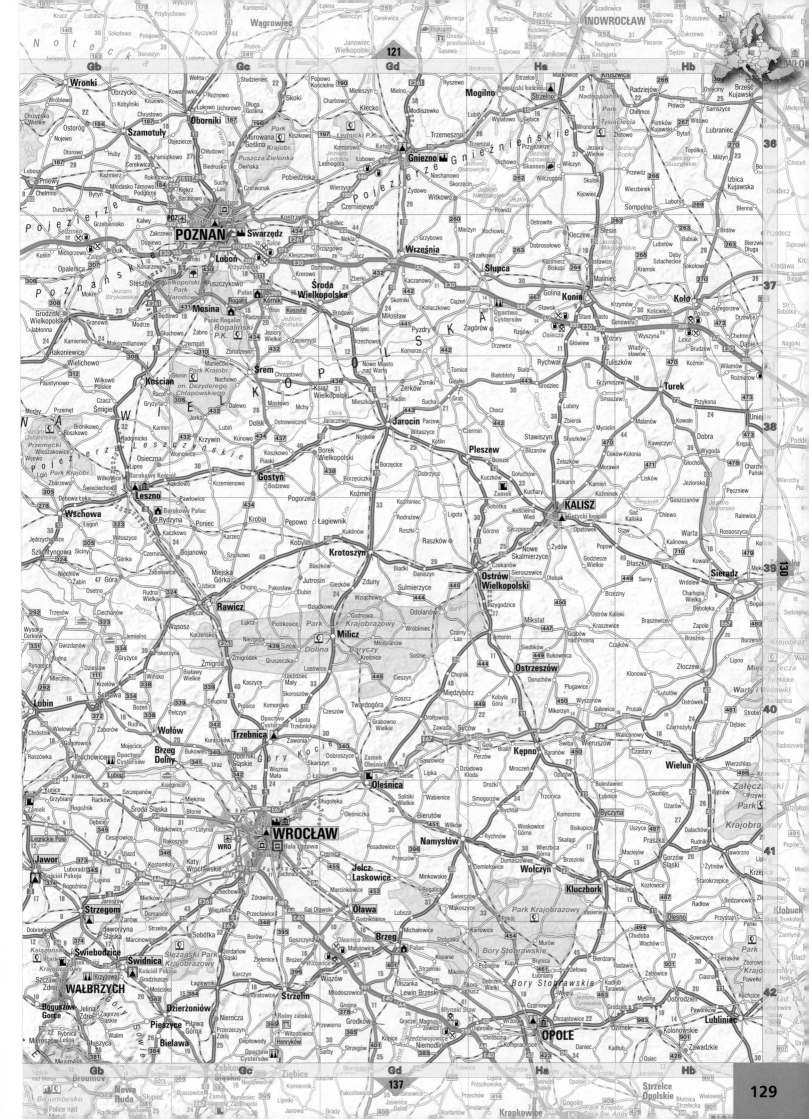

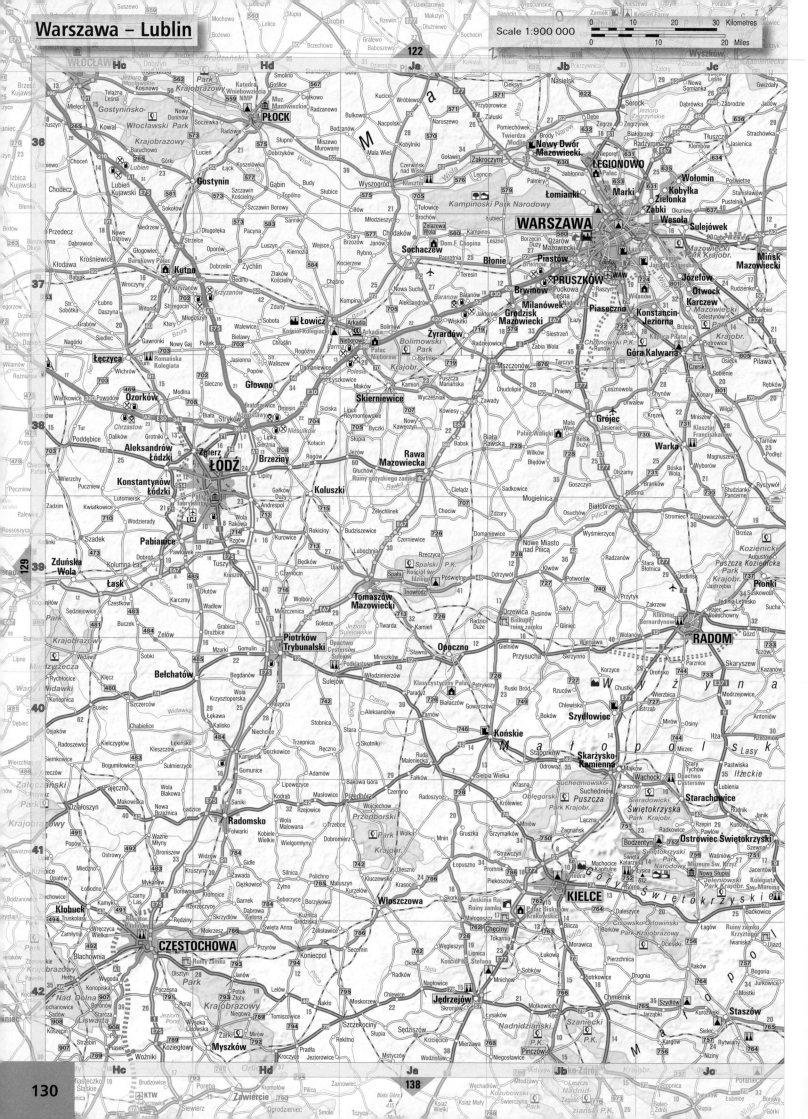

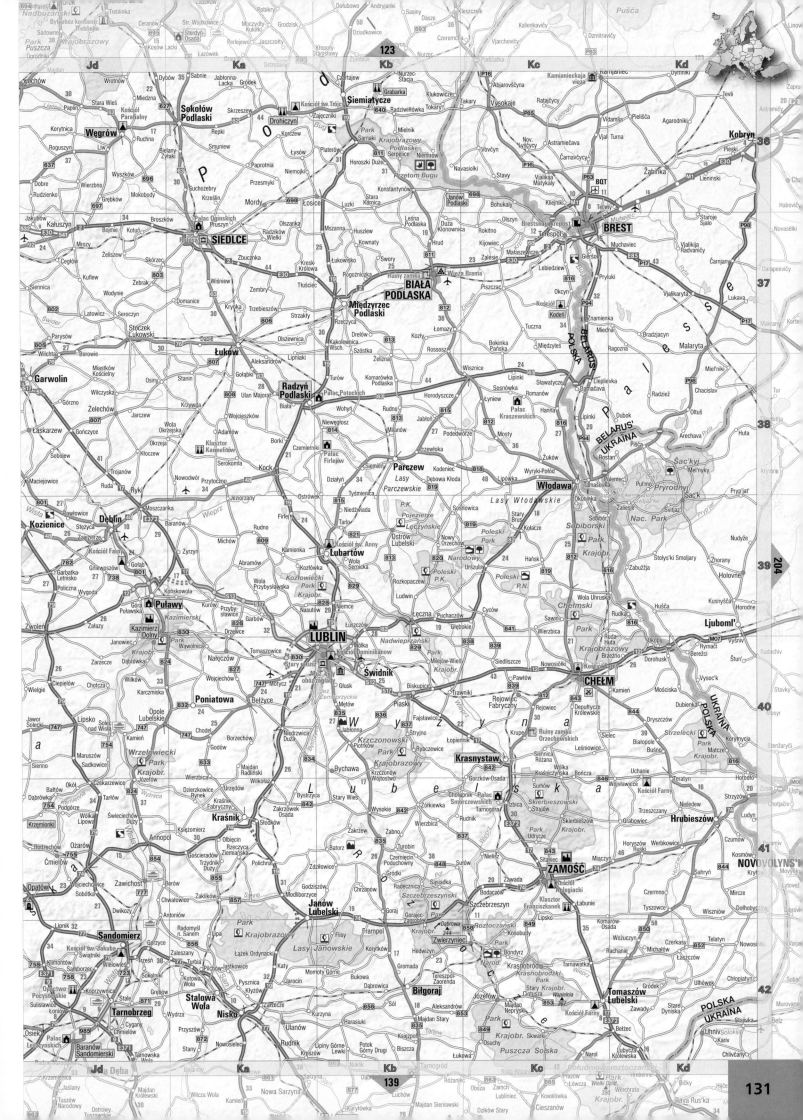

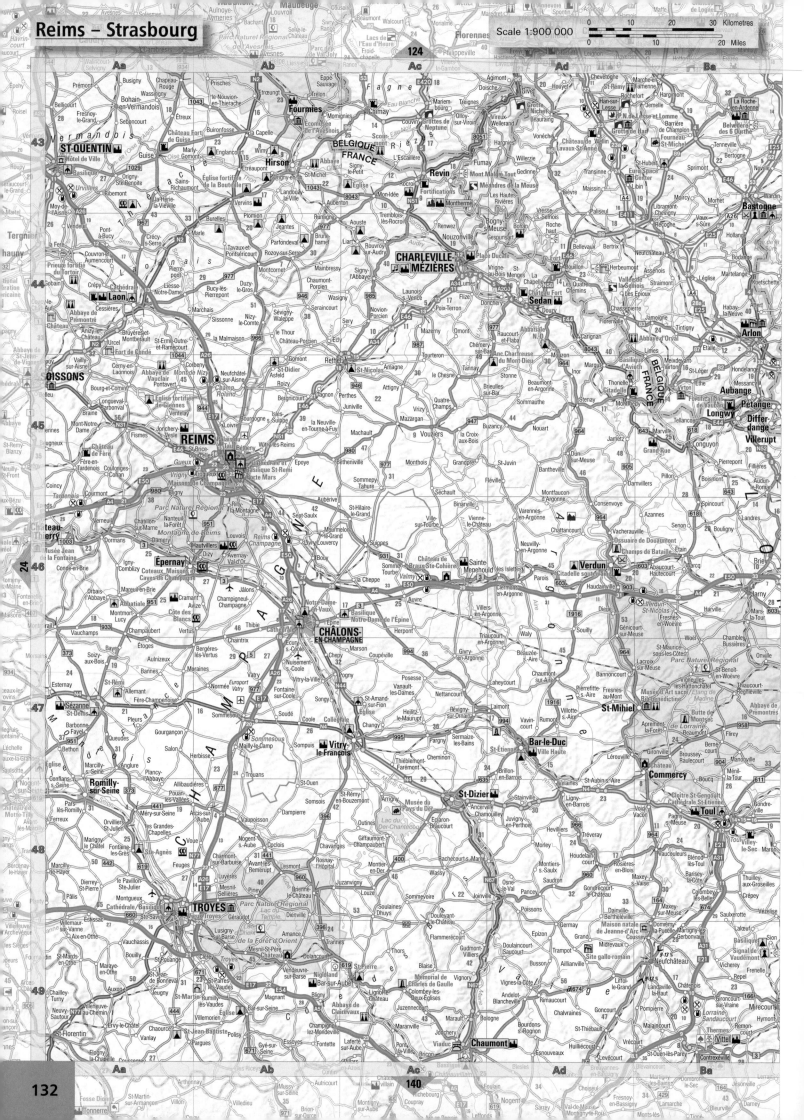

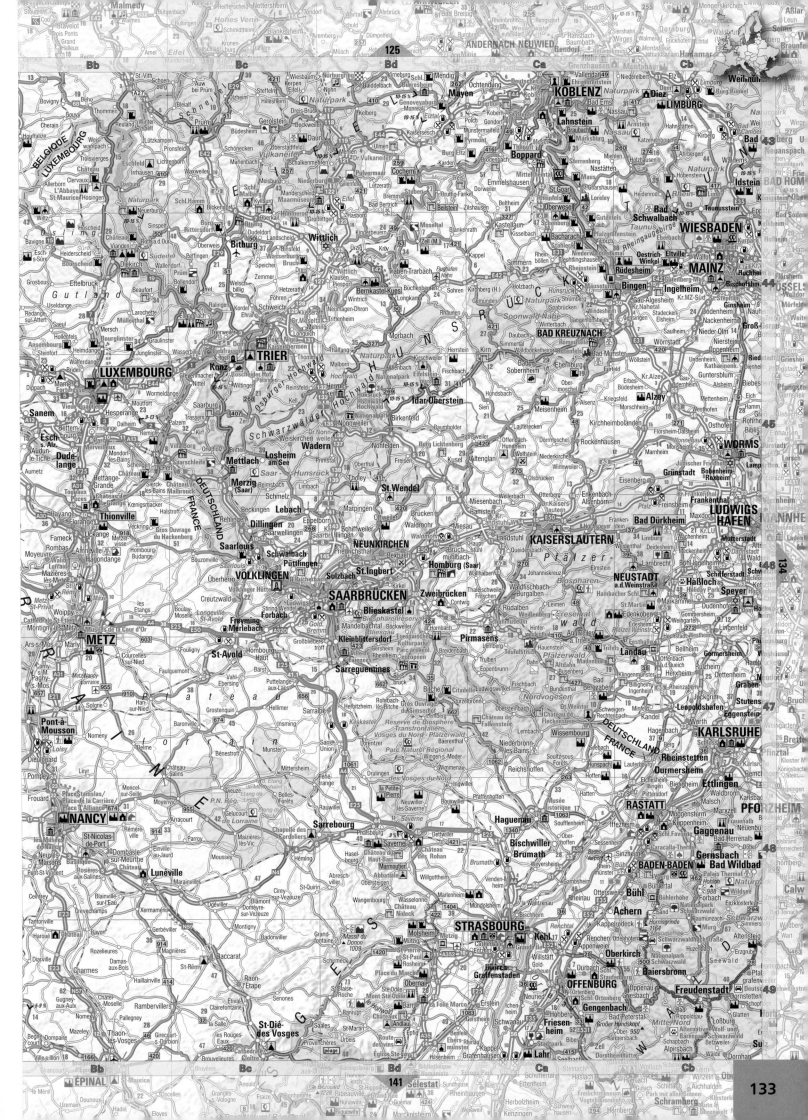

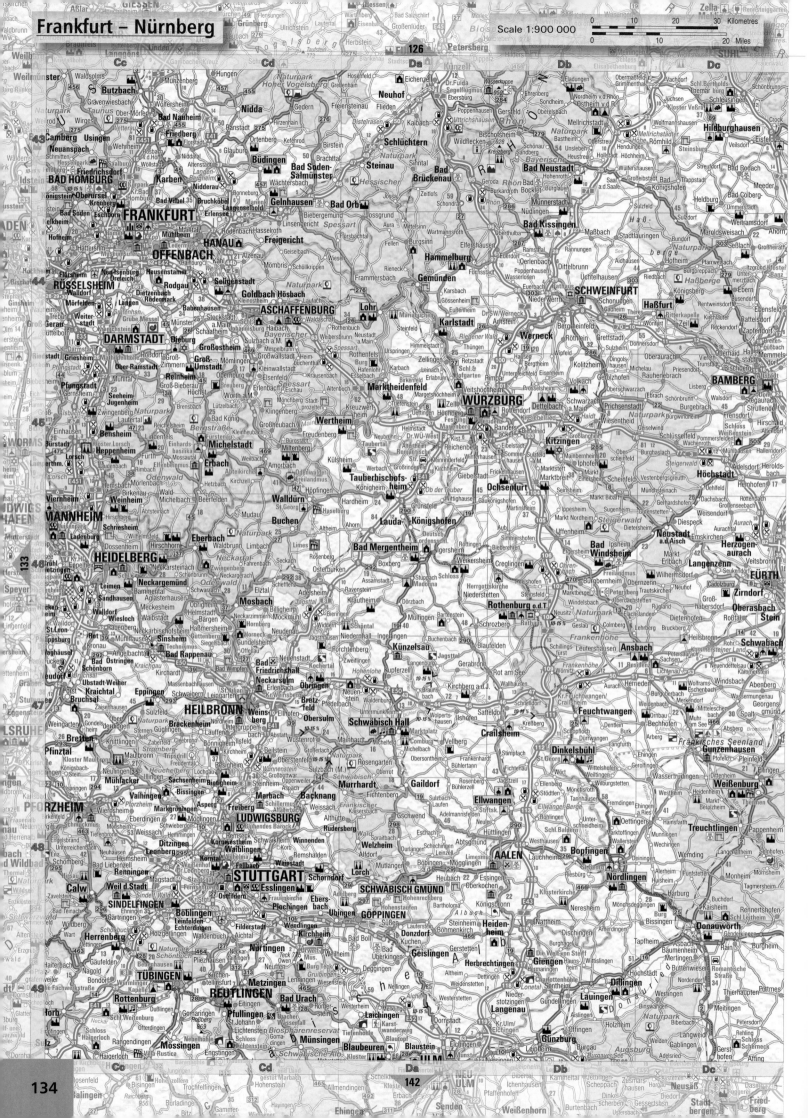

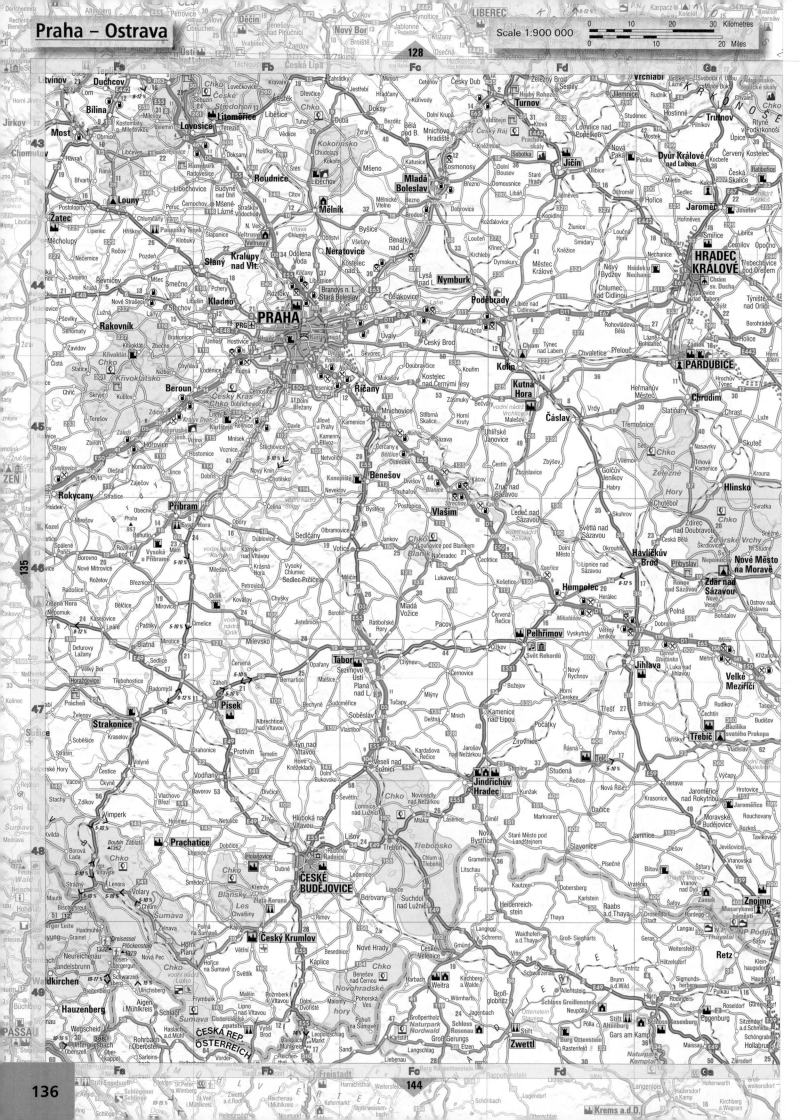

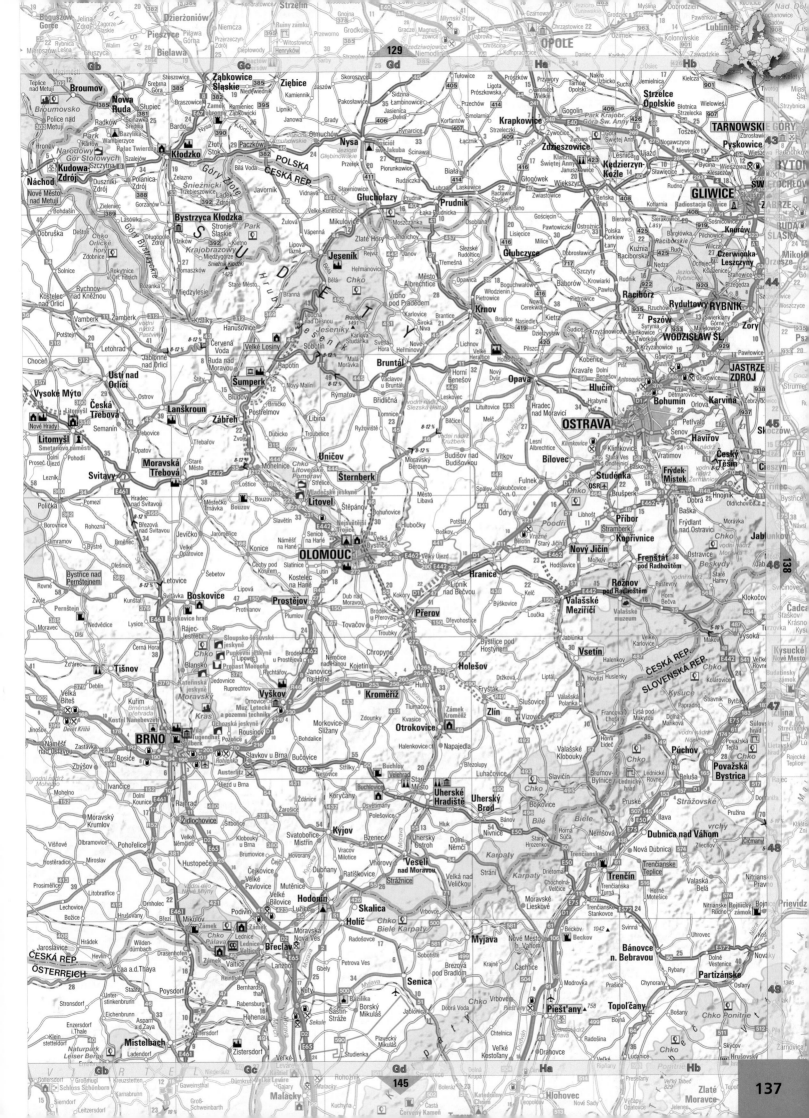

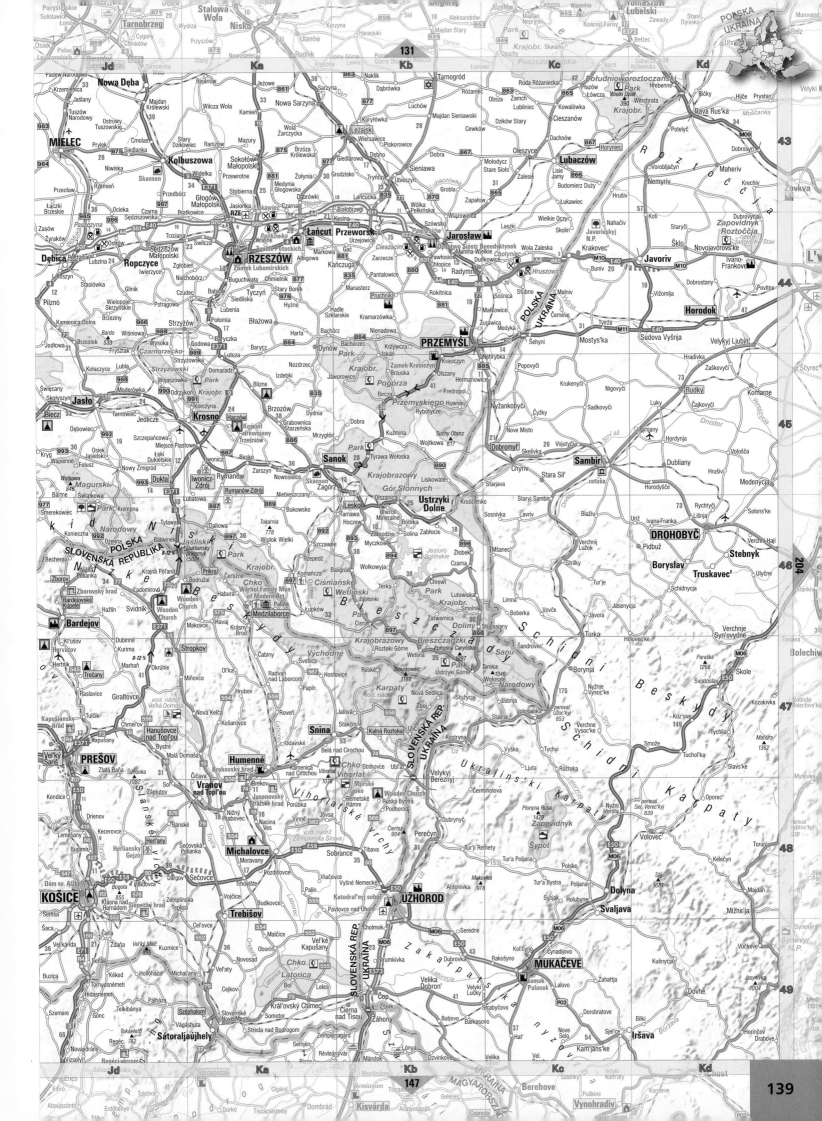

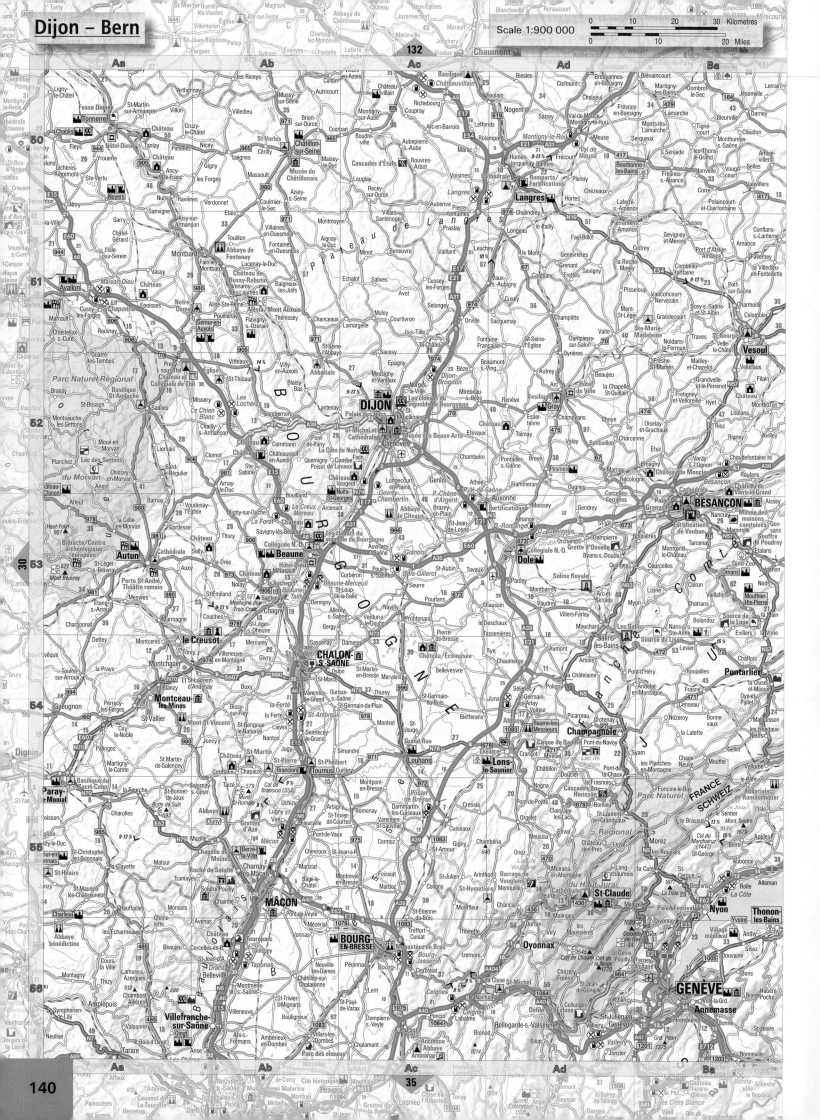

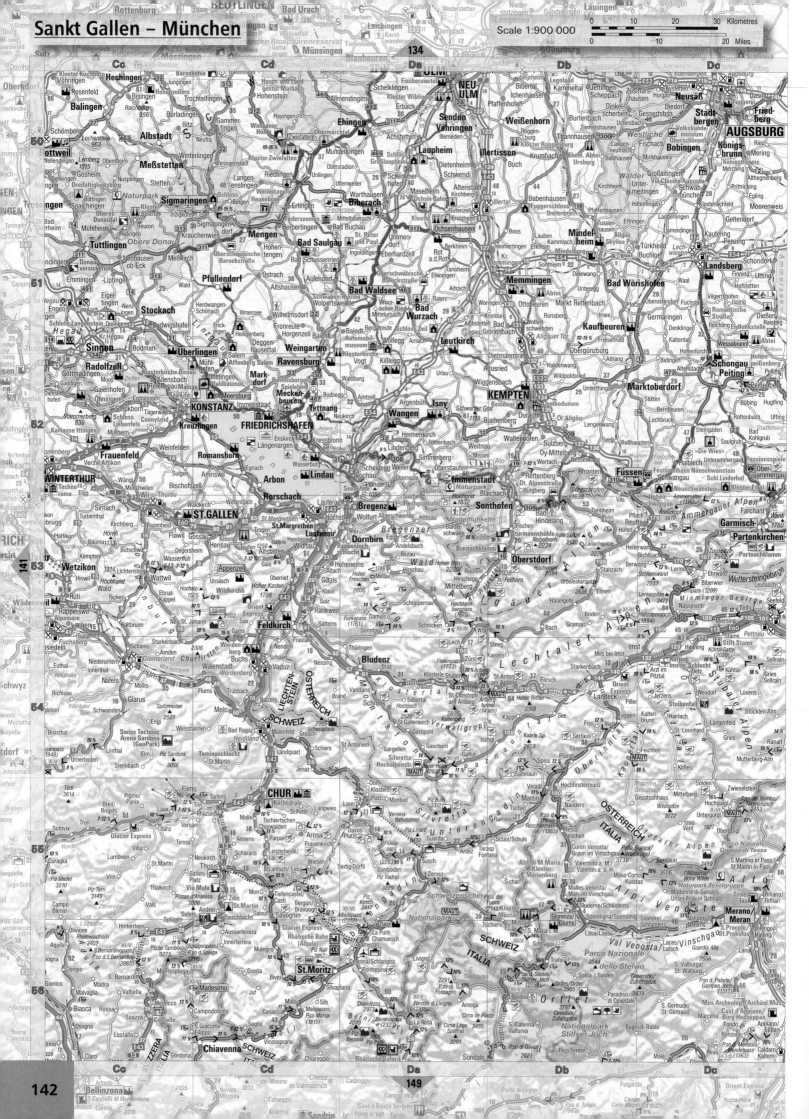

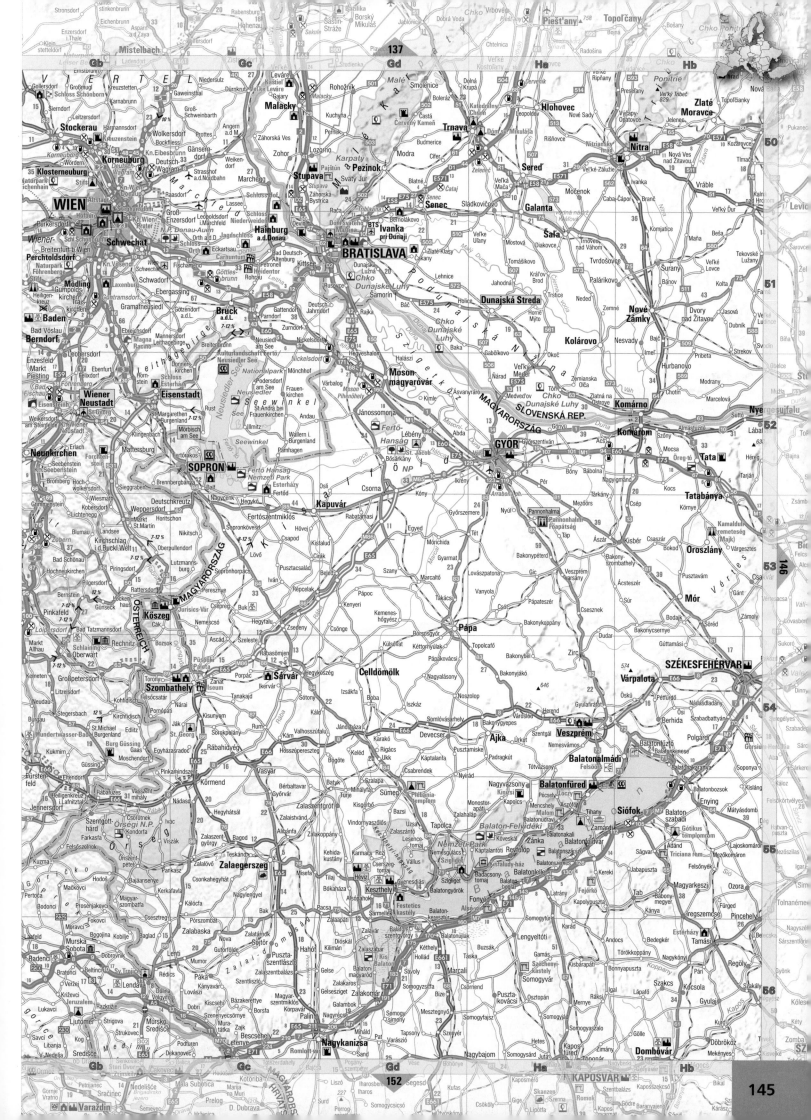

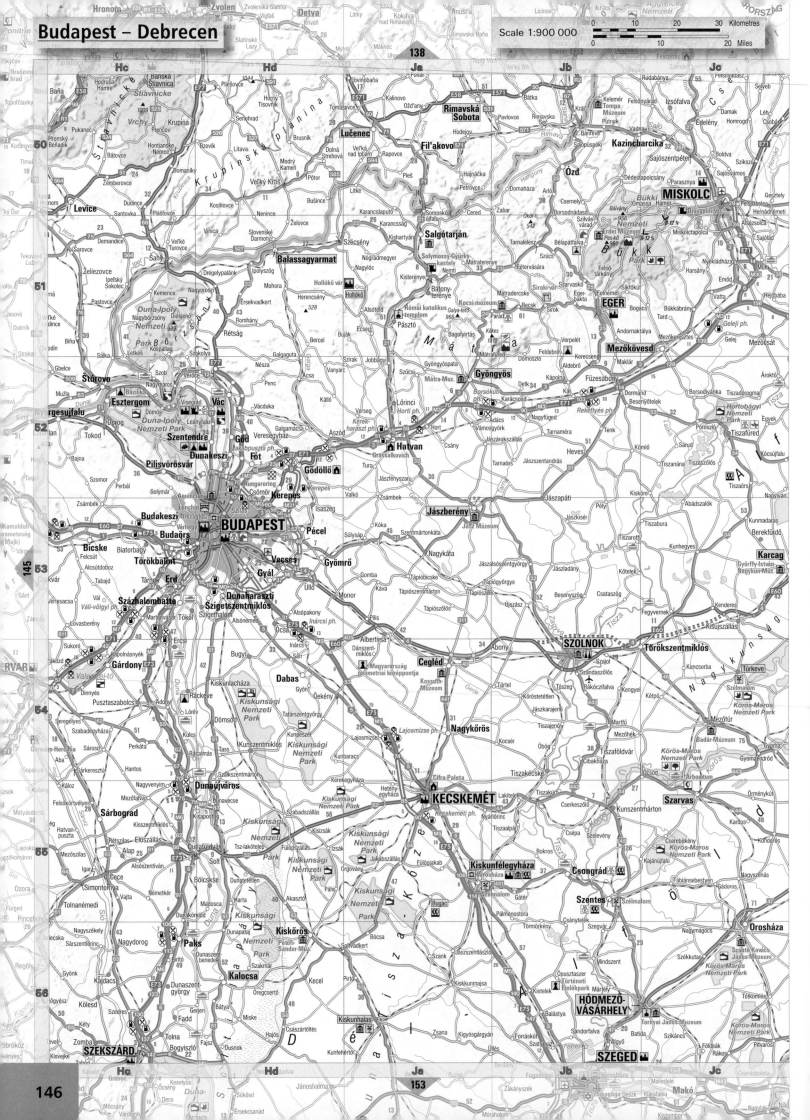

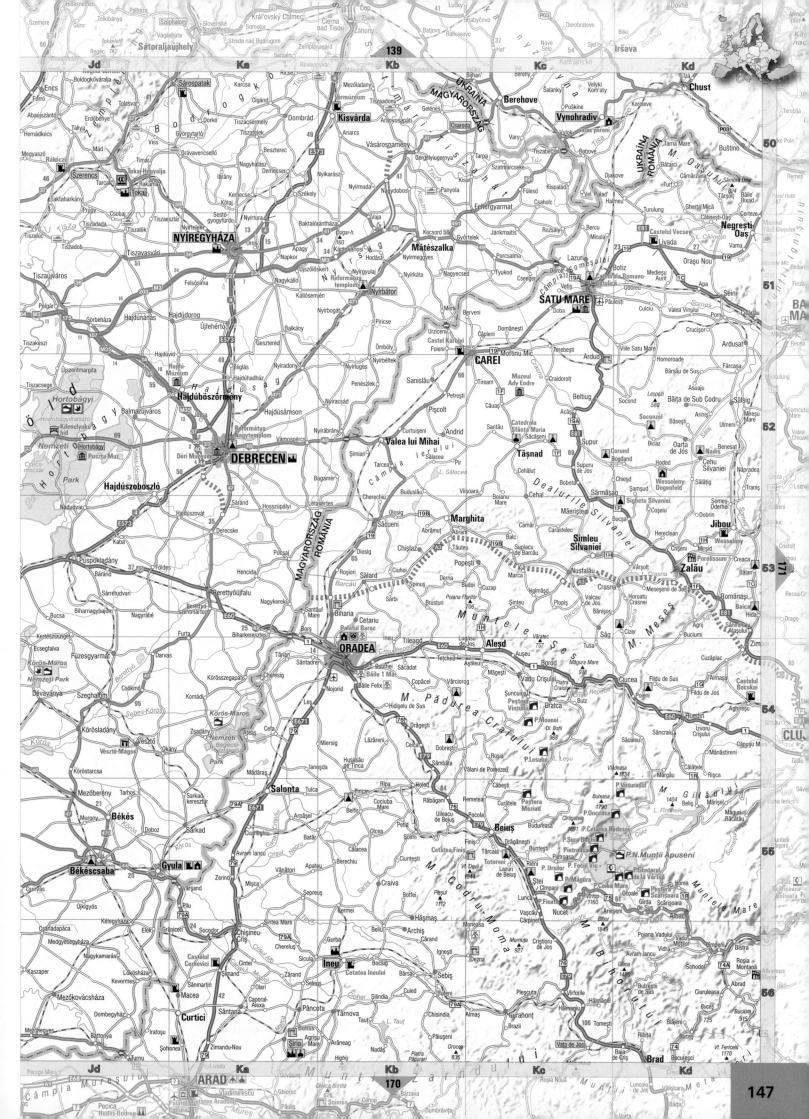

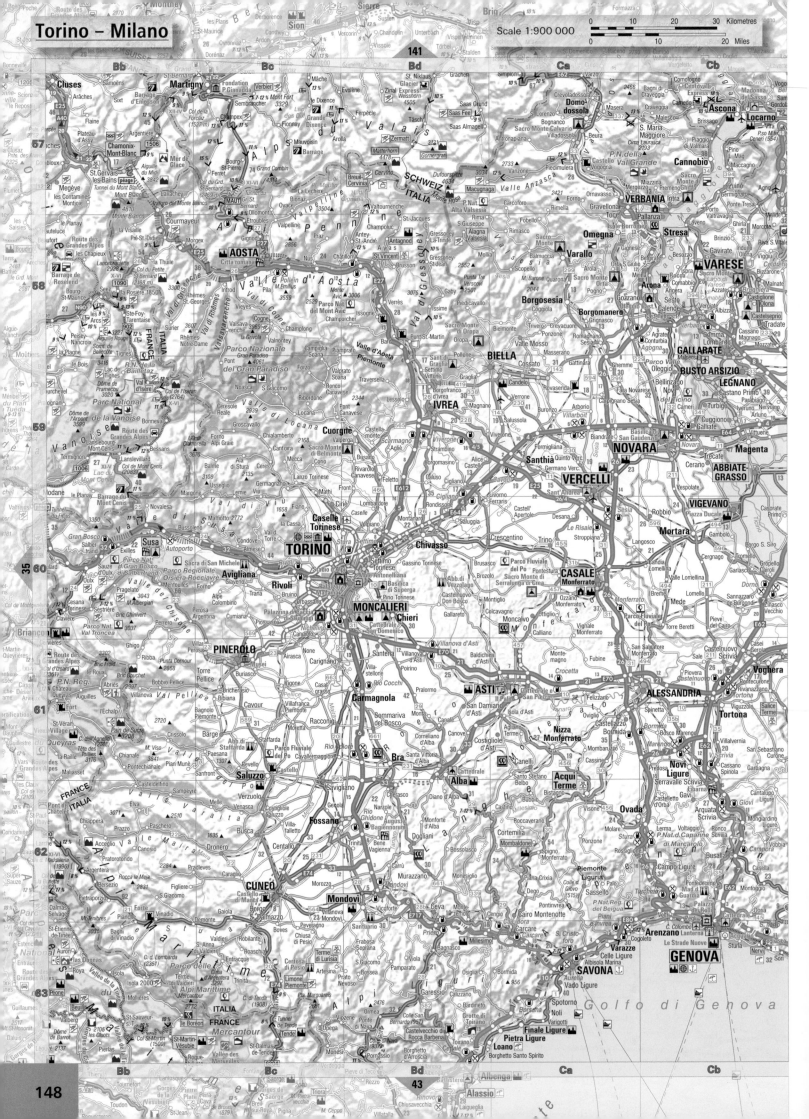

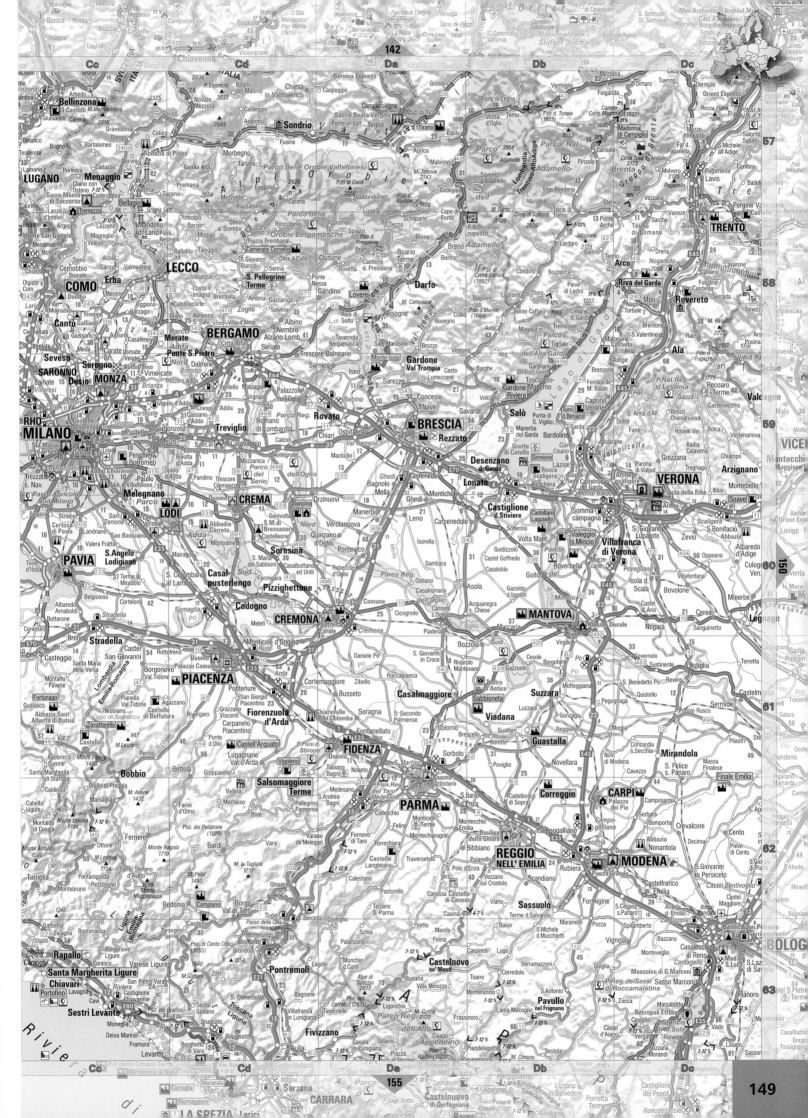

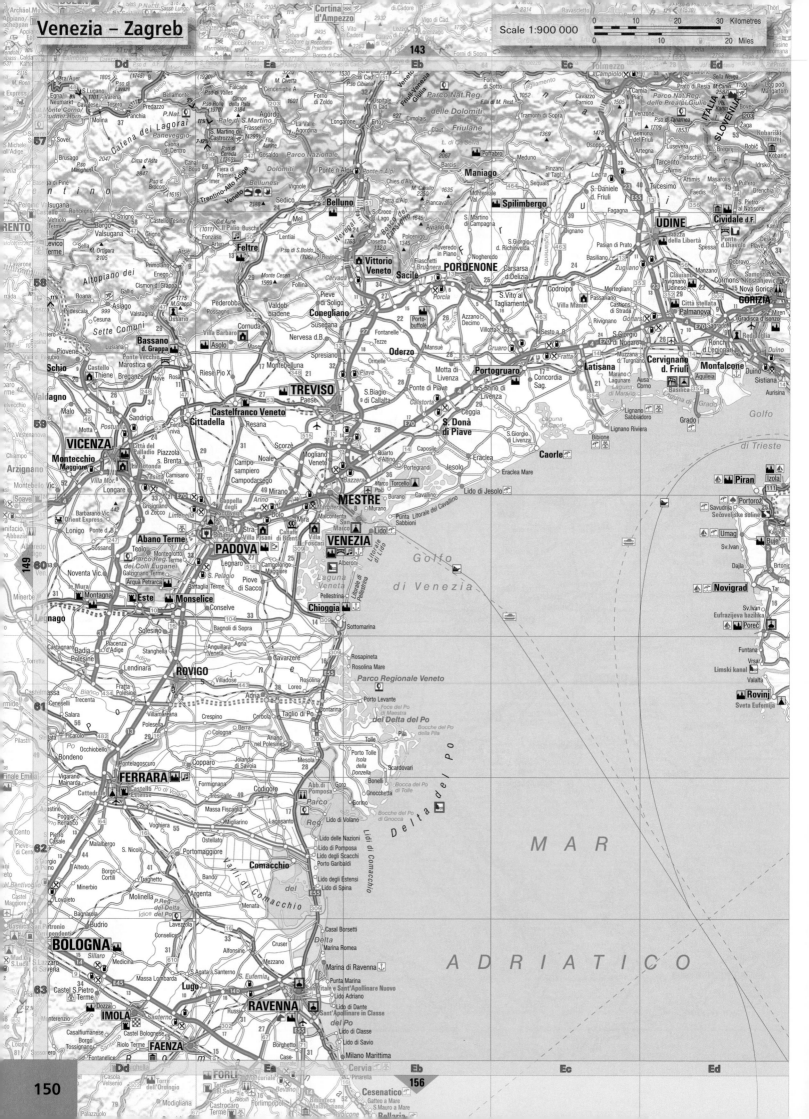

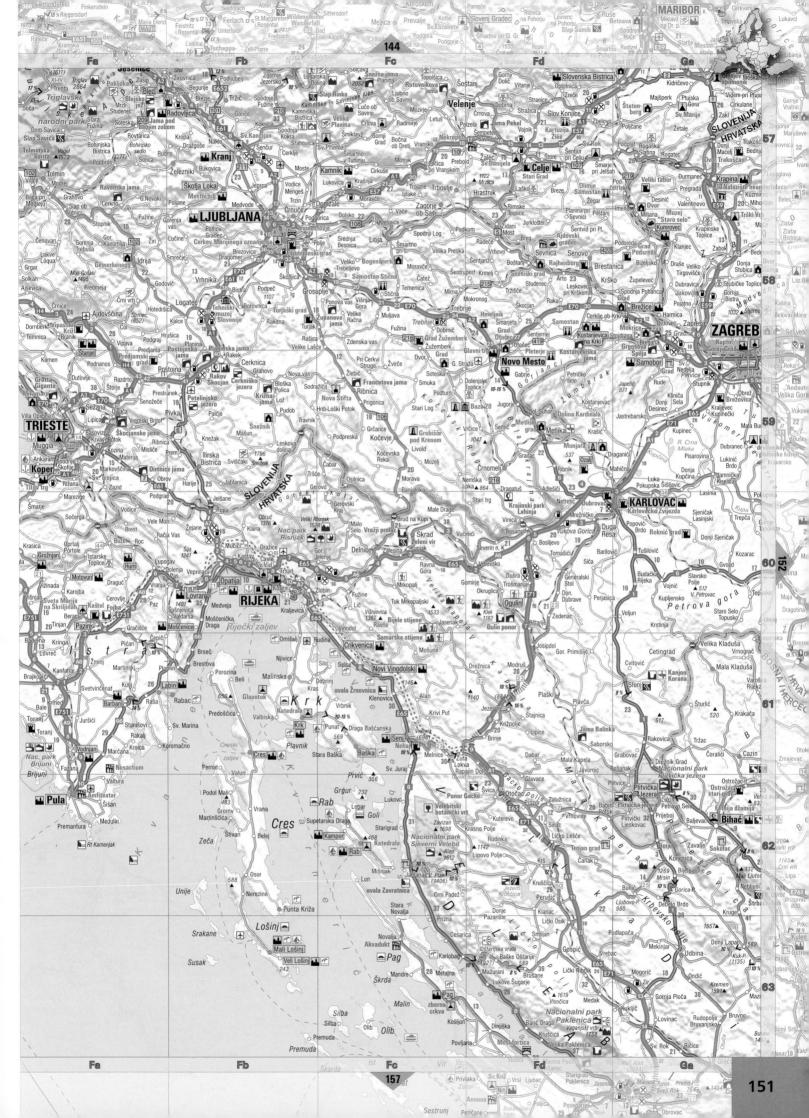

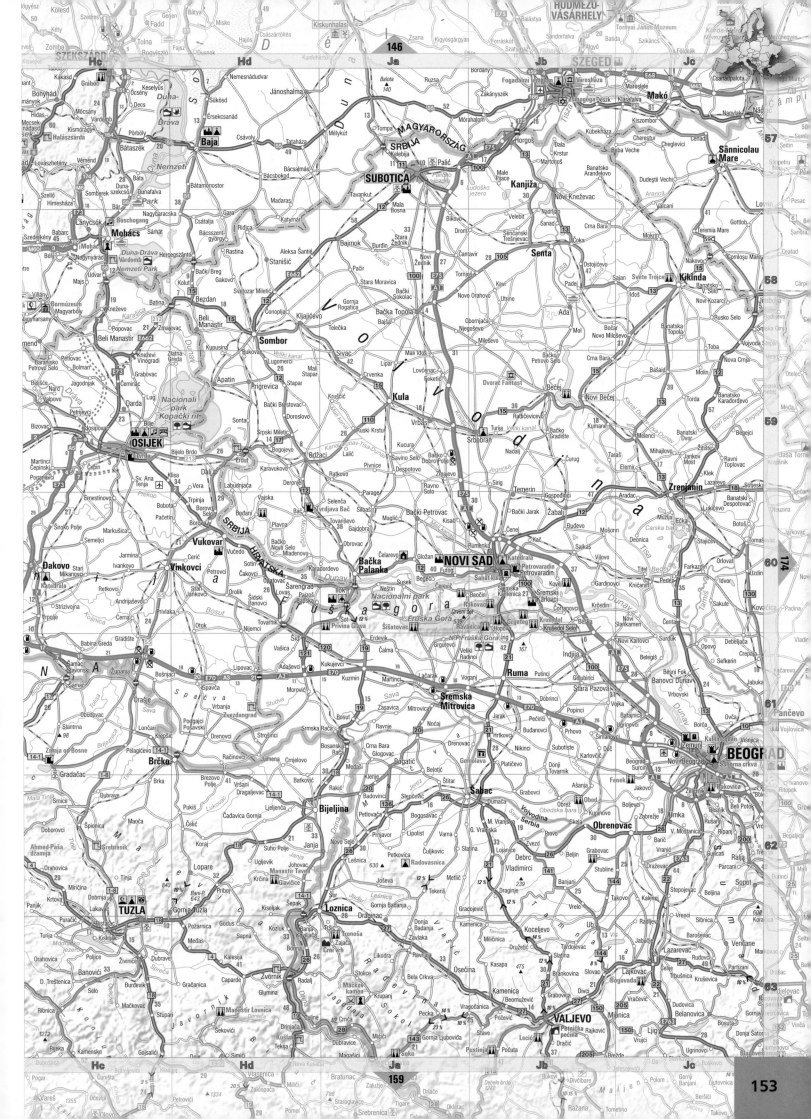

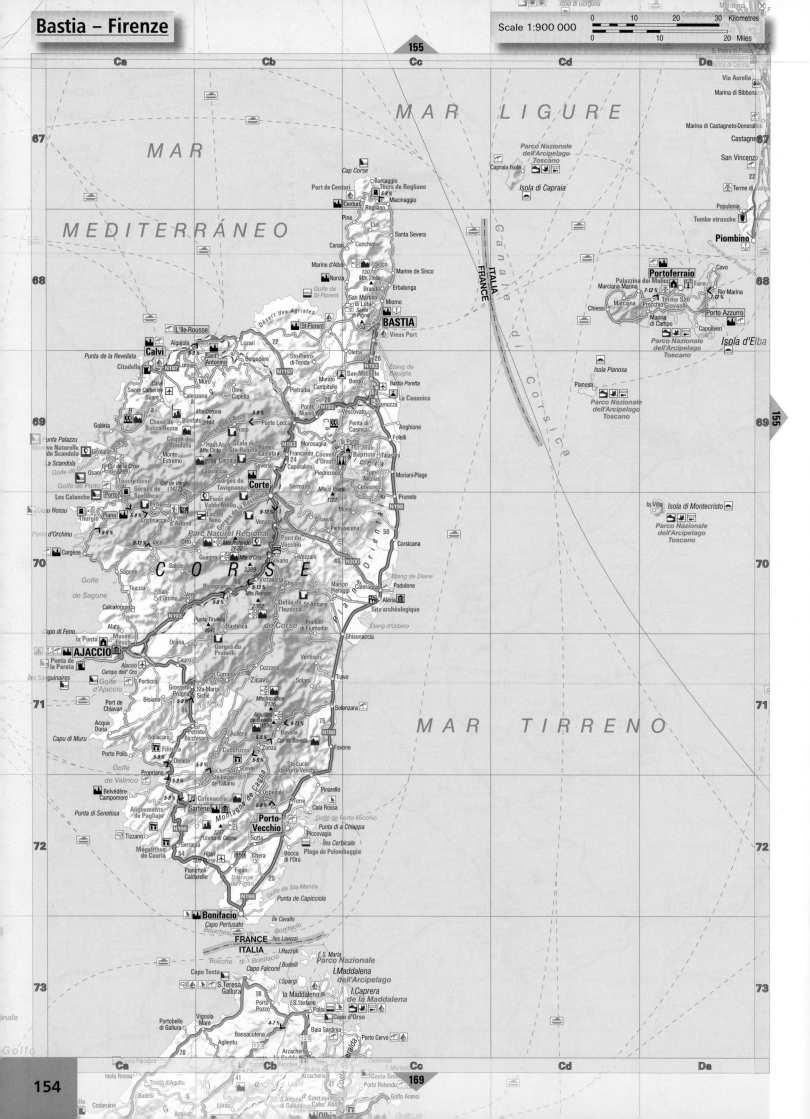

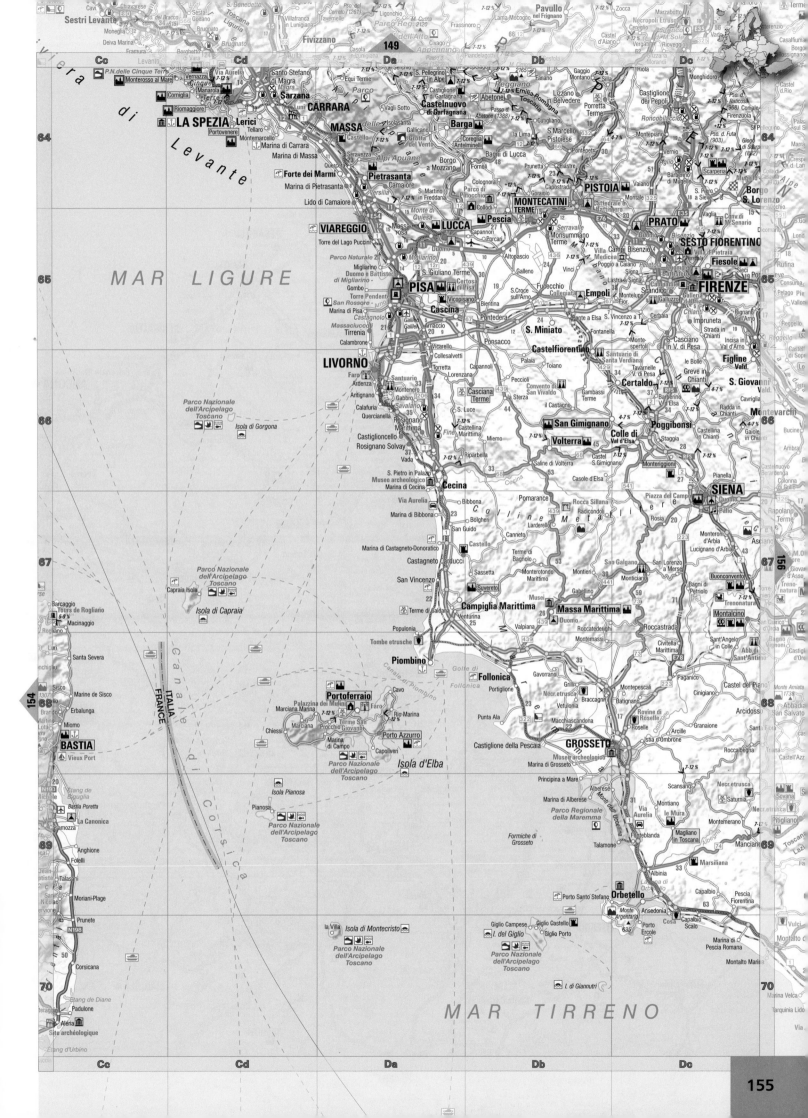

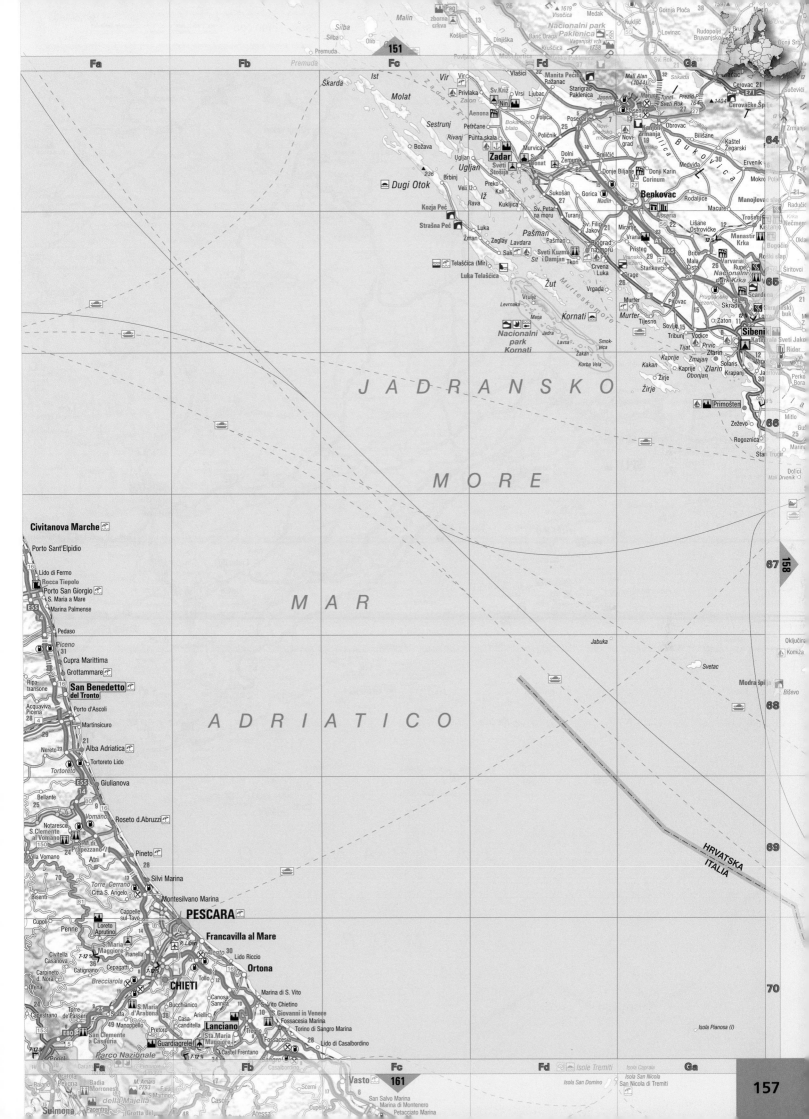

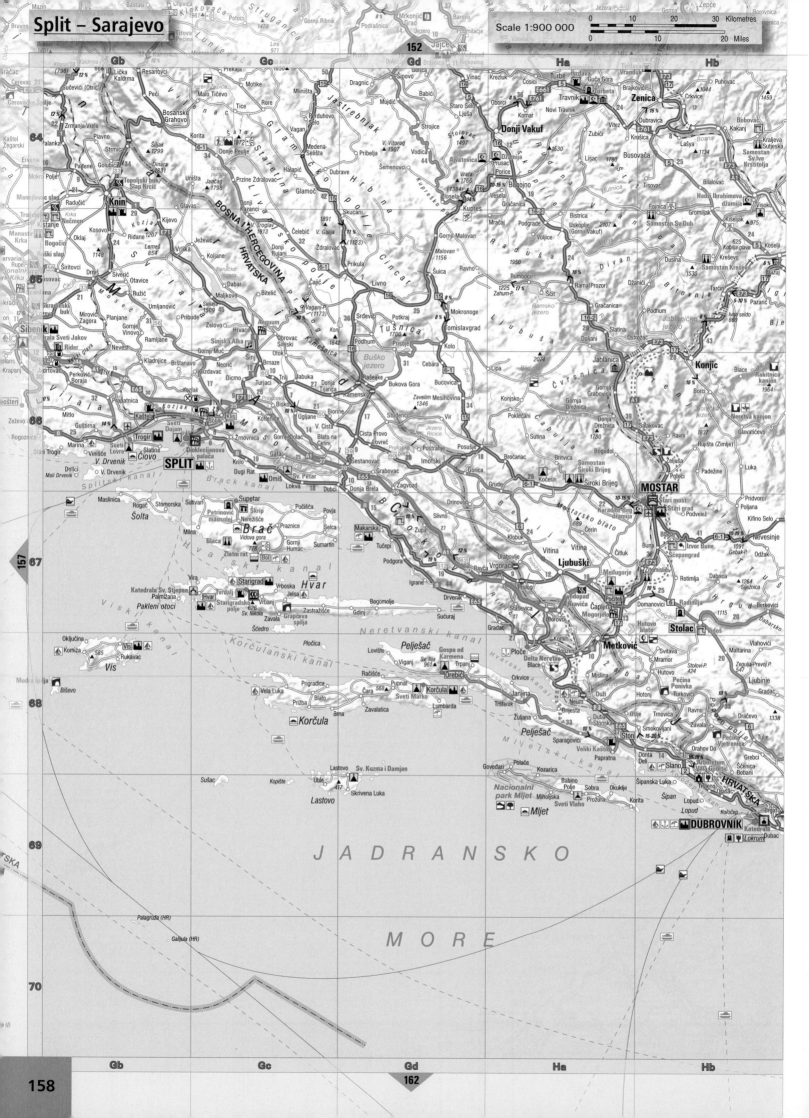

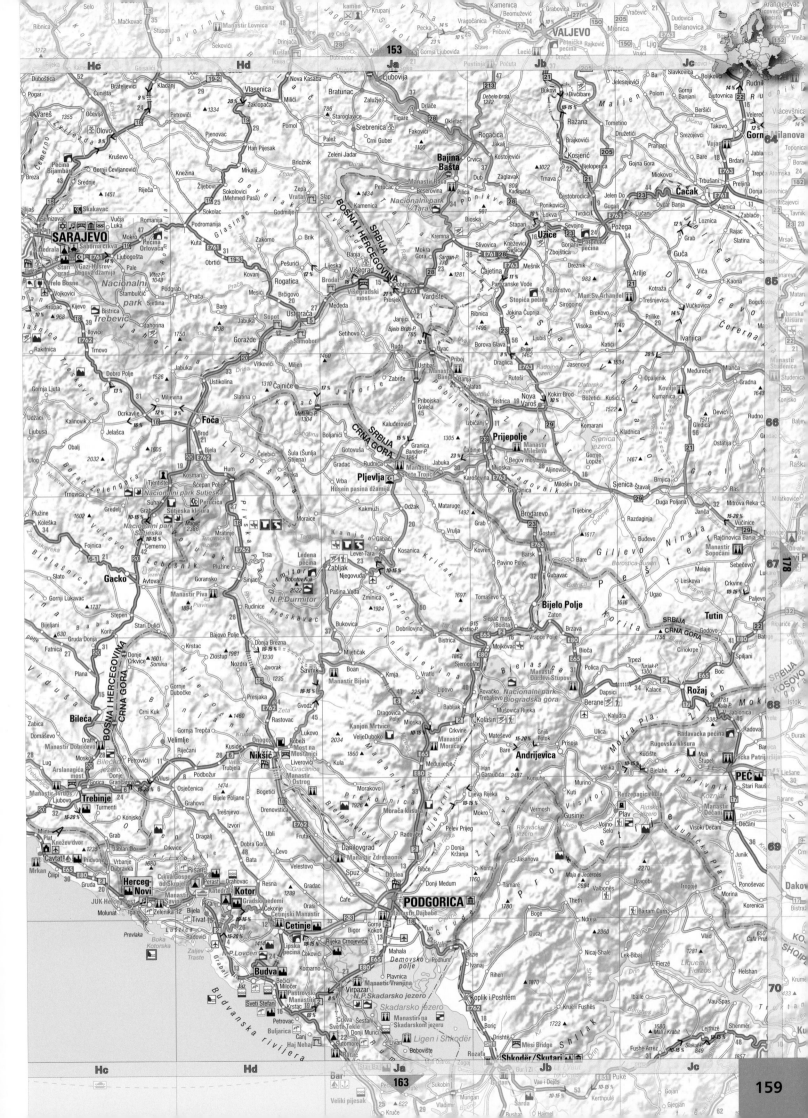

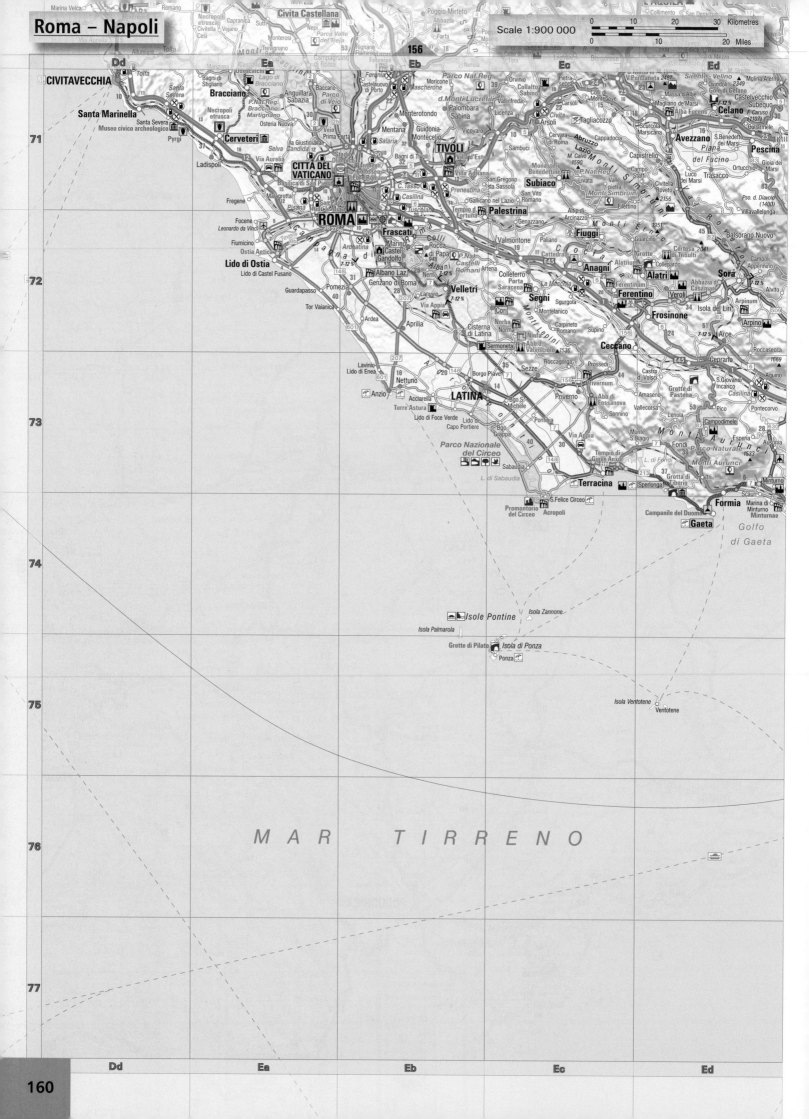

VIENNA TO PRAGUE 181.6 MI CAR
PRAGUE TO SALSBURG 170.0 MI
SALSBURG TO VIENNA 156. MI

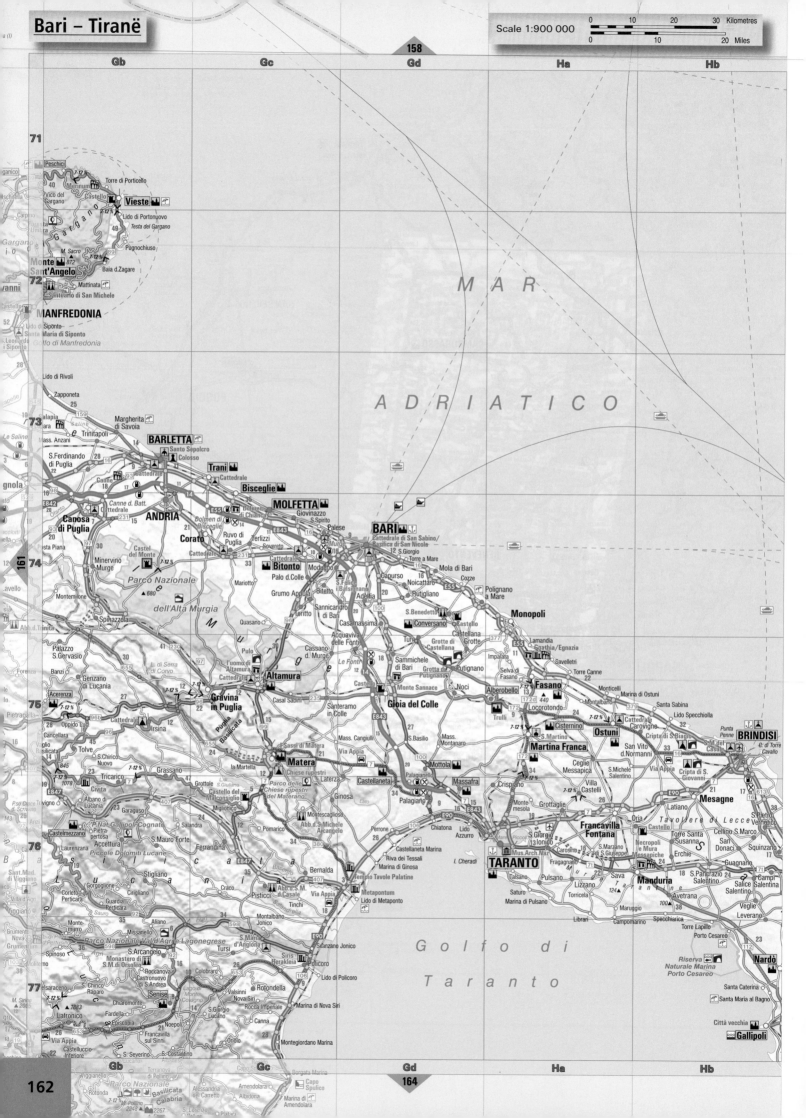

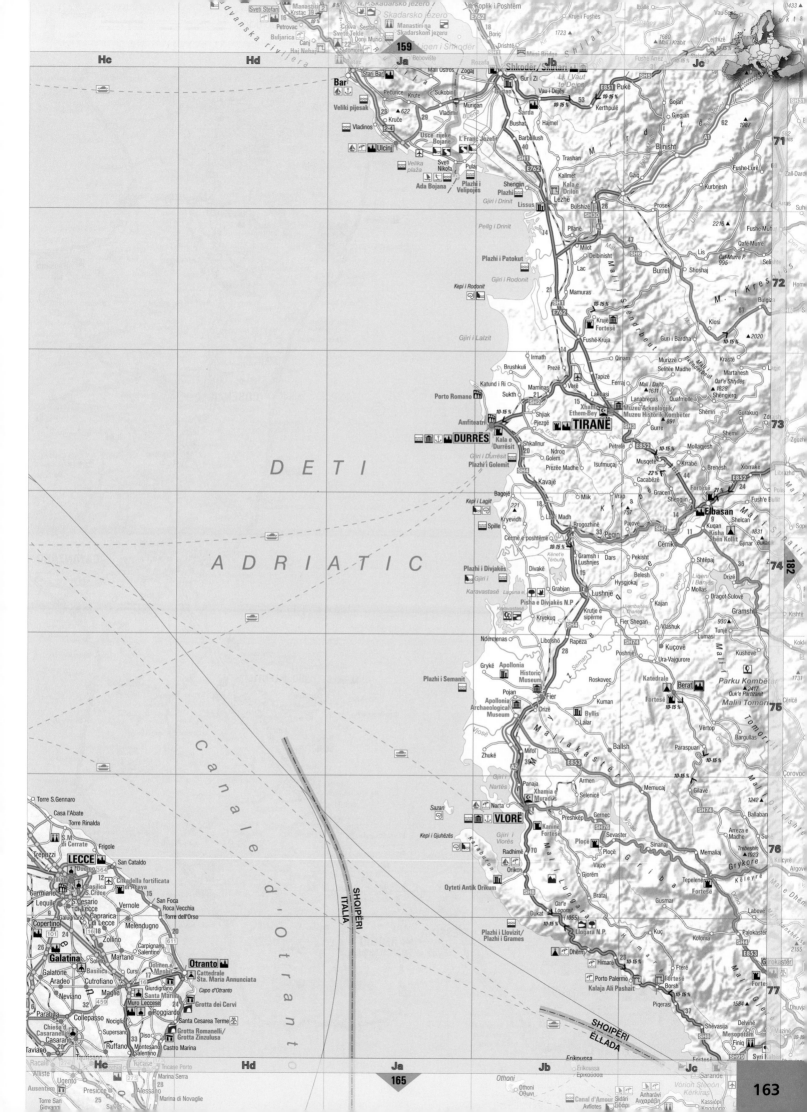

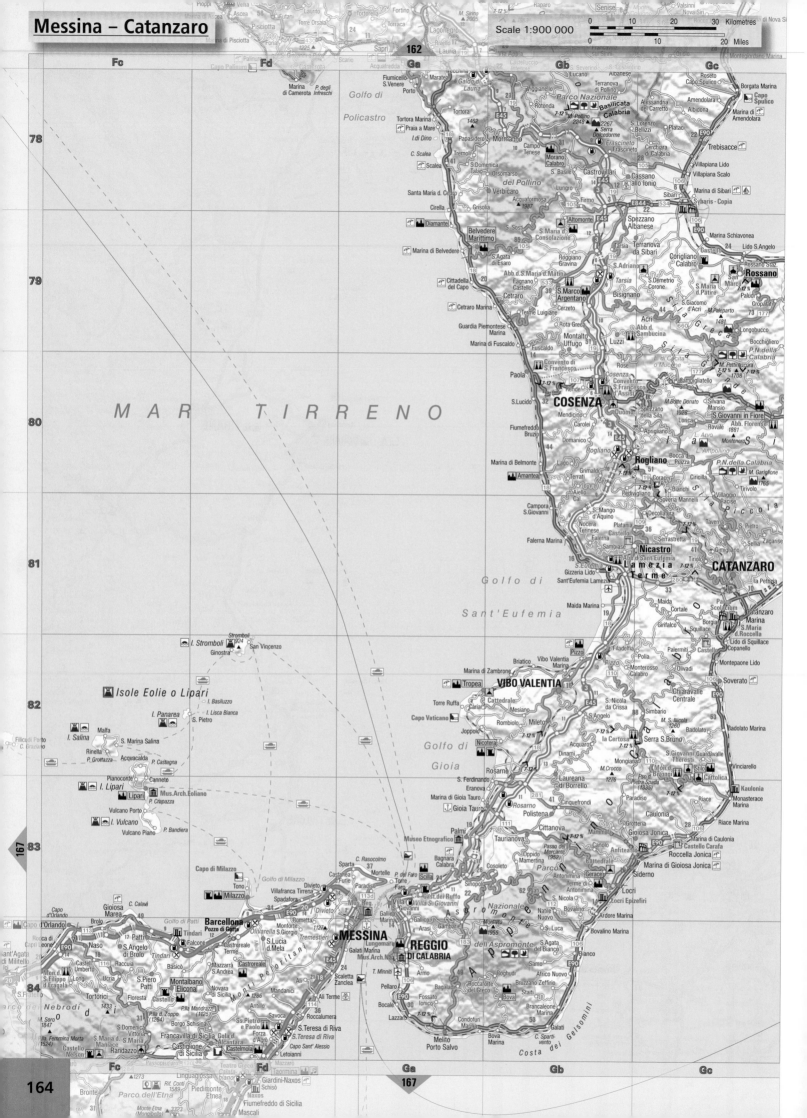

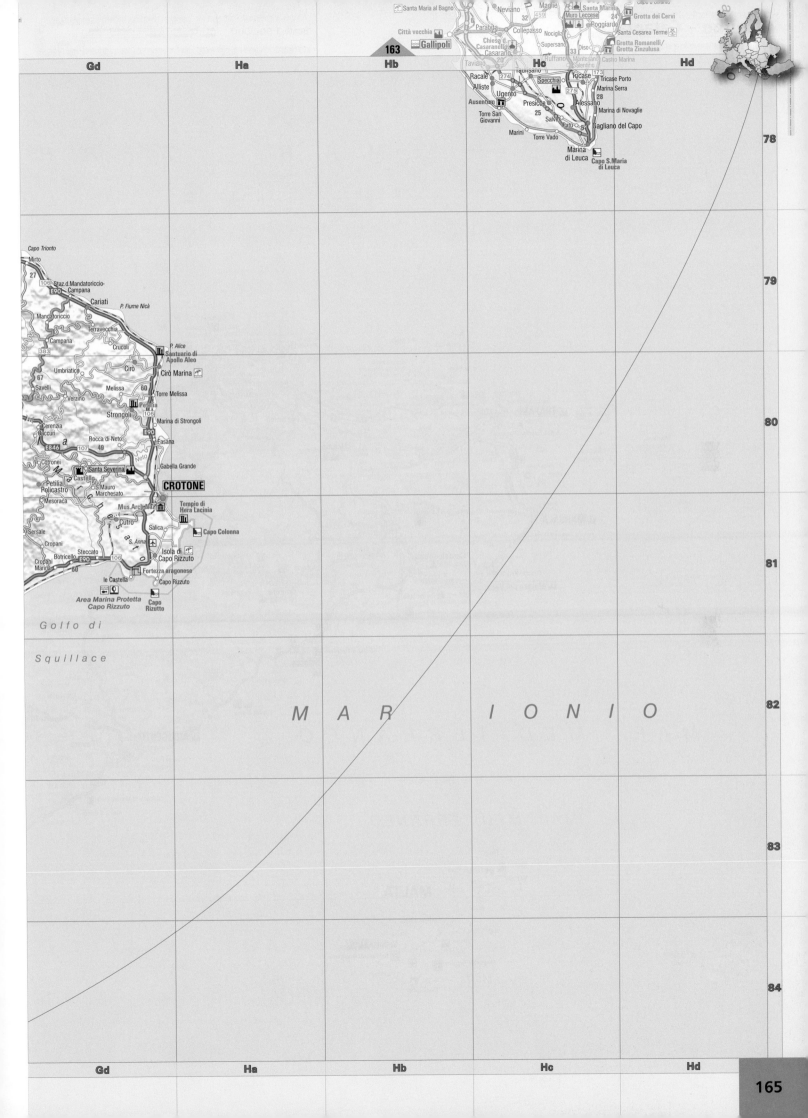

Santa Maria al Bagno
Neviano
Maglie
Santa Maria
Grotta dei Cervi
Città vecchia
Parabita
Collepasso
Muro Leccese
Poggiardo

163

Gallipoli
Chiesa d.
Casaranello
Casarano
Nociglia
Santa Cesarea Terme
Grotta Romanelli/
Grotta Zinzulusa
Taviano
Ruffano
Supersano
Diso
Montesano
Castro Marina
Salentino

Racale
Taurisano
Tricase
Tricase Porto
Alliste
Specchia
Marina Serra
Ugento
Presicce
Alessano
Marina di Novaglie
Ausentum
Salvé
Torre San
Giovanni
Marini
Patù
Gagliano del Capo

Torre Vado
Marina
di Leuca
Capo S.Maria
di Leuca

78

Capo Trionto
Mirto

79

Staz.d.Mandatoriccio-
Campana
Cariati
P. Fiume Nicà
Mandatoriccio
Terravecchia
Campana
Crucoli
P. Alice
Santuario di
Apollo Aleo
Umbriatico
Cirò
Cirò Marina
Savelli
Melissa
Torre Melissa
Verzino
Petilia
Strongoli
Cerenzia
Caccuri
Marina di Strongoli
Rocca di Neto
Fasana
Cotronei
Neto
Gabella Grande
Petilia
Policastro
Santa Severina
Castello
S.Mauro
Marchesato

80

CROTONE

Mesoraca
Mus.Arch.Naz.
Tempio di
Hera Lacinia
Cutro
Salica
Capo Colonna
Sersale
S. Anna
Cropani
Isola di
Capo Rizzuto
Botricello
Steccato
Cropani
Marina
Forteza aragonese
le Castella
Area Marina Protetta
Capo Rizzuto
Capo Rizzuto
Capo
Rizutto

81

Golfo di

Squillace

M A R   I O N I O

82

83

84

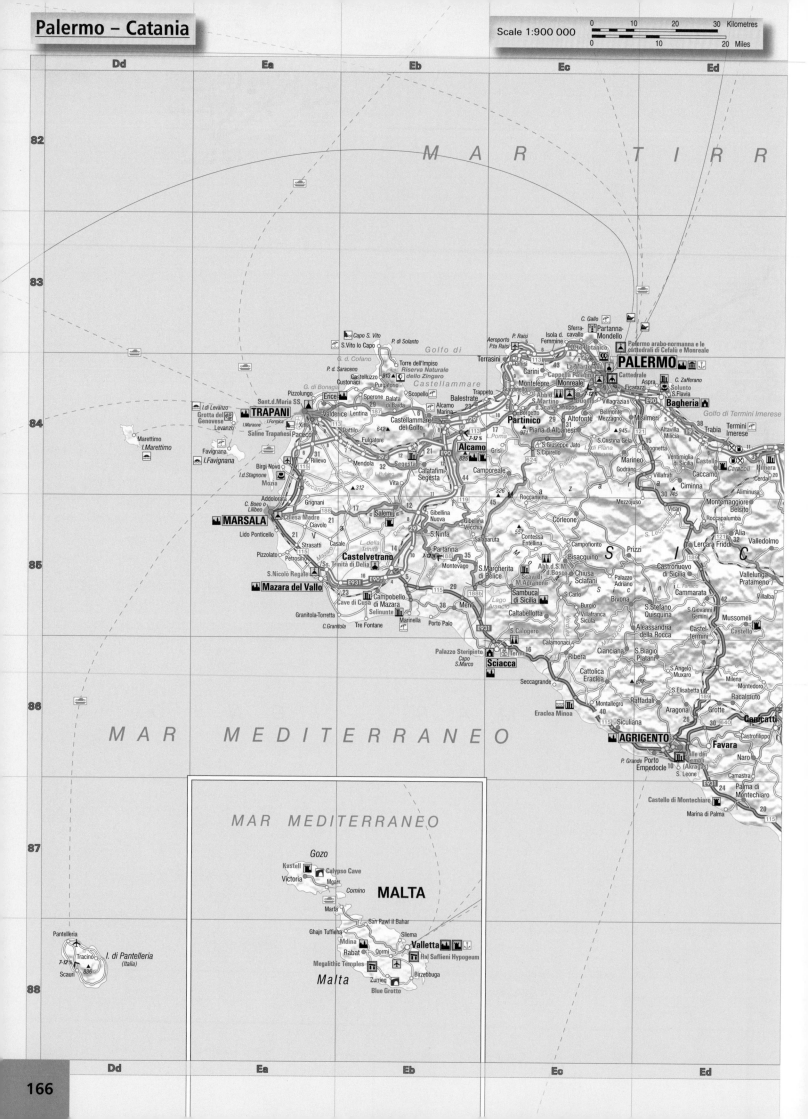

Scale 1:900 000

0   10   20   30 Kilometres
0   10   20 Miles

Dd   Ea   Eb   Ec   Ed

82

M A R   T I R R

83

Capo S. Vito
S.Vito lo Capo
P. di Solanto
Golfo di
Aeroporto
P.ta Raisi
P. Raisi
Isola d.
Femmine
Sferra-
cavallo
C. Gallo
Partanna-
Mondello
Palermo arabo-normanna e le
cattedrali di Cefalù e Monreale
P. d. Saraceno
G. d. Cofano
Terrasini
Cinisi
Carini
Orto Botanico
PALERMO
Riserva Naturale
dello Zingaro
Torre dell'Impiso
Castelluzzo   913
Custonaci   Purgatorio
Castellammare
Montelepre
La Martorana
Cappella Palatina
Cattedrale
C. Zafferano
Aspra
Soluto
S.Flavia
84
Pizzolungo
Sant.d.Maria SS.
Erice
Sperone   Balata
di Baida
Scopello
Alcamo
Marina
Trappeto
Giardinello
S.Martino
d. Scale
Monreale
Duomo
Ficarazzi
Villagrazia
Bagheria
Golfo di Termini Imerese
I.di Levanzo
Grotta del
Genovese
Levanzo
TRAPANI
Valderice   Lentina
Balestrate
Piano
Borgeto
Altofonte
Belmonte
Mezzagno
Misilmeri
Trabia
Termini
Imerese
I.Maraone
I.Formica
Saline Trapanesi
Xitta
Paceco
Dattilo
642
Castellammare
del Golfo
Partinico
Piana d.Albanesi
945
Altavilla
Milicia
Marettimo
I.Marettimo
Favignana
I.Favignana
Rilievo
Fulgatore
Mendola
I.d.Stagnone
Mozia
Grignani
Segesta
Calatafimi-
Segesta
Camporeale
S.Giuseppe Jato
Grisi
Lidi Plana
Marineo
Godrano
Ventimiglia
di Sicilia
Villafrati
Caccamo
Himera
Cerda
85
Addolorata
C. Boeo o
Lilibeo
MARSALA
Chiesa Madre
Ciavolo
Casale
Salemi
Vita
Roccamena
Corleone
Mezzojuso
Vicari
Ciminna
Montemaggiore
Belsito
Roccapalumba
Alia
Lercara Friddi
Valledolmo
S I C I
Lido Ponticello
Strasatti
Pizzolato
Petrosino
S.Nicolò Regale
Castelvetrano
Ss. Trinità di Delia
L. della
Trinità
Gibellina
Nuova
Gibellina
Vecchia
Partanna
Montevago
Salaparuta
S.Ninfa
Contessa
Entellina
Campofiorito
Bisacquino
Prizzi
Castronuovo
di Sicilia
Cammarata
Vallelunga
Pratameno
Villalba
MAZARA del VALLO
Cave di Cusa
Campobello
di Mazara
Selinunte
Menfi
S.Margherita
di Belice
M.Adranone
Scavi di
Abb.d.S.M.
d.Bosco
Chiusa
Sclafani
Palazzo
Adriano
S.Carlo
Burgio
Bivona
S.Stefano
Quisquina
S.Giovanni
Gemini
Mussomeli
Castel-
termini
86
Granitola-Torretta
C.Granitola
Tre Fontane
Marinella
Porto Palo
Sambuca
di Sicilia
Lago
Arancio
Caltabellotta
S.Calogero
Palazzo Steripinto
Capo
S.Marco
Sciacca
Seccagrande
Ribera
Cianciana
Cattolica
Eraclea
Villafranca
Sicula
Aleassandria
della Rocca
S.Biagio
Platani
S.Angelo
Muxaro
Calamonaci
Milena
Montedoro
Racalmuto
Montallegro
Eraclea Minoa
Siculiana
Raffadali
Aragona
Grotte
Canicatti
MAR   MEDITERRANEO
AGRIGENTO
Favara
Castrofilippo
Naro
Camastra
P. Grande Porto
Empedocle
Valle dei
Templi
(Akragas)
S. Leone
Palma di
Montechiaro
87
Castello di Montechiaro
Marina di Palma

M A R   M E D I T E R R A N E O

Gozo
Kastell
Victoria
Calypso Cave
Mgarr
Comino
MALTA
Marfa
Pantelleria
Tracino
I. di Pantelleria
(Italia)
836
Scauri
San Pawl il Bahar
Sliema
Ghajn Tuffieha
Mdina   Valletta
Rabat   Qormi   Hal Saflieni Hypogeum
88
Megalithic Temples
Zurrieq
Birzebbuga
Malta
Blue Grotto

Dd   Ea   Eb   Ec   Ed

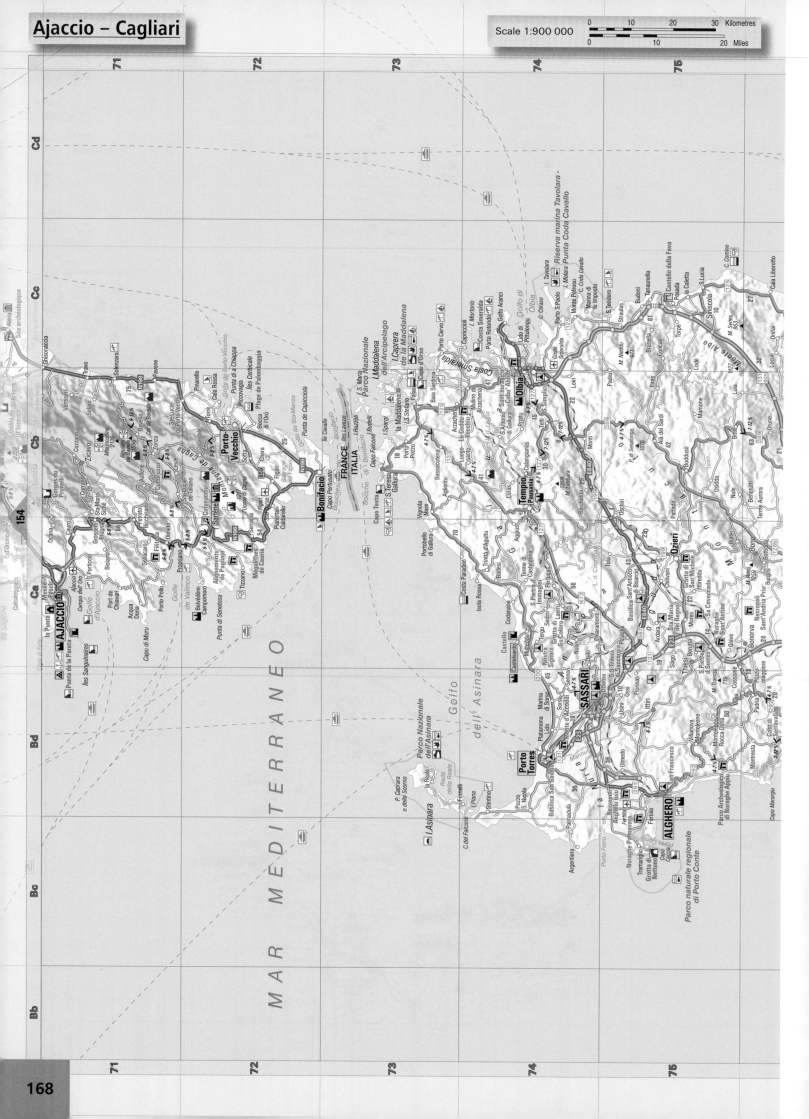

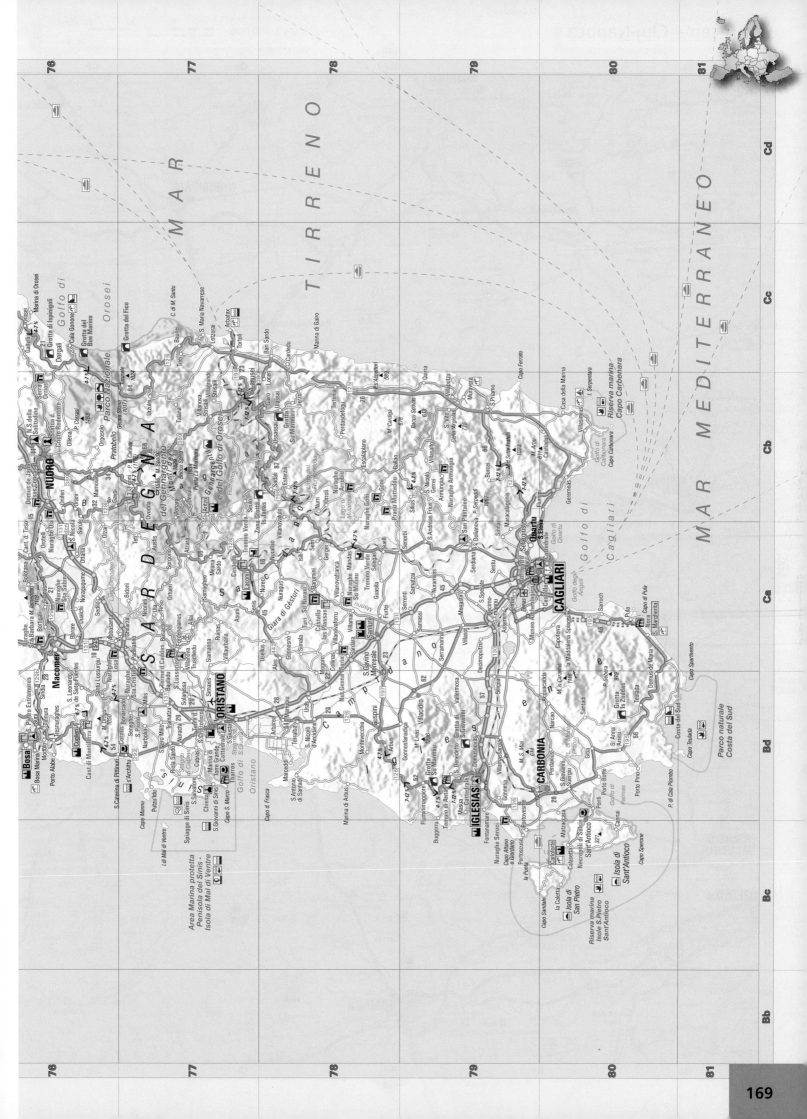

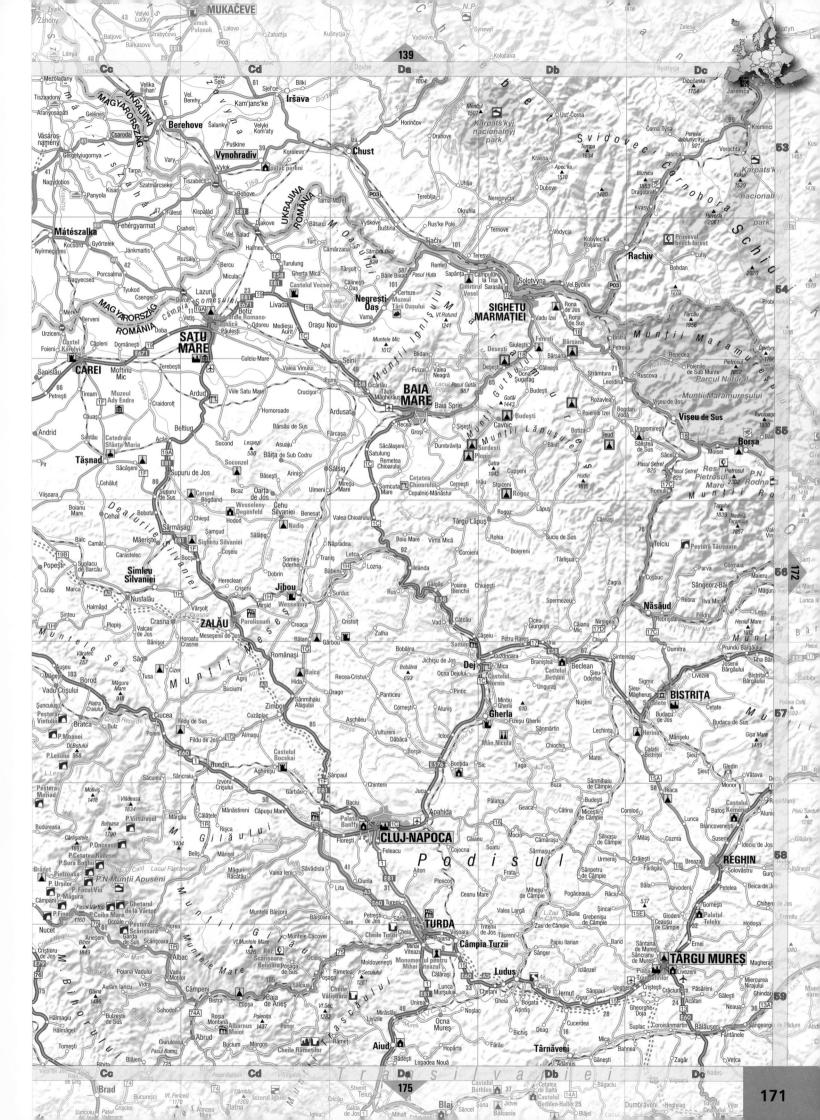

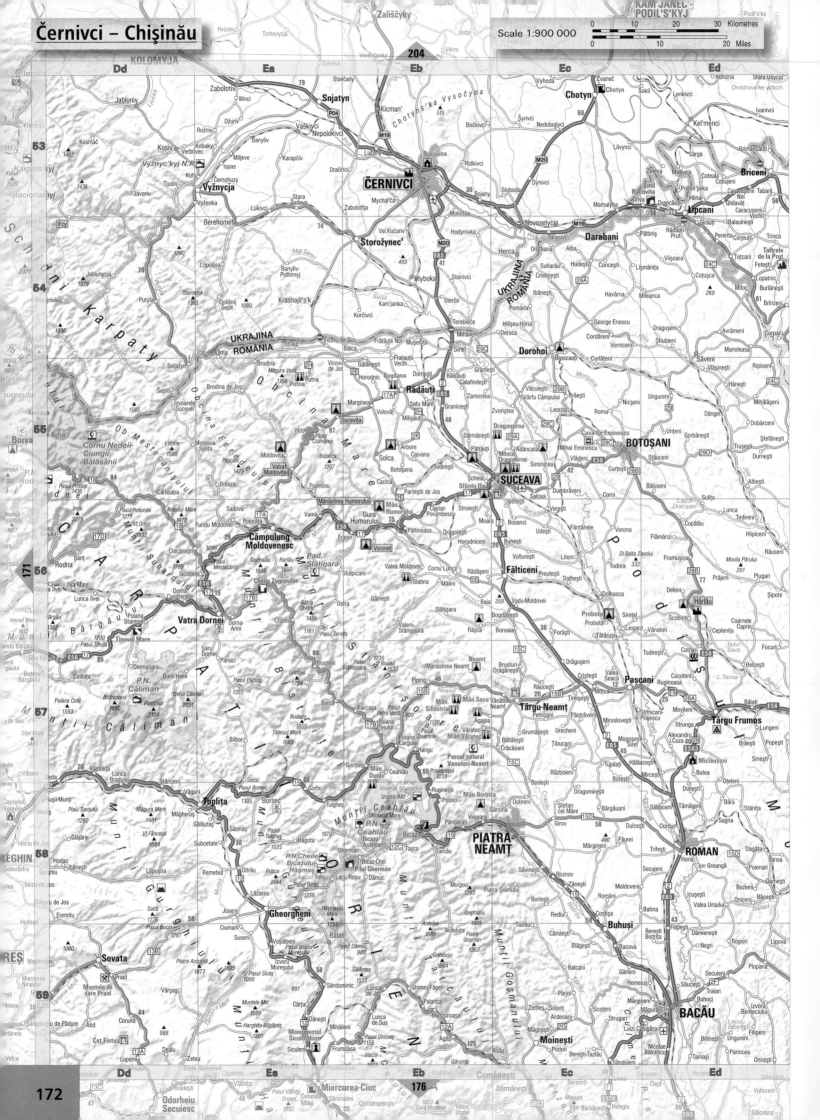

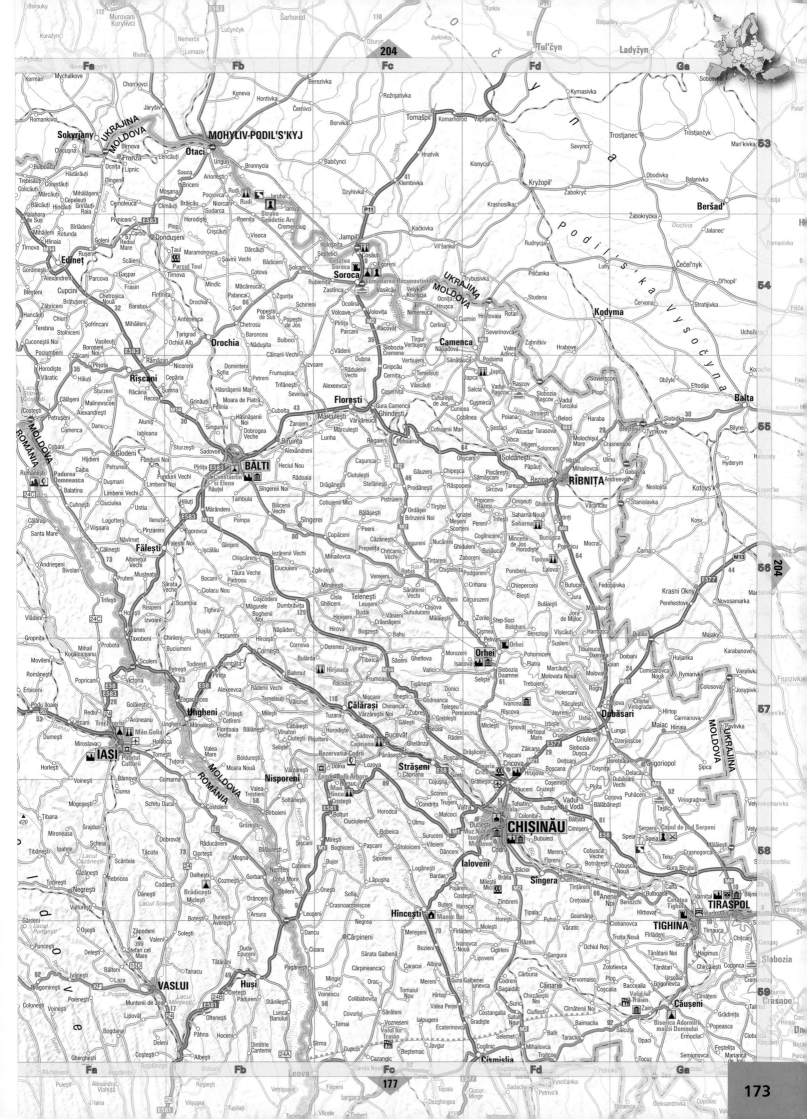

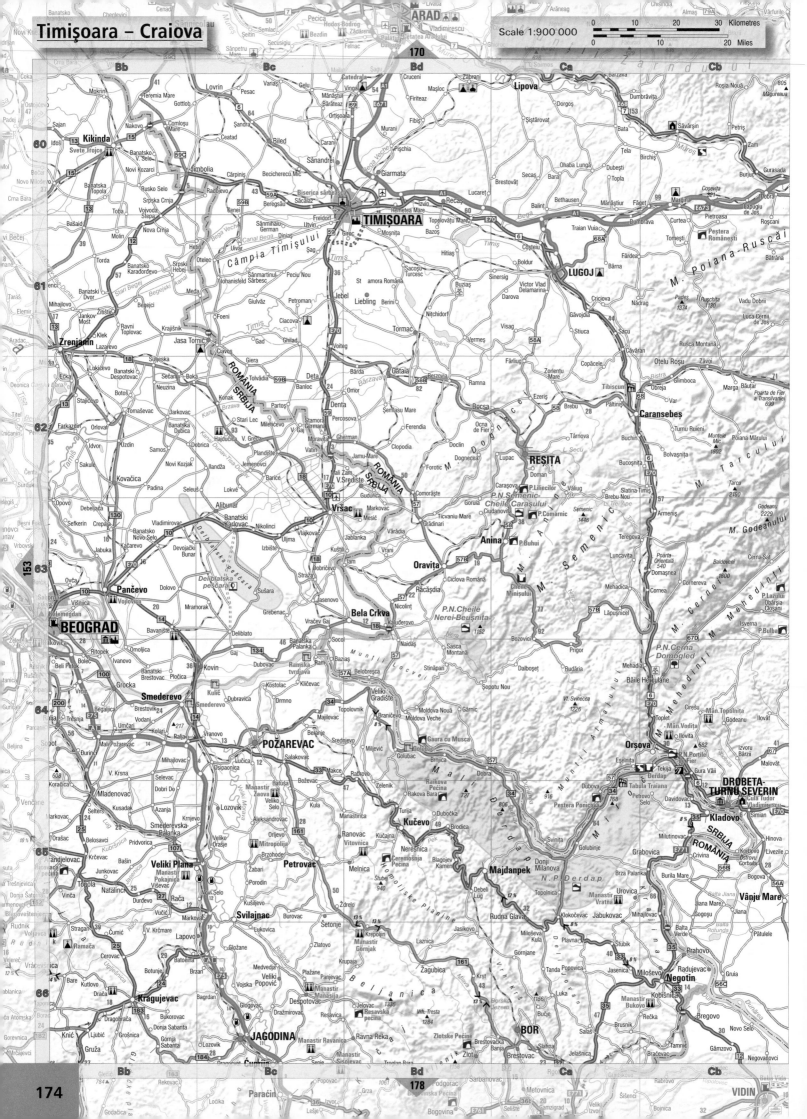

Scale 1:900 000

ARAD

Kilometres
Miles

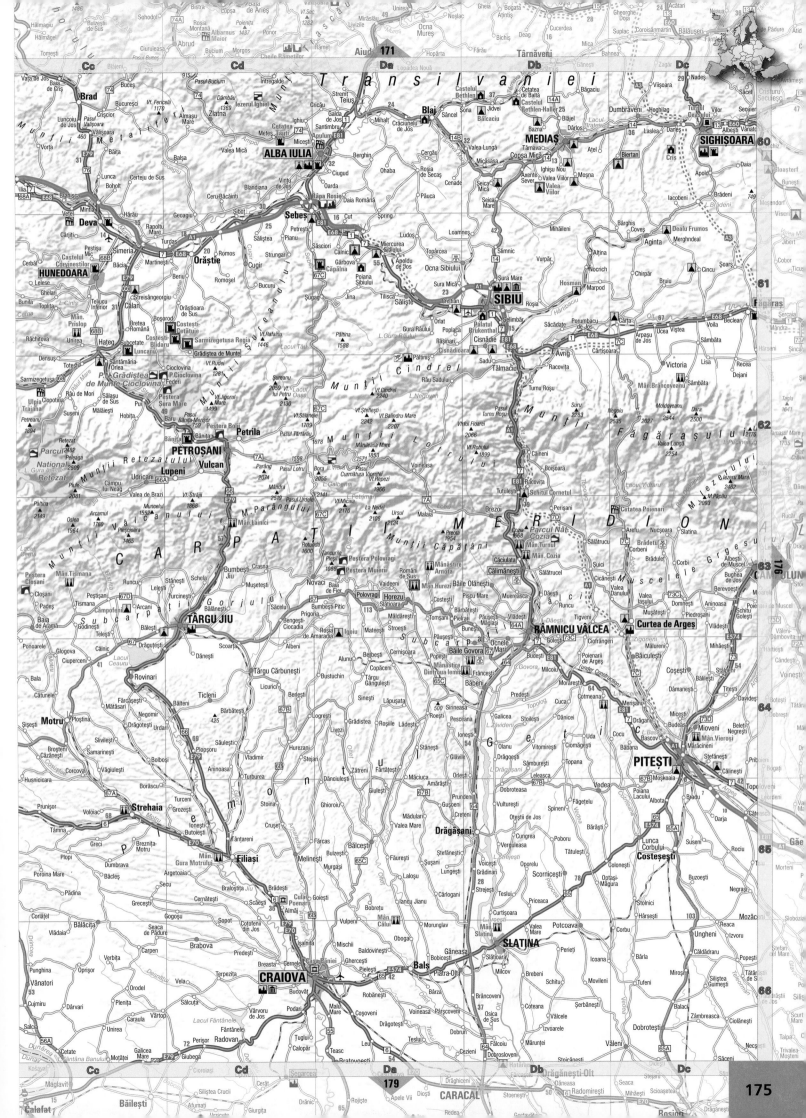

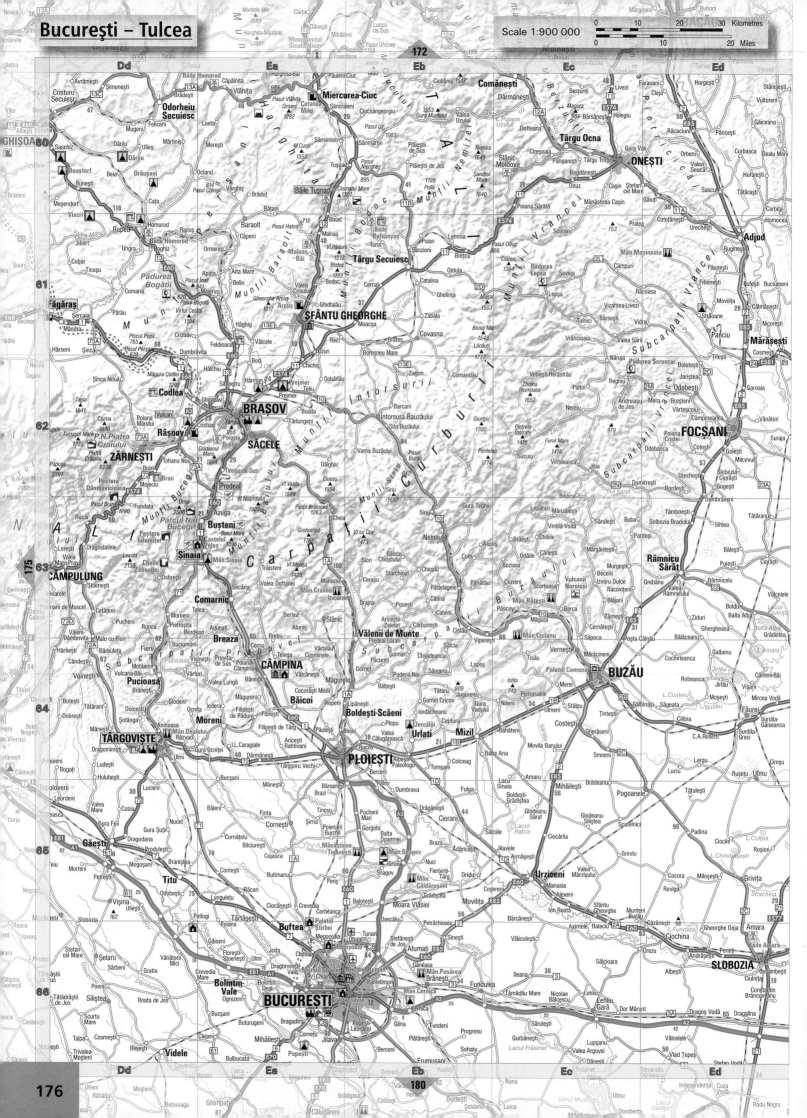

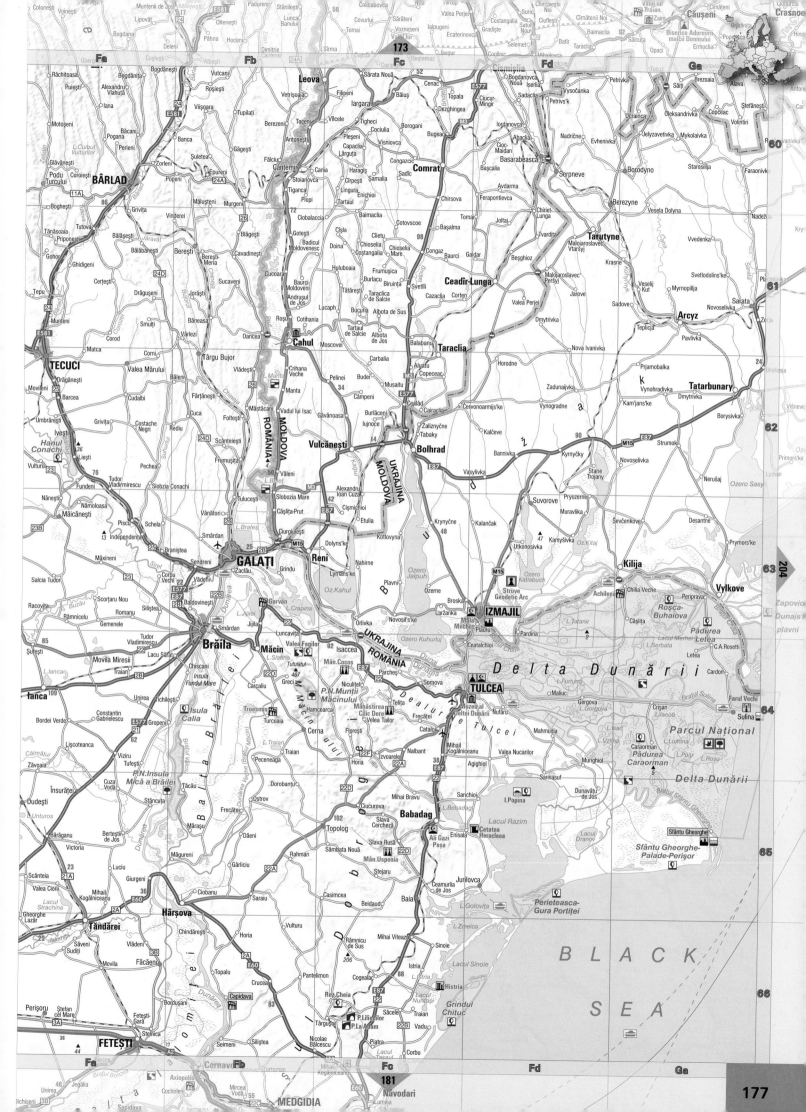

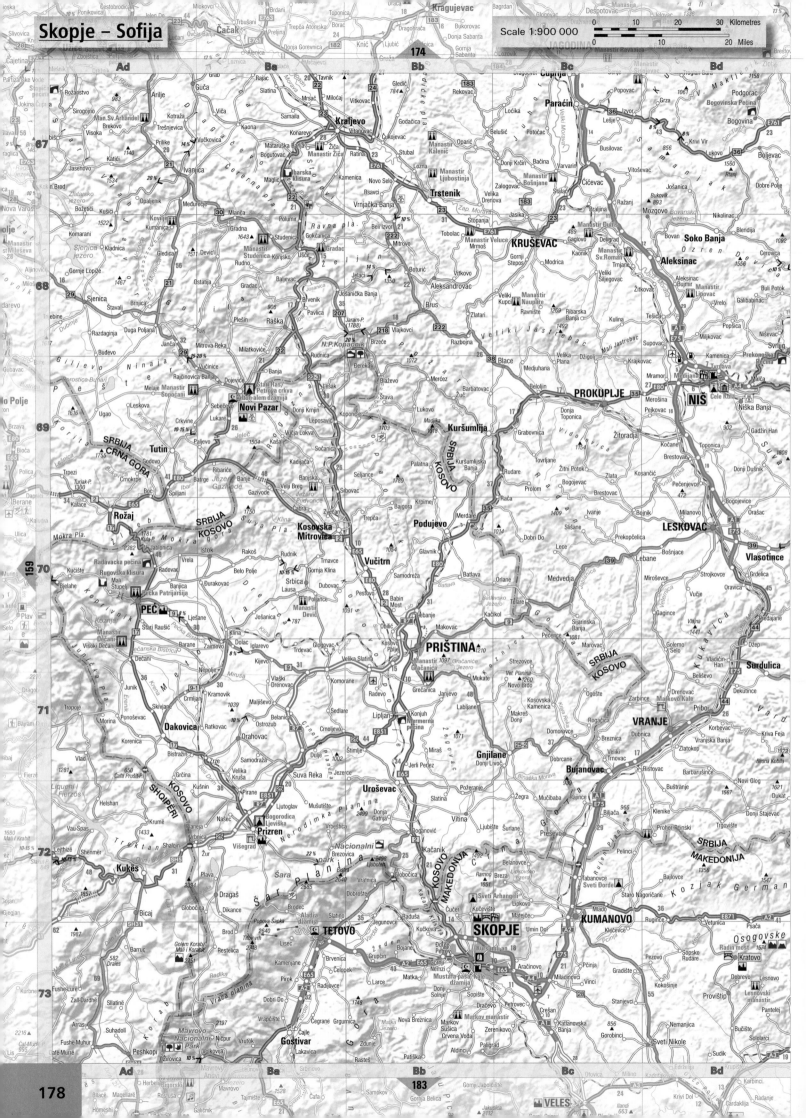

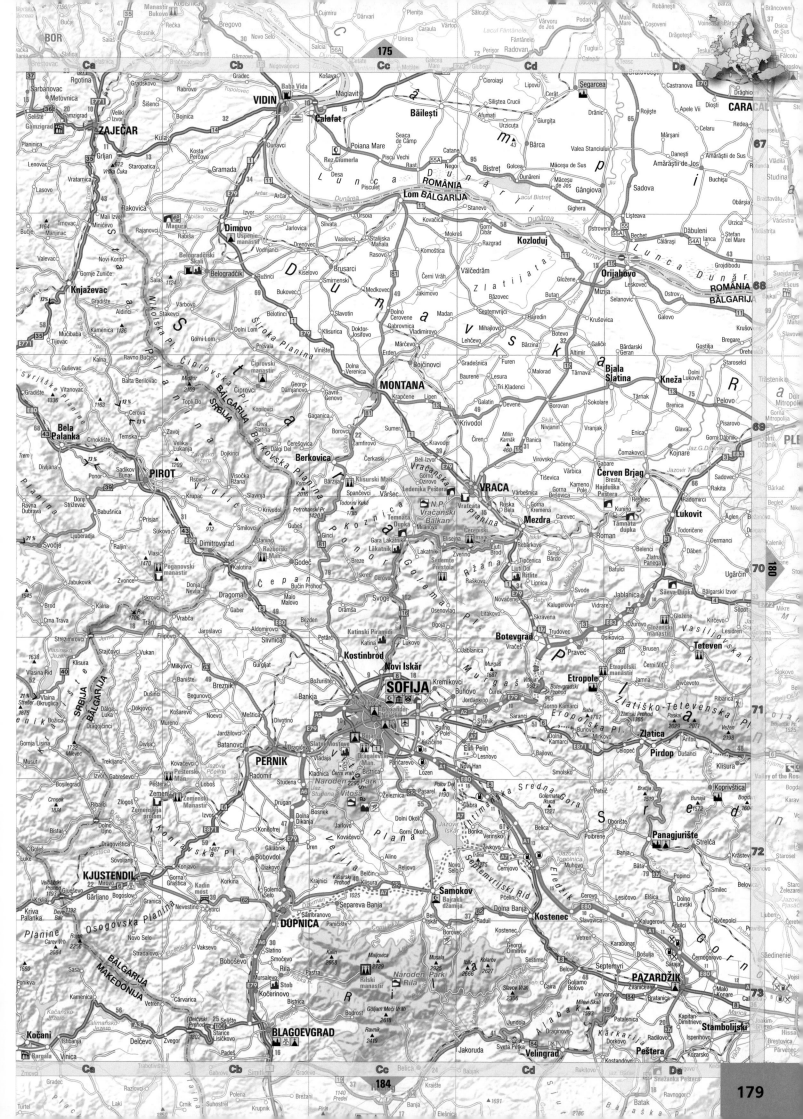

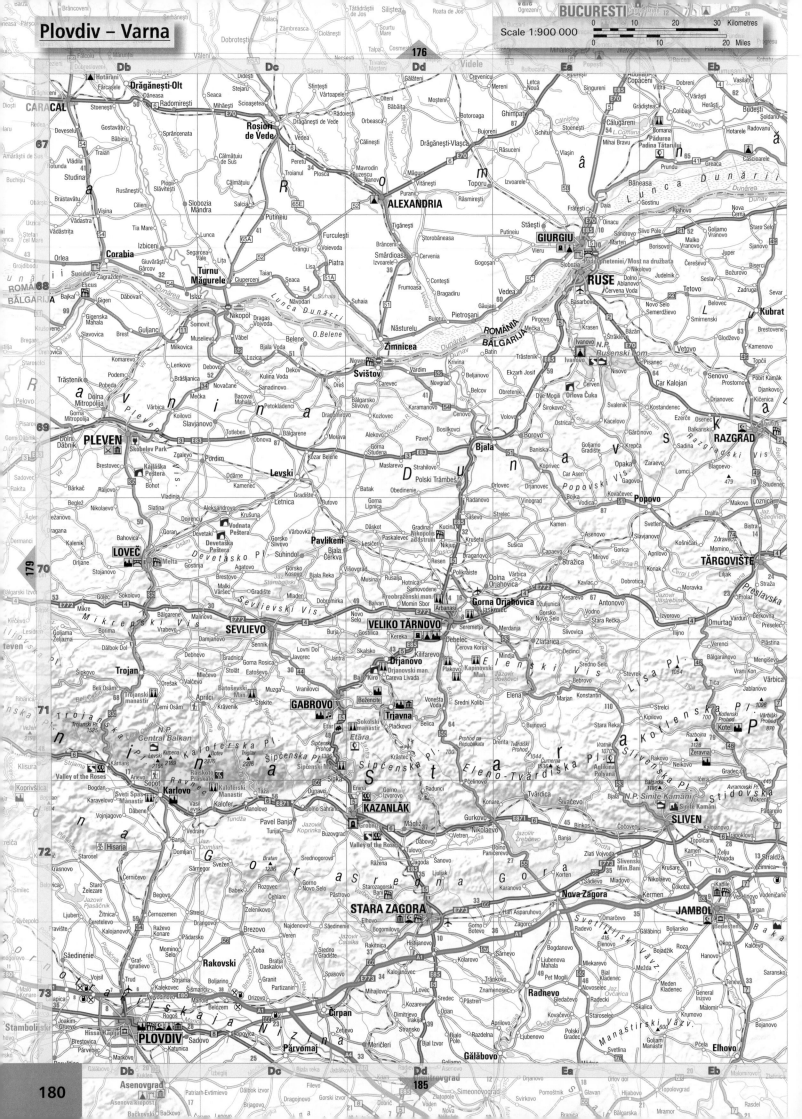

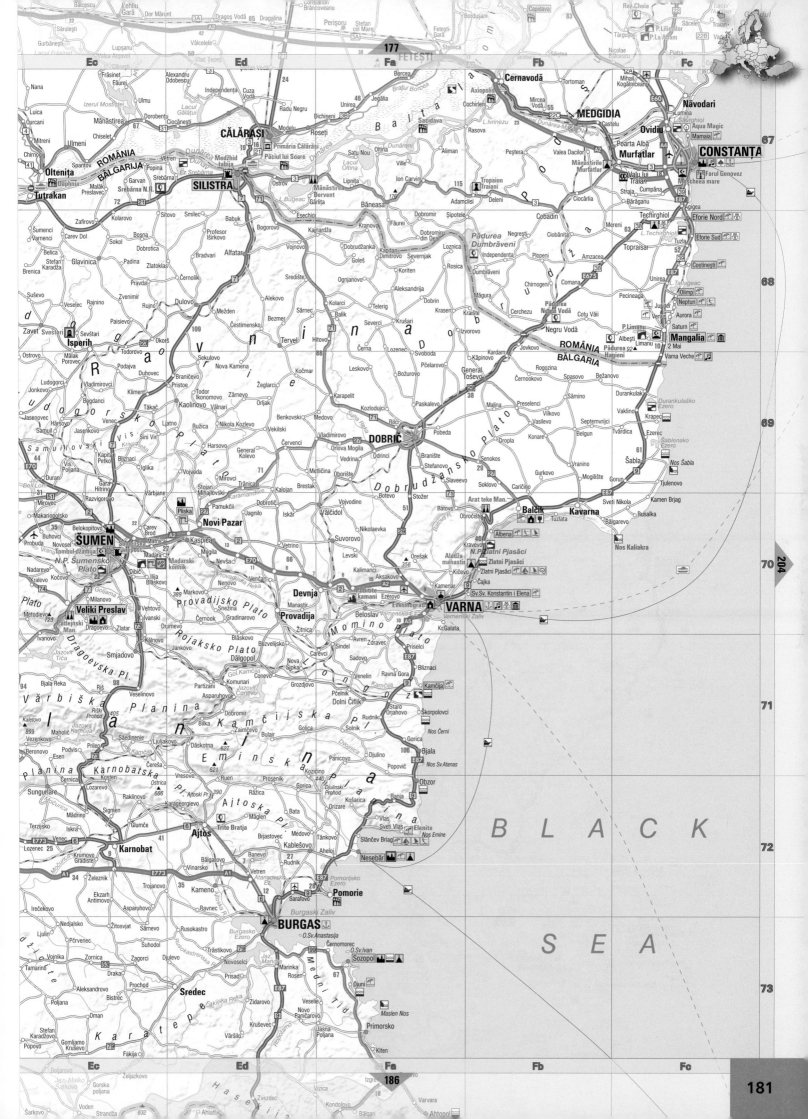

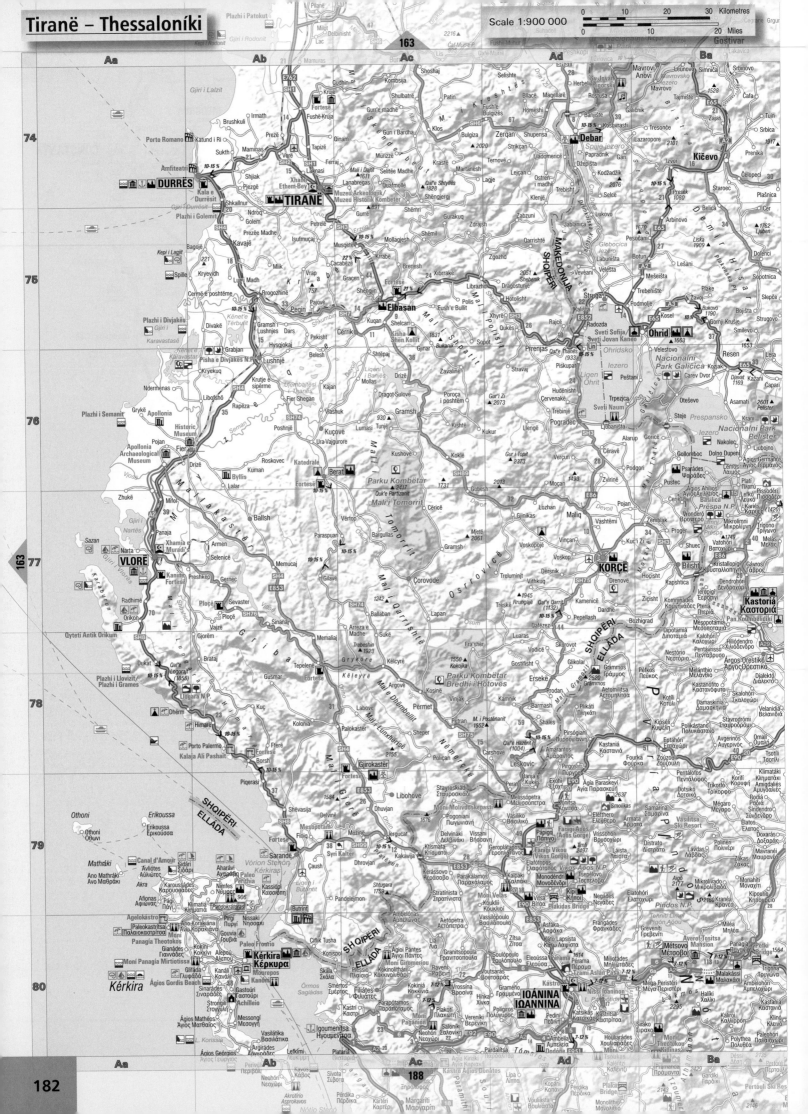

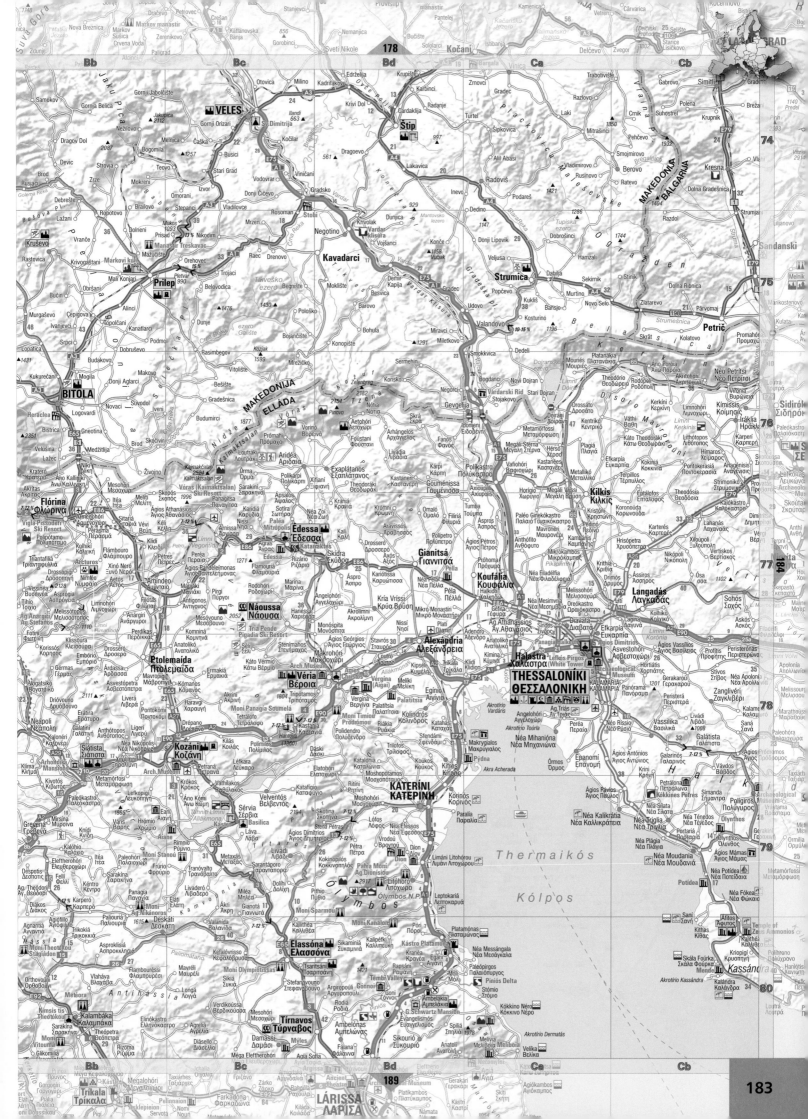

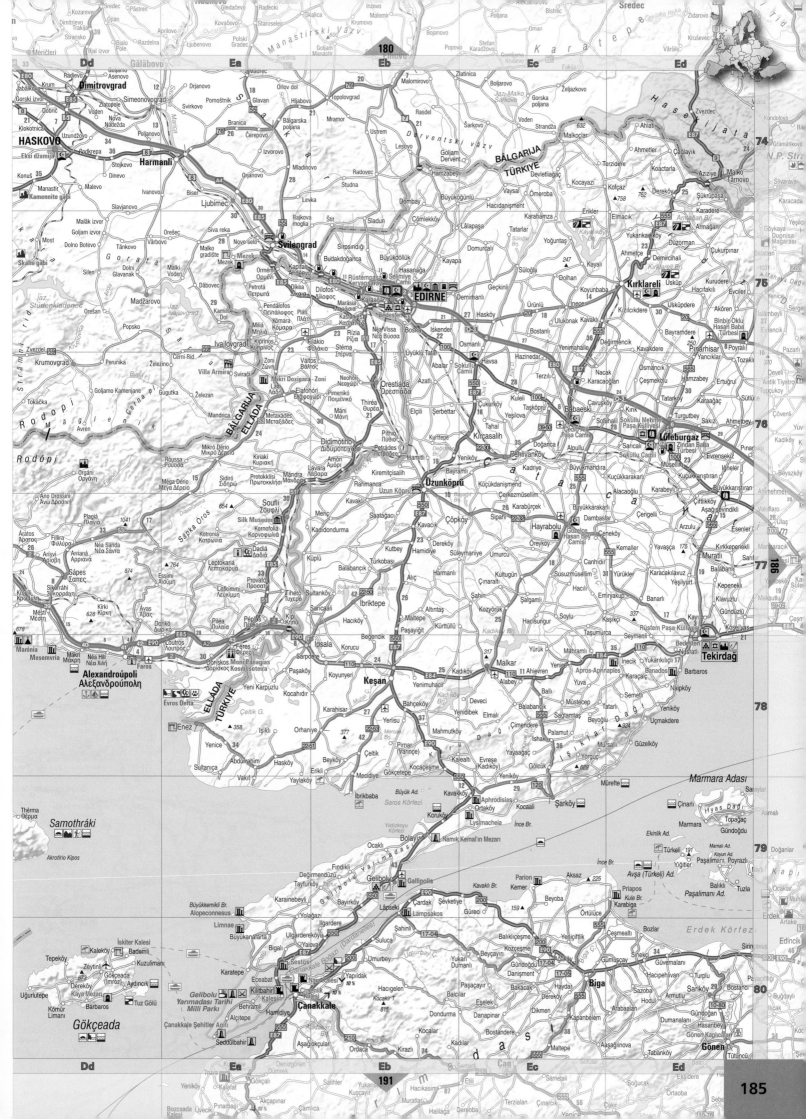

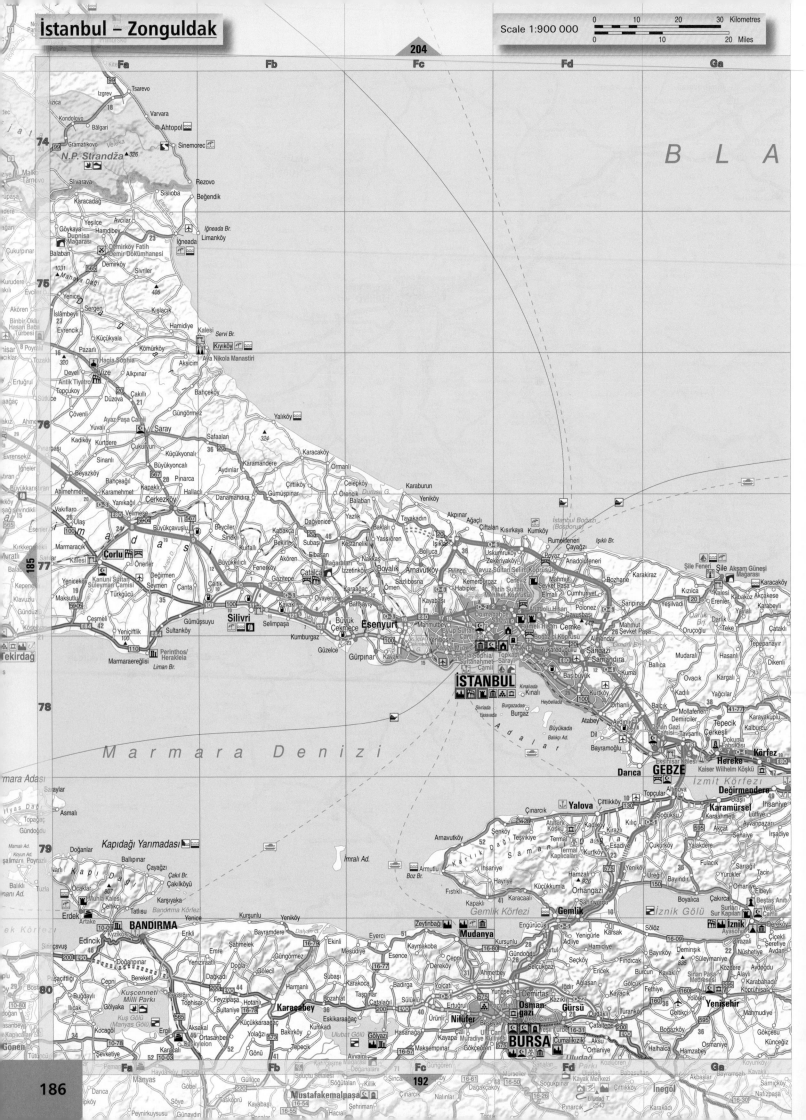

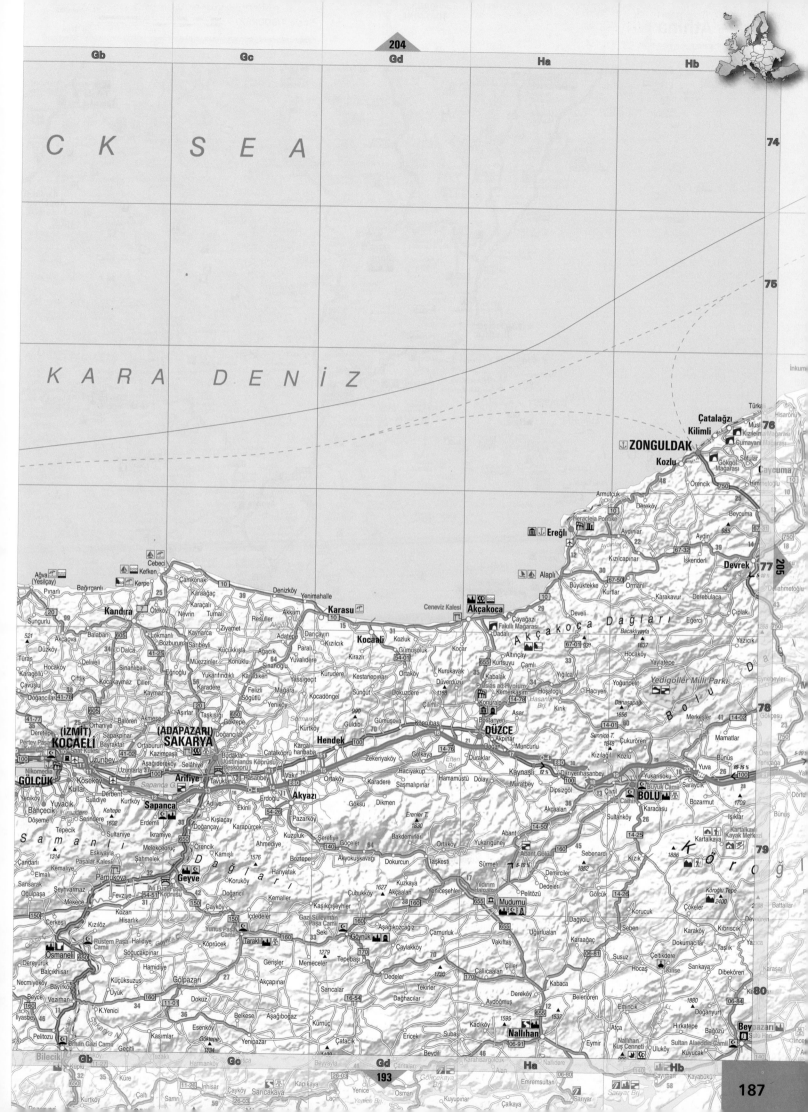

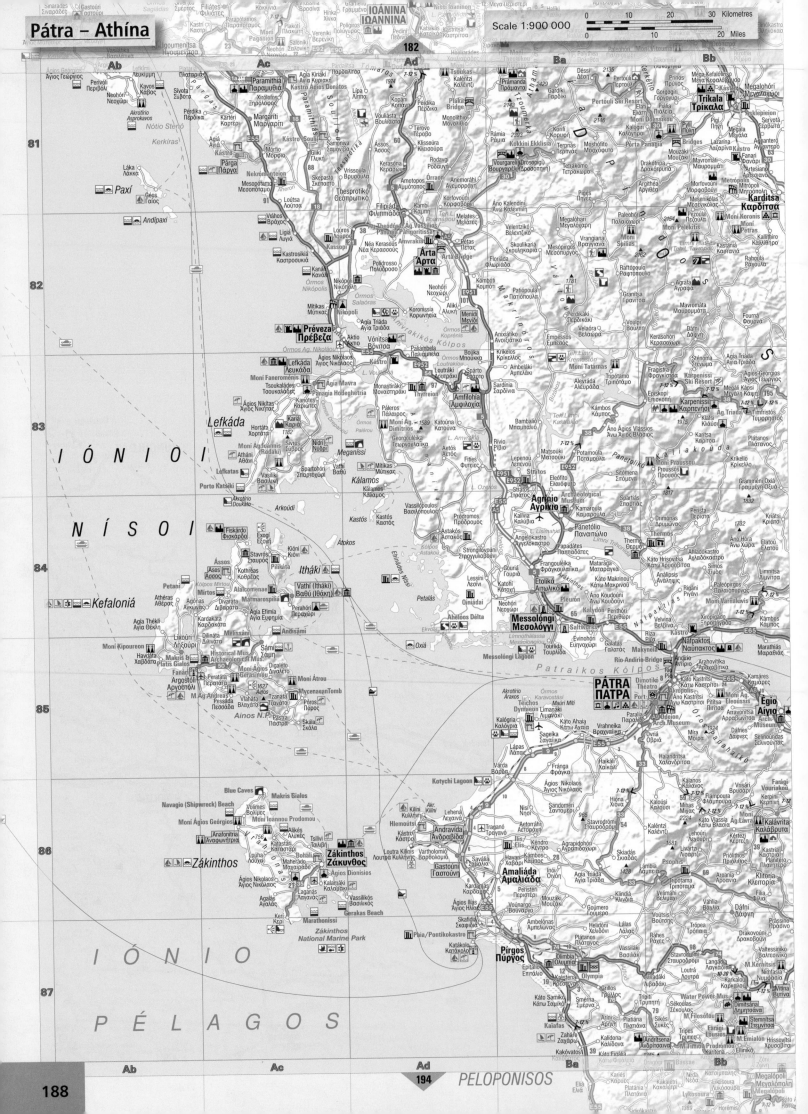

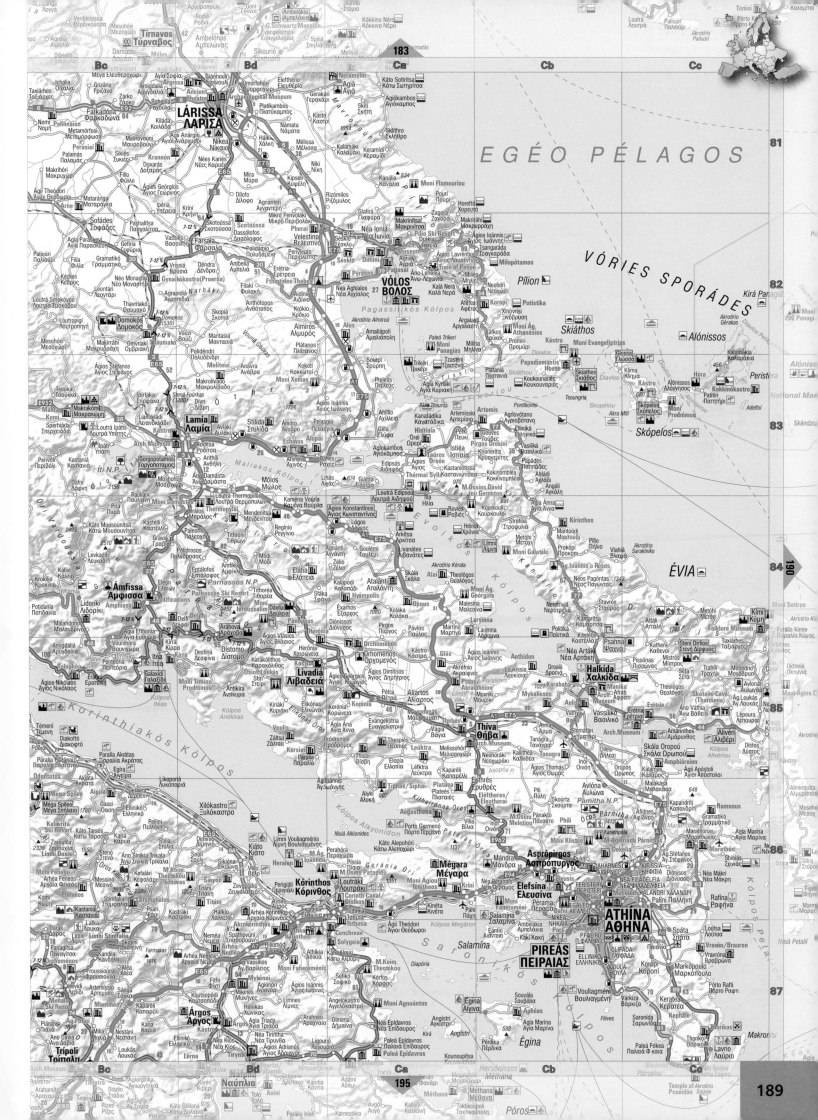

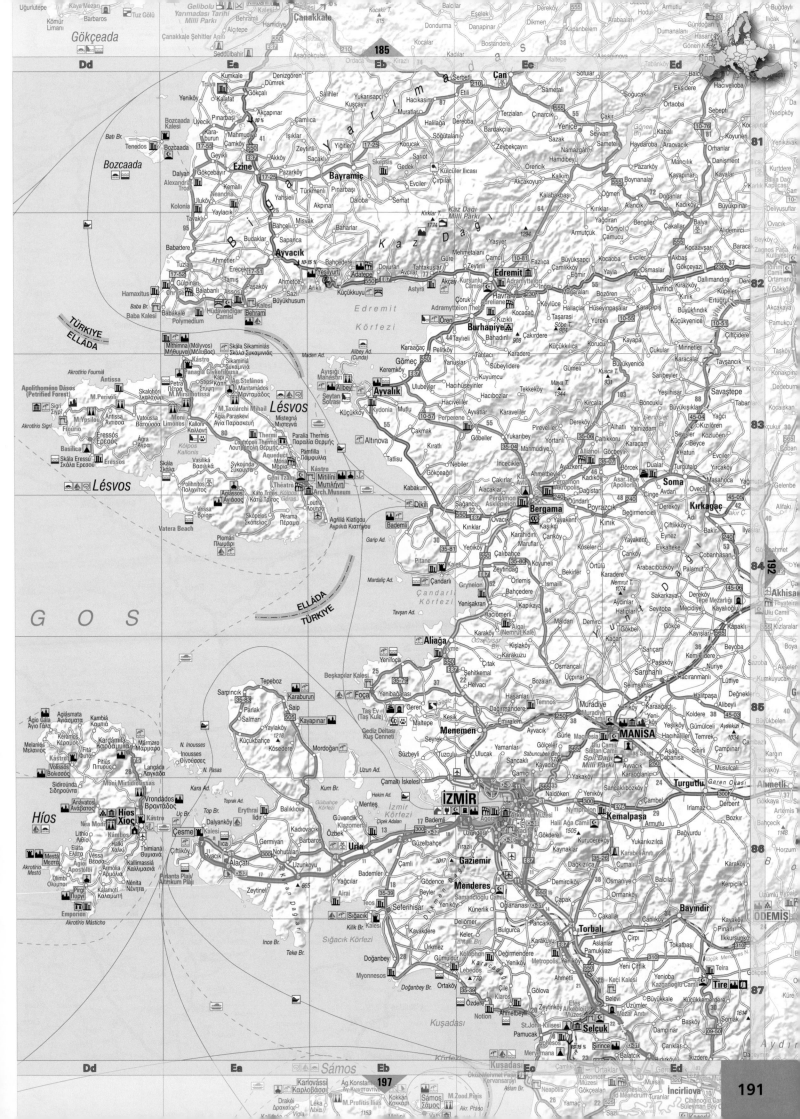

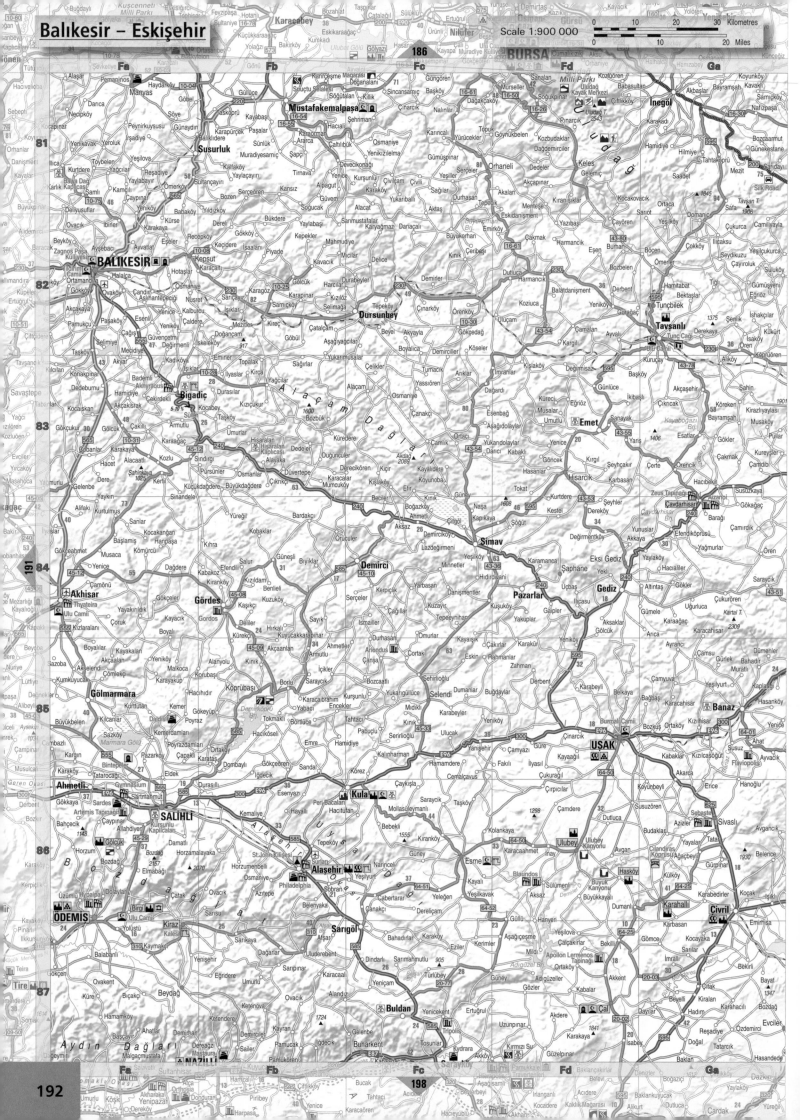

Scale 1:900 000

| 0 | 10 | 20 | 30 Kilometres |

| 0 | 10 | 20 Miles |

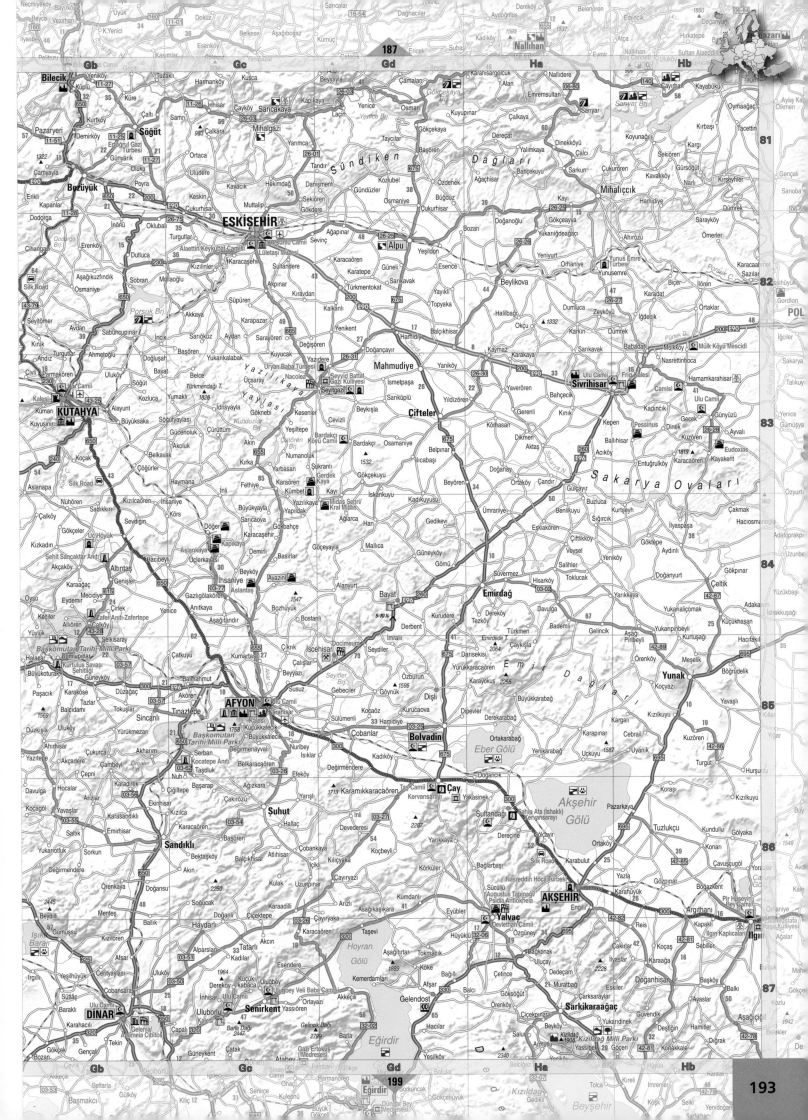

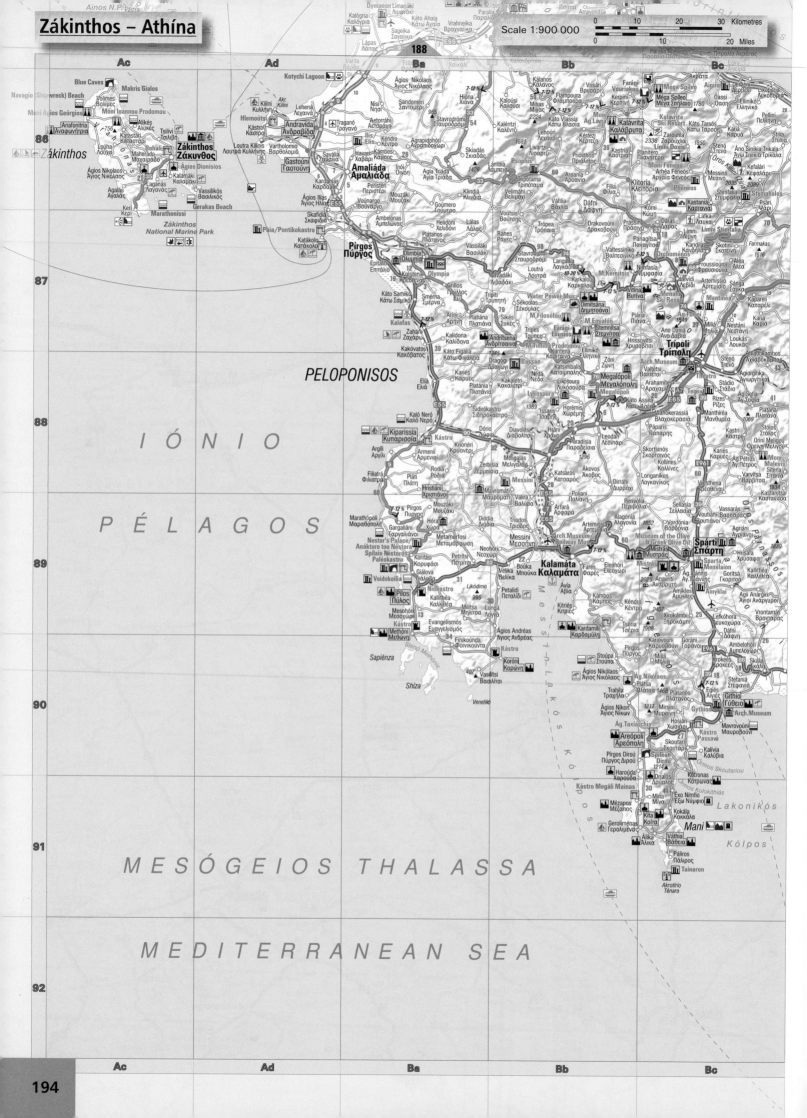

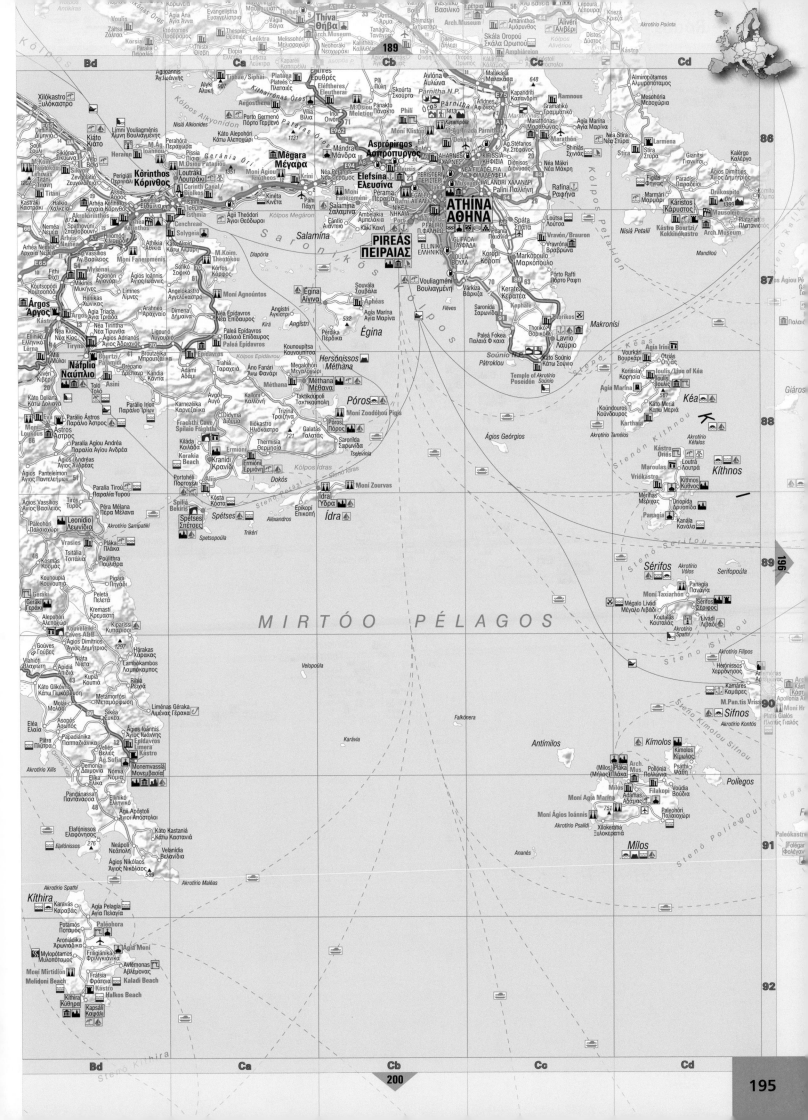

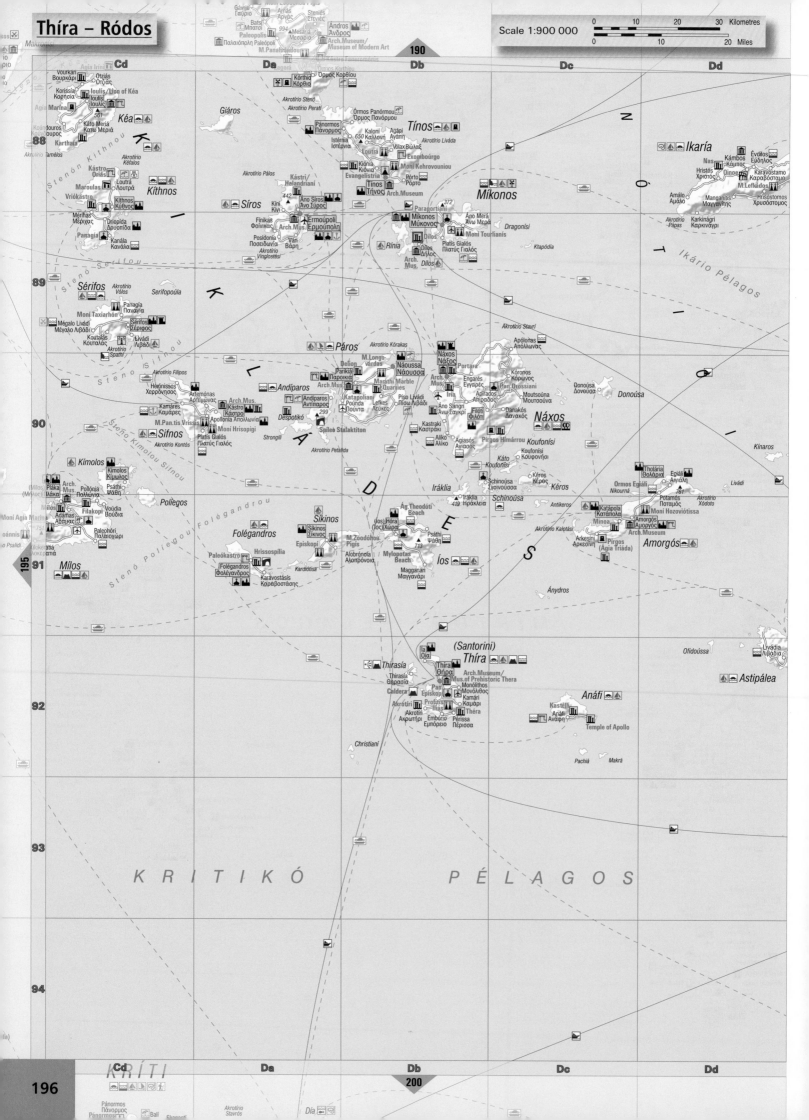

Scale 1:900 000

0 10 20 30 Kilometres
0   10   20 Miles

Makrónisi

Gávrio
Γαύριο
Batsí
Μπατσί
Mesariá
994 Μεσαριά
Paleopolis
Palaiópoli
Παλαιόπολη Παλεόπολι
M.Panahrándou

Steniés
Στενιές
Andros
Ανδρος
Arch.Museum/
Museum of Modern Art

Agora

Kástro Faneroménis

Ormos Kórthiou
Κόρθι Όρμος Κορθίου
Κόρθι

Akrotírio Steno

Akrotírio Peráti

Ormos Panórmou
Ormos Πανόρμου

Panórmou
Πάνορμος

Isternia
Ιστέρνια

Tínos
Τήνος

Kaloní
650 Καλλονή

Agápi
Αγάπη

Akrotírio Livada

N   Ó

Ikaría
Ikaría

Vourkári
Βουρκάρι

Korissía
Κορησσία

Ioulis/Lion of Kéa
Ioulís
Ιουλίς

Agía Marína

Kéa
Κέα

Kato Meriá
Κατω Μεριά

561

Karthaía

Giáros
Γιάρος

Loutrá
Λουτρά

Vólax Βώλαξ

Kiónia
Κιόνια

Evangelistria

Tínos
Τήνος Τήνος

Arch.Museum

Exoubourgo
Εξωμβούργο

Moni Kehrovouniou

Pórto
Πόρτο

Mikonos
Μύκονος

372

Áno Merá
Άνω Μερά

Moni Tourliánis

Dragonisi

Nas

Kámbos
Κάμπος

Éndilos
Εύδηλος

Hristós
Χριστός

Oinoe
Οίνοε

Manganitis
Μαγγανίτης

Karkinágri
Καρκινάγρι

M.Lefkádos

Hrisóstomos
Χρυσόστομος

Akrotírio Kéfalos

Kástro
Oriás

Kástro
Kástro

Loutrá
Λουτρά

Vriókastro

Kíthnos
Κύθνος

Síros
Σίρος

Kastrí/
Halandriani

Kiní Κινί
Κίνι

Áno Síros
Άνο Σύρος

542

Ano Síros
Άνο Σύρος

Ermoúpoli
Ερμούπολη

Paragortiá

Mikonos
Μύκονος

Áno Merá
Άνω Μερά

Dragonísi

Ktapódia

Akrotírio
Pápas

Karkinágri
Καρκινάγρι

Ikário Pélagos

Mérihas
Μέριχας

Driopida
Δρυοπίδα

Panagía

Kanála
Κανάλα

Fínikas
Φοίνικας

Posidonía
Ποσειδωνία

Akrotírio
Vinglostási

Arch.Mus.
Váni
Βάρη

Rínia
Ρήνια

Dílos
Δήλος

Platís Gialós
Πλατύς Γιαλός

Dílos
Δήλος

Arch.
Mus.

88

89

Serifopoúla
Σεριφοπούλα

Akrotírio
Vólos

Sérifos
Σέριφος

Panagía Taxiarhón
Παναγία

Moni Taxiarhón

Sérifos
Σέριφος
Σέριφος

Páros
Πάρος

Akrotírio Kórakas

Akrotírio Stavrí

Náxos
Νάξος

Apólonas
Απόλλωνας

Kóronos
Κόρωνος

Donoúsa
Δονούσα

Donoúsa

Mégalo Livádi
Μέγαλο Λιβάδι

Koutalás
Κουταλάς

Akrotírio
Spathi

Livádi
Λιβάδι

M.Longovárdas

Náoussa
Νάουσσα

Portára

Engarés
Εγγαρές

Pan.Drossiani

Apirados
Απίραθος

Moutsoúna
Μουτσούνα

89

Akrotírio Filipos

Herónissos
Χερρόνησος

Artemónas
Αρτέμωνας

Delion

Parikiá
Παροικιά

Arch.Mus.

Maráthi Marble
Quarries

Lefkés
Λεύκες

Ano Sangri
Άνω Σαγκρί

Filóti
Φιλότι

Iria
Ιρια

Danakós
Δανακός

Kéros
Κέρος

Náxos
Νάξος

Kamáres
Καμάρες

M.Pan.tis Vrissis
Sifnos
Σίφνος

Apollonía Απολλωνία

Kástro
Κάστρο

Moni Hrisopigí

Andíparos
Αντίπαρος

Arch.Mus.

Andiparos
Αντίπαρος

Poúnda
Πούντα

Despotikó

299

Spilea Stalaktiton

Strongili

Kastraki
Καστράκι

Aliko
Αλυκό

Agiasós
Αγιασός

Pírgos Hímárrou

Koufonísi

Koufonísi
Κουφονήσι

Kato
Koufonísi

Koufoníssi
Κουφονήσι

Tholária
Θολάρια

Egiáli
Αιγιάλη

Livádi

90

Akrotírio Kontós

Platís Gialós
Πλατύς Γιαλός

Kímolos
Κίμολος

Kímolos
Κίμολος

Psáthi Ψάθη

Andíparos
Αντίπαρος

Akrotírio Petalida

Irakliá
Ιράκλεια

Schinoúsa
Σχοινούσα

Kéros
Κέρος

Ormos Egiáli

Nikourná

Amorgós
Αμοργός

Náxos
Νάξος

Potamós
Ποταμός

Akrotírio
Xódoto

Kínaros

90

Arch.
Mus.

Pláka
Πλάκα

Pollónia
Πολλώνια

Psáthi
Ψάθη

Kimolos
Κίμολος

Pollegos

Adamas
Αδάμας

Filakopi

Irakliá
419 Ηράκλεια

Iráklia
Ιράκλια

Schinoúsa

Antikeros

Katápola
Κατάπολα

Amorgós
Αμοργός

Moni Hozoviótissa

Arch.Museum

Amorgós
Αμοργός

Mílos
Μήλος

Paleohóri
Παλαιοχώρι

Folégandros
Φολέγανδρος

Síkinos
Σίκινος

Akrotírio Kalotási

Minoa

Arkesíni
Αρκεσίνη

Pírgos
(Agia Triáda)

761

91

Moni Agia Marina
oánnis
o Psalídi

751

Kíkladatá

195

Mílos
Μήλος

Paleókastro

Folégandros
Φολέγανδρος

Karavostásis
Καραβοστάσης

Hrissospília

Sikinos
Σίκινος

Episkopí
Επισκοπή

M.Zoodóhou
Pigís

Kardiótisa

Ág.Theodóti
Beach

(Íos)
(Ίος) Hóra
(Ίος) Χώρα

Piso Livádi
Πίσω Λιβάδι

Psáthi
Ψάθη

713

Íos
Ίος

Ánydros

Amorgós
Αμοργός

91

Alóbronoía
Αλόπρόνοια

Mylopotas
Beach

Magganári
Μαγγανάρι

S

Christiani

(Santorini)
Thíra

Thirasía
Θηρασία

Iá
Η Οία

Thíra
Θήρα

Arch.Museum/
Mus.of Prehistoric Thera

Ofidoússa

Livádia
Λιβάδια

92

Thirasía
Θηρασία

Caldera

Akrotíri
Ακρωτήρι

Akrotíri
Ακρωτήρι

Monólithos
Μονόλιθος

Pan.
Episkopí
Επισκοπή

Profitis
Ilías

Thíra
Θήρα

Embório
Εμπόριο

Kamári
Καμάρι

Périssa
Πέρισσα

Kastélli
Anáfi
Ανάφη

Anáfi
Ανάφη

Temple of Apollo

Astipálea

Anáfi
Ανάφη

92

Pachiá

Makrá

93

K R I T I K Ó   P É L A G O S

94

Kríti
KRÍTI

Pánormos
Πάνορμος

Akrotírio
Stavrós

Día

Balí
Skopóti

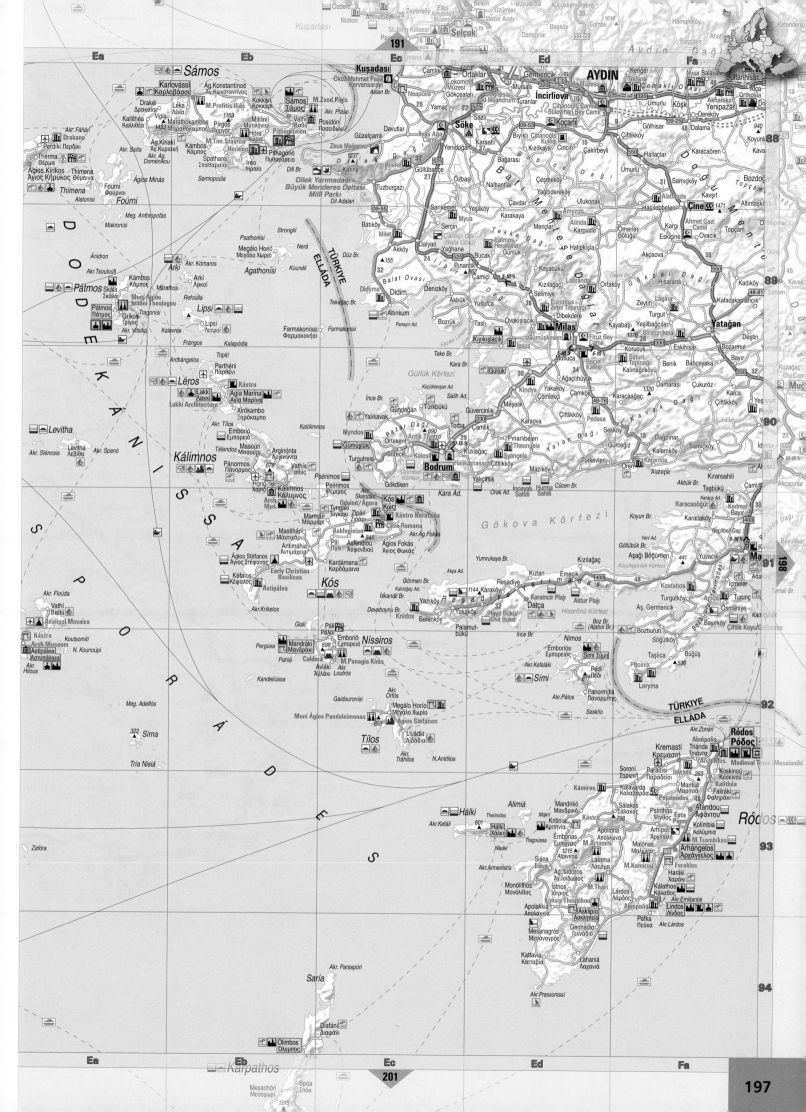

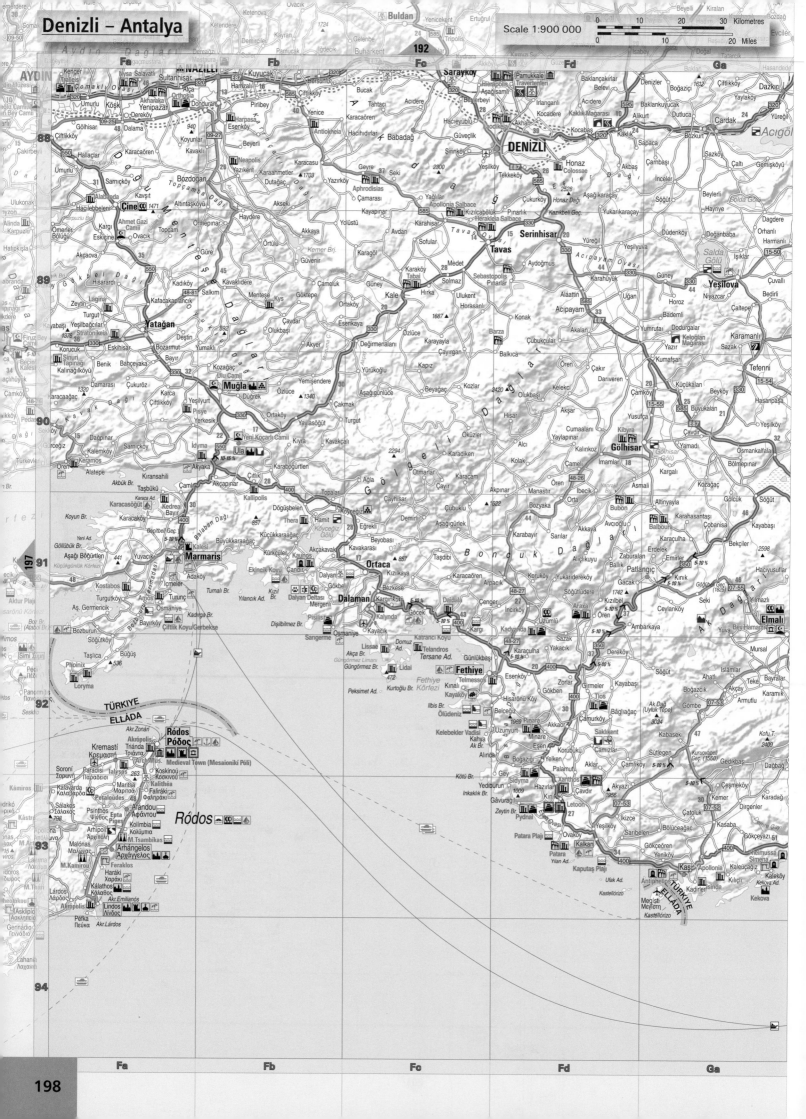

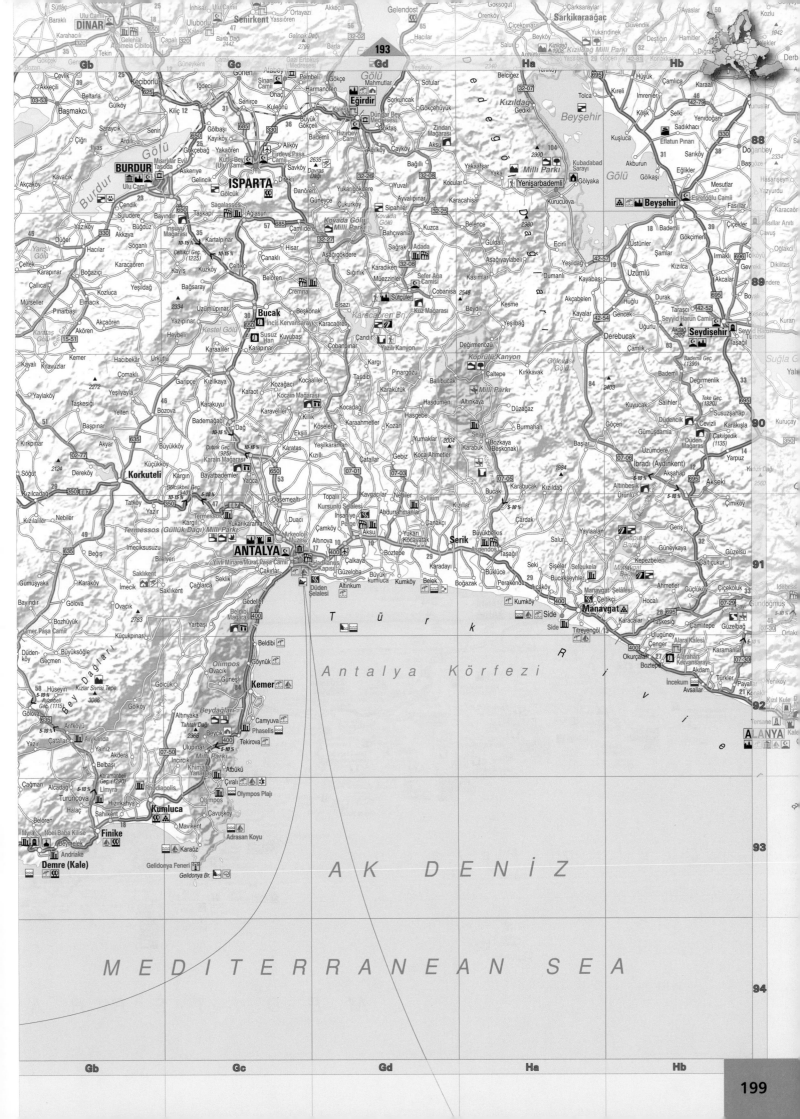

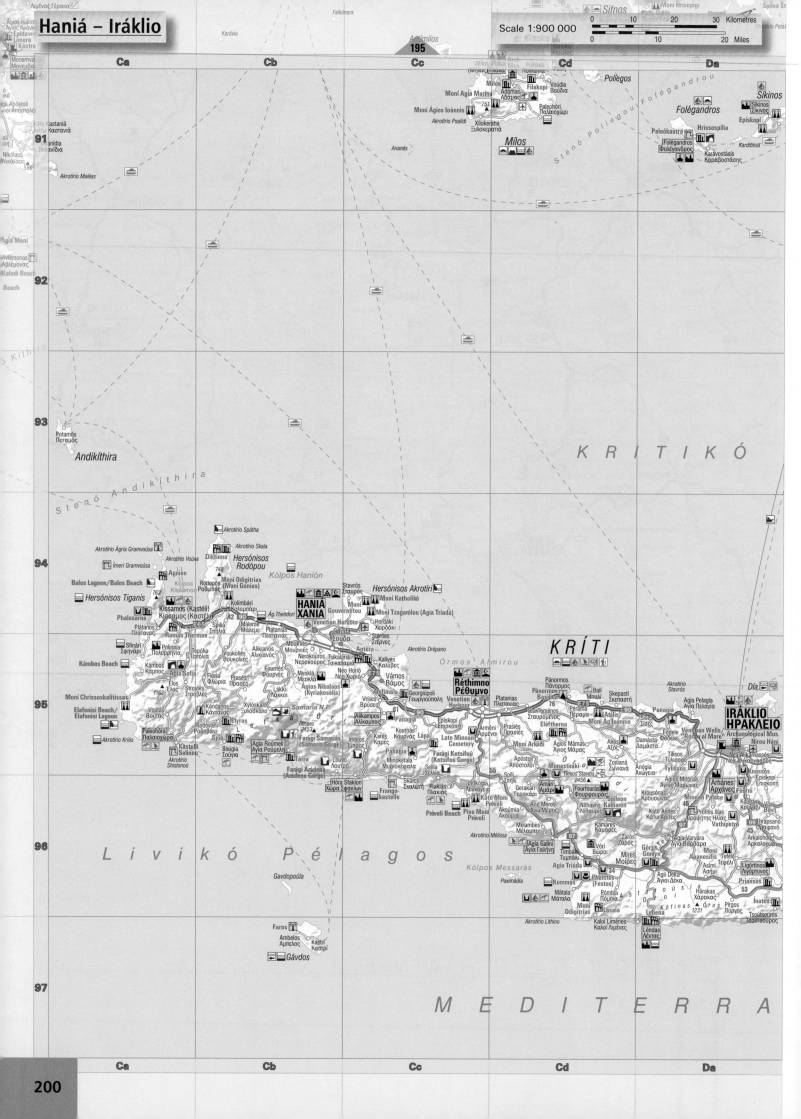

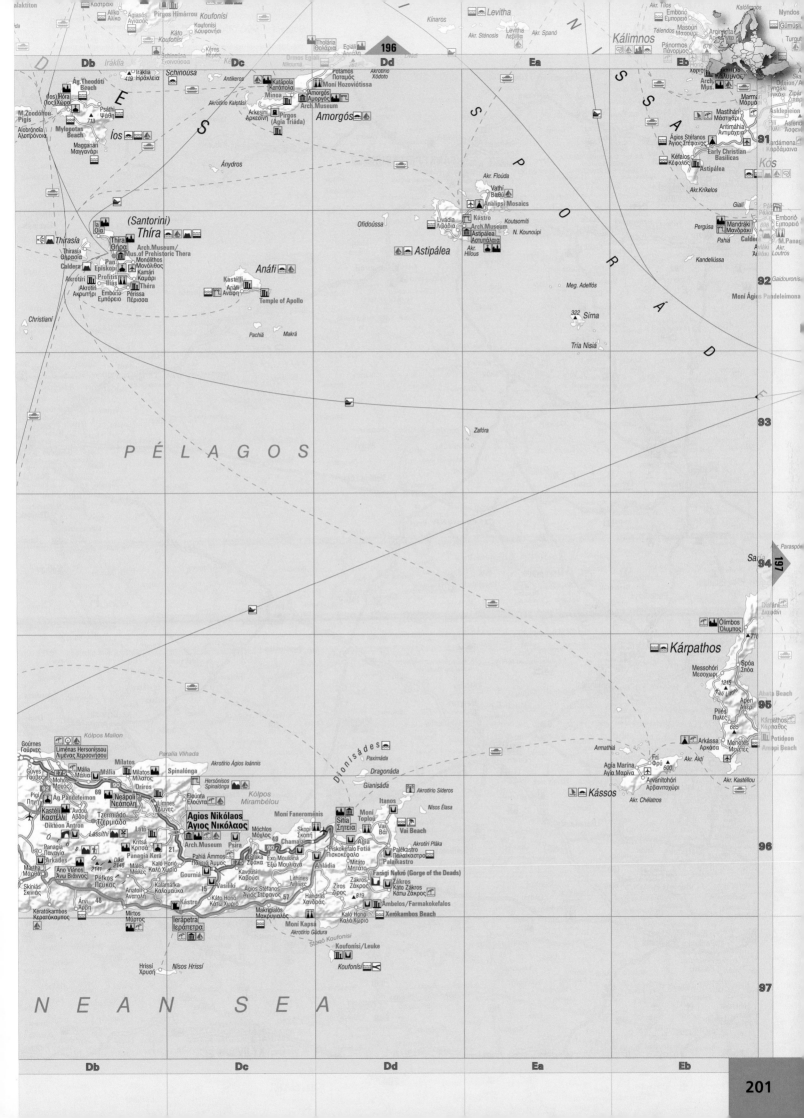

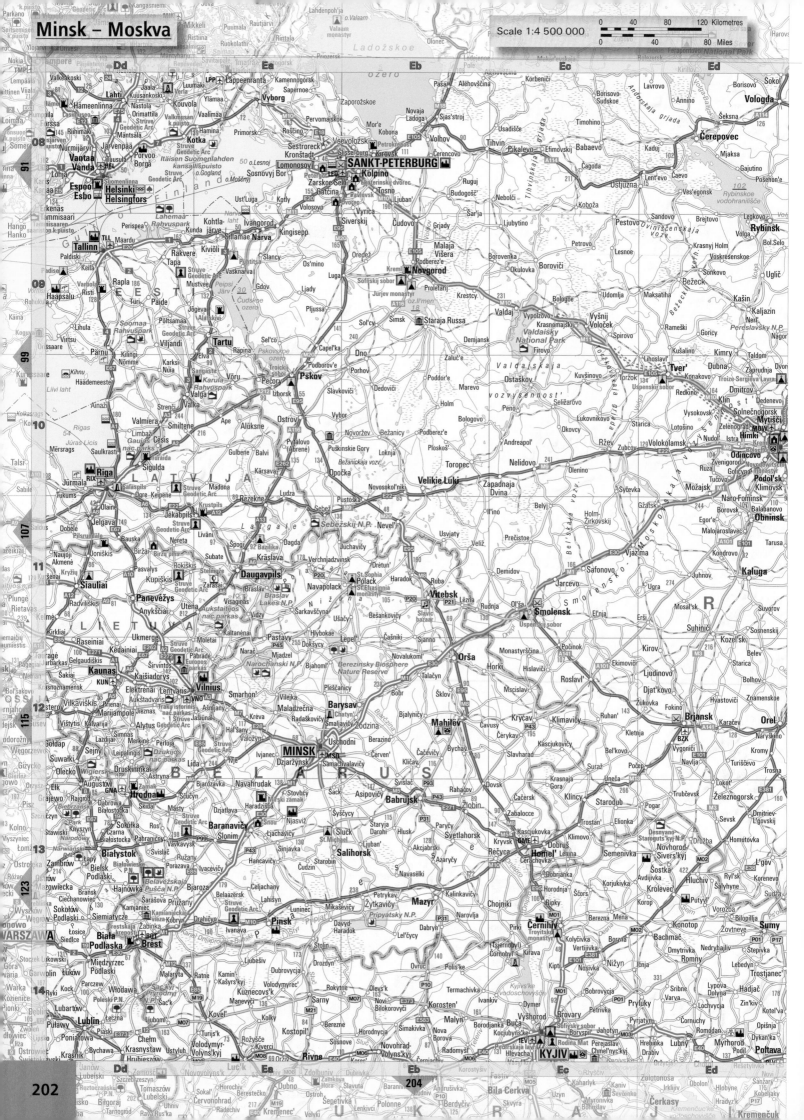

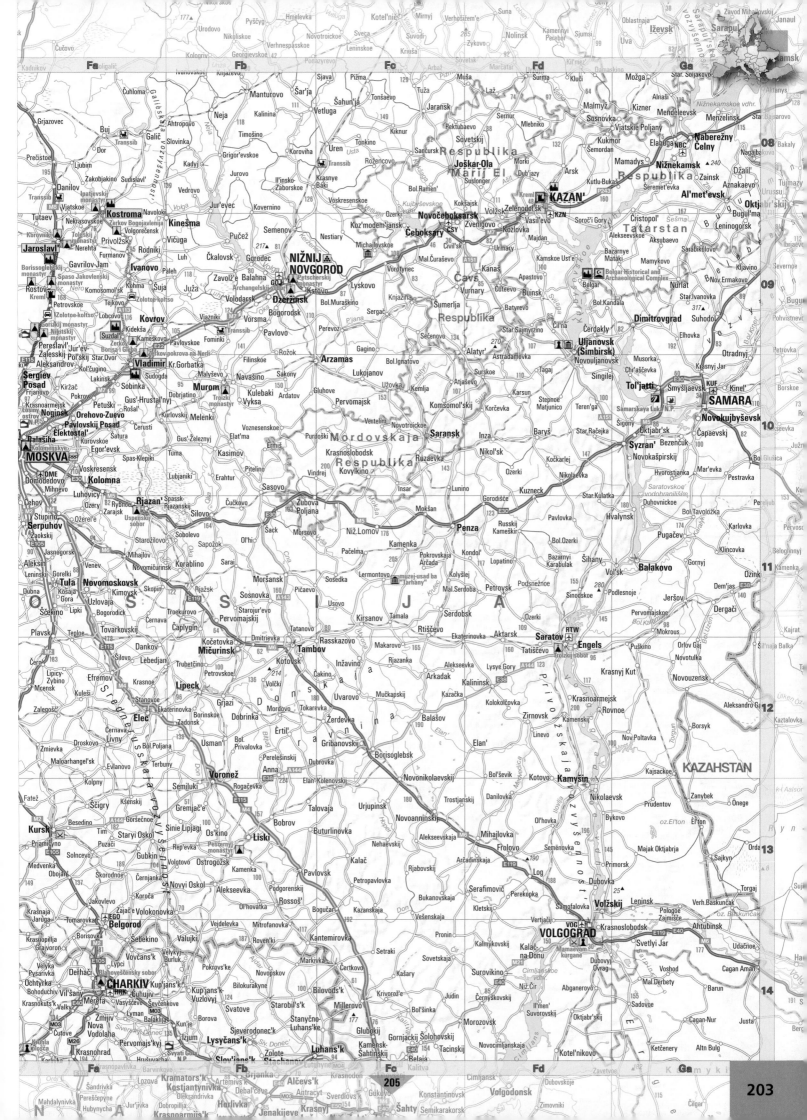

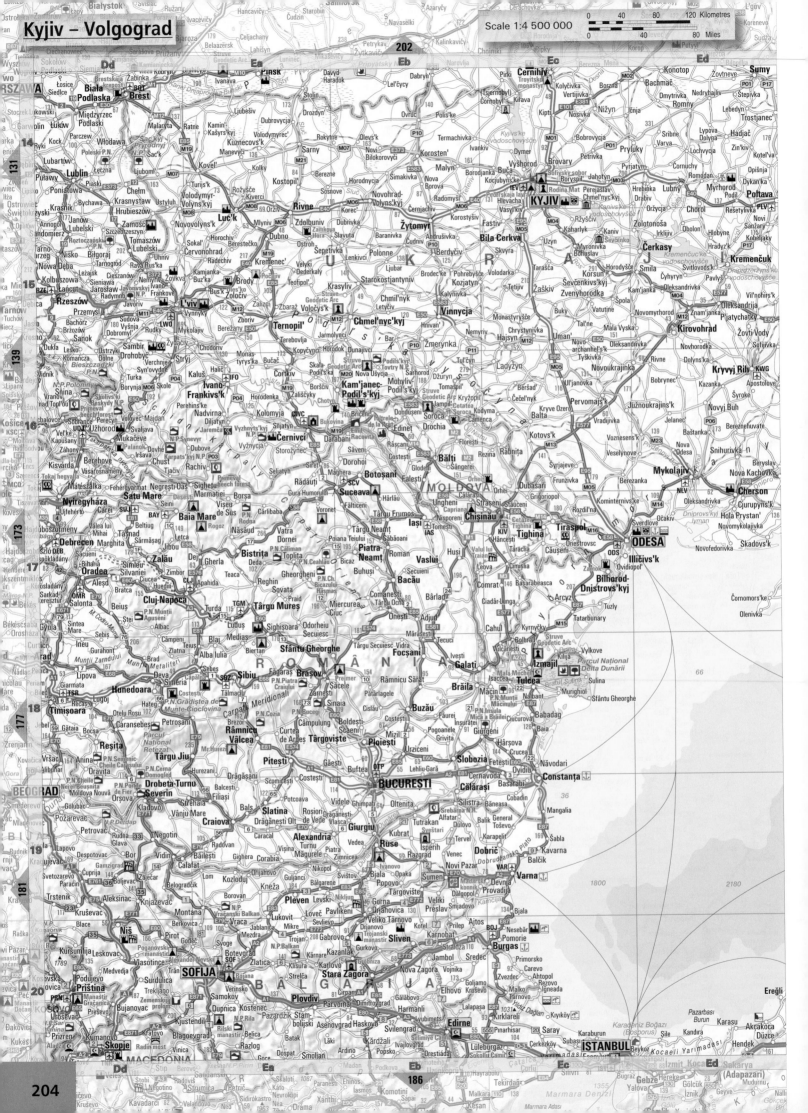

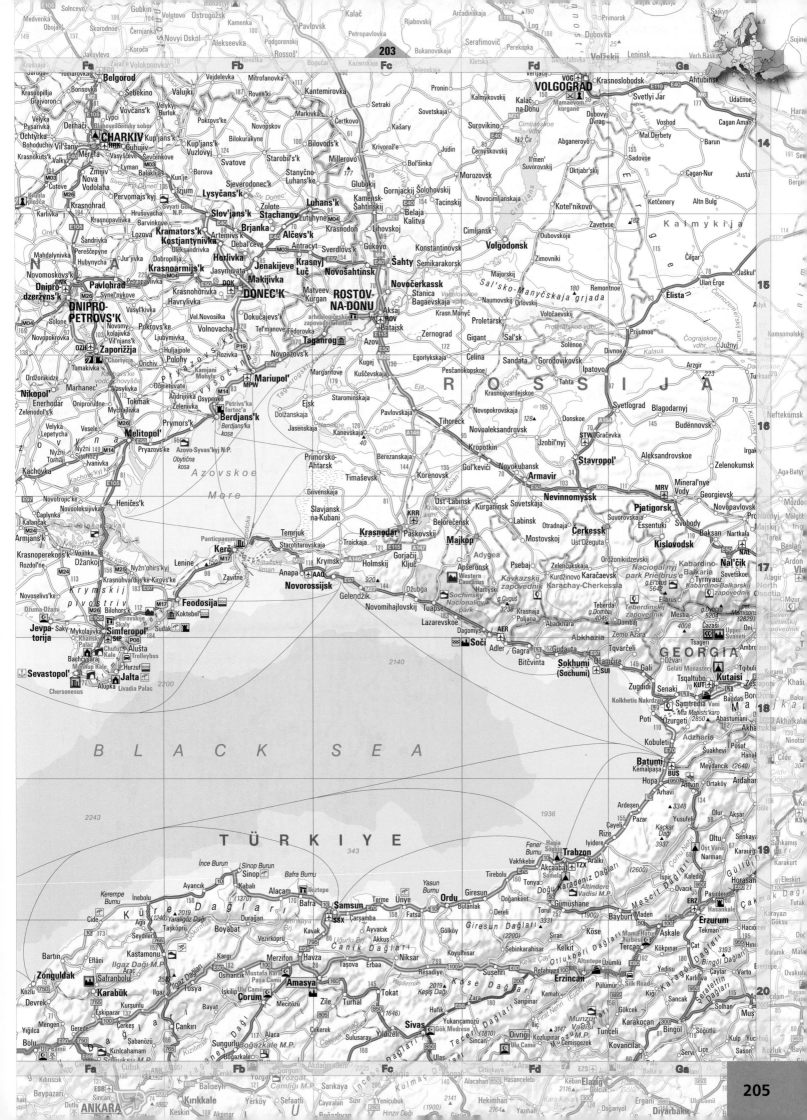

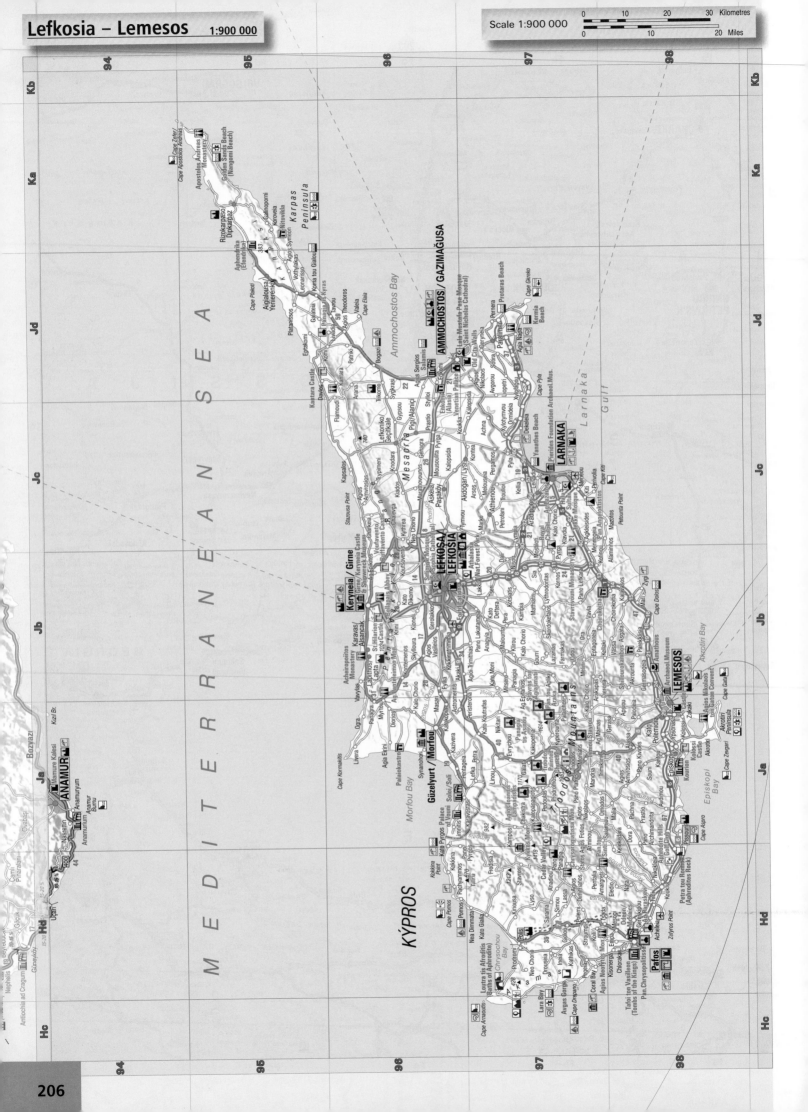

Scale 1:900 000

0   10   20   30   Kilometres
0   10   20   Miles

Aird of Sleat - Almaceda

Aird of Sleat GB 6 Db09
Airdrie GB 10 Ea13
Airel F 22 Fa36
Airėnai LT 114 Kd57
Aire-sur-l'Adour F 40 Fc54
Aire-sur-la-Lys F 23 Gd31
Airisto FIN 97 Jb40
Airola I 161 Fb74
Airolo CH 141 Cb56
Airvault F 28 Fc43
Aisa E 39 Fb57
Aisey-sur-Seine F 30 Ja40
Aislingen D 134 Db49
Aissey F 31 Jd41
Aisy-sur-Armançon F 30 Hd40
Aita Mare RO 176 Ea61
Aiterhofen D 135 Ec48
Aith GB 5 Ec02
Aith GB 5 Fa04
Aitolahti FIN 89 Jd35
Aiton RO 171 Da58
Aitona E 48 Ga61
Aitoniemi FIN 89 Jd35
Aitoo FIN 90 Ka36
Aitrach D 142 Da51
Aitrang D 142 Db52
Aittaniemi FIN 75 Kc19
Aittijoki FIN 64 Jc08
Aittojärvi FIN 74 Kb22
Aittojärvi FIN 82 Kc28
Aittokoski FIN 82 Kd27
Aittokylä FIN 75 Kd23
Aittolahti FIN 91 Ld32
Aittoperä FIN 82 Ka27
Aittovaara FIN 75 Lb23
Aiud RO 171 Da59
Åivo FIN 81 Jb28
Aix-en-Othe F 30 Hc39
Aix-en-Provence F 42 Jc54
Aixe-sur-Vienne F 33 Gb47
Aix-les-Bains F 35 Jd47
Aizdzire LV 105 Jd51
Aizenay F 28 Ed44
Aizkalne LV 107 Lc52
Aizkraukle LV 106 Kd51
Aizkuja LV 107 Lb50
Aizpūre LV 107 Ma51
Aizpute LV 105 Jb52
Aizviki LV 113 Jb53
Ajaccio F 154 Ca71
Ajain F 33 Gd45
Ajaur S 80 Ha25
Ajaureforsen S 71 Fd23
Ajdovščina SLO 151 Fa58
Ajka H 145 Ha54
Ajo E 38 Dc54
Ajofrín E 52 Db66
Ajos FIN 74 Jc21
Ajševica SLO 151 Fa58
Ajtos BG 181 Ed72
Akācijas LV 106 Ka52
Akácliget H 152 Ha58
Akademija LV 114 Kb56
Akaki CY 206 Jb97
Akalan TR 192 Fd81
Akalan TR 198 Fd89
Akarca TR 192 Ga86
Åkarp S 110 Ed56
Äkäsjokisuu FIN 68 Jb16
Äkäslompolo FIN 68 Jb15
Akasztó H 146 Hd55
Akbaş TR 191 Ed82
Akbaş TR 198 Fd88
Akbaşlar TR 192 Ga81
Akbük TR 197 Ec89
Akburun TR 199 Hb88
Akçaabat TR 205 Fd19
Akçaalan TR 187 Gd79
Akçaalan TR 187 Ha79
Akçaalan TR 192 Fa85
Akçaanlan TR 192 Fb85
Akçabelen TR 199 Ha89
Akçadere TR 193 Gb85
Akçakavak TR 198 Fb91
Akçakaya TR 192 Fa82
Akçakese TR 186 Ga77
Akçakisrak TR 192 Fa83
Akçaköy TR 193 Gb84
Akçaköy TR 198 Ga88
Akçakoyun TR 191 Ec81
Akçalar TR 199 Hb89
Akçaören TR 199 Gb89
Akçaova TR 187 Gb78
Akçaova TR 197 Fa89
Akçapınar TR 187 Gc80
Akçapınar TR 191 Ea81
Akçapınar TR 192 Fd81
Akçapınar TR 198 Fb90
Akçaşehir TR 192 Ga83
Akçat TR 186 Ga79
Akçay TR 191 Eb82
Akçay TR 198 Ga92
Akcın TR 193 Gc87
Akcjabrski BY 202 Eb13
Akçokoca TR 187 Ha77
Akdam TR 199 Hb92
Akdera TR 199 Gb90
Akdere TR 192 Fd87
Akdoğan = Lysi CY 206 Jc97
Aken D 127 Eb38
Aken = Aachen D 125 Bb41
Åker S 95 Gb44
Åker S 103 Fb50
Åkerbäck S 80 Hb27
Åkerbränna S 79 Gb28
Åkerby S 73 Hc21
Åkerby S 96 Gc41
Åkerholmen S 73 Hc21
Åkermark S 73 Hc22
Åkernes N 92 Cd45
Åkerö S 88 Gc33
Åkerøya N 70 Ed21
Åkersberga S 96 Gd43
Åkersjön S 79 Fb29
Akersloot NL 116 Ba35
Åkers styckebruk S 95 Gb44
Åkervika N 71 Fb22
Akhan TR 198 Fd88
Akharım TR 193 Gb85
Akhisar TR 192 Fa84
Akin TR 193 Gc83
Akın TR 193 Gc86
Akkala FIN 90 La34
Akkan S 71 Ga23
Akkaor TR 198 Fd92
Akkarfjord N 63 Hd06
Akkarfjord N 63 Hd05
Akkarvik N 62 Ha08
Akkavare S 67 Ha17
Akkavare S 72 Ha22
Akkaya TR 192 Fd84
Akkaya TR 193 Gc82
Akkaya TR 198 Fb89
Akkaya TR 198 Fd91
Akkaya TR 199 Gb89
Akkeçili TR 193 Gd87
Akkeçili TR 199 Gb88
Akkent TR 192 Fd87
Akköy TR 191 Ea81
Akköy TR 192 Fd87
Akköy TR 197 Ec89
Akkrum NL 117 Bc33
Akkum TR 187 Gc77
Akkuş TR 205 Fc20
Akland N 93 Db45
Aklar TR 198 Fd92
Akmeņdziras LV 105 Jb49
Akmenė LT 113 Jd53
Akmeniai LT 114 Kc56
Akmeniši LV 107 Ld52
Akmeņe LV 117 Gb78
Akmeņe TR 187 Gb78
Akniste LV 114 La53
Akoluk TR 193 Gc83
Akonpohja FIN 83 Lb29
Akören TR 185 Ed75
Akören TR 186 Fb77
Akören TR 193 Gc85
Akören TR 199 Gb89
Akoúmia GR 200 Cd96
Akovos GR 194 Bb88
Akpınar TR 186 Fc77
Akpınar TR 187 Ha78
Akpınar TR 191 Eb81
Akpınar TR 193 Gc82
Akpınar TR 198 Fd90
Åkra N 92 Bd43
Åkra N 92 Cb41
Åkrahamn N 92 Bd42
Åkran N 78 Ec28
Akranes IS 2 Ac04
Akráta GR 189 Bc85
Akréfnio GR 189 Ca85
Åkrestrømmen N 86 Eb35
Ákri GR 183 Bc79
Akriní GR 183 Bc78
Akritas GR 183 Bb77
Akritohóri GR 183 Cb76
Akrogiáli GR 184 Cc77
Akrolímni GR 183 Bd77
Akropótamos GR 184 Cd77
Akrotiri CY 206 Ja98
Akrotiri GR 196 Db92
Akrounta CY 206 Jb98
Akşahap TR 199 Hb90
Aksaj RUS 205 Fc15
Aksakal TR 186 Fa80
Aksakalar TR 192 Fd84
Aksakovo BG 181 Fa70
Akşar TR 198 Fd90
Akşar TR 205 Ga19
Aksaz TR 185 Ec79
Aksaz TR 192 Fc84
Aksaz TR 192 Fd86
Aksdal N 92 Ca42
Akşehir TR 193 Ha86
Akseki TR 198 Fb88
Akseki TR 199 Hb90
Akselendi TR 192 Fa85
Akset N 77 Dc29
Äksi EST 99 Lb45
Aksicim TR 186 Fa76
Aksla N 84 Cc35
Akstinai LT 114 Ka56
Aksu TR 186 Fd80
Aksu TR 199 Gd88
Aksu TR 199 Gd91
Aksubaevo RUS 203 Ga09
Aktarsk RUS 203 Fd12
Aktaş TR 192 Fc81
Aktaş TR 193 Ha83
Aktio GR 188 Ad82
Aktse S 67 Gc17
Akujärvi FIN 69 Kb11
Åkullsjön S 80 Hc27
Akureyri IS 2 Ba04
Åkvåg N 93 Db45
Akyaka TR 198 Fb90
Akyar TR 192 Fa82
Akyar TR 199 Gb90
Akyayla TR 192 Fc82
Akyazı TR 187 Gc79
Akyazı TR 198 Fd93
Akyer TR 198 Fb89
Akyokuşkavagı TR 187 Gd79
Ål N 85 Db39
Ala EST 106 Kd46
Ala I 149 Dc58
Ala S 87 Gb37
Ala S 104 Ha50
Aláattin TR 198 Fd89
Alabey TR 185 Ec78
Alaca TR 205 Fb20
Alacaatlı TR 192 Fa83
Alacaklar TR 191 Ec83
Alaçam TR 192 Fc83
Alaçam TR 205 Fb19
Alacant E 55 Fb71
Alacaoğlu TR 185 Ed76
Alacat TR 192 Fc81
Alaçati TR 191 Ea86
Alacón E 48 Fb62
Alà dei Sardi I 168 Cb75
Ala di Stura I 148 Bc59
Alaejos E 45 Cc61
Alafors S 102 Ec48
Alagna Valsesia I 148 Bd58
Alagoa P 50 Ba67
Alagón E 47 Fa60
Alagonía GR 194 Bb89
Alahärmä FIN 81 Jb30
Ala-Honkajoki FIN 89 Jb34
Alainenjoki FIN 89 Jc37
Alaior E 57 Ja66
Alájar E 59 Bc72
Alajärvi FIN 75 La23
Alajärvi FIN 81 Jc30
Alajärvi FIN 82 La26
Alajõe EST 99 Lb43
Alajoki FIN 69 Ka12
Alajoki FIN 82 Ka27
Ala-Jokikylä FIN 74 Jd21
Ala-Keyritty FIN 82 La28
Ala-Kolkki FIN 89 Jd33
Ala-Kuona FIN 91 Lc32
Alakylä FIN 68 Jc16
Alakylä FIN 74 Ka23
Alakylä FIN 81 Jd28
Alakylä FIN 81 Jb31
Alakylä FIN 89 Ja35
Alakylä FIN 89 Ja33
Alakylä FIN 91 Ld33
Ala-Livo FIN 74 Kb22
Alamaa FIN 82 Kb30
Alameda E 60 Cd74
Alameda de la Sagra E 52 Db66
Alamedilla E 60 Dc74
Alaminnos CY 206 Jc98
Alaminos E 47 Ea63
Alamlillo E 52 Cd70
Alan HR 151 Fc61
Alan TR 193 Ha81
Ala-Nampa FIN 74 Ka18
Alanäs S 79 Fd27
Alancık TR 191 Ed81
Åland S 96 Gc42
Alandız TR 192 Fb87
Alandroal P 50 Ba69
Ålandsbro S 88 Gc32
Alange E 51 Bd69
Alaniçi = Pigi CY 206 Jc96
Alaniemi FIN 74 Jd21
Alanis E 59 Ca72
Alanta LT 114 La55
Alanyolu TR 192 Fb85
Alanyurt TR 193 Gd84
Alap H 146 Hc55
Alapää FIN 81 Jd27
Alapitkä FIN 82 Kd29
Alaplı TR 187 Ha77
Alapohja FIN 90 Kb32
Ala-Postojoki FIN 69 Ka15
Alappmo N 67 Gd11
Alaraz E 45 Cc63
Alarcia E 38 Dd58
Alarcón E 53 Eb67
Alar del Rey E 38 Db57
Alaró E 57 Hb67
Alarup AL 182 Ad76
Alaşar TR 192 Fa81
Alaşehir TR 192 Fb86
Ålåsen S 79 Fc28
Ala-Siurua FIN 74 Kb22
Alaskylä FIN 89 Jc34
Alassa CY 206 Ja98
Alassio I 43 La52
Alastaro FIN 89 Jc37
Ala-Sydänmaa FIN 82 Ka27
Alata F 154 Ca70
Ala-Temmes FIN 74 Ka24
Alatepe TR 197 Fa90
Alatornio FIN 74 Jc21
Alatoz E 54 Ed69
Alatri I 160 Ed72
Alatskivi EST 99 Lb44
Alatyr' RUS 203 Fd09
Alava MD 177 Ga60
Alavaara S 73 Hc18
Ala-Valli FIN 89 Jb32
Alavattnet S 79 Fd28
Alaveteli FIN 81 Jc28
Ala-Vieksi FIN 83 Lb25
Alavieska FIN 81 Jd26
Ala-Viirre FIN 81 Jc27
Ala-Vuokki FIN 75 Lb23
Ala-Vuotto FIN 74 Kb23
Alavus FIN 89 Jc32
Alayaka TR 192 Fb83
Alaylı TR 186 Ga80
Alayunt TR 193 Gb83
Alba E 36 Bb54
Alba E 47 Ed64
Alba I 148 Bd61
Alba RO 172 Ec54
Alba Adriatica I 157 Fa68
Albac RO 171 Cc59
Albacete E 53 Ec69
Albacken S 87 Ga32
Alba de Cerrato E 46 Da60
Alba de Tormes E 45 Cc63
Ålbæk DK 101 Dd19
Albaida E 55 Fb70
Albaina E 38 Ea57
Alba Iulia RO 175 Da60
Albaladejo E 53 Ea70
Albalate de Cinca E 48 Fd60
Albalate del Arzobispo E 48 Fb62
Albalate de las Nogueras E 47 Eb65
Albalate de Zorita E 47 Ea65
Alban F 41 Ha53
Albánchez E 61 Eb75
Albánchez de Úbeda E 60 Dc73
Albaneto I 156 Ec69
Albano di Lucania I 162 Gb76
Albano Laziale I 160 Eb72
Albanyà E 41 Hb58
Albarca E 48 Gb62
Albaredo Arnaboldi I 149 Cc60
Albaredo d'Adige I 149 Dc60
Albarellos E 36 Ba56
Albares E 46 Dd65
Albarracín E 47 Ed64
Albarreal de Tajo E 52 Da66
Albas F 33 Gb51
Albatana E 55 Ed70
Albatàrrec E 48 Ga61
Albatera E 55 Fa72
Albbruck D 141 Ca52
Albelda de Iregua E 39 Eb58
Albena BG 181 Fb70
Albendín E 60 Da73
Albenga I 43 La52
Albeni RO 175 Cd64
Albeniz E 39 Eb56
Albens F 35 Jd46
Albentosa E 54 Fb66
Albercastle GB 14 Db26
Alberese I 155 Dc69
Ålberga S 95 Ga44
Alberga S 95 Gb45
Albergaria-a-Nova P 44 Ad62
Albergaria-a-Velha P 44 Ad62
Alberguería E 36 Bb58
Alberique E 54 Fb69
Alberite E 39 Eb58
Albernoa P 58 Ad72
Alberobello I 162 Ha75
Alberona I 161 Fd73
Alberoni I 150 Eb60
Alberschwende A 142 Da53
Albersdorf D 118 Da30
Albert F 23 Ha33
Albertirsa H 146 Ja53
Albertville F 35 Ka47
Albesa E 48 Ga60
Albeşti RO 172 Ed55
Albeşti RO 173 Fb59
Albeşti RO 175 Dc60
Albeşti RO 176 Ed66
Albeşti RO 181 Fc68
Albeştii de Muscel RO 175 Dc63
Albeşti Paleologu RO 176 Eb64
Albi F 41 Gd53
Albias F 40 Gc52
Albidona I 164 Gc78
Albigowa PL 139 Ka44
Albina MD 173 Fc59
Albineţul Vechi MD 173 Fa56
Albinia I 155 Dc69
Albino I 149 Cd58
Albires E 37 Cc58
Albisola Marina I 148 Ca63
Albizzate I 148 Cb58
Alblasserdam NL 124 Ad37
Albocàsser E 54 Fd65
Alboga S 102 Ed48
Alböke S 103 Gb51
Alboloduy E 61 Ea75
Albolote E 60 Db75
Albondón E 60 Dc76
Alborea E 54 Ed68
Albota RO 175 Dc65
Albota de Jos MD 177 Fc61
Albota de Sus MD 177 Fc61
Alboussière F 34 Jb49
Albox E 61 Eb74
Albrechtice nad Vltavou CZ 136 Fb47
Albrighton GB 15 Eb24
Albrighton GB 15 Ec24
Albstadt D 142 Cc50
Albu EST 98 Kd43
Albudeite E 55 Ed72
Albufeira P 58 Ac74
Albujón E 55 Fa73
Albuñol E 60 Dc76
Albuñuelas E 60 Db76
Albuquerque E 51 Bc67
Alby S 87 Fd33
Alby-sur-Chéran F 35 Jd46
Alcácer do Sal P 50 Ac70
Alcáçovas P 50 Ad70
Alcadağ TR 199 Gb93
Alcadozo E 53 Ec70
Alcafozes P 45 Bc65
Alcaine E 48 Fb63
Alcalá de Gurrea E 48 Fb59
Alcalá de Henares E 46 Dd64
Alcalá de la Selva E 54 Fb65
Alcalá de la Vega E 54 Ed66
Alcalá del Júcar E 54 Ed68
Alcalá del Opispo E 48 Fc59
Alcalá de los Gazules E 59 Ca77
Alcalá del Río E 59 Ca73
Alcalá del Valle E 60 Cc75
Alcalà de Xivert E 54 Fd65
Alcalá la Real E 60 Db74
Alcamo I 166 Eb84
Alcamo Marina I 166 Eb84
Alcampell E 48 Fd60
Alcanadre E 39 Ec58
Alcanar E 48 Ga64
Alcanede P 50 Ab66
Alcanena P 50 Ac66
Alcañices E 45 Ca60
Alcañiz E 48 Fc62
Alcántara E 51 Bc66
Alcantarilha P 58 Ac74
Alcantarilla E 53 Ea71
Alcantarilla E 55 Ed72
Alcantud E 47 Eb64
Alcaracejos E 52 Cc71
Alcaraz E 53 Ea70
Alcaria P 44 Bb64
Alcaria Rulva P 58 Ad72
Alcarràs E 48 Ga61
Alcaucín E 60 Da76
Alcaudete E 60 Da73
Alcaudete de la Jara E 52 Cd66
Alcázar del Rey E 47 Ea65
Alcázar de San Juan E 53 Dd68
Alcazarén E 46 Da61
Alceda E 38 Dc55
Alcedar MD 173 Fd55
Alcester GB 20 Ed25
Alčevs'k UA 205 Fb15
Alcı TR 198 Fd90
Alcıtepe TR 185 Ea80
Alcobaça P 50 Ab66
Alcoba de los Montes E 52 Da68
Alcobendas E 46 Dc64
Alcocer E 47 Ea64
Alcochete P 50 Ab68
Alcoentre P 50 Ab67
Alcohujate E 47 Ea64
Alcoi E 55 Fb70
Alcolea E 60 Cd72
Alcolea E 61 Dd75
Alcolea de Calatrava E 52 Da69
Alcolea de Cinca E 48 Fd60
Alcolea del Pinar E 47 Eb62
Alcolea del Río E 59 Ca73
Alcoletge E 48 Ga60
Alcollarín E 51 Cb68
Alconbury GB 20 Fc25
Alconchel E 51 Bb70
Alconera E 51 Bd70
Alcóntar E 61 Ea74
Alcorcón E 46 Db64
Alcorisa E 48 Fc63
Alcoroches E 47 Ec64
Alcossebre E 54 Fd65
Alcoutim P 58 Ba73
Alcover E 48 Gb62
Alcoy E 55 Fb70
Alcsútdoboz H 146 Hc53
Alcubierre E 48 Fb60
Alcubilla de Avellaneda E 46 Dd60
Alcubillas E 53 Dd70
Alcublas E 54 Fb66
Alcúdia E 57 Hc66
Alcudia de Gaudix E 61 Dd75
Alcuéscar E 51 Bd68
Alcuneza E 47 Ea62
Aldborough GB 11 Fa19
Aldbourne GB 20 Ed28
Aldbrough GB 17 Fc20
Aldeacentenera E 51 Cb67
Aldeadávila de la Ribera E 45 Bd61
Aldea del Cano E 51 Bd67
Aldea del Fresno E 46 Db64
Aldea del Obispo E 45 Bd63
Aldea del Rey E 52 Db70
Aldea de Pallarés E 51 Bd71
Aldea de San Esteban E 46 Dd61
Aldeahermosa E 53 Dd71
Aldealafuente E 47 Eb60
Aldealcorvo E 46 Dc62
Aldealengua de Santa Maria E 46 Dc61
Aldeamayor de San Martín E 46 Da61
Aldeanueva de Barbarroya E 52 Cc66
Aldeanueva de la Vera E 45 Cb65
Aldeanueva de San Bartolomé E 52 Cc67
Aldeaquemada E 52 Dc71
Aldea Quintana E 60 Cc73
Aldearrodrigo E 45 Cb62
Aldeaseca de la Frontera E 45 Cc62
Aldeavieja E 46 Da63
Aldebrő H 146 Jb52
Aldeburgh GB 21 Gb26
Aldehuela de la Bóveda E 45 Ca63
Aldehuela de Liestos E 47 Ec62
Aldehuela de Yeltes E 45 Ca63
Aldeia da Mata P 50 Ba67
Aldeia da Ponte P 45 Bc64
Aldeia da Serra P 50 Ba69
Aldeiade João Pires P 45 Bc65
Aldeia dos Palheiros P 58 Ac72
Aldeia Gavinha P 50 Ab67
Aldeia Velha P 50 Ad68
Aldenhoven D 125 Bc41
Aldenueva de Figueroa E 45 Cc62
Aldenueva de la Serrezuela E 46 Dc61
Aldenueva del Codonal E 46 Da62
Aldeonte E 46 Dc61
Alderbury GB 20 Ed29
Aldernäset S 79 Fd27
Aldersbach D 135 Ed49
Aldershot GB 20 Fb29
Aldfield GB 11 Fa19
Aldford GB 15 Eb22
Aldinci MK 178 Bb73
Aldinci SRB 179 Ca68
Aldingen D 142 Cc50
Aldomirovci BG 179 Cb70
Aldover E 48 Ga63
Aldsworth GB 20 Ed27
Aldtsjerk NL 117 Bc33
Aldwincle GB 20 Fc25
Ale S 73 Hd22
Aléa GR 194 Bc87
Åleby S 94 Fa41
Åled S 102 Ed52
Aledo E 55 Ed73
Ålefjær N 92 Cd47
Alegrete P 51 Bb67
Alëhovščina RUS 202 Eb08
Alekovo BG 180 Dd69
Alekovo BG 181 Ed68
Aleksandrevėlė LT 115 Lb53
Aleksandrija BG 181 Fa68
Aleksandrija LT 113 Jb53
Aleksandrov Gaj RUS 203 Ga12
Aleksandrov RUS 203 Fa10
Aleksandrovac SRB 178 Bb68
Aleksandrovo BG 180 Dc70
Aleksandrovo BG 181 Ec73
Aleksandrovskaja RUS 99 Mb40
Aleksandrovskoe RUS 205 Ga16
Aleksandrów PL 130 Ja37
Aleksandrów PL 130 Ja40
Aleksandrów PL 131 Ka38
Aleksandrów PL 131 Kb42
Aleksandrów Kujawski PL 121 Hb35
Aleksandrów Łódzki PL 130 Hc38
Aleksa Šantić SRB 153 Hd58
Alekseevka RUS 99 Ld41
Alekseevka RUS 107 Mb46
Alekseevka RUS 203 Fb13
Alekseevka RUS 203 Fc12
Alekseevskaja RUS 203 Fc13
Alekseevskoe RUS 203 Ga09
Aleksin RUS 202 Ed11
Aleksinac SRB 178 Bd68
Aleksinac Bujmir SRB 178 Bd68
Åleklulla S 102 Ed50
Ålem S 103 Gb51
Ålen N 86 Eb32
Alençon F 28 Fd38
Alenica SRB 159 Jc64
Alenquer P 50 Ab68
Alentisque E 47 Eb61
Alepohóri GR 195 Bd89
Alepoú GR 182 Ab80
Alera E 39 Ed58
Alerheim D 134 Dc48
Aléria F 154 Cc70
Alès F 41 Hd52
Ales I 169 Ca78
Alesanco E 38 Ea58
Aleşd RO 170 Cb57
Alesjaure sameviste S 67 Gc14
Ale-Skövde S 102 Ec48
Alessandria I 148 Cb61
Alessandria del Carretto I 164 Gc78
Alessandria della Rocca I 166 Ec85
Alessano I 165 Hc78
Ålesund N 76 Cc32
Alet-les-Bains F 41 Gd56
Alevráda GR 188 Ba83
Alexain F 28 Fb39
Alexándreni MD 173 Fa54
Alexăndreni MD 173 Fb55
Alexandreşti MD 173 Fa55
Alexándria GR 183 Bd78
Alexandria RO 180 Dd67
Alexandroúpoli GR 185 Dd78
Alexandru Ioan Cuza MD 177 Fc63
Alexandru I.Cuza RO 172 Ed57
Alexandru Odobescu RO 181 Ed67
Alexandru Vlahuţă RO 177 Fa60
Alexeevca MD 173 Fb57
Alexeevca MD 173 Fc55
Alexeni RO 176 Ec65
Alfacar E 60 Dc75
Alfajarín E 48 Fb61
Alfambra E 47 Fa64
Alfambra P 58 Ab73
Alfamén E 47 Fa61
Alfândega da Fé P 45 Bc61
Alfano I 161 Fd77
Alfara de Carles E 48 Fd63
Alfarela de Jales P 44 Bb60
Alfarelos P 44 Ac64
Alfarim P 50 Aa69
Alfarnate E 60 Da75
Alfaro E 47 Ec59
Alfarràs E 48 Ga60
Alfatar BG 181 Ed68
Alfaz del Pi E 55 Fc70
Alfdorf D 134 Da48
Alfedena I 161 Fa72
Alfeld D 126 Db38
Alfeld D 135 Ea46
Alfhausen D 117 Cb36
Alfonsine I 150 Eb63
Alford GB 7 Ec09
Alford GB 17 Fd22
Alforja E 48 Gb62
Ålfoten N 84 Cb34
Alfreton GB 16 Fa23
Alfstedt D 118 Da32
Alfta S 87 Ga37
Älga S 94 Ec42
Algaida E 57 Hb67
Algajola F 154 Ca68
Algallarín E 60 Cd72
Algámitas E 60 Cc75
Älganå S 94 Ec44
Algar E 59 Ca76
Algarås S 95 Fb45
Ålgård N 92 Ca44
Ålgård N 92 Cb46
Algarinejo E 60 Da74
Algarrobo E 60 Da76
Algatocin E 59 Cb76
Algeciras E 59 Cb78
Algemesí E 54 Fb68
Älgered S 87 Gb34
Algermissen D 126 Db37
Algerri E 48 Ga60
Algestrup DK 109 Eb27
Algete E 46 Dc64
Alghero I 168 Bd75
Älghult S 103 Fd51
Algimia de Almonacid E 54 Fb66
Alginet E 54 Fb68
Algodonales E 59 Cb75
Algodor P 58 Ad72
Algora E 47 Ea63
Algoso P 45 Bd60
Algoz P 58 Ac74
Älgsjö S 80 Gc27
Alguaire E 48 Ga60
Alguazas E 55 Ed72
Algueña E 55 Fa71
Algutsboda S 103 Fd52
Algutsrum S 103 Gb52
Algyő H 146 Jb56
Alhabia E 61 Ea75
Alhadas P 44 Ac64
Alhama de Almería E 61 Ea76
Alhama de Aragón E 47 Ec62
Alhama de Granada E 60 Da75
Alhama de Murcia E 55 Ed73
Alhambra E 53 Dd69
Alhamn S 73 Hd23
Alharilla E 52 Da72
Alhatlı TR 191 Ed83
Alhaurín de la Torre E 60 Cd76
Alhaurín el Grande E 60 Cd76
Alhojärvi FIN 90 Kb34
Alholm FIN 89 Ja32
Alhóndiga E 47 Ea64
Ålhus N 84 Cc35
Ali I 167 Fd84
Alia I 166 Ed85
Alía E 52 Cc67
Aliaga E 48 Fb64
Aliağa TR 191 Eb85
Aliaguilla E 54 Ed67
Aliano I 162 Gb77
Aliártos GR 189 Ca85
Alibánfa H 145 Gc55
Alibeyli TR 191 Eb83
Alibeyli TR 191 Ed85
Alibunar SRB 174 Bc63
Aliç TR 185 Eb77
Alicante E 55 Fb71
Alice Castello I 148 Bd59
Aliçlıkuyu TR 198 Fd91
Alicudi Porto I 167 Fb82
Alicún de Ortega E 61 Dd73
Alidemirci TR 191 Ed82
Aliden S 80 Hc25
Alifakı TR 192 Fa84
Alife I 161 Fb73
Alija del Infantado E 37 Cb58
Alijó P 44 Bb61
Alika GR 194 Bc91
Alikampos GR 200 Cc95
Alikés GR 188 Ac86
Alikí GR 184 Db78
Alikí GR 188 Ad82
Alikianós GR 200 Cb95
Aliko GR 196 Db90
Aliköy TR 192 Ga83
Aliköy TR 199 Gc88
Alikurt TR 198 Fd88
Alikylä FIN 81 Jc28
Alil Abasi MK 183 Ca74
Aliman RO 181 Fa67
Alimena I 167 Fa85
Aliminusa I 166 Ed84
Alınca TR 198 Fd92
Alinci MK 183 Bb75
Alingsås S 102 Ec48
Alino BG 179 Cc72
Alins E 40 Gb58
Alinyà E 49 Gc59
Alionys LT 114 La56
Aliseda E 51 Bc67
Alise-Sainte-Reine F 30 Ja41
Alistráti GR 184 Cd77
Ali Terme I 167 Fd84
Alivéri GR 189 Cc85
Alixan F 34 Jb49
Alizava LT 114 Kd53
Aljaraque E 59 Bb74
Aljezur P 58 Ab73
Aljinovići SRB 159 Jb66
Aljucén E 51 Bd68
Aljustrel P 50 Ac71
Alken B 124 Ba40
Alkiškiai LT 113 Jd53
Alkkia FIN 89 Jb33
Alkmaar NL 116 Ba34
Alkoven A 144 Fa50
Alkpınar TR 186 Fa76
Alksėnai LT 114 Ka58
Alksnėnai LT 113 Jc54
Alksnėnai LV 114 Kb55
Alksniupiai LT 114 Kb54
Allahdiyen TR 192 Fa86
Allai I 169 Ca77
Allaines-Mervilliers F 29 Gc39
Allainville-en-Beauce F 29 Gd39
Allaire F 27 Ec41
Allaman CH 140 Ba55
Allanche F 34 Hb49
Allariz E 36 Bb58
Allasac F 33 Gc49
Allauch F 42 Jd55
Allavaara S 67 Ha17
Allažmuiža LV 106 Kc50
Alle CH 141 Bc52
Alle DK 108 Da24
Alleen N 92 Cc47
Alleghe I 143 Ea56
Alleknjarg N 64 Ka07
Allemagne-en-Provence F 42 Ka53
Allemant F 24 Hc37
Allen IRL 13 Cc21
Allenbach D 133 Bd45
Allendale Town GB 11 Ed16
Allendorf D 126 Cd42
Allendorf, Bad Sooden- D 126 Db40
Allenheads GB 11 Ed17
Allensbach D 142 Cc52
Allensteig A 136 Fd49
Allenstein = Olsztyn PL 122 Ja32
Allepuz E 48 Fb64
Allerborn L 133 Bb43
Allerey-sur-Saône F 30 Jb43
Allersberg D 135 Dd47
Allershausen D 143 Ea50
Allerslev DK 109 Eb28
Allerston GB 16 Fb19
Allerum S 110 Ec54
Allés E 38 Da55
Alleuze F 34 Hb49
Allevard F 35 Jd48
Allex F 34 Jb50
Allgunnen S 103 Ga51
Allhallows GB 21 Ga28
Allibaudières F 24 Hd37
Alligny-Cosne F 30 Hb41
Allihies IRL 12 Ba26
Allinge DK 111 Fb57
Allington GB 20 Ed28
Alliören TR 193 Gb84
Alliste I 165 Hc78
Allistragh GB 9 Cd18
Allmendingen D 142 Da50
Allo E 39 Ec57
Alloa GB 7 Ea12
Allogny F 29 Gd42
Ålloluokta S 67 Ha17
Allonby GB 11 Eb17
Allones F 28 Fd40
Allones F 29 Gc38
Allonne F 28 Fc44
Allons F 40 Fc52
Alloon Lower IRL 12 Bd21
Allos F 43 Kb51
Allouе F 33 Ga46
Alloza E 48 Fb63
Allstedt D 127 Ea40
Allumiere I 156 Dd70
Ally F 33 Gd49
Ally F 34 Hc49
Almaça P 44 Ad64
Almaceda P 44 Ba65

Almacelles - Ansnes

Almacelles E 48 Fd60
Almaciles E 61 Eb72
Almada P 50 Aa69
Almadén E 52 Cd69
Almadén de la Plata E 59 Bd72
Almadenejos E 52 Cd70
Almagro E 52 Db69
Almăj RO 175 Cd65
Almajano E 47 Eb60
Almaluez E 47 Eb62
Almancil P 58 Ac74
Almansa E 55 Fa70
Almanza E 37 Cd57
Almaraz E 51 Cb66
Almarda E 54 Fc67
Almargen E 60 Cc75
Almarza E 47 Eb59
Almås N 78 Ed26
Almaş RO 170 Cb59
Almásfüzitő H 145 Hb52
Almassora E 54 Fc66
Almaşu RO 171 Cd57
Almaşu Mare RO 175 Cd60
Almatret E 48 Fd62
Almazán E 47 Eb61
Almazora E 54 Fc66
Almberget S 94 Fa39
Almby S 95 Fd44
Almdalen N 70 Fa22
Alme D 126 Cc39
Almeda de Cervera E 53 Dd68
Almedíjar E 54 Fb66
Almedina E 53 Dd70
Almedinilla E 60 Da74
Almeida E 45 Ca61
Almeida P 45 Bc63
Almeirim P 50 Ac67
Almelo NL 117 Bd36
Almenar E 48 Ga60
Almenara E 54 Fc67
Almenar de Soria E 47 Eb60
Almendar TR 186 Fd77
Almendra E 45 Ca61
Almendral E 51 Bc69
Almendralejo E 51 Bd69
Almendricos E 61 Ec74
Almendros E 53 Ea66
Almenêches F 22 Fd37
Almenno San Salvatore I 149 Cd58
Almens CH 142 Cd55
Almensilla E 59 Bd74
Almere NL 116 Ba35
Almere-Buiten NL 116 Ba35
Almere-Haven NL 116 Ba36
Almería E 61 Ea76
Almerimar E 61 Dd76
Almesåkra S 103 Fc49
Almese I 148 Bc60
Al'met'evsk RUS 203 Ga08
Älmhult S 111 Fb53
Almidar E 61 Dd74
Almind DK 108 Db26
Almiropótamos GR 190 Cd86
Almirós GR 189 Bd82
Almklov N 84 Cb34
Almlia N 78 Eb27
Almlia N 78 Eb28
Ålmo N 77 Db30
Almodôvar P 58 Ac73
Almodóvar del Campo E 52 Da70
Almodóvar del Pinar E 53 Ec67
Almodóvar del Río E 60 Cc72
Almogia E 60 Cd76
Almograve P 58 Ab72
Almoguera E 46 Dd65
Almoharín E 51 Ca68
Almonacid de la Sierra E 47 Ed61
Almonacid del Marquesado E 53 Ea66
Almonacid de Toledo E 52 Db66
Almonacid de Zorita E 47 Ea65
Almonáster la Real E 59 Bc72
Almonte E 59 Bc74
Almoradí E 55 Fb72
Almoraima E 59 Cb77
Almorox E 46 Da65
Almoster P 44 Ac65
Almourol P 50 Ac66
Almsele S 79 Gb27
Älmsta S 96 Ha41
Almstedt D 126 Db37
Almudaina E 55 Fc70
Almudema E 61 Ec72
Almudévar E 48 Fb59
Almuñécar E 60 Db76
Almunge S 96 Gd42
Almunia de San Juan E 48 Fd60
Almuradiel E 52 Dc70
Almussafes E 54 Fb68
Alna N 93 Ea41
Alnaši RUS 203 Ga08
Alnes N 76 Cc32
Alness GB 5 Ea07
Alnö S 88 Gc33
Alnwick GB 11 Fa15
Alobrónoia GR 196 Da91
Alocén E 47 Ea64
Aloja LV 106 Kc47
Alomartes E 60 Db74
Alónissos GR 189 Cc83
Alonsotegi E 38 Ea55
Álora E 60 Cd76
Alosno E 59 Bb73
Alovė LT 114 Kc59
Alovera E 46 Dd64
Alozaina E 60 Cc76
Alp E 41 Gd58
Alpagut TR 192 Fb81
Alpalhão P 50 Ba67
Alparslan TR 193 Gc87
Alpbach A 143 Ea53
Alpe Colombino I 148 Bc60
Alpe di Siusi I 143 Dd56
Alpedrete E 46 Db63
Alpedrinha P 44 Bb65
Alpen D 125 Bc38
Alpera E 54 Ed69
Alphen NL 124 Ad38
Alphen aan de Rijn NL 116 Ad36
Alpheton GB 21 Ga26
Alpiarça P 50 Ac67
Alpicat E 48 Ga60
Alpirsbach D 133 Cb49
Alpnach Dorf CH 141 Ca54
Alpu TR 193 Gd82
Alpua FIN 82 Ka25
Alpuente E 54 Fa66
Alpullu TR 185 Ec76
Alqueva P 50 Ba71
Alquézar E 48 Fd59
Als DK 101 Dd22
Alsån S 73 Ja19
Alsån S 73 Jb21
Alsancak = Karavas CY 206 Jb96
Alsasua E 39 Ec56
Alsdorf D 125 Bc41
Alseda S 103 Fd50
Alsėdžiai LT 113 Jc54
Alsen S 79 Fb30
Alsenz D 133 Ca45
Alsfeld D 126 Cd42
Ålsgårde DK 109 Ec24
Alsheim D 133 Cb45
Ålshult S 111 Fc53
Alsike S 96 Gc42
Alsjärv S 73 Ja19
Alsjö S 87 Ga34
Alskog S 104 Ha50
Alsleben D 127 Ea39
Alslev DK 108 Cd25
Alslev DK 108 Da27
Ålsø DK 101 Dd23
Alsónémedi H 146 Hd53
Alsópáhok H 145 Gd55
Alsópakony H 146 Hd53
Alsószentiván H 146 Hc55
Alsótold H 146 Ja51
Alsózsolca H 146 Jc51
Ålsrode DK 101 Dd23
Alstad N 78 Eb29
Alstadt S 110 Ed56
Alstätte D 125 Bd37
Alster S 94 Fa43
Alsterbro S 103 Ga51
Alsterfors S 103 Fd51
Alstermo S 103 Fd51
Alston GB 11 Ec17
Alstrup DK 109 Dd25
Alsunga LV 105 Jb51
Ålsvåg N 66 Fd12
Alsvik N 66 Fb17
Alsviķi LV 107 Lc48
Alswear GB 19 Dd29
Alta N 63 Hd08
Älta S 96 Gd44
Altach A 142 Cd53
Altamura I 162 Gc75
Altarejos E 53 Eb66
Altaussee A 144 Fa52
Altavilla Irpina I 161 Fc74
Altavilla Milicia I 166 Ed84
Altavilla Silentina I 161 Fd76
Altbüron CH 141 Ca53
Altdöbern D 128 Fb39
Altdorf CH 141 Cb54
Altdorf D 135 Dd46
Altdorf D 135 Eb49
Alt Duvenstedt D 118 Db30
Alte P 58 Ac74
Altea E 55 Fc70
Altedo I 150 Dd62
Alteglofsheim D 135 Eb48
Alteidet N 63 Hc08
Altena D 125 Cb40
Altenahr D 125 Bd42
Altenbeken D 126 Cd38
Altenberg D 128 Fa42
Altenberge D 125 Ca37
Altenbuch D 134 Cd45
Altenburg D 127 Eb41
Altendorf D 135 Dd45
Altendorf D 135 Eb46
Altenfelden A 144 Fa50
Altenglan D 133 Ca45
Altenhausen D 127 Dd37
Altenhof D 119 Ec33
Altenkirchen (Rügen) D 119 Ed29
Altenkirchen (Westerwald) D 125 Ca42
Altenkrempe D 119 Dd31
Altenkunstadt D 135 Dd44
Altenmark bei Sankt Gallen A 144 Fc52
Altenmarkt D 143 Eb51
Altenmarkt an der Triesting A 144 Ga51
Altenmarkt im Isperthale A 144 Fc50
Altenmarkt im Pongau A 143 Ed53
Altenmedingen D 118 Dc34
Altenstadt D 134 Cd43
Altenstadt D 135 Eb45
Altenstadt D 142 Da50
Altenstadt D 142 Dc52
Altensteig D 133 Cb49
Altenthann D 135 Eb48
Altentreptow D 119 Ed32
Altenwalde D 118 Cd31
Altenweddingen D 127 Ea38
Alter do Chão P 50 Ba67
Alteren N 71 Fb20
Altertheim D 134 Da45
Altes Lager D 127 Ed38
Altfraunhofen D 143 Eb50
Altfriesack D 119 Ec35
Althegnenberg D 142 Dc50
Altheim A 143 Ed50
Altheim D 134 Cd46
Altheim D 134 Da49
Althofen A 144 Fb55
Althorne GB 21 Ga27
Althütte D 134 Da48
Altimir BG 179 Cd69
Alţina RO 175 Db61
Altınçay TR 187 Ha78
Altınkaya TR 199 Ha90
Altınkum TR 197 Ec89
Altınkum TR 199 Gd91
Altınova TR 186 Ga79
Altınova TR 191 Eb83
Altınova TR 199 Gd91
Altıntaş TR 185 Eb77
Altıntaş TR 192 Ga84
Altıntaş TR 193 Gb84
Altıntaşköyü TR 198 Fb88
Altınyaka TR 199 Gc92
Altınyayla TR 198 Ga91
Altipiani di Arcinazzo I 160 Ec72
Alt Käbelich D 120 Fa33
Altkalen D 119 Ec32
Altkirch F 31 Kb40
Altlandsberg D 128 Fa36
Altmannstein D 135 Ea48
Altmünster A 144 Fa52
Altnabreac Station GB 5 Eb05
Altnacallich GB 4 Dd05
Altnaharra GB 4 Dd05
Altnamackan GB 9 Cd18
Altn Bulg RUS 203 Ga14
Altnes N 63 Hd07
Altobordo E 61 Ec74
Alto da Serra P 50 Ab67
Alto de la Madera E 37 Cc54
Altofonte I 166 Ec84
Altomonte I 164 Gb79
Altomünster D 143 Dd50
Alton GB 16 Ed23
Alton GB 20 Fb29
Altopascio I 155 Db65
Altorricón E 48 Fd60
Altötting D 143 Ec50
Alträsk S 73 Hc22
Altrip D 134 Cc46
Alt Ruppin D 119 Ec35
Altsasu E 39 Ec56
Alt Schadow D 128 Fa38
Alt Schönau D 119 Ec33
Altshausen D 142 Cd51
Altstätten CH 142 Cd53
Altsvattnets sameviste S 71 Fd21
Alttajärvi S 67 Hb15
Alttojärvi FIN 69 Kb12
Altuna S 95 Gb42
Altura E 54 Fb66
Altusried D 142 Db52
Altwarp D 120 Fb32
Alu EST 98 Kb43
Aluatu MD 177 Fc62
Alūksne LV 107 Lc48
Ålum DK 100 Dc23
Ålund S 73 Hc24
Alunda S 96 Gd41
Aluniş MD 173 Fa55
Aluniş RO 171 Da57
Aluniş RO 171 Dc58
Aluniş RO 176 Ea63
Aluniş RO 176 Eb63
Alunu RO 175 Da64
Aluokta S 67 Gd16
Alupka UA 205 Fa18
Aluskylä FIN 89 Jb35
Alušta UA 205 Fa18
Alustante E 47 Ed64
Alvaiázere P 44 Ad65
Alvajärvi FIN 82 Ka29
Alvalade P 50 Ac71
Älvan S 103 Fd46
Älvängen S 102 Ec48
Alvarado E 51 Bc69
Alvarenga P 44 Ad61
Alvares P 44 Ad65
Álvaro P 44 Ba65
Alvarrões P 51 Bb67
Alvdal N 85 Ea34
Älvdalen S 87 Fb37
Alvegal P 50 Ad66
Alverca do Ribatejo P 50 Ab68
Alversund N 84 Ca38
Alves GB 5 Eb07
Alveslohe D 118 Db32
Alvesta S 103 Fc52
Alvestad N 92 Ca43
Alveston GB 19 Ec28
Alvettula FIN 90 Ka36
Älvho S 87 Fc36
Alviano I 156 Ea69
Alvignac F 33 Gc50
Alvik N 76 Cc32
Ålvik N 84 Cc39
Alvik S 73 Hd22
Alvik S 95 Fc39
Alvitas LT 114 Ka58
Alvito I 160 Ed72
Alvito P 50 Ad70
Älvkarleby S 96 Gc39
Älvkarleö S 96 Gc39
Alvor P 58 Ab74
Alvorge P 44 Ac65
Alvøy N 84 Ca39
Älvros S 87 Fc34
Älvsbacka S 72 Gd21
Älvsbacka S 94 Fa42
Älvsbyn S 73 Hc22
Älvsered S 102 Ed50
Älvsund S 87 Gb34
Alwernia PL 138 Hd44
Alwinton GB 11 Ed15
Alykí GR 189 Ca86
Alyth GB 7 Eb11
Alytus LT 114 Kc59
Alzano Lombardo I 149 Cd58
Alzenau D 134 Cd44
Alzey D 133 Cb45
Alzira E 54 Fb69
Alzola E 39 Eb55
Alzon F 41 Hc53
Amadora P 50 Aa68
Amagne F 24 Hd34
Amailloux F 28 Fc44
Åmål S 94 Ed44
Amalfi I 161 Fb76
Amaliáda GR 188 Ba86
Amaliápoli GR 189 Ca82
Amálo GR 196 Dd88
Amance F 30 Ja38
Amance F 31 Jd40
A Manchica E 36 Ba57
Amandola I 156 Ed68
Amange F 31 Jc42
Amantea I 164 Gb80
Amara RO 176 Ed66
Amarante P 44 Ba61
Amárantos GR 182 Ad78
Amărăşti RO 175 Da65
Amărăştii de Jos RO 179 Da67
Amărăştii de Sus RO 179 Da67
Amareleja P 51 Bb71
Amares P 44 Ad59
Amargeti CY 206 Hd98
Amári GR 200 Cd96
Amárinthos GR 189 Cc85
Amaru RO 176 Ec64
Amaseno I 160 Ec73
Amasya TR 205 Fc20
Amatrice I 156 Ec69
Amay B 124 Ba41
Amaya E 38 Db57
Ambarès-et-Lagrave F 32 Fb50
Ambarkaya TR 198 Fd91
Ambas E 37 Cc54
Ambazac F 33 Gb46
Ambeláki GR 188 Ba83
Ambelákia GR 183 Bd80
Ambelákia GR 195 Cb87
Ambeļi LV 115 Lc53
Ambelía GR 182 Ad80
Ambeliá GR 189 Bd82
Ambelohóri GR 182 Ba80
Ambelohóri GR 194 Bc90
Ambelónas GR 182 Ac80
Ambelónas GR 183 Bd80
Ambelónas GR 194 Ba87
Ambelos GR 200 Cb97
Amberg D 135 Ea46
Ambérieu-en-Bugey F 35 Jc46
Ambérieux-en-Dombes F 34 Jb46
Ambert F 34 Hc47
Ambialet F 41 Ha53
Ambierle F 34 Hd46
Ambiévillers F 31 Jd39
Ambjörby S 94 Fa40
Ambjörnarp S 102 Fa50
Ambla EST 98 Kd43
Amblainville F 23 Gd35
Amble GB 11 Fa15
Ambleside GB 11 Eb18
Ambleteuse F 21 Gb30
Ambleville F 23 Gc36
Amboise F 29 Gb42
Ambon F 27 Eb41
Ämbra EST 98 Kd43
Ambra I 156 Dd66
Ambrault F 29 Gd44
Ambria I 149 Cd58
Ambrières-les-Vallées F 28 Fb38
Ambronay F 35 Jc46
Åmdal N 92 Cd46
Amden CH 142 Cc54
Ameixial P 58 Ad73
Amel B 125 Bb42
Amele LV 105 Jc49
Åmelfot N 84 Cb34
Amelia I 156 Ea69
Amélie-les-Bains-Palalda F 41 Ha58
Amelin PL 122 Jc34
Amelinghausen D 118 Dc34
Amelunxen D 126 Da38
Amendoeira P 58 Ad72
Amendolara I 164 Gc78
Amer E 49 Ha59
Amerang D 143 Eb51
A Merca E 36 Ba58
Amerongen NL 125 Bb37
Amersfoort NL 116 Bb36
Amersham GB 20 Fb27
Amesbury GB 20 Ed29
Amezketa E 39 Ec56
A Mezquita E 36 Bc58
Amfíklia GR 189 Bd84
Amfilohía GR 188 Ad83
Amfípolis GR 184 Cd77
Ámfissa GR 189 Bc84
Amieira P 50 Ba70
Amiens F 23 Gd33
Amieva E 37 Cd55
Amigdaliá GR 189 Bc81
Amigdaliá GR 189 Bc85
Amigdaliés GR 182 Ba79
Amíkles GR 194 Bc89
Amillano E 39 Ec57
Amilly F 29 Ha40
Amíndeo GR 183 Bb77
Äminne FIN 81 Hd31
Äminne S 104 Ha49
Amla N 84 Cd37
Åmli N 93 Da45
Åmliden S 72 Ha24
Amlwch GB 15 Dd21
Amlwch Port GB 15 Dd21
Ämmälä FIN 89 Jb33
Ammanford GB 19 Dd27
Ämmänsaari FIN 75 La23
Ammarnäs S 71 Ga21
Åmmeberg S 95 Fc45
Ammenäs S 102 Eb47
Ammern D 126 Dc40
Ammersbek D 118 Dc32
Ammerthal D 135 Ea46
Ammerzoden NL 124 Ba37
Ammeville F 22 Fd36
Ammochostos CY 206 Jd96
Amnehärad S 95 Fb45
Amnéville F 25 Jd35
Åmnøyhamna N 70 Fa19
Amolianí GR 184 Cd79
Amöneburg D 126 Cd41
Amorbach D 134 Cd45
Amorebieta E 38 Ea55
Amorgós GR 196 Dc91
Amóri GR 185 Eb76
Amorosa P 44 Ac59
Amorosi I 161 Fb74
Åmot N 85 Db38
Åmot N 86 Eb37
Åmot N 93 Dd41
Åmot N 93 Da42
Åmot S 87 Ga38
Åmot S 94 Ed42
Åmotfors S 94 Ec42
Amotopos GR 188 Ad81
Åmotsdal N 93 Da42
Amou F 39 Fb54
Amous F 43 Kb53
Ampezzo I 143 Ec56
Ampfing D 143 Eb50
Ampflwang A 143 Ed51
Ampfurth D 127 Dd38
Ampiala FIN 90 Ka33
Amplepuis F 34 Ja46
Amplier F 23 Gd32
Ampola FIN 97 Jc40
Amposta E 48 Ga64
Ampthill GB 20 Fc26
Ampudia E 46 Cd59
Ampuero E 38 Dd55
Amriswil CH 142 Cd52
Amroth GB 18 Dc27
Åmsele S 80 Ha26
Amsteg CH 141 Cb55
Amstelveen NL 116 Ba35
Amsterdam NL 116 Ba35
Amstetten A 144 Fc51
Amtoft DK 100 Da21
Amtsberg D 127 Ec42
Amtzell D 142 Da52
Amulree GB 7 Ea11
Amurrio E 38 Ea56
Amusco E 38 Da58
Amusquillo E 46 Db60
Amvrossía GR 184 Dc77
Amzacea RO 181 Fb68
Ån S 79 Fb31
Anacapri I 161 Fa76
Anadiou CY 206 Hd97
Anadolufeneri TR 186 Fd77
Anáfi GR 196 Dc92
Anafonitria GR 188 Ac86
Anagénisis GR 183 Cb76
Anagni I 160 Ec72
Anagyia CY 206 Jb97
Análipsis GR 188 Bb84
Anapa RUS 205 Fb17
Anarcs H 147 Kb50
Anárgiri GR 183 Bb77
Anascaul IRL 12 Ba24
Ånäset S 80 Hc27
Åna-Sira N 92 Cb46
Änätinpää FIN 75 Lc24
Anatolí GR 183 Bd80
Anatolí GR 201 Db96
Anatolikó GR 183 Bc78
Anatolikó GR 183 Ca78
Anavainen FIN 97 Ja39
Anávatos GR 191 Dd86
Anávra GR 189 Bd83
Anavrití GR 194 Bc89
Anaya E 46 Da62
Anaya de Alba E 45 Cc63
An Bun Beag IRL 8 Ca15
Ançã P 44 Ac64
An Cabhán IRL 9 Cb19
An Caiseal IRL 8 Bb20
An Caisleán Nua IRL 12 Bc24
An Caisleán Riabhach IRL 8 Bd19
Ance LV 105 Jc49
Ancelle F 35 Ka50
Ancenis F 28 Fa42
Ančenki RUS 107 Ma50
Ancerville F 24 Ja37
An Charraig IRL 8 Ca16
An Chathair IRL 13 Ca24
Anché F 32 Fd45
Anchor GB 15 Eb25
Anchuras E 52 Cd67
Ancín E 39 Eb57
Anciverovo RUS 107 Ld49
Ančkini LV 107 Lc52
An Clochán IRL 8 Bb20
An Clochán IRL 9 Cb16
An Clochán Liath IRL 8 Ca15
An Cloigeann IRL 8 Ba20
An Cóbh IRL 12 Bd26
An Coireán IRL 12 Ba25
Ancona I 156 Ed66
An Creagán IRL 8 Bd20
Ancroft GB 11 Ed14
Ancy-le-Franc F 30 Hd40
An Daingean IRL 12 Ba24
Andalo I 149 Dc57
Åndalseter N 77 Da31
Åndalsnes N 77 Da32
Andance F 34 Jb48
Andåsen S 87 Fc34
Andau A 145 Gc52
Andavías E 45 Cb60
Anddalsvågen N 70 Ed23
Andebu N 93 Dd43
Andechs D 143 Dd51
Andeer CH 142 Cd55
Andelfingen CH 141 Cb52
Andelot-Blancheville F 30 Jb38
Andelot-en-Montagne F 31 Jd43
Andelsbuch A 142 Da53
Andelst NL 125 Bb37
Andenäs S 94 Fa40
Andenes N 66 Ga11
Andeņi LV 107 Ld52
Andenne B 124 Ad42
Andermatt CH 141 Cb55
Andernach D 125 Ca42
Andernos-les-Bains F 32 Fa50
Andersby FIN 90 Kd38
Andersby N 65 Kc06
Anderslöv S 110 Ed56
Anderssskog N 77 Db29
Anderstorp S 102 Fa50
Andersvattnet S 80 Hc26
Andijk NL 116 Bb34
Andilly F 32 Fa45
Andíparos GR 196 Da90
Andírio GR 188 Bb85
Andız TR 193 Gb83
Andlau F 25 Kb37
Andoain E 39 Ec55
Andocs H 145 Ha56
Andoins F 40 Fc55
Andon F 43 Kb53
Andorf A 143 Ed50
Åndørja N 67 Gb12
Andorlia N 67 Gd11
Andornaktálya H 146 Jb51
Andorra E 48 Fb63
Andorra la Vella AND 40 Gc58
Andosilla E 39 Ec58
Andouillé F 28 Fb39
Andover GB 20 Fa29
Andoversford GB 20 Ed27
Andrarum S 111 Fb56
Andrăşeşti RO 176 Ed66
Andratx E 56 Ha67
Andravída GR 188 Ad86
Andreapol' RUS 202 Ec10
Andreas GB 10 Dd18
Andreevca MD 173 Ga55
Andreiaşu de Jos RO 176 Ec62
Andrespol PL 130 Hd39
Andrest F 40 Fd55
Andrésy F 23 Gd36
Andretta I 161 Fd75
Andrézieux-Bouthéon F 34 Ja47
Andria I 162 Gb74
Andrid RO 171 Cc55
Andrieşeni RO 173 Fa56
Andrijaševci HR 153 Hc60
Andrijevica MNE 159 Jb68
Andriïvka UA 205 Fb16
Andrioniškis LT 114 Kd55
Andritsena GR 194 Bb87
An Droichead Nua IRL 13 Cc22
Ándros GR 190 Da87
Andrup DK 108 Cd26
Andrupene LV 107 Ld52
Andrušivka UA 204 Eb15
Andruškoniai LT 114 Kc57
Andruşul de Jos MD 177 Fb61
Andrychów PL 138 Hd45
Andryjanki PL 123 Kb35
Andrzejewo PL 123 Jd34
Andselv N 67 Gc11
Andsnes N 63 Hb07
An Dúchoraidh IRL 8 Ca16
Andújar E 52 Da72
Anduze F 41 Hd52
Andvikgrend N 84 Ca37
Anebakelv N 63 Hb09
Anebjør N 92 Cd44
Aneboda S 103 Fc51
Aneby S 103 Fc48
Anelema EST 98 Kb45
Anemoráhi GR 188 Ad81
Anenii Noi MD 173 Ga58
Anero E 38 Dc55
Ånes N 66 Fd11
Ånessletta N 66 Fd12
Anet F 23 Gb37
Anetjärvi FIN 75 Kd20
Anevo BG 180 Db72
Anfo I 149 Db58
Äng S 103 Fc49
Anga S 104 Ha49
Angáli GR 189 Cb83
Angarn S 96 Gd43
Angé F 29 Gb42
Ånge S 72 Gc21
Ånge S 79 Fb30
Ånge S 87 Fd33
Ängebäck S 94 Ec43
Ängebo S 87 Ga35
Angelbachtal D 134 Cc47
Angelburg D 126 Cc41
Ängelholm S 110 Ed54
Angeli FIN 68 Jc11
Angelniemi FIN 97 Jc40
Angelohóri GR 183 Bd77
Angelohóri GR 183 Ca78
Angelókastro GR 188 Ba84
Angelókastro GR 195 Ca87
Ängelsberg S 95 Ga41
Angelstad S 102 Fa52
Anger A 144 Ga54
Angera I 148 Cb58
Angerdshestra S 103 Fb49
Angered S 102 Ec49
Angerlo NL 125 Bc37
Angermoen N 70 Fa21
Angermünde D 120 Fa35
Angern D 127 Ea37
Angern an der March A 145 Gc50
Angerneset N 70 Ed21
Angers F 28 Fb41
Ängersjö S 80 Hb29
Ängersjö S 87 Fc35
Angerville F 29 Gd38
Ängesån S 73 Hd18
Ängesbyn S 73 Hd22
Ängesleva FIN 74 Ka24
Ängesträsk S 73 Hd21
Anghiari I 156 Ea66
Anghione F 154 Cc69
Angista GR 184 Cd77
Angístri GR 195 Ca87
Angistro GR 184 Cc75
Angla EST 97 Jc45
Anglards-de-Salers F 33 Ha49
Angle GB 18 Db27
An Gleann Garbh IRL 12 Bb26
Anglefort F 35 Jd46
Angles F 32 Fa45
Anglès F 41 Ha54
Anglès E 49 Ha59
Anglesola E 48 Gb60
Angles-sur-l'Anglin F 29 Ga44
Anglet F 39 Ed54
Angliers F 28 Fd43
Anglure F 24 Hc37
Angnäs S 80 Ha28
Angoncillo E 39 Eb58
An Gort IRL 12 Bd22
An Gort Mór IRL 8 Bb20
Angoulême F 32 Fd47
Angri I 161 Fb75
Ängskär S 96 Gd40
Ängsö S 95 Gb43
Angstedt, Gräfinau- D 127 Dd42
Ängsvik S 96 Ha43
Angües E 48 Fc59
Anguiano E 38 Ea58
Anguillara Sabazia I 160 Ea71
Anguillara Veneta I 150 Ea61
Anguita E 47 Eb62
Anguix E 47 Ea64
Anguse EST 98 La42
Angvik N 77 Db31
Anhée B 124 Ad42
Anholt D 125 Bc37
Anholt DK 101 Eb22
Aniane F 41 Hc54
Aniche F 24 Hb32
Ánidro GR 189 Bd83
Aniés E 39 Fb58
Änimskog S 94 Ec45
Anina RO 174 Ca63
Aninoasa RO 175 Cd64
Aninoasa RO 175 Dc63
Aninoasa RO 176 Dd64
Aniñón E 47 Ed61
Anıtkaya TR 193 Gc84
Anixiátiko GR 188 Bd82
Anizy-le-Château F 24 Hb34
Anjala FIN 90 La37
Anjalankoski FIN 90 La37
Anjan S 78 Ed29
Anjum NL 117 Bc32
Ankaran SLO 151 Fa59
Ankarsrum S 103 Ga49
Ankarsund S 71 Ga23
Ankarsvik S 88 Gc33
Ankarvattnet S 79 Fb25
Änkilänsalo FIN 91 Ld34
Anklam D 120 Fa32
Ankum D 117 Cb35
An Leacht IRL 12 Bc22
An Longfort IRL 9 Cb20
Anloo NL 117 Bd34
An Mhala Raithní IRL 8 Bb19
An Móta IRL 13 Cb21
An Muileann gCearr IRL 9 Cb20
Anna E 54 Fb69
Anna EST 98 Kd43
Anna LV 107 Lc48
Anna RUS 203 Fb12
Annaberg A 144 Fd52
Annaberg-Buchholz D 135 Ed43
Annaberg im Lammertal A 143 Ed53
Annaburg D 127 Ed39
Annacloy GB 9 Da18
Annahütte D 128 Fa39
Annalong GB 9 Da19
Annan GB 11 Eb16
Anna Paulowna NL 116 Ba34
An Nás IRL 13 Cc22
Annas LV 106 Kd50
Annayalla IRL 9 Cd18
Anneberg S 102 Ec49
Anneberg S 103 Fc49
Annecy F 35 Jd46
Annel FIN 68 Jc11
Annelund S 102 Ed48
Annemasse F 35 Ka45
Annenieki LV 106 Ka52
Annental A 144 Ga51
Annerstad S 102 Fa52
Annestown IRL 13 Cb25
Annevoie-Rouillon B 124 Ad42
Annfield Plain GB 11 Ed17
Anņi LV 106 La48
Annikvere EST 98 Kd41
Annino RUS 99 Mb39
Annino RUS 202 Ed08
Annonay F 34 Ja48
Annonen FIN 82 Ka26
Annopol PL 131 Jd41
Annot F 43 Kb52
Ånnstad N 66 Fc13
Annweiler amTrifels D 133 Ca47
Áno Ágios Vlássios GR 188 Ba83
Áno Damásta GR 189 Bd83
Áno Daviá GR 194 Bc87
Áno Drossiní GR 185 Dd77
Annœullin F 23 Ha31
Áno Fanári GR 195 Ca88
Anógia GR 200 Da95
Áno Hóra GR 188 Bb84
Áno Kalendíni GR 188 Ba82
Áno Kalliníki GR 183 Bb76
Áno Kariófito GR 184 Db76
Áno Kastrítsi GR 188 Bb85
Áno Kómi GR 183 Bc79
Áno Korakiána GR 182 Ab80
Áno Koudoúni GR 188 Ba84
Áno-Lehónia GR 189 Ca82
Ano Mathráki GR 182 Aa79
Áno Merá GR 196 Db89
Áno Méros GR 200 Cd96
Añón E 47 Ec60
Ånonjalme sameviste S 67 Gb16
Áno Poróia GR 183 Cb76
Añora E 52 Cc71
Áno Sangrí GR 196 Db90
Áno Sinikia Trikala GR 189 Bc86
Áno Síros GR 196 Da88
Anost F 30 Hd42
Anould F 31 Ka38
Áno Váthia GR 189 Cc85
Áno Viános GR 201 Db96
Áno Vrondoú GR 184 Cc76
Anoye F 40 Fc55
Anquela del Ducado E 47 Eb63
An Ráth IRL 12 Bd24
Anröchte D 126 Cc39
An Ros IRL 13 Da21
Ans DK 100 Db23
Ansac-sur-Vienne F 33 Ga46
Ansager DK 108 Da25
Ansalahti FIN 90 Kd36
Ansbach D 134 Dc47
An Scairbh IRL 12 Bd22
An Sciobairín IRL 12 Bb26
Anse F 34 Ja46
An Seanchaisleán IRL 9 Cc20
Ansedonia I 155 Dc69
Anselküla EST 105 Jc47
Anserall E 40 Gc58
Ansião P 44 Ac65
Ansignan F 41 Ha57
Ansio FIN 90 Kc34
Ansku FIN 97 Jd40
Ansnes N 62 Gc10
Ansnes N 77 Dc29

Ansó – Åsenhöga

Ansó E 39 Fb57
An Spidéal IRL 12 Bc21
Anspoki, L. LV 107 Lc52
Anstad N 85 Db35
Anstruther GB 7 Ec12
Antagnod I 148 Bd58
Antakalnis LT 114 Kc57
Antakalnis LT 114 Kd56
Antalieptė LT 115 Lb54
Antalya TR 199 Gc91
Antanavas LV 114 Kb58
An tAonach IRL 13 Ca22
Antas E 61 Ec75
Antas P 44 Bb62
Antašava LT 114 Kd54
Antas de Ulla E 36 Bb56
Antazavė LT 115 Lb54
An Teach Dóite IRL 8 Bb20
An Teampall Mór IRL 13 Ca23
Antegluonis LT 113 Jd56
Antegnate I 149 Cd59
Antemil (Cerceda) E 36 Ba54
Anten S 102 Ec48
Antequera E 60 Cd75
Anterselva di Mezzo I 143 Ea55
Antey-Saint-André I 148 Bd58
Anthée B 124 Ad42
Anthéor F 43 Kc54
Anthí GR 184 Cc77
Anthili GR 189 Bd83
Anthófito GR 183 Ca77
Antholz Mittertal I 143 Ea55
Anthorn GB 11 Eb16
Anthótopos GR 183 Bb78
Anthótopos GR 189 Bd82
Anthy F 31 Ka44
Antibes F 43 Kc53
Antignano I 155 Da66
Antigonos GR 183 Bc77
Antigüedad E 46 Db59
Antíkira GR 189 Bd85
Antilä FIN 89 Jb34
Antillo I 167 Fd84
Antimáhia GR 197 Eb91
An tInbhear Mór IRL 13 Cd23
Antinrova S 68 Ja17
Ántissa GR 191 Db83
Antjärn S 88 Gc32
Antnäs S 73 Hd22
Anton BG 179 Da71
Antonești MD 177 Fb60
Antoneuca MD 173 Fb54
Antonimina I 164 Gb83
Antonin PL 122 Hc32
Antonin PL 129 Ha39
Antoniów PL 130 Jc40
Antoniów PL 131 Jd41
Antonovo BG 180 Ea70
Antonsthal D 135 Ec43
Antracyt UA 205 Fb15
Antraigues-sur-Volane F 34 Ja50
Antrain F 28 Ed38
Antrim GB 9 Da17
Antrodoco I 156 Ec70
Antronapiana I 148 Ca57
Antskog FIN 97 Jd40
Antsla EST 107 Lb47
Anttila FIN 90 La36
Anttila FIN 98 Kc39
Anttis S 68 Ja17
Anttola FIN 90 La34
Anttola FIN 91 Lc33
An Tulach IRL 13 Cc23
Antuži LV 106 La51
Antwerpen B 124 Ac39
An Uaimh IRL 9 Cd20
Anundsjö S 80 Gd30
Anversa di Abruzzi I 161 Fa71
Anvin F 23 Gd31
Anxeriz E 36 Ad54
Anykščiai LT 114 Kd55
Anzat-le-Luguet F 34 Hb48
Anzi I 161 Ga76
Anzin F 24 Hb32
Anzing D 143 Ea51
Anzio I 160 Eb73
Anzlezy F 30 Hc43
Anzola dell'Emilia I 149 Dc62
Anzur E 60 Cd74
Anzy-le-Duc F 34 Hd45
Aoiz E 39 Ed57
Aosta I 148 Bc58
Aouste F 24 Hd33
Aovere EST 99 Lb45
Apa H 146 Hc54
Apa RO 171 Cd54
Apače SLO 144 Ga56
Apagy H 147 Ka51
Apahida RO 171 Da58
Aparhant H 153 Hc57
Apastovo RUS 203 Fd09
Apața RO 176 Ea61
Apateu RO 170 Ca58
Apatin SRB 153 Hd59
Apatovac HR 152 Gc57
Ape LV 107 Lb48
Apecchio I 156 Eb66
Apeldoorn NL 117 Bc36
Apelern D 126 Da37
Apele Vii RO 179 Da67
Apelscha NL 117 Bd34
Apen D 117 Cb33
Apenburg D 119 Dd35
Apensen D 118 Db33
Apéri GR 201 Eb95
A Peroxa E 36 Bb57
Apice I 161 Fc74
Apidiá GR 195 Bd90
Apiés E 48 Fc59
Apírados GR 196 Dc90
Apiro I 156 Ec66
Aplared S 102 Ed49
Apliki CY 206 Jb97
A Pobra de Caramiñal E 36 Ac56
Apolakkiá GR 197 Ed93
Apold RO 175 Dc60
Apolda D 127 Ea41
Apoldu de Jos RO 175 Da61
Apóllona GR 197 Fa93
Apollonia GR 196 Da90
Apólonas GR 196 Dc89
Apolonía GR 184 Cc78
Apóstoli GR 200 Cd95
Apostolove UA 204 Ed16
Appel D 118 Db33
Äppelbo S 95 Fb40
Appeltern NL 125 Bb37
Appenweier D 133 Ca49
Appenzell CH 142 Cd53
Appiano I 142 Dc56
Appingedam NL 117 Ca33
Appleby GB 16 Fb21
Appleby-in-Westmorland GB 11 Ec18
Appleby Magna GB 16 Fa24
Applecross GB 4 Db08
Appledore GB 21 Ga29
Apples CH 140 Ba55
Appletreewick GB 11 Ed19
Äpplö FIN 97 Ja40
Appoigny F 30 Hc40
Apremont F 28 Ed44
Apremont-la-Forêt F 25 Jc36
Apremont-sur-Allier F 30 Hb43
Aprica I 149 Da57
Apricale I 43 Kd52
Apricena I 161 Fd72
Aprigliano I 164 Gc80
Apriķi LV 105 Jb51
Aprilci BG 179 Da73
Aprilci BG 180 Dc71
Aprilia I 160 Eb72
Aprilovo BG 180 Ea73
Aprilovo BG 180 Eb70
Apsalos GR 183 Bc77
Apsella I 156 Eb65
Apšeronsk RUS 205 Fc17
Apsiou CY 206 Ja98
Apšuciems LV 106 Ka50
Apšupe LV 106 Ka51
Apt F 42 Jc53
Aquila CH 142 Cc56
Aquileia I 150 Ed59
Aquilonia I 161 Fd74
Aquino I 160 Ed73
Arabaalan TR 185 Ed80
Arabacıbozköy TR 191 Ed84
Arabba I 143 Ea56
Araç TR 205 Fa20
Aracena E 59 Bc72
Arâches F 35 Ka45
Aračinovo MK 178 Bc73
Arad RO 170 Bd59
Aradac SRB 153 Jc60
Aradeo I 163 Hc77
Aradippou CY 206 Jc97
Aradninkai LV 123 Kb30
Araglin IRL 13 Ca25
Aragnouet F 40 Fd57
Aragona I 166 Ed86
Aragoncillo E 47 Ec63
Aragüés del Puerto E 39 Fb57
Arahamítes GR 194 Bc88
Arahnéo GR 195 Bd87
Aráhova GR 189 Bd84
Arahovítika GR 188 Bb85
Arakapas CY 206 Jb97
Arakste LV 106 Kd47
Aralkı TR 205 Fd19
Aralla E 37 Cb56
Åram N 76 Cb33
A Ramallosa E 36 Ac58
Aramits F 39 Fb56
Aramon F 42 Jb53
Arana CY 206 Jd96
Aranaz E 39 Ec56
Aranda de Duero E 46 Dc60
Aranda de Moncayo E 47 Ec61
Arándiga E 47 Ed61
Arandilla del Arroyo E 47 Eb64
Aráneag RO 170 Ca59
Aranga E 36 Bb54
Aranjuez E 52 Dc66
Arantzazu E 39 Eb56
Aranyosapáti H 147 Kb50
Aranzueque E 46 Dd64
Araovacık TR 191 Ed81
Ararca TR 192 Fb81
Årås N 84 Ca37
Aras de Alpuente E 54 Fa66
Araševo RUS 107 Mb46
Arasi I 164 Ga84
Arasluokta sameviste S 66 Ga17
Aratores E 39 Fb57
Áratos GR 185 Dd77
Arauzo de Miel E 46 Dd60
Aravete EST 98 Kd43
Aravissós GR 183 Bd77
Arazede P 44 Ac64
Arbanasi BG 180 Dd70
Arbas F 40 Gb56
Arbás E 37 Cc56
Arbatax I 169 Cc77
Arbeca E 48 Gb61
Arbedo CH 149 Cc57
Arberg D 134 Dc47
Arbesbach A 144 Fc50
Arbeteta E 47 Eb64
Arbigny F 30 Jb44
Arbing A 144 Fc51
Arbinovo MK 182 Ba75
Arbirlot GB 7 Ec11
Arboga S 95 Ga43
Arbois F 31 Jc43
Arbon CH 142 Cd52
Arbonne-la-Forêt F 29 Ha38
Arbore RO 172 Eb55
Arborea I 169 Bd78
Arborio I 148 Ca59
Årbostad N 67 Gb12
Årbotten S 94 Ed42
Arbrå S 87 Ga36
Arbroath GB 7 Ec11
Arbúcies E 49 Ha60
Arbuniel E 60 Dc73
Arbus I 169 Bd78
Arby S 111 Ga53
Arc F 31 Jc41
Arca P 44 Ad63
Arcachon F 32 Fa51
Arčadinskaja RUS 203 Fd13
Arcallana E 37 Ca54
Arcani RO 175 Cc63
Arčar BG 179 Cb67
Arcas E 53 Eb66
Arce I 160 Ed72
Arcen NL 125 Bc39
Arcenant F 30 Ja42
Arc-en-Barrois F 30 Jb39
Arcens F 34 Ja50
Arcentales E 38 Dd55
Arces-Dilo F 30 Hc39
Arc-et-Senans F 31 Jc42
Arcevia I 156 Ec66
Arcey F 31 Ka40
Archangel'skoje RUS 113 Jd58
Archena E 55 Ed72
Archiac F 32 Fc48
Archiane F 35 Jc50
Archidona E 60 Cd75
Archiestown GB 7 Eb08
Archigny F 29 Ga44
Archiș RO 170 Cb58
Archivel E 61 Eb72
Arcidosso I 156 Dd68
Arciems LV 106 Kc48
Arcille I 155 Dc68
Arcins F 32 Fb49
Arcis-sur-Aube F 30 Hd38
Arco I 149 Dc58
Arco de Baúlhe P 44 Ba60
Arco de las Salinas E 54 Fa66
Arcos E 36 Bb56
Arcos E 38 Dc58
Arcos de Jalón E 47 Eb62
Arcos de la Frontera E 59 Ca76
Arcos de la Sierra E 47 Eb65
Arcos de Valdevez P 44 Ad59
Arcy-sur-Cure F 30 Hc41
Arcyz UA 204 Ec17
Arda BG 184 Db75
Ardagh IRL 12 Bc23
Ardahan TR 205 Ga18
Årdal N 92 Cb43
Årdal N 92 Cd45
Årdala S 95 Gb45
Ardales E 60 Cc76
Årdalstangen N 85 Da37
Ardan IRL 13 Cb21
Ardanairy IRL 13 Cd23
Ardara I 168 Ca75
Ardara IRL 8 Ca16
Árdassa GR 183 Bb78
Ardatov RUS 203 Fb10
Ardbeg GB 9 Da14
Ardcharnich GB 4 Dc06
Ardea I 160 Eb72
Ardee IRL 9 Cd19
Ardeluța RO 172 Eb59
Arden DK 100 Dc22
Ardenno I 149 Cd57
Ardentes F 29 Gc44
Ardentinny GB 6 Dc12
Ardenza I 155 Da66
Ardeoani RO 172 Ec59
Ardes F 34 Hb48
Ardeșen TR 205 Ga19
Ardèvol E 49 Gc60
Ardez CH 142 Da55
Ardfert IRL 12 Bb24
Ardfield IRL 12 Bc27
Ardfinnan IRL 13 Ca24
Ardgartan GB 6 Dc12
Ardgay GB 5 Ea06
Ardglass GB 10 Db18
Ardgroom IRL 12 Ba26
Ardılı TR 199 Gb88
Ardino BG 184 Dc75
Ardisa E 48 Fb59
Ardkeen GB 10 Db18
Ardleigh GB 21 Ga26
Ardlussa GB 6 Db12
Ardminish GB 6 Db13
Ardmore IRL 13 Ca26
Ardon CH 141 Bc56
Ardón E 37 Cc57
Ardore Marina I 164 Gb83
Ardpatrick IRL 12 Bd24
Ardrahan IRL 12 Bd21
Ardre S 104 Ha50
Ardres F 21 Gc30
Ardrishaig GB 6 Db12
Ardrossan GB 10 Dc14
Ardshankill GB 9 Cb17
Ardstraw GB 9 Cc16
Ardtalla GB 6 Da13
Ardtoe GB 6 Db10
Ardu EST 98 Kc43
Arduaine GB 6 Db12
Ardud RO 171 Cd55
Ardusat RO 171 Da55
Ardwell GB 10 Dc17
Åre S 78 Fa30
Areatza E 38 Ea56
Årebrot N 84 Ca35
Arèches F 35 Ka47
Arefu RO 175 Dc63
Aremark N 94 Eb44
Aremberg D 125 Bd42
Arenales de San Gregorio E 53 Dd68
Arenas E 60 Da76
Arenas de Cabrales E 38 Da55
Arenas del Rey E 60 Db75
Arenas de San Juan E 52 Dc68
Arenas de San Pedro E 45 Cc65
Arendal N 93 Da46
Arendonk B 124 Ba39
Arendsee D 119 Ea35
Arengosse F 39 Fb53
Arenshausen D 126 Db40
Arentsminde DK 100 Dc21
Arenys de Mar E 49 Ha61
Arenys de Munt E 49 Ha60
Arenzano I 148 Cb63
Areópoli GR 194 Bc90
Ares E 36 Ba54
Arès F 32 Fa50
Ares del Maestrat E 48 Fc64
Aresing D 135 Dd49
Årestrup DK 100 Dc22
Aresvik N 77 Db30
Areta E 38 Ea55
Aréthoussa GR 184 Cc77
Arette F 39 Fb56
Arevalillo E 45 Cc63
Arévalo E 46 Cd62
Arévalo de la Sierra E 47 Eb59
Arez P 50 Ba66
Arezzo I 156 Dd66
Arfará GR 194 Bb89
Argalastí GR 189 Cb82
Argallón E 51 Cb71
Argamasilla de Alba E 53 Dd69
Argamasilla de Calatrava E 52 Db70
Argamasón E 53 Ec70
Arganda E 46 Dc65
Arganil P 44 Ad64
Argaño E 38 Dc58
Argegno I 149 Cc58
Argein F 40 Gb56
Argelaguer E 49 Ha59
Argelès-Gazost F 40 Fc56
Argelès-Plage F 41 Hb57
Argelès-sur-Mer F 41 Hb57
Argelita E 54 Fc66
Argemil P 44 Bb60
Argenbühl D 142 Da52
Argenta I 150 Dd62
Argentan F 22 Fc37
Argentat F 33 Gd49
Argente E 47 Fa64
Argentera I 148 Bb62
Argenteuil F 23 Gd36
Argentiera I 168 Bc74
Argentière F 35 Kb45
Argentona E 49 Ha61
Argenton-Château F 28 Fc43
Argenton-sur-Creuse F 29 Gc44
Argentré F 28 Fb39
Argentré-du-Plessis F 28 Fa39
Argent-sur-Sauldre F 29 Gd41
Arges E 55 Fb70
Argés E 52 Db66
Argetoaia RO 175 Cd65
Argili GR 194 Ba88
Arginónta GR 197 Eb90
Argirádes GR 182 Ab80
Argiropoúli GR 183 Bd80
Argithani TR 193 Hb86
Argithéa GR 188 Bb81
Árgos GR 195 Bd87
Árgos Orestikó GR 182 Ba78
Argostóli GR 188 Ac85
Argovë AL 182 Ac78
Arguedas E 47 Ed59
Argueil F 23 Gb34
Argüero E 37 Cc54
Arguis E 48 Fc58
Arguisuelas E 53 Ec66
Argy F 29 Gb43
Arhánes GR 200 Da96
Arhángelos GR 183 Bd76
Arhángelos GR 197 Fa93
Arhavi TR 205 Ga19
Arhéa Feneós GR 189 Bc86
Arhéa Kórinthos GR 195 Bd87
Arhéa Neméa GR 195 Bd87
Arhípoli GR 197 Fa93
Ariano Irpino I 161 Fd74
Ariano nel Polesine I 150 Ea61
Arıca TR 192 Ga84
Ariceștii Zeletin RO 176 Eb63
Aricești Rahtivani RO 176 Ea64
Aridéa GR 183 Bc76
Arielli I 157 Fb70
Arienzo I 161 Fb74
Arieșeni RO 171 Cc59
Arifiye TR 187 Gc79
Arifköyü TR 199 Gb92
Arija E 38 Dc56
Arıklar TR 192 Fc83
Arıklı TR 191 Eb82
Arild S 110 Ec54
Arileod GB 6 Da10
Arileod GB 9 Da14
Arilje SRB 178 Ad67
Arinagh IRL 8 Bd18
Arinagour GB 9 Da14
Aringo I 156 Ec69
Aríni GR 194 Ba87
Ariniș RO 171 Cd55
Ariño E 48 Fb62
Arinsal AND 40 Gc57
Arinsal AND 40 Gc57
Arinthod F 31 Jc44
Ariogala LV 114 Kb56
Arionești MD 173 Fb53
Arisaig GB 6 Db09
Ariscal E 59 Bd74
Arisgotas E 52 Db67
Aristava LT 114 Kc56
Aristot E 40 Gc58
Arisvere EST 98 Kd44
Arísvi GR 185 Dd77
Aritzo I 169 Cb77
Arive E 39 Fa56
Arivruaich GB 4 Da05
Ariza E 47 Ec61
Arızlar TR 193 Gb86
Arızlı TR 193 Gd86
Årjäng S 94 Ec43
Arjeplog S 72 Gc21
Árjepluovve S 72 Gc21
Arjona E 52 Da72
Arjonilla E 52 Da72
Arjuzanx F 39 Fb53
Arkadak RUS 203 Fc12
Arkadia PL 130 Ja37
Arkalohóri GR 200 Da96
Arkássa GR 201 Eb95
Arkelstorp S 111 Fb54
Arkesíni GR 196 Dc91
Arkhyttan S 95 Ga40
Arkí GR 197 Eb89
Arkítsa GR 189 Ca84
Arklow IRL 13 Cd23
Arkna EST 98 La42
Arkösund S 103 Gb46
Ärla S 95 Gb44
Arlanc F 34 Hc48
Arlaviškės LT 114 Kc57
Arlempdes F 34 Hd50
Arles F 42 Jb54
Arles-sur-Tech F 41 Ha58
Arleuf F 30 Hd42
Arlingham GB 19 Ec27
Arló H 146 Jb50
Arlon B 132 Ba44
Arlöv S 110 Ed56
Arlucea E 39 Eb57
Arluno I 148 Cb59
Árma GR 189 Cb85
Armação de Pera P 58 Ac74
Armadale GB 6 Db09
Arma di Taggia I 43 La52
Armağan TR 185 Ed75
Armagh GB 9 Cd18
Armallones E 47 Eb63
Armamar P 44 Bb61
Ārmani LV 107 Ld52
Armășești RO 176 Ec65
Armasjärvi S 73 Jb20
Ármata GR 182 Ad79
Armavir RUS 205 Fd16
Armellada E 37 Cb57
Armen AL 182 Ab77
Arméni GR 200 Cc95
Armenií GR 194 Ba88
Armeniș RO 174 Cb63
Armeniškiai LV 114 Kb57
Armenohóri GR 183 Bb77
Armenteira E 36 Ad56
Armentia E 38 Ea57
Armentières F 23 Ha31
Armilla E 60 Db75
Arminou CY 206 Ja97
Armintza E 38 Ea54
Armivesi FIN 90 Kd32
Armjans'k UA 205 Fa17
Armo I 164 Ga84
Armólia GR 191 Dd86
Armonys LT 114 La53
Armoy GB 9 Da15
Armuña de Tajuña E 46 Dd64
Armungia I 169 Cb79
Armutçuk TR 187 Ha77
Armutçuk TR 191 Ec82
Armutlu TR 185 Ed80
Armutlu TR 186 Fc79
Armutlu TR 191 Ed86
Armutlu TR 192 Fa83
Armutlu TR 192 Fb85
Armutlu TR 193 Ha87
Armutlu TR 198 Ga92
Arnabost GB 6 Da10
Arnabost GB 9 Da14
Arnaccio I 155 Da65
Arnach D 142 Da51
Arnac-Pompadour F 33 Gb48
Arnac-sur-Dourdou F 41 Hb54
Arnafjord N 84 Cc37
Arnage F 28 Fd40
Arnager DK 111 Fc58
Arnás GR 190 Da87
Ärnäs S 86 Fa38
Arnäsvall S 80 Ha30
Arnavutköy TR 186 Fc77
Arnavutköy TR 186 Fc79
Arnay-le-Duc F 30 Ja42
Arnberg S 80 Ha25
Arnborg DK 108 Da24
Arnbruck D 135 Ec47
Arncott GB 20 Fa27
Arndrup DK 108 Da27
Arnéa GR 184 Cc78
Arneberg N 86 Ea38
Arneburg D 127 Eb36
Arnedillo E 47 Eb59
Arnedo E 47 Ec59
Arnemark S 73 Hc23
Arnemuiden NL 124 Ab38
Årnes N 62 Gd08
Årnes N 67 Gb14
Årnes N 78 Eb26
Årnes N 94 Eb41
Arnesby GB 16 Fa24
Arnfels A 144 Fd56
Arnhem NL 125 Bb37
Arnionys LT 115 Lb56
Arnis D 108 Dc29
Arnisdale GB 6 Db09
Árnissa GR 183 Bc77
Arnö S 95 Gb45
Arnö S 96 Gc43
Arnoga I 142 Da56
Arnold GB 16 Fa23
Arnoldstein A 144 Fa56
Arnøyhamn N 62 Ha08
Arnprior GB 7 Dd12
Arnsberg D 125 Cb39
Arnschwang D 135 Ec47
Arnsdorf D 128 Fb41
Arnside GB 11 Eb19
Arnstadt D 127 Dd42
Arnstein D 134 Db44
Arnstorf D 135 Ec49
Arnum DK 108 Da27
Aroania GR 188 Bb86
Aroche E 59 Bb72
Aröd S 102 Eb47
Ároktő H 146 Jc52
Arola FIN 64 Ka07
Arola I 148 Ca58
Arolla CH 148 Bc57
Arona I 148 Cb58
Aroneanu RO 173 Fa57
Aroniádika GR 195 Bd92
Aronkylä FIN 89 Ja32
Åros N 93 Dd42
Arosa CH 142 Cd55
Arosa P 44 Ba60
Årosjåkk S 67 Gd15
Årøsund DK 108 Db27
Arouca P 44 Ad62
Arousa E 36 Ac56
Årøysund N 93 Dd44
Arpacık TR 198 Fd91
Arpajon la Norville F 29 Gd38
Arpășel RO 170 Ca57
Arpașu de Jos RO 175 Dc61
Arpela FIN 74 Jc20
Arpino I 160 Ed72
Arquà Petrarca I 150 Dd60
Arquata del Tronto I 156 Ec68
Arquata Scrivia I 148 Cb62
Arques F 21 Gd30
Arques-la-Bataille F 23 Gb33
Arquillos E 52 Dc72
Arrabal (Oia) E 36 Ac58
Arrach D 135 Ec47
Arracourt F 25 Ka37
Arradon F 27 Eb41
Arraiolos P 50 Ad69
Arrakoski FIN 90 Kb35
Arrankorpi FIN 90 Kb37
Arrans F 30 Hd40
Arras AL 178 Ad73
Arras F 23 Ha32
Arrasate Mondragon E 39 Eb56
Arraute-Charritte F 39 Fa55
Arravonítsa GR 188 Bb85
Årre DK 108 Da26
Arreau F 40 Fd56
Arredondo E 38 Dc55
Årrenjarka S 72 Gc18
Arrens F 40 Fc56
Arreza e Madhe AL 182 Ac77
Arrianá GR 185 Dd77
Arriano E 38 Ea56
Arriate E 60 Cc76
Arrie S 110 Ed56
Arrien F 40 Fc55
Arrifana P 44 Ad64
Arrifana P 45 Bc63
Arrifana P 58 Aa73
Arrigny F 24 Ja37
Arrigorriaga E 38 Ea55
Arrild DK 108 Da27
Arriondas (Parres) E 37 Cd54
Arro E 40 Fd58
Arroiabe E 39 Eb56
Arrojo E 37 Cb55
Arromanches-les-Bains F 22 Fb35
Arronches P 51 Bb68
Arróniz E 39 Ec57
Arrou F 29 Gb39
Arrovo del Ojanco E 53 Dd71
Arroyal E 38 Db56
Arroyo E 38 Db56
Arroyo de la Luz E 51 Bd67
Arroyo de la Plata E 59 Bd73
Arroyo de San Serván E 51 Bd69
Arroyomolinos de León E 51 Bd71
Arroyomolinos de Montánchez E 51 Ca68
Arruazu E 39 Ec56
Arryheernabin IRL 9 Cb15
Ars E 40 Gc58
Arsac F 32 Fb50
Årsand N 70 Ed24
Årsballe DK 111 Fc57
Arsbeck D 125 Bc40
Ars-en-Ré F 32 Ed45
Arsgue F 39 Fb54
Arsiè I 150 Dd58
Arsiero I 150 Dd58
Arsk RUS 203 Fd08
Árskógssandur IS 2 Ba03
Årslev DK 109 Dd27
Årsnes N 76 Cc33
Arsoli I 160 Ec71
Arsos CY 206 Jc97
Ars-sur-Formans F 34 Jb46
Ars-sur-Moselle F 25 Jc35
Årsta havsbad S 96 Gd44
Årsunda S 95 Gb39
Arsura RO 173 Fb58
Arsvågen N 92 Ca43
Árta GR 188 Ad82
Artà E 57 Hc67
Artajona E 39 Ec57
Artana E 54 Fc66
Arta Terme I 143 Ec56
Artazu E 39 Ec57
Artegna I 150 Ec57
Artemare F 35 Jc46
Ärtemark S 94 Ec44
Artemisia GR 194 Bb89
Artemíssio GR 189 Ca83
Artemíssio GR 194 Bc87
Artemivs'k UA 205 Fb15
Artemónas GR 196 Da90
Artemovka RUS 113 Jc57
Arten I 150 Ea58
Artena I 160 Ec72
Artenay F 29 Gc39
Artern D 127 Dd40
Artés E 49 Gd60
Artesa de Lleida E 48 Gb61
Artesa de Segre E 48 Gb60
Artesianó GR 188 Bb81
Artesina I 148 Bc63
Arth CH 141 Cb54
Arthez-de-Béarn F 39 Fb55
Arthies F 23 Gc36
Arthon-en-Retz F 27 Ec42
Arthonnay F 30 Hd39
Arthurstown IRL 13 Cc25
Artieda E 39 Ed57
Arties E 40 Ga57
Artiguelouve F 39 Fb55
Artiguillon F 32 Fb49
Artix F 39 Fb55
Artjärvi FIN 90 Kd37
Ärtled S 87 Fd38
Artlenburg D 118 Dc33
Arto SLO 151 Fd58
Artozqui E 39 Ed56
Ärtrik S 79 Gb30
Artvin TR 205 Ga19
Artziniega E 38 Dd56
A Rúa E 36 Bc57
Arudy F 39 Fb56
Arukülä EST 98 Kc42
Arum NL 116 Bb33
Arundel GB 20 Fb30
Aruvalla EST 98 Kc43
Årvåg N 77 Dc30
Arvagh IRL 9 Cb19
Arvån S 80 Ha26
Arvanitohóri GR 201 Eb96
Arvant F 34 Hc48
Arvert F 32 Fa47
Arvesund S 79 Fb30
Árvi GR 201 Db96
Arvidsjaur S 72 Ha22
Arvidsträsk S 73 Hc22
Arvieux F 35 Kb50
Årvik N 76 Ca33
Årvik N 76 Ca33
Arvika S 94 Ed42
Årviksand N 62 Ha08
Årvikstrand N 84 Cb40
Arville F 29 Ga39
Arville F 29 Ha39
Arvola FIN 89 Jb34
Arvospuoli FIN 69 Kb16
Arvträsk S 80 Ha26
Åryd S 103 Fc52
Åryd S 111 Fc54
Arzachena I 168 Cb73
Arzacq-Arraziguet F 39 Fb54
Arzádigos E 45 Bc59
Arzamas RUS 203 Fc10
Arzano F 27 Dd40
Arzberg D 127 Ed39
Arzberg D 135 Eb44
Arzgir RUS 205 Ga16
Arzignano I 149 Dc59
Arzl im Pitztal A 142 Dc54
Arzon F 27 Eb41
Arzúa E 36 Ba55
Arzulu TR 185 Ed77
As B 125 Bb40
Aš CZ 135 Eb44
Ås N 78 Ec31
Ås N 93 Ea42
Ås N 93 Db45
Ås S 79 Fc30
Ås S 111 Gb54
Åsa S 102 Ec50
Asa S 103 Fc51
Asaa DK 101 Dd21
Aşağıboğaz TR 187 Gc80
Aşağı Böğürtlen TR 197 Fa91
Aşağıçeşme TR 192 Fd87
Aşağıçiğil TR 193 Hb87
Aşağı Çobanisa TR 191 Ed85
Aşağıdereköy TR 187 Gc78
Aşağıdolaylar TR 192 Fc83
Aşağı Germencik TR 197 Fa91
Aşağıgökdere TR 199 Gd89
Aşağıgünlüce TR 198 Fc90
Aşağıgürlek TR 198 Fc91
Aşağıkaraçay TR 198 Fd88
Asağıkaşıkara TR 193 Gd86
Aşağıkozcağız TR 187 Gd80
Aşağıkuzfındık TR 193 Gb82
Aşağıokçular TR 185 Ea80
Aşağı Piribeyli TR 193 Hb84
Aşağısamlı TR 198 Fc88
Aşağısevindikli TR 185 Ed77
Aşağıtandır TR 193 Gc84
Aşağıtırtar TR 193 Gd87
Aşağıyağcılar TR 192 Fc82
Aşağıyaylabeli TR 199 Ha89
Asak N 94 Eb44
Asamati MK 182 Ba76
Åsane N 84 Ca39
Åsäng S 88 Gc32
Ašanja SRB 153 Jb62
Asar TR 187 Ha78
Asare LV 115 Lb53
Åsåren N 85 Dc35
Åsarna S 79 Fb25
Åsarna S 87 Fb32
Åsarp S 102 Fa48
Asarum S 111 Fc54
Asasp-Arros F 39 Fb56
Asău RO 172 Ec59
Asbach D 125 Ca42
Asbach-Bäumenheim D 134 Dc49
Åsbro S 95 Fc45
Asby S 103 Fd48
Ásbyrgi IS 3 Bb04
Ascád H 145 Gc54
Ascain F 39 Ed55
Ascea I 161 Fd77
Ascha D 135 Ec48
Aschach an der Donau A 144 Fa50
Aschaffenburg D 134 Cd44
Aschau D 143 Eb51
Aschau D 143 Eb52
Aschbach-Markt A 144 Fc51
Ascheberg D 118 Dc31
Ascheberg D 125 Cb38
Ascheffel D 118 Db30
Aschères-le-Marché F 29 Gd39
Aschersleben D 127 Ea39
Așchileu RO 171 Da57
Asciano I 156 Dd67
Asco F 154 Cb69
Ascó E 48 Ga62
Ascoli Piceno I 156 Ed68
Ascoli Satriano I 161 Ga74
Ascona CH 148 Cb57
Ascot GB 20 Fb28
Ascoux F 29 Gd39
Åse N 66 Fd12
A Seara E 36 Ba57
Åsebyn S 94 Ec43
Åseda S 103 Fd51
Åsele S 79 Gb27
Åselet S 73 Hb24
Åseli N 66 Fc12
Asemankylä FIN 74 Ka23
Asemankylä FIN 90 Lb33
Asemanseutu FIN 81 Jb31
Asemanseutu FIN 89 Jc32
Åsen N 76 Cc33
Åsen N 78 Eb29
Åsen S 80 Hb26
Åsen S 87 Fb38
Åsen S 87 Fb37
Asendorf D 118 Cd35
Asendorf D 118 Db33
Åsenhöga S 102 Fa50

Asenovgrad – Bad Bertrich

Asenovgrad BG 184 Db74
Asenovo BG 180 Ea70
Åsensbruk S 94 Ec45
Åseral N 92 Cc45
Aseri EST 98 La41
Åserud N 94 Eb42
Asevelikylä FIN 89 Jb32
Asfáka GR 182 Ad80
Asfeld F 24 Hd34
Asfendioú GR 197 Ec91
Asferg DK 100 Dc22
Asfordby GB 16 Fb24
Åsgårdstrand N 93 Dd43
Asgata CY 206 Jb98
Ash GB 20 Fd28
Åshagen S 94 Ed41
Åshammar S 95 Gb39
Ashbourne GB 16 Ed23
Ashbourne IRL 13 Cd21
Ashburton GB 19 Dd31
Ashbury GB 20 Ed28
Ashby-de-la-Zouch GB 16 Fa24
Ashdon GB 20 Fd26
Ashford GB 21 Ga29
Ashford IRL 13 Cd22
Ashford-in-the-Water GB 16 Ed22
Ashill GB 17 Ga24
Ashington GB 11 Fa16
Ashington GB 20 Fc30
Ashkirk GB 11 Ec14
Ashley GB 20 Fd26
Ashmore GB 19 Ec30
Ashperton GB 15 Ec26
Ashton-in-Makerfield GB 15 Ec21
Ashton Keynes GB 20 Ed27
Ashton-under-Lyne GB 16 Ed21
Ashwater GB 18 Dc30
Ashwell GB 16 Fb24
Ashwell GB 20 Fc26
Ashwellthorpe GB 17 Gb24
Asiago I 150 Dd58
Asikkala FIN 90 Kc36
Asikkala FIN 91 Lb32
Asila FIN 90 La34
Asími GR 200 Da96
Asipovičy BY 202 Eb13
Aşırlar TR 187 Gc78
Ask N 84 Ca39
Ask N 85 Dd40
Ask N 93 Ea41
Ask S 103 Fc46
Ask S 110 Ed55
Aska FIN 69 Ka16
Askainen FIN 97 Ja39
Aşkale TR 205 Ga20
Askanmäki FIN 75 Kd23
Askeaton IRL 12 Bc23
Askeby S 103 Ga47
Askeia CY 206 Jc96
Asker N 93 Dd42
Askerıye TR 199 Gc88
Askern GB 16 Fa21
Askeröd S 110 Fa55
Askersby S 95 Fd44
Askersund S 95 Fc45
Askerswell GB 19 Eb30
Askeryd S 103 Fc49
Askesta S 87 Gb37
Askett GB 20 Fb27
Åskilje S 80 Gc25
Åskiljeby S 80 Gc25
Askim N 93 Ea42
Askim S 102 Eb49
Asklanda S 102 Ed48
Asklipio GR 197 Ed93
Åskloster S 102 Ec50
Askø By DK 109 Ea28
Askola FIN 90 Kc38
Askome S 102 Ec51
Asköping S 95 Ga44
Askós GR 183 Cb77
Askov DK 108 Da26
Askum S 102 Eb46
Askvoll N 84 Ca36
As Lamas E 36 Bb58
Aslanapa TR 193 Gb83
Aslanlar TR 191 Ec87
Aslestad N 92 Cd43
Aslıhantepeciği TR 192 Fa82
Åsljunga S 110 Fa54
Asma E 36 Bb56
Asmalı TR 186 Fa79
Asmali TR 198 Fd90
Åsmansbo S 95 Fd40
Åsmarka N 86 Ea38
Asmíni GR 189 Ca83
Ašmjany BY 202 Ea12
Asmo N 67 Gd11
Åsmon S 79 Gb30
Asmundtorp S 110 Ed55
Asmunti FIN 74 Kb21
Asmyra N 70 Ed22
Asnæs DK 109 Ea25
Åsnes N 78 Eb27
Åsnes Finnskog N 94 Ec39
As Neves E 36 Ad58
Asnières-sur-Vègre F 28 Fc40
As Nogais E 36 Bc56
Asola I 149 Da60
Asolo I 150 Ea58
Asopós GR 195 Bd90
Asos GR 188 Ac84
Asp DK 100 Da23
Aspach D 134 Cd48
Aspai E 36 Bb55
Aspang Markt A 145 Gb53
Aspariegos E 45 Cc60
Asparn an der Zaya A 137 Gb49
Asparuhovo BG 181 Ec72
Asparuhovo BG 181 Ed71
Aspås S 79 Fc30
Aspåsnäset S 79 Fc30
Aspatria GB 11 Eb17
Aspberget S 86 Ec38
Aspe E 55 Fb71
Aspeå S 80 Ha29
Aspeå S 80 Gc30
Aspeboda S 95 Fd39
Aspenes N 62 Gd10
Aspenstedt D 127 Dd38
Åspered S 102 Ed49
Asperen NL 124 Ba37
Asperg D 134 Cd48
Äsperöd S 110 Fa56
Aspet F 40 Ga56
Aspliden S 72 Ha23
Aspliden S 73 Hc24
Asplund S 72 Gc23
Aspnäs S 88 Gc32
Aspnes N 79 Fb27
Aspö S 95 Gb43
Aspö S 111 Fd54
As Pontes de García Rodríguez E 36 Bb54
Aspoús GR 190 Da84
Aspra I 166 Ed84
Aspremont F 42 Jd51
Aspres-sur-Buëch F 35 Jd50
Åspro GR 183 Bd77
Asprógia GR 183 Bb77
Asproklisiá GR 183 Bb80
Asprópirgos GR 189 Cb86
Áspros GR 183 Ca77
Asproválta GR 184 Cc78
Aspsele S 80 Gd28
Assamalla EST 98 La42
Assamstadt D 134 Da46
Assat F 40 Fc55
Assé-le-Bérenger F 28 Fc39
Assé-le-Boisne F 28 Fc38
Assemini I 169 Ca79
Assen NL 117 Bd34
Assenois B 132 Ba44
Assens DK 100 Dc22
Assens DK 108 Dc27
Assentoft DK 100 Dc23
Assérac F 27 Ec41
Asserbo DK 109 Eb24
Assergi I 156 Ed70
Assesse B 124 Ad42
Assier F 33 Gd51
Assikvere EST 99 Lb44
Ássiros GR 183 Cb77
Assisi I 156 Eb67
Åsskard N 77 Db31
Aßlar D 126 Cc42
Aßling D 143 Ea51
Asso I 149 Cc58
Asson F 40 Fc56
Assoro I 167 Fb85
Ássos GR 188 Ad81
Ássos GR 189 Bd86
Åsta N 86 Eb37
Åstad N 66 Fd15
Astaffort F 40 Ga53
Astakós GR 188 Ad84
Åstan N 77 Dd29
Astašova LV 107 Ld52
Aste EST 105 Jc46
Åsteby S 94 Ed40
Astee IRL 12 Bb23
Asten A 144 Fb51
Asten NL 125 Bb39
Astfeld I 143 Dd56
Asti I 148 Ca61
Aştileu RO 170 Cb57
Astipálea GR 197 Ea92
Åstol S 102 Eb48
Aston GB 16 Fa22
Aston GB 20 Fa27
Astorga E 37 Cb57
Åstorp S 110 Ed54
Astradamovka RUS 203 Fd10
Astráin E 39 Ec57
Åsträsk S 80 Hb26
Astromeritis CY 206 Ja96
Ástros GR 195 Bd88
Astrup DK 100 Dc19
Astrup DK 100 Dc22
Åstrup DK 108 Da24
Åstrup DK 108 Dc27
Astruptunet N 84 Cc35
Astryna BY 202 Dd13
Astudillo E 38 Db58
Asuaju RO 171 Cd55
Asuja EST 106 Kc46
Asūne LV 107 Ld52
Asuni I 169 Ca77
Asunta FIN 90 Ka33
Asuny PL 122 Jc30
Ásvanyráró H 145 Gd52
Asvestohóri GR 183 Cb78
Asvestópetra GR 183 Bb78
Ászár H 145 Ha53
Aszód H 146 Hd52
Aszófő H 145 Ha55
Atabey TR 186 Fd78
Atabey TR 199 Gc88
Atajate E 59 Cb76
Ataki RUS 107 Ma47
Atalánti GR 189 Ca84
Atalaya del Cañavate E 53 Eb67
Atanzón E 46 Dd64
Ataquines E 46 Cd62
Atarte E 60 Db75
Atašiene LV 107 Lb51
Atbükü TR 199 Gc92
Atça TR 187 Hb80
Atça TR 197 Fa88
Atea E 47 Ed62
Ateaş RO 170 Ca57
Ateca E 47 Ec61
Ateham GB 15 Ec24
Aţel RO 175 Db60
Ateleta I 161 Fa71
Atella I 161 Ga75
Atena Lucana I 161 Ga76
Atessa I 161 Fb71
Atháni GR 188 Ac83
Athboy IRL 9 Cc20
Áth Cinn IRL 8 Bc20
Athea IRL 12 Bb23
Athée F 31 Jc42
Athenry IRL 12 Bd21
Athéras GR 188 Ab84
Atherstone GB 16 Fa24
Athesans F 31 Ka40
Athienou CY 206 Jc97
Athies F 23 Ha33
Athíkia GR 195 Bd87
Athína GR 189 Cb86
Athis-de-l'Orne F 22 Fb37
Athleague IRL 8 Ca20
Athlone IRL 13 Ca21
Athy IRL 13 Cc22
Atid RO 172 Dd59
Atienza E 47 Ea62
Atina I 161 Fa72
Aţintiş RO 171 Db59
Atios E 36 Ba53
Atjaševo RUS 203 Fc10
Atla EST 105 Jb46
Atlanterra E 59 Ca78
Atlıhisar TR 193 Gc86
Åtlo N 78 Eb29
Atnbrua N 85 Ea35
Atnmoen N 85 Ea35
Åtran S 102 Ed51
Atrani I 161 Fb75
Åträsk S 73 Hc23
Åträsk S 73 Hc21
Atri I 157 Fa69
Atripalda I 161 Fc75
Atsalama EST 99 Lb42
Attáli GR 189 Cc84
Attendorn D 125 Cb40
Attenkirchen D 135 Ea49
Attersee A 143 Ed52
Attert B 132 Ba44
Attigny F 24 Hd34
Attimis I 150 Ed57
Attiökylä FIN 74 Kb24
Attleborough GB 21 Ga25
Attlebridge GB 17 Gb24
Attmar S 87 Gb33
Attnang-Puchheim A 144 Fa51
Åttonträsk S 80 Gc26
Attrup DK 100 Db21
Attsjö S 103 Fc52
Attu FIN 97 Jb40
Attvika N 66 Ga12
Åtvidaberg S 103 Ga47
Atzara I 169 Ca77
Atzendorf D 127 Ea38
Atzeneta del Maestrat E 54 Fc65
Au D 135 Ea49
Aub D 134 Db46
Aubagne F 42 Jd55
Aubange B 132 Ba45
Aubazine F 33 Gc49
Aubel B 125 Bb41
Aubenas F 34 Ja50
Aubenton F 24 Hd33
Aubepierre-sur-Aube F 30 Jb39
Aubergenville F 23 Gc36
Aubérive F 24 Hd35
Auberive F 30 Jb40
Aubeterre-sur-Dronne F 32 Fd49
Aubiat F 34 Hb46
Aubiet F 40 Ga54
Aubigné F 32 Fc46
Aubigny F 28 Ed44
Aubigny-au-Bac F 24 Hb32
Aubigny-en-Artois F 23 Gd32
Aubigny-sur-Nère F 29 Gd41
Aubin F 33 Gd51
Aubonne CH 140 Ba55
Aubrac F 34 Hb51
Aubusson F 33 Gd46
Auby F 23 Ha31
Auce LV 105 Jd52
Auch F 40 Ga54
Aucharnie GB 7 Ec08
Auchavan GB 7 Eb10
Auchel F 23 Gd31
Auchencairn GB 10 Ea17
Auchenmaig GB 10 Dc16
Auchentiber GB 10 Dd14
Auchronie GB 7 Ec10
Auchterarder GB 7 Ea12
Auchtermuchty GB 7 Eb12
Auchy-au-Bois F 23 Gd31
Aucun F 40 Fc56
Audenge F 32 Fa51
Audenhain D 127 Ec40
Auderville F 22 Ed34
Audevälja EST 98 Ka43
Audierne F 27 Db39
Audincourt F 31 Ka41
Audla EST 105 Jd46
Audlem GB 15 Ec23
Audru EST 106 Kb46
Audruicq F 21 Gc30
Audrupi LV 106 Kc52
Audun-le-Roman F 25 Jc34
Audun-le-Tiche F 25 Jc34
Aue D 135 Ec43
Auer I 150 Dd57
Auerbach D 135 Ea45
Auerbach D 135 Eb43
Auerbach D 135 Ed49
Auerswalde D 127 Ec42
Auetal D 126 Da37
Aufferville F 29 Ha39
Aufhausen D 135 Eb48
Aufles N 70 Fa22
Aufseß D 135 Dd45
Augan F 27 Ec40
Augé F 32 Fc45
Augerolles F 34 Hc47
Augerum S 111 Fd54
Aughacasla IRL 12 Ba24
Augher GB 9 Cc17
Aughils IRL 12 Ba24
Aughnacloy GB 9 Cc18
Aughrim IRL 13 Ca21
Aughrim IRL 13 Cd23
Augland N 93 Da46
Augmėnai LV 114 Kb55
Augsburg D 142 Dc50
Augsligatne LV 106 Kd49
Augstasils LV 107 Ld49
Augstkalne LV 106 Ka52
Augusta I 167 Fd87
Augustdorf D 126 Cd38
Auguste LV 113 Jc53
Augustenborg DK 108 Db28
Augustów PL 123 Ka31
Augustów PL 130 Jc39
Augustowo PL 123 Kb34
Augustusburg D 127 Ed42
Auho FIN 75 Kc23
Auiņi LV 105 Jc52
Aukan N 77 Db30
Aukland N 92 Cd47
Auklandshamn N 92 Ca41
Aukra N 76 Cd31
Aukrug D 118 Db31
Aukštadvaris LT 114 Kd58
Aukštelkai LT 114 Kb54
Aukštelkė LT 114 Ka54
Auktsjaur S 72 Ha22
Auleben D 127 Dd40
Auleja LV 107 Ld52
Aulendorf D 142 Cd51
Aulesti E 39 Eb55
Auletta I 161 Fd76
Aulla I 149 Cd63
Aullène F 154 Cb71
Aulnay F 32 Fc46
Aulnay-la-Riviere F 29 Gd39
Aulnay-sous-Bois F 23 Gd36
Aulnizeux F 24 Hc37
Aulnoye-Aymeries F 24 Hc32
Aulstad N 85 Dd37
Ault F 23 Gb33
Aultbea GB 4 Dc06
Aulum DK 100 Da23
Aulus-les-Bains F 40 Gb57
Auma D 127 Ea42
Aumale F 23 Gc34
Aumeisteri LV 106 La48
Aumetz F 25 Jc34
Aumont F 31 Jc43
Aumont-Aubrac F 34 Hc50
Aumühle D 118 Dc33
Aun N 66 Ga12
Aunay F 29 Gc38
Aunay-en-Bazois F 30 Hc42
Aunay-sur-Odon F 22 Fb36
Aune N 77 Dd30
Auneau F 29 Gc38
Aunebakksetra N 77 Dc31
Aunet N 78 Ec25
Aunet N 78 Ed26
Aunet N 78 Eb27
Aunet N 78 Ea29
Auneuil F 23 Gc35
Auning DK 101 Dd23
Aunslev DK 109 Dd27
Aups F 42 Ka53
Aura D 134 Da44
Aura FIN 89 Jc38
Aurach D 134 Db47
Aurachtal D 134 Dc46
Auray F 27 Ea41
Aurdal N 85 Dc38
Aure N 77 Db30
Aureskoski FIN 89 Jc34
Aurice F 39 Fb53
Aurich D 117 Cb32
Aurignac F 40 Ga55
Aurillac F 33 Ha50
Auriol F 42 Jd54
Aurisina I 151 Fa59
Auritz E 39 Ed56
Aurlandsvangen N 84 Cd38
Aurolzmünster A 143 Ed50
Auron F 43 Kc51
Aurons F 42 Jc53
Auronzo di Cadore I 143 Eb56
Aurora RO 181 Fc68
Auros F 32 Fc51
Aursfjordbotn N 67 Gc11
Aursmoen N 94 Eb41
Ausa Corno I 150 Ed59
Ausås S 110 Ed54
Auschwitz = Oświęcim PL 138 Hd44
Ausdal N 92 Cc44
Ausejo E 39 Eb58
Auşeu RO 171 Cc57
Auskarnes N 64 Ka05
Ausonia I 160 Ed73
Ausserferrera CH 142 Cd56
Ausserfragant A 143 Ec55
Außervillgraten A 143 Eb55
Aussonne F 40 Gb54
Austad N 92 Cd44
Austad N 92 Cc47
Austafjord N 78 Eb25
Austanå N 93 Da45
Austbø N 70 Ed21
Austbygda N 93 Db41
Austefjord N 84 Cc34
Austervika N 67 Gb13
Austevoll N 84 Ca40
Austhasselstrand N 92 Cb47
Austis I 169 Ca77
Austmarka N 94 Ec41
Austnes N 66 Ga12
Austnes N 76 Cc32
Austpollen N 66 Fd13
Austrått N 77 Dd29
Austre Amøy N 92 Ca43
Austreim N 84 Cb36
Austre Moland N 93 Db46
Austre Vikebygd N 92 Ca42
Austrheim N 84 Ca38
Austrumdal N 92 Cb45
Auterive F 40 Gc55
Auteuil F 23 Gd35
Autheuil-Authouillet F 23 Gb36
Authon F 42 Ka51
Authon-du-Perche F 29 Ga39
Authon-la-Plaine F 29 Gc38
Autilla del Pino E 46 Da59
Autio FIN 74 Kb24
Autio FIN 81 Jd31
Autio FIN 82 Kb31
Autionperä FIN 82 Ka30
Autol E 47 Ec59
Autrans F 35 Jc48
Autrèche F 29 Gb41
Autrey F 31 Jc41
Autricourt F 30 Ja39
Autry-le-Châtel F 29 Ha41
Autti FIN 74 Kb19
Auttoinen FIN 90 Kb36
Autun F 30 Hd43
Auvåg N 66 Fc13
Auverse F 28 Fd41
Auvers-sur-Oise F 23 Gd36
Auvillar F 40 Ga53
Auvillars-sur-Saône F 30 Jb42
Auvre F 24 Ja36
Auw bei Prüm D 133 Bc43
Auxerre F 30 Hc40
Auxi-le-Château F 23 Gd32
Auxon F 30 Hc39
Auxonne F 31 Jc42
Auxy F 30 Ja43
Auzances F 33 Ha46
Auzat-la-Combelle F 34 Hc48
Auziņas LV 106 Ka51
Auziņi LV 106 Kd51
Auziņi LV 107 Ld51
Åva FIN 97 Hd39
Ava S 80 Ha29
Avafors S 73 Hd21
Availles-Limouzine F 33 Ga46
Avaldsnes N 92 Bd42
Avallon F 30 Hc41
Avan S 73 Hd22
Avan S 73 Hd24
Avanäs S 80 Ha27
Avant-lès-Marcilly F 30 Hc38
Avant-lès-Remerupt F 30 Hd38
Ávas GR 185 Dd77
Avasjö S 79 Gb27
Avaträsk S 79 Ga27
Avaviken S 72 Gd22
Avcılar TR 186 Fa75
Avcılar TR 191 Eb82
Avcıoğlu TR 198 Fd91
Avdan TR 186 Ga80
Avdan TR 191 Ed83
Avdan TR 193 Gb82
Avdan TR 198 Fc89
Avdarma MD 177 Fd60
Avdebo DK 109 Eb25
Avdijivka UA 202 Ed13
Avdimou CY 206 Ja98
Ávdira GR 184 Db77
Avdoú GR 201 Db96
Avebury GB 20 Ed28
Åvedal N 92 Cb45
Åvedal N 92 Cc46
A Veiga E 36 Bc58
Aveiras de Cima P 50 Ab67
Aveiro P 44 Ac62
Avelengo I 142 Dc56
Avella I 161 Fb74
Avellanosa del Páramo E 38 Dc58
Avellino I 161 Fc75
Avenas F 34 Ja45
Avenches CH 141 Bc54
Avening GB 19 Ec27
Åvensor FIN 97 Ja40
Avereest NL 117 Bd35
Avernak By DK 108 Dc28
Avernay-Val-d'Or F 24 Hd36
A Ver-o-Mar P 44 Ac60
Aversa I 161 Fa74
Averton F 28 Fc38
Aves P 44 Ad60
Avesnes-le-Comte F 23 Gd32
Avesnes-lès-Aubert F 24 Hb32
Avesnes-sur-Helpe F 24 Hc32
Avessac F 27 Ec41
Avesta S 95 Ga41
Avetrana I 162 Hb76
Avezzano I 160 Ed71
Avgan TR 192 Fd86
Avgancık TR 192 Ga86
Avgerinós GR 182 Ba78
Avgó GR 195 Ca88
Avgorou CY 206 Jd97
Avía GR 194 Bb89
Avià E 41 Gd59
Aviano I 150 Eb58
Aviemore GB 7 Ea09
Avigliana I 148 Bc60
Avigliano I 161 Ga75
Avignon F 42 Jb53
Avignonet-Lauragais F 40 Gc55
Ávila E 46 Cd63
Avilés E 37 Cb54
Aviliai LT 115 Lb54
Avilley F 31 Jd41
Avinurme EST 99 Lb43
Avinyó E 49 Gd60
Avio I 149 Dc58
Avion F 23 Ha31
Avión E 36 Ba57
Avirey F 30 Hd39
Avis P 50 Ad68
Åvist FIN 81 Jb29
Avize F 24 Hc36
Avižieniai LT 123 Kc30
Avláki GR 189 Bd83
Avláki GR 197 Ec92
Avlémonas GR 195 Bd92
Avliótes GR 182 Aa79
Avlóna GR 189 Cb86
Avlonári GR 189 Cc85
Avö P 44 Ba64
Avoca IRL 13 Cd23
Avoch GB 5 Ea07
Avoine F 28 Fd42
Avola I 167 Fd88
Avord F 29 Ha43
Avoriaz F 35 Kb45
Avot F 30 Jb40
Avoudrey F 31 Ka42
Avrămeni RO 172 Ed54
Avrămești RO 176 Dd60
Avram Iancu RO 170 Ca58
Avram Iancu RO 171 Cc59
Avranches F 22 Fa37
Avren BG 185 Dd76
Avren BG 181 Fa71
Avrig RO 175 Db61
Avrillé F 28 Fb41
Avrillé F 32 Ed45
Avsallar TR 199 Hb92
Avtovac BIH 159 Hc67
Avtovo RUS 99 Mb39
Avvakajjo S 67 Ha17
Avvakko S 67 Hb17
Avvil FIN 69 Ka11
Avžže N 68 Ja11
Axalp CH 141 Ca55
Axamer Lizum A 143 Dd54
Axams A 143 Dd54
Axat F 41 Gd57
Axberg S 95 Fd43
Axel NL 124 Ab39
Axente Sever RO 175 Db60
Axford GB 20 Fa29
Axintele RO 176 Ec66
Axioúpoli GR 183 Ca76
Ax-les-Thermes F 41 Gd57
Axmarby S 87 Gb38
Axminster GB 19 Eb30
Axós GR 183 Bd77
Axós GR 200 Cd95
Axstedt D 118 Cd33
Axvall S 102 Fa47
Ayamonte E 58 Ba74
Ayancık TR 205 Fb19
Ayas I 148 Bd58
Ayaslar TR 193 Hb87
Ayaz E 36 Bb56
Ayazini TR 193 Gc84
Ayazkent TR 191 Ec83
Aydan TR 193 Gc82
Aydin TR 187 Hb77
Aydın TR 197 Ed88
Aydıncık TR 185 Dd80
Aydınkent = İbradı TR 199 Hb90
Aydınlar TR 186 Fb76
Aydınlar TR 187 Hb77
Aydınlar TR 191 Ed84
Aydınlı TR 186 Fd78
Aydınlı TR 193 Hb84
Aydoğdu TR 186 Ga80
Aydoğmuş TR 187 Ha80
Aydoğmus TR 198 Fd89
Ayen F 33 Gb49
Ayer CH 141 Bd56
Ayerbe E 39 Fb58
Ayguesvives F 40 Gc55
Aylesbury GB 20 Fb27
Aylesham GB 21 Gb29
Ayllón E 46 Dd61
Aylsham GB 17 Gb24
Aylton GB 15 Ec26
Aynac F 33 Gc50
Ayódar E 54 Fc66
Ayora E 54 Fa69
Ayr GB 10 Dd14
Ayrancı TR 192 Ga85
Ayron F 28 Fd44
Ayşebacı TR 192 Fa82
Aysgarth GB 11 Ed19
Äyskoski FIN 82 Kc30
Aystetten D 142 Dc50
Äystö FIN 89 Ja32
Ayton GB 11 Ed13
Ayton GB 17 Fc19
Aytré F 32 Fa46
Ayvacık TR 191 Ea82
Ayvacık TR 191 Ec85
Ayvacık TR 191 Ed85
Ayvacık TR 192 Ga85
Ayvacık TR 205 Fc20
Ayvalı TR 192 Fd82
Ayvalı TR 193 Hb83
Ayvalık TR 191 Eb83
Ayvalıpınar TR 199 Gd88
Ayvanpazarı TR 186 Ga79
Ayvatlar TR 191 Ec83
Ayvatlat TR 192 Fa82
Aywaille B 124 Ba42
Azaila E 48 Fb62
Azambuja P 50 Ab68
Azanja SRB 174 Bb65
Azannes F 24 Jb35
Azanúy E 48 Fd59
Azaruja P 50 Ba69
Azaryčy BY 202 Eb13
Azatlı TR 185 Eb76
Azay-le-Ferron F 29 Gb43
Azay-le-Rideau F 28 Fd42
Azé F 29 Gb40
Azeitada P 50 Ac67
Azincourt F 23 Gd31
Azinhal P 58 Ba74
Azinheira dos Barros P 50 Ac71
Azinhoso P 45 Bd61
Azıtepe TR 192 Fb86
Aziziye BG 185 Ed74
Azizler TR 192 Ga86
Aznakaevo RUS 203 Ga08
Aznalcázar E 59 Bd74
Aznalcóllar E 59 Bd73
Azoia P 44 Ab65
Azov RUS 205 Fc15
Azpeitia E 39 Eb55
Azuaga E 51 Cb71
Azuara E 47 Fa62
Azuel E 52 Da71
Azuga RO 176 Ea63
Ažulaukė LT 114 La57
Ažulolu Būda LV 114 Kb58
Azuoliniai LV 114 Kb59
Azuqueca de Henares E 46 Dd64
Azur F 39 Fa53
Azurara P 44 Ac60
Azy F 29 Ha42
Ažytėnai LV 114 Kb55
Azzano Decimo I 150 Eb58
Azzate I 148 Cb58

B

Ba SRB 159 Jc64
Baak NL 125 Bc37
Baal D 125 Bc40
Baalberge D 127 Ea39
Baamonde E 36 Bb54
Baar CH 141 Cb53
Baarland NL 124 Ab38
Baarle-Nassau B 124 Ad38
Baarlo NL 125 Bc39
Baarn NL 116 Bb36
Baasdorf D 127 Eb39
Baba Ana RO 176 Eb64
Babadag RO 177 Fc65
Babadağ TR 198 Fc88
Babadat TR 193 Hb82
Babadere TR 191 Ea82
Babaeski TR 185 Ec76
Babaevo RUS 202 Ec08
Băbăița RO 180 Dd67
Babakale TR 191 Ea82
Babaköy TR 192 Fa81
Băbana RO 175 Dc64
Babarc H 153 Hc58
Babasultan TR 192 Fd81
Babek BG 180 Dc72
Babenhausen D 134 Cd44
Babenhausen D 142 Db50
Băbeni RO 171 Da56
Băbeni RO 175 Db64
Babensham D 143 Eb51
Babiak PL 122 Ja30
Babiak PL 129 Hb37
Babiak PL 130 Hc37
Babica PL 139 Ka44
Babice PL 138 Hd44
Babići BIH 158 Gd64
Băbiciu RO 180 Db67
Babięta PL 122 Jb32
Babigoszcz PL 120 Fc32
Babilafuente E 45 Cc62
Babimost PL 128 Ga37
Babina Greda HR 153 Hc61
Babin Most KSV 178 Bb70
Babino RUS 99 Ld40
Babino Polje HR 158 Ha69
Babin Potok HR 151 Fd62
Babjak BG 184 Cd74
Babljak MNE 159 Ja68
Babócsa H 152 Gd58
Bábolna H 145 Ha52
Bábonymegyer H 145 Hb55
Baborów PL 137 Ha44
Baboszewo PL 122 Ja35
Babriškės LT 114 Kd59
Babrujsk BY 202 Eb13
Babrungas LT 113 Jc54
Babsk PL 130 Ja38
Babtai LV 114 Kb57
Babuk BG 181 Ed68
Babušnica SRB 179 Ca70
Bač SRB 153 Hd60
Băcani RO 177 Fa60
Bača pri Modreju SLO 151 Fa57
Bacares E 61 Ea75
Bacău RO 172 Ed59
Bačavani BIH 152 Gc61
Baccano I 160 Ea71
Baccarat F 25 Ka37
Baccealia MD 173 Ga59
Baccon F 29 Gc40
Baceno I 141 Ca56
Băcești RO 172 Ed58
Bach A 142 Db53
Bach D 135 Eb48
Bach F 40 Gc52
Bachant F 24 Hc32
Bacharach D 133 Ca44
Bachčysaraj UA 205 Fa18
Bachmač UA 202 Ed14
Bachórz PL 139 Ka44
Bachórzec PL 139 Kb44
Bachotek PL 122 Hc33
Băcia RO 175 Cc61
Bačina SRB 178 Bc67
Băcioi MD 173 Fd58
Baciu RO 171 Da58
Baciuty PL 123 Kb34
Back GB 4 Db05
Bäck S 103 Fb46
Backa S 87 Fc38
Backa S 96 Ha41
Backa S 102 Eb49
Bäckaby S 103 Fc50
Backaland GB 5 Ec02
Bačka Palanka SRB 153 Ja60
Backaryd S 111 Fd53
Bačka Topola SRB 153 Ja58
Backberg S 95 Gb39
Backbodarna S 95 Fc40
Bäckby FIN 81 Jb28
Backe S 79 Ga28
Bäcke S 94 Ec45
Bäckebo S 103 Ga52
Bäckefors S 94 Ec45
Backen S 87 Gb32
Backen S 87 Ga33
Backgränd FIN 97 Jd40
Bački Breg SRB 153 Hd58
Bački Brestovac SRB 153 Hd59
Bački Jarak SRB 153 Jb60
Bačkininkai LT 114 Kc58
Bački Petrovac SRB 153 Ja60
Bački Sokolac SRB 153 Ja58
Bäckmark S 72 Gb23
Backnang D 134 Cd48
Bäcknäs S 72 Gd23
Bačko Dobro Polje SRB 153 Ja59
Bačko Gradište SRB 153 Jb59
Bačko Novo Selo SRB 153 Hd60
Bačko Petrovo Selo SRB 153 Jb59
Bačkovo BG 184 Db74
Bäckseda S 103 Fc50
Bäckträsk S 73 Hc22
Băcleș RO 175 Cc65
Bacoli I 161 Fa75
Bacor Olivar E 61 Dd74
Bacova Mahala BG 180 Dc69
Bacquepuis F 23 Gb36
Bácsalmás H 153 Hd57
Bácsbokod H 153 Hd57
Bácsszentgyörgy H 153 Hd58
Bacton GB 21 Ga25
Bacup GB 16 Ed20
Bad Abbach D 135 Ea48
Badachro GB 4 Db07
Badacsonytomaj H 145 Ha55
Bad Aibling D 143 Ea52
Badajoz E 51 Bc69
Badalona E 49 Ha61
Badalucco I 43 La52
Badarán E 38 Ea58
Bad Arolsen D 126 Cd40
Bad Aussee A 144 Fa53
Bad Bederkesa D 118 Cd32
Bad Bentheim D 117 Ca36
Badbergen D 117 Cc35
Bad Bergzabern D 133 Ca47
Bad Berka D 127 Dd41
Bad Berleburg D 126 Cc40
Bad Berneck im Fichtelgebirge D 135 Ea44
Bad Bertrich D 133 Bd43

Bad Bevensen – Balsthal

Bad Bevensen D 118 Dc34
Bad Bibra D 127 Ea40
Bad Birnbach D 143 Ec50
Bad Blankenburg D 127 Dd42
Bad Bleiberg A 144 Fa56
Bad Blumau A 144 Ga54
Bad Bocklet D 134 Db43
Bad Bodenteich D 118 Dc35
Bad Boll D 134 Da49
Bad Brambach D 135 Eb44
Bad Bramstedt D 118 Db31
Bad Breisig D 125 Ca42
Bad Brückenau D 134 Da43
Bad Buchau D 142 Cd51
Badby GB 20 Fa25
Bad Camberg D 133 Cb43
Badcaul GB 4 Dc06
Bad Colberg-Heldburg D 134 Dc43
Badderen N 63 Hc08
Bad Deutsch-Altenburg A 145 Gc51
Bad Doberan D 119 Eb31
Bad Driburg D 126 Cd38
Bad Düben D 127 Ec39
Bad Dürkheim D 133 Cb46
Bad Dürrenberg D 127 Eb40
Bad Dürrheim D 141 Cb51
Badeborn D 127 Dd38
Bądecz PL 121 Gc34
Bad Eilsen D 126 Cd37
Badellou E 48 Ga60
Bad Elster D 135 Eb44
Badelunda S 95 Gb42
Bademağacı TR 199 Gc90
Bademler TR 191 Eb86
Bademli TR 185 Dd80
Bademli TR 191 Eb84
Bademli TR 191 Eb86
Bademli TR 192 Fa83
Bademli TR 193 Ha84
Bademli TR 198 Ga89
Bademli TR 199 Gd88
Bademli TR 199 Hb89
Bademli TR 199 Hb90
Bad Ems D 133 Ca43
Baden A 145 Gb51
Baden CH 141 Cb52
Baden-Baden D 133 Cb48
Bad Endbach D 126 Cc41
Badendiek D 119 Eb32
Bad Endorf D 143 Eb51
Badenhausen D 126 Db38
Badenscoth GB 7 Ec08
Badenweiler D 141 Bd51
Baderna HR 151 Fa61
Badersleben D 127 Dd38
Badesi I 168 Ca74
Bad Essen D 117 Cc36
Bad Feilnbach D 143 Ea52
Bad Frankenhausen D 127 Dd40
Bad Freienwalde D 120 Fb35
Bad Friedrichshall D 134 Cd47
Bad Fusch A 143 Ec54
Bad Füssing D 143 Ed50
Bad Gandersheim D 126 Db38
Bad Gastein A 143 Ec54
Bad Gleichenberg A 144 Ga55
Bad Gögging D 135 Ea48
Bad Goisern A 143 Ed52
Bad Gottleuba-Berggießhübel D 128 Fa42
Bad Griesbach D 143 Ed50
Bad Grund D 126 Db38
Bad Hall A 144 Fb51
Bad Harzburg D 126 Dc38
Bad Heilbrunn D 143 Dd52
Bad Herrenalb D 133 Cb48
Bad Hersfeld D 126 Da41
Bad Hindelang D 142 Db53
Bad Hofgastein A 143 Ec54
Bad Homburg D 134 Cc43
Bad Honnef D 125 Bd42
Bad Hönningen D 125 Ca42
Badia I 143 Ea56
Badia Calavena I 149 Dc59
Badia Gran E 57 Hb68
Badia Polesine I 150 Dd61
Badia Prataglia I 156 Dd65
Badia Tedalda I 156 Ea65
Bad Iburg D 125 Cb37
Bădiceni MD 173 Fb54
Badicul Moldovenesc MD 177 Fb61
Badingen D 127 Ea36
Badirga TR 186 Fc80
Bad Ischl A 143 Ed52
Badje-Sohppar S 68 Hc14
Bad Karlshafen D 126 Da39
Bad Kemmeriboden CH 141 Ca54
Bądki PL 121 Hb32
Bad Kissingen D 134 Db44
Bad Kleinen D 119 Ea32
Bad Kleinkirchheim A 144 Fa55
Bad Klosterlausnitz D 127 Ea41
Bad Kohlgrub D 142 Dc52
Bad König D 134 Cd45
Bad Königshofen D 134 Dc43
Bad Kösen D 127 Ea41
Bad Köstritz D 127 Eb41
Bądkowo PL 121 Hb35
Bad Kreuzen A 144 Fc50
Bad Kreuznach D 133 Ca44
Bad Krozingen D 141 Bd51
Bad Laasphe D 126 Cc41
Bad Laer D 126 Cc37
Bad Langensalza D 126 Dc41
Bad Lauchstädt D 127 Ea40
Bad Lausick D 127 Ec41
Bad Lauterberg D 126 Dc39
Bad Leonfelden A 144 Fb50
Bad Liebenstein D 126 Db42
Bad Liebenwerda D 127 Ed40
Bad Liebenzell D 134 Cc48
Bad Lippspringe D 126 Cd38
Badljevina HR 152 Gd59
Bad Lobenstein D 135 Ea43
Bad Marienberg D 125 Cb42
Bad Meinberg, Horn- D 126 Cd38
Bad Mergentheim D 134 Da46
Badminton GB 19 Ec28
Bad Mitterndorf A 144 Fa53
Bad Münder D 126 Da37
Bad Münster-Ebernburg D 133 Ca45
Bad Münstereifel D 125 Bd42
Bad Muskau D 128 Fc39
Bad Nauheim D 134 Cc43
Bad Neuenahr-Ahrweiler D 125 Bd42
Bad Neustadt D 134 Db43
Bad Oeynhausen D 126 Cd37
Badolato I 164 Gc82
Badolato Marina I 164 Gc82
Badolatosa E 60 Cd74
Bad Oldesloe D 118 Dc32
Badonviller F 25 Ka37
Bad Orb D 134 Cd43
Badovinci SRB 153 Ja62
Bad Peterstal-Griesbach D 133 Cb49
Bad Pyrmont D 126 Da38
Bad Radkersburg A 144 Ga56
Bad Ragaz CH 142 Cd54
Bad Rappenau D 134 Cd47
Bad Reichenhall D 143 Ec52
Bad Rippoldsau-Schapbach D 133 Cb49
Bad Rodach D 134 Dc43
Bad Rothenfelde D 126 Cc37
Bad Saarow-Pieskow D 128 Fb37
Bad Sachsa D 126 Dc39
Bad Säckingen D 141 Ca52
Bad Salzdetfurth D 126 Db37
Bad Salzschlirf D 126 Da42
Bad Salzschlirf D 126 Da42
Bad Salzuflen D 126 Cd37
Bad Salzungen D 126 Db42
Bad Sankt Leonhard im Lavanttal A 144 Fc55
Bad Sassendorf D 126 Cc39
Bad Saulgau D 142 Cd51
Bad Schallerbach A 144 Fa50
Bad Schandau D 128 Fb42
Bad Schmiedeberg D 127 Ec39
Bad Schönau A 145 Gb53
Bad Schönborn D 134 Cc47
Bad Schussenried D 142 Cd51
Bad Schwalbach D 133 Cb43
Bad Schwartau D 119 Dd31
Bad Schwarzsee CH 141 Bc55
Bad Segeberg D 118 Dc31
Bad Sobernheim D 133 Ca45
Bad Soden D 134 Cc44
Bad Soden-Salmünster D 134 Cd43
Bad Sooden-Allendorf D 126 Db40
Bad Staffelstein D 135 Dd44
Bad Steben D 135 Ea43
Bad Suderode D 127 Dd39
Bad Sulza D 127 Ea41
Bad Sülze D 119 Ec31
Bad Tatzmannsdorf A 145 Gb54
Bad Teinach-Zavelstein D 134 Cc48
Bad Tennstedt D 126 Dc41
Bad Tölz D 143 Dd52
Bad Überkingen D 134 Da49
Badules E 47 Ed62
Bad Urach D 134 Cd49
Bad Vellach A 144 Fb56
Bad Vilbel D 134 Cc43
Bad Vöslau A 145 Gb51
Bad Waldsee D 142 Da51
Bad Wiessee D 143 Ea52
Bad Wildbad D 133 Cb48
Bad Wildungen D 126 Cd40
Bad Wilsnack D 119 Eb35
Bad Wimpfen D 134 Cd47
Bad Windsheim D 134 Db46
Bad Wörishofen D 142 Db51
Bad Wurzach D 142 Da51
Bad Zell A 144 Fc50
Bad Zwesten D 126 Cd41
Bad Zwischenahn D 118 Cc33
Baek D 119 Eb34
Bække DK 108 Da26
Bækmarksbro DK 100 Cd23
Bælum DK 100 Dc22
Baena E 60 Da73
Baerenthal F 25 Kb35
Baesweiler D 125 Bc41
Baeza E 52 Dc72
Bafra TR 205 Fb19
Bagà E 41 Gd58
Băgaciu RO 175 Db60
Bagaladi I 164 Ga84
Bagamér H 147 Kb52
Bağarası TR 197 Ed88
Bagart PL 122 Hc31
Bagaslaviškis LT 114 Kd56
Bağbaşı TR 192 Ga85
Bagdononys LT 114 Kd58
Bågede S 79 Fc27
Bâgé-le-Châtel F 34 Jb45
Bagenalstown IRL 13 Cc23
Bagenkop DK 109 Dd29
Bages F 41 Hb57
Baggböle S 80 Hb28
Baggbrod S 95 Fd42
Baggetorp S 95 Ga45
Bagheria I 166 Ed84
Bagienice PL 123 Jd32
Bağıllı TR 193 Gd87
Bağıllı TR 199 Gd88
Bağırganlı TR 187 Gb77
Bağkonak TR 193 Ha87
Baglad H 145 Gb56
Bağlarbaşı TR 193 Ha86
Bagley GB 15 Eb23
Bağlıağaç TR 198 Fd92
Baglicy RUS 99 Ld45
Bagn N 85 Dc38
Bagnac-sur-Célé F 33 Gd51
Bagnaia I 156 Ea70
Bagnara Calabra I 164 Ga83
Bagnarola I 150 Dd62
Bagnasco I 148 Bd63
Bagnères-de-Bigorre F 40 Fd56
Bagnères-de-Luchon F 40 Ga57
Bagneux-la-Fosse F 30 Hd39
Bagni Contursi I 161 Fd75
Bagni del Masino I 149 Cd57
Bagni di Craveggia I 148 Cb57
Bagni di Lucca I 155 Db64
Bagni di Mondragone I 161 Fa74
Bagni di Petriolo I 155 Dc67
Bagni di Rabbi I 142 Dc56
Bagni di Stigliano I 160 Ea71
Bagni di Tivoli I 160 Eb71
Bagni di Vinadio I 148 Bb63
Bagni San Cataldo I 161 Ga75
Bagnity PL 122 Hd31
Bagno I 161 Ga72
Bagno di Romagna I 156 Ea65
Bagnoles-de-l'Orne F 28 Fc38
Bagnoli di Sopra I 150 Ea60
Bagnoli Irpino I 161 Fc75
Bagnolo Mella I 149 Da59
Bagnolo Piemonte I 148 Bc61
Bagnols F 33 Ha48
Bagnols-en Forêt F 43 Kb54
Bagnols-les-Bains F 34 Hc51
Bagnols-sur-Cèze F 42 Jb52
Bagnone I 149 Cd63
Bagnoregio I 156 Ea69
Bagny PL 123 Kb32
Bågø By DK 108 Db27
Bagod H 145 Gc55
Bagojë AL 182 Ab75
Bagolino I 149 Db58
Bagolyirtás H 146 Ja51
Bagotoji LV 114 Kb58
Bağözü TR 187 Hb80
Bagrationovsk RUS 122 Ja30
Bagrdan SRB 174 Bc66
Bağsaray TR 199 Gc89
Báguena E 47 Ed62
Bagüés E 39 Fa58
Bağyurdu TR 191 Ed86
Bahabón de Esgueval E 46 Dc60
Bahadınlı TR 191 Ec82
Bahadır TR 192 Ga85
Bahadırlar TR 192 Fc87
Baharlar TR 191 Eb82
Bahçeağlı TR 186 Fa76
Bahçecik TR 187 Gb79
Bahçecik TR 192 Fa86
Bahçecik TR 193 Ha83
Bahçedere TR 191 Eb82
Bahçedere TR 191 Ec84
Bahçeköy TR 185 Eb78
Bahçeköy TR 186 Fa76
Bahçekuyu TR 193 Ha81
Bahçeli TR 191 Ea82
Bahçeyaka TR 197 Fa90
Bahçıvanlar TR 199 Gd89
Bahillo (Loma del Ucieza) E 38 Da57
Bahmut MD 173 Fb57
Bahna RO 172 Ec58
Bahnea RO 171 Dc59
Bahovica BG 180 Db70
Bahrdorf D 127 Dd36
Bahrenborstel D 126 Cd36
Bahrendorf D 127 Ea38
Bahşayış TR 186 Fc77
Bahu MD 173 Fc56
Baia I 161 Fa75
Baia RO 172 Eb56
Baia RO 177 Fc65
Baia de Aramă RO 175 Cc63
Baia de Criş RO 175 Cc60
Baia de Fier RO 175 Da63
Baia delle Zagare I 162 Gb72
Baia Domizia I 161 Fa74
Baia Mare RO 171 Da55
Baiano I 161 Fb74
Baiardo I 43 Kd52
Baia Sardinia I 168 Cb73
Baia Sprie RO 171 Da55
Băicoi RO 176 Ea64
Băiculeşti RO 175 Dc64
Baides E 47 Ea62
Baienfurt D 142 Cd51
Baierbrunn D 143 Dd51
Baiersbronn D 133 Cb49
Baiersdorf D 135 Dd46
Baierz D 142 Da51
Baigneaux F 29 Gc39
Baigneux-les-Juifs F 30 Ja41
Baile an Fheirtearaigh IRL 12 Ad24
Baile an Mhóta IRL 8 Bd18
Baile an Róba IRL 8 Bc20
Baile an Sceilg IRL 12 Ad25
Baile Átha IRL 13 Cc22
Baile Átha an Rí IRL 12 Bd21
Baile Átha Cliath IRL 13 Cd21
Baile Átha Fhirdhia IRL 9 Cd19
Baile Átha Luain IRL 13 Ca21
Baile Átha Troim IRL 9 Cc20
Băile Bixad RO 171 Da54
Băile Borşa RO 171 Dc55
Baile Brigín IRL 9 Cd20
Baile Chláir IRL 12 Bc21
Băile Felix RO 170 Cb57
Băile Govora RO 175 Db64
Băile Herculane RO 174 Cb64
Baile Locha Riach IRL 12 Bd21
Baile Mhic Andáin IRL 13 Cb24
Baile Mhistéala IRL 12 Bd24
Baile Mór GB 6 Da11
Bailén E 52 Db72
Baile na Finne IRL 8 Ca16
Baile na Lorgan IRL 9 Cd19
Băile Olăneşti RO 175 Db63
Băileşti RO 179 Cc67
Baile Tuşnad RO 176 Ea60
Baile Uí Fhiacháin IRL 8 Bc19
Baile Ui Mhatháin IRL 9 Cb20
Bailieborough IRL 9 Cc19
Baillé F 28 Fa38
Bailleau-le-Pin F 29 Gb38
Bailleul F 21 Ha30
Bailo E 39 Fb58
Bailyhaugh GB 6 Da10
Bailyhaugh GB 9 Da14
Baimaclia MD 173 Fd59
Baimaclia MD 177 Fc61
Baiñas E 36 Ac55
Bainbridge GB 11 Ed18
Bain-de-Bretagne F 28 Ed40
Baindt D 142 Da51
Bains F 34 Hd49
Bains-les-Bains F 31 Jd39
Bainton GB 17 Fc20
Baio E 36 Ac54
Baiona E 36 Ac58
Bairro P 50 Ac66
Bais F 28 Fc39
Baiso I 149 Db63
Băişoara RO 171 Cd58
Baisogala LV 114 Kb55
Băiţa RO 175 Cc60
Băiţa de Sub Codru RO 171 Cd55
Băiuş MD 177 Fc60
Băiuţ RO 171 Db55
Baix F 34 Jb50
Baja H 153 Hd57
Bajáansenye H 145 Gb55
Baja de Arieş RO 171 Cd59
Bajāri LV 114 La53
Bajč SK 145 Hb51
Bajćsa H 152 Gc57
Bajdyty PL 122 Jb30
Bajevka RUS 113 Ja58
Bajgora KSV 178 Bb70
Bajina Bašta SRB 159 Ja64
Bajkal BG 180 Db68
Bajki-Zalesie PL 123 Ka33
Bajlovce MK 178 Bd72
Bajlovo BG 179 Cd71
Bajmok SRB 153 Ja58
Bajna H 146 Hc52
Bajorai LT 114 La53
Bajovo Polje MNE 159 Hd67
Bajram Curr AL 159 Jc69
Bajša SRB 153 Ja58
Bak H 145 Gc55
Baka SK 145 Gd51
Bakacak TR 185 Ec80
Bakałarzewo PL 123 Ka30
Bakar HR 151 Fb60
Bakdemirler TR 187 Gd79
Bakel NL 125 Bb38
Bakewell GB 16 Ed22
Bakır TR 191 Ed84
Bakırköy TR 186 Fb80
Bakka N 92 Cb46
Bakka N 93 Db41
Bakkafjörður IS 3 Bc04
Bakkagerði IS 3 Bc05
Bakke N 84 Cb40
Bakke N 92 Cb46
Bakke N 93 Dd42
Bakke N 93 Db45
Bakkeby N 63 Hb09
Bakkejord N 62 Gc10
Bakkejord N 67 Gb13
Bakken N 77 Dc29
Bakken N 78 Eb30
Bakken N 79 Fb27
Bakketun N 71 Fb22
Bakkeveen NL 117 Bd33
Bakko N 93 Db41
Baklalı TR 186 Fc77
Baklan TR 192 Ga87
Baklançakırlar TR 198 Fd88
Baklankuyucak TR 198 Ga88
Baklia N 85 Dc36
Bakonybél H 145 Ha54
Bakonycsernye H 145 Hb53
Bakonygyepes H 145 Ha54
Bakonyjákó H 145 Ha54
Bakonykoppány H 145 Ha53
Bakonypéterd H 145 Ha53
Bakonyszombathely H 145 Ha53
Bąków PL 129 Hb41
Bąkowa Góra PL 130 Ja41
Baksan RUS 205 Ga17
Baksjöberg S 80 Gd27
Baksjöliden S 80 Gd27
Baktakék H 146 Jc50
Baktalórántháza H 147 Kb51
Baktsjaur S 72 Ha23
Bakum D 117 Cc35
Bakvattnet S 79 Fb28
Bäl S 104 Ha49
Bala GB 15 Ea23
Bala RO 171 Dc58
Bala RO 175 Cc64
Balaban TR 186 Fa75
Balaban TR 186 Fc77
Balaban TR 187 Gb78
Balabancık TR 185 Eb77
Balabancık TR 185 Ec78
Bălăbăneşti MD 173 Fd58
Bălăbăneşti RO 177 Fa61
Balabanlı TR 185 Ed77
Balabanlı TR 191 Ea82
Balabanlı TR 192 Fa87
Balabanovo RUS 202 Ed11
Balabanu MD 177 Fc61
Bălăceanu RO 176 Ed63
Balaci RO 175 Dd66
Bălăciţa RO 175 Cc66
Balaciu RO 176 Ec66
Balaguer E 48 Ga60
Balahna RUS 203 Fb09
Balahoncevo RUS 107 Mb50
Balaklija UA 203 Fa14
Balakovo RUS 203 Ga11
Bălan RO 171 Cd56
Bălan RO 172 Ea59
Balanegra E 61 Dd76
Bălăneşti MD 173 Fb57
Bălăneşti RO 175 Cd63
Balaruc-les-Bains F 41 Hd54
Bålaryd S 103 Fc49
Bălăşeşti MD 173 Fc56
Bălăşeşti RO 177 Fa61
Balašiha RUS 203 Fa10
Balasineşti MD 172 Ed54
Balašov RUS 203 Fc12
Balassagyarmat H 146 Hd51
Balástya H 146 Jb56
Balata di Baida I 166 Eb84
Balata di Modica I 167 Fc87
Balatcık TR 191 Ed87
Balatdanişment TR 192 Fd82
Balaţi RO 172 Ed57
Balatina MD 173 Fa55
Balatonakali H 145 Ha55
Balatonakarattya H 145 Hb54
Balatonalmádi H 145 Hb54
Balatonboglár H 145 Ha55
Balatonbozsok H 145 Hb55
Balatonföldvár H 145 Ha55
Balatonfüred H 145 Ha55
Balatonfűzfő H 145 Hb54
Balatongyörök H 145 Gd55
Balatonkenese H 145 Hb54
Balatonkeresztúr H 145 Gd56
Balatonlelle H 145 Ha55
Balatonmagyaród H 145 Gd56
Balatonszabadi H 145 Hb55
Balatonszárszó H 145 Ha55
Balatonszemes H 145 Ha55
Balatonszentgyörgy H 145 Gd56
Balatonudvari H 145 Ha55
Balatonújlak H 145 Gd56
Bălăureşti MD 173 Fb58
Bălăuşeri RO 171 Dc59
Balazote E 53 Eb69
Balazuc F 34 Ja51
Balbeggie GB 7 Eb11
Balbieriškis LT 114 Kc59
Balbigny F 34 Hd46
Balbiši LV 107 Ld51
Balblair GB 5 Ea07
Balboa E 37 Bd56
Balbriggan IRL 9 Cd20
Balc RO 171 Cc56
Bâlca RO 172 Eb54
Balcani RO 172 Ec59
Bălcăuţi MD 173 Fa53
Bălcăuţi RO 172 Eb55
Balceşti RO 175 Da65
Balcı TR 191 Ed81
Balcı TR 193 Gd87
Balcıdamı TR 193 Gb85
Balčik BG 181 Fb70
Balçık TR 186 Ga78
Balçıkhisar TR 187 Gb80
Balçıkhisar TR 193 Gc86
Balçıkhisar TR 193 Gd82
Balcılar TR 185 Eb80
Balcılar TR 191 Ed86
Balcombe GB 20 Fc29
Balderschwang D 142 Da53
Baldichieri d'Asti I 148 Bd61
Baldock GB 20 Fc26
Baldone LV 106 Kc51
Baldos P 44 Bb62
Baldovineşti RO 175 Da66
Baldovineşti RO 177 Fb63
Bale HR 151 Fa61
Baleix F 40 Fc55
Baleizão P 50 Ad71
Balen B 124 Ba39
Băleni RO 176 Ea65
Băleni RO 177 Fb62
Balenos LT 113 Jd53
Balerma E 61 Dd76
Băleşti RO 175 Cc63
Băleşti RO 176 Ed63
Balestrand N 84 Cc36
Balestrate I 166 Eb84
Balf H 145 Gc52
Balfour GB 5 Ec03
Balfron GB 7 Dd12
Balgale LV 105 Jd50
Bălgaranovo BG 180 Eb71
Bălgarene BG 180 Db70
Bălgarene BG 180 Dc69
Bălgarevo BG 181 Fb70
Bălgari BG 186 Fa74
Bălgarin BG 185 Ea74
Bălgarovo BG 181 Ed72
Bălgarska poljana BG 185 Ea74
Bălgarski Izvor BG 179 Da70
Bălgarsko Slivovo BG 180 Dd69
Balge D 118 Da35
Bälgviken S 95 Gb44
Bali GR 200 Cd95
Balice PL 138 Ja44
Baligród PL 139 Kb46
Balik BG 181 Fa68
Balıkesir TR 192 Fa82
Balıklı TR 185 Ed79
Balıklıçeşme TR 185 Ec80
Balıklıdere TR 192 Fb81
Balıklıova TR 191 Ea86
Bălileşti RO 175 Dc64
Balinderry IRL 13 Ca22
Bälinge S 73 Hd22
Bälinge S 96 Gc41
Bälinge S 96 Gc45
Bälinge S 102 Ec48
Bälinge S 110 Fa54
Balingen D 142 Cc50
Bälingsta S 96 Gc42
Balinţ RO 174 Ca60
Balintore GB 5 Ea07
Baliskės LV 114 Kb58
Balivanich GB 6 Cd07
Balizac F 32 Fb51
Balje D 118 Da31
Baljevac BIH 151 Ga62
Baljevac SRB 178 Ba68
Balk NL 116 Bb34
Balka DK 111 Fd58
Balkanski BG 180 Eb69
Balkány H 147 Ka51
Balkasodis LT 114 Kc59
Balkbrug NL 117 Bd35
Balkı TR 193 Hb87
Balkıca TR 198 Fd89
Balla IRL 8 Bc19
Ballaban AL 182 Ac77
Ballabio Inferiore I 149 Cd58
Ballachullish GB 6 Dc10
Ballagh IRL 12 Bc24
Ballaghaderreen IRL 8 Bd19
Ballancourt-sur-Essone F 29 Gd38
Ballangen N 66 Ga14
Ballantrae GB 10 Dc16
Ballao I 169 Cb78
Ballasalla GB 10 Dc19
Ballasviken S 71 Ga20
Ballater GB 7 Ec09
Balle DK 101 Dd23
Balle Bhuirne IRL 12 Bb25
Ballefors S 103 Fb46
Ballen DK 109 Dd25
Ballenstedt D 127 Dd39
Balleroy F 22 Fb36
Ballerup DK 109 Ec25
Ballesteros E 52 Db68
Ballesteros de Calatrava E 52 Db69
Ballı TR 185 Ec78
Ballıbucak TR 199 Gd90
Ballıca TR 186 Ga78
Ballickmoyler IRL 13 Cc23
Ballıhisar TR 193 Hb83
Ballık TR 193 Gb86
Ballık TR 198 Fd91
Ballina IRL 8 Bc18
Ballina IRL 12 Bd23
Ballinafad IRL 8 Ca19
Ballinagleragh IRL 8 Ca18
Ballinakill IRL 13 Cb23
Ballinalee IRL 9 Cb20
Ballinamore IRL 9 Cb19
Ballinascarty IRL 12 Bc26
Ballinasloe IRL 13 Ca21
Ballinclea IRL 13 Cd22
Ballincollig IRL 12 Bd26
Ballincurrig IRL 12 Bd25
Ballindine IRL 8 Bd20
Balling DK 100 Da22
Ballingarry IRL 12 Bc24
Ballingarry IRL 13 Ca22
Ballingarry IRL 13 Cb23
Ballingeary IRL 12 Bc26
Ballingslöv S 110 Fa54
Ballingurteen IRL 12 Bc26
Ballinhassig IRL 12 Bd26
Ballinlough IRL 8 Bd19
Ballino I 149 Db58
Ballinrobe IRL 8 Bc20
Ballinspittle IRL 12 Bc26
Ballintogher IRL 8 Ca18
Ballinunty IRL 13 Ca23
Ballinure IRL 13 Ca24
Ballıpınar TR 186 Fa79
Ballivor IRL 9 Cc20
Ballobar E 48 Fd61
Balloch GB 10 Dd13
Balloch GB 10 Dd15
Ballon F 28 Fd39
Ballon IRL 13 Cc23
Balloo Cross Roads GB 10 Db18
Ballota E 37 Ca54
Ballots F 28 Fa40
Ballsh AL 182 Ab77
Ballsnes N 66 Ga14
Ballstad N 66 Fb15
Ballvengland IRL 12 Bc23
Ballybay IRL 9 Cc18
Ballybofey IRL 9 Cb16
Ballyboghill IRL 13 Cd21
Ballybogy GB 9 Cd15
Ballybrittas IRL 13 Cc22
Ballybunnion IRL 12 Bb23
Ballycanew IRL 13 Cd24
Ballycastle GB 9 Da15
Ballycastle IRL 8 Bc17
Ballyclare GB 9 Da17
Ballyclare IRL 8 Ca20
Ballycolla IRL 13 Cb22
Ballyconneely IRL 8 Ba20
Ballyconnell IRL 9 Cb18
Ballycorick IRL 12 Bc23
Ballycotton IRL 13 Ca26
Ballydangan IRL 13 Ca21
Ballydehob IRL 12 Bb26
Ballydesmond IRL 12 Bb24
Ballyduff IRL 12 Bb23
Ballyduff IRL 13 Ca25
Ballyfad IRL 13 Cd23
Ballyfeard IRL 12 Bd26
Ballyferriter IRL 12 Ad24
Ballygalley GB 9 Da16
Ballygarrett IRL 13 Cd24
Ballygawley GB 9 Cc17
Ballyglass IRL 8 Bc19
Ballygowan GB 9 Da17
Ballygrant GB 6 Da13
Ballyhahill IRL 12 Bc23
Ballyhalbert GB 10 Db17
Ballyhaunis IRL 8 Bd19
Ballyhean IRL 8 Bc19
Ballyheerin IRL 9 Cb15
Ballyheige IRL 12 Ba24
Ballyhillin IRL 9 Cc14
Ballyhooly IRL 12 Bd25
Ballyhornan GB 10 Db18
Ballyjamesduff IRL 9 Cc19
Ballykeel GB 9 Da18
Ballylanders IRL 12 Bd24
Ballylongford IRL 12 Bb23
Ballylooby IRL 13 Ca24
Ballylynan IRL 13 Cc22
Ballymacarbry IRL 13 Ca25
Ballymack IRL 13 Cb24
Ballymacoda IRL 13 Ca26
Ballymacrevan GB 9 Da17
Ballymahon IRL 9 Cb20
Ballymena GB 9 Da16
Ballymoe IRL 8 Bd20
Ballymoney GB 9 Cc16
Ballymoney GB 9 Cd15
Ballymore IRL 9 Cb20
Ballymore Eustace IRL 13 Cd22
Ballymote IRL 8 Bd18
Ballymurphy IRL 13 Cc24
Ballynabola IRL 13 Cc24
Ballynacarrigy IRL 9 Cb20
Ballynacourty IRL 13 Ca25
Ballynagore IRL 13 Cb21
Ballynagree IRL 12 Bc25
Ballynahinch GB 9 Da18
Ballynahown IRL 12 Bb21
Ballynahown IRL 13 Ca21
Ballynakilla IRL 12 Ba26
Ballynakilly Upper IRL 12 Ba25
Ballynamona IRL 12 Bd25
Ballynamult IRL 13 Ca25
Ballynana IRL 12 Ad24
Ballynaskreena IRL 12 Bb23
Ballyneety IRL 12 Bd23
Ballynure GB 9 Da16
Ballypatrick IRL 13 Cb24
Ballyporeen IRL 13 Ca24
Ballyquin IRL 12 Ba24
Ballyragget IRL 13 Cb23
Ballyroebuck IRL 13 Cd23
Ballyroon IRL 12 Ba26
Ballysadare IRL 8 Ca18
Ballyshannon IRL 8 Ca17
Ballyshannon IRL 13 Cc22
Ballysteen IRL 12 Bc23
Ballytoohy IRL 8 Bb19
Ballyvaughan IRL 12 Bc21
Ballyvourney IRL 12 Bb25
Ballyvoy GB 9 Da15
Ballywater GB 10 Db17
Ballywilliam IRL 13 Cc24
Balmacara GB 4 Da05
Balmahmut TR 193 Gc85
Balmaseda E 38 Dd55
Balmazújváros H 147 Jd52
Balme I 148 Bc59
Balmedie GB 7 Ed09
Balmerino GB 7 Eb11
Balminnoch GB 10 Dc16
Balmonte E 37 Bd54
Balmuccia I 148 Ca58
Balnafoich GB 7 Ea08
Balnahard GB 6 Da11
Balnapaling GB 5 Ea07
Balneario de Panticosa E 40 Fc57
Balninkai LT 114 La56
Baloira E 36 Ad56
Bálojotnjálbmi FIN 68 Ja13
Balören TR 187 Gb78
Baloteşti RO 176 Eb65
Baloži LV 106 Kb51
Balquhidder GB 7 Dd11
Balrath IRL 9 Cd20
Balş RO 175 Da66
Balsa P 44 Bb60
Balşa RO 175 Cd60
Balsa de Ves E 54 Fa68
Balsareny E 49 Gd60
Balsfjord N 62 Gd10
Balsham GB 20 Fd26
Balsicas E 55 Fa73
Balsièges F 34 Hc51
Balsjö S 80 Ha28
Balsorano Nuovo I 160 Ed72
Balsovo RUS 99 Lc45
Bålsta S 96 Gc43
Balsthal CH 141 Bd53

Balsupiai – Bebertal

Balsupiai LV 114 Kb59
Balta UA 204 Ec16
Balta Albă RO 176 Ed63
Balta Berilovac SRB 179 Ca69
Balta Doamnei RO 176 Eb65
Baltanás E 46 Db59
Baltar E 36 Bb58
Baltasound GB 5 Fa03
Băltata MD 173 Fd58
Băltătești RO 172 Ec57
Balta Verde RO 174 Cb66
Bălteni RO 173 Fa59
Bălteni RO 175 Cd64
Bălțești RO 176 Eb64
Bălti MD 173 Fb55
Baltijsk RUS 113 Hd59
Baltimore IRL 12 Bb27
Baltinava LV 107 Ld49
Baltinglass IRL 13 Cc22
Bal'tino RUS 107 Ma50
Baltoji Vokė LT 114 La58
Bałtów PL 131 Jd41
Baltrušaičiai LT 113 Jd57
Balugães P 44 Ad59
Băluseni RO 172 Ed55
Balvan BG 180 Dd70
Balve D 125 Cb39
Balvi LV 107 Lc49
Balya TR 191 Ed82
Balze I 156 Ea65
Balzers FL 142 Cd54
Balzo I 156 Ed68
Bambalió GR 188 Ba83
Bamberg D 134 Dc45
Bamble N 93 Dc44
Bamburgh GB 11 Fa14
Bamford GB 16 Ed22
Bammental D 134 Cc46
Bampton GB 19 Ea29
Banafjäl S 80 Ha30
Banagher IRL 13 Ca21
Banarlı TR 185 Ed77
Banatska Dubica SRB 174 Bb62
Banatska Palanka SRB 174 Bc64
Banatska Topola SRB 153 Jc58
Banatska Topola SRB 174 Bb60
Banatski Despotovac SRB 174 Bb62
Banatski Dvor SRB 153 Jc59
Banatski Karlovac SRB 174 Bc63
Banatsko Aranđelovo SRB 170 Bb59
Banatsko Karađorđevo SRB 153 Jc59
Banatsko Novo Selo SRB 174 Bb63
Banatsko Veliko Selo SRB 174 Bb60
Banaz TR 192 Ga85
Banbridge GB 9 Da18
Banbury GB 20 Fa26
Banca RO 177 Fb60
Band RO 171 Db59
Bande E 36 Ba58
Bandeira E 36 Ba56
Bandenitz D 119 Ea33
Bandholm DK 109 Ea28
Bandirma TR 186 Fa80
Bando I 150 Ea62
Bandol F 42 Jd55
Bandon IRL 12 Bc26
Băneasa RO 177 Fb61
Băneasa RO 180 Ea67
Băneasa RO 181 Fa67
Bañeres E 55 Fb70
Bånes N 63 Hc08
Bănești RO 176 Ea64
Banevo BG 181 Ed72
Banff GB 5 Ec07
Bångnäs S 79 Fd25
Bangor GB 10 Db17
Bangor GB 15 Dd22
Bangor IRL 8 Bb18
Bangor-is-y-coed GB 15 Eb23
Bangsund N 78 Ec26
Bangueses E 36 Ba58
Banica BG 179 Cd69
Banie PL 120 Fc34
Banie Mazurskie PL 123 Jd30
Baniewice PL 120 Fc34
Baniska BG 180 Ea69
Bănișor RO 171 Cc57
Banište BG 179 Cb71
Bănița RO 175 Cd62
Banja BG 184 Cc74
Banja BG 179 Da72
Banja BG 180 Db72
Banja BG 180 Ea72
Banja BG 181 Fa72
Banja BIH 159 Ja65
Banja SRB 159 Ja66
Banja e Kukës AL 182 Ad79
Banja Koviljača SRB 153 Hd63
Banjaloka SLO 151 Fc60
Banja Luka BIH 152 Gd62
Banjani SRB 153 Jb62
Banja Vrućica BIH 152 Hb62
Banje KSV 178 Ba69
Banjica KSV 178 Ad70
Banjica SRB 159 Jc68
Banjište MK 182 Ad74
Banjska KSV 178 Ba69
Bankekind S 103 Ga47
Bankeryd S 103 Fb48
Bankja BG 179 Cc71
Banloc RO 174 Bc62
Bannalec F 27 Dd40
Bännbäck S 95 Gb41
Bannegon F 29 Ha43
Bannes F 24 Hc37
Bannes F 30 Jb39
Bannewitz D 128 Fa41
Bannockburn GB 7 Ea12
Bannoncourt F 24 Jb36
Bannow IRL 13 Cc25
Banon F 42 Jd52
Bañón E 47 Fa63
Banos de Alicún de las Torres E 61 Dd74
Baños de Benasque E 40 Ga57
Baños de Fuente de la Encina E 52 Db72
Baños de la Encina E 52 Db71
Baños de Molgas E 36 Bb58
Baños de Montemayor E 45 Cb64
Baños de Río Tobía E 38 Ea58
Baños de Valdearados E 46 Dc60
Baños de Valdeganga E 53 Eb66
Bánov CZ 137 Ha48
Bánov SK 145 Hb51
Banova Jaruga HR 152 Gc60
Bánovce nad Bebravou SK 137 Hb49
Banovci Dunav SRB 153 Jc61
Banovići BIH 153 Hc63
Bánréve H 146 Jb50
Bansha IRL 13 Ca24
Bansin D 120 Fb31
Bansjo MK 183 Ca75
Banská Bystrica SK 138 Hd49
Banská Stiavnica SK 146 Hc50
Banské SK 139 Jd48
Bansko BG 184 Cc74
Banstead GB 20 Fc29
Banteer IRL 12 Bc25
Banteln D 126 Db37
Bantheville F 24 Ja35
Bantry IRL 12 Bb26
Bantzenheim F 31 Kc39
Bañuelos de Bureba E 38 Dd58
Bañugues E 37 Cc53
Bānūži LV 106 Kd49
Banwell GB 19 Eb28
Banyalbufar E 56 Ha67
Banyoles E 49 Hb59
Banyuls-sur-Mer F 41 Hb58
Banzi I 162 Gb75
Banzkow D 119 Ea33
Bapaume F 23 Ha32
Bár H 153 Hc57
Bar MNE 163 Ja71
Bar UA 204 Eb15
Băra RO 172 Ed58
Bara RO 174 Ca60
Bara S 110 Ed56
Barabany RUS 107 Mb50
Baraboi MD 173 Fa54
Baracak TR 191 Ed82
Bărăganu RO 177 Fa65
Bărăganu RO 181 Fc67
Baragem da Aguieira P 44 Ad63
Barağı TR 192 Ga84
Barago E 38 Da55
Barahona E 47 Ea62
Barajas E 46 Dc64
Barajas de Melo E 47 Ea65
Barakaldo E 38 Ea55
Baraklı TR 193 Gb87
Baranavičy BY 202 Ea13
Baránd H 147 Jd53
Barane KSV 178 Ad71
Baranivka UA 204 Eb15
Baranjsko Petrovo Selo HR 153 Hc59
Barano d'Ischia I 161 Fa75
Baranovka LV 107 Ld50
Baranów PL 129 Ha40
Baranów PL 130 Ja37
Baranów PL 131 Ka39
Baranowo PL 122 Jc31
Baranowo PL 122 Jc33
Baranowo PL 129 Gc36
Baranów Sandomierski PL 131 Jd42
Baranyajenő H 152 Hb57
Baraolt RO 176 Ea61
Baraque-Saint-Jean F 41 Ha52
Baraqueville F 41 Ha52
Bårared S 102 Ed52
Barásoain E 39 Ed57
Bărăști RO 175 Db65
Bărăteaz RO 174 Bc60
Barbacena P 51 Bb68
Barbadillo E 45 Cb62
Barbadillo de Herreros E 46 Dd59
Barbadillo del Mercado E 46 Dd59
Barbadillo del Pez E 46 Dd59
Barbalimpia E 53 Eb66
Barban HR 151 Fa61
Barbantes E 36 Ba57
Barbarano Vicentino I 150 Dd60
Barbaros TR 185 Dd80
Barbaros TR 185 Ed78
Barbaros TR 191 Ea86
Barbarušince SRB 178 Bd71
Barbaste F 40 Fd52
Barbastro E 48 Fd59
Barbate E 59 Bd77
Bărbătești RO 175 Cd64
Bărbătești RO 175 Da63
Barbatovac SRB 178 Bb69
Barbâtre F 27 Ec43
Barbazan F 40 Ga56
Barbeitos E 37 Bd55
Bārbele LV 106 Kc52
Barber Booth GB 16 Ed22
Barberino di Mugello I 155 Dc64
Barberino Val d'Elsa I 155 Dc66
Barbezieux-Saint-Hilaire F 32 Fc48
Barbières F 35 Jc49
Barbing D 135 Eb48
Barbizon F 29 Ha38
Bärbo S 95 Gb45
Bárboles E 47 Fa60
Barbonne-Fayel F 24 Hc37
Barbotan-les-Thermes F 40 Fc53
Barbu N 93 Db46
Bărbulețu RO 176 Dd64
Barbullush AL 163 Jb71
Barbuñales E 48 Fc59
Barby D 127 Eb38
Barca E 47 Ea61
Bârca RO 179 Cd67
Barca de Alva P 45 Bc62
Barcaggio F 154 Cc67
Barcaldine GB 6 Dc11
Bărcănești RO 176 Ec65
Barcani RO 176 Eb62
Barcarrota E 51 Bc70
Barcea RO 177 Fa62
Barcellona Pozzo di Gotto I 167 Fd84
Barcelona E 49 Ha61
Barcelonne-du-Gers F 40 Fc54
Barcelonnette F 43 Kb51
Barcelos P 44 Ad60
Bárcena de Ebro E 38 Db56
Bárcena del Monasterio E 37 Ca54
Bárcena de Pie de Concha E 38 Db55
Bárcena Mayor E 38 Db55
Barchem NL 125 Bd37
Barchín del Hoyo E 53 Eb67
Barčiai LT 114 Kd59
Barcial del Barco E 45 Cb59
Barciany PL 122 Jb30
Barcillonnette F 42 Jd51
Barcin PL 121 Ha35
Barcis I 150 Eb57
Barco P 44 Ba64
Barcones E 47 Ea61
Barcos P 44 Bb61
Barcs H 152 Ha58
Barcus F 39 Fb55
Barczewko PL 122 Ja31
Barczewo PL 122 Ja31
Bard I 148 Bd58
Bârda RO 174 Bd62
Bardakçı TR 192 Fb84
Bardakçı TR 193 Gd83
Bardakçılar TR 191 Ec81
Bardal N 70 Fa21
Bardallur E 47 Fa60
Bardar MD 173 Fc58
Bărdarski Geran BG 179 Da68
Barde DK 108 Da24
Bardejov SK 139 Jd46
Bardejovské Kúpele SK 139 Jd46
Bårdesø DK 109 Dd26
Bardi I 149 Cd62
Bardineto I 148 Bd63
Bard-le-Régulier F 30 Hd42
Bardney GB 17 Fc22
Bardo PL 137 Gc43
Bardolino I 149 Db59
Bardonecchia I 148 Ba60
Bardowick D 118 Dc33
Bardsea GB 11 Eb19
Bardsey GB 16 Fa20
Bardu bygdetun N 67 Gc12
Bardujord N 67 Gc12
Bare BIH 159 Hd65
Bare MNE 159 Jb68
Bare SRB 174 Bb66
Băreanești RO 176 Eb65
Bäreberg S 102 Ed47
Barèges F 40 Fd56
Bärenbad A 143 Ea54
Barenburg D 118 Cd35
Barendrecht NL 124 Ad37
Bärenstein D 128 Fa42
Bärenstein D 135 Ed43
Barentin F 23 Ga34
Barenton F 28 Fb38
Barevo BIH 152 Gd63
Bärfendal S 102 Eb46
Barfleur F 22 Fa34
Barford GB 17 Ga24
Barford Saint Martin GB 20 Ed29
Barga I 155 Da64
Bargas E 52 Db66
Bârgăuani RO 172 Ec58
Barge I 148 Bc61
Bargême F 43 Kb53
Bargemon F 43 Kb53
Bargen, Helmstadt- D 134 Cd46
Bargeshagen D 119 Eb31
Bargfeld-Stegen D 118 Dc32
Barghe I 149 Db59
Bărghis RO 175 Dc61
Bargłówka PL 137 Hb44
Bargłów Kościelny PL 123 Ka31
Bargoed GB 19 Ea27
Bargrennan GB 10 Dd16
Bargstedt D 118 Da33
Bargteheide D 118 Dc32
Bargullas AL 182 Ac77
Bar Hill GB 20 Fd25
Bari I 162 Gd74
Barić SRB 153 Jc62
Barić Draga HR 151 Fd63
Barice SRB 174 Bc62
Barilović HR 151 Fd60
Barinas E 55 Fa71
Båring DK 108 Dc26
Bari Sardo I 169 Cc78
Barisciano I 156 Ed70
Barisey-la-Côte F 25 Jc37
Barjac F 34 Hc51
Barjac F 34 Ja51
Bårjås S 72 Ha18
Barjols F 42 Ka54
Bark D 118 Dc31
Bărkač BG 180 Db69
Barkåker N 93 Dd43
Barkarö S 95 Gb43
Barkava LV 107 Lb50
Barkelsby D 108 Db29
Barkeryd S 103 Fc49
Barkestad N 66 Fc12
Barking GB 20 Fd28
Barklainiai LT 114 Kc55
Barkowo PL 120 Fd32
Barkowo PL 121 Gc32
Barkston GB 16 Fb23
Barkway GB 20 Fd26
Bârla RO 175 Dc66
Barla TR 193 Gd87
Bârlad RO 177 Fa60
Barleben D 127 Ea37
Bar-le-Duc F 24 Jb37
Barles F 42 Ka51
Barletta I 162 Gb73
Barlinek PL 120 Fd35
Barlingbo S 104 Ha49
Barlo D 125 Bd37
Barlow GB 16 Fa22
Barmash AL 182 Ad78
Barmouth GB 15 Dd24
Barmstedt D 118 Db32
Barna IRL 12 Bc21
Bârna RO 174 Ca61
Barnaderg IRL 8 Bd20
Barnard Castle GB 11 Ed18
Barnarp S 103 Fb49
Bärnau D 135 Eb45
Barnave F 35 Jc50
Barnay F 30 Hd42
Barne-Åsaka S 102 Ed47
Barneberg D 127 Dd37
Barnes GB 20 Fc28
Barnesmore IRL 9 Cb16
Barnetby le Wold GB 17 Fc21
Barneveld NL 116 Bb36
Barneville-Carteret F 22 Ed35
Barnewitz D 127 Ec36
Barney GB 17 Ga23
Barnim PL 120 Fc34
Bärnkopf A 144 Fc50
Barnoldswick GB 16 Ed20
Bârnova RO 173 Fa58
Barnówko PL 120 Fc35
Barnsley GB 16 Fa21
Barnsley GB 20 Ed27
Barnstädt D 127 Ea40
Barnstaple GB 19 Dd29
Barnstorf D 118 Cd35
Barntrup D 126 Cd38
Baron F 23 Ha36
Baroncea MD 173 Fb54
Baronissi I 161 Fc75
Baronville F 25 Ka36
Baroševac SRB 153 Jc63
Barösund FIN 98 Ka40
Barovo MK 183 Bd75
Barqueiro P 44 Ad65
Barqueiros P 44 Ac60
Barquilla de Pinares E 45 Cc65
Barr F 25 Kb37
Barracas E 54 Fb66
Barrachina E 47 Fa63
Barraco E 46 Da64
Barra de Mira P 44 Ac63
Barrado E 45 Cb65
Barraduff IRL 12 Bb25
Barrafranca I 167 Fa86
Barral (Castrelo de Miño) E 36 Ba57
Barrancos P 51 Bb71
Barranco Velho P 58 Ad74
Barranda E 61 Ec72
Barrax E 53 Eb69
Barrea I 161 Fa72
Barreiro P 50 Aa69
Barrême F 42 Ka52
Barret-le-Bas F 42 Jd51
Barrhead GB 10 Dd13
Barrhill GB 10 Dc16
Barriada de Jarana E 59 Bd76
Barriada Las Canteras E 61 Eb75
Barrière de Champlon B 132 Ba43
Barrigone IRL 12 Bc23
Barri Mar E 54 Fc67
Barrio de Nuestra Señora E 37 Cc57
Barrit DK 108 Dc25
Barro E 38 Da54
Barrô P 44 Ba61
Barroca P 44 Ba64
Barroças e Taias P 36 Ad58
Barros E 38 Db55
Barroselas P 44 Ac59
Barrosinha P 50 Ac70
Barrou F 29 Ga42
Barrowby GB 16 Fb23
Barrow-in-Furness GB 11 Eb19
Barrow-upon-Soar GB 16 Fa24
Barruç AL 178 Ad73
Barruecopardo E 45 Bd62
Barruelo de Santullán E 38 Db56
Barry GB 19 Ea28
Bârsa RO 170 Cb59
Bârsana RO 171 Db54
Bârsănești RO 176 Ec60
Barsanges F 33 Gd48
Bârsău de Sus RO 171 Cd55
Barsbüttel D 118 Dc32
Bårse DK 109 Eb27
Barsebäckshamn S 110 Ed55
Barsele S 72 Gc24
Bârsești RO 176 Ec61
Barsinghausen D 126 Da36
Barsinghausen D 126 Da37
Barsk MNE 159 Jb67
Barßel D 117 Cb33
Barst F 25 Ka35
Barstyčiai LT 113 Jc53
Bar-sur-Aube F 30 Ja38
Bar-sur-Seine F 30 Hd39
Barsviken S 88 Gc33
Barszczewo PL 123 Kb33
Bārta LV 113 Jb53
Bartąg PL 122 Ja32
Bartenheim F 31 Kc40
Bartenstein D 134 Da46
Barth D 119 Ec30
Bartholomä D 134 Da48
Bartın TR 205 Fa20
Bartne PL 139 Jd45
Bartniki PL 130 Ja38
Bartninkai LT 114 Ka59
Bartołtły Wielkie PL 122 Jb31
Barton GB 16 Ed24
Barton Mills GB 20 Fd25
Barton-upon-Humber GB 17 Fc21
Bartoszyce PL 122 Jb30
Barty PL 122 Hd31
Baru RO 175 Cc62
Baruchowo PL 130 Hc36
Barum D 118 Dc34
Barumini I 169 Ca78
Barun RUS 203 Ga14
Baruth/Mark D 128 Fa38
Barutin BG 184 Da75
Barva S 95 Gb43
Barvas GB 4 Da04
Barvaux B 124 Ba42
Barvaux-Condroz B 124 Ba42
Barver D 118 Cd35
Bårvik N 63 Hc06
Barvinkove UA 205 Fb15
Barwice PL 121 Gb32
Barwinek PL 139 Jd46
Barwino PL 121 Gc30
Barycz PL 139 Ka44
Baryczka PL 139 Ka44
Baryš RUS 203 Fd10
Barysav BY 202 Eb12
Bârza RO 175 Da66
Barzago I 149 Cc58
Bârzava RO 174 Ca60
Barzdai LV 114 Kb58
Barzdžiūnai LT 123 Kc30
Bârzija BG 179 Cc69
Bârzina BG 179 Cd68
Barzio I 149 Cd58
Bås N 93 Da45
Bašaid SRB 174 Bb61
Başalma MD 177 Fc61
Basarabeasca MD 177 Fd60
Basarabi RO 181 Fc67
Başarap TR 193 Gd82
Basarbovo BG 180 Ea68
Basardilla E 46 Db62
Basauri E 38 Ea55
Basavžže N 65 Kb06
Bâsca Chiojdului RO 176 Eb63
Başcalia MD 177 Fd60
Bàscara E 49 Hb59
Başçayır TR 192 Fa87
Baschi I 156 Ea68
Baschurch GB 15 Eb24
Basconcillos del Tozo E 38 Db57
Bascones de Ojeda E 38 Da57
Bascov RO 175 Dc64
Basdahl D 118 Da33
Basdorf D 119 Ed35
Basel CH 141 Bd52
Båseland N 93 Da46
Baselga di Piné I 149 Dc57
Baselice I 161 Fc73
Băsești RO 171 Cd55
Başgöze TR 199 Hb88
Båsheim N 93 Dc41
Basi LV 105 Jb51
Başıbüyük TR 186 Fd78
Basicò I 167 Fc84
Basigo de Bakio E 38 Ea55
Basildon GB 20 Fd28
Basiliano I 150 Ec58
Basilique de Hennebont F 27 Ea40
Bašin SRB 174 Bb65
Bäsinge S 95 Ga41
Basingstoke GB 20 Fa29
Basırlar TR 193 Gc84
Bäsjösätern S 86 Fa38
Baška CZ 137 Hb46
Baška HR 151 Fc61
Baskas FIN 81 Ja30
Baskemölla S 111 Fb56
Baške Oštarije HR 151 Fd63
Başköy TR 191 Ed87
Başköy TR 192 Fc81
Başköy TR 192 Fd83
Başköy TR 193 Hb87
Bäsksele S 79 Gb26
Bäsksjö S 79 Gb26
Başlamiş TR 192 Fa84
Başlar TR 199 Ha90
Baslow GB 16 Fa22
Başmakçı TR 199 Gb88
Bäsna S 95 Fd39
Basonys LT 114 Kc58
Başören TR 193 Gc82
Başören TR 193 Gc86
Başören TR 193 Gd81
Basovizza I 151 Fa59
Başpınar TR 199 Gb90
Bassac F 32 Fc47
Bassacutena I 168 Cb73
Bassano del Grappa I 150 Dd59
Basse D 119 Ec31
Bassella E 48 Gb59
Bassenthwaite GB 11 Eb17
Bassevuovdde N 68 Jc11
Bassignac F 33 Ha48
Bassignac-le-Haut F 33 Gd49
Bassilac F 33 Ga49
Bassingham GB 16 Fb22
Bassou F 30 Hc40
Bassoues F 40 Fd54
Bassum D 118 Cd35
Bast FIN 81 Jb28
Båstad N 94 Eb42
Båstad S 110 Ed53
Baštanka UA 204 Ed16
Bastardo I 156 Eb68
Bastasi BIH 152 Gb63
Bästdal S 88 Gc35
Bastelica F 154 Cb70
Bastheim D 134 Db43
Bastia F 154 Cc68
Bastia Umbra I 156 Eb67
Båstlund DK 108 Da25
Bastnäs S 94 Ed41
Bastogne B 132 Ba43
Baston GB 17 Fc24
Bastorf D 119 Eb31
Bastuträsk S 80 Hb25
Bastuträsk S 80 Ha28
Bastuträsk by S 80 Hb25
Bastwick GB 17 Gb24
Baszków PL 129 Gd39
Băta BG 179 Da72
Bata BG 181 Ed72
Báta H 153 Hc57
Bata MNE 159 Hd69
Bata RO 174 Ca60
Batajnica SRB 153 Jc61
Batajsk RUS 205 Fc15
Batak BG 184 Da74
Batak BG 180 Dd69
Batakiai LT 113 Jd56
Batalha P 50 Ab66
Bátamonostor H 153 Hd57
Bățani RO 176 Ea60
Batanovci BG 179 Cb71
Batăr RO 170 Ca58
Bătarci RO 171 Cd54
Båtas S 79 Fd25
Bátaszék H 153 Hc57
Batea E 48 Fd62
Båteng N 64 Ka07
Baterno E 52 Cd69
Bath GB 19 Ec28
Bathgate GB 10 Ea13
Bathmen NL 117 Bc36
Batida H 146 Jc56
Batignano I 155 Dc68
Batıköy TR 197 Ec89
Batin BG 180 Dd68
Batina HR 153 Hc58
Batır MD 173 Fd59
Bátka SK 146 Jb50
Batković BIH 153 Hd62
Batlava KSV 178 Bb70
Batley GB 16 Ed20
Batnfjordsøra N 77 Da31
Batočina SRB 174 Bb66
Bátonyterenye H 146 Ja51
Batorz PL 131 Kb41
Batoș RO 171 Dc58
Bátovce SK 146 Hc50
Batovo BG 181 Fa70
Batowo PL 120 Fc34
Bătrâna RO 174 Cb61
Batrge SRB 178 Ad69
Batrina HR 152 Ha60
Båtsfjord N 65 Kc05
Batsi GR 190 Da87
Båtsjaur S 72 Gb21
Båtskärsnäs S 73 Jb21
Battaglia Terme I 150 Dd60
Battenberg D 126 Cc41
Bätterkinden CH 141 Bd53
Battipaglia I 161 Fc76
Battle GB 20 Fd30
Battonya H 147 Jd56
Batulci BG 179 Da70
Batuša SRB 174 Bc65
Båtvik S 73 Hc24
Bátya H 146 Hd56
Batyk H 145 Gd55
Batyrevo RUS 203 Fd09
Baud F 27 Ea40
Baudreville F 29 Gc38
Bauduen F 42 Ka53
Baugé F 28 Fc41
Baugy F 29 Ha42
Bauladu I 169 Bd77
Baulmes CH 141 Bb54
Bauma CH 142 Cc53
Baumbach, Ransbach- D 125 Ca42
Baumber GB 17 Fc22
Baume-les-Doubs F 31 Ka41
Baume-les-Messieurs F 31 Jc43
Baumholder D 133 Bd45
Baunatal D 126 Da40
Baunei I 169 Cc77
Bauņi LV 106 Kd47
Baurci MD 177 Fc61
Baurci-Moldoveni MD 177 Fb61
Baurene BG 179 Cd69
Bauska LV 106 Kc52
Băuțar RO 174 Cb62
Bautzen D 128 Fb41
Bavanište SRB 174 Bb63
Bavay F 24 Hc32
Bavella F 154 Cb72
Bavigne L 133 Bb44
Bavorov CZ 136 Fa48
Bawdeswell GB 17 Ga24
Bawdsey GB 21 Gb26
Bawinkel D 117 Cb35
Bawnboy IRL 9 Cb18
Bawtry GB 16 Fb21
Bayat TR 192 Ga87
Bayat TR 193 Gb83
Bayat TR 193 Gd84
Bayat TR 205 Fb20
Bayatbademler TR 199 Gc90
Bayburt TR 205 Ga19
Baye F 24 Hc37
Bayerbach D 135 Eb49
Bayerbach D 143 Ed50
Bayerisch Eisenstein D 135 Ed48
Bayeux F 22 Fb35
Bayındır TR 186 Ga79
Bayındır TR 191 Ed86
Bayındır TR 199 Gb91
Bayındır TR 199 Gc89
Bayır TR 197 Fa90
Bayır TR 197 Fa91
Bayırköy TR 185 Eb79
Bayırköy TR 186 Ga80
Bayırköy TR 187 Gb80
Bayırköy TR 197 Fa91
Bayo E 37 Cb54
Bayon F 25 Jd37
Bayonne F 39 Ed54
Bayons F 42 Ka51
Bayraktar TR 187 Gb78
Bayralar TR 198 Ga92
Bayramdere TR 185 Ed75
Bayramdere TR 186 Fb80
Bayramiç TR 191 Eb81
Bayramlı TR 185 Ec76
Bayramoğlu TR 186 Fd78
Bayramşah TR 192 Ga81
Bayramşah TR 192 Ga83
Bayreuth D 135 Ea45
Bayrischzell D 143 Ea52
Bayubas de Abajo E 47 Ea61
Baza E 61 Ea74
Băzăn BG 180 Ea68
Bazán E 52 Dc70
Bazarnye Mataki RUS 203 Ga09
Bazarnyi Karabulak RUS 203 Fd11
Bazas F 32 Fc51
Bazenheid CH 142 Cc53
Baziaș RO 174 Bc64
Bazicourt F 23 Ha35
Bazie AL 159 Ja70
Bazièges F 40 Gc55
Bazna RO 175 Db60
Bazoches F 30 Hc41
Bazoches-les-Gallerandes F 29 Gd39
Bazoches-sur-Hoëne F 28 Fd38
Bazolles F 30 Hc42
Bazoques F 23 Ga36
Bazoș RO 174 Bd61
Bazouges-la-Perouse F 28 Ed38
Băzovec BG 179 Cd68
Bazsi H 145 Gd55
Bazzano I 149 Dc63
Beaconsfield GB 20 Fb28
Beal IRL 12 Bb23
Bealach an Doirín IRL 8 Bd19
Bealach Conglais IRL 13 Cc22
Bealach Féich IRL 9 Cb16
Bealaha IRL 12 Bb23
Bealalaw Bridge IRL 12 Ba25
Béal an Átha IRL 8 Bc18
Béal an Átha Móir IRL 9 Cb19
Béal an Mhuirthead IRL 8 Bb17
Béal Átha an Ghaorthaidh IRL 12 Bb26
Béal Átha hAmhnais IRL 8 Bd19
Béal Átha na Muice IRL 8 Bd19
Béal Átha na Sluaighe IRL 13 Ca21
Béal Átha Seanaidh IRL 8 Ca17
Béal Deirig IRL 8 Bc17
Bealdovuobmi FIN 68 Jb13
Bealnablath IRL 12 Bc26
Beaminster GB 19 Eb30
Beanntrai IRL 12 Bb26
Béard F 30 Hb43
Beardsen GB 10 Dd13
Beare Green GB 20 Fc29
Beariz E 36 Ba57
Bearna IRL 12 Bc21
Béar Tairbirt IRL 9 Cb18
Beas E 59 Bc73
Beasain E 39 Eb56
Beas de Segura E 53 Dd71
Beateberg S 103 Fb46
Beatenberg CH 141 Bd55
Beaucaire F 42 Jb53
Beaucamps-le-Vieux F 23 Gc33
Beauchamps F 22 Fa37
Beauchamps F 23 Gb33
Beauchastel F 34 Jb50
Beauche F 23 Ga37
Beauchêne F 22 Fb37
Beaufay F 28 Fd39
Beaufort F 35 Ka46
Beaufort IRL 12 Bb25
Beaufort L 133 Bb44
Beaugency F 29 Gc40
Beaujeu F 31 Jc41
Beaujeu F 34 Ja45
Beaujeu F 42 Ka51
Beaulard I 148 Bb60
Beaulieu F 23 Ga37
Beaulieu F 29 Ha41
Beaulieu GB 20 Fa30
Beaulieu-sur-Dordogne F 33 Gc50
Beauly GB 7 Dd08
Beaumaris GB 15 Dd22
Beaumesnil F 22 Fa37
Beaumesnil F 23 Ga36
Beaumetz-lès-Loges F 23 Ha32
Beaumont B 124 Ac42
Beaumont F 25 Jc36
Beaumont-de-Lomagne F 40 Gb53
Beaumont-du-Gâtinais F 29 Ha39
Beaumont-du-Périgord F 33 Ga50
Beaumont-en-Argonne F 24 Ja34
Beaumont-Hague F 22 Ed34
Beaumont-Hamel F 23 Ha33
Beaumont-la-Ronce F 29 Ga41
Beaumont-le-Roger F 23 Ga36
Beaumont-lès-Valence F 34 Jb50
Beaumont-sur-Oise F 23 Gd36
Beaumont-sur-Sarthe F 28 Fd39
Beaumont-sur-Vingeanne F 30 Jb41
Beaune F 30 Ja42
Beaune-la-Rolande F 29 Gd39
Beaupréau F 28 Fa42
Beauquesne F 23 Gd33
Beauraing B 132 Ad43
Beaurainville F 23 Gc31
Beauregard F 40 Gc52
Beaurepaire F 34 Jb48
Beaurières F 35 Jc50
Beauvais F 23 Gd35
Beauval F 23 Gd33
Beauvezer F 43 Kb52
Beauvoir-sur-Mer F 27 Ec43
Beauvoir-sur-Niort F 32 Fb46
Beauzac F 34 Hd48
Beauzée-sur-Aire F 24 Jb36
Bebares E 37 Ca54
Beba Veche RO 170 Bb59
Bebe LV 105 Jb52
Bebekli TR 192 Fc86
Bebertal D 127 Ea37

Bebington – Bettola

Bebington GB 15 Eb22
Bebra D 126 Da41
Bebrene LV 115 Lb53
Bebrininkai LV 114 Kb59
Bebrovo BG 180 Ea71
Beccles GB 21 Gb25
Becedas E 45 Cb64
Beceite E 48 Fd63
Bečej SRB 153 Jb59
Béceleuf F 32 Fb45
Beceni RO 176 Ec63
Becerreá E 36 Bc56
Becerril E 46 Dd61
Becerril de Campos E 46 Da59
Bécherel F 28 Ed39
Becherov SK 139 Jd46
Bechet RO 179 Da68
Bechhofen D 134 Dc47
Becicherecu Mic RO 174 Bc60
Bečići MNE 159 Hd70
Beciler TR 192 Fc84
Becilla de Valderaduey E 46 Cd59
Beckdorf D 118 Db33
Beckedorf D 126 Da36
Beckenham GB 20 Fc28
Beckfoot GB 11 Eb17
Beckingen D 133 Bc46
Beckingen D 133 Bd47
Beckingham GB 16 Fb22
Beckinghausen D 125 Ca38
Beckington GB 19 Ec29
Beckov SK 137 Ha49
Beck Side GB 11 Eb19
Beckum D 125 Cb38
Beclean RO 171 Db57
Beclean RO 175 Dc61
Bécon-les-Granits F 28 Fb41
Bečov nad Teplou CZ 135 Ec44
Bečváry CZ 136 Fc45
Bedale GB 11 Fa19
Bédarieux F 41 Hb54
Bédarrides F 42 Jb52
Bedburg D 125 Bc40
Bedburg-Hau D 125 Bc38
Beddau GB 19 Ea28
Beddgelert GB 15 Dd23
Beddinge läge S 110 Fa57
Beddingestrand S 110 Fa57
Beddwas GB 19 Ea27
Bedée F 28 Ed39
Bedegkér H 145 Hb56
Bedekovčina HR 151 Ga58
Beden BG 184 Da75
Bédenac F 32 Fc49
Bedenica HR 152 Gb58
Bedenik HR 152 Gd58
Beder DK 108 Dc24
Bedford GB 20 Fc26
Będgoszcz PL 120 Fc34
Bedirli TR 198 Ga89
Będków PL 130 Hd39
Będlewo PL 129 Gb37
Bedlington GB 11 Fa16
Bedlno PL 130 Hd37
Bedmar E 60 Dc73
Bednja HR 151 Ga57
Bédoin F 42 Jc52
Bedonia I 149 Cd62
Bedous F 39 Fb56
Bedretto CH 141 Cb56
Bedsted DK 100 Da21
Bedsted DK 108 Da27
Bedum NL 117 Bd33
Bedworth GB 20 Fa25
Będzin PL 138 Hc43
Będzino PL 120 Ga31
Beedenbostel D 126 Dc36
Beeford GB 17 Fc20
Beek NL 125 Bb40
Beekbergen NL 117 Bc36
Beek en Donk NL 125 Bb38
Beelen D 126 Cc38
Beelitz D 127 Ed37
Beer GB 19 Eb30
Beerfelden D 134 Cd46
Beerse B 124 Ad39
Beerta NL 117 Ca33
Beesel NL 125 Bb39
Beesenstedt D 127 Ea39
Beeskow D 128 Fb37
Beesten D 117 Cb36
Beeston GB 16 Fa23
Beeswing GB 10 Ea16
Beetsterzwaag NL 117 Bc33
Beetz D 119 Ed35
Beetzendorf D 119 Dd35
Begaljica SRB 174 Bb64
Bégard F 26 Ea37
Begeč SRB 153 Ja60
Begejci SRB 174 Bb61
Beğendik TR 185 Eb78
Beğendik TR 186 Fa74
Beget E 41 Ha58
Beggerow D 119 Ed32
Begijar E 52 Dc72
Begış TR 199 Gb91
Begles F 32 Fb50
Beglež BG 180 Db70
Beg-Meil F 27 Dc40
Begnecourt F 31 Jd38
Begnins CH 140 Ba55
Begnište MK 183 Bc75
Begonte E 36 Bb55
Begov most SRB 159 Jb66
Begovo BG 180 Db72
Begues E 49 Gd61
Begunicy RUS 99 Ma40
Begunje SLO 151 Fb57
Begunovci BG 179 Cb71
Begur E 49 Hc59
Beho B 133 Bb43
Behram TR 191 Ea82
Behramli TR 185 Ea80
Behren-Lübchin D 119 Ec31
Behringen D 126 Dc41
Béhuard F 28 Fb42
Beia RO 176 Dd60
Beian N 77 Dd29
Beica de Jos RO 171 Dc58
Beidaud RO 177 Fc65
Beiersdorf D 128 Fb41
Beignon F 27 Ec40
Beigondo E 36 Ba55
Beilen NL 117 Bd34
Beilngries D 135 Dd48
Beilrode D 127 Ed39
Beilstein D 133 Bd43
Beilstein D 134 Cd47
Beirã P 51 Bb67
Beisfjord N 67 Gb14
Beisland N 93 Da46
Beistad N 78 Eb28
Beith GB 10 Dd13
Beitostølen N 85 Db37
Beiuş RO 170 Cb58
Beižionys LT 114 Kd58
Beja LV 107 Lc48
Beja P 50 Ad71
Béjar E 45 Cb64
Bejís E 54 Fb66
Bejsce PL 138 Jb43
Bejsnap DK 108 Da25
Bekçiler TR 198 Ga91
Békés H 147 Jd55
Békéscsaba H 147 Jd55
Bekilli TR 192 Fd87
Bekirler TR 191 Ec84
Bekirli TR 186 Fb77
Bekirli TR 192 Ga87
Bekkarfjord N 64 Jd05
Bekken N 86 Ec36
Bekkestrand N 62 Gd08
Bekkevoll N 65 Kd08
Bekkevoort B 124 Ad40
Bekkjarvik N 84 Ca40
Bektaşköy TR 193 Gc86
Bektaşlar TR 192 Ga82
Bělá CZ 135 Ed45
Bělá CZ 137 Gd44
Belá SK 138 Hc47
Belaazërsk BY 202 Ea13
Beląbino RUS 113 Jc59
Bélâbre F 29 Gb44
Bela Crkva SRB 174 Bd63
Bel-Air F 27 Eb41
Belaja Kalitva RUS 203 Fc14
Belajevo RUS 107 Ma48
Bela Krajina SLO 151 Fd59
Belalcázar E 52 Cc70
Belá nad Cirochou SK 139 Ka47
Bělá nad Radb. CZ 135 Ec46
Belanica KSV 178 Ba71
Belanovce MK 178 Bc72
Belanovica SRB 153 Jc63
Belante E 36 Bc56
Bela Palanka SRB 179 Ca69
Bélapátfalva H 146 Jb51
Bělá pod B. CZ 136 Fc43
Belascoáin E 39 Ec57
Belava LV 107 Lb49
Belava LV 107 Lb51
Bélavár H 152 Gd57
Belbaşı TR 199 Gb92
Belbroughton GB 20 Ed25
Belca SLO 144 Fa56
Belcaire F 41 Gd57
Belcastel F 33 Ha51
Belce TR 193 Gc83
Belceğiz TR 198 Fc92
Belceşti RO 172 Ed57
Bełchatów PL 130 Hd40
Belchite E 48 Fb62
Bělčice CZ 136 Fa46
Belciğez TR 199 Ha88
Belcoo GB 9 Cb18
Belcov BG 180 Dd69
Bełda PL 123 Ka32
Belderrig IRL 8 Bc17
Beldibi TR 199 Gc92
Belec HR 152 Gb57
Belecke D 126 Cc39
Belecska H 145 Hb56
Beled H 145 Gc53
Belegiš SRB 153 Jc61
Belej HR 151 Fb62
Belek TR 199 Gd91
Belén E 36 Bc53
Belén E 37 Ca54
Belence TR 192 Ga86
Belence TR 199 Ha89
Belenci BG 179 Da70
Belene BG 180 Dc68
Belenköy TR 197 Ec91
Beleño E 37 Cd55
Belenören TR 187 Ha80
Belenyaka TR 192 Fb86
Belesh AL 182 Ab76
Beleţi-Negreşti RO 175 Dc64
Beletovo RUS 99 Ld42
Belev RUS 202 Ed12
Belevi TR 191 Ed87
Belevi TR 198 Fd88
Belfast GB 9 Da17
Belfir RO 170 Ca57
Belford GB 11 Ed14
Belfort F 31 Ka40
Belgern D 127 Ed40
Belgioioso I 149 Cc60
Belgirate I 148 Cb58
Belgodère F 154 Cb69
Belgorod RUS 203 Fa14
Belgun BG 181 Fb69
Belhade F 39 Fb52
Belhomert-Guéhouville F 29 Gb38
Beli HR 151 Fb61
Belianes E 48 Gb61
Belica BG 184 Cc74
Belica BG 179 Cd72
Belica BG 180 Dd71
Belica BG 181 Ec68
Belica HR 152 Gc57
Belica MK 182 Ba75
Beli Iskăr BG 179 Cc72
Beli Izvor BG 179 Cc69
Beli Izvor SRB 178 Bb68
Beli Manastir HR 153 Hc58
Beli Manastir SRB 153 Hd58
Belin RO 176 Ea61
Belin-Béliet F 32 Fb51
Belinchón E 53 Dd66
Beli Osăm BG 180 Db71
Beli plast BG 185 Dd74
Beli Potok SRB 174 Bb64
Beliş RO 171 Cd58
Belišće HR 153 Hc59
Beliševo SRB 178 Bd71
Beliu RO 170 Ca58
Beljanovo BG 180 Dd69
Beljin SRB 153 Jb62
Beljina SRB 153 Jc62
Belkaracaören TR 193 Gc85
Belkavak TR 193 Gb83
Belkaya TR 192 Fd85
Belkese TR 187 Gc80
Belkino RUS 113 Jc59
Belkino RUS 113 Jd58
Bel'kovo RUS 202 Ec12
Bell D 125 Bd42
Bella I 161 Ga75
Bellac F 33 Gb46
Bellacorick IRL 8 Bc18
Bellagio I 149 Cc57
Bellamonte I 150 Dd57
Bellanaboy Bridge IRL 8 Bc17
Bellanacargy IRL 9 Cc19
Bellananagh IRL 9 Cb19
Bellano I 149 Cc57
Bellante I 157 Fa69
Bellarena GB 9 Cd15
Bellaria I 156 Eb64
Bellavary IRL 8 Bc19
Bellavista E 59 Ca74
Bellcaire d'Urgell E 48 Gb60
Belleben D 127 Ea39
Bellechaume F 30 Hc39
Belle Croix B 125 Bb42
Belle-Eglise F 23 Gd35
Belleek GB 8 Ca17
Bellegarde F 29 Gd39
Bellegarde F 42 Ja53
Bellegarde-en-Marche F 33 Gd46
Bellegarde-sur-Valserine F 35 Jd45
Belleherbe F 31 Ka41
Bellême F 29 Ga38
Bellenaves F 34 Hb45
Bellencombre F 23 Gb34
Bellerive-sur-Allier F 34 Hc46
Bellersen D 126 Da38
Belles-Forêts F 25 Ka36
Belleu F 24 Hb35
Bellevaux B 132 Ad44
Bellevesvre F 31 Jc43
Belleville F 34 Ja45
Belleville-sur-Vie F 28 Ed44
Bellevue-la-Montagne F 34 Hd49
Belley F 35 Jc46
Bellheim D 133 Cb47
Bellicourt F 24 Hb33
Bellifallim E 55 Fb70
Belligné F 28 Fa41
Bell-lloc d'Urgell E 48 Ga61
Bellinge DK 108 Dc27
Bellingham GB 11 Ed16
Bellingwolde D 117 Ca33
Bellingwolde NL 117 Ca33
Bellinzago Novarese I 148 Cb59
Bellinzona CH 149 Cc57
Bellizzi I 161 Fc76
Bello E 47 Ed63
Bellö S 103 Fd49
Belloc F 40 Fc54
Bellocq F 39 Fa54
Bellosguardo I 161 Fd76
Bellot F 24 Hb37
Bellou F 22 Fd36
Bellpuig E 48 Gb61
Bellreguart E 54 Fc69
Belluno I 150 Ea57
Bellvik S 79 Ga27
Bellvika N 62 Gc09
Bellvís E 48 Ga60
Bellwald CH 141 Ca56
Belm D 117 Cc36
Bélmez E 52 Cc71
Bélmez de la Moraleda E 60 Dc73
Belmont GB 5 Fa03
Belmont GB 15 Ec21
Belmonte E 53 Ea67
Belmonte P 44 Bb64
Belmonte Castello I 161 Fa72
Belmonte de Campos E 46 Cd59
Belmonte del Sannio I 161 Fb72
Belmonte de Miranda E 37 Cb54
Belmontejo E 53 Eb66
Belmonte Mezzagno I 166 Ec84
Belmont-sur-Rance F 41 Hb53
Belmullet IRL 8 Bb17
Belobreşca RO 174 Bd64
Beloci MD 173 Fd55
Belœil B 124 Ab41
Belogradčik BG 179 Cb68
Belokopitovo BG 181 Ec70
Beloljin SRB 178 Bc69
Belomorskoje RUS 113 Jb58
Belo Polje KSV 178 Ba70
Belorado E 38 Dd58
Belorečensk RUS 205 Fc17
Belören TR 199 Gb93
Belören TR 199 Gc89
Belosavci SRB 174 Bb65
Beloslav BG 181 Fa70
Belotić SRB 153 Ja61
Belotín CZ 137 Ha46
Belotinci BG 179 Cb68
Belovar Moravče HR 152 Gb58
Belovec BG 180 Eb68
Belovica BG 180 Db72
Belovo BG 179 Cd73
Belovodica MK 183 Bc75
Belozem BG 180 Dc73
Belpasso I 167 Fc85
Belpech F 40 Gc55
Belper GB 16 Fa23
Belpınar TR 193 Gd83
Belsay GB 11 Ed16
Belsk Duży PL 130 Jb38
Beltarla TR 199 Gb88
Beltheim D 133 Ca43
Beltinci SLO 145 Gb56
Beltiug RO 171 Cd55
Beltra IRL 8 Bc19
Beltra IRL 8 Bd18
Belturbet IRL 9 Cb18
Belum D 118 Da31
Beluša SK 137 Hb48
Belušić SRB 178 Bb67
Beluso E 36 Ac57
Belvédère-Campomoro F 154 Ca72
Belvedere Marittimo I 164 Ga79
Belver E 48 Fd60
Belver P 50 Ad66
Belver de los Montes E 45 Cc60
Belvès F 33 Gb50
Belvèze-du-Razès F 41 Gd56
Belvezet F 34 Hd51
Belville IRL 8 Bc18
Belvís de la Jara E 52 Cd66
Belvis de Monroy E 51 Cb66
Belvoir F 31 Ka41
Belvoir GB 16 Fb23
Belyj RUS 202 Ec11
Belz F 27 Ea40
Bełżec PL 131 Kd42
Belzig D 127 Ec37
Bełżyce PL 131 Ka40
Bembibre E 37 Ca57
Bembibre (Val do Dubra) E 36 Ad55
Bembridge GB 20 Fa31
Bemmel NL 125 Bb37
Bemowo Piskie PL 123 Jd31
Bemposta P 45 Bd61
Bemposta P 50 Ad67
Benabarre E 48 Ga59
Benacazón E 59 Bd74
Benadresa E 54 Fc66
Benafim Grande P 58 Ac74
Benaguasil E 54 Fb67
Benahadux E 61 Ea76
Benahavís E 60 Cc77
Benajarafe E 60 Da76
Ben Alder Lodge GB 7 Dd10
Benalí E 54 Fa69
Benalmádena E 60 Cd76
Benalmádena E 60 Cd77
Benalúa de Guadix E 61 Dd74
Benalúna de la Villas E 60 Db74
Benalup de Sidonia E 59 Ca77
Benamargosa E 60 Da76
Benamaurel E 61 Ea73
Benamejí E 60 Cd74
Benamocarra E 60 Da76
Benaoján E 59 Cb76
Benasal E 54 Fc65
Benasau E 55 Fc70
Benasque E 40 Ga57
Benassay F 28 Fd44
Benatae E 53 Ea71
Benátky nad Jizera CZ 136 Fc44
Benavent E 48 Gb59
Benavente E 45 Cb59
Benavente E 51 Bb68
Benavente P 50 Ab68
Benavides E 37 Cb57
Bendestorf D 118 Db33
Bendorf D 125 Ca42
Bēne LV 106 Ka52
Beneden-Leeuwen NL 125 Bb37
Benediktbeuern D 143 Dd52
Benedita P 50 Ab66
Benefield GB 20 Fb25
Benejama E 55 Fb70
Benejúzar E 55 Fa72
Benesat RO 171 Cd56
Benešov CZ 136 Fc45
Benešovice CZ 135 Ec45
Benešov nad Černou CZ 136 Fc49
Benešov nad Ploučnici CZ 128 Fb42
Bénesse-lès-Dax F 39 Fa54
Benesse-Maremne F 39 Fa54
Benestad S 103 Fc52
Bénestroff F 25 Ka36
Benet F 32 Fb45
Benetutti I 168 Cb76
Beneuvre F 30 Jb40
Bene Vagienna I 148 Bd62
Bénévent-l'Abbaye F 33 Gc46
Benevento I 161 Fc74
Benfeld F 31 Kc38
Bengeşti-Ciocadia RO 175 Cd63
Bengiler TR 191 Ed82
Bengtsby FIN 98 Kc39
Bengtsfors S 94 Ec44
Bengtsheden S 95 Ga39
Benia (Onís) E 37 Cd55
Beniarrés E 55 Fb70
Benicanci HR 152 Hb59
Benicarló E 48 Fd64
Benicasim E 54 Fd66
Benicàssim E 54 Fd66
Benidorm E 55 Fc71
Beniel E 55 Fa72
Benifaió E 54 Fb68
Benifallet E 48 Ga63
Benigànim E 54 Fb69
Benik TR 197 Fa90
Benilloba E 55 Fb70
Benimaurell E 55 Fc70
Beninar E 61 Dd76
Benington GB 17 Fd23
Benissa E 55 Fd70
Benitachell E 55 Fd70
Benkovac HR 157 Ga64
Benkovski BG 181 Eb69
Benlieli TR 192 Fb84
Benlikuyu TR 193 Ha84
Benllech GB 15 Dd22
Benlloch E 54 Fd65
Benløse DK 109 Eb26
Benmore GB 7 Dd11
Benneckenstein D 126 Dc39
Bennettsbridge IRL 13 Cb24
Bennstedt D 127 Ea40
Bennungen D 127 Dd40
Bénodet F 27 Dc40
Benquerenicia E 36 Bc53
Bensafrim P 58 Ab74
Bensbyn S 73 Hd22
Bensdorf D 127 Eb36
Bensersiel D 117 Cb32
Bensheim D 134 Cc45
Bensjö S 87 Fd32
Bensnes N 62 Ha09
Benson GB 20 Fa28
Bentpath GB 11 Eb15
Bentraces E 36 Ba57
Bentwisch D 119 Eb31
Benwick GB 20 Fc25
Benzú E 59 Cb79
Beočin SRB 153 Ja60
Beograd SRB 153 Jc61
Beograd- Surcin SRB 153 Jc61
Beomužević SRB 153 Jb63
Bera E 39 Ed55
Beram HR 151 Fa60
Berane MNE 159 Jb68
Beranje SRB 174 Bc64
Beranuy E 40 Ga58
Berastegi E 39 Ec56
Berat AL 182 Ab76
Bérat F 40 Gb55
Beratón E 47 Ec60
Beratzhausen D 135 Ea47
Berazino BY 202 Eb12
Bérbaltavar H 145 Gc55
Berbegal E 48 Fc59
Berbes E 37 Cd54
Berbeşti RO 175 Da64
Berbinzana E 39 Ec58
Berca RO 176 Ec63
Bercedo E 38 Dd56
Bercel H 146 Hd51
Bercenay-le-Hayer F 30 Hc38
Berceni RO 176 Eb64
Berceni RO 176 Eb66
Berceto I 149 Cd62
Berchères-sur-Vesgre F 23 Gc37
Berchidda I 168 Cb74
Berching D 135 Dd47
Berchtesgaden D 143 Ec52
Bérchules E 60 Dc75
Bercianos de Aliste E 45 Ca59
Bercianos del Páramo E 37 Cc58
Bercimuel E 46 Dc61
Berck F 23 Gb32
Berck-Plage F 23 Gb32
Bercu RO 171 Cd54
Berdal N 77 Dc30
Berdalen N 92 Cd42
Berd'huis F 29 Ga38
Berdía E 36 Ad55
Berdjans'k UA 205 Fb16
Berdoias E 36 Ac54
Berducedo E 37 Bd55
Berdún E 39 Fa57
Berdyčiv UA 204 Eb15
Berechiu RO 170 Ca58
Beregsău RO 174 Bc60
Berehove UA 204 Dd16
Berek HR 152 Gc59
Bereketli TR 186 Fa80
Berekfürdő H 146 Jc53
Beremend H 153 Hc58
Bere Regis GB 19 Ec30
Berestečko UA 204 Ea15
Bereşti RO 177 Fc61
Bereşti Bistriţa RO 172 Ed59
Bereşti-Meria RO 177 Fb61
Bereşti-Tazlău RO 172 Ec59
Beretinec HR 152 Gb57
Berettyószentmárton H 147 Ka53
Berettyóújfalu H 147 Ka53
Berevoeşti RO 175 Dc63
Berezanka UA 204 Ec16
Berezanskaja RUS 205 Fc16
Berežany UA 204 Ea15
Berezeni RO 177 Fb60
Berežkovskoe RUS 113 Jc59
Berezlogi MD 173 Fd56
Berezna UA 202 Ec13
Berezne UA 202 Ea14
Bereznehuvate UA 204 Ed16
Berezno RUS 99 Ld43
Berezovka RUS 113 Ja59
Berezovo RUS 113 Jb59
Berfay F 29 Ga40
Berg D 133 Cb47
Berg D 135 Dd47
Berg D 135 Dd49
Berg D 135 Ea43
Berg D 143 Db51
Berg N 70 Ed23
Berg N 93 Dc44
Berg N 94 Eb44
Berg S 87 Fc32
Berg S 94 Ec45
Berg S 95 Ga43
Berg S 102 Fa46
Berg S 103 Ga47
Berg S 103 Fc51
Berga D 127 Dd40
Berga D 127 Eb42
Berga E 49 Gd59
Berga S 94 Eb42
Berga S 95 Fb45
Berga S 103 Ga50
Bergaland N 92 Cb43
Bergama TR 191 Ec84
Bergamo I 149 Cd58
Bergara E 39 Eb56
Bergatreute D 142 Da51
Bergdala S 103 Fd52
Berge D 117 Cb35
Berge D 119 Eb34
Berge D 127 Ec36
Berge E 48 Fb63
Berge N 77 Da31
Berge N 93 Da44
Bergeforsen S 88 Gc33
Bergen D 118 Db35
Bergen D 120 Fa30
Bergen D 135 Eb43
Bergen D 143 Eb52
Bergen N 84 Ca39
Bergen NL 116 Ba34
Bergen aan Zee NL 116 Ad34
Bergendal N 93 Db45
Bergen (Dumme) D 119 Dd35
Bergen = Mons B 124 Ab41
Bergen op Zoom NL 124 Ac38
Berger N 93 Dd43
Bergerac F 32 Fd50
Bergéres-lès-Vertus F 24 Hc36
Berget N 71 Fb20
Berget N 78 Ea28
Bergeyk NL 124 Ba39
Bergfors S 67 Ha14
Bergfors S 87 Ga36
Berggießhübel, Bad Gottleuba- D 128 Fa42
Bergheim D 125 Bc40
Berghem S 102 Ec50
Berghin RO 175 Da60
Bergholz-Rehbrücke D 127 Ed37
Bergisch Gladbach D 125 Bd40
Bergkamen D 125 Cb38
Bergkarlås S 87 Fc38
Bergkvara S 111 Ga53
Bergland S 71 Ga24
Berglern D 143 Ea50
Bergli N 77 Db29
Berglia N 78 Fa27
Bergliden S 80 Hb25
Berglund N 62 Ha09
Berglunda S 80 Gd26
Bergmo N 63 Hb09
Bergnäs S 72 Gb22
Bergnäs S 79 Gb25
Bergnäset S 73 Hd22
Bergnäsudden S 72 Gc22
Bergnäsviken S 72 Gc20
Bergndal N 85 Dd39
Bergneset N 67 Gd11
Bergneustadt D 125 Ca40
Bergnicourt F 24 Hd34
Bergnicourt F 24 Hd35
Bergö FIN 81 Hd31
Bergrheinfeld D 134 Db44
Bergsäng S 94 Fa41
Bergsäter S 79 Gb25
Bergsbyn S 80 Hc25
Bergseng N 86 Ea38
Bergshammar S 95 Gb45
Bergshamra S 96 Ha42
Bergsjö S 79 Ga28
Bergsjö S 87 Gb35
Bergsmoen N 78 Ed26
Bergstad FIN 98 Kb40
Bergstrøm N 94 Eb43
Bergsviken S 73 Hc23
Bergtheim D 134 Db45
Bergues F 21 Gd30
Bergün CH 142 Cd55
Bergunda S 103 Fc52
Bergundhaugen N 85 Ea37
Bergvik S 87 Gb37
Bergviken S 72 Gd20
Bergwitz D 127 Ec39
Berhida H 145 Hb54
Berill N 77 Da33
Beringel P 50 Ad71
Beringen B 124 Ba40
Berini RO 174 Bd61
Beriozchi MD 173 Ga58
Berisal CH 141 Ca56
Beriu RO 175 Cd61
Berja E 61 Dd76
Berka D 126 Db41
Berkåk N 77 Dd32
Berkatal D 126 Db40
Berkel NL 116 Ad36
Berkeley GB 19 Ec27
Berkenbrück D 127 Ed37
Berkenthin D 119 Dd32
Berkhamsted GB 20 Fb27
Berkheim D 142 Da51
Berknes N 76 Cc33
Berkovica BG 179 Cc69
Berkovici BIH 158 Hb67
Berkswell GB 20 Ed25
Berlanga E 51 Ca71
Berlanga de Duero E 47 Ea61
Berlanga del Bierzo E 37 Ca56
Berlangas de Roa E 46 Dc60
Berle N 84 Ca34
Berleşti RO 175 Cd64
Berlevåg N 65 Kb04
Berlin D 127 Ed36
Berlingerode D 126 Db39
Berlstedt D 127 Dd41
Bermeo E 38 Ea55
Bermés E 36 Ba56
Bermillo de Sayago E 45 Ca61
Bern CH 141 Bd54
Bernalda I 162 Gc76
Bernardos E 46 Da62
Bernartice CZ 136 Fb47
Bernāti LV 113 Ja53
Bernau D 128 Fa36
Bernau D 141 Ca51
Bernau D 143 Eb52
Bernaville F 23 Gd32
Bernay F 23 Ga36
Bernay F 28 Fc39
Bernbeuren D 142 Dc52
Bernburg D 127 Ea38
Berndorf A 145 Gb51
Berne D 118 Cd33
Bernécourt F 25 Jc36
Bernedo E 39 Eb57
Berngau D 135 Dd47
Bernhardswald D 135 Eb48
Bernhardthal A 137 Gc49
Bernin F 35 Jd48
Bernkastel-Kues D 133 Bd44
Bernolákovo SK 145 Gd51
Bernon F 30 Hd39
Bernried D 135 Ec48
Bernried D 143 Dd51
Bernsdorf D 128 Fb40
Bernstadt D 128 Fc41
Bernstein A 145 Gb53
Bernués E 39 Fb58
Beromünster CH 141 Ca53
Beronovo BG 181 Ec71
Beroun CZ 136 Fb45
Berovo MK 183 Cb74
Berra I 150 Ea61
Berre-l'Étang F 42 Jc54
Berric F 27 Eb41
Berriedale GB 5 Eb05
Berrien F 26 Dd38
Berriew GB 15 Eb24
Berro E 53 Eb70
Berrocal E 59 Bc73
Berrocal de Salvatierra E 45 Cb63
Berrocalejo E 52 Cc66
Berrocalejo de Aragona E 46 Da63
Beršad' UA 204 Ec16
Bersagel N 92 Ca44
Bersbo S 103 Ga47
Bersenbrück D 117 Cb35
Bersezio I 148 Bb62
Beršići SRB 159 Jc64
Bertamiráns (Ames) E 36 Ad55
Bertea RO 176 Ea63
Berteroda D 126 Dc41
Berteškiai LV 114 Kb56
Berteştii de Jos RO 177 Fa65
Berthelsdorf D 128 Fb41
Berthelsdorf D 128 Fc41
Bertincourt F 23 Ha32
Bertingen D 127 Eb37
Bertinoro I 156 Ea64
Bertogne B 132 Ba43
Bertrix B 132 Ad44
Berven F 26 Dc37
Berveni RO 171 Cc54
Berville-sur-Mer F 22 Fd35
Berwang A 142 Dc53
Berwick-upon-Tweed GB 11 Ed14
Beryslav UA 204 Ed16
Bērzaune LV 106 La50
Berzé-la-Ville F 34 Ja45
Berzence H 152 Gd57
Bērzgale LV 107 Ld51
Bērzi LV 105 Jd52
Bērziems LV 106 Ka50
Bērziņi LV 107 Ma52
Berżniki PL 123 Kb30
Berzocana E 51 Cb67
Berzosa E 46 Dd60
Berzovia RO 174 Bd62
Bērzpils LV 107 Lc50
Berzunţi RO 176 Ec60
Bērzupe LV 106 Ka51
Beša SK 145 Hb51
Besalú E 49 Hb59
Besançon F 31 Jd42
Besande E 37 Cd56
Bešankovičy BY 202 Eb11
Bescanó E 49 Hb59
Bescaran E 40 Gc58
Bescsehely H 145 Gc56
Besedino RUS 203 Fa13
Besednice CZ 136 Fb49
Besenyőtelek H 146 Jb52
Besenyszög H 146 Jb53
Beserovina SRB 159 Ja64
Beşevler TR 186 Fc80
Beşghioz MD 177 Fd61
Bęsia PL 122 Jb31
Besigheim D 134 Cd47
Běšiny CZ 135 Ed47
Bešište MK 183 Bc76
Beška SRB 153 Jb60
Beškino RUS 99 Lc44
Besko PL 139 Ka45
Beşkonak TR 199 Gc89
Beşkonak = Bozkaya TR 199 Ha90
Beslé F 28 Ed41
Besni Fok SRB 153 Jc61
Besozzo I 148 Cb58
Bessais-le-Fromental F 29 Ha44
Bessaker N 78 Ea27
Bessan F 41 Hc55
Bessans F 35 Kb48
Bessbrook GB 9 Cd18
Besse F 35 Ka49
Besse-et-Saint-Anastaise F 34 Hb48
Bessèges F 41 Hd52
Bessenay F 34 Ja47
Bessenbach D 134 Cd44
Bessé-sur-Braye F 29 Ga40
Bessières F 40 Gc53
Besson F 30 Hb44
Best NL 124 Ba38
Besteland N 92 Cd44
Beştemac MD 173 Fc59
Bestensee D 128 Fa37
Bestwig D 126 Cc39
Besullo E 37 Ca55
Besvica MK 183 Bd75
Beszterec H 147 Ka50
Betanzos E 36 Ba54
Betelu E 39 Ec56
Bétera E 54 Fb67
Beteta E 47 Ec64
Bethausen RO 174 Ca60
Betheln D 126 Db37
Bétheniville F 24 Hd35
Betheny F 24 Hc35
Bethersden GB 21 Ga29
Bethesda GB 15 Dd22
Béthines F 29 Ga44
Béthisy-Saint-Pierre F 23 Ha35
Bethmale F 40 Gb56
Bethon F 24 Hc37
Béthune F 23 Ha31
Betliar SK 138 Jb48
Betsele S 80 Gd26
Bettembourg L 133 Bb45
Bettens CH 141 Bb55
Bettna S 95 Gb45
Bettola I 149 Cd61

Blumau – Bösdorf

Blumau I 143 Dd56
Blumberg D 141 Cb51
Blumberg, Ahrensfelde- D 128 Fa36
Blumenhagen D 120 Fa33
Blumenthal D 119 Ec34
Blyberg S 87 Fb37
Blynki RUS 99 Ld43
Blyth GB 11 Fa16
Blyth Bridge GB 11 Eb14
Bnin PL 129 Gc37
Bø N 62 Gc09
Bø N 66 Fc13
Bø N 66 Fd13
Bø N 77 Db31
Bø N 84 Ca36
Bø N 92 Ca43
Bø N 92 Cd45
Bø N 93 Db43
Bo N 93 Dc43
Bo S 95 Fd45
Bo'Ness GB 10 Ea13
Boadilla del Monte E 46 Db64
Boadilla de Rioseco E 37 Cd58
Boal E 37 Bd54
Boalt S 111 Fb53
Boan MNE 159 Ja68
Boario Terme I 149 Da58
Boat of Garten GB 7 Ea08
Boa Vista P 44 Ac65
Boba H 145 Gd54
Bobadilla del Campo E 46 Cd62
Bobadilla Estación E 60 Cd75
Bobâlna RO 171 Da57
Bobbau D 127 Eb39
Bobbio I 149 Cc61
Bobbio Pellice I 148 Bb61
Bobeica MD 173 Fc58
Bobenheim-Roxheim D 133 Cb45
Boberg S 79 Fd30
Bobicești RO 175 Da66
Bobigny F 23 Gd36
Böbing D 142 Dc52
Bobingen D 142 Dc50
Böbingen an der Rems D 134 Da48
Bobitz D 119 Ea32
Böblingen D 134 Cc48
Bobolice PL 121 Gb31
Boboševo BG 179 Cb73
Bobota HR 153 Hd60
Bobota RO 171 Cc56
Bobovdol BG 179 Cb72
Boboviště MNE 159 Ja70
Bobowa PL 138 Jc45
Bobowo PL 121 Hb31
Bobr BY 202 Eb12
Bobrețu RO 175 Da65
Bóbrka PL 139 Kb46
Bobrov RUS 203 Fb13
Bobrovec SK 138 Hd47
Bobrovycja UA 202 Ec14
Bobrowice PL 128 Fc38
Bobrówko PL 120 Fd35
Bobrówko PL 122 Jc32
Bobrowniki PL 122 Hc35
Bobrowniki PL 123 Kc33
Bobrowniki Wielkie PL 138 Jc44
Bobrynec' UA 204 Ed16
Boc MNE 159 Jc68
Boc MNE 178 Ad69
Bóč SK 145 Gd51
Boca de Huérgano E 37 Cd56
Bocairent E 55 Fb70
Bocale I 164 Ga84
Bocani MD 173 Fb56
Bočar SRB 153 Jb58
Bocca di l'Orù F 154 Cb72
Bocca di Piazza I 164 Gc80
Bocchigliero I 164 Gc79
Boceguillas E 46 Dc61
Böçen TR 192 Ga82
Bochnia PL 138 Jb44
Bocholt B 125 Bb39
Bocholt D 125 Bd38
Bochov CZ 135 Ed44
Bochum D 125 Ca39
Bocigas E 46 Da61
Bockara S 103 Ga50
Bockau D 135 Ec43
Bockenem D 126 Db38
Bockfliess A 145 Gc50
Bockhorn D 118 Cc33
Bockhorn D 143 Ea50
Böcki PL 123 Kb35
Böckstein A 143 Ec54
Bockträsk S 72 Gc23
Böckweiler D 133 Bd46
Bočna ob Dreti SLO 151 Fc57
Bocognano F 154 Cb70
Bócsa H 146 Ja56
Bocșa RO 171 Cd56
Bocșa RO 174 Bd62
Bocsig RO 170 Ca59
Boczów PL 128 Fc37
Bod RO 176 Ea62
Boda S 87 Fd38
Boda S 87 Gb32
Boda S 94 Ed43
Boda S 94 Ed43
Böda S 104 Gc50
Bodaczów PL 131 Kc41
Boda glasbruk S 103 Fd52
Bodajk H 145 Hb53
Bødal N 84 Cd35
Bodange B 132 Ba44
Bođani SRB 153 Hd60
Bodaño E 36 Ba56
Bodators S 103 Fc50
Bodbacka FIN 89 Hd32
Bodbyn S 80 Hb28
Boddam GB 5 Fa08
Boddensdorf A 144 Fa56
Boddum DK 100 Da22
Bodegraven NL 116 Ad36
Boden A 142 Db53
Boden D 125 Cb42
Boden S 73 Hd21
Bodenfelde D 126 Da39
Bodenheim D 133 Cb44
Bodenkirchen D 143 Eb50
Bodenmais D 135 Ed48
Bodenwerder D 126 Da38
Bodenwöhr D 135 Eb47
Bodești RO 172 Ec57
Bodfari GB 15 Ea22
Bodilsker DK 111 Fc58
Bodman D 142 Cc51
Bodmin GB 18 Db31
Bodnegg D 142 Da52
Bodö FIN 81 Jb28
Bodø N 66 Fc17
Bodoc RO 176 Ea61
Bodom N 78 Ec28
Bodonal de la Sierra E 51 Bc71
Bodonci SLO 145 Gb55
Bodorgan Station GB 15 Dd22
Bodrost BG 179 Cc73
Bodrum TR 197 Ec90
Bodsjö S 87 Fc32
Bodsjöedet S 78 Ed30
Bodträskfors S 73 Hc21
Bodyke IRL 12 Bd22
Bodzanów PL 130 Ja36
Bodzanowice PL 129 Hb41
Bodzechów PL 131 Jd41
Bodzentyn PL 130 Jc41
Bodzewo PL 129 Gc38
Boé F 40 Ga52
Boecillo E 46 Da60
Boedapest = Budapest H 146 Hd53
Boëge F 35 Ka45
Boekel NL 125 Bb38
Boekelo NL 117 Bd36
Boën F 34 Hd47
Boen N 93 Da47
Boeslunde DK 109 Ea27
Boeza E 37 Ca56
Bofara S 87 Ga37
Boffzen D 126 Da38
Bofin IRL 8 Ba19
Bofors S 95 Fc43
Boftsa N 64 Ka06
Bogács H 146 Jc51
Bogaczów PL 128 Fd38
Bogádmindszent H 152 Hb58
Bogan N 78 Ed25
Bøgard N 66 Fd11
Bogarra E 53 Eb70
Bogata RO 171 Db59
Bogați RO 176 Dd64
Bogatić SRB 153 Ja61
Bogatovo RUS 113 Jb58
Bogatovo RUS 122 Ja30
Bogatynia PL 128 Fc42
Boğazak TR 199 Ha91
Boğazcık TR 198 Ga92
Bogazi CY 206 Jd96
Boğaziçi TR 198 Ga88
Boğaziçi TR 199 Gb89
Boğaziği TR 198 Fd92
Boğazkale TR 205 Fb20
Boğazkent TR 193 Hb86
Boğazköy TR 186 Ga80
Boğazköy TR 192 Fc84
Bogdan BG 180 Db72
Bogdana RO 173 Fa59
Bogdanci BG 181 Ec69
Bogdanci MK 183 Ca76
Bogdand RO 171 Cd56
Bogdănești RO 172 Ec56
Bogdănești RO 176 Ec60
Bogdănești RO 177 Fa60
Bogdaniec PL 128 Fc36
Bogdănița RO 177 Fa60
Bogdanovca Nouă MD 177 Fd60
Bogdanovo BG 180 Ea73
Bogdanowo PL 130 Hd40
Bogdan Vodă RO 171 Db55
Bogë AL 159 Jb69
Boge S 104 Ha49
Bogen D 135 Ec48
Bogen N 66 Fd15
Bogen N 67 Gb13
Bogen S 94 Ed41
Bogense DK 108 Dc26
Bogetići MNE 159 Hd69
Boggan IRL 9 Cc19
Bogheni Noi MD 173 Fb56
Boghești RO 177 Fa61
Boghiceni MD 173 Fc58
Bogliasco I 148 Cb63
Boglösa S 96 Gc43
Bognanco Fonti I 148 Ca57
Bognelv N 63 Hc08
Bognelvdalen N 63 Hc08
Bognes N 66 Ga14
Bogno CH 149 Cc57
Bognor Regis GB 20 Fb30
Bogny-sur-Meuse F 24 Ja33
Bogø By DK 109 Eb28
Bogodol BIH 158 Ha66
Bogojevac SRB 178 Bc69
Bogojevice SRB 178 Bd70
Bogojevo SRB 153 Hd59
Bogojina SLO 145 Gb56
Bogomila MK 183 Bb74
Bogomilovo BG 180 Dd73
Bogomolje HR 158 Gd67
Bogoria PL 130 Jc42
Bogorodick RUS 203 Fa11
Bogorodsk RUS 203 Fb09
Bogorovo BG 181 Ed68
Bogosavac SRB 153 Ja62
Bogoslov BG 179 Ca72
Bögöte H 145 Gd54
Bogova RO 174 Cb65
Bogovina SRB 178 Bd67
Böğrüdelik TR 193 Hb85
Bogsta S 96 Gc45
Bogstad N 84 Cc35
Bogsund N 92 Cb43
Bogučar RUS 203 Fc13
Boguchwałów PL 137 Ha44
Boguchwały PL 122 Hd31
Bogue GB 10 Dd16
Bogumiłów PL 129 Hb39
Bogumiłowice PL 130 Hc40
Boguszewo PL 121 Hb33
Boguszów-Gorce PL 129 Gb42
Bogutovac SRB 178 Ba67
Boguty-Pianki PL 123 Ka35
Bogyiszló H 146 Hc56
Bogzești MD 173 Fc56
Bohain-en-Vermandois F 24 Hb33
Bohan B 132 Ad44
Bohdalice CZ 137 Gc47
Bohdalov CZ 136 Ga46
Bohdašin CZ 137 Gb43
Boheden S 73 Ja20
Böheimkirchen A 144 Ga51
Boherboy IRL 12 Bc25
Boherlalan IRL 13 Ca23
Bohinjska Bistrica SLO 151 Fa57
Böhl-Iggelheim D 133 Cb46
Böhme D 118 Da35
Böhmenkirch D 134 Da49
Bohmte D 117 Cc36
Bohoduchiv UA 203 Fa14
Boholt RO 175 Cc60
Bohonal de Ibor E 51 Cb66
Böhönye H 145 Gd56
Bohot BG 180 Db69
Bohukaly PL 131 Kc36
Bohula MK 183 Bd75
Bohumín CZ 137 Hb45
Bohuňovice CZ 137 Gd46
Bohus S 102 Ec48
Bohuslav UA 204 Ec15
Bohutín CZ 136 Fa46
Boialvo P 44 Ad63
Boianu Mare RO 171 Cc56
Boiereni RO 171 Db56
Boiro E 36 Ac56
Boiry-Saint-Matin F 23 Ha32
Boiscommun F 29 Gd39
Bois-de-Céné F 28 Ed43
Bois-le-Roi F 29 Ha38
Boismont F 25 Jc34
Boișoara RO 175 Db62
Boisredon F 32 Fb48
Boisseron F 41 Hd53
Boisson F 42 Ja52
Boišta = Slepač most MNE 159 Jb67
Boisville F 29 Gc38
Boitzenburg D 120 Fa34
Boiu Mare RO 171 Da56
Bóixols E 48 Gb59
Boizenburg D 119 Dd33
Böja S 102 Fa46
Bojadła PL 128 Ga38
Bojadžik BG 180 Eb73
Bojančište MK 183 Bc75
Bojane MK 178 Bb73
Bojano I 161 Fb73
Bojanovo BG 180 Eb73
Bojanów PL 139 Ka43
Bojanowo PL 129 Gc39
Bojas LV 105 Jb52
Bojčinovci BG 179 Cc69
Bøjden DK 108 Dc27
Bojewyan GB 18 Cd32
Bojišta MK 182 Ba75
Bojka BG 180 Ea70
Bojkovice CZ 137 Ha48
Bojmie PL 131 Jd37
Bojná SK 137 Ha49
Bojnica BG 179 Cb67
Bojnice SK 137 Hb48
Bojnik SRB 178 Bc70
Bojszowy PL 138 Hc44
Bojtiken S 71 Fc23
Boka SRB 174 Bb62
Bókaháza H 145 Gd55
Bokel D 118 Cd33
Bokenäs S 102 Eb47
Bokinka Pańska PL 131 Kc37
Böklund D 108 Db29
Bokod H 145 Hb53
Boków PL 130 Jb40
Bokros H 146 Jb55
Böksholm S 103 Fc51
Boksjok N 64 Ka05
Boksjön S 71 Fd22
Bol HR 158 Gc67
Bol' SK 139 Ka49
Bolandoz F 31 Jd42
Bolaños de Calatrava E 52 Dc69
Bolaños de Campos E 45 Cc59
Bolayır TR 185 Eb79
Bolbec F 22 Fd34
Bölberget S 86 Fa34
Bolboși RO 175 Cc64
Bolca I 149 Dc59
Bölcske H 146 Hd55
Bolderaja LV 106 Kb50
Boldești-Grădiștea RO 176 Ec65
Boldești-Scăeni RO 176 Ea64
Boldogkőváralja H 147 Jd50
Boldon GB 11 Fa16
Boldu RO 176 Ed63
Boldur RO 174 Ca61
Boldurești MD 173 Fb57
Boldva H 146 Jc50
Böle FIN 98 Ka40
Bøle N 78 Eb26
Böle S 73 Hc23
Böle S 73 Hd21
Böle S 79 Fb30
Böle S 79 Gb31
Böle S 87 Fb33
Bolea E 39 Fb58
Boleč SRB 153 Jc62
Boleč SRB 174 Bb64
Bolemin PL 128 Fd36
Boleráz SK 145 Gd50
Bolesław PL 138 Hd43
Bolesławiec PL 128 Fd40
Bolesławiec PL 129 Ha40
Boleszkowice PL 128 Fc36
Boleszyn PL 122 Hd33
Bolewice PL 128 Ga37
Bolewicko PL 128 Ga37
Bolfan HR 152 Gc57
Bolfoss N 94 Eb41
Bolga N 70 Fa19
Bolgatovo RUS 107 Mb49
Bolgheri I 155 Db67
Bolhás H 152 Gd57
Bolhó H 152 Gd58
Bolhov RUS 202 Ed12
Bolhrad UA 204 Ec18
Boliden S 80 Hb25
Bolimów PL 130 Ja37
Bolinglanna IRL 8 Bb19
Bolintin-Deal RO 176 Ea66
Bolintin-Vale RO 176 Ea66
Boljanic BIH 152 Hb62
Boljanići MNE 159 Ja66
Boljarino BG 180 Dc73
Boljarovo BG 185 Ec74
Boljarsko BG 180 Eb73
Boljevac SRB 178 Bd67
Boljevci SRB 153 Jc62
Boljkovci SRB 159 Jc64
Bolkesjø N 93 Dc42
Bölkow D 119 Eb31
Bolków PL 128 Ga42
Boll, Bad D 134 Da49
Bollebygd S 102 Ec49
Bollendorf D 133 Bc44
Bollène F 42 Jb52
Bollermoen N 71 Fb21
Bollezeele F 21 Gd30
Bólliga E 47 Eb65
Bollnäs S 87 Ga37
Bollosetra N 63 Ja08
Bollsbyn S 94 Ec44
Bollstabruk S 80 Gc31
Bolluca TR 186 Fc77
Bollullos de la Mitación E 59 Bd74
Bollullos par del Condado E 59 Bc74
Bolman HR 153 Hc59
Bolmen S 102 Fa52
Bölmepınar TR 198 Ga90
Bolmsö S 102 Fa51
Bolnhurst GB 20 Fc26
Bolnuevo E 55 Ed74
Bologna I 149 Dc63
Bologne F 30 Jb39
Bolognetta I 166 Ed84
Bolognola I 156 Ec68
Bologoe RUS 202 Ec09
Bologovo RUS 202 Eb10
Bolohani MD 173 Fd56
Bolotana I 169 Ca76
Bolotești RO 176 Ed62
Bolotovo RUS 107 Ma47
Bol'šaja Polja RUS 99 Lc42
Bol'šaja Poljana RUS 113 Jb59
Bol'šakovo RUS 113 Jc58
Bolsena I 156 Ea69
Bol'ševik RUS 203 Fd12
Bol'šie Berežki RUS 113 Jb57
Bol'šinka RUS 203 Fc14
Bol'šoe Zareč'e RUS 99 Mb41
Bol'šoj Borovnja RUS 99 Ld42
Bol'šoj Ižora RUS 99 Ma39
Bol'šoj Jamno RUS 99 Ld44
Bol'šoj Kolpany RUS 99 Mb40
Bol'šoj Kuzemkino RUS 99 Lc41
Bol'šoj L'zi RUS 99 Mb44
Bol'šoj Ozerticy RUS 99 Ma41
Bol'šoj Pustomerža RUS 99 Ld41
Bol'šoj Rožki RUS 99 Ld43
Bol'šoj Ruddilovo RUS 99 Ld40
Bol'šoj Sabicy RUS 99 Ma43
Bol'šoj Sabsk RUS 99 Ma42
Bol'šoj Selo RUS 113 Jd57
Bol'šoj Stremlenie RUS 99 Ld40
Bol'šoj Taglino RUS 99 Mb40
Bol'šoj Teškovo RUS 99 Ma40
Bol'šoj Vruda RUS 99 Ma41
Bol'šoj Zagorje RUS 107 Ma46
Bol'šoj Zahon'e RUS 99 Mb44
Bolsover GB 16 Fa22
Bolstad S 102 Ec46
Bolsward NL 116 Bb33
Bolszewo PL 121 Ha29
Boltaña E 40 Fd58
Boltenhagen D 119 Ea31
Boltigen CH 141 Bc55
Bolton GB 15 Ec21
Bolton Abbey GB 16 Ed20
Bolton-le-Sand GB 11 Ec19
Bolțun MD 173 Fc58
Bolu TR 187 Hb79
Bölüceağac TR 198 Ga93
Bolungarvík IS 2 Ac02
Bolvadin TR 193 Gd85
Bolvașnița RO 174 Cb62
Bóly H 153 Hc58
Bolzano I 143 Dd56
Bomal B 124 Ba42
Bomarken S 94 Eb44
Bomba I 161 Fb71
Bombarral P 50 Aa67
Bominaco I 156 Ed70
Bomlitz D 118 Db35
Bømlo N 92 Bd41
Bompas F 41 Hb57
Bomporto I 149 Dc62
Bomsund S 79 Fd31
Bona F 30 Hc43
Bona S 103 Fc46
Bonac F 40 Gb56
Bönan S 96 Gc39
Bonanza E 59 Bd75
Boñar E 37 Cc56
Bonar Bridge GB 5 Ea06
Bonarcado I 169 Bd77
Bonares E 59 Bc74
Bonäs S 87 Fb38
Bonäset S 78 Fa30
Bonäset S 79 Fd28
Bonåsjøen N 66 Fd16
Bonawe GB 6 Dc11
Bonboillon F 31 Jc41
Boncath GB 14 Dc26
Bonchester Bridge GB 11 Ec15
Boncuklu TR 191 Ed83
Bończa PL 131 Kc40
Bondari RUS 107 Mb52
Bondary PL 123 Kc34
Bondeborg S 73 Ja21
Bondemon S 94 Eb45
Bondeno I 150 Dd61
Bonderup DK 100 Db21
Bondorf D 134 Cc49
Bondstorp S 103 Fb49
Bondyrz PL 131 Kc42
Bönebüttel D 118 Dc31
Bonefro I 161 Fc72
Bonelli I 150 Eb62
Bönen D 125 Cb39
Bones N 67 Gc13
Bonese D 119 Dd35
Bonete E 55 Ed70
Bönhamn S 80 Gd31
Bonhill GB 10 Dd13
Bonhomme F 31 Kb38
Boniches E 54 Ed66
Boniewo PL 129 Hb36
Bonifacio F 154 Cb72
Bonifato F 154 Ca69
Bonilla de la Sierra E 45 Cc64
Bonin PL 120 Fd34
Bonlieu F 31 Jd44
Bonn D 125 Bd41
Bonnat F 33 Gc45
Bonndorf D 141 Cb51
Bonne F 35 Ka45
Bonnebosq F 22 Fd36
Bønnerup Strand DK 101 Dd23
Bonnet DK 100 Cd22
Bonnétable F 28 Fd39
Bonneuil-Matours F 29 Ga44
Bonneval F 29 Gb39
Bonneval F 35 Kb47
Bonneval-en-Diois F 35 Jd50
Bonnevaux F 31 Jd43
Bonnevaux F 31 Ka44
Bonneville F 35 Ka45
Bonneville-la-Louvet F 22 Fd35
Bonnières-sur-Seine F 23 Gc36
Bonnieux F 42 Jc53
Bönnigheim D 134 Cd47
Bönningstedt D 118 Db32
Bonnyapuszta H 145 Ha56
Bonny-sur-Loire F 29 Ha41
Bono E 40 Ga58
Bono I 168 Ca76
Bonorva I 168 Ca76
Bonrepaux F 40 Gc53
Bons F 35 Ka45
Bonsecours F 23 Gb35
Bønsnes N 93 Dd41
Bønsvig DK 109 Eb27
Bontgoch Elerch GB 15 Dd24
Bonțida RO 171 Da57
Bonvilston GB 19 Ea28
Bőny H 145 Ha52
Bonyhád H 153 Hc57
Boo S 96 Gd43
Boock D 119 Ea35
Boolakennedy IRL 13 Ca24
Boos D 142 Db51
Boos F 23 Gb35
Boostedt D 118 Dc31
Bootle GB 11 Eb18
Bopfingen D 134 Db48
Boppard D 133 Ca43
Boquiñeni E 47 Fa60
Bor CZ 135 Ec46
Bor S 103 Fb51
Bor SRB 174 Ca66
Boraja HR 158 Gb66
Borås S 102 Ed49
Borăscu RO 175 Cc65
Borawe PL 122 Jc34
Borawskie PL 123 Ka30
Borba P 50 Ba69
Borca RO 172 Ea57
Borča SRB 153 Jc61
Borca di Cadore I 143 Eb56
Borcea RO 181 Fa67
Börcek TR 191 Ed83
Borchen D 126 Cd39
Borci BIH 152 Ha63
Borci BIH 158 Hb66
Borculo NL 125 Bd37
Bordalba E 47 Ec61
Bordalen N 78 Eb30
Bordány H 146 Jb56
Bordeaux F 32 Fb50
Bordeira P 58 Aa73
Bordei Verde RO 177 Fa64
Bordelum D 108 Da29
Bordères-Louron F 40 Fd57
Bordesholm D 118 Dc30
Bordessoule F 33 Gd45
Bordești RO 176 Ed62
Borðeyri IS 2 Ad03
Bordighera I 43 Kd52
Bording DK 108 Db24
Bordon GB 20 Fb29
Bords F 32 Fb47
Bordușani RO 177 Fa66
Bore I 149 Cd62
Borehamwood GB 20 Fc27
Borek PL 138 Jb44
Borek Wielkopolski PL 129 Gc38
Boreland GB 11 Eb15
Borello I 156 Ea64
Borensberg S 103 Fd46
Boretto I 149 Db61
Bore Verdalen N 92 Ca44
Borg N 66 Fb14
Borgå FIN 98 Kc39
Borgafjäll S 79 Fc25
Borgan N 78 Eb25
Borgarnes IS 2 Ac04
Borgata Marina I 164 Gc78
Borge N 93 Ea44
Borgen N 92 Cd43
Borgen S 80 Gc27
Borgentreich D 126 Da39
Börger D 117 Cb34
Börger D 117 Cb34
Borger NL 117 Bd34
Borger NL 117 Ca34
Borgetto I 166 Ec84
Borggård S 95 Fd45
Borghamn S 103 Fc47
Borghetto I 150 Ea63
Borghetto d'Arroscia I 148 Bd63
Borghetto di Vara I 149 Cd63
Borghetto Santo Spirito I 148 Bd63
Borgholm S 103 Gb52
Borgholzhausen D 126 Cc37
Borghorst D 125 Ca37
Borghusseter N 77 Dd33
Borgia I 164 Gc81
Borgloon B 124 Ba41
Børglum DK 100 Dd20
Borgo F 154 Cc69
Borgo a Mozzano I 155 Da64
Borgo Cortili I 150 Dd62
Borgoforte I 149 Db61
Borgofranco d'Ivrea I 148 Bd59
Borgo Grappa I 160 Ec73
Borgo Libertà I 161 Ga74
Borgomanero I 148 Ca58
Borgomasino I 148 Bd59
Borgonovo Ligure I 149 Cc63
Borgonovo Val Tidone I 149 Cc61
Borgo Piave I 160 Eb73
Borgorose I 156 Ec70
Borgo San Dalmazzo I 148 Bc63
Borgo San Giusto I 161 Fd73
Borgo San Lorenzo I 155 Dc64
Borgo San Michele I 160 Ec73
Borgo San Siro I 148 Cb60
Borgo Schisina I 167 Fd84
Borgo Segezia I 161 Fd73
Borgosesia I 148 Ca58
Borgo Tossignano I 150 Dd63
Borgo Val di Taro I 149 Cd62
Borgo Valsugana I 150 Dd58
Borgsdorf D 127 Ed36
Borgsjö S 80 Gc27
Borgsjö S 87 Ga33
Borgstena S 102 Ed48
Borgund N 85 Da37
Borgunda S 102 Fa47
Borgvattnet S 79 Fd30
Borgvik S 94 Ed43
Bori RUS 99 Ma43
Boriç AL 159 Jb70
Borika BG 179 Cd72
Borima BG 180 Db70
Borina SRB 153 Hd63
Borino BG 184 Da75
Borinskoe RUS 203 Fb12
Borisenki RUS 107 Ma51
Borisoglebsk RUS 203 Fc12
Borisovka RUS 203 Fa14
Borisovo BG 180 Eb68
Borisovo RUS 202 Ed08
Borisovo-Sudskoe RUS 202 Ec08
Borja E 47 Ed60
Børja N 94 Ec41
Borje HR 151 Ga62
Börjelsbyn S 73 Ja21
Börjelslandet S 73 Hd22
Borkan S 71 Fd24
Borkel NL 124 Ba39
Borken D 125 Bd38
Borken (Hessen) D 126 Cd41
Borkheide D 127 Ec37
Borki PL 131 Ka38
Borki PL 138 Jc43
Borki RUS 99 Ma39
Børkop DK 108 Db25
Borków PL 130 Jb42
Borkowo PL 123 Jd33
Borkum D 117 Bd32
Borlänge S 95 Fd40
Borlaug N 85 Da37
Borlești RO 172 Ec58
Børlja N 86 Ea32
Borlu TR 192 Fb85
Bormes-les Mimosas F 43 Kb55
Bormida I 148 Ca63
Bormio I 142 Db56
Born D 119 Ec30
Born NL 125 Bb40
Born S 87 Fd38
Borna D 127 Ec41
Borna D 127 Ed40
Borne D 127 Ea38
Borne F 34 Hd49
Borne NL 117 Bd36
Borne GB 10 Dd17
Borne Sulinowo PL 121 Gb33
Bornheim D 125 Bd41
Bornhöved D 118 Dc31
Börnichen D 127 Ed42
Børnnes N 64 Jc05
Borno I 149 Da58
Bornos E 59 Ca76
Börnsen D 118 Dc33
Bornstedt D 127 Ea39
Boroaia RO 172 Ec56
Borobia E 47 Ec60
Borod RO 171 Cc57
Borodino RUS 113 Jc59
Borodjanka UA 202 Ec14
Borogani MD 177 Fc60
Borohrádek CZ 136 Ga44
Boronów PL 130 Hc42
Borore I 169 Ca77
Boroseni Noi MD 173 Fa54
Boroșneu Mare RO 176 Eb61
Borotin CZ 136 Fc46
Borotno RUS 99 Mb45
Borova UA 203 Fb14
Borova Glava SRB 159 Jb65
Borová Lada CZ 136 Fa48
Borovan BG 179 Cd69
Borovany CZ 136 Fc48
Borovci BG 179 Cc69
Borovci HR 158 Ha67
Borovec BG 179 Cc73
Borovenka RUS 202 Ec09
Boroviči RUS 202 Ec09
Borovik HR 152 Hb60
Borovik RUS 99 Ld45
Borovnica BIH 152 Hb63
Borovnica SLO 151 Fb58
Borovnice CZ 137 Gb46
Borovno CZ 136 Fa46
Borovo BG 180 Ea69
Borovo HR 153 Hd60
Borovo Selo HR 153 Hd60
Borovsk RUS 202 Ed11
Borovye RUS 107 Mb52
Borów PL 129 Gc42
Borów PL 131 Jd41
Borowa PL 138 Jc43
Borowie PL 131 Jd37
Borowiec PL 128 Ga39
Borowina PL 128 Fd39
Borówno PL 121 Ha33
Borowno PL 130 Hc41
Borowo PL 121 Ha30
Borox E 46 Dc65
Borrby S 111 Fb56
Borrby strandbad S 111 Fb57
Borre N 93 Dd43
Borredà E 49 Gd59
Borres E 37 Ca54
Borrèze F 33 Gb50
Borriana E 54 Fc66
Börringe S 110 Fa56
Borriol E 54 Fc66
Borris DK 108 Da24
Borris IRL 13 Cc24
Borris in Ossory IRL 13 Cb22
Borrisokane IRL 13 Ca22
Borrisoleigh IRL 13 Ca23
Börrum S 103 Gb47
Borș RO 170 Ca56
Børsa N 77 Ea30
Borșa RO 171 Da57
Borșa RO 171 Dc55
Borsækoia N 92 Cd43
Borščiv UA 204 Ea16
Borsdorf D 127 Ec40
Borsec RO 172 Ea58
Børselv N 64 Jc06
Borsfa H 145 Gc56
Borsh AL 182 Ab78
Borsk PL 121 Gd31
Borskoe RUS 113 Jb59
Borský Mikuláš SK 137 Gd49
Borsodivánka H 146 Jc52
Borsodnádasd H 146 Jb51
Borsosgyőr H 145 Gd53
Borssele NL 124 Ab38
Börßum D 126 Dc37
Børsted DK 109 Eb27
Borstel D 118 Cd35
Börstig S 102 Fa48
Börstil S 96 Gd40
Bortan S 94 Ed41
Borth D 125 Bd38
Borth GB 15 Dd24
Bortigali I 169 Ca76
Bort-les-Orgues F 33 Ha48
Börtlüce TR 192 Fb85
Börtnan S 87 Fb32
Bortnen N 84 Cb34
Boruja PL 128 Ga37
Boruja Kościelna PL 128 Ga37
Borum DK 108 Dc24
Borup DK 100 Db21
Borup DK 109 Eb26
Boruszyn PL 121 Gb35
Borutta I 168 Ca75
Borve GB 4 Cd06
Borynja UA 204 Ed16
Boryspil' UA 202 Ec14
Boryszyn PL 128 Fd37
Borzechów PL 131 Ka40
Borzechowo PL 121 Ha31
Borzęcice PL 129 Gd38
Borzęciczki PL 129 Gd38
Borzecin PL 138 Jb44
Borzęcin Duży PL 130 Jb37
Borzna UA 202 Ec14
Borzonasca I 149 Cc63
Borzykowa PL 130 Hd41
Borzymy PL 123 Ka31
Borzysław PL 121 Gc31
Borzytuchom PL 121 Gc31
Bosa I 169 Bd76
Bosa Marina I 169 Bd76
Bosanci RO 172 Ec56
Bosanic HR 151 Fd60
Bosanka Kostajnica BIH 152 Gc60
Bosanki Dubočac BIH 152 Hb61
Bosanska Bojna BIH 151 Ga61
Bosanska Krupa BIH 152 Gb62
Bosanska Rača BIH 153 Ja61
Bosanski Brod BIH 152 Hb61
Bosanski Kobaš BIH 152 Ha61
Bosanski Petrovac BIH 152 Gb63
Bosansko Grahovo BIH 158 Gb64
Bošany SK 137 Hb49
Bősárkány H 145 Gd52
Bosau D 118 Dc31
Bosbury GB 15 Ec26
Boscamnant F 32 Fc49
Boșcana MD 173 Fd57
Boscastle GB 18 Db30
Bosco I 156 Eb67
Bosco/Gurin CH 141 Cb56
Bosco Chiesanuova I 149 Dc59
Bosco Marengo I 148 Cb61
Boscotrecase I 161 Fb75
Bösdorf D 118 Dc31

Bosebo – Brisley

Bosebo S 102 Fa50
Bosebyn S 94 Ed42
Bösel D 117 Cc34
Bösenbrunn D 135 Eb43
Bosherston GB 18 Db27
Bosilegrad SRB 179 Ca72
Bosiljevo HR 151 Fd60
Bosilkovci BG 180 Dd69
Bosjön S 95 Fb42
Boskic HR 152 Hb59
Boskoop NL 116 Ad36
Boškov CZ 137 Gd46
Boskovice CZ 137 Gc46
Bosley GB 16 Ed22
Bosna BG 181 Ec68
Bosna TR 185 Eb75
Bosnek BG 179 Cc72
Bošnjace SRB 178 Bd70
Bošnjaci HR 153 Hc61
Boşorod RO 175 Cc61
Bossbøen N 93 Da42
Bossbu N 92 Cc43
Bossea I 148 Bd63
Bossée F 29 Ga42
Bossolasco I 148 Bd62
Bossòst E 40 Ga57
Bostanci TR 185 Ed80
Bostandere TR 185 Ec80
Bostandere TR 199 Hb89
Boštanj SLO 151 Fd58
Bostanlı TR 185 Ec75
Bostanlı TR 193 Gc84
Bostanyeri TR 187 Ha78
Böste läge S 110 Ed57
Boston GB 17 Fc23
Bostrak N 93 Db44
Bošulja BG 179 Da73
Bosund FIN 81 Jb28
Bosundet S 79 Ga28
Bosut SRB 153 Ja61
Bosuta SRB 153 Jc63
Böszénfa H 152 Ha57
Boszkowo PL 129 Gb38
Bot E 48 Fd63
Bote S 80 Gc31
Botesdale GB 21 Ga25
Boteşti RO 172 Ec57
Boteşti RO 173 Fb58
Boteşti RO 176 Dd64
Botevgrad BG 179 Cd70
Botevo BG 179 Cd68
Botevo BG 181 Fa70
Botfei RO 170 Cb58
Bothel D 118 Da34
Bothel GB 11 Eb17
Bothenheilingen D 126 Dc40
Boticas P 44 Bb59
Botilsäter S 94 Ed44
Botiz RO 171 Cd54
Botiza RO 171 Db55
Botley GB 20 Fa30
Botn N 62 Ha09
Botn N 67 Gb13
Botnăreşti MD 173 Fd58
Botne N 92 Ca44
Botne N 93 Dd43
Botnen N 84 Cc34
Botngård N 77 Dd28
Botnlia N 86 Ec32
Bótoa E 51 Bc68
Botoroaga RO 180 Dd67
Botorrita E 47 Fa61
Botoš SRB 153 Jc60
Botoš SRB 174 Bb62
Botoşana RO 172 Eb55
Botoşani RO 172 Ec55
Botrange B 125 Bb42
Botricello I 165 Gd81
Botsmark S 80 Hb27
Bottarone I 149 Cc60
Botteghelle I 167 Fb87
Botten S 94 Ed43
Bottesford GB 16 Fb23
Bottheim N 85 Dc34
Bottidda I 168 Ca76
Böttingen D 142 Cc50
Bottna S 102 Eb46
Bottnaryd S 102 Fa49
Bottrop D 125 Bd39
Bottsfjord N 63 Hd06
Botun MK 182 Ba75
Botunje SRB 174 Bb66
Boturić SRB 178 Bb68
Bötzingen D 141 Ca50
Bötzow D 127 Ed36
Bouaye F 28 Ed42
Bouça P 45 Bc60
Bouce F 22 Fc37
Bouchain F 24 Hb32
Bouçoães P 45 Bc59
Boucq F 25 Jc37
Boudin F 35 Ka46
Boudreville F 30 Ja39
Boudry CH 141 Bb54
Boueilho F 40 Fc54
Bouessay F 28 Fc40
Bouesse F 29 Gc44
Bouges-le-Château F 29 Gc43
Bouglainval F 29 Gb38
Bouguenais F 28 Ed42
Bouilland F 30 Ja42
Bouillargues F 42 Ja53
Bouillé-Ménard F 28 Fa40
Bouillon B 132 Ad43
Bouillon B 132 Ad44
Bouilly F 30 Hd39
Bouin F 27 Ec43
Boujailles F 31 Jd43
Boúka GR 188 Ad83
Boúka GR 194 Bb89
Bouladuff IRL 13 Ca23
Boulay-Moselle F 25 Jd35
Bouligneux F 34 Jb46
Bouligny F 25 Jc35
Bouloc F 41 Hb52
Boulogne-Billancourt F 23 Gd37
Boulogne-sur-Gesse F 40 Ga55
Boulogne-sur-Mer F 21 Gc30
Bouloire F 29 Ga40
Bouloz CH 141 Bb55
Bouniagues F 33 Ga50
Bouray sur-Juine F 29 Gd38
Bourbon-Lancy F 30 Hc44
Bourbon-l'Archambault F 30 Hb44
Bourbonne-les-Bains F 31 Jc39
Bourbourg F 21 Gd30
Bourbriac F 26 Ea38
Bourdeaux F 35 Jc50
Bourdeilles F 33 Ga48
Bourdon F 23 Gc33
Bourdons-sur-Rognon F 30 Jb39
Bouresse F 33 Ga45
Bourg F 32 Fb49
Bourg-Achard F 23 Ga35
Bourganeuf F 33 Gc46
Bourg-Archambault F 33 Gb45
Bourg-Argental F 34 Ja48
Bourg-Beaudouin F 23 Gb35
Bourg-Blanc F 26 Db38
Bourg-de-Péage F 34 Jb49
Bourg-des Comptes F 28 Ed40
Bourg-de-Visa F 40 Gb52
Bourg-d'Oueil F 40 Ga57
Bourg-en-Bresse F 34 Jb45
Bourges F 29 Gd43
Bourg-et-Comin F 24 Hc35
Bourg-Lastic F 33 Ha47
Bourg-Madame F 41 Gd58
Bourgneuf F 29 Gd42
Bourgneuf F 35 Ka47
Bourgneuf-en-Retz F 27 Ec43
Bourgogne F 24 Hd35
Bourgoin-Jallieu F 35 Jc47
Bourg-Saint-Andéol F 42 Jb51
Bourg-Saint-Maurice F 35 Kb47
Bourg-Saint Pierre CH 148 Bc57
Bourgthéroulde-Infreville F 23 Ga35
Bourgueil F 28 Fd42
Bourn GB 20 Fc26
Bournand F 28 Fd43
Bourne GB 17 Fc24
Bournemouth GB 20 Ed31
Bourneville F 23 Ga35
Bournezeau F 28 Fa44
Bournos F 40 Fc55
Bouro P 44 Ad59
Bourriot-Bergonce F 40 Fc52
Bourron F 29 Ha38
Bourtange NL 117 Ca34
Bourth F 23 Ga37
Bourton-on-the-Water GB 20 Ed27
Bousières F 31 Jd42
Boussac F 33 Gd45
Boussais F 28 Fc43
Boussens F 40 Gb56
Bousses F 40 Fd52
Boussière-Poitevine F 33 Ga45
Bouvières F 42 Jc51
Bouville F 29 Gd38
Bouvron F 28 Ed41
Bouxwiller F 25 Kb36
Bouy F 24 Hd36
Bouzas E 36 Ad57
Bouzonville F 25 Jd35
Bouzov CZ 137 Gc46
Bova I 164 Gb84
Bøvær N 62 Gb10
Bovalino I 164 Gb83
Bovalino Marina I 164 Gb84
Bovallstrand S 102 Eb46
Bova Marina I 164 Gb84
Bovan SRB 178 Bd68
Bovec SLO 150 Ed57
Bóveda E 36 Bc56
Bóveda E 38 Dd56
Bovegno I 149 Da58
Bovenau D 118 Db30
Bovenden D 126 Db39
Bovense DK 109 Dd26
Bøverdal N 85 Db35
Bøverfjord N 77 Db31
Boves F 23 Gd33
Boves I 148 Bc63
Bovey Tracey GB 19 Dd31
Boviel GB 9 Cd16
Bovigny B 133 Bb43
Bovik FIN 96 Hb40
Boviken S 80 Hc25
Bovingdon GB 20 Fb27
Bovino I 161 Fd74
Bøvlingbjerg DK 100 Cd23
Bovolone I 149 Dc60
Bovrup DK 108 Db28
Bowburn GB 11 Fa17
Bowes GB 11 Ed18
Bowmore GB 6 Da13
Bowness-on-Solway GB 11 Eb16
Box FIN 98 Kc39
Box GB 19 Ec28
Boxberg D 128 Fb40
Boxberg D 134 Da46
Boxford GB 20 Fa28
Boxholm S 103 Fc47
Boxmeer NL 125 Bb38
Boxtel NL 124 Ba38
Boyabat TR 205 Fb20
Boyalı TR 192 Fa84
Boyalı TR 199 Hb89
Boyalıca TR 186 Ga79
Boyalıca TR 192 Fc82
Boyalık TR 186 Fc77
Boyalılar TR 192 Fa85
Boyardville F 32 Fa46
Boyle IRL 8 Ca19
Bøylestad N 93 Da46
Boynanalar TR 191 Ed81
Boynes F 29 Gd39
Boynton GB 17 Fc19
Bøyum N 84 Cc36
Bozahlat TR 186 Fb80
Bozalan TR 191 Ec85
Bozan TR 193 Gb87
Bozan TR 193 Gd82
Bożanka PL 121 Gc31
Bozarmut TR 187 Hb79
Bozarmut TR 197 Fa89
Božava HR 157 Fc64
Bozbelen TR 192 Fd82
Bozbük TR 192 Fb83
Bozburun TR 187 Gb78
Bozburun TR 197 Fa91
Bozcaada TR 191 Ea81
Bozcaarmut TR 192 Ga81
Bozcaatlı TR 192 Fc85
Bozdağ TR 192 Fa86
Bozdağ TR 192 Ga87
Bozdoğan TR 198 Fb88
Bożejewo PL 123 Jd33
Božejov CZ 136 Fd47
Bozel F 35 Kb47
Bozen I 143 Dd56
Bożeń PL 129 Gb40
Bozen TR 192 Fb81
Božencite BG 180 Dd71
Bożepole Wielkopolski PL 121 Gd29
Božetići SRB 178 Ad67
Boževac SRB 174 Bc65
Bożewo PL 122 Hd35
Bozhane TR 186 Fd77
Bozhigrad AL 182 Ba77
Bozhüyük TR 193 Gc84
Bozhüyük TR 199 Gb91
Božica SRB 179 Ca71
Božice CZ 137 Gb48
Bozieni MD 173 Fc59
Bozieni RO 172 Ed58
Bozioru RO 176 Ec63
Bozkaya TR 199 Ha90
Bozkır TR 191 Ed86
Bozkurt TR 198 Ga88
Bozkuş TR 192 Ga85
Bozlar TR 185 Ed80
Bozören TR 191 Ed82
Bozouls F 33 Ha51
Bozova TR 199 Gb90
Bozovici RO 174 Ca64
Bozürk TR 197 Ec89
Bozsok H 145 Gb54
Boztepe TR 187 Gc79
Boztepe TR 199 Gd91
Boztepe TR 199 Hb92
Božurište BG 179 Cc71
Božurovo BG 180 Eb68
Božurovo BG 181 Fa69
Bozüyük TR 193 Gb81
Bozvelijsko BG 181 Ed71
Bozyaka TR 198 Fd91
Bozzecca I 149 Db58
Bozzolo I 149 Db61
Bra B 124 Ba42
Bra I 148 Bd61
Braaid GB 10 Dc19
Braak D 118 Dc32
Braås S 103 Fc51
Brabova RO 175 Cd66
Bracadale GB 4 Da08
Braccagni I 155 Db68
Bracciano I 160 Ea71
Bracebridge Heath GB 17 Fc22
Braćevac SRB 174 Cb66
Brach F 32 Fa49
Brachlewo PL 121 Hb32
Brachstedt D 127 Eb39
Bracht D 125 Bc39
Brachttal D 134 Cd43
Bracieux F 29 Gc41
Bracigliano I 161 Fc75
Bracigovo BG 184 Da74
Brackagh IRL 13 Cc21
Bräcke S 87 Fd32
Bräcke S 94 Ec44
Brackel D 118 Db33
Brackenheim D 134 Cd47
Brackley GB 20 Fa26
Bracknell GB 20 Fb28
Braco GB 7 Ea12
Brad RO 175 Cc60
Bradaiž LV 107 Ld51
Brădeanu RO 176 Ec65
Brădeni RO 175 Dc60
Bradesiai LT 115 Lb54
Brădeşti RO 175 Cc65
Brădeşti RO 176 Dd60
Bradfield GB 20 Fa28
Bradford GB 16 Ed20
Bradford-on-Avon GB 19 Ec28
Brådland N 92 Cb44
Brádno SK 138 Ja49
Bradu RO 175 Dc65
Brăduleţ RO 175 Dc63
Brăduţ RO 176 Ea60
Bradvari BG 181 Ed68
Bradwell-on-Sea GB 21 Ga27
Bradworthy GB 18 Dc30
Brae GB 5 Fa04
Brædstrup DK 108 Db24
Braemar GB 7 Eb09
Brændstrup DK 108 Da26
Brăeşti RO 172 Ec55
Brăeşti RO 172 Ed57
Brăeşti RO 176 Ec63
Braeswick GB 5 Ec02
Braga P 44 Ad60
Bragadiru RO 176 Ea66
Bragadiru RO 180 Dd68
Bragança P 45 Bd59
Bragayrac F 40 Gb54
Brăicău MD 173 Fb53
Braies I 143 Ea55
Brail CH 142 Da55
Brăila MD 173 Fd58
Brăila RO 177 Fb64
Brailes GB 20 Fa26
Brailovo MK 183 Bb74
Braine F 24 Hb35
Braintree GB 20 Fd27
Braives B 124 Ba41
Brajkovići BIH 158 Ha64
Brajkovići HR 151 Fa61
Brajkovići SRB 159 Jb64
Brake D 118 Cd33
Brakel D 126 Cd38
Brakel NL 124 Ba37
Bräkne-Hoby S 111 Fd54
Brålanda S 102 Ec46
Bralin PL 129 Ha40
Braljina SRB 178 Bc67
Brallo di Pregola I 149 Cc62
Brálos GR 189 Bd84
Braloştiţa RO 175 Cd65
Bram F 41 Gd55
Bramberg A 143 Eb54
Bramhope GB 16 Fa20
Brämhult S 102 Ed49
Bramming DK 108 Da26
Brampton GB 11 Ec16
Brampton GB 21 Gb25
Bramsche D 117 Cb36
Bramstedt D 118 Cd33
Bran RO 176 Dd62
Brånaberg S 71 Ga23
Branäs S 94 Ed39
Braña Vieja E 38 Db56
Branč SK 145 Hb50
Branca I 156 Eb67
Brancaleone Marina I 164 Gb84
Br'ančaninovo RUS 107 Ma48
Brancaster GB 17 Ga23
Brânceni RO 180 Dd68
Brancion F 30 Ja44
Brâncoveneşti RO 171 Dc58
Brâncoveni RO 175 Db66
Brand A 142 Cd54
Brandal N 76 Cc32
Brandåsen S 86 Ed33
Brandasund N 84 Bd40
Brandberg A 143 Ea54
Brandbu N 85 Ea40
Brande DK 108 Da24
Brände S 80 Hc26
Brandenberg A 143 Ea53
Brandenburg D 127 Ec36
Brand-Erbisdorf D 127 Ed42
Branderup DK 108 Da27
Brandeso E 36 Ba55
Brandis D 127 Ec40
Brandlecht D 117 Ca36
Brando F 154 Cc68
Brandö FIN 97 Hd39
Brandomil E 36 Ac55
Brandon GB 11 Fa17
Brandon GB 21 Ga25
Brändön S 73 Ja22
Brändövik FIN 81 Hd30
Brandsby GB 16 Fb19
Brandshagen D 119 Ed30
Brandsøy N 84 Ca35
Brandstad N 77 Db32
Brandstorp S 103 Fb48
Brandsvoll N 92 Cd46
Brandval N 94 Ec40
Brandýs nad Labem-Stará Boleslav CZ 136 Fc44
Brăneşti RO 176 Dd64
Brăneşti RO 176 Eb66
Branica BG 185 Ea74
Branice PL 137 Ha44
Braničevo BG 181 Ed69
Braničevo SRB 174 Bd64
Braniewo PL 122 Hd30
Branik SLO 151 Fa58
Brănişca RO 175 Cc60
Branište BG 181 Fa69
Braniştea RO 171 Db57
Braniştea RO 176 Dd65
Braniştea RO 177 Fa63
Brankovina SRB 153 Jb63
Branków PL 130 Jc38
Branná CZ 137 Gc44
Bränna S 94 Ec45
Brännåker S 79 Fd25
Brännan FIN 81 Jb29
Brannan N 78 Ec29
Brännan S 73 Hb23
Brännan S 73 Hd21
Brännäs S 73 Hb24
Brännås S 87 Ga34
Brannay F 30 Hb39
Brännberg S 73 Hc22
Branne F 32 Fc50
Brannenburg D 143 Ea52
Brännfors S 73 Hc24
Brännholmen S 72 Gd21
Brännkälen S 80 Hc25
Brännland S 80 Hb28
Brännland S 80 Ha28
Brännö S 102 Eb49
Brännvattnet S 80 Hb26
Brännvattnet S 80 Hc26
Brañosera E 38 Db56
Brańsk PL 123 Kb35
Bransles F 29 Ha39
Brańszczyk PL 122 Jc35
Brant Broughton GB 16 Fb23
Brantevik S 111 Fb56
Branti LV 106 La49
Brantice CZ 137 Gd44
Brantôme F 33 Ga48
Braset N 71 Fb19
Braskereidfoss N 94 Ec39
Braslav BY 202 Ea11
Brăšljanica BG 180 Db69
Braşov RO 176 Ea62
Brasparts F 26 Dc38
Brassac F 41 Ha54
Brasschaat B 124 Ad39
Brassempouy F 39 Fb54
Brassy F 30 Hd42
Brastad N 70 Ed22
Brastad S 102 Eb46
Brastavăţu RO 180 Db67
Břasy CZ 136 Fa45
Brąszewice PL 129 Hb39
Braszewice PL 137 Gc43
Brataj AL 182 Ab78
Bratca RO 171 Cc57
Brateljevici BIH 159 Hc64
Brateş RO 176 Eb61
Bratian PL 122 Hd33
Bratislava SK 145 Gd51
Bratja Daskalovi BG 180 Dc73
Bratkowice PL 139 Ka44
Bratonci SLO 145 Gb56
Bratoszewice PL 130 Hd38
Bratovoeşti RO 175 Da66
Bratronice CZ 136 Fa44
Brattåker S 71 Ga24
Bråttas S 81 Hd26
Brattbäcken S 79 Fd27
Brattby S 71 Ga24
Brattby S 80 Hb28
Bratteborg S 103 Fb49
Bratten N 66 Fc17
Bratten S 80 Gd26
Brattfors S 80 Hb29
Brattfors S 95 Fb42
Bratthøvollseter N 77 Ea33
Brattli N 65 Kd08
Brattli N 67 Gc12
Brattmon S 94 Ed39
Brättö FIN 96 Hc41
Bratto I 149 Da58
Bratton GB 19 Ec29
Brattsbäcken S 80 Ha28
Brattsele S 79 Gb28
Brattset N 77 Dc31
Brattvåg N 76 Cc32
Bratunac BIH 159 Ja64
Brătuşeni MD 173 Fa54
Braubach D 133 Ca43
Braughing GB 20 Fd27
Braunau a.Inn A 143 Ec50
Braunfels D 126 Cc42
Braunlage D 126 Dc39
Bräunlingen D 141 Cb51
Braunsbach D 134 Da47
Braunsbedra D 127 Ea40
Braunschweig D 126 Dc37
Bräunsdorf-Langhennersdorf D 127 Ed41
Braunton GB 19 Dd29
Brauteseter N 94 Eb41
Bravães P 44 Ad59
Bravnica BIH 152 Gd63
Bravuogn CH 142 Cd55
Bray IRL 13 Cd22
Bray Shop GB 18 Dc31
Bray-sur-Seine F 30 Hb38
Bray-sur-Somme F 23 Ha33
Braz A 142 Da54
Brazatortas E 52 Da70
Brazey-en-Plain F 30 Jb42
Brazi RO 176 Ea65
Brazii RO 170 Cb59
Brazii RO 176 Eb65
Brbinj HR 157 Fc64
Brčigovo BIH 159 Hd65
Brčko BIH 153 Hc61
Brdani SRB 159 Jc64
Brdovec HR 151 Ga58
Brdów PL 129 Hb37
Bré IRL 13 Cd22
Brea de Aragón E 47 Ed61
Breakish GB 4 Db08
Brean GB 19 Eb29
Breasclete GB 4 Da05
Breasta RO 175 Cd66
Bréau F 29 Ha38
Breaza RO 171 Dc58
Breaza RO 172 Ea55
Breaza RO 176 Ea63
Brebeni RO 175 Db66
Brebu RO 174 Ca62
Brebu RO 176 Ea64
Brebu Nou RO 174 Ca62
Brécey F 22 Fa37
Brechfa GB 15 Dd26
Brechin GB 7 Ec10
Brecht B 124 Ad39
Breckerfeld D 125 Ca40
Břeclav CZ 137 Gc49
Brecon GB 15 Ea26
Bred S 95 Gb42
Breda E 49 Ha60
Breda NL 124 Ad38
Bredablikk N 92 Cd45
Bredal DK 108 Db25
Bredared S 102 Ed48
Bredaryd S 102 Fa51
Bredballe DK 108 Db25
Bredbyn S 79 Fb29
Bredbyn S 80 Gd30
Breddin D 119 Eb35
Breddorf D 118 Da33
Bredebro DK 108 Da27
Bredenbury GB 15 Ec25
Bredene B 21 Ha29
Bredenfelde D 119 Ed33
Bredereiche D 119 Ed34
Bredestad S 103 Fc49
Bredevad DK 108 Da28
Bredgar GB 21 Ga29
Bredkälen S 79 Fd28
Bredon GB 20 Ed26
Bredsäter S 102 Fa46
Bredsätra S 103 Gb52
Bredsel S 73 Hb22
Bredsjö S 95 Fc42
Bredsjön S 87 Gb32
Bredstedt D 108 Da29
Bredsten DK 108 Db25
Bredstrup DK 108 Db26
Bredträsk S 80 Gd28
Bredvik S 80 Hb29
Bredviken S 73 Jb21
Bredwardine GB 15 Eb26
Bredynki PL 122 Jb31
Bree B 125 Bb40
Breg SLO 151 Fd58
Bregana HR 151 Ga58
Breganze I 150 Dd59
Bregare BG 179 Da68
Bregenz A 142 Da53
Breginj SLO 150 Ed57
Bregninge DK 108 Dc28
Bregninge DK 109 Dd28
Bregovo BG 174 Cb66
Bréhal F 22 Ed37
Bréhand F 26 Eb38
Bréhec-en-Plouha F 26 Eb37
Brehme D 126 Dc39
Brehna D 127 Eb39
Breibuktnes N 68 Hd11
Breidablik N 85 Da34
Breiðdalsvík IS 3 Bc06
Breidenbach D 126 Cc41
Breidenbach F 25 Kb35
Breidvik N 78 Eb28
Breidvik N 93 Da44
Breidvika N 66 Fc13
Breiholz D 118 Db30
Breil CH 142 Cc55
Breil F 28 Fd41
Breil-sur-Roya F 43 Kd52
Brein N 84 Cc35
Breisach D 141 Bd50
Breistein N 84 Ca39
Breitenaich A 144 Fa50
Breitenau A 144 Fb52
Breitenbach CH 141 Bd52
Breitenbach D 126 Da42
Breitenbach D 126 Da42
Breitenberg D 136 Fa49
Breitenbrunn A 145 Gc51
Breitenbrunn D 135 Ea48
Breitenbrunn D 135 Ec43
Breitenbrunn D 142 Db50
Breitenfelde D 119 Dd32
Breitenfurth bei Wien A 145 Gb51
Breitengüßbach D 134 Dc44
Breitenworbis D 126 Dc40
Breitscheid D 125 Cb42
Breitungen D 126 Db42
Breivik N 63 Hc06
Breivik N 64 Ka05
Breivik N 66 Ga12
Breivik N 66 Fd17
Breivik N 66 Ga11
Breivik N 92 Cb43
Breivikbotn N 63 Hd05
Breivikeidet N 62 Gd09
Breja RUS 99 Ma42
Brejning DK 108 Db25
Brejtovo RUS 202 Ed09
Brekka N 70 Fa22
Brekke N 84 Ca37
Brekken N 78 Eb29
Brekken N 86 Ec32
Brekkestø N 93 Da47
Brekkhus N 84 Cb38
Brekko N 92 Ca44
Brekkvasselv N 78 Fa25
Breklum D 108 Da29
Brekov SK 139 Ka48
Brekovo SRB 178 Ad67
Brekstad N 77 Dd29
Brembilla I 149 Cd58
Breme I 148 Cb60
Bremen D 118 Cd34
Bremen D 125 Cb39
Bremerhaven D 118 Cd32
Bremervörde D 118 Da33
Bremgarten CH 141 Cb53
Bremm D 133 Bd43
Bremnes N 66 Fd12
Bremnes N 92 Bd41
Bremsnes N 77 Da30
Brem-sur-Mer F 28 Ed44
Breń PL 120 Ga34
Brénaz F 35 Jd46
Brence E 36 Bc57
Brenderup DK 108 Dc26
Brenes E 59 Ca73
Brenesh AL 182 Ac75
Brenguļi LV 106 Kd48
Brenica BG 179 Da69
Brenica BG 181 Ec68
Brenish GB 4 Cd05
Brenna N 66 Fc14
Brenna PL 138 Hc45
Brennan N 78 Ec30
Brennberg D 135 Eb48
Brennbergbánya H 145 Gb52
Brennfjell N 62 Ha10
Brennsvik N 63 Ja06
Breno I 149 Da58
Brenod F 35 Jc46
Brensbach D 134 Cc45
Breńsk PL 121 Gc32
Brentonico I 149 Dc58
Brentwood GB 20 Fd28
Brény F 24 Hb35
Brenzett GB 21 Ga30
Brenzone I 149 Db59
Bres E 37 Bd54
Brescello I 149 Db61
Brescia I 149 Da59
Bresinchen D 128 Fc38
Breskens NL 124 Ab38
Breslau = Wrocław PL 129 Gc41
Bresles F 23 Gd35
Bressanone I 143 Dd55
Bressuire F 28 Fb43
Brest BG 180 Db68
Brèst BY 202 Dd14
Brest F 26 Db38
Brest HR 151 Fa60
Brestak BG 181 Ed69
Brestanica SLO 151 Fd58
Breste BG 179 Da69
Brestova HR 151 Fb61
Brestovac SRB 174 Ca66
Brestovac SRB 178 Bd69
Brestovačka Banja SRB 174 Ca66
Brestovac Požeški HR 152 Ha60
Brestovăţ RO 174 Ca60
Brestovec BG 180 Db69
Brestovene BG 180 Eb68
Brestovica BG 180 Db73
Brestovik SRB 174 Bb64
Brestovo BG 180 Dc70
Breţcu RO 176 Eb61
Bretea Română RO 175 Cc61
Breteau F 29 Ha40
Bretenoux F 33 Gc50
Breteuil F 23 Gd34
Breteuil-sur-Iton F 23 Ga37
Bretford GB 20 Fa25
Bretforton GB 20 Ed26
Bretignolles-sur-Mer F 28 Ed44
Bretigny-sur-Orge F 23 Gd37
Bretnig-Hauswalde D 128 Fb41
Bretoncelles F 29 Ga38
Bretstein A 144 Fb53
Bretten D 134 Cc47
Brettesnes N 66 Fc14
Bretteville-sur-Ay F 22 Ed35
Bretteville-sur-Laize F 22 Fc36
Bretzfeld D 134 Cd47
Breuil-Cervinia I 148 Bd57
Breuillet F 29 Gd38
Breuilpont F 23 Gb36
Breukelen NL 116 Ba36
Breum DK 100 Db22
Breuna D 126 Cd39
Breuvannes-en-Bassigny F 31 Jc39
Brevens bruk S 95 Fd45
Brevik N 93 Dc44
Brevik S 96 Gd43
Brevik S 96 Gd44
Brevik S 103 Fb46
Breza BIH 158 Hb64
Breza MK 178 Bc72
Brežani BG 183 Cb74
Brežde SRB 153 Jb63
Breze BG 179 Cc70
Breze SLO 151 Fd57
Březí CZ 137 Gb49
Brežice SLO 151 Ga58
Brézins F 35 Jc48
Brezje pri Tržič SLO 151 Fb57
Breznica KSV 178 Bc71
Breźnica PL 122 Jc30
Breznica Đakovačka HR 152 Hb60
Breznica Našička HR 152 Hb59
Březnice CZ 136 Fa46
Breznički Hum HR 152 Gb58
Breznik BG 179 Cb71
Brezniţa-Motru RO 175 Cc65
Brezno CZ 136 Fc43
Brezno SK 138 Ja48
Brezno SLO 144 Fd56
Brezoaia MD 177 Ga60
Brezoi RO 175 Db63
Brezolles F 23 Gb37
Březolupy CZ 137 Gd47
Březová CZ 135 Ec44
Březová nad Svitavou CZ 137 Gb46
Brezová pod Bradlom SK 137 Gd49
Brezovica KSV 178 Ba72
Brezovica SK 138 Jc47
Brezovica SLO 151 Fb58
Brezovo BG 180 Dc73
Brezovo Polje BIH 153 Hd62
Brezovo Polje HR 152 Gb61
Brgat HR 158 Hb69
Briançon F 35 Kb49
Briare F 29 Ha41
Briatexte F 41 Gd54
Briatico I 164 Gb82
Bribir HR 157 Ga65
Briceni MD 172 Ed53
Briceni MD 173 Fb53
Bricherasio I 148 Bc61
Bricon F 30 Jb39
Bricquebec F 22 Ed35
Bricqueville F 22 Fb35
Bridaga LV 106 Kb48
Bride GB 10 Dd18
Bridel L 133 Bb45
Brideswell IRL 8 Ca20
Bridge End IRL 9 Cc15
Bridgend GB 19 Ea28
Bridgent GB 6 Da13
Bridge of Baldie GB 7 Dd11
Bridge of Ericht GB 7 Dd10
Bridge of Orchy GB 7 Dd11
Bridgetown IRL 13 Cc25
Bridgnorth GB 15 Ec24
Bridgwater GB 19 Eb29
Břidličná CZ 137 Gd45
Bridlington GB 17 Fc19
Bridport GB 19 Eb30
Briec F 27 Dc39
Brie-Comte-Robert F 23 Ha37
Brielle NL 124 Ac37
Brienne-le-Château F 30 Ja38
Briénon-sur-Armançon F 30 Hc39
Brienz CH 141 Ca55
Brienza I 161 Ga76
Brienzwiler CH 141 Ca55
Brieselang D 127 Ed36
Briesen D 128 Fb37
Brieskow-Finkenheerd D 128 Fb37
Brietlingen D 118 Dc33
Brieulles-sur-Bar F 24 Ja34
Brieva de Cameros E 47 Ea59
Brieves E 37 Ca54
Briey F 25 Jc35
Brig CH 141 Ca56
Brigachtal D 141 Cb51
Brigels CH 142 Cc55
Brigg GB 17 Fc21
Brighouse GB 16 Ed20
Brightlingsea GB 21 Ga27
Brighton GB 18 Db31
Brighton GB 20 Fc30
Brigi LV 107 Ma51
Brignais F 34 Jb47
Brignogan-Plage F 26 Dc37
Brignoles F 42 Ka54
Brignoud F 35 Jd48
Brig o'Turk GB 7 Dd12
Brigueuil F 33 Ga46
Brihuega E 47 Ea63
Brijesta HR 158 Ha68
Brik BIH 159 Hd65
Briksdal N 84 Cd35
Brillon-en-Barrois F 24 Jb37
Brilon D 126 Cc39
Brimfield GB 15 Ec25
Brimnes N 84 Cc39
Brinches P 50 Ba71
Brindisi I 162 Hb75
Bringetofta S 103 Fc50
Brinje HR 151 Fd61
Brinkum D 118 Cd34
Brinkworth GB 20 Ed28
Brinlack IRL 8 Ca15
Brinon-sur-Beuvron F 30 Hc42
Brinon-sur-Sauldre F 29 Gd41
Brintbodarna S 95 Fb39
Brinzeni MD 172 Ed54
Brînzenii Noi MD 173 Fc56
Brinzio I 148 Cb58
Brion F 29 Gc43
Briones E 38 Ea57
Brione Verzasca CH 141 Cb56
Brionne F 23 Ga36
Brion-près-Thouet F 28 Fc43
Brion-sur-Ource F 30 Ja39
Brioude F 34 Hc48
Brioux-sur-Boutonne F 32 Fc46
Briouze F 22 Fc37
Briscous F 39 Ed55
Brisighella I 156 Dd64
Brisley GB 17 Ga24

Brismene – Busachi

Brismene S 102 Fa48
Brissac-Quince F 28 Fc42
Brissago CH 148 Cb57
Bristen CH 141 Cb55
Bristol GB 19 Ec28
Briston GB 17 Ga23
Britiande P 44 Ba61
Brittas IRL 13 Cd22
Britten D 133 Bc45
Britvica BIH 158 Ha66
Britz D 120 Fa35
Brive-la-Gaillarde F 33 Gc49
Brives F 29 Ga40
Briviesca E 38 Dd57
Brivio I 149 Cd58
Brixen I 143 Dd55
Brixen im Thale A 143 Eb53
Brixham GB 19 Ea31
Brixlegg A 143 Ea53
Brize Norton GB 20 Fa27
Brjagovo BG 184 Dc74
Brjanka UA 205 Fb15
Brjansk RUS 202 Ed12
Brjastovec BG 181 Ed72
Brka BIH 153 Hc62
Brložnik BIH 159 Hd64
Brmyan GB 5 Ec02
Brna HR 158 Gc68
Brnaze HR 158 Gc66
Brněnec CZ 137 Gb46
Brničko CZ 137 Gc45
Brniště CZ 128 Fc42
Brnjica SRB 178 Ad68
Brno CZ 137 Gb47
Bro S 94 Ed44
Bro S 96 Gc43
Bro S 104 Ha49
Broad Chalke GB 20 Ed29
Broadford GB 4 Db08
Broadford IRL 12 Bc24
Broadford IRL 12 Bd22
Broad Haven GB 18 Db27
Broad Hinton GB 20 Ed28
Broad Oak GB 21 Ga30
Broadstairs GB 21 Gb28
Broadwas GB 15 Ec25
Broadway GB 19 Eb30
Broadway GB 20 Ed26
Broadwell Ho GB 11 Ed17
Broadwey GB 19 Ec31
Broadwindsor GB 19 Eb30
Broager DK 108 Db28
Broaryd S 102 Ed51
Broby S 111 Fb54
Brobyværk DK 108 Dc27
Broćanac BIH 158 Ha66
Brocas F 39 Fb53
Brocēni LV 105 Jd52
Brochel GB 4 Db08
Brochów PL 130 Ja37
Broćice HR 152 Gc60
Brock D 125 Cb37
Brockel D 118 Da34
Bröckel D 126 Dc36
Brockenhurst GB 20 Ed30
Brockhagen D 126 Cc37
Broczyno PL 121 Gb33
Brod BIH 159 Hd66
Brod KSV 178 Ba73
Brod MK 183 Bb74
Brod MK 183 Bb76
Brod SRB 179 Ca70
Brodalen S 102 Eb46
Brodarevo SRB 159 Jb67
Brodce CZ 136 Fc44
Broddarp S 102 Fa48
Broddbo S 95 Ga41
Broddetorp S 102 Fa47
Brodec MK 178 Ba72
Brodec'ke UA 204 Eb15
Brodek u Přerova CZ 137 Gd46
Brodek u Prostějova CZ 137 Gc47
Brodenbach D 133 Ca43
Broderstorf D 119 Eb31
Broderup DK 108 Da28
Brodica SRB 174 Bd65
Brodick GB 10 Dc14
Brodie Castle GB 5 Eb07
Brodina RO 172 Ea55
Brodina de Jos RO 172 Ea55
Brod na Kupi HR 151 Fc60
Brodnica PL 122 Hc34
Brodowe Łąki PL 122 Jb33
Brodowo PL 129 Gd37
Brodski Stubnik HR 152 Ha61
Brody PL 128 Fc39
Brody PL 128 Fd38
Brody PL 130 Jb36
Brody UA 204 Ea15
Broglie F 23 Ga36
Brojce PL 120 Fd31
Brok PL 123 Jd35
Brokdorf D 118 Da31
Brokęcino PL 121 Gc33
Brokefjell N 93 Da43
Brokind S 103 Fd47
Brokke N 92 Cd44
Brokstedt D 118 Db31
Brolo I 167 Fc84
Bromarv FIN 97 Jc41
Bromberg A 145 Gb52
Bromberg = Bydgoszcz PL 121 Ha34
Brome D 127 Dd36
Brome GB 21 Gb25
Bromley GB 20 Fd28
Bromma N 85 Dc39
Brommösund S 94 Fa45
Bromnes N 62 Gd08
Bromölla S 111 Fb54
Brompton GB 17 Fc19
Brömsebro S 111 Ga54
Bromsgrove GB 20 Ed25
Bromskirchen D 126 Cc40
Bromyard GB 15 Ec26
Bron F 34 Jb47
Brönäs S 94 Ed39
Bronchales E 47 Ed64
Brøndby Strand DK 109 Ec26
Brønderslev DK 100 Dc20
Broni I 149 Cc61
Bronice PL 128 Fc39
Bronikowo PL 120 Ga34
Bronikowo PL 129 Gb38
Broniszew PL 130 Hc41
Bronken N 94 Eb39
Bronkow D 128 Fa39
Brönnestad S 110 Fa54
Brønnøysund N 70 Ed23
Bronowo PL 123 Jd33
Brøns DK 108 Da27
Bronte I 167 Fc85
Bronzani BIH 152 Gc62
Brook GB 20 Ed30
Brookhouse GB 11 Ec19
Broomfield GB 20 Fd27
Broomfield IRL 9 Cd19
Broomhaugh GB 11 Ed16
Broons F 26 Ec38
Brora GB 5 Ea06
Brørup DK 108 Da26
Brösarp S 111 Fb56
Broscauți RO 172 Ec54
Brossac F 32 Fc48
Brøstadbotn N 67 Gb11
Broșteni MD 173 Ga55
Broșteni RO 172 Ea57
Broșteni RO 175 Cc64
Broșteni RO 176 Ed62
Broszków PL 131 Jd37
Brotas P 50 Ad68
Broto E 40 Fc57
Broträsk S 80 Hc26
Brottby S 96 Gd43
Brøttem N 77 Ea30
Brotterode D 126 Dc42
Brøttum N 86 Ea38
Brou F 29 Gb39
Brouage F 32 Fa47
Broué F 23 Gb37
Brough GB 11 Ec18
Brough Lodge GB 5 Fa03
Broughshane GB 9 Da16
Broughton GB 11 Eb17
Broughton GB 15 Eb22
Broughton GB 15 Ec20
Broughton GB 16 Fb21
Broughton GB 20 Fa29
Broughton Astley GB 16 Fa24
Broughton-in-Furness GB 11 Eb18
Broughton Poggs GB 20 Ed27
Broumov CZ 137 Gb43
Brousse-le-Château F 41 Ha53
Broussey-Raulecourt F 25 Jc36
Broutzéika GR 195 Bd87
Brouvelieures F 31 Ka38
Brouwershaven NL 124 Ac37
Brouzet-lès-Alès F 42 Ja52
Brovary UA 202 Ec14
Brovst DK 100 Db21
Brown Candover GB 20 Fa29
Brownhills GB 16 Ed24
Brownston GB 19 Dd32
Broxton GB 15 Eb23
Broye F 31 Jc41
Brozas E 51 Bc66
Brożec PL 129 Gc42
Brozolo I 148 Bd60
Brozzo I 149 Da58
Brseč HR 151 Fb61
Brštanavo HR 158 Gb66
Brtnice CZ 136 Ga47
Brtonigla HR 150 Ed60
Brú IS 2 Ad04
Brua N 86 Eb34
Bruay-la-Buissière F 23 Gd31
Bruay-sur-les-Eaux F 24 Hb31
Brubakk N 78 Eb30
Bruchhausen-Vilsen D 118 Cd35
Bruchköbel D 134 Cd43
Bruchmühlbach-Miesau D 133 Bd46
Bruchsal D 134 Cc47
Bruck A 143 Ec54
Brück D 127 Ec37
Bruck/Opf. D 135 Eb47
Bruck an der Leitha A 145 Gc51
Bruck an der Mur A 144 Fd53
Bruckberg D 134 Dc46
Bruckberg D 135 Ea49
Brücken D 133 Bd46
Brückl A 144 Fb55
Bruckmühl D 143 Ea52
Brucoli I 167 Fd86
Bruc-sur-Aff F 27 Ec40
Brudzeń Duży PL 122 Hc35
Brudzew PL 129 Hb37
Brudzowice PL 138 Hc43
Brue-Auriac F 42 Ka54
Brüel D 119 Ea32
Bruès E 36 Ba57
Bruff IRL 12 Bd24
Bruflat N 85 Dc38
Brugg CH 141 Ca52
Brugge B 124 Aa39
Brüggen D 125 Bc39
Brüggen D 126 Db37
Brugnato I 149 Cd63
Bruhagen N 77 Da31
Bruheim N 84 Cd35
Brühl D 125 Bd41
Brühl D 134 Cc46
Bruinisse NL 124 Ac37
Bruino I 148 Bc60
Bruino I 148 Bc60
Bruiu RO 175 Dc61
Bruksvallarna S 86 Ed32
Brullés E 38 Dc57
Brûlon F 28 Fc40
Brumath F 25 Kc36
Brumby D 127 Ea38
Brummen NL 125 Bc37
Brumov-Bylnice CZ 137 Ha48
Brumovice CZ 137 Gc48
Brumundal N 86 Ea38
Brunate I 149 Cc58
Brunau D 119 Ea35
Brunava LV 106 Kc52
Brundby DK 109 Dd25
Brune N 76 Cd33
Bruneck I 143 Ea55
Brunehamel F 24 Hd33
Brunella I 168 Cc75
Brünen D 125 Bd38
Brunet F 42 Ka53
Brunete E 46 Db64
Bruneval F 22 Fd34
Brunflo S 79 Fc31
Brunhosinho P 45 Bd61
Brunico I 143 Ea55
Bruniquel F 40 Gc53
Brunkeberg N 93 Da43
Brunmyrheden S 72 Gd23
Brunn D 119 Ed32
Brunn S 96 Ha43
Brunn S 102 Fa49
Brünn = Brno CZ 137 Gb47
Brunna S 96 Gc43
Brunnalm A 144 Fd53
Brunn an der Wild A 136 Fd49
Brunnen CH 141 Cb54
Brunnsberg S 87 Fb37
Brunnthal D 143 Ea51
Brunsbüttel D 118 Da31
Brunskog S 94 Ed42
Brunssum NL 125 Bb40
Brunswijk = Braunschweig D 126 Dc37
Bruntál CZ 137 Gd45
Bruree IRL 12 Bd24
Brus SRB 178 Bb68
Brusago I 150 Dd57
Brusand N 92 Ca45
Brušane HR 151 Fd63
Brusarci BG 179 Cc68
Brusasco I 148 Bd60
Brusen BG 179 Da71
Brüsewitz D 119 Ea32
Brushkuli AL 182 Ab74
Bruskowo Wielkopolski PL 121 Gc30
Brusnik SRB 174 Ca66
Brusnik SK 146 Hd50
Brusno-kúpele SK 138 Hd48
Br'usovo RUS 113 Jd59
Brušperk CZ 137 Hb45
Brusque F 41 Hb53
Brussel B 124 Ac40
Brusson I 148 Bd58
Brüssow D 120 Fb33
Brusturi RO 170 Cb56
Brusturi-Drăgănești RO 172 Ec57
Brusturoasa RO 172 Eb59
Brusy PL 121 Gd32
Brutelles F 23 Gb32
Bruton GB 19 Ec29
Brutovce SK 138 Jc47
Bruttig-Fankel D 133 Bd43
Brutuli LV 106 La48
Bruvik N 84 Cb39
Bruvno HR 151 Ga63
Bruvoll N 94 Eb40
Bruxelles B 124 Ac40
Bruyères F 31 Ka38
Bruyères-et-Montberault F 24 Hc34
Bruz F 28 Ed39
Bruzaholm S 103 Fd49
Bruzilas LV 105 Jd52
Bruzzano Zeffirio I 164 Gb84
Břvarty CZ 136 Fa43
Brvenica MK 178 Ba73
Brvenik SRB 178 Ba68
Brwinow PL 130 Jb37
Brydalen N 86 Eb34
Bryggesåk N 92 Cc46
Bryggia N 84 Cb34
Brylle DK 108 Dc27
Bryn N 93 Dd41
Brynamman GB 19 Dd27
Bryncethin GB 19 Ea28
Bryne N 92 Ca44
Bryngwran GB 14 Dc22
Bryngwyn GB 15 Eb26
Bryn-henllan GB 14 Db26
Brynica PL 129 Ha42
Brynje S 79 Fc31
Brynmawr GB 19 Eb27
Bryrup DK 108 Db24
Bryzgiel PL 123 Kb30
Brzączowice PL 138 Ja45
Brzan SRB 174 Bc66
Brza Palanka SRB 174 Cb65
Brzava MNE 159 Jb67
Brzeće SRB 178 Bb68
Brzechowo PL 122 Hd35
Brzeg PL 129 Gd42
Brzeg Dolny PL 129 Gc40
Brzeg Głogowski PL 128 Ga39
Brzemiona PL 121 Ha33
Brześce PL 130 Jc37
Brześć Kujawski PL 129 Hb36
Brzesko PL 138 Jb44
Brzeszcze PL 138 Hc44
Brzezie PL 121 Gc32
Brzezie PL 129 Ha38
Brzezina PL 120 Fd34
Brzezinki PL 129 Ha41
Brzeziny PL 120 Ga34
Brzeziny PL 129 Ha39
Brzeziny PL 130 Hd38
Brzeziny PL 139 Jd44
Brzeźnica PL 138 Hd44
Brzeźnica Krajeńska PL 121 Gb33
Brzeźnio PL 129 Hb39
Brzeźno PL 120 Ga32
Brzeźno PL 121 Hb34
Brzeźno PL 128 Fc37
Brzeźno PL 131 Kd40
Brzeźno Lęborskie PL 121 Gd29
Brzeźno Szlacheckie PL 121 Gd31
Brzezówka PL 138 Jc43
Brzohode SRB 174 Bc65
Brzostek PL 139 Jd44
Brzotín SK 138 Jb49
Brzoza PL 121 Ha34
Brzóza PL 130 Jc39
Brzóza Królewska PL 139 Ka43
Brzozie PL 122 Hd33
Brzozie Lubawskie PL 122 Hc33
Brzózka PL 128 Fc38
Brzozów PL 139 Ka45
Brzozowa PL 123 Kb32
Brzozowiec PL 128 Fd36
Brzozowo PL 122 Ja34
Brzozowo PL 123 Kb32
Brzuska PL 139 Kb45
Brzuze PL 122 Hc34
Bšezno CZ 135 Ed43
Bû F 23 Gb37
Bua S 102 Ec50
Buais F 28 Fb38
Buar S 94 Eb45
Buavåg N 92 Ca41
Buba RO 176 Ec63
Bubakken N 77 Ea33
Bubbio I 148 Ca62
Bubenreuth D 135 Dd46
Buberget S 80 Hb27
Bubiai LT 114 Ka54
Bublava CZ 135 Ec43
Bubnevo RUS 107 Ld48
Bubry F 27 Ea40
Bubuieci MD 173 Fd58
Bubwith GB 16 Fb20
Buc F 23 Gd37
Buča UA 202 Ec14
Bučač UA 204 Ea16
Bucak TR 197 Ed89
Bucak TR 198 Fc88
Bucak TR 199 Gc89
Bucak TR 199 Ha91
Bucakşeyhler TR 199 Ha91
Buccheri I 167 Fc87
Bucchianico I 157 Fa70
Buccino I 161 Fd75
Buccleuch GB 11 Eb15
Bucelas P 50 Aa68
Buceş RO 175 Cc60
Buch D 142 Db50
Buch D 143 Ea50
Buchanty GB 7 Ea11
Buchau, Bad D 142 Cd51
Buchbach D 143 Eb50
Buchdorf D 134 Dc48
Bucheben A 143 Ec54
Bücheloh D 127 Dd42
Büchen D 118 Dc33
Buchen D 134 Cd46
Buchenbach D 134 Da47
Büchenbach D 135 Dd47
Buchenberg D 142 Db52
Büchenbeuren D 133 Bd44
Buchholz D 118 Db33
Buchholz D 118 Db35
Buchholz D 127 Ed37
Buchholz (Westerwald) D 125 Ca41
Buchin RO 174 Ca62
Buchișu RO 179 Da67
Büchlberg D 135 Ed49
Buchloe D 142 Dc51
Buchlovice CZ 137 Gd48
Buchs CH 142 Cd54
Buchy F 23 Gb34
Bučin MK 183 Bb75
Bucine I 156 Dd66
Bučin Prohod BG 179 Cc70
Bučionys LT 114 Kd57
Bučište MK 178 Bd73
Bucium RO 171 Cd59
Buciumeni MD 173 Fa57
Buciumeni RO 176 Ed61
Buciumi RO 171 Cd57
Buciumoni RO 176 Dd64
Bučiūnai LT 114 Kb53
Buciușca MD 173 Fd56
Bučje HR 152 Gd60
Bučje SRB 174 Ca66
Buckarby S 95 Gb41
Buckden GB 11 Ed19
Buckden GB 20 Fc25
Bückeburg D 126 Cd37
Bücken D 118 Da35
Buckfastleigh GB 19 Dd31
Buckhaven GB 7 Eb12
Buckie GB 5 Ec07
Buckingham GB 20 Fb26
Buckland GB 20 Fa27
Bucklay GB 15 Eb22
Buckminster GB 16 Fb24
Bucknell GB 15 Eb25
Buckow D 128 Fb36
Bucks Green GB 20 Fc29
Bucoșnița RO 174 Cb62
Bucov RO 176 Eb64
Bucovăț MD 173 Fc57
Bucovăț RO 175 Cd66
Bucovica BIH 158 Gd66
Bučovice CZ 137 Gc47
Bucquoy F 23 Ha32
Bucsa H 147 Jd53
Bucșani RO 176 Ea64
Bucșani RO 176 Ea66
Bucureșci RO 175 Cc60
București RO 176 Eb66
Bucuria MD 177 Fc61
Bucuru RO 175 Cd61
Bucy-lès-Pierrepont F 24 Hc34
Buczek PL 130 Hc39
Buczkowice PL 138 Hc45
Bud N 76 Cd31
Budachów PL 128 Fc37
Budačka Rijeka HR 151 Ga60
Budacu de Jos RO 171 Dc57
Budacu de Sus RO 171 Dc57
Budăi MD 173 Fc56
Budakdoğanca TR 185 Eb75
Budakeszi H 146 Hc53
Budaklar TR 187 Gc78
Budaklar TR 191 Ea82
Budaklar TR 192 Ga86
Budakovo MK 183 Bb76
Buđanovci SRB 153 Jb61
Budaörs H 146 Hc53
Budapest H 146 Hd53
Búðardalur IS 2 Ac03
Budby GB 16 Fb22
Buddbyn S 73 Hd21
Büddenstedt D 127 Dd37
Buddusò I 168 Cb75
Bude GB 18 Dc30
Budeasa RO 175 Dc64
Budei MD 177 Fc62
Budel NL 125 Bb39
Büdelsdorf D 118 Db30
Budënnovsk RUS 205 Ga16
Budens P 58 Aa74
Büderich D 125 Bd38
Büdesheim D 133 Bc43
Budești MD 173 Fd58
Budești RO 171 Db55
Budești RO 171 Db58
Budești RO 175 Db64
Budești RO 180 Eb67
Budevo SRB 178 Ad68
Budia E 47 Ea64
Budila RO 176 Ea62
Budilovo RUS 99 Ma43
Budimci HR 152 Hb60
Budimír SK 139 Jd48
Budimlić Japra BIH 152 Gb62
Büdingen D 134 Cd43
Budišov CZ 136 Ga47
Budišov nad Budišovkou CZ 137 Gd45
Budkovce SK 139 Ka48
Budleigh Salterton GB 19 Ea31
Budmerice SK 145 Gd50
Budogošč' RUS 202 Eb08
Budoi RO 170 Cb56
Budomierz Duży PL 139 Kc43
Budoni I 168 Cc75
Budoviž RUS 107 Ld46
Budraičiai LT 114 Ka55
Budrio I 150 Dd63
Budry PL 122 Jc30
Budumirci MK 183 Bc76
Budureasa RO 171 Cc58
Buduslău RO 170 Cb55
Budva MNE 159 Hd70
Būdviečiai LT 113 Jc56
Būdviečiai LT 114 Ka59
Būdviečiai LT 114 Ka59
Būdvietis LV 114 Kb59
Budweis = České Budějovice CZ 136 Fb48
Budy PL 130 Hd36
Budyně CZ 136 Fb43
Budzeń PL 120 Fc33
Budziska PL 123 Jd30
Budzisz PL 122 Hc31
Budziszewice PL 130 Ja39
Budzyń PL 121 Gc35
Buenache de Alarcón E 53 Eb67
Buenache de la Sierra E 47 Ec65
Buenaventura E 46 Cd65
Buenavista de Valdavia E 38 Da57
Buendía E 47 Ea65
Buer D 126 Cc37
Buerås S 102 Eb50
Bueres E 37 Cd55
Bueu E 36 Ad57
Buftea RO 176 Ea66
Bugac H 146 Ja55
Bugarra E 54 Fb67
Buğdaylar TR 192 Fd85
Buğdaylı TR 186 Fa80
Buğdüz TR 193 Gd81
Buğdüz TR 199 Gb89
Bugeac MD 177 Fc60
Bugeat F 33 Gd47
Bugeniai LT 113 Jc53
Buggerru I 169 Bd79
Bughea de Jos RO 175 Dc63
Buginiai LT 114 Kd53
Buglose F 39 Fa54
Bugnara I 161 Fa71
Bugojno BIH 158 Ha64
Bugøyfjord N 65 Kc07
Bugøynes N 65 Kc07
Bugraz TR 186 Fd78
Buguchwała PL 139 Ka44
Bugul'ma RUS 203 Ga09
Bugurzyn PL 122 Ja34
Büğüş TR 197 Fa92
Bugyi H 146 Hd54
Buharkent TR 192 Fc87
Bühl D 133 Cb48
Bühlertal D 133 Cb48
Bühlertann D 134 Da47
Bühlerzell D 134 Da48
Buhoci RO 172 Ed59
Buhølen N 92 Cc47
Buholmen N 65 Kc07
Buhovci BG 181 Ec70
Buhovo BG 179 Cc71
Buhuși RO 172 Ec59
Builth Wells GB 15 Ea26
Buinsk RUS 203 Fd09
Buiríos Uí Chéin IRL 13 Ca22
Buironfosse F 24 Hc33
Buis-les-Baronnies F 42 Jc51
Buitenpost NL 117 Bc33
Buitrago del Lozoya E 46 Dc62
Buivydžiai LT 115 Lb57
Buj RUS 203 Fa08
Buják H 146 Ja51
Bujalance E 52 Da72
Bujanicy RUS 99 Ma40
Bujanovac KSV 178 Bc71
Bujaraloz E 48 Fc61
Buje HR 150 Ed60
Bujnovci BG 180 Ea71
Bujor MD 173 Fc58
Bujoreni RO 180 Dd67
Bujoru RO 180 Dd68
Buk H 145 Gc53
Buk PL 129 Gb37
Bukaiši LV 106 Ka52
Bukanovskaja RUS 203 Fc13
Bukas LV 106 Kd48
Bükdere TR 192 Fb82
Bükkábrány H 146 Jc51
Bukkemoen N 62 Gb10
Bükkösd H 152 Hb57
Büklüce TR 199 Hb91
Bukonys LT 114 Kc56
Bukorovac SRB 174 Bb66
Bukovac SRB 153 Hd59
Bukova Gora BIH 158 Gd66
Bukovec BG 179 Cb68
Bukovi SRB 159 Jb64
Bukovica HR 152 Ha59
Bukovica MNE 159 Ja67
Bukovica SLO 151 Fb57
Bukowa PL 131 Kb42
Bukowiec PL 129 Gc40
Bukowiec PL 121 Ha33
Bukowiec PL 128 Ga37
Bukowina Tatrzańska PL 138 Ja46
Bukówko PL 120 Ga31
Bukownica PL 129 Ha40
Bukowno PL 138 Hd43
Bukowsko PL 139 Ka46
Buksnes N 66 Fd12
Bukta N 64 Jd05
Bukta N 78 Ea29
Buky UA 204 Ec15
Bülach CH 141 Cb52
Bulăiești MD 173 Fd56
Bulair BG 181 Ed71
Bulanlak TR 205 Fd19
Bulărda MD 173 Fc57
Bulavėnai LT 114 Ka55
Bulboaca MD 173 Fa53
Bulboaca MD 173 Ga58
Bulboci MD 173 Fb54
Bulbucata RO 176 Ea66
Bulbuente E 47 Ed60
Buldan TR 192 Fc87
Bulduri LV 106 Kb50
Bulgar RUS 203 Fd09
Bulgiza AL 163 Jc72
Bulgiza AL 182 Ac74
Bulgurca TR 191 Ec87
Buli Potok SRB 178 Bd68
Bülkau D 118 Da32
Bulken N 84 Cb38
Bulkowo PL 130 Ja36
Bull N 92 Cc46
Bullas E 61 Ec72
Bullaun IRL 12 Bd21
Bulle CH 141 Bc55
Bullerup DK 109 Dd26
Büllingen B 125 Bc42
Bullmark S 80 Hc27
Bully-les-Mines F 23 Ha31
Bulnes E 38 Da55
Bulshizë AL 163 Jb71
Bultei I 168 Ca75
Bulz RO 171 Cc57
Bulzești RO 175 Da65
Bulzeștii de Sus RO 171 Cc59
Bumbăta MD 173 Fb57
Bumbești-Jiu RO 175 Cd63
Bumbești-Pitic RO 175 Da63
Buna BIH 158 Hb67
Bun an Phobail IRL 9 Cc15
Bunarkaig GB 6 Dc09
Bunbeg IRL 8 Ca15
Bunbrosna IRL 9 Cb20
Bunclody IRL 13 Cc23
Buncrana IRL 9 Cc15
Bun Cranncha IRL 9 Cc15
Bunde D 117 Ca33
Bünde D 126 Cd37
Bundenthal D 133 Ca47
Bun Dobhráin IRL 8 Ca17
Bundoran IRL 8 Ca17
Bundorf D 134 Dc44
Bunes N 65 Kb06
Bunessan GB 6 Da11
Bunești RO 172 Ec56
Bunești RO 175 Db63
Bunești RO 176 Dd60
Bunești-Averești RO 173 Fb59
Bungay GB 21 Gb25
Bunge S 104 Ha48
Bunić HR 151 Ga62
Bunila RO 175 Cc61
Bunka LV 105 Jb52
Bunkeflostrand S 110 Ed56
Bunken DK 101 Dd19
Bunkris S 86 Fa36
Bunmahon IRL 13 Cb25
Bun na hAbhna IRL 8 Bb18
Bunnahowen IRL 8 Bb18
Bun na Leaca IRL 8 Ca15
Bunnyconnellan IRL 8 Bd18
Buño E 36 Ad54
Buñol E 54 Fb68
Bunovo BG 179 Cd71
Bunschoten NL 116 Bb36
Bunteşti RO 170 Cb58
Buntingford GB 20 Fc26
Buntowo PL 121 Gc34
Buñuel E 47 Ed59
Bünüs TR 187 Hb78
Bunyola E 57 Hb67
Buochs CH 141 Cb54
Buoldavárre S 68 Hc16
Buonabitacolo I 161 Ga77
Buonalbergo I 161 Fc74
Buonconvento I 155 Dc67
Bur DK 100 Cd23
Burano I 150 Eb60
Burbach D 125 Cb41
Burbáguena E 47 Ed63
Burbia E 37 Bd56
Burbiškiai LV 114 Kb56
Burcei I 169 Cb79
Burcin F 35 Jc48
Burcun TR 186 Ga80
Burdąg PL 122 Jb32
Burdnomohkki FIN 69 Ka13
Burdur TR 199 Gb88
Bureå S 72 Gc23
Bureå S 80 Hc25
Bureåborg S 80 Gc30
Burela E 36 Bc53
Burelles F 24 Hc33
Büren D 126 Cc39
Buren NL 117 Bc32
Buren NL 124 Ba37
Büren an der Aare CH 141 Bd53
Bures GB 21 Ga26
Burfjord N 63 Hc08
Burford GB 20 Ed27
Burg D 118 Da31
Burg D 127 Eb37
Burg D 128 Fb38
Burgas BG 181 Ed73
Burgau A 145 Gb54
Burgau D 134 Db49
Burg auf Fehmarn D 119 Ea30
Burgberg D 142 Db52
Burgbernheim D 134 Db46
Burgbrohl D 125 Bd42
Burgdorf CH 141 Bd54
Burgdorf D 126 Db36
Burgdorf D 126 Db37
Burgebrach D 134 Dc45
Bürgel D 127 Ea41
Burgess Hill GB 20 Fc30
Burghagel D 134 Db49
Burghammer D 128 Fb40
Burghaslach D 134 Dc45
Burghaun D 126 Da42
Burghausen D 127 Eb40
Burghausen D 143 Ec51
Burghead GB 5 Eb07
Burgheim D 134 Dc49
Burgh-Haamstede NL 124 Ab37
Burgh le Marsh GB 17 Fd22
Burgh Saint Peter GB 21 Gb25
Burgillos del Cerro E 51 Bc70
Burgio I 166 Ec85
Burgio I 167 Fc86
Burgkirchen A 143 Ec51
Burgkirchen D 143 Ec51
Burgkunstadt D 135 Dd44
Burg Lauenstein D 135 Dd43
Burglauer D 134 Db43
Burglengenfeld D 135 Ea47
Burgo E 36 Bb55
Burgo P 44 Ad62
Burgoberbach D 134 Dc47
Burgohondo E 46 Cd64
Burgos E 38 Dc58
Burgos I 168 Ca76
Burgpreppach D 134 Dc44
Burgsalach D 135 Dd48
Burgsinn D 134 Da44
Burgstädt D 127 Ec41
Bürgstadt D 134 Cd45
Burg Stargard D 119 Ed33
Burgsteinfurt D 125 Ca37
Burgsvik S 104 Gd51
Burgthann D 135 Dd47
Burgueira E 36 Ac58
Burguete E 39 Ed56
Burgui E 39 Fa57
Burguillos E 59 Ca73
Burguillos de Tajo E 52 Db66
Burgum NL 117 Bb33
Burgwald D 126 Cc41
Burgwedel D 126 Db36
Burgwindheim D 134 Dc45
Burhan TR 192 Fd82
Burhaniye TR 191 Ec82
Buriasco I 148 Bc61
Burie F 32 Fc47
Burila Mare RO 174 Cb65
Burja BG 180 Dc70
Burjassot E 54 Fb67
Burjuc RO 174 Cb60
Burk D 134 Db47
Burkal DK 108 Da28
Burkardroth D 134 Db43
Burkat PL 122 Ja33
Burkaty PL 122 Jb35
Burkhardtsdorf D 127 Ec42
Burlăceni MD 177 Fc62
Burlacu MD 177 Fc61
Burladingen D 142 Cc50
Burlănești MD 172 Ed54
Burley in Wharfedale GB 16 Ed20
Burlo D 125 Bd37
Burlton GB 15 Eb23
Burmahan TR 199 Ha90
Burness GB 5 Ed02
Burnham-on-Crouch GB 21 Ga27
Burnham-on-Sea GB 19 Eb29
Burnley GB 16 Ed20
Burntisland GB 11 Eb13
Buronzo I 148 Ca59
Burovac SRB 174 Bc65
Burow D 119 Ed32
Burøysund N 62 Gd07
Burrafirth GB 5 Fa03
Burravoe GB 5 Fa04
Burrel AL 163 Jc72
Burren IRL 12 Bc21
Burres E 36 Ba55
Burringham GB 16 Fb21
Burry Port GB 19 Dd27
Burs S 104 Ha50
Bursa TR 186 Fd80
Burscheid D 125 Bd40
Burscough GB 15 Eb21
Burseryd S 102 Fa51
Bursiljum S 80 Hc26
Bürstadt D 134 Cc45
Bursuc MD 173 Fc58
Burszewo PL 122 Jb31
Burtenbach D 142 Db50
Burtnieki LV 106 Kd48
Burton Agnes GB 17 Fc19
Burton Constable GB 17 Fc20
Burton-in-Kendal GB 11 Ec19
Burton Latimer GB 20 Fb25
Burtonport IRL 8 Ca15
Burton-upon-Stather GB 16 Fb21
Burton-upon-Trent GB 16 Fa23
Burträsk S 80 Hc26
Burujón E 52 Da66
Burvik S 81 Hd26
Burwash GB 20 Fd30
Burwell GB 17 Fd22
Burwell GB 20 Fd25
Burwick GB 5 Ec04
Bury GB 15 Ec21
Bury Saint Edmunds GB 21 Ga25
Burzenin PL 129 Hb40
Burzyn PL 123 Ka33
Busachi I 169 Ca77

Busalla – Cañaveral de León

Busalla I 148 Cb62
Busana I 149 Da63
Busano I 148 Bd59
Bușăuca MD 173 Fd56
Busca I 148 Bc62
Busche I 150 Ea58
Busdorf D 108 Db29
Buseck D 126 Cc42
Busemarke DK 109 Ec28
Busenberg D 133 Ca47
Busendorf D 134 Dc44
Bušetina HR 152 Gd58
Buševec HR 152 Gb59
Bushat AL 163 Jb71
Bushey GB 20 Fc27
Bushfield IRL 12 Bd23
Bushmills GB 9 Cd15
Busici MK 183 Bc74
Busigny F 24 Hb33
Bușila MD 173 Fb56
Busilovac SRB 178 Bc67
Bušince SK 146 Hd50
Bus'k UA 204 Ea15
Buske DK 109 Eb27
Buskhyttan S 103 Gb46
Busko-Zdrój PL 138 Jb43
Bušletić BIH 152 Hb62
Buśno PL 131 Kd40
Busnovi HR 152 Ha60
Busot E 55 Fb71
Busovača BIH 158 Hb64
Bussac-Forêt F 32 Fc49
Bussang F 31 Ka39
Busséol F 34 Hb47
Busseto I 149 Da61
Bussière-Badil F 33 Ga47
Bussières F 24 Hb36
Büßleben D 127 Dd41
Bussö FIN 96 Hc40
Bussoleno I 148 Bb60
Busson F 30 Jb38
Bussum NL 116 Ba36
Bussy-le-Repos F 30 Hb39
Bustadmon S 78 Fa30
Bustares E 46 Dd62
Bustarviejo E 46 Dc63
Bușteni RO 176 Ea63
Bustidoño E 38 Db56
Bustillo de Páramo E 37 Cb57
Bustnes N 71 Fb20
Busto E 37 Ca53
Busto Arsizio I 148 Cb59
Buštranje SRB 178 Bd72
Bustuchin RO 175 Da64
Büsum D 118 Da30
Buszkowo PL 121 Gd33
Buszów PL 120 Fd35
Butan BG 179 Cd68
Butea RO 172 Ed57
Buțeni MD 173 Fc58
Buteni RO 170 Cb59
Butera I 167 Fa87
Bütgenbach B 125 Bb42
Butimanu RO 176 Ea65
Bütingė LT 113 Jb54
Butjadingen D 117 Cc32
Butkaičiai I LT 114 Ka56
Butkiškė LT 114 Ka55
Butkiškiai LT 114 Kc55
Butler's Bridge IRL 9 Cb19
Butlerstown IRL 12 Bc26
Butley GB 21 Gb26
Butniūnai LT 114 Kd53
Butoiești RO 175 Cd65
Butovo BG 180 Dc70
Butrimonys LT 114 Kc59
Butrint AL 182 Ab79
Butron E 38 Ea55
Butryny PL 122 Ja32
Butryny PL 122 Ja32
Bütschwil CH 142 Cc53
Büttelborn D 134 Cc44
Buttenheim D 135 Dd45
Buttenwiesen D 134 Dc49
Buttevant IRL 12 Bd24
Buttington GB 15 Eb24
Buttlar D 126 Db42
Buttle S 104 Ha50
Buttlerstown IRL 13 Cb25
Buttstädt D 127 Ea41
Büttstedt D 126 Db40
Butuceni MD 173 Fd56
Buturlinovka RUS 203 Fb13
Buturugeni RO 176 Ea66
Butzbach D 134 Cc43
Bützow D 119 Eb32
Buurse NL 125 Bd37
Buvåg N 66 Fd14
Buvarp N 78 Eb27
Buvik N 77 Da32
Buvika N 70 Fa19
Buvika N 70 Fa20
Buvika N 77 Ea30
Buvika N 86 Ec34
Buxières-les-Mines F 30 Hb44
Buxtehude D 118 Db33
Buxton GB 16 Ed22
Buxy F 30 Ja43
Büyükalan TR 198 Ga90
Büyükanafarta TR 185 Ea80
Büyükbelen TR 192 Fa85
Büyükbelkıs TR 199 Ha91
Büyükçavuşlu TR 185 Ed76
Büyükçavuşlu TR 186 Fa77
Büyük Çekmece TR 186 Fc77
Büyükdağdere TR 192 Fb83
Büyükdöllük TR 185 Eb75
Büyükfındık TR 191 Ed82
Büyük Gökçeli TR 199 Gd88
Büyükhusum TR 191 Ea82
Büyükışıklar TR 191 Ed83
Büyükkale TR 191 Ed87
Büyükkalecik TR 193 Gc85
Büyükkaraağaç TR 198 Fb91
Büyükkarabağ TR 193 Ha85
Büyükkarıştıran TR 185 Ed77
Büyükkayalı TR 192 Fd86
Büyükkılıcılı TR 186 Fb77
Büyükköy TR 199 Gb90
Büyükkumluca TR 199 Gd91
Büyükmandıra TR 185 Ec76
Büyüköğünlü TR 185 Eb74
Büyükorhan TR 192 Fc82
Büyükoturak TR 193 Gb85
Büyükpınar TR 191 Ed81
Büyüksaka TR 193 Gb83
Büyükşapçı TR 191 Ec82
Büyüksöğle TR 199 Gb92
Büyüktekke TR 187 Ha77
Büyükyayla TR 193 Gc84
Büyükyenice TR 191 Ed83
Büyükyoncalı TR 186 Fa76
Buza RO 171 Db57
Buzançais F 29 Gb43
Buzancy F 24 Ja34
Buzău RO 176 Ec64
Buzescu RO 180 Dd67
Buzet HR 151 Fa60
Buziaș RO 174 Bd61
Buzica SK 138 Jc49
Bužim BIH 152 Gb61
Buzluca TR 193 Ha84
Buzoești RO 175 Dc65
Buzovgrad BG 180 Dd72
Buzsák H 145 Ha56
Bweeng IRL 12 Bc25
Bwlch GB 15 Ea26
Bwlchllan GB 15 Dd25
Bwlch-y-ffridd GB 15 Ea24
Bwlch-y-Sarnau GB 15 Ea25
By N 78 Ea28
By S 94 Ed42
By S 94 Ed44
By S 95 Ga41
Byans-sur-Doubs F 31 Jd42
Byarum S 103 Fb49
Byberget S 87 Fd33
Bybjerg DK 109 Eb25
Bychav BY 202 Eb12
Bychawa PL 131 Kb40
Bycina PL 137 Hb43
Byczki PL 130 Ja38
Byczyna PL 129 Ha41
Byczyna PL 138 Hd44
Bydalen S 79 Fb31
Bydgoszcz PL 121 Ha34
Bydlin PL 121 Gc29
Bye S 88 Gc33
Byford GB 15 Eb26
Bygdeå S 80 Hc27
Bygdeträsk S 80 Hc26
Bygdsiljum N 85 Db36
Bygdsiljum S 80 Hc26
Bygget S 102 Ed52
Bygland N 92 Cd45
Byglandsfjord N 92 Cd45
Bykle N 92 Cd43
Byklestøylane N 92 Cd43
Bykovo RUS 203 Fd13
Bylchau GB 15 Ea22
Byluft N 65 Kb07
Byn S 94 Ed42
Byneset N 77 Ea30
Byremo N 92 Cc46
Byrkjedal N 92 Cb44
Byrkjelo N 84 Cc35
Byrness GB 11 Ec15
Byrudstua N 85 Ea40
Byrum DK 101 Ea20
Byšice CZ 136 Fc44
Byske S 73 Hc24
Byškovice CZ 137 Ha46
Bysław PL 121 Ha33
Bysträsk S 80 Ha27
Býšť CZ 136 Ga44
Bysting N 77 Dd29
Bystrá SK 138 Hd48
Bystré CZ 137 Gb46
Bystré SK 139 Jd47
Bystrecovo RUS 107 Ma47
Bystřice CZ 136 Fc46
Bystřice CZ 138 Hc46
Bystřice nad Pernštejnem CZ 137 Gb46
Bystřice pod Hostýnem CZ 137 Ha47
Bystrzyca PL 131 Ka41
Bystrzyca Kłodzka PL 137 Gc44
Byszyno PL 120 Ga31
Bytča SK 137 Hb47
Bytnica PL 128 Fd37
Bytom PL 138 Hc43
Bytom Odrzański PL 128 Ga39
Bytoń PL 129 Hb36
Bytów PL 121 Gd31
Bytyń PL 129 Gb36
Byvattnet S 80 Gc30
Byxelkrok S 104 Gc50
Bzenec CZ 137 Gd48
Bzovík SK 146 Hd50

C

Căbăiești MD 173 Fb57
Cabaj-Cápor SK 145 Ha50
Cabaleiros (Tordoia) E 36 Ad54
Cabanac F 32 Fb51
Cabañaquinta (Aller) E 37 Cc55
Cabañas de la Dornilla E 37 Ca57
Cabanes E 54 Fd65
Cabañes de Esgueva E 46 Dc60
Cabanillas E 47 Ed59
Cabanillas de la Sierra E 46 Dc63
Čabar HR 151 Fc59
Cabasse F 42 Ka54
Cabdella E 40 Gb58
Cabeça de Carneiro P 50 Ba70
Cabeça Gorda P 50 Ad71
Cabeço de Vide P 50 Ba68
Cabella Ligure I 149 Cc62
Cabertarar TR 192 Fc86
Căbești RO 170 Cb57
Cabezabellosa E 45 Ca65
Cabeza del Buey E 52 Cc69
Cabeza la Vaca E 51 Bd71
Cabezamesada E 53 Dd66
Cabezarados E 52 Da69
Cabezarrubias E 52 Da70
Cabezas del Villar E 45 Cc63
Cabezas Rubias E 59 Bb72
Cabezón E 46 Da60
Cabezón de la Sal E 38 Db55
Cabezón de Liébana E 38 Da55
Cabezuela E 46 Db62
Cabezuela del Valle E 45 Cb65
Cabia E 38 Dc58
Čabiny SK 139 Ka47
Caboalles de Arriba E 37 Ca56
Cabourg F 22 Fc35
Cabra E 60 Cd74
Čabra KSV 178 Ba70
Cabrach GB 7 Ec08
Cabra del Santo Cristo E 60 Dc73
Cabra de Mora E 54 Fb65
Cabragh GB 9 Cc17
Cabrahigos E 59 Ca77
Cabras I 169 Bd77
Cabredo E 39 Eb57
Cabreiros E 36 Bb54
Cabrejas del Pinar E 47 Ea60
Cabrela P 50 Ac69
Cabrerets F 33 Gc51
Cabrières F 41 Hc54
Cabrillas E 45 Ca63
Cabruñana E 37 Cb54
Cabuna HR 152 Ha59
Cacabelos E 37 Bd57
Cacabézë AL 182 Ab75
Čačak SRB 159 Jc64
Caccamo I 166 Ed84
Caccuri I 165 Gd80
Cacela Velha P 58 Ba74
Cáceres E 51 Bd67
Čačėrsk BY 202 Ec13
Čačëvičy BY 202 Eb12
Cachafeiro E 36 Ba56
Cachão P 45 Bc60
Cachopo P 58 Ad73
Cachtice SK 137 Ha49
Cacia P 44 Ac62
Cacica RO 172 Eb55
Cacin E 60 Db75
Čaćinci HR 152 Ha59
Căciulata RO 175 Db63
Cádabo (Baleira) E 36 Bc55
Cadafresnas E 37 Bd57
Cadagua E 38 Dd56
Cadalen F 41 Gd53
Cadalso de los Vidrios E 46 Da65
Cadaqués E 41 Hc58
Cadaval P 50 Ab67
Cadavedo E 37 Ca54
Čadavica BIH 152 Gd63
Čadavica HR 152 Ha59
Čadavica Gornja BIH 153 Hd62
Čadca SK 138 Hc46
Cadelbosco di Sopra I 149 Db62
Caden F 27 Ec41
Cadenabbia I 149 Cc57
Cadenberge D 118 Da32
Cadenet F 42 Jc53
Cádiar E 60 Dc76
Cadillac F 32 Fc51
Cadillon F 40 Fc54
Čadinje SRB 159 Jb66
Cadis F 41 Gd54
Cádiz E 59 Bd76
Cadolzburg D 134 Dc46
Cadouin F 33 Ga50
Cadreita E 47 Ed59
Cadzand NL 124 Ab38
Caen F 22 Fc36
Caerleon GB 19 Eb27
Caernarfon GB 15 Dd22
Caerphilly GB 19 Eb28
Caersws GB 15 Ea24
Čaevo RUS 202 Ed08
Čafa MK 182 Ba74
Ćafe MNE 159 Ja69
Cagan Aman RUS 203 Ga14
Cagan-Nur RUS 203 Ga14
Caggiano I 161 Fd76
Çağıllar TR 192 Fc84
Çağış TR 192 Fa82
Cagitán E 61 Ec72
Çağlarca TR 199 Gc91
Çağlayık TR 185 Ed74
Cagli I 156 Eb66
Cagliari I 169 Ca80
Čaglin HR 152 Hb60
Çağman TR 199 Gb93
Cagnano Varano I 161 Ga72
Cagnes-sur-Mer F 43 Kc53
Cagnotte F 39 Fa54
Čagoda RUS 202 Ec08
Caher IRL 8 Bc20
Cahir IRL 13 Ca24
Caherdaniel IRL 12 Ba26
Cahersiveen IRL 12 Ba25
Cahors F 33 Gc51
Cahul MD 177 Fb61
Cahuzac-sur-Vére F 41 Gd53
Căianu RO 171 Da58
Căianu Mic RO 171 Db56
Caiazzo I 161 Fb74
Caín E 38 Da55
Căinari MD 173 Fd59
Căinarii Vechi MD 173 Fb54
Câineni RO 175 Db62
Câineni-Băi RO 176 Ed64
Caión E 36 Ad54
Čaira BG 179 Cd73
Cairaclia MD 177 Fc62
Cairnborrow GB 7 Ec08
Cairndow GB 6 Dc12
Cairnryan GB 10 Dc16
Cairo Montenotte I 148 Ca62
Caiseal IRL 13 Ca24
Caisleán an Bharraigh IRL 8 Bc19
Caisleán an Chomair IRL 13 Cb23
Caister-on-Sea GB 17 Gc24
Caistor GB 17 Fc21
Caivano I 161 Fb74
Cajarc F 33 Gc51
Cajba MD 173 Fa55
Čajetina SRB 159 Jb65
Čajić BIH 158 Gc65
Čajka BG 181 Fb70
Čajle MK 178 Ba73
Čajniče BIH 159 Hd66
Cajvana RO 172 Eb55
Cák H 145 Gb53
Çakallar TR 191 Ec86
Çakallar TR 191 Ed82
Čakany SK 145 Gd51
Çakılköyü TR 186 Fa79
Çakıllı TR 186 Fa76
Çakıllı TR 192 Fa83
Čakino RUS 203 Fc12
Çakır TR 191 Ed81
Çakır TR 198 Fd90
Çakırbeyli TR 197 Ed88
Çakırca TR 186 Ga79
Çakırdere TR 191 Ec82
Çakırlar TR 191 Ec83
Çakırlar TR 192 Fc85
Çakırlar TR 193 Hb87
Çakırlar TR 199 Gc91
Çakırözü TR 193 Gc86
Çakmak TR 191 Eb83
Çakmak TR 192 Fd82
Çakmak TR 192 Ga83
Çakmak TR 193 Hb84
Çakmak TR 198 Fb90
Čakovci HR 153 Hd60
Čakovec HR 152 Gb57
Çal TR 192 Fd87
Cala E 59 Bd72
Cala P 51 Bb69
Cala Antena E 57 Hc67
Calabernardo I 167 Fd88
Cala Blanca E 57 Ja66
Cala Blava E 57 Hb67
Calabritto I 161 Fd75
Călacea RO 170 Ca58
Calaceite E 48 Fd63
Calacuccia F 154 Cb69
Cala de Mijas E 60 Cd77
Cala d'Or E 57 Hc68
Cala en Porter E 57 Ja66
Calaf E 49 Gc60
Calafat RO 179 Cc67
Calafell E 49 Gc62
Cala Figuera E 57 Hc68
Calafindești RO 172 Eb55
Calafort Ros Láir IRL 13 Cd25
Calafuria I 155 Da66
Cala Galdana E 57 Ja66
Cala Gonone I 169 Cc76
Calahonda E 60 Cd77
Calahonda E 60 Dc76
Calahora de Boedo E 38 Db57
Calahorra E 39 Ec58
Calais F 21 Gc30
Cala Liberotto I 168 Cc76
Cala Llonga E 56 Gc69
Calalzo di Cadore I 143 Eb56
Cala Major E 57 Hb67
Calambrone I 155 Da65
Cala Mesquida E 57 Jb66
Cala Millor E 57 Hd67
Calamocha E 47 Ed63
Calamonaci I 166 Ec86
Calamonte E 51 Bd69
Cala Morell E 57 Ja65
Călan RO 175 Cc61
Calañas E 59 Bb72
Calanda E 48 Fc63
Calangianus I 168 Cb74
Cala Pi E 57 Hb68
Calapica BG 180 Db73
Cala Rajada E 57 Hd67
Călărași MD 173 Fc57
Călărași RO 171 Da59
Călărași RO 173 Fa56
Călărași RO 179 Da68
Călărași RO 181 Ed67
Cala Rossa F 154 Cb72
Cala Sant Vicenç E 56 Gc69
Cala Sant Vicenç E 57 Hc66
Calascibetta I 167 Fa85
Călășeni MD 173 Fa55
Calasetta I 169 Bc80
Calasparra E 61 Ec72
Calatafimi-Segesta I 166 Eb84
Calatañazor E 47 Ea60
Calatayud E 47 Ed61
Călățele RO 171 Cd58
Calații Bistriței RO 171 Dc57
Calatorao E 47 Ed61
Cala Turqueta E 57 Ja66
Calau D 128 Fa39
Cala Vedella E 56 Gb69
Calbe D 127 Ea38
Calberlah D 126 Dc36
Çalçakırlar TR 192 Fd87
Calcatoggio F 154 Ca70
Calcena E 47 Ec60
Çalcı TR 193 Ha81
Calcinelli I 156 Ec65
Calcio I 149 Cd59
Calco I 149 Cc58
Căldăraru RO 175 Dc66
Caldaro I 142 Dc56
Caldarola I 156 Ec67
Caldas da Felgueira P 44 Ba63
Caldas da Rainha P 50 Ab66
Caldas de Monchique P 58 Ab73
Caldas de Reis E 36 Ad56
Caldas de Vizela P 44 Ad60
Caldbeck GB 11 Eb17
Calde E 36 Bb55
Caldearenas E 39 Fb58
Caldebarcos E 36 Ac55
Caldelas E 36 Ad58
Caldelas P 44 Ad60
Caldelas P 44 Ad59
Calden D 126 Da39
Calderari I 167 Fb86
Çaldere TR 192 Fb82
Calder Mains GB 5 Eb04
Calders E 49 Gd60
Caldes de Boí E 40 Ga58
Caldes de Malavella E 49 Hb60
Caldes de Montbui E 49 Gd60
Caldirola I 149 Cc62
Caldueño E 38 Da54
Caleao E 37 Cc55
Caledon GB 9 Cd18
Calella E 49 Hb60
Calella de Palafrugell E 49 Hc60
Calenzana F 154 Ca69
Calera de León E 51 Bd71
Calera y Chozas E 52 Cd66
Caleruega E 46 Dc60
Caleruela E 52 Cc66
Cales de Mallorca E 57 Hc67
Calestano I 149 Da62
Calfa MD 173 Ga58
Calfsound GB 5 Ec02
Calgary GB 6 Da10
Çalı TR 186 Fc80
Çalıbahçe TR 191 Ec84
Càlig E 48 Fd64
Calignac F 40 Fd52
Călimănești RO 175 Db63
Călinești MD 173 Fa56
Călinești RO 171 Db55
Călinești RO 175 Dc64
Călinești RO 180 Dd67
Călinești-Oaș RO 171 Da54
Çalışlar TR 193 Gc85
Calitri I 161 Fd75
Calizzano I 148 Bd63
Çalkara TR 193 Gc81
Çalkaya TR 193 Ha81
Çalkaya TR 199 Gd91
Çalköy TR 193 Gb84
Çalköy TR 193 Gb84
Callac F 26 Ea38
Callainn IRL 13 Cb24
Callan IRL 13 Cb24
Callander GB 7 Dd12
Callanish GB 4 Da05
Callantsoog NL 116 Ba34
Callas F 43 Kb53
Callelongue F 42 Jc55
Calliano I 148 Ca60
Calliano I 149 Dc58
Çallıca TR 199 Gb89
Çallıcaalan TR 187 Ha80
Callington GB 18 Dc31
Callosa d'En Sarrià E 55 Fc70
Callosa de Segura E 55 Fa72
Callow IRL 8 Bd19
Callús E 49 Gd60
Čalma SRB 153 Ja61
Călmănești RO 176 Ed61
Călmățuiu RO 180 Dc67
Călmățuiu de Sus RO 180 Dc67
Calne GB 20 Ed28
Calnegre y Los Curas E 55 Ed74
Călnic RO 175 Cc64
Călnic RO 175 Da61
Calolziocorte I 149 Cd58
Calonge E 49 Hc60
Calonge E 57 Hc68
Calonne-Ricouart F 23 Gd31
Calopăr RO 175 Cd66
Calp E 55 Fd70
Calpe E 55 Fd70
Caltabellotta I 166 Ec85
Caltagirone I 167 Fb87
Caltanissetta I 167 Fa86
Caltavuturo I 167 Fa85
Çaltepe TR 198 Ga89
Çaltepe TR 199 Ha90
Çaltı TR 193 Gb81
Çaltı TR 198 Ga88
Çaltıçukur TR 199 Hb91
Çaltıkkoru TR 191 Ec83
Çaltılıbük TR 192 Fc81
Caltojar E 47 Ea61
Călugăreni RO 180 Ea67
Caluso I 148 Bd59
Calvão P 44 Ac63
Calvarrasa de Abajo E 45 Cb62
Calvello I 161 Ga76
Calver GB 16 Fa21
Calvering GB 20 Fd26
Calverrasa de Arriba E 45 Cb62
Calvi F 154 Ca69
Calvià E 56 Ha67
Calviac F 33 Gd50
Calvi dell' Umbria I 156 Eb70
Calvine GB 7 Ea10
Calvinet F 33 Ha50
Calvini RO 176 Eb63
Calvisson F 42 Ja53
Calvos de Randín E 36 Ba58
Calw D 134 Cc48
Calzada de Bureba E 38 Dd57
Calzada de Calatrava E 52 Db70
Calzada del Coto E 37 Cd58
Calzada de los Molinos E 38 Da58
Calzada de Valdunciel E 45 Cb62
Calzadilla E 45 Bd65
Calzadilla de los Barros E 51 Bd71
Camaiore I 155 Da64
Çamalan TR 192 Fd82
Çamalan TR 193 Gd81
Camaldoli I 156 Dd65
Camaleño E 38 Da55
Çamaltı İskelesi TR 191 Eb86
Camañas E 47 Fa64
Camăr RO 171 Cc56
Camarasa E 48 Ga60
Camarası TR 198 Fc88
Cămărașu RO 171 Db58
Camarena E 46 Db65
Camarena de la Sierra E 47 Fa65
Camarenilla E 52 Db66
Camarès F 41 Hb53
Camaret-sur-Mer F 26 Db38
Camarinal E 59 Ca78
Camariñas E 36 Ac54
Camarles E 48 Ga63
Camarma de Esteruelas E 46 Dc64
Camarmeña E 38 Da55
Cămărzana RO 171 Da54
Camarzana de Tera E 45 Cb59
Camas E 59 Bd74
Camastra I 166 Ed86
Cambados E 36 Ad56
Cambas P 44 Ba65
Cambazlı TR 192 Fa85
Çambel TR 191 Ed86
Cambela E 36 Bc58
Cambeo E 36 Bb57
Camber GB 21 Ga30
Çambeyli TR 193 Gb85
Cambil E 60 Dc73
Camblesforth GB 16 Fb20
Cambo GB 11 Ed16
Cambo-les-Bains F 39 Ed55
Camborne GB 18 Da32
Cambra P 44 Ad62
Cambrai F 24 Hb32
Cambre E 36 Ba54
Cambres P 44 Ba61
Cambridge GB 20 Fd26
Cambrils E 48 Gb62
Cambs D 119 Ea32
Camburg D 127 Ea41
Çamcı TR 191 Ec82
Çamdere TR 192 Fd86
Çamdibi TR 192 Ga83
Camedo CH 148 Cb57
Camelford GB 18 Dc31
Çameli TR 198 Fd90
Camelle E 36 Ac54
Camenca MD 173 Fa55
Camenca MD 173 Fd54
Camerano I 156 Ed66
Camerata Cornello I 149 Cd58
Cameri I 148 Cb59
Camerino I 156 Ec67
Camerota I 161 Fd77
Çamiçi TR 191 Ec85
Çamiçi TR 197 Ed89
Camiers F 23 Gc31
Çamiliyayla TR 192 Ga82
Caminha P 36 Ac58
Caminomorisco E 45 Ca64
Caminreal E 47 Ed63
Çamırdık TR 192 Ga84
Camisano Vicentino I 150 Dd59
Camızlar TR 198 Fd92
Çamkonak TR 187 Gc77
Çamköy TR 191 Ea81
Çamköy TR 197 Ed90
Çamköy TR 198 Ga90
Çamköy TR 199 Gd91
Çamlı TR 187 Ha78
Çamlı TR 191 Eb86
Çamlı TR 197 Fa90
Çamlıca TR 191 Ea81
Çamlıca TR 199 Hb88
Çamlıdere TR 199 Gc89
Çamlık TR 192 Fc83
Çamlık TR 197 Ec88
Çamlık TR 197 Ed90
Çamlik TR 199 Hb89
Çamlıkköy TR 191 Ec82
Çamlıköy TR 198 Fd92
Çamlitepe TR 199 Hb91
Cammarata I 166 Ed85
Camogli I 149 Cc63
Camolin IRL 13 Cd24
Çamoluk TR 198 Fb89
Çamönü TR 192 Fa84
Camors F 27 Ea40
Camp IRL 12 Ba24
Campagna I 161 Fd75
Campagnano di Roma I 156 Ea70
Campagne F 39 Fb53
Campana I 165 Gd79
Campanario E 51 Cb69
Campanas E 39 Ed57
Campanet E 57 Hb66
Câmpani RO 171 Cc58
Campanillas E 60 Cd76
Campaspero E 46 Db61
Campbeltown GB 10 Db14
Campel F 27 Ec40
Campénéac F 27 Ec40
Câmpeni MD 177 Fc62
Câmpeni RO 171 Cd59
Camperduin NL 116 Ba34
Campia P 44 Ad62
Campi Bisenzio I 155 Dc65
Câmpie Turzii RO 171 Da59
Campiglia Marittima I 155 Da67
Campiglia Soana I 148 Bc59
Campigliatello Silano I 164 Gc80
Campigna I 156 Dd65
Campillo E 45 Cb60
Campillo E 47 Fa65
Campillo de Altobuey E 53 Ec67
Campillo de Arenas E 60 Db74
Campillo de Azaba E 45 Bd63
Campillo de Deleitosa E 51 Cb66
Campillo de Dueñas E 47 Ed63
Campillo de las Doblas E 53 Ec70
Campillo de Llerena E 51 Ca70
Campillos E 60 Cc75
Campillos Sierra E 47 Ec65
Câmpina RO 176 Ea64
Çampınar TR 191 Ed85
Câmpineanca RO 176 Ed62
Campisábalos E 46 Dd62
Campi Salentina I 162 Hb76
Campitello F 154 Cb69
Campitello di Fassa I 143 Dd56
Campitello Matese I 161 Fb73
Campli I 156 Ed69
Camplongo E 37 Cc56
Campo E 40 Fd58
Campo Arcis E 54 Fa68
Campobasso I 161 Fc72
Campobecerros E 36 Bc58
Campobello di Licata I 167 Fa86
Campobello di Mazara I 166 Eb85
Campo Blénio CH 142 Cc55
Campocologno CH 149 Da57
Campodarsego I 150 Ea59
Campo de Besteiros P 44 Ad63
Campo de Caso E 37 Cd55
Campo de Criptana E 53 Dd68
Campo del Hospital E 36 Bb53
Campo de San Pedro E 46 Dc61
Campo de Víboras P 45 Bd60
Campo di Giove I 161 Fa71
Campodimele I 160 Ed73
Campo do Gerês P 44 Ba59
Campodolcino I 142 Cd56
Campo Felice I 156 Ed70
Campofelice di Roccella I 167 Fa84
Campofiorito I 166 Ec85
Campofrío E 59 Bc72
Campogalliano I 149 Db62
Campohermoso E 61 Eb76
Campolasta I 143 Dd56
Campolattaro I 161 Fc73
Campoli Appennino I 160 Ed72
Campo Ligure I 148 Cb62
Campolongo E 36 Ba54
Campolongo Maggiore I 150 Ea60
Campo Lugar E 51 Cb68
Campo Maior P 51 Bb68
Campomarino I 161 Fc71
Campomarino I 162 Ha76
Camponaraya E 37 Bd57
Campora San Giovanni I 164 Gb81
Campo Real E 46 Dc65
Camporeale I 166 Ec84
Campo Redondo P 58 Ab72
Camporrells E 48 Ga59
Camporrobles E 54 Ed67
Campos E 57 Hc68
Camposampiero I 150 Ea59
Camposancos E 36 Ac58
Camposanto I 149 Dc62
Campo Staffi I 160 Ed71
Campotéjar E 60 Db74
Campo Tenese I 164 Gb78
Campotosto I 156 Ed69
Campo Tures I 143 Ea55
Campo Vallemaggia CH 141 Cb56
Campo Xestada E 36 Ad54
Camprodon E 41 Ha58
Camps-en-Amiénois F 23 Gc33
Camptown GB 11 Ec15
Câmpu lui Neag RO 175 Cc62
Câmpulung RO 175 Dc63
Câmpulung la Tisa RO 171 Db54
Câmpulung Moldovenesc RO 172 Ea56
Câmpuri RO 176 Ec61
Camrose GB 14 Db26
Çamsu TR 192 Ga85
Çamucu TR 191 Ed82
Camuñas E 52 Dc68
Çamurköy TR 198 Fd92
Çamurluk TR 187 Gd80
Çamyayla TR 193 Gb81
Çamyazı TR 192 Fd85
Çamyuva TR 192 Ga85
Çamyuva TR 199 Gc92
Çan TR 191 Ec81
Čaňa SK 139 Jd49
Canabal E 36 Bb57
Cañada E 55 Fa70
Cañada de la Cruz E 61 Eb72
Cañada del Hoyo E 53 Ec66
Cañada del Rosal E 60 Cc73
Cañadajuncosa E 53 Eb67
Cañada Vellida E 47 Fa64
Cañadillas E 60 Cd74
Čanak HR 151 Fd62
Çanakçı TR 192 Fc83
Çanakçı TR 192 Fc86
Çanakçı TR 199 Gd91
Çanakkale TR 185 Ea80
Çanaklı TR 199 Gc89
Canale I 148 Bd61
Canalejas del Arroyo E 47 Eb65
Canals E 54 Fb69
Canal San Bovo I 150 Dd57
Cañamares E 47 Eb64
Cañamares E 53 Ea70
Cañamero E 51 Cb67
Canaples F 23 Gd33
Canara E 61 Ec72
Canari F 154 Cc68
Canas de Senhorim P 44 Ba63
Cañaveral E 51 Bd66
Cañaveral de León E 51 Bc71

Chalamera – Čioiškiai

Chalamera E 48 Fd60
Chalamont F 34 Jb46
Chale GB 20 Fa31
Châlette-sur-Loing F 29 Ha39
Chalevga CY 206 Jc96
Chalindrey F 30 Jb40
Chalivoy-Milon F 29 Ha43
Challacombe GB 19 Dd29
Challain-la-Potherie F 28 Fa41
Challans F 28 Ed43
Challock GB 21 Ga29
Chalmazel F 34 Hd47
Chalmoux F 30 Hc44
Chalonnes-sur-Loire F 28 Fb42
Châlons-en-Champagne F 24 Hd36
Chalon-sur-Saône F 30 Jb43
Chalou-Moulineux F 29 Gd38
Chałupy PL 121 Ha29
Châlus F 33 Gb47
Chalvraines F 30 Jb38
Cham CH 141 Cb53
Cham D 135 Ec47
Chamalières-sur-Loire F 34 Hd49
Chamaloc F 35 Jc50
Chambeire F 30 Jb42
Chambellay F 28 Fb41
Chamberet F 33 Gc47
Chambéria F 31 Jc44
Chambéry F 35 Jd47
Chambilly F 34 Hd45
Chamblet F 33 Ha45
Chambley-Bussières F 25 Jc36
Chambly F 23 Gd36
Chambois F 22 Fd37
Chambon-la-Forêt F 29 Gd39
Chambon-sur-Voueize F 33 Ha45
Chambord F 29 Gc41
Chamborigaud F 41 Hd52
Chambost-Allières F 34 Ja46
Chambray F 23 Gb36
Chamdeniers-Saint-Denis F 32 Fc45
Chamerau D 135 Ec47
Chammes F 28 Fc39
Chamonix-Mont-Blanc F 35 Kb46
Chamouilley F 24 Jb37
Chamoy F 30 Hc39
Champagnac F 33 Ha48
Champagnac-le-Vieux F 34 Hc48
Champagné-les-Marais F 32 Fa45
Champagne-Mouton F 32 Fd46
Champagnole F 31 Jd43
Champaubert F 24 Hc36
Champdieu F 34 Hd47
Champeaux F 28 Fa39
Champeix F 34 Hb47
Champéry CH 141 Bb56
Champex CH 148 Bc57
Champier F 35 Jc48
Champigne F 28 Fb41
Champignelles F 30 Hb40
Champigneul-Champagne F 24 Hd36
Champignol-lez-Mondeville F 30 Ja39
Champigny F 23 Ha37
Champigny-le-Sec F 28 Fd44
Champigny-sur-Veude F 28 Fd43
Champlemy F 30 Hb42
Champlitte F 31 Jc40
Champlong I 148 Bc58
Champmotteux F 29 Gd38
Champniers F 32 Fd47
Champoluc I 148 Bd58
Champorcher I 148 Bd58
Champrond-en-Gâtine F 29 Gb38
Champs-sur-Yonne F 30 Hc40
Champtoceaux F 28 Fa42
Champvans F 31 Jc41
Chamrousse F 35 Jd49
Chamsk PL 122 Hd34
Chamusca P 50 Ac67
Chana E 37 Ca57
Chanac F 34 Hc51
Chança P 50 Ba67
Chanceaux F 30 Ja41
Chancelade F 33 Ga49
Chancelaria P 50 Ac66
Chancelaria P 50 Ac66
Chancery GB 15 Dd25
Chancia F 35 Jc45
Chancy CH 140 Ad56
Chandai F 23 Ga37
Chandler's Ford GB 20 Fa30
Chandolin CH 141 Bd56
Chandrexa E 36 Bc58
Chañe E 46 Da61
Changé F 28 Fb39
Changé F 28 Fd40
Changy F 24 Ja37
Changy F 34 Hd45
Chaniers F 32 Fc47
Channay-sur-Lathan F 28 Fd41
Chantada E 36 Bb56
Chantelle F 34 Hb45
Chanteloup F 28 Fb44
Chantemerle F 35 Kb49
Chantenay-Villedieu F 28 Fc40
Chantepie F 28 Ed39
Chantilly F 23 Gd35
Chantonnay F 28 Fa44
Chão de Codes P 50 Ad66
Chaon F 29 Gd41
Chaource F 30 Hd39
Chapaize F 30 Ja44
Chapeau-Rouge F 24 Hc33
Chapeauroux F 34 Hd50
Chapela E 36 Ad57
Chapel-en-le Frith GB 16 Ed22
Chapelle-Royale F 29 Gb39
Chapel Saint Leonards GB 17 Fd22
Chappes F 34 Hb46
Charbonnat F 30 Hd43
Charbowo PL 129 Gd36
Charcenne F 31 Jc41
Charches E 61 Dd74
Charchów Pański PL 130 Hc38
Chard GB 19 Eb30
Charenton-du-Cher F 29 Ha44
Charing GB 21 Ga29
Charkeia CY 206 Jc96
Charkiv UA 203 Fa14
Charlbury GB 20 Fa27
Charleroi B 124 Ac42
Charles GB 19 Dd29
Charlestown GB 9 Cd17
Charlestown IRL 8 Bd19
Charleval F 23 Gb35
Charleville-Mézières F 24 Ja33
Charlieu F 34 Hd45
Charlottenberg S 94 Ec42
Charlton Kings GB 20 Ed27
Charłupia Wielka PL 129 Hb39
Charly F 24 Hb36
Charmant F 32 Fd48
Charmé F 32 Fd46
Charmes F 31 Jd38
Charmes-sur-Rhône F 34 Jb50
Charmey CH 141 Bc55
Charmoille F 31 Jd40
Charmont-en-Beauce F 29 Gd39
Charmont-sur-Barbuise F 30 Hd38
Charnay-lès-Mâcon F 34 Ja45
Charney Bassett GB 20 Fa27
Charny F 23 Ha36
Charny F 30 Hb40
Charolles F 30 Hd44
Chârost F 29 Gd43
Charpey F 34 Jb49
Charquemont F 31 Ka41
Charras F 32 Fd48
Charritte-de-Bas F 39 Fa55
Charron F 32 Fa45
Charroux F 32 Fd46
Chars F 23 Gc36
Charsonville F 29 Gc40
Chartów PL 128 Fc36
Chartres F 29 Gb38
Chartridge GB 20 Fb27
Charzykowy PL 121 Gd32
Chasné F 28 Ed39
Chąśno PL 130 Hd37
Chasseneuil-sur-Bonnieure F 32 Fd47
Chassenon F 33 Ga47
Chassepierre B 132 Ad44
Chasse-sur-Rhône F 34 Jb47
Chassillé F 28 Fc39
Chastanier F 34 Hd50
Chastellux-sur-Cure F 30 Hc41
Chastleton GB 20 Ed26
Chatain F 32 Fd46
Château-Arnoux F 42 Ka52
Châteaubernard F 32 Fc47
Château-Bernard F 35 Jc49
Châteaubourg F 28 Fa39
Châteaubriant F 28 Fa40
Château-Chervix F 33 Gb47
Château-Chinon F 30 Hd42
Château-des-Prés F 31 Jd44
Château-d'Oex CH 141 Bc55
Château d'Olonne F 28 Ed44
Château-du-Loir F 28 Fd41
Châteaudun F 29 Gb39
Châteaufort F 42 Ka51
Château-Garnier F 32 Fd45
Châteaugiron F 28 Ed39
Château-Gontier F 28 Fb40
Château-Landon F 29 Ha39
Château-Larcher F 32 Fd45
Château-la-Vallière F 28 Fd41
Château-l'Evêque F 33 Ga49
Châteaulin F 27 Dc39
Châteaumeillant F 29 Gd44
Châteauneuf-de-Galaure F 34 Jb48
Châteauneuf-de-Randon F 34 Hc50
Châteauneuf-d'Ille-et-Vilaine F 28 Ed38
Châteauneuf-du-Faou F 27 Dd39
Châteauneuf-du-Pape F 42 Jb52
Châteauneuf-en-Auxois F 30 Ja42
Châteauneuf-en-Thymerais F 29 Gb38
Châteauneuf-la-Forêt F 33 Gc47
Châteauneuf-les-Bains F 34 Hb46
Châteauneuf-sur-Charente F 32 Fc48
Châteauneuf-sur-Cher F 29 Gd43
Châteauneuf-sur-Loire F 29 Gd40
Châteauneuf-sur-Sarthe F 28 Fb41
Châteauneuf-Val-de-Bargis F 30 Hb42
Châteauponsac F 33 Gb46
Château-Porcien F 24 Hd34
Château-Queyras F 35 Kb50
Châteauredon F 42 Ka52
Château-Renard F 29 Ha40
Châteaurenard F 42 Jb53
Château-Renault F 29 Ga41
Châteauroux F 29 Gc43
Châteauroux F 35 Kb50
Château-Salins F 25 Jd36
Château-Thierry F 24 Hb36
Châteauvillain F 30 Ja39
Châtel F 35 Kb45
Châtelaillon-Plage F 32 Fa46
Châtelard F 35 Ka47
Châtelaudren F 26 Ea38
Châtel-Censoir F 30 Hc41
Châtel-de-Neuvre F 34 Hb45
Châtel-Gérard F 30 Hd41
Châtelguyon F 34 Hb46
Châtellerault F 29 Ga44
Châtel-Montagne F 34 Hc46
Châtel-sur-Moselle F 31 Jd38
Châtelus-le-Marcheix F 33 Gc46
Châtelus-Malvaleix F 33 Gd45
Châtenois F 31 Jc38
Châtenoy F 29 Gd40
Chatham GB 20 Fd28
Châtillon F 30 Hb44
Châtillon F 31 Jc44
Châtillon I 148 Bd58
Châtillon-Coligny F 29 Ha40
Châtillon-en-Bazois F 30 Hc42
Châtillon-en-Diois F 35 Jc50
Châtillon-en-Vendelais F 28 Fa39
Châtillon-la-Palud F 35 Jc46
Châtillon-sur-Chalaronne F 34 Jb45
Châtillon-sur-Colmont F 28 Fb38
Châtillon-sur-Indre F 29 Gb43
Châtillon-sur-Loire F 29 Ha41
Châtillon-sur-Marne F 24 Hc36
Châtillon-sur-Seine F 30 Ja40
Châtillon-sur-Thouet F 28 Fc44
Chatrans F 31 Jd42
Châtres-sur-Cher F 29 Gc42
Chattancourt F 24 Jb35
Chatteris GB 20 Fd25
Chatton GB 11 Ed14
Chauchina E 60 Db75
Chaudefontaine F 31 Jd41
Chaudes-Aigues F 34 Hb50
Chaudieu F 35 Jd46
Chauffailles F 34 Ja45
Chaulnes F 23 Ha33
Chaumard F 30 Hd42
Chaumergy F 31 Jc43
Chaumes-en-Brie F 23 Ha37
Chaumont F 30 Jb39
Chaumont-en-Vexin F 23 Gc35
Chaumont-Porcien F 24 Hd34
Chaumont-sur-Aire F 24 Jb36
Chaumont-sur-Loire F 29 Gb41
Chaumont-sur-Tharonne F 29 Gc41
Chaunay F 32 Fd46
Chauny F 24 Hb34
Chauray F 32 Fc45
Chaussin F 31 Jc43
Chauvé F 27 Ec42
Chauvigné F 29 Gd44
Chauvigny F 29 Ga44
Chaux-Neuve F 31 Jd43
Chavagnes-en-Paillers F 28 Fa43
Chavanay F 34 Ja48
Chavanges F 30 Ja38
Chaves P 44 Bb59
Chawleigh GB 19 Dd30
Chazelles-sur-Lyon F 34 Ja47
Chazeuil F 34 Hc45
Cheadle GB 15 Ec22
Cheadle GB 16 Ed23
Cheb CZ 135 Eb44
Checa E 47 Ec64
Chechło PL 138 Hd43
Chęciny PL 130 Jb42
Checkendon GB 20 Fb28
Cheddar GB 19 Eb29
Cheddleton GB 16 Ed23
Chedworth GB 20 Ed27
Chef-Boutonne F 32 Fc46
Chef-du-Pont F 22 Fa35
Cheglevici RO 170 Bb59
Cheia RO 171 Da59
Cheia RO 176 Ea63
Cheissoux F 33 Gc47
Cheles E 51 Bb70
Chelford GB 15 Ec22
Chełm PL 131 Kc40
Chełm PL 138 Hd43
Chełmce PL 129 Hb36
Chełmek PL 128 Ga38
Chełmek PL 138 Hd44
Chełmno PL 121 Ha33
Chełmno PL 129 Gb36
Chełmno PL 129 Hb37
Chelmsford GB 20 Fd27
Chełmsko Śląskie PL 128 Ga42
Chełmża PL 121 Hb34
Chełst PL 120 Ga35
Chelsworth GB 21 Ga26
Cheltenham GB 20 Ed27
Chelun F 28 Fa40
Chelva E 54 Fa67
Chemazé F 28 Fb40
Chémeré-le-Roi F 28 Fc40
Chémery F 29 Gc42
Chémery-sur-Bar F 24 Ja34
Chemillé F 28 Fb42
Chemillé-sur-Dême F 29 Ga41
Cheminon F 24 Ja37
Chemiré-le-Gaudin F 28 Fc40
Chemnitz D 127 Ec42
Chenay F 32 Fc45
Chenay-le-Châtel F 34 Hd45
Chénelette F 34 Ja45
Chénerailles F 33 Gd46
Chenies GB 20 Fc27
Chennebrun F 23 Ga37
Chennevières F 23 Gb37
Chenoise F 24 Hb37
Chenonceaux F 29 Gb42
Chenôve F 30 Jb42
Chepoix F 23 Gd34
Chepstow GB 19 Eb27
Chepy F 24 Hd36
Chera E 54 Fa67
Chera F 154 Cb72
Cherain B 133 Bb43
Cherasco I 148 Bd62
Cherbonnières F 32 Fc46
Cherbourg-Octeville F 22 Ed34
Cherechiu RO 170 Cb55
Chereluş RO 170 Ca58
Chérencé-le-Roussel F 22 Fa37
Cheresig RO 170 Ca56
Cherestur RO 170 Bb59
Cheriton GB 20 Fa29
Chéroy F 29 Ha39
Cherson UA 204 Ed16
Chertsey GB 20 Fb28
Cherves-Richemont F 32 Fc47
Cheseaux CH 141 Bb55
Chesham GB 20 Fb27
Cheshunt GB 20 Fc27
Chesley F 30 Hd39
Chesney's Corner GB 9 Cd16
Cheste E 54 Fb67
Chester GB 15 Eb22
Chesterfield GB 16 Fa22
Chester-le-Street GB 11 Fa17
Cheţani RO 171 Db59
Chetroşica Nouă MD 173 Fa54
Chetrosu MD 173 Fb54
Chetrosu MD 173 Fd58
Chevagnes F 30 Hc44
Chevanceaux F 32 Fc49
Chevenez CH 141 Bc52
Cheverny F 29 Gb41
Chevetogne B 132 Ad43
Chevillon F 30 Hb40
Chevilly F 29 Gc39
Cheviré-le-Rouge F 28 Fc41
Chevreuse F 23 Gd37
Chevroux F 34 Jb45
Chew Magna GB 19 Ec28
Cheylade F 33 Ha49
Chezal-Benoît F 29 Gd43
Chézeaux F 31 Jc39
Chézery-Forens F 35 Jd45
Chiajna RO 176 Ea66
Chialamberto I 148 Bc59
Chiampo I 149 Dc59
Chianale I 148 Bb61
Chianciano Terme I 156 Dd67
Chiappera I 148 Bb62
Chiaramonte Gulfi I 167 Fc87
Chiaramonti I 168 Ca74
Chiaravalle I 156 Ed66
Chiaravalle Centrale I 164 Gc82
Chiareggio I 142 Cd56
Chiari I 149 Cd59
Chiaromonte I 162 Gb77
Chiasso I 149 Cc58
Chiatona I 162 Gd76
Chiauci I 161 Fb72
Chiavari I 149 Cc63
Chiavenna I 142 Cd56
Chiché F 28 Fc44
Chicheley GB 20 Fb26
Chichester GB 20 Fb30
Chichilianne F 35 Jc50
Chichiş RO 176 Ea62
Chichy PL 128 Fd39
Chiclana de la Frontera E 59 Bd77
Chiclana de Segura E 53 Dd71
Chiddingfold GB 20 Fb29
Chiddingstone GB 20 Fd29
Chieming D 143 Eb52
Chieperceni MD 173 Fd56
Chieri I 148 Bd60
Chiesa in Valmalenco I 149 Cd57
Chieşd RO 171 Cd56
Chies d'Alpago I 150 Eb57
Chiessi I 155 Cd68
Chieti I 157 Fa70
Chieuti I 161 Fd72
Chiggiogna CH 141 Cb56
Chigné F 28 Fd41
Chigwell GB 20 Fd28
Chiheru de Jos RO 171 Dc58
Chilcompton GB 19 Ec29
Childrey GB 20 Fa28
Chilham GB 21 Ga29
Chilia Veche RO 177 Ga63
Chiliile RO 176 Ec63
Chilivani I 168 Ca75
Chillarón de Cuenca E 47 Eb65
Chilleurs-aux-Bois F 29 Gd39
Chillón E 52 Cd69
Chilluevar E 61 Dd72
Chilmark GB 20 Ed29
Chiloeches E 46 Dd64
Chilsworthy GB 18 Dc30
Chimay B 132 Ac43
Chimeneas E 60 Db75
Chimparra E 36 Bb53
Chinchilla de Monte Aragón E 53 Ec69
Chinchón E 46 Dc65
Chindăreşti RO 177 Fb66
Chingford GB 20 Fc27
Chinnor GB 20 Fb27
Chinon F 28 Fd42
Chinteni RO 171 Da58
Chiochiş RO 171 Db57
Chioggia I 150 Ea60
Chiojdeanca RO 176 Eb64
Chiojdu RO 176 Eb63
Chioselia MD 177 Fc61
Chioselia Mare MD 177 Fc61
Chipeşca MD 173 Fc55
Chipiona E 59 Bc76
Chippenham GB 19 Ec28
Chipping GB 15 Ec20
Chipping Campden GB 20 Ed26
Chipping Norton GB 20 Fa26
Chipping Ongar GB 20 Fd27
Chiprana E 48 Fc62
Chirbury GB 15 Eb24
Chircăieşti MD 173 Ga59
Chircăieştii Noi MD 173 Fb59
Chirens F 35 Jc48
Chirianca MD 173 Fc57
Chiriet-Lunga MD 177 Fd60
Chirileni MD 173 Fb57
Chirivel E 61 Eb74
Chirnogeni RO 181 Fb68
Chirnogi RO 181 Eb67
Chirnside GB 11 Ed13
Chirols F 34 Ja50
Chirpăr RO 175 Dc61
Chirsova MD 177 Fc60
Chiscani RO 177 Fb64
Chişcăreni MD 173 Fb56
Chiselet RO 181 Ec67
Chişinău MD 173 Fd58
Chisindia RO 170 Cb59
Chişineu-Criş RO 170 Bd58
Chişlaz RO 170 Cb56
Chissey-en-Morvan F 30 Hd42
Chiştelniţa MD 173 Fc56
Chiţcani MD 173 Ga59
Chiţcanii Vechi MD 173 Fc56
Chitila RO 176 Ea66
Chiuieşti RO 171 Db56
Chiurt MD 173 Fa54
Chiusa I 143 Dd56
Chiusa di Pesio I 148 Bc63
Chiusaforte I 150 Ed57
Chiusa Sclafani I 166 Ec85
Chiusavecchia I 43 La52
Chiusi I 156 Dd68
Chiusi della Verna I 156 Ea65
Chiuza RO 171 Db56
Chiva E 54 Fb68
Chivasso I 148 Bd60
Chizé F 32 Fc46
Chłapowo PL 112 Ha58
Chlebiotki PL 123 Ka33
Chlebówka PL 122 Hc31
Chlebowo PL 128 Fc38
Chlewice PL 130 Ja42
Chlewiska PL 130 Jb40
Chlewnica PL 121 Gd30
Chlewo PL 129 Hb39
Chłopiatyn PL 131 Kd42
Chłopice PL 139 Kb44
Chlorakas CY 206 Hd98
Chłudowo PL 129 Gc36
Chlum CZ 136 Fa48
Chlumčany CZ 135 Ed46
Chlumčany CZ 136 Fa44
Chlumec nad Cidlinou CZ 136 Fd44
Chlumin CZ 136 Fb44
Chlum u Třebňe CZ 136 Fc48
Chmel'nyc'kyj UA 204 Eb15
Chmel'ov SK 139 Jd47
Chmieleń PL 128 Fd41
Chmielnik PL 130 Jb42
Chmielnik PL 139 Ka44
Chmielno PL 121 Ha30
Chmielów PL 131 Jd42
Chmil'nyk UA 204 Eb15
Chobienice PL 128 Ga37
Choceň CZ 137 Gb45
Choceń PL 130 Hc36
Chocholná-Velčice SK 137 Ha48
Chochołów PL 138 Ja46
Chocianów PL 128 Ga40
Chociw PL 130 Ja39
Chociwel PL 120 Fd33
Chocz PL 129 Ha38
Choczewo PL 121 Gd29
Chodaków PL 130 Ja37
Chodecz PL 130 Hc36
Chodel PL 131 Ka40
Chodoriv UA 204 Ea15
Chodorówka PL 123 Kb32
Chodov CZ 135 Ec44
Chodová Planá CZ 135 Ec45
Chodský Újezd CZ 135 Ec45
Chodzież PL 121 Gc35
Choiny Młode PL 123 Jd33
Choirokoitia CY 206 Jb98
Choiseul F 31 Jc39
Choisy-au-Bac F 23 Ha35
Choisy-en-Brie F 24 Hb37
Chojewo PL 123 Kb35
Chojna PL 120 Fb35
Chojnice PL 121 Gd32
Chojnik PL 129 Gd40
Chojniki BY 202 Eb13
Chojno PL 129 Gc39
Chojnow PL 128 Ga40
Chojnowo PL 122 Jb34
Cholderton GB 20 Ed29
Cholesbury GB 20 Fb27
Cholet F 28 Fb43
Chollerford GB 11 Ed16
Chomérac F 34 Jb50
Chomutov CZ 135 Ed43
Chorges F 35 Ka50
Chorley GB 15 Ec21
Chorol UA 202 Ed14
Choroszcz PL 123 Kb33
Chorupnik PL 131 Kb41
Chorzele PL 122 Jb33
Chorzów PL 138 Hc43
Choszczno PL 120 Fd34
Chotcza PL 131 Jd40
Chotěboř CZ 136 Ga46
Chotěšov CZ 135 Ed46
Chotilsko CZ 136 Fb45
Chotín SK 145 Hb52
Chouvigny F 34 Hb46
Choye F 31 Jc41
Chozas de Canales E 46 Db65
Chraboły PL 123 Kb33
Chr'aščevka RUS 203 Ga10
Chrást CZ 135 Ed45
Chrast CZ 136 Ga45
Chrastava CZ 128 Fc42
Chrewt PL 139 Kb46
Chřibská CZ 128 Fb42
Chrisí Ammoudiá GR 184 Db78
Christchurch GB 20 Ed30
Christiansfeld DK 108 Db26
Chropyne CZ 137 Gd47
Chróścina PL 121 Ha35
Chroślice PL 128 Ga41
Chrostkowo PL 122 Hc35
Chróstnik PL 128 Ga40
Chrudim CZ 136 Ga45
Chruściel PL 122 Hd30
Chruślin PL 130 Hd37
Chrustowo PL 129 Gb36
Chrystynivka UA 204 Ec15
Chrzanów PL 131 Kb41
Chrzanów PL 138 Hd44
Chrzanowo PL 121 Gd29
Chrząstowice PL 129 Ha42
Chrząstowo PL 129 Gc38
Chrzypsko Wielkie PL 129 Gb36
Chtelnica SK 137 Ha49
Chucena E 59 Bd74
Chudoba PL 129 Hb42
Chudolazy CZ 136 Fb43
Chudolipie PL 130 Jb38
Chuelles F 29 Ha39
Chulilla E 54 Fa67
Chulmleigh GB 19 Dd30
Chur CH 142 Cd55
Church Cross IRL 12 Bb26
Church Eaton GB 15 Ec24
Churchill GB 20 Fa26
Church Lench GB 20 Ed26
Church Stoke GB 15 Eb24
Churchstow GB 19 Dd32
Church Stretton GB 15 Eb24
Churchtown GB 10 Dd18
Churchtown IRL 13 Cd25
Churwalden CH 142 Cd55
Chust UA 204 Dd16
Chustki PL 130 Jb40
Chvaleč CZ 136 Ga43
Chvaletice CZ 136 Fd45
Chvalšiny CZ 136 Fb48
Chwałowice PL 131 Jd41
Chwarstnica PL 120 Fc34
Chwarszczany PL 128 Fc36
Chwaszczyno PL 121 Ha30
Chwiram PL 121 Gb34
Chyňava CZ 136 Fb45
Chynorany SK 137 Hb49
Chýnov CZ 136 Fc47
Chynów PL 130 Jc38
Chynowie PL 121 Ha29
Chyše CZ 135 Ed44
Chyšky CZ 136 Fb46
Ciacova RO 174 Bc61
Cianciana I 166 Ec86
Ciasna PL 129 Hb42
Ciavolo I 166 Ea85
Ciavoş RO 174 Bc61
Ciążeń PL 129 Gd37
Cibakháza H 146 Jb54
Cibla LV 107 Ma51
Ciborro P 50 Ad69
Cibourg CH 141 Bc53
Cicagna I 149 Cc63
Cicăneşti RO 175 Db63
Cicârlău RO 171 Da55
Čičava SK 139 Ka48
Çiçekler TR 199 Hb89
Çiçekli TR 186 Ga80
Çiçekoluk TR 199 Hb91
Çiçekpınar TR 193 Ha87
Çiçektepe TR 193 Gc86
Cicero E 38 Dd54
Ciceu-Giurgeşti RO 171 Db56
Ćićevac SRB 178 Bc67
Cichy PL 123 Jd30
Ciclova Română RO 174 Bd63
Čičmany SK 137 Hb48
Cicognolo I 149 Da60
Cide TR 205 Fa20
Cidones E 47 Ea60
Ciechanów PL 122 Ja35
Ciechanów PL 129 Gb39
Ciechanowiec PL 123 Ka35
Ciechocin PL 121 Hb34
Ciechocinek PL 121 Hb35
Cieksyn PL 130 Jb36
Cielądz PL 130 Ja38
Ciemnik PL 120 Fd33
Ciemnoszyje PL 123 Ka32
Ciempozuelos E 46 Dc65
Cieniawa PL 138 Jc45
Ciepielów PL 131 Jd40
Cieplice Śląskie-Zdrój PL 128 Ga42
Ciepłowody PL 129 Gc42
Čierna nad Tisou SK 139 Kb49
Čierny Balog SK 138 Ja48
Cierznie PL 121 Gc33
Cierzpięty PL 122 Jc31
Ciesina PL 122 Jc32
Cieśków PL 129 Gd39
Cieśle PL 129 Gd40
Cieszanów PL 139 Kc43
Cieszyn PL 129 Gd40
Cieszyn PL 137 Hb45
Cieszyno PL 120 Fd33
Cieux F 33 Gb46
Cieza E 55 Ed72
Ciężkowice PL 130 Hd41
Ciężkowice PL 138 Jc45
Čifer SK 145 Gd50
Ciflik Tusha AL 182 Ab80
Çiftalan TR 186 Fc77
Çiftçidere TR 191 Ed82
Çifteler TR 193 Gd83
Çiftlik TR 187 Gb78
Çiftlikköy TR 185 Ed77
Çiftlikköy TR 186 Fd79
Çiftlikköy TR 191 Ed84
Çiftlikköy TR 192 Fd81
Çiftlikköy TR 193 Ha84
Çiftlikköy TR 197 Ed90
Çiftlikköy TR 197 Ed90
Çiftlikköy TR 197 Fa88
Çiftlikköy TR 197 Fa90
Çiftlikköy TR 198 Fb88
Çiftlikköy TR 198 Ga88
Çiftliköy TR 186 Fb76
Çiftliköy TR 191 Ea86
Cifuentes E 47 Ea63
Cigales E 46 Da60
Cigánd H 147 Ka50
Cigel'ka SK 138 Jc46
Çiğiltepe TR 193 Gb86
Cigirleni MD 173 Fd59
Cigliano I 148 Bd59
Čigoč HR 152 Gc60
Çığrı TR 199 Gb88
Ciguñuela E 46 Cd60
Cihangazi TR 193 Gb82
Cihetu MD 177 Fc61
Cijara E 52 Cc67
Çıkrıcak TR 192 Ga83
Çıkrık TR 193 Gc85
Çıkrıkçı TR 192 Fb83
Çile TR 191 Ec87
Cilibia RO 176 Ed64
Cilieni RO 180 Db67
Çilimli TR 187 Gd78
Čilipi HR 159 Hc69
Čilipina LV 107 Ld49
Cill Airne IRL 12 Bb25
Cillamayor E 38 Db56
Cillas E 47 Ec63
Cill Chainnigh IRL 13 Cb23
Cill Chaoi IRL 12 Bb23
Cill Chiaráin IRL 8 Bb20
Cill Chiaráin IRL 12 Bb21
Cill Dalua IRL 12 Bd23
Cill Dara IRL 13 Cc22
Çiller TR 187 Gb78
Çiller TR 187 Ha80
Cilleros E 45 Bc65
Cilleruelo de Abajo E 46 Dc59
Cillervelo de Bezana E 38 Dc56
Cill Mhantáim IRL 13 Da22
Cill Mocheallog IRL 12 Bd24
Cill Orglan IRL 12 Ba25
Cill Rois IRL 12 Bb23
Cilmery GB 15 Ea26
Čil'na RUS 203 Fd09
Cimanes de la Vega E 37 Cc58
Cimanes del Tejar E 37 Cb57
Cimăteni MD 173 Ga59
Cimelice CZ 136 Fa46
Çimendere TR 185 Ec78
Čimeř CZ 136 Fc48
Çimiköy TR 199 Hb91
Ciminna I 166 Ed84
Cimişeni MD 173 Fd58
Cimitile I 161 Fb74
Cimljansk RUS 205 Fd15
Cimolais I 150 Eb57
Cimoszki PL 123 Ka31
Çınaraltı TR 185 Ec77
Çınarcık TR 186 Fd79
Çınarcık TR 191 Ec81
Çınarcık TR 192 Fc81
Çınarcık TR 192 Fd85
Çınarköy TR 192 Fc82
Çınarlı TR 185 Ed79
Cincin TR 197 Ed88
Cinco Casas E 53 Dd68
Cinctorres E 48 Fc64
Cincu RO 175 Dc61
Cinderford GB 19 Ec27
Çine TR 197 Fa88
Ciñera E 37 Cc56
Ciney B 124 Ad42
Cinfães P 44 Ba61
Cinge TR 191 Ed83
Cingoli I 156 Ec66
Cinigiano I 155 Dc68
Cinişeuţi MD 173 Fd56
Cinisi I 166 Ec84
Cinobaňa SK 138 Ja49
Cinovec CZ 128 Fa42
Cinq-Mars-la-Pile F 28 Fd42
Cinquefrondi I 164 Gb83
Cintegabelle F 40 Gc55
Cintei RO 170 Ca58
Cintrey F 31 Jc40
Cintruénigo E 47 Ec59
Cioara MD 173 Fb59
Ciobalaccia MD 177 Fc61
Ciobăniş RO 176 Eb60
Ciobăniţa RO 181 Fb68
Ciobanovca MD 173 Fd59
Ciobanu RO 177 Fb65
Ciobiškis LT 113 Kd57
Ciocăneşti RO 172 Dd56
Ciocăneşti RO 176 Ea65
Ciocăneşti RO 181 Eb67
Ciocârlia RO 176 Ec65
Ciocârlia RO 181 Fb67
Ciochina RO 176 Ed66
Ciocile RO 176 Ed65
Ciocîlteni MD 173 Fc56
Cioclovina RO 175 Cd62
Cioc-Maidan MD 177 Fd60
Ciofrângeri RO 175 Db64
Čioiškiai LT 113 Jd54

Czerwone – Diakovo

Czerwone PL 123 Jd33
Czerwonka PL 122 Jb31
Czerwonka PL 122 Jc34
Czerwonki PL 123 Ka32
Czerwony Dwór PL 123 Jd30
Czestków PL 130 Hc39
Częstochowa PL 130 Hc42
Czeszów PL 129 Gd40
Człopa PL 120 Ga34
Człuchów PL 121 Gc32
Czorsztyn PL 138 Jb46
Czudec PL 139 Ka44
Czumów PL 131 Kd41
Czyczkowy PL 121 Gd32
Czyże PL 123 Kc34
Czyżew-Osada PL 123 Ka35
Czyżkowo PL 121 Gc33

D

Daaden D 125 Cb41
Dăbâca RO 171 Da57
Dabar HR 151 Fd61
Dabar HR 158 Gc65
Dabas H 146 Hd54
Dabbnäs S 79 Fd25
Dabel D 119 Eb32
Dăben BG 179 Da70
Dăbene BG 180 Db72
Dąbie PL 120 Fd32
Dąbie PL 128 Fd38
Dąbie PL 129 Hb37
Dąbie PL 131 Ka37
Dabilja MK 183 Ca75
Dąbki PL 121 Gb30
Dăbnica BG 184 Cd75
Dăbovan BG 180 Db68
Dăbovec BG 185 Ea75
Dăbovo BG 180 Dd72
Dabrac BIH 152 Gd63
Dabrica BIH 158 Hb67
Dąbrowa PL 120 Fc35
Dąbrowa PL 121 Ha35
Dąbrowa PL 122 Hc30
Dąbrowa PL 129 Ha42
Dąbrowa Białostocka PL 123 Kb31
Dąbrowa Biskupia PL 121 Hb35
Dąbrowa Chełmińska PL 121 Ha34
Dąbrowa Górnicza PL 138 Hc43
Dąbrowa Tarnowska PL 138 Jc44
Dąbrowa Zielona PL 130 Hd41
Dąbrowica PL 131 Kb42
Dąbrowice PL 130 Hc37
Dąbrówka PL 122 Hc33
Dąbrówka PL 122 Jc33
Dąbrówka PL 130 Jc36
Dąbrówka PL 131 Jd40
Dąbrówka PL 131 Jd41
Dąbrówka PL 139 Kb43
Dąbrówka-Kościelna PL 123 Ka34
Dąbrówka Wielkopolska PL 128 Ga37
Dąbrówki PL 139 Ka43
Dąbrówno PL 122 Hd33
Dąbrowy PL 122 Jc33
Dabryn' BY 202 Eb14
Dăbuleni RO 179 Da68
Dachau D 143 Dd50
Dachnów PL 139 Kc43
Dachsbach D 134 Dc46
Dačice CZ 136 Fd48
Dacón E 36 Ba57
Dadalı TR 187 Ha77
Dädesjö S 103 Fc51
Dadiá GR 185 Ea77
Dådran S 87 Fd38
Dăeni RO 177 Fb65
Dăești RO 175 Db63
Dafjord N 62 Gd08
Dáfnes GR 188 Bb85
Dafni GR 184 Cd79
Dáfni GR 188 Bb82
Dáfni GR 188 Bb86
Dáfni GR 189 Bc83
Dáfni GR 194 Bc89
Dağ TR 199 Gc90
Dağakçaköy TR 192 Fc81
Dagali N 85 Db39
Dağardı TR 192 Fc83
Dağarlar TR 192 Fb87
Dagâța RO 172 Ed58
Dağbağ TR 199 Gb92
Dagda LV 107 Ld52
Dağdemirciler TR 192 Fd81
Dağdere TR 192 Fa84
Dağdere TR 198 Ga88
Dagebüll D 108 Cd28
Dagenham GB 20 Fd28
Dağeymiri TR 191 Ed87
Dağhacılar TR 187 Gd80
Dağırmandere TR 191 Ec85
Dağıstan TR 191 Ec83
Dağkadı TR 186 Fb80
Dağkızılca TR 191 Ec86
Daglingworth GB 20 Ed27
Dagomys RUS 205 Fd17
Dağpınar TR 197 Fa90
Dagsås S 102 Ec51
Dagsmark FIN 89 Ja33
Dağyenice TR 186 Fb77
Dağyolu TR 187 Ha80
Dahlem D 125 Bc42
Dahlen D 127 Ed40
Dahlenburg D 119 Dd34
Dahme D 119 Dd30
Dahme D 127 Ed38
Dahn D 133 Ca47
Dähre D 119 Dd35
Daia RO 175 Dc60
Daia RO 180 Ea67
Daia Română RO 175 Da60
Daikanberg S 71 Ga24
Daikanvik S 71 Ga24
Dailly GB 10 Dc15
Dailučiai LT 114 Ka58
Daimiel E 52 Dc69
Dainville-Bertheléville F 30 Jb38
Dairsie GB 7 Ec12
Dajla HR 150 Ed60
Dakovica KSV 178 Ad71
Đakovo HR 153 Hc60
Daksti LV 106 Kd47
Dal N 93 Db41
Dal N 93 Db44
Dal N 94 Eb40
Dal S 80 Gc31
Dala S 102 Fa47
Đala SRB 153 Jb57
Dalaas A 142 Da54
Dalachów PL 129 Hb41
Dalama TR 197 Fa88
Dalaman TR 198 Fc91
Dalarö S 96 Ha44
Dalasjö S 79 Gb26
Dalavardo S 71 Fd21
Dalavich GB 6 Dc12
Dalbe LV 106 Kb51
Dalbeattie GB 10 Ea16
Dălbok Dol BG 180 Db71
Dălbok izvor BG 184 Dc74
Dalboşeţ RO 174 Ca64
Dalby DK 109 Eb27
Dalby DK 109 Dd26
Dalby S 94 Ed39
Dalby S 96 Gc42
Dalby S 110 Fa56
Dalbyn S 87 Fc37
Dalbyover DK 100 Dc22
Dalca TR 187 Gb78
Dalchalloch GB 7 Ea10
Dalchruin GB 7 Ea12
Dale GB 18 Db27
Dale N 66 Ga12
Dale N 84 Ca36
Dale N 84 Cb38
Dale N 84 Cc34
Dale N 84 Cd36
Dale N 92 Cd45
Dale N 93 Da44
Dale N 93 Da44
Dale N 93 Da46
Dalen N 77 Db32
Dalen N 92 Cb43
Dalen N 93 Da43
Dalen N 94 Eb42
Dalen NL 117 Bd35
Dalen S 78 Fa30
Daleng N 67 Gd12
Dalesjukhus N 92 Ca44
Daleszyce PL 130 Jb41
Dalewo PL 129 Gc38
Dalfors S 87 Fd37
Dalfsen NL 117 Bc35
Dălga Luka BG 179 Ca71
Dalghiu RO 176 Ea62
Dălgi Del BG 179 Cb69
Dălgopol BG 181 Ed71
Dalhavaig GB 5 Ea04
Dalheim L 133 Bb45
Dalheim N 62 Ha10
Dalheim N 70 Ed21
Dalhem B 125 Bb41
Dalhem S 103 Ga48
Dalhem S 104 Ha49
Dalholen N 85 Dd34
Dali CY 206 Jb97
Dalías E 61 Dd76
Daliburgh GB 6 Cd08
Dalików PL 130 Hc38
Daliowa PL 139 Ka46
Dalj HR 153 Hd59
Dalkarlså S 80 Hc27
Dalkarsberg S 95 Fc43
Dalkeith GB 11 Eb13
Dallas GB 5 Eb07
Dalleagles GB 10 Dd15
Dallgow-Döberitz D 127 Ed36
Dallımandıra TR 191 Ed82
Dallmin D 119 Eb34
Dállogilli S 73 Ja18
Dall Villaby DK 100 Dc21
Dalmally GB 6 Dc11
Dalmellington GB 10 Dd15
Dalmine I 149 Cd59
Dalmose DK 109 Ea27
Dal'nee RUS 113 Jc58
Dalness GB 6 Dc10
Daloba TR 191 Eb81
Dalry GB 10 Dc14
Dalsbruk FIN 97 Jc41
Dalselv N 71 Fb20
Dalsetra N 77 Dd33
Dalsfjord N 76 Cc33
Dalshult S 102 Ed52
Dalsjöfors S 102 Ed49
Dalskog S 94 Ec45
Dals Långed S 94 Ec45
Dalsøyra N 84 Ca37
Dals Rostock S 94 Ec45
Dalston GB 11 Eb17
Dalstorp S 102 Fa49
Dalstuga S 87 Fd38
Dalton GB 11 Eb16
Dalton-in-Furness GB 11 Eb19
Daluis F 43 Kb52
Dalum S 102 Fa48
Dalvík IS 2 Ba03
Dálvvadis S 72 Ha19
Dalyan TR 191 Ea81
Dalyan TR 197 Ec89
Dalyan TR 198 Fb91
Dalyanköy TR 191 Ea86
Damak H 146 Jc50
Dâmanești RO 175 Dc64
Damarası TR 197 Fa90
Damas-aux-Bois F 31 Jd38
Damaskinía GR 182 Ba78
Damasławek PL 121 Gd35
Damássi GR 183 Bc80
Damásta GR 200 Da95
Damatlı TR 192 Fa86
Damazan F 40 Fd52
Dambaslar TR 185 Ed77
Damelang-Freienthal D 127 Ec37
Dameliai LT 114 Ka53
Damerey F 30 Jb43
Damerham GB 20 Ed30
Damery F 24 Hc36
Damgan F 27 Eb41
Dămienești RO 172 Ed59
Damjanovo BG 180 Dc70
Dammarie F 29 Gb38
Dammarie-les-Lys F 29 Ha38
Dammartin-en-Goële F 23 Ha36
Damme B 124 Aa39
Damme D 117 Cc36
Dammen N 93 Dc43
Dammet S 73 Ja21
Damnica PL 121 Gc30
Damno PL 121 Gc29
Damp D 108 Dc29
Dampierre F 24 Hd37
Dampierre F 31 Jc42
Dampierre-en-Bray F 23 Gc34
Dampierre-en-Burly F 29 Ha40
Dampierre-en-Yvelines F 23 Gc37
Dampierre-Saint-Nicolas F 23 Gb33
Dampierre-sur-Boutonne F 32 Fc46
Dampierre-sur-Salon F 31 Jc41
Dampınar TR 191 Ed87
Damprichard F 31 Kb41
Damsdorf D 127 Ec37
Damsdorf D 127 Ed38
Damsholte DK 109 Ec28
Dămuc RO 172 Eb58
Damüls A 142 Da53
Damville F 23 Gb37
Damvillers F 24 Jb35
Damwoude NL 117 Bc33
Danaçalı TR 192 Fc82
Danakós GR 196 Dc90
Danamandıra TR 186 Fb77
Danapınar TR 185 Ec80
Danasjö S 71 Ga23
Danbury GB 21 Ga27
Danby GB 11 Fb18
Dănceni MD 173 Fc58
Dănciulești RO 175 Da65
Dancu MD 173 Fb59
Dăneasa RO 180 Db67
Daneș RO 175 Dc60
Danesfort IRL 13 Cb24
Dănești RO 172 Ea59
Dănești RO 173 Fa58
Dănești RO 175 Cd64
Dănești RO 176 Ec66
Dănești RO 179 Da67
Dangast D 118 Cc33
Dangeau F 29 Gb39
Dångebo S 111 Fd53
Dăngeni RO 172 Ed55
Dangé-Saint-Romain F 29 Ga43
Dangy F 22 Fa36
Danholn S 95 Fd39
Dănicei RO 175 Db64
Daniec PL 129 Ha42
Danilov RUS 203 Fa08
Danilova RUS 99 Ma42
Danilovgrad MNE 159 Ja69
Danilovka RUS 203 Fd13
Dänischenhagen D 118 Dc30
Danişment TR 185 Ec80
Danişment TR 191 Ed81
Danişment TR 193 Gd81
Danişmentler TR 192 Fc84
Daniszyn PL 129 Gd39
Dankov RUS 203 Fa12
Danków PL 120 Fd35
Dannäs S 102 Fa51
Danndorf D 127 Dd36
Dannemare DK 109 Ea29
Dannemarie F 31 Kb40
Dannemora S 96 Gc41
Dannenberg D 119 Dd34
Dannenwalde D 119 Ed34
Dannike S 102 Ed49
Danören TR 199 Gd88
Dánszentmiklós H 146 Ja54
Danu MD 173 Fa55
Danzé F 29 Gb40
Danzig = Gdańsk PL 121 Hb30
Daoulas F 26 Dc38
Dapšiai LT 114 Kd54
Dapsici MNE 159 Jb68
Dapšioniai LT 114 Kb54
Darabani RO 172 Ec54
Darány H 152 Ha58
Dáras GR 194 Bc87
Darbėnai LT 113 Jb54
Dărcăuți MD 173 Fb54
Darda HR 153 Hc59
Dardesheim D 127 Dd38
Dardhë AL 182 Ad77
Darenth GB 20 Fd28
Daretorp S 103 Fb47
Darfo I 149 Da58
Dargosław PL 120 Fd31
Dargov SK 139 Jd48
Dargun D 119 Ec32
Darıca TR 186 Fd78
Darıca TR 192 Fa81
Darıçayırı TR 187 Gc78
Darıcı TR 192 Fc83
Darısekisi TR 193 Ha85
Darıveren TR 198 Fd90
Darıyerihasanbey TR 187 Ha78
Dârjiu RO 176 Dd60
Darlaston GB 16 Ed24
Darlık TR 186 Ga77
Darlington GB 11 Fa18
Dârlos RO 175 Db60
Darłówko PL 121 Gb30
Darłowo PL 121 Gb30
Darlton GB 16 Fb22
Dărmănești RO 172 Eb55
Dărmănești RO 176 Ea64
Dărmănești RO 176 Ec60
Darmstadt D 134 Cc44
Darneke sameviste S 71 Fc23
Darnétal F 23 Gb35
Darney F 31 Jd39
Darnowo PL 121 Gc31
Daroca E 47 Ed62
Darova RO 174 Ca61
Darque E 44 Ac59
Darragh IRL 12 Bc22
Darro E 60 Dc74
Dars AL 182 Ab75
Darsūniškis LT 114 Kc58
Dārte LV 105 Jd49
Dartford GB 20 Fd28
Dartmouth GB 19 Ea32
Dartsel S 73 Hb23
Daruvar HR 152 Gd59
Dârvari RO 175 Cc66
Darvas H 147 Jd54
Darvel GB 10 Dd14
Darwen GB 15 Ec20
Daržininkai LT 114 Ka58
Darzininkai LT 114 La58
Dasburg D 133 Bb43
Dascălu RO 176 Eb65
Daseburg D 126 Cd39
Dasing D 142 Dc50
Dáski GR 183 Bc78
Dăskot BG 180 Dd70
Dăskotna BG 181 Ed71
Dassel D 126 Da38
Dassendorf D 118 Dc33
Dassólofos GR 189 Bd82
Dassow D 119 Dd31
Dasze PL 123 Kb35
Daszyna PL 130 Hc37
Datça TR 197 Ed91
Datchworth GB 20 Fc27
Datteln D 125 Ca38
Dattilo I 166 Eb84
Daubach D 133 Ca44
Daudzese LV 106 Kd52
Daudzeva LV 106 Kd52
Daugai LT 114 Kd59
Daugailiai LT 115 Lb54
Daugård DK 108 Db25
Daugavpils LV 115 Lc53
Daugbjerg DK 100 Db23
Daugelišiai LV 114 Kb57
Daugėliškis LT 115 Lc55
Dauginčiai LT 113 Jb54
Dauglaukis LT 113 Jd57
Daugstad N 76 Cb33
Dauguļi LV 106 Kd48
Daujėnai LT 114 Kc54
Daukšiai LT 113 Jb53
Daukšiai LV 114 Kb59
Daukstes LV 107 Lb49
Daumazan-sur-Arize F 40 Gb56
Daumeray F 28 Fc41
Daun D 133 Bd43
Dausse F 40 Ga52
Dautphetal D 126 Cc41
Daužnagiai LV 114 Kb55
Dava GB 7 Eb08
Daventry GB 20 Fa25
Davézieux F 34 Jb48
Davidești RO 175 Dc64
Davidovac SRB 174 Cb65
Davidstow GB 18 Dc30
Davik N 84 Cb34
Davle CZ 136 Fb45
Dávlia GR 189 Bd84
Davlos CY 206 Jd95
Davor HR 152 Ha61
Davos CH 142 Da55
Davulga TR 193 Gb86
Davulga TR 193 Ha84
Davutlar TR 197 Ec88
Davyd-Haradok BY 202 Ea14
Dawley GB 15 Ec24
Dawlish GB 19 Ea31
Dax F 39 Fa54
Dayılar TR 192 Ga87
Dazkırı TR 198 Ga88
D. Bijelo Bučje BIH 152 Ha63
D. Dubrava HR 152 Gc57
Deag RO 171 Db59
Deal GB 21 Gb29
Dealu RO 172 Dd59
Dealu Morii RO 176 Ed60
Deanich Lodge GB 4 Dd06
Deanshanger GB 20 Fb26
Dearggel S 68 Hd17
Deauville F 22 Fd35
Deba E 39 Eb55
Debal'ceve UA 205 Fb15
Débanos E 47 Ec60
Debar MK 182 Ad74
Dębe PL 130 Jb36
Debeikiai LT 114 La55
Debel DK 100 Da21
Debelec BG 180 Dd70
Debeli Lug SRB 174 Bd65
Debeljača SRB 153 Jc61
Debeljača SRB 174 Bb63
Debelo Brdo HR 151 Ga62
Dębe Wielkie PL 130 Jc37
Dębica PL 120 Fd31
Dębica PL 139 Jd44
Dębice PL 129 Gb41
Dębiec PL 129 Hb40
Dębień PL 122 Hd33
Dębieniec PL 121 Hb33
De Bilt NL 116 Ba36
De Blesse NL 117 Bc34
Dęblin PL 131 Jd39
Deblín CZ 137 Gb47
Debnevo BG 180 Db71
Dębnica Kaszubska PL 121 Gc30
Dębno PL 120 Fc35
Dębno PL 121 Gd34
Dębno PL 138 Jb44
Dębno PL 138 Jb46
Dębno PL 139 Kb43
Dębołęka PL 129 Hb39
Debovo BG 180 Dc69
Dębowa Kłoda PL 131 Kb38
Debowa Łąka PL 122 Hc34
Dębowa Łęka PL 129 Gb39
Dębowiec PL 139 Jd45
Dębowo PL 123 Ka32
Debrc SRB 153 Jb62
Debrecen H 147 Ka52
Debrešte MK 183 Bb74
Debrznica PL 128 Fc37
Debrzno PL 121 Gc33
Dębsk PL 122 Ja34
Debsko PL 120 Ga34
Dęby Szlacheckie PL 129 Hb37
Deč SRB 153 Jb61
Dečani KSV 178 Ad71
Dečani SRB 159 Jc69
Decazeville F 33 Gd51
Decima I 149 Dc62
Decimomannu I 169 Ca79
Decimoputzu I 169 Ca79
Děčín CZ 128 Fb42
Decize F 30 Hc43
De Cocksdorp NL 116 Ba33
Decollatura I 164 Gc81
Decs H 153 Hc57
Deda RO 172 Dd57
Deddington GB 20 Fa26
Dedeburnu TR 192 Fa83
Dedeçam TR 193 Ha87
Dedeleben D 127 Dd38
Dedeler TR 187 Gd80
Dedeler TR 187 Ha79
Dedeler TR 192 Fb83
Dedeler TR 192 Fd81
Dedeli MK 183 Ca75
Dedelow D 120 Fa33
Dedelstorf D 118 Dc35
Dedems-vaart NL 117 Bd35
Dedenevo RUS 202 Ed10
Dédestapolcsány H 146 Jb50
Dedinci BG 180 Ea71
Dedinky SK 138 Jb48
Dedino MK 183 Ca74
Dedoviči RUS 202 Eb10
Deelish IRL 12 Bb26
Deensen D 126 Da38
Deeping Saint Nicholas GB 17 Fc24
Deetz D 127 Eb38
Deetz D 127 Ec36
Defurovy Lažany CZ 136 Fa47
Dég H 145 Hb55
Degaña E 37 Ca55
Degeberga S 111 Fb55
Degerbäcken S 73 Hc21
Degerby FIN 96 Hc41
Degerby FIN 98 Ka40
Degerfors S 80 Hc26
Degerfors S 95 Fb44
Degerhamn S 111 Gb53
Degernes N 94 Eb43
Degerö FIN 98 Ka40
Degersheim CH 142 Cc53
Degersjö S 80 Gc29
Degerträsk S 73 Hb24
Deggendorf D 135 Ec48
Deggenhausertal D 142 Cd51
Deggingen D 134 Da49
Degionys LT 114 Kd55
Değirmen TR 186 Fa77
Değirmenalanı TR 198 Fc89
Değirmenayvalı TR 193 Gc85
Değirmencieli TR 191 Ed84
Değirmencik TR 185 Ed75
Değirmendere TR 186 Ga79
Değirmendere TR 191 Ec87
Değirmendere TR 193 Gb86
Değirmendere TR 193 Gd85
Değirmendüzü TR 185 Eb79
Değirmenli TR 192 Fa82
Değirmenlik TR 199 Hb90
Değirmenözü TR 199 Ha89
Değirmentköy TR 192 Fd84
Değirmisaz TR 192 Fd83
Değişören TR 193 Gc82
Değnekler TR 192 Fa85
Dego I 148 Ca62
Degolados P 51 Bb68
Degole LV 106 Ka51
Degučiai LT 113 Jc56
Degučiai LT 114 Kb54
Degučiai LT 115 Lb54
De Haan B 21 Ha29
Dehesa de Campoamor E 55 Fb73
Dehesa Mayor E 46 Db61
Dehesas E 37 Bd57
Deià E 57 Hb67
Deidesheim D 133 Cb46
Deifontes E 60 Db74
Deining D 135 Dd47
Deining D 135 Ea47
Deiningen D 134 Dc48
Deinste D 118 Da32
Deißlingen D 141 Cb50
Deiva Marina I 149 Cc63
Dej RO 171 Da57
Dejani RO 175 Dc62
Deje S 94 Fa43
Dejret DK 109 Dd24
Dekanovec HR 145 Gc56
Dekeleia CY 206 Jc97
Deknepollen N 84 Ca34
Dekov BG 180 Dd69
Dekutince SRB 178 Bd71
Delacău MD 173 Ga57
Delamere GB 15 Ec22
Delary S 111 Fb53
Délasse F 22 Fd37
Delbinisht AL 163 Jb72
Delbrück D 126 Cc38
Delčevo MK 179 Ca73
Delden NL 117 Bd36
Delecke D 125 Cb39
Deleitosa E 51 Cb66
Đelekovec HR 152 Gc57
Delémont CH 141 Bd53
Deleni RO 172 Ed56
Deleni RO 173 Fa59
Deleni RO 181 Fb67
Delești RO 173 Fa59
Delfí GR 189 Bd84
Delft NL 116 Ad36
Delfzijl NL 117 Ca33
Delia I 167 Fa86
Deliblato SRB 174 Bb63
Delice TR 192 Fc82
Deliceto I 161 Fd74
Deligrad SRB 178 Bc68
Deliler TR 192 Fb84
Deliömer TR 191 Ec87
Delitzsch D 127 Eb39
Deliveli TR 187 Gb78
Deliyusuflar TR 192 Fa81
Dellach A 143 Ea56
Dellach A 143 Ed55
Dellach im Drautal A 143 Ec55
Delle F 31 Kb40
Delligsen D 126 Db38
Delme F 25 Jd36
Delmenhorst D 118 Cd34
Delnice HR 151 Fc60
Delphi IRL 8 Bb19
Delsbo S 87 Gb35
Deltebre E 48 Ga63
Deltuva LT 114 Kd56
Delvin IRL 9 Cc20
Delvináki GR 182 Ac79
Delvinë AL 182 Ab79
Demandice SK 146 Hc51
Demandolx F 43 Kb53
Dem'anka RUS 107 Mb46
Demanová SK 138 Hd47
de Meca E 59 Bd77
Demecser H 147 Ka50
Demen D 119 Eb32
Demene LV 115 Lc54
Demeškino RUS 107 Ma48
Demidov RUS 202 Ec11
Demigny F 30 Jb43
Demirci TR 191 Ec84
Demirci TR 192 Fc84
Demircihali TR 185 Ed75
Demirciköy TR 191 Ec86
Demirciköy TR 192 Fc84
Demirciler TR 186 Ga78
Demirciler TR 187 Ha79
Demirciler TR 192 Fb87
Demirciller TR 192 Fc82
Demirhan TR 192 Fa87
Demirhanlı TR 185 Eb75
Demirışık TR 186 Ga80
Demir Kapija MK 183 Bd75
Demirköy TR 186 Fa75
Demirköy TR 193 Gb81
Demirler TR 187 Gb79
Demirler TR 192 Fc82
Demirli TR 193 Gc84
Demirli TR 198 Fc91
Demirtaş TR 186 Fd80
Demitz-Thumitz D 128 Fb41
Demjansk RUS 202 Eb09
Dem'jas RUS 203 Ga11
Demmin D 119 Ed32
Demonía GR 195 Bd90
Demonte I 148 Bb63
Demre TR 199 Gb93
Demstrup DK 100 Db23
Dena E 36 Ac56
Denain F 24 Hb32
Denbigh GB 15 Ea22
Den Burg NL 116 Ba33
Denby Dale GB 16 Fa21
Dencsháza H 152 Ha58
Dendermonde B 124 Ac40
Déndra GR 189 Bd82
Dendrohóri GR 182 Ba77
Denekamp NL 117 Ca36
Den Haag NL 116 Ad36
Den Ham NL 117 Bd35
Den Helder NL 116 Ba33
Denholm GB 11 Ec15
den Hoorn NL 117 Bd32
Denia E 55 Fd70
Denizgören TR 191 Ea81
Denizköy TR 187 Gc77
Denizköy TR 197 Ec89
Denizler TR 198 Fd88
Denizli TR 198 Fd88
Denkendorf D 135 Dd48
Denkingen D 142 Cc50
Denklingen D 142 Dc51
Denkte D 126 Dc37
Dennebrœucq F 23 Gd31
Dennington GB 21 Gb25
Denny GB 10 Ea13
Densuș RO 175 Cc62
Denta RO 174 Bc62
Dentlein D 134 Db47
Denzlingen D 141 Ca50
Deonica SRB 153 Jc60
De Panne B 21 Gd29
Děpoltovice CZ 135 Ec44
Depułtycze Królewskie PL 131 Kc40
Derben D 127 Eb36
Derbent TR 187 Gb79
Derbent TR 191 Ed86
Derbent TR 192 Fd82
Derbent TR 192 Fd85
Derbent TR 193 Gd84
Derborence CH 141 Bc56
Derby GB 16 Fa23
Dere TR 192 Fa83
Dereağzı TR 192 Fb87
Derebucak TR 199 Ha89
Derebulaca TR 187 Hb77
Dereçat TR 193 Ha81
Derecikören TR 192 Fb83
Dereçine TR 193 Ha86
Derecske H 147 Ka53
Derekarabağ TR 193 Ha85
Đerekari SRB 178 Bb69
Derekaya TR 192 Ga82
Dereköy TR 185 Dd80
Dereköy TR 185 Eb77
Dereköy TR 185 Ec80
Dereköy TR 185 Ed74
Dereköy TR 186 Fc80
Dereköy TR 186 Ga80
Dereköy TR 187 Ha80
Dereköy TR 187 Hb77
Dereköy TR 191 Ec83
Dereköy TR 191 Ed82
Dereköy TR 191 Ed84
Dereköy TR 191 Fd84
Dereköy TR 192 Fa84
Dereköy TR 193 Gc87
Dereköy TR 193 Ha84
Dereköy TR 197 Fa88
Dereköy TR 198 Fd92
Dereköy TR 199 Gb90
Dereli TR 192 Fb82
Dereli TR 205 Fd19
Dereliçam TR 192 Fc86
Derenburg D 127 Dd38
Dereneu MD 173 Fc57
Dereoba TR 191 Ec81
Deretepe TR 187 Gb78
Derevkovo RUS 107 Mb46
Dereyürük TR 187 Gb80
Dergači RUS 203 Ga11
Derhači UA 203 Fa14
Dermanci BG 179 Da70
Dermbach D 126 Db42
Dermulo I 149 Dc57
Derna RO 170 Cb56
Dernau D 125 Bd42
Dernbach D 125 Cb42
Deronje SRB 153 Hd59
Derreen IRL 8 Bc18
Derreendarragh IRL 12 Ba25
Derringstone GB 21 Gb29
Derry GB 9 Cc16
Derrybrien IRL 12 Bd22
Derrydruel IRL 8 Ca16
Derryerglinna IRL 8 Bc20
Derrygonelly GB 9 Cb17
Derrykeevan GB 9 Cd17
Derrylin GB 9 Cb18
Derrynawilt GB 9 Cc18
Dersca RO 172 Ec54
Dersekow D 119 Ed31
Dersingham GB 17 Fd23
Dërsnik AL 182 Ad77
Dersum D 117 Ca34
Dertini RUS 99 Mb45
Deruta I 156 Eb68
Dervaig GB 6 Da10
Derval F 28 Ed41
Derveliai LT 114 Kb54
Dervéni GR 189 Bc86
Derventa BIH 152 Hb61
Dervio I 149 Cc57
Deryneia CY 206 Jd97
Deržavino RUS 113 Jc59
Desa RO 179 Cc67
Désaignes F 34 Ja49
Desana I 148 Ca60
Desborough GB 20 Fb25
Descargamaría E 45 Bd64
Descartes F 29 Ga43
Desenzano del Garda I 149 Db59
Désertines F 28 Fb38
Desertmartin GB 9 Cd16
Deșești RO 171 Db55
Deset N 86 Eb37
Desfina GR 189 Bd85
Desinić HR 151 Ga57
Desio I 149 Cc59
Deskáti GR 183 Bb80
Deskle SLO 150 Ed58
Desna CZ 128 Fd42
Desno Trebarjevo HR 152 Gb59
Dešov CZ 136 Ga48
Despeñaperros E 61 Ec74
Despetal D 126 Db37
Despotis GR 183 Bb79
Despotovac SRB 174 Bc66
Despotovo SRB 153 Ja59
Dessau-Roßlau D 127 Eb38
Dessel B 124 Ba39
Déssi GR 188 Ba81
Deştiğin TR 193 Hb87
Deştin TR 197 Fa89
Deštná CZ 136 Fc47
Deštné CZ 137 Gb44
Destriana E 37 Cb58
Desulo I 169 Cb77
Desvres F 23 Gc31
Deszczno PL 128 Fd36
Deszk H 153 Jb57
Deta RO 174 Bc62
Detern D 117 Cb33
Detk H 146 Jb52
Detkovo RUS 99 Ma43
Dětmarovice CZ 137 Hb45
Detmold D 126 Cd38
Dettelbach D 134 Db45
Dettenheim D 133 Cb47
Dettey F 30 Hd43
Dettmannsdorf D 119 Ec31
Dettwiller F 25 Kb36
Detva SK 138 Hd49
Deuerling D 135 Ea48
Deuna D 126 Dc40
Deurne NL 125 Bb39
Deutsch-Evern D 118 Dc34
Deutsch-Griffen A 144 Fa55
Deutsch Jahrndorf A 145 Gd51
Deutschkreuz A 145 Gc53
Deutschlandsberg A 144 Fd55
Deutsch-Wagram A 145 Gb50
Deux-Chaises F 34 Hb45
Deva RO 175 Cc61
Devauden GB 19 Eb27
Dévaványa H 147 Jd54
Deveci TR 185 Ec78
Devecikonağı TR 192 Fb81
Devecser H 145 Gd54
Devederesi TR 193 Gd86
Develi TR 186 Fa76
Develi TR 187 Ha77
Devene BG 179 Cd69
Deventer NL 117 Bc36
Deveören TR 187 Hb80
Devesa E 37 Bd53
Deveselu RO 180 Db67
Deveso E 36 Bb53
Devesos E 36 Bb53
Devetaki BG 180 Dc70
Deviat F 32 Fd48
Devic MK 183 Bb74
Devic'i SRB 178 Ba68
Devil's Bridge GB 15 Dd25
Devin BG 184 Da74
Devin SK 145 Gc51
Devizes GB 20 Ed28
Devletliağaç TR 185 Ec74
Devnja BG 181 Fa70
Devojački Bunar SRB 174 Bb63
Devrek TR 187 Hb77
Devynduoniai LV 114 Kb55
De Wijk NL 117 Bc35
Dewsbury GB 16 Fa21
Deza E 47 Ec61
Dežanovac HR 152 Gd59
Dezghingea MD 177 Fc60
Dezna RO 170 Cb59
Dezzo I 149 Da58
Dhërm AL 182 Aa78
Dhrovjan AL 182 Ac79
Dhuizon F 29 Gc41
Dhuvjan AL 182 Ac79
Diablerets CH 141 Bc56
Diafáni GR 197 Ec94
Diakoftó GR 189 Bc85
Diákos GR 183 Bb79
Diakovce SK 145 Ha51
Diakovo BG 179 Cb72

Dornie – East Haddon

Dornie GB 6 Dc08
Dornişoara RO 172 Dd57
Dornoch GB 5 Ea06
Dornstadt D 134 Da49
Dornstetten D 133 Cb49
Dornum D 117 Cb32
Dornumersiel D 117 Cb32
Dorobanţu RO 177 Fb65
Dorobenţu RO 181 Ec67
Dorog H 146 Hc52
Dorohoi RO 172 Ec54
Dorohusk PL 131 Kd40
Dorolţ RO 171 Cd54
Doroslovo SRB 153 Hd59
Dorotea S 79 Ga27
Doroţcaia MD 173 Ga57
Dörpen D 117 Ca34
Dorras N 63 Hc08
Dorrås N 78 Eb27
Dorrington GB 15 Eb24
Dorris S 79 Fd25
Dörrmoschel D 133 Ca45
Dorsten D 125 Bd38
Dortan F 35 Jc45
Dortmund D 125 Ca39
Dörtyol TR 191 Ed82
Doruchów PL 129 Ha40
Dorum D 118 Cd32
Dorupe LV 106 Ka52
Dörverden D 118 Da35
Dorvinjargga N 64 Jc09
Dorweiler D 133 Ca43
Dörzbach D 134 Da46
Dos Aguas E 54 Fb68
Dosbarrios E 52 Dc66
Döşeme TR 187 Gb79
Döşemealtı TR 199 Gc91
Dos Hermanas E 59 Ca74
Dösjebro S 110 Ed55
Dospat BG 184 Da75
Dossenheim D 134 Cc46
Dos Torres E 52 Cc70
Døstrup DK 100 Dc22
Døstrup DK 108 Da27
Dotkomyrene N 65 Kb06
Dötlingen D 117 Cc34
Dotnuva LV 114 Kb56
Dotsikó GR 182 Ba79
Döttingen CH 141 Cb52
Douai F 23 Ha32
Douarnenez F 27 Dc39
Doubravčice CZ 136 Fc45
Douchy F 30 Hb40
Douchy-les-Mines F 24 Hb32
Doucier F 31 Jd44
Doudeville F 23 Ga34
Doue F 24 Hb37
Doué-la-Fontaine F 28 Fc42
Douglas GB 10 Dd19
Doulaincourt-Saucourt F 30 Jb38
Doulevant-le-Château F 30 Ja38
Doullens F 23 Gd32
Dounby GB 5 Ec02
Doune GB 7 Ea12
Dounoux F 31 Jd39
Dourdan F 29 Gd38
Dourgne F 41 Gd54
Douriez F 23 Gc32
Dournazac F 33 Ga47
Doussard F 35 Ka46
Douvaine F 35 Ka45
Douvres-la-Délivrande F 22 Fc35
Douzy F 24 Ja34
Dovadola I 156 Dd64
Dovatorovka RUS 113 Jc59
Dover GB 21 Gb29
Dovhe UA 204 Dd16
Døvik N 92 Cb43
Dovilai LT 113 Jb55
Døvling DK 108 Da24
Dovre N 85 Dc34
Dovreskogen N 85 Dc34
Dovsk BY 202 Eb13
Downham GB 20 Fd25
Downhill GB 9 Cd15
Downpatrick GB 9 Da18
Dowra IRL 8 Ca18
Dowsby GB 17 Fc23
Doxarás GR 182 Ba79
Doxarás GR 189 Bc81
Doxáto GR 184 Da77
Doyuran TR 191 Eb82
Dozulé F 22 Fc36
Dozza I 150 Dd63
Drabeši LV 106 Kd49
Drabiv UA 202 Ed14
Dråby DK 109 Dd24
Drača SRB 174 Bb66
Dračevo BIH 158 Hb68
Dračevo MK 178 Bc73
Drachselsried D 135 Ec48
Drachten NL 117 Bc33
Dračić SRB 153 Jb63
Drag N 66 Ga15
Drag N 78 Eb25
Draga Baščanska HR 151 Fc61
Dragacz PL 121 Hb33
Dragalina RO 176 Ed66
Dragalj MNE 159 Hd69
Dragaljevac BIH 153 Hd62
Dragalovci BIH 152 Ha62
Dragana BG 179 Da70
Drăgăneşti MD 173 Fc55
Drăgăneşti RO 170 Cb58
Drăgăneşti RO 176 Eb65
Drăgăneşti RO 177 Fa62
Drăgăneşti de Vede RO 180 Dc67
Drăgăneşti-Olt RO 180 Db67
Drăgăneşti-Vlaşca RO 180 Dd67
Draganići HR 151 Ga59
Draganovo BG 180 Dd70
Drăganu RO 175 Dc64
Dragaryd S 102 Fa52
Dragaš KSV 178 Ba72
Drăgăşani RO 175 Db65
Dragas Vojvoda BG 180 Dc68
Dragatuš SLO 151 Fd59
Drage D 118 Dc33
Drage HR 157 Ga65
Dragedal N 92 Cc47
Drăgeşti RO 170 Cb57
Drăghiceni RO 179 Da67
Dragičevo BG 179 Cc71
Draginac SRB 153 Ja63
Draginje SRB 153 Jb62
Draginovo BG 179 Cd73
Dragland N 66 Ga13
Draglica SRB 159 Jb66
Dragnic BIH 158 Gd64
Drago RO 171 Cd57
Dragobi AL 159 Jc69
Dragobrača SRB 174 Bb66
Dragočaj BIH 152 Gd62
Dragocvet SRB 174 Bb66
Dragodana RO 176 Dd65
Drăgoeşti RO 175 Db64
Dragoevo BG 181 Ec70
Dragoevo MK 183 Bd74
Dragógi GR 194 Bb88
Drăgoieşti RO 172 Eb56
Dragojčinci BG 179 Ca71
Dragojnovo BG 184 Dc74
Dragoman BG 179 Cb70
Dragomer SLO 151 Fb58
Dragomireşti RO 171 Dc55
Dragomireşti RO 172 Ec58
Dragomireşti RO 173 Fa59
Dragomireşti RO 176 Dd64
Dragomirovo BG 180 Dc69
Dragør DK 109 Ec26
Dragomireşti-Vale RO 176 Ea66
Dragoslavele RO 176 Dd63
Dragostunjë AL 182 Ad75
Dragoş Vodă RO 176 Ed66
Drăgoteşti RO 175 Cc64
Drăgoteşti RO 175 Da66
Dragotina HR 152 Gb60
Dragot-Sulovë AL 182 Ac76
Dragov Dol MK 183 Bb74
Dragovica Polje MNE 159 Ja68
Dragoviština BG 179 Ca72
Dragsmark S 102 Eb47
Dragsvik FIN 97 Jd40
Dragsvik N 84 Cc36
Draguć HR 151 Fa60
Draguignan F 43 Kb54
Drăguşeni RO 172 Ec57
Drăguşeni RO 172 Ed54
Drăguşeni RO 177 Fa61
Drăguteşti RO 175 Cc64
Drahičyn BY 202 Ea14
Drahnsdorf D 128 Fa38
Drahonice CZ 136 Fa47
Drajna RO 176 Eb63
Draka BG 181 Ec73
Drakéi GR 197 Ea88
Drakenburg D 118 Da35
Drákia GR 189 Ca82
Drakótripa GR 188 Bb81
Drakovoúni GR 194 Bb87
Drakšenić BIH 152 Gc60
Dralfa BG 180 Eb70
Dráma GR 184 Cd76
Drammen N 93 Dd42
Drămša BG 179 Cc70
Drânceni RO 173 Fb58
Drangan IRL 13 Cb24
Drange N 92 Cb46
Drangedal N 93 Db44
Drangovo BG 180 Dc73
Drängsered S 102 Ed51
Drängsmark S 80 Hc25
Drangsnes IS 2 Ad03
Drangstedt D 118 Cd32
Drănic RO 179 Da67
Dransfeld D 126 Da39
Dranske D 119 Ed29
Drarović HR 152 Gd60
Draše HR 151 Ga58
Drasenhofen A 137 Gc49
Drăşliceni MD 173 Fd57
Drasučiai LT 114 Ka54
Drávafok H 152 Ha58
Drávaszabolcs H 152 Hb58
Drávaszentes H 152 Gd58
Drávasztára H 152 Ha58
Draveil F 23 Gd37
Draviskos GR 184 Cd77
Dravograd SLO 144 Fc56
Dravovce SK 137 Ha49
Drawno PL 120 Ga34
Drawsko PL 120 Ga35
Drawsko Pomorskie PL 120 Ga33
Drążdżewo PL 122 Jb34
Draženov CZ 135 Ec46
Draževac SRB 153 Jc62
Dražgoše SLO 151 Fb57
Dražice HR 151 Fb60
Dražmirovac SRB 174 Bc66
Drebber D 117 Cc35
Drebkau D 128 Fb39
Dreenagh IRL 12 Ba23
Dreetz D 119 Ec35
Drégelypalánk H 146 Hd51
Dreieich D 134 Cc44
Dreierwalde D 117 Cb36
Dreis D 133 Bc44
Dreis-Brück D 133 Bc43
Dreißigacker D 126 Db42
Drejø By DK 108 Dc28
Drelnes DK 3 Ca07
Drelów PL 131 Kb37
Drem GB 11 Ec13
Dren BG 179 Cb72
Drena I 149 Dc58
Drenchia I 150 Ed57
Drenovac SRB 178 Bd71
Drenovci HR 153 Hd61
Drenovë AL 182 Ad77
Drenovec BG 179 Cb68
Drenovo MK 183 Bc75
Drenovstica MNE 159 Hd69
Drensteinfurt D 125 Cb38
Drenta BG 180 Ea71
Drentwede D 118 Cd35
Drépano GR 183 Bc78
Drépano GR 195 Bd88
Drepcăuţi MD 172 Ed53
Dresden D 128 Fa41
Drëtun' BY 202 Eb11
Dretyń PL 121 Gc31
Dreux F 23 Gb37
Dřevčice CZ 136 Fb43
Drevdagen S 86 Ed35
Dreverna LT 113 Jb56
Dřevohostice CZ 137 Gd46
Drevsjø N 86 Ec35
Drevvatn N 70 Fa21
Drewitz D 127 Eb37
Drewnica PL 121 Hb30
Drezdenko PL 120 Ga35
Drežnica HR 151 Fd61
Drežnik SRB 159 Jb65
Drežnik Grad HR 151 Ga61
Drialos GR 194 Bc91
Dricāni LV 107 Lc51
Dridu RO 176 Eb65
Driebergen-Rijsenburg NL 116 Ba36
Driebes E 46 Dd65
Driedorf D 125 Cb42
Drieliņi LV 106 Kc48
Drienov SK 139 Jd48
Driesum NL 117 Bc33
Drietoma SK 137 Ha48
Driffield GB 17 Fc20
Drimnin GB 6 Db10
Drimoleague IRL 12 Bb26
Drimónas GR 188 Bb84
Drimós GR 183 Ca77
Drimpton GB 19 Eb30
Drinagh IRL 13 Cd25
Drinić BIH 152 Gc63
Drinjača BIH 153 Hd63
Drinovci BIH 158 Gd67
Drionville F 23 Gc31
Driopída GR 195 Cd89
Drióvouno GR 183 Bb78
Drishtë AL 159 Jb70
Drizë AL 182 Aa76
Drizë AL 182 Ac76
Drjanovec BG 180 Ea69
Drjanovec BG 180 Eb69
Drjanovo BG 185 Ea74
Drjanovo BG 180 Dd71
Drjažno RUS 99 Ma44
Drlače SRB 159 Ja64
Drmno SRB 174 Bc64
Drnholec CZ 137 Gb48
Drniš HR 158 Gb65
Drnje HR 152 Gc57
Drnovice CZ 137 Gc47
Dro I 149 Dc58
Drøbak N 93 Ea42
Drobeta-Turnu Severin RO 174 Cb65
Drobin PL 122 Hd35
Drochia MD 173 Fb54
Drochia MD 173 Fb54
Drochow D 128 Fa39
Drochtersen D 118 Da32
Drogheda IRL 9 Cd20
Drogomin PL 128 Fc36
Drogosze PL 122 Jb30
Drohiczyn PL 131 Ka36
Drohobyč UA 204 Dd16
Droichead Átha IRL 9 Cd20
Droichead na Bandan IRL 12 Bc26
Droisy F 23 Gb37
Droitwich GB 20 Ed25
Drolshagen D 125 Cb40
Drołtowice PL 129 Gd40
Drom SRB 153 Jb58
Droman GB 4 Dc04
Dromcolliher IRL 12 Bc24
Dromina IRL 12 Bc25
Drommahane IRL 12 Bc25
Drömme S 80 Gd30
Dromod IRL 8 Ca19
Dromore GB 9 Cb17
Dromore GB 9 Da18
Dromore West IRL 8 Bd18
Dronero I 148 Bc62
Dronfield GB 16 Fa22
Dronninglund DK 101 Dd20
Dronningmølle DK 109 Ec25
Dronten NL 116 Bb35
Dropkovec HR 152 Gb58
Dropla BG 181 Fb69
Drosbacken S 86 Ed35
Drosendorf Stadt A 136 Ga48
Drosiá GR 189 Cb85
Droskovo RUS 203 Fa12
Drosopigí = Vourgareli GR 188 Ba81
Drossáto GR 183 Ca76
Drosseró GR 183 Bb78
Drosseró GR 183 Bd77
Drossopigí GR 183 Bb77
Drottninghaug N 76 Cd33
Drottningskär S 111 Fd54
Droué F 29 Gb39
Drouseia CY 206 Hd97
Drozdowo PL 121 Gb30
Drozdowo PL 123 Jd33
Drozdyn' UA 202 Ea14
Drożki PL 129 Ha41
Drübeck D 126 Dc38
Drugan BG 179 Cb72
Drugnia PL 130 Jb42
Drulingen F 25 Kb36
Drumbeg GB 4 Dc05
Drumcliff IRL 8 Ca17
Drumclog GB 10 Dd14
Drumcondra IRL 9 Cd19
Drume MNE 159 Ja70
Drumevo BG 181 Ed70
Drumfin IRL 8 Ca18
Drumfree IRL 9 Cc15
Drumgoft IRL 13 Cd22
Drumkeen IRL 9 Cb16
Drumkeeran IRL 8 Ca18
Drumlegagh GB 9 Cb17
Drumlish IRL 9 Cb19
Drummannon GB 9 Cd17
Drummore GB 10 Dc17
Drumnadrochit GB 7 Dd08
Drumnakilly GB 9 Cc17
Drumreagh IRL 8 Bb18
Drumrunie GB 4 Dc06
Drumsallie GB 6 Dc10
Drumshanbo IRL 8 Ca19
Drunen NL 124 Ba38
Druskininkai LT 123 Kc30
Drusti LV 106 La49
Druten NL 125 Bb37
Druva LV 105 Jd52
Druvas LV 105 Jd52
Druviena LV 107 Lb49
Druyes-les-Belles-Fontaine F 30 Hb41
Družba RUS 113 Jb59
Družba UA 202 Ed13
Drużbice PL 130 Hd40
Druževac SRB 153 Jb63
Družetići SRB 159 Jc64
Družnaja Gorka RUS 99 Mb41
Drvar BIH 152 Gb63
Drvenik HR 158 Gd67
Drwalew PL 130 Jb38
Drwęczno PL 122 Hd31
Drybrook GB 19 Ec27
Drygały PL 123 Jd32
Drymen GB 7 Dd12
Dryszczów PL 131 Kd40
Drzązgowo PL 129 Gc37
Drzecin PL 128 Fc37
Drzewce PL 129 Ha37
Drzewce PL 129 Hb37
Drzewce PL 131 Ka39
Drzewiany PL 121 Gb31
Drzewica PL 130 Jb39
Držková CZ 137 Ha47
Drzonów PL 128 Fd38
Drzonowo PL 120 Fd31
Drzonowo PL 121 Gc32
Drzycim PL 121 Ha33
Duacı TR 199 Gc91
Duagh IRL 12 Bb24
Dualar TR 191 Ed83
Dualchi I 169 Ca76
Duas Igrejas P 45 Ca60
Dub SRB 159 Jb64
Dubá CZ 136 Fb43
Dubac HR 158 Hb69
Dubăsari MD 173 Fd57
Dubăsarii Vechi MD 173 Ga57
Duba Stonska HR 158 Ha68
Dubău MD 173 Ga56
Dub-Bor RUS 99 Ld45
Dubci HR 158 Gc66
Dubeni LV 105 Jb52
Dubeni LV 105 Jb52
Dubeniniki PL 123 Ka30
Dubeşti RO 174 Ca60
Dubí CZ 128 Fa42
Dubicko CZ 137 Gc45
Dubicze Cerkiewne PL 123 Kc35
Dubienka PL 131 Kd40
Dubin PL 129 Gc39
Dubingiai LT 114 La56
Dubinné SK 139 Jd47
Dubiny PL 123 Kc34
Dub'jazy RUS 203 Fd08
Dubki RUS 107 Ma49
Dubleva LV 107 Lc49
Dublin IRL 13 Cd21
Dublovice CZ 136 Fb46
Dubna LV 115 Lc53
Dubna MD 173 Fc55
Dubna RUS 202 Ed10
Dubna RUS 203 Fa11
Dub nad Moravou CZ 137 Gd46
Dubňany CZ 137 Gc48
Dubné CZ 136 Fb48
Dubnica SRB 178 Bd71
Dubnica nad Váhom SK 137 Hb48
Dubník SK 145 Hb51
Dubno UA 204 Ea15
Dubočka SRB 174 Bd65
Duboštica BIH 153 Hc63
Dubova RO 174 Ca65
Dubovac KSV 178 Ba70
Dubovac SRB 174 Bc64
Dubovac Okučanski HR 152 Gd60
Dubovka RUS 203 Fd13
Dubovskoje RUS 113 Jd58
Dubovskoje RUS 205 Fd15
Dubovyj Ovrag RUS 203 Fd14
Dubranec HR 151 Ga59
Dubrava BIH 152 Ha62
Dubrava HR 152 Gb58
Dubrava HR 152 Gc58
Dubrava RUS 113 Jd59
Dubrave BIH 153 Hc62
Dubrave BIH 153 Hc63
Dubravica BIH 158 Hb64
Dubravica HR 151 Ga58
Dubravica SRB 174 Bc64
Dubravice BIH 153 Ja63
Dubravka HR 159 Hc69
Dubrivka UA 204 Eb15
Dubrovka RUS 107 Mb51
Dubrovka RUS 203 Fc12
Dubrovnik HR 158 Hb69
Dubrovno RUS 107 Mb46
Dubrovy RUS 107 Mb49
Dubrovycja UA 202 Ea14
Dubuļi LV 107 Ld52
Dubulti LV 106 La52
Ducaj AL 159 Jb70
Ducey F 28 Fa38
Duchally GB 4 Dd05
Duchcov CZ 136 Fa43
Ducherow D 120 Fa32
Duclair F 23 Ga35
Duda-Epureni RO 173 Fb59
Dudaklı TR 186 Fd80
Dudar H 145 Ha53
Duddington GB 16 Fb24
Dudelange L 133 Bb45
Dudeldorf D 133 Bc44
Dudenhofen D 133 Cb46
Düdenköy TR 198 Ga89
Düdenköy TR 199 Gb92
Duderstadt D 126 Db39
Dudeşti RO 177 Fa65
Dudeştii Vechi RO 170 Bb59
Đuđevo SRB 153 Jb60
Dudince SK 146 Hc50
Dudley GB 16 Ed24
Dudovica SRB 153 Jc63
Dueñas E 46 Da59
Duesund N 84 Ca37
Dufftown GB 7 Eb08
Duffus GB 5 Eb07
Duga Poljana SRB 178 Ad68
Duga Resa HR 151 Fd60
Düğer TR 199 Gb89
Duggendorf D 135 Ea47
Dugi Rat HR 158 Gc66
Dugo Selo HR 152 Gb59
Düğrek TR 198 Fb90
Duğüncüler TR 192 Fb83
Duhnen D 118 Cd31
Duhnovo RUS 107 Mb49
Duhovec BG 181 Ec69
Duhovnickoe RUS 203 Ga11
Duingen D 126 Da38
Duingt F 35 Ka46
Duinkerken = Dunkerque F 21 Gd29
Duino I 150 Ed59
Duirinish GB 4 Db08
Duisburg D 125 Bd39
Duiven NL 125 Bc37
Dukat AL 182 Aa78
Dukat SRB 178 Bd72
Dukla PL 139 Jd45
Dūkštas LT 115 Lb55
Dūkštos LT 114 La57
Dukuļava LV 107 Ld49
Dulceşti RO 172 Ed58
Dulcza Wielka PL 138 Jc43
Duleek IRL 9 Cd20
Duljci BIH 152 Gd63
Dulje KSV 178 Ba71
Dullingham GB 20 Fd26
Dülmen D 125 Ca38
Dulovka RUS 107 Ma47
Dulovo BG 181 Ed68
Dulverton GB 19 Ea29
Duły PL 123 Jd30
Dumača SRB 153 Jb62
Dumanalanı TR 185 Ed80
Dumanlar TR 192 Fc85
Dumanlı TR 192 Fd86
Dumanlı TR 199 Ha89
Dumbarton GB 10 Dd13
Dumbleton GB 20 Ed26
Dumbrava RO 174 Ca61
Dumbrava RO 175 Cc65
Dumbrava RO 176 Eb65
Dumbrăveni RO 172 Ec55
Dumbrăveni RO 175 Dc60
Dumbrăveni RO 176 Ed62
Dumbrăveni RO 181 Fb68
Dumbrăviţa MD 173 Fb56
Dumbrăviţa RO 171 Da55
Dumbrăviţa RO 174 Ca60
Dumbrăviţa RO 176 Dd62
Dümenler TR 192 Ga85
Dumeşti RO 172 Ed58
Dumeşti RO 173 Fa57
Dumfries GB 10 Ea16
Dumha Eige IRL 8 Bb18
Dumitra RO 171 Dc57
Dumitreşti RO 176 Ec62
Dumluca TR 193 Ha82
Dumlupınar TR 193 Gb85
Dummerstorf D 119 Eb31
Dümpelfeld D 125 Bd42
Dümrek TR 191 Ea81
Dümrek TR 193 Hb81
Dümrek TR 193 Hb82
Duna N 78 Ec26
Dunafalva H 153 Hc57
Dunaff IRL 9 Cc15
Dunaföldvár H 146 Hc55
Dunaharaszti H 146 Hd53
Dunajivci UA 204 Eb16
Dunajská Lužná SK 145 Gd51
Dunajská Streda SK 145 Ha51
Dunakeszi H 146 Hd52
Dunakömlőd H 146 Hc55
Dunalka LV 105 Jb52
Dunapataj H 146 Hd56
Dunăreni RO 179 Cd67
Dūņas LV 107 Lb52
Dunaszekcső H 153 Hc57
Dunaszentbenedek H 146 Hd56
Dunaszentgyörgy H 146 Hc56
Dunatetétlen H 146 Hd55
Dunaújváros H 146 Hc54
Dunava LV 107 Lb52
Dunavăţu de Jos RO 177 Fd65
Dunavci BG 179 Cb67
Dunavci BG 180 Dc72
Dunavecse H 146 Hd55
Dunbar GB 11 Ec13
Dunblane GB 7 Ea12
Dunboyne IRL 13 Cd21
Dún Chaoin IRL 12 Ad24
Dunchurch GB 20 Fa25
Duncormick IRL 13 Cc25
Dundaga LV 105 Jc49
Dundalk IRL 9 Cd19
Dündarlı TR 191 Ec84
Dun Dealgan IRL 9 Cd19
Dundee GB 7 Ec11
Dunderland N 71 Fc20
Dunderrow IRL 12 Bc26
Dundonald GB 9 Da17
Dundonnell GB 4 Dc06
Dundrennan GB 10 Ea17
Dundrum IRL 13 Ca23
Dunecht GB 7 Ed09
Dunes F 40 Ga53
Dunfanaghy IRL 9 Cb15
Dunfermline GB 7 Eb12
Dungannon GB 9 Cd17
Dún Garbhán IRL 13 Ca25
Dungarvan IRL 13 Ca25
Dungiven GB 9 Cd16
Dunglow IRL 8 Ca15
Dungourney IRL 12 Bd25
Dunholme GB 17 Fc22
Dunières F 34 Ja48
Dunika LV 113 Jb53
Duninowo PL 121 Gb29
Dunje MK 183 Bc75
Dunjica MK 183 Bd75
Dunkeld GB 7 Eb11
Dunker S 95 Gb44
Dunkerque F 21 Gd29
Dunkerrin IRL 13 Ca22
Dunkeswell GB 19 Ea30
Dunkineely IRL 8 Ca17
Dünkirchen = Dunkerque F 21 Gd29
Dunkirk GB 19 Ec28
Duńkowice PL 139 Kc44
Dun Laoghaire IRL 13 Cd21
Dunlavin IRL 13 Cc22
Dunleer IRL 9 Cd20
Dun-le-Palestel F 33 Gc45
Dunlop GB 10 Dd14
Dún Manmhaí IRL 12 Bc26
Dunmanus IRL 12 Ba26
Dunmanway IRL 12 Bc26
Dún Mór IRL 8 Bd20
Dunmore GB 9 Da19
Dunmore IRL 8 Bd20
Dunmore East IRL 13 Cc25
Dunnamanagh GB 9 Cc16
Dunnamore GB 9 Cc17
Dun na nGall IRL 8 Ca16
Dunnet GB 5 Eb04
Dunningen D 141 Cb50
Dunoon GB 6 Dc13
Dunquin IRL 12 Ad24
Duns GB 11 Ed14
Dunscore GB 10 Ea16
Dünsen D 118 Cd34
Dunsford GB 19 Dd30
Dunshaughlin IRL 13 Cd21
Dunstable GB 20 Fb27
Dunster GB 19 Ea29
Dun-sur-Auron F 29 Ha43
Dun-sur-Meuse F 24 Jb34
Dunte LV 106 Kc49
Duntish GB 19 Ec30
Dunum D 117 Cb32
Dunure GB 10 Dc15
Dunvegan GB 4 Da07
Dupnica BG 179 Cb72
Durabeyler TR 192 Fc82
Durach D 142 Db52
Đurađ HR 152 Hb59
Durağan TR 205 Fb20
Durak TR 199 Hb89
Duraklar TR 187 Ha78
Đurakovac KSV 178 Ba70
Duran BG 181 Ec69
Durance F 40 Fd52
Durango E 39 Eb55
Durankulak BG 181 Fc69
Duras F 32 Fd51
Durasılar TR 192 Fb83
Durasıllı TR 192 Fb86
Durbach D 133 Ca49
Durban-Corbières F 41 Hb56
Durbe LV 105 Jb52
Durbuy B 124 Ba42
Dúrcal E 60 Db75
Durdat-Larequille F 33 Ha45
Đurđenovac HR 152 Hb59
Đurđevac HR 152 Gd58
Đurđevik BIH 153 Hc63
Đurđevo SRB 174 Bb65
Đurđin SRB 153 Ja58
Dūre LV 106 Kd48
Düren D 125 Bc41
Durfort F 41 Hd53
Durfort-Lacapelette F 40 Gb52
Durham GB 11 Fa17
Durhasan TR 192 Fc81
Durhasan TR 192 Fc84
Đurinci SRB 174 Bb64
Durlangen D 134 Da48
Durlas IRL 13 Ca23
Durleşti MD 173 Fd58
Đurmanec HR 151 Ga57
Durmersheim D 133 Cb47
Durness GB 4 Dd04
Durneşti RO 172 Ed55
Dürnholz I 143 Dd55
Dürnkrut A 145 Gc50
Dürnstein A 144 Fb55
Dürnstein A 144 Fd50
Duronia I 161 Fb72
Dürrboden CH 142 Da55
Durrës AL 182 Ab74
Dürrhennersdorf D 128 Fc41
Durrington GB 20 Ed29
Dürröhrsdorf-Dittersbach D 128 Fb41
Durrow IRL 13 Cb23
Durrus IRL 12 Bb26
Dürrwangen D 134 Db47
Dursunbey TR 192 Fc82
Durtal F 28 Fc41
Duruelo de la Sierra E 47 Ea59
Durup DK 100 Da22
Dūrupe LV 105 Jc51
Dury F 23 Gd33
Dušanci BG 179 Da71
Dūseikiai LT 113 Jd54
Dusetos LT 115 Lb54
Dusina BIH 158 Hb65
Dušinci BG 179 Ca71
Duşmani MD 173 Fa55
Dusmenys LT 114 Kd59
Dusnok H 146 Hd56
Dusocin PL 121 Hb32
Düsseldorf D 125 Bd40
Dussen NL 124 Ba37
Dußlingen D 134 Cc49
Duston GB 20 Fb25
Duszniki PL 129 Gb36
Duszniki-Zdrój PL 137 Gb43
Dutağaç TR 198 Fb88
Duthil GB 7 Ea08
Dutka LV 106 Kd48
Dutluca TR 192 Fd82
Dutluca TR 192 Fd86
Dutluca TR 193 Gb82
Dutluca TR 198 Ga88
Dutovlje SLO 151 Fa59
Duvberg S 87 Fb34
Duved S 78 Ed30
Düverdüzü TR 187 Gd78
Düvertepe TR 192 Fb83
Düzağaç TR 193 Gb85
Düzağaç TR 199 Ha90
Duża Klonownica PL 131 Kb37
Düzce TR 187 Ha78
Duži BIH 158 Ha68
Dužica HR 152 Gb59
Düzkışla TR 193 Gb85
Düzköy TR 187 Gb78
Düzorman TR 185 Ed75
Düzova TR 186 Fa76
Duzy-le-Gros F 24 Hc34
Dvärsätt S 79 Fc30
Dve Mogili BG 180 Ea69
Dverberg N 66 Fd11
Dviete LV 115 Lb53
Dvor HR 152 Gb61
Dvor SLO 151 Fc59
Dvorčani LV 115 Ld53
Dvoriki RUS 203 Fa10
Dvorišče RUS 99 Ld42
Dvorišče RUS 107 Mb51
Dvory nad Žitavou SK 145 Hb51
Dvůr Králové nad Labem CZ 136 Ga43
Dwikozy PL 131 Jd41
Dwingeloo NL 117 Bd34
Dwórzno PL 122 Ja30
Dyan GB 9 Cd18
Dyblin PL 122 Hc35
Dybów PL 131 Jd36
Dyce GB 7 Ed09
Dydnia PL 139 Ka45
Dyffryn Ardudwy GB 15 Dd23
Dyfjord N 64 Jd04
Dygowo PL 120 Ga31
Dykan'ka UA 202 Ed14
Dyke GB 18 Dc29
Dykehead GB 7 Ec10
Dykends GB 7 Eb10
Dylewo PL 122 Jc33
Dylicy RUS 99 Mb40
Dylife GB 15 Ea24
Dymchurch GB 21 Ga29
Dymer UA 202 Ec14
Dymock GB 15 Ec26
Dymokury CZ 136 Fd44
Dynów PL 139 Ka44
Dyping N 66 Fd15
Dypvåg N 93 Db45
Dyranut N 84 Cd39
Dyrham GB 19 Ec28
Dyrkorn N 76 Cd33
Dyrnes N 77 Db29
Dyrøy N 67 Gb11
Dysberg S 87 Fb37
Dysbodarna S 86 Fa38
Dysna LT 115 Lc55
Dywity PL 122 Ja31
Džalil' RUS 203 Ga08
Džanići BIH 158 Hb65
Džankoj UA 205 Fa17
Dzbonie PL 122 Jb34
Džebel BG 184 Dc75
Dzedri LV 105 Jd50
Dzelda LV 105 Jc52
Dzelmes LV 106 Kd51
Dzelzava LV 107 Lb50
Dzeņi LV 106 La48
Džep SRB 178 Bd71
Džepišta MK 182 Ad74
Dzērbene LV 106 Lc49
Dzerjinscoe MD 173 Ga57
Dzeržinsk RUS 203 Fb09
Dzeržinskoje RUS 113 Jc58
Dziadkowice PL 123 Kb35
Dziadkowo PL 129 Gd39
Dziadowa Kłoda PL 129 Gd40
Działdowo PL 122 Ja33
Działoszyce PL 138 Jb43
Działoszyn PL 130 Hc41
Działyń PL 131 Kb38
Dziekanowice PL 138 Ja45
Dziektarzewo PL 122 Ja35
Dziemiany PL 121 Gd31
Dzierążnia PL 122 Ja35
Dzierżążno Wielkie PL 121 Gb35
Dzierzgoń PL 122 Hc31
Dzierzgowo PL 122 Jb34
Dzierzkowice Rynek PL 131 Ka41
Dzierżoniów PL 129 Gb42
Dzierżysław PL 137 Ha44
Dziesław PL 129 Gb40
Dzietrzychowo PL 122 Jb30
Dziewin PL 138 Jb44
Džigolj SRB 178 Bc69
Dzikowo PL 120 Fd35
Dzikowo PL 121 Gb34
Dzików Stary PL 139 Kc43
Dzirciems LV 105 Jd50
Dziwnów PL 120 Fc31
Dziwnówek PL 120 Fc31
Dzjaržynsk BY 202 Ea12
Dzjatlava BY 202 Ea13
Džubga RUS 205 Fc17
Džūkste LV 106 Ka51
Džuljunica BG 180 Ea70
Džurkovo BG 184 Db74
Džurovo BG 179 Da70
Džuryn UA 204 Eb16
Dźwierszno Wielkie PL 121 Gd34
Dźwierzno PL 121 Hb34
Dźwierzuty PL 122 Jb32
Dźwiżyno PL 120 Fd31

E

Ea E 39 Eb55
Éadan Doire IRL 13 Cc21
Eaglesfield GB 11 Eb16
Eani GR 183 Bc79
Eanodat FIN 68 Ja13
Eántio GR 195 Cb87
Earby GB 16 Ed20
Earls Barton GB 20 Fb25
Earls Colne GB 21 Ga26
Earlsferry GB 7 Ec12
Earlston GB 11 Ec14
Easdale GB 6 Db11
Easington GB 11 Fa17
Easington GB 17 Fd21
Easington GB 20 Fb27
Easingwold GB 11 Fa19
Easky IRL 8 Bd18
Eastbourne GB 20 Fd30
East Brent GB 19 Eb29
Eastchurch GB 21 Ga28
Eastcote GB 20 Fc28
East Cowes GB 20 Fa30
East Dereham GB 17 Ga24
Eastergate GB 20 Fb30
East Grafton GB 20 Ed28
East Grinstead GB 20 Fc29
East Haddon GB 20 Fb25

East Hanningfield - Emersleben

East Hanningfield GB 21 Ga27
East Horsley GB 20 Fc29
East Ilsley GB 20 Fa28
East Kilbride GB 10 Dd13
East Leake GB 16 Fa23
Eastleigh GB 20 Fa30
East Linton GB 11 Ec13
East Morden GB 19 Ec30
East Norton GB 16 Fb24
Eastoft GB 16 Fb21
Easton GB 17 Gb24
Easton GB 19 Ec31
Easton Grey GB 19 Ec27
East Poringland GB 17 Gb24
East Portlemouth GB 19 Dd32
East Ravendale GB 17 Fc21
East Rudham GB 17 Ga24
East Tisted GB 20 Fb29
Eastville GB 17 Fd23
East Winch GB 17 Fd24
Eastwood GB 16 Fa23
Eatoševo BG 180 Dc71
Eaux-Bonnes F 40 Fc56
Eauze F 40 Fd53
Ebberup DK 108 Dc27
Ebbo FIN 98 Kc39
Ebbw Vale GB 19 Eb27
Ebchester GB 11 Ed17
Ebeleben D 126 Dc40
Ebeltoft DK 109 Dd24
Eben A 143 Ea53
Ebene Reichenau A 144 Fa55
Ebenfurt A 145 Gb52
Ebensee A 144 Fa52
Ebensfeld D 134 Dc44
Eberbach D 134 Cd46
Eberdingen D 134 Cc48
Ebergassing A 145 Gb51
Ebergötzen D 126 Db39
Eberhardzell D 142 Da51
Ebermannsdorf D 135 Ea47
Ebermannstadt D 135 Dd45
Ebern D 134 Dc44
Ebernburg D 133 Ca45
Eberndorf A 144 Fc56
Ebersbach D 127 Ed41
Ebersbach D 128 Fa40
Ebersbach D 128 Fc41
Ebersbach D 128 Fc41
Ebersbach D 134 Cd48
Ebersberg D 143 Ea51
Ebersburg D 134 Da43
Eberschwang A 143 Ed51
Ebersdorf D 135 Dd44
Ebersdorf, Saalburg- D 135 Ea43
Eberswalde D 120 Fa35
Ebnat-Kappel CH 142 Cc53
Eboli I 161 Fc76
Ebrach D 134 Dc45
Ebreichsdorf A 145 Gb51
Ebreuil F 34 Hb46
Ebsdorfergrund D 126 Cd42
Ebstorf D 118 Dc34
Ecaterinovca MD 173 Fd59
Écaussinnes-Lalaing B 124 Ac41
Eccles GB 11 Ec14
Eccleshall GB 15 Ec23
Eceabat TR 185 Ea80
Echalar E 39 Ed55
Echallens CH 141 Bb55
Echalot F 30 Ja41
Echarri- E 39 Ec56
Echassières F 34 Hb45
Echauri E 39 Ec57
Eching D 135 Ea49
Eching D 143 Ea50
Echiré F 32 Fc45
Echourgnac F 32 Fd49
Echt GB 7 Ed09
Echt NL 125 Bb40
Echteld NL 125 Bb37
Echterdingen, Leinfelden- D 134 Cd49
Echternach L 133 Bc44
Écija E 60 Cc73
Ecirli TR 199 Ha89
Ečka SRB 174 Bb62
Eckartsau A 145 Gc51
Eckartsberga D 127 Ea41
Eckental D 135 Dd46
Eckernförde D 108 Db29
Eckerö FIN 96 Hb40
Eckersdorf D 135 Dd45
Eckington GB 16 Fa22
Eclaron-Braucourt F 24 Ja37
Ecly F 24 Hd34
Écommoy F 28 Fd40
Ecouché F 22 Fc37
Ecouflant F 28 Fb41
Écouis F 23 Gb35
Ecoyeux F 32 Fb47
Ecques F 23 Gd31
Ecseg H 146 Ja51
Ecsegfalva H 147 Jd54
Ecueillé F 29 Gb43
Écury-sur-Coole F 24 Hd36
Ed S 79 Gb30
Ed S 94 Ec45
Eda S 94 Ec42
Eda Glasbruck S 94 Ec41
Edam NL 116 Ba35
Edane S 94 Ed42
Ēdas LV 105 Jc51
Eddelak D 118 Da31
Edderton GB 5 Ea07
Eddleston GB 11 Eb14
Ede NL 125 Bb37
Ede S 79 Fd29
Ede S 87 Ga33
Edebäck S 94 Fa41
Edebo S 96 Ha41
Edeby S 96 Ha41
Edefors S 73 Hc21
Edelave By DK 108 Dc25
Edelény H 146 Jc50
Edelschrott A 144 Fc55
Edelsfeld D 135 Ea46
Edemissen D 126 Db38
Edemissen D 126 Dc36
Eden S 79 Gb29
Edenbridge GB 20 Fd29
Edenderry IRL 13 Cc21
Edenkoben D 133 Cb46
Edersleben D 127 Dd40
Edertal D 126 Cd40
Edesbyn S 87 Fd37
Edesheim D 133 Cb46
Édessa GR 183 Bc77
Edestad S 113 Fd54
Edevik S 78 Ed28
Edewecht D 117 Cc34
Edgbaston GB 20 Ed25
Edgeworthstown = Mostrim IRL 9 Cb20
Edhem S 103 Fb47
Edinburgh GB 11 Eb13
Edincik TR 186 Fa80
Edineț MD 173 Fa54
Edipsós GR 189 Ca83
Edırne TR 185 Eb75
Edith Weston GB 16 Fb24
Edlingham GB 11 Ed15
Edlitz A 145 Gb54
Edmundbyers GB 11 Ed17
Édole LV 105 Jb51
Edolo I 149 Da57
Edremit TR 191 Ec82
Edrželija MK 183 Bd74
Edsberg S 95 Fc44
Edsbro S 96 Ha41
Edsbruk S 103 Gb48
Edsele S 79 Ga30
Edshult S 103 Fd49
Edshultshall S 102 Eb47
Edsleskog S 94 Ec44
Edsta S 87 Gb35
Edsvalla S 94 Fa43
Edsvära S 102 Ed47
Edsvik FIN 89 Hd32
Edzell GB 7 Ec10
Eeklo B 124 Ab39
Eelde NL 117 Bd33
Eemshaven NL 117 Ca32
Eemsmond NL 117 Ca32
Eerbeek NL 125 Bc37
Eernegem B 21 Ha29
Eersel NL 124 Ba39
Efeköy TR 193 Gc86
Efendiköprüsü TR 192 Ga84
Efendili TR 192 Fb84
Eferding A 144 Fa50
Effelder D 135 Dd43
Effretikon CH 141 Cb53
Efimovskij RUS 202 Ec08
Efir TR 192 Fc83
Efkarpía GR 183 Ca76
Efkarpía GR 183 Ca77
Efkarpía GR 184 Cc77
Eflâni TR 205 Fa20
Eforie Nord RO 181 Fc68
Eforie Sud RO 181 Fc68
Efremov RUS 203 Fa12
Efteløt N 93 Dc42
Eg DK 108 Da25
Egáleo GR 189 Cb86
Egáni GR 183 Bd80
Egby S 103 Gb52
Egebæk DK 108 Da27
Egebjerg DK 108 Dc25
Egebjerg DK 109 Eb25
Egeln D 127 Ea38
Egense DK 101 Dd21
Eger H 146 Jb51
Egerbakta H 146 Jb51
Eğerci TR 187 Hb77
Egeris DK 108 Da24
Egersund N 92 Ca45
Egeskov DK 108 Db26
Egestorf D 118 Db34
Eggby S 102 Fa46
Eggebek D 108 Da29
Eggedal N 85 Dc40
Eggemoen N 85 Kd07
Eggenburg A 136 Ga49
Eggenfelden D 143 Ec50
Eggenstein-Leopoldshafen D 133 Cb47
Eggerding A 143 Ed50
Eggermühlen D 117 Cb35
Eggersdorf, Fredersdorf- D 128 Fa36
Eggesin D 120 Fb32
Eggingen D 141 Cb52
Eggiwil CH 141 Bd54
Eggkleiva N 77 Ea30
Egglescliffe GB 11 Fa18
Egglham D 135 Ec49
Egglkofen D 143 Eb50
Eggolsheim D 135 Dd45
Eggstätt D 143 Eb51
Eggum N 66 Fb14
Egham GB 20 Fb28
Eghezée B 124 Ad41
Egiáli GR 196 Dd90
Egiertowo PL 121 Ha30
Egiés GR 194 Bc90
Egileta E 39 Eb57
Egilsstaðir IS 3 Bc05
Égina GR 195 Cb87
Eging am See D 135 Ed49
Egínio GR 183 Bd78
Égio GR 188 Bb85
Egira GR 189 Bc85
Eğirdir TR 199 Gd88
Égiros GR 184 Dc77
Egkomi CY 206 Jd96
Églaine LV 115 Lb53
Égletons F 33 Gd48
Eğlikler TR 199 Hb88
Egling D 142 Dc50
Egling D 143 Dd51
Eglingham GB 11 Ed15
Eglisau CH 141 Cb52
Égliseneuve-d'Antraigues F 33 Ha48
Egloffstein D 135 Dd45
Eglwysfach GB 15 Dd24
Eglwyswrw GB 14 Dc26
Eğmir TR 191 Ec82
Egmond aan Zee NL 116 Ad34
Egna I 150 Dd57
Egnach CH 142 Cd52
Egor'e RUS 202 Ed11
Egoreni MD 173 Fc54
Egor'evsk RUS 203 Fa10
Egorlykskaja RUS 205 Fc16
Egorovca MD 173 Fb56
Eğrekli TR 198 Fc91
Egremont GB 10 Ea18
Égreville F 29 Ha39
Eğridere TR 192 Fb87
Eğrioğlu TR 187 Gc78
Eğriöz TR 192 Fd83
Eğriöz TR 192 Ga82
Egsmark DK 109 Dd24
Egton GB 11 Fb18
Egtved DK 108 Db26
Éguilles F 42 Jc54
Eguisheim F 31 Kb39
Eguzon F 33 Gc45
Egyed H 145 Gd53
Egyek H 146 Jc52
Egyházasradoc H 145 Gc54
Egyptinkorpi FIN 83 Lc27
Ehekirchen D 134 Dc49
Ehingen D 134 Dc47
Ehingen am Ries D 134 Dc48
Ehingen (Donau) D 142 Da50
Ehinos GR 184 Db76
Ehningen D 134 Cc48
Ehra-Lessien D 127 Dd36
Ehrang D 133 Bc44
Ehrenberg D 134 Db43
Ehrenburg D 118 Cd35
Ehrenfriedersdorf D 127 Ec42
Ehrenhain D 127 Ec41
Ehrenhausen A 144 Fd55
Ehrenkirchen D 141 Ca51
Ehringshausen D 126 Cc42
Ehrwald A 142 Dc53
Ehtamo FIN 89 Jb37
Eia N 92 Cb45
Eiane N 92 Cb44
Eibar E 39 Eb55
Eibau D 128 Fc41
Eibelstadt D 134 Db45
Eibenstock D 135 Ec43
Eibergen NL 125 Bd37
Eibiswald A 144 Fd56
Eiby N 63 Hd08
Eich D 133 Cb45
Eichenbarleben D 127 Ea37
Eichenbrunn A 137 Gb49
Eichendorf D 135 Ec49
Eichenzell D 134 Da43
Eichstätt D 135 Dd48
Eichstetten D 141 Ca50
Eichwalde D 128 Fa37
Eičiai LT 113 Jd57
Eicklingen D 126 Dc36
Eid N 77 Dc29
Eid N 77 Da32
Eid N 78 Ea28
Eidanger N 93 Dc44
Eidapere EST 98 Kc44
Eiðar IS 3 Bc05
Eidbukt N 66 Fd12
Eidbukta N 71 Fb19
Eide N 66 Fc14
Eide N 77 Da31
Eide N 84 Ca36
Eide N 84 Cc39
Eide N 92 Cb45
Eide N 93 Da47
Eidem N 70 Ec23
Eidesund N 92 Ca43
Eidet N 62 Gc10
Eidet N 65 Fd12
Eidet N 66 Ga14
Eidet N 77 Dd30
Eidet N 93 Db45
Eidevik N 84 Cb36
Eidfjord N 84 Cd39
Eiði DK 3 Ca06
Eidkjosen N 62 Gc09
Eidnes N 63 Ja04
Eidså N 76 Cb33
Eidsberg N 94 Eb43
Eidsborg N 93 Da42
Eidsdal N 76 Cd33
Eidsfoss N 93 Dd42
Eidskog N 94 Ec41
Eidslandet N 84 Cb38
Eidsnes N 63 Hd08
Eidsøra N 77 Db31
Eidsvåg N 77 Db32
Eidsvåg N 92 Ca41
Eidsvoll N 94 Eb40
Eidvågeid N 63 Hd06
Eiesland N 92 Cc45
Eige N 92 Ca45
Eigebrekk N 92 Cd47
Eigeland N 92 Ca44
Eigeland N 92 Ca45
Eigeltingen D 142 Cc51
Eigirdonys LT 114 Kd58
Eigirdžiai LT 113 Jd54
Eigirgala LT 114 Kc57
Eijsden NL 125 Bb41
Eik N 92 Ca43
Eik N 92 Cb45
Eikange N 84 Ca38
Eikåsgrend N 92 Cb46
Eikefjord N 84 Cb35
Eikeland N 92 Cb46
Eikeland N 92 Cd46
Eikeland N 93 Db45
Eikelandsosen N 84 Cb40
Eiken N 92 Cc46
Eikenes N 84 Ca36
Eikla EST 105 Jc46
Eiknes N 84 Cb40
Eilenburg D 127 Ec40
Èilgar RUS 205 Ga15
Eilsleben D 127 Dd37
Eime D 126 Db37
Eimen D 126 Db38
Eimisjärvi FIN 83 Ma30
Eimke D 118 Dc34
Eina N 85 Ea39
Einastrand N 85 Ea39
Einavoll N 85 Ea39
Einbeck D 126 Db38
Eindhoven NL 125 Bb39
Einhausen D 134 Cc45
Einola FIN 83 Lb28
Einsiedel D 127 Ec42
Einsiedeln CH 141 Cb54
Einville-au-Jaurd F 25 Jd37
Eisden B 125 Bb40
Eisenach D 126 Db41
Eisenbach D 141 Cb51
Eisenberg D 127 Ea41
Eisenberg D 133 Cb45
Eisenerz A 144 Fc53
Eisenheim D 134 Db45
Eisenhüttenstadt D 128 Fc37
Eisenkappel A 144 Fb56
Eisenstadt A 145 Gb52
Eisentratten A 143 Ed55
Eisfeld D 134 Dc43
Eisgarn A 136 Fd48
Eišiškės LT 114 La59
Eisķene LV 105 Jb50
Eisma EST 98 Kd41
Eitensheim D 135 Dd48
Eiterfeld D 126 Da42
Eitorf D 125 Ca41
Eitrheimsnes N 84 Cc40
Eitting D 143 Ea50
Eivere EST 98 Kd43
Eivindvik N 84 Ca37
Eivissa E 56 Gc69
Eixo P 44 Ac62
Ejby DK 108 Dc26
Ejby DK 109 Eb26
Ejea de los Caballeros E 47 Fa59
Ejheden S 87 Fd37
Ejsing DK 100 Da22
Ejsk RUS 205 Fb16
Ejstrupholm DK 108 Db24
Ejulve E 48 Fb63
Ek S 102 Fa46
Ekängen S 103 Fd46
Ekaterinovka RUS 203 Fa12
Ekaterinovka RUS 203 Fc12
Ekby S 102 Fa46
Eke S 104 Ha50
Ekeberga S 103 Fd52
Ekeby S 96 Gd41
Ekeby S 96 Gc44
Ekeby S 103 Fc47
Ekeby S 104 Ha49
Ekeby S 110 Ed55
Ekeby-Almby S 95 Fd44
Ekebyborna S 103 Fd46
Ekedalen S 102 Fa47
Ekenäs FIN 97 Jd40
Ekenässjön S 103 Fc50
Eker S 95 Fc44
Ekerö S 96 Gd44
Ekeskog S 103 Fb46
Eket S 110 Ed54
Eketånga S 102 Ed52
Ekfors S 73 Jb20
Ekimoviči RUS 202 Ec12
Ekinhisar TR 193 Gb86
Ekinli TR 186 Fb80
Ekinli TR 187 Gc79
Ekkerøy N 65 Kc06
Eknäs FIN 97 Jc40
Ekne N 78 Eb29
Ekola FIN 81 Jb30
Ekorrsele S 80 Ha26
Ekorrträsk S 80 Ha26
Ekså N 92 Cd45
Ekshärad S 94 Fa41
Ekşidere TR 191 Ed81
Eksı Gediz TR 192 Fd84
Ekşili TR 199 Gc90
Eksingedal N 84 Cb38
Eksjö S 103 Fc49
Ekskogen S 96 Gd42
Eksta S 104 Gd50
Ekträsk S 80 Hb26
Ekzarh Antimovo BG 181 Ec72
Ekzarh Josif BG 180 Ea69
Elabuga RUS 203 Ga08
Elafohóri GR 184 Da77
Elafohóri GR 185 Ea76
Elafónissos GR 195 Bd91
Elafótopos GR 182 Ad79
El Álamo E 46 Db65
El Álamo E 59 Bd73
El Álamo E 59 Cb73
El Algar E 55 Fa73
El Aljibe y las Brencas de Sicilia E 61 Ec73
El Alquián E 61 Eb76
Elämäjärvi FIN 82 Kb28
Elan' RUS 203 Fd12
El Ángel E 60 Cc77
Elan'-Kolenovskij RUS 203 Fc13
Elantxobe E 39 Eb55
El Arahal E 59 Cb74
El Arenal E 45 Cc65
Elassóna GR 183 Bc80
El Astillero E 38 Dc55
Eláta GR 191 Dd86
Eláti GR 183 Bc79
Elati GR 188 Bb81
Elátia GR 189 Bd84
Elat'ma RUS 203 Fb10
Elatohóri GR 182 Ba79
Elatohóri GR 183 Bd78
Élatos GR 182 Ba79
Elatoú GR 188 Bb84
El Azagador E 54 Fa67
El Ballestero E 53 Ea70
El Barco de Ávila E 45 Cb64
Elbasan AL 182 Ac75
Elbasan TR 186 Fb77
El Batán E 45 Bd65
El Baúl E 61 Dd74
El Bayo E 47 Fa59
Elbe D 126 Dc37
El Bercial E 52 Cc66
Elbeuf F 23 Ga35
Elbeyli TR 186 Ga79
Elbingerode D 126 Dc38
Elbląg PL 122 Hc30
El Bocal E 47 Ed59
El Bodón E 45 Bd64
El Bonillo E 53 Ea69
El Bosque E 59 Cb76
El'brus RUS 205 Ga17
Elbtal D 125 Cb42
El Bujeo E 59 Ca78
El Bullaque E 52 Da68
Elburg NL 117 Bc35
El Burgo E 60 Cc76
El Burgo de Ebro E 48 Fb61
El Burgo de Osma E 46 Dd60
El Burgo Ranero E 37 Cd57
El Buste E 47 Ed60
El Cabaco E 45 Ca63
El Cabo de Gata E 61 Eb76
El Calonge E 59 Cb73
El Campamento E 59 Cb78
el Campello E 55 Fb71
El Campillo E 53 Dd71
El Campillo E 53 Ea71
El Campillo de la Jara E 52 Cc67
El Campo de Peñaranda E 45 Cc62
El Cañavate E 53 Eb67
El Cardoso de la Sierra E 46 Dc62
El Carpio E 60 Cd72
El Carpio de Tajo E 52 Da66
El Casar de Escalona E 46 Da65
El Casar de Talamanca E 46 Dc63
El Castaño E 59 Ca77
El Castellar E 47 Fa65
El Castillo de las Guardas E 59 Bd73
El Centenillo E 52 Db71
El Cerro de Andévalo E 59 Bb72
El Chaparral E 60 Cd77
Elche E 55 Fb71
Elche de la Sierra E 53 Eb71
Elchesheim-Illingen D 133 Cb47
Elchingen D 134 Da49
Elciego E 39 Eb58
Elçili TR 185 Eb76
Elcóaz E 39 Fa57
El Cobo E 61 Ec72
el Cogul E 48 Ga61
El Collado E 54 Fa66
El Colmenar E 59 Cb76
El Colmenar E 59 Cb77
El Colorado E 59 Bd77
El Corchuelo E 59 Bc74
El Coronil E 59 Ca75
El Crucero E 37 Ca54
El Cuartón E 59 Ca78
El Cubillo de Uceda E 46 Dc63
El Cubo de Don Sancho E 45 Ca62
El Cubo de la Tierra del Vino E 45 Cb61
El Cuervo E 59 Bd75
Elda E 55 Fa71
Elda N 66 Ga12
Eldalen N 92 Cd46
Eldek TR 192 Fa85
Eldena D 119 Ea34
Eldforsen S 95 Fb40
Eldingen D 118 Dc35
Eldsberga S 110 Ed53
Eléa GR 195 Bd90
Elec RUS 203 Fa12
Eledio CY 206 Hd98
Elefsína GR 189 Cb86
Elefthério GR 189 Bd81
Eléfthero GR 182 Ad79
Eleftherohóri GR 183 Bb79
Eleftheroúpoli GR 184 Da77
Eleja LV 106 Kb52
El Ejido E 61 Dd76
Elek H 147 Jd56
Èlektostal' RUS 203 Fa10
Elektrėnai LT 114 Kd58
Elemir SRB 153 Jc59
Elemno RUS 99 Ma43
Elena BG 180 Ea71
Elenovo BG 180 Ea73
Eleófito GR 188 Ba83
Eleohóri GR 184 Cd77
Eleohóri GR 194 Bb89
Eleón GR 184 Cc76
Eleón GR 189 Bc84
Eleoússa GR 182 Ad80
El Escorial E 46 Db64
Elešnica BG 184 Cc74
El Espinar E 46 Da63
Elfershausen D 134 Db44
Elford GB 16 Ed24
El Frago E 39 Fa58
El Frasno E 47 Ed61
Elgå N 86 Ec34
Elganowo PL 121 Ha31
El Gargantón E 52 Da69
El Garrobo E 59 Bd73
El Gastor E 59 Cb76
Elgg CH 142 Cc52
Elgin GB 5 Eb07
Elgiszewo PL 121 Hb34
Elgoibar E 39 Eb55
Elgol GB 6 Db09
El Grado E 48 Fd59
El Granado E 58 Ba73
el Grau de Castelló E 54 Fc66
el Grau de Gandia E 54 Fc69
Elgsmyra N 86 Ec36
Elgsnes N 66 Ga12
El Guijar E 46 Db62
El Guijo E 52 Cd70
Elham GB 21 Gb29
El Haza del Riego E 61 Ea75
El Herrumblar E 54 Ed68
El Higuerón E 60 Cc72
El Hijate E 61 Ea74
Elhovka RUS 203 Ga09
Elhovo BG 180 Dd73
Elhovo BG 180 Eb73
El Hoyo E 52 Db71
El Hoyo de Pinares E 46 Da64
Eliá GR 194 Ba88
Elijärven kaivos FIN 74 Jc21
Elika GR 195 Bd91
Elikónas GR 189 Bd85
Elimäki FIN 90 Kd37
Elincourt-Sainte-Marguerite F 23 Ha34
Elinókastro GR 183 Bb80
Elin Pelin BG 179 Cd71
Elionka RUS 202 Ec13
Elisejna BG 179 Cc70
Èlista RUS 205 Ga15
Elizarovo RUS 107 Ld46
Elizavetino RUS 99 Mb40
Elizondo E 39 Ed56
El Jardín E 53 Eb70
El Jardón E 60 Cd73
Eljaröd S 111 Fb56
El Jautor E 59 Ca77
Ełk PL 123 Jd31
Elkeland N 92 Cc46
Elkenroth D 125 Cb41
Elkšņi LV 106 La52
Elkšņukrogs LV 106 La52
Elkstone GB 20 Ed27
Ellamaa EST 98 Ka43
El Lance de la Virgen E 61 Dd76
Ellastone GB 16 Ed23
Elleholm S 111 Fc54
Ellenberg D 134 Db48
Ellen's Green GB 20 Fc29
El Lentiscal E 59 Ca78
Ellerau D 118 Db32
Ellesmere GB 15 Eb23
Ellesmere Port GB 15 Eb22
Ellewoutsdijk NL 124 Ab38
Ellhofen D 134 Cd47
Elliant F 27 Dd39
Ellidshøj DK 100 Dc21
Elling DK 101 Dd19
Ellingen D 134 Dc47
Elliniká GR 189 Cb83
Ellinikó GR 189 Bc86
Ellinikó GR 194 Bb87
Ellinikó GR 194 Bc87
Ellinikó GR 195 Bd91
Ellinikó GR 195 Cb87
El Llano (San Tirso de Abres) E 37 Bd54
Ellmau A 143 Eb53
Ellon GB 5 Ed08
Ellös S 102 Eb47
Ellrich D 126 Dc39
Ellwangen D 142 Da51
Ellwangen/Jagst D 134 Db48
Elm CH 142 Cc54
Elmabağı TR 192 Fa86
Elmacık TR 185 Ed74
Elmacık TR 199 Gb89
El Maderal E 45 Cb61
El Madroño E 59 Bc73
Elmalı TR 185 Ec78
Elmalı TR 186 Fd77
Elmalı TR 187 Gb79
Elmalı TR 198 Ga91
El Manantial E 59 Bd76
Elmas I 169 Ca79
el Masnou E 49 Ha61
Elmdon GB 20 Fd26
Elmelunde DK 109 Ec28
Elmen A 142 Db53
Elmenhorst D 118 Dc32
Elmenhorst D 119 Eb31
Elmley Castle GB 20 Ed26
El Molar E 46 Dc63
el Molar E 48 Ga62
El Molar E 61 Dd72
El Molinillo E 52 Da67
El Moncayo E 55 Fb72
El Moral E 61 Eb72
Elmore GB 19 Ec27
el Morell E 48 Gb62
Elmshorn D 118 Db32
Elmstein D 133 Ca46
El Musel E 37 Cc54
Elne F 41 Hb57
Elnesvågen N 76 Cd31
El Niño E 55 Ed72
El'nja RUS 202 Ec11
Elopía GR 189 Ca85
Elorrio E 39 Eb56
Élos GR 200 Ca95
Előszállás H 146 Hc55
Eloúnta GR 201 Dc96
Eloyes F 31 Ka39
el Palmar E 54 Fc68
El Palmar E 55 Fa72
El Palmar de Troya E 59 Ca75
El Parador de las Hortichuelas E 61 Ea76
El Paraíso E 60 Cc77
El Pardo E 46 Dc64
el Pas de la Casa AND 40 Gc58
el Pas de la Casa AND 40 Gc58
El Pedernoso E 53 Ea67
El Pedregal E 47 Ed63
El Pedroso E 37 Cc54
El Pedroso E 59 Ca72
El Pedroso de la Armuña E 45 Cc62
El Peral E 53 Ec67
El Perdigón E 45 Cb61
el Perelló E 48 Ga63
el Perelló E 54 Fc68
Elphin GB 4 Dc06
Elphin IRL 8 Ca19
el Pla de Santa Maria E 48 Gb61
El Picazo E 53 Eb68
el Pi de Sant Just E 49 Gc59
El Pilar de la Horadada E 55 Fb73
el Pinell de Brai E 48 Ga63
El Piñero E 45 Cc61
El Pintado E 59 Ca72
el Poblenou del Delta E 48 Ga64
El Pobo E 47 Fa64
El Pobo de Dueñas E 47 Ed63
el Pont d'Armentera E 49 Gc61
el Pont de Suert E 40 Ga58
el Pont de Vilomara E 49 Gd60
El Portal E 59 Bd76
el Port de Borriana E 54 Fc66
el Port de la Selva E 41 Hc58
el Port de Sagunt E 54 Fc67
El Portil E 59 Bb74
El Pozo de los Frailes E 61 Eb76
El Priorato E 59 Cb73
El Provencio E 53 Ea68
El Puente del Arzobispo E 52 Cc66
El Puente del Rio E 61 Dd76
El Puente (Guriezo) E 38 Dd55
El Puerto E 37 Cb55
El Puerto E 51 Bc71
El Puerto de Santa María E 59 Bd76
El Pulpillo E 55 Ed70
El Puntal E 37 Cd54
El Real de la Jara E 59 Bd72
El Real de San Vicente E 46 Cd65
El Rincón E 61 Ec74
El Robledo E 52 Da68
El Rocío E 59 Bc74
el Rodriguillo E 55 Fa71
El Romeral E 52 Dc67
El Rompido E 59 Bb74
El Ronquillo E 59 Bd72
El Royo E 47 Ea60
El Rubio E 60 Cc74
El Sabinar E 47 Fa59
El Sabinar E 61 Eb72
el Sahuco E 61 Ea74
el Saler E 54 Fc68
El Salobral E 53 Ec69
El Saltador E 61 Ec74
El Santiscal E 59 Ca76
els Arcs E 48 Fd61
El Saucejo E 60 Cc75
Elsazı TR 199 Gd89
Elsdon GB 11 Ed15
Elsdorf D 118 Da33
Elsdorf D 125 Bc40
Elsdorf-Westermühlen D 118 Db30
Elsenborn B 125 Bb42
Elsenfeld D 134 Cd45
Elsenham GB 20 Fd27
el Serrat AND 40 Gc57
el Serrat AND 40 Gc57
Elsfjord N 71 Fb21
Elsfleth D 118 Cd33
els Hostalets d'en Bas E 49 Ha59
Elšica BG 179 Da72
Elsing D 127 Ec39
Elsing GB 17 Ga24
Elsinvaara FIN 83 Lc25
el Soleràs E 48 Ga61
Elspeet NL 116 Bb36
els Prats de Rei E 49 Gc60
Elsrickle GB 11 Eb14
Elst NL 125 Bb37
Elstad N 78 Ed26
Elstal D 127 Ed36
Elstead GB 20 Fb29
Elster D 127 Ec38
Elstertrebnitz D 127 Eb41
Elsterwerda D 128 Fa40
Elstow GB 20 Fc26
Elstra D 128 Fb41
Eltendorf A 145 Gb55
Elterlein D 135 Ec43
Eltham GB 20 Fd28
El Tiemblo E 46 Da64
El Toboso E 53 Dd67
Elton IRL 12 Bd24
Èl'ton RUS 203 Ga13
El Torno E 59 Bd76
El Toro E 54 Fa66
El Toro E 54 Fb66
El Tricheto E 52 Da68
El Trobal E 59 Ca75
El Tumbalejo E 59 Bc73
Eltvik N 76 Ca33
Eltville D 133 Cb44
Elva EST 106 La46
Elva I 148 Bb62
El Vacar E 60 Cc72
Elvanfoot GB 10 Ea15
Elvas P 51 Bb68
Elvåsen N 78 Ec25
Elvdal N 86 Ec36
Elve N 92 Cb46
Elvebakken N 62 Gd08
Elvebakken N 63 Hd08
Elveden GB 21 Ga25
Elvedjupkroken N 64 Ka06
Elvegården N 67 Gb14
El Vellón E 46 Dc63
Elvemund N 64 Jc09
Elven F 27 Eb40
el Vendrell E 49 Gc62
Elvenes N 65 Kd07
Elvenes N 66 Fc12
Elvenheim N 65 La07
El Ventorillo E 38 Db56
Elverum N 67 Gc11
Elverum N 86 Eb38
Elvestad N 93 Ea42
Elvevollen N 62 Ha10
El Villar de Arnedo E 39 Ec58
el Vilosell E 48 Gb61
Elviria E 60 Cc77
El Viso E 52 Cc70
El Viso del Alcor E 59 Ca74
Elvkroken N 66 Fd16
Elvran N 78 Eb30
Elwick GB 11 Fa17
Elworthy GB 19 Ea29
Elx E 55 Fb71
Elxleben D 127 Dd41
Ely GB 20 Fd25
Elz D 133 Cb43
Elzach D 141 Ca50
Elze D 126 Db37
Elztal D 134 Cd46
Emagny F 31 Jc41
Emanville F 23 Ga36
Embid E 47 Ec63
Embid de Ariza E 47 Ec61
Émbonas GR 197 Ed93
Embório GR 183 Bb78
Embório GR 196 Db92
Emborió GR 197 Eb90
Emborió GR 197 Ec92
Emboriós GR 197 Ed92
Embrach CH 141 Cb52
Embrun F 35 Kb50
Embsen D 118 Dc34
Embún E 39 Fb57
Emburga LV 106 Kb52
Embūte LV 105 Jc52
Emden D 117 Ca33
Emecik TR 197 Ed91
Emerando E 38 Ea55
Emersleben D 127 Dd38

Emet – Fåker

Emet TR 192 Fd83
Emincik TR 187 Hb80
Emiralem TR 191 Ec85
Emirdağ TR 193 Ha84
Emirhisa TR 192 Ga86
Emirhisar TR 193 Gb86
Emirköy TR 192 Fd82
Emirler TR 192 Fb83
Emirler TR 198 Ga91
Emiryakup TR 185 Ec77
Emkendorf D 118 Db30
Emlichheim D 117 Bd35
Emly IRL 12 Bd24
Emmaboda S 111 Fd53
Emmaljunga S 110 Fa53
Emmaste EST 97 Jc45
Emmeloord NL 117 Bc34
Emmelsbüll-Horsbüll D 108 Cd28
Emmelshausen D 133 Ca43
Emmen NL 117 Ca34
Emmendingen D 141 Ca50
Emmer-Compascuum NL 117 Ca34
Emmerich D 125 Bc37
Emmerik = Emmerich D 125 Bc37
Emmerthal D 126 Da37
Emmerting D 143 Ec51
Emmingen-Liptingen D 142 Cc51
Emmoo IRL 8 Ca20
Emo IRL 13 Cb22
Emőd H 146 Jc51
Emoniemi FIN 82 Kb28
Empa CY 206 Hd98
Empessós GR 188 Ba82
Empfingen D 134 Cc49
Empo FIN 97 Jb39
Empoli I 155 Db65
Empuriabrava E 41 Hc58
Emre TR 186 Fb80
Emre TR 192 Fb85
Emremsultan TR 193 Ha81
Emsbüren D 117 Ca36
Emsdetten D 125 Cb37
Emsfors S 103 Gb51
Emskirchen D 134 Dc46
Emstek D 117 Cc35
Emtinghausen D 118 Cd34
Emyvale IRL 9 Cc18
Ena E 39 Fb58
Enafors S 78 Ed30
Enäjärvi FIN 90 La37
Enåker S 95 Gb41
Enånger S 87 Gb36
Enarsvedjan S 79 Fb29
Enåsa S 95 Fb45
Encekler TR 192 Fb85
Encima-Angulo E 38 Dd56
Encinas E 46 Dc61
Encinas de Abajo E 45 Cc62
Encinas de Esgueva E 46 Db60
Encinasola E 51 Bc71
Encinasola de los Comendadores E 45 Bd62
Encinas Reales E 60 Cd74
Encío E 38 Dd57
Enciso E 47 Eb59
Encs H 147 Jd50
Endach A 143 Eb53
Endingen CH 141 Cb52
Endingen D 141 Ca50
Endla EST 98 La44
Endon GB 16 Ed23
Endre S 104 Ha49
Endriejavas LT 113 Jc55
Endrinal E 45 Cb63
Endrup DK 108 Da26
Enebakk N 93 Ea42
Enego I 150 Dd58
Enerhodar UA 205 Fa16
Eneryda S 103 Fb52
Enez TR 185 Ea78
Enfesta E 36 Ad56
Engan N 70 Ed21
Engarés GR 196 Db90
Engdal N 77 Dc30
Enge N 77 Dc30
Engelberg CH 141 Cb55
Engelhartszell A 144 Fa50
Engeln D 118 Cd35
Engels RUS 203 Fd12
Engelsberg D 143 Eb51
Engelsbrand D 134 Cc48
Engelskirchen D 125 Ca41
Engelst DK 100 Db21
Engelsviken N 93 Ea43
Engelthal D 135 Dd46
Engen D 142 Cc51
Engene N 93 Da46
Engenes N 67 Gb12
Enger D 126 Cc37
Enger N 85 Dd39
Engerdal N 86 Ec35
Engerneset N 86 Ec36
Engesland N 93 Da46
Engesvang DK 108 Db24
Enghien B 124 Ab41
Engi CH 142 Cc54
Engilli TR 193 Ha86
Engis B 124 Ba41
Englancourt F 24 Hc33
Englefontaine F 24 Hc32
Engstingen D 134 Cd49
Engstlenalp CH 141 Cb55
Enguera E 54 Fb69
Enguídanos E 54 Ed67
Engure LV 106 Ka50
Engürücük TR 186 Fd80
Engvik N 62 Gc08
Engvoll N 85 Ea34
Enica BG 179 Da69
Enichioi MD 177 Fc60
Enina BG 180 Dd72
Eningen D 134 Cd49
Enisala RO 177 Fc65
Enix E 61 Ea76
Enkenbach-Alsenborn D 133 Ca46
Enkhausen D 126 Cc40
Enkhuizen NL 116 Bb34
Enklinge FIN 97 Hd40
Enköping S 95 Gb42
Enköpings-Näs S 95 Gb43
Enmo N 86 Ea32
Enna I 167 Fa86
Enneberg I 143 Ea56
Ennepetal D 125 Ca39
Enney CH 141 Bc55
Ennezat F 34 Hb46
Ennigerloh D 125 Cb38
Enningdal N 94 Eb44
Ennis IRL 12 Bc22
Enniscorthy IRL 13 Cc24
Enniskean IRL 12 Bc26
Enniskerry IRL 13 Cd22
Enniskillen GB 9 Cb18
Ennistimon IRL 12 Bc22
Enns A 144 Fb51
Ennyinen FIN 97 Ja39
Eno FIN 83 Ld30
Enodden N 78 Ea31
Enokunta FIN 89 Jd35
Enonkoski FIN 91 Lc32
Enonkylä FIN 82 Kc25
Enonlahti FIN 82 La30
Enontekiö FIN 68 Ja13
Ens NL 117 Bc35
Enschede NL 117 Bd36
Ensdorf D 135 Ea47
Ense D 125 Cb39
Ensen S 87 Fd38
Ensisheim F 31 Kb39
Enskogen S 87 Fd35
Enstone GB 20 Fa26
Enter NL 117 Bd36
Entlebuch CH 141 Ca54
Entracque I 148 Bc63
Entradas P 58 Ad72
Entrages F 42 Ka52
Entraigues F 29 Gc43
Entraigues F 35 Jd49
Entrains-sur-Nohain F 30 Hb41
Entrambasmestas E 38 Dc55
Entrammes F 28 Fb40
Entraunes F 43 Kb51
Entraygues-sur-Truyère F 33 Ha51
Entrecasteaux F 42 Ka54
Entrechaux F 42 Jc52
Entrena E 39 Eb58
Entre-os-Rios P 44 Ad61
Entrevaux F 43 Kb52
Entrín Bajo E 51 Bc69
Entroncamento P 50 Ac66
Entuğrulköy TR 193 Hb83
Entzheim F 25 Kc37
Envendos P 50 Ba66
Envermeu F 23 Gb33
Envernallas E 37 Bd55
Enviken S 95 Fd39
Enville GB 15 Ec25
Enying H 145 Hb55
Enzenkirchen A 144 Fa50
Enzersdorf im Thale A 137 Gb49
Enzesfeld A 145 Gb52
Enzinger Boden A 143 Eb54
Enzklösterle D 133 Cb48
Eochaill IRL 13 Ca26
Čohkkiras S 67 Hb15
Epagny F 24 Hb35
Epagny F 30 Jb41
Epaignes F 22 Fd35
Epáno Fellós GR 190 Da87
Epanomí GR 183 Ca78
Epaux-Bézu F 24 Hb36
Epe NL 117 Bc36
Épehy F 24 Hb33
Épernay F 24 Hc36
Epernon F 29 Gc38
Epfig F 31 Kb38
Epieds F 24 Hb36
Epierre F 35 Ka47
Epikopí GR 195 Ca89
Épila E 47 Fa61
Épinal F 31 Jd38
Epineuil-le-Fleuriel F 29 Ha44
Epiry F 30 Hc42
Episcopia I 162 Gb77
Episkopí CY 206 Ja98
Episkopí GR 188 Bb83
Episkopí GR 200 Cc95
Episkopí GR 200 Da96
Epitálio GR 194 Ba87
Epizon F 30 Jb38
Époisses F 30 Hd41
Epoo FIN 98 Kc39
Epoye F 24 Hd35
Eppan I 142 Dc56
Eppelborn D 133 Bd46
Eppenbrunn D 133 Ca47
Eppendorf D 127 Ed42
Eppe-Sauvage F 24 Hd32
Epping GB 20 Fd27
Eppingen D 134 Cc47
Eppstein D 134 Cc44
Epsom GB 20 Fc28
Eptagoneia CY 206 Jb97
Eptahóri GR 182 Ba78
Eptakomi CY 206 Jd95
Eptálofos GR 183 Cb76
Eptálofos GR 189 Bd84
Epuisay F 29 Ga40
Epureni RO 177 Fb60
Epworth GB 16 Fb21
Équeurdreville-Hainneville F 22 Ed34
Equihen-Plage F 23 Gb31
Equi Terme I 155 Da64
Eraclea I 150 Eb59
Eraclea Mare I 150 Ec59
Erahtur RUS 203 Fb10
Eräjärvi FIN 90 Ka35
Eräjärvi FIN 91 Lc34
Eranova I 164 Gb83
Eräslahti FIN 90 Ka34
Erastvere EST 107 Lb46
Eratiní GR 189 Bc85
Erátira GR 183 Bb78
Erba I 149 Cc58
Erbaa TR 205 Fc20
Erbach D 134 Cd45
Erbach D 142 Da50
Erbajolo F 154 Cb70
Erbalunga F 154 Cc68
Erbedeiro E 36 Bb57
Erbendorf D 135 Eb45
Ērberge LV 106 Kd52
Erbes-Büdesheim D 133 Cb45
Erbiceni RO 173 Fa57
Ercheu F 23 Ha34
Erchie I 162 Hb76
Erco E 39 Ed56
Ercolano I 161 Fb75
Ercsi H 146 Hc54
Erd H 146 Hc53
Erdal N 63 Ja06
Erdal N 84 Cd34
Erdal N 84 Cb35
Erdeborn D 127 Ea40
Erdek TR 186 Fa79
Erdelek TR 198 Ga91
Erdemli TR 187 Gb79
Erden BG 179 Cc69
Erdeven F 27 Ea41
Erdevik SRB 153 Ja61
Erding D 143 Ea50
Erdington GB 16 Ed24
Erdőbénye H 147 Jd50
Erdoğlu TR 187 Gc79
Erdut HR 153 Hd59
Erdweg D 143 Dd50
Éréac F 27 Ec39
Erecek TR 191 Ea82
Ereğli TR 187 Ha77
Erehnovo RUS 107 Ld46
Ereira P 50 Ab67
Eremitu RO 172 Dd58
Erenköy TR 193 Gb82
Erenler TR 186 Ga77
Eresfjord N 77 Db32
Eressós GR 191 Dd83
Erétria GR 189 Bd82
Erétria GR 189 Cc85
Erezée B 124 Ba42
Erfde D 118 Da30
Erfjord N 92 Cb42
Erftstadt D 125 Bd41
Erfurt D 127 Dd41
Ērgeme LV 106 La47
Ergersheim D 134 Db46
Ergili TR 186 Fa80
Ērgli LV 106 La50
Ergolding D 135 Eb49
Ergoldsbach D 135 Eb49
Ergué-Gabéric F 27 Dc39
Eriboll GB 4 Dd04
Erice I 166 Ea84
Erice TR 192 Ga86
Ericeira P 50 Aa68
Ericek TR 186 Fd80
Ericek TR 187 Gd80
Erikler TR 185 Ec75
Erikli TR 185 Eb78
Erikli TR 186 Fa80
Erikli TR 193 Gb81
Erikoussa GR 182 Aa79
Eriksberg S 71 Fd24
Eriksberg S 102 Eb47
Erikslund S 87 Ga33
Eriksmåla S 103 Fd52
Eriksrud N 85 Ea39
Erikstad N 66 Fd13
Erikstad S 102 Ec46
Ering D 143 Ed50
Eringsboda S 111 Fd53
Ériškiai LT 114 Kc55
Eriskirch D 142 Cd52
Eriswell GB 20 Fd25
Eriswil CH 141 Ca54
Erithrés GR 189 Ca86
Erka N 85 Db34
Erkelenz D 125 Bc40
Erkheikki S 68 Ja17
Erkheim D 142 Db51
Erkner D 128 Fa36
Erla E 47 Fa59
Erlabrunn D 134 Da45
Erlach A 145 Gb52
Erlangen D 135 Dd46
Erlau D 127 Ec41
Erlbach D 143 Ec50
Erle D 125 Bd38
Erlėnai LT 113 Jb54
Erlenbach D 134 Cd45
Erlenbach D 134 Cd47
Erlensee D 134 Cd44
Erligheim D 134 Cd47
Erlinsbach CH 141 Ca53
Erlsbach A 143 Eb55
Erm NL 117 Bd35
Ermakiá GR 183 Bc78
Ermakovo RUS 122 Jb30
Ermakovo RUS 203 Ga09
Erma reka BG 184 Db76
Ermatingen CH 142 Cc52
Ermelo NL 116 Bb36
Ermelo P 44 Ba60
Ermenonville F 23 Ha36
Ermesinde P 44 Ad61
Ermida P 44 Ac63
Ermidas-Aldeia P 50 Ac71
Ermióni GR 195 Ca88
Ermiš RUS 203 Fb10
Ermita de Carrión E 51 Bb68
Ermita del Ramonete E 55 Ed74
Ermoclia MD 173 Ga59
Ermoúpoli GR 196 Da89
Ermsleben D 127 Dd39
Ermua E 39 Eb55
Erndtebrück D 126 Cc41
Ernée F 28 Fb39
Ernei RO 171 Dc59
Ernestinovo HR 153 Hc60
Ernsgaden D 135 Ea49
Ernstbrunn A 137 Gb49
Erolzheim D 142 Da51
Erôme F 34 Jb49
Erp NL 125 Bb38
Erpingham GB 17 Gb23
Erquy F 26 Eb37
Erriff Bridge IRL 8 Bb19
Erril IRL 13 Cb23
Errindlev DK 109 Ea29
Erritsø DK 108 Db26
Erro E 39 Ed56
Errol GB 7 Eb11
Erschwil CH 141 Bd53
Érsekcsanád H 153 Hd57
Ersekë AL 182 Ad78
Érsekvadkert H 146 Hd51
Ersfjordbotn N 62 Gc09
Erši RUS 202 Ed11
Erska S 102 Ec47
Erslev DK 100 Da21
Ersmark S 72 Gb24
Ersmark S 80 Hc25
Ersmark S 80 Hb28
Ersnäs S 73 Hd22
Eršovo RUS 107 Ld46
Erstein F 25 Kc37
Erstfeld CH 141 Cb55
Ersvika N 66 Fc17
Ertingen D 142 Cd50
Erto I 150 Eb57
Ertsjärv S 73 Hd19
Ertuğrul TR 185 Ed76
Ertuğrul TR 186 Fc80
Ertuğrul TR 191 Ed82
Ertuğrul TR 192 Fc87
Ervalla S 95 Fd43
Ervasti FIN 75 Kc22
Ervauville F 29 Ha39
Ervedal P 50 Ba68
Ervedosa do Douro P 44 Bb61
Ervelä FIN 97 Jd40
Ervenik HR 157 Ga64
Ervidel P 50 Ad71
Ervik N 76 Ca33
Ervita EST 98 Kd43
Ervy-le-Châtel F 30 Hc39
Erwitte D 126 Cc39
Erwood GB 15 Ea26
Erxleben D 127 Dd37
Erzgrube D 133 Cb49
Erzincan TR 205 Fd20
Erzurum TR 205 Ga19
Eržvilkas LT 114 Ka56
Esadiye TR 186 Fd79
Esanos E 38 Da55
Esatlar TR 192 Ga83
Esbjerg DK 108 Cd26
Esbo FIN 98 Kb39
Esbønderup DK 109 Ec24
Escairón (Saviñao) E 36 Bb56
Escalada E 38 Dc56
Escalaplano I 169 Cb78
Escalhão P 45 Bc62
Escalles F 21 Gc30
Escalona E 40 Fd58
Escalona E 46 Dd65
Escalona del Prado E 46 Db62
Escalonilla E 52 Da66
Escalos de Baixo P 44 Bb65
Escalos de Cima P 44 Bb65
Escamplero E 37 Cb54
Escañuela E 52 Da72
es Capdella E 56 Ha67
Escarabote E 36 Ac56
Escariche E 46 Dd64
Escároz E 39 Fa56
Escarrilla E 40 Fc57
es Castell E 57 Jb66
Escatalens F 40 Gb53
Escatrón E 48 Fc62
Eschach D 134 Da48
Eschau D 134 Cd45
Eschborn D 134 Cc44
Escheburg D 118 Dc33
Eschede D 118 Dc35
Eschenau A 144 Fd51
Eschenbach D 135 Ea45
Eschenburg D 126 Cc41
Eschenfelden D 135 Ea46
Eschenlohe D 143 Dd52
Eschershausen D 126 Da38
Eschlkam D 135 Ec47
Esch-s.-Alz. L 133 Bb45
Esch-sur-Sûre L 133 Bb44
Eschwege D 126 Db40
Eschweiler D 125 Bc41
Escombreras E 55 Fa74
Escorihuela E 47 Fa64
Escos F 39 Fa55
Escot F 39 Fb56
Escouloubre F 41 Gd57
Escource F 39 Fa52
Escrennes F 29 Gd39
es Cubells E 56 Gb69
Escucha E 48 Fb63
Escudeiros P 44 Ad60
Escuderos E 46 Db59
Escurial E 51 Ca68
Escusa P 50 Ad67
Esechioi RO 181 Ed68
Eşelek TR 185 Ec80
Eşelniţa RO 174 Ca64
Esen BG 181 Ec71
Eşen TR 192 Fd82
Eşen TR 198 Fd92
Esenbağ TR 192 Fc83
Esence TR 186 Fc80
Esence TR 193 Gd82
Esendere TR 193 Gc87
Esenkaya TR 198 Fb89
Esenköy TR 187 Gc80
Esenköy TR 198 Fb88
Esenköy TR 198 Fd92
Esenler TR 185 Ed77
Esenli TR 192 Fa82
Esens D 117 Cb32
Esenyazı TR 192 Fb86
Esenyurt TR 186 Fc77
Esgos E 36 Bb57
es Grau E 57 Jb66
Esguevillas de Esgueva E 46 Da60
Esher GB 20 Fc28
Esh Winning GB 11 Fa17
Eskdale Green GB 11 Eb18
Eskdalemuir GB 11 Eb15
Eskebjerg DK 109 Ea25
Eskelhem S 104 Gd49
Eskiakören TR 193 Ha84
Eskiçine TR 197 Fa89
Eskidanişment TR 192 Fd81
Eskifjörður IS 3 Bc05
Eskihisar TR 197 Fa89
Eskikaraağaç TR 186 Fc80
Eskiler TR 193 Ha87
Eskilsäter S 94 Ed45
Eskilstrup DK 109 Eb28
Eskilstuna S 95 Gb43
Eskin TR 192 Fc85
Eskipazar TR 205 Fa20
Eskişehir TR 193 Gc82
Eskisığırcı TR 186 Fa80
Eskiyayla TR 187 Gb79
Eskola FIN 81 Jd27
Eskragh GB 9 Cc17
Esku EST 98 Kd44
Eslared S 102 Fa52
Eslarn D 135 Eb46
Eslida E 54 Fc66
es Llombards E 57 Hc68
Eslohe D 125 Cb40
Eslöv S 110 Ed55
Esmared S 102 Ed52
Esme TR 192 Fc86
es Mercadal E 57 Ja65
es Migjorn Gran E 57 Ja66
es Molinar E 57 Hb67
Esmoriz P 44 Ac61
Esna EST 98 Kd43
Esnandes F 32 Fa45
Esneux B 124 Ba42
Esnouveaux F 30 Jb39
Espadañedo E 37 Ca58
Espalion F 33 Ha51
Esparragal E 61 Ec74
Esparragalejo E 51 Bd68
Esparragosa de la Serena E 51 Cb70
Esparreguera E 49 Gd61
Esparron F 42 Jd54
Esparron-de-Verdon F 42 Ka53
Espås N 77 Ea30
Espe DK 108 Dc27
Espe N 84 Cc40
Espejo E 38 Ea56
Espejo E 60 Cd73
Espel NL 116 Bb34
Espeland N 84 Ca39
Espeland N 92 Cb45
Espeli N 92 Cd45
Espelkamp D 126 Cd36
Espeluche F 42 Jb51
Espenau D 126 Da40
Espera E 59 Ca75
Esperança P 51 Bb68
Espéraza F 41 Gd56
Esperia I 160 Ed73
Esperstedt D 127 Dd40
Espetøl N 93 Da44
Espevær N 92 Bd41
Espezel F 41 Gd57
Espiel E 52 Cc71
Espinama E 38 Da55
Espiñaredo E 36 Bb53
Espinasses F 42 Ka51
Espinhal P 44 Ad65
Espinho P 44 Ac61
Espinilla E 38 Db56
Espinosa de Cerrato E 46 Db59
Espinosa de Cervera E 46 Dc59
Espinosa de Henares E 46 Dd63
Espinosa de los Monteros E 38 Dc56
Espinoso del Rey E 52 Cd67
Espírito Santo P 58 Ba73
Esplantas F 34 Hc50
Esplús E 48 Fd60
Espoey F 40 Fc55
Espolla E 41 Hb58
Espoo FIN 98 Kb39
Esporles E 57 Hb67
es Port E 57 Hb68
Esposende P 44 Ac59
Esprels F 31 Jd40
es Pujols E 56 Gc70
Esquedas E 48 Fb59
Esquivias E 46 Db65
Esrange S 67 Hb15
Esrum DK 109 Ec24
Essay F 28 Fd38
Esse FIN 81 Jb29
Esselbach D 134 Da45
Essen B 124 Ad38
Essen D 117 Cb35
Essen D 125 Bd39
Essenbach D 135 Eb49
Essenniki RUS 107 Mb50
Essentuki RUS 205 Ga17
Essertaux F 23 Gd34
Essertenne F 31 Jc41
Essími GR 185 Dd77
Essing D 135 Ea48
Essingen D 134 Da48
Esslingen D 134 Cd48
Essômes-sur-Marne F 24 Hb36
Essoyes F 30 Ja39
Essunga S 102 Ed47
Essvik S 88 Gc33
Establet F 42 Jc51
Estação de Ourique P 58 Ac72
Estacas E 36 Ad57
Estación de Cártama E 60 Cd76
Estación de Páramo E 37 Ca56
Estación de Salinas E 60 Da75
Estadilla E 48 Fd59
Estagel F 41 Ha57
Estaing F 33 Ha51
Estaires F 23 Ha31
Estang F 40 Fc53
Estarreja P 44 Ac62
Estavayer-le-Lac CH 141 Bb54
Este I 150 Dd60
Estedt D 127 Ea36
Estela P 44 Ac60
Estella E 39 Ec57
Estellencs E 56 Ha67
Estenfeld D 134 Db45
Esteng F 43 Kb51
Estepa E 60 Cc74
Estépar E 38 Dc58
Estepona E 59 Cb77
Estercuel E 48 Fb63
Esternay F 24 Hc37
Esternberg A 135 Ed49
Esterri d'Àneu E 40 Gb57
Estersmark S 80 Hc26
Esterwegen D 117 Cb34
Esterzili I 169 Cb78
Estiche de Cinca E 48 Fd60
Estissac F 30 Hc38
Estivella E 54 Fc67
Estorf D 118 Da32
Estorf D 126 Da36
Estoril P 50 Aa68
Estorninhos P 58 Ad74
Estrées-Saint-Denis F 23 Ha35
Estrée-Wamin F 23 Gd32
Estreito P 44 Ba65
Estremera E 46 Dd65
Estremoz P 50 Ba69
Estrup DK 109 Eb26
Estry F 22 Fb37
Estuna S 96 Ha42
Estvad DK 100 Da22
Esztergom H 146 Hc52
Étain F 25 Jc35
Etais F 30 Ja40
Étalans F 31 Jd42
Étalle B 132 Ba44
Étampes F 29 Gd38
Étang-sur-Arroux F 30 Hd43
Étaples F 23 Gc31
Etauliers F 32 Fb49
Etel F 27 Ea41
Eteläinen FIN 90 Ka37
Eteläkylä FIN 90 Kd34
Etelälahti FIN 82 Ka27
Etelä-Niskamäki FIN 90 Kd32
Eteläpää FIN 89 Hd33
Etelä Varisala FIN 97 Ja39
Etelhem S 104 Ha50
Eterna E 38 Dd58
Etevaux F 30 Jb41
Etili TR 191 Ec81
Etival F 31 Jd44
Etival-Clairefontaine F 31 Ka38
Etne N 92 Cb41
Étoges F 24 Hc36
Etoile-Rhône F 34 Jb50
Etola FIN 90 Kb37
Etolikó GR 188 Ba84
Etouy F 23 Gd35
Étréaupont F 24 Hc33
Étréchy F 29 Gd38
Etrembières F 35 Jd45
Etrépagny F 23 Gc35
Étretat F 22 Fd34
Étreux F 24 Hc33
Etrœungt F 24 Hc33
Etropole BG 179 Cd71
Etroubles I 148 Bc58
Etsaut F 39 Fb56
Ettelbruck L 133 Bb44
Ettenheim D 141 Ca50
Etten-Leur NL 124 Ad38
Ettiswil CH 141 Ca53
Ettlingen D 133 Cb48
Ettrickbridge GB 11 Eb14
Ettringen D 142 Dc51
Etu-Ikola FIN 90 Kc33
Etulia MD 177 Fc63
Etusson F 28 Fb43
Etuz F 31 Jd41
Etxano E 38 Ea55
Etzen A 136 Fc49
Etzenricht D 135 Eb46
Eu F 23 Gb33
Euerbach D 134 Db44
Euerdorf D 134 Db44
Eugénie-les-Bains F 40 Fc54
Eulatal D 127 Ec41
Eupen B 125 Bb41
Eura FIN 89 Jb37
Eurajoki FIN 89 Ja37
Euratsfeld A 144 Fc51
Eursinge NL 117 Bd34
Euskirchen D 125 Bd42
Eußenheim D 134 Da44
Euston GB 21 Ga25
Euthal CH 142 Cc54
Eutin D 119 Dd31
Euzet F 42 Ja52
Evaillé F 29 Ga40
Eväjärvi FIN 90 Ka34
Evangelismós GR 183 Bd80
Evangelismós GR 194 Ba89
Evangelistria GR 189 Ca85
Evanger N 84 Cb38
Evanton GB 5 Ea07
Evaux-les-Bains F 33 Ha45
Evciler TR 185 Ed75
Evciler TR 191 Eb81
Evciler TR 191 Ed82
Evciler TR 191 Ed83
Evciler TR 192 Ga87
Évdilos GR 196 Dd88
Évele LV 106 Kd48
Evelix GB 5 Ea06
Evenhus N 78 Ea29
Evenskjer N 66 Ga13
Evenstad N 86 Eb36
Evercreech GB 19 Ec29
Everleigh GB 20 Ed29
Everöd S 111 Fb55
Eversley GB 20 Fb28
Everswinkel D 125 Cb38
Evertsberg S 87 Fb37
Evesham GB 20 Ed26
Évian-les-Bains F 31 Ka44
Evijärvi FIN 81 Jc29
Evillers F 31 Jd42
Evinohóri GR 188 Ba85
Evisa F 154 Ca70
Evitskog FIN 98 Ka40
Evja N 66 Fc17
Evje N 92 Cd45
Evkafteke TR 191 Ed84
Évlalo GR 184 Db77
Evlanovo RUS 203 Fa12
Évora P 50 Ad69
Évora Monte P 50 Ba69
Evran F 26 Ec38
Evrecy F 22 Fb36
Evrencik TR 186 Fa75
Evrensekiz TR 185 Ed76
Evreşe TR 185 Ec78
Évreux F 23 Gb36
Evrieu F 35 Jc47
Evriguet F 27 Ec39
Évron F 28 Fc39
Évry F 23 Gd37
Evrychou CY 206 Ja97
Ewell GB 20 Fc28
Examilia GR 195 Bd87
Exaplátanos GR 183 Bd76
Exarhos GR 189 Ca84
Exbourne GB 19 Dd30
Excideuil F 33 Gb48
Exeter GB 19 Ea30
Exford GB 19 Ea29
Exilles I 148 Bb60
Exloo NL 117 Ca34
Exmes F 22 Fd37
Exmouth GB 19 Ea31
Exogí GR 188 Ac84
Exohí GR 182 Ad79
Exohí GR 184 Cd75
Exohí GR 184 Db77
Éxo Moulianá GR 201 Dc96
Éxo Nímfio GR 194 Bc91
Extertal D 126 Cd37
Extremo P 36 Ad58
Eyam GB 16 Ed22
Eydehavn N 93 Db46
Eydelstedt D 118 Cd35
Eydemir TR 193 Gb84
Eye GB 17 Fc24
Eye GB 21 Gb25
Eyerci TR 186 Fc80
Eyeries IRL 12 Ba26
Eygalières F 42 Jb53
Eygluy-Escoulin F 35 Jc50
Eyguians F 42 Jd51
Eyguières F 42 Jb53
Eygurande F 33 Ha47
Eygurande-et-Gardedeuil F 32 Fd49
Eymet F 32 Fd51
Eymir TR 187 Ha80
Eymoutiers F 33 Gc47
Eynez TR 191 Ed84
Eyrarbakki IS 2 Ac05
Eyrecourt IRL 13 Ca21
Eyrein F 33 Gd48
Eystrup D 118 Da35
Eyübler TR 193 Gd87
Ezaro E 36 Ac55
Ezcaray E 38 Ea58
Ezcurra E 39 Ec56
Eze F 43 Kd53
Ezerče BG 180 Eb69
Ezere LV 113 Jd53
Ezerec BG 181 Fc69
Ežerėlis LV 114 Kb57
Ezeriş RO 174 Ca62
Ezermala LV 107 Ld51
Ezernieki LV 107 Ld52
Ezerovo BG 181 Fa70
Eziler TR 192 Fc87
Ezine TR 191 Eb81
Ezy-sur-Eure F 23 Gb37

F

Faaborg DK 108 Dc27
Faak am See A 144 Fa56
Fabara E 48 Fd62
Fabas F 40 Ga55
Fabas F 40 Gb56
Fabbrica Curone I 149 Cc61
Fåberg N 84 Cd35
Fåberg N 85 Ea37
Fabero E 37 Bd56
Fábiánsebestyén H 146 Jc55
Fäboda FIN 81 Jb28
Fäbodliden S 80 Gc26
Fåborg DK 108 Da26
Fabrègues F 41 Hd54
Fabrezan F 41 Ha56
Fabriano I 156 Ec67
Fabrica di Roma I 156 Ea70
Fabro Scalo I 156 Ea68
Făcăeni RO 177 Fa66
Facho P 50 Ab66
Facinas E 59 Ca78
Fadd H 146 Hc56
Fadón E 45 Cb61
Faedis I 150 Ed57
Faenza I 150 Dd63
Færvik N 93 Db46
Faeto I 161 Fd73
Fafe P 44 Ba60
Fafleralp CH 141 Bd56
Fagagna I 150 Ec57
Făgăraş RO 175 Dc61
Fågelberget S 79 Fc27
Fågelfors S 103 Ga51
Fågelmara S 111 Ga54
Fågelsjö S 87 Fc35
Fågelsta S 79 Ga27
Fågelsta S 103 Fc46
Fågelsundet S 96 Gd39
Fågeltofta S 111 Fb56
Fagerås S 94 Fa43
Fagerdal S 79 Fd29
Fagerhaug N 64 Jb04
Fagerhaug N 77 Dd32
Fagerhult S 94 Eb45
Fagerhult S 102 Ec46
Fagerhult S 103 Fb48
Fagerhult S 103 Fd51
Fagermoen N 71 Fb21
Fagernes N 62 Gd10
Fagernes N 67 Gb13
Fagernes N 85 Dc38
Fagersanna S 103 Fb46
Fagersta S 95 Fd41
Fagerstrand N 93 Ea42
Fagertun N 67 Gc12
Fagervik FIN 98 Ka40
Fagervik N 78 Eb28
Fagervika N 70 Fa21
Fagerviken S 96 Gc39
Făget RO 174 Cb60
Făgeţelu RO 175 Db65
Fåggeby S 95 Ga40
Faggen A 142 Db54
Fåglavik S 102 Ed47
Fåglum S 102 Ed47
Fagnano Castello I 164 Gb79
Fägre S 103 Fb46
Fagurhólsmýri IS 2 Ba06
Fahan IRL 9 Cc15
Fahrenbach D 134 Cd46
Fahrenkrug D 118 Dc31
Fahrenwalde D 120 Fb33
Fahrenzhausen D 143 Dd50
Fährhafen Sassnitz D 120 Fa30
Fahrland D 127 Ed36
Fahrwangen CH 141 Ca53
Fai della Paganella I 149 Dc57
Faido CH 141 Cb56
Fain-lès-Montbard F 30 Hd41
Fairbourne GB 15 Dd24
Fairford GB 20 Ed27
Fairlight GB 21 Ga30
Fairy Cross GB 18 Dc29
Fajsławice PL 131 Kb40
Fajsz H 146 Hd56
Fakenham GB 17 Ga23
Fåker S 79 Fc31

Fakija – Fobello

Fakija BG 181 Ec73
Fakılı TR 192 Fd85
Fakovići BIH 159 Ja64
Faksdal N 78 Eb26
Fakse DK 109 Eb27
Fakse Ladeplads DK 109 Eb27
Falaise F 22 Fc37
Fálana GR 183 Bd80
Fålasjö S 80 Gc31
Falcade I 150 Ea57
Falces E 39 Ec58
Falciano del Massico I 161 Fa74
Fălciu RO 177 Fb60
Fălcoiu RO 175 Db66
Falconara I 167 Fa87
Falconara Marittima I 156 Ed66
Falcone I 167 Fc84
Faldsled DK 108 Dc27
Falerna I 164 Gb81
Falerna Marina I 164 Gb81
Falerum S 103 Ga47
Fălești MD 173 Fa56
Faleștii Noi MD 173 Fb56
Falfield GB 19 Ec27
Falileevo RUS 99 Ld41
Faliráki GR 197 Fa93
Falkelva N 66 Ga15
Falkenberg D 120 Fa35
Falkenberg D 127 Ed39
Falkenberg D 143 Ec50
Falkenberg S 102 Ec52
Falkenhagen D 128 Fb37
Falkenhain D 127 Ec40
Falkensee D 127 Ed36
Falkenstein D 135 Eb43
Falkenstein D 135 Eb48
Falkenthal D 119 Ed35
Falkerslev DK 109 Eb28
Falkirk GB 10 Ea13
Falköping S 102 Fa47
Fałków PL 130 Ja40
Falla S 103 Fd46
Fållen S 103 Fb52
Falleron F 28 Ed43
Fallet N 85 Dd34
Fallford GB 11 Eb16
Fällfors S 73 Hc24
Fallingbostel D 118 Db35
Fälloheden S 72 Gd22
Fallon F 31 Ka41
Fällträsk S 73 Hd22
Falmouth GB 18 Db32
Falnes N 92 Bd43
Falset E 48 Ga62
Falsnes N 62 Ha10
Falsterbo S 110 Ed57
Fălticeni RO 172 Ec56
Falträsk S 80 Gd25
Falun S 95 Fd39
Famagusta = Ammochostos CY 206 Jd96
Fambach D 126 Db42
Fameck F 25 Jd35
Fana N 84 Ca39
Fanagmore GB 4 Dc04
Fanano I 155 Db64
Fanári GR 184 Dc77
Fanari GR 188 Bb81
Fandrup DK 100 Db22
Fane I 149 Dc59
Fångåmon S 78 Fa31
Fangel DK 108 Dc27
Fanjeaux F 41 Gd55
Fanlo E 40 Fc57
Fannerup DK 101 Dd23
Fänneslunda S 102 Ed48
Fannrem N 77 Dd30
Fano I 156 Ec65
Fanore IRL 12 Bc21
Fanós GR 183 Bd76
Fänsta S 87 Ga33
Fântânele RO 170 Bd59
Fântânele RO 171 Dc59
Fântânele RO 172 Ec56
Fântânele RO 175 Cd66
Fanthyttan S 95 Fc42
Fantoft N 84 Ca39
Fao E 36 Ba55
Fărăgău RO 171 Dc58
Fara in Sabina I 156 Eb70
Faramontanos de Tábara E 45 Cb59
Fara Novarese I 148 Ca59
Faraoani RO 176 Ed60
Fara San Martino I 161 Fa71
Farasdués E 47 Fa59
Fărău RO 171 Db59
Fårberget S 80 Ha27
Fårbo S 103 Gb50
Fărcaș RO 175 Cd65
Fărcașa RO 171 Da55
Fărcașa RO 172 Eb57
Fărcașele RO 180 Db67
Fărcășești RO 175 Cc64
Farchant D 142 Dc53
Fărdea RO 174 Ca61
Fardella I 162 Gb77
Fardhem S 104 Gd50
Färdkällan S 86 Ed37
Farndum IRL 13 Ca21
Fåred S 95 Fb45
Fareham GB 20 Fa30
Faremoutiers F 23 Ha37
Färentuna S 96 Gc43
Farés GR 194 Bb89
Farestad N 92 Cc47
Fårevejle DK 109 Ea25
Fårevejle Stationsby DK 109 Ea25
Farfa I 156 Eb70
Färgaryd S 102 Fa51
Färgelanda S 102 Ec46
Fargues-Saint-Hilaire F 32 Fb50
Fargues-sur-Ourbise F 40 Fd52
Farhult S 110 Ec54
Färila S 87 Fd35
Faringdon GB 20 Ed27
Faringe S 96 Gd41
Färingtofta S 110 Fa54
Farini d'Olmo I 149 Cd62
Fariza E 45 Ca61
Färjestaden S 103 Gb52
Farkadóna GR 189 Bc81
Farkaševac HR 152 Gc58
Farkasfa H 145 Gb55
Farkazdin SRB 153 Jc60
Farkazdin SRB 174 Bb62
Farlete E 48 Fb60
Fårliug RO 174 Ca62
Färlöv S 111 Fb54
Farmakas CY 206 Jb97
Farmakonissi GR 197 Eb89
Farmborough GB 19 Ec28
Farmtown GB 7 Ec08
Färna S 95 Ga42
Farná SK 145 Hb51
Farnanes Cross Roads IRL 12 Bc26
Färnäs S 87 Fc38
Farnborough GB 20 Fb29
Farnborough GB 20 Fd28
Farnese I 156 Dd69
Farnham GB 20 Fb29
Färnigen CH 141 Cb55
Farnstädt D 127 Ea40
Farnworth GB 15 Ec21
Faro P 58 Ad74
Fårö S 104 Hb48
Fårösund S 104 Hb48
Farra d'Alpago I 150 Eb57
Farranfore IRL 12 Bb24
Farre DK 108 Dc24
Farre DK 108 Db25
Fársala GR 189 Bd82
Farsø DK 100 Db22
Farstad N 77 Da31
Farstorp S 110 Fa54
Farstrup DK 100 Db21
Farsund N 92 Cb47
Fârțănești RO 177 Fb62
Fârțățești RO 175 Da64
Farum DK 109 Ec25
Fårup DK 100 Dc23
Fårvang DK 100 Dc23
Faryny PL 122 Jc32
Fasana I 165 Gd80
Fasano I 162 Ha75
Fasgar E 37 Ca56
Fasillar TR 199 Hb88
Fáskrúðsfjörður IS 3 Bc05
Fasnacloich GB 6 Dc11
Faßberg D 118 Dc35
Fåssjödal S 87 Fd34
Faster DK 108 Da24
Fasterholt DK 108 Da24
Fasterna S 96 Gd42
Fastias E 37 Ca54
Fastiv UA 204 Ec15
Fasty PL 123 Kb33
Fatež RUS 203 Fa13
Fátima P 50 Ac66
Fatjas S 73 Hb19
Fatmomakke S 71 Fd24
Fatnica BIH 159 Hc68
Fatsa TR 205 Fc19
Fättjaur S 71 Fd24
Faucogney-et-la-Mer F 31 Ka39
Faugères F 41 Hb54
Fauguerolles F 32 Fd51
Fauldhouse GB 10 Ea13
Faulenrost D 119 Ec32
Faulquemont F 25 Ka35
Fauquembergues F 23 Gd31
Faura E 54 Fc67
Făurei RO 172 Ec58
Făurei RO 176 Ed64
Făurei RO 181 Ec67
Făurei RO 181 Fa68
Făurești RO 175 Da65
Fausing DK 100 Dc23
Fauske N 66 Fd17
Faustynowo PL 129 Gb38
Fauville-en-Caux F 23 Ga34
Faux F 33 Ga50
Faux F 34 Hc51
Favaios P 44 Bb61
Fåvang N 85 Dd36
Fåvangfjellet N 85 Ea36
Favara E 54 Fc69
Favara I 166 Ed86
Faverges F 35 Ka46
Faverney F 31 Jd40
Faverolles F 23 Ga36
Faverolles F 23 Gc37
Faversham GB 21 Ga29
Favignana I 166 Ea84
Favone F 154 Cb72
Favrholt DK 108 Db24
Fawley GB 20 Fa30
Fay-aux-Loges F 29 Gd40
Fay-de-Bretagne F 28 Ed41
Fayence F 43 Kb53
Fayet F 41 Hb53
Fayl-Billot F 31 Jc40
Fayón E 48 Fd62
Fay-sur-Lignon F 34 Ja49
Fažana HR 151 Fa61
Fazlıca TR 191 Ec82
Feakle IRL 12 Bd22
Fearnan GB 7 Ea11
Fearn Lodge GB 5 Ea06
Feas E 36 Bb53
Fécamp F 22 Fd34
Feces de Abaixo P 44 Bb59
Feckenham GB 20 Ed25
Feda N 92 Cb46
Fedamore IRL 12 Bd23
Federi RO 175 Cd62
Fedje N 84 Bd37
Fedkovščyna RUS 99 Ld43
Fëdorovka RUS 205 Fb15
Fedosino RUS 107 Ma48
Fedotovo RUS 113 Jb59
Fegen S 102 Ed51
Fegyvernek H 146 Jc53
Fehérgyarmat H 147 Kc50
Fehmarn D 119 Ea30
Fehrbellin D 119 Ec35
Fehring A 144 Ga55
Feichten A 142 Dc54
Feignies F 24 Hc32
Feilitz D 135 Ea43
Feimaņi LV 107 Lc52
Feins F 28 Ed38
Feira do Monte E 36 Bc54
Feiring N 85 Ea40
Feiring N 94 Eb39
Feistritz im Rosental A 144 Fb56
Feiteira P 58 Ad74
Feketić SRB 153 Ja59
Felanitx E 57 Hc67
Felchow D 120 Fb34
Felcsút H 146 Hc53
Feldafing D 143 Dd51
Feld am See A 144 Fa55
Feldatal D 126 Cd42
Feldbach A 144 Ga55
Feldbach F 31 Kb40
Feldballe DK 101 Dd23
Feldberg D 119 Ed33
Feldberger Seenlandschaft D 119 Ed33
Feldborg DK 100 Da23
Feldioara RO 176 Ea61
Feldkirch A 142 Cd53
Feldkirchen D 135 Eb48
Feldkirchen D 143 Ea51
Feldkirchen in Kärnten A 144 Fa56
Feldkirchen-Westerham D 143 Ea51
Feldru RO 171 Dc56
Feleacu RO 171 Da58
Felechosa E 37 Cc55
Feletto I 148 Bd59
Felgueiras P 44 Ba60
Feliceni RO 176 Dd60
Felina I 149 Da63
Felindre GB 15 Eb25
Felindre GB 19 Dd27
Félines-Minervois F 41 Ha55
Félines-Termenès F 41 Ha56
Felinfach GB 15 Ea26
Felino I 149 Da62
Felitto I 161 Fd76
Félix E 61 Ea76
Felixdorf A 145 Gb52
Felixstowe GB 21 Gb26
Felizli TR 187 Gc78
Felizzano I 148 Ca61
Fell A 143 Ed54
Fellabær IS 3 Bc05
Fellbach D 134 Cd48
Fellegrenda N 93 Db44
Fellen D 134 Da44
Felletin F 33 Gd46
Fellí GR 183 Bb79
Fellingfors N 70 Fa23
Fellingsbro S 95 Fd43
Felm D 118 Dc30
Felmín E 37 Cc56
Felnac RO 170 Bd59
Felnémet H 146 Jb51
Felsberg D 126 Da40
Felsőcsatar H 145 Gb54
Felsőkörtvélyes H 146 Hc55
Felsőnyárád H 146 Jc50
Felsőnyék H 145 Hb55
Felsősima H 147 Ka51
Felsőszolnok H 145 Gb55
Felsőtárkány H 146 Jb51
Felsővadász H 146 Jc50
Felsőzsolca H 146 Jc50
Felsted GB 20 Fd27
Feltham GB 20 Fc28
Felton GB 15 Ec26
Feltre I 150 Ea58
Femanger N 84 Cb40
Femsjö S 102 Fa52
Femundssundet N 86 Ec35
Fenagh IRL 9 Cb19
Fendeille F 41 Gd55
Fene E 36 Ba53
Fenerköy TR 186 Fb77
Fenes N 66 Fb17
Fénétrange F 25 Ka36
Feneu F 28 Fb41
Fengersfors S 94 Ec45
Fenioux F 28 Fb44
Fenioux F 32 Fb47
Fenit IRL 12 Ba24
Fennagh IRL 13 Cc23
Fensmark DK 109 Eb27
Fenstad N 94 Eb40
Fenstanton GB 20 Fc26
Fensterbach D 135 Eb46
Fenwick GB 10 Dd14
Fenwick GB 11 Ed14
Feodosija UA 205 Fb17
Feohanagh IRL 12 Bc24
Féole F 28 Fa44
Feolin Ferry GB 6 Da13
Feragen N 86 Ec33
Ferapontievca MD 177 Fd60
Ferbane IRL 13 Ca21
Ferdinandovac HR 152 Gd58
Ferdinandshof D 120 Fa32
Fère-Champenoise F 24 Hc37
Fère-en-Tardenois F 24 Hb35
Ferendia RO 174 Bd62
Ferentillo I 156 Eb69
Ferentino I 160 Ec72
Féres GR 185 Ea78
Férez E 53 Ec71
Feria E 51 Bc70
Feričanci HR 152 Hb59
Ferla I 167 Fc87
Ferlach A 144 Fb56
Fermignano I 156 Eb65
Fermo I 156 Ed67
Fermoselle E 45 Ca61
Fermoy IRL 12 Bd25
Fernáncaballero E 52 Db68
Fernán-Núñez E 60 Cd73
Ferndown GB 20 Ed30
Ferness GB 7 Ea08
Ferney-Voltaire F 35 Jd45
Fernhurst GB 20 Fb29
Ferns IRL 13 Cd24
Fernwald D 126 Cc42
Ferovac HR 152 Ha60
Ferpècle CH 148 Bd57
Ferraj AL 182 Ac74
Ferrandina I 162 Gc76
Ferrão Ferro P 50 Aa69
Ferrara I 150 Dd62
Ferrara di Monte Baldo I 149 Db59
Ferrazzano I 161 Fc73
Ferreira E 36 Bb55
Ferreira do Alentejo P 50 Ad71
Ferreira do Zêzere P 50 Ad66
Ferreira (Valadouro) E 36 Bc53
Ferreiros E 36 Bc55
Ferreras de Abajo E 45 Cb59
Ferreras de Arriba E 45 Ca59
Ferreries E 57 Ja66
Ferreruela de Huerva E 47 Fa62
Ferret CH 148 Bc57
Ferrette F 31 Kb40
Ferreux F 30 Hc38
Ferriere I 149 Cc62
Ferrières F 41 Ha54
Ferrières-en-Brie F 23 Ha37
Ferrières-en-Gâtinais F 29 Ha39
Ferrières-Saint-Mary F 34 Hb49
Ferrières-sur-Sichon F 34 Hc46
Ferring DK 100 Cd22
Ferritslev DK 109 Dd27
Ferrol E 36 Ba53
Ferry Bridge IRL 12 Bc23
Ferryhill GB 11 Fa17
Fertilia I 168 Bd75
Fertőd H 145 Gc52
Fertőrakos H 145 Gc52
Fertőszentmiklós H 145 Gc53
Fervaques F 22 Fd36
Ferwerd NL 117 Bc32
Fessenheim F 31 Kc39
Feștelița MD 173 Ga59
Festøy N 76 Cc33
Festvåg N 66 Fc17
Fetești MD 172 Ed54
Fetești RO 177 Fa66
Fetești-Gară RO 177 Fa66
Fethard IRL 13 Ca24
Fethard IRL 13 Cc25
Fethiye TR 186 Ga80
Fethiye TR 193 Gc83
Fethiye TR 198 Fc92
Fetsund N 94 Eb41
Fettercairn GB 7 Ec10
Fettwell GB 20 Fd25
Feucht D 135 Dd46
Feuchtwangen D 134 Db47
Feudingen D 126 Cc41
Feuerleiten A 143 Ec54
Feugarolles F 40 Fd52
Feuges F 30 Hd38
Feuquières F 23 Gc34
Feuquières-en-Vimeu F 23 Gc33
Feurs F 34 Hd47
Fevik N 93 Da46
Fevral'skoje RUS 113 Jd58
Fevzipaşa TR 186 Fb80
Fevziye TR 187 Gb79
Feytiat F 33 Gb47
Ffestiniog GB 15 Dd23
Ffostrasol GB 14 Dc26
Fiane N 93 Db46
Fiano I 148 Bc60
Fiaschetti I 150 Eb58
Fibiș RO 174 Bd60
Ficarazzi I 166 Ed84
Ficarolo I 150 Dd61
Fichtelberg D 135 Ea44
Fichtenau D 134 Db47
Fichtenberg D 127 Ed40
Fichtenberg D 134 Da48
Ficulle I 156 Ea68
Fiddleton GB 11 Eb15
Fiddown IRL 13 Cb24
Fide S 104 Gd51
Fidenza I 149 Da61
Fidjastølen N 92 Cb44
Fidjeland N 92 Cc44
Fidjetun N 93 Da46
Fieberbrunn A 143 Eb53
Fielbmatgiedde N 64 Jc08
Fieni RO 176 Dd64
Fienvillers F 23 Gd32
Fier AL 182 Ab76
Fiera di Primiero I 150 Ea57
Fierbinți-Târg RO 176 Eb65
Fier Shegan AL 182 Ab76
Fierzë AL 159 Jc70
Fiesch CH 141 Ca56
Fiesole I 155 Dc65
Figaredo E 37 Cc55
Figari F 154 Cb72
Figeac F 33 Gd51
Figeholm S 103 Gb50
Figgjo N 92 Ca44
Figiás GR 190 Cd86
Figliere I 148 Bb62
Figline Valdarno I 155 Dc66
Figueira da Foz P 44 Ab64
Figueira de Castelo Rodrigo P 45 Bc62
Figueira dos Cavaleiros P 50 Ac71
Figueiró dos Vinhos P 44 Ad65
Figueras E 37 Bd53
Figueres E 41 Hb58
Figuerola d' Orcau E 48 Gb59
Figueroles E 54 Fc65
Fijnaart NL 124 Ad38
Fiksdal N 76 Cd32
Filadélfi GR 184 Cc77
Filadelfia I 164 Gb82
Filain F 31 Jd41
Filakí GR 189 Bd82
Filakió GR 185 Ea75
Fil'akovo SK 146 Ja50
Filatova Gora RUS 107 Ld47
Filderstadt D 134 Cd49
Fildu de Jos RO 171 Cd57
Fildu de Sus RO 171 Cd57
Filettino I 160 Ec71
Filevo BG 184 Dc74
Filey GB 17 Fc19
Filí GR 189 Cb86
Filia GR 188 Bb86
Filía GR 189 Bc82
Filiași RO 175 Cd65
Filiátes GR 182 Ac80
Filiatrá GR 194 Ba88
Filicudi Porto I 167 Fb82
Filinskoe RUS 203 Fb10
Filipeni MD 177 Fc60
Filipeni RO 172 Ed59
Filipești RO 172 Ed59
Filipeștii de Pădure RO 176 Ea64
Filipeștii de Târg RO 176 Ea64
Fílipi GR 184 Da77
Filipiáda GR 188 Ad82
Filipovci BG 179 Cb70
Filipów PL 123 Ka30
Filippovka RUS 113 Jb59
Filipstad S 95 Fb42
Filiriá GR 183 Bd77
Fillan N 77 Dc29
Fillières F 25 Jc34
Fillingsnes N 77 Dc29
Fillingtveit N 93 Da46
Fillira GR 185 Dd77
Fillo GR 189 Bc81
Film S 96 Gd40
Filótas GR 183 Bb77
Filóti GR 196 Db90
Filottrano I 156 Ed66
Filsbäck S 102 Fa46
Filskov DK 108 Da25
Filsnes N 76 Cc32
Filsum D 117 Cb33
Filzmoos A 143 Ed53
Finale Emilia I 149 Dc62
Finale Ligure I 148 Ca63
Finaña E 61 Dd75
Finbo FIN 96 Hc40
Finby FIN 97 Jc40
Finchingfield GB 20 Fd26
Finchley GB 20 Fc28
Finderup DK 100 Db23
Finderup DK 108 Cd24
Findhorn GB 5 Eb07
Fındıcak TR 186 Fd80
Fındıklı TR 185 Eb79
Findochty GB 5 Ec07
Findon GB 20 Fc30
Finelv N 63 Hd05
Finhan F 40 Gb53
Finikas GR 196 Da89
Finike TR 199 Gb93
Finikoúnda GR 194 Ba90
Finiq AL 182 Ab79
Finiș RO 170 Cb58
Finja S 110 Fa54
Finkenstein A 144 Fa56
Finmere GB 20 Fa26
Finnäs FIN 81 Jb28
Finnasand N 92 Ca43
Finnbacka S 87 Fd38
Finnea IRL 9 Cb20
Finneby S 87 Fd34
Finneidfjord N 71 Fb21
Finnentrop D 125 Cb40
Finnerödja S 95 Fb45
Finnes N 63 Ja04
Finnes N 71 Fb18
Finnfjordeidet N 67 Gc11
Finnforsfallet S 80 Hb25
Finngruvan S 95 Fb39
Finnhöle S 95 Gb40
Finning D 142 Dc51
Finnisglin IRL 8 Bb20
Finnkroken N 62 Gd09
Finnliden S 73 Hb23
Finnøya N 66 Fd15
Finnsäter S 79 Fb29
Finnsjå N 63 Hd08
Finnsnes N 67 Gc11
Finnsta S 87 Ga33
Finnstad N 78 Ec28
Finnstad N 86 Eb34
Finnstuga S 87 Fd37
Finntorp S 94 Ec43
Finnträsk S 73 Hc24
Finnvelta N 94 Ec40
Finnvollan N 78 Fa25
Finny IRL 8 Bc20
Fino Mornasco I 149 Cc58
Finowfurt D 120 Fa35
Fins F 23 Ha33
Finse N 84 Cd39
Finsjö S 103 Ga51
Finsland N 92 Cd46
Finspång S 103 Fd46
Finsterau D 135 Ed48
Finsterwalde D 128 Fa39
Finstown GB 5 Ec03
Finström FIN 96 Hc40
Finta RO 176 Ea65
Fintel D 118 Db34
Fintînița MD 173 Fb54
Fintona GB 9 Cc17
Fintown IRL 8 Ca16
Finvik N 63 Hd05
Finvoy GB 9 Cd16
Fiodh Ard IRL 13 Ca24
Fiolleda E 36 Bb56
Fionnaithe IRL 8 Bc20
Fionnay CH 148 Bc57
Fionnphort GB 6 Da11
Fiorenzuola d'Arda I 149 Cd61
Firenze I 155 Dc65
Firenzuola I 155 Dc64
Firiteaz RO 174 Bd60
Firizza RO 171 Da55
Firkeel IRL 12 Ba26
Firlădeni MD 173 Fc59
Firlădeni MD 173 Ga59
Firlej PL 131 Ka39
Firminy F 34 Ja48
Firmo I 164 Gb78
Firoga PL 121 Ha30
Firovo RUS 202 Ec09
Fischach D 142 Dc50
Fischamend A 145 Gc51
Fischbach A 144 Ga53
Fischbach D 133 Bd45
Fischbach D 133 Ca47
Fischbachau D 143 Ea52
Fischen D 142 Db53
Fischering A 144 Fc55
Fishbourne GB 20 Fb30
Fishburn GB 11 Fa17
Fishguard GB 14 Db26
Fishsätra S 96 Gd43
Fiskå N 76 Cb33
Fiskå N 92 Bd42
Fiskárdo GR 188 Ac84
Fiskarheden S 86 Fa38
Fiskari FIN 97 Jd40
Fiskars FIN 97 Jd40
Fiskavaig GB 4 Da08
Fiskebäckskil S 102 Eb47
Fiskebøl N 66 Fc13
Fiskefjord N 66 Ga13
Fiskenes N 66 Ga11
Fisketjønnbu N 92 Ca44
Fiskevik N 63 Ja06
Fiskevollen N 86 Eb35
Fiskö FIN 97 Hd39
Fiskum N 93 Dc42
Fislisbach CH 141 Cb53
Fismes F 24 Hc35
Fiss A 142 Db54
Fister N 92 Cb43
Fisterra E 36 Ac55
Fistéus E 36 Bc57
Fıstıklı TR 186 Fc79
Fitá GR 191 Dd85
Fitero E 47 Ec59
Fithi GR 195 Bd87
Fities GR 188 Ad83
Fitionești RO 176 Ed61
Fitjar N 84 Ca40
Fitou F 41 Hb56
Fittja S 96 Gc43
Fittleton GB 20 Ed29
Fiuggi I 160 Ec72
Fiumata I 156 Ec70
Fiumefreddo Bruzio I 164 Gb80
Fiumefreddo di Sicilia I 167 Fd85
Fiumicello-San Venere I 164 Ga78
Fiumicino I 160 Ea72
Fiveally IRL 13 Ca22
Five Ashes GB 20 Fd30
Fivelanes GB 18 Dc31
Fivemiletown GB 9 Cc18
Five Oaks GB 20 Fc29
Fivizzano I 149 Da63
Fivlered S 102 Fa48
Fixin F 30 Jb42
Fizeșu Gherlii RO 171 Db57
Fjær N 66 Fc16
Fjæra N 92 Cb41
Fjærland N 84 Cc36
Fjågesund N 93 Db43
Fjäl S 79 Fc30
Fjälbyn S 81 Hd26
Fjälkinge S 111 Fb54
Fjällåsen S 67 Ha16
Fjällbacka S 102 Ea46
Fjällbonäs S 72 Ha22
Fjällgården S 87 Fb33
Fjällnäs S 72 Gc22
Fjällnäs S 86 Ec32
Fjällsjönäs S 71 Ga23
Fjaltring DK 100 Cd22
Fjärås S 102 Ec50
Fjärdhundra S 95 Gb42
Fjelberg N 92 Ca41
Fjelde DK 109 Eb29
Fjell N 78 Eb26
Fjell N 84 Ca39
Fjellbu N 67 Gb14
Fjellbu N 85 Dc38
Fjellbygda N 86 Ed37
Fjelldal N 66 Ga13
Fjellerad DK 100 Dc21
Fjellerup DK 101 Dd23
Fjellheim N 85 Db38
Fjellkjøsa N 77 Dd30
Fjellså N 92 Cb46
Fjellstad N 67 Gc12
Fjellstrand N 93 Ea42
Fjelltoten N 94 Eb41
Fjelsø DK 100 Db22
Fjelsted DK 108 Dc26
Fjelstervang DK 108 Da24
Fjelstrup DK 108 Db27
Fjerritslev DK 100 Db21
Fjølvika N 70 Ec24
Fjon N 84 Cb37
Fjordgård N 62 Gb10
Fjotland N 92 Cc45
Fjugesta S 95 Fc44
Flåbygd N 93 Db43
Flaca E 49 Hb59
Flachau A 143 Ed53
Flachslanden D 134 Dc46
Fläckebo S 95 Ga42
Fladan FIN 89 Hd34
Fladbury GB 20 Ed26
Flade DK 100 Da21
Fladungen D 134 Db43
Flagy F 29 Ha38
Flaine F 35 Kb45
Flaka FIN 96 Hc41
Flakaberg S 73 Hd19
Flakaträsk S 72 Gb23
Flakaträsk S 80 Gd27
Flakeberg S 102 Ed47
Flakk N 78 Ea29
Flakkstadvåg N 67 Gb11
Flaknan N 78 Eb31
Flakstad N 66 Fa14
Flåm N 84 Cd38
Flămânzi RO 172 Ed56
Flamatt CH 141 Bc54
Flamborough GB 17 Fc19
Flambouréssi GR 183 Bb80
Flámbouro GR 183 Bb77
Flámbouro GR 184 Cc77
Flammerans F 31 Jc42
Flammerécourt F 30 Jb38
Flammersfeld D 125 Ca42
Flamoudi CY 206 Jc96
Flamouriá GR 183 Bc77
Flámpoura GR 188 Bb86
Flamstead GB 20 Fc27
Flärke S 80 Ha29
Flarken S 80 Hc27
Flash GB 16 Ed22
Flassans-sur-Issole F 42 Ka54
Flatdal N 93 Db42
Flateby N 93 Ea42
Flateland N 92 Cd43
Flateland N 93 Da45
Flåten N 63 Hb08
Flaten N 93 Da45
Flåtestøa N 86 Eb37
Flatøydegard N 85 Dc38
Flatraket N 84 Ca34
Flåtsbo S 87 Fd37
Flått N 78 Ed26
Flattach A 143 Ec55
Flattnitz A 144 Fa55
Flatvoll N 62 Gc10
Flauenskjold DK 101 Dd20
Flaugeac F 32 Fd50
Flavigny-sur-Ozerain F 30 Ja41
Flavin F 41 Ha52
Flavy-le Martel F 24 Hb34
Flawil CH 142 Cc53
Flayat F 33 Ha47
Flayosc F 43 Kb54
Flechtdorf D 126 Cd40
Flechtingen D 127 Dd37
Fleckeby D 108 Db29
Fleet GB 20 Fb29
Fleetmark D 119 Ea35
Fleetwood GB 15 Eb20
Fleines N 66 Fc13
Flekke N 84 Ca36
Flekkefjord N 92 Cb46
Flem N 76 Cc32
Flemløse DK 108 Dc27
Flemma N 77 Db31
Flen S 95 Gb44
Flen S 95 Fc40
Flensburg D 108 Db28
Flensungen D 126 Cd42
Fleres I 143 Dd55
Fleringe S 104 Ha48
Flerohopp S 103 Ga52
Flers F 22 Fb37
Flesberg N 93 Dc41
Flesnes N 66 Fd13
Flessau D 119 Ea35
Fleurance F 40 Ga53
Fleuré F 33 Ga45
Fleurier CH 141 Bb54
Fleurville F 30 Jb44
Fleury F 41 Hb55
Fleury-la-Vallée F 30 Hb40
Fleury-les-Aubrais F 29 Gc40
Fleury-sur-Andelle F 23 Gb35
Fléville F 24 Ja35
Fleys F 30 Hc40
Flieden D 134 Da43
Flikka N 92 Cb46
Flims CH 142 Cc55
Flimwell GB 20 Fd29
Flines-les-Raches F 24 Hb31
Flint GB 15 Eb22
Flintbek D 118 Dc30
Flintnes N 63 Hd08
Flirey F 25 Jc36
Flirsch A 142 Db54
Flisa N 94 Ec39
Flisberget N 86 Ec38
Flisby S 103 Fc49
Fliseryd S 103 Ga51
Flistad S 103 Fd46
Flisy PL 131 Kb42
Flitwick GB 20 Fc26
Flix E 48 Ga62
Flixecourt F 23 Gd33
Flixton GB 21 Gb25
Flize F 24 Ja34
Flø N 76 Cc32
Flo N 84 Cd34
Flo S 102 Ec47
Floby S 102 Fa47
Floda S 80 Hb26
Floda S 95 Ga44
Floda S 95 Fc40
Floda S 95 Fd40
Floda S 102 Ec48
Flodigarry GB 4 Da07
Flogny-la-Chapelle F 30 Hc39
Flöha D 127 Ed42
Floh-Seligenthal D 126 Dc42
Flon S 86 Ed32
Flor S 87 Fc34
Florac F 34 Hc51
Florange F 25 Jd35
Flor da Rosa P 50 Ba67
Florence = Firenze I 155 Dc65
Floreni MD 173 Fd58
Florensac F 41 Hc55
Florenville B 132 Ad44
Florenz = Firenze I 155 Dc65
Flores de Ávila E 46 Cd62
Floresta I 167 Fc84
Florești MD 173 Fc55
Florești RO 171 Da58
Florești RO 176 Ea64
Florești RO 177 Fc64
Florești-Stoenești RO 176 Ea66
Flória GR 200 Cb95
Floriáda GR 188 Ba82
Floridia I 167 Fd87
Flórina GR 183 Bb77
Florinas I 168 Ca75
Florițoaia Veche MD 173 Fb57
Flornes N 78 Eb30
Florø N 84 Ca35
Flörsbachtal D 134 Cd44
Flörsheim D 133 Cb44
Flörsheim-Dalsheim D 133 Cb45
Florstadt D 134 Cc43
Florvåg N 84 Ca39
Florynka PL 138 Jc46
Floß D 135 Eb45
Flossenbürg D 135 Eb45
Flosta N 93 Db46
Flostrand N 70 Fa20
Flöthe D 126 Dc37
Flötningen S 86 Ec35
Fluberg N 85 Dd38
Flúðir IS 2 Ac05
Flüelen CH 141 Cb54
Flühli CH 141 Ca54
Flumet F 35 Ka46
Flumini I 169 Cb80
Fluminimaggiore I 169 Bd79
Flums CH 142 Cd54
Fluorn-Winzeln D 141 Cb50
Fluren S 87 Ga36
Flurkmark S 80 Hb28
Flutbukt N 63 Ja06
Flyggsjö S 80 Ha29
Flygsandsvær N 84 Ca40
Flygsfors S 103 Ga52
Flyinge S 110 Fa55
Flykälen S 79 Fc28
Flymen S 111 Ga53
Flyn S 79 Ga29
Flytåsen S 87 Fd37
Fobello I 148 Ca58

Foča – Furset

Foča BIH 159 Hd66
Foça TR 191 Eb85
Focene I 160 Ea72
Fochabers GB 5 Ec07
Fockbek D 118 Db30
Focșani RO 176 Ed62
Focuri RO 172 Ed57
Fódele GR 200 Da95
Foeni RO 174 Bc61
Fogdö S 95 Gb43
Foggia I 161 Ga73
Föglö FIN 96 Hc41
Fohnsdorf A 144 Fc54
Föhren D 133 Bc44
Foiano della Chiana I 156 Dd67
Foiano di Val Fortore I 161 Fc73
Foieni RO 171 Cc54
Foissiat F 34 Jb45
Foix F 40 Gc56
Fojnica BIH 158 Hb64
Fojnica BIH 159 Hc67
Fokino RUS 202 Ed12
Fokovci SLO 145 Gb55
Føland N 92 Cc46
Folby DK 100 Dc23
Földeák H 146 Jc56
Foldereid N 78 Ed25
Földes H 147 Jd53
Foldingbro DK 108 Da26
Fole S 104 Ha49
Folégandros GR 196 Da91
Folelli F 154 Cc69
Folgaria I 149 Dc58
Folgarida I 149 Dc57
Folgensbourg F 31 Kc40
Folgosinho P 44 Bb63
Folgoso E 36 Ba56
Folgoso de la Ribera E 37 Ca57
Folgoso do Courel E 36 Bc56
Folgueiro E 36 Bc53
Foliá GR 184 Cd77
Foligno I 156 Eb68
Føling N 78 Ec27
Folkestad N 76 Cc33
Folkestone GB 21 Gb29
Folkingham GB 17 Fc23
Folladal N 78 Eb28
Follafoss N 78 Eb28
Folldal N 85 Dd34
Følle DK 101 Dd23
Follebu N 85 Dd37
Follina I 150 Ea58
Follingbo S 104 Ha49
Föllinge S 79 Fc29
Follonica I 155 Db68
Fölsbyn S 94 Ec43
Folsztyn PL 121 Gb35
Foltești RO 177 Fb62
Folusz PL 139 Jd45
Folven N 84 Cd34
Folwarki PL 130 Hd41
Fombellida E 38 Db56
Fominki RUS 203 Fb09
Fompedraza E 46 Db61
Fon N 93 Dd43
Foncebadón E 37 Ca57
Foncine-le-Bas F 31 Jd44
Foncquevillers F 23 Ha32
Fondi I 160 Ed73
Fondo I 142 Dc56
Fondón E 61 Dd75
Föne S 87 Ga35
Fönebo S 87 Gb35
Fonelas E 60 Dc74
Fonfría E 36 Bc56
Fonfría E 45 Ca60
Fonn N 84 Cc35
Fonni I 169 Cb77
Fonollosa E 49 Gc60
Fons F 42 Ja53
Fonsorbes F 40 Gb54
Fontainebleau F 29 Ha38
Fontaine-Chalendray F 32 Fc46
Fontaine-de-Vaucluse F 42 Jc53
Fontaine-Française F 30 Jb41
Fontaine-la-Gaillarde F 30 Hb39
Fontaine-le-Bourg F 23 Gb34
Fontaine-le-Dun F 23 Ga34
Fontaine-les-Grès F 30 Hc38
Fontaines-en-Duesmois F 30 Ja40
Fontaine-sur-Coole F 24 Hd37
Fontainhas P 44 Ac60
Fontainhas P 50 Ab70
Fontan F 43 Kd52
Fontanamare I 169 Bd79
Fontanar E 46 Dd63
Fontanar E 61 Dd73
Fontanarejo E 52 Da68
Fontanars dels Alforins E 55 Fb70
Fontane Bianche I 167 Fd87
Fontanelice I 150 Dd63
Fontanella I 155 Db65
Fontanellato I 149 Da61
Fontanelle I 150 Eb58
Fontanes-du Causse F 33 Gc51
Fontanières F 33 Ha46
Fontanigorda I 149 Cc62
Fontaniva I 150 Dd59
Fontanosas E 52 Cd69
Fontdepou E 48 Ga59
Fonteblanda I 155 Dc69
Fontecchio I 156 Ed70
Fontecha E 37 Cc57
Fonte da Telha P 50 Aa69
Fontenai-les-Louvets F 28 Fc38
Fontenay-le-Comte F 32 Fb45
Fontenay-le-Marmion F 22 Fc36
Fontenay-Trésigny F 23 Ha37
Fontenelle-en-Brie F 24 Hb36
Fontet F 32 Fc51
Fontette F 30 Ja39
Fontevraud-l'Abbaye F 28 Fd42
Fontibre E 38 Db56
Fontioso E 46 Dc59
Fontiveros E 46 Cd62
Font-Romeu F 41 Gd58
Fontstown IRL 13 Cc22
Fontvieille F 42 Jb53
Fonyód H 145 Ha55
Fonz E 48 Fd59
Fonzaso I 150 Ea58
Foppiano I 141 Ca56
Foppolo I 149 Cd57
Föra S 103 Gb51
Forăști RO 172 Ec56
Forbach D 133 Cb48
Forbach F 25 Ka35
Förby FIN 97 Jc40
Forcall E 48 Fc64
Forcalqueiret F 42 Ka54
Forcalquier F 42 Jd52
Forcarei E 36 Ba56
Forchheim D 135 Dd45
Forchtenberg D 134 Da47
Ford GB 6 Db12
Ford GB 11 Ed14
Ford GB 20 Ed26
Førde N 84 Cb36
Førde N 84 Cc35
Førde N 92 Ca41
Förderstedt D 127 Ea38
Førdesfjorden N 92 Ca42
Fordham GB 20 Fd25
Fordingbridge GB 20 Ed30
Fordongianus I 169 Ca77
Fordoun GB 7 Ed10
Fordstown IRL 9 Cc20
Fore N 71 Fb18
Forenza I 161 Ga75
Forestburn Gate GB 11 Ed15
Forest Green GB 20 Fc29
Forest-Montiers F 23 Gc32
Forest Row GB 20 Fd29
Forfar GB 7 Ec11
Forgès F 33 Gc49
Forges-les-Eaux F 23 Gb34
Foria I 161 Fd77
Forio I 161 Fa75
Forkärla S 111 Fd54
Förlanda S 102 Ec50
Forlev DK 109 Ea27
Forlì I 156 Ea64
Forlimpopoli I 156 Ea64
Formazza I 141 Ca56
Formby GB 15 Eb21
Formentor E 57 Hc66
Formerie F 23 Gc34
Formia I 160 Ed73
Formiche Alto E 47 Fa65
Formicola I 161 Fb74
Formigara I 149 Cd60
Formigine I 149 Db62
Formigliana I 148 Ca59
Formignana I 150 Ea62
Formigny F 22 Fb35
Formiguères F 41 Gd57
Formofoss N 78 Ed27
Fornalhas Novas P 58 Ac72
Fornåsa S 103 Fd46
Fornazzo I 167 Fd85
Forneby S 95 Gb41
Fornelli I 168 Bd74
Fornells E 57 Ja65
Fornelos E 36 Ad58
Fornelos P 44 Ad59
Fornelos de Montes E 36 Ad57
Fornes N 67 Gb12
Forneset N 62 Ha09
Forni Avoltri I 143 Ec56
Forni di Sopra I 143 Eb56
Forni di Sotto I 150 Eb57
Forno I 148 Bc60
Forno I 148 Ca57
Forno Alpi Graie I 148 Bc59
Forno di Zoldo I 150 Ea57
Fornoli I 155 Db64
Fornos de Algodres P 44 Bb63
Fornovo di Taro I 149 Da62
Foros da Fonte de Pau P 50 Ac68
Foros de Vale de Figueira P 50 Ac69
Foros do Arrão P 50 Ad67
Foros do Cortiço P 50 Ad69
Forotic RO 174 Bd62
Førøya N 70 Fa19
Forráskút H 146 Jb56
Forres GB 5 Eb07
Forronda E 38 Ea56
Fors S 80 Gd30
Fors S 95 Ga41
Fors S 102 Ec47
Forsa N 66 Ga14
Forsa S 87 Gb35
Forsand N 92 Cb44
Forsås S 79 Gb30
Forsbacka S 80 Hb25
Forsbacka S 87 Gb37
Forsbacka S 95 Gb39
Forsby FIN 81 Jb29
Forsby FIN 90 Kd38
Forsby S 103 Fb47
Forsby Koskenkyla FIN 90 Kc38
Forsen N 71 Fb21
Forserum S 103 Fb49
Forset N 85 Dd37
Forshaga S 94 Fa43
Forshälla S 102 Eb47
Forshed S 73 Hd20
Forsheda S 102 Fa51
Forshem S 102 Fa46
Forsholm S 80 Ha25
Forsinard GB 5 Ea05
Forsland N 70 Fa20
Förslöv S 110 Ed53
Forsmark S 71 Fd23
Forsmark S 96 Gd40
Forsmo S 79 Gb30
Forsmo S 79 Gb29
Forsmoen N 70 Fa21
Forsnäs S 72 Gd20
Forsnäs S 72 Gb22
Forsnäs S 73 Hd21
Forsnäs S 73 Hc20
Forsnäs S 79 Gb27
Forsnes N 77 Db29
Forsøl N 63 Ja05
Forssa FIN 89 Jd38
Forssa S 95 Gb45
Forssjö S 95 Ga45
Forst D 128 Fc39
Forst D 134 Cc47
Forstau A 143 Ed53
Forstern D 143 Ea51
Forstinning D 143 Ea51
Forstranda N 71 Fb18
Forsträskhed S 73 Hd21
Forsvik S 72 Gb24
Forsvik S 103 Fb46
Fortan F 29 Ga40
Fortanete E 48 Fb64
Fort Augustus GB 7 Dd09
Forte dei Marmi I 155 Da64
Fortezza I 143 Dd55
Forth GB 10 Ea13
Förtha D 126 Db41
Fortino I 161 Ga77
Fort-Mahon-Plage F 23 Gb32
Forton GB 15 Ec24
Fortrose GB 5 Ea07
Fortun N 85 Da36
Fortuna E 55 Fa72
Fortunago I 149 Cc61
Fortuneswell GB 19 Ec31
Fort William GB 6 Dc10
Forvika N 70 Ed22
Forza d'Agrò I 167 Fd84
Forzo I 148 Bc59
Fos F 40 Ga56
Fösked S 94 Fa42
Foskros S 86 Ed34
Foskvallen S 86 Ed35
Fosnavåg N 76 Cb33
Fosnes N 78 Ec25
Foss S 102 Eb46
Fossacesia I 157 Fb70
Fossacesia Marina I 157 Fb70
Fossano I 148 Bc62
Fossato di Vico I 156 Eb67
Fossato Ionico I 164 Ga84
Fossbakken N 67 Gc12
Fossbua N 67 Ha12
Fosse N 84 Cb39
Fossegården N 85 Ea37
Fossemagne F 33 Gb49
Fossen N 84 Cd36
Fossen N 94 Eb42
Fosses F 23 Gd36
Fosses-la-Ville B 124 Ad42
Fossestrand N 64 Jb07
Fosshaug N 67 Gc12
Fossheim N 62 Ha10
Fossheim N 65 Kc09
Fossheim N 85 Db35
Fossholm N 64 Ka07
Fossli N 84 Cd39
Fossmoen N 78 Fa25
Fossombrone I 156 Eb65
Fos-sur-Mer F 42 Jb54
Föt H 146 Hd52
Fotheringhay GB 17 Fc24
Fotiní GR 183 Bb77
Fotinovo BG 184 Da74
Fotlandsvåg N 84 Ca38
Fotolívos GR 184 Cd77
Fouesnant F 27 Dc40
Fougeré F 28 Fc41
Fougères F 28 Fa38
Fougères-sur-Bièvre F 29 Gb41
Fougerolles F 31 Jd39
Fougerolles-du-Plessis F 28 Fb38
Fouilloy F 23 Gc34
Foulain F 30 Jb39
Foulayronnes F 40 Ga52
Fouligny F 25 Jd35
Foulsham GB 17 Ga24
Foulum DK 100 Db23
Fountain Cross IRL 12 Bc22
Fountainhal GB 11 Ec14
Fouquerolles F 23 Gd35
Fouras F 32 Fa46
Fourcamont F 23 Gb33
Fourcès F 40 Fd53
Fourchambault F 30 Hb43
Four Crosses GB 15 Eb24
Fourfourás GR 200 Cd96
Fourka GR 182 Ad78
Fourmies F 24 Hc33
Four Mile House IRL 8 Ca20
Fourná GR 188 Bb82
Fournaudin F 30 Hc39
Fournels F 34 Hb50
Fournés GR 200 Cb95
Fournet F 31 Kb42
Fourni GR 197 Ea88
Fourques F 41 Hb57
Fours F 30 Hc43
Fousing Kirkeby DK 100 Cd23
Foussais F 28 Fb44
Foústani GR 183 Bd76
Fovrfeld DK 108 Cd26
Fowey GB 18 Dc31
Fownhope GB 15 Ec26
Foxford IRL 8 Bc18
Foxhall IRL 8 Bc20
Foxo E 36 Ba56
Foxup GB 11 Ed19
Foynes IRL 12 Bc23
Foz E 36 Bc53
Foz de Arouce P 44 Ad64
Foz de Odeleite P 58 Ba73
Foz do Arelho P 50 Aa66
Foz Giraldo P 44 Ba65
Frabosa Soprana I 148 Bd63
Frącki PL 123 Kb30
Fraddon GB 18 Db31
Frades de la Sierra E 45 Cb63
Fraga E 48 Fd61
Fragagnano I 162 Ha76
Fragístra GR 188 Bb83
Frahier-et-Châtebier F 31 Ka40
Frailes E 60 Db74
Frais F 31 Kb40
Fraisse-sur-Agout F 41 Hb54
Fraize F 31 Kb38
Framlev DK 108 Dc24
Framlingham GB 21 Gb25
Frammersbach D 134 Da44
Främmestad S 102 Ed47
Framnäs S 72 Ha19
Frampol PL 131 Kb42
Framura I 149 Cc63
França P 45 Bd59
Francaltreff F 25 Ka36
Francavilla al Mare I 157 Fb70
Francavilla di Sicilia I 167 Fd84
Francavilla Fontana I 162 Ha76
Francavilla sul Sinni I 162 Gb77
Francescas F 40 Fd53
Frâncești RO 175 Db64
Franciszkowo PL 122 Hd34
Francofonte I 167 Fc87
Francolise I 161 Fa74
Francorchamps B 125 Bb42
Francos E 46 Dd61
Francova Lhota CZ 137 Ha47
Frändefors S 102 Ec46
Franeker NL 116 Bb33
Franekeradeel NL 116 Bb33
Fránga GR 188 Ba85
Frangádes GR 182 Ad80
Frangouléika GR 188 Ba84
Frangy F 35 Jd46
Frankenau D 126 Cd40
Frankenberg D 126 Cd41
Frankenberg D 127 Ed42
Frankenburg A 143 Ed51
Frankenförde D 127 Ed38
Frankenhardt D 134 Da47
Frankenmarkt A 143 Ed51
Frankenstein D 133 Cb46
Frankenthal D 133 Cb46
Frankfurt am Main D 134 Cc44
Frankfurt (Oder) D 128 Fb37
Frankleben D 127 Ea40
Franknowo PL 122 Ja31
Frankrike S 78 Fa29
Frånö S 80 Gc31
Franqueville F 40 Ga56
Františkovy Lázně CZ 135 Eb44
Franzburg D 119 Ed31
Franzensfeste I 143 Dd55
Frascati I 160 Eb72
Frascineto I 164 Gb78
Frasdorf D 143 Eb52
Fraserburgh GB 5 Ed07
Fra'shër AL 182 Ac78
Frasin MD 173 Fa54
Frasin RO 172 Eb56
Frăsinet RO 181 Ec67
Frasne F 31 Jd43
Frassene I 150 Ea57
Frassinoro I 149 Db63
Frasso Telesino I 161 Fb74
Frastanz A 142 Cd54
Frata RO 171 Db58
Frătăuții Noi RO 172 Eb54
Frătăuții Vechi RO 172 Eb54
Fratel P 50 Ba66
Frătești RO 180 Ea67
Frátsia GR 195 Bd92
Frattamaggiore I 161 Fb74
Fratta Polesine I 150 Dd61
Frauenau D 135 Ed48
Frauenfeld CH 142 Cc52
Frauenhain D 127 Ed40
Frauenkirch CH 142 Cd55
Frauenkirchen A 145 Gc52
Frauensee D 126 Db41
Frauenstein D 128 Fa42
Frauenwald D 126 Dc42
Fraugde DK 109 Dd27
Fraunberg D 143 Ea50
Frayssinet-le-Gélat F 33 Gb51
Frecăței RO 177 Fb65
Frecăței RO 177 Fc64
Frechen D 125 Bd41
Frechilla E 37 Cd58
Freckenhorst D 125 Cb38
Freckleben D 127 Ea39
Freckleton GB 15 Eb20
Frécourt F 31 Jc39
Freden D 126 Db38
Fredenbeck D 118 Da32
Fredensborg DK 109 Ec25
Fredericia DK 108 Db26
Frederiks DK 100 Db23
Frederiksberg DK 109 Ec26
Frederiksberg DK 109 Ea26
Frederikshavn DK 101 Dd20
Frederikssund DK 109 Eb25
Frederiksværk DK 109 Eb25
Fredersdorf-Eggersdorf D 128 Fa36
Frednowy PL 122 Hd32
Fredrika S 80 Gd28
Fredriksberg S 95 Fb41
Fredriksli N 77 Dd30
Fredrikstad N 93 Ea44
Fredriksten N 94 Eb44
Fredropol PL 139 Kb45
Fredros S 94 Ed41
Fredsberg S 95 Fb45
Fredvang N 66 Fa14
Freeland GB 20 Fa27
Freemount IRL 12 Bc24
Freethorpe GB 17 Gb24
Fregenal de la Sierra E 51 Bc71
Fregene I 160 Ea71
Fréhel F 26 Ec37
Frei N 77 Da31
Freiamt D 141 Ca50
Freibach A 144 Fb56
Freiberg D 127 Ed42
Freiberg (Neckar) D 134 Cd48
Freiburg D 118 Da31
Freiburg D 141 Ca51
Freidorf RO 174 Bc61
Freiensteinau D 134 Da43
Freienwill D 108 Db29
Freigericht D 134 Cd44
Freihung D 135 Ea46
Freila E 61 Dd74
Freilassing D 143 Ec52
Freisen D 133 Bd45
Freising D 143 Ea50
Freissinières F 35 Kb50
Freistadt A 144 Fb50
Freistatt D 118 Cd35
Freiston GB 17 Fd23
Freital D 128 Fa41
Freixedas P 45 Bc63
Freixeiro E 36 Bc57
Freixianda P 44 Ac65
Freixo de Espada à Cinta P 45 Bd61
Fréjairolles F 41 Gd53
Frejlev DK 100 Dc21
Frejlev DK 109 Eb29
Fréjus F 43 Kb54
Fremdingen D 134 Db48
Frenchpark IRL 8 Ca19
Frencq F 23 Gc31
Frende P 44 Ba61
Frenelle F 31 Jd38
Frenelles F 23 Gb35
Frensdorf D 134 Dc45
Frensham GB 20 Fb29
Frenštát pod Radhoštěm CZ 137 Hb46
Freren D 117 Cb36
Freshford IRL 13 Cb23
Freshwater GB 20 Fa31
Fresnay-sur-Sarthe F 28 Fd39
Fresneda E 38 Db58
Fresneda E 53 Eb66
Fresnedillas E 46 Db64
Fresnedo de Valdellorma E 37 Cd56
Fresnedoso de Ibor E 51 Cb66
Fresne-Léguillon F 23 Gc35
Fresne-Saint-Mamès F 31 Jc41
Fresnes-au-Mont F 24 Jb36
Fresnes-en-Woëvre F 25 Jc35
Fresnes-sur-Apance F 31 Jc39
Fresnes-sur-les-Eaux F 24 Hb31
Fresno-Alhándiga E 45 Cb63
Fresno de Cantespino E 46 Dc61
Fresno de Caracena E 46 Dd61
Fresno de la Ribera E 45 Cc60
Fresno de la Vega E 37 Cc58
Fresno de Sayago E 45 Cb61
Fresno el Viejo E 45 Cc61
Fresnoy-en-Bassigny F 31 Jc39
Fresnoy-Folny F 23 Gb33
Fresnoyrand F 24 Hb33
Fresselines F 33 Gc45
Fressingfield GB 21 Gb25
Fresvik N 84 Cd37
Freswick GB 5 Ec04
Fretigney-et-Velloreille F 31 Jd41
Frétigny F 29 Ga38
Frettes F 31 Jc40
Fretzdorf D 119 Ec34
Freudenberg D 125 Cb41
Freudenberg D 134 Cd45
Freudenberg D 135 Ea46
Freudenstadt D 133 Cb49
Freudental D 134 Cc47
Frévent F 23 Gd32
Freyburg D 127 Ea40
Freyenstein D 119 Ec34
Freyming-Merlebach F 25 Ka35
Freystadt D 135 Dd47
Freyung D 135 Ed49
Frí GR 201 Eb95
Frías E 38 Dd57
Frías de Albarracín E 47 Ed65
Fribourg CH 141 Bc54
Frick CH 141 Ca52
Frička SK 138 Jc46
Frickenhausen D 134 Db45
Frickhofen D 125 Cb42
Frickingen D 142 Cd51
Fričovce SK 138 Jc47
Fridafors S 111 Fc53
Fridaythorpe GB 16 Fb19
Fridene S 103 Fb47
Fridhem S 102 Ed47
Fridingen D 142 Cc51
Fridlevstad S 111 Fd54
Fridolfing D 143 Ec51
Friedberg A 144 Ga53
Friedberg D 134 Cc43
Friedberg D 142 Dc50
Friedberg A 143 Ed51
Friedeburg D 117 Cc32
Friedenfels D 135 Eb45
Friedenweiler D 141 Cb51
Friedersdorf D 127 Eb39
Friedersdorf D 128 Fa37
Friedewald D 126 Db41
Friedland D 120 Fa32
Friedland D 126 Db40
Friedland D 128 Fb38
Friedrichroda D 126 Dc41
Friedrichsbrunn D 127 Dd39
Friedrichsdorf D 134 Cc43
Friedrichshafen D 142 Cd52
Friedrichshain D 128 Fb39
Friedrichskoog D 118 Da31
Friedrichsruhe D 119 Eb33
Friedrichstadt D 118 Da30
Friedrichsthal D 119 Ed35
Friedrichsthal D 133 Bd46
Friedrichswalde D 120 Fa34
Friel S 102 Ed46
Frielendorf D 126 Da41
Friera E 37 Bd57
Friesach A 144 Fb55
Friesack D 119 Ec35
Friesenheim D 133 Ca49
Friesenried D 142 Db51
Friesoythe D 117 Cb34
Frifelt DK 108 Da27
Friggesund S 87 Ga35
Frigiliana E 60 Db76
Frigole I 163 Hc76
Frihetsli N 67 Ha12
Frilford GB 20 Fa27
Friligiánika GR 195 Bd92
Frillesås S 102 Ec50
Frimley GB 20 Fb29
Frinnaryd S 103 Fc48
Frinton-on-Sea GB 21 Gb27
Friockheim GB 7 Ec11
Friol E 36 Bb55
Frisange L 133 Bb45
Friskney GB 17 Fd23
Fristad S 102 Ed48
Frithville GB 17 Fc23
Fritsla S 102 Ed49
Fritzlar D 126 Cd40
Friville-Escarbotin F 23 Gb33
Frjanovo RUS 203 Fa10
Froan N 77 Dd28
Fröderyd S 103 Fc50
Frödinge S 103 Ga49
Frodisia CY 206 Hd97
Frogn N 93 Ea42
Frogner N 93 Ea41
Frogner (Oslo) N 93 Ea41
Frohburg D 127 Ec41
Frohen-le-Grand F 23 Gd32
Frohnleiten A 144 Fd54
Froissy F 23 Gd34
Fröjel S 104 Gd50
Fröjered S 103 Fb47
Froland N 93 Da46
Frolovo RUS 203 Fd13
Frombork PL 122 Hc30
Frome GB 19 Ec29
Fromentel F 22 Fc37
Fromentine F 27 Ec43
Frómista E 38 Da58
Fröndenberg D 125 Cb39
Fronhausen D 126 Cc42
Fronreute D 142 Cd51
Front I 148 Bd59
Fronteira P 50 Ba68
Frontenard F 30 Jb43
Frontenay-Rohan-Rohan F 32 Fb45
Frontenex F 35 Ka47
Frontenhausen D 135 Eb49
Frontignan F 41 Hd54
Fronton F 40 Gb53
Frørup DK 109 Dd27
Frose D 127 Ea38
Fröseke S 103 Ga51
Frosinone I 160 Ed72
Frøskeland N 66 Fc12
Fröskog S 94 Ec45
Frøslev DK 100 Da21
Fröslunda S 96 Gc42
Frösö S 79 Fc31
Frosolone I 161 Fb72
Frossay F 27 Ec42
Frosta N 78 Eb29
Frösthult S 95 Gb42
Frostkåge S 80 Hc25
Frøstrup DK 100 Db21
Frösunda S 96 Gd42
Frösve S 103 Fb46
Frötuna S 96 Ha42
Frouard F 25 Jd36
Froussioúna GR 194 Bc87
Frövi S 95 Fd43
Frövifors S 95 Fd43
Froxfield GB 20 Ed28
Frøyset N 84 Ca37
Frøysnes N 92 Cd44
Frufällan S 102 Ed49
Fruges F 23 Gd31
Frula E 48 Fb60
Frumoasa MD 173 Fc57
Frumoasa RO 172 Ea59
Frumoasa RO 180 Dd68
Frumosu RO 172 Ea55
Frumușani RO 180 Eb67
Frumușica MD 173 Fb55
Frumușica MD 177 Fc61
Frumușica RO 172 Ed56
Frumușița RO 177 Fb62
Fruniz E 38 Ea55
Frunză MD 173 Fa53
Frunzivka UA 204 Ec16
Frúrio GR 183 Bc79
Frutak MNE 159 Hd69
Frutigen CH 141 Bd55
Fruzenskoe RUS 113 Jc59
Frýdek-Místek CZ 137 Hb45
Frýdlant CZ 128 Fc42
Frýdlant nad Ostravicí CZ 137 Hb46
Fryele S 103 Fb50
Frygnowo PL 122 Hd33
Frykerud S 94 Ed43
Fryksände S 94 Ed41
Fryksås S 87 Fc37
Frymburk CZ 136 Fb49
Fryšták CZ 137 Ha47
Frysztak PL 139 Jd44
Fterë AL 182 Ab78
Fuans F 31 Ka42
Fubine I 148 Ca61
Fucecchio I 155 Db65
Fuchsmühl D 135 Eb45
Fuchsstadt D 134 Da44
Fuchstal D 142 Dc51
Füchtorf D 125 Cb37
Fuencaliente E 52 Da71
Fuendejalón E 47 Ed60
Fuendetodos E 47 Fa62
Fuengirola E 60 Cd77
Fuenlabrada E 46 Dc65
Fuenlabrada de los Montes E 52 Cd68
Fuensalida E 46 Da65
Fuensanta E 53 Eb68
Fuensanta E 61 Ec73
Fuensanta de Martos E 60 Db73
Fuente-Álamo E 55 Fa73
Fuente-Álamo E 55 Ed70
Fuentealbilla E 54 Ed68
Fuentearmegil E 46 Dd60
Fuente-Blanca E 55 Fa71
Fuentecaliente de Lucio E 38 Db57
Fuente Carreteros E 60 Cc73
Fuentecén E 46 Dc60
Fuente Dé E 38 Da55
Fuente de Cantos E 51 Bd71
Fuente del Arco E 51 Ca71
Fuente del Maestre E 51 Bd70
Fuente del Pino E 55 Ed71
Fuente de Pedro Naharro E 53 Dd66
Fuente de Piedra E 60 Cd75
Fuente de Reina E 54 Fb66
Fuente el Fresno E 52 Db68
Fuente el Olmo de Íscar E 46 Da61
Fuente el Saz de Jarama E 46 Dc64
Fuente el Sol E 46 Cd62
Fuente Encalada E 37 Cb58
Fuenteheridos E 59 Bc72
Fuentelapeña E 45 Cc61
Fuentelcésped E 46 Dc60
Fuentelespino deHaro E 53 Ea67
Fuentelespino de Moya E 54 Ed66
Fuentelmonje E 47 Eb61
Fuentelsaz E 47 Ec62
Fuentemilanos E 46 Db63
Fuente Obejuna E 51 Cb71
Fuente Palmera E 60 Cc73
Fuentepelayo E 46 Db62
Fuentepinilla E 47 Ea61
Fuenterrebollo E 46 Db61
Fuenterrobles E 54 Ed67
Fuentes E 53 Ec66
Fuentesaúco E 45 Cc61
Fuentesaúco de Fuentidueña E 46 Db61
Fuentes Claras E 47 Ed63
Fuentes de Andalucía E 59 Cb73
Fuentes de Béjar E 45 Cb64
Fuentes de Carbajal E 37 Cc58
Fuentes de Cesna E 60 Da74
Fuentes de Ebro E 48 Fb61
Fuentes de León E 51 Bc71
Fuentes de Nava E 46 Da59
Fuentes de Oñoro E 45 Bc63
Fuentes de Ropel E 45 Cc59
Fuentes de Valdepero E 46 Da59
Fuentespalda E 48 Fd63
Fuentespina E 46 Dc60
Fuente Tójar E 60 Da74
Fuentidueña E 46 Db61
Fuentidueña E 60 Da73
Fuentidueña de Tajo E 46 Dd65
Fuerte del Rey E 60 Db72
Fuestrup D 125 Cb37
Fügen A 143 Ea53
Fugleberg N 67 Gb12
Fuglebjerg DK 109 Ea27
Fuglestad N 92 Ca45
Fuglsø DK 109 Dd24
Fuglstad N 70 Ed24
Fuhrberg D 126 Db36
Fulacık TR 186 Ga79
Fulda D 126 Da42
Fülesd H 147 Kc50
Fulga RO 176 Eb65
Fulgatore I 166 Eb84
Fullerton GB 20 Fa29
Fullestad S 102 Ed48
Fullösa S 102 Fa46
Fulnek CZ 137 Ha45
Fülöpjakab H 146 Ja55
Fülöpszállás H 146 Hd55
Fulpmes A 143 Dd54
Fulunäs S 86 Ed37
Fumay F 24 Ja33
Fumel F 33 Gb51
Funäsdalen S 86 Ed33
Funbo S 96 Gd42
Funchal P
Fundão P 44 Bb64
Fundata RO 176 Dd63
Fundeni RO 176 Eb66
Fundeni RO 177 Fa62
Fundres I 143 Ea55
Fundulea RO 176 Eb66
Fundu Moldovei RO 172 Ea56
Fundurii Noi MD 173 Fa55
Fundurii Vechi MD 173 Fb55
Funes E 39 Ec58
Fünfstetten D 134 Dc48
Funtana HR 150 Ed61
Funzie GB 5 Fa03
Furadouro P 44 Ac62
Furco E 36 Bb56
Furculești RO 180 Dc68
Furen BG 179 Cd69
Fürfeld D 134 Cb46
Fürged H 145 Hb55
Furingstad S 103 Ga46
Furiz- E 38 Db55
Furlo I 156 Eb66
Furmanov RUS 203 Fa09
Furmanovo RUS 113 Jd59
Furore I 161 Fb76
Furset N 77 Da31

Fürstenau – Geriş

Fürstenau D 117 Cb36
Fürstenberg D 119 Ed34
Fürstenberg D 126 Da38
Fürstenfeld A 145 Gb54
Fürstenfeldbruck D 143 Dd50
Fürstenstein D 135 Ed49
Fürstenwalde D 128 Fb37
Fürstenwerder D 120 Fa33
Fürstenzell D 143 Ed50
Furta H 147 Ka54
Furtan S 94 Ed42
Furtei I 169 Ca78
Furth A 144 Ga50
Fürth D 134 Cc45
Fürth D 134 Dc46
Furth D 135 Ea49
Furth im Wald D 135 Ec47
Furtwangen D 141 Cb50
Furuby S 103 Fc52
Furudal S 87 Fc37
Furuflaten N 62 Ha10
Furulund S 110 Ed55
Furuly N 65 Kd08
Furunäs S 73 Hb20
Furuögrund S 73 Hc24
Furusjö S 103 Fb48
Furusund S 96 Ha42
Furuvik S 96 Gc39
Fusa N 84 Ca40
Fuscaldo I 164 Gb79
Fuschl am See A 143 Ed52
Fushë-Arrëz AL 159 Jc70
Fush'e Bullit AL 182 Ac75
Fush'e Bulqizës AL 182 Ad74
Fushë-Kruja AL 182 Ab74
Fushe-Lurë AL 163 Jc71
Fushë-Muhur AL 178 Ad73
Fusine I 149 Cd57
Fusine in Valromana I 143 Ed56
Fusio CH 141 Cb56
Füssen D 142 Dc52
Fussy F 29 Ha42
Fustiñana E 47 Ed59
Futani I 161 Fd77
Futog SRB 153 Ja60
Futrikelv N 62 Gd09
Fuurtti FIN 90 Kd35
Füzesabony H 146 Jb52
Füzesgyarmat H 147 Jd54
Fužina SLO 151 Fc58
Fužine HR 151 Fc60
Fužine SLO 151 Fa58
Fyfield GB 20 Fd27
Fyllia CY 206 Jb96
Fyllinge S 102 Ed52
Fynshav DK 108 Dc28
Fyrås S 79 Fd29
Fyresdal N 93 Da43
Fyrudden S 103 Gb47
Fyrunga S 102 Ed47
Fyvie GB 5 Ed08

G

Gaaldorf A 144 Fc54
Gaanderen NL 125 Bc37
Gaas A 145 Gb54
Gabaldón E 53 Ec67
Gabare BG 179 Cd69
Gabarret F 40 Fc53
Gabas F 39 Fb56
Gabbro I 155 Da66
Gabčikovo SK 145 Ha51
Gabella Grande I 165 Gd80
Gabellino I 155 Db67
Gaber BG 179 Cb70
Gabicce Mare I 156 Eb65
Gąbin PL 130 Hd36
Gąbino PL 121 Gc29
Gablenz D 128 Fc40
Gablingen D 134 Dc49
Gabøl DK 108 Da27
Gabra BG 179 Cd72
Gabreševci BG 179 Ca71
Gabriac F 34 Hb51
Gabrje SLO 151 Fd59
Gabrovnica BG 179 Cc68
Gabrovo BG 180 Dc71
Gabrovo BG 183 Cb74
Gabrowo PL 123 Jd32
Gabšiai LT 114 Ka56
Gaby I 148 Bd58
Gać PL 123 Jd34
Gać PL 139 Kb44
Gacak TR 198 Fd91
Gacé F 22 Fd37
Gać Kaliska PL 129 Hb39
Gacko BIH 159 Hc67
Gad RO 174 Bc61
Gadbjerg DK 108 Db25
Gäddede S 79 Fb26
Gaddesby GB 16 Fb24
Gäddträsk S 80 Gd26
Gäddvik S 73 Hd22
Gadebusch D 119 Dd32
Gädheim D 134 Db44
Gądków PL 128 Fc37
Gadmen CH 141 Cb55
Gádor E 61 Ea76
Gádoros H 146 Jc55
Gadow D 119 Ec34
Gadūnavas LT 113 Jc54
Gadžin Han SRB 178 Bd69
Gæidno N 64 Ka07
Gæidnovuoppe N 63 Ja10
Gaël F 27 Ec39
Gærum DK 101 Dd20
Găești RO 176 Dd65
Gaeta I 160 Ed74
Gættevægie N 64 Jc09
Gafanha de Boa Hora P 44 Ac63
Gáfete P 50 Ba67
Gaflenz A 144 Fc52
Gaganica BG 179 Cc69
Gägelow D 119 Ea31
Găgești RO 177 Fb60
Gaggenau D 133 Cb48
Gaggio Montano I 155 Db64
Gagince SRB 178 Bd70
Gagino RUS 203 Fc09
Gagliano Castelferrato I 167 Fb85
Gagliano del Capo I 165 Hc78
Gaglovo SRB 178 Bc68
Gagnef S 95 Fc39
Gagovo BG 180 Eb69
Gagsmark S 73 Hc24
Găiceana RO 176 Ed60
Gaick Lodge GB 7 Ea09
Gaidar MD 177 Fd61
Gaideliai LT 113 Jc56
Gaidūnai LT 115 Lb58
Gaienhofen D 142 Cc52
Gaifana I 156 Eb67
Gaigalava LV 107 Lc50
Gaiķi LV 105 Jd51
Gaildorf D 134 Da48
Gailey GB 16 Ed24
Gailingen D 142 Cc52
Gailiūnai LT 114 La56
Gaillac F 41 Gd53
Gaillefontaine F 23 Gc34
Gaillimh IRL 12 Bc21
Gaillon F 23 Gb36
Gailmuiža LV 107 Lc52
Gailumi LV 107 Ld50
Gaimersheim D 135 Dd48
Găinești RO 172 Eb56
Gainsborough GB 16 Fb22
Gaiola I 148 Bc62
Gaiole in Chianti I 155 Dc66
Gaipler TR 192 Fd84
Gairloch GB 4 Db07
Gairlochy GB 6 Dc09
Gairo I 169 Cb78
Gais CH 142 Cd53
Găiseni RO 176 Ea66
Gaishorn A 144 Fb53
Gaitsgill GB 11 Eb17
Găiuți RO 176 Ed60
Gaj HR 152 Gd60
Gaj SRB 174 Bc64
Gajary SK 145 Gc50
Gajdobra SRB 153 Ja60
Gajewo PL 121 Gb35
Gaj Oławski PL 129 Gd41
Gajtaninovo BG 184 Cc75
Gajutino RUS 202 Ed08
Gakkovo RUS 99 Lc40
Gakovo SRB 153 Hd58
Gålå N 85 Dd36
Gala P 44 Ab64
Gălăbinci BG 180 Ea73
Gălăbnik BG 179 Cb72
Galåbodarna S 87 Fb32
Gălăbovo BG 180 Ea73
Gălăbovo BG 184 Db74
Galåen N 86 Eb33
Gałajny PL 122 Ja30
Galambok H 145 Gd56
Galamuiža LV 105 Jd51
Galan F 40 Fd55
Galanito N 68 Hd11
Galanta SK 145 Ha50
Galapagar E 46 Db64
Gălăriești RO 172 Eb55
Galarinós GR 183 Cb78
Galaroza E 59 Bc72
Galashiels GB 11 Ec14
Galata CY 206 Ja97
Galata, Kr. BG 181 Fa70
Galatás GR 188 Ba85
Galatás GR 195 Cb88
Galateia CY 206 Jd95
Gălăteni RO 180 Dd67
Galati I 164 Gb84
Galați RO 177 Fb63
Galati Marina I 164 Ga84
Galatin BG 179 Cd69
Galatina I 163 Hc77
Galatiní GR 183 Bb78
Galátista GR 183 Cb78
Galatone I 163 Hc77
Gălăuțaș RO 172 Ea58
Galaxídi GR 189 Bc85
Galbally IRL 12 Bd24
Galbenu RO 176 Ed64
Gålberget S 80 Gd29
Gălbinași RO 176 Ec64
Galda de Jos RO 175 Da60
Galeata I 156 Ea64
Galera E 61 Ea73
Galéria F 154 Ca69
Găleşti MD 173 Fc57
Găleşti RO 171 Dc59
Galewice PL 129 Ha40
Galgaguta H 146 Hd51
Galgamácsa H 146 Hd52
Galgate GB 11 Ec19
Gălgău RO 171 Da56
Galgauska LV 107 Lb49
Galgenen CH 142 Cc53
Galibabinac SRB 178 Bd68
Galič RUS 203 Fa08
Galiče BG 179 Cd68
Galicea RO 175 Db64
Galicea Mare RO 175 Cc66
Galičnik MK 182 Ad74
Galinduste E 45 Cb63
Galiniai LV 123 Kb30
Galinoporni CY 206 Ka95
Galiny PL 122 Jb30
Galipsós GR 184 Cd77
Galisteo E 45 Ca65
Galizano E 38 Dc54
Galizes P 44 Ba64
Gałków Duży PL 130 Hd39
Gallarate I 148 Cb58
Gallardon F 29 Gc38
Gällared S 102 Ed51
Gallareto I 148 Bd60
Gallargues F 42 Ja53
Gallartu E 38 Ea56
Gällaryd S 103 Fb51
Gallegos de Argañán E 45 Bd63
Gallegos de Solmirón E 45 Cc64
Gallejaur S 72 Ha24
Galleno I 155 Db65
Gällersta S 95 Fd44
Galliate I 148 Cb59
Gallicano I 155 Da64
Gallicano nel Lazio I 160 Eb71
Gallico I 164 Ga84
Gallico Marina I 164 Ga84
Gallinge S 102 Ec50
Gallio I 150 Dd58
Gallipoli I 162 Hb77
Gallisancho E 45 Cb63
Gällivare S 67 Hb17
Gallneukirchen A 144 Fb50
Gallo I 156 Eb65
Gällö S 79 Fd31
Gallo Matese I 161 Fb73
Gallspach A 144 Fa51
Gällstad S 102 Fa49
Gallur E 47 Ed60
Galluzzo I 155 Dc65
Galmenai LT 113 Jd56
Galovo BG 179 Da68
Galston GB 10 Dd14
Galtby FIN 97 Ja40
Galteland N 92 Cd45
Galtelli I 169 Cc76
Galten DK 108 Dc24
Galtisjaur S 72 Gc21
Gåltjärn S 87 Gb33
Galtseter N 86 Ec35
Galtström S 88 Gc34
Galtür A 142 Da54
Galugnano I 163 Hc77
Galve de Sorbe E 46 Dd62
Galveias P 50 Ad67
Gálvez E 52 Da66
Galway IRL 12 Bc21
Gałwuny PL 122 Jb30
Galzignano Terme I 150 Dd60
Gamaches F 23 Gb33
Gamalseter N 67 Gb11
Gamás H 145 Ha56
Gambais F 23 Gc37
Gambara I 149 Da60
Gambarie I 164 Ga84
Gambassi Terme I 155 Db66
Gambatesa I 161 Fc73
Gambettola I 156 Ea64
Gambolò I 148 Cb60
Gamborg DK 108 Db26
Gambsheim F 25 Kc36
Gamil P 44 Ad60
Gaming A 144 Fc52
Gamla Uppsala S 96 Gc41
Gamleby S 103 Gb48
Gamlingay GB 20 Fc26
Gammalkil S 103 Fd47
Gammalsälen S 94 Fa39
Gammalstorp S 111 Fc54
Gammelbo S 95 Fd42
Gammelby S 95 Ga42
Gammelgården S 73 Ja21
Gammelgarn S 104 Ha50
Gammelheimen N 63 Hd08
Gammel-Homna S 87 Fd37
Gammel Østerby DK 101 Ea20
Gammel Rye DK 108 Db24
Gammelsdorf D 135 Ea49
Gammelskolla N 85 Ea37
Gammelstaden S 73 Hd22
Gammertingen D 142 Cd50
Gamnes N 62 Gd08
Gamonal E 52 Cd66
Gamonero E 52 Cd67
Gampel CH 141 Bd56
Gams CH 142 Cd53
Gams bei Hieflau A 144 Fc52
Gamvik N 63 Hd05
Gamvik N 63 Hc07
Gamvik N 64 Ka04
Gamzigrad SRB 179 Ca67
Gămzovo BG 174 Cb66
Gan F 40 Fc55
Gándara E 36 Ba55
Gándara de Espariz P 44 Ba64
Gandarela E 36 Ba57
Gandarela P 44 Ba60
Ganddal N 92 Ca44
Ganderkesee D 118 Cd34
Gandesa E 48 Fd62
Gandia E 54 Fc69
Gandino I 149 Da58
Gandra P 44 Ad59
Gandrup DK 100 Dc21
Gandvik N 65 Kb07
Găneasa RO 175 Db66
Găneasa RO 176 Eb66
Gănești RO 171 Db59
Gangelt D 125 Bb40
Ganges F 41 Hd53
Gånghester S 102 Ed49
Gangi I 167 Fa85
Gângiova RO 179 Cd67
Gangkofen D 143 Eb50
Gangloffsömmern D 127 Dd40
Gangsei N 93 Da45
Gangura MD 173 Fd59
Gañinas E 38 Da57
Ganllwyd GB 15 Dd23
Gannat F 34 Hb46
Gannay-sur-Loire F 30 Hc44
Gänsbrunnen CH 141 Bd53
Gänsen S 95 Fc40
Gänserndorf A 145 Gc50
Gånsvik S 88 Gd32
Gánt H 145 Hb53
Ganthem S 104 Ha49
Ganthorpe GB 16 Fb19
Gañuelas E 55 Ed73
Gañuelas E 55 Ed73
Ganuza E 39 Ec57
Gaoth Saile IRL 8 Bb18
Gap F 35 Ka50
Gaperhult S 94 Fa45
Gara H 153 Hd58
Garaballa E 54 Ed66
Garaguso I 162 Gb76
Gara Hitrino BG 181 Ec69
Gara Lakatnik BG 179 Cc70
Garancières F 23 Gc37
Gárasavvon FIN 68 Hd13
Garbagna I 148 Cb61
Garbatka-Letnisko PL 131 Jd39
Gârbău RO 171 Cd58
Garbayuela E 52 Cc68
Garberg N 78 Eb30
Garbno PL 122 Jb30
Gârbou RO 171 Da56
Gârbova RO 175 Da61
Garbów PL 131 Ka39
Garbsen D 126 Da36
Gârceni RO 173 Fa59
Garching D 143 Ea50
Garching D 143 Eb51
Garcia E 48 Ga62
Garciaz E 51 Cb67
Garciems LV 106 Kb50
Garcihernández E 45 Cc63
Garcilgalindo E 45 Cb63
Garčin HR 152 Hb60
Gârcina RO 172 Ec58
Garcinarro E 47 Ea65
Gărčinovo BG 180 Ea69
Gârcov RO 180 Db68
Garda I 149 Db59
Gârda de Sus RO 171 Cc59
Gardamas LT 113 Jc56
Gardanne F 42 Jd54
Gardawice PL 138 Hc44
Gårdby S 111 Gb53
Garde E 39 Fa57
Garde S 104 Ha50
Gårdeby S 103 Ga46
Gardeja PL 121 Hb32
Gardelegen D 127 Ea36
Gardenstown GB 5 Ed07
Garderen NL 116 Bb36
Gardermoen N 85 Ea40
Gardete P 50 Ba66
Gardhem S 102 Ec47
Gardíki GR 188 Ba81
Garding D 118 Cd30
Gardinovci SRB 153 Jb60
Gardna PL 121 Gc29
Gärdnäs S 79 Fd27
Gardno PL 120 Fc34
Gardone Riviera I 149 Db59
Gardone Val Trompia I 149 Da59
Gardonne F 32 Fd50
Gárdony H 146 Hc54
Gardouch F 40 Gc55
Gårdsby S 103 Fc51
Gärdserum S 103 Ga47
Gärdsjö S 80 Gc27
Gårdsjö S 95 Fb45
Gardsjöbäcken S 71 Ga23
Gardsjönäs S 71 Ga23
Gårdskär S 96 Gc39
Gårdskär fiskehamn S 96 Gc39
Gärds Köpinge S 111 Fb55
Gärdslösa S 103 Gb52
Gårdstånga S 110 Fa55
Gardur IS 2 Ab04
Gardyny PL 122 Ja33
Gardzień PL 122 Hc32
Garein F 39 Fb53
Garel F 23 Gb36
Garelehöjden S 79 Gb29
Garelochhead GB 6 Dc12
Gares E 39 Ec57
Garešnica HR 152 Gc59
Garessio I 148 Bd63
Garfin E 37 Cd57
Garforth GB 16 Fa20
Gargaliáni GR 194 Ba89
Gargallo E 48 Fb63
Gargantiel E 52 Cd69
Gargaur S 72 Gc22
Gargellen A 142 Da54
Gargia fjellstue N 63 Ja08
Gargilesse-Dampierre F 29 Gc44
Gargnano I 149 Db59
Gargnäs S 72 Gc23
Gárgoles de Abajo E 47 Ea63
Gargrave GB 16 Ed20
Gargüera E 45 Ca65
Gargždai LT 113 Jb55
Gari MK 182 Ad74
Garino RUS 107 Mb49
Garipçe TR 199 Gc90
Garitz D 127 Eb38
Garkalne LV 106 Kc50
Garkleppvollen N 78 Ec31
Garkolovo RUS 99 Ld40
Garlasco I 148 Cb60
Gârleni RO 172 Ec59
Garliava LT 114 Kc58
Gârliciu RO 177 Fb65
Garliestown GB 10 Dd17
Garlin F 40 Fc54
Gârlița RO 181 Ed67
Garlitos E 52 Cc69
Gărljano BG 179 Ca72
Garmisch-Partenkirchen D 142 Dc53
Garmo N 85 Dc35
Garnat-sur-Engièvre F 30 Hc44
Garnek PL 130 Hd41
Gârnic RO 174 Bd64
Garoaia RO 176 Ed62
Garons F 42 Ja53
Garoza LV 106 Kb52
Garpenberg S 95 Ga40
Garphyttan S 95 Fc44
Garpom FIN 90 Kd38
Garraf E 49 Gd62
Garrafe de Torío E 37 Cc56
Garragie Lodge GB 7 Dd09
Garrapinillos E 47 Fa60
Garray E 47 Eb60
Garrel D 117 Cc34
Garrigill GB 11 Ec17
Garrison GB 8 Ca17
Garrobillo E 55 Ed74
Garrovillas E 51 Bd66
Garrucha E 61 Ec75
Gars D 143 Eb51
Gars am Kamp A 136 Ga49
Garsås S 87 Fc38
Garsdale Head GB 11 Ec18
Gārsene LV 114 La53
Garsjøen N 85 Ea39
Gårslev DK 108 Db25
Garsnäs S 111 Fb56
Garssnitz A 144 Fd53
Garstang GB 15 Ec20
Garsten A 144 Fb51
Garsūnai LT 114 Kc53
Garten N 77 Dd29
Gartland N 78 Ed26
Gartow D 119 Ea34
Gärtringen D 134 Cc49
Gartz D 120 Fb34
Garusovo RUS 107 Mb50
Gårva N 64 Jb10
Garvagh GB 9 Cd16
Garvaghy GB 9 Cc17
Garvald GB 11 Ec13
Garvan BG 181 Ec67
Garvão P 58 Ac72
Garve GB 4 Dd07
Garvin E 52 Cc66
Garvock GB 6 Dc13
Garwolin PL 131 Jd38
Garynahine GB 4 Da05
Garz D 119 Ed30
Gąsawa PL 121 Gd35
Gåsbakken N 77 Dd31
Gåsborn S 95 Fb42
Gåsbu N 77 Db33
Gaschurn A 142 Da54
Gaschwitz D 127 Eb40
Gascueña E 47 Ea65
Gąsewo Poduchowne PL 122 Jc34
Gashy F 23 Gc36
Gaskeluokt S 72 Gb24
Gąski PL 123 Jd31
Gasmyr N 67 Gc11
Gåsnäs S 79 Gb30
Gåsnes N 63 Ja04
Gąsocin PL 122 Jb35
Gaşpar MD 173 Fa54
Gaspoltshofen A 144 Fa51
Gasselte NL 117 Ca34
Gasselternijveen NL 117 Ca34
Gassino Torinese I 148 Bd60
Gässjö S 79 Ga30
Gasteiz E 38 Ea56
Gastellovo RUS 113 Jc57
Gastes F 39 Fa52
Gastiáin E 39 Eb57
Gastins F 24 Hb37
Gastoúni GR 188 Ad86
Gastoúri GR 182 Ab80
Gaszowice PL 129 Gd40
Gata E 45 Bd64
Gata HR 158 Gc66
Gata N 94 Eb39
Gata de Gorgos E 55 Fd70
Gătaia RO 174 Bd62
Gatarta LV 106 La49
Gatčina RUS 99 Mb40
Gatčina RUS 202 Ea08
Gatehouse of Fleet GB 10 Dd16
Gátér H 146 Jb55
Gateshead GB 11 Fa16
Gatheme F 22 Fb37
Gátova E 54 Fb67
Gatten DK 100 Db21
Gattendorf A 145 Gc51
Gatteo a Mare I 156 Eb64
Gattinara I 148 Ca59
Gattorna I 149 Cc63
Gau-Algesheim D 133 Cb44
Gaubert F 29 Gc39
Gaucín E 59 Cb77
Gauernitz D 127 Ed41
Gäufelden D 134 Cc49
Gauja LV 106 Kb50
Găujani RO 180 Ea68
Gaujiena LV 107 Lb48
Gaukås N 93 Da44
Gaukheihytta N 92 Cc44
Gaukönigshofen D 134 Db46
Gaukönigshofen D 134 Db46
Gaulėniai LT 113 Jd54
Gaulstad N 78 Ec28
Gau-Odernheim D 133 Cb45
Gaupne N 84 Cd36
Gaurė LT 113 Jd56
Gaußig D 128 Fb41
Gausvik N 66 Ga13
Gautefall N 93 Db44
Gautestad N 92 Cd45
Gauting D 143 Dd51
Gauto S 71 Ga20
Găuzeni MD 173 Fc55
Gavà E 49 Gd62
Găvănoasa MD 177 Fc62
Gavardo I 149 Db59
Gavarnie F 40 Fc57
Gavelli I 156 Ec69
Gavėniai LT 114 La56
Gavi I 148 Cb62
Gavião P 50 Ad66
Gavieze LV 105 Jb52
Gavilanes E 46 Cd65
Gavirate I 148 Cb58
Gävle S 95 Gb39
Gavoi I 169 Cb76
Găvojdia RO 174 Ca61
Gavorrano I 155 Db68
Gavray F 22 Fa37
Gâvres F 27 Ea40
Gavril-Genovo BG 179 Cc69
Gavrilov-Jam RUS 203 Fa09
Gavrilovka RUS 99 Mb45
Gavrilovo RUS 113 Jd59
Gávrio GR 190 Da87
Gávros GR 182 Ba77
Gavry RUS 107 Ld49
Gavry RUS 107 Ma50
Gåvsta S 96 Gd41
Gâvurağılı TR 198 Fd93
Gaweinstal A 145 Gc50
Gawliki Wielkie PL 123 Jd31
Gaworzyce PL 128 Ga39
Gawroniec PL 120 Ga32
Gawronki PL 130 Hc37
Gawrychy PL 122 Jc33
Gawthrop GB 11 Ec18
Gawthwaite GB 11 Eb19
Gåxsjö S 79 Fc29
Gazeran F 23 Gc37
Gaziemir TR 191 Ec86
Gazimağusa = Ammochostos CY 206 Jd96
Gazitepe TR 186 Fb77
Gazivode KSV 178 Ba69
Gazlıgölakören TR 193 Gc84
Gazoldo degli Ippoliti I 149 Db60
Gazzaniga I 149 Cd58
Gazzuolo I 149 Db61
Gbelce SK 146 Hc52
Gbely SK 137 Gd49
Gdańsk PL 121 Hb30
Gdingen = Gdynia PL 121 Ha29
Gdinj HR 158 Gd67
Gdov RUS 99 Lc44
Gdov RUS 202 Ea09
Gdów PL 138 Ja45
Gdynia PL 121 Ha29
Gea de Albarracín E 47 Ed64
Geamăna MD 173 Fd58
Geashill IRL 13 Cb21
Geaune F 40 Fc54
Geay F 28 Fc43
Gebałka PL 123 Jd30
Gebeciler TR 193 Gd85
Gebesee D 127 Dd41
Gebhardshagen D 126 Dc37
Gebhardshain D 125 Cb41
Gębice PL 121 Gb35
Gębice PL 128 Fc38
Gębice PL 129 Ha36
Gebiz TR 199 Gd90
Gebra D 126 Dc40
Gebze TR 186 Ga78
Gecek TR 193 Hb83
Geçitkale = Lefkoniko CY 206 Jc96
Geçitli TR 187 Gb80
Geçkinli TR 185 Ec75
Geçmen TR 199 Gb92
Gedek TR 191 Eb81
Gedeller TR 199 Gc91
Gedern D 134 Cd43
Gedesby DK 109 Eb29
Gedikbaşı TR 198 Ga92
Gedikevi TR 193 Gd84
Gedikli TR 199 Ha88
Gedinne B 132 Ad43
Gediz TR 192 Fd84
Gedney Dove End GB 17 Fd23
Gedre F 40 Fc57
Gedser DK 109 Eb29
Gedsted DK 100 Db22
Gedved DK 108 Dc25
Geel B 124 Ba39
Geertruidenberg NL 124 Ad38
Geesala IRL 8 Bb18
Geeste D 117 Ca35
Geesthacht D 118 Dc33
Geevagh IRL 8 Ca18
Gefell D 135 Ea43
Géfira GR 183 Ca77
Gefíria GR 189 Bc82
Gefrees D 135 Ea44
Gegiedžiai LT 114 Kb53
Gehofen D 127 Dd40
Gehrde D 117 Cc35
Gehrden D 126 Da37
Gehren D 127 Dd42
Gehren D 128 Fa39
Geibi LV 115 Ld53
Geidžiūnai LT 114 Kd53
Geilenkirchen D 125 Bb40
Geilo N 85 Da39
Geinberg A 143 Ed50
Geiranger N 84 Cd34
Geisa D 126 Db42
Geiselbach D 134 Cd44
Geiselhöring D 135 Eb48
Geiselwind D 134 Dc45
Geisenfeld D 135 Ea49
Geisenheim D 133 Cb44
Geising D 128 Fa42
Geisingen D 141 Cb51
Geisleden D 126 Db40
Geislingen D 134 Da49
Geismar D 126 Db40
Geisnes N 78 Ec25
Geistthal A 144 Fd54
Geisvika N 67 Gb13
Geithain D 127 Ec41
Geithus N 93 Dd41
Geitvågen N 66 Fc17
Gela I 167 Fa87
Gelbensande D 119 Ec31
Geldermalsen NL 124 Ba37
Geldern D 125 Bc38
Geldrop NL 125 Bb39
Geleen NL 125 Bb40
Gelej H 146 Jc51
Gelemiç TR 192 Fd81
Gelenau D 127 Ec42
Gelenbe TR 192 Fa83
Gelenbe TR 192 Fc87
Gelendost TR 193 Gd87
Gelendžik RUS 205 Fc17
Gelénes H 147 Kb50
Geležiai LT 114 Kd54
Gelfingen CH 141 Ca53
Gelgaudiškis LT 114 Ka57
Gelibolu TR 185 Eb79
Gelida E 49 Gd61
Gelincik TR 193 Ha84
Gelincik TR 199 Gc88
Gelles F 33 Ha47
Gellin F 31 Jd43
Gelnhausen D 134 Cd43
Gelnica SK 138 Jc48
Gelnmassan GB 6 Dc12
Gelsa E 48 Fb61
Gelse H 145 Gd56
Gelsenkirchen D 125 Ca39
Gelsesziget H 145 Gd56
Geltendorf D 142 Dc51
Gelterkinden CH 141 Ca52
Gelting D 108 Db29
Geltow D 127 Ed37
Gelu RO 174 Bc60
Gelucourt F 25 Ka36
Gėluva LT 114 Kb56
Gelvonai LT 114 Kd57
Gembloux sur-Orneau B 124 Ad41
Gemenele RO 177 Fa63
Gemer SK 138 Jb49
Gemerská Panica SK 138 Jb49
Gemerská Poloma SK 138 Jb48
Gemert NL 125 Bb38
Gemişköyü TR 198 Ga88
Gemla S 103 Fc52
Gemlik TR 186 Fd79
Gemona del Friuli I 150 Ec57
Gémozac F 32 Fb48
Gemträsk S 73 Hd21
Gemünd D 125 Bc42
Gemünden D 126 Cd41
Gemünden D 126 Cd42
Gemünden D 133 Ca44
Gemünden D 134 Da44
Genagra CY 206 Jc96
Genarp S 110 Fa56
Genas F 34 Jb47
Génave E 53 Ea71
Genazzano I 160 Ec72
Gençali TR 193 Gb87
Gençay F 32 Fd45
Gencek TR 199 Hb89
Genderkingen D 134 Dc49
Gendrey F 31 Jc42
Gendringen NL 125 Bc37
Gendt NL 125 Bc37
Genemuiden NL 117 Bc35
Génerac F 42 Ja53
General Inzovo BG 180 Eb73
General Kolevo BG 181 Ed69
Generalski Stol HR 151 Fd60
General Toševo BG 181 Fb69
Geneston F 28 Ed43
Genevad S 110 Ed53
Genève CH 140 Ba56
Genevrières F 31 Jc40
Genf = Genève CH 140 Ba56
Gengenbach D 133 Ca49
Genicera E 37 Cc56
Génicourt-sur-Meuse F 24 Jb36
Genillé F 29 Gb42
Génis F 33 Gb48
Genişler TR 193 Gb84
Genisséa GR 184 Db77
Genivolta I 149 Cd60
Genk B 124 Ba40
Genlis F 30 Jb42
Gennádio GR 197 Ed94
Gennep NL 125 Bc38
Genner DK 108 Db27
Gennes F 28 Fc42
Genola I 148 Bc62
Génolhac F 34 Hd51
Genouillac F 33 Gd45
Genouillé F 32 Fd46
Genova I 148 Cb63
Genowefa PL 129 Hb37
Gensac F 32 Fd50
Gensingen D 133 Cb44
Gent B 124 Ab39
Genthin D 127 Eb37
Gentioux-Pigerolles F 33 Gd47
Gentofte DK 109 Ec25
Genua = Genova I 148 Cb63
Genzano di Lucania I 162 Gb75
Genzano di Roma I 160 Eb72
Geoagiu RO 175 Cd61
George Enescu RO 172 Ec54
Georgenberg D 135 Eb46
Georgenberg D 135 Eb46
Georgensgmünd D 134 Dc47
Georgenthal D 126 Dc42
Georgi-Damjanovo BG 179 Cb69
Georgi Dimitrov BG 179 Cd73
Georgievsk RUS 205 Ga17
Georgioúpoli GR 200 Cc95
Georgouléika GR 188 Ad83
Georgsdorf D 117 Ca35
Georgsmarienhütte D 126 Cc37
Georth GB 5 Ec02
Géos GR 188 Ab81
Gepatschhaus A 142 Db55
Ger F 22 Fb37
Gera D 127 Eb42
Gera E 37 Ca54
Geraardsbergen B 124 Ab40
Gerabronn D 134 Da47
Gerace I 164 Gb83
Geraci Siculo I 167 Fa85
Gerahies IRL 12 Bb26
Gerakári GR 189 Bd81
Gerakári GR 200 Cd96
Gerakaroú GR 183 Cb78
Geráki GR 195 Bd89
Gerakiní GR 183 Cb79
Gérardmer F 31 Ka39
Geras A 136 Ga49
Geras E 37 Cc56
Gerasa CY 206 Ja98
Géraudot F 30 Hd38
Gerberoy F 23 Gc34
Gerbéviller F 25 Ka37
Gerbini I 167 Fc86
Gerbstedt D 127 Ea39
Gerby FIN 81 Hd30
Gerdašiai LT 123 Kc30
Gerdau D 118 Dc34
Gerdshagen D 119 Eb34
Gerede TR 205 Fa20
Geremeas I 169 Cb80
Geren TR 191 Eb85
Gerena E 59 Bd73
Gerenli TR 193 Ha83
Gereñu E 39 Eb57
Geretsried D 143 Dd51
Gérgal E 61 Ea75
Gergei I 169 Ca78
Gergelyiugornya H 147 Kb50
Gergova RO 177 Fd64
Gergy F 30 Jb43
Gerhardshofen D 134 Dc46
Geringswalde D 127 Ec41
Geriş TR 199 Hb91

Gerişler – Gonnesa

Gerişler TR 187 Gc80
Gerjen H 146 Hc56
Ģērķēni LV 107 Lb52
Gerlev DK 109 Eb25
Gerlos A 143 Ea54
Germagnano I 148 Bc59
Germaringen D 142 Dc51
Germasogeia CY 206 Jb98
Germay F 30 Jb38
Germencik TR 197 Ed88
Germendorf D 119 Ed35
Germering D 143 Dd51
Germersheim D 133 Cb47
Germignaga I 148 Cb57
Germigny-des-Prés F 29 Gd40
Germiyan TR 191 Ea86
Gernec AL 182 Ab77
Gernika E 38 Ea55
Gernrode D 127 Dd39
Gernsbach D 133 Cb48
Gernsheim D 134 Cc45
Geroda D 134 Da43
Gerola Alta I 149 Cd57
Gerolakkos CY 206 Jb96
Geroldsgrün D 135 Ea43
Gerolfingen D 134 Db47
Gerolimenas GR 194 Bc91
Gerolsbach D 135 Dd49
Gerolstein D 133 Bc43
Gerolzhofen D 134 Db45
Gerona = Girona E 49 Hb59
Geroplátanos GR 182 Ad79
Geroskipou CY 206 Hd98
Gerovo HR 151 Fc59
Gerovski Kraj HR 151 Fc60
Gerri de la Sal E 40 Gb58
Gerrikaiz E 39 Eb55
Gersdorf D 127 Ec41
Gersdorf D 127 Ec42
Gersfeld D 134 Db43
Gersheim D 133 Bd47
Gersten A 144 Fc51
Gersten D 117 Cb35
Gerstetten D 134 Da49
Gerstheim F 25 Kc37
Gersthofen D 134 Dc49
Gerstungen D 126 Db41
Gerswalde D 120 Fa34
Gerum S 104 Gd50
Gervelės LT 115 Lc55
Gerviškes LT 114 La59
Gerwisch D 127 Ea37
Gerzen D 135 Eb49
Gesäter S 94 Eb45
Gescher D 125 Ca37
Geschwenda D 126 Dc42
Geseke D 126 Cc39
Geslau D 134 Db46
Gespunsart F 24 Ja33
Gessertshausen D 142 Dc50
Gestad S 102 Ec46
Gestalgar E 54 Fa67
Gesté F 28 Fa42
Gesten DK 108 Da26
Gesties F 40 Gc57
Gestingthorpe GB 21 Ga26
Gęstowice PL 128 Fc37
Gesualdo I 161 Fc74
Gesunda S 87 Fc38
Gesves B 124 Ad42
Gesztely H 146 Jc50
Geszteréd H 147 Ka51
Geta FIN 96 Hb40
Getafe E 46 Dc65
Getaria E 39 Eb55
Getelo D 117 Bd36
Getinge S 102 Ed52
Gettorf D 118 Dc30
Getxo E 38 Ea55
Gevelsberg D 125 Ca39
Gevensleben D 127 Dd37
Gévezé F 28 Ed39
Gevgelija MK 183 Ca76
Gevigney-et-Mercey F 31 Jc40
Gévora del Caudillo E 51 Bc68
Gevrekli TR 199 Hb89
Gevsjön S 78 Ed30
Gex F 35 Jd45
Gey TR 198 Fd92
Geyre TR 198 Fc88
Geyve TR 187 Gc79
Gföhl A 144 Fd50
Ghajn Tuffieha M 166 Eb88
Ghedi I 149 Da60
Gheia RO 171 Db59
Ghelănza MD 173 Fc57
Ghelari RO 175 Cc61
Ghelința RO 176 Eb61
Ghemme I 148 Ca59
Gheorghe Doja RO 171 Dc59
Gheorghe Doja RO 176 Ed66
Gheorghe Lazăr RO 177 Fa66
Gheorgheni RO 172 Ea58
Gherăseni RO 176 Ec64
Ghercești RO 175 Da66
Ghergheasa RO 176 Ed63
Gherghești RO 173 Fa59
Gherla RO 171 Db57
Gherman RO 172 Eb58
Gherman RO 174 Bd62
Gherța Mică RO 171 Cd54
Ghetlova MD 173 Fc57
Ghiare I 149 Cd62
Ghidfalău RO 176 Ea61
Ghidigeni RO 177 Fa61
Ghidirim MD 173 Fd56
Ghiduleni MD 173 Fd56
Ghigo I 148 Bb61
Ghilad RO 174 Bc61
Ghilarza I 169 Ca77
Ghilavăț MD 172 Ed53
Ghiliceni MD 173 Fc56
Ghimbav RO 176 Ea62
Ghimeș-Făget RO 172 Eb59
Ghimpați RO 180 Ea67
Ghindari RO 172 Dd59
Ghindești MD 173 Fc55
Ghioroc RO 170 Bd59
Ghioroiu RO 175 Da65
Ghirla I 148 Cb58
Ghisonaccia F 154 Cc71
Ghisoni F 154 Cb70
Giálova GR 194 Ba89
Giáltra GR 189 Ca83
Gianádes GR 182 Aa80
Gianitsá GR 183 Bd77
Gianítsi GR 190 Cd86
Giánnouli GR 189 Bd81
Gianotá GR 183 Bc79
Giardinello I 166 Ec84
Giardinetto Vecchio I 161 Fd73
Giardini-Naxos I 167 Fd85
Giarmata RO 174 Bd60
Giarratana I 167 Fc87
Giarre I 167 Fd85
Giat F 33 Ha47
Giave I 168 Ca75
Giaveno I 148 Bc60
Giazza I 149 Dc59
Giba I 169 Bd80
Gibaldin E 59 Ca75
Gibellina Nuova I 166 Eb85
Gibellina Vecchia I 166 Eb85
Gibostad N 62 Gc10
Gibraleón E 59 Bb73
Gibraltar GB 59 Cb78
Ģibuļi LV 105 Jc50
Giby PL 123 Kb30
Gibzde LV 105 Jc49
Gic H 145 Ha53
Gidböle S 80 Ha30
Gideå S 80 Ha29
Gideå S 80 Gd29
Gideå bruk S 80 Ha29
Gideåkroken S 80 Gc26
Gidle PL 130 Hd41
Giebelstadt D 134 Da45
Gieboldehausen D 126 Db39
Giecz PL 129 Gd37
Gieczno PL 130 Hd38
Giedlarowa PL 139 Kb43
Giedraičiai LT 114 La56
Giekau D 118 Dc30
Gielas S 71 Fc23
Gielde D 126 Dc38
Gielniów PL 130 Jb40
Gielow D 119 Ec32
Gien F 29 Ha40
Giengen D 134 Db49
Giens F 42 Ka55
Giera RO 174 Bc62
Gierdingen N 85 Ea40
Giersleben D 127 Ea39
Gierzwałd PL 122 Hd32
Giesen D 126 Db37
Giessen D 126 Cc42
Gietelo NL 117 Bc36
Gieten NL 117 Ca34
Giethoorn NL 117 Bc34
Gietrzwałd PL 122 Ja32
Giffaumont-Champaubert F 24 Ja37
Giffers CH 141 Bc54
Gifford GB 11 Ec13
Gifhorn D 126 Dc36
Gigant RUS 205 Fd15
Gige H 152 Ha57
Gigean F 41 Hd54
Gigen BG 180 Db68
Gigenska Mahala BG 180 Db68
Gighera RO 179 Cd67
Giglio Campese I 155 Db70
Giglio Castello I 155 Db70
Giglio Porto I 155 Db70
Gignac F 41 Hc54
Gignese I 148 Cb58
Gignod I 148 Bc58
Gigny F 30 Hd40
Gigny F 31 Jc44
Gigors F 42 Ka51
Gigors-et-Luzeron F 34 Jb50
Gijano E 38 Dd55
Gijón E 37 Cc54
Ģikši LV 106 Kd49
Gilău RO 171 Cd58
Gilavë AL 182 Ab77
Gilbbesjavri FIN 67 Hb11
Gilberdyke GB 16 Fb20
Gilching D 143 Dd51
Gilcrux GB 11 Eb17
Gilena E 60 Cc74
Gilgenberg A 143 Ec51
Gilja N 92 Cb44
Gillanda S 94 Eb45
Gillberga S 94 Ed43
Gillberga S 95 Ga44
Gilleleje DK 109 Ec24
Gillenfeld D 133 Bd43
Gilley F 31 Ka42
Gillhov S 87 Fc32
Gillingham GB 19 Ec29
Gillingham GB 21 Ga28
Gillstad S 102 Ed46
Gilocourt F 23 Ha35
Gilserberg D 126 Cd41
Gilten D 118 Da35
Gilučiai LT 114 Kd57
Gilūtos LT 115 Lc55
Gilvrazino P 58 Ac74
Gilwern GB 19 Eb27
Gilze NL 124 Ad38
Gim S 87 Ga33
Gimåfors S 87 Ga32
Gimbsheim D 133 Cb45
Gimdalen S 87 Fd32
Gimel-les-Cascades F 33 Gc48
Gimenells E 48 Fd60
Gimigliano I 164 Gc81
Gimileo E 38 Ea57
Gimmestad N 84 Cc35
Gimo S 96 Gd41
Gimont F 40 Ga54
Gimsøy N 66 Fb14
Ginasservis F 42 Jd53
Ginci BG 179 Cc70
Gindulai LT 113 Jb55
Ginestas F 41 Hb55
Ginestra degli Schiavoni I 161 Fc73
Gingelom B 124 Ba41
Gingst D 119 Ed30
Ginosa I 162 Gc76
Ginostra I 167 Fd82
Ginsheim D 133 Cb44
Gintališkė LT 113 Jc54
Ginzling A 143 Ea54
Gio E 37 Bd54
Gioi I 161 Fd77
Gioia dei Marsi I 160 Ed71
Gioia del Colle I 162 Gd75
Gioia Sannitica I 161 Fb73
Gioia Tauro I 164 Gb83
Gioiosa Jonica I 164 Gc83
Gioiosa Marea I 167 Fc84
Giolou CY 206 Hd97
Giornico CH 142 Cc56
Giovinazzo I 162 Gc74
Ģipka LV 105 Jd49
Giraltovce SK 139 Jd47
Girancourt F 31 Jd38
Girdiškė LT 113 Jd56
Girdvainiai LT 113 Jc55
Girdžiai LT 114 Ka57
Girecourt-sur-Durbion F 31 Ka38
Girėnai LT 113 Jc55
Girėnai LT 114 Ka59
Giresun TR 205 Fd19
Girifalco I 164 Gc81
Girininai LT 115 Lb56
Girininkai LT 113 Jb55
Girkalnis LT 114 Ka56
Girmeler TR 198 Fd92
Girne = Keryneia CY 206 Jb96
Giroc RO 174 Bd61
Girolata F 154 Ca69
Giromagny F 31 Ka40
Giron S 67 Ha15
Girona E 49 Hb59
Gironcourt-sur-Vraine F 31 Jc38
Gironella E 49 Gd59
Gironville F 25 Jc36
Girov RO 172 Ec58
Giruliai LT 113 Jb55
Girvan GB 10 Dc15
Gisburn GB 15 Ec20
Gisca MD 173 Ga59
Gisholt N 93 Dc44
Giske N 76 Cc32
Gislaved S 102 Fa50
Gislev DK 109 Dd27
Gislingham GB 21 Ga25
Gislövsläge S 110 Ed57
Gisløy N 66 Fd12
Gisors F 23 Gc35
Gisselås S 79 Fd29
Gisslarbo S 95 Ga42
Gissträsk S 72 Ha24
Gistad S 103 Ga46
Gistel B 21 Ha29
Gistel B 124 Aa39
Gistrup DK 100 Dc21
Giswil CH 141 Ca54
Githio GR 194 Bc90
Gittelde D 126 Db38
Gittun S 72 Gd20
Giubega RO 175 Cd66
Giubiasco CH 149 Cc57
Giugliano in Campania I 161 Fa75
Giulești RO 171 Db54
Giulești RO 175 Da65
Giulianova I 157 Fa69
Giulvăz RO 174 Bc61
Giumarra I 167 Fb86
Giurdignano I 163 Hc77
Giurgeni RO 177 Fa65
Giurgița RO 179 Cd67
Giurgiu RO 180 Ea68
Giussano I 149 Cc58
Giuvărăști RO 180 Db68
Give DK 108 Db25
Giverny F 23 Gc36
Givet F 24 Ja32
Givors F 34 Jb47
Givry F 30 Ja43
Givry-en-Argonne F 24 Ja36
Givskud DK 108 Db25
Gižai LV 114 Kb58
Giżałki PL 129 Gd38
Gizdavac HR 158 Gc66
Gizeux F 28 Fd42
Giżycko PL 122 Jc31
Giżynek PL 122 Hc34
Gizzeria Lido I 164 Gb81
Gjæsingen N 77 Dc28
Gjegjan AL 163 Jc71
Gjelbuneset N 66 Fd17
Gjelleråsen N 93 Ea41
Gjellerup DK 108 Da24
Gjelsvik N 84 Ca35
Gjemnes N 77 Da31
Gjengstøa N 77 Dc29
Gjerde N 84 Cd35
Gjerdemyro N 93 Dc44
Gjerlev DK 100 Dc22
Gjermundshamn N 84 Cb40
Gjern DK 108 Dc24
Gjerrild DK 101 Dd23
Gjerstad N 66 Fd13
Gjerstad N 84 Ca39
Gjerstad N 93 Db45
Gjersvika N 78 Fa25
Gjesdal N 92 Ca44
Gjesing DK 108 Cd26
Gjesvær N 64 Jb04
Gjevaldshaugen N 86 Ec37
Gjevdeli N 93 Da44
Gjinar AL 182 Ac75
Gjinikas AL 182 Ad77
Gjirokastër AL 182 Ac78
Gjøl DK 100 Dc21
Gjølga N 78 Ea28
Gjølme N 77 Dd30
Gjøra N 77 Dc32
Gjorëm AL 182 Ab78
Gjøvdal N 93 Da45
Gjøvik N 67 Gb11
Gjøvik N 86 Ea38
Gjueševo BG 179 Ca72
Gladbach D 125 Bc41
Gladbeck D 125 Bd38
Gladenbach D 126 Cc41
Gladhammer S 103 Gb49
Gladstad N 70 Ec22
Glafirá GR 183 Ca81
Glainans F 31 Ka41
Glăjărie RO 172 Dd58
Glamis GB 7 Ec11
Glamoč BIH 158 Gc64
Glamsbjerg DK 108 Dc27
Glanaman GB 19 Dd27
Glandieu F 35 Jc47
Glandore IRL 12 Bb26
Glandorf D 125 Cb37
Glanegg A 144 Fb56
Glanerbrug NL 117 Ca36
Glanet F 28 Ed41
Glangevlin IRL 9 Cb18
Glanoe IRL 12 Bb24
Glanshammar S 95 Fd43
Glanworth IRL 12 Bd25
Glarryford GB 9 Da16
Glarus CH 142 Cc54
Glasbach, Mellenbach- D 127 Dd42
Glasgow GB 10 Dd13
Glashütte D 120 Fb33
Glashütte D 128 Fa42
Glashütten A 144 Fc55
Glashütten D 135 Dd45
Glassan IRL 8 Ca20
Glastonbury GB 19 Eb29
Glattbrugg CH 141 Cb53
Glatten D 133 Cb49
Glaubitz D 127 Ed40
Glauburg D 134 Cd43
Glauchau D 127 Ec42
Glava BG 179 Da69
Glava S 94 Ed43
Glavace HR 151 Fd62
Glava glasbruk S 94 Ec43
Glavan BG 185 Ea74
Glăvănești RO 177 Fa60
Glavas HR 158 Gb64
Glavatićevo BIH 158 Hb66
Glavičice BIH 153 Hd62
Glăvile RO 175 Da64
Glavinica BG 181 Ec68
Glavnik KSV 178 Bb71
Glāžškūnis LV 106 Kc51
Gleann Cholm Cille IRL 8 Bd16
Gleba PL 122 Jc33
Głębock PL 122 Hd30
Głębock PL 122 Ja30
Głębocz Wielki PL 123 Jd34
Głębokie PL 128 Fd36
Głębokie PL 131 Kc39
Gledačevo BG 180 Ea73
Gledić SRB 178 Bb67
Gledica SRB 178 Ad68
Gledin RO 171 Dc57
Gleichen D 126 Db39
Glein N 70 Ed21
Gleinstätten A 144 Fd55
Gleisdorf A 144 Ga54
Glejbjerg DK 108 Da26
Glemsford GB 21 Ga26
Glenade IRL 8 Ca17
Glenariff or Waterfoot GB 9 Da16
Glenarm GB 9 Da16
Glenbarr GB 10 Db14
Glenbeigh IRL 12 Ba25
Glenborrodale GB 6 Db10
Glenbrittle GB 4 Da08
Glencolumbkille IRL 8 Bd16
Glendalough IRL 13 Cd22
Glendorragha IRL 8 Ca16
Glenealy IRL 13 Cd22
Gleneely IRL 9 Cc15
Glenegedale GB 6 Da13
Glenelg GB 4 Db08
Glenfarne IRL 8 Ca18
Glenfeshie Lodge GB 7 Ea09
Glenfinnan GB 6 Dc10
Glengarriff IRL 12 Bb26
Glénic F 33 Gc45
Glenkindie GB 7 Ec09
Glenlivet GB 7 Eb08
Glenluce GB 10 Dc16
Glenmaye GB 10 Dc19
Glenmore IRL 12 Bc22
Glenmore IRL 13 Cc24
Glennamaddy IRL 8 Bd20
Glenridding GB 11 Eb18
Glenrothes GB 7 Eb12
Glenties IRL 8 Ca16
Glen Trool Lodge GB 10 Dd16
Glère F 31 Kb41
Glesborg DK 101 Dd23
Glesien D 127 Eb40
Glesne N 93 Dc41
Glespin GB 10 Ea14
Gletness GB 5 Fa05
Gletsch CH 141 Ca55
Glewe, Neustadt- D 119 Ea33
Glewitz D 119 Ed31
Glibaći MNE 159 Ja67
Glienicke D 127 Ed36
Glifa GR 189 Ca83
Glifáda GR 182 Ab80
Glifáda GR 195 Cb87
Glikí GR 188 Ac81
Glikolar AL 182 Ad78
Glikomiliá GR 183 Bb80
Glimåkra S 111 Fb54
Glimboca RO 174 Cb62
Glin IRL 12 Bc23
Glina HR 152 Gb60
Glina RO 176 Eb66
Glinde D 118 Dc33
Glindow D 127 Ec37
Gliniec PL 130 Jb39
Glinik PL 139 Jd44
Glinjeni MD 173 Fb56
Glinka PL 129 Gb39
Glinojeck PL 122 Ja35
Glinsce IRL 8 Bb20
Glinsk IRL 8 Bb20
Glisno PL 128 Fd36
Glissjöberg S 87 Fb34
Gliwice PL 137 Hb43
Gljadino RUS 99 Mb40
Globicy RUS 99 Ma40
Globočica KSV 178 Ba72
Globočica KSV 178 Bb72
Głochów PL 129 Hb38
Glodeanu Sărat RO 176 Ec65
Glodeanu-Siliștea RO 176 Ec65
Glodeni MD 173 Fa55
Glodeni RO 171 Dc58
Glodeni RO 176 Dd64
Glödnitz A 144 Fa55
Głodowa PL 121 Gb31
Głodówko PL 122 Hd31
Glodževo BG 180 Eb68
Gloggnitz A 144 Ga52
Glogova RO 175 Cc64
Glogovac KSV 178 Ba71
Glogovac SRB 174 Bc66
Glogovnica HR 152 Gc58
Głogów PL 128 Ga39
Głogówek PL 137 Ha43
Głogowiec PL 130 Hc37
Głogów Małopolski PL 139 Ka43
Glomel F 27 Ea39
Glomfjord N 71 Fb19
Glommen S 102 Ec51
Glommersträsk S 72 Ha23
Glömminge S 103 Gb52
Glomno PL 122 Ja30
Głomsk PL 121 Gc33
Glonn D 143 Ea51
Glorenza I 142 Db55
Glória do Ribatejo P 50 Ac68
Glösa S 79 Fb30
Glos-la-Ferrière F 23 Ga37
Glossa GR 189 Cb83
Glössbo S 87 Gb37
Glossop GB 16 Ed21
Glostrup DK 109 Ec26
Glöte S 86 Fa34
Glottertal D 141 Ca50
Gloucester GB 19 Ec27
Gloup GB 5 Fa03
Głowaczów PL 130 Jc39
Głowczyce PL 121 Gc29
Glowe D 120 Fa29
Glöwen D 119 Eb35
Główiew PL 129 Ha37
Głowno PL 130 Hd38
Gložan SRB 153 Ja60
Gložane SRB 174 Bc66
Gložene BG 179 Cd68
Gložene BG 179 Da70
Głubczyce PL 137 Ha44
Głubczyn PL 121 Gc34
Glubokij RUS 203 Fc14
Glubokoe RUS 107 Mb50
Głuchołazy PL 137 Gd43
Głuchów PL 130 Ja38
Głuchowo PL 128 Fc36
Głuchowo PL 129 Gb37
Glücksburg D 108 Db28
Glückstadt D 118 Da32
Glud DK 108 Dc25
Gludsted DK 108 Db24
Gluhove RUS 203 Fb10
Gluhovo RUS 99 Mb40
Glumče BG 181 Ec72
Glumina BIH 153 Hd63
Glumslöv S 110 Ed55
Glumsø DK 109 Eb27
Glurns I 142 Db55
Glusburn GB 16 Ed20
Głusk PL 131 Kb40
Gluškovo RUS 113 Jb59
Głuszyca PL 129 Gb42
Glutt Lodge GB 5 Eb05
Glyn Ceiriog GB 15 Eb23
Glyncorrwg GB 19 Ea27
Glyngøre DK 100 Da22
Glyn-neath GB 19 Ea27
Glyxnäs S 96 Ha42
Gmünd A 136 Fc49
Gmünd A 143 Ed55
Gmund D 143 Ea52
Gmunden A 144 Fa52
Gmyrino RUS 99 Mb45
Gnarp S 87 Gb34
Gnarrenburg D 118 Da33
Gnas A 144 Ga55
Gneevgullia IRL 12 Bb25
Gneisenaustadt Schildau D 127 Ec40
Gneotina MK 183 Bb76
Gnesau A 144 Fa55
Gnesta S 96 Gc44
Gniazdowo PL 123 Jd34
Gniebing A 144 Ga55
Gniechowice PL 129 Gc41
Gniew PL 121 Hb32
Gniewino PL 121 Ha29
Gniewkowo PL 121 Hb35
Gniewoszów PL 131 Jd39
Gniezno PL 129 Gd36
Gnilišče RUS 99 Ld44
Gnissau D 118 Dc31
Gnisvärd S 104 Gd49
Gnjilane KSV 178 Bc71
Gnjili Potok MNE 159 Jb68
Gnocchetta I 150 Eb62
Gnoien D 119 Ec31
Gnojewo PL 121 Hb31
Gnojna PL 129 Gd42
Gnojnik PL 138 Jb45
Gnosall GB 15 Ec24
Gnosjö S 102 Fa50
G. Novaki SLO 151 Fa57
Goathland GB 11 Fb18
Gob an Choire IRL 8 Bb18
Gobasna MD 173 Ga55
Göbel TR 192 Fa81
Göbeller TR 191 Ec83
Gobesh AL 182 Ac77
Gobowen GB 15 Eb23
Göbül TR 192 Fb82
Göçbeyli TR 191 Ed83
Goce Delčev BG 184 Cc74
Goce Delčev BG 184 Cc75
Göcek TR 198 Fc91
Göçeler TR 187 Gd79
Göçeri TR 193 Hb87
Göçeri TR 199 Ha90
Göçeyayla TR 193 Gd84
Goch D 125 Bc38
Goch GB 19 Ea27
Gockenholz D 118 Dc35
Goczałki PL 137 Ha43
Goczałkowice-Zdrój PL 138 Hc45
Göd H 146 Hd52
Göda D 128 Fb41
Godačica SRB 178 Bb67
Godalming GB 20 Fb29
Godby FIN 96 Hc40
Goddelsheim D 126 Cd40
Godeanu RO 174 Cb64
Godeč BG 179 Cb70
Godegård S 95 Fd45
Godejorda N 78 Ed26
Godelleta E 54 Fb68
Gödence TR 191 Eb86
Gödenstorf D 118 Dc34
Goderville F 22 Fd34
Gödestad S 102 Ec51
Godętowo PL 121 Gd29
Godfjordbotn N 66 Fd12
Godiasco I 148 Cb61
Godinești RO 175 Cc63
Godkowo PL 122 Hd31
Godlaukis LT 114 Ka56
Godlewo PL 123 Ka35
Godmanchester GB 20 Fc25
Godmilje BIH 159 Hd64
Godnowa PL 129 Gd39
Gödöllő H 146 Hd52
Godovič SLO 151 Fa58
Godovo SRB 178 Ad69
Godów PL 131 Ka40
Godowa PL 139 Ka44
Godøynes N 66 Fc17
Godrano I 166 Ec84
Gödre H 152 Hb57
Godsted DK 109 Ea29
Godstone GB 20 Fd29
Godus BIH 153 Hd63
Godziesze Wielkie PL 129 Ha39
Godzikowice PL 129 Gd41
Godziszewo PL 121 Hb31
Godziszów PL 131 Kb41
Goente E 36 Bb53
Goes NL 124 Ab38
Goglio I 141 Ca56
Gogolin PL 137 Ha43
Gogołowice PL 129 Gb40
Gogoșari RO 180 Ea68
Gogoșu RO 174 Cb65
Gogoșu RO 175 Cd65
Göhl D 119 Dd30
Gohor RO 177 Fa61
Göhren D 120 Fa30
Goian MD 173 Fd57
Goián E 36 Ac58
Goiești RO 175 Cd65
Goirle NL 124 Ba38
Góis P 44 Ad64
Goito I 149 Db60
Goizueta E 39 Ec55
Gojan AL 163 Jc71
Gojna Gora SRB 159 Jc64
Gojsalići BIH 153 Hc63
Gójsk PL 122 Hd35
Gökağaç TR 192 Ga84
Gökbahçe TR 193 Gc84
Gökbel TR 191 Ed84
Gökbel TR 198 Fb91
Gökben TR 198 Fd92
Gökçalı TR 191 Ea81
Gokčanica SRB 178 Ba68
Gökçe TR 191 Ed84
Gökçe TR 199 Gd88
Gökçeada TR 185 Dd80
Gökçeağıl TR 191 Eb83
Gökçeahmet TR 192 Fa84
Gökçeağaç TR 197 Ec88
Gökçeayva TR 193 Ha82
Gökçebağ TR 199 Gc88
Gökçebayır TR 191 Ea81
Gökçedağ TR 192 Fc82
Gökçehüyük TR 199 Gd88
Gökçek TR 193 Gb87
Gökçek TR 205 Ga20
Gökçekaya TR 193 Gd81
Gökçekuyu TR 193 Gd83
Gökçeler TR 192 Fa84
Gökçeler TR 193 Gb84
Gökçen TR 192 Fa87
Gökçeören TR 186 Fc80
Gökçeören TR 192 Fb85
Gökçeören TR 198 Ga93
Gökçesu TR 186 Ga80
Gökçetepe TR 185 Eb78
Gökçeyazı TR 191 Ed82
Gökçeyazı TR 198 Ga93
Gökçimen TR 199 Hb89
Gökçukur TR 192 Fa83
Gökdere TR 191 Ec86
Gökdere TR 193 Gc81
Gökdiken TR 197 Ec90
Gökeyüp TR 192 Fb85
Gökhem S 102 Fa47
Gökkaya TR 192 Fa86
Gökköy TR 192 Fa82
Gökköy TR 192 Fb82
Gökler TR 192 Ga83
Gökler TR 192 Ga84
Göknebi TR 193 Gc83
Gökpınar TR 193 Hb84
Göksöğüt TR 193 Ha87
Göksu TR 187 Gd79
Göktaş TR 199 Gd88
Göktepe TR 187 Gc78
Göktepe TR 193 Hb84
Göktepe TR 198 Fb89
Gol N 85 Db38
Gola HR 152 Gd57
Gola PL 129 Ha40
Gołąb PL 131 Jd39
Gołąbki PL 131 Ka38
Golada E 36 Ba56
Golăiești RO 173 Fa57
Gołańcz PL 121 Gc35
Golany PL 122 Jb34
Goławin PL 130 Ja36
Gölbaşı TR 199 Gc88
Golborne GB 15 Ec21
Gölby FIN 96 Hc40
Gölçayır TR 193 Ha86
Golce PL 121 Gb33
Golcea RO 179 Cd67
Gölçeler TR 191 Ec85
Gölcük TR 185 Ec78
Gölcük TR 186 Fd80
Gölcük TR 186 Ga79
Gölcük TR 187 Ha79
Gölcük TR 192 Fa83
Gölcük TR 192 Fa86
Gölcük TR 192 Fb82
Gölcük TR 192 Fd84
Gölcük TR 198 Ga90
Gölcük TR 199 Gc92
Golčův Jeníkov CZ 136 Fd45
Golczewo PL 120 Fc32
Gołdap PL 123 Jd30
Goldbach D 126 Dc41
Goldbach D 134 Cd44
Goldbeck D 119 Eb35
Goldberg D 119 Eb33
Goldcliff GB 19 Eb28
Golden N 63 Ja10
Goldelund D 108 Da29
Golden IRL 13 Ca24
Golden Cross GB 20 Fd30
Goldenstedt D 117 Cc35
Goldkronach D 135 Ea44
Goldsborough GB 11 Fb18
Goldscheuer D 133 Ca49
Göle TR 205 Ga19
Golec BG 180 Db70
Gölecil TR 186 Fb80
Goleen IRL 12 Ba27
Golegã P 50 Ac67
Golem AL 182 Ab75
Golemo Selo BG 179 Cb72
Golemo Selo SRB 178 Bd71
Goleni MD 173 Fa54
Golenice PL 120 Fc35
Goleniów PL 120 Fc33
Goleš BG 181 Fa68
Goleš SRB 179 Ca72
Golești RO 175 Db63
Golești RO 176 Ed62
Golesze PL 130 Hd39
Goleszyn PL 122 Hd35
Golfe-Juan F 43 Kc53
Golfo Aranci I 168 Cc74
Gölhisar TR 197 Fa88
Gölhisar TR 198 Ga90
Golica BG 181 Ed71
Golicyno RUS 202 Ed10
Golina PL 129 Ha37
Goliševo LV 107 Ld50
Goljama Željazna BG 180 Db70
Goljam Dervent BG 185 Ec74
Goljam izvor BG 185 Dd75
Goljam Manastir BG 180 Eb73
Goljamo Asenovo BG 185 Dd74
Goljamo Belovo BG 179 Cd73
Goljamo Gradište BG 180 Ea69
Goljamo Kamenjane BG 185 Dd76
Goljamo Vranovo BG 180 Eb68
Gölkaşı TR 199 Hb88
Gölkaya TR 187 Gd78
Gołkowice PL 138 Jb46
Gölköy TR 199 Gb92
Gölköy TR 205 Fc20
Gölle H 145 Hb56
Göllersdorf A 145 Gb50
Gollin D 120 Fa34
Golling an der Salzach A 143 Ed52
Göllingen D 127 Dd40
Gollomboc AL 182 Ba76
Gollrad A 144 Fd52
Golm D 127 Ed37
Golma N 77 Db30
Gölmarmara TR 192 Fa85
Golmbach D 126 Da38
Golokino RUS 113 Jb58
Gološčapy RUS 107 Mb50
Gölova TR 191 Ec87
Gölova TR 199 Gb91
Gölova TR 199 Gb92
Gölpazarı TR 187 Gc80
Golpejas E 45 Cb62
Golspie GB 5 Ea06
Golßen D 128 Fa38
Golubac SRB 174 Bd64
Golub-Dobrzyń PL 122 Hc34
Golubevo RUS 113 Ja59
Golubic HR 158 Gb64
Golubinci SRB 153 Jb61
Golubinje SRB 174 Ca65
Golubovicy RUS 99 Ma40
Gołuchów PL 129 Ha38
Golvari LV 107 Lc50
Gölyaka TR 186 Fa80
Gölyaka TR 193 Hb86
Gölyaka TR 199 Ha88
Gölyazı TR 186 Fc80
Gołymin-Ośrodek PL 122 Jb35
Golzow D 127 Ec37
Golzow D 128 Fb36
Gomadingen D 134 Cd49
Gomagoi I 142 Db56
Gomantlaukis LT 113 Jc55
Gómara E 47 Eb60
Gomaringen D 134 Cc49
Gomáti GR 184 Cc79
Gomba H 146 Ja53
Gömbe TR 198 Ga92
Gombergean F 29 Gb41
Gombo I 155 Da65
Gombrèn E 41 Gd58
Gömce TR 192 Ga87
Gömeç TR 191 Eb83
Gomecello E 45 Cc62
Gomes Aires P 58 Ac73
Gomezserracín E 46 Da61
Gomirje HR 151 Fd60
Gomljamo Kruševo BG 181 Ec73
Gommern D 127 Ea38
Gommersheim D 133 Cb46
Gomont F 24 Hd34
Gömü TR 193 Gd84
Gomulin PL 130 Hd40
Gomunice PL 130 Hd40
Gonäs S 95 Fc41
Gönc H 139 Jd49
Göncek TR 192 Fd83
Goncelin F 35 Jd48
Goncourt F 31 Jc38
Gończyce PL 131 Jd38
Gondelsheim D 134 Cc47
Gondomar E 36 Ad58
Gondomar P 44 Ad61
Gondorf D 133 Ca43
Gondrame E 36 Bb56
Gondrecourt-le-Château F 25 Jc37
Gondreville F 25 Jc37
Gondrin F 40 Fd53
Gönen TR 185 Ed80
Gönen TR 199 Gc88
Gonfaron F 42 Ka54
Gonfreville l'Orcher F 22 Fd35
Goni GR 183 Bd80
Goni I 169 Cb78
Goniądz PL 123 Ka32
Gonnesa I 169 Bd79

Gonnosfanadiga – Grenči

Gonnosfanadiga I 169 Bd79
Gonnosnò I 169 Ca78
Gonsans F 31 Jd42
Gontán E 36 Bc54
Gönü TR 186 Fb80
Gőnyü H 145 Ha52
Gonzaga I 149 Db61
Gonzar E 36 Bb56
Gooderstone GB 17 Ga24
Goodwick GB 14 Db26
Goole GB 16 Fb21
Goor NL 117 Bd36
Gopegi E 38 Ea56
Goppenstein CH 141 Bd56
Göppingen D 134 Da49
Gor E 61 Dd74
Gora HR 152 Gb60
Góra PL 122 Ja35
Góra PL 129 Gb39
Gora RUS 107 Ma47
Gora Bobyli RUS 107 Mb47
Gorafe E 61 Dd74
Gorai RUS 107 Ma49
Gorainiai LT 113 Jc56
Goraiolo I 155 Db64
Goraj PL 131 Kb41
Gorajec-Zagroble PL 131 Kb42
Góra Kalwaria PL 130 Jc37
Goran BG 180 Db70
Goráni GR 194 Bc89
Goransko MNE 159 Hd67
Góra Puławska PL 131 Jd39
Góra Świętej Anny PL 137 Ha43
Gorawino PL 120 Fd31
Goražde BIH 159 Hd65
Gorban RO 173 Fb58
Gorbănești RO 172 Ed55
Görbeháza H 147 Jd51
Gorbovo RUS 107 Ld47
Gorbunova Gora RUS 107 Ld48
Görcsöny H 152 Hb58
Gorczenica PL 122 Hc34
Gördalen S 86 Ed36
Gordaliza del Pino E 37 Cd58
Gordes F 42 Jc53
Gördes TR 192 Fb84
Gordinești MD 173 Fa54
Gørding DK 108 Da26
Gordoa E 39 Eb56
Gordoe RUS 113 Jb59
Gordola CH 148 Cb57
Gordon GB 11 Ec14
Gordona I 142 Cc56
Gordoncillo E 37 Cc58
Gördsbyn S 94 Ed42
Gorelki RUS 203 Fa11
Gorelovo RUS 99 Mb39
Gorenja Kanomlja SLO 151 Fa58
Gorenja Trebuša SLO 151 Fa58
Gorenja vas SLO 151 Fb58
Gorey GBJ 26 Ec36
Gorey IRL 13 Cd23
Gorgast D 128 Fb36
Görgeteg H 152 Gd57
Gorgogiri GR 188 Bb81
Gorgoglione I 162 Gb76
Gorgonzola I 149 Cc59
Gorgopotamos GR 189 Bc83
Gorgota RO 176 Eb65
Gorica BG 180 Ea70
Gorica BG 181 Ed72
Gorica BG 181 Fa71
Gorica BIH 158 Gd64
Gorica BIH 158 Gd66
Gorica BIH 159 Hc69
Gorica HR 157 Fd64
Goricë AL 182 Ba76
Gorice SLO 151 Fb57
Goricy RUS 202 Ed09
Gorinchem NL 124 Ba37
Goring GB 20 Fa28
Gorino I 150 Eb62
Goritsá GR 194 Bc89
Goritz D 119 Ec31
Gorizia I 150 Ed58
Gorjačevo RUS 107 Mb50
Gorjačij Ključ RUS 205 Fc17
Gorjani SRB 159 Jb65
Gorjão P 50 Ad67
Gorka RUS 99 Lc44
Gorka RUS 99 Ma42
Górki PL 130 Hc36
Górki PL 138 Jc43
Gorki RUS 99 Mb40
Gorki RUS 99 Mb40
Gorki RUS 107 Mb47
Górki Noteckie PL 120 Fd35
Gørlev DK 109 Ea26
Gorlice PL 138 Jc45
Görlitz D 128 Fc41
Gørløse DK 109 Ec25
Görmar D 126 Dc40
Gormaz E 46 Dd61
Görmin D 119 Ed31
Gorna Bešovica BG 179 Cd70
Gorna Graštica BG 179 Cb72
Gorna Kremena BG 179 Cd70
Gorna Lipnica BG 180 Dd70
Gorna Mitropolija BG 180 Db69
Gorna Orjahovica BG 180 Dd70
Gorna Rosica BG 180 Dc71
Gorna Studena BG 180 Dd69
Gornau D 127 Ed42
Gornești RO 171 Dc58
Gornet RO 176 Eb64
Gornet Cricov RO 176 Eb64
Gorni Cibăr BG 179 Cd68
Gorni Dăbnik BG 179 Da69
Gorni Lom BG 179 Cb68
Gorni Okol BG 179 Cc72
Gornja Badanja SRB 153 Ja62
Gornja Belica MK 183 Bb74
Gornja Bistra HR 151 Ga58
Gornjackij RUS 203 Fc14
Gornja Deržnica BIH 158 Ha66
Gornja Golubinja BIH 152 Hb63
Gornja Grabovica BIH 158 Ha66
Gornja Klina KSV 178 Ba70
Gornja Lisina SRB 179 Ca71
Gornja Ljubovida SRB 153 Ja63
Gornja Ljuta BIH 159 Hc66
Gornjane SRB 174 Ca66
Gornja Ploča HR 151 Ga63
Gornja Radgona SLO 144 Ga56
Gornja Rogatica SRB 153 Ja58
Gornja Sabanta SRB 174 Bb66
Gornja Stubica HR 151 Ga58
Gornja Suvaja BIH 152 Gb62
Gornja Trepča MNE 159 Hd68
Gornja Trešnjevica SRB 153 Jc63
Gornja Tuzla BIH 153 Hc62
Gornja Vranjska SRB 153 Jb62
Gornje Dubočke MNE 159 Hc68
Gornje Jelenje HR 151 Fc60
Gornje Komarevo HR 152 Gb60
Gornje Lopiže SRB 159 Jb66
Gornje Lopiže SRB 178 Ad68
Gornje Ratkovo BIH 152 Gc63
Gornje Taborište HR 151 Ga60
Gornje Vinovo HR 158 Gb65
Gornje Vratno HR 152 Gb57
Gornje Zuniče SRB 179 Ca68
Gornji Banjani SRB 159 Jc64
Gornji Čevljanovići BIH 159 Hc64
Gornji Dolac HR 158 Gc66
Gornji Dolič SLO 151 Fd57
Gornji Grad SLO 151 Fc57
Gornji Humac HR 158 Gc67
Gornji Jabolčište MK 183 Bb74
Gornji Kamengrad BIH 152 Gc62
Gornji Kokoti MNE 159 Ja70
Gornji Kraljevec HR 152 Gb57
Gornji Krušje MK 182 Ba75
Gornji Lapac HR 152 Gb63
Gornji Lukavac BIH 159 Hc67
Gornji Malovan BIH 158 Gd65
Gornji Miklouš HR 152 Gc59
Gornji Milanovac SRB 159 Jc64
Gornji Muć HR 158 Gc66
Gornji Nemzi MK 178 Bb73
Gornji Orizari MK 183 Bc74
Gornji Podgradci BIH 152 Gd61
Gornji Rajić HR 152 Gd60
Gornji Ribnik BIH 152 Gc63
Gornji Stepos SRB 178 Bc68
Gornji Vakuf = Uskoplje BIH 158 Ha65
Górno PL 130 Jb41
Gorno Botevo BG 180 Dd73
Gorno Izvorovo BG 180 Dd72
Gorno Kamarci BG 179 Cd71
Gorno Novo Selo BG 180 Dc72
Gorno Ozirovo BG 179 Cc69
Gornyj RUS 203 Ga11
Goro I 150 Ea62
Gorobinci MK 178 Bc73
Gorodec RUS 99 Mb44
Gorodec RUS 203 Fb09
Gorodenka EST 99 Lc42
Gorodišče RUS 203 Fd11
Gorodkovo RUS 113 Jc57
Gorodovikovsk RUS 205 Fd16
Górowo Iławeckie PL 122 Ja30
Gor. Primišlje HR 151 Fd61
Gorran Heaven GB 18 Db32
Gorre F 33 Gb47
Gorredijk NL 117 Bc34
Gorron F 28 Fb38
Görsbach D 127 Dd40
Görsdorf D 127 Ed38
Goršečnoe RUS 203 Fa13
Gorseinon GB 19 Dd27
Górsk PL 121 Ha34
Gorska poljana BG 185 Ec74
Gorski izvor BG 184 Dc74
Gorsko Kosovo BG 180 Dc70
Gorsko Novo Selo BG 180 Ea70
Gorsko Slivovo BG 180 Dc70
Gørslev DK 109 Eb26
Gorssel NL 117 Bc36
Gort IRL 12 Bd22
Gortaclare GB 9 Cc17
Gortahork IRL 9 Cb15
Gort an Choirce IRL 9 Cb15
Gorteen IRL 8 Bd19
Gortin GB 9 Cc16
Gortipohl A 142 Da54
Gortmore IRL 8 Bb20
Gortymadden IRL 12 Bd21
Goruia RO 174 Bd63
Gorun BG 181 Fc69
Gorv N 84 Cb35
Görvik S 79 Fd29
Görwihl D 141 Ca52
Gorzanów PL 137 Gb43
Görzig D 127 Eb39
Görzig D 128 Fb37
Görzke D 127 Eb37
Gorzkowice PL 130 Hd40
Gorzków-Osada PL 131 Kc40
Górzna PL 121 Gc33
Górzno PL 122 Hd34
Górzno PL 129 Ha39
Górzno PL 131 Jd38
Gorzów Śląski PL 129 Hb41
Gorzów Wielkopolski PL 128 Fd36
Gorzupia PL 128 Fd39
Górzyca PL 120 Fd31
Górzyca PL 128 Fc36
Gorzyce PL 131 Jd42
Gorzyce PL 137 Hb45
Górzyn PL 128 Fc39
Gorzyń PL 128 Ga36
Goržžam N 64 Jd07
Gosaldo I 150 Ea57
Gosau A 143 Ed53
Gosberton GB 17 Fc23
Göschenen CH 141 Cb55
Göscheneralp CH 141 Cb55
Gościcino PL 121 Ha29
Gościęcin PL 137 Ha44
Gościeradów PL 131 Ka41
Gościkowo Jordanowo PL 128 Fd37
Gościm PL 120 Ga35
Gościno PL 120 Fd31
Gościsław PL 129 Gb41
Gościszewo PL 121 Hb31
Gościszów PL 128 Fd41
Gosdorf A 144 Ga55
Goseck D 127 Ea41
Gosen-Neu Zittau D 128 Fa37
Gosforth GB 10 Ea18
Gosheim D 142 Cc50
Goslar D 126 Dc38
Gosławice PL 129 Ha37
Goślice PL 130 Hd36
Gospić HR 151 Fd63
Gospodinci BG 184 Cd75
Gospodinci SRB 153 Jb60
Gospori LV 107 Lb52
Gosport GB 20 Fa30
Gossa D 127 Ec39
Gössäter S 102 Fa46
Gossau CH 142 Cd53
Gössel A 144 Fa52
Gössenheim D 134 Da44
Gossensass I 143 Dd55
Gösslunda S 102 Ed46
Gößnitz D 127 Eb42
Gößweinstein D 135 Dd45
Gostavățu RO 180 Db67
Gosticy RUS 99 Lc42
Gostifisht AL 182 Ad78
Gostilica BG 180 Dd70
Gostilicy RUS 99 Ma40
Gostilja BG 179 Da68
Gostiņi LV 106 La51
Gostinja BG 180 Db70
Gostinu RO 180 Ea67
Gostivar MK 178 Ba73
Göstling an der Ybbs A 144 Fc52
Gostomia PL 121 Gb34
Gostun SRB 159 Jb67
Gostycyn PL 121 Gd33
Gostyń PL 129 Gc38
Gostynin PL 130 Hd36
Goszcz PL 129 Gd40
Goszczanów PL 129 Hb39
Goszczanówko PL 128 Fd36
Goszczyn PL 130 Jb38
Goszczyna PL 129 Gc42
Göta S 102 Ec47
Göteborg S 102 Eb49
Götene S 102 Fa46
Gotești MD 177 Fb61
Göteve S 102 Fa47
Gotha D 126 Dc41
Gotham GB 16 Fa23
Gothem S 104 Ha49
Götlunda S 95 Fd43
Gotlybiškiai LT 114 Ka57
Gotovuša MNE 159 Ja66
Gottböle FIN 89 Hd33
Gottby FIN 96 Hb41
Göttersdorf D 135 Ec49
Gotteszell D 135 Ec48
Gottfrieding D 135 Eb49
Göttingen D 126 Db39
Gottlob RO 174 Bb60
Gottmadingen D 142 Cc52
Gottne S 80 Gd30
Gottow D 127 Ed38
Gottröra S 96 Gd42
Gøttrup DK 100 Db21
Gottsdorf A 144 Fa50
Gottskär S 102 Eb50
Götzendorf an der Leitha A 145 Gc51
Götzis A 142 Cd53
Gouarec F 27 Ea39
Gouda NL 116 Ad36
Goudargues F 42 Ja52
Goudhurst GB 20 Fd29
Gouesnou F 26 Db38
Goulémi GR 189 Ca84
Goulven F 26 Dc37
Gouménissa GR 183 Bd77
Goúmero GR 188 Ba86
Gourdon F 33 Gb50
Gourdon F 43 Kc53
Gourgançon F 24 Hc37
Gourgé F 28 Fc44
Gouriá GR 188 Ba84
Gourin F 27 Dd39
Gournay-en-Bray F 23 Gc35
Goúrnes GR 200 Da95
Gournier F 35 Ka50
Gourock GB 6 Dc13
Gourri CY 206 Jb97
Gourville F 32 Fc47
Goussainville F 23 Gd36
Gouveia P 44 Bb63
Goúves GR 189 Cb83
Goúves GR 195 Bd90
Gouvia GR 182 Ab80
Gouvy B 133 Bb43
Gouzeaucourt F 24 Hb33
Gouzon F 33 Gd45
Goveđari HR 158 Ha68
Goven F 28 Ed39
Governolo I 149 Dc61
Gowarczów PL 130 Jb40
Gowidlino PL 121 Gd30
Goworowo PL 122 Jc34
Gowran IRL 13 Cc23
Göykaya TR 186 Fa75
Göynük TR 187 Gd80
Göynük TR 193 Gd85
Göynük TR 199 Gb92
Göynükbelen TR 192 Fd81
Gózd PL 130 Jc39
Gozdnica PL 128 Fc40
Gozdowice PL 120 Fb35
Gözler TR 192 Fd87
Gozon = Luanco E 37 Cc53
Gözpınar TR 193 Hb86
Gozzano I 148 Ca58
Graal-Müritz D 119 Eb30
Graauw NL 124 Ac39
Grab BIH 159 Hc67
Grab BIH 159 Hc69
Grab MNE 159 Jb67
Grab PL 129 Gd38
Grabarka PL 131 Kb36
Grabbskog FIN 97 Jd40
Grabe D 126 Dc40
Gräben D 127 Ec37
Graben-Neudorf D 133 Cb47
Grabenstätt D 143 Eb52
Grabica PL 130 Hd39
Grabice PL 128 Fc38
Grabjan AL 182 Ab76
Grabnik PL 123 Jd31
Gräbo S 102 Ec48
Graboszyce PL 138 Hd45
Grabovac HR 151 Ga61
Grabovac HR 153 Hc59
Grabovac HR 158 Gd66
Grabovac SRB 153 Jb62
Grabovci SRB 153 Jb62
Grabovica SRB 174 Cb65
Grabovnica SRB 178 Bc69
Grabow D 119 Ea34
Grabow D 127 Eb37
Grabów PL 130 Hc37
Grabowhöfe D 119 Ec33
Grabowiec PL 123 Kb35
Grabowiec PL 131 Kd41
Grabówka PL 123 Kb33
Grabów nad Prosną PL 129 Ha39
Grabownica Starzeńska PL 139 Ka45
Grabowno PL 121 Gc34
Grabowno Wielkie PL 129 Gd40
Grabowo PL 121 Gc35
Grabowo PL 122 Jb31
Grabowo PL 123 Jd30
Grabowo-Skorupki PL 122 Jb33
Grabowskie PL 123 Jd32
Grabupiai LT 113 Jc56
Gračac HR 157 Ga64
Gračanica BIH 152 Hb62
Gračanica BIH 153 Hd63
Gračanica BIH 158 Ha64
Gračanica BIH 158 Ha65
Gračanica SRB 159 Jb66
Graçay F 29 Gc42
Gracciano I 156 Dd67
Gracen AL 182 Ac75
Gračenica HR 152 Gc59
Gračevka RUS 205 Fd16
Grächen CH 141 Bd56
Gračišće HR 151 Fa60
Gracze PL 129 Gd42
Gradac BIH 158 Hb68
Gradac HR 158 Ha67
Gradac MNE 159 Hd69
Gradac MNE 159 Ja66
Gradac SLO 151 Fd59
Gradac SRB 178 Ba68
Gradačac BIH 153 Hc61
Gradara I 156 Eb65
Graddis N 71 Fd19
Gräddö S 96 Ha42
Gradec BG 179 Cb67
Gradec BG 180 Eb71
Gradec HR 152 Gb58
Gradec MK 183 Bd75
Gradec MK 183 Ca74
Gradefes E 37 Cd57
Grades A 144 Fb55
Gradešnica BG 179 Cd69
Gradešnica MK 183 Bc76
Gradevo BG 183 Cb74
Gradina BG 180 Dd70
Grădinari RO 174 Bd63
Grădinari RO 175 Db65
Gradinarovo BG 181 Ed70
Grădinița MD 173 Ga59
Gradisca d'Isonzo I 150 Ed58
Gradiška BIH 152 Gd61
Gradište BG 180 Dc69
Gradište BG 180 Dc70
Gradište HR 153 Hc61
Gradiște MD 173 Fd59
Gradište MK 178 Bc73
Gradište SRB 179 Ca68
Gradište SRB 179 Ca69
Grădiștea RO 175 Da64
Grădiștea RO 176 Eb65
Grădiștea RO 176 Ed63
Grădiștea RO 180 Eb67
Grădiștea RO 181 Ed67
Grădiștea de Munte RO 175 Cd61
Gradki PL 122 Ja31
Gradna SRB 178 Ba68
Gradnica BG 180 Dc71
Grado E 37 Cb54
Grado I 150 Ed59
Grådö S 95 Ga40
Gradojević SRB 153 Ja62
Gradoli I 156 Dd69
Gradsko MK 183 Bc74
Gradskovo SRB 179 Ca67
Grad Straža SLO 151 Fc59
Grady PL 137 Gd43
Grądy-Woniecko PL 123 Ka33
Graena E 60 Dc74
Græsted DK 109 Ec24
Gräfelfing D 143 Dd51
Grafenau D 135 Ed48
Gräfenberg D 135 Dd46
Grafengehaig D 135 Ea44
Gräfenhainichen D 127 Ec39
Grafenhausen D 141 Cb51
Gräfenroda D 126 Dc42
Grafenstein A 144 Fb56
Gräfenthal D 135 Dd43
Gräfentonna D 126 Dc41
Grafenwiesen D 135 Ec47
Grafenwöhr D 135 Ea45
Grafhorst D 127 Dd36
Graf-Ignatievo BG 180 Db73
Gräfinau-Angstedt D 127 Dd42
Grafing D 143 Ea51
Grafling D 135 Ec48
Grafrath D 143 Dd51
Gräfsnäs S 102 Ec48
Gräftåvallen S 79 Fb31
Graglia I 148 Bd59
Gragnague F 40 Gc54
Gragnano I 161 Fb75
Grahovo MNE 159 Hd69
Grahovo SLO 151 Fa57
Grahovo SLO 151 Fb59
Graig na Manach IRL 13 Cc24
Graigue Hill IRL 13 Cc23
Graiguenamanagh IRL 13 Cc24
Grain GB 21 Ga28
Grainet D 136 Fa49
Grainville-Langannerie F 22 Fc36
Graja de Iniesta E 53 Ec67
Grajal de Campos E 37 Cd58
Grajduri RO 173 Fa58
Grajewo PL 123 Ka32
Grajvoron RUS 203 Fa14
Gralewo PL 122 Ja35
Gralhos P 44 Bb59
Gralhos P 45 Bd60
Gralla A 144 Fd55
Gram DK 108 Da27
Gramada BG 179 Cb67
Gramais A 142 Db53
Gramastetten A 144 Fb50
Gramat F 33 Gc50
Gramatikó GR 189 Bc82
Gramatikó GR 189 Cc86
Gramatikovo BG 186 Fa74
Gramatsneusiedl A 145 Gb51
Grambow D 120 Fb33
Graméni GR 184 Cd76
Graméno GR 182 Ad80
Grămești RO 172 Eb55
Grametten A 136 Fd48
Grammendorf D 119 Ed31
Gramméni Oxiá GR 188 Bb83
Grammichele I 167 Fb87
Grámmos GR 182 Ad78
Gramont F 40 Ga53
Gramsdale GB 6 Cd07
Gramsh AL 182 Ac76
Gramsh AL 182 Ac77
Gramsh i Lushnjes AL 182 Ab75
Gramzda LV 113 Jb53
Gramzow D 120 Fb34
Gran N 85 Ea40
Granabeg IRL 13 Cd22
Granada E 60 Db75
Granaione I 155 Dc68
Gran Alacant E 55 Fb72
Granard IRL 9 Cb20
Gránard IRL 9 Cb20
Granås S 71 Fd22
Granåsen N 86 Ec36
Granåsen S 79 Gb28
Granátula de Calatrava E 52 Db70
Granberg S 73 Hb23
Granberget S 72 Gc23
Granberget S 79 Gb27
Granbergsträsk S 73 Hb24
Granbo S 79 Fc30
Granboda FIN 96 Hc41
Granby GB 16 Fb23
Grand F 30 Jb38
Grandas de Salime E 37 Bd55
Grand-Auverne F 28 Fa41
Grand-Bornand F 35 Ka46
Grandcamp-Maisy F 22 Fa35
Grand-Champ F 27 Eb40
Grandchamps F 30 Hb40
Grandcour CH 141 Bc54
Grand-Couronne F 23 Ga35
Grand Crohot Océan F 32 Fa50
Grandecourt F 31 Jc40
Grandes E 46 Cd63
Grandfontaine F 25 Kb37
Grand-Fort-Philippe F 21 Gc30
Grand-Fougeray F 28 Ed40
Grand Halleux B 125 Bb42
Grândola P 50 Ab70
Grandpré F 24 Ja35
Grandrieu F 34 Hc50
Grand-Rullecourt F 23 Gd32
Grandson CH 141 Bb54
Grandtully GB 7 Ea10
Grand-Vabre F 33 Ha51
Grandvelle-et-le-Perrenot F 31 Jd41
Grandvillars F 31 Kb40
Grandvilliers F 23 Gc34
Grane F 34 Jb50
Grane N 70 Fa23
Grañén E 48 Fb60
Grañena E 60 Db73
Grangärde S 95 Fc40
Grangärdes Hästberg S 95 Fc40
Grange IRL 13 Ca25
Grangeford IRL 13 Cc23
Grange-le-Bocage F 30 Hb38
Grangemouth GB 10 Ea13
Grängesberg S 95 Fc41
Granges-sur-Aube F 24 Hc37
Granges-sur-Vologne F 31 Ka38
Grängshyttan S 95 Fc42
Grängsjö S 87 Gb36
Granheim N 92 Cd44
Granhult S 68 Hc17
Granica BG 179 Ca72
Granica SRB 159 Ja66
Gräniceri RO 170 Bd58
Granicești RO 172 Eb55
Gränichen CH 141 Ca53
Granieri I 167 Fb87
Graninge S 79 Gb31
Granit BG 180 Dc73
Granítis GR 184 Cd76
Granitola Torretta I 166 Eb85
Granítsa GR 188 Ba82
Granitsopoúla GR 182 Ac80
Granja P 51 Bb70
Granja de Moreruela E 45 Cb59
Granja de Torrehermosa E 51 Cb71
Grankulla FIN 98 Kb39
Grankullavik S 104 Gc50
Granliden S 79 Ga25
Granmoen N 70 Fa21
Gränna S 103 Fb48
Grannäs S 71 Ga24
Grannäs S 72 Gb22
Granne PL 123 Ka35
Grannes N 71 Fb23
Granö S 80 Ha27
Granollers E 49 Ha61
Granowo PL 129 Gb37
Grańs E 36 Bb53
Grans F 42 Jc54
Gransee D 119 Ed35
Gränsfors S 87 Gb34
Gränsgård S 72 Gc23
Gransha GB 10 Db16
Gransherad N 93 Db42
Gransholm S 103 Fc52
Gransjö S 72 Gd24
Gransjö S 73 Hc21
Gransjøbergstra N 86 Eb37
Gränsjön S 94 Ec42
Grantham GB 16 Fb23
Grantown-on-Spey GB 7 Eb08
Granträsk S 73 Hc22
Granträsk S 80 Gd27
Granträskmark S 73 Hc23
Grantshouse GB 11 Ed13
Granucillo E 45 Cb59
Granum S 111 Fc54
Granusjön S 86 Fa36
Granvik S 103 Fc46
Granvika N 85 Ea35
Granville F 22 Ed37
Granvin N 84 Cc39
Granzin D 119 Eb33
Grapska BIH 152 Hb62
Grasbakken N 65 Kb07
Grasberg D 118 Cd34
Gräsbrickan S 86 Ed38
Graševo BG 184 Cd74
Gräsgård S 111 Gb54
Grasleben D 127 Dd37
Gräsmark S 94 Ed41
Grasmere GB 11 Eb18
Gräsmyr S 80 Hb28
Gräsö S 96 Gd40
Grassano I 162 Gb75
Grassau D 127 Ed39
Grassau D 143 Eb52
Grasse F 43 Kc53
Grassington GB 11 Ed19
Gråssjön S 87 Fd32
Gråsten DK 108 Db28
Grästorp S 102 Ed47
Gratallops E 48 Ga62
Gråtånes N 71 Fc18
Gratangsbotn N 67 Gb13
Gråtanliden S 79 Gb25
Gratens F 40 Gb55
Gratentour F 40 Gc54
Gratia RO 176 Dd66
Grătiești MD 173 Fd58
Gratkorn A 144 Fd54
Gråträsk S 72 Ha23
Gratteri I 167 Fa84
Grattersdorf D 135 Ed49
Gratwein A 144 Fd54
Grauballe DK 108 Db24
Grau-d'Agde F 41 Hc55
Graulhet F 41 Gd54
Graulinster L 133 Bb44
Graun im Vinschgau I 142 Db55
Graupa D 128 Fa41
Graus E 48 Fd59
Grava S 94 Fa43
Grávalos E 47 Ec59
Gravås S 94 Ed42
Grávavencsellő H 147 Ka50
Gravberget N 86 Ec38
Gravdal N 66 Fb14
Grave NL 125 Bb38
Gräve S 95 Fc44
Gravedona I 149 Cc57
Graveley GB 20 Fc25
Gravelines F 21 Gd30
Gravellona Toce I 148 Ca57
Gravenhage, 's- NL 116 Ad36
Gravens DK 108 Db26
Gravenwiesbach D 134 Cc43
Graveri LV 115 Ld53
Gravesend GB 20 Fd28
Graveson F 42 Jb53
Graviá GR 189 Bc84
Gravigny F 23 Gb36
Gravina di Puglia I 162 Gc75
Gravmark S 80 Hb27
Gravoúna GR 184 Da77
Gravvik N 78 Ec25
Gray F 31 Jc41
Grays GB 20 Fd28
Graz A 144 Fd54
Grazalema E 59 Cb76
Grążawy PL 122 Hd33
Gražiškiai LT 114 Ka59
Grazzanise I 161 Fa74
Grazzano Visconti I 149 Cd61
Grčarice SLO 151 Fc59
Grčina KSV 178 Ad71
Grdelica SRB 178 Bd70
Greaca RO 180 Eb67
Greåker N 93 Ea44
Great Ayton GB 11 Fb18
Great Bentley GB 21 Ga27
Great Bircham GB 17 Ga23
Great Cornard GB 21 Ga26
Great Cubley GB 16 Ed23
Great Dalby GB 16 Fb24
Great Dunmow GB 20 Fd27
Great Eccleston GB 15 Eb20
Great Ellingham GB 17 Ga24
Great Glen GB 16 Fb24
Great Grimsby GB 17 Fc21
Great Hanwood GB 15 Eb24
Great Harwood GB 15 Ec20
Great Hockham GB 21 Ga25
Great Horkesley GB 21 Ga26
Great Langton GB 11 Fa18
Great Malvern GB 15 Ec26
Great Milton GB 20 Fa27
Great Ponton GB 16 Fb23
Great Shefford GB 20 Fa28
Great Smeaton GB 11 Fa18
Great Snoring GB 17 Ga23
Greatstone-on-Sea GB 21 Ga30
Great Tew GB 20 Fa26
Great Torrington GB 19 Dd29
Great Totham GB 21 Ga27
Great Wakering GB 21 Ga28
Great Yarmouth GB 17 Gc24
Great Yeldham GB 20 Fd26
Grebănu RO 176 Ed63
Grebbestad S 94 Ea45
Grebci BIH 158 Hb68
Grebenac SRB 174 Bc63
Grebenau D 126 Da42
Grebenhain D 134 Cd43
Grebenişu de Câmpie RO 171 Db58
Grebenstein D 126 Da39
Grebin D 118 Dc30
Grębków PL 131 Jd36
Greblești MD 173 Fc57
Grebneva LV 107 Ld50
Grebo S 103 Ga47
Grębocin PL 121 Hb34
Grębów PL 131 Jd42
Grečanica KSV 178 Bb71
Greccio I 156 Eb70
Grecești RO 175 Cc65
Greci I 161 Fd73
Greci RO 175 Cc65
Greci RO 177 Fb64
Gredelj BIH 159 Hc67
Greding D 135 Dd48
Gredstedbro DK 108 Da26
Greencastle GB 9 Da19
Greencastle IRL 9 Cd15
Greenfield GB 15 Eb22
Green Hammerton GB 11 Fa19
Green Hammerton GB 16 Fa20
Greenhead GB 11 Ec16
Greenlaw GB 11 Ec14
Greenock GB 6 Dc13
Greenodd GB 11 Eb19
Greenway GB 19 Ea31
Greenwich GB 20 Fc28
Greetland GB 16 Ed21
Greetsiel D 117 Ca32
Greffen D 126 Cc37
Grefrath D 125 Bc39
Gregurovec HR 152 Gb58
Greifenberg D 120 Fa34
Greifenberg D 143 Dd51
Greifenburg A 143 Ed55
Greifswald D 119 Ed31
Grein A 144 Fc51
Greipstad N 62 Gc10
Greipstad N 92 Cd47
Greiskani LV 107 Ld51
Greith A 144 Fd52
Greiz D 127 Eb42
Gremersdorf D 119 Dd30
Gremjač'e RUS 203 Fb13
Grenaa DK 101 Dd23
Grenaa Strand DK 101 Ea23
Grenade F 40 Gb54
Grenade-sur-l'Adour F 39 Fb54
Grenant F 31 Jc40
Grenås S 79 Fd29
Grenchen CH 141 Bd53
Grenči LV 105 Jd51

Grenctāle – Gutowiec

Grenctāle LV 114 Kc53
Grendavė LT 114 Kd58
Grenivík IS 2 Ba03
Grenoble F 35 Jd48
Grense Jakobselv N 65 Kd07
Grentzingen F 31 Kb40
Grenzhausen, Höhr- D 125 Ca42
Gréolières F 43 Kc53
Gréoux-les-Bains F 42 Jd53
Greppin D 127 Eb39
Gresse-en-Vercors F 35 Jc49
Gressoney-La-Trinité I 148 Bd58
Gressoney-Saint-Jean I 148 Bd58
Gressvik N 93 Ea44
Grésy-sur-Isère F 35 Ka47
Gretna GB 11 Eb16
Grettstadt D 134 Db44
Greußen D 127 Dd40
Grevbäck S 103 Fb47
Greve DK 109 Ec26
Greve in Chianti I 155 Dc66
Greven D 125 Cb37
Grevená GR 183 Bb79
Grevenbroich D 125 Bc40
Greveníti GR 182 Ba80
Grevenmacher L 133 Bc45
Grevesmühlen D 119 Ea32
Greve Strand DK 109 Ec26
Grevie S 110 Ed53
Grevnäs FIN 90 Kc38
Greyabbey GB 10 Db17
Greysteel GB 9 Cc15
Greystoke GB 11 Eb17
Greystone GB 9 Cd17
Greystones IRL 13 Da22
Grézels F 33 Gb51
Grez-en-Bouère F 28 Fb40
Grèzes F 33 Gc51
Grezzana I 149 Dc59
Grgar SLO 151 Fa58
Grgurevci SRB 153 Ja61
Grgurnica MK 178 Bb73
Gribanovskij RUS 203 Fc12
Gribuli RUS 107 Ld48
Gridino RUS 99 Ld45
Grieben D 127 Eb36
Griebenow D 119 Ed31
Griem'ačje RUS 113 Jc58
Gries A 142 Dc54
Griesalp CH 141 Bd55
Gries am Brenner A 143 Dd54
Griesbach, Bad Peterstal- D 133 Cb49
Griesheim D 134 Cc45
Gries im Sellrain A 142 Dc54
Grieskirchen A 144 Fa50
Griesstätt D 143 Eb51
Griffen A 144 Fc56
Grigale LV 114 Kd53
Grigiškes LT 114 La58
Grignan F 42 Jb51
Grignani I 166 Ea85
Grignasco I 148 Ca58
Grigno I 150 Dd58
Grignols F 33 Ga49
Grignols F 40 Fc52
Grigor'evskoe RUS 203 Fb08
Grigorievca MD 173 Ga59
Grigoriopol MD 173 Ga57
Grijota E 46 Da59
Grijpskerk NL 117 Bd33
Griķi LV 105 Jc51
Grikos GR 197 Ea89
Grillby S 96 Gc42
Grilli I 155 Db68
Grillos GR 194 Ba87
Grimaldi I 164 Gb80
Grimăncăuţi MD 172 Ed53
Grimaud F 43 Kb54
Grimbråten S 94 Ed44
Grimdalen N 93 Da43
Grimentz CH 141 Bd56
Grimeton S 102 Ec51
Grimma D 127 Ec40
Grimmen D 119 Ed31
Grimmenstein A 145 Gb53
Grimmialp CH 141 Bd55
Grimnäs S 87 Fd32
Grimo N 84 Cc39
Grimsås S 102 Fa50
Grimsey IS 3 Bb03
Grimslöv S 103 Fc52
Grímsstaðir IS 3 Bb04
Grimstad N 93 Da46
Grimston GB 17 Fd24
Grimstorp S 103 Fc49
Grimstrup DK 108 Da26
Grimzdai LT 113 Jc55
Grinăuţi MD 173 Fb55
Grinăuţi-Raia MD 173 Fa53
Grindavík IS 2 Ab05
Grinde N 84 Cc37
Grindelwald CH 141 Ca55
Grinder N 94 Ec40
Grindheim N 92 Cb41
Grindheim N 92 Cc46
Grindholmen FIN 81 Jb29
Grindjorda N 67 Gb14
Grindon GB 16 Ed23
Grindsted DK 108 Da25
Grindu RO 176 Ec65
Grindu RO 177 Fb63
Gringley on the Hill GB 16 Fb21
Griniai LT 114 Ka55
Grinkiškis LV 114 Kb55
Grinneröd S 102 Eb47
Griñón E 46 Db65
Grinstad S 102 Ec46
Grinţieş RO 172 Eb57
Grip N 77 Da30
Gripenberg S 103 Fc48
Grisi I 166 Ec84
Grisignano di Zocco I 150 Dd60
Griškabūdis LV 114 Kb58
Grisolia I 164 Ga78
Grisolles F 40 Gb53
Grisselören FIN 81 Ja29
Grisslehamn S 96 Ha41
Grīva LV 115 Lc53
Grivaši LV 105 Jd52
Grivenskaja RUS 205 Fc16
Griviţa RO 176 Ed65
Griviţa RO 177 Fa61
Griviţa RO 177 Fa62
Grizáno GR 189 Bc81
Grizebeck GB 11 Eb19
Grizic HR 152 Ha60
Grizzana Morandi I 149 Dc63
Grjadišče RUS 99 Ld45
Grjady RUS 202 Eb09
Grjazi RUS 203 Fb12
Grjazovec RUS 203 Fa08
Grljan SRB 179 Ca67
Grøa N 77 Dc32
Gröbers D 127 Eb40
Grobiņa LV 105 Jb52
Grobla PL 138 Jb44
Grobla PL 139 Kb43
Gröbming A 144 Fa53
Gröbzig D 127 Ea39
Grocka SRB 174 Bb64
Grodås N 84 Cc34
Gródek PL 121 Gb33
Gródek PL 123 Kc33
Gródek PL 131 Ka36
Gródek PL 131 Kd42
Gródek nad Dunajcem PL 138 Jc45
Gröden D 128 Fa40
Gröding A 143 Ec52
Grödinge S 96 Gd44
Gröditsch D 128 Fa38
Gröditz D 127 Ed40
Gródki PL 122 Hd33
Gródki PL 131 Kb41
Grodków PL 129 Gd42
Grodziczno PL 122 Hd33
Grodziec PL 128 Ga41
Grodziec PL 129 Ha38
Grodziec PL 129 Hb42
Grodziec PL 138 Hc45
Grodzisk PL 123 Jd34
Grodzisk PL 123 Ka35
Grodzisk Mazowiecki PL 130 Jb37
Grodzisko PL 123 Jd30
Grodzisko PL 139 Kb43
Grodzisk Wielkopolski PL 129 Gb37
Grodziszcze PL 129 Gb42
Groeningen NL 125 Bc38
Groenlo NL 125 Bd37
Groesbeek NL 125 Bb38
Grogan IRL 13 Cb21
Grohotno BG 184 Da75
Groitzsch D 127 Eb41
Groix F 27 Ed41
Grojdibodu RO 179 Da68
Grójec PL 129 Gd37
Grójec PL 130 Jb38
Grolanda S 102 Fa48
Grom PL 122 Jb32
Gromada PL 131 Kb42
Gromadka PL 128 Ga40
Gromadno PL 121 Gd34
Gromandcyzna PL 123 Ka29
Gromiljak BIH 158 Hb64
Grömitz D 119 Dd31
Gromnik PL 138 Jc45
Gromo I 149 Da58
Gromovo RUS 113 Jb58
Gron F 30 Hb39
Grøna N 85 Db35
Grönahög S 102 Fa49
Gronau (Leine) D 126 Db37
Gronau (Westfalen) D 117 Ca36
Grønbæk DK 100 Db23
Grønbjerg DK 108 Cd24
Grønbjerg DK 108 Da25
Grönbo S 73 Hb24
Grönbo S 95 Fc43
Grønbua N 85 Db35
Grøndal N 84 Cb35
Gröndal S 71 Fc22
Grondola I 149 Cd63
Grönenbach D 142 Db51
Grönfjäll S 71 Fd24
Grong N 78 Ed26
Grönhögen S 111 Gb54
Grønhøj DK 100 Db23
Gröningen D 127 Dd38
Groningen NL 117 Bd33
Grønlia N 78 Ea28
Grönliden S 80 Hb25
Grønnemose DK 108 Dc26
Grono CH 149 Cc57
Gronów PL 128 Fc36
Gronowo PL 122 Hd30
Gronowo Elbląskie PL 122 Hc31
Grönskara S 103 Fd51
Grönskåra S 103 Ga51
Grönwohld D 118 Dc32
Grootegast NL 117 Bd33
Gropello Cairoli I 148 Cb60
Gropen S 95 Fc44
Gropeni RO 177 Fa64
Gropniţa RO 173 Fa57
Gropparello I 149 Cd61
Grornv HR 151 Fb62
Grosbliederstroff F 25 Ka35
Grosbous L 133 Bb44
Grosbreuil F 28 Ed44
Groscavallo I 148 Bc59
Grosebay GB 4 Da06
Groşi RO 171 Da55
Grosio I 149 Da57
Grošnica SRB 174 Bb66
Großaitingen D 142 Dc50
Großalmerode D 126 Db40
Großalsleben D 127 Dd38
Groß Ammensleben D 127 Ea37
Großarl A 143 Ed54
Großbeeren D 127 Ed37
Groß-Bieberau D 134 Cc45
Großbodungen D 126 Dc39
Großbothen D 127 Ec41
Großbottwar D 134 Cd47
Großbreitenbach D 127 Dd42
Großburgwedel D 126 Db36
Groß Dölln D 120 Fa35
Großdubrau D 128 Fb40
Großefehn D 117 Cb33
Großeibstadt D 134 Dc43
Grosselfingen D 142 Cc50
Großenaspe D 118 Db31
Großenbrode D 119 Dd30
Großenehrich D 126 Dc40
Großenhain D 128 Fa40
Großenkneten D 117 Cc34
Großenlüder D 126 Da42
Großenlüder D 126 Da42
Großenlupnitz D 126 Dc41
Großensee D 118 Dc32
Großenseebach D 134 Dc46
Großenwiehe D 108 Da29
Grossenzersdorf A 145 Gb51
Grossepeterdorf A 145 Gb54
Großerlach D 134 Cd47
Grosseto I 155 Dc68
Grosseto Prugna F 154 Ca71
Großfurra D 126 Dc40
Groß Gaglow D 128 Fb39
Groß Garz D 119 Ea35
Groß-Gerau D 134 Cc44
Großgerungs A 136 Fc49
Groß Glienicke D 127 Ed36
Großglobnitz A 136 Fd49
Großgörschen D 127 Eb40
Groß Grönau D 119 Dd32
Großhabersdorf D 134 Dc46
Großhansdorf D 118 Dc32
Großharthau D 128 Fb41
Großhartmannsdorf D 127 Ed42
Großheide D 117 Cb32
Großheirath D 135 Dd44
Großhennersdorf D 128 Fc41
Großheubach D 134 Cd45
Großhöchstetten CH 141 Bd54
Groß Ippener D 118 Cd34
Großkarolinenfeld D 143 Ea52
Groß Kiesow D 120 Fa31
Groß Kölzig D 128 Fc39
Groß Köris D 128 Fa37
Großkoschen D 128 Fb40
Groß Kreutz D 127 Ec37
Großkugel D 127 Eb40
Großlangheim D 134 Db45
Großlehna D 127 Eb40
Groß Leine D 128 Fb38
Großlittgen D 133 Bc44
Großlohra D 126 Dc40
Groß Miltzow D 120 Fa33
Groß Muckrow D 128 Fb38
Grossmugl A 145 Gb50
Groß Mühlingen D 127 Ea38
Groß Naundorf D 127 Ed39
Groß Oesingen D 126 Dc36
Großostheim D 134 Cd44
Grossouvre F 30 Hb43
Groß Pankow D 119 Eb34
Großpertholz A 136 Fc49
Groß Pösna D 127 Ec40
Großpostwitz D 128 Fb41
Groß Quenstedt D 127 Dd38
Großraming A 144 Fb52
Großräschen D 128 Fa39
Großreifling A 144 Fc52
Großrinderfeld D 134 Da45
Groß Rodensleben D 127 Ea37
Groß-Rohrheim D 134 Cc45
Großröhrsdorf D 128 Fa41
Groß Rosenburg D 127 Eb38
Groß-Sankt-Florian A 144 Fd55
Groß Särchen D 128 Fb40
Groß Schacksdorf D 128 Fc39
Großschirma D 127 Ed41
Großschönau D 128 Fc42
Groß Schönebeck D 120 Fa35
Groß Schwechten D 127 Ea36
Großschweidnitz D 128 Fc41
Gross-Schweinparth A 145 Gc50
Groß-Siegharts A 136 Fd49
Großsölk A 144 Fa53
Großsolt D 108 Db29
Großsteinberg D 127 Ec40
Großthiemig D 128 Fa40
Großtreben D 127 Ed39
Groß Twülpstedt D 127 Dd36
Groß-Umstadt D 134 Cc45
Großwallstadt D 134 Cd45
Groß Warnow D 119 Ea34
Grossweikersdorf A 144 Ga50
Großweitzschen D 127 Ed41
Groß Wokern D 119 Ec32
Großwudicke D 127 Eb36
Groß Ziescht D 128 Fa38
Grostenquin F 25 Ka36
Grosuplje SLO 151 Fc58
Grøtavær N 66 Ga12
Grote LV 107 Lb49
Grotle N 84 Ca34
Grotli N 85 Da34
Grötlingbo S 104 Ha51
Grøtnes N 63 Hd06
Grøtnesdalen N 62 Gd09
Grotniki PL 130 Hc38
Grotów PL 120 Ga35
Grötsch D 128 Fb39
Grottaglie I 162 Ha76
Grottaminarda I 161 Fc74
Grottammare I 157 Fa68
Grotte I 166 Ed86
Grotte di Castro I 156 Dd69
Grotteria I 164 Gb83
Grotte Santo Stefano I 156 Ea69
Grottole I 162 Gc76
Grötvågen N 77 Dc30
Grou NL 117 Bc33
Grov N 67 Gb13
Grova N 93 Db43
Grozas LV 107 Lc51
Grozdjovo BG 181 Ed71
Grozeşti RO 173 Fb58
Grozeşti RO 175 Cd65
Grožnjan HR 151 Fa60
Grua N 85 Ea40
Grub D 135 Dd44
Grubben N 71 Fb22
Grubbenvorst NL 125 Bc39
Grubišno Polje HR 152 Gd59
Grucno PL 121 Ha33
Gruda HR 159 Hc69
Gruda Donja BIH 159 Hc68
Grude BIH 158 Ha66
Grudusk PL 122 Ja34
Grudziądz PL 121 Hb33
Grues F 32 Fa45
Gruffy F 35 Jd46
Gruia RO 174 Cb66
Gruissan F 41 Hb56
Gruissan-Plage F 41 Hb56
Gruiu RO 176 Eb65
Grumăzeşti RO 172 Ec57
Grumento Nova I 161 Ga77
Grumo Appula I 162 Gc74
Grums S 94 Ed43
Grünau im Almtal A 144 Fa52
Grünbach D 135 Eb43
Grünbach am Schneeberg A 144 Ga52
Grünberg D 126 Cd42
Grünberg PL 128 Fd38
Grünburg A 144 Fb51
Grundarfjörður IS 2 Ab03
Grundfors S 71 Fc24
Grundfors S 80 Gc25
Grundforsen S 86 Ed37
Grundsel S 73 Hb22
Grundsjö S 79 Ga28
Grundsjö S 79 Gb25
Grundsjön S 87 Fd33
Grundsund S 102 Eb47
Grundsunda FIN 96 Hc40
Grundsunda S 80 Ha30
Grundtjärn S 79 Gb29
Grundträsk S 72 Ha23
Grundträsk S 72 Ha24
Grundträsk S 73 Hd20
Grundträsk S 73 Hb24
Grundvattnet S 73 Hb22
Grundzāle LV 106 La48
Grüneberg D 119 Ed35
Grunewald D 125 Bc38
Grünewalde D 128 Fa40
Grungedal N 92 Cd42
Grünhain D 135 Ec43
Grünheide D 128 Fa37
Grunnerud S 94 Eb44
Grunnfjord N 62 Gd08
Grunnfjordbotn N 66 Ga15
Grünsfeld D 134 Da46
Grünstadt D 133 Cb45
Grüntal D 120 Fa35
Grünwald D 143 Dd51
Grunwald PL 122 Hd33
Grupčin MK 178 Bb73
Grury F 30 Hd44
Grüsch CH 142 Cd54
Grūšlaukė LT 113 Jb54
Gruszeczka PL 129 Gc40
Gruszka PL 130 Ja41
Gruta PL 121 Hb33
Grūtas LT 123 Kc30
Gruvbyn S 87 Fc35
Gruyères CH 141 Bc55
Gruža SRB 174 Bb66
Gruzdiškė LT 114 Ka56
Grūzdžiai LT 114 Ka53
Grybėnai LT 115 Lb55
Grybów PL 138 Jc45
Grycksbro S 95 Fd39
Gryfice PL 120 Fd32
Gryfino PL 120 Fb34
Gryfów Śląski PL 128 Fd41
Grykë AL 182 Aa76
Gryllefjord N 62 Gb10
Grymyr N 85 Dd40
Grynberget S 79 Gb27
Gryt S 95 Gb44
Gryt S 103 Gb47
Gryta N 77 Dc29
Gryta S 96 Gc42
Grytåa N 70 Ed22
Gryteryd S 102 Ed51
Grytgöl S 95 Fd45
Grythyttan S 95 Fc42
Grytnäs S 95 Ga41
Grytsjö S 79 Fd25
Gryttjom S 96 Gc40
Gryzavino RUS 107 Ma48
Gryzy PL 123 Jd30
Gryżyce PL 129 Gb40
Gryżyna PL 129 Gb38
Grza SRB 178 Bd67
Grzebienisko PL 129 Gb37
Grzechotki PL 122 Hd30
Grzęda PL 122 Jb30
Grzegorzew PL 129 Hb37
Grzegrzółki PL 122 Jb32
Grzmiąca PL 121 Gb32
Grzybiany PL 129 Gb41
Grzybno PL 120 Fc35
Grzybno PL 122 Hc33
Grzybowo PL 129 Gd37
Grzymałków PL 130 Jb41
Grzymiszew PL 129 Hb38
Grzywna Biskupia PL 121 Hb34
Gschnitz A 143 Dd54
Gschwandt A 144 Fa51
Gschwend D 134 Da48
Gstaad CH 141 Bc55
Gsteig CH 141 Bc56
Guadahortuna E 60 Dc74
Guadalajara E 46 Dd64
Guadalaviar E 47 Ec65
Guadalcanal E 51 Ca71
Guadalcázar E 60 Cc73
Guadalix de la Sierra E 46 Dc63
Guadalmedina E 60 Cd76
Guadalmez E 52 Cc70
Guadalupe E 52 Cc67
Guadalupe E 61 Eb73
Guadamur E 52 Db66
Guadarrama E 46 Db63
Guadassuar E 54 Fb69
Guadiana del Caudillo E 51 Bc68
Guadix E 61 Dd74
Guadramil P 45 Bd59
Guagno F 154 Cb70
Guaire IRL 13 Cd23
Guájar-Faragüit E 60 Db76
Gualachulain GB 6 Dc11
Gualdo Tadino I 156 Eb67
Gualöv S 111 Fb54
Gualtieri I 149 Db61
Guarcino I 160 Ec72
Guarda CH 142 Da55
Guarda P 44 Bb63
Guardalfiera I 161 Fc72
Guardamar del Segura E 55 Fb72
Guardapasso I 160 Ea72
Guardavalle I 164 Gc82
Guardea I 156 Ea69
Guardia de Tremp E 48 Ga59
Guardiagrele I 157 Fb70
Guardia Lombardi I 161 Fd75
Guardia Perticara I 162 Gb76
Guardia Piemontese Marina I 164 Gb79
Guardiaregia I 161 Fb73
Guardia Sanframondi I 161 Fb73
Guardias Viejas E 61 Dd76
Guardiola de Berguedà E 49 Gd59
Guardiola de Font-rubí E 49 Gc61
Guardo E 38 Da56
Guareña E 51 Ca69
Guaro E 60 Cc76
Guarromán E 52 Db71
Guasila I 169 Ca78
Guastalla I 149 Db61
Guaza de Campos E 37 Cd58
Gubanicy RUS 99 Ma40
Gubavac MNE 159 Jb67
Gubbhögen S 79 Fd27
Gubbio I 156 Eb67
Gubbmyran S 86 Fa37
Gubbträsk S 72 Gc24
Guben D 128 Fc38
Gubeš BG 179 Cb70
Gubin PL 128 Fc38
Gubkin RUS 203 Fa13
Guča SRB 178 Ad67
Guča Gora BIH 158 Ha64
Gücenoluk TR 193 Gc83
Güçlüköy TR 199 Hb91
Gudai LT 113 Jc57
Gúdar E 48 Fb64
Gudbjerg DK 109 Dd27
Guddal N 84 Cb36
Guddalbru N 92 Cb45
Gudeliai LT 123 Kc30
Gudeliai LV 114 Kb59
Gudenieki LV 105 Jb51
Gudensberg D 126 Da40
Guderup DK 108 Db28
Gudhjem DK 111 Fc57
Gudin N 78 Ec27
Gudinge S 96 Gd39
Gudkaimis LT 114 Ka58
Gudme DK 109 Dd27
Gudmindrup DK 109 Ea25
Gudmont-Villiers F 30 Jb38
Gudmundrå S 80 Gc31
Gudmuntorp S 110 Fa55
Gudow D 119 Dd33
Gudowo PL 120 Ga33
Gudum DK 100 Cd22
Gudumholm DK 100 Dc21
Gudurica SRB 174 Bd62
Gudvangen N 84 Cc38
Gudžiūnai LV 114 Kb55
Guebwiller F 31 Kb39
Güéjar Sierra E 60 Dc75
Guémar F 31 Kb38
Guémené-Penfao F 28 Ed41
Guémené-sur-Scorff F 27 Ea39
Guengat F 27 Dc39
Guenrout F 27 Ec41
Guer F 27 Ec40
Guérande F 27 Eb42
Guéret F 33 Gc46
Guérigny F 30 Hb42
Guernica = Gernika E 38 Ea55
Güesa E 39 Fa57
Gües-d'Oloron F 39 Fb55
Gueugnon F 30 Hd44
Güevejar E 60 Db74
Gugalj SRB 159 Jc64
Gugeşti RO 176 Ed62
Güglingen D 134 Cc47
Guglionesi I 161 Fc71
Gugney-aux-Aulx F 31 Jd38
Gugny PL 123 Ka33
Gugutka BG 185 Ea76
Guhttás S 68 Hd13
Guia P 44 Ac65
Guichen F 28 Ed40
Guidizzolo I 149 Db60
Guidonia-Montecelio I 160 Eb71
Guiglia I 149 Db63
Guignen F 28 Ed40
Guignes F 23 Ha37
Guijo de Coria E 45 Bd65
Guijosa E 47 Ea62
Guijuelo E 45 Cb63
Guildford GB 20 Fb29
Guilheta P 44 Ac59
Guillar E 36 Ba56
Guillaumes F 43 Kb52
Guillena E 59 Bd73
Guillestre F 35 Kb50
Guillos F 32 Fb51
Guilsfield GB 15 Eb24
Guilvinec F 27 Dc40
Guimarães P 44 Ad60
Guimiliau F 26 Dc38
Guînes F 21 Gc30
Guingamp F 26 Ea38
Guipavas F 26 Dc38
Guipry F 28 Ed40
Guipy F 30 Hc42
Guisando E 45 Cc65
Guisborough GB 11 Fb18
Guiscard F 23 Ha34
Guiscriff F 27 Dd39
Guise F 24 Hc33
Guissona E 48 Gb60
Guist GB 17 Ga24
Guitalens F 41 Gd54
Guiting Power GB 20 Ed26
Guitiriz E 36 Bb54
Guîtres F 32 Fc49
Guizan E 36 Ad57
Gujan-Mestras F 32 Fa51
Gukovo RUS 205 Fc15
Gulbene LV 107 Lb49
Gulbēris LV 106 La50
Gulbji LV 105 Ja51
Gülçayır TR 193 Ha83
Gulcz PL 121 Gb35
Güldalı TR 199 Ha89
Guldborg DK 109 Eb28
Güldibi TR 187 Gd78
Guldrupe S 104 Ha50
Gulen N 84 Ca37
Gulgofjorden N 65 Kb05
Gulholmen N 66 Fd13
Guljanci BG 180 Db68
Gul'keviči RUS 205 Fd16
Gülköy TR 199 Gb88
Gulla N 77 Dc31
Gullabo S 111 Ga53
Gulladuff GB 9 Cd16
Gullan GB 11 Ec13
Gullaskruv S 103 Fd52
Gullberg S 87 Fd37
Gullbrandstorp S 102 Ed52
Gulleråsen S 87 Fd38
Gullered S 102 Fa49
Gullesfjordbotn N 66 Fd13
Gullgammen N 64 Jb04
Gullhaug N 93 Dd43
Gullholmen N 64 Ka05
Gullholmen S 102 Eb47
Gullön S 72 Gd22
Gullringen S 103 Fd49
Gullsby S 94 Ed41
Gullspång S 95 Fb45
Gulltjärn S 80 Hb27
Gullträsk S 73 Hc20
Güllü TR 192 Fd86
Güllübahçe TR 197 Ec88
Güllüce TR 192 Fb81
Güllük TR 197 Ed90
Gullvik S 80 Gd30
Gülpınarı TR 191 Ea82
Gulsele S 79 Gb28
Gulsrud N 93 Dd41
Gulstøa N 84 Ca34
Gulsvik N 85 Dc40
Gumboda S 73 Hb24
Gumboda S 80 Hc27
Gumbodahamn S 80 Hc27
Gümele TR 192 Ga84
Gümeli TR 191 Ec83
Gumiel de Hizán E 46 Dc60
Gumiel de Mercado E 46 Dc60
Gumlösa S 111 Fb54
Gummark S 80 Hc25
Gummersbach D 125 Ca40
Gumowo PL 122 Ja35
Gumpelstadt D 126 Db42
Gumpersdorf D 143 Ec50
Gumpoldskirchen A 145 Gb51
Gumtow D 119 Eb35
Gümülceli TR 191 Ed85
Gümüldür TR 191 Eb87
Gümüşçay TR 185 Ec80
Gümüşdamla TR 199 Hb90
Gümüşhane TR 205 Fd19
Gümüşkent TR 197 Ec90
Gümüşoluk TR 187 Gd78
Gümüşova TR 187 Gd78
Gümüşpınar TR 186 Fb77
Gümüşpınar TR 192 Fc81
Gümüşsu TR 193 Gb87
Gümüşsuyu TR 186 Fa77
Gümüşyaka TR 199 Gb91
Gümüşyeni TR 192 Ga82
Günaydın TR 192 Fa81
Guncati SRB 153 Jc62
Gundelfingen D 134 Db49
Gundelfingen D 141 Ca50
Gundelsheim D 134 Cd47
Gundelsheim D 134 Dc45
Gundertshausen A 143 Ec51
Gunderup DK 108 Cd25
Gündoğan TR 185 Ed80
Gündoğan TR 197 Ec90
Gündoğdu TR 185 Ec80
Gündoğdu TR 185 Ed79
Gündoğdu TR 186 Fd80
Gündüzler TR 193 Gd81
Gündüzlü TR 185 Ed77
Günekestane TR 192 Ga81
Güneli TR 193 Gd82
Güneşli TR 192 Fb84
Güneşlı TR 199 Gc92
Güney TR 192 Fc83
Güney TR 192 Fc86
Güney TR 192 Fc87
Güney TR 198 Fc89
Güney TR 198 Ga89
Güneyce TR 199 Gd88
Güneykaya TR 199 Hb91
Güneykent TR 193 Gc87
Güneyköy TR 193 Gb85
Güneyköy TR 193 Gd84
Güngören TR 192 Fc81
Güngörmez TR 186 Fa76
Güngörmez TR 186 Fb80
Gunhåberget S 94 Fa39
Günlüce TR 192 Fd83
Günlük TR 197 Ed89
Günlükbaşı TR 198 Fd92
Gunnarn S 80 Gc25
Gunnarnes N 63 Ja05
Gunnarp S 102 Ed51
Gunnarsbyn S 73 Hd21
Gunnarsjö S 102 Ec50
Gunnarskog S 94 Ed42
Gunnarskulla FIN 98 Kb40
Gunnarsnäs S 94 Ec45
Gunnarvattnet S 79 Fb27
Gunnebo S 103 Gb49
Gunnfarnes N 66 Ga11
Gunnilbo S 95 Ga42
Gunnislake GB 18 Dc31
Günseck A 145 Gb53
Gunskirchen A 144 Fa51
Gunsta S 96 Gd42
Günstedt D 127 Dd40
Gunten CH 141 Bd55
Guntersblum D 133 Cb45
Gunter's Bridge GB 20 Fb30
Guntersdorf A 136 Ga49
Günthersleben D 126 Dc41
Gunthorpe GB 16 Fb23
Guntín de Pallares E 36 Bb55
Günyarık TR 193 Gb81
Günyüzü TR 193 Hb83
Günzburg D 134 Db49
Gunzenhausen D 134 Dc47
Guovdageaidnu N 68 Hd11
Gura Bîcului MD 173 Ga58
Gura Camencii MD 173 Fc55
Gura Foii RO 176 Dd65
Gürağaç TR 192 Fd82
Gura Galbenei MD 173 Fc59
Gura Haitii RO 172 Dd57
Gurahonţ RO 170 Cb59
Gura Humorului RO 172 Eb56
Gurakuq AL 182 Ac75
Gura Ocniţei RO 176 Dd64
Gura Râului RO 175 Da61
Gurasada RO 174 Cb60
Gura Şuţii RO 176 Dd65
Gura Teghii RO 176 Eb63
Gura Vadului RO 176 Eb64
Gura Văii RO 174 Cb64
Gura Văii RO 176 Ec60
Gurb E 49 Gd59
Gurba RO 170 Ca58
Gurbăneşti RO 176 Ec66
Gürceğiz TR 197 Ed90
Güre TR 191 Eb82
Güre TR 192 Fd85
Güre TR 198 Fb89
Gürece TR 197 Ec90
Güreci TR 185 Ec79
Gur'evsk RUS 113 Ja58
Gurghiu RO 171 Dc58
Gurgljat BG 179 Cb71
Guri i Bardha AL 182 Ac74
Gur i Zi AL 163 Jb71
Gurk A 144 Fb55
Gurkovo BG 180 Dd72
Gurkovo BG 181 Fb69
Gürle TR 191 Ec85
Gürlek TR 192 Ga85
Gurnos GB 19 Dd27
Gürpınar TR 186 Fc78
Gürpınar TR 192 Ga86
Gurrë AL 182 Ac75
Gurre DK 109 Ec24
Gurrea de Gállego E 48 Fb59
Gurr'e madhë AL 182 Ac74
Gursken N 76 Cb33
Gürsöğüt TR 193 Hb81
Gürsü TR 186 Fd80
Gurteen IRL 8 Ca18
Gurteen IRL 12 Bd21
Gurten A 143 Ed50
Gurunhuel F 26 Ea38
Gurviksdalen N 77 Dc28
Gusborn D 119 Dd34
Gušće HR 152 Gc60
Güsen D 127 Eb37
Gusendo de los Oteros E 37 Cc58
Gusev RUS 113 Jd59
Guševac SRB 179 Ca69
Gusevo RUS 107 Mb51
Gusevo RUS 113 Jc59
Gus'-Hrustal'nyj RUS 203 Fa10
Gusinje MNE 159 Jb69
Gusmar AL 182 Ab78
Guşoeni RO 175 Da65
Gusow D 128 Fb36
Guspini I 169 Bd78
Gusselby S 95 Fd42
Güsselfeld D 119 Ea35
Güssing A 145 Gb54
Gusswerk A 144 Fd52
Gustav Adolf S 95 Fb41
Gustav Adolf S 103 Fb48
Gustavsberg S 80 Ha25
Gustavsberg S 96 Gd43
Gustavsfors S 94 Fa41
Gustavsfors S 94 Ec44
Güsten D 127 Ea38
Guštirna HR 158 Gb66
Güstrow D 119 Eb32
Gusum S 103 Gb47
Gusvattnet S 79 Fb26
Gus'-Železnyj RUS 203 Fb10
Gutach D 141 Ca50
Gutach D 141 Cb50
Gutar E 61 Dd72
Gutau A 144 Fb50
Gutcher GB 5 Fa03
Gutenbrunn A 144 Fd50
Gutenstein A 144 Ga52
Gutenstetten D 134 Dc46
Gutenswegen D 127 Ea37
Gutenzell D 142 Da50
Güterfelde D 127 Ed37
Gütersloh D 126 Cc38
Gutorfölde H 145 Gc56
Gutowiec PL 121 Gd32

Gúttamási H 145 Hb54
Guttannen CH 141 Ca55
Guttaring A 144 Fb55
Gützkow D 119 Ed31
Guvåg N 66 Fc13
Güveçlik TR 198 Fc88
Güvem TR 192 Fb81
Güvemalanı TR 185 Ed80
Güvençetmi TR 192 Fa82
Güvendik TR 191 Eb86
Güvendik TR 193 Hb87
Güvenir TR 198 Fb89
Güvercinlik TR 197 Ed90
Gúves GR 201 Db95
Guxhagen D 126 Da40
Guxinde E 36 Ba58
Guyancourt F 23 Gd37
Guyhirn GB 17 Fd24
Güzelbağ TR 199 Hb91
Güzelbahçe TR 191 Eb86
Güzelçamlı TR 197 Ec88
Güzelce TR 186 Fb78
Güzelköy TR 185 Ed78
Güzeloba TR 199 Gd91
Güzelpınar TR 192 Fd87
Güzelsu TR 199 Hb91
Güzelyurt = Morfou CY 206 Ja96
Guzmán E 46 Db60
Gvardejskoe RUS 113 Ja59
Gvarv N 93 Db43
Gvozd HR 151 Ga60
Gvozdansko HR 152 Gb60
Gwalchmai GB 15 Dd22
Gwardejsk RUS 113 Jb59
Gwbert GB 14 Dc26
Gwda Wielka PL 121 Gc32
Gweek GB 18 Da32
Gwieździn PL 121 Gc32
Gwizdały PL 130 Jc36
Gwizdanów PL 129 Gb40
Gwyddgrug GB 15 Dd26
Gwytherin GB 15 Ea22
Gy F 31 Jc41
Gya N 92 Cb45
Gyál H 146 Hd53
Gyarmat H 145 Gd53
Gyékényes H 152 Gd57
Gyenesdiás H 145 Gd55
Gyé-sur-Seine F 30 Hd39
Gyhum D 118 Da33
Gyl N 77 Db31
Gyland N 92 Cb46
Gyliai LT 114 Ka56
Gyljen S 73 Ja20
Gylling DK 108 Dc25
Gyltvika N 66 Fd17
Gymnich D 125 Bd41
Gyoma H 146 Jc54
Gyömrő H 146 Hd53
Gyón H 146 Hd54
Gyöngyös H 146 Ja52
Gyöngyöspata H 146 Ja52
Gyönk H 146 Hc56
Győr H 145 Ha52
Györgytarló H 147 Ka50
Györszemere H 145 Ha53
Győrszentiván H 145 Ha52
Györtelek H 147 Kb51
Győrvár H 145 Gc55
Gypsou CY 206 Ja96
Gysinge S 95 Gb40
Gyttorp S 95 Fc43
Gyula H 147 Jd55
Gyulafirátot H 145 Ha54
Gyulaj H 145 Hb56
Gžatsk RUS 202 Ed11
Gziq AL 163 Jc71
Gzy PL 122 Jb35

H

Haabneeme EST 98 Kb42
Haabsaare EST 107 Lb47
Häädemeeste EST 106 Kb47
Haag A 144 Fa51
Haag A 144 Fb51
Haag D 143 Eb51
Haag a.d.Amper D 143 Ea50
Haajainen FIN 82 Kc28
Haaksbergen NL 125 Bd37
Haan D 125 Bd40
Haanja EST 107 Lc47
Haapaharju FIN 82 La29
Haapajärvi FIN 82 Ka28
Haapajärvi FIN 82 Kd27
Haapajärvi FIN 11 Lc36
Haapajoki FIN 81 Jc28
Haapa Kimola FIN 90 Kd37
Haapakoski FIN 81 Jc31
Haapakoski FIN 90 Kd32
Haapakumpu FIN 69 Kc16
Haapakylä FIN 81 Jc29
Haapakylä FIN 82 Kc31
Haapala FIN 74 Kb22
Haapala FIN 81 Jc28
Haapala FIN 90 Kd32
Haapalahti FIN 64 Ka10
Haapalankylä FIN 90 Kc32
Haapaluoma FIN 89 Jc32
Haapamäki FIN 82 La29
Haapamäki FIN 82 Kb28
Haapamäki FIN 90 Kc33
Haapaniemi FIN 91 Lb32
Haapasaari FIN 98 La39

Haapasalmi FIN 91 Ld32
Haapavaara FIN 91 Ma32
Haapavesi FIN 82 Ka26
Haapimaa FIN 89 Jc35
Haapola FIN 75 La24
Haapovaara FIN 83 Mb30
Haapsalu EST 98 Ka44
Haar D 143 Ea51
Haarajoki FIN 90 Kd33
Haarajoki FIN 90 Kb33
Haarala FIN 82 Kc30
Haarala FIN 90 Kb32
Haaraoja FIN 82 Kb25
Haarasajo FIN 74 Jc19
Haarbach D 143 Ed50
Haarbrück D 126 Da39
Haarby DK 108 Dc27
Haarjärvi FIN 97 Jd39
Haarlem NL 116 Ad35
Haaroinen FIN 89 Jd36
Haataja FIN 75 Kd19
Haatajankylä FIN 83 Lc25
Haavisto FIN 81 Jc28
Haavisto FIN 90 Kb33
Haavisto FIN 98 Ka42
Habaja EST 98 Kc43
Habartice CZ 128 Fc41
Habartov CZ 135 Ec44
Habas F 39 Fa54
Habay-la-Neuve B 132 Ba44
Häbersliden S 73 Hb24
Habère-Poche F 35 Ka45
Habernau A 144 Fa52
Habichtswald D 126 Da40
Habipler TR 186 Fc77
Habkern CH 141 Bd55
Hablingbo S 104 Gd50
Habo S 103 Fd48
Hábol S 94 Ec45
Hábo-Tibble kyrkby S 96 Gc44
Habry CZ 136 Fd45
Habura SK 139 Ka46
Håby S 102 Eb46
Hacet TR 192 Fa83
Hachenburg D 125 Cb42
Hacıali TR 192 Fb81
Hacıaliler TR 192 Ga84
Hacıbekår TR 199 Gb90
Hacıbekir TR 192 Ga82
Hacıbeyli TR 193 Gb84
Hacıbozlar TR 191 Ec83
Hacıdanişment TR 185 Ec74
Hacienda 2 Mares E 55 Fb73
Hacıeyüblü TR 198 Fc88
Hacıfakılı TR 185 Ed75
Hacıfakılı TR 193 Hb85
Hacıgelen TR 185 Eb80
Hacıhaliller TR 191 Ed85
Hacıhıdırlar TR 198 Fc88
Hacıhüseyinler TR 191 Eb83
Hacıkasım TR 191 Eb81
Hacıköseli TR 192 Fb85
Hacıköy TR 185 Eb77
Hacılar TR 193 Gd87
Hacılar TR 199 Gb89
Hacılebbeleni TR 197 Fa88
Hacılı TR 185 Ec77
Hacınas E 46 Dd59
Hacıömer TR 205 Ga20
Hacıpehlivan TR 185 Ed80
Hacıranmanlı TR 191 Ed85
Hacısungur TR 185 Ec77
Hacıtufan TR 192 Fc86
Hacıveli TR 191 Eb83
Hacıvelioba TR 191 Ed81
Hacıyakup TR 187 Gd78
Hacıyeri TR 187 Ha78
Haciyusuflar TR 198 Ga91
Hackås S 79 Fc31
Hacksjö S 79 Fd29
Hacksta S 96 Gc43
Håcksvik S 102 Ed50
Hackvad S 95 Fc44
Haczów PL 139 Ka45
Hadamar D 125 Cb42
Hädanberg S 80 Gd29
Hädäräuţi MD 173 Fa53
Hadbjerg DK 100 Dc23
Haddal N 76 Cb33
Haddeland N 92 Cc45
Haddenham GB 17 Fb27
Haddenham GB 20 Fd31
Haddington GB 11 Ec13
Hadersdorf am Kamp A 144 Ga51
Haderslev DK 108 Db27
Hadım TR 192 Ga87
Hadjač UA 202 Ed14
Hadleigh GB 21 Ga26
Hadle Szklarskie PL 139 Ka44
Hadmersleben D 127 Dd38
Hadol F 31 Ka39
Hadsel N 66 Fc13
Hadsten DK 100 Dc23
Hadsund DK 100 Dc22
Hadsund Syd DK 100 Dc22
Hægebostad N 92 Cc46
Hægeland N 92 Cd46
Haelen NL 125 Bb39

Hærland N 94 Eb43
Haeska EST 98 Ka44
Haeska EST 105 Jc46
Hafenlohr D 134 Da45
Hafik TR 205 Fc20
Hafling I 142 Dc56
Hafnarfjörður IS 2 Ac04
Hafnir IS 2 Ab04
Hafslo N 84 Cd36
Hafslund N 93 Ea44
Hafsmo N 77 Dd30
Haga N 94 Eb41
Haga S 96 Gc42
Haganj HR 152 Gc58
Hagby S 96 Gc42
Hagby S 111 Ga53
Hage D 117 Cb32
Hage N 78 Ea31
Hagebro DK 100 Da23
Hagebyhöga S 103 Fd46
Hagelberg S 103 Fb47
Hagen D 118 Cd33
Hagen D 125 Ca39
Hagen D 125 Cb37
Hagenbach D 133 Cb47
Hagenburg D 126 Da36
Hagenow D 119 Dd33
Hageri EST 98 Kb43
Hagestad N 93 Da46
Hagetmau F 39 Fb54
Hagfors S 94 Fa41
Häggås S 79 Ga27
Häggdånger S 88 Gc33
Häggeby S 96 Gc42
Häggemåla S 103 Ga51
Häggenås S 79 Fc30
Häggesled S 102 Ed47
Häggnäs S 80 Hb27
Häggnäset S 79 Fb27
Häggsjön S 79 Fb28
Häggsjövik S 79 Fb28
Häggum S 102 Fa47
Häggvik S 80 Gd31
Häghig RO 176 Ea61
Hägline S 110 Fa55
Hagondange F 25 Jd35
Hagota RO 172 Ea58
Hagshult S 103 Fb50
Haguenau F 25 Kc36
Hahausen D 126 Db38
Håhellarhytta N 92 Cc44
Hähler N 92 Cd44
Hahmajärvi FIN 90 Kb35
Hahnbach D 135 Ea46
Hahnstätten D 133 Cb43
Hahót H 145 Gc56
Haibach D 134 Cd44
Haibach D 135 Ec48
Haidmühle D 136 Fa49
Haiger D 125 Cb42
Haigerloch D 134 Cc49
Häijää FIN 89 Jc35
Haikáli TR 188 Ba85
Haikkaanlahti FIN 91 Lb35
Haillainville F 31 Ka38
Hailsham GB 20 Fd30
Hailuoto FIN 74 Jd24
Haimburg A 144 Fc56
Haimhausen D 143 Dd50
Haiming A 142 Dc54
Haiming D 143 Ec50
Haimoo FIN 98 Ka39
Haina D 126 Cd41
Hainburg D 134 Cd44
Hainburg an der Donau A 145 Gc51
Hainfeld A 144 Ga51
Hainford GB 17 Gb24
Hainichen D 127 Ed41
Hainsfarth D 134 Db48
Hainton GB 17 Fc22
Hairlach A 142 Dc54
Haiterbach D 134 Cc49
Hajala FIN 97 Jc39
Hajdúbagos H 147 Ka52
Hajdúdorog H 147 Ka51
Hajdúhadház H 147 Ka51
Hajdúnánás H 147 Jd51
Hajdúsámson H 147 Ka52
Hajdúszoboszló H 147 Jd52
Hajdúszovát H 147 Ka53
Hajdúvid H 147 Ka51
Hajmel AL 163 Jb71
Hajnáčka SK 146 Ja50
Hajnówka PL 123 Kc34
Hajom S 102 Ec50
Hajós H 146 Hd56
Hajredin BG 179 Cd68
Hajsyn UA 204 Ec15
Håkafot N 79 Fc27
Hakarp S 103 Fb49
Hakenstedt D 127 Dd37
Hakkas S 73 Hc18
Hakkenpää FIN 97 Ja39
Häkkilä FIN 82 Kb31
Häkkilä FIN 90 Kd33
Häkkiskylä FIN 90 Ka33
Hakkstabben N 63 Hd07
Hall S 104 Ha48
Hall Green GB 20 Ed25
Håknäs S 80 Hb29
Hakojärvi FIN 89 Jd32
Hakokylä FIN 75 La29
Hakola FIN 82 La25

Hakola FIN 82 Kb30
Hakomäki FIN 89 Jd32
Håkøybotn N 62 Gc09
Håksberg S 95 Fd41
Hakuni FIN 89 Ja32
Hakvåg N 66 Fd15
Håkvika N 67 Gb13
Halaç TR 199 Gb93
Halaçar TR 193 Gb85
Halåforsen N 79 Fc44
Halahora de Sus MD 173 Fa54
Halalca TR 192 Fa82
Håland N 92 Cb46
Håland N 92 Cc47
Hålanda S 102 Ec48
Halándri GR 189 Cc86
Halandritsa GR 188 Bb85
Halástra GR 183 Ca78
Halászi H 145 Gd52
Hälăuceşti RO 172 Ed57
Halbe D 128 Fa38
Halbenrain A 144 Ga55
Halbjerg DK 101 Dd20
Hålberg S 72 Ha23
Halberstadt D 127 Dd38
Halblech D 142 Dc52
Haldern D 125 Bc38
Haldrup DK 108 Dc25
Halen B 124 Ba40
Halenbeck D 119 Eb34
Halenkov CZ 137 Hb47
Halenkovice CZ 137 Gd47
Halesowen GB 20 Ed25
Halesworth GB 21 Gb25
Håle-Täng S 102 Ed47
Halfing D 143 Eb51
Halford GB 20 Ed26
Halhalca TR 186 Ga80
Halhjem N 84 Ca40
Halič UA 204 Ea16
Halidiye TR 187 Gb80
Halifax GB 16 Ed20
Halikko FIN 97 Jc39
Halilağa TR 191 Eb81
Halilbağı TR 193 Ha82
Halitpaşa TR 191 Ed85
Haljala EST 98 La42
Håljarp S 110 Ed55
Halk DK 108 Db27
Hálki GR 189 Bd81
Hálki GR 190 Db86
Halki GR 190 Ed93
Halkia FIN 90 Kc38
Halkida GR 189 Cb85
Halkidó GR 183 Ca77
Halkio GR 189 Bd86
Halkirk GB 5 Eb04
Halkivaha FIN 89 Jc37
Halkokari FIN 74 Jd23
Halkokumpu FIN 90 Kd33
Halkosaari FIN 81 Jb31
Hälla S 79 Gb28
Halla-aho FIN 82 Kd26
Halla-aho FIN 90 La33
Hallabro S 111 Fc53
Hällabrottet S 95 Fd44
Hallaç TR 193 Gc86
Hallaçlar TR 191 Ec82
Hallaçlar TR 197 Fa88
Hallaçlı TR 186 Fa76
Hällan S 79 Fb29
Halland GB 20 Fd30
Hallapuro FIN 81 Jd30
Halle B 124 Ac41
Halle D 124 Cd37
Halle D 126 Da38
Halle (Saale) D 127 Eb40
Hälleberga S 103 Fd52
Hälleforsnäs S 95 Gb44
Hallein A 143 Ec52
Hällekis S 102 Fa46
Hallen S 79 Fb31
Hallenberg D 126 Cd40
Hallenberg, Steinbach- D 126 Dc42
Hallencourt F 23 Gc33
Hallerndorf D 134 Dc45
Hällesjö S 79 Ga31
Hällestad S 95 Fd45
Hällestad S 102 Fa48
Hälleström S 73 Hd23
Hällevadsholm S 102 Eb46
Hälleviksstrand S 102 Eb47
Hall-Håxåsen S 79 Fd29
Halli FIN 90 Ka34
Hallila FIN 90 Kc38
Hallingby N 85 Dd40

Hallingeberg S 103 Ga48
Hallingsjö S 102 Ec49
Hall in Tirol A 143 Dd53
Halliste EST 106 Kd46
Hällnäs S 72 Gc20
Hällnäs S 80 Ha27
Hällnäs S 80 Gd39
Hallormsstaður IS 3 Bb05
Hallsberg S 95 Fc44
Hallschlag D 125 Bc42
Hallsta S 87 Fd33
Hållsta S 95 Ga44
Hällstad S 102 Fa47
Hallstadt D 134 Dc45
Hallstahammar S 95 Ga43
Hallstatt A 144 Fa53
Hallstavik S 96 Ha41
Halltal A 143 Dd53
Halltorp S 111 Ga53
Hällvattnet S 79 Ga28
Hällvik S 72 Gc21
Hällviken S 79 Fb29
Hälmägel RO 171 Cc59
Halmagiu RO 171 Cc59
Halmåsd RO 171 Cc56
Halmeniemi FIN 90 La35
Halmeu RO 171 Cd54
Halmstad S 102 Ed52
Halna S 103 Fb46
Halosenkylä FIN 90 La34
Halosenniemi FIN 74 Jd23
Hals DK 101 Dd21
Halsa N 77 Db31
Halsbrücke D 127 Ed41
Halsskov DK 109 Ea27
Halsted DK 109 Ea28
Halstenbek D 118 Dc32
Halsteren NL 124 Ac38
Halsua FIN 81 Jd29
Haltdalen N 78 Eb31
Haltern D 125 Ca38
Haltie FIN 90 Ka36
Halttula FIN 91 Lb33
Haltwhistle GB 11 Ec16
Haluna FIN 82 La29
Halvari FIN 69 Jd17
Halvarsgårdarna S 95 Fd40
Halver D 125 Ca40
Halvorstorp S 102 Ec47
Halvrimmen DK 100 Db21
Halwell GB 19 Dd31
Halwill GB 18 Dc30
Halže CZ 135 Ec45
Ham F 23 Ha34
Hämäläinen FIN 90 La36
Hamamdere TR 192 Fc85
Hamamkarahisar TR 193 Hb83
Hamamköy TR 192 Fa87
Hamamüstü TR 187 Gd79
Hamar N 86 Eb38
Hambergen D 118 Cd33
Hambledon GB 20 Fa30
Hambleton GB 16 Fa20
Hambrücken D 133 Cb47
Hambühren D 126 Db36
Hamburg D 118 Db32
Hamburgsund S 102 Ea46
Hambye F 22 Fa36
Hamcearca RO 177 Fc64
Hamdibey TR 186 Fa75
Hamdibey TR 191 Ec81
Hamdorf D 118 Db30
Hämeenkoski FIN 90 Kc37
Hämeenkylä FIN 83 Lb26
Hämeenkyrö FIN 89 Jc35
Hämeenlinna FIN 90 Ka37
Hameln D 126 Da37
Hamersleben D 127 Dd38
Hamidiye TR 185 Ea80
Hamidiye TR 185 Eb77
Hamidiye TR 186 Fa75
Hamidiye TR 187 Gb80
Hamidiye TR 187 Gd80
Hamidiye TR 192 Fa83
Hamidiye TR 192 Fa85
Hamidiye TR 192 Ga81
Hamidiye TR 192 Ga82
Hamidiye TR 193 Gd82
Hamidiye TR 193 Gd83
Hamidiye TR 193 Hb81
Hamilton GB 10 Ea13
Hamina FIN 90 La38
Hamit TR 198 Fb91
Hamitabat TR 192 Ga82
Hamitler TR 193 Hb87
Hamitli TR 185 Eb76
Hamlot N 66 Fd14
Hamm D 125 Ca41
Hamm D 134 Cd45
Hamm/ Westf. D 125 Cb38
Hammah D 118 Da32
Hammar N 78 Eb28
Hammar S 95 Fc44
Hammarby S 96 Gd43
Hammarland FIN 96 Hb40
Hammarnäs S 79 Fb31
Hammarnes N 64 Jd06
Hammarö S 94 Fa43
Hammarstrand S 79 Ga31
Hammarvika N 77 Dd29
Hammaslahti FIN 83 Ld31
Hammel DK 100 Dc23
Hammelburg D 134 Da44

Hammelev DK 108 Db27
Hammelspring D 119 Ed34
Hammenhög S 111 Fb56
Hammer DK 108 Db25
Hammer N 78 Eb29
Hammer N 78 Ec26
Hammer N 78 Ec27
Hammerdal S 79 Fd29
Hammerfest N 63 Hd06
Hämmern D 135 Dd43
Hammershøj DK 100 Dc23
Hammerum DK 108 Da24
Hamminkeln D 125 Bd38
Hamn N 70 Ed22
Hamna N 77 Dc29
Hamnavoe GB 5 Fa05
Hamnbukt N 64 Jb07
Hamneda S 102 Fa52
Hamneidet N 63 Hb08
Hamnes N 66 Ga13
Hamnes N 70 Ed22
Hamnes N 78 Eb26
Hamnøy N 66 Fa15
Hamnsund N 76 Cc32
Hamnvågnes N 62 Gd10
Hamnvik N 67 Gb12
Hamoir B 124 Ba42
Hamois B 124 Ad42
Hamont B 124 Ba39
Hámor H 146 Jc50
Hamra N 84 Ca38
Hamra N 92 Cd47
Hamra S 86 Ec33
Hamra S 87 Fc36
Hamra S 104 Gd51
Hamrånge S 87 Gb38
Hamrångefjärden S 87 Gb38
Hamre N 84 Ca38
Hamre N 92 Cd47
Hamre S 87 Gb38
Hamremoen N 85 Dc40
Hamstreet GB 21 Ga29
Hamsund N 66 Fd14
Hamula FIN 82 Kc30
Hamula FIN 82 Kc30
Hamýšký RUS 205 Fd17
Hamzabey TR 185 Ed76
Hamzabey TR 186 Fc79
Hamzabeyli TR 185 Eb74
Hamzali MK 183 Ca75
Hamzali TR 186 Fb79
Hamzalı TR 198 Fb88
Hån S 95 Fb41
Han TR 193 Gd84
Hana N 65 Kb06
Hanadal N 64 Ka06
Hanak TR 205 Ga18
Hánánbihen F 26 Ec38
Hanaskog S 111 Fb54
Han Asparuhovo BG 180 Ea72
Hanau D 134 Cd44
Hanbury GB 20 Ed25
Hançalar TR 192 Fd86
Hancavičy BY 202 Ea13
Handbjerg DK 100 Da23
Handegg CH 141 Ca55
Handeland N 92 Cb45
Handeloh D 118 Db33
Handenberg A 143 Ec51
Händene S 102 Fa47
Handest DK 100 Dc22
Handewitt D 108 Da28
Handlová SK 138 Hc49
Handog S 79 Fc30
Handöl S 78 Ed30
Handrás GR 201 Dd96
Handrup D 117 Cb35
Handstein N 70 Fa20
Hanebo S 87 Gb37
Hanekamhaug N 77 Db32
Hanerau-Hademarschen D 118 Da30
Hanestad N 85 Ea35
Häneşti RO 172 Ed55
Hang N 85 Dd40
Han Garaučića MNE 159 Jd68
Hangaskylä FIN 89 Ja32
Hangastenmaa FIN 90 La34
Hängelsberg S 103 Fb51
Hangö FIN 97 Jc41
Hangu RO 172 Eb57
Hangvar S 104 Ha48
Hanhals S 102 Ec50
Hanhijärvi FIN 91 Lb35
Hanhimaa FIN 68 Jc14
Hanhisalo FIN 81 Jd28
Hanho FIN 89 Jd34
Haniá GR 200 Cb94
Hankamäki FIN 82 Kd31
Hankamäki FIN 83 Lb29
Hankasalmen asema FIN 90 Kc32
Hankasalmi FIN 90 Kc32
Hankavaara FIN 83 Lc29
Hanken S 103 Fb46
Hankensbüttel D 118 Dc35

Han Knežica BIH 152 Gc61
Hanko FIN 97 Jc41
Hanmer GB 15 Eb23
Hanna PL 131 Kc38
Hannäs S 103 Ga47
Hannemyr N 93 Db45
Hännilä FIN 91 Lc35
Hannington GB 20 Ed27
Hannover D 126 Db36
Hannoversch Münden D 126 Da40
Hannukainen FIN 68 Jb16
Hannut B 124 Ad41
Hanoğlu TR 192 Ga85
Hanovo BG 180 Eb73
Hanøy N 66 Fd13
Hanpaşa TR 192 Fa84
Han Pijesak BIH 159 Hd64
Hansca MD 173 Fd58
Hansjö S 87 Fc36
Hańsk PL 131 Kc39
Hansnes N 62 Gd08
Hanstedt D 118 Db33
Hanstedt D 118 Dc34
Hanstholm DK 100 Da20
Hanstorf D 119 Eb31
Han-sur-Lesse B 132 Ad43
Han-sur-Nied F 25 Jd36
Hantos H 146 Hc54
Hanušovce nad Topľou SK 139 Jd47
Hanušovice CZ 137 Gc44
Hanyatak TR 187 Gc79
Hanyeri TR 192 Fd86
Haparanda S 74 Jc21
Haparanda hamn S 74 Jc21
Hapert NL 124 Ba39
Happakylä FIN 90 Kc33
Häppälä FIN 90 Kc33
Happurg D 135 Dd46
Hapträsk S 73 Hb21
Hapua FIN 89 Jb35
Hara N 79 Fc31
Haraba MD 173 Fd55
Harads S 73 Hc21
Häradsbäck S 111 Fb53
Häradsbygden S 95 Fc39
Häradshammar S 103 Gb46
Haradziśča BY 202 Ea13
Haragiş MD 177 Fc60
Hárakas GR 195 Bd90
Hárakas GR 200 Da94
Haraker S 95 Ga42
Haráki GR 197 Fa93
Haraldseng N 63 Hc06
Haraldshaugen N 92 Bd42
Harasiuki PL 131 Kb42
Hárau RO 175 Cc61
Haravgi GR 183 Bc78
Harbach D 136 Fc49
Harbak N 78 Ea27
Hårberg N 78 Ea27
Harbergsdalen S 79 Fb26
Harbke D 127 Dd37
Harbo S 96 Gc41
Hårbølle DK 109 Ec28
Harboøre DK 100 Cd22
Harborg N 86 Eb32
Harburg D 134 Dc48
Harby GB 16 Fb23
Harcılar TR 192 Fb82
Harcourt F 23 Ga36
Hardegg A 136 Ga48
Hardegsen D 126 Db39
Hardelot-Plage F 23 Gb31
Hardemo S 95 Fc44
Hardenberg NL 117 Bd35
Hardenberg, Nörten- D 126 Db39
Hardheim D 134 Da46
Hardinghen F 21 Gc30
Hardom FIN 90 Kd38
Hareid N 76 Cc33
Haren NL 117 Bd33
Haren (Ems) D 117 Ca35
Harestad S 102 Eb48
Harestua N 85 Ea40
Harewood GB 16 Fa20
Harg S 96 Gd40
Harghita-Băi RO 176 Ea60
Hargimont B 132 Ad43
Hargla EST 107 Lb48
Hargnies F 24 Ja32
Hargrave GB 20 Fc25
Hargrave Green GB 21 Ga26
Hargshamn S 96 Gd41
Harhala FIN 90 Ka36
Hariéssa GR 183 Bc77
Harije SLO 151 Fb59
Harivaara FIN 83 Lc29
Härja S 103 Fb48
Härjåsjön S 87 Fb35
Harjakangas FIN 89 Ja35
Harjakoski FIN 89 Jb35
Harjankylä FIN 89 Jb33
Härjevad S 102 Ed47
Harjavalta FIN 89 Jb36
Harju FIN 75 Kc24
Harju FIN 82 La26
Harjula FIN 74 Ka21
Harjunmaa FIN 90 Kd34
Harjunpää FIN 89 Ja35
Harjunsalmi FIN 90 Kb34
Harju-Risti EST 98 Ka43

Härkäjoki FIN 69 Kb16
Harkány H 152 Hb58
Härkäpää FIN 98 Kd39
Härkeberga S 96 Gc42
Harken DK 100 Dc20
Härkki FIN 91 Lc32
Harkmark N 92 Cd47
Härkmeri FIN 89 Hd34
Härkmyran S 73 Hc19
Harku EST 98 Kb42
Härlau RO 172 Ed56
Harlaug N 85 Dc35
Harlech GB 15 Dd23
Harlesiel D 117 Cc32
Harleston GB 21 Gb25
Härlev DK 109 Dd27
Harlingen NL 116 Bb33
Harlösa S 110 Fa56
Harlow GB 20 Fd27
Harmaalanranta FIN 82 Kb29
Harmaasalo FIN 83 Lc30
Härman RO 176 Ea62
Harmancık TR 192 Fd82
Harmancık TR 192 Fd82
Harmanec SK 138 Hc48
Harmånger S 87 Gb35
Harmanköy TR 193 Gc81
Härmänkylä FIN 83 Lb25
Harmanli BG 185 Ea74
Harmanlı TR 185 Eb77
Harmanlı TR 186 Fb80
Harmatca MD 173 Fd56
Harmica HR 151 Ga58
Harmoinen FIN 90 Kb35
Härna S 102 Ed48
Harndrup DK 108 Dc26
Harnes F 23 Ha31
Härnösand S 88 Gc32
Haro E 38 Ea57
Harola FIN 89 Jb37
Háromfa H 152 Gd57
Haroué F 25 Jd37
Härpe FIN 98 Kd39
Harpefoss N 85 Dd36
Harpenden GB 20 Fc27
Harplinge S 102 Ed52
Harpstedt D 118 Cd34
Harpswell GB 16 Fb22
Harra D 135 Ea43
Harrå S 67 Ha16
Harrachov CZ 128 Fd42
Harrachsthal A 144 Fc50
Harre DK 100 Da22
Harrejaur S 73 Hb19
Harres DK 108 Da27
Harrested DK 109 Ea27
Harridslev DK 100 Dc23
Harrislee D 108 Db28
Harrogate GB 16 Fa20
Harrow GB 20 Fc28
Harrsele S 80 Ha28
Harrsjö S 71 Ga24
Harrsjö S 79 Ga26
Harrsjön S 79 Fd25
Harrström FIN 89 Hd32
Harrvik S 71 Ga24
Harrviken S 73 Ja22
Härryda S 102 Ec49
Harsa S 87 Ga36
Harsängen S 102 Ec46
Harsány H 146 Jc51
Harsefeld D 118 Da33
Hârseşti RO 175 Dc65
Harsewinkel D 126 Cc37
Harskamp NL 116 Bb36
Harsleben D 127 Dd38
Hârşova BG 177 Fb65
Hârsovo BG 181 Ec69
Harsovo BG 181 Ed69
Harsprånget S 72 Ha18
Hårstad N 62 Gc10
Harstad N 66 Ga12
Harsum D 126 Db37
Harsvika N 78 Ea27
Harsz PL 122 Jc30
Harta H 146 Hd55
Hartaanselkä FIN 82 Ka25
Hartberg A 144 Ga54
Hårte S 88 Gc35
Hartenholm D 118 Db31
Hartennes F 24 Hb35
Hartenstein D 127 Ec42
Hartenstein D 135 Ea46
Hartfield GB 20 Fd29
Harth D 126 Cc39
Hartha D 127 Ec41
Hartheim D 141 Bd51
Hartland GB 18 Dc30
Hartlebury GB 15 Ec25
Hartlepool GB 11 Fa17
Hartley GB 20 Fd28
Hartmanice CZ 135 Ed47
Hartmannsdorf A 144 Ga54
Hartmannsdorf D 127 Ec42
Hartola FIN 90 Kc35
Hartola FIN 90 Kb35
Hartpury GB 15 Ec26
Hårup DK 100 Dc23
Harvaluoto FIN 97 Jb39
Harvanmäki FIN 82 Kd28
Harvassdua N 71 Fc24
Harviala FIN 90 Ka37
Harville F 25 Jc35

Harwell – Hiirijärvi

Harwell GB 20 Fa28
Harwich GB 21 Gb26
Harworth GB 16 Fb21
Harzgerode D 127 Dd39
Hasanağa TR 185 Eb75
Hasanağa TR 186 Fc80
Hasanbey TR 185 Ed80
Hasanbey TR 187 Gc78
Håsand N 66 Fc16
Hasandede TR 192 Ga87
Hasanköy TR 192 Ga85
Hasanlar TR 191 Ec85
Hasanlar TR 192 Fd83
Hasanlı TR 186 Ga78
Hasanpaşa TR 198 Ga90
Hasbergen D 125 Cb37
Hasborn D 133 Bd44
Hasdümen TR 199 Gd90
Haselbach D 135 Ec48
Haselbourg F 25 Kb36
Häselgehr A 142 Db53
Haselund D 108 Da29
Haselünne D 117 Cb35
Hasfjord N 63 Hc06
Hasgebe TR 199 Gd90
Håsjö S 79 Ga31
Haskovo BG 185 Dd74
Hasköy TR 185 Ea78
Hasköy TR 185 Ec75
Hasköy TR 192 Fd86
Hasla N 93 Da46
Haslach D 141 Ca50
Haslach an der Mühl A 126 Fa49
Hasle CH 141 Bd54
Hasle DK 111 Fc57
Haslemere GB 20 Fb29
Haslemoen N 94 Ec39
Haslev DK 109 Eb27
Haslingden GB 15 Ec20
Hasloch D 134 Da45
Hasloh D 118 Db32
Håslöv S 110 Ed56
Hasmark DK 109 Dd26
Hăşmaş RO 170 Cb58
Hăsnăşenii Mari MD 173 Fb55
Hăsnăşenii Noi MD 173 Fb55
Hasparren F 39 Fa55
Haßbergen D 118 Da35
Hassel D 118 Da35
Hassel S 87 Gb34
Hassela S 87 Gb34
Hasselfelde D 127 Dd39
Hasselfors S 95 Fc44
Hasselösund S 102 Ea47
Hasselroth D 134 Cd44
Hasselt B 124 Ba40
Hasselt NL 117 Bc35
Haßfurt D 134 Dc44
Hassi FIN 90 Kb34
Hässjö S 88 Gc33
Hasslarp S 110 Ed54
Hassle S 95 Fb45
Haßleben D 120 Fa34
Hässleholm S 110 Fa54
Hasslö S 111 Fd54
Haßloch D 133 Cb46
Hasslösa S 102 Fa46
Haßmersheim D 134 Cd46
Håstad N 78 Eb26
Hästbacka FIN 81 Jc29
Hästbo S 95 Gb39
Hästbo S 95 Ga40
Haste D 126 Da36
Hästhagen S 96 Gd43
Hästholmen S 103 Fc47
Hastière-Lavaux B 124 Ad42
Hastings GB 21 Ga30
Hästö FIN 97 Jc40
Hästveda S 111 Fb54
Håsum DK 100 Da22
Hasvik N 63 Hc06
Haţeg RO 175 Cc61
Hatfield GB 15 Ec25
Hatfield GB 16 Fb21
Hatfield GB 20 Fc27
Hatfield Heath GB 20 Fd27
Hatfield Peverel GB 21 Ga27
Hatherleigh GB 19 Dd30
Hathersage GB 16 Fa22
Hätila FIN 90 Ka37
Hatipkışla TR 197 Ed89
Hatıplar TR 191 Ed84
Hatlestrand N 84 Cb40
Hatlinghus N 78 Ec27
Hatrik N 84 Ca40
Hatsola FIN 90 La33
Hattem NL 117 Bc35
Hatten D 117 Cc34
Hatten F 25 Kc36
Hattersheim D 134 Cc44
Hattert D 125 Cb42
Hattevik N 77 Dc29
Hattfjelldal N 71 Fb23
Hatting DK 108 Db25
Hattingen D 125 Ca39
Hattorf D 126 Db39
Hättorp S 95 Fb45
Hattstedt D 108 Da29
Hattula FIN 90 Ka37
Hattusaari FIN 83 Lc28
Hattuselkonen FIN 83 Ld27
Hatu EST 98 Ka43
Hatulanmäki FIN 82 Kd26
Hatun TR 191 Ed83
Håtuna S 96 Gc42
Hatunkylä FIN 83 Ld28
Hatvan H 146 Ja52
Hatvanpuszta H 146 Hc55
Hatzfeld D 126 Cc41
Haubourdin F 23 Ha31
Haudainville F 24 Jb35
Hauenstein D 133 Ca47
Haug N 67 Gb11
Haug N 85 Da36
Haug N 93 Dd42
Haugastøl N 85 Da39
Hauge N 65 Kc09
Hauge N 84 Cd37
Hauge N 92 Cb46
Haugen N 92 Cc44
Haugesund N 92 Bd42
Haugeveit N 92 Cd44
Haugfoss N 93 Da43
Haughom N 92 Cb45
Haugland N 70 Fa20
Haugli N 67 Gc12
Haugnes N 62 Ha08
Haugsdorf A 136 Ga49
Haugsvik N 84 Cc38
Hauho FIN 90 Ka36
Hauhuu FIN 89 Jd33
Haukanmaa FIN 90 Kc33
Haukedal N 84 Cc36
Haukeligrend N 92 Cd41
Haukeliseter N 92 Cc41
Haukijärvi FIN 75 Kd22
Haukijärvi FIN 89 Jc35
Haukilahti FIN 83 Lb25
Haukilahti FIN 91 Lc35
Haukiniemi FIN 91 Lc32
Haukipudas FIN 74 Ka23
Haukitaipale FIN 74 Ka20
Haukivaara FIN 83 Ma30
Haukivuori FIN 90 La33
Haukkilahti FIN 81 Jd29
Hauklappi FIN 91 Lc34
Hauknes N 71 Fb20
Hauneck D 126 Da41
Haunetal D 126 Da42
Haunia FIN 89 Jb35
Haunsheim D 134 Db49
Hauptstuhl D 133 Ca46
Haurida S 103 Fc48
Haurukylä FIN 74 Ka24
Haus N 84 Ca39
Hausach D 141 Cb50
Hausen D 134 Db45
Hausen D 135 Ea48
Hausen D 141 Ca52
Häusern D 141 Ca51
Hausham D 143 Ea52
Hausjärvi FIN 90 Kb38
Hausmannstätten A 144 Fd55
Haustreisa N 70 Fa23
Hausvik N 92 Cc47
Hauta-Aho FIN 83 Lb31
Hautajärvi FIN 74 Kd18
Hautajoki FIN 82 Kb27
Hautajoki FIN 82 Kc28
Hautakylä FIN 81 Jd31
Hautaranta FIN 75 La19
Haut-Asco F 154 Cb69
Hautefort F 33 Gb49
Hauteluce F 35 Ka46
Haute-Nendaz CH 141 Bc56
Hauterives F 34 Jb48
Hauteville-Lompnès F 35 Jc46
Hauteville-Plage F 22 Ed36
Hautjärvi FIN 90 Kc38
Hautmont F 24 Hc32
Hautolahti FIN 82 Kc30
Hautvillers F 24 Hc36
Hauzenberg D 136 Fa49
Havaj SK 139 Ka46
Havant GB 20 Fb30
Havari GR 188 Ba86
Havârna RO 172 Ec54
Håvberget S 95 Fc40
Havbro DK 100 Db22
Havdáta GR 188 Ab85
Havdhem S 104 Gd51
Havdrup DK 109 Eb26
Håve S 94 Eb45
Havelange B 124 Ba42
Havelberg D 119 Eb35
Havelte NL 117 Bc34
Havenbuurt NL 116 Ba35
Haverdal S 102 Ec52
Haverdalsstrand S 102 Ec52
Haverfordwest GB 18 Db27
Haverhill GB 20 Fd26
Haverö S 87 Fc33
Häverö S 96 Ha41
Haversin B 124 Ad42
Haverslev DK 100 Dc22
Håverud S 94 Ec45
Havířov CZ 137 Hb45
Havixbeck D 125 Ca37
Hävla S 95 Ga45
Havlíčkův Brod CZ 136 Ga46
Havnbjerg DK 108 Db27
Havndal DK 100 Dc22
Havneby DK 108 Cd27
Havnemark DK 109 Dd26
Havnsø DK 109 Ea25
Havnstrup DK 108 Da24
Havøysund N 63 Ja04
Havraň CZ 136 Fa43
Havran TR 191 Ec82
Håvre S 87 Fd35
Havrebjerg DK 109 Ea26
Havrylivka UA 205 Fb15
Havsa TR 185 Ec76
Havsnäs S 79 Fd28
Havstenssund S 94 Ea45
Havumäki FIN 90 Kc33
Havusalmi FIN 82 Kb30
Havusalmi FIN 90 Kc32
Havvness N 62 Ha09
Havza TR 205 Fb20
Hawes GB 11 Ed18
Hawick GB 11 Ec15
Hawkhurst GB 20 Fd29
Hawkinge GB 21 Gb29
Hawkshead GB 11 Eb18
Hawsker GB 11 Fb18
Haxey GB 16 Fb21
Hayalli TR 192 Fb86
Hayange F 25 Jc35
Haydar TR 185 Ec80
Haydarköy TR 192 Fa81
Haydarlı TR 193 Gc87
Haydaroba TR 191 Ed81
Haydere TR 198 Fb89
Haydon Bridge GB 11 Ed16
Hayes GB 20 Fc28
Hayfield GB 16 Ed22
Häyhtiönmaa FIN 89 Jb36
Hayingen D 142 Cd50
Hayle GB 18 Da32
Haymana TR 193 Gc83
Hay-on-Wye GB 15 Eb26
Hayrabolu TR 185 Ec77
Hayriye TR 186 Fc79
Hayriye TR 198 Ga88
Hayscastle GB 14 Db26
Haywards Heath GB 20 Fc30
Haza del Lino E 60 Dc76
Hazebrouck F 21 Gd30
Hazelbank GB 10 Ea14
Hazinedar TR 185 Ec76
Hazırlar TR 198 Fd93
Hažlín SK 139 Jd46
Hazlov CZ 135 Eb44
Heacham GB 17 Fd23
Headcorn GB 21 Ga29
Headford IRL 8 Bc20
Headley GB 20 Fb29
Heager DK 108 Cd24
Heanor GB 16 Fa23
Heath End GB 20 Fa28
Heather GB 16 Fa24
Heathfield GB 20 Fd30
Heath Hayes GB 16 Ed24
Heber D 118 Db34
Heberg S 102 Ec52
Hebertsfelden D 143 Ec50
Hebnes N 92 Cb42
Heby S 95 Gb41
Hèches F 40 Fd56
Hechingen D 142 Cc50
Hecho E 39 Fb57
Hechtel-Eksel B 124 Ba40
Hechthausen D 118 Da32
Heciul Nou MD 173 Fb55
Heckelberg D 120 Fa35
Heckfield GB 20 Fb28
Heckington GB 17 Fc23
Hecklingen D 127 Ea38
Hed S 95 Fd42
Heda S 103 Fc47
Hedalen N 85 Dc39
Hedared S 102 Ed48
Hedås S 94 Fa43
Hedben Bridge GB 16 Ed20
Hedberg S 72 Gd23
Hedby S 95 Fc39
Hedbyn S 95 Fd41
Heddal N 93 Db42
Hedderen N 92 Cc44
Hédé F 28 Ed39
Hede S 86 Fa33
Hede S 95 Ga40
Hede S 95 Gb41
Hede S 102 Eb46
Hedegård DK 108 Db25
Hedehusene DK 109 Ec26
Hedekas S 102 Eb46
Hedemora S 95 Ga40
Heden DK 108 Dc27
Heden S 73 Hd22
Heden S 86 Ed35
Heden S 87 Fb37
Hedenäset S 73 Jb20
Hedenstad N 93 Dc42
Hedensted DK 108 Db25
Hedersleben D 127 Dd38
Hedersleben D 127 Ea39
Hedesunda S 95 Gb40
Hedeviken S 86 Fa33
Hedon GB 17 Fc20
Hedon GB 17 Fc21
Hedrum N 93 Dc44
Hedwiżyn PL 131 Kb42
Hee DK 108 Cd24
Heede D 117 Ca34
Heek D 125 Ca37
Heel NL 125 Bb40
Heemsen D 118 Da35
Heemskerk NL 116 Ad35
Heemstede NL 116 Ad35
Heerbrugg CH 142 Cd53
Heerde NL 117 Bc36
Heere D 126 Dc37
Heerenveen NL 117 Bc34
Heerhugowaard NL 116 Ba34
Heerlen NL 125 Bb41
Heers B 124 Ba41
Heesch NL 125 Bb38
Heeslingen D 118 Da33
Heestrand S 102 Ea46
Heeten NL 117 Bc36
Heeze NL 125 Bb39
Hegge N 85 Dc37
Heggelia N 67 Gc11
Heggen N 93 Dd41
Heggenes N 67 Gd11
Heggheim N 84 Cb36
Heggmoen N 66 Fc17
Heglesvollen N 78 Ec29
Hegra N 78 Eb30
Hegyeshalom H 145 Gd51
Hegyfalu H 145 Gc53
Hegyhátsál H 145 Gc55
Hegykő H 145 Gc53
Hegyközség H 145 Gc54
Hehlen D 126 Da38
Heia N 67 Gd11
Heia N 78 Ed27
Heidal N 85 Dc35
Heide D 118 Da30
Heideck D 135 Dd47
Heidelberg D 134 Cc46
Heiden D 125 Bd38
Heidenau D 118 Db33
Heidenau D 128 Fa41
Heidenheim D 134 Db49
Heidenheim D 134 Dc48
Heidenreichstein A 136 Fd48
Heidenrod D 133 Cb43
Heiderscheid L 133 Bb44
Heidersdorf D 127 Ed42
Heidgraben D 118 Db32
Heigrestad N 92 Ca45
Heikendorf D 118 Dc30
Heikinkylä FIN 90 Kd38
Heikkil N 68 Hd11
Heikkilä FIN 75 La19
Heikkilä FIN 75 Kd21
Heikkilä FIN 81 Jc29
Heikkilä FIN 82 Kb28
Heikkilä FIN 83 Lb25
Heikkilä FIN 89 Ja33
Heikkilä FIN 89 Jb37
Heikkurila FIN 91 Lb33
Heikola FIN 89 Ja38
Heilbronn D 134 Cd47
Heilevong N 84 Cb35
Heiligenberg D 142 Cd51
Heiligenblut A 143 Ec54
Heiligendamm D 119 Eb31
Heiligenfelde D 119 Ea35
Heiligengrabe D 119 Ec34
Heiligenhafen D 119 Dd30
Heiligenhaus D 125 Bd39
Heiligenkreuz A 144 Ga55
Heiligenkreuz A 145 Gb51
Heiligenkreuz im Lafnitztal A 145 Gb55
Heiligenstadt D 126 Db40
Heiligenstadt D 135 Dd45
Heiligenthal D 127 Ea39
Heiligerlee NL 117 Ca33
Heilitz-le-Maurupt F 24 Ja37
Heiloo NL 116 Ba35
Heilsbronn D 134 Dc47
Heim N 77 Dc30
Heimbuchenthal D 134 Cd45
Heimburg D 127 Dd38
Heimdal N 62 Gd10
Heimdal N 77 Ea30
Heimenkirch D 142 Da52
Heimertingen D 142 Db51
Heimola FIN 69 Kb15
Heimsheim D 134 Cc48
Heimsnes N 78 Ed25
Heinäaho FIN 83 Ma30
Heinade D 126 Da38
Heinajoki FIN 90 Kb37
Heinälahti FIN 83 Lb25
Heinämaa FIN 90 Kc37
Heinämäki FIN 82 Kc29
Heinämäki FIN 82 La25
Heinäperä FIN 89 Jd32
Heinävaara FIN 83 Ld30
Heinävesi FIN 83 Lb31
Heinebach D 126 Da41
Heinersdorf D 128 Fb36
Heinijärvi FIN 74 Ka24
Heinijoki FIN 89 Jb38
Heinikoski FIN 74 Jd22
Heinilä FIN 89 Ja35
Heiningen D 126 Dc37
Heiniranta FIN 82 Kd26
Heinisuo FIN 74 Kb20
Heinlahti FIN 90 La38
Heino NL 117 Bc35
Heinola FIN 90 Kc36
Heinolanperä FIN 82 Ka25
Heinoniemi FIN 91 Ld32
Heinoo FIN 89 Jc36
Heinsberg D 125 Bc40
Heinsen D 126 Da38
Heistad N 93 Dc44
Heiste EST 97 Jc44
Heitersheim D 141 Bd51
Heiterwang A 142 Dc53
Heituinlahti FIN 90 La36
Hejde S 104 Gd50
Hejls DK 108 Db26
Hejlsminde DK 108 Db26
Hejnice CZ 128 Fd42
Hejnsvig DK 108 Da25
Hejnum S 104 Ha49
Hejőbába H 146 Jc51
Hejsager DK 108 Db27
Hekimdağ TR 193 Gc81
Heksem N 78 Eb31
Hel PL 121 Hb29
Helbra D 127 Ea39
Heldburg, Bad Colberg- D 134 Dc43
Helden NL 125 Bb39
Heldrungen D 127 Dd40
Helechal E 51 Cb70
Helechosa E 52 Cd68
Helegiu RO 176 Ec60
Helenelund FIN 89 Hd32
Helensburgh GB 10 Dd13
Helfenberg A 136 Fb49
Helgarö S 95 Gb43
Helgatun N 84 Cc38
Helgen N 93 Dc43
Helgeroa N 93 Dc44
Helgerød N 93 Dd44
Helgesta S 95 Gb44
Helgheim N 84 Cc35
Helgøy N 62 Gd08
Helgøy N 85 Ea39
Helgøysund N 92 Ca43
Helgum S 79 Gb31
Heli N 93 Ea43
Helidóni GR 194 Ba87
Heligfjäll S 79 Ga25
Héliopolis F 43 Kb55
Hell N 78 Eb30
Hella IS 2 Ac05
Hella N 84 Cc36
Hellamaa EST 97 Jd44
Hellamaa EST 97 Jd45
Helland N 66 Ga15
Helland N 77 Dc30
Hellandsbygd N 92 Cb41
Hellanmaa FIN 81 Jb30
Helle N 92 Cb44
Helle N 92 Cd44
Hellebæk DK 109 Ec24
Hellefjord N 63 Hd06
Helleland N 92 Ca45
Hellendoorn NL 117 Bd36
Hellenthal D 125 Bc42
Hellesøy N 84 Bd38
Hellesvikan N 77 Dc28
Hellesylt N 84 Cd34
Hellevad DK 108 Da27
Hellevik N 84 Ca36
Hellevoetsluis NL 124 Ac37
Helligvær N 66 Fb17
Hellimer F 25 Ka36
Hellin E 53 Ec71
Hellissandur IS 2 Ab03
Hellmobotn N 66 Ga15
Hellmonsödt A 144 Fb50
Hellnar IS 2 Ab03
Hellnes N 63 Hb08
Hellsö FIN 97 Hd41
Helmbrechts D 135 Ea44
Helmdange L 133 Bb44
Helme EST 106 La46
Helminghausen D 126 Cd39
Helmküla EST 98 Ka45
Helmond NL 125 Bb38
Helmsdale GB 5 Eb06
Helmsley GB 16 Fb19
Helmstadt D 134 Da45
Helmstadt-Bargen D 134 Cd46
Helmstedt D 127 Dd37
Helnæs By DK 108 Dc27
Helnessund N 66 Fc16
Hel'pa SK 138 Ja48
Helpfau-Uttendorf A 143 Ed51
Helppi FIN 68 Jc17
Helsa D 126 Da40
Helsby GB 15 Ec22
Helse D 118 Da31
Helshan AL 178 Ad72
Helsingborg S 110 Ec54
Helsingby FIN 81 Ja31
Helsinge DK 109 Ec24
Helsingfors FIN 98 Kb39
Helsingør DK 109 Ec24
Helsinki FIN 97 Ja39
Helsinki FIN 98 Kb39
Helstad N 70 Ed24
Helston GB 18 Da32
Heltermaa EST 97 Jd44
Helvacı TR 191 Ec85
Hem N 93 Dd43
Hemau D 135 Ea48
Hemavan S 71 Fc22
Hemden D 125 Bd37
Hemeiuş RO 172 Ed59
Hemel Hempstead GB 20 Fc27
Hemer D 125 Cb39
Hemfjällstangen S 86 Fa38
Hemfurth D 126 Cd40
Hemhofen D 134 Dc45
Héming F 25 Ka37
Hemingbrough GB 16 Fb20
Hemling S 80 Gd29
Hemmesjö S 103 Fc52
Hemmesta S 96 Ha43
Hemmet DK 108 Cd25
Hemmingen D 126 Db37
Hemmingen D 134 Cc48
Hemmingen S 80 Ha25
Hemmingsjord N 67 Gc11
Hemmingsmark S 73 Hc23
Hemmingstedt D 118 Da30
Hemmonranta FIN 82 La30
Hemmoor D 118 Da32
Hemnes N 94 Eb42
Hemnesberget N 71 Fb21
Hemsbach D 134 Cc45
Hemse S 104 Ha50
Hemsedal N 85 Db38
Hemsjö S 102 Ec48
Hemslingen D 118 Db34
Hemsö S 88 Gd32
Hemyock GB 19 Ea30
Hen N 85 Dd40
Henån S 102 Eb47
Henarejos E 54 Ed66
Hencida H 147 Ka53
Henclová SK 138 Jb48
Hendaye F 39 Ec55
Hendek TR 187 Gd78
Hendungen D 134 Db43
Henfield GB 20 Fc30
Henfort GB 18 Dc30
Hengelo NL 117 Bd36
Hengelo NL 125 Bc37
Hengersberg D 135 Ec49
Hengevelde NL 117 Bd36
Heni N 93 Ea41
Heničes'k UA 205 Fa17
Hénin-Beaumont F 23 Ha31
Henley GB 20 Ed25
Henley-on-Thames GB 20 Fb28
Henllys GB 19 Eb27
Hennan S 87 Ga34
Hennebont F 27 Ea40
Hennef D 125 Ca41
Henne Stationsby DK 108 Cd25
Henne Strand DK 108 Cd25
Hennickendorf D 128 Fa36
Hennigsdorf D 127 Ed36
Henning N 78 Ec28
Henningen D 119 Dd35
Henningskälen S 79 Fc28
Henningsvær N 66 Fb14
Hennstedt D 118 Da30
Henrichemont F 29 Ha42
Henriksdal FIN 89 Hd34
Henryków PL 129 Gc42
Henrykowo PL 122 Hd30
Hensås N 85 Db37
Henstedt-Ulzburg D 118 Db32
Henstridge GB 19 Ec30
Hentorp S 102 Fa47
Hentula FIN 91 Lb35
Heol Senni GB 15 Ea26
Hepberg D 135 Dd48
Hepojoki FIN 97 Jc39
Hepola FIN 74 Jc21
Heppenheim D 134 Cc45
Herad N 85 Dc38
Herad N 92 Cb47
Heradsbygd N 86 Eb38
Herajärvi FIN 83 Ma30
Herajoki FIN 83 Ld29
Herajoki FIN 90 Kb38
Heraklion = Iráklio GR 200 Da95
Herakulma FIN 90 Ka34
Herálec CZ 136 Fd46
Herand N 84 Cc39
Heraniemi FIN 83 Ld29
Herăşti RO 180 Eb67
Herbault F 29 Gb41
Herbeli AL 182 Ad74
Herbern D 125 Cb38
Herbertingen D 142 Cd51
Herbertstown IRL 12 Bd23
Herbeumont B 132 Ad44
Herbignac F 27 Ec41
Herbisse F 24 Hd37
Herbitzheim F 25 Kb35
Herbolzheim D 141 Ca50
Herborn D 126 Cc42
Herbrechtingen D 134 Db49
Herbsleben D 126 Dc41
Herbstein D 126 Cd42
Herby PL 130 Hc42
Herceg-Novi MNE 159 Hc69
Hercegovac HR 152 Gd59
Hercegszántó H 153 Hd58
Herdal N 76 Cd33
Herdecke D 125 Ca39
Herdla N 84 Bd38
Herdorf D 125 Cb41
Herdwangen-Schönach D 142 Cd51
Hereclean RO 171 Cd56
Hereford GB 15 Eb26
Héreg H 145 Hb52
Hereke TR 186 Ga78
Herencia E 52 Dc68
Herencsény H 146 Hd51
Herend H 145 Ha54
Herentals B 124 Ad39
Hérepian F 41 Hb54
Herfølge DK 109 Eb26
Herford D 126 Cd37
Herguijuela E 51 Cb67
Héric F 28 Ed41
Héricourt F 31 Ka40
Hericourt-en-Caux F 23 Ga34
Hérimoncourt F 31 Kb41
Heringen D 126 Db41
Heringsdorf D 119 Dd30
Heringsdorf D 120 Fb31
Heriot GB 11 Ec13
Herisau CH 142 Cd53
Hérisson F 29 Ha44
Herjangen N 67 Gb13
Herk-de-Stad B 124 Ba40
Herl'any SK 139 Jd48
Herleshausen D 126 Db41
Herlev DK 109 Ec25
Herlies F 23 Ha31
Herlufmagle DK 109 Eb27
Herm F 39 Fa53
Hermagor A 143 Ed56
Hermannsburg D 118 Db35
Heřmanova Hut' CZ 135 Ed46
Heřmanovice CZ 137 Gd44
Hermanowice PL 139 Kc45
Hermansverk N 84 Cd37
Heřmanův Městec CZ 136 Ga45
Hermaringen D 134 Db49
Hérmedes de Cerrato E 46 Db60
Herment F 33 Ha47
Hermes F 23 Gd35
Hermeskeil D 133 Bd45
Hermsdorf D 127 Ea42
Hermsdorf D 128 Fa40
Hermsdorf D 128 Fa42
Hernádkécs H 147 Jd50
Hernádnémeti H 146 Jc51
Hernani E 39 Ec55
Hernansancho E 46 Cd63
Herne D 125 Ca39
Herne Bay GB 21 Gb28
Herning DK 108 Da24
Herold D 127 Ec42
Heroldsbach D 134 Dc45
Heroldsberg D 135 Dd46
Herongen D 125 Bc39
Herónia GR 189 Bd85
Herónissos GR 195 Cd90
Herøyholmen N 70 Ed21
Herpont F 24 Ja36
Herråkra S 103 Fd52
Herrala FIN 90 Kc37
Herräng S 96 Ha41
Herraskylä FIN 89 Jd33
Herrberga S 103 Fd47
Herre N 93 Dc44
Herrefoss N 93 Da46
Herrenberg D 134 Cc49
Herrera E 60 Cc74
Herrera de Alcántara E 51 Bb66
Herrera del Duque E 52 Cc68
Herrera de los Navarros E 47 Fa62
Herrera de Pisuerga E 38 Db57
Herrere F 39 Fb56
Herreros de Jamuz E 37 Cb58
Herreros de Suso E 46 Cd63
Herreruela E 51 Bb67
Herreruela de Castillería E 38 Db56
Herrestad S 102 Eb47
Herrestrup DK 109 Eb25
Herrieden D 134 Db47
Herrischried D 141 Ca52
Herrljunga S 102 Ed48
Herrngiersdorf D 135 Eb49
Herrnhut D 128 Fc41
Herrö S 87 Fb34
Herröskaten FIN 96 Hc41
Herrsching D 143 Dd51
Herrskog S 80 Gc31
Herrstein D 133 Bd45
Herrup DK 100 Da23
Herry F 30 Hb42
Hersbruck D 135 Dd46
Herschbach D 125 Ca42
Herscheid D 125 Cb40
Herselt B 124 Ad40
Hérso GR 183 Ca76
Herstadberg S 103 Ga46
Hersvik N 84 Ca36
Herten D 125 Ca38
Hertford GB 20 Fc27
Hertnik SK 139 Jd47
Hertsånger S 80 Hc27
Herttuansaari FIN 91 Ld33
Herukka FIN 74 Ka23
Hervanta FIN 89 Jd36
Hervás E 45 Cb64
Herve B 125 Bb41
Herveland N 92 Cb46
Herves E 36 Ba54
Hervik N 92 Ca42
Herxheim D 133 Cb47
Herzberg D 119 Ed35
Herzberg D 127 Ed39
Herzberg am Harz D 126 Db39
Herzebrock-Clarholz D 126 Cc38
Herzfeld D 126 Cc38
Herzfelde D 128 Fa36
Herzhorn D 118 Db32
Herzlake D 117 Cb35
Herzogenaurach D 134 Dc46
Herzogenbuchsee CH 141 Bd53
Herzogenburg A 144 Ga50
Herzogenrath D 125 Bb41
Herzsprung D 119 Ec34
Hesby N 92 Ca43
Hesdin F 23 Gc32
Hesel D 117 Cb33
Heskestad N 92 Cb45
Hesnæs DK 109 Eb28
Hespe D 126 Cd36
Hesperange L 133 Bb45
Hesselager DK 109 Dd27
Hesselbjerg DK 100 Da21
Hessellund DK 100 Db23
Hessen D 126 Dc38
Hesseng N 65 Kd07
Hessfjord N 62 Gd08
Hessisch Lichtenau D 126 Da40
Hessisch Oldendorf D 126 Da37
Hessvik N 84 Cb40
Hestad N 84 Cb36
Hestad N 92 Cb45
Hesteneset N 64 Jb09
Hestenesøyri N 84 Cc34
Hestmona N 70 Fa20
Hestnes N 64 Jb06
Hestnes N 66 Ga14
Heston GB 20 Fc28
Hestra S 102 Fa50
Hestra S 103 Fc48
Hestvika N 63 Hb08
Hestvika N 77 Dc29
Hetekylä FIN 74 Kb23
Hetényegyháza H 146 Ja55
Hetes H 145 Ha56
Hethpool GB 11 Ed14
Hetin SRB 174 Bc61
Hetta FIN 68 Ja13
Hettange-Grande F 25 Jd34
Hettensen D 126 Db39
Hetton-le-Hole GB 11 Fa17
Hettstedt D 127 Ea39
Hettstedt, Dienstedt- D 127 Dd42
Hetvehely H 152 Hb57
Hetzbach D 134 Cd45
Hetzerath D 133 Bc44
Heubach D 134 Da48
Heuchelheim D 126 Cc42
Heuchin F 23 Gd31
Heuchlingen D 134 Da48
Heudeber D 127 Dd38
Heumen NL 125 Bb38
Heusden NL 124 Ba38
Heusden-Zolder B 124 Ba40
Heusenstamm D 134 Cc44
Heustreu D 134 Db43
Heves H 146 Jb52
Hevilliers F 24 Jb37
Hevingham GB 17 Gb24
Héviz H 145 Gd55
Hevlín CZ 137 Gb49
Hevosmäki FIN 82 Kd28
Hevosoja FIN 90 Ka38
Hevosoja FIN 90 La36
Hevossuo FIN 90 Kd37
Hewas Water GB 18 Db32
Hexham GB 11 Ed16
Heybeli TR 199 Gc89
Heybrook Bay GB 19 Dd32
Heyerode D 126 Db40
Heygendorf D 127 Dd40
Heyrieux F 34 Jb47
Heysham GB 11 Eb19
Heytesbury GB 19 Ec29
Hickling GB 16 Fb23
Hickling Green GB 17 Gb24
Hickstead GB 20 Fc30
Hida RO 171 Cd57
Hidas H 153 Hc57
Hidasnémeti H 139 Jd49
Hiddenhausen D 126 Cd37
Hidinge S 95 Fc44
Hıdırdivani TR 192 Fc84
Hıdırköylü TR 197 Ed88
Hidişelu de Sus RO 170 Cb57
Hieflau A 144 Fc53
Hiekkaniemi FIN 75 Kc24
Hiendelaencina E 46 Dd62
Hierden NL 116 Bb36
Hiersac F 32 Fc47
Hietakylä FIN 82 La31
Hietalanperä FIN 82 Ka26
Hietana FIN 90 Kd37
Hietanen FIN 90 La34
Hietaniemi FIN 69 Kd15
Hietaniemi FIN 90 Kd35
Hietaperä FIN 83 Lb25
Hietaranta FIN 75 La21
Hietoinen FIN 90 Kb37
Higham GB 21 Ga26
Higham Ferrers GB 20 Fb25
Highampton GB 19 Dd30
High Bentham GB 11 Ec19
Highbridge GB 19 Eb29
Highclere GB 20 Fa28
High Easter GB 20 Fd27
High Ercall GB 15 Ec24
Higher Town GB 18 Cc32
High Halden GB 21 Ga29
High Hesket GB 11 Ec17
Highworth GB 20 Ed27
High Wycombe GB 20 Fb27
Higuera de Arjona E 60 Db72
Higuera de Calatrava E 60 Da73
Higuera de las Dueñas E 46 Da65
Higuera de la Serena E 51 Ca70
Higuera de la Sierra E 59 Bd72
Higuera de Llerena E 51 Ca70
Higuera de Vargas E 51 Bb70
Higuera la Real E 51 Bc71
Higueruela E 54 Ed69
Higueruelas E 54 Fa67
Hihnavaara FIN 69 Kc15
Hiidenkylä FIN 82 Kb28
Hiidenlahti FIN 83 Lb30
Hiidensaari FIN 90 Kd36
Hiirijärvi FIN 89 Jb36

Hiirola – Horodyszcze

Hiirola FIN 90 La34
Hiisi FIN 82 La27
Hiisijärvi FIN 82 La25
Hiitelä FIN 90 Kc37
Hiittinen FIN 97 Jc41
Hijar E 48 Fb62
Hijdieni MD 173 Fa55
Hijosa E 38 Db57
Hikiä FIN 90 Kb38
Hilchenbach D 125 Cb41
Hildburghausen D 134 Dc43
Hilden D 125 Bd40
Hilders D 126 Db42
Hildesheim D 126 Db37
Hildre N 76 Cc32
Hilgermissen D 118 Da35
Hilgertshausen D 143 Dd50
Hiliódendro GR 182 Ba78
Hiliomódi GR 195 Bd87
Hilișeu-Horia RO 172 Ec54
Hiliuți MD 173 Fa55
Hiliuți MD 173 Fb56
Hill GB 19 Ec27
Hilla FIN 98 Ka40
Hillared S 102 Ed49
Hille D 126 Cd36
Hille S 95 Gb39
Hillegom NL 116 Ad35
Hillerød DK 109 Ec25
Hillersboda S 95 Ga39
Hillerse D 126 Dc36
Hillerslev DK 100 Da21
Hillerslev DK 108 Dc27
Hillerstorp S 102 Fa50
Hillesheim D 133 Bc43
Hilleshög S 96 Gc43
Hillesøy N 62 Gc10
Hillestad N 93 Dd43
Hillested DK 109 Ea29
Hillhead GB 10 Dd16
Hilliilä FIN 81 Jc27
Hilliilä FIN 90 Kb36
Hillington GB 17 Ga24
Hillion F 26 Eb38
Hillmersdorf D 128 Fa39
Hillo FIN 90 La38
Hill of Fearn GB 5 Ea07
Hillosensalmi FIN 90 Kd36
Hillringsberg S 94 Ed43
Hillsand S 79 Fd28
Hillsborough GB 9 Da18
Hillswick GB 5 Ed04
Hilltown GB 9 Da18
Hilmiye TR 192 Ga81
Hilok RUS 99 Ma42
Hilovo RUS 107 Mb46
Hilpoltstein D 135 Dd47
Hilsenheim F 31 Kc38
Hiltenfingen D 142 Dc50
Hilter D 126 Cc37
Hiltpoltstein D 135 Dd46
Hiltula FIN 91 Lb33
Hiltulanlahti FIN 82 La30
Hiltunen FIN 75 Lb20
Hiltusen vaara FIN 75 La22
Hilvarenbeek NL 124 Ba38
Hilversum NL 116 Ba36
Hilzingen D 142 Cc51
Himalansaari FIN 90 La35
Himanka FIN 81 Jc27
Himankakylä FIN 81 Jc27
Himarë AL 182 Ab78
Himaros GR 183 Cb76
Himbergen D 119 Dd34
Himesháza H 153 Hc57
Himki RUS 202 Ed10
Himmelberg A 144 Fa55
Himmelkron D 135 Ea44
Himmelpforten D 118 Da32
Himmelstadt D 134 Da44
Himmeta S 95 Ga43
Himmetoğlu TR 187 Hb76
Hinbjørgen N 78 Eb31
Hincăuți MD 173 Fa53
Hincești MD 173 Fc58
Hinckley GB 16 Fa24
Hindår FIN 98 Kc39
Hindås S 102 Ec49
Hindelang, Bad D 142 Db53
Hindeloopen NL 116 Bb34
Hindersby FIN 90 Kd38
Hindersön S 73 Ja22
Hindhead GB 20 Fb29
Hindsby FIN 98 Kc39
Hindsig DK 108 Cd25
Hınıs TR 205 Ga20
Hinișeni MD 173 Fc56
Hinka GR 182 Ad80
Hinna N 92 Ca44
Hinnerjoki FIN 89 Jb37
Hinnerup DK 100 Dc23
Hinneryd S 110 Fa53
Hinojal E 51 Bd66
Hinojales E 51 Bc71
Hinojar E 55 Ed73
Hinojares E 61 Dd73
Hinojos E 59 Bd74
Hinojosa de la Sierra E 47 Ea60
Hinojosa del Duque E 52 Cb70
Hinojosa del Valle E 51 Bd70
Hinojosas de Calatrava E 52 Da70
Hinova RO 174 Cb65
Hinsala FIN 89 Jd36
Hinstock GB 15 Ec23
Hinte D 117 Ca32
Hinterbichl A 143 Eb54
Hinterrhein CH 142 Cc56
Hinterriß A 143 Dd53
Hintersee A 143 Ed52
Hintersee D 120 Fb33
Hinterstoder A 144 Fb52
Hintertux A 143 Dd54
Hinterweidenthal D 133 Ca47
Hinterzarten D 141 Ca51
Hinthaara FIN 98 Kc39
Hinwil CH 142 Cc53
Hio E 36 Ac57
Hióna GR 188 Ba86
Híos GR 191 Dd86
Hippolytushoef NL 116 Ba34
Hipstedt D 118 Da33
Hirbovaț MD 173 Ga58
Hircești MD 173 Fb56
Hird H 152 Hb57
Hirel F 28 Ed38
Hirjău MD 173 Fd55
Hırka TR 198 Fc89
Hırkalı TR 192 Fb84
Hırkatepe TR 187 Hb80
Hirla EST 98 La43
Hirova MD 173 Fc56
Hirsala FIN 98 Kb40
Hirschaid D 134 Dc45
Hirschau A 142 Da53
Hirschau D 135 Ea46
Hirschbach D 135 Ea46
Hirschberg D 134 Cc46
Hirschegg A 142 Da53
Hirschegg-Rein A 144 Fc55
Hirschfeld D 128 Fa40
Hirschfelde D 128 Fc42
Hirschhorn D 134 Cc46
Hirsijärvi FIN 74 Kb24
Hirsikangas FIN 83 Lb27
Hirsilä FIN 90 Ka34
Hirsingue F 31 Kb40
Hirsjärvi FIN 89 Jd38
Hirson F 24 Hc33
Hirtolahti FIN 90 Ka35
Hirtop MD 173 Fc59
Hirtop MD 173 Fd53
Hirtopul Mare MD 173 Fd57
Hirtshals DK 100 Dc19
Hirtzfelden F 31 Kc39
Hirvaanmäki FIN 82 Kb31
Hirvälä FIN 97 Jd39
Hirvas FIN 74 Jd19
Hirvaskoski FIN 75 Kc22
Hirvasniemi FIN 74 Ka24
Hirvassalmi FIN 69 Jd12
Hirvasvaara FIN 74 Kd18
Hirvelä FIN 83 Lc25
Hirvelä FIN 90 La37
Hirvelänpää FIN 89 Ja32
Hirvenlahti FIN 90 Kd34
Hirvensalmi FIN 90 Kd34
Hirviäkuru FIN 69 Ka16
Hirvihaara FIN 90 Kb38
Hirvijärvi FIN 82 Kd27
Hirvijärvi FIN 82 Kd30
Hirvijärvi FIN 89 Ja34
Hirvijärvi FIN 90 Ka38
Hirvijärvi S 73 Ja19
Hirvijoki FIN 81 Jc31
Hirvikangas FIN 90 Kb32
Hirvikoski FIN 90 Kd38
Hirvikylä FIN 90 Ka32
Hirvilahti FIN 82 Kd30
Hirvimäki FIN 90 Kb33
Hirviperä FIN 89 Jc34
Hirvipohja FIN 90 Kc34
Hirvisalo FIN 90 Kd36
Hirvivaara FIN 75 Lb24
Hirvlax FIN 81 Ja29
Hirwaun GB 19 Ea27
Hirzenhain D 134 Cd43
Hisar TR 198 Fd90
Hisar TR 199 Gc89
Hisaralan TR 192 Fb83
Hisarardı TR 197 Fa89
Hisarcık TR 192 Fd83
Hisarja BG 180 Db72
Hisarköy TR 193 Ha84
Hisarlık TR 187 Gb80
Hisarönü Köy TR 198 Fd92
Hischberg D 135 Ea43
Hishult S 110 Fa53
Hisingen S 102 Eb49
Hiski RUS 99 Lb40
Hislaviči RUS 202 Ec12
Hisøy N 93 Da46
Hissjön S 80 Hb28
Histijanovo BG 180 Dd73
Hita E 46 Dd63
Hitcham GB 21 Ga26
Hitchin GB 20 Fc26
Hitiaș RO 174 Bd61
Hitis FIN 97 Jc41
Hitovo BG 181 Fa68
Hitra N 77 Dc29
Hittarp S 110 Ec54
Hittisau A 142 Da53
Hitzacker D 119 Dd34
Hitzhofen D 135 Dd48
Hiukamaa FIN 89 Jd33
Hiukkaa FIN 90 Ka34
Hiukkajoki FIN 91 Ld33
Hızırkahya TR 199 Gb93
Hjäggsjö S 80 Hb28
Hjallerup DK 100 Dc20
Hjällstad S 94 Ed39
Hjälmseryd S 103 Fc50
Hjälmsjö S 110 Ed54
Hjälsta S 96 Gc42
Hjälstad S 103 Fb46
Hjältevad S 103 Fd49
Hjärnarp S 110 Ed53
Hjärsås S 111 Fb54
Hjartdal N 93 Db42
Hjärtum S 102 Ec47
Hjarup DK 108 Db26
Hjelle N 84 Cc34
Hjelle N 85 Da36
Hjellestad N 84 Ca39
Hjelm DK 109 Eb28
Hjelmeland N 92 Cb43
Hjelmset N 70 Ed24
Hjelset N 77 Da31
Hjemås N 66 Fd17
Hjerkinn N 85 Dd34
Hjerm DK 100 Da23
Hjerpsted DK 108 Cd27
Hjerting DK 108 Cd26
Hjo S 103 Fb47
Hjøllund DK 108 Db24
Hjordkær DK 108 Db27
Hjørring DK 100 Dc19
Hjortdal DK 100 Db20
Hjorte DK 108 Dc26
Hjorted S 103 Ga49
Hjorteset N 84 Cb35
Hjortkvarn S 95 Fd45
Hjortsberga S 103 Fb52
Hjortshøj DK 100 Dc23
Hjulsbro S 103 Fd47
Hjulsjö S 95 Fc42
Hlebine HR 152 Gc57
Hlevacha UA 202 Ec14
Hligeni MD 173 Fd55
Hlina MD 172 Ed53
Hlinaia MD 173 Fa54
Hlinaia MD 173 Ga57
Hlinky CZ 135 Ec44
Hlinsko CZ 136 Ga45
Hlipiceni RO 172 Ed56
Hljabovo BG 185 Ea74
Hlobyne UA 204 Ed15
Hlohovec SK 145 Ha50
Hlubočky CZ 137 Gd46
Hluboká nad Vltavou CZ 136 Fb48
Hluchiv UA 202 Ed13
Hlučín CZ 137 Ha45
Hluk CZ 137 Gd48
Hlusk BY 202 Eb13
Hlybokae BY 202 Ea11
Hniezdne SK 138 Jb46
Hnilec SK 138 Jb48
Hnivan' UA 204 Eb15
Hnjótur IS 2 Ab02
Hnojník CZ 137 Hb45
Hnúšťa SK 138 Ja49
Hobeck D 127 Eb38
Hõbesalu EST 98 Ka45
Hobița RO 175 Cc62
Hobol H 152 Ha58
Hobro DK 100 Dc22
Hocaköy TR 187 Gb78
Hocaköy TR 187 Hb78
Hocalar TR 193 Gb86
Hocalı TR 199 Hb91
Hocaş TR 187 Hb80
Hoceni RO 173 Fb59
Höchberg D 134 Da45
Hochburg A 143 Ec51
Hochdonn D 118 Da31
Höchenschwand D 141 Ca51
Hochfinstermünz A 142 Db55
Hochgurgl A 142 Dc55
Hochheim D 133 Cb44
Höchheim D 134 Db44
Hochnaukirchen A 145 Gb53
Hochspeyer D 133 Ca46
Höchst CH 142 Cd53
Höchst D 134 Cd45
Hochstadt D 133 Cb46
Höchstadt D 134 Db49
Höchstadt D 134 Dc45
Höchstadt D 135 Dd44
Höchstädt D 135 Eb44
Hochwolkersdorf A 145 Gb52
Hoçisht AL 182 Ba77
Hockenheim D 134 Cc46
Hockley Heath GB 20 Ed25
Hoczew PL 139 Kb46
Hodac RO 172 Dd58
Hodal N 86 Eb33
Hodász H 147 Kb51
Hodde DK 108 Da25
Hoddesdon GB 20 Fc27
Hoddevika N 76 Ca33
Hodejov SK 146 Ja50
Hodenhagen D 118 Da35
Hodkovice nad Mohelkou CZ 128 Fc42
Hódmezővásárhely H 146 Jb56
Hodnanes N 92 Ca41
Hodnet GB 15 Ec23
Hodod RO 171 Cd56
Hodøl N 86 Ec33
Hodonín CZ 137 Gd48
Hodoš SLO 145 Gb55
Hodoșa RO 171 Dc59
Hodošan HR 152 Gc57
Hodrua-Hámre SK 146 Hc50
Hodsager DK 100 Da23
Hodslavice CZ 137 Ha46
Hodul TR 185 Ed80
Hoegaarden B 124 Ad41
Hoek NL 124 Ab38
Hoek van Holland NL 116 Ac36
Hoenderloo NL 117 Bc36
Hoeselt B 124 Ba41
Hoetmar D 125 Cb38
Hof D 135 Ea43
Hof N 93 Dd42
Hof N 93 Dd43
Hofbieber D 126 Da42
Höfen A 142 Db53
Höfen D 134 Cc48
Höfer D 118 Dc35
Hoff N 76 Cc32
Hoffen F 25 Kc36
Hofgeismar D 126 Da39
Hofheim D 134 Cc44
Hofheim D 134 Dc44
Hofkirchen A 144 Fa51
Hofkirchen D 135 Ed49
Hofkirchen im Traunkreis A 144 Fb51
Hofles N 78 Ec25
Höfn IS 3 Bb06
Hofors S 95 Ga39
Hofsós IS 2 Ba03
Hofsøy N 67 Gb11
Hofstad N 78 Ea27
Hofstätten A 144 Ga54
Hofstetten D 142 Dc51
Hofsvík IS 2 Ac04
Hög S 87 Gb35
Höga S 102 Eb48
Höganäs S 110 Ec54
Högås S 80 Gc26
Högås S 102 Eb47
Högbo S 95 Gb39
Högbränna S 72 Gc23
Högbränna S 72 Ha23
Högby S 104 Gc51
Hogdal S 93 Ea44
Høgebru N 84 Cd36
Högen S 94 Eb45
Högerund S 94 Ed43
Høgeset N 85 Da37
Högfors S 95 Fc41
Högfors S 95 Ga41
Hoggais FIN 97 Jb40
Höggeröd S 102 Eb47
Högheden S 73 Hb24
Hoghilag RO 175 Dc60
Hoghiz RO 176 Db61
Høgild DK 108 Da24
Hogland RUS 98 La39
Högland S 79 Fd26
Högland S 80 Ha29
Högland S 87 Gb35
Höglekardalen S 79 Fb31
Höglunda S 79 Fd31
Högnabba FIN 81 Jc29
Hogne B 124 Ba42
Hognes N 78 Ed25
Högsåra FIN 97 Jb41
Högsäter S 102 Ec46
Högsätter S 94 Ec42
Högsbo S 95 Gb41
Högsby S 103 Ga51
Högsjö S 88 Gc32
Högsjö S 95 Fd44
Högsön S 73 Ja21
Hogstad S 103 Fc47
Høgstadgård N 67 Gd12
Högstena S 102 Fa47
Högträsk S 73 Hb19
Högvålen S 86 Ed34
Högvalta S 94 Ed42
Hőgyész H 146 Hc56
Hohberg D 133 Ca49
Hohburg D 127 Ec40
Hoheleye D 126 Cc40
Hohen D 128 Fa36
Hohenahr D 126 Cc42
Hohenaspe D 118 Db31
Hohenau A 137 Gc49
Hohenau D 135 Ed48
Hohenberg A 144 Ga52
Hohenberg D 135 Eb44
Hohenbocka D 128 Fa40
Hohenbrunn D 143 Ea51
Hohenbucko D 127 Ed39
Hohenems A 142 Cd53
Hohenfels D 135 Ea47
Hohenfurch D 142 Dc51
Hohengörsdorf D 127 Ed38
Hohenhameln D 126 Db37
Hohenkirchen D 143 Ea51
Hohenleipisch D 128 Fa40
Hohenleuben D 127 Eb42
Hohenlinden D 143 Ea51
Hohenlobese D 127 Eb37
Hohenlockstedt D 118 Db31
Hohenmocker D 119 Ed32
Hohenmölsen D 127 Eb41
Hohennauen D 127 Eb36
Hohen Neuendorf D 127 Ed36
Hohenpolding D 143 Eb50
Hohenroth D 134 Db43
Hohensaaten D 120 Fb35
Hohenseeden D 127 Eb37
Hohenseefeld D 127 Ed38
Hohenselchow D 120 Fb34
Hohen Sprenz D 119 Eb31
Hohenstein D 133 Cb43
Hohenstein D 142 Cd50
Hohenstein-Ernstthal D 127 Ec42
Hohentauern A 144 Fb53
Hohentengen D 142 Cd51
Hohenthann D 135 Eb49
Hohen Wangelin D 119 Ec32
Hohenwarsleben D 127 Ea37
Hohenwart D 135 Dd49
Hohenwarth A 144 Ga50
Hohenwarth D 135 Ec47
Hohenwestedt D 118 Db31
Hohenziatz D 127 Eb37
Hohn D 118 Db30
Hohne D 126 Dc36
Höhnhart A 143 Ed51
Höhnhart A 143 Ed52
Höhnstedt D 127 Ea39
Hohnstein D 128 Fb41
Hohnstorf D 118 Dc33
Hoho FIN 90 Kc32
Höhr-Grenzhausen D 125 Ca42
Hohwacht D 119 Dd30
Høiby DK 109 Eb25
Hoikankylä FIN 82 Kd31
Hoikka FIN 75 La24
Hoilola FIN 83 Ma31
Hoisko FIN 81 Jd30
Højby DK 109 Dd27
Højen DK 101 Dd19
Højer DK 108 Cd28
Højerup DK 109 Ec27
Højmark DK 108 Cd24
Højslev DK 100 Db22
Højslev Stationsby DK 100 Db22
Hojsova Stráž CZ 135 Ed47
Hok S 103 Fb50
Hökåsen S 95 Gb42
Hökhuvud S 96 Gd40
Hokka FIN 90 Kd33
Hokkåsen N 94 Ec40
Hokkaskylä FIN 89 Jd33
Hokksund N 93 Dd42
Hokland N 66 Ga12
Hökmark S 81 Hd26
Hökön S 111 Fb53
Hököpinge S 110 Ed56
Hokstad N 78 Eb28
Hökvattnet S 79 Fc28
Hol N 77 Dd31
Hol N 85 Da39
Holand N 66 Fc14
Holand N 79 Fb26
Holandsvika N 70 Fa21
Holapantörmä FIN 75 Kc23
Hola Prystan' UA 204 Ed17
Hólar IS 2 Ba03
Holasovice CZ 137 Ha44
Holbæk DK 101 Dd22
Holbæk DK 109 Eb25
Holbeach GB 17 Fd24
Holbeach Saint Matthew GB 17 Fd23
Holboca RO 173 Fa57
Holbøl DK 108 Db28
Holdenstedt D 127 Ea40
Holdorf D 117 Cc35
Holdre EST 106 Kd47
Hole N 92 Ca44
Hole N 93 Dd41
Hole S 94 Fa41
Holeby DK 109 Ea29
Holen N 93 Ea43
Holercani MD 173 Fd57
Holešov CZ 137 Gd47
Holevik N 84 Ca35
Holford GB 19 Ea29
Holguera E 45 Bd65
Holič SK 137 Gd49
Holice CZ 136 Ga44
Holice SK 145 Gd51
Hölick S 88 Gc36
Holiseva FIN 90 Ka34
Holja FIN 90 Ka36
Höljäkkä FIN 83 Lc28
Höljes S 86 Ed38
Holkestad N 66 Fc15
Holkonkylä FIN 89 Jd32
Holla N 77 Dc30
Hollabrunn A 136 Ga49
Hollád H 145 Gd56
Hollandstoun GB 5 Ed02
Hollange B 132 Ba44
Holle D 126 Db37
Holleben D 127 Ea40
Høllen N 92 Cd47
Hollenfels L 133 Bb44
Hollenstedt D 118 Db33
Hollerath D 125 Bc42
Hollern-Twielenfleth D 118 Db32
Hollersbach A 143 Eb54
Hollfeld D 135 Dd45
Hollingsholm N 76 Cd31
Hollóháza H 139 Jd49
Hollókő H 146 Ja51
Hollola FIN 90 Kc37
Hollolan FIN 90 Kb37
Hollstadt D 134 Db43
Hollum NL 117 Bc32
Höllviken S 110 Ed57
Hollybush GB 10 Dd15
Hollyford IRL 13 Ca23
Hollyfort IRL 13 Cd23
Hollymount IRL 8 Bc20
Hollywood IRL 13 Cd22
Holm D 118 Db32
Holm DK 108 Db27
Holm FIN 81 Jb28
Holm N 66 Fd12
Holm N 70 Ed24
Holm N 77 Da32
Holm N 93 Ea44
Holm RUS 202 Eb10
Holm S 87 Gb32
Holm S 94 Ec45
Holm S 96 Gc42
Holma FIN 90 Ka35
Hólmavík IS 2 Ad03
Holme S 79 Gb30
Holmedal N 92 Cb41
Holmedal S 94 Ec43
Holmegil N 94 Eb44
Holmen N 70 Fa23
Holmenkollen N 93 Ea41
Holme-Olstrup DK 109 Eb27
Holme-on-Spalding-Moor GB 16 Fb20
Holmes Chapel GB 15 Ec22
Holmestad S 102 Fa46
Holmestrand N 93 Dd43
Holmfirth GB 16 Ed21
Holmfors S 72 Gc24
Holmfors S 73 Hb23
Holmfors S 73 Hc24
Holmisperä FIN 82 Ka29
Holmmo N 78 Fa25
Holmön S 80 Ja28
Holmøyane N 84 Cc34
Holmsbu N 93 Dd42
Holmsjö S 72 Gd24
Holmsjö S 79 Fd31
Holmsjö S 80 Gc29
Holmsjö S 111 Fd53
Holmskij RUS 205 Fc17
Holmstrand N 64 Jb09
Holmsund S 80 Hc29
Holmsvattnet S 80 Hc26
Holmsveden S 87 Gb37
Holmträsk S 73 Hc23
Holmträsk S 80 Hb25
Holmträsk S 80 Ha26
Holmträsk S 80 Gc28
Holmudden S 104 Hb48
Holmvassdalen N 70 Fa23
Holm-Žirkovskij RUS 202 Ec11
Hölö S 96 Gc44
Holod RO 170 Cb57
Holoșnița MD 173 Fc54
Holøydal N 86 Eb34
Holsbybrunn S 103 Fd50
Holsen N 84 Cc36
Holsljunga S 102 Ed50
Hølstad N 78 Eb27
Holstebro DK 100 Da23
Holsted DK 108 Da26
Holsted Stationsby DK 108 Da26
Holstinmäki FIN 74 Ka23
Holsworthy GB 18 Dc30
Holt GB 17 Ga23
Holt N 93 Db45
Holtdalsvollen N 78 Eb31
Holte N 78 Ea31
Holten NL 117 Bd36
Holtet DK 101 Dd21
Holtgast D 117 Cb32
Holt Heath GB 15 Ec25
Holtsee D 118 Db30
Holtslåtten N 94 Eb39
Holum N 92 Cc47
Holungen D 126 Dc39
Holven N 84 Cc39
Holvika N 78 Eb26
Holwerd NL 117 Bc32
Holy Cross IRL 13 Ca23
Holyhead GB 14 Dc22
Holýšov CZ 135 Ed46
Holywell GB 15 Eb22
Holywell GB 19 Eb30
Holywood GB 9 Da17
Holzbach D 133 Ca44
Holzdorf D 127 Ed39
Holzgerlingen D 134 Cc49
Holzhausen D 133 Cb43
Holzheim D 134 Db49
Holzkirchen D 143 Ea52
Holzminden D 126 Da38
Holzthaleben D 126 Dc40
Holzweiler D 125 Bc40
Holzweißig D 127 Eb39
Holzwickede D 125 Ca39
Hömb S 103 Fb47
Homberg (Efze) D 126 Da41
Homberg (Ohm) D 126 Cd42
Homborsund N 93 Da47
Hombourg-Budange F 25 Jd35
Hombourg-Haut F 25 Ka35
Hombukt N 63 Hc08
Homburg am Main D 134 Da45
Homburg (Saar) D 133 Bd46
Homel' BY 202 Ec13
Homeshi AL 182 Ad74
Homme N 92 Cd46
Homme N 92 Cd46
Hommelstø N 70 Ed23
Hommelvik N 78 Eb30
Hommerts NL 116 Bb34
Homocea RO 176 Ed61
Homokszentgyörgy H 152 Ha57
Homoroade RO 171 Cd55
Homorod RO 176 Db61
Hompland N 92 Cb45
Homps F 41 Ha55
Homrogd H 146 Jc50
Homstad N 78 Ec26
Homstean N 92 Cd46
Homutovka RUS 202 Ed13
Hømvejle DK 108 Da26
Hömyrfors S 73 Jb21
Honaz TR 198 Fd88
Hondarribia E 39 Ec55
Hondelange B 132 Ba45
Hondón de las Nieves E 55 Fa71
Hondón de los Frailes E 55 Fa71
Hondschoote F 21 Gd30
Hønefoss N 85 Dd40
Honfleur F 22 Fd35
Høng DK 109 Ea26
Hongisto FIN 90 Ka38
Hongset N 70 Ed23
Hónikas GR 195 Bd87
Honing GB 17 Gb24
Honiton GB 19 Ea30
Honkajärvi FIN 89 Ja34
Honkajoki FIN 89 Jb34
Honkakoski FIN 82 Kd28
Honkakoski FIN 89 Ja35
Honkakylä FIN 89 Jb32
Honkalahti FIN 91 Lc35
Honkamäki FIN 83 Lb31
Honkamukka FIN 69 Kd15
Honkaperä FIN 82 Kb26
Honkaperä FIN 82 Kb28
Honkaranta FIN 82 Ka29
Honkilahti FIN 89 Jb37
Honkola FIN 82 Kb31
Honkola FIN 89 Jd37
Hønning DK 108 Da27
Honningsvåg N 64 Jc04
Hönö S 102 Eb49
Honrubia E 53 Eb67
Hønseby N 63 Hd06
Hontalbilla E 46 Db61
Hontanares E 46 Cd65
Hontanaya E 53 Ea67
Hontangas E 46 Dc60
Hontianske Nemce SK 146 Hc50
Hontoria del Pinar E 46 Dd60
Hoofddorp NL 116 Ad35
Hoofdplaat NL 124 Ab38
Hoogerheide NL 124 Ac38
Hoogersmilde NL 117 Bd34
Hoogeveen NL 117 Bd35
Hoogezand-Sappemeer NL 117 Ca33
Hooge Zwaluwe NL 124 Ad37
Hooghalen NL 117 Bd34
Hoogkarspel NL 116 Ba34
Hoogkerk NL 117 Bd33
Hoogstade B 21 Ha30
Hoogstede D 117 Ca35
Hoogstraten B 124 Ad38
Hook GB 20 Fb29
Hook Norten GB 20 Fa26
Hooksiel D 117 Cc32
Höör S 110 Fa55
Hoorn NL 116 Ba34
Hopa TR 205 Ga19
Hopârta RO 171 Da59
Hope GB 4 Dd04
Hope GB 15 Eb22
Hope GB 19 Dd32
Hope N 93 Db45
Hope Bowdler GB 15 Eb24
Hopen N 66 Fc14
Hopen N 66 Fd15
Hopen N 77 Db29
Hopfgarten A 143 Ea53
Hopfgarten A 143 Eb55
Höpfingen D 134 Cd46
Hôpital-Camfrout F 26 Dc38
Hopovo SRB 153 Jb60
Hoppegarten D 128 Fa36
Hoppula FIN 74 Kb19
Hopseidet N 64 Ka05
Hopsten D 117 Cb36
Hopsu FIN 90 Kb34
Hopton GB 17 Gc24
Hopton Wafers GB 15 Ec25
Hoptrup DK 108 Db27
Hóra GR 194 Ba89
Hóra GR 196 Db91
Hóra GR 197 Eb88
Horam GB 20 Fd30
Horasan TR 205 Ga19
Horasanlı TR 198 Fc89
Hóra Sfakion GR 200 Cc95
Hora Svatého Kateřiny CZ 135 Ed43
Hora Svaté Šebestiána CZ 135 Ed43
Horaždovice CZ 136 Fa47
Horb am Neckar D 134 Cc49
Horbelev DK 109 Eb28
Horbury GB 16 Fa21
Hørby DK 100 Dc22
Hørby DK 101 Dd20
Hörby S 110 Fa55
Horcajada de la Torre E 53 Ea66
Horcajo de las Torres E 46 Cc62
Horcajo de los Montes E 52 Cd68
Horcajo de Santiago E 53 Dd66
Horcajo Medianero E 45 Cc63
Horche E 46 Dd64
Horda S 103 Fb51
Hörda S 103 Fb51
Hordabø N 84 Ca38
Hordáki GR 200 Cc94
Hörden D 126 Dc39
Hordorf D 127 Dd38
Hørdum DK 100 Da21
Høre N 85 Db37
Horea RO 171 Cc59
Horeb GB 14 Dc26
Höreda S 103 Fc49
Horeftó GR 189 Ca81
Horémis GR 194 Bb88
Horești MD 173 Fa56
Horești MD 173 Fd58
Horezu RO 175 Da63
Horgau D 142 Dc50
Horgen CH 141 Cb53
Horgenzell D 142 Cd51
Hörgertshausen D 135 Ea49
Horgești RO 176 Ed60
Horgevik N 93 Da43
Horgheim N 77 Da33
Horgoš SRB 153 Jb57
Horhausen D 125 Ca42
Höri CH 141 Cb52
Horia RO 172 Ed58
Horia RO 177 Fb66
Horia RO 177 Fc64
Hořice CZ 136 Ga43
Hořice na Šumavě CZ 136 Fb49
Horigio GR 183 Ca76
Hořiněves CZ 136 Ga44
Horió GR 197 Eb90
Horistí GR 184 Cd76
Hörja S 110 Fa54
Horka D 128 Fc40
Horki BY 202 Eb12
Hörkkölä FIN 91 Lc35
Horlești RO 173 Fa57
Horley GB 20 Fc29
Horlivka UA 205 Fb15
Hörlösa S 103 Gb51
Hormakumpu FIN 68 Jc15
Hormanloukko FIN 81 Jb31
Hormigos E 46 Da65
Horn A 136 Ga49
Horn N 70 Ed23
Horn N 70 Fa21
Horn S 103 Fb46
Horn S 103 Ga48
Horna E 55 Ed70
Hornachos E 51 Ca70
Hornachuelos E 60 Cc72
Horná Súča SK 137 Ha48
Hornbach D 133 Bd46
Horn-Bad Meinberg D 126 Cd38
Hornbæk DK 109 Ec24
Hornberg D 141 Cb50
Hornberga S 87 Fc37
Hornburg D 126 Dc38
Horncastle GB 17 Fc22
Horndal S 95 Ga40
Horne DK 100 Dc19
Horne DK 108 Dc27
Hörnebo S 103 Fb47
Horneburg D 118 Db33
Hörnefors S 80 Hb29
Horné Motešice SK 137 Hb48
Horné Mýto SK 145 Ha51
Hornesund N 92 Cd46
Horní Bečva CZ 137 Hb46
Horní Benešov CZ 137 Gd45
Horní Blatná CZ 135 Ec43
Horní Bříza CZ 135 Ed45
Horní Cerekev CZ 136 Fd47
Horní Jelení CZ 136 Ga44
Horní Jiřetín CZ 135 Ed43
Horní Kněžeklady CZ 136 Fb47
Horní Kruty CZ 136 Fc45
Horní Lideč CZ 137 Ha47
Hornillatorre E 38 Dc56
Hornillos de Cerrato E 46 Db59
Hornindal N 84 Cc34
Hørning DK 108 Dc24
Horning GB 17 Gb24
Horninglow GB 16 Ed23
Hornio FIN 89 Jc36
Horní Planá CZ 136 Fa49
Horní Slavkov CZ 135 Ec44
Horní Vítavice CZ 136 Fa48
Hornmyr S 80 Gd26
Hornnes N 92 Cd45
Hornoy-le-Bourg F 23 Gc33
Hornsea GB 17 Fc20
Hornsjø N 85 Ea37
Hörnsjö S 80 Ha28
Hornslet DK 100 Dc23
Hornstein A 145 Gb52
Hornsträsk S 73 Hb24
Hornsyld DK 108 Dc25
Hörnum D 108 Cd28
Hornum DK 100 Db21
Horný Tisovník SK 146 Hd50
Horoatu Crasnei RO 171 Cc56
Horochiv UA 204 Ea15
Horodca MD 173 Fc58
Horodenka UA 204 Ea16
Horodiște MD 173 Fa55
Horodiște MD 173 Fb54
Horodiște MD 173 Fc57
Horodiște MD 173 Fd56
Horodło PL 131 Kd40
Horodnic RO 172 Eb55
Horodniceni RO 172 Eb56
Horodnja UA 202 Ec13
Horodnycja UA 202 Eb14
Horodok UA 204 Ea15
Horodyšče UA 204 Ec15
Horodyszcze PL 131 Kb38

Horonkylä FIN 82 Kc30
Horonkylä FIN 89 Ja32
Horoszki Duże PL 131 Kb36
Hořovice CZ 136 Fa45
Hořovičky CZ 135 Ed44
Horoz TR 198 Ga89
Horrabridge GB 19 Dd31
Horred S 102 Ec50
Hörröd S 111 Fb55
Horrskog S 95 Gb40
Horsdal N 71 Fb18
Horse and Jockey IRL 13 Ca23
Horseleap IRL 13 Cb21
Horsens DK 108 Dc25
Horsham GB 20 Fc29
Hørsholm DK 109 Ec25
Horslunde DK 109 Ea28
Horsmanaho FIN 83 Lc30
Hörsne S 104 Ha49
Horšovský Týn CZ 135 Ec46
Horst D 118 Db32
Horst NL 125 Bc39
Hörstel D 117 Cb36
Horstmar D 125 Ca37
Horstwalde D 127 Ed38
Horsunlu TR 198 Fb88
Hort H 146 Ja52
Horta de Sant Joan E 48 Fd63
Hortas E 36 Ba55
Hortáta GR 188 Ac83
Hørte N 93 Da46
Horten N 93 Dd43
Hortes F 31 Jc40
Hortezuela E 47 Ea61
Hortiátis GR 183 Cb78
Hortigüela E 46 Dd59
Hortlax S 73 Hd23
Hortobágy H 147 Jd52
Horton GB 20 Fc30
Horton GB 20 Fb26
Horton-cum-Studley GB 20 Fa27
Horton in Ribbledale GB 11 Ec19
Hörup D 108 Da28
Hørup DK 108 Dc28
Hørve DK 109 Ea25
Horven N 78 Ec25
Hörvik S 111 Fc54
Horwich GB 15 Ec21
Horyniec PL 139 Kc43
Horyszów Ruski PL 131 Kd41
Horzamalayaka TR 192 Fb86
Horzum TR 192 Fa86
Horzumenbelli TR 192 Fb86
Hoşafoglu TR 187 Ha78
Hosanger N 84 Ca34
Hösbach D 134 Cd44
Hosby DK 102 Ec50
Hoscheid L 133 Bb44
Hosena D 128 Fa40
Hosenfeld D 134 Da43
Hoset N 66 Fc17
Hoset N 77 Da31
Hosiári GR 194 Bc90
Hosingen L 133 Bb43
Hosio FIN 74 Ka21
Hoslemo N 92 Cd42
Hospice de France F 40 Ga57
Hospital E 36 Bc56
Hospital E 40 Fd58
Hospital IRL 12 Bd24
Hospital de Órbigo E 37 Cb57
Hossa FIN 75 Lb21
Hossegor F 39 Ed54
Hössjö S 80 Hb28
Hössjön S 79 Fd28
Hössna S 102 Fa48
Hosszúhetény H 152 Hb57
Hosszúpályi H 147 Ka53
Hosszúpereszteg H 145 Gc54
Hostal de Ispiés E 40 Fc58
Hostalric E 49 Hb60
Hostens F 32 Fb51
Hostěradice CZ 137 Gb48
Hostikka FIN 91 Lb37
Hostinné CZ 136 Ga43
Hostivice CZ 136 Fb44
Hošt'ka CZ 136 Fb43
Hostomice CZ 136 Fa45
Höstoppen S 79 Fd28
Hostouň CZ 135 Ec46
Hostrupskov DK 108 Db27
Hotanlı TR 186 Fb80
Hotarele RO 180 Eb67
Hotaşlar TR 192 Fa82
Hotedršica SLO 151 Fa58
Hötensleben D 127 Dd37
Hoticy RUS 107 Ld46
Hoting S 79 Ga27
Hotneža RUS 99 Ma42
Hotnica BG 180 Dd70
Hotolisht AL 182 Ad75
Hotonj BIH 158 Hb68
Hotton B 124 Ba42
Hötzelsdorf A 136 Ga49
Hou DK 101 Dd21
Hou DK 108 Dc25
Houdain F 23 Gd31
Houdan F 23 Gc38
Houdelaincourt F 24 Jb37
Houeillès F 40 Fd52
Houetteville F 23 Gb36
Houffalize B 133 Bb43

Houghton-le-Spring GB 11 Fa17
Houhajärvi FIN 89 Jc36
Houlbjerg DK 100 Dc23
Houlgate F 22 Fc35
Houliarádes GR 182 Ad80
Houmnikó GR 184 Cc77
Hourtin F 32 Fa49
Hourtin-Plage F 32 Fa49
Houssay F 28 Fb40
Housukoski FIN 90 Ka32
Houten NL 124 Ba37
Houthalen-Helchteren B 124 Ba40
Houtsala FIN 97 Ja40
Houtsklär FIN 97 Ja40
Houyet B 132 Ad43
Hov N 62 Gd09
Hov N 66 Ga13
Hov N 78 Eb26
Hov N 85 Dd39
Hov S 103 Fc47
Hov S 110 Ed53
Hova S 95 Fb45
Høvåg N 93 Da47
Hovås S 102 Ec49
Hovborg DK 108 Da26
Hovda N 92 Cb45
Hovden N 66 Fc12
Hove GB 20 Fc30
Hove N 84 Cb35
Hovedgård DK 108 Dc24
Hövej H 145 Gc53
Hövelhof D 126 Cd38
Hoven DK 108 Da25
Hovenäset S 102 Ea46
Hovet N 85 Da39
Hovězí CZ 137 Ha47
Hovi FIN 82 La30
Hovid S 88 Gc33
Hovika N 78 Ec26
Höviken S 94 Ed41
Höviksnäs S 102 Eb48
Hovin N 78 Ea31
Hovin N 93 Db41
Hovin N 93 Ea42
Hovinmäki FIN 90 La34
Hovinsalo FIN 90 Kd33
Hovland N 92 Cb45
Hovmantorp S 103 Fd52
Hovsherad N 92 Cb45
Hovslätt S 103 Fb49
Hovslund Stationsby DK 108 Db27
Hovsta S 95 Fd43
Hovsund N 66 Fb14
Hovsvågen N 70 Ed21
Howden GB 16 Fb21
Howmore GB 6 Cd08
Hownam GB 11 Ec15
Howth IRL 13 Da21
Höxter D 126 Da38
Hoya D 118 Da35
Hoya de Santa María E 59 Bd72
Hoya-Gonzalo E 54 Ed69
Høyanger N 84 Cb36
Høydalsmo N 93 Da42
Hoyerswerda D 128 Fb40
Høyholm N 70 Ed22
Høyjord N 93 Dd43
Höykkylä FIN 81 Jc30
Höylä FIN 83 Lb28
Hoylake GB 15 Eb21
Høylandet N 78 Ec26
Hoyland Nether GB 16 Fa21
Hoym D 127 Dd38
Hoyocasero E 46 Cd64
Hoyo de Manzanares E 46 Db64
Hoyos E 45 Bd64
Höytiä FIN 90 Kb32
Høyvåk N 63 Hc06
Høyvik N 84 Ca35
Hoz E 40 Fc57
Hozabejas E 38 Dc57
Hrabrovo RUS 113 Ja58
Hrabušice SK 138 Jb48
Hrabyně CZ 137 Ha45
Hradčany CZ 136 Fc43
Hradec Králové CZ 136 Ga44
Hradec nad Moravicí CZ 137 Ha45
Hradec nad Svitavou CZ 137 Gd46
Hrádek CZ 136 Fa46
Hrádek CZ 137 Gb49
Hrádek nad Nisou CZ 128 Fc42
Hradyz'k UA 204 Ed15
Hrafnagil IS 2 Ba03
Hrafnseyri IS 2 Ac02
Hráni GR 194 Bb88
Hranice CZ 135 Eb43
Hranice CZ 137 Ha46
Hraničné SK 138 Jc46
Hranovnica SK 138 Jb48
Hrastelnica HR 152 Gb60
Hrastje HR 152 Gb58
Hrastnik SLO 151 Fd57
Hrebenne PL 139 Kd43
Hrebinka UA 202 Ed14
Hredino RUS 99 Mb45
Hřensko CZ 128 Fb42
Hrhov SK 138 Jc49
Hrib-Loški Potok SLO 151 Fb59
Hriňová SK 138 Hd49
Hrisafa GR 194 Bc89
Hrisey IS 2 Ba03
Hrískov CZ 136 Fa44
Hrisópetra GR 183 Cb77

Hrisóstomos GR 196 Dd88
Hrissi GR 201 Db97
Hrissó GR 184 Cc76
Hrissoúpoli GR 184 Db77
Hrissovítsi GR 194 Bb87
Hristiáni GR 194 Ba88
Hristós GR 196 Dd88
Hristovaia MD 173 Fd54
Hrnjadi BIH 152 Gb63
Hrochův Týnec CZ 136 Ga45
Hrodna BY 202 Dd13
Hrómio GR 183 Bb79
Hrónia GR 189 Cb84
Hronov CZ 137 Gb43
Hronský Beňadik SK 146 Hc50
Hrostovice SK 139 Ka47
Hrotovice CZ 136 Ga48
Hroznětín CZ 135 Ec44
Hrtkovci SRB 153 Jb61
Hrubieszów PL 131 Kd41
Hrubov SK 139 Ka47
Hrud PL 131 Kb37
Hruşca MD 173 Fc54
Hrušica SLO 144 Fa56
Hrušica SLO 151 Fa58
Hrušova MD 173 Fd57
Hruštín SK 138 Hd47
Hrušuvacha UA 203 Fa14
Hrvaćani BIH 152 Ha62
Hrvace HR 158 Gc65
Hrvatska Dubica HR 152 Gc60
Hrvatska Kostajnica HR 152 Gc60
Hrženica HR 152 Gc57
Huaröd S 111 Fb55
Hubbo S 95 Gb42
Huben A 143 Eb55
Huby PL 129 Gb42
Hubynycha UA 205 Fa15
Huchet F 39 Ed53
Hückelhoven D 125 Bc40
Hückeswagen D 125 Ca40
Hucknall GB 16 Fa23
Hucqueliers F 23 Gc31
Huddersfield GB 16 Ed21
Hudding GB 20 Fb27
Hüde D 117 Cc36
Hude D 118 Cd34
Hudene S 102 Ed48
Hudënisht AL 182 Ad76
Hudeşti RO 172 Ec54
Hudiksvall S 87 Gb35
Huedin RO 171 Cd57
Huélago E 60 Dc74
Huélamo E 47 Ec65
Huelgoat F 26 Dd38
Huelma E 60 Dc73
Huelva E 59 Bb74
Huéneja E 61 Dd75
Huércal-Overa E 61 Ec74
Huércanos E 38 Ea58
Huergas E 37 Cc56
Huergas E 37 Cc56
Huérmeces E 38 Dc57
Huerta de Arriba E 46 Dd59
Huerta de la Obispalía E 53 Eb66
Huerta del Rey E 46 Dd60
Huerta de Valdecarábanos E 52 Dc66
Huertahernado E 47 Eb63
Huérteles E 47 Eb59
Huerto E 48 Fc60
Huesa E 61 Dd73
Huesa del Común E 47 Fa63
Huesca E 48 Fc59
Huéscar E 61 Ea73
Huete E 47 Ea65
Huétor Santillán E 60 Dc75
Huétor Tajar E 60 Da75
Hüfingen D 141 Cb51
Hugh Town GB 18 Cc32
Hugla N 70 Fa21
Hugley GB 15 Ec24
Huglfing D 143 Dd52
Huglu TR 199 Hb89
Huhmarkoski FIN 81 Jc30
Huhtaa FIN 89 Jc36
Huhtala FIN 74 Jd21
Huhtalanniemi FIN 74 Jd18
Huhtamo FIN 89 Jc37
Huhtapuhto FIN 81 Jd27
Huhti FIN 89 Jd37
Huhtia FIN 90 Kb33
Huhtijärvi FIN 90 Ka33
Huhtilampi FIN 83 Ma31
Huhus FIN 83 Ma29
Huikkola FIN 83 Ma31
Huilliécourt F 31 Jc39
Huisheim D 134 Dc48
Huissen NL 125 Bc37
Huissinkylä FIN 81 Jb31
Huizen NL 116 Ba36
Hujakkala FIN 91 Lb37
Hukanmaa S 68 Hd16
Hukkajärvi FIN 83 Lc30
Hukkala FIN 83 Lc30
Hukkala FIN 89 Jc32
Hulby DK 109 Ea27
Hulderbu N 85 Dc34
Hulín CZ 137 Gd47
Huljajpole UA 205 Fb15
Huljen S 87 Gb33
Hullbridge GB 21 Ga27
Hüllhorst D 126 Cd38

Hullo EST 97 Jd44
Hülsede D 126 Da37
Hulsig DK 101 Dd19
Hulst NL 124 Ac39
Hult S 95 Fb44
Hult S 103 Fd49
Hultafors S 102 Ed49
Hulterstad S 111 Gb53
Hultsfred S 103 Ga50
Hultsjö S 103 Fc50
Huluboaia MD 177 Fc61
Huluboaia MD 177 Fc61
Hum BIH 159 Hd66
Hum HR 151 Fa60
Humada E 38 Db57
Humanby GB 17 Fc19
Humanes E 46 Dd63
Humberston GB 17 Fc21
Humble GB 11 Ec13
Humble DK 109 Dd28
Humenné SK 139 Ka47
Humes-Jorquenay F 30 Jb39
Humilladero E 60 Cd75
Humla S 102 Fa48
Humlebæk DK 109 Ec25
Humljani HR 152 Ha59
Humlum DK 100 Da22
Hummelholm S 80 Ha29
Hummelo NL 125 Bc37
Hummelsta S 95 Gb42
Hummelvik N 63 Hc07
Hummersö FIN 96 Hc41
Hummuvaara FIN 91 Ld32
Hummuli EST 106 La47
Humpolec CZ 136 Fd46
Humppi BG 82 Ka31
Humppila FIN 89 Jd37
Hunawihr F 31 Kb38
Hundåla N 70 Fa22
Hundberg N 62 Gd10
Hundberg S 72 Gd23
Hundborg DK 100 Da21
Hundeidvik N 76 Cc33
Hundelev DK 100 Dc20
Hundeluft D 127 Eb38
Hunderdorf D 135 Ec48
Hundeshagen D 126 Db40
Hundested DK 109 Eb25
Hundholmen N 66 Ga14
Hundisburg D 127 Ea37
Hundorp N 85 Dd36
Hundred House GB 15 Ea25
Hundsangen D 125 Cb38
Hundsbach D 133 Ca45
Hundsjö S 80 Ha29
Hundsjön S 73 Hd21
Hundslund DK 108 Dc24
Hundsnes N 76 Cb33
Hundvin N 84 Ca38
Hunedoara RO 175 Cc61
Hünfeld D 126 Da42
Hunge S RF 32
Hungen D 134 Cd43
Hungerford GB 20 Fa28
Hunnebostrand S 102 Ea46
Hunnefossen N 92 Ca46
Hunnestad S 102 Ec51
Hunspach F 25 Kc35
Hunstanton GB 17 Fd23
Huntingdon GB 20 Fc27
Huntley GB 19 Ec27
Huntly GB 7 Ec08
Huopana FIN 82 Kb30
Huopanankoski FIN 82 Kb30
Huparlac F 33 Ha50
Huppy F 23 Gc33
Hüpstedt D 126 Dc40
Hurbanovo SK 145 Hb52
Hurdal N 85 Ea40
Hurezani RO 175 Cc64
Huriel F 33 Ha45
Hurissalo FIN 91 La34
Hurlers Cross IRL 12 Bc23
Hurliness GB 5 Eb03
Hurones E 38 Dc58
Hurskaala FIN 90 La32
Hurstbourne Priors GB 20 Fa29
Hurstbourne Tarrant GB 20 Fa29
Hurst Green GB 20 Fd30
Hurşunlu TR 193 Hb85
Hürtgenwald D 125 Bc41
Hürth D 125 Bd41
Hurttala FIN 91 Lb37
Huruiești RO 176 Ed60
Hurum N 93 Da45
Hurum N 93 Dd42
Hurup DK 100 Da21
Hurva S 110 Fa55
Hurworth-on-Tees GB 11 Fa18
Hurzuf UA 205 Fa18
Husa N 84 Cb40
Husa S 78 Fa30
Hukanmaa S 68 Hd16
Hukkajärvi FIN 91 Ld36
Húsafell IS 2 Ac04
Husasău de Tinca RO 170 Ca57
Husbondliden S 80 Gd25
Husby D 108 Db28
Husby DK 100 Cd23
Husby N 70 Fa21
Husby S 95 Ga41

Husby-Ärlinghundra S 96 Gd42
Husby-Rekarne S 95 Ga43
Husby-Sjuhundra S 96 Ha42
Husby-Sjutolft S 96 Gc42
Hüseyin TR 199 Gb92
Hüseyinpaşalar TR 191 Ec82
Hushinish GB 4 Cd06
Huşi RO 173 Fb59
Husinec CZ 136 Fa48
Huskvarna S 103 Fb49
Huslenky CZ 137 Ha47
Husnes N 92 Ca41
Husnicioara RO 175 Cc64
Husøy N 62 Gb10
Hustad N 76 Cd31
Hustopeče CZ 137 Gc48
Husula FIN 90 La38
Husula FIN 91 Lb36
Husum D 108 Da29
Husum D 126 Da36
Husum S 80 Ha30
Husum-Ballum DK 108 Cd27
Husvika N 70 Ed22
Huszlew PL 131 Kb37
Hutovo BIH 158 Hb68
Hüttenberg A 144 Fb55
Hüttenberg D 126 Cc42
Hüttenrode D 127 Dd39
Hutthurm D 135 Ed49
Hüttlingen D 134 Db48
Hutton Sessay GB 11 Fa19
Hüttschlag A 143 Ed54
Huttukylä FIN 74 Ka23
Huttwil CH 141 Ca54
Huuhilo FIN 90 La36
Huuhilonkylä FIN 83 Lb25
Huuhkala FIN 69 Ka11
Huukki S 68 Jb16
Huutijärvi FIN 89 Jd36
Huutokoski FIN 83 Lc29
Huutokoski FIN 90 La32
Huutoperä FIN 82 Kb28
Huuttila FIN 90 Kc35
Huwniki PL 139 Kd45
Huy B 124 Ba41
Hüyük TR 199 Hb88
Hüyüklü TR 193 Ha87
Huzenbach D 133 Cb49
Hvåle N 85 Dc40
Hvaler N 93 Ea44
Hvalpsund DK 100 Db22
Hvalvik DK 3 Lae
Hvalynsk RUS 203 Ga11
Hvam DK 100 Da23
Hvam Mejeriby DK 100 Da23
Hvammstangi IS 2 Ad03
Hvam Stationsby DK 100 Db22
Hvanneyri IS 2 Ac04
Hvar HR 158 Gc67
Hvarnes N 93 Dd43
Hvastoviči RUS 202 Ed12
Hveragerði IS 2 Ac05
Hvidbjerg DK 100 Da22
Hvide Sande DK 108 Cd24
Hvilsom DK 100 Db22
Hvirring DK 108 Db25
Hvitsten N 93 Ea42
Hvittingfoss N 93 Dd43
Hvitträsk FIN 98 Kb39
Hvojna BG 184 Db74
Hvolsvöllur IS 2 Ac05
Hvornum DK 100 Dc22
Hvorslev DK 100 Dc23
Hybo S 87 Ga35
Hycklinge S 103 Ga48
Hyde GB 16 Ed21
Hyen N 84 Cb35
Hyenville F 22 Fa36
Hyères F 42 Ka55
Hyères-Plage F 42 Ka55
Hyet F 31 Jd41
Hylestad N 92 Cd44
Hylke DK 108 Dc24
Hylla N 78 Eb28
Hyllested Skovgårde DK 109 Dd24
Hyllinge DK 109 Eb27
Hyltebruk S 102 Ed51
Hyltinge S 95 Gb44
Hymont F 31 Jd38
Hynish GB 9 Da14
Hynnekle N 93 Da45
Hyönölä FIN 98 Ka39
Hyötyy FIN 90 La33
Hyrkäs FIN 74 Kb24
Hyrkkälä FIN 91 Lb35
Hyrsyla FIN 98 Ka39
Hyrvälä FIN 90 Kb37
Hyry FIN 74 Ka21
Hyrylä FIN 98 Kb39
Hyrynsalmi FIN 75 Kd25
Hysgjokaj AL 182 Ab76
Hysnes N 77 Dd29
Hyssna S 102 Ec49
Hythe GB 20 Fa30
Hythe GB 21 Ga30
Hytölä FIN 82 Kc31
Hytti FIN 91 Lc36
Hyväniemi FIN 75 Kd19
Hyvikkälä FIN 90 Ka37
Hyvinkää FIN 90 Kb38

Hyvölänranta FIN 82 Kb26
Hyvönmäki FIN 91 Ld32
Hyyniliä FIN 89 Jc35
Hyypiö FIN 74 Kb18
Hyyppä FIN 89 Ja34
Hyyrylä FIN 90 Ka34
Hyytiälä FIN 90 Ka34
Hyžne PL 139 Ka44

I

Ía GR 196 Db92
Iabloana MD 173 Fa55
Iacobeni RO 172 Ea56
Iacobeni RO 175 Dc60
Ialoveni MD 173 Fd58
Ialpugeni MD 173 Fc59
Iam RO 174 Bd63
Iana RO 177 Fa60
Ianca RO 177 Fa64
Ianca RO 179 Da68
Iancu Jianu RO 175 Da65
Ianoşda RO 170 Ca57
Iare RO 171 Da58
Iargara MD 177 Fc60
Iarova MD 173 Fb53
Iaşi RO 173 Fa57
Iásmos GR 184 Dc77
Ibahernando E 51 Ca67
Iballë AL 159 Jc70
Ibănești RO 172 Dd58
Ibănești RO 172 Ec54
Ibarra E 39 Ec56
Ibbenbüren D 117 Cb36
Ibdes E 47 Ec62
Ibeas de Juarros E 38 Dc58
Ibecik TR 198 Fd90
Ibi E 55 Fb70
İbirler TR 192 Fa82
Ibiza E 56 Gc69
İbradı TR 199 Hb90
Ibramowice PL 138 Ja43
İbrány H 147 Ka50
İbrikbaba TR 185 Eb79
İbriktepe TR 185 Eb77
Ibros E 52 Dc72
Ibstone GB 20 Fb27
İçalalia GR 189 Bc81
İçdere TR 187 Gc79
İçera BG 180 Eb72
İçhalia GR 189 Bc81
İchenhausen D 142 Db50
Ichenheim D 133 Ca49
İchtershausen D 127 Dd41
İçikler TR 192 Fb85
İçikli TR 193 Gc86
Icking D 143 Dd51
İcklingham GB 21 Ga25
İcksjö S 87 Fc38
İçlänzel RO 171 Db59
İclod RO 171 Da57
İçmeler TR 197 Fa91
İcna UA 202 Ed14
Icoana RO 175 Db66
İcusești RO 172 Ed58
Idala S 102 Ec50
Idala S 110 Fa56
İdanha-a-Nova P 44 Bb65
Idar-Oberstein D 133 Bd45
İdbacka S 79 Gb26
İdd N 94 Eb44
Ideciu de Jos RO 171 Dc58
Iden D 119 Eb35
Iden GB 21 Ga30
İdeņa LV 107 Lc50
İdivuoma S 68 Hd13
İdkerberget S 95 Fd40
İdom DK 100 Cd23
Idomeni GR 183 Ca76
İdoš SRB 174 Bb60
İdre S 86 Ed35
İdre S 86 Ed35
İdrija SLO 151 Fa58
İdrisyayla TR 193 Gc83
Idro I 149 Db58
İdrsko SLO 150 Ed57
Idstein D 133 Cb44
Idus LV 106 Kc47
İdvattnet S 79 Gb26
İdvor SRB 153 Jc60
İdvor SRB 174 Bb62
İdzikow PL 137 Gc44
İecava LV 106 Kb52
İeclelnieki LV 107 Lc50
İedera RO 176 Ea64
İeper B 21 Ha30
İepurești RO 180 Ea67
İerapetra GR 201 Dc96
İeras LV 105 Jc51
İeriki LV 106 Kd49
İerissós GR 184 Cd79
İernut RO 171 Db59
İle de Fédrun F 27 Ec42
İlenuța MD 173 Fb56
İl' eši RUS 99 Ma41
İlfeld D 126 Dc39
İlfeldorf D 143 Dd52
İlgaz TR 205 Fb20
İlgın TR 193 Hb87
İlgıziai LV 114 Kb57
İlguva LV 114 Kb57
İlhavo P 44 Ac63
İlia GR 189 Ca83
İlia RO 175 Cc60
İlıca TR 191 Ea86
İlıca TR 192 Fa81
İlıca TR 192 Fd80

İğdecik TR 192 Fb85
İğdecik TR 192 Fb87
İğdecik TR 193 Hb82
İğdır TR 186 Fd80
İgé F 34 Ja45
İgea E 47 Ec59
İgea Marina I 156 Eb64
İgel D 133 Bc45
İgelfors S 95 Fd45
İgelstorp S 103 Fb47
İgensdorf D 135 Dd46
İgerøy N 70 Ed22
İgersheim D 134 Da46
İggaldas N 64 Jb07
İggensbach D 135 Ed49
İggesund S 87 Gb36
İghiu RO 175 Cd60
İghtham GB 20 Fd29
İglarevo KSV 178 Ba71
İglesiarrubia E 46 Dc59
İglesias I 169 Bd79
İgliauka LV 114 Kb58
İglika BG 181 Ec70
İgliškėliai LV 114 Kb58
İgls A 143 Dd54
İgnaberga S 110 Fa54
İgnalina LT 115 Lb55
İgnaţei MD 173 Fc56
İğneada TR 186 Fa75
İğneler TR 185 Ed79
İgnești RO 170 Cb59
İgny-Comblizy F 24 Hc36
İgofomia PL 138 Ja44
İgomel' RUS 99 Ma44
İgoumenítsa GR 182 Ac80
İgrane HR 158 Gd67
İgrejinha P 50 Ad69
İgualada E 49 Gc61
İgualeja E 60 Cc76
İgüeña E 37 Ca56
İhamäki FIN 89 Jd38
İhamaniemi FIN 91 Lc32
İhamaru EST 107 Lb46
İhari FIN 90 Ka36
İharos H 152 Gd57
İharosberény H 152 Gd57
İhasalu EST 98 Kc42
İhaste EST 99 Lb45
İhastjärvi FIN 90 La33
İhlienworth D 118 Cd32
İhlow D 117 Cb33
İholdy F 39 Ja37
İhova SLO 144 Ga56
İhrlerstein D 135 Ea48
İhsaniye TR 186 Fc79
İhsaniye TR 186 Ga79
İhsaniye TR 193 Gc83
İhsaniye TR 193 Gc84
İhsaniye TR 199 Gd91
İi FIN 74 Ka23
İidir TR 191 Ea86
İigaste EST 106 La47
İijärvi FIN 64 Ka09
İiksenvaara FIN 83 Ld30
İinattijärvi FIN 75 Kc22
İinattiniemi FIN 75 Kc22
İiroonranta FIN 81 Jd31
İisalmi FIN 82 Kd28
İisinki FIN 74 Jd18
İisvesi FIN 82 Kd31
İitin FIN 90 Kd37
İittala FIN 90 Ka37
İisofd D 134 Cd47
İiskov DK 100 Da23
İlükste LV 115 Lb53
İittula FIN 97 Jc39
İlva Mare RO 172 Dd56
İlva Mică RO 171 Db57
İlvesjoki FIN 89 Jb33
İlyas TR 199 Gb88
İlyasbey TR 187 Gb80
İlyaslı TR 192 Fd85
İlyaslar TR 191 Ed84
İlyaslar TR 192 Fd83
İlyaspaşa TR 193 Hb84
İlža PL 130 Jc40
İzene LV 107 Lb48
İmamlar TR 198 Fd90
İmatra FIN 91 Lc35
İmatrankoski FIN 91 Lc35
İmavere EST 98 Kd44
İmbaré LT 113 Jb54
İmbradas LT 115 Lb54
İmbros GR 200 Cc95
İmecik TR 199 Gb91
İmeciksusuzu TR 199 Gb91
İmel' SK 145 Hb51
İmenicy RUS 99 Mb42
İmer I 150 Ea57
İmeros GR 184 Dc77
İmielin PL 138 Hc44
İmirzalıdı E 39 Fd71
İmjärvi FIN 90 Kd36
İmmeln S 111 Fb54
İmmendingen D 142 Cc51
İmmenhausen D 126 Da40
İmmenreuth D 135 Ea45
İmmenstaad D 142 Cd52
İmmenstadt D 142 Db52
İmmilä FIN 90 Kd37
İmmingham GB 17 Fc21
İmmolanmäki FIN 91 Lb32
İmola I 150 Dd63
İmón E 47 Ea62
İmotski HR 158 Gd66
İmpalata I 162 Ha75

Imperia – Jasanova

Imperia I 43 La52
Imphy F 30 Hb43
Impiö FIN 75 Kc20
Imposte I 156 Ed69
Impruneta I 155 Dc65
İmrallı TR 192 Ga87
İmrallı TR 193 Gd85
İmranlar TR 192 Fd83
Imrenler TR 199 Hb88
İmroz = Gökçeada TR 185 Dd80
Ims N 92 Ca44
Imsland N 92 Cb42
Imst A 142 Dc54
Ina FIN 81 Jc29
Iňačovce SK 139 Ka48
Inagh IRL 12 Bc22
Ináres H 146 Hd54
Inari FIN 69 Ka11
Inău RO 171 Db55
İnay TR 192 Fd86
Inca E 57 Hb67
İncecikler TR 191 Ec83
İncehisar TR 193 Gd85
İnceler TR 198 Ga88
Inch IRL 12 Ba24
Inch IRL 13 Cd23
Inchenhofen D 135 Dd49
Inchnadamph GB 4 Dd05
Inchree GB 6 Dc10
Inciems LV 106 Kc49
İncik TR 193 Gb82
Incinillas E 38 Dc56
İncirck TR 199 Gc92
İnciröy TR 198 Fd91
İnciriova TR 197 Ed88
Incisa in Val d'Arno I 155 Dc65
Incourt B 124 Ad41
Inčukalns LV 106 Kc50
Indal S 87 Gb33
Independența RO 177 Fa63
Independența RO 181 Ed67
Independența RO 181 Fb68
Indjija SRB 153 Jb61
Indor S 87 Fb37
Indra LV 115 Ld53
Indrāni LV 106 La50
Indre N 65 Kd05
Indre N 93 Db45
Indreabhán IRL 12 Bc21
Indre Arna N 84 Ca39
Indre Brenna N 64 Jc06
Indreeide N 76 Cd33
Indre Leirpollen N 64 Jb06
Indre Vieluft N 63 Hd07
Induno Olona I 148 Cb58
İnebolu TR 205 Fa19
İnece TR 185 Ec75
İnecik TR 185 Ed78
İnegöl TR 192 Ga81
Ineia CY 206 Hd97
Ineši LV 106 La50
Ineu RO 170 Ca58
Ineu RO 170 Cb56
Inevo MK 183 Ca74
Infantado P 50 Ab68
Infiesto (Piloña) E 37 Cc54
Ingå FIN 98 Ka40
Ingå station FIN 98 Ka40
Ingatestone GB 20 Fd27
Ingatrop S 103 Fd49
Ingavangis LT 114 Kc58
Ingdalen N 77 Dd29
Ingedal N 93 Ea44
Ingelfingen D 134 Da47
Ingelheim D 133 Cb44
Ingelstad S 103 Fc52
Ingelsvatnet N 78 Fa26
Ingevallsbo S 95 Fd40
Ingham GB 21 Ga25
Ingleton GB 11 Ec19
Ingoldingen D 142 Da51
Ingoldmells GB 17 Fd22
Ingoldsby GB 17 Fc23
Ingolstadt D 135 Dd48
Ingøy N 63 Ja04
Ingrandes F 28 Fb42
Ingrandes F 29 Ga44
Ingstrup DK 100 Dc20
Ingwiller F 25 Kb36
Inha FIN 89 Jd32
İnhisar TR 193 Gc81
İnhisar TR 193 Gc87
Iniesta E 53 Ec68
Iniö FIN 97 Ja39
Inis IRL 12 Bc22
Inis Córthaidh IRL 13 Cc24
Inis Díomáin IRL 12 Bc22
Inishannon IRL 12 Bc26
Inishcrone IRL 8 Bd18
Inistioge IRL 13 Cc24
Inkaliai LT 113 Jc56
Inkberrow GB 20 Ed25
Inke H 152 Gd57
Inkee FIN 75 Kd20
Inkere FIN 97 Jd39
Inkeriä FIN 90 La36
Inkernen FIN 90 La37
Inkilä FIN 90 La34
Inkilä FIN 90 La36
Inkoo FIN 98 Ka40
Inkoon asema FIN 98 Ka40
İnli TR 193 Gc83
İnli TR 193 Gd86
Innala FIN 89 Jd33
Innamo FIN 97 Ja40
Innansjön S 80 Hc26
Inndyr N 71 Fb18
Innellan GB 6 Dc13
Innerdalen N 71 Fb21
Inner-Eriz CH 141 Bd55
Innerferrera CH 142 Cd56
Innerkrems A 144 Fa55
Innerleithen GB 11 Eb14
Innermessan GB 10 Dc16
Innernzell D 135 Ed48
Innertällmo S 80 Gc29
Innertavle S 80 Hc28
Innerthal CH 142 Cc54
Innertkirchen CH 141 Ca55
Inner-Torga N 70 Ed23
Innervik S 72 Gc22
Innervillgraten A 143 Eb55
Innfield IRL 13 Cc21
Innfjorden N 77 Da32
Innfjorden N 77 Da32
Innhavet N 66 Fd15
Innichen I 143 Eb55
Inning D 143 Dd51
Innsbruck A 143 Dd53
Innset N 67 Gd13
Innset N 77 Dd32
Innvik N 84 Cc34
Inói GR 188 Ba86
Inói GR 189 Cb85
İnönü TR 191 Ec82
İnönü TR 193 Gb82
Inor F 24 Jb34
Inousses GR 191 Ea85
Inowłódz PL 130 Ja39
Inowrocław PL 121 Ha35
Ins CH 141 Bc54
Insar RUS 203 Fc10
Insch GB 7 Ec08
Insel Poel D 119 Ea31
Insjön S 95 Fc39
Ińsko PL 120 Fd33
Insming F 25 Ka36
Instefjord N 84 Ca37
Însurăței RO 177 Fa65
Interlaken CH 141 Bd55
Întorsura Buzăului RO 176 Eb62
Intra I 148 Cb57
Întregalde RO 175 Cd60
Introbio I 149 Cd58
Introd I 148 Bd58
Introdacqua I 161 Fa71
Inturkė LT 114 La56
Inver IRL 8 Ca16
Inveran GB 4 Dd06
Inveraray GB 6 Dc12
Inverarnan GB 7 Dd11
Inverbervie GB 7 Ed10
Invercassley GB 4 Dd06
Inverchapel GB 6 Dc12
Inverdruie GB 7 Ea09
Inverey GB 7 Eb09
Invergarry GB 7 Dd09
Inverigo I 149 Cc58
Inverin IRL 12 Bc21
Inverkeilor GB 7 Ec11
Inverkeithing GB 11 Eb13
Inverlochlarig GB 7 Dd11
Invermoriston GB 7 Dd08
Inverness GB 7 Ea08
Inveruglas GB 7 Dd12
Inveruno I 148 Cb59
Inverurie GB 5 Ed08
Inviken S 79 Fc26
Inwałd PL 138 Hd45
Inza RUS 203 Fd10
Inžavino RUS 203 Fc12
Inzell D 143 Ec52
Inzigkofen D 142 Cd51
Ioánina GR 182 Ad80
Iohanisfeld RO 174 Bc61
Ion Corvin RO 181 Fa67
Ionești RO 175 Cd65
Ionești RO 175 Db64
Ion Creangă RO 172 Ed58
Ion Roată RO 176 Ec65
Iordăcheanu RO 176 Eb64
Iordanovca MD 177 Fd60
Íos = Hóra GR 196 Db91
Ioulís GR 195 Cd88
Ipatele RO 173 Fa58
Ipáti GR 189 Bc83
Ipatovo RUS 205 Fd16
Ipeľský Sokolec SK 146 Hc51
Ipéria GR 189 Bc81
Iphofen D 134 Db45
Ipiķi LV 106 Kc47
Ipolyszög H 146 Hd51
Ipotești RO 172 Ec56
Ippesheim D 134 Db46
Ipplepen GB 19 Dd31
İpsala TR 185 Eb78
Ipsheim D 134 Db46
Ipsilí Ráhi GR 184 Da76
Ipswich GB 21 Gb26
Iráklia GR 183 Cb76
Iráklia GR 196 Db91
Iráklio GR 200 Da95
Irase EST 105 Jc46
Iratoșu RO 170 Bd59
Irbene LV 105 Jb49
Irbes LV 105 Jc49
Irchenrieth D 135 Eb46
Irchester GB 20 Fb25
Irdning A 144 Fa53
Irečekovo BG 181 Ec72
Iregszemcse H 145 Hb55
Iréo GR 197 Eb88
Irevik S 104 Ha48
Irgıllı TR 193 Gb87
Irig SRB 153 Jb61
Irissarry F 39 Fa55
Irixo E 36 Ba56
Irixoa E 36 Bb54
Irjanne FIN 89 Ja37
Irklijiv UA 204 Ed15
Irlamaz TR 191 Ed86
Irlanganlı TR 198 Fd88
Irlava LV 105 Jd51
Irmaklı TR 199 Hb89
Irmath AL 182 Ab74
Irnfritz A 136 Fd49
Irninniemi FIN 75 La21
Iron Acton GB 19 Ec28
Iron Bridge GB 15 Ec24
Irrel D 133 Bc44
Irrhausen D 133 Bb43
İrşadiye TR 186 Ga79
İrşadiye TR 192 Fa81
Iršava UA 204 Dd16
Irschenberg D 143 Ea52
Irsee D 142 Db51
Irsi LV 105 Jb50
Irši LV 106 La51
Irsina I 162 Gb75
Irthington GB 11 Ec16
Irthlingborough GB 20 Fb25
Iru EST 98 Kb42
Iruecha E 47 Ec62
Irujo E 39 Ec57
Irun E 39 Ec55
Iruña E 39 Ed57
Irurita E 39 Ed56
Irurtzun E 39 Ec56
Irús E 38 Dd56
Irvillac F 26 Dc38
Irvine GB 10 Dd14
Irvinestown GB 9 Cb17
İsaalanı TR 192 Fb82
Isaba E 39 Fa57
İsabey TR 192 Fd87
Isaccea RO 177 Fc64
Isacova MD 173 Fd57
Ísafjörður IS 2 Ac02
Isaki RUS 107 Mb50
Isakka FIN 82 La28
İsaköy TR 192 Ga81
İsaköy TR 192 Ga82
Isaku EST 99 La42
Işalnița RO 175 Cd66
Isane N 84 Cb34
Isaszeg H 146 Hd53
Isbister GB 5 Fa03
Işcălău MD 173 Fb56
Íscar E 46 Da61
Ischgl A 142 Db54
Ischia I 161 Fa75
Ischia di Castro I 156 Dd69
Ischitella I 161 Ga71
Isdes F 29 Gd41
Iselvmo N 67 Gd12
Isen D 143 Ea50
Isenbüttel D 126 Dc36
Isenvad DK 108 Db24
Iseo I 149 Da59
Iserlia MD 177 Fd60
Iserlohn D 125 Cb39
Isernhagen D 126 Db36
Isernia I 161 Fb72
İshakçılar TR 192 Ga82
İshaklı TR 185 Ec78
Isigny-le-Buat F 28 Fa38
Isigny-sur-Mer F 22 Fa35
Işıklar TR 187 Hb79
Işıklar TR 191 Ea81
Işıklar TR 191 Ec86
Işıklar TR 192 Fa83
Işıklar TR 192 Fb82
Işıklar TR 193 Gc85
Işıklar TR 198 Ga89
Işıklı TR 185 Ea78
Işıklı TR 192 Ga86
Isili I 169 Ca78
İskânkuyu TR 193 Gd83
Iskăr BG 181 Ed70
İskeleköy TR 192 Fa82
İskender TR 185 Eb75
İskenderli TR 187 Hb77
İskilip TR 205 Fb20
İskitler TR 193 Gc82
Iskra BG 181 Ec72
Iskra BG 184 Dc74
Iskrec BG 179 Cc70
Iskrovci SRB 179 Ca70
Iškuras N 64 Jc10
Isla E 38 Dd54
Isla Canela E 58 Ba74
Isla Cristina E 58 Ba74
Islallana E 39 Eb58
İslâmbeyli TR 186 Fa75
İslâmlar TR 198 Ga92
Islares E 38 Dd55
Išlaužas LT 114 Kc58
Islaz RO 180 Db68
Isle of Whithorn GB 10 Dd17
Isleornsay GB 6 Db09
Isles-sur-Suippe F 24 Hd35
Islip GB 20 Fa27
Ismailler TR 192 Fc84
Ismailli TR 191 Ec84
Ismaning D 143 Ea50
Ismeri LV 107 Ld51
İsmetpaşa TR 193 Gd83
Isna P 44 Ba65
Isnäs FIN 98 Kd39
Isnauda LV 107 Ld51
Isnello I 167 Fa84
Isnestoften N 63 Hd07
Işnovăț MD 173 Fd57
Isny im Allgäu D 142 Da52
Isoaho FIN 74 Kb20
Iso-Äiniö FIN 90 Kb36
Isoba E 37 Cd55
Iso-Evo FIN 90 Kb36
Isohalme FIN 69 Kc17
Iso-Hiisi FIN 97 Jd39
Isojoki FIN 89 Ja34
Isokumpu FIN 75 Kd21
Isokylä FIN 74 Kc18
Isokylä FIN 81 Jb31
Isokylä FIN 81 Jc29
Isokylä FIN 81 Ja31
Isokylä FIN 82 Ka31
Isokylä FIN 82 Ka25
Isokylä FIN 90 Kd32
Isokylä S 68 Hd17
Isokyrö FIN 81 Ja31
Isola F 43 Kc51
Isola 2000 F 43 Kc51
Isola d'Asti I 148 Ca61
Isola del Gran Sasso d'Italia I 156 Ed69
Isola della Scala I 149 Dc60
Isola delle Femmine I 166 Ec83
Isola del Liri I 160 Ed72
Isola di Capo Rizzuto I 165 Gd81
Isolahti FIN 90 Kb33
Isola Maggiore I 156 Ea67
Isola Rossa I 168 Ca74
Isolasanta I 155 Da64
Iso-Leppijärvi FIN 89 Ja34
Isomäki FIN 82 Kc27
Isona E 48 Gb59
Isoperä FIN 89 Jc38
Isorella I 149 Da60
Iso-Vimma FIN 89 Jb37
Isparta TR 199 Gc88
Isperih BG 181 Ec68
Isperihovo BG 179 Da73
Ispica I 167 Fc88
İspir TR 205 Ga19
Ispra I 148 Cb58
Ispringen D 134 Cc48
Issa RUS 107 Mb49
Issakka FIN 82 La28
Issakka FIN 83 Ma30
,Issaris GR 194 Bb88
Isselburg D 125 Bc38
Issigau D 135 Ea43
Issigeac F 33 Ga50
Issime I 148 Bd58
Issing D 142 Dc51
Isso E 53 Ec71
Issogne I 148 Bd58
Issoire F 34 Hb47
Issoudun F 29 Gd43
Issum D 125 Bc38
Is-sur-Tille F 30 Jb41
Issy-l'Evêque F 30 Hd44
Istalsna LV 107 Ma51
Istán E 60 Cc76
İstanbul TR 186 Fd78
Istarske Toplice HR 151 Fa60
Istebna PL 138 Hc46
Istérnia GR 196 Db88
Istfjorden N 77 Da32
Istha D 126 Cd40
Isthmía GR 189 Ca86
Istia d'Ombrone I 155 Dc68
Istibanja MK 179 Ca73
Istiéa GR 189 Ca83
Istok KSV 178 Ba70
Istorp S 102 Ec50
Istra RUS 202 Ed10
Isträsk S 73 Hc22
Istres F 42 Jb54
Istria RO 177 Fc66
Istrios GR 197 Ed93
Istruala FIN 90 Kd34
Istunmäki FIN 82 Kc31
Isufmuçaj AL 182 Ab75
Isverna RO 174 Cb63
Iszkáz H 145 Gd54
Itääho FIN 82 La28
Itä-Ähtäri FIN 81 Jd31
Itä-Aure FIN 89 Jc34
Itä-Karttula FIN 82 Kd30
Itäkeskus FIN 98 Kb39
Itäkoski FIN 74 Jc21
Itäkylä FIN 81 Jc30
Itämeri FIN 89 Jd33
Itä-Peräinne FIN 89 Jd32
Itäranta FIN 74 Kb18
Itäranta FIN 82 Kd26
Itäsalmi FIN 98 Kb39
Itéa GR 183 Bb77
Itéa GR 183 Bb79
Itéa GR 189 Bc85
Itháki = Vathí GR 188 Ac84
Itrabo E 60 Db76
Itri I 160 Ed73
Itterbeck D 117 Bd35
Ittireddu I 168 Ca75
Ittiri I 168 Bd75
Iturmendi E 39 Ec56
Itzehoe D 118 Db31
Itzgrund D 134 Dc44
Itziar E 39 Eb55
Iujnoe MD 177 Fc62
Iurievca MD 173 Fd59
Iváć H 145 Gb55
Ivacėvičy BY 202 Ea13
Ivajlovgrad BG 185 Ea75
Ivalo FIN 69 Ka11
Ivalon Matti FIN 69 Jd13
Iván H 145 Gc53
Ivanaj AL 159 Ja70
Ivanava BY 202 Ea14
Ivancea MD 173 Fd57
Ivančice CZ 137 Gb48
Ivande LV 105 Jb51
Ivanec HR 152 Gb57
Ivănești RO 173 Fa59
Ivangorod RUS 99 Ld41
Ivangorod RUS 202 Ea09
Ivanić Grad HR 152 Gb59
Ivanivka UA 205 Fa16
Ivanja Reka HR 152 Gb59
Ivanje SRB 178 Bc70
Ivanjevci MK 183 Bb75
Ivanjica SRB 178 Ad67
Ivanka SK 145 Hb50
Ivanka pri Dunaji SK 145 Gd51
Ivankiv UA 202 Ec14
Ivankovo HR 153 Hc60
Ivano-Frankivs'k UA 204 Ea16
Ivano-Frankove UA 204 Dd15
Ivanovca Nouă MD 173 Fc59
Ivanovka RUS 99 Mb40
Ivanovka RUS 113 Jb58
Ivanovka RUS 203 Ga09
Ivanovo BG 180 Ea68
Ivanovo BG 181 Ec71
Ivanovo BG 185 Ea74
Ivanovo RUS 203 Fa09
Ivanovo SRB 174 Bb64
Ivanovskoe RUS 99 Ma41
Ivanovskoe RUS 203 Fb08
Ivanska HR 152 Gc59
Ivanskaja BIH 152 Gd61
Ivanski BG 181 Ec70
Ivarrud N 71 Fb23
Ivarsberg S 94 Ec42
Ivars de Noguera E 48 Ga60
Ivedal N 92 Cd46
Iveland N 92 Cd46
Iveni MK 183 Bb76
Iversfjord N 64 Ka04
Ivești RO 177 Fa62
Ivetofta S 111 Fb54
Ivgolova LV 107 Ld51
Iville F 23 Ga36
Ivinghoe GB 20 Fb27
Ívira GR 184 Cc77
Ivjanec BY 202 Ea12
Ivje BY 202 Ea12
Ivö S 111 Fb54
Ivoskai LV 123 Kb30
Ivrea I 148 Bd59
İvrindi TR 191 Ed82
Ivry-la-Bataille F 23 Gb37
Ivybridge GB 19 Dd31
Iwaniska PL 130 Jc42
Iwanowice Dworskie PL 138 Ja44
Iwierzyce PL 139 Jd44
Iwiny PL 128 Ga41
Iwkowa PL 138 Jb45
Iwonicz PL 139 Ka45
Iwonicz-Zdrój PL 139 Ka45
Iwuy F 24 Hb32
Iyidere TR 205 Fd19
Izarra E 38 Ea56
Izbeglij BG 184 Dc74
Izbica PL 121 Gd29
Izbica PL 131 Kc41
Izbica Kujawska PL 129 Hb36
Izbičanj SRB 159 Jb66
Izbice PL 129 Gc39
Izbiceni RO 180 Db68
Izbicko PL 137 Ha43
Izbiște MD 173 Fd57
Izbiște SRB 174 Bc63
Izborsk RUS 107 Ld47
Izborsk RUS 202 Ea10
Izdebki PL 139 Ka45
Izeaux F 35 Jc48
Izeda P 45 Bd60
Izernore F 35 Jc45
Izgrev BG 186 Fa74
Izjum UA 203 Fb14
Izlake SLO 151 Fc57
Izmajil UA 204 Ec18
İzmir TR 191 Ec86
İzmit = Kocaeli TR 187 Gb78
Iznájar E 60 Da74
Iznalloz E 60 Dc74
İznik TR 186 Ga80
Izola SLO 150 Ed59
Izon F 32 Fc50
Ižora, Mal. RUS 99 Ma39
Izsák H 146 Hd55
Izsákfa H 145 Gd54
Izsófalva H 146 Jc50
Izvalta LV 115 Lc53
Izvara RUS 99 Ma41
Izvin RO 174 Bd60
Izvoare MD 173 Fa56
Izvoare MD 173 Fb55
Izvoarele RO 175 Db66
Izvoarele RO 176 Eb63
Izvoarele RO 177 Fc64
Izvoarele RO 180 Dd68
Izvoarele RO 180 Ea67
Izvoarele Sucevei RO 172 Dd55
Izvor BG 179 Cb68
Izvor BG 179 Cb72
Izvor MK 182 Ba74
Izvor MK 183 Bc74
Izvor SRB 178 Bc67
Izvor SRB 179 Ca71
Izvori MNE 159 Hd69
Izvorovo BG 180 Eb70
Izvorovo BG 182 Fa68
Izvorovo BG 185 Ea74
Izvoru RO 175 Dc66
Izvoru Alb RO 172 Ec57
Izvoru Bârzii RO 174 Cb64
Izvoru Berheciului RO 172 Ed59
Izvoru Crișului RO 171 Cd57
Izvoru Dulce RO 176 Ec63
Izvoru Mureșului RO 172 Ea59
Izvoz RUS 99 Ma42
İzzetinköy TR 186 Fb77
Jääjoki FIN 82 Ka29

J

Jaakkolankylä FIN 89 Jc34
Jaakonvaara FIN 83 Ld29
Jaala FIN 90 Kd36
Jaalanka FIN 75 Kc22
Jaalanka FIN 82 Kc25
Jääli FIN 74 Ka23
Jaama FIN 91 Ld32
Jäärja EST 106 Kc47
Jääskä FIN 81 Jc28
Jääskö FIN 68 Jc17
Jääskö FIN 68 Jc17
Jaatila FIN 74 Jd20
Jabălkovo BG 185 Dd74
Jabalquinto E 60 Db72
Jabapuszta H 145 Hb55
Jabbeke B 21 Ha29
Jablanac HR 151 Fc62
Jablan Do MNE 159 Hc69
Jablanica BG 179 Cd71
Jablanica BG 179 Da70
Jablanica BIH 158 Ha66
Jablanica MK 182 Ad75
Jablanica SLO 151 Fb59
Jablanica SRB 159 Jc64
Jablanka SRB 174 Bd63
Jablanovo BG 180 Eb71
Jabłoń PL 122 Jc32
Jabłoń PL 131 Kb38
Jablonec nad Nisou CZ 128 Fd42
Jablonevka RUS 113 Ja59
Jablonica SK 137 Gd49
Jabłonka PL 122 Ja33
Jabłonka PL 138 Ja46
Jabłonka Kościelne PL 123 Ka34
Jabłonki PL 139 Kb46
Jabłon-Kościelna PL 123 Ka34
Jabłonna PL 129 Gb37
Jabłonna PL 130 Jb36
Jabłonna PL 131 Kb40
Jabłonna-Lacka PL 131 Ka36
Jablonné nad Orlicí CZ 137 Gb44
Jablonné v. Podještědí CZ 128 Fc42
Jabłonowo PL 121 Gb35
Jabłonowo Pomorskie PL 122 Hc33
Jabłowo PL 121 Hb31
Jablůnka CZ 137 Ha46
Jablunkov CZ 138 Hc46
Jabučje SRB 153 Jc63
Jabugo E 59 Bc72
Jabuka BIH 159 Hd65
Jabuka BIH 159 Hd66
Jabuka HR 158 Gc66
Jabuka SRB 153 Jc61
Jabuka SRB 159 Ja66
Jabukovac HR 152 Gb60
Jabukovac SRB 174 Ca65
Jabukovik SRB 179 Ca70
Jaca E 39 Fb57
Jacentów PL 130 Jc41
Jáchymov CZ 135 Ec43
Jacinki PL 121 Gb31
Jackarby FIN 90 Kc38
Jackerath D 125 Bc40
Jadagoniai LV 114 Kb57
Jade D 118 Cc33
Jäder S 95 Gb43
Jaderberg D 118 Cc33
Jäderfors S 95 Gb39
Jadów PL 130 Jc36
Jadowniki PL 138 Jb44
Jädraås S 87 Ga38
Jadraque E 47 Ea63
Jadrtovac HR 157 Ga66
Jægerspris DK 109 Eb25
Jægervatn N 62 Ha09
Jaén E 60 Db73
Jagare BIH 152 Gd62
Jagel D 108 Db29
Jagėlonys LT 114 Kd58
Jagenbach A 136 Fc49
Jägerberg A 144 Ga55
Jagnilo BG 181 Ed70
Jagoda BG 180 Dd72
Jagodina SRB 174 Bc66
Jagodnja RUS 99 Mb45
Jagodne Małe PL 122 Jc31
Jagodnjak HR 153 Hc59
Jagsthausen D 134 Cd46
Jagstzell D 134 Db47
Jähdyspohja FIN 89 Jd33
Jahkola FIN 90 Kb37
Jahna-Löthain D 127 Ed41
Jahodná SK 145 Ha51
Jahorina BIH 159 Hc65
Jahotyn UA 202 Ec14
Jajce BIH 152 Gd63
Jajkowo PL 122 Hc33
Ják H 145 Gc54
Jakabszállás H 146 Ja55
Jäkälätieva FIN 68 Hc12
Jäkäläväara FIN 75 Kc20
Jakalj SRB 159 Jb64
Jakari FIN 90 Kc38
Jakėnai LT 115 Lb55
Jāķi LV 105 Jc49
Jakimovo BG 179 Cc68
Jakkukylä FIN 74 Ka23
Jakkula FIN 81 Ja31
Jakkula FIN 97 Jd39
Jäkkvik S 72 Gb20
Jaklovce SK 138 Jc48
Jakobsbyn S 94 Ed44
Jakobsfors S 73 Hc24
Jakobshagen D 120 Fa34
Jakobsnes N 65 Kd07
Jakobstad FIN 81 Jb28
Jakokoski FIN 83 Ld30
Jakola FIN 91 Lc35
Jakoruda BG 179 Cd73
Jakovlevo RUS 203 Fa13
Jakovo SRB 153 Jc62
Jaksamo FIN 75 Kd19
Jaksice PL 121 Ha35
Jaktorów PL 130 Jb37
Jakubany SK 138 Jc47
Jakubčovice n. O. CZ 137 Ha45
Jakubów PL 131 Jd37
Jakubowo Lubińskie PL 128 Ga40
Jakunówko PL 123 Jd30
Jäla S 102 Fa48
Jalance E 54 Fa68
Jalasjärvi FIN 89 Jb32
Jalasjoki FIN 89 Jc37
Jaligny-sur-Besbre F 34 Hc45
Jalkala FIN 82 Kd31
Jallais F 28 Fb42
Jällby S 102 Ed48
Jälluntofta S 102 Fa51
Jalón E 55 Fc70
Jalón de Cameros E 47 Eb59
Jâlons F 24 Hd36
Jalová SK 139 Kb47
Jałówka PL 123 Kb32
Jałówka PL 123 Kc33
Jalta UA 205 Fa18
Jämaja EST 105 Jc47
Jamali FIN 83 Lc28
Jämäs FIN 83 Lb26
Jambol BG 180 Eb72
Jameln D 119 Dd34
Jamena SRB 153 Hd61
Jametz F 24 Jb34
Jämijärvi FIN 89 Jb35
Jamilena E 60 Db73
Jäminkipohja FIN 89 Jd34
Jämjö S 111 Ga54
Jamkino RUS 107 Mb46
Jamm RUS 99 Ld44
Jammerdal N 94 Ec41
Jamna BG 179 Da71
Jamnice CZ 136 Fd48
Jamnička Kiselica HR 151 Ga59
Jamno PL 120 Ga30
Jamoigne B 132 Ba44
Jampil' UA 204 Eb16
Jämsä FIN 81 Jd28
Jämsä FIN 90 Kb34
Jämsänkoski FIN 90 Kb34
Jämshög S 111 Fc54
Jämton S 73 Ja21
Jamu-Mare RO 174 Bd62
Janaillat F 33 Gc46
Janakkala FIN 90 Ka37
Janapole LT 113 Jd55
Janča SRB 178 Ad68
Jandelsbrunn D 136 Fa49
Janderup DK 108 Cd25
Jäneda EST 98 Kd42
Janežovci SLO 144 Ga56
Jänhiälä FIN 91 Lc35
Janiewice PL 121 Gb30
Janik PL 130 Jc41
Janikowo PL 121 Ha35
Jäniskylä FIN 90 Kd35
Janiszewo PL 122 Hc35
Janiszowice PL 128 Fc38
Janja BIH 153 Hd62
Janjevo KSV 178 Bb71
Janjici BIH 159 Jb65
Janjina HR 158 Ha68
Jankai LV 114 Kb58
Jänkisjärvi S 73 Ja19
Jánkmajtis H 147 Kc51
Jankov CZ 136 Fc46
Jankov Most SRB 174 Bb61
Jankovo BG 181 Ed71
Jännevirta FIN 82 La30
Janopole LV 107 Ld51
Jánoshalma H 153 Hd57
Jánosháza H 145 Gd54
Jánossomorja H 145 Gd52
Janov CZ 137 Gd44
Janova Lehota SK 138 Hc49
Janovice nad Úhl. CZ 135 Ed47
Janovice na Hane CZ 137 Gc47
Janów PL 123 Kb32
Janów PL 130 Hd42
Janów PL 130 Ja37
Janowa PL 137 Gc43
Janowiec PL 131 Jd40
Janowiec Wielkopolski PL 121 Gd35
Janówka PL 123 Ka31
Janówko PL 122 Hd33
Janów Lubelski PL 131 Ka41
Janowo PL 122 Ja33
Janowo PL 123 Jd33
Janów Podlaski PL 131 Kb36
Jänschwalde D 128 Fb38
Jansjö S 79 Ga28
Janské Lazně CZ 136 Ga43
Jänsmässholmen S 79 Fb29
Jantar PL 121 Hb30
Jantarnyi RUS 113 Hd58
Jantra BG 180 Dc71
Januszkowice PL 137 Ha43
Janville F 29 Gc39
Janzé F 28 Ed40
Japca MD 173 Fd55
Jäppilä FIN 90 La32
Jaraba E 47 Ec62
Jarabá SK 138 Ja48
Jaraczewo PL 129 Gd38
Jarafuel E 54 Fa69
Jaraicejo E 51 Cb66
Jaraiz de la Vera E 45 Cb65
Jarak SRB 153 Jb61
Järämä lappläger S 67 Hb13
Jarandilla de la Vera E 45 Cb65
Jaransk RUS 203 Fc08
Jarantowice PL 121 Hb33
Järbo S 94 Ec45
Järbo S 95 Gb39
Jarceley E 37 Ca55
Jarcevo RUS 202 Ec11
Jarcieu F 34 Jb48
Jarczew PL 131 Jd38
Jard-sur-Mer F 32 Ed45
Jardžilovci BG 179 Cb71
Jarek HR 152 Gb58
Jaren N 85 Ea40
Jargeau F 29 Gd40
Jarhoinen FIN 68 Jb17
Jarhois S 68 Jb17
Järise EST 105 Jc46
Jariștea RO 176 Ed62
Jårkastaka S 68 Hc13
Jarkovac SRB 174 Bb62
Järkvissle S 87 Gb32
Järlåsa S 96 Gc42
Järlepa EST 98 Kc43
Jarlovica BG 179 Cb68
Jarlovo BG 179 Cc72
Jarmen D 119 Ed32
Jarmenovci SRB 153 Jc63
Jarmina HR 153 Hc60
Jarmolynci UA 204 Eb15
Järn S 102 Ec46
Järna S 95 Fb39
Järna S 96 Gc44
Jarnac F 32 Fc47
Jarnages F 33 Gd45
Järnes S 80 Hb29
Järnesklubb S 80 Hb30
Järnforsen S 103 Fd50
Järnskog S 94 Ec42
Jarny F 25 Jc35
Jarocin PL 129 Gd38
Jarocin PL 131 Ka42
Jaroměř CZ 136 Ga43
Jaroměřice CZ 137 Gc46
Jaroměřice nad Rokytnou CZ 136 Ga48
Jaroslavci BG 179 Cb70
Jaroslavice CZ 137 Gb49
Jaroslavl' RUS 203 Fa09
Jarosław PL 139 Kb44
Jarosławiec PL 121 Gb29
Jarosławsko PL 120 Fd35
Jarošov nad Nežárkou CZ 136 Fc47
Jaroszów PL 129 Gb41
Järpås S 102 Ed47
Järpen S 78 Fa30
Järpliden S 94 Ec39
Jarplund-Weding D 108 Db28
Järrestad S 111 Fb56
Jars F 29 Ha41
Järsnäs S 103 Fc49
Jarszewko PL 120 Fc32
Jarszewo PL 120 Fc32
Jarszówka PL 128 Ga40
Järva-Jaani EST 98 Kc43
Järvakandi EST 98 Kc44
Järva-Madise EST 98 Kd43
Järvberget S 80 Gc29
Järvelä FIN 90 Kb37
Järvelänranta FIN 75 Lb23
Järvenpää FIN 82 Kd27
Järvenpää FIN 82 Kb31
Järvenpää FIN 82 La28
Järvenpää FIN 89 Ja32
Järvenpää FIN 90 La35
Järvenpää FIN 90 Kb38
Järvenpää FIN 91 Lb33
Järvenpää FIN 97 Jd39
Järvenperä FIN 97 Ja39
Järventaus FIN 91 Ma32
Järventausta FIN 81 Jd28
Järventausta FIN 89 Jb36
Järvikäinen FIN 69 Jd11
Järvikylä FIN 81 Jd27
Järvikylä FIN 82 Kc26
Järvikylä FIN 82 Kc25
Järvikylä FIN 82 Ka27
Järvikylä FIN 89 Ja36
Järvirova FIN 68 Jb17
Järvsand S 79 Fd28
Järvselja EST 99 Lc45
Järvsjö S 79 Gb26
Järvsö S 87 Ga36
Järvsta S 96 Gc39
Järvtjärn S 80 Hc26
Järvträsk S 72 Ha24
Jarząbki PL 130 Jc42
Jarzé F 28 Fc41
Jasanova AL 159 Jb69

Jasa Tornič SRB 174 Bc61
Jaščera RUS 99 Mb41
Jasenak HR 151 Fc60
Jasenica BIH 152 Gb62
Jasenica SRB 174 Ca66
Jasenice HR 157 Ga64
Jasenie SK 138 Hd48
Jasenik HR 152 Gd58
Jasenkovo BG 181 Ec69
Jasenovac HR 152 Gc60
Jasenovec BG 181 Ec69
Jasenovo SRB 174 Bc63
Jasenovo SRB 158 Ad67
Jasenskaja RUS 205 Fc16
Jasień PL 121 Gd30
Jasień PL 121 Hb30
Jasień PL 128 Fc39
Jasienica PL 120 Fb33
Jasienica PL 128 Fc38
Jasienica PL 130 Jc36
Jasienica PL 138 Hc45
Jasienica Dolna PL 137 Gd43
Jasienie PL 129 Ha41
Jasieniec PL 130 Jb46
Jasika SRB 178 Bd66
Jasionka PL 139 Ka43
Jasionna PL 121 Gb35
Jasionna PL 130 Hd38
Jasionów PL 138 Ja46
Jasionówka PL 123 Kb32
Jasionowo PL 123 Ka30
Jašiūnai LT 114 La58
Jaškul' RUS 205 Ga15
Jaślany PL 139 Jd43
Jasło PL 139 Jd45
Jasná SK 138 Hd48
Jasnaja Poljana RUS 113 Jd59
Jasna Poljana BG 181 Fa73
Jasnoe RUS 113 Jc57
Jasnogorsk RUS 203 Fa11
Jasov SK 138 Jc48
Jásová SK 145 Hb51
Jastarnia PL 121 Hb29
Jastkowice PL 131 Ka42
Jastrebarsko HR 151 Ga59
Jastrebino RUS 99 Ma41
Jastrowie PL 121 Gc33
Jastrząb PL 130 Jc40
Jastrząbka PL 122 Jc34
Jastrzębia PL 130 Jc39
Jastrzębia PL 138 Jc45
Jastrzębia Góra PL 112 Ha58
Jastrzębie-Zdrój PL 137 Hb45
Jaświły PL 123 Kb32
Jasynuvata UA 205 Fb15
Jászalsószentgyörgy H 146 Jb53
Jászapáti H 146 Ja52
Jászárokszállás H 146 Ja52
Jászberény H 146 Ja53
Jaszczołty PL 123 Ka35
Jászfényszaru H 146 Ja52
Jászkarajenő H 146 Jb54
Jászkisér H 146 Jb53
Jászladány H 146 Jb53
Jászszentandrás H 146 Jb52
Jászszentlászló H 146 Ja56
Jät S 103 Fc52
Játar E 60 Db75
Jatko FIN 75 Kc22
Jättendal S 87 Gb35
Jättensö S 87 Ga33
Jättölä FIN 96 Ka39
Jatwieź PL 123 Kb32
Jatznick D 120 Fa33
Jauge F 32 Fb51
Jauhojärvi FIN 68 Jc16
Jauja E 60 Cd74
Jaulin E 47 Ec45
Jaulnay F 28 Fd43
Jaun CH 141 Bc55
Jaunaglona LV 107 Lc52
Jaunalūksne LV 107 Lc48
Jaunanna LV 107 Lc49
Jaunauce LV 105 Jd52
Jaunbērze LV 105 Jd51
Jaunciems LV 105 Jc48
Jaunciems LV 105 Jd49
Jaundziras LV 105 Jd51
Jaungulbene LV 107 Lb49
Jauniūnai LT 114 La57
Jaunjelgava LV 106 Kd51
Jaunjērčēni LV 106 Kd48
Jaunkalsnava LV 106 La51
Jaunlaicene LV 107 Lb48
Jaunlutriņi LV 105 Jc51
Jaunmuiža LV 105 Jc51
Jaunpasts LV 105 Jd50
Jaunpiebalga LV 106 La51
Jaunpils LV 106 Ka51
Jaunsaras E 39 Ec56
Jaunsāti LV 105 Jd51
Jaunsaule LV 106 Kc52
Jaunsmiltene LV 106 La48
Jaunsvirlauka LV 106 Kb52
Jaurakkajärvi FIN 75 Kc23
Jausa EST 97 Jc45
Jausiers F 43 Kb51
Javárus FIN 69 Kb17
Jávea E 55 Fd70
Jävenitz D 127 Ea36
Javerlhac-et-la-Chapelle-Saint-Robert F 33 Ga48

Javgur MD 173 Fc59
Javier E 39 Fa57
Javierre E 40 Fc58
Javorani BIH 152 Gd62
Javorec BG 180 Dc71
Javorie SK 138 Ja47
Javoriv UA 204 Dd15
Javorná CZ 135 Ec44
Javorná CZ 135 Ed47
Javornic HR 151 Fd61
Javornik CZ 137 Gc43
Jävre S 73 Hd24
Javron F 28 Fc38
Jawor PL 129 Gb41
Jaworki PL 138 Jb46
Jawornik PL 138 Ja45
Jaworze PL 138 Hc45
Jaworzno PL 129 Hb41
Jaworzno PL 138 Hd47
Jaworzyna Śląska PL 129 Gb42
Jayena E 60 Db75
Jaywick GB 21 Gb27
Jaz MNE 159 Hd70
Jazente P 44 Ba61
Jeantes F 24 Hc33
Jebel RO 174 Bc61
Jedburgh GB 11 Ec15
Jedlicze PL 139 Jd46
Jedlina-Zdrój PL 129 Gb42
Jedliňsk PL 130 Jc39
Jedlnia-Letnisko PL 130 Jc39
Jednorożec PL 122 Jb34
Jedovnice CZ 137 Gc47
Jędrychowo PL 122 Hc32
Jędrychowo PL 122 Hd32
Jędrzejów PL 130 Ja42
Jędrzychowice PL 129 Gb39
Jédula E 59 Ca76
Jedwabne PL 123 Jd33
Jedwabno PL 122 Jb32
Jeesiö FIN 69 Jd15
Jeesiöjärvi FIN 69 Jd15
Jegălia RO 181 Fa67
Jegerup DK 108 Db27
Jeggau D 127 Dd36
Jegind DK 100 Da22
Jegłownik PL 122 Hc31
Jégun F 40 Fd54
Jegunovce MK 178 Bb72
Jēkabpils LV 106 La52
Jeksen DK 108 Dc24
Jektvika N 70 Fa19
Jektvika N 70 Fa19
Jelaci SRB 178 Bb68
Jelah BIH 152 Hb62
Jelanec' UA 204 Ed16
Jelašca BIH 159 Hc66
Jelašnica SRB 174 Ca66
Jelcz-Laskowice PL 129 Gd41
Jelen Do SRB 159 Jc64
Jelenec SK 145 Hb50
Jelenia Gora PL 128 Ga42
Jeleniewo PL 123 Ka30
Jelenin PL 128 Fd39
Jelenino PL 121 Gb32
Jelesejevići SRB 159 Jb64
Jelésnia PL 138 Hd46
Jelgava LV 106 Kb51
Jelgavkrasti LV 106 Kc49
Jelling DK 108 Db25
Jelonki PL 123 Jd34
Jelovac SRB 174 Bd66
Jelovoje RUS 113 Jd58
Jełowa PL 129 Ha42
Jels DK 108 Da26
Jelsa HR 158 Gc67
Jelsa N 92 Cb42
Jelšane SLO 151 Fb60
Jelšava SK 138 Jb49
Jelsi I 161 Fc73
Jemelle B 132 Ba43
Jemenovci SRB 174 Bc62
Jemenuño E 46 Da62
Jemeppe-sur-Meuse B 124 Ad42
Jemgum D 117 Cb33
Jemielnica PL 137 Hb43
Jemielno PL 129 Gb39
Jena D 127 Ea41
Jenakijeve UA 205 Fb15
Jenaz CH 142 Cd54
Jenbach A 143 Ea53
Jenikowo PL 120 Fd33
Jénlain F 24 Hc33
Jennersdorf A 145 Gb55
Jenny S 103 Gb49
Jensåsvoll N 86 Ec32
Jenstad N 77 Dc33
Jenzat F 34 Hb45
Jeppo FIN 81 Jb29
Jeprca SLO 151 Fb57
Jepua FIN 81 Jb29
Jerez de la Frontera E 59 Bd76
Jerez del Marquesado E 61 Dd75
Jerez de los Caballeros E 51 Bc70
Jergucat AL 182 Ac79
Jérica E 54 Fb66
Jerichow D 127 Eb36
Jerka PL 129 Gc38
Jerli Perlez KSV 178 Bb71
Jerpåsen N 70 Fa20
Jerretspass GB 9 Cd18
Jersika LV 107 Lb52
Jerslev DK 100 Dc20

Jeršov RUS 203 Ga11
Jeršovo RUS 113 Jb58
Jerte E 45 Cb65
Jerup DK 101 Dd19
Jerxheim D 127 Dd37
Jerzens A 142 Dc54
Jerzmanowa PL 128 Ga39
Jerzmanowice PL 138 Hd44
Jerzu I 169 Cb78
Jerzwałd PL 122 Hc32
Jesberg D 126 Cd41
Jesenice CZ 135 Ed44
Jesenice CZ 136 Fb45
Jesenice SLO 144 Fa56
Jeseník CZ 137 Gd44
Jeserig D 127 Ec37
Jesewitz D 127 Ec40
Jesi I 156 Ec66
Jesico I 150 Eb59
Jésonville F 31 Jd39
Jessen D 127 Ed39
Jessheim N 94 Eb41
Jeßnitz D 127 Eb39
Jesteburg D 118 Db33
Jestetten D 141 Cb52
Jestřebí CZ 136 Fc43
Jeti EST 106 La47
Jettingen D 134 Cc49
Jettingen-Scheppach D 142 Db50
Jetzendorf D 143 Dd50
Jeugny F 30 Hd39
Jeumont F 24 Hc32
Jeurre F 31 Jc44
Jevenstedt D 118 Db30
Jever D 117 Cc32
Jevíčko CZ 137 Gc46
Jevišovice CZ 136 Ga48
Jevnaker N 85 Dd40
Jevpatorija UA 205 Fa17
Jevreni MD 173 Fd57
Ježe PL 123 Jd32
Jezera RO 174 Ba63
Jezerane HR 151 Fd61
Jezerce KSV 178 Bb71
Jezero BIH 152 Gd63
Ježević HR 158 Gc65
Ježevo HR 152 Gb58
Ježewo PL 121 Hb33
Jeżewo PL 122 Hd35
Jezierany PL 122 Ja31
Jezierzyce Wielkie PL 129 Ha36
Jeziorki Wałeckie PL 120 Ga34
Jeziorko PL 123 Jd33
Jeziorowice PL 130 Hd42
Jeziorsko PL 129 Hb38
Jezierzany PL 131 Ka39
Jeżów PL 130 Ja38
Jeżowe PL 139 Ka43
Jiana RO 174 Cb65
Jiana Mare RO 174 Cb65
Jibert RO 176 Ea61
Jibou RO 171 Cd56
Jichișu de Jos RO 171 Da57
Jičín CZ 136 Fd43
Jičíněves CZ 136 Fd43
Jidvei RO 175 Db60
Jierijärvi S 73 Ja18
Jieznas LT 114 Kc58
Jihlava RO 177 Fb63
Jijona E 55 Fb71
Jilava RO 176 Ea66
Jilemnice CZ 136 Fd43
Jílové CZ 128 Fa42
Jílové u Prahy CZ 136 Fb45
Jiltjaur S 72 Gb23
Jimbolia RO 174 Bb60
Jimena E 60 Dc73
Jimena de la Frontera E 59 Cb77
Jiménez de Jamuz E 37 Cb58
Jimramov CZ 137 Gb46
Jina RO 175 Da61
Jince CZ 136 Fa45
Jindřichov CZ 137 Gd44
Jindřichovice CZ 135 Ec44
Jindřichovice pod Smŕkem CZ 128 Fd43
Jindřichův Hradec CZ 136 Fc48
Jinošov CZ 137 Gb47
Jirkov CZ 135 Ed43
Jirlău RO 176 Ed64
Jistebnice CZ 136 Fb46
Jitia RO 176 Ec62
Jivjany CZ 135 Ec46
Joachimsthal D 120 Fa35
Joakim-Gruevo BG 180 Db73
João Serra P 58 Ad72
Joarilla de las Matas E 37 Cd68
Jobbágyi H 146 Ja52
Jochberg A 143 Eb53
Jocketa D 135 Eb43
Jockfall S 73 Ja19
Jockgrim D 133 Cb47
Jódar E 60 Dc73
Jodłowa PL 139 Jd44
Jodłowo PL 123 Kb30
Jodoigne B 124 Ad41
Jõelähtme EST 98 Kc42
Joensuu FIN 83 Ld30

Joesjö S 71 Fc22
Jõgeva EST 98 La44
Johampolis LT 114 Ka55
Johannesfors S 80 Hc28
Johann-Georgenstadt D 135 Ec43
Johannishus S 111 Fd54
Johanniskirchen D 135 Ec49
Johanniskreuz D 133 Ca46
Johansfors S 102 Ed52
Johansfors S 103 Fd52
John o'Groats GB 5 Ec04
Johnsbach A 144 Fb53
John's Cross GB 20 Fd30
Johnshaven GB 7 Ed10
Johnstone GB 10 Dd13
Johnstown IRL 13 Cb23
Johnstown IRL 13 Cd23
Johovac BIH 152 Hb62
Johovac BIH 153 Hd62
Jöhstadt D 135 Ed43
Jõhvi EST 99 Lb42
Joigny F 30 Hb39
Joinville F 30 Jb38
Joița RO 176 Ea66
Jokela FIN 74 Ka19
Jokela FIN 82 Kc27
Jokela FIN 90 Kb38
Jokijärvi FIN 75 Kd21
Jokijärvi FIN 82 Kc30
Jokikunta FIN 98 Ka39
Jokikylä FIN 74 Ka23
Jokikylä FIN 75 La24
Jokikylä FIN 81 Jd27
Jokikylä FIN 81 Jc29
Jokikylä FIN 81 Ja31
Jokikylä FIN 82 Kb27
Jokikylä FIN 82 Ka25
Jokikylä FIN 89 Jc33
Jokina Čuprija SRB 159 Jb65
Jokiniemi FIN 90 Ka38
Jokioinen FIN 89 Jd38
Jokiperä FIN 81 Ja31
Jokipii FIN 89 Jb32
Jokisalo FIN 81 Ja31
Jokivarsi FIN 81 Jd31
Jokivarsi FIN 89 Jb34
Jokivarsi FIN 89 Jc32
Jokikylä FIN 83 Ld27
Jokkmokk S 72 Ha19
Jokůbavas LT 113 Jb55
Jola E 51 Bb67
Jolanda di Savoia I 150 Ea61
Jolda P 44 Ad59
Jolkka FIN 81 Jc28
Jølle N 92 Cb47
Jöllen S 87 Fb37
Joloskylä FIN 74 Kb23
Jolstad N 86 Ea32
Joltai MD 177 Fd61
Jomås N 93 Da45
Jonai LV 114 Kd59
Jönåker S 95 Gb45
Jonasvollen N 86 Ec34
Jonava LT 114 Kc57
Jonchery F 31 Kb40
Jonchery F 30 Jb39
Jonchery-sur-Vesle F 24 Hc35
Joncy F 30 Ja44
Jondal N 84 Cb39
Jondalen N 93 Dc42
Joniec PL 121 Gb32
Joniškis LT 114 Kb53
Joniškis LT 115 Lb56
Joniškėlis LT 114 Kc53
Jonkeri FIN 83 Lc26
Jönköping S 103 Fb49
Jonkovo BG 181 Ec69
Jonkowe PL 122 Ja31
Jonku FIN 75 Kc22
Jonquières F 42 Jb52
Jonsa FIN 82 La28
Jonsberg S 103 Gb46
Jonsdorf D 128 Fc42
Jonsered S 102 Ec49
Jonsnyttan S 95 Fc42
Jønsrud N 86 Eb38
Jonsrud N 94 Eb39
Jonstorp S 110 Ec54
Jonvelle F 31 Jc39
Jonzac F 32 Fc48
Jonzier F 35 Jd45
Jöpiste EST 97 Jd45
Joppolo I 164 Ga82
Jora de Mijloc MD 173 Fd56
Jorăști RO 177 Fb61
Jordanów PL 138 Ja45
Jordanów Śląski PL 129 Gc42
Jordbro S 96 Gd44
Jordet N 86 Ec36
Jordløse DK 108 Dc27
Jörgastak N 64 Jc10
Jork D 118 Db33
Jörlanda S 102 Eb48
Jørlunde DK 109 Dd25
Jormasjokisuu FIN 82 La26
Jormlien S 79 Fb25
Jormua FIN 82 Kd25
Jormvattnet S 79 Fb26

Jörn S 73 Hb24
Jornini LV 105 Jc49
Jörpeland N 92 Ca44
Jorquera E 54 Ed69
Jørstad N 78 Ed27
Jørstad N 92 Ca43
Jørstadmoen N 85 Ea37
Jørundland N 93 Da44
Jorvas FIN 98 Kb40
Jošanica BIH 159 Hc65
Jošanica KSV 178 Ba70
Jošanica SRB 178 Bd67
Jošanička Banja SRB 178 Ba68
Joseni RO 172 Ea58
Joseni Bârgăului RO 171 Dc57
Joševa SRB 153 Ja62
Josipdol HR 151 Fd61
Josipovac HR 153 Hc59
Joskaudai LT 113 Jd54
Joškar-Ola RUS 203 Fc08
Josnes F 29 Gc40
Jøsok N 76 Cb33
Jossa D 134 Da43
Jössefors S 94 Ec42
Josselin F 27 Eb40
Jøssenøya N 77 Dc29
Jossgrund D 134 Da44
Jøsund N 78 Be27
Jostaji LV 105 Jd51
Jósvafő H 138 Jb49
Josvainiai LT 114 Kb56
Jotainiai LT 114 Kc55
Jou P 44 Bb60
Joudeikiai LT 114 Ka53
Joudeikiai LT 113 Jd55
Joué-Etiau F 28 Fb42
Joué-lès-Tours F 29 Ga42
Joué-sur-Erdre F 28 Fa41
Jouet-sur-l'Aubois F 30 Hb43
Jõuga EST 99 Lb42
Jougne F 31 Ka43
Jouhenvaara FIN 91 Ld32
Jouhet F 33 Ga45
Jouix F 33 Gd48
Joukio FIN 91 Ld34
Joukokylä FIN 75 Kd23
Jouques F 42 Jd53
Joure NL 117 Bc34
Journy F 21 Gc30
Joutenniva FIN 82 Ka27
Joutsa FIN 90 Kc34
Joutsenkylä FIN 75 La20
Joutsenlampi FIN 90 Kc34
Joutseno FIN 91 Lc36
Joutsijärvi FIN 74 Kc18
Joutsjärvi FIN 90 Kd35
Joux-la-Ville F 30 Hc41
Jouy F 29 Gc42
Jouy-le-Châtel F 24 Hb37
Jouy-le-Potier F 29 Gc40
Jovkovo BG 181 Fb68
Jovnes N 93 Db45
Jovsa SK 139 Ka48
Joyeuse F 34 Ja51
Józefów PL 130 Jc37
Józefów PL 131 Jd41
Józefów PL 131 Kc42
Józsa H 147 Ka52
Juankoski FIN 83 Lb29
Juan-les-Pins F 43 Kc53
Jübar D 119 Dd35
Jübek D 108 Db29
Jublains F 28 Fb39
Jubrique E 59 Cb76
Jučaičiai LT 113 Jd56
Jüchen D 125 Bc40
Jüchnov RUS 202 Ed11
Juchnowiec Dolny PL 123 Kb34
Juchowo PL 121 Gb32
Jüchsen D 134 Dc43
Jucu RO 171 Da58
Judaberg N 92 Ca43
Judaš LV 106 Kd50
Judelnik BG 180 Eb68
Judenau A 144 Ga50
Judenburg A 144 Fc54
Judin RUS 203 Fc14
Judino RUS 107 Ma48
Judino RUS 113 Jb58
Judinsalo FIN 90 Kb34
Judrėnai LT 113 Jc56
Juelsminde DK 108 Dc25
Juf CH 142 Cd56
Juggijaur S 72 Ha19
Jugon-les-Lacs F 26 Ec38
Jugorje SLO 151 Fd59
Jugureni RO 176 Eb64
Jugy F 30 Jb44
Juhnov RUS 202 Ed11
Juhonpieti S 68 Ja17
Juhtimäki FIN 89 Jc34
Juigné-des-Moutiers F 28 Fa41
Juillac F 33 Gb48
Juillan F 40 Fd55
Juist D 117 Ca32
Jukajärvi FIN 91 Lc36
Jukkasjärvi S 67 Hb15
Juknaičiai LT 113 Jc56
Juksjaur S 71 Fd22
Juktån S 72 Gb22
Jule N 79 Fb27
Jülich D 125 Bc41
Julianadorp NL 116 Ba34
Julianstown IRL 9 Cd20
Julita S 95 Ga44
Jullouville F 22 Ed37
Julnes N 78 Ed28
Julo FIN 83 Ld28
Jumaliskylä FIN 75 La24
Jumeaux F 34 Hc48

Jumesniemi FIN 89 Jc35
Jumilhac-le-Grand F 33 Gb48
Jumilla E 55 Ed71
Juminda EST 98 Kc41
Juminen FIN 82 La28
Jumisko FIN 75 Kc19
Jumkil S 96 Gc41
Jumo FIN 97 Ja39
Jumprava LV 106 Kd51
Jumurda LV 106 La50
Juncosa E 48 Ga61
Jundola BG 179 Cd73
Juneda E 48 Ga61
Jung S 102 Ed47
Jungėnai LV 114 Kb59
Jungingen D 142 Cc50
Junglinster L 133 Bb44
Jungsund FIN 81 Hd30
Junik KSV 178 Ad71
Junik SRB 159 Jc69
Juniskär S 88 Gb33
Juniville F 24 Hd35
Junkerdal N 71 Fd19
Junkerdal turistcenter N 71 Fd19
Junkovac SRB 174 Bb65
Junnikkala FIN 91 Lc35
Junnonoja FIN 82 Kb26
Junnunperä FIN 81 Jd27
Junosando S 68 Hd16
Junquera F 44 Ad62
Junquera de Tera E 45 Ca59
Junsele S 79 Gb29
Juntinaapa FIN 69 Ka16
Juntinvaara FIN 83 Lc29
Juntusranta FIN 75 Lb22
Juodaičiai LV 114 Kb56
Juodainiai LT 113 Jd55
Juodeikiai LT 113 Jc56
Juodkrantė LT 113 Jb56
Juodpėnai LT 114 Kd54
Juodupė LT 114 La53
Juojärvi FIN 83 Lc31
Juoksenki S 73 Jb19
Juokslahti FIN 90 Kb34
Juokuanvaara FIN 74 Jd21
Juonto FIN 83 Lb25
Juopuli FIN 74 Kb23
Juorkuna FIN 75 Kc23
Juornankylä FIN 90 Kc38
Juostininkai LT 114 Kd55
Juotasjärvi FIN 74 Kb19
Juper BG 180 Eb68
Jupilles F 28 Fd40
Jupiter RO 181 Fd68
Juprelle B 124 Ba41
Jura MD 173 Fd56
Jurata FIN 121 Hb29
Jurbarkas LT 114 Ka57
Juré F 34 Hd46
Jūrė LV 114 Kb58
Jurignac F 32 Fc48
Jurilovca RO 177 Fd65
Jur'evec RUS 203 Fb08
Jur'ev-Pol'skij RUS 203 Fa10
Jurgelionys LT 115 Lb59
Jurgežeriai LT 114 Kb59
Jurgi LV 105 Jd51
Jüri EST 98 Kd42
Jürkalne LV 105 Jb51
Jurki PL 122 Hd31
Jurklošter SLO 151 Fd58
Jurkowice PL 130 Jc42
Jurkowo Węgrzewskie PL 123 Kb34
Jürmaliciems LV 113 Ja53
Jurmo FIN 97 Hd39
Jurmo FIN 97 Ja41
Jurmu FIN 75 Kd21
Juromenha P 51 Bb69
Jurovo RUS 203 Fb08
Jurowce PL 123 Kb33
Juršići HR 151 Fa61
Juršinci SLO 144 Ga56
Jursla S 103 Ga46
Jurva FIN 89 Ja32
Jurvala FIN 91 Lc36
Jurvansalo FIN 82 Kb30
Juseu E 48 Fd59
Juškino RUS 99 Lc44
Juškovo RUS 107 Ld48
Jussac F 33 Ha49
Jussey F 31 Jc40
Jussy-Champagne F 29 Ha43
Jussy-le-Chaudrier F 30 Hb42
Justa RUS 203 Ga14
Justøy N 93 Da47
Jüterbog D 127 Ed38
Jutigny F 30 Hb38
Jutis S 72 Gb20
Jutrosin PL 129 Gc39
Jutsajaure S 72 Ha18
Juttila FIN 90 Kb34
Juttuanvaara FIN 83 Lc25
Juuansaari FIN 74 Kb19
Juujärvi FIN 74 Kb19
Juuka FIN 83 Lc28
Juukskylä FIN 83 Lb31
Juupajoki FIN 90 Ka34
Juupakylä FIN 89 Jb32
Juurikka FIN 83 Ld31
Juurikka FIN 91 Ma32
Juurikkalahti FIN 82 La26

Juurikkamäki FIN 83 Lb30
Juurikkasalmi FIN 91 Ld32
Juurikorpi FIN 90 La38
Juuru EST 98 Kc43
Juurussuo FIN 74 Ka24
Juutinen FIN 82 Kc26
Juva FIN 89 Jb38
Juva FIN 91 Lc33
Juvigné F 28 Fa39
Juvigny-en-Perthois F 24 Jb37
Juvigny-le-Tertre F 22 Fa37
Juvola FIN 91 Lc32
Juvre DK 108 Cd27
Juža RUS 203 Fb09
Juzanvigny F 30 Ja39
Juzennecourt F 30 Ja39
Juzet-d'Izaut F 40 Ga56
Jūžintai LT 114 La53
Južnoukrajins'k UA 204 Ec16
Južnyj RUS 113 Ja59
Južnyj RUS 205 Ga15
Jyderup DK 109 Ea26
Jylhä FIN 82 Kc29
Jylhämä FIN 82 Kc25
Jyllinge DK 109 Eb25
Jyllinkoski FIN 89 Jb34
Jyllintaival FIN 89 Jb32
Jyrinki FIN 81 Jd27
Jyrkänkoski FIN 75 La19
Jyrkkä FIN 82 Kc27
Jyry FIN 81 Ja31
Jyväskylä FIN 90 Kb33
Jyväskylän maalaiskunta FIN 90 Kb32

K

Kaagjärve EST 106 La47
Kaagvere EST 99 Lb45
Kaagvere EST 107 Lb46
Kaakamo FIN 74 Jc21
Kaalasjärvi S 67 Ha15
Kaali EST 105 Jc46
Kaali EST 105 Jd46
Kaamanen FIN 64 Ka10
Kaamasjoki FIN 64 Jd09
Kaamasmukka FIN 64 Jd09
Kaanaa FIN 89 Jd34
Kaanaa FIN 90 Kb38
Kaananvaara FIN 75 Lc21
Käännänmäki FIN 82 Ka28
Kaansoo EST 98 Kb45
Kääntöjärvi S 68 Hc16
Kääpa EST 107 Lc47
Kaarakkala FIN 82 Kd27
Kaarela FIN 74 Ka23
Kaarepere EST 98 La44
Kaaresuvanto FIN 68 Hd13
Kääriälä FIN 90 La34
Käärlänperä FIN 74 Kb23
Kaarina FIN 97 Jb39
Kaarlela FIN 81 Jb28
Kaarma EST 105 Jc46
Kaarnalampi FIN 83 Lc30
Kaarnevaara S 68 Ja15
Kaarnijärvi FIN 74 Kb19
Kaaro FIN 89 Ja37
Kaarßen D 119 Dd34
Kaarst D 125 Bd40
Kaarto FIN 75 Kc22
Kaartotienperä FIN 74 Jd23
Kaartunen FIN 81 Jc30
Kaasmarkku FIN 89 Ja36
Kaavere EST 98 Kd45
Kaavi FIN 83 Lb29
Kaba H 147 Jd53
Kabaağaç TR 198 Fb88
Kabaca TR 187 Ha80
Kabakça TR 186 Fd77
Kabaklar TR 192 Ga85
Kabaklı TR 193 Gc87
Kabakoz TR 186 Ga77
Kabakoz TR 192 Fb84
Kabala EST 98 Kd44
Kabalak TR 187 Ha78
Kabalar TR 192 Fd87
Kabalı TR 205 Fb19
Kabalı TR 191 Ed81
Kabala LV 105 Jc51
Kabdalis S 73 Hb21
Kabeliai LT 114 Kd60
Kabelvåg N 66 Fc14
Kabile BG 180 Eb72
Kabile LV 105 Jc51
Kabkešovo BG 181 Fa72
Kabli EST 106 Kb47
Kabmasmohkki FIN 64 Jd09

Kačanik = Kaçaniku KSV 178 Bb72
Kačarevo SRB 174 Bc63
Kačergiškė LT 115 Lc55
Kačikol KSV 178 Bb70
Kachovka UA 205 Fa16
Kácov CZ 136 Fc45
Kaczanowo PL 129 Gd37
Kaczkowo PL 129 Gb39
Kaczorów PL 128 Ga42
Kaczory PL 121 Gc34
Kadaga LV 106 Kc50
Kadaň CZ 135 Ed43
Kadıdondurma TR 185 Eb77
Kadijača KSV 178 Ba69
Kadiki LV 106 Kb51
Kadıköy TR 186 Fa76
Kadıköy TR 186 Fd79
Kadıköy TR 187 Ha80
Kadıköy TR 191 Ec83
Kadıköy TR 191 Ed81
Kadıköy TR 193 Gd85
Kadıköy = Evreşe TR 185 Ec78
Kadıkuyusu TR 193 Gd84
Kadılar TR 185 Eb80
Kadılar TR 193 Gc87
Kadıllı TR 186 Ga78
Kadıncık TR 193 Hb83
Kadıovacık TR 191 Ea86
Kadirler TR 198 Ga93
Kadłub PL 129 Hb42
Kadłubówka PL 123 Kb35
Kadłub Turawski PL 129 Ha42
Kadrifakovo MK 183 Bd74
Kadrina EST 98 Kd42
Kadriye TR 185 Ec76
Kaduj RUS 202 Ed08
Kädva EST 98 Kc44
Kady RUS 203 Fb08
Kadymka RUS 113 Jd59
Kædeby DK 109 Dd28
Kaelase EST 98 Kb45
Kafacakaplancık TR 197 Fa89
Kåfjord N 62 Ha09
Kåfjord N 64 Jc05
Kåfjordbotn N 63 Hb10
Kåfjorddalen N 63 Hb10
Kağan TR 191 Ed85
Kaharlyk UA 204 Ec15
Kähkölä FIN 83 Lc26
Kahl D 134 Cd44
Kahla D 127 Ea42
Kähtävä FIN 81 Jd27
Kahya TR 198 Fd92
Kaidankylä FIN 89 Jd34
Kaikino RUS 99 Lc41
Kåikul S 73 Hb20
Käina EST 97 Jc44
Kainach A 144 Fc54
Kainasto FIN 89 Ja32
Kaindorf A 144 Ga54
Kainu FIN 81 Jc29
Kainulasjärvi S 73 Hd18
Kainuunkylä FIN 73 Jb20
Kainuunmäki FIN 82 Kd27
Kaipiainen FIN 90 La37
Kaipola FIN 90 Kb34
Kairahta FIN 90 Kc33
Kairala FIN 69 Kb16
Kairala FIN 75 Kd20
Kairėnai LT 114 Kd55
Kairila FIN 89 Jb35
Kairiškiai LT 113 Jd53
Kaisepakte S 67 Gd14
Kaisersbach D 134 Da48
Kaisersesch D 133 Bd43
Kaiserslautern D 133 Ca46
Kaisheim D 134 Dc48
Kaišiadorys LT 114 Kd57
Kaitainsalmi FIN 82 La26
Kaitajärvi FIN 74 Jc19
Kaitsor FIN 81 Ja30
Kaitum S 67 Ha16
Kaiu EST 98 Kc43
Kaivanto FIN 82 Kc25
Kaive LV 105 Jd50
Kaive LV 106 La50
Kaivomäki FIN 90 La33
Kajaani FIN 82 Kd26
Kajan AL 182 Ab76
Kajánújfalu H 146 Jc55
Kajbolovo RUS 99 Lc40
Kajdacs H 146 Hc56
Kajoo FIN 83 Lb29
Kajov CZ 136 Fb49
Kakalétri GR 194 Bb88
Kakanj BIH 158 Hb64
Kakasd H 146 Hc56
Kakavija AL 182 Ac79
Kakerbeck D 127 Ea36
Kaki GR 195 Cb87
Kakilahti FIN 82 Kc26
Kakkisenvaara FIN 83 Ld29
Kaklık TR 198 Fd88
Kąkol PL 121 Hb34
Kąkolewnica Wschodnia PL 131 Kb37

Kakolewnica Wschodnia – Karjalaisenniemi

Kakolewnica Wschodnia PL 131 Kb37
Kąkolewo PL 129 Gb38
Kakopetria CY 206 Ja97
Kakóvatos GR 194 Ba87
Kakskerta FIN 97 Jb39
Kakslauttanen FIN 69 Ka12
Kakuåsen S 79 Fc29
Kál H 146 Jb52
Kälä FIN 90 Kc34
Kalabakbaşı TR 191 Ec81
Kålaboda S 80 Hc26
Kalač RUS 203 Fc13
Kalace MNE 159 Jc68
Kalace MNE 178 Ad70
Kalač-na-Donu RUS 203 Fd14
Kalafat TR 191 Ea81
Kalafati SRB 159 Ja66
Kalaja FIN 82 Ka28
Kalajoki FIN 81 Jc26
Kalak N 64 Jd05
Kalakoski FIN 89 Jc32
Kalamáfka GR 201 Db96
Kalamáki GR 188 Ac86
Kalamáki GR 189 Ca81
Kalamákia GR 189 Cc83
Kalamariá GR 183 Ca78
Kalamark S 73 Hc23
Kalamáta GR 194 Bb89
Kalambáka GR 183 Bb80
Kalambáki GR 184 Cd77
Kalamítsi GR 184 Cd80
Kálamos GR 188 Ad83
Kálamos GR 189 Cc85
Kalamoti GR 191 Dd86
Kalamotó GR 183 Cb78
Kalana EST 97 Jb44
Kalana EST 98 La44
Kalančak UA 205 Fa17
Kalándra GR 183 Cb80
Kalá Nerá GR 189 Ca82
Kálanos GR 188 Bb86
Kalanti FIN 89 Ja38
Kalapódi GR 189 Ca84
Kälarne S 79 Ga31
Kálathos GR 197 Fa93
Kalavárda GR 197 Ed93
Kalavasos CY 206 Jb98
Kalávrita GR 188 Bb86
Kalax FIN 89 Hd32
Kalbach D 134 Da43
Kalbe D 127 Ea36
Kalbensteinberg D 134 Dc47
Kalburcu TR 186 Ga78
Kalburcu TR 192 Fa82
Kalce SLO 151 Fb58
Kalčevo BG 180 Eb73
Kalchreuth D 135 Dd46
Káld H 145 Gd54
Kaldal N 79 Fb26
Kaldenkirchen D 125 Bc39
Kaldfarnes N 67 Gb11
Kaldfjord N 62 Gc09
Kaldvika N 66 Ga14
Kale TR 198 Fc89
Kalealtı TR 185 Eb78
Kale = Demre TR 199 Gb93
Kaledibi TR 205 Ga19
Kalefeld D 126 Db38
Kalekovec BG 180 Db73
Kaleköy TR 185 Dd80
Kaleköy TR 198 Ga93
Kalela FIN 89 Jb38
Kalemköy TR 197 Fa90
Kälen S 73 Hc24
Kalenci SRB 153 Jc62
Kalenik BG 180 Db70
Kaléntzi GR 188 Ad81
Kaléntzi GR 188 Bb86
Kalérgo GR 190 Cd86
Kalesi EST 98 Kc42
Kalesija BIH 153 Hd63
Kalesninkai LT 114 Kc59
Kalesninkai LT 114 La59
Kaleste EST 97 Jb44
Kalēti LV 113 Jb53
Kaletnik PL 123 Kb30
Kalety PL 138 Hc43
Kaleüçağız TR 198 Ga93
Kaleva FIN 97 Jc39
Kalfaköy TR 192 Fb81
Kalho FIN 90 Kc35
Kalí GR 183 Bd77
Kali HR 157 Fd64
Kalidona GR 194 Ba87
Kalífitos GR 184 Da76
Kalimanci BG 181 Fa70
Kálimnos GR 197 Eb90
Kalina FIN 83 Ld28
Kalınağılköyü TR 197 Fa90
Kalınharman TR 192 Fc85
Kalinina RUS 203 Fb08
Kaliningrad RUS 113 Ja58
Kalininsk RUS 203 Fd12
Kalininskoe RUS 113 Jd59
Kalinkavičy BY 202 Eb13
Kalınkoz TR 198 Fd90
Kalinovik BIH 159 Hc66
Kalinovka RUS 113 Jc58
Kalinovo SK 146 Ja50
Kalinowa PL 129 Hb39
Kalinówka Kościelna PL 123 Kb32
Kalinowo PL 123 Ka31
Kalipéfki GR 183 Bd80
Kaliroi GR 182 Ba80
Kaliska PL 121 Ha31
Kalisko PL 130 Hd40
Kališta MK 182 Ad75
Kalisty PL 122 Hd31
Kalisz PL 121 Gd31
Kalisz PL 129 Ha39
Kaliszki PL 123 Jd32
Kalisz Pomorski PL 120 Ga34
Kalithéa GR 183 Cb80
Kalithía GR 184 Cd76
Kalīti LV 105 Jc50
Kalitino RUS 99 Mb41
Kalivári GR 190 Da87
Kalíves GR 184 Da78
Kalíves GR 200 Cc95
Kalívia GR 188 Ba84
Kalívia GR 194 Bc90
Kalí Vrissi GR 184 Cd76
Kalix S 73 Jb21
Kalixforsbron S 67 Ha15
Kaljazin RUS 202 Ed09
Kaljord N 66 Fd13
Kaljunen FIN 91 Ld34
Kalkan TR 198 Fd93
Kalkanlı TR 193 Gd82
Kalkar D 125 Bc38
Kalkhorst D 119 Dd31
Kalķi LV 105 Jc49
Kalkım TR 191 Ec81
Kalkkiainen FIN 69 Kc17
Kalkkikangas FIN 68 Jb16
Kalkkimaa FIN 74 Jc21
Kalkkinen FIN 90 Kc36
Kalkstein A 143 Eb55
Kalkstrand FIN 98 Kc39
Kalkūne LV 115 Lc53
Kall D 125 Bc42
Kall S 78 Fa30
Källa S 104 Gc51
Kalland N 92 Cd46
Kållands-Åsaka S 102 Ed46
Kallarberg N 93 Da45
Källarbo S 95 Fd40
Kallaste EST 99 Lb44
Kallax S 73 Hd22
Källbäcken S 95 Fc40
Källbomark S 73 Hc24
Kållby FIN 81 Jb29
Källby S 102 Fa46
Kållered S 102 Ec49
Kallernäs S 95 Fd42
Källerstad S 102 Fa51
Kalletal D 126 Cd37
Källfallet S 95 Fd42
Kallham A 144 Fa50
Kallholen S 87 Fc37
Kalli EST 98 Ka45
Kallimassiá GR 191 Dd86
Kallinge S 111 Fd54
Kallio FIN 83 Lb26
Kallio FIN 89 Jd34
Kállio GR 189 Bc84
Kalliojoki FIN 83 Lc25
Kalliokylä FIN 82 Kc28
Kalliola FIN 90 Kc36
Kallioluoma FIN 75 Lb20
Kalliomäki FIN 82 Kd27
Kallislahti FIN 91 Lc33
Kallithéa GR 183 Bc80
Kallithéa GR 189 Cb85
Kallithéa GR 194 Ba89
Kallithéa GR 194 Bc89
Kallithéa GR 197 Ea88
Kallíthiro GR 188 Bb82
Kallivere EST 99 Lc41
Kallmet AL 163 Jb71
Kallmora S 87 Fc37
Kallmünz D 135 Ea47
Kallo FIN 68 Jc16
Källö H 146 Hd52
Källö-Knippla S 102 Eb49
Kallön S 72 Gc22
Kalloní GR 191 Ea83
Kalloní GR 195 Ca88
Kállósemjén H 147 Ka51
Kall-Rör S 78 Fa29
Källsjö S 102 Ec50
Källsjön S 87 Ga38
Kallträsk FIN 89 Ja34
Källunga S 102 Ed48
Källunge S 104 Ha49
Källvik S 103 Gb48
Kallviken S 81 Hd26
Kalmaküla EST 99 Lb43
Kalmar S 96 Gc43
Kalmar S 103 Gb52
Kalmari FIN 82 Ka31
Kalmonmäki FIN 82 La27
Kalmthout B 124 Ad38
Kalmykovskij RUS 203 Fd14
Kalna SRB 179 Ca69
Kalna SRB 179 Ca70
Kalnaberže LT 114 Kc56
Kalnamuiža LV 105 Jc52
Kálna nad Hronom SK 145 Hb50
Kalná Roztoka SK 139 Kb47
Kalnbirze LV 107 Lb51
Kalncempji LV 107 Lb48
Kalnciems LV 106 Ka51
Kalniena LV 107 Lc49
Kalnik PL 122 Hd31
Kalniški LV 113 Jb53
Kalniškiai LT 113 Jb54
Kálnovo BG 181 Ec71
Kalnujai LT 114 Ka56
Kálócfa H 145 Gc55
Kalo Chorio CY 206 Ja96
Kalo Chorio CY 206 Ja97
Kalo Chorio CY 206 Jb97
Kalo Chorio CY 206 Jc97
Kalocsa H 146 Hd56
Kalofer BG 180 Dc72
Kalógiri GR 188 Bb81
Kalógria GR 188 Ba85
Kalóhio GR 183 Bb79
Kalohóri GR 182 Ba78
Kaló Horió GR 201 Dc96
Kaló Horió GR 201 Dd96
Kaloí Liménes GR 200 Cd96
Kalojan BG 181 Ed69
Kalojanovec BG 180 Dd73
Kalojanovo BG 180 Db73
Kalojanovo BG 180 Eb72
Kalókastro GR 183 Cb77
Kälom S 79 Fb30
Kalonéri GR 183 Bb78
Kaló Neró GR 194 Ba88
Kaloní GR 196 Db88
Kalopanagiotis CY 206 Ja97
Kalopsida CY 206 Jc96
Kalopsida CY 206 Jc97
Kalotina BG 179 Cb70
Kaloúsi GR 188 Bb86
Káloz H 146 Hc55
Kalożicy RUS 99 Ma41
Kalpáki GR 182 Ad79
Kalpio FIN 75 Kd24
Kals A 143 Eb54
Kalsdorf bei Graz A 144 Fd55
Kälsjärv S 73 Jb21
Kalsko PL 128 Fd36
Kaltanėnai LT 115 Lb56
Kaltbrunn CH 142 Cc53
Kaltenbach A 143 Ea53
Kaltenbrunn A 142 Dc54
Kaltene LV 105 Jd49
Kaltenkirchen D 118 Db32
Kaltennordheim D 126 Db42
Kaltensundheim D 126 Db42
Kaltental D 142 Dc51
Kaltern I 142 Dc56
Kaltesluokta S 67 Gd17
Kaltinėnai LT 113 Jd55
Kaltsila FIN 89 Jc36
Kalttonen FIN 82 Kc29
Kaluderovići SRB 159 Ja66
Kaluderovo SRB 174 Bd63
Kaludra MNE 159 Jb68
Kaluga RUS 202 Ed11
Kalugerovc BG 179 Da72
Kalugerovo BG 179 Cd70
Kalundborg DK 109 Ea25
Kalupe LV 115 Lc53
Kaluš UA 204 Ea16
Kałuszyn PL 131 Jd37
Kalužskoe RUS 113 Jc58
Kalv S 102 Ed50
Kalvåg N 84 Ca34
Kalvarija LV 114 Kb59
Kalvatn N 84 Cc34
Kalvbäcken S 80 Gc28
Kalvehave DK 109 Eb28
Kalvene LV 105 Jb52
Kälvene S 102 Fa48
Kalvi EST 98 La41
Kälviä FIN 81 Jc28
Kalviai LT 114 Kc58
Kalvitsa FIN 90 La33
Kalvjärv S 73 Ja20
Kalvola FIN 90 Ka37
Kalvslund DK 108 Da26
Kalvträsk S 80 Hb25
Kalwang A 144 Fc53
Kalwaria Zebrzydowska PL 138 Hd45
Kalwy PL 129 Gb37
Kalynivka UA 204 Eb15
Kám H 145 Gc54
Kamajai LT 114 La54
Kämäränkylä FIN 83 Lc25
Kamārde LV 114 Kc53
Kamáres GR 188 Bb85
Kamáres GR 195 Cd90
Kamáres GR 200 Cd96
Kamári GR 196 Db92
Kamarino RUS 99 Mb45
Kamariótissa GR 184 Dc79
Kamarítsa GR 189 Cb84
Kamaroúla GR 188 Ba84
Kambánis GR 183 Ca77
Kambí GR 188 Ad81
Kambiá GR 191 Dd85
Kambja EST 107 Lb46
Kambo N 93 Ea43
Kámbos GR 188 Ba83
Kámbos GR 188 Ba86
Kámbos GR 188 Bb84
Kámbos GR 194 Bb89
Kámbos GR 196 Dd88
Kámbos GR 197 Ea89
Kámbos GR 197 Eb88
Kámbos GR 200 Ca95
Kámbos GR 201 Dd96
Kamčija BG 181 Fa71
Kamçılı TR 192 Fa81
Kamen BG 180 Ea70
Kamen BG 180 Eb72
Kamen D 125 Cb39
Kamenar BG 181 Fa70
Kaména Voúrla GR 189 Bd84
Kamen Brjag BG 181 Fc70
Kamenec BG 180 Dc69
Kamenec RUS 99 Ld43
Kamenica BIH 152 Gb63
Kamenica BIH 152 Hb63
Kamenica BIH 159 Ja64
Kamenica MK 179 Ca73
Kamenica SK 138 Jc47
Kamenica SRB 178 Ba67
Kamenica SRB 178 Bd69
Kamenica SRB 179 Ca68
Kamenica nad Cirochou SK 139 Ka47
Kamenicë AL 182 Ad77
Kamenice CZ 136 Fc45
Kamenice nad Lipou CZ 136 Fc47
Kamenjane MK 178 Ba73
Kamenka RUS 99 Ld43
Kamenka RUS 107 Ld46
Kamenka RUS 203 Fb13
Kamenka RUS 203 Fc11
Kamennogorsk RUS 202 Ea08
Kamennyj Konec RUS 99 Lc43
Kamenný Přívoz CZ 136 Fb45
Kameno BG 181 Ed72
Kameno Pole BG 179 Cd69
Kamenovo BG 180 Eb68
Kamenskij RUS 203 Fd12
Kamenski Vučjak HR 152 Ha60
Kamensko BIH 153 Hc63
Kamensko HR 152 Ha60
Kamensko HR 158 Gd66
Kamenskoe RUS 113 Jc59
Kamensk-Šahtinskij RUS 203 Fc14
Kamenz D 128 Fb40
Kames GB 6 Dc13
Kameškovo RUS 203 Fa09
Kamičak BIH 152 Gc62
Kamień PL 122 Jc32
Kamień PL 128 Fc36
Kamień PL 129 Ha38
Kamień PL 130 Ja39
Kamień PL 131 Jd40
Kamień PL 131 Kd40
Kamień PL 139 Ka43
Kamienica PL 121 Gc35
Kamienica PL 128 Fd42
Kamienica PL 138 Jb46
Kamienica Dolna PL 139 Jd44
Kamieniec PL 122 Hc32
Kamieniec PL 129 Gb37
Kamieniec Ząbkowicki PL 137 Gc43
Kamienka SK 138 Jb46
Kamień Krajeński PL 121 Gd33
Kamienna Góra PL 128 Ga42
Kamiennik PL 137 Gc43
Kamiennik Wielkopolski PL 122 Hc30
Kamień Pomorski PL 120 Fc31
Kamieńsk PL 130 Hd40
Kamilski Dol BG 185 Ea75
Kamin'-Kašyrs'kyj UA 202 Ea14
Kamion PL 130 Ja38
Kamionek Wielki PL 122 Jc30
Kamionka PL 131 Ka39
Kamionka Wielka PL 138 Jc46
Kamionna PL 128 Ga36
Kamışlı TR 187 Gc79
Kam'janec-Podil's'kyj UA 204 Eb16
Kamjaniec BY 202 Dd13
Kam'janka UA 204 Ed15
Kamjanka-Buz'ka UA 204 Ea15
Kamlunge S 73 Ja21
Kämmäkka FIN 89 Jc36
Kammela FIN 89 Hd38
Kammeltal D 142 Db50
Kämmenniemi FIN 89 Jd35
Kammerstein D 134 Dc47
Kamminke D 120 Fb32
Kammlach D 142 Db51
Kamnik AL 182 Ad78
Kamnik SLO 151 Fc57
Kamniška Bistrica SLO 151 Fb57
Kamorūnai LT 114 Kd59
Kamøyvær N 64 Jc04
Kampen D 108 Cd28
Kampen NL 117 Bc35
Kampertal A 144 Fb52
Kampevoll N 67 Gb11
Kampia CY 206 Jb97
Kampinkylä FIN 89 Ja32
Kampinos PL 130 Ja37
Kamp-Lintfort D 125 Bc39
Kampor HR 151 Fc62
Kampos CY 206 Ja97
Kamsdorf D 127 Dd42
Kamsjö S 80 Hb27
Kamskoe Ust'e RUS 203 Fd09
Kamula FIN 82 Kb27
Kamyk PL 130 Hc41
Kamýk nad Vltavou CZ 136 Fb46
Kamyšin RUS 203 Fd13
Kanaküla EST 106 Kc46
Kanal SLO 150 Ed58
Kanala FIN 81 Jd29
Kanála GR 195 Cd89
Kanáli GR 182 Ab80
Kanáli GR 188 Ac82
Kanália GR 189 Ca81
Kanan S 71 Fd23
Kanaš RUS 113 Jc57
Kanaš RUS 113 Jc58
Kanaš RUS 203 Fd09
Kanatádika GR 189 Ca83
Kanatlarci MK 183 Bb75
Kańczuga PL 139 Kb44
Kandakjulja RUS 99 Ld39
Kandakopšino RUS 99 Mb40
Kándanos GR 200 Cb95
Kandava LV 105 Jd50
Kandel D 133 Cb47
Kandergrund CH 141 Bd55
Kandern D 141 Bd51
Kandersteg CH 141 Bd55
Kandestederne DK 101 Dd19
Kándia GR 195 Bd88
Kandila GR 194 Bc87
Kandıra TR 187 Gb77
Kandle EST 98 Kd41
Kandyty PL 122 Ja30
Kanepi EST 107 Lb46
Kånešštohpu FIN 64 Jd08
Kanevskaja RUS 205 Fc16
Kanfanar HR 151 Fa61
Kangarisi LV 106 Kc50
Kangas FIN 81 Jd26
Kangas FIN 81 Jb30
Kangas FIN 81 Jb31
Kangasaho FIN 82 Ka31
Kangasala FIN 89 Jd35
Kangasalan asema FIN 89 Jd35
Kangashäkki FIN 90 Kb32
Kangaskylä FIN 82 Kc25
Kangaskylä FIN 82 Kb26
Kangaskylä FIN 82 Ka28
Kangaskylä FIN 82 Ka29
Kangaslahti FIN 82 La28
Kangaslampi FIN 91 Lb32
Kangasniemi FIN 90 Kd33
Kangasoja FIN 81 Jd28
Kangasperä FIN 82 Kc25
Kangasvieri FIN 81 Jd29
Kangos S 68 Hd16
Kangosjärvi FIN 68 Ja15
Kania PL 120 Fd33
Kania PL 121 Ha35
Kanigowo PL 122 Ja33
Kaniów PL 128 Fc38
Kaniv UA 204 Ec15
Kanjiža SRB 153 Jb57
Kankaanpää FIN 89 Jb35
Kankaanpää FIN 89 Jb37
Kankaanpää FIN 90 Ka33
Kankainen FIN 90 Kd32
Kankainen FIN 90 Kc33
Kankari FIN 82 Kc25
Kankberg S 80 Hb25
Kankböle FIN 90 Kc38
Kankkula FIN 82 Kd29
Känna S 102 Fa52
Kannas FIN 91 Ld34
Kannawurf D 127 Dd40
Kannonkoski FIN 82 Ka30
Kannonsaha FIN 82 Ka30
Kannus FIN 81 Jc27
Kannusjärvi FIN 90 La37
Kannuskoski FIN 90 La36
Kansız TR 192 Fb81
Kanstad N 66 Fd13
Kantala FIN 90 La33
Kantara CY 206 Jd96
Kanteenmaa FIN 89 Jc37
Kantele FIN 90 Kc38
Kantemirovka RUS 203 Fb14
Kantii FIN 89 Jb34
Kantinieki LV 107 Lc51
Kantküla EST 98 La44
Kantojärvi FIN 74 Jc21
Kantojoki FIN 75 La19
Kantokylä FIN 81 Jd27
Kantola FIN 74 Jd22
Kantomaanpää FIN 73 Jb19
Kantoperä FIN 89 Jc33
Kántorjánosi H 147 Kb51
Kantornes N 62 Gd10
Kantou CY 206 Ja98
Kantsjö S 80 Gd29
Kanturk IRL 12 Bc24
Kánya H 145 Hb55
Kányavár H 145 Gc56
Kaolinovo BG 181 Ed69
Kaona SRB 178 Ba67
Kaonik SRB 178 Bc68
Kapaklı TR 186 Fa76
Kapaklı TR 186 Fc79
Kapaklı TR 191 Ed84
Kapaklı TR 193 Hb87
Kapanbelem TR 185 Ec80
Kapandríti GR 189 Cc86
Kapanlar TR 193 Gb81
Kaparéli GR 189 Ca85
Kaparéli GR 194 Bc87
Kapčiamiestis LT 123 Kc30
Kapee FIN 89 Jd34
Kapela HR 152 Gc58
Kapellen A 144 Ga52
Kapellen B 124 Ac39
Kapellen D 125 Bc38
Kapelln A 144 Ga50
Kapera EST 107 Lc47
Kāpessils LV 107 Ld50
Kapfenberg A 144 Fd53
Kápi GR 191 Ea83
Kapice PL 123 Ka32
Kapıkaya TR 191 Ec84
Kapıkaya TR 192 Fd84
Kapıkaya TR 193 Gd81
Kapiņi LV 107 Ld52
Kăpinovo BG 181 Fb69
Kapitan Andeevo BG 185 Ea75
Kapitan-Dimitrievo BG 179 Da73
Kapitan Dimitrovo BG 181 Fa68
Kapitan Petko BG 181 Ec69
Kapız TR 198 Fc90
Kapłan PL 123 Ka35
Kaplangı TR 192 Ga85
Kaplice CZ 136 Fb49
Kapljuh BIH 152 Gb63
Kapolcs H 145 Ha55
Kápolna H 146 Jb52
Kápolnásnyék H 146 Hc54
Kapolypuszta H 145 Ha55
Kaposfüred H 145 Ha56
Kaposgyarmat H 152 Ha57
Kaposmérő H 152 Ha57
Kaposszekcső H 152 Hb57
Kaposvár H 152 Ha57
Kapp N 85 Ea39
Kappel D 133 Bd44
Kappel D 133 Ca44
Kappel DK 109 Dd28
Kappel Grafenhausen D 141 Ca50
Kappeln D 108 Dc29
Kappelrodeck D 133 Cb49
Kappelshamn S 104 Ha48
Kappelskär S 96 Ha42
Kappl A 142 Db54
Kåpponis S 73 Hb20
Kaprije HR 157 Ga66
Kaprun A 143 Ec54
Kapsajoki FIN 68 Jc14
Kapsáli GR 195 Bd92
Kapsalos CY 206 Jc96
Kapsēde LV 105 Ja52
Kapshtica AL 182 Ba77
Káptalanfa H 145 Gd54
Káptalantóti H 145 Ha55
Kaptol HR 152 Ha60
Kapūne LV 107 Lc50
Kapušany SK 139 Jd47
Kapuvár H 145 Gc53
Käpysalo FIN 82 Kd30
Karáad H 145 Ha55
Karaadilli TR 193 Gc86
Karaağa TR 193 Hb87
Karaağaç TR 185 Eb75
Karaağaç TR 185 Ed76
Karaağaç TR 186 Fc77
Karaağaç TR 187 Gc77
Karaağaç TR 187 Ha80
Karaağaç TR 191 Eb82
Karaağaç TR 192 Fa83
Karaağaç TR 192 Ga84
Karaağaç TR 193 Gb84
Karaağaçlı TR 191 Ed85
Karaahmetler TR 198 Fb90
Karaahmetler TR 199 Gd90
Karaahmetli TR 186 Ga79
Karaali TR 199 Hb88
Karaaliler TR 199 Gc89
Karaatlı TR 197 Ed88
Karabahadır TR 186 Ga80
Karabayır TR 198 Fd91
Karabedirler TR 192 Ga86
Karabeyler TR 192 Fc85
Karabeyli TR 185 Ed76
Karabeyli TR 186 Ga77
Karabeyli TR 192 Fd85
Karabiga TR 185 Ed79
Karaböğürtlen TR 198 Fb90
Karabucak TR 199 Ha90
Karabük TR 199 Ha90
Karabük TR 205 Fa20
Karabulut TR 193 Hb86
Karabunar BG 179 Da73
Karabürçek TR 185 Ec77
Karaburun TR 186 Fc76
Karaburun TR 191 Ea81
Karaburun TR 191 Ea85
Karaby S 102 Ed46
Karacaağaç TR 197 Fa90
Karacaahmet TR 192 Fd86
Karacaahmet TR 193 Hb82
Karacaali TR 186 Fd79
Karacaali TR 192 Fb87
Karacabey TR 186 Fb80
Karacadağ TR 186 Fa74
Karačaevsk RUS 205 Ga17
Karacahisar TR 192 Ga84
Karacahisar TR 192 Ga85
Karacahisar TR 199 Ha88
Karacaibrahim TR 192 Fb85
Karacakılavuz TR 185 Ed77
Karacaköy TR 186 Fb76
Karacaköy TR 186 Ga77
Karacaköy TR 197 Fa91
Karacalar TR 191 Ed83
Karacalar TR 192 Fb83
Karacalar TR 199 Hb91
Karaçalç TR 185 Ed78
Karacalı TR 186 Fa80
Karaçalı TR 187 Gc77
Karaçaltı TR 192 Fb82
Karaçam TR 191 Ed83
Karaçam TR 198 Fc90
Karacaoğlan TR 185 Ec76
Karacaören TR 193 Gc86
Karacaören TR 193 Gc87
Karacaören TR 193 Gd82
Karacaören TR 193 Hb83
Karacaören TR 197 Fa88
Karacaören TR 198 Fb88
Karacaören TR 198 Fc91
Karacaören TR 199 Gb89
Karacaören TR 199 Gd89
Karacaşehir TR 193 Gc82
Karacaşehir TR 193 Gc84
Karacasu TR 187 Hb79
Karacasu TR 198 Fb88
Karaçepiş TR 191 Ed82
Karačev RUS 202 Ed12
Karácsond H 146 Jb52
Karaçulha TR 198 Fd92
Karaçulha TR 198 Ga91
Karadağ TR 198 Ga93
Karadat TR 193 Hb82
Karadayı TR 199 Gd91
Karadere TR 185 Ed74
Karadere TR 187 Gc78
Karadere TR 187 Gd79
Karadere TR 191 Ec82
Karadere TR 191 Ed84
Karadiken TR 187 Gc78
Karadiken TR 198 Fc90
Karadiken TR 199 Gd89
Karadirek TR 193 Gb86
Karadordevo SRB 153 Ja60
Karageorgievo BG 181 Ed72
Karagöl TR 198 Fc89
Karagöllü TR 186 Ga78
Karagöz TR 192 Fb82
Karahacılı TR 192 Ga87
Karahacılı TR 193 Gb87
Karahallı TR 192 Ga86
Karahamza TR 185 Ec75
Karahasantaşı TR 198 Ga91
Karahıdırlı TR 191 Ec84
Karahisar TR 185 Eb78
Karahisar TR 198 Fc89
Karahisargölcük TR 193 Ha81
Karahka FIN 74 Ka21
Karahka FIN 74 Kb23
Karahüyük TR 193 Ha86
Karahüyük TR 198 Fd89
Karainebeyli TR 185 Ea79
Karakadı TR 192 Ga81
Karakavur TR 187 Hb77
Karakaya TR 192 Fa82
Karakaya TR 192 Fa83
Karakaya TR 192 Fd87
Karakaya TR 193 Ha83
Karakaya TR 197 Ed89
Karakiraz TR 186 Fd77
Karakışla TR 199 Hb90
Karako H 145 Gd54
Karakoca TR 186 Fb80
Karakoçan TR 205 Ga20
Karakólithos GR 189 Bd85
Karaköse TR 193 Gb85
Karaköy TR 187 Hb80
Karaköy TR 191 Ec84
Karaköy TR 191 Ed86
Karaköy TR 192 Fa85
Karaköy TR 192 Fc81
Karaköy TR 192 Fc87
Karaköy TR 197 Ed91
Karaköy TR 198 Fc89
Karaköy TR 199 Gb91
Karakür TR 192 Fd85
Karakütük TR 199 Gd90
Karakuyu TR 191 Ec87
Karakuyu TR 199 Gc90
Karakuzu TR 191 Ec85
Karala EST 105 Jb46
Karalaks N 64 Jb08
Karališkiai LT 114 Ka57
Karališkiai LT 114 La56
Karalkreslis LT 114 Ka59
Karamanca TR 192 Fd84
Karamanci BG 184 Dc74
Karamandere TR 186 Fb76
Karamanlar TR 199 Hb92
Karamanlı TR 198 Ga89
Karamanovo BG 180 Dd69
Karamehmet TR 186 Fa76
Karamık TR 198 Ga92
Karamıkkaracaören TR 193 Gd86
Karamürsel TR 186 Ga79
Karamyševo RUS 107 Ma46
Karamyševo RUS 113 Jd59
Karancslapujtő H 146 Ja50
Karancsság H 146 Ja51
Karankamäki FIN 82 Kc27
Karanovo BG 180 Ea72
Karaoğlanlı TR 191 Ed85
Karaören TR 193 Gc83
Karaorman TR 192 Fb81
Karaot TR 199 Gc90
Karaova TR 197 Ed90
Karaöz TR 199 Gc93
Karapazar TR 193 Gc82
Karapelit BG 181 Fa69
Karapınar TR 192 Fb82
Karapınar TR 193 Ha85
Karapınar TR 199 Gb89
Karapınar TR 199 Gc89
Karapürçek TR 187 Gc79
Karapürçek TR 192 Fb81
Kararkút H 152 Ha57
Karasandıklı TR 193 Gb86
Kárášjohka N 64 Jc09
Karasjok N 64 Jc09
Karasu TR 187 Gd77
Kárász H 152 Hb57
Karataş TR 192 Fb85
Karataş TR 199 Gc90
Karatepe TR 185 Ea80
Karatepe TR 193 Gd82
Karats S 72 Gd19
Karaurgan TR 205 Ga19
Karavas CY 206 Jb96
Karavás GR 195 Bd91
Karaveliler TR 191 Ec83
Karaveliler TR 199 Gc90
Karavelovo BG 180 Db72
Karavóstamo GR 196 Dd88
Karavostasi CY 206 Ja96
Karavostásis GR 196 Da91
Karavukovo SRB 153 Hd59
Karayakup TR 192 Fa85
Karayakuplu TR 186 Ga78
Karayayla TR 198 Fc89
Karayokuş TR 193 Ha85
Karbach D 134 Da45
Karbasan TR 192 Fd83
Karbasan TR 192 Ga87
Karben D 134 Cc43
Karbenning S 95 Ga41
Karbinci MK 183 Bd74
Kårböle S 87 Fd35
Karbowo PL 122 Hc33
Karbow-Vietlübbe D 119 Eb33
Karby DK 100 Da22
Karby S 96 Gd43
Karca TR 197 Fa90
Karcag H 146 Jc53
Karcsa H 147 Ka50
Karczew PL 130 Jc37
Karczmiska PL 131 Jd40
Karczmy PL 130 Hc39
Karczyn PL 129 Gc42
Kärda S 103 Fb51
Kardakáta GR 188 Ab84
Kardam BG 181 Fb69
Kardamás GR 188 Ad86
Kardámena GR 197 Ec91
Kardámila GR 191 Dd85
Kardamíli GR 194 Bb89
Kardašova Řečice CZ 136 Fc47
Kärde EST 98 La44
Kardis S 68 Jb17
Karditsa GR 188 Bb81
Kärdla EST 97 Jc44
Kardos H 146 Jc55
Kărdžali BG 184 Dc75
Kareby S 102 Eb48
Karegasnjarga FIN 64 Jc09
Kårehamn S 103 Gb51
Käremo S 103 Gb52
Karepa EST 98 La41
Karés GR 200 Cc95
Karesuando S 68 Hd13
Kärevere EST 98 Kd44
Kärevere EST 98 La45
Kärevete EST 98 Kd43
Kargalı TR 186 Ga78
Kargalı TR 193 Hb85
Kargalı TR 198 Ga90
Kargalıhanbaba TR 187 Gc78
Kargersee I 143 Dd56
Kargı TR 193 Hb81
Kargı TR 197 Fa89
Kargı TR 198 Fc91
Kargı TR 199 Gd90
Kargı TR 205 Fb20
Kargılı TR 192 Fd82
Kargılı TR 199 Gc91
Kargın TR 192 Fa85
Kargın TR 199 Gc90
Kargınkürü TR 198 Fc91
Kargów PL 130 Jc42
Kargowa PL 128 Ga38
Kärgula EST 107 Lb47
Karhe FIN 89 Jc35
Karhi FIN 81 Jc27
Karhila FIN 90 Ka32
Karhujärvi FIN 74 Kd18
Karhukangas FIN 82 Ka26
Karhula FIN 89 Jc38
Karhula FIN 90 La38
Karhunkylä FIN 89 Jd33
Karhunoja FIN 89 Jc38
Karhunpää FIN 83 Lb27
Karhusjärvi FIN 91 Lc36
Karhuvaara FIN 75 Kd22
Karhuvaara FIN 75 Lb24
Kari FIN 83 Lb28
Kariá GR 188 Ac83
Kariá GR 189 Bc86
Kariá GR 194 Bc87
Karianí GR 184 Cd78
Karidiá GR 183 Bc77
Karidohóri GR 184 Cc76
Kariés GR 182 Ba77
Kariés GR 184 Cd79
Kariés GR 194 Ba88
Kariés GR 194 Bc88
Karigasniemi FIN 64 Jc09
Karihaugen N 66 Ga14
Karijoki FIN 89 Ja33
Karilatsi EST 107 Lb46
Karinainen FIN 89 Jc38
Karıncalı TR 192 Fc81
Karine TR 197 Ec88
Käringön S 102 Ea47
Karinkanta FIN 74 Jd24
Kariótes GR 188 Ac83
Kariótissa GR 183 Bd77
Karivouni GR 194 Bc90
Karırçeşme TR 192 Fb81
Karis FIN 97 Jd40
Karise DK 109 Ec27
Karisjärvi FIN 98 Ka39
Káristos GR 195 Cd87
Karítena GR 194 Bb87
Karitsa GR 188 Bb83
Karja EST 97 Jc45
Karjaa FIN 97 Jd40
Karjala FIN 89 Jb38
Karjalaisenniemi FIN 75 Kd19

Karjalan – Kičenica

Karjalan FIN 89 Jb38
Karjalankylä FIN 74 Ka22
Karjalanvaara FIN 74 Kb19
Karjalohja FIN 97 Jd40
Karjatnurme EST 106 Kd47
Kärjenkoski FIN 89 Ja34
Kärjenniemi FIN 89 Jd36
Karjula FIN 89 Jd34
Karjulanmäki FIN 81 Jd28
Karkaloú GR 194 Bb87
Karkažiškė LT 115 Lb57
Karkeamaa FIN 90 La33
Kärkelä FIN 97 Jd39
Karken D 125 Bb40
Kārķi LV 106 Kd47
Karkın TR 193 Ha82
Karkinágri GR 196 Dd88
Kärkkäälä FIN 82 Kc31
Karkkila FIN 90 Ka38
Karkku FIN 89 Jc36
Karkkula FIN 90 Kc37
Karklampi FIN 90 Kb35
Kärklax FIN 81 Ja30
Karklėnai LT 113 Jd55
Karkliniai LV 114 Kb59
Kärkna EST 99 Lb45
Kärkölä FIN 90 Kb37
Kärkölä FIN 90 Ka38
Karksi EST 106 Kd46
Karksi-Nuia EST 106 Kd46
Karkučiai LT 114 Kd58
Kärla EST 105 Jc46
Karlanda S 94 Ec43
Karlbo S 95 Ga41
Karlby FIN 97 Hd41
Karleby FIN 81 Jb28
Karleby FIN 81 Jb28
Karleby S 102 Fa46
Karlewo PL 122 Hd35
Karl Gustav S 102 Ec50
Karlholmsbruk S 96 Gc39
Kārļi LV 106 Kc51
Kārļi LV 106 Kd49
Karlık TR 191 Ed81
Karlino PL 120 Ga31
Karlıova TR 205 Ga20
Karlivka UA 203 Fa14
Karlobag HR 151 Fc63
Karlovac HR 151 Ga60
Karlovássi GR 197 Eb88
Karlova Studánka CZ 137 Gd44
Karlovčić SRB 153 Jb61
Karlovice CZ 137 Gd44
Karlovka RUS 203 Ga11
Karlovo BG 180 Db72
Karlovy Vary CZ 135 Ec44
Karłów PL 137 Gb43
Karłowice PL 129 Gd42
Karlsbäck S 80 Gd28
Karlsbad D 133 Cb48
Karlsbad = Karlovy Vary CZ 135 Ec44
Karlsberg S 87 Fd36
Karlsberg S 103 Fb47
Karlsborg S 73 Jb21
Karlsborg S 103 Fc46
Karlsburg D 120 Fa31
Karlsby S 103 Fc46
Karlsfeld D 143 Dd50
Karlshagen D 120 Fa31
Karlshamn S 111 Fc54
Karlshuld D 135 Dd49
Karlskoga S 95 Fc43
Karlskrona S 111 Fd54
Karlslunda S 111 Ga53
Karlslunde Strand DK 109 Ec26
Karlsøy N 62 Ha08
Karlsruhe D 133 Cb47
Karlstad N 67 Gc11
Karlstad S 94 Fa43
Karlstadt D 134 Da44
Karlstein A 136 Fd48
Karlstift A 136 Fc49
Karlstorp S 103 Fd50
Karmacs H 145 Gd55
Karmannsbo S 95 Fd42
Karmas S 67 Gd17
Karmėlava LT 114 Kc57
Karmin PL 129 Gb38
Kärna FIN 81 Jc30
Kärnä FIN 82 Kb29
Kärna S 102 Eb48
Karnabrunn A 145 Gb50
Karnare BG 180 Db71
Kärne S 95 Fc43
Karnezéika GR 195 Ca88
Karnice PL 120 Fc31
Karniewo PL 122 Jb35
Karnjarga N 64 Jd07
Karnkowo PL 122 Hc35
Karnobat BG 181 Ec72
Karojba HR 151 Fa60
Karolewo PL 121 Ha33
Karonsbo S 80 Gd26
Karoševina SRB 159 Ja66
Karoussádes GR 182 Aa79
Karow D 119 Eb33
Karpacz PL 128 Ga42
Kärpänkylä FIN 75 Lb20
Karpássi GR 184 Dc80
Karpbukt N 65 Kd07
Karpenísi GR 188 Bb83
Karperí GR 183 Cb76
Karperö FIN 81 Hd30
Karperó GR 183 Bb79
Kárpi GR 183 Bd76
Karpicko PL 128 Ga37
Karpinvaara FIN 75 La24
Karpowicze PL 123 Kb32
Kärppälä FIN 89 Jc36
Kärppäsuo FIN 74 Ka22
Karpuzlu TR 197 Ed89
Kärra FIN 97 Jb40
Kärråkra S 102 Fa48
Kärrbäck S 95 Gb41
Kärrbackstrand S 86 Ed38
Kärrbo S 95 Fd42
Kärrbo S 95 Gb43
Karrebæksminde DK 109 Eb27
Karrsjö S 80 Gd29
Karsak TR 186 Fd80
Karsakiškis LT 114 Kc54
Kärsämä FIN 82 Ka25
Kärsämäki FIN 82 Kb27
Karsanlahti FIN 82 La28
Kärsava LV 107 Ld50
Karsbach D 134 Da44
Karsdorf D 127 Ea40
Karsibór PL 120 Fb32
Karsikas FIN 82 Ka27
Karsikko FIN 74 Jd22
Karsikkovaara FIN 82 Kd26
Karsin PL 121 Gd31
Karşıyaka TR 186 Fa79
Karsjö S 87 Ga36
Karskog FIN 98 Ka40
Kårsta S 96 Gd42
Karstädt D 119 Ea34
Kärstna EST 106 Kd46
Karstula FIN 82 Ka31
Karsun RUS 203 Fd10
Kartalkaya TR 187 Hb79
Kartalpınar TR 199 Gc89
Kartena LT 113 Jb54
Karterés GR 183 Cb77
Karterés GR 183 Cb77
Kartéri GR 188 Ac81
Kårtjevuolle sameviste S 67 Gc15
Kartno PL 120 Fc34
Karttiperä FIN 89 Jc34
Karttula FIN 82 Kd30
Kartuzy PL 121 Ha30
Käru EST 98 Ka45
Käru EST 98 Kc44
Karula EST 106 La47
Karulõpe EST 98 La41
Karuna FIN 97 Jc40
Karungi S 73 Jb20
Karunki FIN 74 Jc20
Karup DK 100 Db23
Karvala FIN 81 Jc30
Karvasalmi FIN 82 Kd29
Kärväskylä FIN 82 Kb29
Karvia FIN 89 Jb33
Karviankylä FIN 89 Jb33
Karvila FIN 91 Lc32
Karviná CZ 137 Hb45
Karvio FIN 83 Lb31
Karvoskylä FIN 82 Ka27
Karvys LT 114 La57
Karwica PL 112 Ha58
Karwica PL 122 Jc32
Karwin PL 120 Ga31
Karwowo-Wszebory PL 123 Jd33
Karyağmaz TR 192 Fc82
Karzec PL 129 Gc39
Kås DK 100 Dc20
Kaş TR 198 Ga93
Kåsa N 77 Dc32
Kasaba TR 198 Ga93
Kasaböle FIN 89 Hd34
Kasala FIN 89 Hd34
Kašalj SRB 178 Ba69
Kasapa SRB 153 Jb63
Kašary RUS 203 Fc14
Kascjukovičy BY 202 Ec12
Kascjukovka BY 202 Ec13
Kåseberga S 111 Fb57
Kasejovice CZ 136 Fa46
Kasendorf D 135 Dd44
Kasepää EST 99 Lb44
Kasfjord N 66 Ga12
Kaşıkçı TR 185 Ec77
Kaşıkçı TR 191 Ec84
Kaşıkçı TR 192 Fb84
Kaşıkçışeyhler TR 187 Gc79
Kasımlar TR 187 Gb80
Kasımlar TR 199 Ha89
Kasimov RUS 203 Fb10
Kašin RUS 202 Ed09
Kašina HR 152 Gb58
Kasina Wielka PL 138 Ja45
Kasiniemi FIN 90 Kb35
Kasinka Mała PL 138 Ja45
Kaširskoe RUS 113 Ja58
Kåskats S 73 Hb19
Kaskii FIN 91 Lb33
Kaskinen FIN 89 Hd33
Kaskö FIN 89 Hd33
Kas'kovo RUS 99 Ma40
Käsma FIN 75 La20
Käsmänlatva FIN 69 Kd17
Käsmu EST 98 Kd41
Kasnäs FIN 97 Jb41
Káspakas GR 190 Db81
Kašperské Hory CZ 135 Ed47
Kaspičan BG 181 Ed70
Kassa S 68 Jb17
Kassari EST 97 Jd45
Kassari saar EST 97 Jd45
Kasseedorf D 119 Dd31
Kassel D 126 Da40
Kassiópi GR 182 Ab79
Kassjö S 80 Hb28
Kastamonu TR 205 Fa20
Kastanées GR 183 Ca76
Kastaneri GR 183 Bd76
Kastaniá GR 182 Ad78
Kastaniá GR 182 Ba80
Kastaniá GR 183 Bc78
Kastaniá GR 188 Bb82
Kastaniá GR 189 Bc83
Kastaniá GR 189 Bc86
Kastaniés GR 185 Eb75
Kastaniótissa GR 189 Ca83
Kastanitsa GR 194 Bc88
Kastanófito GR 182 Ba78
Kastav HR 151 Fb60
Kastel HR 150 Ed60
Kaštela HR 158 Gb66
Kastelev DK 109 Eb28
Kastéli GR 201 Db96
Kastellaun D 133 Ca44
Kastélli GR 189 Bc84
Kastelruth I 143 Dd56
Kastelyosdombó H 152 Ha58
Kaštel Žegarski HR 157 Ga64
Kasterlee B 124 Ad39
Kastl D 143 Ec51
Kastlösa S 111 Gb53
Kastneshamn N 67 Gb12
Kastoriá GR 182 Ba77
Kastós GR 188 Ad84
Kastráki GR 189 Bd86
Kastraki GR 196 Db90
Kastre EST 99 Lb45
Kastrí GR 182 Ac80
Kastrí GR 189 Bd81
Kastrí GR 194 Bc88
Kastrí GR 200 Cb97
Kastria GR 188 Bb86
Kastritsa GR 182 Ad80
Kástro GR 188 Ad86
Kástro GR 189 Ca85
Kástro GR 196 Da90
Kastrosikiá GR 188 Ac82
Kastrup DK 109 Eb28
Kašučiai LT 113 Jb54
Kasukkala FIN 91 Lc36
Kaszaper H 147 Jd56
Kasztanowo PL 122 Hd31
Kaszyce PL 129 Gc40
Katafígio GR 183 Bc79
Katáfito GR 184 Cc76
Katahás GR 183 Bd78
Katajamäki FIN 83 Lb28
Katajamäki FIN 90 La32
Katákolo GR 194 Ad87
Kåtaliden S 72 Gc23
Kataloinen FIN 90 Kb37
Katalónia GR 183 Bd78
Kätänjoki FIN 81 Jc31
Katápola GR 196 Dc91
Kåtaselet S 73 Hb23
Katastári GR 188 Ac86
Katauskiai LT 114 Ka55
Kåtaviken S 71 Fc21
Katęczyn PL 122 Jb32
Katerini GR 183 Bd79
Katerma FIN 83 Lb26
Katesbridge GB 9 Da18
Katheni GR 189 Cc85
Kathikas CY 206 Hd97
Katići SRB 178 Ad67
Kåtilla S 87 Fb37
Katina BG 179 Cc71
Katinac HR 152 Gd59
Katinhänta FIN 89 Ja38
Kätkäsuvanto FIN 68 Ja14
Kätkävaara FIN 74 Jd20
Kätkesuando S 68 Ja14
Katko FIN 89 Jb34
Katlanovska Banja MK 178 Bc73
Katlenburg-Lindau D 126 Db39
Katleši LV 107 Ld48
Káto Ahaía GR 188 Ba85
Káto Alepohóri GR 189 Ca86
Káto Almirí GR 195 Ca87
Káto Asítes GR 200 Da96
Káto Asséa GR 194 Bc88
KatoDeftera CY 206 Jb97
Káto Dikomo CY 206 Jb96
Káto Doliana GR 195 Bd88
Káto Figália GR 194 Ba88
Káto Gialia CY 206 Hd97
Káto Glikóvrisi GR 195 Bd90
Katohí GR 188 Ba84
Káto Horió GR 201 Dc96
Káto Hrisovitsa GR 188 Bb84
Káto Kastaniá GR 195 Bd91
Káto Kastrítsi GR 188 Bb85
Katokopia CY 206 Ja96
Káto Koutrafas CY 206 Ja97
Káto Lapsísta GR 182 Ad80
Káto Makrinoú GR 188 Ba84
Káto Meriá GR 195 Cd88
Káto Moni CY 206 Jb97
Káto Mousounítsa GR 189 Bc84
Káto Nevrokópi GR 184 Cd76
Káto Polemidia CY 206 Ja98
Káto Pyrgos CY 206 Ja96
Káto Samikó GR 194 Ba87
Káto Sotirítsa GR 189 Ca81
Káto Soúnio GR 195 Cc88
Katosranta FIN 75 La21
Káto Tarsós GR 189 Bc86
Káto Theodoráki GR 183 Cb76
Káto Tritos GR 191 Ea83
Katoúna GR 188 Ad83
Káto Vérmio GR 183 Bc78
Káto Vlassía GR 188 Bb86
Kátó Vrontoú GR 184 Cc76
Katowice PL 138 Hc44
Káto Zákros GR 201 Dd96
Katriņa LV 106 La50
Katrineholm S 95 Ga45
Katsarós GR 194 Bb88
Katsch an der Mur A 144 Fb54
Katsikás GR 182 Ad80
Katsimbalis GR 194 Bb88
Kattarp S 110 Ed54
Kattavía GR 197 Ed94
Kättbo S 87 Fb38
Kattelus FIN 89 Jd32
Katterat N 67 Gc13
Katterjåkk S 67 Gc13
Katthammarsvik S 104 Ha50
Kattilainen FIN 91 Lb38
Kattilakoski FIN 81 Jc29
Kattilasaari S 73 Jb21
Kattisavan S 80 Gc25
Kattisberg S 80 Ha25
Kattlunds S 104 Ha51
Kattowitz = Katowice PL 138 Hc44
Kattuvuoma S 67 Ha14
Katunci BG 184 Cc75
Katund i Ri AL 182 Ab74
Katunica BG 180 Db73
Katusice CZ 136 Fc43
Katvari LV 106 Kc48
Katwijk aan Zee NL 116 Ad36
Kąty PL 123 Jd33
Katy PL 131 Ka42
Katyčiai LT 113 Jc56
Katymár H 153 Hd58
Kąty Rybackie PL 122 Hc30
Katy Wrocławskie PL 129 Gc41
Katzenelnbogen D 133 Cb43
Katzhütte D 135 Dd43
Kaub D 133 Ca44
Kaufbeuren D 142 Db51
Kaufering D 142 Dc51
Kaufungen D 126 Da40
Kauhajärvi FIN 81 Jc30
Kauhajärvi FIN 89 Jb33
Kauhajoki FIN 89 Ja33
Kauhanoja FIN 89 Jc38
Kauhava FIN 81 Jb30
Kauhee FIN 83 Ld29
Kauk- FIN 98 Kb40
Kaukalampi FIN 90 Kc38
Kaukas FIN 90 Kb38
Kaukassalo FIN 97 Jc40
Kaukela FIN 90 Kb35
Kauklainen FIN 89 Ja37
Kaukola FIN 97 Jd39
Kaukolikai LT 113 Jc53
Kaukonen FIN 68 Jc16
Kauksi EST 99 Lb43
Kaukuri FIN 97 Jd40
Kaulaci LV 105 Jd51
Kaulakiai LT 114 Ka56
Kaulinranta FIN 73 Jb19
Kaulio FIN 90 La36
Kaunas LT 114 Kc57
Kaunata LV 107 Ld52
Kaunatava LT 113 Jd54
Kauniainen FIN 98 Kb39
Kaunisjoensuu S 68 Jb16
Kaunisvaara S 68 Ja16
Kaunitz D 126 Cc38
Kaupanger N 84 Cd37
Kauppila FIN 90 Kd32
Kauppilanmäki FIN 82 Kd27
Kaupuži LV 107 Ld50
Kaurajärvi FIN 81 Jb30
Kauria FIN 90 La35
Kaurissalo FIN 97 Ja39
Kauronkylä FIN 83 Lc25
Kauša LV 107 Lc52
Kausala FIN 90 Kd37
Kausen D 125 Cb41
Kausland N 84 Bd39
Kaustajärvi FIN 83 Ma31
Kaustari FIN 81 Jb28
Kaustinen FIN 81 Jc29
Kautokeino N 68 Hd11
Kauttua FIN 89 Jb37
Kautzen A 136 Fd48
Kauvatsa FIN 89 Jb36
Káva H 146 Ja53
Kavacık TR 185 Eb77
Kavacık TR 192 Fb82
Kavacık TR 193 Gc81
Kavacık TR 199 Gb88
Kavadarci MK 183 Bd75
Kavajë AL 182 Ab75
Kavak TR 205 Fc20
Kavakarası TR 198 Fc91
Kavakçalı TR 198 Fb90
Kavakdere TR 185 Ed75
Kavakdere TR 191 Eb87
Kavakköy TR 185 Ec79
Kavakköy TR 193 Hb81
Kavaklı TR 185 Eb77
Kavaklı TR 185 Ec75
Kavaklı TR 186 Fb77
Kavaklı TR 186 Fc78
Kavaklı TR 186 Ga80
Kavaklı TR 192 Ga81
Kavaklı TR 198 Fb88
Kavaklıdere TR 198 Fb89
Kavala FIN 90 Ka34
Kavála GR 184 Da77
Kavarna BG 181 Fb70
Kavarskas LT 114 Kd55
Kavelstorf D 119 Eb31
Kåvenvallen S 86 Ed33
Kavgacılar TR 199 Gd91
Kavlac BG 180 Ea70
Kävlinge S 110 Ed55
Kavos GR 188 Ab81
Kavoúsi GR 201 Dc96
Kavşıt TR 197 Fa88
Kavslunde DK 108 Db26
Kawęczyn PL 129 Hb38
Kawice PL 129 Gb40
Kaxås S 79 Fb30
Kaxholmen S 103 Fb48
Kayaağıl TR 192 Fd85
Kayabaşı TR 186 Fc77
Kayabaşı TR 192 Fb81
Kayabaşı TR 197 Ed89
Kayabaşı TR 198 Fd92
Kayabaşı TR 198 Ga91
Kayabaşı TR 199 Ha89
Kayabükü TR 193 Hb81
Kayabükü TR 197 Ed89
Kayacık TR 186 Fd80
Kayacık TR 192 Fa84
Kayacık TR 198 Fc91
Kayadibi TR 191 Ec85
Kayaışık TR 192 Fc84
Kayakalan TR 192 Fa85
Kayakent TR 193 Hb83
Kayaköy TR 191 Ed87
Kayaköy TR 198 Fc92
Kayalar TR 191 Ed81
Kayalar TR 199 Ha89
Kayalı TR 185 Ec75
Kayalı TR 192 Fc86
Kayalı TR 199 Gb90
Kayalıdere TR 192 Fc83
Kayalıoğlu TR 191 Ed84
Kayapa TR 185 Eb75
Kayapa TR 186 Fc80
Kayapa TR 191 Ed82
Kayapınar TR 191 Ea85
Kayapınar TR 191 Ed81
Kayapınar TR 198 Fc89
Kayı TR 185 Ed77
Kayı TR 193 Gd83
Kayı TR 193 Ha81
Kayıköy TR 199 Gc88
Kayış TR 199 Gc89
Kayışlar TR 191 Ed84
Käylä FIN 74 La18
Käymäjärvi S 68 Ja16
Kaymakçı TR 192 Fa87
Kaymakoba TR 186 Fc80
Kaymaz TR 187 Gb78
Kaymaz TR 193 Ha83
Kayna D 127 Eb41
Kaynaklar TR 191 Ec86
Kaynarca TR 187 Gc78
Kaynaşlı TR 187 Ha78
Käyppälä FIN 81 Ja31
Käyrämö FIN 69 Ka17
Kayran TR 192 Fb87
Kaysersberg F 31 Kb38
Kazačka RUS 203 Fc12
Kazan' RUS 203 Fd08
Kažani MK 182 Ba76
Kazanka UA 204 Ed16
Kazanlăk BG 180 Dd72
Kazanów PL 130 Jc40
Kazanskaja RUS 203 Fc13
Kazdanga LV 105 Jb52
Kazičene BG 179 Cc71
Kazıklı TR 186 Fd80
Kazimierza Wielka PL 138 Jb43
Kazimierz Biskupi PL 129 Ha37
Kazimierz Dolny PL 131 Jd40
Kazimierzewo PL 121 Hb35
Kazimierzewo PL 122 Hc30
Kazımpaşa TR 187 Gc78
Kazincbarcika H 146 Jc50
Kazitiškis LT 115 Lb55
Kazivera CY 206 Ja96
Kazliškis LT 114 La53
Kazlų Rūda LV 114 Kb58
Kaźmierz PL 129 Gb36
Kaznějov CZ 135 Ed45
Kcynia PL 121 Gd35
Kdyně CZ 135 Ed47
Keadew IRL 8 Ca18
Keady GB 9 Cd18
Keal GB 17 Fd22
Kealkil IRL 12 Bb26
Keava EST 98 Kc44
Keb RUS 107 Ma46
Kecel H 146 Hd56
Kecerovce SK 139 Jd48
Keçiborlu TR 199 Gc88
Keçidere TR 192 Fb82
Keçiler TR 193 Gb84
Kecskemét H 146 Ja55
Kėdainiai LT 114 Kc56
Kédros GR 189 Bc82
Kędrzyno PL 120 Fd31
Kędzierzyn-Koźle PL 137 Ha43
Keeagh IRL 12 Bc21
Keeken D 125 Bc37
Keel IRL 8 Bb18
Keelby GB 17 Fc21
Keeni EST 106 La47
Kefalári GR 189 Bc86
Kéfalos GR 197 Eb91
Kefalóvrisso GR 183 Bc80
Kefenrod D 134 Cd43
Kefermarkt A 144 Fb50
Kefferhausen D 126 Db40
Kefken TR 187 Gb77
Keflavík IS 2 Ab04
Ķegums LV 106 Kc51
Kegworth GB 16 Fa23
Kehidakustány H 145 Gd55
Kehl D 133 Ca49
Kehra EST 98 Kc42
Kehrigk D 128 Fa37
Kehrókambos GR 184 Da76
Kehtna EST 98 Kc44
Keighley GB 16 Ed20
Keihärinkoski FIN 82 Kb30
Keihäskoski FIN 89 Jb38
Keihäsniemi FIN 90 Kb34
Keikyä FIN 89 Jb36
Keila EST 98 Kb42
Keila-Joa EST 98 Kb42
Keillmore GB 6 Db13
Keimola FIN 98 Kb39
Keinäsperä FIN 75 Kc23
Keinojärvi FIN 65 Kb10
Keino sameviste S 67 Gd17
Keinovuopio S 67 Hb12
Keinton Mandeville GB 19 Eb29
Ķeipene LV 106 Kd50
Keisala FIN 81 Jd31
Keistiö FIN 97 Ja40
Keitele FIN 82 Kc29
Keitelepohja FIN 82 Kb29
Keith GB 7 Ec08
Keitjärvi FIN 90 La37
Keituri FIN 90 Kc37
Ķekava LV 106 Kb51
Kéked H 139 Jd49
Kekkilä FIN 82 Kb31
Kekkonen FIN 89 Jd34
Kelankylä FIN 74 Kb21
Kelberg D 133 Bd43
Kelbra D 127 Dd40
Kelč CZ 137 Ha46
Kelchsau A 143 Ea53
Kėlcyrë AL 182 Ac78
Keld GB 11 Ed18
Keldbylille DK 109 Ec28
Keldernæs DK 109 Ea28
Keldinge FIN 97 Jb40
Kelebija SRB 153 Ja57
Keléd H 145 Gd54
Kelekcı TR 198 Fd90
Kelemér H 146 Jb50
Keler TR 191 Ec87
Keles TR 192 Fd81
Kelheim D 135 Ea48
Kéli GR 183 Bb77
Kelionkangas FIN 90 Kb33
Kelkheim D 134 Cc44
Kelkit TR 205 Fd20
Kelkkala FIN 97 Jd40
Kellahti FIN 89 Ja35
Kellaki CY 206 Jb97
Kellenhusen D 119 Dd30
Kellerberg A 144 Fa56
Kellia CY 206 Jc97
Kelling GB 17 Gb23
Kellinghusen D 118 Db31
Kello FIN 74 Ka23
Kellokoski FIN 90 Kb38
Kelloniemi FIN 74 Kc18
Kellosalmi FIN 90 Kb35
Kelloselkä FIN 69 Kd17
Kells IRL 9 Cc20
Kells IRL 12 Ba25
Kellybray GB 18 Dc31
Kelmė LT 114 Ka55
Kelmis B 125 Bb41
Kelokedara CY 206 Hd98
Kelontekemä FIN 69 Jd15
Kelottijärvi FIN 68 Hc13
Kelovaara FIN 68 Ja14
Kelsale GB 21 Gb25
Kelsall GB 15 Ec22
Kelso GB 11 Ec14
Kelstrup DK 108 Db27
Keltakangas FIN 90 La37
Keltaniemi FIN 90 Kc36
Keltiäinen FIN 89 Jd38
Keltti FIN 90 Kd37
Kelty GB 7 Eb12
Kelujärvi FIN 69 Ka15
Kelvä FIN 83 Ld29
Kelvedon GB 21 Ga27
Kemah TR 205 Fd20
Kemaliye TR 187 Gb79
Kemaliye TR 192 Fb86
Kemaller TR 185 Ed77
Kemaller TR 187 Gc79
Kemallı TR 191 Ea81
Kemalpaşa TR 191 Ec86
Kemalpaşa TR 205 Ga18
Ķemari LV 106 Ka51
Kematen A 144 Fc51
Kemberg D 127 Ec39
Kemble GB 20 Ed27
Kemecse H 147 Ka50
Kemence H 146 Hc51
Kemeneshőgyész H 145 Gd53
Kemer TR 185 Ec79
Kemer TR 192 Fa85
Kemer TR 198 Ga93
Kemer TR 199 Gb89
Kemer TR 199 Gc92
Kemerburgaz TR 186 Fc77
Kemerdamları TR 192 Fa85
Kemerdamları TR 193 Gd87
Kemerkasım TR 187 Ha78
Kémes H 152 Hb58
Kemeten A 145 Gb54
Kemi FIN 74 Jc21
Kemie FIN 83 Ma31
Kemihaara FIN 69 Kc13
Kemijärvi FIN 74 Kb18
Kemiklidere TR 191 Ed85
Kemilä FIN 75 La20
Keminmaa FIN 74 Jc21
Keminperä FIN 75 La21
Kemiö FIN 97 Jc40
Kemlja RUS 203 Fc10
Kemmel B 21 Ha30
Kemnath D 135 Ea45
Kemnay GB 7 Ed09
Kemnitz D 120 Fa31
Kemnitz D 127 Ed37
Kempele FIN 74 Ka24
Kempen D 125 Bc39
Kempenich D 125 Bd42
Kempsey GB 15 Ec26
Kempston GB 20 Fc26
Kempten CH 142 Cc53
Kempten D 142 Db52
Kemtau D 127 Ec42
Kena LT 115 Lb58
Kendal GB 11 Ec18
Kenderes H 146 Jc53
Kendice SK 139 Jd48
Kéndro GR 188 Ba86
Kéndro GR 194 Bb89
Kenestupa FIN 64 Jd08
Kenfig GB 19 Dd28
Kenger TR 197 Fa88
Kengis S 68 Ja17
Kengyel H 146 Jb54
Kenilworth GB 20 Fa25
Kenknock GB 7 Dd11
Kenmare IRL 12 Bb25
Neidín IRL 12 Bb25
Kenmore GB 7 Ea11
Kenn GB 19 Ea31
Kennää FIN 82 Kb30
Kennacraig GB 6 Db13
Kenninghall GB 21 Ga25
Kenraalinkylä FIN 83 Ma31
Kentisbury Ford GB 19 Dd29
Kentmere GB 11 Ec18
Kentrikó GR 183 Ca76
Kéntro GR 183 Bb79
Kenttan N 64 Jc09
Kenyeri H 145 Gd53
Kenzingen D 141 Ca50
Kepaliai LT 114 Kb53
Kepekler TR 192 Fb82
Kepen TR 193 Ha83
Kepenekli TR 185 Ed77
Kepezbeleni TR 199 Hb91
Kępice PL 121 Gc30
Kępno PL 129 Ha40
Kepsut TR 192 Fa82
Kerälä FIN 82 Ka25
Keramídi GR 189 Ca81
Kéramos GR 191 Dd85
Keramotí GR 184 Db77
Keränen FIN 75 Kd19
Keräntöjärvi S 68 Ja15
Kerasohóri GR 188 Bb82
Kerasóna GR 188 Ad81
Keräs-Sieppi FIN 68 Jb14
Kerássovo GR 182 Ac79
Keratea GR 195 Cc87
Keratókambos GR 201 Db96
Kerauzern F 26 Ea37
Kerava FIN 98 Kb39
Keravere EST 98 Ka44
Kerbanlar TR 187 Hb80
Kerč UA 205 Fb17
Kerecsend H 146 Jb52
Kereka BG 180 Dd70
Kerekegyháza H 146 Ja55
Kereki H 145 Ha55
Keremköy TR 191 Eb83
Kerepestarcsa H 146 Hd52
Kergrist-Moëlou F 26 Ea38
Kergu EST 98 Kc45
Kerí GR 188 Ac86
Kérien F 26 Ea38
Kerimäki FIN 91 Ld33
Kerimler TR 192 Fc87
Keriniemi FIN 91 Lb34
Kerisalo FIN 91 Lb32
Kérity F 27 Dc40
Kerkafavla H 145 Gb55
Kerken D 125 Bc39
Kerkini GR 183 Cb76
Kerkira GR 182 Ab80
Kerkkoo FIN 90 Kc38
Ķerkliņi LV 105 Jd52
Kerko FIN 90 Kc38
Kerkola FIN 89 Jd38
Kerkonkoski FIN 82 Kc31
Kerkow D 120 Fa34
Kerkrade NL 125 Bb41
Kerma FIN 83 Lc31
Kermen BG 180 Ea72
Kernascléden F 27 Ea39
Kernavė LT 114 Kd57
Kernhof A 144 Fd52
Kernovo RUS 99 Ld40
Kerns CH 141 Ca54
Kernu EST 98 Kb43
Kéros GR 196 Dc90
Kerpe TR 187 Gb77
Kerpen D 125 Bc41
Kerpen (Eifel) D 133 Bc43
Kerpiçlik TR 191 Ed86
Kerpiçlik TR 192 Fc84
Kerpini GR 188 Bb86
Kerry GB 15 Eb24
Kersalu EST 98 Ka42
Kersilö FIN 69 Ka15
Kersleti EST 97 Jd44
Kerstovo RUS 99 Ld41
Kerstovo RUS 99 Ld41
Kerteminde DK 109 Dd26
Kertészsziget H 147 Jd54
Kértezi GR 188 Bb86
Kerthpulë AL 163 Jb71
Kertil TR 192 Fa83
Kerttuankylä FIN 81 Jc29
Keryneia CY 206 Jb96
Kerzers CH 141 Bc54
Kesälahti FIN 91 Ld33
Kesämäki FIN 82 La29
Keşan TR 185 Eb78
Kesäpuro FIN 64 Ka07
Kesarevo BG 180 Ea70
Kesasjärv S 73 Hd20
Kesčiai LT 113 Jd56
Kesecik TR 199 Hb89
Keselyüs H 153 Hc57
Kesenler TR 193 Gc83
Kesh GB 9 Cb17
Kesh IRL 8 Ca18
Keshcarigan IRL 8 Ca19
Kesik TR 191 Eb85
Keskijärvi FIN 83 Ld30
Keskikylä FIN 74 Ka22
Keskikylä FIN 74 Jd24
Keskikylä FIN 74 Ka24
Keskikylä FIN 81 Jd31
Keskikylä FIN 81 Jd26
Keskikylä FIN 89 Jb33
Keskikylä FIN 91 Lb33
Keskin TR 193 Gc81
Keskinen FIN 75 Lb24
Keski-Nurmo FIN 81 Jb31
Keski-Palokka FIN 90 Kb32
Keskipiiri FIN 74 Ka24
Keskisaari FIN 91 Lb32
Keski-Valli FIN 89 Jb32
Keski-Vuokko FIN 83 Lb28
Kesme TR 199 Ha89
Kesnacken S 94 Ec44
Kęsowo PL 121 Gd33
Kessel NL 125 Bc39
Kesselfall A 143 Ec54
Kesselinkylä FIN 83 Lc26
Kesselsdorf D 128 Fa41
Kessingland GB 21 Gc25
Kessock GB 7 Ea08
Kestad S 102 Fa46
Kestanelik TR 186 Fb77
Kestanepınarı TR 187 Gd78
Kestel TR 192 Fd84
Ķesterciems LV 106 Ka50
Kesteren NL 125 Bb37
Kesteri LV 113 Jb53
Kesti FIN 89 Ja32
Kestilä FIN 74 Jd23
Kestilä FIN 82 Kb26
Kesusmaa FIN 91 Ld33
Keswick GB 11 Eb17
Keszthely H 145 Gd55
Ketčenery RUS 203 Ga14
Kétegyháza H 147 Jd56
Ketelhaven NL 117 Bc35
Ketendere TR 192 Fb87
Ketenova TR 192 Fb87
Kéthely H 145 Gd56
Ketola FIN 74 Kb18
Ketomella FIN 68 Jb13
Kétpó H 146 Jc54
Keträvaara FIN 75 La22
Kętrzyn PL 122 Jc30
Ketsch D 134 Cc46
Kettenkamp D 117 Cb35
Kettering GB 20 Fb25
Kettilsbyn S 94 Ed44
Kettinge DK 109 Eb29
Kettletoft GB 5 Ed02
Kettlewell GB 11 Ed19
Kéttornyúlak H 145 Gd54
Kettula FIN 97 Jd39
Ketūnai LT 113 Jc53
Keturkaimis LT 114 Ka58
Keturvalakiai LV 114 Kb59
Kéty H 146 Hc56
Kęty PL 138 Hd45
Ketzin D 127 Ec36
Ketzür D 127 Ec36
Keula D 126 Dc40
Keula D 126 Dc40
Keuruu FIN 90 Ka33
Keväjärvi FIN 69 Kb11
Kevastu EST 99 Lb45
Kevelaer D 125 Bc38
Kevele LV 105 Jd52
Kevermes H 147 Jd56
Kevi SRB 153 Jb58
Kewstoke GB 19 Eb28
Kexby GB 16 Fb22
Keynsham GB 19 Ec28
Keyritty FIN 82 La28
Keyston GB 20 Fc25
Keyworth GB 16 Fb23
Kežmarok SK 138 Jb47
Kiaby S 111 Fb54
Kiados CY 206 Jc96
Kiannanniemi FIN 75 La22
Kiáto GR 189 Bd86
Kiaunoriai LT 114 Ka55
Kibæk DK 108 Da24
Kiberg N 62 Gc09
Kiberg N 65 Kd05
Kıbrıscık TR 187 Hb80
Kiburi LV 113 Jb53
Kiby N 65 Kc06
Kibyšiai LT 123 Kc30
Kičenica BG 180 Eb69

Kičevo – Klenovec

Kičevo BG 181 Fa70
Kičevo MK 182 Ba74
Kiçir TR 192 Fc83
Kidderminster GB 15 Ec25
Kidekša RUS 203 Fa09
Kidelv N 63 Hd08
Kidričevo SLO 151 Ga57
Kidsgrove GB 15 Ec23
Kiduliai LT 114 Ka57
Kidwelly GB 18 Dc27
Kiefersfelden D 143 Eb52
Kiekinkoski FIN 83 Ld26
Kiekrz PL 129 Gc36
Kieksiäisvaara S 68 Jb17
Kiel D 118 Dc30
Kielajoki FIN 64 Jd09
Kielce PL 130 Jb41
Kielcza PL 137 Hb43
Kietczygłów PL 130 Hc40
Kielder GB 11 Ec15
Kielkenes N 84 Ca34
Kiełpiny PL 122 Hd33
Kieměnai LT 114 Kc53
Kiemunkivaara FIN 69 Kb17
Kienberg A 144 Fd51
Kienberg D 143 Eb51
Kienes LV 106 Kd49
Kiental CH 141 Bd55
Kierinki FIN 69 Jd16
Kiernozia PL 130 Hd37
Kierspe D 125 Ca40
Kiesen CH 141 Bd54
Kiesilä FIN 90 La35
Kiesimä FIN 82 Kc31
Kietävälä FIN 91 Lb35
Kietävälä FIN 91 Lb34
Kietrz PL 137 Ha44
Kietz D 128 Fc36
Kiewłaki PL 123 Ka34
Kifino Selo BIH 158 Hb67
Kifissiá GR 189 Cc86
Kifjord N 64 Jd04
Kiği TR 205 Ga20
Kigyósgárgyán H 146 Ja56
Kihelkonna EST 105 Jb46
Kihlanki FIN 68 Ja15
Kihlanki S 68 Ja16
Kihlepa EST 106 Kb46
Kihlevere EST 98 Kd42
Kihniä FIN 89 Jc32
Kihniö FIN 89 Jc33
Kihniön asema FIN 89 Jc33
Kıhra TR 192 Fb84
Kiideva EST 98 Ka44
Kiihtelysvaara FIN 83 Ma30
Kiikala FIN 97 Jd39
Kiikka FIN 89 Jc36
Kiikla EST 99 Lb42
Kiikoinen FIN 89 Jb36
Kiiholma FIN 89 Ja35
Kiimajärvi FIN 89 Jb36
Kiiminki FIN 74 Ka23
Kiipu FIN 89 Jd38
Kiisa EST 98 Kb43
Kiiskilä FIN 81 Jd28
Kiistala FIN 68 Jc14
Kiiu EST 98 Kc42
Kije PL 130 Jb42
Kijevo BIH 159 Hc65
Kijevo HR 158 Gb65
Kijevo KSV 178 Ba71
Kijewo PL 123 Ka31
Kijewo Królewskie PL 121 Ha34
Kijowiec PL 129 Ha36
Kijowiec PL 131 Kc37
Kikerino RUS 99 Mb41
Kikersy RUS 99 Ld41
Kikinda SRB 153 Jc58
Kiknur RUS 203 Fc08
Kikoł PL 122 Hc35
Kikorze PL 120 Fc33
Ķikuri LV 105 Jb51
Kil N 93 Db45
Kil S 94 Fa43
Kil S 95 Fc43
Kila S 94 Ed44
Kila S 95 Gb42
Kiláda GR 189 Bc81
Kiláda GR 195 Ca88
Kilafors S 87 Gb37
Kilan N 78 Eb26
Kilanda S 102 Ec48
Kilás GR 183 Bc78
Kılavuzlar TR 199 Gb90
Kilb A 144 Fd51
Kilbaha IRL 12 Ba23
Kilbarry IRL 12 Bc26
Kilbeheny IRL 12 Bd24
Kilberry GB 6 Db13
Kilberry IRL 13 Cc22
Kilbirnie GB 10 Dd13
Kilboghamn N 70 Fa20
Kilbotn N 66 Ga12
Kilbreedy IRL 12 Bc23
Kilbride IRL 13 Cd22
Kilbride IRL 13 Cd23
Kilbrien IRL 13 Ca25
Kilcanlar TR 192 Fa85
Kilcar IRL 8 Ca16
Kilcarn IRL 9 Cd20
Kilchattan GB 6 Dc13
Kilchberg CH 141 Cb53
Kilchoan GB 6 Da10
Kilchoman GB 6 Da13
Kilchreest IRL 12 Bd21
Kilchrenan GB 6 Dc11
Kılcılan TR 192 Fa83
Kilclonfert IRL 13 Cb21
Kilcock IRL 13 Cd21
Kilcolgan IRL 12 Bd21
Kilcoo GB 9 Da18
Kilcormac IRL 13 Cb21
Kilcullen IRL 13 Cc22
Kilcummin IRL 8 Bc17
Kilcummin IRL 12 Ba24
Kilcurry IRL 9 Cd19
Kildal N 63 Hb09
Kildare IRL 13 Cc22
Kildavanan GB 6 Dc13
Kildavin IRL 13 Cc23
Kildebrønde DK 109 Ec26
Kildermmorie Lodge GB 4 Dd07
Kildonan GB 10 Dc14
Kildonan Lodge GB 5 Ea05
Kildorrery IRL 12 Bd24
Kildress GB 9 Cd17
Kildrum GB 9 Da16
Kildrummy GB 7 Ec09
Kile S 94 Ea45
Kilebygd N 93 Dc44
Kilefjorden N 92 Cd46
Kilegrend N 93 Da44
Kilen N 93 Db43
Kilfeakle IRL 13 Ca24
Kilgarvan IRL 12 Bb25
Kilgi EST 106 Ka46
Kilglass IRL 13 Ca21
Kilgobnet IRL 12 Ba25
Kilham GB 11 Ed14
Kilham GB 17 Fc19
Kılıç TR 186 Fd79
Kılıç TR 199 Gc88
Kılıçlı TR 198 Ga93
Kılıçyaka TR 193 Gd86
Kilifarevo BG 180 Dd71
Kilija UA 204 Ec18
Kilimán H 145 Gd56
Kilimli TR 187 Hb76
Kilingi-Nõmme EST 106 Kc46
Kilini GR 188 Ad86
Kilitbahir TR 185 Ea80
Kilkcowan GB 10 Dd16
Kilkeary IRL 13 Ca23
Kilkee IRL 12 Bb23
Kilkeel GB 9 Da19
Kilkenny IRL 13 Cb23
Kilkhampton GB 18 Dc30
Kilkieran IRL 8 Bb20
Kilkieran IRL 12 Bb21
Kilkinkylä FIN 90 Kd34
Kilkís GR 183 Ca76
Kilkishen IRL 12 Bd22
Kill IRL 13 Cb25
Kill IRL 13 Cd21
Killadeas GB 9 Cb17
Killadysert IRL 12 Bc23
Killagan Bridge GB 9 Da16
Killakee IRL 13 Cd22
Killala IRL 8 Bc18
Killaloe IRL 12 Bd23
Killamery IRL 13 Cb24
Killanena IRL 12 Bd22
Killarga IRL 8 Ca18
Killarney IRL 12 Bb25
Killashandra IRL 9 Cb19
Killbeggan IRL 13 Cb21
Killderry IRL 13 Cb23
Killea IRL 9 Cc16
Killea IRL 13 Ca23
Killeagh IRL 13 Ca25
Killeany IRL 12 Bb21
Killearn GB 7 Dd12
Killeberg S 111 Fb53
Killeen IRL 12 Bd22
Killeigh IRL 13 Cb21
Killen GB 9 Cb17
Killeter GB 9 Cb17
Killiecrankie GB 7 Ea10
Killik TR 192 Fc81
Killik TR 199 Gc90
Killimor IRL 13 Ca21
Killin GB 7 Dd11
Killinge S 67 Hb16
Killinkoski FIN 89 Jd32
Killkelly IRL 8 Bd19
Killmuckridge IRL 13 Cd24
Killorglin IRL 12 Ba25
Killough IRL 13 Cd22
Killukin IRL 8 Ca19
Killurin IRL 13 Cc24
Killybegs IRL 8 Ca16
Killyleagh GB 10 Db18
Kilmacrenan IRL 9 Cb15
Kilmacthomas IRL 13 Cb25
Kilmaganny IRL 13 Cb24
Kilmaine IRL 8 Bc20
Kilmaley IRL 12 Bc22
Kilmallock IRL 12 Bd24
Kilmanagh IRL 13 Cb23
Kilmarnock GB 10 Dd14
Kilmartin GB 6 Db12
Kilmeadan IRL 13 Cb25
Kilmeelickin IRL 8 Bb20
Kilmessan IRL 9 Cd20
Kilmichael IRL 12 Ad26
Kilmichael IRL 12 Bc26
Kilmington GB 19 Eb30
Kilmona IRL 12 Bd25
Kilmoon IRL 12 Bb27
Kilmorack GB 7 Dd08
Kilmore Quay IRL 13 Cc25
Kilmory GB 10 Dc14
Kilmurry IRL 12 Bd23
Kilmurvy IRL 12 Bb21
Kilnalag IRL 8 Bd20
Kilnaleck IRL 9 Cc19
Kilninver GB 6 Db11
Kilnsea GB 17 Fd21
Kilpeck GB 15 Eb26
Kilpilahti FIN 98 Kc39
Kilpisjärvi FIN 67 Hb11
Kilpola FIN 90 La33
Kilpoole IRL 13 Da23
Kilpua FIN 81 Jd26
Kilrea GB 9 Cd16
Kilreekill IRL 12 Bd21
Kilrush IRL 12 Bb23
Kilshanchoe IRL 13 Cc21
Kilshannig IRL 12 Ba24
Kilsheelan IRL 13 Cb24
Kilskeery GB 9 Cb17
Kilsmo S 95 Fd44
Kilsund N 93 Db46
Kilsyth GB 10 Ea13
Kiltealy IRL 13 Cc24
Kiltimagh IRL 8 Bd19
Kiltoom IRL 8 Ca20
Kiltsi EST 98 La43
Kiltullagh IRL 12 Bd21
Kilvakkala FIN 89 Jc35
Kilve GB 19 Ea29
Kilvo S 73 Hc18
Kilwaughter GB 9 Da16
Kilwinning GB 10 Dd14
Kilworth Camp IRL 12 Bd25
Kimberley GB 17 Ga24
Kimbolton GB 20 Fc25
Kiméria GR 184 Db77
Kími GR 189 Cc84
Kímina GR 183 Ca78
Kiminki FIN 82 Kb30
Kiminki FIN 82 Ka30
Kímissis GR 183 Cb76
Kimito FIN 97 Jc40
Kimle H 145 Gd52
Kimo FIN 81 Ja30
Kimola FIN 90 Kd36
Kimolos GR 195 Cd90
Kimonkylä FIN 90 Kd37
Kimovsk RUS 203 Fa11
Kimpton GB 20 Fc27
Kimry RUS 202 Ed09
Kimstad S 103 Ga46
Kinahmo FIN 83 Lc30
Kınalı TR 186 Fd78
Kınalı TR 198 Fc92
Kinbrace GB 5 Ea05
Kincasslagh IRL 8 Ca15
Kincraig GB 7 Ea09
Kindberg A 144 Fd53
Kindelbrück D 127 Dd40
Kinderbeuern D 133 Bd44
Kinderdijk NL 124 Ad37
Kinding D 135 Dd48
Kindsjön S 94 Ed39
Kinel' RUS 203 Ga10
Kinešma RUS 203 Fb09
Kinéta GR 189 Ca86
Kineton GB 20 Fa26
Kingarth GB 6 Dc13
Kingersheim F 31 Kb39
Kingham GB 20 Ed26
Kinghorn GB 7 Eb12
Kingisepp RUS 99 Ld41
Kingisepp RUS 202 Ea09
Kingsbarns GB 7 Ec12
Kingsbridge GB 19 Dd32
Kingsbury GB 16 Ed24
Kingsclere GB 20 Fa28
King's Cliffe GB 17 Fc24
Kingscote GB 19 Ec27
Kingscourt IRL 9 Cc19
Kingsdown GB 21 Gb29
Kingskerswell GB 19 Ea31
Kingsland IRL 8 Ca19
King's Lynn GB 17 Fd24
Kingsmill GB 9 Cd17
King's Somborne GB 20 Fa29
King's Sutton GB 20 Fa26
Kingsteignton GB 19 Ea31
Kingstone GB 15 Eb26
Kingston Seymour GB 19 Eb28
Kingston-upon-Hull GB 17 Fc20
Kingston-upon-Hull GB 17 Fc21
Kingstown IRL 8 Ba20
King's Walden GB 20 Fc27
Kingswear GB 19 Ea32
Kingswood GB 15 Eb24
Kingswood GB 19 Ec27
Kings Worthy GB 20 Fa29
Kington GB 15 Eb25
Kington Langley GB 20 Ed28
Kingussie GB 7 Ea09
Kini GR 196 Da88
Kınık TR 191 Ed82
Kınık TR 191 Ed84
Kınık TR 192 Fb85
Kınık TR 192 Fc83
Kınık TR 192 Fc85
Kınık TR 193 Gb82
Kınık TR 193 Ha83
Kınık TR 198 Ga91
Kınıklı TR 198 Fd93
Kinisjärvi FIN 68 Jc16
Kinkiai LT 114 Ka53
Kinknockie GB 5 Ed08
Kinkomaa FIN 90 Kb33
Kinlet GB 15 Ec25
Kinloch GB 4 Dd05
Kinloch GB 6 Da09
Kinlochard GB 7 Dd12
Kinlochbervie GB 4 Dd04
Kinlochewe GB 4 Dc07
Kinloch Hourn GB 6 Dc09
Kinlochleven GB 6 Dc10
Kinlochmoidart GB 6 Db10
Kinloch Rannoch GB 7 Ea10
Kinloss GB 5 Eb07
Kinlough IRL 8 Ca17
Kinmel Bay GB 15 Ea22
Kinn N 66 Fd12
Kinn N 85 Dd38
Kinna S 102 Ed49
Kinnadoohy IRL 8 Bb19
Kinnakyrkja N 84 Ca35
Kinnared S 102 Ed51
Kinnarp S 102 Fa48
Kinnarumma S 102 Ed49
Kinnasniemi FIN 83 Ma30
Kinnbäck S 73 Hd24
Kinnegad IRL 13 Cc21
Kinnerley GB 15 Eb24
Kinne-Vedum S 102 Fa46
Kinni FIN 90 La35
Kinnitty IRL 13 Cb22
Kinnula FIN 82 Ka29
Kinnulanlahti FIN 82 Kd29
Kinousa CY 206 Hd97
Kinrooi B 125 Bb40
Kinsale IRL 12 Bd26
Kinsalebeg IRL 13 Ca25
Kinsarvik N 84 Cc39
Kintai LT 113 Jb56
Kintaus FIN 90 Kb33
Kintilloch GB 10 Ea13
Kintore GB 7 Ed09
Kintra GB 6 Da13
Kintus FIN 89 Jc35
Kinvarra IRL 8 Bb20
Kinvarra IRL 12 Bb21
Kinvarre IRL 12 Bc21
Kioneli CY 206 Jb96
Kióni GR 188 Ac84
Kiónia GR 196 Db88
Kiparíssi GR 195 Bd89
Kiparissía GR 194 Ba88
Kiparluoto FIN 97 Ja39
Kipeacan Cross Roads IRL 12 Ba25
Kipen' RUS 99 Mb40
Kipfenberg D 135 Dd48
Kipi EST 105 Jb47
Kípi GR 182 Ad79
Kípi GR 185 Ea77
Kipia GR 184 Cd77
Kipilovo BG 180 Eb71
Kipinä FIN 74 Kb22
Kipourío GR 182 Ba79
Kippel CH 141 Bd56
Kiprínos GR 185 Ea75
Kipséli GR 182 Ba78
Kipséli GR 183 Bd78
Kipséli GR 189 Bd81
Kipti UA 202 Ec14
Kirakkajärvi FIN 65 Kb08
Kirakkaköngäs FIN 69 Ka11
Kiralan TR 192 Ga87
Királyegyháza H 152 Hb58
Kiran N 78 Ea27
Kıranısıklar TR 192 Fd81
Kıranköy TR 192 Fb84
Kıranköy TR 192 Fc86
Kıransahili TR 197 Fa90
Kıratlı TR 191 Eb83
Kirava UA 202 Ec14
Kıravdan TR 193 Gc82
Kiraz TR 192 Fa87
Kirazköy TR 191 Ed82
Kirazlı TR 185 Eb80
Kirazlı TR 186 Fd79
Kirazlı TR 187 Gd78
Kirazlıyaylası TR 192 Ga83
Kırbaşı TR 193 Hb81
Kirberg D 133 Cb43
Ķirbiži LV 106 Kc48
Kirbla EST 98 Ka45
Kirby Bellars GB 16 Fb24
Kirby Hill GB 11 Fa19
Kirby Lonsdale GB 11 Ec19
Kirby Misperton GB 16 Fb19
Kirby Underwood GB 17 Fc23
Kirca TR 192 Fb83
Kircalar TR 191 Ec83
Kırcasalih TR 185 Ec76
Kirčevo BG 179 Da70
Kirchardt D 134 Cc47
Kirchbach A 143 Ed56
Kirchbach in der Steiermark A 144 Ga55
Kirchberg A 143 Eb53
Kirchberg CH 141 Bd53
Kirchberg CH 142 Cc53
Kirchberg D 127 Ec42
Kirchberg D 135 Ed48
Kirchberg D 142 Da50
Kirchberg am Wagram A 144 Ga50
Kirchberg am Walde A 136 Fc49
Kirchberg am Wechsel A 144 Ga53
Kirchberg an der Jagst D 134 Da47
Kirchberg an der Pielach A 144 Fd51
Kirchberg (Hunsrück) D 133 Ca44
Kirchbichl A 143 Ea53
Kirchbrak D 126 Da38
Kirchdorf A 144 Fd53
Kirchdorf D 118 Cd35
Kirchdorf D 143 Ea50
Kirchdorf am Inn D 143 Ec50
Kirchdorf an der Krems A 144 Fb52
Kirchdorf im Wald D 135 Ed48
Kirchehrenbach D 135 Dd45
Kirchen D 125 Cb41
Kirchendemenreuth D 135 Eb45
Kirchenlamitz D 135 Ea44
Kirchenpingarten D 135 Ea45
Kirchensittenbach D 135 Dd46
Kirchentellinsfurt D 134 Cd49
Kirchenthumbach D 135 Ea45
Kirchenthurnen CH 141 Bd54
Kirchfidisch A 145 Gb54
Kirchgellersen D 118 Dc34
Kirchhain D 126 Cd41
Kirchham D 143 Ed50
Kirchhasel, Uhlstädt- D 127 Dd42
Kirchheim D 126 Da41
Kirchheim D 134 Cd47
Kirchheim D 134 Cd49
Kirchheim D 134 Da45
Kirchheim D 142 Db50
Kirchheim D 143 Ea51
Kirchheimbolanden D 133 Cb45
Kirchhellen D 125 Bd38
Kirchhundem D 125 Cb40
Kirchlauter D 134 Dc44
Kirchlengern D 126 Cd37
Kirchlinteln D 118 Da34
Kirch Mulsow D 119 Eb31
Kirchroth D 135 Eb48
Kirchsahr D 125 Bd42
Kirchschlag in der Buckligen Welt A 145 Gb53
Kirchseelte D 118 Cd34
Kirchseeon D 143 Ea51
Kirchwalsede D 118 Da34
Kirchweidach D 143 Ec51
Kirchzarten D 141 Ca51
Kirchzell D 134 Cd45
Kircubbin GB 10 Db18
Kirdeikiai LT 115 Lb55
Kireç TR 192 Fb82
Kirehasjärvi FIN 65 Kb08
Kireli TR 199 Hb88
Kiremitçisalih TR 185 Eb76
Kirf D 133 Bc45
Kırgıl TR 192 Fd83
Kiriakí GR 185 Ea76
Kiriáki GR 189 Bd85
Kırık TR 185 Ed76
Kırık TR 187 Ha78
Kirikküla EST 98 Ka43
Kırıklar TR 191 Ec81
Kırıklar TR 191 Ec84
Kirimäe EST 98 Ka44
Kirjais FIN 97 Jb40
Kirjakkala FIN 97 Jc40
Kirjaluokta S 67 Gd17
Kirjamo RUS 99 Lc40
Kirjavala FIN 91 Ld33
Kirjavalansalo FIN 91 Ld33
Kırka TR 193 Gc83
Kırkağaç TR 191 Ed84
Kirkbean GB 10 Ea16
Kirkbride GB 11 Eb16
Kirkbuddo GB 7 Ec11
Kirkby GB 15 Eb21
Kirkby-in Ashfield GB 16 Fa23
Kirkby-la-Thorpe GB 17 Fc23
Kirkby Mallory GB 16 Fa24
Kirkbymoorside GB 16 Fb19
Kirkby Stephen GB 11 Ec18
Kirkcaldy GB 7 Eb12
Kirkcolm GB 10 Dc16
Kirkconnel GB 10 Ea15
Kirkcudbright GB 10 Dd17
Kirkeby DK 108 Cd25
Kirkeby DK 109 Dd27
Kirkeby N 78 Ec30
Kirkehamn N 92 Cb46
Kirke Helsinge DK 109 Ea26
Kirke Hvalsø DK 109 Eb26
Kirke Hyllinge DK 109 Eb25
Kirkel D 133 Bd46
Kirkenær N 94 Ec40
Kirkenes N 65 Kd07
Kirke Såby DK 109 Eb26
Kirke Stillinge DK 109 Ea26
Kirkham GB 15 Eb20
Kirkholt DK 100 Dc20
Kirkhope GB 10 Eb15
Kirki GR 185 Dd77
Kirk Ireton GB 16 Fa23
Kirkjubæjarklaustur IS 2 Ad06
Kirkjubøur DK 3 Ca07
Kırkkavak TR 199 Ha90
Kırkkepenekli TR 185 Ed77
Kirkkokangas FIN 74 Ka23
Kirkkonummi FIN 98 Ka40
Kirkkovo RUS 99 Ld41
Kirkland GB 10 Ea15
Kırklareli TR 185 Ed75
Kirkliai LT 113 Jd56
Kirklington GB 11 Fa19
Kirk Michael GB 10 Dc18
Kirkonkylä FIN 82 Kb28
Kirkonkylä FIN 89 Jb38
Kirkonkylä FIN 89 Jc39
Kirkonkylä FIN 90 La33
Kirkonkylä FIN 91 Lc34
Kirkoswald GB 11 Ec17
Kırkpınar TR 199 Gb90
Kirkton of Culsaimond GB 7 Ec08
Kirkton of Largo GB 7 Ec12
Kirkwall GB 5 Ec03
Kirkwhelpington GB 11 Ed16
Kirn D 133 Ca44
Kirnujärvi S 68 Ja17
Kirnula FIN 69 Jd17
Kirov RUS 202 Ed12
Kirovohrad UA 204 Ed15
Kirovsk RUS 202 Eb08
Kirovs'ke UA 205 Fa17
Kirra GR 189 Bc85
Kirriemuir GB 7 Ec10
Kirsanov RUS 203 Fc11
Kirschau D 128 Fb41
Kirschweiler D 133 Bd45
Kırşeyhler TR 193 Hb81
Kirtik S 73 Hb20
Kirtlebridge GB 11 Eb16
Kirton End GB 17 Fc23
Kirton in Lindsey GB 16 Fb21
Kirtorf D 126 Cd42
Kiruna S 67 Ha15
Kiržač RUS 203 Fa10
Kisa S 103 Fd48
Kisač SRB 153 Ja60
Kisapostag H 146 Hd55
Kisar H 147 Kc50
Kisbárapáti H 145 Ha56
Kisbér H 145 Hb53
Kiscsehi H 145 Gc56
Kisdorf D 118 Db32
Kiseljak BIH 153 Hc63
Kiseljak BIH 153 Hd62
Kiseljak BIH 158 Hb65
Kiselovo BG 179 Cb68
Kisfalud H 145 Gd53
Kisgörbő H 145 Gd55
Kishajmás H 152 Hb57
Kishartyán H 146 Ja51
Kishtë AL 182 Ac76
Ķiši LV 106 Kc47
Kisielice PL 122 Hc32
Kisielin PL 128 Fd38
Kisielnica PL 123 Jd33
Kısırkaya TR 186 Fd77
Kisizsák H 146 Hd55
Kiškino RUS 107 Mb50
Kiskunmajsa H 146 Ja56
Kisko FIN 97 Jd40
Kisköre H 146 Jc52
Kiskőrös H 146 Hd56
Kiskunfélegyháza H 146 Ja55
Kiskunhalas H 146 Ja56
Kiskunlacháza H 146 Hd54
Kışlaçay TR 187 Gc79
Kışlacık TR 186 Fa75
Kışlaköy TR 191 Ec85
Kışlaköy TR 192 Fc83
Kışlaköy TR 192 Fd83
Kislang H 145 Hb55
Kislovodsk RUS 205 Ga17
Kismórágy H 153 Hc57
Kisonerga CY 206 Hd98
Kissakoski FIN 90 Kd34
Kissakoski FIN 91 Lb33
Kíssamos (Kastéli) GR 200 Ca94
Kisselbach D 133 Ca44
Kissenbrück D 126 Dc37
Kissleberg S 102 Eb47
Kißlegg D 142 Da52
Kisszentmiklós H 146 Hc55
Kist D 134 Da45
Kistanje HR 157 Ga65
Kistelek H 146 Jb56
Kisterenye H 146 Ja51
Kistrand N 64 Jb06
Kisújszállás H 146 Jc53
Kisunyom H 145 Gc54
Kisvárda H 147 Kb50
Kisvejke H 146 Hc56
Kiszewo PL 129 Gb36
Kiszkowo PL 129 Gc36
Kiszombor H 153 Jc57
Kíta GR 194 Bc91
Kitee FIN 91 Ma32
Kiten BG 181 Fa73
Kithas GR 183 Cb80
Kíthira GR 195 Bd92
Kíthnos GR 195 Cd88
Kiti CY 206 Jc97
Kitinoja FIN 81 Jb31
Kitka FIN 75 La19
Kitkiöjärvi S 68 Ja15
Kitkiöjoki S 68 Ja15
Kitriés GR 194 Bb89
Kítros GR 183 Bd78
Kitsi FIN 83 Ma28
Kittajaur S 72 Ha20
Kittelfjäll S 71 Fd24
Kittendorf D 119 Ed32
Kittilä FIN 68 Jc15
Kittilä FIN 97 Ja40
Kittlitz D 128 Fc41
Kittsee A 145 Gc51
Kitula FIN 90 Kc34
Kitula FIN 97 Jd39
Kitzbühel A 143 Eb53
Kitzingen D 134 Db45
Kitzscher D 127 Ec41
Kiukainen FIN 89 Jb37
Kiurujärvi FIN 69 Kb15
Kiuruvesi FIN 82 Kc28
Kiutaköngäs FIN 74 La18
Kivarinjärvi FIN 75 Kc23
Kivenmäki FIN 81 Jc31
Kiverci UA 202 Ea14
Kivéri GR 195 Bd88
Kivesjärvi FIN 82 Kd25
Kiveskylä FIN 82 Kd25
Kiveslahti FIN 82 Kc25
Kiviapaja FIN 91 Lc34
Kivijärvi FIN 82 Ka30
Kivijärvi S 73 Ja18
Kivik S 111 Fb56
Kivikangas FIN 81 Jd29
Kivilahti FIN 83 Ma29
Kivilompolo FIN 68 Ja12
Kivilompolo FIN 74 Jc19
Kiviloo EST 98 Kc42
Kivilöppe EST 106 La46
Kivimäki FIN 82 Kd26
Kiviniemenkulma FIN 89 Jb35
Kiviniemi FIN 90 La38
Kivioja FIN 74 Jd20
Kiviõli EST 99 Lb42
Kiviperä FIN 75 Lb19
Kivisalmi FIN 82 Kc31
Kivisuo FIN 90 Kc34
Kivitaipale FIN 74 Ka19
Kivivaara FIN 75 Kd22
Kivivaara FIN 83 Ld27
Kivi-Vigala EST 98 Kb44
Kivotós GR 183 Bb79
Kivyliai LT 113 Jc56
Kiwajny PL 122 Ja30
Kiwity PL 122 Ja30
Kiwity PL 122 Ja30
Kıyıkışlacık TR 197 Ed89
Kıyıköy TR 186 Fb75
Kıyra TR 198 Fb90
Kızıçukur TR 192 Fb83
Kizielany PL 123 Kb32
Kızık TR 187 Hb79
Kızıklı TR 191 Ec82
Kızılağaç TR 197 Ec90
Kızılağaç TR 197 Ed89
Kızılağaç TR 197 Ed91
Kızılağıl TR 187 Ha78
Kızılaliler TR 199 Gb91
Kızılbel TR 198 Fd91
Kızılca TR 186 Ga77
Kızılca TR 193 Gc86
Kızılca TR 199 Hb89
Kızılcabölük TR 198 Fc89
Kızılcadağ TR 199 Gb91
Kızılcahamam TR 205 Fa20
Kızılcaören TR 193 Gb84
Kızılcapınar TR 187 Hb77
Kızılcasöğüt TR 192 Ga85
Kızılcık TR 187 Gd78
Kızılcıkdere TR 185 Ed75
Kızıldağ TR 199 Ha90
Kızıldam TR 192 Fb84
Kızılhisar TR 192 Ga85
Kızılinler TR 193 Gc82
Kızılkaya TR 197 Ed88
Kızılkaya TR 198 Fc91
Kızılkaya TR 199 Gc90
Kızılkuyu TR 193 Hb85
Kızılkuyu TR 193 Hb86
Kızıllar TR 199 Gd91
Kızıllı TR 199 Gc90
Kızılören TR 191 Ed83
Kızılören TR 193 Gb87
Kızılöz TR 187 Gb80
Kızılöz TR 192 Fb82
Kızkadın TR 193 Gb84
Kızlan TR 197 Ed91
Kızlaralanı TR 192 Fa84
Kizner RUS 203 Ga08
Kjærnes N 79 Fb25
Kjelda N 70 Ed24
Kjeldal N 93 Db43
Kjeldbjerg DK 100 Da23
Kjeldebotn N 66 Ga13
Kjelkvika N 66 Ga14
Kjellerup DK 100 Db23
Kjellmyra N 94 Ec39
Kjelstraumen N 84 Ca37
Kjengsnes N 66 Fd13
Kjenstad N 78 Ed27
Kjerag N 92 Cb44
Kjerknesvågen N 78 Eb28
Kjerkøya N 70 Ec22
Kjernmoen N 86 Ec37
Kjerr N 66 Ga15
Kjerringholmen N 63 Hd06
Kjerringøy N 66 Fc16
Kjerringvåg N 77 Dc29
Kjerringvik N 64 Jb06
Kjerringvik N 66 Fc12
Kjerringvik N 93 Dd44
Kjerringvika N 66 Ga14
Kjøllefjord N 64 Jd04
Kjølsdal N 84 Cb34
Kjøpmannskjær N 93 Dd44
Kjøpstad N 71 Fb18
Kjøpsvik N 66 Ga14
Kjøra N 77 Dd30
Kjos N 84 Cd36
Kjose N 93 Dc44
Kjosen N 62 Ha09
Kjøtta N 66 Ga12
Kjulaås S 95 Gb43
Kjustendil BG 179 Ca72
Klaaswaal NL 124 Ad37
Klacka-Lerberg S 95 Fc43
Kläckeberga S 103 Ga52
Kladanj BIH 159 Hc64
Kläden D 127 Ea36
Klädesholmen S 102 Eb48
Kladnica BG 179 Cc71
Kladnica SRB 178 Ad68
Kladnjice HR 158 Gb66
Kladno CZ 136 Fb44
Kladovo SRB 174 Cb65
Klæbu N 77 Ea30
Klafsi GR 188 Bb83
Klagenfurt A 144 Fb56
Klågerup S 110 Ed56
Klagstorp S 110 Fa57
Klaipėda LT 113 Jb55
Kłaj PL 138 Jb44
Kłajpeda PL 123 Ka30
Kľak SK 138 Hc49
Klakar Donji BIH 152 Hb61
Klakegg N 84 Cc35
Klakring DK 108 Dc25
Klaksvík DK 3 Ca06
Klamila FIN 91 Lb38
Klämmesbo S 103 Fb47
Klampju ciems LV 113 Ja53
Klana HR 151 Fb60
Klanac HR 151 Fd62
Kłanino PL 121 Gb31
Klanjec HR 151 Ga58
Klapkalnciems LV 106 Ka50
Kläppen S 72 Gd22
Kläppen S 80 Hc25
Kläppsjö S 79 Gb29
Kläppvik S 87 Gb34
Klárafalva H 153 Jc57
Klarup DK 100 Dc21
Klašnice BIH 152 Gd62
Klässbol S 94 Ed43
Klášterec nad Ohří CZ 135 Ed43
Kláštor pod Znievom SK 138 Hc48
Klatovy CZ 135 Ed47
Klattrup DK 101 Dd20
Klaukkala FIN 98 Kb39
Klaus A 142 Cd53
Klaus an der Phyrnbahn A 144 Fb52
Klausdorf D 118 Dc30
Klausdorf D 119 Ed30
Klausdorf D 127 Ed37
Klausen D 133 Bd44
Klausen I 143 Dd56
Klausgalvai LT 113 Jb54
Klauvnes N 63 Hb08
Klavdia CY 206 Jc97
Klāvi LV 106 Kb51
Klavreström S 103 Fd51
Klavuzlu TR 185 Ed77
Klębanowice PL 128 Ga39
Kleblach A 143 Ed55
Klečevce MK 178 Bc73
Klecko PL 129 Gd36
Klęcz PL 130 Hc40
Kleczew PL 129 Ha37
Kleczkowo PL 123 Jd34
Kleef = Kleve D 125 Bc38
Kleemola FIN 81 Jd28
Kleinarl A 143 Ed54
Klein Berßen D 117 Cb35
Kleinblittersdorf D 133 Bd47
Kleinbrembach D 127 Dd41
Klein Bünzow D 120 Fa32
Kleinenberg D 126 Cd39
Klein-Glödnitz A 144 Fb55
Kleinhaugsdorf A 136 Ga49
Kleinheubach D 134 Cd45
Kleinjena D 127 Ea41
Kleinlobming A 144 Fc54
Kleinmachnow D 127 Ed37
Klein Offenseth D 118 Db32
Klein Oschersleben D 127 Ea38
Kleinostheim D 134 Cd44
Kleinpaschleben D 127 Eb39
Kleinraming A 144 Fb51
Kleinrinderfeld D 134 Da45
Klein Sankt Paul A 144 Fb55
Kleinschmalkalden D 126 Dc42
Klein Sien D 119 Eb31
Kleinsölk A 144 Fa53
Kleinstetteldorf A 137 Gb49
Kleinwallstadt D 134 Cd45
Klein Wanzleben D 127 Ea38
Kleinzell A 144 Ga51
Kleiva N 92 Cb46
Kleive N 77 Da31
Kleivegrend N 92 Cd43
Klejniki PL 123 Kc34
Klejtrup DK 100 Db22
Klek SRB 174 Bb61
Klembów PL 130 Jc36
Klemensker DK 111 Fc57
Klemetsrud N 93 Ea42
Klemetstad N 64 Jb08
Klempenow D 119 Ed32
Klenčí pod Č. CZ 135 Ec46
Klenica PL 128 Ga38
Klenike SRB 178 Bd72
Klenjë AL 182 Ad74
Klenje SRB 153 Ja62
Klenovec SK 138 Ja49

Klenovica - Korita

Klenovica HR 151 Fc61
Kleosin PL 123 Kb33
Kleppe N 85 Dc35
Kleppe N 92 Ca44
Kleppenes N 84 Cb34
Kleppestø N 84 Ca39
Klępsk PL 128 Ga38
Klepstad N 66 Fb14
Klėriškės LT 114 Kd58
Kleśno PL 120 Ga35
Kleszczele PL 123 Kb35
Kleszczewo PL 129 Gc37
Kleszczów PL 130 Hc40
Kleszczów PL 137 Hb43
Kleszewo PL 122 Jb35
Klėtiškė LT 113 Jd55
Kletnja RUS 202 Ec12
Kletno PL 137 Gc44
Kletskij RUS 203 Fd13
Klettgau D 141 Cb52
Klettwitz D 128 Fa39
Kleve D 125 Bc38
Kleven N 92 Cc47
Klevmarken S 94 Eb45
Klevshult S 103 Fb50
Klewianka PL 123 Ka32
Klewki PL 122 Ja32
Klezeno RUS 107 Lc47
Kličav BY 202 Eb12
Kličevac SRB 174 Bc64
Kliczków PL 128 Fd40
Klidí GR 183 Bb77
Klidí GR 183 Ca78
Klieken D 127 Eb38
Kliening A 144 Fc55
Klietz D 127 Eb36
Kligene LV 106 Kd50
Klíma GR 183 Bb78
Klíma GR 189 Cc83
Klimaszewnica PL 123 Ka32
Klimatáki GR 182 Ba79
Klimatiá GR 182 Ab79
Klimavičy BY 202 Ec12
Kliment BG 181 Ec69
Klimkovice CZ 137 Ha45
Klimontów PL 131 Jd42
Klimontów PL 138 Jb43
Klimovo RUS 107 Ma47
Klimovo RUS 202 Ec13
Klimovsk RUS 202 Ed10
Klimpfjäll S 71 Fc24
Klin RUS 202 Ed10
Klina KSV 178 Ba70
Klincovka RUS 113 Ja58
Klincovka RUS 203 Ga11
Klincy RUS 202 Ec13
Klindiá GR 188 Ba86
Klinga N 78 Ec26
Klingenbach A 145 Gb52
Klingenberg D 134 Cd45
Klingenmünster D 133 Cb47
Klingenthal D 135 Eb43
Klingersel S 73 Hc20
Klingnau CH 141 Cb52
Klinića Sela HR 151 Ga59
Klink D 119 Ec33
Klinkby DK 100 Cd22
Klinó GR 182 Ba80
Klintebjerg DK 109 Dd26
Klintehamn S 104 Gd50
Klippan S 110 Ed54
Klippen S 71 Fc22
Klippen S 80 Gc28
Klippinge DK 109 Ec27
Klirou CY 206 Jb97
Klis HR 158 Gc66
Klisa HR 153 Hd59
Klisino PL 137 Ha44
Klissoúra GR 183 Bb78
Klissoúra GR 188 Ad81
Klisura BG 179 Cc72
Klisura BG 179 Da71
Klisura SRB 179 Ca71
Klisurica BG 179 Cc68
Klitmøller DK 100 Da21
Klitoría GR 188 Bb86
Klitten D 128 Fc40
Klitten S 87 Fb37
Klivi LV 106 Kc52
Kljajićevo SRB 153 Hd58
Kljasino RUS 99 Ma40
Kljavino RUS 203 Ga09
Ključ BIH 152 Gc63
Klo N 66 Fd12
Klobouky u Brna CZ 137 Gc48
Kłobuck PL 130 Hc41
Klobuk BIH 158 Ha67
Klobuky CZ 136 Fa44
Klöch A 144 Ga55
Klockestrand S 88 Gc32
Klockrike S 103 Fd46
Klockträsk S 73 Hb24
Kłoczew PL 131 Jd38
Kłodawa PL 120 Fd35
Kłodawa PL 130 Hc37
Klöden D 127 Ec39
Kłodzko PL 137 Gc43
Kløfta N 93 Ea41
Klokk N 76 Cd32
Klokkarvik N 84 Ca39
Klokkarvollen N 62 Ha08
Klokkerholm DK 100 Dc20
Klokočevac SRB 174 Ca65
Klokočevci HR 152 Hb59
Klokočov SK 137 Hb46
Klokotnica BG 185 Dd74
Kłomnice PL 130 Hd41
Klonowa PL 129 Hb40
Klooga EST 98 Ka43
Kloogaranna EST 98 Ka42
Klopicy RUS 99 Ma40
Kłopoty-Stanisławy PL 123 Kb35
Klos AL 182 Ac74
Klosi AL 163 Jc72
Kloštar HR 152 Gd58
Kloštar Ivanic HR 152 Gb59
Kloster DK 108 Cd24
Klosterfelde D 120 Fa35
Klosterhaar NL 117 Bd35
Klösterle A 142 Da54
Klosterlechfeld D 142 Dc50
Klostermansfeld D 127 Ea39
Klosterneuburg A 145 Gb50
Klosters CH 142 Da55
Kloster Zinna D 127 Ed38
Kloten CH 141 Cb53
Kloten S 95 Fd42
Klötze D 127 Dd36
Klovainiai LT 114 Kb54
Klövborg DK 108 Db24
Klövedal S 102 Eb48
Klöverfors S 73 Hc24
Klöverträsk S 73 Hc22
Kløvimoen N 71 Fb23
Klövsjö S 87 Fb33
Kløvstad N 86 Eb37
Klubben N 65 Kc06
Klubben N 84 Ca34
Klubbfors S 73 Hc24
Klubbukt N 63 Ja06
Klubbvik N 65 Kb06
Kluczbork PL 129 Ha41
Klucze PL 138 Hd43
Kluczewo PL 120 Ga32
Kluczewsko PL 130 Ja41
Kluki PL 121 Gc29
Klukowa Huta PL 121 Gd30
Klukowicze PL 131 Kb36
Klukowo PL 122 Jb35
Klukowo PL 123 Ka35
Kluksdal N 78 Ec30
Klund N 94 Eb43
Klundert NL 124 Ad38
Klungland N 92 Ca45
Klupe BIH 152 Ha62
Kluse D 117 Ca34
Kl'ušov SK 139 Jd47
Klüsserath D 133 Bc44
Klusy PL 123 Jd31
Klutmark S 80 Hc25
Klutsjön S 86 Ed34
Klütz D 119 Ea31
Klwów PL 130 Jb39
Klykoliai LT 113 Jd53
Kłyżów PL 131 Ka42
Knaben N 92 Cc45
Knaften S 80 Gd26
Knäm S 94 Ea45
Knaphill GB 20 Fb29
Knappenrode D 128 Fb40
Knapphus N 92 Ca42
Knapstad N 93 Ea42
Knapton GB 16 Fb19
Knäred S 110 Fa53
Knaresborough GB 11 Fa19
Knarvik N 84 Ca38
Knätte S 102 Fa48
Knebel DK 109 Dd24
Kneesall GB 16 Fb22
Kneese D 119 Dd32
Kneesworth GB 20 Fc26
Knesebeck D 118 Dc35
Kneža BG 179 Da69
Knežak SLO 151 Fb59
Kneževici Sušica SRB 159 Jb65
Kneževi Vinogradi HR 153 Hc59
Kneževo HR 153 Hc58
Knežice CZ 136 Fd44
Knežina BIH 159 Hd64
Knežmost CZ 136 Fc43
Knić SRB 174 Bb66
Knićanin SRB 153 Jc60
Knidi GR 183 Bb79
Knighton GB 15 Eb25
Knight's Town IRL 12 Ad25
Knin HR 158 Gb64
Knislinge S 111 Fb54
Knista S 95 Fc44
Knittelfeld A 144 Fc54
Knittlingen D 134 Cc47
Knivert LV 105 Jb52
Kniveton GB 16 Ed23
Knivsta S 96 Gc42
Knjaževac SRB 179 Ca68
Knjazevo RUS 107 Mb51
Knjaževo RUS 203 Fb08
Knjažica RUS 99 Ma45
Knock IRL 8 Bd19
Knock IRL 12 Bb23
Knockalough IRL 12 Bc23
Knockaunalour IRL 12 Bd25
Knockaunnaglashy IRL 12 Ba24
Knockbrandon IRL 13 Cd23
Knockcroghery IRL 8 Ca20
Knockdrin IRL 9 Cb20
Knockeen Cross Roads IRL 12 Bb24
Knockferry IRL 8 Bc20
Knockin GB 15 Eb23
Knocknabul Cross IRL 12 Bb24
Knocknagashel IRL 12 Bb24
Knocks IRL 12 Bc26
Knocktopher IRL 13 Cb24
Knockvicar IRL 8 Ca19
Knodara CY 206 Jc96
Knokke-Heist B 124 Aa38
Knopkägra FIN 97 Jc40
Knoppe S 87 Gb34
Knorydy PL 123 Kb35
Knottingley GB 16 Fa20
Knowehead GB 10 Dd15
Knowl Hill GB 20 Fb28
Knudby DK 100 Db22
Knudshoved DK 109 Dd27
Knurów PL 137 Hb44
Knurowiec PL 122 Jc35
Knutby S 96 Gd41
Knutsford GB 15 Ec22
Knutsvik N 92 Cb43
Knyszyn PL 123 Ka33
Koactarla TR 185 Ed74
Kobaklar TR 192 Fb84
Kobarid SLO 150 Ed57
Kobbevåg N 62 Gd10
Kobbevåg N 63 Hc06
Kobbfoss N 65 Kc09
Kobela EST 107 Lb47
Købelev DK 109 Ea28
Kobeljaky UA 204 Ed15
København DK 109 Ec26
Kobeřice CZ 137 Ha45
Kobern-Gondorf D 133 Ca43
Kobiele Wielkie PL 130 Hd41
Kobiljane BG 184 Dc75
Kobilje SLO 145 Gb56
Kobiór PL 138 Hc44
Kobišnica SRB 174 Cb66
Koblenz D 133 Ca43
Kobona RUS 202 Eb08
Koboža RUS 202 Ec08
Kobrinskoe RUS 99 Mb40
Kobryn BY 202 Dd14
Kobyla Góra PL 129 Ha40
Kobylanka PL 120 Fc33
Kobylin PL 123 Jd33
Kobylin PL 129 Gc39
Kobylin-Borzymy PL 123 Ka34
Kobyłka PL 130 Jc36
Kobylnica PL 121 Gc30
Kobylniki PL 129 Gb36
Kobylniki PL 130 Ja36
Koca Ahmetler TR 199 Gd90
Kocaali TR 185 Ec79
Kocaali TR 187 Gd78
Kocaaliler TR 199 Gd90
Kocaavşar TR 191 Ed82
Kocabaş TR 198 Fd88
Kocabey TR 192 Fb83
Kocaçeşme TR 185 Eb78
Kocadağ TR 191 Ec82
Kocadağ TR 199 Gd90
Kocadere TR 198 Fd88
Kocadöngel TR 187 Gc78
Kocaeli TR 187 Gb78
Kocagöl TR 186 Fa80
Kocagöl TR 193 Gb86
Kocahıdır TR 185 Ea78
Kocaiskan TR 192 Fa83
Koçak TR 192 Ga86
Koçak TR 193 Gb83
Kocakanğan TR 192 Fa84
Kocakaymaz TR 187 Gb78
Kocakovacık TR 192 Fd81
Kocalar TR 185 Eb80
Kočane SRB 178 Bb69
Kočani MK 179 Ca73
Kocaoba TR 191 Ed82
Kocaöz TR 193 Gd85
Kocapınar TR 191 Ed81
Koçar TR 187 Gd78
Koçarlı TR 197 Ed88
Koçaş TR 193 Hb87
Kocayaka TR 192 Ga87
Kocayazı TR 185 Ec74
Koçbeyli TR 193 Gd86
Koceljevo SRB 153 Jb63
Kočėnai LT 106 Kd52
Kočeni LV 106 Kd48
Kočerin BIH 158 Ha66
Kočerinovo BG 179 Cb73
Kočetovka RUS 203 Fb12
Kočevje SLO 151 Fc59
Kočevska Reka SLO 151 Fc59
Kochanowice PL 129 Hb42
Kochcice PL 129 Hb42
Kochel am See D 143 Dd52
Kochfidisch A 145 Gb54
Kochowo PL 129 Ha37
Kocień Wielkie PL 121 Gb35
Kocierzew PL 130 Ja37
Kočilar MK 183 Bc74
Kočiołek Szlachecki PL 122 Jc32
Kock PL 131 Ka38
Kočkarlej RUS 203 Fd10
Kočmar BG 181 Ed69
Kočov CZ 135 Ec45
Kočovo BG 181 Ec70
Kocs H 145 Hb52
Kocsér H 146 Jb54
Kocsola H 145 Hb56
Kocsord H 147 Kb51
Kócsújfalu H 146 Jc52
Kocular TR 199 Ha88
Koçyazı TR 193 Hb85
Koczała PL 121 Gc32
Kodal N 93 Dd44
Kodavere EST 99 Lb44
Kode S 102 Eb48
Kodeń PL 131 Kc37
Kodeniec PL 131 Kb38
Kodersdorf D 128 Fc41
Kodesjärvi FIN 89 Ja34
Kodiksami FIN 89 Ja37
Kodisjoki FIN 89 Ja37
Köditz D 135 Ea43
Kodjala FIN 89 Ja38
Kodrąb PL 130 Hd41
Kodyma UA 204 Ec16
Kodžadžik MK 182 Ad74
Koekelare B 21 Ha29
Kœnigsmacker F 25 Jd34
Koersel B 124 Ba40
Koeru EST 98 Kd43
Koetschette L 132 Ba44
Kœtzingue F 31 Kc40
Kofçaz TR 185 Ec74
Kofinou CY 206 Jb97
Köflach A 144 Fc54
Köfles A 142 Dc54
Kog SLO 145 Gb56
Køge DK 109 Ec26
Kogula EST 105 Jc46
Koguva EST 97 Jd45
Kohila EST 98 Kb43
Köhkörö FIN 89 Jc35
Kohlberg D 135 Eb46
Köhlen D 118 Cd32
Kohma RUS 203 Fa09
Kohmu FIN 82 Kb31
Kohren-Sahlis D 127 Ec41
Kohtla-Järve EST 99 Lb41
Kohtla Nõmme EST 99 Lb42
Koigi EST 98 Kd43
Koigi EST 98 Kd44
Koijärvi FIN 89 Jd37
Koikkala FIN 91 Lb34
Koikkula FIN 105 Jd46 — see note
Koikküla EST 106 La47
Koili CY 206 Hd97
Koilovci BG 180 Db69
Kõima EST 106 Kb46
Koimäki FIN 90 Kd32
Koimla EST 105 Jc47
Köinge S 102 Ec51
Koirakoski FIN 82 La28
Koirasalmi FIN 82 Ka29
Koiravaara FIN 75 La21
Koisjärvi FIN 98 Ka39
Koisko SLO 150 Ed58
Koitila FIN 75 Kd21
Koitsanlahti FIN 91 Ld34
Koivisto FIN 90 Kb32
Koivistonpää FIN 73 Jb19
Koivu FIN 74 Jd20
Koivujärvi FIN 82 Kc28
Koivukylä FIN 82 Kd26
Koivulahti FIN 81 Ja30
Koivumäki FIN 81 Jd30
Koivumäki FIN 82 La29
Koivumäki FIN 89 Jb33
Koivuniemi FIN 74 Ka21
Kojanlahti FIN 83 Lb30
Kojdalen N 86 Ec32
Kojetín CZ 137 Gd47
Kojnare BG 179 Da69
Kojola FIN 81 Jb31
Kojola FIN 82 Ka28
Kojonperä FIN 89 Jc37
Kóka H 146 Ja53
Kokála GR 194 Bc91
Kokanin PL 129 Ha38
Kökar FIN 97 Hd41
Kokava nad Rimavicou SK 138 Ja49
Köke TR 193 Gd87
Kokelv N 63 Ja06
Kokemäki FIN 89 Jb36
Kokin Brod SRB 159 Jb66
Kokíni GR 182 Ab80
Kokiniá GR 182 Ac80
Kokiniá GR 183 Cb76
Kokinolithári GR 182 Ac80
Kokinombléa GR 189 Cb83
Kokinopilós GR 183 Bd79
Kokinvaara FIN 83 Ma30
Kokkári GR 197 Eb88
Kokkila FIN 90 Ka36
Kokkila FIN 97 Jc39
Kokkina CY 206 Hd96
Kókkino Néro GR 183 Ca80
Kokkinotrimithia CY 206 Jb96
Kokkokylä FIN 74 Kb21
Kokkola FIN 75 Lb24
Kokkola FIN 81 Jb28
Kokkola FIN 90 Ka35
Kokkolahti FIN 91 Lc32
Kokkoniemi FIN 75 Lb22
Kokkosenlahti FIN 90 La34
Kokkovaara FIN 68 Jc16
Koklë AL 182 Ac76
Köklot FIN 81 Hd30
Koknese LV 106 Kd51
Koknese LV 106 La51
Kokonkylä FIN 90 Kd33
Kokonniemi FIN 75 Lb24
Kokonvaara FIN 83 Lc30
Kokora EST 99 Lb44
Kokořín CZ 136 Fb43
Kokory CZ 137 Gd46
Kokošinje MK 178 Bd73
Kokotí GR 189 Bd83
Kökpınar TR 205 Ga20
Kokrica SLO 151 Fb57
Koksijde-Bad B 21 Gd29
Kokšino RUS 107 Ma49
Koktebel' UA 205 Fb17
Kokträsk S 72 Gd23
Kola BIH 152 Gd62
Kola FIN 81 Jc28
Köla S 94 Ec42
Kölaby S 102 Fa48
Kołacin PL 130 Hd38
Kołacze PL 131 Kc39
Kołaczkowo PL 129 Gd37
Kołaczyce PL 139 Jd45
Kolak TR 198 Fd90
Koláka GR 189 Ca84
Kołaki Kościelne PL 123 Ka34
Koland N 92 Cd45
Kolankaya TR 192 Fc86
Kolarci BG 181 Fa68
Kolari FIN 68 Jb16
Kolari SRB 174 Bb64
Kolárovice SK 137 Hb47
Kolarovo BG 180 Dd73
Kolarovo BG 181 Ec68
Kolárovo SK 145 Ha51
Kolås N 76 Cc33
Kolåsen S 78 Fa29
Kolašin MNE 159 Jb68
Kolatovo BG 183 Cb75
Kolbäck S 95 Ga43
Kolbermoor D 143 Ea52
Kołbiel PL 130 Jc37
Kolbnitz A 143 Ed55
Kolbu N 85 Ea39
Kolbudy Grn. PL 121 Ha30
Kolbulia N 86 Eb38
Kolbuszowa PL 139 Jd43
Kølby DK 100 Db21
Kolby DK 109 Dd25
Kolby Kås DK 109 Dd25
Kol'čugino RUS 203 Fa10
Kołczewo PL 120 Fc31
Kołczygłowy PL 121 Gc30
Koldby DK 100 Da21
Koldere TR 191 Ed85
Kolding DK 108 Db26
Kołdrąb PL 121 Gd35
Koler S 73 Hb23
Kölesd H 146 Hc56
Koleška BIH 159 Hc67
Kolešovice CZ 136 Fa44
Kolga-Jaani EST 98 Kd45
Kolgaküla EST 98 Kd42
Kolgomp'a RUS 99 Ld40
Kolhikí GR 183 Bb77
Kolhikó GR 183 Cb77
Kolho FIN 90 Ka33
Koli FIN 83 Lc29
Kolimbári GR 200 Cb94
Kolímbia GR 197 Fa93
Kolín CZ 136 Fd45
Kolind DK 101 Dd23
Kolindrós GR 183 Bd78
Kolinec CZ 135 Ed47
Kölingared S 102 Fa48
Kolisevo FIN 90 Kd37
Kolitzheim D 134 Db45
Köljala EST 105 Jd46
Koljane HR 158 Gc65
Kolka LV 105 Jc48
Kølkær DK 108 Da24
Kolkanlahti FIN 82 Ka31
Kolkja EST 99 Lb44
Kolkku FIN 82 Kb29
Kolko FIN 97 Ja39
Kolkonjärvi FIN 75 La21
Kolkonpää FIN 91 Lb33
Kolkontaipale FIN 91 Lb33
Kolkwitz D 128 Fb39
Kolky UA 202 Ea14
Kollaja FIN 74 Kb22
Kölleda D 127 Dd40
Kollersdorf A 144 Ga50
Kollerud S 94 Ed40
Kollerup DK 100 Db21
Kölliken CH 141 Ca53
Kollínes GR 194 Bc88
Kollinmäki FIN 89 Jb33
Kollinperä FIN 90 Ka32
Kollnburg D 135 Ec48
Kölln-Reisiek D 118 Db32
Kollum NL 117 Bc33
Kollund DK 108 Db28
Kollungeröd S 102 Eb47
Kolma FIN 90 La32
Kolmården S 103 Ga46
Kolmjärv S 73 Hd20
Kolm-Saigurn A 143 Ec54
Köln D 125 Bd41
Kolno PL 122 Jb31
Kolno PL 122 Jd33
Kolo BIH 158 Gd65
Koło PL 129 Hb37
Kołobrzeg PL 120 Fd31
Kołodzież PL 123 Ka33
Kolokolčovka RUS 203 Fd12
Kolokolovo RUS 99 Lc44
Kolomna RUS 203 Fa10
Kolomyja UA 204 Ea16
Kolonia AL 182 Ab78
Kolonowskie PL 129 Hb42
Kolossi CY 206 Ja98
Koloveč CZ 135 Ed46
Kolpino RUS 107 Lc46
Kolpino RUS 202 Eb08
Kolpny RUS 203 Fa12
Kolppi FIN 81 Jb29
Kolrep D 119 Eb34
Kolsätter S 87 Fc34
Kölsillre S 87 Fd33
Kolsjön S 87 Ga34
Kolsko PL 128 Ga38
Kolta SK 145 Hb51
Kolu FIN 81 Jd31
Kolumna PL 130 Hc39
Kolunić BIH 152 Gb63
Koluszki PL 130 Hd38
Kolut SRB 153 Hd58
Koluvere EST 98 Ka44
Kolvereid N 78 Ec25
Kolvik N 64 Jb07
Kolyčivka UA 202 Ec14
Kolyšlej RUS 203 Fc11
Komádi H 147 Ka54
Komagfjord N 63 Hd07
Komagvær N 65 Kd06
Komagvik N 62 Gd08
Komańcza PL 139 Ka46
Kómanos GR 183 Bc78
Komar BIH 158 Ha64
Kómara GR 185 Ea75
Komarani SRB 178 Ad68
Komarevo BG 180 Db69
Komarno MNE 159 Ja70
Komárno SK 145 Hb52
Komárom H 145 Hb52
Komárov CZ 136 Fa45
Komarówka Podlaska PL 131 Kb38
Komarów-Osada PL 131 Kc41
Koma tou Gialou CY 206 Jd95
Kombóti GR 188 Ad82
Kombsija AL 182 Ac74
Kombuļi LV 115 Ld53
Komen SLO 151 Fa59
Komi CY 206 Jd96
Komi FIN 89 Jc35
Kómi GR 189 Bc86
Komin HR 158 Ha68
Kominternivs'ke UA 204 Ec17
Kómito GR 190 Cd86
Komiža HR 158 Gb68
Komjatice SK 145 Hb51
Kömlő H 146 Jb52
Komló H 152 Hb57
Kommerniemi FIN 91 Lc33
Komnes N 93 Dd43
Komniná GR 183 Bc77
Komniná GR 184 Db76
Komninádes GR 182 Ba77
Komorane KSV 178 Ba71
Komorniki PL 129 Gc37
Komorowo PL 122 Jc35
Komorowo PL 129 Gc40
Komorowo PL 129 Gd36
Komorze PL 129 Gd37
Komorzno PL 129 Ha41
Komosomol's'k RUS 203 Fa09
Komossa FIN 81 Jb30
Komoštica BG 179 Cc68
Komotiní GR 184 Dc77
Kompakka FIN 83 Ld31
Kompelusvaara S 68 Hd17
Kompina PL 130 Ja37
Komprachcice PL 129 Ha42
Kõmsi EST 98 Ka45
Komsi FIN 89 Ja33
Komsomol'sk RUS 113 Hd59
Komsomol'sk RUS 113 Ja59
Komsomol'skij RUS 203 Fc10
Komsomol'sk Zappvednik RUS 113 Ja59
Komu FIN 82 Kb28
Komula FIN 82 La26
Komunari BG 181 Ed71
Komuniga BG 184 Dc74
Kömürcü TR 192 Fa84
Kömürköy TR 186 Fa75
Kömür Limanı TR 185 Dd80
Konak BG 180 Eb70
Konak SRB 174 Bc62
Konak TR 198 Fd89
Konakkale TR 193 Hb87
Konaklı TR 199 Hb92
Konakovo RUS 202 Ed10
Konakpınar TR 192 Fa83
Konare BG 180 Ea72
Konare BG 181 Fb69
Konarevo SRB 178 Ba67
Konarı TR 193 Hb86
Konary PL 130 Jc38
Konarzewo PL 129 Gb37
Konarzyce PL 123 Jd33
Konarzyny PL 121 Gd32
Konäs S 78 Fa29
Končanica HR 152 Gd59
Konče MK 183 Bd75
Kończewice PL 121 Hb34
Kondiás GR 190 Db81
Kondofrej BG 179 Cb72
Kondolovo BG 186 Fa74
Kondopoúli GR 190 Dc81
Kondorfa H 145 Gb55
Kondoros H 146 Jc55
Kondratovo RUS 107 Ma47
Kondratów PL 128 Ga41
Kondratowice PL 129 Gc42
Kondrić HR 152 Hb60
Kondrovo RUS 202 Ed11
Køng DK 109 Eb27
Konga S 111 Fd53
Köngäs FIN 64 Jd07
Köngäs FIN 68 Jc14
Köngäs FIN 69 Ka14
Köngäs FIN 69 Kb17
Kongasmäki FIN 75 Kd24
Kongens Lyngby DK 109 Ec25
Kongerslev DK 100 Dc21
Konginkangas FIN 82 Kb31
Kongsberg N 93 Dc42
Kongselva N 66 Fd13
Kongsfjord N 65 Kb04
Kongshavn N 93 Db46
Kongsli N 67 Gd11
Kongsmark DK 108 Cd27
Kongsmoen N 78 Ed25
Kongsvika N 66 Ga13
Kongsvinger N 94 Ec40
Koņi LV 106 Kd47
Koniaków PL 138 Hc46
Konice CZ 137 Gc46
Koniecpol PL 130 Hd42
Konieczna PL 139 Jd46
Koniewo PL 120 Fc32
Königerode D 127 Dd39
Königgrätz = Hradec Králové CZ 136 Ga44
Königheim D 134 Da45
Königsaue D 127 Ea38
Königsbach-Stein D 134 Cc47
Königsberg D 134 Dc44
Königsbronn D 134 Db48
Königsbrück D 128 Fa40
Königsbrunn D 142 Dc50
Königsdorf D 143 Dd52
Königsee D 127 Dd42
Königsfeld D 135 Dd45
Königsfeld D 141 Cb50
Königshain-Wiederau D 127 Ec41
Königshofen D 134 Da46
Königslutter D 127 Dd37
Königsmoos D 135 Dd49
Königstein D 128 Fb42
Königstein D 134 Cc43
Königstein D 135 Ea46
Königswartha D 128 Fb40
Königswiesen A 144 Fc50
Königswinter D 125 Bd41
Königs Wusterhausen D 128 Fa37
Konin PL 129 Ha37
Konina PL 138 Ja46
Koniņciems LV 105 Jb51
Konispol AL 182 Ab80
Kónitsa GR 182 Ad79
Köniz CH 141 Bd54
Konjavo BG 179 Cb72
Konjic BIH 158 Hb66
Konjsko BIH 158 Ha66
Konjsko BIH 159 Hc69
Konjsko SRB 178 Ba68
Konju EST 99 Lc41
Konjuh KSV 178 Bb71
Konjuhe MNE 159 Jb68
Konnekoski FIN 82 Kd31
Könnern D 127 Ea39
Konnersreuth D 135 Eb44
Konnerud N 93 Dd42
Konnevesi FIN 82 Kc31
Könni FIN 81 Jb31
Konnovo RUS 99 Lc40
Kõnnu EST 98 Kc44
Kõnnu EST 105 Jd46
Konnunsuo FIN 91 Lc36
Konnuslahti FIN 82 La31
Konohovicy RUS 99 Ma41
Könölä FIN 74 Jc20
Konopiska PL 130 Hc42
Konopište MK 183 Bd75
Konopki PL 122 Ja34
Konopnica PL 130 Hc40
Konotop PL 120 Ga33
Konotop PL 128 Ga38
Konotop UA 202 Ed14
Konradsreuth D 135 Ea44
Końskie PL 130 Jb40
Konsko MK 183 Bd76
Końskowola PL 131 Ka39
Konsmo N 92 Cc46
Konstancin-Jeziorna PL 130 Jc37
Konstantin BG 180 Ea71
Konstantinova LV 107 Ld52
Konstantinovka RUS 113 Ja58
Konstantinovsk RUS 205 Fc15
Konstantinovy Lázně CZ 135 Ec45
Konstantynów PL 131 Kb36
Konstantynów Łódzki PL 130 Hc39
Konstanz D 142 Cc52
Kontea CY 206 Jc97
Kontemenos CY 206 Jb96
Kontiainen FIN 81 Jc30
Kontiainen FIN 89 Jc32
Kontinjoki FIN 82 Kd26
Kontiolahti FIN 83 Ld30
Kontiomäki FIN 82 La25
Kontioranta FIN 83 Ld30
Kontiovaara FIN 83 Ma29
Kontiovaara FIN 83 Ld28
Kontkala FIN 83 Lc30
Konttajärvi FIN 74 Jc18
Konttimäki FIN 83 Lb29
Konttimäki FIN 83 Lb31
Konttimäki FIN 90 Ka32
Kontu FIN 91 Lc36
Konuklu TR 187 Gc78
Konuralp TR 187 Ha78
Konuš BG 185 Dd74
Kóny H 145 Gd52
Konz D 133 Bc45
Konzell D 135 Ec48
Kõo EST 98 Kd44
Koobassaare EST 107 Lb47
Koonga EST 98 Kb45
Kooraste EST 107 Lb46
Koorküla EST 106 La47
Kööritilä FIN 89 Ja35
Koosa EST 99 Lb44
Kootwijk NL 116 Bb36
Kopáni GR 188 Ad81
Kopanica PL 128 Ga38
Kopanie PL 129 Gd42
Koparnes N 76 Cb33
Kópasker IS 3 Bb03
Kópavogur IS 2 Ac05
Kopciówka PL 123 Kb32
Kopdarbs LV 105 Ja52
Kopenhagen = København DK 109 Ec26
Koper SLO 151 Fa59
Kopervik N 92 Bd42
Kopfing A 144 Fa50
Kopice PL 120 Fc32
Kopice PL 129 Gd42
Kopidlno CZ 136 Fd44
Kopilovci BG 179 Cb69
Köping S 95 Ga43
Köpingebro S 110 Fa56
Köpingsvik S 103 Gb52
Kopisk PL 123 Kb33
Koplik i Poshtëm AL 159 Ja70
Köpmanholm S 96 Ha42
Köpmanholmen S 80 Gd31
Kopor'e RUS 99 Ld40
Koporic'e KSV 178 Bb69
Koposperä FIN 82 Ka27
Koppang N 86 Eb36
Koppangen N 62 Ha09
Kopparåsen S 67 Gc13
Kopparberg S 95 Fc42
Koppardal N 70 Ed21
Kopparmora S 96 Ha43
Koppelo FIN 69 Kb11
Koppelo FIN 83 Lb27
Kopperå N 78 Ec30
Koppom S 94 Ec42
Koprivec BG 180 Ea69
Koprivlen BG 184 Cd75
Koprivna SLO 144 Fc56
Koprivnica HR 152 Gc57
Kopřivnice CZ 137 Ha46
Koprivštica BG 179 Da72
Köprübaşı TR 187 Gd78
Köprübaşı TR 192 Fb85
Köprücek TR 187 Gc80
Köprühisar TR 186 Ga80
Köprüören TR 192 Ga82
Koprzywnica PL 131 Jd42
Kopsa FIN 81 Jd25
Kopstad N 93 Dd43
Kõpu EST 97 Jc44
Kõpu EST 106 Kd46
Kopyčynci UA 204 Ea16
Korablino RUS 203 Fb11
Koračica SRB 174 Bb65
Koraj BIH 153 Hd62
Koraşı TR 193 Hb86
Korb D 134 Cd48
Korbach D 126 Cd40
Korbeniči RUS 202 Ec08
Korbevac SRB 178 Bd71
Korbielów PL 138 Hd46
Korbøl N 71 Fc18
Korbovo SRB 174 Cb65
Korčanica BIH 152 Gb62
Korçë AL 182 Ad77
Korčevka RUS 203 Fd10
Korčula HR 158 Gd68
Korczew PL 131 Ka36
Korczyna PL 139 Ka45
Kordel D 133 Bc44
Korec' UA 202 Eb14
Köreken TR 192 Ga83
Korenevo RUS 202 Ed13
Korenica HR 151 Ga62
Korenica KSV 178 Ad71
Korenica SRB 159 Jc69
Korenovsk RUS 205 Fc16
Korentokylä FIN 75 Kc22
Korentovaara FIN 83 Mb29
Kõrez TR 192 Fc85
Korfantów PL 137 Gd43
Körfez TR 186 Ga78
Kórfos GR 195 Ca87
Korfovoúni GR 188 Ad81
Korfu = Kérkira GR 182 Ab80
Korgen N 71 Fb21
Korgene LV 106 Kc48
Körgepalu EST 107 Lb47
Körgessaare EST 97 Jc44
Körhasan TR 193 Ha83
Korholanmäki FIN 82 Kd31
Korhosenniemi FIN 75 Kd20
Korhoskylä FIN 81 Jd27
Korhoskylä FIN 89 Jc33
Koria FIN 90 Kd37
Korifási GR 194 Ba89
Korifí GR 182 Ba79
Korifí GR 188 Ba81
Korinós GR 183 Bd79
Korinth DK 108 Dc27
Korinth = Kórinthos GR 189 Bd86
Kórinthos GR 189 Bd86
Koriseva FIN 83 Lc28
Korissía GR 195 Cd88
Korissós GR 183 Bb78
Korita BIH 158 Gb64
Korita BIH 159 Hc67
Korita HR 152 Gd60
Korita HR 158 Ha69
Korita MNE 159 Jb69

Kronach – Kyselka

Kronach D 135 Dd44
Kronan S 94 Ed42
Kronau D 134 Cc47
Kroņauce LV 106 Ka52
Kronberg D 134 Cc43
Kronburg D 142 Db51
Kronenburg D 125 Bc42
Kröning D 135 Eb49
Kronoby FIN 81 Jb28
Kronowo PL 122 Ja31
Kronprinzenkoog D 118 Da31
Kronsdorf A 144 Fb51
Kronshagen D 118 Db30
Kronshagen D 118 Dc30
Kronštadt RUS 202 Ea08
Kron-Vike S 79 Ga27
Krootuse EST 107 Lb46
Kropa SLO 151 Fb57
Kröpelin D 119 Eb31
Kropotkin RUS 205 Fd16
Kropp D 118 Db30
Kroppenstedt D 127 Dd38
Kropstädt D 127 Ec38
Krościenko PL 139 Kb46
Krościenko nad Dunajcem PL 138 Jb46
Kroševo Brdo BIH 152 Ha63
Kröslin D 120 Fa31
Krosna LV 114 Kb59
Krośnice PL 129 Gd40
Krośniewice PL 130 Hc37
Krosno PL 122 Hc31
Krosno PL 139 Ka45
Krosno Odrzańskie PL 128 Fc38
Krössbach A 143 Dd54
Krossen N 92 Cc47
Krossen N 93 Da42
Krossli N 93 Da43
Krostitz D 127 Ec40
Krote LV 105 Jb52
Krotoszyce PL 128 Ga41
Krotoszyn PL 129 Gd39
Krottendorf A 144 Fd54
Krouna CZ 136 Ga45
Krousónas GR 200 Da96
Kröv D 133 Bd44
Krovili GR 185 Dd77
Krowiarki PL 137 Ha44
Krpimej KSV 178 Bb70
Krrabë AL 182 Ac75
Krš HR 151 Fd62
Krško SLO 151 Fd58
Krst SRB 174 Bd66
Krstac MNE 159 Hd68
Krstac MNE 159 Hd70
Krstinja HR 151 Ga60
Krstur SRB 153 Jb57
Krtova BIH 153 Hc62
Kruče MNE 163 Ja71
Krucz PL 121 Gb35
Kruë i Fushës AL 159 Jb70
Kruge HR 151 Ga62
Krügersdorf D 128 Fb37
Kruglovka RUS 113 Jb59
Kruglovo RUS 113 Hd58
Kruishoutem B 124 Ab40
Krujë AL 163 Jb72
Krujë AL 182 Ab74
Kruk N 85 Dc37
Kruklanki PL 123 Jd30
Krukowo PL 122 Jb33
Krum BG 185 Dd74
Krumbach (Schwaben) D 142 Db50
Krumë AL 178 Ad72
Krummennaab D 135 Eb45
Krummesse D 119 Dd32
Krummhörn D 117 Ca32
Krumovgrad BG 185 Dd76
Krumovo BG 180 Eb73
Krumovo Gradiste BG 181 Ec72
Krumpendorf A 144 Fb56
Krün D 143 Dd53
Krunderup DK 100 Da23
Kruonis LT 114 Kc58
Kruopiai LT 113 Jc54
Kruopiai LT 114 Ka53
Krupá CZ 136 Fa44
Krupac BIH 159 Hc65
Krupac SRB 179 Cb70
Krupaja SRB 174 Bd66
Krupa na Vrbasu BIH 152 Gd62
Krupanj SRB 153 Ja63
Krupe PL 131 Kc40
Krupina SK 146 Hc50
Krupište MK 183 Bd74
Krupka CZ 128 Fa42
Krupnik BG 183 Cb74
Krupovo RUS 107 Ma52
Krupp RUS 107 Ld46
Kruså DK 108 Db28
Krušare BG 180 Eb72
Krušari BG 181 Fa68
Kruščić SRB 153 Ja59
Kruščica HR 151 Fd62
Kruščica HR 151 Fd63
Krušedol Selo SRB 153 Jb60
Krušeto BG 180 Dd70
Kruševac SRB 178 Bc68
Kruševec BG 181 Ed73
Kruševica SRB 153 Jc63
Kruševo BIH 159 Hc64
Kruševo MK 183 Bb75
Krušica BIH 158 Ha64
Krusin PL 121 Hb33
Krušovene BG 180 Db68
Krušovica BG 179 Cd68
Krustpils LV 106 La51
Krušuna BG 180 Dc70
Kruszewo PL 121 Gb35
Kruszewo PL 123 Ka33
Kruszki PL 123 Ka30
Kruszów PL 130 Hd39
Kruszwica PL 129 Ha36
Kruszyn PL 130 Hc36
Kruszyna PL 130 Hc41
Kruszyniany PL 123 Kc33
Kruszyny PL 122 Hc33
Krūte LV 113 Jb53
Krute MNE 163 Ja71
Kruth F 31 Kb39
Kruti LV 107 Ld48
Krutje e sipërme AL 182 Ab76
Krutneset N 71 Fb22
Krutyń PL 122 Jc32
Kruunupyy FIN 81 Jb28
Kruusila FIN 97 Jd39
Kruuvinkylä FIN 89 Jb36
Krużlowa Wyżna PL 138 Jc45
Krvavi Potok SLO 151 Fa59
Kryčav BY 202 Ec12
Kryekuq AL 182 Ab76
Kryevidh AL 182 Ab75
Kryg PL 139 Jd45
Kryle DK 100 Cd23
Krylovo RUS 122 Jc30
Krymsk RUS 205 Fc17
Krynica PL 138 Jc46
Krynica Morska PL 122 Hc30
Krynka PL 131 Ka37
Krynki PL 123 Kc33
Krypno Wielkie PL 123 Ka33
Kryry CZ 135 Ed44
Kryve Ozero UA 204 Ec16
Kryvsk BY 202 Ec13
Kryvyj Rih UA 204 Ed16
Kryżanów PL 130 Hc37
Kryžopil' UA 204 Eb16
Krzęcięcice PL 130 Ja42
Krzczonów Wójtostwo PL 131 Kb40
Krzęcin PL 120 Fd34
Krzeczów PL 129 Hb40
Krzelów PL 129 Gb40
Krzemienica PL 139 Jd43
Krzemieniewo PL 121 Gc32
Krzemienowo PL 129 Gc38
Krzemlin PL 120 Fc34
Krzepice PL 129 Hb41
Krzepielów PL 128 Ga39
Krzepów PL 128 Ga39
Krześlin PL 131 Ka36
Krzeszów PL 139 Kb43
Krzeszowice PL 138 Hd44
Krzeszyce PL 128 Fc36
Krzewiny PL 121 Hb32
Krzywe PL 122 Jb34
Krzymów PL 129 Hb37
Krzynowłoga Mała PL 122 Jb34
Krzystkowice PL 128 Fd39
Krzyszkowice PL 138 Ja45
Krzywa PL 128 Ga40
Krzywcza PL 139 Kb44
Krzywda PL 131 Ka38
Krzywe PL 123 Ka30
Krzywin PL 129 Gc38
Krzyż PL 120 Ga35
Krzyż PL 138 Jb43
Krzyżanowice PL 137 Ha44
Krzyżowa PL 128 Ga40
Krzyżowa PL 129 Gb42
Krzyżówka PL 138 Jc46
Kšenskij RUS 203 Fa13
Książenice PL 137 Hb44
Książki PL 122 Hc33
Książ Mały PL 138 Ja43
Książ Wielki PL 138 Ja43
Książ Wielkopolski PL 129 Gc38
Księginice PL 129 Gc41
Księżomierz PL 131 Ka41
Księżpol PL 131 Kb42
Księży Lasek PL 122 Jb33
Kstovo RUS 203 Fb09
Ktery PL 130 Hc37
Ktísmata GR 182 Ac79
Ktová CZ 136 Fd43
Kubanovka RUS 113 Jd58
Kubbe S 80 Gc29
Kübekháza H 153 Jb57
Kublov CZ 136 Fa45
Kubrat BG 180 Eb68
Kubuļi LV 107 Lc49
Kuç AL 182 Ab78
Kučajna SRB 174 Bd65
Kućanci HR 152 Hb59
Kučeviste MK 178 Bb72
Kučevo SRB 174 Bd65
Kučgalys LT 114 Kd53
Kuchary PL 129 Ha38
Kuchen D 134 Da49
Kuchl A 143 Ed52
Kuchyňa SK 145 Gd50
Kucice PL 130 Ja36
Kucina BG 180 Dd70
Kućište KSV 178 Ad70
Kućište SRB 159 Jc68
Kučiūnai LV 123 Kb30
Kuc'i Zi AL 182 Ad77
Kučkova MK 178 Bb73
Kuçovë AL 182 Ab76
Küçükalan TR 198 Ga90
Küçükbahçe TR 191 Ea85
Küçükdağdere TR 192 Fb83
Küçükdanişmend TR 185 Ec76
Küçükhasan TR 193 Hb84
Küçükkabaca TR 193 Gc87
Küçükkalecik TR 193 Gc85
Küçükkaraağaç TR 186 Fb80
Küçükkaraağaç TR 198 Fb91
Küçükkarakarlı TR 185 Ed76
Küçükkarıştıran TR 185 Ed76
Küçükkemerdere TR 191 Ed87
Küçükkılıca TR 191 Ec82
Küçükkışla TR 187 Gc78
Küçükköy TR 191 Eb83
Küçükköy TR 199 Gb90
Küçükkumla TR 186 Fd79
Küçükkuyu TR 191 Eb82
Küçükpınar TR 199 Gb92
Küçüksuzus TR 187 Gb80
Küçükyala TR 186 Fa75
Küçükyenice TR 191 Ed82
Küçükyonalı TR 186 Fa76
Kucura SRB 153 Ja59
Kuczbork-Osada PL 122 Hd34
Kuczków PL 129 Ha38
Kuczyn PL 123 Ka35
Kuddby S 103 Gb46
Kudinava LV 107 Lc48
Kudirkos Naumiestis LT 114 Ka58
Kudowa-Zdrój PL 137 Gb43
Kūdums LV 106 Kd49
Kufas H 152 Gd57
Kuflew PL 131 Jd37
Kufstein A 143 Eb53
Kugej RUS 205 Fc16
Kūgeliai LT 113 Jc57
Kuggeboda S 111 Fd54
Kuha FIN 74 Kb20
Kuhakoski FIN 91 Lb33
Kuhalankylä FIN 82 Kb29
Kuhanen FIN 82 La30
Kühbach D 135 Dd49
Kuhfelde D 119 Dd35
Kühlungsborn D 119 Eb31
Kuhmalahti FIN 90 Ka35
Kuhmirn A 145 Gb54
Kuhmo FIN 83 Lb25
Kuhmoinen FIN 90 Kb35
Kühnhausen D 127 Dd41
Kühnsdorf A 144 Fc56
Kuhnusta FIN 83 Lc29
Kühren-Burkartshain D 127 Ec40
Kühsen D 119 Dd32
Kühtai A 142 Dc54
Kuhtur FIN 69 Jd12
Kuijõe EST 98 Ka43
Kuikkalampi FIN 83 Ma29
Kuimetsa EST 98 Kc43
Kuinre NL 117 Bc34
Kuišiai LT 114 Kc58
Kuisma FIN 83 Ma30
Kuittua FIN 83 Lb31
Kuivainen FIN 91 Lb35
Kuivajärvi FIN 75 Lc24
Kuivajõe EST 98 Kc43
Kuivakangas S 73 Jb19
Kuivalahti FIN 89 Ja36
Kuivaniemi FIN 74 Jd22
Kuivanto FIN 90 Kc37
Kuivas järvi FIN 74 Ka23
Kuivasjärvi FIN 89 Jc33
Kuivaskylä FIN 89 Jc32
Kuivasmäki FIN 90 Kb32
Kuivastu EST 97 Jd45
Kuiviži LV 106 Kb48
Kujan PL 121 Gc33
Kujduzi RUS 99 Mb40
Kükas LV 107 Lb51
Kukasjärvi FIN 69 Jd16
Kukasjärvi S 73 Jb20
Kukës AL 178 Ad72
Kukkaperä FIN 74 Kb23
Kukkaro FIN 90 Kb33
Kukko FIN 90 Ka32
Kukkola FIN 74 Jc21
Kukkola FIN 82 Kb25
Kukkola FIN 90 Ka36
Kukkola S 74 Jc21
Kukkolanmäki FIN 91 Lb32
Kukkolanvaara FIN 75 Lb20
Kuklen BG 184 Db74
Kuklin PL 122 Ja34
Kuklinów PL 129 Gd39
Kukliš MK 183 Ca75
Kukljić HR 151 Ga63
Kukljica HR 157 Fd64
Kukmor RUS 203 Fd08
Kukohijoki FIN 90 Ka36
Kukonharja FIN 89 Jc37
Kukonkylä FIN 81 Jd27
Kukonkylä FIN 81 Jd31
Kuks CZ 136 Ga43
Kuktiškės LT 114 La55
Kukujevci SRB 153 Ja61
Kukulje BIH 152 Ha61
Kukur AL 182 Ac76
Kukurečani MK 183 Bb76
Kukuri LV 106 Ka52
Kükürt TR 192 Ga82
Kula BG 179 Cb67
Kula HR 152 Hb60
Kula MNE 159 Ja68
Kula SRB 153 Ja59
Kula TR 192 Fc86
Kulak TR 193 Gc86
Kulaši BIH 152 Ha62
Kulata BG 184 Cc75
Kulautuva LV 114 Kb57
Kuļciems LV 105 Jd50
Kulcs H 146 Hc54
Kuldīga LV 105 Jc51
Kul'e RUS 107 Lc46
Kulebaki RUS 203 Fb10
Kuleli TR 185 Ec76
Kulennoinen FIN 91 Ld33
Kulen Vakuf BIH 152 Gb63
Kuleönü TR 199 Gc88
Kuleši RUS 203 Fa12
Kulesze PL 123 Ka32
Kulesze Kościelne PL 123 Ka34
Kuleszewo PL 121 Gc30
Kulho FIN 83 Ld30
Kulhuse DK 109 Eb25
Kulikovo RUS 113 Ja58
Kulina SRB 178 Bc68
Kulina Voda BG 180 Dc69
Kulju FIN 89 Jd35
Kulju FIN 89 Jd36
Külköy TR 192 Ga86
Kulkwitz D 127 Eb40
Kulla EST 106 Kd46
Kullaa FIN 89 Jb36
Kullaberg S 110 Ec54
Kulla kap S 103 Fc49
Kullamaa EST 98 Ka44
Kullar TR 187 Gb79
Kullavik S 102 Eb49
Kullen S 79 Ga26
Kullenga EST 98 La42
Kullerstad S 103 Ga46
Kullo FIN 98 Kc39
Kulloo FIN 98 Kc39
Küllstedt D 126 Db40
Kulltorp S 102 Fa50
Kullunki FIN 69 Kd17
Kulmain D 135 Ea45
Kulmbach D 135 Dd44
Kulmenai LT 113 Jc57
Kuloharju FIN 75 Kd20
Kulp TR 205 Ga20
Külsheim D 134 Da45
Külsővat H 145 Gd54
Kultima FIN 68 Hd13
Kultugün TR 185 Ec77
Kultukka FIN 74 Kb20
Kuluntalahti FIN 82 Kd25
Kulupėnai LT 113 Jb54
Kulva LT 114 Kc57
Kulvemäki FIN 82 Kd27
Kuma TR 186 Fd78
Kumafşarı TR 198 Ga90
Kuman AL 182 Ab76
Kumane SRB 153 Jb59
Kumanica SRB 178 Ad68
Kumanovo MK 178 Bc72
Kumarı TR 193 Gb83
Kumartaş TR 193 Gc85
Kümbet TR 193 Gc83
Kumbuli LV 115 Lc54
Kumburgaz TR 186 Fb77
Kumdanlı TR 193 Gd86
Kumelsk PL 123 Jd32
Kumhausen D 143 Eb50
Kumielsk PL 123 Jd32
Kumilä FIN 89 Jc38
Kumio FIN 97 Jc39
Kumiseva FIN 82 Ka28
Kumja FIN 90 Kc37
Kumkadı TR 186 Fb80
Kumkale TR 191 Ea81
Kumköy TR 186 Fd77
Kumköy TR 199 Gd91
Kumköy TR 199 Ha91
Kumkuyucak TR 192 Fa85
Kumla S 95 Fd44
Kumla Kyrkby S 95 Gb42
Kumlinge FIN 97 Hd40
Kumluca TR 199 Gb93
Kummavuopio S 67 Hb12
Kummelnäs S 96 Gd43
Kümmersbruck D 135 Ea46
Kummunkylä FIN 82 Kc30
Kumpu FIN 91 Ld33
Kumpula FIN 82 Ka30
Kumpumäki FIN 82 Kb29
Kumpuranta FIN 91 Ld32
Kumpuselkä FIN 82 Kb29
Kumpuvaara FIN 74 Kb20
Kumrags LV 106 Kd50
Kumrovec HR 151 Ga58
Kumu FIN 90 Kc35
Kunbaracs H 146 Hd54
Künceğiz TR 186 Ga80
Kuncsorba H 146 Jc54
Kunda EST 98 La41
Kundl A 143 Ea53
Kundullu TR 193 Hb86
Künerlik TR 191 Ec86
Kunes N 64 Jd06
Kunfehértó H 146 Ja56
Kungälv S 102 Eb48
Kungas FIN 81 Jc27
Kungbäck S 93 Ea44
Kungsängen S 96 Gc43
Kungsåra S 95 Gb43
Kungsäter S 102 Ec50
Kungsbacka S 102 Ec50
Kungsberg S 95 Ga39
Kungsfors S 95 Gb39
Kungsgarden S 95 Gb39
Kungshamn S 102 Ea47
Kungs-Husby S 96 Gc43
Kungsör S 95 Ga43
Kunhegyes H 146 Jc53
Kunice PL 129 Gb41
Kunigiškiai LT 114 Ka59
Kuningaküla EST 99 Lc42
Kuninkaanlähde FIN 89 Jb35
Kunino BG 179 Da70
Kunioniai LV 114 Kb56
Kunj HR 151 Fa61
Kun'je UA 203 Fb14
Kunmadaras H 146 Jc53
Kunnasniemi FIN 83 Ld30
Kunow D 119 Eb35
Kunów PL 130 Jc41
Kunowice PL 128 Fc37
Kunowo PL 129 Gc38
Kunpeszér H 146 Hd54
Kunrau D 127 Dd36
Kunreuth D 135 Dd45
Kunštat CZ 137 Gb46
Kunszentmárton H 146 Jb55
Kunszentmiklós H 146 Hd54
Kunžak CZ 136 Fd48
Künzell D 126 Da42
Künzelsau D 134 Da47
Künzing D 135 Ec49
Kuohatti FIN 83 Lc27
Kuohenmaa FIN 89 Jd36
Kuohu FIN 90 Kb33
Kuoksu S 68 Hc16
Kuolio FIN 75 La20
Kuomiokoski FIN 90 La35
Kuomiolahti FIN 90 La35
Kuona FIN 82 Kb28
Kuopio FIN 82 La30
Kuoppala FIN 82 Ka31
Kuora FIN 83 Ld29
Kuormuvaara FIN 83 Lc29
Kuorpak sameviste S 72 Gd18
Kuorsuma FIN 89 Jb35
Kuortane FIN 81 Jc31
Kuortti FIN 90 Kd35
Kuosku FIN 69 Kc16
Kup PL 129 Ha42
Kuparivaara FIN 75 La20
Kupčino RUS 99 Mb39
Küpeler TR 191 Ed82
Kupeli RUS 99 Mb43
Kupferberg D 135 Ea44
Kupferzell D 134 Da47
Kupiá GR 195 Bd90
Kupiainen FIN 91 Lb32
Kupinec HR 151 Ga59
Kupinovo SRB 153 Jb62
Kupiski PL 123 Jd33
Kupiškis LT 114 Kd54
Kupjak HR 151 Fc60
Kup'jans'k UA 203 Fb14
Kup'jans'k- Vuzlovyj UA 203 Fb14
Kupljensko HR 151 Ga60
Küplü TR 185 Ea77
Küplü TR 193 Gb81
Kupovo RUS 99 Lc43
Kuppenheim D 133 Cb48
Kuprava LV 107 Ld49
Kupreliškis LT 114 Kd53
Kupres BIH 158 Gd64
Küps D 135 Dd44
Kupusina SRB 153 Hd59
Kuqan AL 182 Ac75
Kuraszków PL 129 Gc40
Kurbnesh AL 163 Jc71
Kurd H 145 Hb56
Kurdžinovo RUS 205 Fd17
Küre TR 192 Fa87
Küre TR 193 Gb81
Küreci TR 192 Fd83
Küredere TR 192 Fb83
Kurejoki FIN 81 Jc30
Kürekçi TR 192 Fb84
Kureküla EST 98 La45
Kuremaa EST 98 La44
Kuremäe EST 99 Lc42
Kuressaare EST 105 Jc46
Kurevere EST 98 Ka44
Kurevere EST 105 Jb46
Kureyşler TR 192 Ga83
Kurfallı TR 186 Fb77
Kurganinsk RUS 205 Fd17
Kurgja EST 98 Kc44
Kurgolovo RUS 99 Lc40
Kurhila FIN 90 Kb36
Kurianka PL 123 Kb31
Kurikka FIN 89 Jb32
Kurikkala FIN 81 Jc27
Kuřim CZ 137 Gb47
Kurima SK 139 Jd47
Kurisjärvi FIN 89 Jd37
Kuřivody CZ 136 Fc43
Kurjala FIN 83 Lb31
Kurjenkylä FIN 89 Jc33
Kürkçüler TR 198 Fb91
Kurkela FIN 97 Jd39
Kurkevicy RUS 99 Mb41
Kurki FIN 75 Kc22
Kurki PL 122 Ja32
Kurkikylä FIN 75 Kd22
Kurkimäki FIN 82 La30
Kurkkio FIN 68 Jb14
Kurkkio S 68 Hd16
Kurkse EST 98 Ka43
Kurlovskij RUS 203 Fa10
Kurmale LV 105 Jc51
Kurmelionys LT 115 Lb59
Kurmene LV 106 Kd52
Kürnüç TR 187 Gd80
Kurola FIN 91 Lb32
Kurolanlahti FIN 82 Kd29
Kurortnoe RUS 113 Jb59
Kurovicy RUS 99 Lc41
Kurovicy RUS 99 Mb41
Kurovskoe RUS 203 Fa10
Kurów PL 131 Ka39
Kurowice PL 130 Hd39
Kurowo PL 121 Gb31
Kurozwęki PL 130 Jc42
Kurravaara S 67 Hb15
Kurrokvejk S 72 Gc21
Kuršai LT 113 Jd54
Kürse TR 192 Fa82
Kuršėnai LT 114 Ka54
Kursi EST 98 La44
Kuršiai LT 114 Kc55
Kursiši LV 105 Jd52
Kursk RUS 99 Ma41
Kursk RUS 203 Fa13
Kursu FIN 69 Kc17
Kuršumlija SRB 178 Bc69
Kuršumlijska Banja SRB 178 Bb69
Kurşunlu TR 186 Fb80
Kursunlu TR 186 Fd80
Kurşunlu TR 192 Fc81
Kurşunlu TR 192 Fc85
Kurşunlu TR 205 Fa20
Kurtakko FIN 68 Jb16
Kurtdere TR 186 Fa76
Kurtdere TR 192 Fa81
Kurtdere TR 192 Fd84
Kürten D 125 Ca40
Kurtköy TR 186 Fd78
Kurtköy TR 186 Fd79
Kurtköy TR 187 Gb79
Kurtköy TR 187 Gc78
Kurtköy TR 193 Gb81
Kurtlar TR 187 Ha77
Kurtna EST 99 Lb42
Kurtşeyh TR 193 Hb84
Kurtsuyu TR 187 Ha78
Kurttepe TR 185 Eb76
Kurtti FIN 75 Kd21
Kurtto FIN 75 Kd24
Kürttüllü TR 185 Eb77
Kurttutan TR 192 Fa85
Kurtul TR 186 Fd80
Kurtulmus TR 192 Fa84
Kurtuşağı TR 193 Hb85
Kurtuvėnai LT 114 Ka54
Kuru FIN 89 Jd34
Kuru FIN 89 Jd36
Kuru FIN 90 Kb38
Kurucaova TR 193 Gd85
Kuruçay TR 192 Ga83
Kurucuova TR 199 Ha88
Kurudere TR 185 Ed75
Kurudere TR 187 Gd78
Kurudere TR 193 Gd84
Kurudereköy TR 191 Ed86
Kurukavak TR 187 Gd78
Kurvinen FIN 75 Lb21
Kuryłówka PL 139 Kb43
Kurzelów PL 130 Ja41
Kurzętnik PL 122 Hd33
Kurzras I 142 Dc55
Kurzyna PL 131 Ka42
Kusadak SRB 174 Bb65
Kuşadası TR 197 Ec88
Kušalino RUS 202 Ed09
Kuşca TR 193 Gc81
Kuşçayır TR 191 Eb81
Kuščevskaja RUS 205 Fc16
Kuścince PL 123 Kc32
Kusel D 133 Bd45
Kušela RUS 99 Ld42
Kusey D 127 Dd36
Kushovë AL 182 Ac76
Kušići SRB 178 Ad68
Kuside MNE 159 Hd68
Kušiljevo SRB 174 Bc65
Kuslin PL 129 Gb37
Kuşluca TR 199 Hb88
Kusmark S 80 Hc25
Küsnacht CH 141 Cb53
Kušnin KSV 178 Ad72
Kusowo PL 121 Gb32
Küssaberg D 141 Cb52
Kussjö S 80 Ha27
Küssnacht am Rigi CH 141 Cb54
Kustavi FIN 97 Ja39
Küstelberg D 126 Cc40
Küsten D 119 Dd35
Kuštili SRB 174 Bd63
Kustovo RUS 107 Ma48
Kuşuköy TR 192 Fc84
Kusuri FIN 83 Mb29
Kusva RUS 107 Ld46
Kuta BIH 159 Hd65
Kütahya TR 193 Gb83
Kutajoki FIN 90 Kc36
Kutala FIN 89 Jc36
Kutbey TR 185 Eb77
Kutemainen FIN 82 Kb30
Kutemajärvi FIN 90 Kd33
Kutenholz D 118 Da33
Kuterevo HR 151 Fd62
Kuti MNE 159 Jb69
Küti EST 98 La42
Kutila FIN 90 Ka37
Kutina HR 152 Gc60
Kutinica HR 152 Gc59
Kutiškiai LT 114 Kb54
Kutjevo HR 152 Ha60
Kutlovo SRB 174 Bb66
Kutlu-Bukaš RUS 203 Ga08
Kutná Hora CZ 136 Fd45
Kutno PL 130 Hc37
Kutsu FIN 83 Ma31
Kuttainen S 68 Hd13
Kuttanen FIN 68 Hd13
Küttigen CH 141 Ca53
Kuttura FIN 69 Jd12
Kutumäki FIN 82 Kd31
Kutuzovo RUS 113 Jd59
Kutuzovo RUS 114 Ka58
Kuty PL 123 Jd30
Kúty SK 137 Gc49
Kutzleben D 127 Dd40
Kuukanniemi FIN 91 Lb36
Kuukasjärvi FIN 74 Kb21
Kuuksenvaara FIN 83 Ma30
Kuuminainen FIN 89 Ja36
Kuumu FIN 75 Lb24
Kuurna FIN 91 Ma32
Kuurtola FIN 75 La23
Kuurusenvaara FIN 68 Jb17
Kuusa FIN 90 Kc32
Kuusaa FIN 82 Ka27
Kuusajoki FIN 68 Jc15
Kuusalu EST 98 Kc42
Kuusamo FIN 75 La20
Kuusankoski FIN 90 Kd37
Kuusela FIN 75 Lb24
Kuusijärvi S 73 Jb19
Kuusijoki FIN 89 Jb34
Kuusikinkumpu FIN 69 Ka16
Kuusiku EST 98 Kb44
Kuusilaki S 73 Ja18
Kuusiniemi S 68 Ja15
Kuusiranta FIN 82 Kc26
Kuusirati FIN 82 Ka25
Kuusivaara FIN 74 Kb18
Kuusjärvi FIN 83 Lc30
Kuusjoenperä FIN 97 Jd39
Kuusjoki FIN 89 Jc38
Kuusjoki FIN 97 Jd39
Kuuskanlahti FIN 82 Kc25
Kuuslahti FIN 82 Kc30
Kuuslahti FIN 82 La29
Kuutsi EST 107 Lb48
Kuuttila FIN 81 Ja31
Kuvala FIN 90 La34
Kuvaskangas FIN 89 Ja34
Kuvšinovo RUS 202 Ec10
Kuyubaşı TR 199 Gc89
Kuyucak TR 187 Hb80
Kuyucak TR 193 Gc82
Kuyucak TR 198 Fb88
Kuyucak TR 199 Hb90
Kuyucakkarapınar TR 192 Fb84
Kuyumcu TR 191 Ec83
Kuyupınar TR 193 Gd81
Kuyusinir TR 193 Gb83
Kuzayır TR 192 Fc84
Kuzca TR 199 Gd89
Kužiai LT 114 Ka54
Kuzie PL 122 Jc33
Kuzkaya TR 187 Gd79
Kuzköy TR 199 Gc89
Kuzma SLO 145 Gb55
Kuzmica HR 152 Ha60
Kuzmice SK 139 Jd49
Kuzmin SRB 153 Ja61
Kuźmina PL 139 Kb45
Kuzminec HR 151 Ga57
Kuzminec HR 152 Gc57
Kuzneck RUS 203 Fd10
Kuznecovka RUS 107 Mb51
Kuznecovo RUS 99 Mb41
Kuznecovs'k UA 202 Ea14
Kuźnia Raciborska PL 137 Hb44
Kuźnica PL 121 Hb29
Kuźnica PL 123 Kc32
Kuźnica Czarnkowska PL 121 Gb35
Kuźnica Grodziska PL 130 Hd41
Kuźnica Zbąska PL 128 Ga37
Kuźnica Żelichowska PL 120 Ga35
Kuzören TR 193 Hb83
Kuzören TR 193 Hb85
Kuzovo RUS 107 Mb46
Kuzuköy TR 192 Fb84
Kuzulimanı TR 185 Dd80
Kuzuluk TR 187 Gc79
Kvačany SK 138 Hd47
Kvæfjord N 66 Ga12
Kvæl N 71 Fd18
Kvænangsbotn N 63 Hc09
Kværkeby DK 109 Eb26
Kværndrup DK 109 Dd27
Kværs DK 108 Db28
Kväkköl S 87 Fc37
Kvål N 77 Ea30
Kvalavåg N 92 Bd42
Kvale N 92 Cc46
Kvalfjord N 63 Hd07
Kvalnes N 66 Fb14
Kvalnes N 70 Fa21
Kvaløysætra N 78 Eb26
Kvaløysletta N 62 Gd09
Kvalsund N 63 Ja06
Kvalsund N 76 Cb33
Kvalsvik N 76 Cb32
Kvalvåg N 77 Db31
Kvam N 85 Dd35
Kvammen N 77 Dc31
Kvanløse DK 109 Eb26
Kvanndal N 84 Cc39
Kvanne N 77 Db31
Kvantorp S 80 Ha27
Kvänum S 102 Ed47
Kvarnåsen S 80 Ha25
Kvarnbyn S 80 Hb26
Kvarnriset S 80 Hc26
Kvarnsjö S 87 Fb33
Kvarsätt S 87 Gb33
Kvarsebo S 103 Gb46
Kvarstadseter N 85 Ea37
Kvås N 92 Cc46
Kvasice CZ 137 Gd47
Kveaunet N 78 Fa27
Kvėdarna LT 113 Jc55
Kveina N 70 Ed24
Kvelde N 93 Dd44
Kvelia N 79 Fb26
Kvennland N 78 Eb27
Kvenvær N 77 Db29
Kvernes N 77 Da31
Kvernessetra N 86 Eb36
Kvernhaugen N 94 Ec39
Kvernmo N 86 Ed37
Kvernstad N 77 Dd29
Kvetkai LT 114 Kd53
Kvevlax FIN 81 Ja30
Kvi N 66 Fc17
Kvibille S 102 Ed52
Kviby N 63 Hd07
Kvicksund S 95 Ga43
Kvidinge S 110 Ed54
Kvien N 76 Cc33
Kvikkjokk S 72 Gc18
Kvikne N 85 Dd36
Kvikstad N 66 Fc17
Kvilda CZ 136 Fa48
Kvilldal N 92 Cc42
Kville S 102 Eb46
Kvillinge S 103 Ga46
Kvillsfors S 103 Fd50
Kvimo FIN 81 Ja30
Kvinen N 92 Cc44
Kvinesdal N 92 Cc46
Kvinlog N 92 Cc45
Kvinnestad S 102 Ed48
Kvinnherad N 84 Cb40
Kvisler N 94 Ec39
Kvissleby S 88 Gc34
Kvistbro S 95 Fc44
Kvisvik N 77 Db31
Kvitberget N 63 Hd06
Kvitblik N 66 Fd17
Kviteberg N 62 Ha09
Kviteseid N 93 Da43
Kvitfors N 66 Ga13
Kvitlen N 92 Cb45
Kvitnes N 66 Fd13
Kvitnes N 77 Da31
Kvitno N 84 Cc40
Kvitsøy N 92 Ca43
Kvitten N 86 Eb33
Kvitvik N 63 Hd07
Kvívík DK 3 Ca06
Kvong DK 108 Cd25
Kvorning DK 100 Dc23
Kwakowo PL 121 Gc30
Kwiatkowice PL 130 Hc39
Kwidzyn PL 121 Hb32
Kwiecewo PL 122 Ja31
Kwilcz PL 128 Ga36
Kybartai LT 114 Ka58
Kycklingvattnet S 79 Fb26
K. Yenici TR 187 Gb80
Kyjiv UA 202 Ec14
Kyjov CZ 137 Gd48
Kylämä FIN 90 Kb35
Kylänlahti FIN 83 Lc28
Kylänpää FIN 81 Ja31
Kyläsaari FIN 89 Ja36
Kyle of Lochalsh GB 4 Db08
Kylerhea GB 4 Db08
Kylestrome GB 4 Dd05
Kyllaj S 104 Ha49
Kylland N 92 Cc45
Kyllburg D 133 Bc43
Kylmäkoski FIN 89 Jd37
Kylmälä FIN 74 Ka21
Kylmälä FIN 82 Kb25
Kylmämäki FIN 90 Kd32
Kymbo S 102 Fa48
Kymentaka FIN 90 Kd37
Kymi FIN 90 La38
Kyminlinna FIN 90 La38
Kymönkoski FIN 82 Kb30
Kymstad S 94 Ed41
Kynsikangas FIN 89 Jb36
Kynsivaara FIN 75 Kd20
Kynšperk nad Ohří CZ 135 Ec44
Kyöstilä FIN 89 Jd35
Kypärjärvi FIN 83 Lb31
Kypärävaara FIN 75 La24
Kypasjärv S 73 Ja20
Kyperounta CY 206 Ja97
Kyre Park GB 15 Ec25
Kyritz D 119 Ec35
Kyrkås S 79 Fc30
Kyrkberg S 72 Gb24
Kyrkesund S 102 Eb48
Kyrkhult S 111 Fc53
Kyrkjestølane N 85 Da37
Kyrkjeteig N 84 Cb35
Kyrkosund S 94 Ea45
Kyrksæterøra N 77 Dc30
Kyrkslätt FIN 98 Ka40
Kyrksten S 95 Fb43
Kyrnyčky UA 204 Ec17
Kyrönlahti FIN 89 Jd35
Kyröskoski FIN 89 Jc35
Kyrospohja FIN 89 Jc35
Kyrping N 92 Cb41
Kyrsyä FIN 91 Lb33
Kyselka CZ 135 Ec44

Launois-sur-Vence - Lera

Launois-sur-Vence F 24 Hd34
Launonen FIN 90 Ka38
Laupa EST 98 Kc44
Laupen CH 141 Bc54
Laupheim D 142 Da50
Laupstad N 66 Fc14
Laupunen FIN 97 Ja39
Laura I 161 Fc76
Lauragh IRL 12 Ba26
Laurbjerg DK 100 Dc23
Laureana di Borrello I 164 Gb82
Laurenan F 27 Eb39
Laurencekirk GB 7 Ec10
Laurencetown IRL 13 Ca21
Laurenzana I 162 Gb76
Lauri EST 107 Lb47
Lauria I 161 Ga77
Laurière F 33 Gc46
Laurieston GB 10 Dd16
Laurino I 161 Fd76
Laurito I 161 Fd77
Lauritsala FIN 91 Lc36
Lauro I 161 Fb75
La Urz E 37 Cb56
Lausa KSV 178 Ba70
Lausanne CH 141 Bb55
Lauscha D 135 Dd43
Laussac F 33 Ha50
Laußig D 127 Ec39
Laußnitz D 128 Fa41
Lauta D 128 Fb40
Lautakoski S 68 Hd16
Lautaporras FIN 89 Jd37
Lauteala FIN 91 Lb33
Lautela FIN 97 Jd39
Lautenbach F 31 Kb39
Lauter D 135 Ec43
Lauterach A 142 Cd53
Lauterbach D 126 Da42
Lauterbourg F 133 Cb47
Lauterbrunnen CH 141 Bd55
Lautere LV 106 La50
Lauterecken D 133 Ca45
Lauterhofen D 135 Ea47
Lauterstein D 134 Da48
Lautertal D 126 Cd42
Lautertal D 134 Cc45
Lautertal D 135 Dd43
Lautiosaari FIN 74 Jc21
Lautrec F 41 Gd54
Lauttakulma FIN 89 Jd34
Lauttakylä FIN 75 Kd24
Lauttijärvi FIN 89 Ja34
Lauvåsen N 78 Ea31
Lauvdal N 92 Cd45
Lauvdalen N 66 Fb14
Lauve N 93 Dd44
Lauvsjølia N 79 Fb27
Lauvsnes N 78 Eb26
Lauvstad N 76 Cc33
Lauvuskylä FIN 83 Lc26
Lauvvik N 92 Ca44
Lauwersoog NL 117 Bd32
Lauzerte F 40 Gb52
Lauzun F 32 Fd51
Láva GR 183 Bc79
la Vacherie F 35 Jc49
Lavachey I 148 Bb57
Lavad S 102 Ed46
Lavadáki GR 194 Bb87
Lavagna I 149 Cc63
Lavajärvi FIN 89 Jc35
Laval F 28 Fb39
Laval-Atger F 34 Hd50
Lavaldens F 35 Jd49
la Valette F 35 Jd49
la Valette-du-Var F 42 Ka55
La Vall d'Alba E 54 Fc65
la Vall d'Uixó E 54 Fc66
La Valle Agordina I 150 Ea57
la Vallivana E 48 Fd64
Laval-Roquecézière F 41 Ha53
Lavamünd A 144 Fc56
Lavangen N 66 Ga13
Lavangen N 67 Gc12
Lávara GR 185 Eb76
Lavardac F 40 Fd52
Lavardens F 40 Ga54
Lavardin F 29 Ga40
Lavaré F 29 Ga39
la Varenne F 28 Fa42
Lavarone I 149 Dc58
Lavassaare EST 98 Kb45
Lavaudieu F 34 Hc48
Lavaufranche F 33 Gd45
Lavaur F 40 Gc54
Lavau-sur-Loire F 27 Ec42
Lávdas GR 182 Ba79
La Vecilla E 37 Cc56
La Vega de Almanza E 37 Cd57
La Vega (Riosa) E 37 Cb55
La Vega (Vega de Liébana) E 38 Da55
Lavelanet F 41 Gd56
La Vellés E 45 Cb62
Lavello I 161 Ga74
Lavendon GB 20 Fb26
Lavenham GB 21 Ga26
Laveno I 148 Cb58
la Venta del Poio E 54 Fb67
Laventie F 23 Ha31
La Ventosa E 47 Eb65
Lavercantière F 33 Gb51
la Verdière F 42 Ka53
la Verna I 156 Ea65
la Verrie F 28 Fa43
Laversines F 23 Gd35
Lavertezzo CH 141 Cb56
Laveyssière F 32 Fd50
Lavezzola I 150 Dd63
Lavia FIN 89 Jb35
Laviano I 161 Fd75
La Victoria E 60 Cc73
La Vid E 46 Dc60
La Vid de Ojeda E 38 Db57
la Vieille-Lyre F 23 Ga37
Lavik N 84 Ca37
Lavikko FIN 90 Ka32
La Vila Joiosa E 55 Fc71
La Vilavella E 54 Fc66
la Vilella Baixa E 48 Ga62
La Villa I 143 Ea56
la Villa I 155 Da70
La Villa de Don Fadrique E 53 Dd67
la Ville-aux-Clercs F 29 Gb40
la Villedieu F 32 Fc46
la Villedieu F 33 Gc47
Lavilledieu F 34 Ja51
la Villedieu-du-Clain F 32 Fd45
la Villedieu-en-Fontenette F 31 Jd40
la Villeneuve F 33 Ha46
Lavinio-Lido di Enea I 160 Eb73
La Virgen del Camino E 37 Cc57
Lavis I 149 Dc57
la Visaille I 148 Bb58
Lavit-de-Lomagne F 40 Ga53
Lavoriškės LT 115 Lb57
la Voulte-sur-Rhône F 34 Jb50
Lavoûte-Chilhac F 34 Hc49
Lavoûte-sur-Loire F 34 Hd49
Lavoux F 29 Ga44
Lavra P 44 Ac60
Lavra P 50 Ac69
Lavre S 73 Hb20
la Vrine F 31 Ka42
Lavrio GR 195 Cc87
Lavrovo RUS 107 Mb51
Lavrovo RUS 202 Ed08
Lavry RUS 107 Lc47
Lavsjö S 79 Gb27
la Wantzenau F 25 Kc36
Ławy PL 120 Fc35
Laxå S 95 Fc45
Laxarby S 94 Ec44
Laxbäcken S 79 Ga26
Laxe E 36 Ac54
Laxede S 73 Hc20
Laxey GB 10 Dd19
Laxfield GB 21 Gb25
Laxford Bridge GB 4 Dd05
Laxforsen S 67 Hb15
Laxnäs S 71 Fd22
Laxo GB 5 Fa04
Laxsjö S 79 Fc28
Laxsjön S 87 Gb32
Laxviken S 79 Fc29
Layer-de-la-Haye GB 21 Ga27
La Yesa E 54 Fa66
Läyliäinen FIN 90 Ka38
Layna E 47 Eb62
Layrac F 40 Ga52
Laytown IRL 9 Cd20
La Yunta E 47 Ed63
Laž RUS 203 Fd08
Laza E 36 Bb58
Laza RO 173 Fa59
Lazagurria E 39 Eb58
Lažani MK 183 Bb75
Lazanias CY 206 Jb97
Lăzarea RO 172 Ea58
Lăzăreni RO 170 Cb57
Lazarevac SRB 153 Jc63
Lazarevo SRB 153 Jc59
Lazarevskoe RUS 205 Fc17
Lazarína GR 188 Bb81
Lazaropore MK 182 Ba74
La Zarza E 46 Cd61
Lāzberģi LV 107 Lc48
Laz Bistrički HR 152 Gb58
Lazdeğirmeni TR 192 Fc84
Lazdijai LV 123 Kb30
Lazdininkai LT 113 Jb54
Lazdona LV 107 Lb50
Lazdynai LT 114 La58
Lažec MK 183 Bb76
Łążek Ordynacki PL 131 Ka42
Lazise I 149 Db59
Łaziska Górne PL 138 Hc44
Lazisko SK 138 Hd48
Łaziuki PL 123 Ka33
Lazkao E 39 Ea56
Lázně Bohdaneč CZ 136 Ga44
Lázně Kynžvart CZ 135 Ec44
Laznica SRB 174 Bd66
Lazovskoe RUS 113 Ja58
Łazówek PL 123 Ka35
Lazuri RO 171 Cd54
Lazuri de Beiuș RO 170 Cb58
Lazy CZ 135 Ec44
Łazy PL 120 Ga30
Łazy PL 130 Jb37
Łazy PL 138 Hd43
Lazzaro I 164 Ga84
Leabgarrow IRL 8 Ca15
Leadburn GB 11 Eb13
Leadenham GB 16 Fb23
Leaden Roding GB 20 Fd27
Lealt GB 6 Db12
Leányfalu H 146 Hd52
Leatherhead GB 20 Fc29
Łeba PL 121 Gd29
Lebach D 133 Bc46
Lebane SRB 178 Bc70
Lebanje KSV 178 Bb70
le Barcarès F 41 Hb57
le Barp F 32 Fb51
le Bastit F 33 Gc50
Łebcz PL 121 Ha29
le Béage F 34 Hd50
le Beausset F 42 Jd55
le Bec-Hellouin F 23 Ga35
Lebedjan RUS 203 Fa12
Lebedyn UA 202 Ed14
le Bégude-de Mazenc F 42 Jb51
Lebeña E 38 Da55
Lebeniškiai LT 114 Kc54
Lebeniškiai LT 114 Kd54
Lébény H 145 Gd52
Lebesby N 64 Jd05
le Bessat F 34 Ja48
Lebiedziew PL 131 Kc37
Lebiez F 23 Gc31
le Biot F 35 Ka45
Lebjaž'e RUS 99 Ma39
le Blanc F 29 Gb44
le Bleymard F 34 Hd51
le Bleymard-Mont-Lozère F 34 Hd51
Łebno PL 121 Ha30
Le Bodéo F 26 Eb38
le Bois F 35 Kb47
le Bois-d'Oingt F 34 Ja46
le Bolle I 155 Dc66
Leboreiro E 36 Bb55
le Boréon F 43 Kc52
Lębork PL 121 Gd29
le Bosquet-d'Orb F 41 Hb54
le Boulay F 28 Fa41
le Boulou F 41 Hb57
le Bourg F 33 Gd50
le Bourg-d'Oisans F 35 Jd49
le Bourget-du-Lac F 35 Jd47
le Bourgneuf-la-Forêt F 28 Fb39
le Bourg-Saint-Léonard F 22 Fd37
Lebrade D 118 Dc30
le Brassus CH 140 Ba55
le Breil-sur-Mérize F 28 Fd40
le Breuil F 29 Gb38
le Breuil F 34 Hc45
le Breuil-en-Auge F 22 Fd35
Lebrija E 59 Bd75
le Broc F 43 Kc53
le Bugue F 33 Ga50
le Buisson-de-Cadouin F 33 Ga50
Łebunia PL 121 Gd30
Lebus D 128 Fb37
Lebusa D 127 Ed39
le Busseau F 28 Fb44
le Caloy F 40 Fc53
le Camp-du-Castellet F 42 Jd55
le Cap d'Agde F 41 Hc55
le Castella I 165 Gd81
le Castellet F 42 Jd55
le Cateau-Cambrésis F 24 Hb32
le Catelet F 24 Hb33
le Caylar F 41 Hc53
Lecce I 163 Hc76
Lecco I 149 Cc58
Lece SRB 178 Bc70
le Cendre F 34 Hb47
Lécera E 48 Fb62
Lech A 142 Da54
l'Echalp F 35 Kc50
le Chambon-Feugerolles F 34 Ja48
le Chambon-sur-Lignon F 34 Ja49
le Champ-Saint-Père F 28 Fa44
le Charme F 30 Hb40
le Château-d'Oléron F 32 Fa47
le Châtelet F 29 Gd44
le Châtelet-en-Brie F 29 Ha38
le Châtenet-en-Dognon F 33 Gc46
Lechbruck D 142 Dc52
Léchelle F 24 Hb37
le Chesne F 24 Ja34
le Cheylard F 34 Ja50
Lechința RO 171 Db57
Lechlade GB 20 Ed27
Lechovice CZ 137 Gb48
Lechowo PL 122 Ja30
Lēči LV 105 Jb50
Lecina E 48 Fb59
Leciñena E 48 Fb60
Leck D 108 Da28
Leckanvy IRL 8 Bb19
Leckaun IRL 8 Ca18
Leckava LT 113 Jc53
le Conquet F 26 Db38
le Corbier F 35 Ka48
le Coteau F 34 Hd46
le Creusot F 30 Ja43
le Croisic F 27 Eb42
Le Crotoy F 23 Gc32
Lectoure F 40 Ga53
Lecumberri E 39 Ec56
Łęczna PL 131 Kb39
Łęczyca PL 120 Fc33
Łęczyca PL 130 Hc38
Łęczyce PL 121 Gd29
Ledai LT 114 Kc56
Ledal N 77 Dc30
Ledaña E 53 Ec68
Ledbury GB 15 Ec26
Ledeč nad Sázavou CZ 136 Fd46
Ledenice CZ 136 Fc48
le Deschaux F 31 Jc43
le Désert F 35 Ka49
Ledesma E 45 Ca62
Lédignan F 41 Hd53
Leding S 80 Gd29
le Dixence CH 148 Bc57
Lēdmane LV 106 Kd51
Ledmore GB 4 Dd06
Lednice CZ 137 Gc49
Lednické Rovne SK 137 Hb48
Lednogóra PL 129 Gd36
le Donjon F 34 Hc45
le Dorat F 33 Gb45
le Douhet F 32 Fb47
Łędowo PL 121 Hb30
Ledrada E 45 Cb64
Lēdurga LV 106 Kc49
Łędyczek PL 121 Gc33
Łędziny PL 138 Hc44
Leebiku EST 106 La46
Leeds GB 16 Fa20
Leedstown GB 18 Da32
Leek GB 16 Ed22
Leek NL 117 Bd33
Leek Wooton GB 20 Fa25
Leenaun IRL 8 Bb20
Leende NL 125 Bb39
Leer D 117 Cb33
Leerdam NL 124 Ba37
Leersum NL 125 Bb37
Leese D 126 Da36
Leesi EST 98 Kc41
Leeuwarden NL 117 Bc33
Leevi EST 107 Lc46
Leezdorf D 117 Cb32
Leezen D 118 Dc31
le Faou F 26 Dc38
le Faouët F 27 Dd39
le Ferté-Villeneuil F 29 Gb40
Leffonds F 30 Jb39
Lefka CY 206 Ja97
Lefkáda GR 188 Ac83
Léfkara GR 183 Bc78
Lefkes GR 196 Db90
Léfki GR 184 Da77
Lefkími GR 188 Ab81
Lefkimmi GR 185 Ea77
Lefkó GR 182 Ba77
Lefkógia GR 200 Cc96
Lefkóhora GR 194 Bc89
Lefkónas GR 184 Cc76
Lefkoniko CY 206 Jc96
Lefkopigí GR 183 Bb78
Lefkoșa = Lefkosia CY 206 Jb96
Lefkosia CY 206 Jb96
Léfktra GR 189 Ca85
le Fleix F 32 Fd50
le Folgoët F 26 Dc37
le-Fond-de-France F 35 Jd48
le Fossat F 40 Gc55
le Fousseret F 40 Gb55
le Frasnois F 31 Jd44
le Frêche F 40 Fc53
le Fret F 26 Db38
Leganés E 46 Db65
Leganiel E 46 Dd65
Legau D 142 Da51
le Gault-Perche F 29 Ga39
Legazpi E 39 Eb56
Legbąd PL 121 Ha32
Legden D 125 Ca37
Legé F 28 Ed43
Lège F 32 Fa50
Legečiai LV 114 Kb55
Leginy PL 122 Jb30
Legionowo PL 130 Jb36
Legkovo RUS 202 Ed09
Léglise B 132 Ba44
Legnago I 149 Dc60
Legnano I 148 Cb59
Legnaro I 150 Ea60
Legnica PL 128 Ga41
Legnickie Pole PL 129 Gb41
Łęgoń PL 129 Gb39
Legorreta E 39 Ec56
le Gouray F 26 Eb38
Łęgowo PL 121 Hb30
Łęgowo PL 122 Hc32
Legrad HR 152 Gc57
le Grand-Bourg F 33 Gc46
le Grand- Lucé F 28 Fd40
le Grand-Madieu F 32 Fd46
le Grand-Piquey F 32 Fa50
le Grand-Pressigny F 29 Ga43
Le Grand-Quevilly F 23 Ga35
le Grand-Serre F 34 Jb48
le Grau-du-Roi F 42 Ja54
le Grotte I 161 Ga72
Léguevin F 40 Gb54
le Gurp F 32 Fa48
Legutiano E 39 Eb56
Łęguty PL 122 Hd32
Léh H 146 Jc50
Le Havre F 22 Fd35
Lehčevo BG 179 Cd68
Lehená GR 188 Ad86
Lehesten D 135 Ea43
Lehliu RO 176 Ec66
Lehliu-Gară RO 176 Ec66
Lehmäjoki FIN 81 Jb30
Lehmikumpu FIN 74 Jd20
Lehmja EST 98 Kb42
Lehmo FIN 83 Ld30
Lehnice SK 145 Gd51
Lehnin D 127 Ec37
Lehnitz D 119 Ed35
Lehnsdorf D 127 Ec38
le Houga F 40 Fc54
le Houlme F 23 Gb35
Le Hourdel F 23 Gb32
Lehoúri GR 188 Bb86
Lehrberg D 134 Db46
Lehre D 126 Dc37
Lehrte D 126 Db36
Lehtimäki FIN 81 Jd31
Lehtiniemi FIN 75 Kc19
Lehtiniemi FIN 91 Lc33
Lehtma EST 97 Jc44
Lehto FIN 75 La19
Lehtoi FIN 83 Ld30
Lehtola FIN 74 Kc18
Lehtomäki FIN 82 La29
Lehtomäki FIN 82 Ka31
Lehtomäki FIN 82 La27
Lehtovaara FIN 75 Lb22
Lehtovaara FIN 82 Kd26
Lehtovaara FIN 83 Lb27
Lehtovaara FIN 83 Lc29
Lehtovaara FIN 83 Ma29
Lehtse EST 98 Kd42
Leiblfing D 135 Eb49
Leibnitz A 144 Fd55
Leicester GB 16 Fa24
Leichlingen (Rheinland) D 125 Bd40
Leiden NL 116 Ad36
Leiderdorp NL 116 Ad36
Leie EST 98 La45
Leiferde D 126 Dc36
Leifers I 143 Dd56
Leigh GB 15 Ec21
Leighinbridge IRL 13 Cc23
Leigh Sinton GB 15 Ec26
Leighton-Buzzard GB 20 Fb27
Leignes-sur-Fontaine F 33 Ga45
Leignon B 124 Ad42
Leikanger N 76 Cb33
Leikanger N 84 Cc37
Leimbach D 126 Db42
Leimen D 133 Ca46
Leimen D 134 Cc46
Leina EST 106 Kb46
Leinach D 134 Da45
Leinburg D 135 Dd46
Leine N 76 Cb33
Leinefelde-Worbis D 126 Dc40
Leinelä FIN 90 Kb37
Leineperi FIN 89 Jb36
Leines N 70 Ed21
Leinfelden-Echterdingen D 134 Cd49
Leingarten D 134 Cd47
Leino FIN 75 La22
Leinolanlahti FIN 82 Kd30
Leinzell D 134 Da48
Leipalingis LT 123 Kc30
Leipämäki FIN 91 Lc32
Leipheim D 134 Db49
Leipivaara FIN 75 Kd24
Leipojärvi S 73 Hc18
Leippe-Torno D 128 Fb40
Leipsland N 92 Cd46
Leipzig D 127 Eb40
Leira N 70 Fa21
Leira N 71 Fb23
Leira N 77 Db30
Leira N 85 Dc38
Leiranger N 92 Ca42
Leirbakken N 78 Fa26
Leirbotn N 63 Hd07
Leiria P 44 Ac65
Leirmoen N 71 Fc19
Leiro E 36 Ba57
Leirosa P 44 Ab64
Leirpollskogen N 65 Kb05
Leirskogen N 85 Dd38
Leirsund N 93 Ea41
Leirvåg N 84 Ca37
Leirvik N 63 Hc07
Leirvik N 67 Gb13
Leirvik N 92 Ca41
Leirvik DK 3 Ca06
Leirvika N 70 Fa21
Leirvika N 78 Ec26
Leirviklandet N 77 Dc30
Leisi EST 97 Jc45
Leisnig D 127 Ec41
Leiston GB 21 Gb26
Leisu EST 97 Jc45
Leitariegos E 37 Ca55
Leiten A 143 Ea53
Leitir Ceanainn IRL 9 Cb16
Leitir Meallain IRL 12 Bb21
Leitrim IRL 8 Ca19
Leitza E 39 Ec56
Leitzersdorf A 145 Gb50
Leitzkau D 127 Eb38
Leiva E 38 Ea58
Leivadia CY 206 Jc97
Leiviskänranta FIN 82 Kb25
Leivonmäki FIN 90 Kc34
Leivset N 64 Jb06
Leivset N 66 Fd17
Leixlip IRL 13 Cd21
Lejasciems LV 107 Lb49
Lejçan AL 182 Ad74
Lejkowo PL 121 Gb30
Lejkowo PL 122 Jb33
Lejre DK 109 Eb26
Lejthizë AL 159 Jc70
Lejthizë AL 178 Ad72
Léka GR 197 Eb88
Lekangsund N 67 Gb11
Lekáni GR 184 Da76
Lekaryd S 103 Fc51
Lekåsa S 102 Ed47
Łękawa PL 130 Hd40
Łękawica PL 138 Hd45
Lek-Bibaj AL 159 Jc70
Leke B 21 Ha29
Lekėčiai LV 114 Kb57
Lekeitio E 39 Eb55
Lekenik HR 152 Gb59
Lekeryd S 103 Fb49
Łęki Dukielskie PL 139 Jd45
Łęki Górne PL 138 Jc44
Łękińsko PL 130 Hd40
Lekkerkerk NL 124 Ad37
Leknes N 66 Fb14
Leknes N 70 Ec24
Leknes N 76 Cc33
Łęknica PL 128 Fc40
Łękno PL 121 Gd35
Leksa N 77 Dd29
Leksand S 95 Fc39
Leksberg S 102 Fa46
Leksdalen N 78 Ec28
Leksvik N 78 Ea29
Lekvattnet S 94 Ed41
le Lac-d'Issarlès F 34 Hd50
Leland N 70 Fa21
le Landreau F 28 Fa42
le Lardin-Saint-Lazere F 33 Gb49
le Lauzet-Ubaye F 42 Ka51
le Lavandou F 43 Kb55
Lel'čycy BY 202 Eb14
Leleasca RO 175 Db65
Lelenai LT 113 Jc55
Leles SK 139 Ka49
Lelese RO 175 Cc61
Lelești RO 175 Cc63
l'Eliana E 54 Fb67
Lelice PL 122 Hd35
le Liège F 29 Gb42
le Lion-d'Angers F 28 Fb41
Lelis PL 122 Jc33
Leliūnai LT 114 La55
Leliūnai LT 114 La55
Lelkowo PL 122 Hd30
Lellainen FIN 89 Jb38
Lelle EST 98 Kc44
Le Locle CH 141 Bb53
le Logis-de-Nans F 42 Jd54
le Loroux F 28 Fa38
le Loroux-Bottereau F 28 Fa42
le Louroux-Béconnais F 28 Fb41
Lelów PL 130 Hd42
le Luc F 42 Ka54
le Lude F 28 Fd41
le Luthier F 31 Ka42
Lelystad NL 116 Bb35
Lem DK 100 Da22
Lem DK 108 Cd24
le Malzieu-Ville F 34 Hc50
Leman PL 122 Jc32
Le Mans F 28 Fd40
le Markstein F 31 Kb39
le Mas F 43 Kc53
le Mas-d'Agenais F 32 Fd51
le Mas-d'Azil F 40 Gc56
le Massegros F 41 Hb52
le Mayet-de-Montagne F 34 Hc46
Lembach F 25 Kc35
Lembeck D 125 Bd38
Lemberg D 133 Ca47
Lemberg F 25 Kb35
Lembeye F 40 Fc55
Lembruch D 117 Cc36
Lemele NL 117 Bd35
Lemelerveld NL 117 Bc35
le Mêle-sur-Sarthe F 28 Fd38
le Ménil F 31 Jd39
le Merlerault F 22 Fd37
Lemešany SK 139 Jd48
Lemesjö S 80 Ha29
le Mesnil-Vigot F 22 Fa36
Lemesos CY 206 Ja98
le Meux F 23 Ha35
Lemförde D 117 Cc36
Lemgo D 126 Cd37
Lemgow D 119 Ea35
Lemi FIN 91 Lb36
Lemie I 148 Bc59
Lemierzyce PL 128 Fc36
Lemlahti FIN 89 Ja36
Lemland FIN 96 Hc41
Lemmenjoki FIN 69 Jd11
Lemmer NL 117 Bc34
Lemmikküla EST 98 Ka44
Lemnhult S 103 Fd50
Lemnia RO 176 Eb61
le Molay-Littry F 22 Fb35
le Monastier-sur-Gazeille F 34 Hd49
le Monêtier-les-Bains F 35 Kb49
le Mont F 30 Jb40
le Montat F 40 Gc52
le Mont-Dore F 33 Ha47
le Montet F 34 Hb45
Lemós GR 182 Ba76
le Mouret CH 141 Bc54
le Moutchic F 32 Fa49
Lemovza RUS 99 Ma42
Lempää FIN 90 Kc34
Lempäälä FIN 89 Jd36
Lempdes F 34 Hb47
Lempdes F 34 Hb48
Lempiälä FIN 91 Lc36
Lempyy FIN 82 Kd31
Lemreway GB 4 Da06
Lemsi EST 106 Kb47
Lemu FIN 97 Jb39
le Muret F 32 Fb51
le Muy F 43 Kb54
Lemvig DK 100 Cd22
Lemwerder D 118 Cd34
Lemybrien IRL 13 Cb25
Lēna LV 105 Jc52
Lena N 85 Ea39
Lena S 102 Ec48
Lenart v. Slovenske gorice SLO 144 Ga56
Lenarty PL 123 Ka30
Lėnas LT 114 Kd55
Lencăuți MD 173 Fb53
Lences E 38 Dd57
Lenči LV 106 Kd49
Lencloitre F 28 Fd44
l'Enclus F 35 Jd50
Lencouacq F 40 Fc52
Lend A 143 Ec54
Lendak SK 138 Jb47
Léndas GR 200 Da97
Lendava SLO 145 Gb56
Lendinara I 150 Dd61
Lendínez E 60 Da73
Lendum DK 101 Dd20
Lendži LV 107 Ld51
Lenes N 77 Dc30
Le Neubourg F 23 Ga36
Lengdorf D 143 Ea50
Lengede D 126 Dc37
Lengefeld D 127 Ed42
Lengenes N 67 Gb14
Lengenfeld D 126 Db40
Lengenfeld D 135 Eb43
Lengenwang D 142 Db52
Lengerich D 117 Cb35
Lengerich D 125 Cb37
Lenggries D 143 Dd52
Lengronne F 22 Fa36
Lengyeltóti H 145 Ha56
Lenham GB 21 Ga29
Lenhovda S 103 Fd51
Lenina BY 202 Ec13
Lenine UA 205 Fb17
Leningrad = Sankt-Peterburg RUS 99 Mb39
Leninogorsk RUS 203 Ga09
Leninsk RUS 203 Ga13
Leninskij RUS 203 Fa11
Leninskoje RUS 113 Jc57
Lenk CH 141 Bd56
Lenkimai LT 113 Jb53
Lenkivci UA 204 Eb15
Lenkovo BG 180 Db69
Lennartsfors S 94 Ec43
Lenne D 126 Da38
Lennestadt D 125 Cb40
Lenningen D 134 Cd49
Leno I 149 Da60
Lenola I 160 Ed73
Lenora CZ 136 Fa48
le Nouvion-en-Thiérache F 24 Hc33
Lenovac SRB 179 Ca67
Lenovo BG 184 Dc74
Lens F 23 Ha31
Lensahn D 119 Dd30
Lensvik N 77 Dd29
Lent F 34 Jb45
Lentate sul Seveso I 149 Cc58
Lentellais E 36 Bc57
Lent'evo RUS 202 Ed08
Lentföhrden D 118 Db31
Lenti H 145 Gc56
Lentiira FIN 83 Lc25
Lentina I 166 Eb84
Lenting D 135 Dd48
Lentini I 167 Fc86
Lentuankoski FIN 83 Lc25
Lentvaris LT 114 La58
Lenungen S 94 Ec43
Lenungshammar S 94 Ec43
Lenz CH 142 Cd55
Lenzburg CH 141 Ca53
Lenzen D 119 Ea34
Lenzerheide CH 142 Cd55
Lenzkirch D 141 Ca51
Leoben A 144 Fc53
Leoberghe F 21 Gd30
Leobersdorf A 145 Gb52
Leodári GR 194 Bb88
Leofreni I 156 Ec70
Leogang A 143 Ec53
Léognan F 32 Fb50
Leominster GB 15 Eb25
Léon F 39 Fa53
León E 37 Cc57
Leonarisso CY 206 Jd95
Leonberg D 134 Cc48
Leonberg D 135 Eb45
Leoncin PL 130 Ja36
Leonding A 144 Fb50
Leonessa I 156 Ec69
Leonforte I 167 Fb85
Leonídio GR 195 Bd89
Leonstein A 144 Fb52
Leontári GR 189 Bc82
Leopoldov SK 145 Ha50
Leopoldsburg B 124 Ba39
Leopoldschlag Markt A 136 Fb49
Leopoldsdorf im Marchfelde A 145 Gc51
Leopoldshafen D 133 Cb47
Leopoldshagen D 120 Fa32
Leopoldshöhe D 126 Cd37
Leorda RO 172 Ec55
Leordeni RO 176 Dd65
Leordina RO 171 Db55
Léouvé F 43 Kc52
Leova MD 177 Fc60
Leoz E 39 Ed57
Lepaa FIN 90 Ka37
le Pailly F 30 Jb40
le Palais F 27 Ea42
le Parcq F 23 Gd32
Lepassaare EST 107 Lc47
Lépaud F 33 Ha45
le Pavillon-Sainte-Julie F 30 Hc38
Lepe E 59 Bb74
le Péage-de-Roussillon F 34 Jb48
Lepel' BY 202 Eb12
le Pellerin F 28 Ed42
Lepenoú GR 188 Ba83
le Perray-en-Yvelines F 23 Gc37
le Perthus F 41 Hb58
le Pertuis F 34 Hd49
Łępice PL 122 Jb35
l'Épine F 24 Hd36
l'Épine F 27 Ec43
le Pin-en-Mauges F 28 Fb42
le Pin-la-Garenne F 29 Ga38
Lepistö FIN 69 Kd16
Lepistönmäki FIN 81 Jc29
le Planay F 35 Kb46
le Planay F 35 Kb48
le Plessis-Belleville F 23 Ha36
Le Plessis-Grimoult F 22 Fb36
le Plot F 35 Ka46
Lepno PL 122 Hc31
le Poët F 42 Jd51
Lepoglava HR 152 Gb57
le Poinçonnet F 29 Gc44
le Poiré-sur-Vie F 28 Ed44
Lepola FIN 74 Ka18
le Pompidou F 41 Hc52
le Pont CH 140 Ba55
le Pont-Béranger F 28 Ed42
le Pont-d'Agris F 32 Fd47
le Pont-de-Beauvoisin F 35 Jd47
le Pont-de-Claix F 35 Jd49
le Pont-de-Montvert F 34 Hd51
le Pontet F 32 Fb49
Lepooskangas FIN 90 Kc35
le Porge F 32 Fa50
le-Porge-Océan F 32 Fa50
le Portel F 23 Gb31
Leposavić KSV 178 Ba69
le Pouldu F 27 Dd40
le Pouliguen F 27 Eb42
Lépoura GR 189 Cc85
le Pouzin F 34 Jb50
Leppäjärvi FIN 68 Ja13
Leppäkorpi FIN 97 Jd39
Leppäkoski FIN 89 Jc37
Leppäkoski FIN 90 Ka35
Leppäkoski FIN 90 Kc34
Leppälä FIN 75 Kd22
Leppälä FIN 91 Lc36
Leppälahti FIN 82 Kd29
Leppälahti FIN 83 Ka28
Leppälahti FIN 83 Lc31
Leppälänkylä FIN 81 Jc31
Leppämäki FIN 82 La31
Leppäniemi FIN 83 Ld31
Leppäselkä FIN 82 Kc30
Leppävesi FIN 90 Kb32
Leppävirta FIN 82 La31
Leppiniemi FIN 74 Kb24
Leppneeme EST 98 Kb42
le Pradet F 42 Ka55
Lepşa RO 176 Ec61
Lepsala FIN 90 Kb36
Lepsäma FIN 98 Kb39
Lepste LV 106 Ka49
Leptokaria GR 183 Bd79
Leptokariá GR 185 Ea77
le Puy-en-Velay F 34 Hd49
le Puy-Notre-Dame F 28 Fc42
le Puy-Saint-Réparade F 42 Jc53
le Quesnel F 23 Ha33
le Quesnoy F 24 Hb32
Lequile I 163 Hc76
le Quilho F 27 Eb39
Ler N 77 Ea30
Lera MK 182 Ba76

Lindshammar - Loobu

Lindshammar S 103 Fd51
Lindstedt D 127 Ea36
Lindum DK 100 Dc22
Lindved DK 108 Db25
Lindwedel D 126 Db36
Líně CZ 135 Ed46
Linevo RUS 203 Fd12
Lingbo S 87 Gb38
Lingen D 117 Ca35
Lingen GB 15 Eb25
Lingenfeld D 133 Cb46
Lingfield GB 20 Fc29
Linghed S 95 Ga39
Linghem S 103 Ga46
Linguaglossa I 167 Fd85
Lingura MD 177 Fc60
Linhamari FIN 97 Jd40
Linia PL 121 Gd30
Liniewo PL 121 Ha31
Liniez F 29 Gc43
Linkmenys LT 115 Lb55
Linköping S 103 Fd47
Linksmakalnis LT 114 Kc58
Linksness GB 5 Eb03
Linkuva LT 114 Kb53
Linlithgow GB 10 Ea13
Linna EST 106 La46
Linna FIN 82 Kb31
Linnamäe EST 98 Ka44
Linnankylä FIN 89 Jc34
Linnanperä FIN 82 Kb29
Linnarnäs FIN 97 Jc40
Linnaste RUS 107 Ld46
Linnerud N 86 Eb37
Linneryd S 103 Fd52
Linnes N 86 Ed36
Linneset N 79 Fb28
Linnich D 125 Bc40
Linnunpää FIN 97 Jc39
Linnuse EST 97 Jd45
Linou CY 206 Ja97
Linovo RUS 107 Ld48
Linowo PL 122 Hc33
Linsburg D 126 Da36
Linsell S 87 Fb34
Linsengericht D 134 Cd44
Linthal CH 142 Cc54
Lintig D 118 Cd32
Lintrup DK 108 Da26
Lintula FIN 68 Jc14
Linxe F 39 Fa53
Linyola E 48 Gb60
Linz A 144 Fb50
Linz D 125 Ca42
Lioliai LT 113 Jc55
Lioni I 161 Fd75
Lion-sur-Mer F 22 Fc35
Liopetri CY 206 Jd97
Lios Dúin Bhearna IRL 12 Bc22
Lios Mor IRL 13 Ca25
Lios Tuathail IRL 12 Bb23
Lipa BIH 152 Gb62
Lipa BIH 158 Ha66
Lipa EST 98 Kb44
Lipa GR 188 Ad81
Lipa PL 122 Jb34
Lipa PL 128 Ga41
Lipa PL 131 Ka42
Lipa RUS 99 Ma42
Lipănești RO 176 Ea64
Lipany SK 138 Jc47
Lipar SRB 153 Ja59
Lipari I 167 Fc83
Lipasvaara FIN 83 Lc29
Lipcani MD 172 Ed53
Lipce Reymontowskie PL 130 Ja38
Lipczynek PL 121 Gc32
Lipeck RUS 203 Fb12
Lipen BG 179 Cc69
Lipenec CZ 136 Fa44
Liperi FIN 83 Lc31
Liperin asema FIN 83 Lc30
Liperinsalo FIN 83 Lc31
Liperonmäki FIN 90 Kd32
Liphook GB 20 Fb29
Lipia Góra PL 121 Gc34
Lipiany PL 120 Fc35
Lipica PL 122 Jb30
Lipica SLO 151 Fa59
Lipice HR 151 Fd61
Lipicy-Zybino RUS 203 Fa12
Lipie PL 130 Hc41
Lipik HR 152 Gd60
Lipiniški LV 115 Lc53
Lipinki PL 121 Ha32
Lipinki PL 131 Kc38
Lipinlahti FIN 83 Lc27
Lipiny PL 130 Hd38
Lipiny Górne-Lewki PL 131 Kb42
Lipka PL 121 Gc33
Lipka PL 129 Gd41
Lipka PL 130 Hd38
Lipki RUS 203 Fa11
Lipkovo MK 178 Bc72
Lipljan KSV 178 Bb71
Lipniak PL 123 Ka30
Lipniak PL 123 Kb30
Lipniaki PL 131 Ka37
Lipnic MD 173 Fa51
Lipnica BG 179 Cd70
Lipnica PL 121 Gd31
Lipnica PL 122 Hc34
Lipnica PL 130 Ja42
Lipnica Murowana PL 138 Jb45
Lipnica Wielka PL 138 Hd46
Lipnice CZ 136 Fc48
Lipnice nad Sázavou CZ 136 Fd46
Lipnik PL 131 Jd42
Lipniki PL 122 Jc33
Lipniki PL 137 Gc43
Lipniki Łużyckie PL 128 Fc39
Lipník nad Bečvou CZ 137 Gd46
Lipnița RO 181 Fa67
Lipnjaki RUS 113 Jb59
Lipno PL 122 Hc35
Lipno PL 129 Gb38
Lipno PL 129 Hb40
Lipno nad Vltavou CZ 136 Fb49
Lipolist SRB 153 Ja62
Liposthey F 39 Fb52
Lipótfa H 152 Ha57
Lipová CZ 137 Gc46
Lipova RO 172 Ed59
Lipova RO 174 Ca60
Lipovac HR 153 Hd61
Lipová-lázně CZ 137 Gc44
Lipovăț RO 173 Fa59
Lipovce SK 138 Jc47
Lipovec CZ 137 Gc47
Lipoveni MD 173 Fd59
Lipovljani HR 152 Gc60
Lipovo MNE 159 Ja68
Lipovo RUS 99 Lc40
Lipovo RUS 99 Ld39
Lipovo RUS 113 Jd59
Lipovo Polje HR 151 Fd62
Lipovu RO 179 Cd67
Lipowa PL 138 Hc45
Lipowczyce PL 130 Hd41
Lipowiec PL 122 Jb33
Lipowiec Kościelny PL 122 Ja34
Lipowina PL 122 Hd30
Lipówka PL 131 Kc38
Lippborg D 125 Cb38
Lippetal D 125 Cb38
Lippi FIN 83 Lc27
Lippstadt D 126 Cc38
Lipsí GR 197 Eb89
Lipsk PL 123 Kb31
Lipsko PL 131 Jd40
Lipsko PL 131 Kc41
Liptál CZ 137 Ha47
Liptingen, Emmingen- D 142 Cc51
Liptovská Lúžna SK 138 Hd48
Liptovská Osada SK 138 Hd48
LiptovskáTeplička SK 138 Ja48
Liptovské Revúce SK 138 Hd48
Liptovský Hrádok SK 138 Ja47
Liptovský Mikuláš SK 138 Hd47
Lipuški LV 107 Ld52
Lipusz PL 121 Gd31
Lira E 36 Ac55
Liré F 28 Fa42
Lis AL 163 Jc72
Lisa RO 175 Dc62
Lisa RO 180 Dc68
Lisac BIH 158 Ha64
Lisacul IRL 8 Bd19
Lišane Ostrovičke HR 157 Ga65
Lisberg D 134 Dc45
Lisboa P 50 Aa68
Lisburn GB 9 Da17
Liscannor IRL 12 Bc22
Liscarney IRL 8 Bc19
Liscarroll IRL 12 Bc24
Lișcoteanca RO 177 Fa64
Lisdoonvarna IRL 12 Bc22
Lisduff IRL 9 Cc20
Lisec MK 178 Ba73
Liseleje DK 109 Eb24
Lisewo PL 121 Hb33
Lisia Góra PL 138 Jc44
Lisięcice PL 137 Ha44
Lisie Jamy PL 139 Kc43
Lisieux F 22 Fd36
Lisino RUS 99 Ma41
Lisje RUS 107 Ld46
Liskeard GB 18 Dc31
Liski PL 123 Jd32
Liski RUS 203 Fb13
Liškiava LT 123 Kc30
Lisków PL 129 Hb38
Liskowate PL 139 Kb45
l'Isle CH 140 Ba55
Lisle F 33 Ga49
Lislea GB 9 Cd16
Lislea GB 9 Cd18
l'Isle-Adam F 23 Gd36
l'Isle-d'Abeau F 35 Jc47
l'Isle-deNoé F 40 Fd54
l'Isle-en-Dodon F 40 Ga55
Lisleherad N 93 Dc42
l'Isle-Jourdain F 33 Ga45
l'Isle-Jourdain F 40 Gb54
l'Isle-sur-la-Sorgue F 42 Jc53
l'Isle-sur-le-Doubs F 31 Ka43
l'Isle-sur-Serein F 30 Hd41
Lisle-sur-Tarn F 40 Gc53
Lisma FIN 68 Jc13
Lismacaffry IRL 9 Cb20
Lismanaapa FIN 69 Ka16
Lișmănița RO 172 Ec54
Lismore IRL 13 Ca25
Lisnagry IRL 12 Bd23
Lisnaskea GB 9 Cb18
Lišov CZ 136 Fc48
Lisów PL 128 Fc37
Lisowo PL 120 Fd33
Lisronagh IRL 13 Ca24
Liss GB 20 Fb29
Lissamona IRL 12 Bb27
Lisse NL 116 Ad36
Lissett GB 17 Fc20
Lissy F 23 Ha37
Lissycasey IRL 12 Bc23
List D 108 Cd27
Lista S 95 Ga43
Lișteava RO 179 Da68
Listellick IRL 12 Bb24
Listerby S 111 Fd54
Listowel IRL 12 Bb23
Lisvane GB 19 Eb28
Liszki PL 138 Ja44
Liszkowo PL 121 Gc34
Liszó H 152 Gd57
Lit S 79 Fc30
Lita RO 171 Da58
Lița RO 180 Dc68
Litakovo BG 179 Cd70
Litava SK 146 Hd50
Litcham GB 17 Ga24
Liteň CZ 136 Fb45
Litene LV 107 Lc49
Liteni RO 172 Ec56
Lit-et-Mixe F 39 Fa53
Lith NL 125 Bb37
Lithines GR 201 Dc96
Lithio GR 191 Dd86
Lithótopos GR 183 Cb76
Liti GR 183 Cb77
Litija SLO 151 Fc58
Litke H 146 Ja50
Litmalahti FIN 82 La30
Litmaniemi FIN 83 Lb30
Litobratřice CZ 137 Gb48
Litóhoro GR 183 Bd79
Litoměřice CZ 136 Fb43
Litomyšl CZ 137 Gb45
Litos E 45 Cb59
Litovel CZ 137 Gc46
Litovo RUS 99 Mb39
Litschau A 136 Fc48
Litslena S 95 Gc42
Littiäinen S 73 Jb20
Little Barningham GB 17 Gb23
Littleborough GB 16 Ed21
Little Brington GB 20 Fb25
Littleferry GB 5 Ea06
Little Glenshee GB 7 Ea11
Littlehampton GB 20 Fb30
Little Langdale GB 11 Eb18
Little Mill GB 19 Eb27
Littleport GB 20 Fd25
Littleton IRL 13 Ca23
Little Torrington GB 19 Dd30
Little Walsingham GB 17 Ga23
Little Weighton GB 17 Fc20
Little Weighton GB 17 Fc21
Little Wenlock GB 15 Ec24
Littoinen FIN 97 Jb39
Lituénigo E 47 Ec60
Litultovice CZ 137 Ha45
Litvínov CZ 136 Fa43
Litzelsdorf A 145 Gb54
Litzendorf D 135 Dd45
Liu EST 106 Kb46
Liubavas LT 114 Ka59
Liudvinavas LV 114 Kb59
Liukko FIN 81 Jd30
Liukonys LT 114 Kd57
Liutonys LT 114 Kd58
Livada RO 170 Bd59
Livada RO 171 Cd54
Livaderó GR 183 Bc79
Livaderó GR 184 Dd76
Livádi GR 183 Bc79
Livádi GR 183 Cb78
Livádi GR 195 Cd89
Livadia CY 206 Jd96
Livádia GR 183 Bd76
Livádia GR 189 Bd85
Livádia GR 196 Dd92
Livádia GR 197 Ec92
Livadohóri GR 190 Db81
Livanátes GR 189 Ca84
Livāni LV 107 Lb52
Livari MNE 159 Ja70
Livarot F 22 Fd36
Livártzi GR 188 Bb86
Livata I 160 Ec71
Livbērze LV 106 Ka51
Livenskoje RUS 113 Jd57
Livera CY 206 Ja96
Liverá GR 183 Bb78
Livernon F 33 Gc51
Liverovići MNE 159 Hd68
Liverpool GB 15 Eb21
Livezeni RO 171 Dc59
Livezi RO 175 Da64
Livezi RO 176 Ec60
Livezile RO 171 Dc57
Livezile RO 174 Cb65
Livigno I 142 Da56
Livingston GB 11 Eb13
Liviöjärvi S 68 Ja17
Livizile RO 171 Da59
Livno BIH 158 Gd65
Livny RUS 203 Fa12
Livø DK 100 Db21
Livo FIN 74 Kb21
Livold SLO 151 Fc59
Livonniska FIN 75 Kc20
Livonsaari FIN 97 Ja39
Livorno I 155 Da66
Livorno Ferraris I 148 Ca60
Livov SK 138 Jc47
Livré-sur-Changeon F 28 Fa39
Livron-sur-Drôme F 34 Jb50
Livry-Louvercy F 24 Hd36
Liw PL 131 Jd36
Lixa P 44 Ba60
Lixnaw IRL 12 Bb24
Lixoúri GR 188 Ab85
Lizard GB 18 Da33
Lizarra E 39 Ec57
Lizarraga E 39 Ec56
Lizēre LV 106 La50
Lizespasts LV 107 Lb48
Lizine F 31 Jd42
Lizio F 27 Eb40
Lizums LV 107 Lb49
Lizy-sur-Ourcq F 23 Ha36
Lizzano I 162 Ha76
Lizzano in Belvedere I 155 Db64
Lizzola I 149 Da57
Ljachavičy BY 202 Ea13
Ljady RUS 99 Ma44
Ljady RUS 202 Ea09
Ljahovo RUS 107 Ma52
Ljamcevo RUS 99 Mb44
Ljaskovec BG 180 Dd70
Ljatno BG 181 Ed69
Ljeljenča BIH 153 Hd62
Lješane KSV 178 Ad70
Lješkove Vode BIH 152 Hb62
Ljig SRB 153 Jc63
Ljørdalen N 86 Ed37
Ljosland N 92 Cc45
Ljosland N 92 Cd45
Ljubac HR 157 Fd64
Ljuban' BY 202 Eb13
Ljuban' RUS 202 Eb08
Ljubaništa MK 182 Ad76
Ljubar UA 204 Eb15
Ljuben BG 180 Db72
Ljubenova Mahala BG 180 Ea73
Ljubenovo BG 180 Ea73
Ljuberadja SRB 179 Ca70
Ljubešiv UA 202 Ea14
Ljubić SRB 174 Bb66
Ljubija BIH 152 Gc61
Ljubim RUS 203 Fa08
Ljubimec BG 185 Ea74
Ljubinje BIH 158 Hb68
Ljubiš SRB 159 Jb65
Ljubište KSV 178 Bb72
Ljubljana SLO 151 Fb58
Ljubno ob Savinji SLO 151 Fc57
Ljubogošta BIH 159 Hc65
Ljubojno MK 182 Ba76
Ljuboml' UA 202 Dd14
Ljubovija SRB 159 Ja64
Ljubovo BIH 159 Hc69
Ljubusa BIH 159 Hc66
Ljubuški BIH 158 Ha67
Ljubymivka UA 205 Fb15
Ljubytino RUS 202 Ec09
Ljuder S 103 Fd52
Ljudinovo RUS 202 Ed12
Ljugarn S 104 Ha50
Ljulin BG 181 Ec73
Ljuljak BG 180 Dd72
Ljuljakovo BG 181 Ec71
Ljung S 102 Ed48
Ljung S 103 Fd46
Ljunga S 103 Ga46
Ljungaverk S 87 Ga33
Ljungby S 103 Fb52
Ljungbyhed S 110 Ed54
Ljungbyholm S 103 Ga52
Ljungdalen S 86 Ed32
Ljunghusen S 110 Ed57
Ljungsarp S 102 Fa49
Ljungsbro S 103 Fd46
Ljungskile S 102 Eb47
Ljusă BIH 158 Gd64
Ljusa S 73 Hd21
Ljušci Palanka BIH 152 Gb62
Ljusdal S 87 Ga35
Ljusfallshammar S 95 Fd45
Ljusfors S 103 Ga46
Ljushult S 102 Ed49
Ljusne S 87 Gb37
Ljusnedal S 86 Ed33
Ljusterö S 96 Ha43
Ljustorp S 88 Gc32
Ljusträsk S 72 Ha22
Ljusvattnet S 80 Hb26
Ljuti Brod BG 179 Cd70
Ljuti Dol BG 179 Cd70
Ljutoglav KSV 178 Ba72
Ljutomer SLO 145 Gb56
Ljutovnica SRB 159 Jc64
Ljutye Bolota RUS 107 Mb47
Llaberia E 48 Ga62
Lladó E 41 Hb58
Lladomericë AL 182 Ad74
Lladorre E 40 Gb57
Lladurs E 49 Gc59
Llagostera E 49 Hb60
Llamas de de Rueda E 37 Cd57
Llamas del Mouro E 37 Ca55
Llanallgo GB 15 Dd22
Llanarmon Dyffryn Ceiriog GB 15 Eb23
Llanarthney GB 15 Dd26
Llánaves de la Reina E 38 Da56
Llanbadarn Fawr GB 15 Dd25
Llanberis GB 15 Dd22
Llanbister GB 15 Ea25
Llanboidy GB 14 Dc26
Llanddarog GB 19 Dd27
Llanddewi Ystradenni GB 15 Ea25
Llanddona GB 15 Dd22
Llandegla GB 15 Eb23
Llandeilo GB 15 Dd26
Llandenny GB 19 Eb27
Llandinam GB 15 Ea24
Llandissilio GB 14 Dc26
Llandovery GB 15 Dd26
Llandrillo GB 15 Ea23
Llandrindod-Wells GB 15 Ea25
Llandrinio GB 15 Eb24
Llandudno GB 15 Ea22
Llandyfaelog GB 18 Dc27
Llanelidan GB 15 Ea23
Llanelli GB 19 Dd27
Llanelltyd GB 15 Dd23
Llanerchymedd GB 15 Dd22
Llanerfyl GB 15 Ea24
Llanes E 38 Da54
Llanfaethlu GB 14 Dc21
Llanfair-Caereinion GB 15 Ea24
Llanfair-fechan GB 15 Dd22
Llanfair Talhaiarn GB 15 Ea22
Llanfair-yn-Neubwll GB 14 Dc22
Llanfihangel GB 15 Ea26
Llanfihangel-nant-Melan GB 15 Eb25
Llanfihangel-y-Creuddyn GB 15 Dd25
Llanfihangel-yng-Ngwynfa GB 15 Ea24
Llanfyllin GB 15 Eb24
Llanfynydd GB 15 Dd26
Llanfyrnach GB 14 Dc26
Llangadog GB 15 Dd26
Llangaffo GB 15 Dd22
Llangain GB 18 Dc27
Llangammarch Wells GB 15 Ea26
Llangedwyn GB 15 Eb23
Llangefni GB 15 Dd22
Llangeinor GB 19 Ea27
Llangeler GB 14 Dc26
Llangenith GB 18 Dc27
Llangernyw GB 15 Ea22
Llangollen GB 15 Eb23
Llangorse GB 15 Ea26
Llangrannog GB 14 Dc25
Llangurig GB 15 Ea25
Llangwm GB 15 Ea23
Llangwm GB 18 Db27
Llangwm GB 19 Eb27
Llangwnnadl GB 14 Dc25
Llangybi GB 15 Dd25
Llangybi GB 19 Eb27
Llangynidr GB 19 Ea27
Llangynog GB 15 Ea23
Llangywer GB 15 Ea23
Llanharan GB 19 Ea28
Llanhilleth GB 19 Eb27
Llanidloes GB 15 Ea25
Llanillo E 38 Db57
Llanmadoc GB 19 Dd27
Llanon GB 15 Dd25
Llanrhaeadr-ym-Mochnant GB 15 Ea23
Llanrhystud GB 15 Dd25
Llanrug GB 15 Dd22
Llanrwst GB 15 Ea22
Llansilin GB 15 Eb23
Llansoy GB 19 Eb27
Llansteffan GB 18 Dc27
Llanthony GB 15 Eb26
Llantwit Major GB 19 Ea28
Llanuwchllyn GB 15 Ea23
Llanvetherine GB 19 Eb27
Llanwddyn GB 15 Ea24
Llanwrog GB 15 Dd22
Llanwrtyd Wells GB 15 Ea26
Llanybydder GB 15 Dd26
Llanynghenedl GB 14 Dc22
Llanystumdwy GB 15 Dd23
Llardecans E 48 Ga61
Llavorsí E 40 Gb58
Llechryd GB 14 Dc26
Lleida E 48 Ga61
Llengë AL 182 Ad76
Llera E 51 Ca70
Llessui E 40 Gb58
Llimiana E 48 Gb59
Llinars E 49 Gc59
Llinars del Vallès E 49 Ha60
Llíria E 54 Fb67
Llithfaen GB 14 Dc23
L'Ile-Rousse F 154 Cb68
Llobera E 49 Gc59
Llodio E 38 Ea55
Lloggerheads GB 15 Ec23
Llorac E 48 Gb61
Llorenç del Penedès E 49 Gc62
Lloret de Mar E 49 Hb60
Lloret de Vistalegre E 57 Hc67
Llosa de Ranes E 54 Fb69
Lloseta E 57 Hb67
Llovio E 37 Cd54
Llubí E 57 Hc67
Lluçà E 49 Gd59
Llucena E 54 Fc65
Llucmajor E 57 Hb67
Llutxent E 54 Fc69
Llwyngwril GB 15 Dd24
Llyswen GB 15 Ea26
Lnáře CZ 136 Fa46
Lniano PL 121 Ha33
Lo B 21 Ha30
Löa S 95 Fd42
Loamneș RO 175 Db61
Loanhead GB 11 Eb13
Loano I 148 Bd63
Loan-Villegruis-Fontaine F 24 Hb37
Loarre E 39 Fb58
Löbau D 128 Fc41
Lobcovo RUS 203 Fa09
Łobdowo PL 122 Hc34
Lobe LV 106 Kd51
Lobeiras E 36 Bc53
Löbejün D 127 Eb39
Lobera de Onsella E 39 Fa58
Lobērgi LV 106 La48
Löberitz D 127 Eb39
Löberöd S 110 Fa55
Łobez PL 120 Fd32
Lobinstown IRL 9 Cd20
Löbnitz D 119 Ec30
Löbnitz D 127 Ec39
Łobodno PL 130 Hc41
Lobón E 51 Bc69
Lobonäs S 87 Fd36
Loboš BG 179 Cb72
Loburg D 127 Eb37
Łobżenica PL 121 Gc34
Locana I 148 Bc59
Locarno CH 148 Cb57
Loccum, Rehburg- D 126 Da36
Loceri I 169 Cb78
Lochailort GB 6 Db10
Lochaline GB 6 Db11
Lochau A 142 Da52
Lochbuie GB 6 Db11
Lochcarron GB 6 Dc08
Lochdrum GB 4 Dd07
Lochearnhead GB 7 Dd11
Lochem NL 117 Bc36
Loches F 29 Gb42
Loché-sur-Indrois F 29 Gb43
Loch Garman IRL 13 Cd25
Löchgau D 134 Cd47
Lochgelly GB 7 Eb12
Lochgilphead GB 6 Db12
Lochinver GB 4 Dc05
Lochmaben GB 11 Eb16
Lochmaddy GB 6 Cd07
Lochore GB 7 Eb12
Łochów PL 131 Jd36
Lochranza GB 6 Dc13
Lochskipport GB 6 Cd08
Lochton GB 7 Ed09
Lochuisge GB 6 Db10
Lochvycja UA 202 Ed14
Lochwinnoch GB 10 Dd13
Ločica pri Vranskem SLO 151 Fc57
Loćika SRB 178 Bc67
Lociki LV 115 Lc53
Lockenhaus A 145 Gb53
Lockerbie GB 11 Eb16
Locketorp S 103 Fb46
Lockne S 79 Fc31
Locknevi S 103 Ga49
Löcknitz D 120 Fb33
Locmaria F 27 Ea42
Locmariaquer F 27 Ea41
Locminé F 27 Eb40
Locoal-Mendon F 27 Ea40
Locorotondo I 162 Ha75
Locquémeau F 26 Dd37
Locquirec F 26 Dd37
Locri I 164 Gb83
Locronan F 27 Dc39
Loctudy F 27 Dc40
Loculi I 168 Cc76
Löddeköpinge S 110 Ed55
Loddin D 120 Fb31
Lødding N 78 Eb25
Loddon GB 17 Gb24
Lode GB 20 Fd25
Lodè I 168 Cc75
Lode LV 106 Kd47
Lode LV 106 La49
Loděnice CZ 136 Fb45
Löderburg D 127 Ea38
Lodersleben D 127 Ea40
Löderup S 111 Fb57
Löderups strandbad S 111 Fb57
Lodève F 41 Hc53
Lodi I 149 Cd60
Lødingen N 66 Fc17
Lødingen N 66 Fd13
Lodi Vecchio I 149 Cc60
Lodosa E 39 Ec58
Lödöse S 102 Ec48
Lodrino CH 142 Cc56
Lodrone I 149 Db58
Łódź PL 130 Hd38
Loeches E 46 Dc64
Lockton GB 16 Fb19
Loen N 84 Cd34
Loenen NL 117 Bc36
Lõetsa EST 97 Jd45
Løfallstrand N 84 Cb40
Lofer A 143 Ec53
Löffingen D 141 Cb51
Lófos GR 183 Bd79
Lofsdalen S 86 Fa34
Lofta S 103 Gb48
Loftahammar S 103 Gb48
Lofthouse GB 11 Ed19
Lofthus N 84 Cc39
Loftus GB 11 Fb18
Log RUS 203 Fd13
Loga N 92 Cb46
Logănești MD 173 Fc58
Logarska Dolina SLO 151 Fc57
Logatec SLO 151 Fb58
Lögda S 80 Gd27
Lögdeå S 80 Ha29
Loghill IRL 12 Bc23
Logi RUS 99 Ld40
Lognvik N 93 Da42
Logofteni MD 173 Fa56
Lógos GR 189 Ca84
Logovardi MK 183 Bb76
Logovo RUS 107 Ld48
Log pod Mangartom SLO 150 Ed57
Logrești RO 175 Cd64
Logron F 29 Gb39
Logroño E 39 Eb58
Logrosán E 51 Cb67
Løgstør DK 100 Db21
Løgstrup DK 100 Db23
Løgten DK 100 Dc23
Løgumgårde DK 108 Da27
Løgumkloster DK 108 Da27
Logvino RUS 113 Hd58
Lohals DK 109 Dd27
Lohärad S 96 Ha42
Lohberg D 135 Ed47
Lohéac F 28 Ed40
Lohfelden D 126 Da40
Lohheide D 118 Db35
Lohijärvi FIN 74 Jc19
Lohikoski FIN 91 Lc34
Lohilahti FIN 91 Lc34
Lohiluoma FIN 89 Ja32
Lohiniva FIN 68 Jc17
Lohiranta FIN 75 Kd19
Lohja FIN 98 Ka39
Lohjantaipale FIN 97 Jd39
Lohm D 119 Eb35
Lohmar D 125 Ca41
Lohmen D 128 Fa41
Löhnberg D 125 Cb42
Lohne D 117 Cc35
Löhne D 126 Cd37
Lohnsburg A 143 Ed51
Lohr D 134 Da44
Lohra D 126 Cc42
Lohsa D 128 Fb40
Lohtaja FIN 81 Jc27
Lohusalu EST 98 Ka42
Lohusuu EST 99 Lb43
Lohvanperä FIN 82 Kb27
Loiano I 149 Dc63
Loibltal A 144 Fb56
Loiching D 135 Eb49
Loima FIN 89 Jc37
Loimaa FIN 89 Jc38
Loimaankunta FIN 89 Jc38
Loiré F 28 Fa41
Loiri I 168 Cb74
Loisach A 143 Ec55
Loitsche D 127 Ea37
Loitz D 119 Ed31
Loivre F 24 Hc35
Loja E 60 Da75
Lojanice SRB 153 Jb62
Lojo FIN 98 Ka39
Lojsta S 104 Ha50
Løjt Kirkeby DK 108 Db27
Lokakylä FIN 82 Ka30
Lokalahti FIN 89 Ja38
Lokča SK 138 Hd46
Loke S 79 Fc31
Løken N 93 Ea41
Løken N 94 Eb42
Løkeng N 63 Hc08
Loket CZ 135 Ec44
Lokka FIN 69 Kb14
Løkken DK 100 Dc20
Løkken N 77 Dd31
Lokkiperä FIN 81 Jd28
Lokmanlı TR 187 Gb78
Loknja RUS 202 Eb10
Lökönen FIN 91 Lb36
Lőkösháza H 147 Jd56
Lokot RUS 107 Mb46
Lokot' RUS 202 Ed13
Łokowica PL 138 Jb45
Lokrume S 104 Ha49
Loksa EST 98 Kd41
Løksa N 67 Gb12
Lokuta EST 98 Kc44
Lokva HR 158 Gc66
Lokva SRB 159 Jb65
Lokvé SRB 174 Bc62
Lokve Lóqua SLO 151 Fa58
Løkvoll N 62 Ha10
Lollar D 126 Cc42
l'Olleria E 54 Fb69
Lölling A 144 Fc55
Lom BG 179 Cc67
Lom CZ 136 Fa43
Lom N 85 Db35
Lomas del Mar E 55 Fb72
Lomåsen S 79 Fc29
Łomazy PL 131 Kb37
Lombardore I 148 Bd60
Lomben S 73 Ja20
Lombez F 40 Ga55
Lombheden S 73 Ja20
Lomborg DK 100 Cd22
Lombreuil F 29 Ha40
Lombron F 28 Fd39
Lomci BG 180 Eb69
Lomello I 148 Cb60
Lomen N 85 Db37
Lomi LV 107 Lc51
Lomiai LT 113 Jd56
Łomianki PL 130 Jb36
Lomma S 110 Ed56
Lommel B 124 Ba39
Lommeland S 94 Eb44
Lom nad Rimavicou SK 138 Ja49
Łomnica PL 121 Gb34
Łomnica PL 128 Ga37
Lomnice CZ 135 Ec44
Lomnice CZ 137 Gd45
Lomnice nad Lužnicí CZ 136 Fc48
Lomnice nad Popelkou CZ 136 Fd43
Lomonosov RUS 99 Ma39
Lomonosov RUS 202 Ea08
Lomovo RUS 113 Jd58
Lompolo FIN 68 Jc14
Lompolo FIN 68 Jb16
Lomselenäs S 72 Gc24
Lomsjö S 79 Gb27
Lomträsk S 72 Ha22
Lomträsk S 73 Ja19
Łomy PL 122 Ja31
Lomy RUS 107 Ma48
Łomża PL 123 Jd33
Lonato I 149 Db59
Lønborg DK 108 Cd24
Lončari BIH 153 Hc61
Lončarica HR 152 Gd59
Londa I 156 Dd65
Londinières F 23 Gb33
London GB 20 Fc28
Londonderry = Derry GB 9 Cc16
Lone LV 106 La52
Lonevåg N 84 Ca38
Long S 102 Ed47
Longá GR 183 Bc80
Longá GR 194 Bb89
Longaníkos GR 194 Bc88
Longare I 150 Dd59
Longares E 47 Fa61
Longarone I 150 Eb57
Longbridge Deverill GB 19 Ec29
Longchamp F 35 Ka48
Longchaumois F 31 Jd44
Long Crendon GB 20 Fb27
Long Eaton GB 16 Fa23
Longeau F 30 Jb40
Longecourt-en-Plaine F 30 Jb42
Longega I 143 Ea55
Longeville-sur-Mer F 32 Ed45
Longford GB 16 Ed23
Longford IRL 9 Cb20
Longformacus GB 11 Ec13
Longhorsley GB 11 Ed15
Longhoughton GB 11 Fa15
Longi I 167 Fc84
Longkamp D 133 Bd44
Longmanhill GB 5 Ed07
Long Melford GB 21 Ga26
Longnes F 23 Gc36
Longno GB 15 Eb24
Longnor GB 16 Ed22
Longny-au-Perche F 29 Ga38
Longobucco I 164 Gc79
Longos Vales P 36 Ad58
Longpont F 24 Hb35
Long Preston GB 11 Ed19
Longra P 44 Ad60
Longré F 32 Fc46
Longriddry GB 11 Ec13
Longride GB 15 Ec20
Longroiva P 45 Bc62
Longset N 70 Fa20
Long Stratton GB 21 Gb25
Long Sutton GB 17 Fd24
Long Sutton GB 19 Eb29
Longtown GB 11 Eb16
Longué-Jumelles F 28 Fc42
Longueval-Barbonval F 24 Hc35
Longueville F 30 Hb38
Longueville-sur-Scie F 23 Gb34
Longuich D 133 Bc44
Longuyon F 24 Jb34
Longwy F 25 Jc34
Lonigo I 150 Dd60
Lonin N 78 Ea27
Löningen D 117 Cb35
Löningsberg S 87 Fd32
Łoniów PL 131 Jd42
Lonja HR 152 Gc60
Lonkan N 66 Fd13
Lönnånger S 88 Gc35
Lönneberga S 103 Fd49
Lönnskog S 94 Ed43
Lönsboda S 111 Fb53
Lønsdal N 71 Fd19
Lønset N 77 Dc32
Lønset N 77 Da31
Lons-le-Saunier F 31 Jc44
Lønstrup DK 100 Dc19
Lónya H 139 Kb49
Lonzac F 32 Fc48
Lõo EST 98 Ka45
Loobu EST 98 Kd42

Looe – Luzaga

Looe GB 18 Dc31
Loon op Zand NL 124 Ba38
Loon-Plage F 21 Gd30
Lõõpõllu EST 105 Jc47
Loos F 23 Ha31
Loosdorf A 144 Fd51
Loosdrecht NL 116 Ba36
Loose D 108 Db29
Lopadea Nouă RO 171 Da59
Lopar HR 151 Fc62
Lopare BIH 153 Hd62
Lopătari RO 176 Ec63
Lopatica MK 183 Bb75
Lopatino RUS 107 Ma47
Lopatino RUS 203 Fd11
Łopatki PL 122 Hc33
Lopatnic MD 172 Ed54
Lopatovo RUS 107 Ma46
Lopcombe Corner GB 20 Ed29
Lõpe EST 98 Ka45
Lopera E 52 Da72
Łopiennik PL 131 Kc40
Loppa N 63 Hb07
Loppersum NL 117 Ca33
Loppi FIN 90 Ka38
Loppula FIN 74 Ka23
Lopud HR 158 Hb69
Lopuhinka RUS 99 Ma40
Łopuszna PL 138 Ja46
Łopuszno PL 130 Ja41
Loqueffret F 26 Dd38
Lora de Estepa E 60 Cc74
Lora del Río E 59 Cb73
Loranca de Tajuña E 46 Dd64
Lorbé E 36 Ba54
Lörby S 111 Fc54
Lorca E 61 Ec73
Lorch D 133 Ca44
Lorch D 134 Da48
Lorcha E 55 Fc70
Lordolo P 44 Ad61
Lordosa P 44 Ba62
Lørenfallet N 94 Eb41
Lorentzer F 25 Kb36
Lorenzago di Cadore I 143 Eb56
Lorenzana E 37 Cc57
Lorenzana I 155 Da66
Loreo I 150 Ea61
Loreto I 156 Ed66
Loreto Aprutino I 157 Fa70
Lórév H 146 Hc54
Lorgues F 43 Kb54
Lorguichon F 22 Fc36
Lorica I 164 Gc80
Lorient F 27 Ea40
Loriga P 44 Ba64
Loriguilla E 54 Fa67
Lőrinci H 146 Ja52
Loriol-sur-Drôme F 34 Jb50
Lormaison F 23 Gd35
Lormes F 30 Hc42
Loro Ciuffenna I 156 Dd66
Lorquí E 55 Ed72
Lörrach D 141 Bd52
Lorrez-le-Bocage F 29 Ha39
Lorris F 29 Ha40
Lorsch D 134 Cc45
Lørslev DK 100 Dc20
Lorton GB 11 Eb17
Lorup D 117 Cb34
l'Orxa E 55 Fc70
Lörzweiler D 133 Cb44
Loś PL 130 Jb38
Los S 87 Fd35
Losa del Obispo E 54 Fa67
Los Alares E 52 Cd67
Los Alazdres E 60 Da75
Los Alcázares E 55 Fa73
Los Algarbes E 60 Cc73
Los Arcos E 39 Eb57
Losar de la Vera E 45 Cb65
Los Arejos E 61 Ec74
Los Arenales E 59 Cb74
Los Ausines E 38 Dc58
Los Badalejos E 59 Ca77
Los Barrios E 59 Ca78
Los Barrios de Luna E 37 Cb56
Los Bayos E 37 Cb56
Los Belmontes E 53 Eb71
Los Belones E 55 Fb74
Los Blázquez E 51 Cb70
Los Caños E 59 Bd77
Los Castaños E 61 Eb75
Los Centenaros E 61 Ea72
Los Cerezos E 54 Fa66
Los Cerralbos E 52 Da66
Los Clementes E 61 Dd76
Los Corrales E 60 Cc75
Los Corrales de Buelna E 38 Db55
Los Cortijos de Arriba E 52 Db68
Loscos E 47 Fa62
Los Dolores E 55 Fa73
Losenstein A 144 Fb52
Los Escoriales E 52 Db71
Los Estrechos E 61 Ec74
Løsetdalen N 86 Ec36
Łosewo PL 123 Jd33
Los Gallardos E 61 Ec75
Los Guadalperales E 51 Cb68
Los Guiraos E 61 Eb74
Losheim am See D 133 Bc45
Los Hinojoso E 53 Ea67
Losi RUS 107 Ma49
Łosice PL 131 Kb36
Losicy RUS 99 Ma44
Losilla E 54 Fa66
Łosinka PL 123 Kc34
Łosino PL 121 Gc30
Los Isidros E 54 Ed68
Los Jinetes E 59 Ca73
Loskeran IRL 13 Ca25
Loškovicy RUS 99 Ma40
Los Lobos E 61 Ec74
Los Maldonados E 55 Ed73
Los Molares E 59 Ca74
Los Molinos E 46 Db63
Los Monteros E 60 Cc77
Los Montesinos E 55 Fb72
Los Morones E 60 Dc76
Los Navalmorales E 52 Cd66
Los Navalucillos E 52 Cd67
Los Nietos E 55 Fb73
Løsning DK 108 Db25
Los Nogueroneses E 60 Da73
Los Ojuelos E 59 Cb74
Losomäki FIN 83 Lb29
Losovaara FIN 75 Kd23
Los Palacios y Villafranca E 59 Ca74
Los Pastores E 59 Cb78
l'Ospedale F 154 Cb72
Los Pedrones E 54 Fa68
Los Piedros E 60 Cd74
Los Pozuelos de Calatrava E 52 Da69
Los Rábanos E 47 Eb60
Los Rosales E 59 Ca73
Los Ruices E 54 Ed67
Lossa D 127 Ea40
Los Santos E 45 Cb63
Los Santos de Maimona E 51 Bd70
Loßburg D 133 Cb49
Losse F 40 Fc52
Losser NL 117 Ca36
Losset IRL 9 Cb15
Lossiemouth GB 5 Eb07
Los Silos E 59 Bc72
Lößnitz D 135 Ec43
Los Tablones E 60 Dc76
Lostallo CH 142 Cc56
Loštice CZ 137 Gc45
Los Tonosas E 61 Eb74
Los Tuelas E 55 Ed73
Lostwithiel GB 18 Dc31
Los Villaesteres E 45 Cc60
Los Villares E 60 Db73
Los Villares E 60 Da74
Los Yébenes E 52 Db67
Los Yesos E 61 Eb75
Löt S 96 Gc43
Löt S 103 Gb51
Lote N 84 Cc34
Løten N 86 Eb38
Lothmore GB 5 Eb06
Lotlax FIN 81 Ja30
Lotorp S 95 Ga45
Lotošino RUS 202 Ed10
Lotovicy RUS 107 Mb50
Lotte D 117 Cb36
Lottefors S 87 Ga36
Löttorp S 104 Gc51
Lottum NL 125 Bc39
Lotyń PL 121 Gc33
Lotzorai I 169 Cc77
Louans F 29 Ga42
Louargat F 26 Ea38
Loubillé F 32 Fc46
Loučeň CZ 136 Fc44
Louchats F 32 Fb51
Loučka CZ 137 Ha46
Loučná Hora CZ 136 Fd44
Loučná nad Desnou CZ 137 Gc44
Loudéac F 27 Eb39
Loudun F 28 Fd43
Loué F 28 Fc40
Loue FIN 74 Jd20
Louejärvi FIN 74 Jd19
Louejoki FIN 74 Jd19
Loughanavally IRL 9 Cb20
Loughborough GB 16 Fa24
Lougher IRL 12 Ba24
Loughglinn IRL 8 Bd19
Lough Gowna IRL 9 Cb19
Loughlinstown IRL 13 Cd22
Loughmoe IRL 13 Ca23
Loughrea IRL 12 Bd21
Loughton GB 20 Fd27
Lougratte F 33 Ga51
Loúha GR 188 Ac86
Louhans F 30 Jb44
Louhioja FIN 83 Ld29
Louhivaara FIN 83 Ma28
Louisburgh IRL 8 Bb19
Loukás GR 194 Bc87
Loukee FIN 90 La33
Loukinainen FIN 97 Jb39
Loukíssia GR 189 Cb85
Loukkojärvi FIN 74 Ka23
Loukunvaara FIN 91 Ma32
Loukusa FIN 75 Kd21
Loulans F 31 Jd41
Loulay F 32 Fb46
Loulé P 58 Ac74
Lõunaküla EST 98 Kb42
Lounovice CZ 136 Fc46
Louny CZ 136 Fa43
Lourdes F 40 Fc56
Louredo P 44 Ad61
Loures P 50 Aa68
Louriçal P 44 Ac64
Lourinhã P 50 Aa67
Lourmarin F 42 Jc53
Louro E 36 Ac55
Louro P 44 Ad60
Loúros GR 188 Ad82
Lourosa P 44 Ad61
Loury F 29 Gd39
Lousã P 44 Ad64
Lousa P 45 Bc61
Lousada E 36 Bb55
Lousada P 44 Ad60
Louth GB 17 Fd22
Louth IRL 9 Cd19
Loutrá GR 184 Cc76
Loutrá GR 184 Cc80
Loutrá GR 191 Ea84
Loutrá GR 194 Bb87
Loutrá GR 195 Cd88
Loutrá Edipsoú GR 189 Ca83
Loutrá Eleftherón GR 184 Cd78
Loutrá Ipátis GR 189 Bc83
Loutráki GR 183 Bc76
Loutráki GR 188 Ad83
Loutráki GR 189 Ca86
Loutra Kilinis GR 188 Ad86
Loutrá Smokóvou GR 189 Bc82
Loutrá Thermopilón GR 189 Bd83
Loutró GR 183 Bd78
Loutró GR 200 Cb95
Loutropigí GR 189 Bc82
Loutrópoli Thermís GR 191 Ea83
Loutrós GR 185 Ea78
Loútsa GR 188 Ac81
Loútsa GR 195 Cd87
Louvankylä FIN 89 Ja33
Louverné F 28 Fb39
Louvie-Juzon F 40 Fc56
Louviers F 23 Gb36
Louvigné-de-Bais F 28 Fa39
Louvigné-du-Desert F 28 Fa38
Louvois F 24 Hd36
Louvroil F 24 Hc32
Louze F 30 Ja38
Lovagny F 35 Jd46
Lövånger S 81 Hd26
Lovas HR 153 Hd60
Lövås S 80 Gd27
Lovasberény H 146 Hc53
Lövåsen S 79 Ga30
Lovászhetény H 153 Hc57
Lovászi H 145 Gc56
Lovászpatona H 145 Ha53
Lövberg S 71 Fc24
Lövberga S 79 Fd28
Lövberget S 95 Fc40
Lovćenac SRB 153 Ja59
Lovćić HR 152 Ha60
Loveč BG 180 Db70
Lovec BG 180 Dd73
Lovečkovice CZ 136 Fb43
Løvel DK 100 Db22
Lovelhe P 36 Ad58
Lovere I 149 Da58
Lövestad S 110 Fa56
Loviisa FIN 90 Kd38
Lovik N 66 Fd12
Løvik N 76 Cd31
Lovikka S 68 Hd16
Lovinac HR 151 Ga63
Lovinobaňa SK 146 Ja50
Lovisa FIN 90 Kd38
Lovište HR 158 Gd68
Lövliden S 79 Ga26
Lövnäs S 72 Gc20
Lövnäs S 79 Ga25
Lövnäs S 80 Gc27
Lövnäs S 86 Fa37
Lövnäsvallen S 86 Fa35
Lovni Dol BG 180 Dc71
Lövő H 145 Gc53
Lovoleto I 150 Dd62
Lovosice CZ 136 Fa43
Lovran HR 151 Fb60
Lóvreč HR 151 Fa61
Lovreć HR 158 Gd66
Lovrenc na Pohorju SLO 144 Fd56
Lovrin RO 174 Bc60
Lovrup DK 108 Da27
Lövsjö S 79 Fd25
Lövsjön S 95 Fc40
Løvskal DK 100 Dc23
Lövstabruk S 96 Gd40
Lövstalöt S 96 Gc41
Lövstrand S 79 Ga27
Lovund N 70 Ed20
Lövvik S 79 Ga27
Łówcza PL 139 Kc43
Löwenberg D 119 Ed35
Löwenberger Land D 119 Ed35
Lower Beeding GB 20 Fc29
Lower Boddington GB 20 Fa26
Lower Cam GB 19 Ec27
Lower Diabaig GB 4 Db07
Lower Killeyan GB 9 Da14
Lowestoft GB 21 Gc25
Lowgill GB 11 Ec19
Łowicz PL 130 Hd37
Łowicz Wałecki PL 120 Ga33
Low Row GB 11 Ec16
Łowyń PL 128 Ga36
Loxstedt D 118 Cd33
Loyers GB 7 Dd08
Loyettes F 35 Jc46
Löytänä FIN 82 Kb29
Löytö FIN 90 La34
Löytökylä FIN 74 Kb23
Löytölä FIN 83 Lb25
Löytövaara FIN 75 Kd20
Löytty FIN 90 Kd37
Löyttymäki FIN 90 Kb37
Lož SLO 151 Fb59
Lozarevo BG 181 Ec72
Lozari F 154 Cb68
Lozen B 125 Bb39
Lozen BG 179 Cc71
Lozenec BG 181 Ec72
Lozenec BG 181 Fa68
Lozhan AL 182 Ad77
Lozica BG 180 Dc69
Łozina PL 129 Gc40
Lozna RO 171 Da56
Lozna SRB 178 Bb67
Loznica BG 180 Eb70
Loznica BG 181 Fa68
Łożnica PL 120 Fc32
Loznica SRB 153 Ja62
Łoznik PL 122 Ja30
Lozorno SK 145 Gc50
Lozova MD 173 Fc57
Lozova UA 205 Fa15
Lozovac HR 157 Ga65
Lozovik SRB 174 Bc65
Lozovik SRB 174 Bc66
Lozoya E 46 Dc62
Lozoyuela E 46 Dc63
Lozzo di Cadore I 143 Eb56
Luaces E 36 Bc55
Luanco (Gozon) E 37 Cc53
Luaras AL 182 Ad78
Luarca E 37 Ca54
Lubaczów PL 139 Kc43
Lubań PL 128 Fd41
Lubāna LV 107 Lb50
Lubanie PL 121 Hb35
Lubanowo PL 120 Fc34
Lübars D 127 Eb37
Lubartów PL 131 Kb39
Lubasz PL 121 Gb35
Lubatowa PL 139 Ka45
Lubawa PL 122 Hd33
Lubawka PL 128 Ga42
Lübbecke D 126 Cd36
Lübben/Spreewald D 128 Fa38
Lübbenau/Spreewald D 128 Fa38
Lübbow D 119 Dd35
Lubcroy GB 4 Dd06
Lubczyna PL 120 Fc33
Lübeck D 119 Dd32
Lubenec CZ 135 Ed44
Lubenia PL 139 Ka44
Lubersac F 33 Gb48
Lubes LV 105 Jd49
Lubián E 37 Bd58
Łubianka PL 120 Fd35
Łubianka PL 121 Hb34
Lubiatów PL 128 Fd38
Lubiatowo PL 120 Fc34
Lubiąż PL 129 Gb40
Lubichowo PL 121 Ha32
Lubicz PL 121 Hb34
Łubiec PL 130 Jb37
Lubień PL 128 Fc37
Lubień PL 138 Ja45
Lubień Kujawski PL 130 Hc36
Lubieszewo PL 120 Ga33
Lubiewo PL 121 Ha33
Lubiewo Zalesie PL 120 Fb32
Lubimec RUS 99 Lc43
Lubin PL 120 Fb32
Lubin PL 129 Gb40
Lubiń PL 129 Gc38
Lubiń PL 129 Ha36
Łubin-Kościelny PL 123 Kb35
Lubiny PL 129 Ha38
Lubjaniki RUS 203 Fb10
Lubla PL 139 Jd45
Lublewo Gdańskie PL 121 Ha30
Lublin PL 131 Kb40
Lubliniec PL 129 Hb42
Lubliniec PL 139 Kc43
Lubmin D 120 Fa31
Lubnia PL 121 Gd31
Łubniany PL 129 Ha42
Łubnice PL 129 Ha41
Łubnice PL 138 Jc43
Lubniewice PL 128 Fd36
Lubno PL 120 Fc35
Łubno PL 121 Gb33
Łubno PL 121 Gc31
Łubno PL 130 Hc37
Lubny UA 202 Ed14
L'ubochňa SK 138 Hd47
Lubochnia PL 130 Ja39
Lubomierz PL 128 Fd41
Lubomierz PL 138 Ja45
Lubomino PL 122 Ja31
Luboń PL 129 Gc37
Luboradz PL 129 Gb41
Luborzyca PL 138 Ja44
Lubostroń PL 121 Ha35
Lubosz PL 128 Ga36
L'ubotín SK 138 Jc47
Lubotyń PL 129 Hb36
Lubowidz PL 122 Hd34
Łubowo PL 121 Gb33
Łubowo PL 129 Gd36
Lubraniec PL 129 Hb36
Lubrín E 61 Eb75
Lubrza PL 128 Fd37
Lubrza PL 137 Gd43
Lubsko PL 128 Fc39
Lübstorf D 119 Ea32
Lubstów PL 129 Hb37
Lubsza PL 129 Gd41
Lübtheen D 119 Dd33
Lubuczewo PL 121 Gc29
Luby CZ 135 Eb44
Łuby PL 121 Ha32
Lubycza Królewska PL 131 Kd42
Lübz D 119 Eb33
Lubzina PL 139 Jd44
Luc F 34 Hd50
Luc F 41 Ha52
Luca Cernii de Jos RO 174 Cb61
Lucainena de las Torres E 61 Eb75
Lucan IRL 13 Cd21
Lucaph MD 177 Fc61
Lúcar E 61 Ea74
Lucareț RO 174 Bd60
Lučatin SK 138 Hd48
Luçay-le-Malle F 29 Gb42
Lucca I 155 Da65
Lucena E 60 Cd74
Lucena del Puerto E 59 Bc74
Lucenay-le-Duc F 30 Ja41
Luc-en-Diois F 35 Jc50
Lučenec SK 146 Ja50
Luceni E 47 Fa60
Lucens CH 141 Bb55
Lucenza E 36 Bb58
Luče ob Savinji SLO 151 Fc57
Lucera I 161 Fd73
Lucéram F 43 Kd52
Lucey F 35 Jd46
Luché-Pringé F 28 Fd41
Lucheux F 23 Gd32
Lüchow D 119 Dd35
Luchów PL 139 Kb43
Luchy F 23 Gd34
Luciana E 52 Da69
Lučica SRB 174 Bc64
Lucień PL 130 Hd36
Lucieni RO 176 Dd65
Lucignano I 156 Dd67
Lucignano d' Arbia I 155 Dc67
Lucillos E 52 Cd66
Lučine SLO 151 Fb58
Lucito I 161 Fc72
Luciu RO 176 Ed64
Luciu RO 177 Fa65
Luc'k UA 204 Ea15
Lucka D 127 Eb41
Luckau D 128 Fa38
Luckenbach D 125 Cb42
Luckenwalde D 127 Ed38
Lucker GB 11 Fa14
Lucksta S 87 Gb34
Lückstedt D 119 Ea35
Lúčky SK 138 Hd47
Lucmau F 40 Fc52
Luco dei Marsi I 160 Ed71
Luçon F 32 Fa45
Luc-sur-Mer F 22 Fc35
Ludanice SK 137 Hb49
Ludborough GB 17 Fc21
Ludbreg HR 152 Gc57
Lüdelsen D 119 Dd35
Lüdenhausen D 126 Cd37
Lüdenscheid D 125 Ca40
Lüder D 118 Dc35
Lüderitz D 127 Ea36
Lüderode, Weißenborn- D 126 Dc39
Lüdersdorf D 119 Dd32
Ludești RO 176 Dd64
Ludford GB 17 Fc22
Ludgershall GB 20 Ed29
Ludgershall GB 20 Fb27
Ludgo S 96 Gc45
Ludiente E 54 Fc66
Lüdinghausen D 125 Ca38
Ludlow GB 15 Eb25
Ludogorci BG 181 Ec69
Ludomy PL 121 Gc35
Luduș RO 175 Da61
Luduș RO 171 Db59
Ludvigsborg S 110 Fa55
Ludvika S 95 Fd41
Ludwigsburg D 134 Cd48
Ludwigsfelde D 127 Ed37
Ludwigshafen D 142 Cc51
Ludwigshafen a. Rh. D 133 Cb46
Ludwigslust D 119 Ea33
Ludwigsstadt D 135 Dd43
Ludwigswinkel D 133 Ca47
Ludwin PL 131 Kb39
Ludza LV 107 Ld51
Lüe F 39 Fa52
Luesia E 39 Fa58
Luesma E 47 Fa62
Lueta RO 176 Ea60
Lug BIH 159 Hc68
Lug HR 153 Hc59
Lug RUS 107 Mb46
Luga RUS 99 Mb43
Luga RUS 202 Ea09
Lugagnano Val d'Arda I 149 Cd61
Lugán E 37 Cc56
Lugano CH 149 Cc57
Lugasu de Jos RO 170 Cb57
Lugaži LV 106 La47
Lügde D 126 Da38
Lüge D 119 Ea35
Lugendorf A 144 Fd50
Ługi PL 122 Hd34
Luglon F 39 Fb53
Lugnano in Teverina I 156 Ea69
Lugnås S 102 Fa46
Lugnvik S 80 Gc31
Lugny F 30 Jb44
Lugo E 36 Bb55
Lugo I 149 Db63
Lugo I 150 Ea63
Lugo de Llanera E 37 Cc54
Lugoj RO 174 Ca61
Lugomerci SRB 153 Hd59
Lugones E 37 Cb54
Lugovoe RUS 113 Ja59
Lugovskoe RUS 99 Ma42
Lugros E 60 Dc75
Lugton GB 10 Dd13
Luh RUS 203 Fb09
Luhačovice CZ 137 Ha47
Luhalahti FIN 89 Jc35
Luhamaa EST 107 Lc47
Luhanka FIN 90 Kc34
Luhans'k UA 203 Fb14
Luhe-Wildenau D 135 Eb46
Lühmannsdorf D 120 Fa31
Luhovicy RUS 203 Fa10
Luhtaanmaa FIN 90 Kc36
Luhtanen FIN 90 Kd35
Luhtapohja FIN 83 Ma30
Luhtikylä FIN 90 Kc37
Luib GB 4 Db08
Luica RO 181 Ec67
Luidja EST 97 Jc44
Luige EST 98 Kb42
Luigny F 29 Gb39
Luik = Liège B 124 Ba41
Luikonlahti FIN 83 Lb30
Luimneach IRL 12 Bd23
Luino I 148 Cb57
Luintra (Nogueira de Ramuín) E 36 Bb57
Luiro FIN 69 Kb16
Luisant F 29 Gb38
Luisenthal D 126 Dc42
Luizi Călugăra RO 172 Ed59
Lújar E 60 Dc76
Luka BIH 158 Hb66
Luka HR 157 Fd65
Luka SRB 174 Ca66
Lukač HR 152 Gd58
Luka nad Jihlavou CZ 136 Ga47
Lukanja SLO 144 Fd56
Luka Pokupska HR 151 Ga59
Lukare SRB 178 Ba69
Lukaši RUS 99 Mb40
Lukavac BIH 153 Hc62
Lukavci SLO 145 Gb56
Lukavec CZ 136 Fc46
Łukawiec PL 139 Kc43
Luke MK 179 Ca72
Lukeswell IRL 13 Cb24
Lukićevo SRB 153 Jc60
Lukićevo SRB 174 Bb62
Lukinić Brdo HR 151 Ga59
Lukkaroistenperä FIN 81 Jd25
Luknės LT 113 Jb53
Lukojanov RUS 203 Fc10
Lukovica SLO 151 Fc57
Lukovica SRB 174 Bc66
Lukovit BG 179 Da70
Lukovnikovo RUS 202 Ec10
Lukovo BG 179 Cc71
Lukovo HR 151 Fc62
Lukovo MK 182 Ad75
Lukovo MNE 159 Hd68
Lukovo SRB 178 Bb69
Lukovo SRB 178 Bd67
Lukovo Šugarje HR 151 Fd63
Łuków PL 131 Ka37
Łukowa PL 130 Jb42
Łukowa PL 131 Kc42
Łukowica PL 138 Jb45
Łukowisko PL 131 Kb37
Łukowo PL 122 Jb35
Łukowo PL 129 Gc36
Lukšiai LT 114 Ka57
Lukštai LT 114 La53
Łukta PL 122 Hd32
Luktvatnet N 70 Fa21
Lula I 168 Cb75
Luleå S 73 Hd22
Lüleburgaz TR 185 Ed76
Lüllemäe EST 106 La47
Lullymore IRL 13 Cc21
Łułowo PL 121 Gd33
Lümanda EST 105 Jb46
Lumasi AL 182 Ac76
Lumbarda HR 158 Gd68
Lumbier E 39 Ed57
Lumbrales E 45 Bd62
Lumbrein CH 142 Cc55
Lumbres F 23 Gd31
Lumby DK 108 Dc26
Lumes F 24 Ja33
Lumezzane I 149 Da59
Lumijoki FIN 74 Ka24
Lumikylä FIN 82 Kd25
Lumimetsä FIN 82 Ka26
Lumina RO 181 Fc67
Lumio F 154 Ca69
Lummelunda S 104 Ha49
Lummen B 124 Ba40
Lummukka FIN 81 Jc30
Lumparland FIN 96 Hc41
Lumpiaque E 47 Ed60
Lumpzig D 127 Eb41
Lumsås DK 109 Ea25
Lumsheden S 95 Ga39
Lun HR 151 Fc62
Luna E 47 Fa59
Lunano I 156 Eb65
Lunas F 41 Hc54
Lunca RO 170 Cb58
Lunca RO 171 Dc58
Lunca RO 172 Ed56
Lunca RO 175 Cc60
Lunca RO 180 Dc68
Lunca Banului RO 173 Fb59
Lunca Bradului RO 172 Dd58
Lunca Corbului RO 175 Dc65
Lunca de Jos RO 172 Eb59
Lunca de Sus RO 172 Eb59
Lunca Ilvei RO 172 Dd56
Lunca Mureșului RO 171 Da59
Luncavița RO 174 Ca63
Luncavița RO 177 Fb63
Luncoiu de Jos RO 175 Cc60
Lund DK 108 Db25
Lund N 78 Ec25
Lund N 92 Cb46
Lund S 110 Ed56
Lunda S 96 Gd42
Lundamo N 78 Ea31
Lundbjörken S 95 Fc39
Lundby DK 100 Db21
Lundby DK 109 Dd28
Lundby DK 109 Eb27
Lundby S 95 Ga43
Lunde DK 108 Cd25
Lunde DK 108 Dc26
Lunde N 67 Gc12
Lunde N 84 Cd34
Lunde N 85 Dd38
Lunde N 93 Db43
Lunde S 88 Gc32
Lundeborg DK 109 Dd27
Lundebyvollen N 86 Ec38
Lunden D 118 Da30
Lunden N 93 Db45
Lundenes N 66 Ga12
Lundersæter N 94 Ec40
Lunderskov DK 108 Db26
Lundsbrunn S 102 Fa46
Lundsjön S 79 Fc29
Lüneburg D 118 Dc34
Lunel F 42 Ja53
Lünen D 125 Ca38
Lunestedt D 118 Cd33
Lunéville F 25 Jd37
Lunevščina RUS 99 Lc44
Lunga MD 173 Fd57
Lungeni RO 172 Ed57
Lungern CH 141 Ca55
Lungești RO 175 Da65
Lungön S 88 Gd32
Lungro I 164 Gb78
Lungsjön S 79 Ga30
Lungsund S 95 Fb43
Lunguleţu RO 176 Ea65
Lunha MD 173 Fc55
Luninec BY 202 Ea13
Lunino RUS 113 Jd58
Lunino RUS 203 Fc10
Lunkkaus FIN 69 Kc16
Lünne D 117 Ca36
Lunneborg N 67 Gc11
Lunner N 85 Ea40
Lunning GB 5 Fa04
Lunow D 120 Fb35
Lunteren NL 116 Bb36
Lunz am See A 144 Fc52
Lunzenau D 127 Ec41
Luoba LT 113 Jc53
Luode FIN 89 Jc34
Luoftjok N 64 Ka06
Luogosanto I 168 Cb74
Luohua FIN 82 Ka25
Luohuan Ylipää FIN 82 Ka25
Luoke LT 113 Jd54
Luoma FIN 89 Jc32
Luoma-aho FIN 81 Jc30
Luomala FIN 82 Kb30
Luomankylä FIN 89 Ja33
Luonaala FIN 81 Ja31
Luonetjärvi FIN 90 Kb32
Luopa FIN 89 Jb32
Luopajärvi FIN 89 Jb32
Luopioinen FIN 90 Ka36
Luosto FIN 69 Kb16
Luosu FIN 68 Jb16
Luotakko FIN 82 Kb27
Luoto FIN 81 Jb28
Luotojärvi FIN 91 Lc32
Luotola FIN 91 Lb37
Luotolahti FIN 90 La35
Lupac RO 174 Ca62
Lupara I 161 Ga73
Łupawa PL 121 Gd30
Lupėnai LT 113 Jc57
Lupeni RO 172 Dd59
Lupeni RO 175 Cd62
Lupersat F 33 Gd46
Lupiac F 40 Fd54
Lupiana E 46 Dd64
Lupiñén E 48 Fb59
Łupków PL 139 Ka46
Luplanté F 29 Gb39
Lupogav HR 151 Fa60
Luppa D 127 Ec40
Luppoperä FIN 75 Kc23
Lupșa RO 171 Cd59
Lupșanu RO 176 Ec66
Lüptitz D 127 Ec40
Luque E 60 Da73
Luquin E 39 Ec57
Lur S 94 Eb45
Luras I 168 Cb74
Lurcy-Lévis F 30 Hb44
Lure F 31 Ka40
Lurgan GB 9 Cd17
Luri F 154 Cc68
Lurøy N 70 Fa20
Lurs F 42 Jd52
Lury-sur-Arnon F 29 Gd42
Lusanger F 28 Ed41
Lūšė LT 113 Jc53
Lüsen I 143 Ea55
Lüsens A 142 Dc54
Lusevera I 150 Ed57
Lushnjë AL 182 Ab76
Lusi FIN 90 Kc35
Lusiana I 150 Dd58
Lusignan F 32 Fd45
Lusigny F 30 Hc44
Lusigny-sur-Barse F 30 Hd38
Lusina PL 129 Gb41
Lusk IRL 13 Cd21
Luskovicy RUS 99 Mb40
Lus-la-Croix-Haute F 35 Jd50
Luso P 44 Ad63
Luson I 143 Ea55
Luspebryggan S 72 Ha18
Luspeholmen S 72 Gb24
Luss GB 7 Dd12
Lussac F 32 Fc50
Lussac-les-Châteaux F 33 Ga45
Lussac-les-Eglises F 33 Gb45
Lussan F 42 Ja52
Lussat F 33 Gd45
Lusta GB 4 Da07
Lustenau A 142 Cd53
Lustila FIN 89 Ja33
Łuszczów PL 131 Kb39
Łuszkowo PL 121 Ha33
Luszyn PL 130 Hd37
Lutago I 143 Ea55
Lutcza PL 139 Ka45
Lutepää LV 107 Ld46
Lütersheim D 126 Cd40
Lütfiye TR 186 Ga79
Lütfiye TR 191 Ed85
Luthenay-Uxeloup F 30 Hb43
Luthern-Bad CH 141 Ca54
Lutherstadt Eisleben D 127 Ea39
Lutherstadt Wittenberg D 127 Ec38
Lutin CZ 137 Gc46
Lütjenburg D 119 Dd30
Lütjensee D 118 Dc32
Lutocin PL 122 Hd34
Lutol Suchy PL 128 Ga37
Lutomiersk PL 130 Hc39
Luton GB 20 Fc27
Lütow D 120 Fa31
Lutowiska PL 139 Kb46
Lutówko PL 121 Gd33
Lutriņi LV 105 Jd51
Lutry PL 122 Jb31
Lütschental CH 141 Ca55
Lutsi N 92 Ca44
Lutta FIN 89 Ja37
Luttach I 143 Ea55
Lütte D 127 Ec37
Lutter am Barenberge D 126 Dc38
Lutterworth GB 20 Fa25
Lüttich = Liège B 124 Ba41
Lutuhyne UA 205 Fb15
Lututów PL 129 Hb40
Lutynia PL 129 Gc41
Lützelbach D 134 Cd45
Lützen D 127 Eb40
Lutzerath D 133 Bd43
Lützkampen D 133 Bb43
Lutzmannsburg A 145 Gc53
Lützow D 119 Dd32
Luujoki FIN 74 Jd21
Luukkola FIN 91 Lb35
Luukkonen FIN 91 Lb34
Luumäen kirkonkylä FIN 91 Lb36
Luumäki FIN 91 Lb36
Luupujoki FIN 82 Kc28
Luupuvesi FIN 82 Kc27
Luusniemi FIN 90 Kd33
Luusua FIN 74 Kb18
Luutalahti FIN 83 Ma31
Luutsniku EST 107 Lc47
Luvelahti FIN 82 Kd30
Luvia FIN 89 Ja36
Luvos S 72 Gd19
Luxaondo E 38 Ea56
Luxembourg L 133 Bb45
Luxeuil-les-Bains F 31 Jd40
Luxey F 39 Fb52
Luyando E 38 Ea56
Luyères F 30 Hd38
Luynes F 29 Ga42
Luz P 50 Ba70
Luzaga E 47 Eb63

Luzaide-Valcarlos – Mandelbachtal

Luzaide-Valcarlos E 39 Ed56
Lužani HR 152 Ha61
Luzarches F 23 Gd36
Luz de Tavira P 58 Ad74
Luže CZ 136 Ga45
Luzech F 33 Gb51
Luzern CH 141 Ca54
Luzianes P 58 Ab72
Lužice CZ 137 Gc48
Lužicy RUS 99 Ld40
Luz i Madh AL 182 Ab75
Luzino PL 121 Ha29
Luzki PL 131 Kb36
Lužki RUS 113 Jc59
Lužná CZ 136 Fa44
Lūžņa LV 105 Jb49
Łużna PL 138 Jc45
Luz-Saint-Sauveur F 40 Fc57
Luzy F 30 Hd43
Luzzara I 149 Db61
Luzzi I 164 Gb79
L'viv UA 204 Dd15
L'vovskoe RUS 113 Jc59
Lwówek PL 128 Ga36
Lwówek Śląski PL 128 Fd41
Lybiskiai LT 113 Jd56
Lybster GB 5 Eb05
Lychen D 119 Ed34
Lycke S 102 Eb48
Lyckeby S 111 Fd54
Lycksaberg S 72 Gc24
Lycksele S 80 Gd26
Lydbury North GB 15 Eb25
Lydd GB 21 Ga30
Lydersholm DK 108 Da28
Lydney GB 19 Ec27
Lyduokiai LT 114 Kd56
Lyduvėnai LT 114 Ka55
Lye S 104 Ha50
Lygna N 85 Ea40
Lygudai LT 114 Ka54
Lygumai LT 114 Kb54
Lykling N 92 Bd41
Lyly FIN 90 Ka34
Lylykylä FIN 75 Kd23
Lyman UA 203 Fa14
Lyme Regis GB 19 Eb30
Lyminge GB 21 Gb29
Lymington GB 20 Fa30
Lymm GB 15 Ec22
Lympia CY 206 Jc97
Lympne GB 21 Ga29
Łyna PL 122 Ja33
Lyndby DK 109 Eb26
Lyndhurst GB 20 Ed30
Lyndlich GB 19 Ec30
Lyne DK 108 Cd25
Lyne GB 11 Eb14
Lyneham GB 20 Ed28
Lyness GB 5 Ec03
Lyngby DK 100 Cd21
Lyngby DK 101 Dd23
Lyngdal N 92 Cc47
Lyngdal N 93 Dc41
Lynge DK 109 Ec25
Lyngerup DK 109 Eb25
Lyngmoen N 66 Fc15
Lyngså DK 101 Dd20
Lyngseidet N 62 Ha10
Lyngsjö S 111 Fb55
Lyngstad N 77 Da31
Lyngvoll N 84 Cd34
Łyniew PL 131 Kc38
Lynmouth GB 19 Dd29
Lynton GB 19 Dd29
Lyø By DK 108 Dc27
Lyoffans F 31 Ka40
Lyökki FIN 89 Hd38
Lyon F 34 Jb47
Lyons-la-Forêt F 23 Gb35
Lyöttilä FIN 90 Kd37
Lypci UA 203 Fa14
Lypova Dolyna UA 202 Ed14
Lyrestad S 95 Fb45
Łysaków PL 130 Ja42
Lysá nad Labem CZ 136 Fc44
Lysá pod Makytou SK 137 Hb47
Łysa Polana PL 138 Ja47
Łyse PL 122 Jc33
Lyse S 102 Eb47
Lysebotn N 92 Cb44
Lysekil S 102 Eb47
Lysi CY 206 Jc97
Lysice CZ 137 Gb46
Lyski PL 137 Hb44
Lyskovo RUS 203 Fc09
Lysnes N 62 Gc10
Lyšnicy RUS 99 Mb44
Lyso CY 206 Hd97
Łysomice PL 121 Hb34
Łysów PL 131 Ka36
Lysøysundet N 77 Dd28
Lyss CH 141 Bc53
Lystbæk DK 100 Cd23
Lysthaugen N 78 Ec29
Lystrup DK 108 Dc24
Lystrup Strand DK 101 Dd23
Lysvik S 94 Fa41
Lysvoll N 66 Ga14
Lysyčans'k UA 203 Fb14
Lysye Gory RUS 203 Fd12
Łyszkowice PL 130 Hd38
Lytham GB 15 Eb20
Lytham Saint Anne's GB 15 Eb20
Lythrodontas CY 206 Jb97
Lyttylä FIN 89 Ja35

M

Maakeski FIN 90 Kb36
Maalahti FIN 81 Hd31
Maalismaa FIN 74 Ka23
Maam Cross IRL 8 Bb20
Maaninka FIN 82 Kd29
Maaninkavaara FIN 74 Kd18
Maanselkä FIN 82 La27
Maaralanperä FIN 82 Kb27
Maardu EST 98 Kc42
Maarheeze NL 125 Bb39
Maaria FIN 97 Jb39
Maarianhamina FIN 96 Hc41
Maarianvaara FIN 83 Lb30
Maaritsa EST 107 Lb46
Maarja EST 99 Lb44
Maarn NL 116 Bb36
Maarssen NL 116 Ba36
Maas IRL 8 Ca16
Maasbracht NL 125 Bb40
Maasbree NL 125 Bc39
Maaseik B 125 Bb40
Maasmechelen B 125 Bb40
Maassluis NL 124 Ac37
Maastricht NL 125 Bb41
Määttälä FIN 81 Jd28
Määttälänvaara FIN 75 La19
Maavehmaa FIN 90 Kb37
Maavesi FIN 90 La32
Maavuskylä FIN 90 La32
Mablethorpe GB 17 Fd22
Macael E 61 Eb74
Maçaínhas P 44 Bb64
Maçanet de Cabrenys E 41 Hb58
Maçanet de la Selva E 49 Hb60
Mação P 50 Ad66
Măcăreuca MD 173 Fb54
Macau F 32 Fb49
Maccagno I 148 Cb57
Macchiascandona I 155 Db68
Macclesfield GB 16 Ed22
Macduff GB 5 Ed07
Mače HR 152 Gb58
Mace IRL 8 Bc19
Macea RO 170 Bd58
Maceda E 36 Bb57
Macedo de Cavaleiros P 45 Bc60
Maceira E 36 Ad57
Macerata I 156 Ed67
Macerata Feltria I 156 Eb65
Măceşu de Jos RO 179 Cd67
Măceşu de Sus RO 179 Cd67
Mac Gregor's Corner GB 9 Da16
Long Bennington GB 16 Fb23
Machault F 24 Hd35
Mâche CH 148 Bc57
Machecoul F 28 Ed43
Machern D 127 Ec40
Machliny PL 121 Gb33
Machocice Kapitulne PL 130 Jb41
Machowa PL 138 Jc44
Machrihanish GB 10 Db14
Machynlleth GB 15 Dd24
Mącice PL 122 Jb33
Maciejów PL 129 Hb41
Maciejowice PL 131 Jd38
Măcin RO 177 Fb64
Macinaggio F 154 Cc67
Macisvenda E 55 Fa71
Măciuca RO 175 Da64
Mackan GB 9 Cb18
Mačkovac BIH 153 Hc63
Mačkovci SLO 145 Gb55
Maćkowa Ruda PL 123 Kb30
Maclas F 34 Ja48
Maclodio I 149 Da59
Macomer I 169 Ca76
Mâcon F 34 Jb45
Macotera E 45 Cc63
Macqueville F 32 Fc47
Macroom IRL 12 Bc25
Macugnaga I 148 Bd57
Macure HR 157 Ga64
Maczków PL 128 Fc37
Mád H 147 Jd50
Madan BG 179 Cc68
Madan BG 184 Db75
Mädängsholm S 103 Fb47
Madara BG 181 Ec70
Madaras H 153 Hd57
Mădăraş RO 170 Ca57
Madariaga E 39 Eb55
Maddalena Spiaggia, la I 169 Ca80
Maddaloni I 161 Fb74
Made NL 124 Ad38
Madekoski FIN 74 Ka24
Madeley GB 15 Ec23
Maden TR 205 Ga19
Maderuelo E 46 Dc61
Madesimo I 142 Cd56
Madetkoski FIN 69 Ka14
Madières F 41 Hc53
Madiran F 40 Fc54
Madise EST 98 Ka43
Madiswil CH 141 Bd53
Madla N 92 Ca44
Madliena LV 106 Kd50
Madona LV 107 Lb50
Madonna di Campiglio I 149 Dc57
Madonna di Senales I 142 Dc55
Madonna di Tirano I 149 Da57
Madosca H 146 Hd55
Madra CH 142 Cc56
Mădrec BG 185 Ea74
Madrid E 46 Dc64
Madridejos E 52 Dc67
Madrigal de las Altas Torres E 46 Cd62
Madrigal de la Vera E 45 Cc65
Madrigalejo E 51 Cb68
Madrigalejo del Monte E 46 Dc59
Madrigueras E 53 Ec68
Mădrino BG 181 Ec72
Madrona E 46 Db63
Madroñera E 51 Cb67
Madsøygrenda N 70 Ec24
Mădulari RO 175 Da65
Madžarovo BG 185 Dd75
Madžiūnai LT 114 La58
Mäebe EST 105 Jc47
Mæbø N 92 Cd47
Mæl N 93 Db41
Maël-Carhaix F 26 Ea38
Mælen N 78 Ea28
Maella E 48 Fd62
Maello E 46 Da63
Mælum N 93 Dc44
Maenclochog GB 14 Dc26
Mäentaka FIN 97 Jc39
Maerdy GB 15 Ea23
Mære N 78 Ec28
Măerişte RO 171 Cc56
Maesteg GB 19 Ea27
Maestrello I 156 Ea67
Maestu E 39 Eb57
Mäetaguse EST 99 Lb42
Maevka RUS 113 Jc58
Mafalda I 161 Fc71
Maffe B 124 Ba42
Maffiotto I 148 Bc60
Mafra P 50 Aa68
Magacela E 51 Cb69
Magallón E 47 Ed60
Magaluf E 57 Hb67
Magaña E 47 Eb60
Maganey IRL 13 Cc23
Mağara TR 187 Gc78
Mağaraları TR 191 Ec82
Măgari EST 98 Ka44
Magasa I 149 Db58
Magašići BIH 153 Ja63
Magaz E 46 Da59
Magdala D 127 Ea41
Magdeburg D 127 Ea37
Magenta I 148 Cb59
Magerholm N 76 Cc32
Magerøystua N 64 Jb04
Magescq F 39 Fa54
Măgeşti RO 171 Cc57
Magganári GR 196 Db91
Maggia CH 141 Cb56
Maghanlawaun IRL 12 Ba25
Maghera GB 9 Cd16
Magherabane IRL 9 Cc15
Magherafelt GB 9 Cd16
Magheralin GB 9 Da17
Magheramason GB 9 Cc16
Magheramorne GB 9 Da16
Magherani RO 171 Dc59
Măgheruş RO 172 Dd58
Maghull GB 15 Eb21
Magione I 156 Ea67
Măgireşti RO 172 Ec59
Maglaj BIH 152 Hb63
Maglavit RO 179 Cc67
Maglebrænde DK 109 Eb28
Magleby DK 109 Ec28
Maglehem S 111 Fb55
Maglehøj Strand DK 109 Ea29
Măglen BG 181 Ed72
Magliano de'Marsi I 160 Ed71
Magliano in Toscana I 155 Dc69
Magliano Sabina I 156 Eb70
Maglić SRB 153 Ja60
Maglic SRB 178 Ba67
Maglie I 163 Hc77
Măgliž BG 180 Dd72
Magnac-Bourg F 33 Gb47
Magnac-Laval F 33 Gb45
Magnano I 148 Bd59
Magnant F 30 Hd39
Magnat-l'Etrange F 33 Gd47
Magnières F 25 Ka37
Magnillseter N 77 Ea33
Magnor N 94 Ec41
Magnuszew PL 130 Jc38
Magnuszowice PL 129 Gd42
Magny-Cours F 30 Hb43
Magny-en-Vexin F 23 Gc36
Mágocs H 152 Hb57
Magra S 102 Ed47
Magreglio I 149 Cc58
Magstadt D 134 Cc48
Magueija P 44 Ba61
Maguelone F 41 Hd54
Maguilla E 51 Ca71
Maguiresbridge GB 9 Cb18
Măgūnai LT 115 Lb57
Măgura RO 172 Ed59
Măgura RO 176 Ec63
Măgura RO 180 Dd67
Măgura RO 181 Fb68
Măgura Ilvei RO 172 Dd56
Măgurele MD 173 Fb56
Măgurele RO 176 Eb64
Măgureni RO 176 Ea64
Măgureni RO 177 Fb65
Măguri-Răcătău RO 171 Cd58
Magyarbóly H 153 Hc58
Magyarkeszi H 145 Hb55
Magyarmecske H 152 Hb58
Magyarszék H 152 Hb57
Magyarszentmiklós H 145 Gc56
Magyarszombatfa H 145 Gb55
Mahala MNE 159 Ja70
Mahdalynivka UA 205 Fa15
Maherádo GR 188 Ac86
Mahično HR 151 Fd59
Mahide E 45 Ca59
Mahilëv BY 202 Eb12
Mahlow, Blankenfelde- D 127 Ed37
Mahlu FIN 82 Ka31
Mahlwinkel D 127 Ea36
Mahmudia RO 177 Fd64
Mahmudiye TR 186 Ga80
Mahmudiye TR 191 Ea81
Mahmudiye TR 191 Ec83
Mahmudiye TR 192 Fb82
Mahmudiye TR 193 Gd83
Mahmutbey TR 186 Fc77
Mahmutköy TR 185 Eb78
Mahmutlar TR 199 Gd88
Mahmut Şevket Paşa TR 186 Fd77
Mahmut Şevket Paşa TR 186 Fd77
Mahnala FIN 89 Jc35
Mahnovka RUS 107 Mb47
Maholič BG 181 Ec71
Mahón E 57 Jb66
Mahon Bridge IRL 13 Cb25
Mahora E 53 Ec68
Mahovo HR 152 Gb59
Mahramlı TR 185 Ec78
Mähring D 135 Eb45
Mahtra EST 98 Kc43
Mahu EST 98 La41
Maia P 44 Ad61
Maiac MD 173 Ga57
Maials E 48 Ga61
Măicăneşti RO 177 Fa63
Maiche F 31 Ka41
Maida I 164 Gc81
Maida Marina I 164 Gb81
Maiden Bradley GB 19 Ec29
Maidenhead GB 20 Fb28
Maiden Newton GB 19 Eb30
Maidstone GB 20 Fd29
Maienfeld CH 142 Cd54
Maiern I 143 Dd55
Maieru RO 171 Dc56
Măieruş RO 176 Ea61
Maigh Chromtha IRL 12 Bc25
Maigh Cuilinn IRL 12 Bc21
Maigh Nuad IRL 13 Cd21
Maignelay-Montigny F 23 Gd34
Maijanen FIN 68 Jc17
Maijanen FIN 68 Jc17
Maikammer D 133 Cb46
Mailand = Milano I 149 Cc59
Mailat RO 174 Bc60
Maillas F 40 Fc52
Maillé F 32 Fb45
Mailley-et-Chazelot F 31 Jd41
Maillezais F 32 Fb45
Mailly-le-Camp F 24 Hd37
Mailly-Maillet F 23 Gd33
Mainar E 47 Ed62
Mainbernheim D 134 Db45
Mainbressy F 24 Hd34
Mainburg D 135 Ea49
Mainhardt D 134 Da47
Mainiemi FIN 90 Kd34
Mainistir Fhear Maí IRL 12 Bd25
Mainistir Laoise IRL 13 Cb22
Mainistir na Búille IRL 8 Ca19
Mainistir na Corann IRL 12 Bd26
Mainleus D 135 Dd44
Mainsat F 33 Ha46
Mainstockheim D 134 Db45
Mainstone GB 15 Eb24
Maintal D 134 Cc44
Maintenay F 23 Gc32
Maintenon F 29 Gc38
Mainua FIN 82 Kd26
Mainvilliers F 29 Gb38
Mainz D 133 Cb44
Maiori I 161 Fb76
Mairago I 149 Cd60
Mairena del Alcor E 59 Ca74
Maisach D 143 Dd50
Maisey-le-Duc F 30 Ja40
Maišiagala LT 114 La57
Maison-Neuve F 34 Ja51
Maison Pieraggi F 154 Cb70
Maison-Rouge F 30 Hb38
Maisons F 41 Ha56
Maisons-Laffitte F 23 Gd36
Maissau A 136 Ga49
Maisse F 29 Gd38
Maissin B 132 Ad43
Máistir Gaoithe IRL 12 Ba25
Maitenbeth D 143 Ea51
Maitoinen FIN 90 Kb38
Maivala FIN 75 Lb19
Maivala FIN 90 La34
Maizières F 22 Fc36
Maizières-lès-Vic F 25 Ka36
Maja HR 152 Gb60
Majadahonda E 46 Db64
Majadas E 45 Cb65
Majaelrayo E 46 Dd62
Majak Oktjabrja RUS 203 Ga13
Majakovo RUS 99 Mb45
Majakovske RUS 113 Jd59
Majaneque E 60 Cc72
Majava FIN 75 Kd20
Majavaoja FIN 68 Jb14
Majavatn N 70 Fa24
Majbølle DK 109 Eb28
Majdan PL 123 Jd35
Majdan RUS 203 Fd09
Majdan SK 138 Jc47
Majdan UA 204 Dd16
Majdan Królewski PL 139 Jd43
Majdan Nepryski PL 131 Kc42
Majdanpek SRB 174 Bd65
Majdan Radliński PL 131 Ka40
Majdan Sieniawski PL 139 Kb43
Majdan Stary PL 131 Kb42
Majilovac SRB 174 Bc64
Majkop RUS 205 Fd17
Majków PL 130 Jb40
Majori LV 106 Kb50
Majorskij RUS 205 Fd15
Majs H 153 Hc58
Majskoe RUS 113 Jd58
Majšperk SLO 151 Ga57
Majtum S 72 Ha20
Makariopolsko BG 181 Ec70
Makarovo RUS 203 Fc12
Makarska HR 158 Gd67
Makce SRB 174 Bc64
Mäkelä FIN 75 La19
Mäkelänperä FIN 89 Jc33
Mäkiänen FIN 89 Jc38
Makijivka UA 205 Fb15
Mäkikylä FIN 82 Kd29
Mäkipää FIN 82 Kb29
Makirráhi GR 189 Bc82
Makita EST 107 Lb46
Mäkitalo FIN 68 Jc16
Mäkkarkoski FIN 89 Jb38
Mäkkikylä FIN 89 Jd32
Mäkkikylä FIN 90 Kb33
Makkola FIN 90 Kc33
Makkola FIN 91 Lc33
Makkum NL 116 Bb33
Maklár H 146 Jb52
Makljenovac BIH 152 Hb62
Makmūnai LT 114 Kc59
Makó H 153 Jc57
Mąkoszyce PL 129 Gd41
Makov SK 137 Hb47
Makovac KSV 178 Bb70
Makovce SK 139 Ka46
Makovo BG 180 Eb70
Makovo MK 183 Bb76
Maków PL 130 Ja38
Maków PL 138 Ja43
Mąkowarsko PL 121 Gd33
Makowiska PL 121 Hb34
Makowiska PL 130 Hc41
Makowlany PL 123 Kb32
Maków Mazowiecki PL 122 Jb35
Makowo PL 122 Hd32
Maków Podhalanski PL 138 Hd45
Makrakómi GR 189 Bc83
Makreš Donji KSV 178 Bc71
Mákri GR 185 Dd78
Makríamos GR 184 Db78
Makrigialós GR 201 Dc96
Makrihóri GR 184 Da77
Makrihóri GR 189 Bc81
Makrinitsa GR 189 Ca82
Makriplágio GR 184 Da76
Makrirráhi GR 189 Ca82
Makrohóri GR 183 Bd78
Makrolívado GR 189 Bd83
Makrygialos GR 183 Ca78
Mäksa EST 99 Lb45
Maksamaa FIN 81 Ja30
Maksatiha RUS 202 Ed09
Makşempınar TR 186 Fc80
Maksniemi FIN 74 Jd21
Maksutlu TR 186 Fa77
Mäksy FIN 81 Jd30
Maksymilianowo PL 121 Ha34
Maksymilianowo PL 129 Gb37
Makušino RUS 107 Ma50
Makuži LV 107 Lc51
Mala IRL 12 Bc25
Malå S 72 Gd24
Malá E 60 Db75
Mala Bosna SRB 153 Ja57
Mala Buna HR 152 Gb59
Mala Čista HR 157 Ga65
Malacky SK 145 Gc50
Malá Domaša SK 139 Ka47
Maladzečna BY 202 Ea12
Malaf'evka RUS 99 Ld43
Málaga E 60 Cd76
Málaga del Fresno E 46 Dd63
Malagón E 52 Db68
Malagrotta I 160 Ea71
Malaguilla E 46 Dd63
Malahide IRL 13 Cd21
Malahvianvaara FIN 75 Lc23
Malaia RO 175 Da63
Mălăieşti MD 173 Fc56
Mălăieşti MD 173 Ga58
Mălăieşti RO 175 Cc62
Malaincourt F 31 Jc38
Málainn Bhig IRL 8 Bd16
Malaja Višera RUS 202 Eb09
Mala Kapela HR 151 Fd61
Malakása GR 189 Cc86
Malakássi GR 182 Ba80
Malăk izvor BG 185 Dd75
Mala Kladuša BIH 151 Ga61
Mălak Porovec BG 181 Ec68
Mălak Preslavec BG 181 Ec67
Malalbergo I 150 Dd62
Malá Morávka CZ 137 Gd45
Malandrino GR 189 Bc84
Målång S 79 Fc31
Malangen N 62 Gc10
Malangseidet N 62 Gd10
Malanów PL 129 Hb38
Mälarhusen S 111 Fb57
Malarrif IS 2 Ab03
Malaryta BY 202 Dd14
Mäläskä FIN 82 Kb25
Mala Subotica HR 152 Gc57
Małaszewicze PL 131 Kc37
Malaucène F 42 Jc52
Malåvännäs S 72 Gd24
Mala Vyska UA 204 Ed15
Mala Wieś PL 130 Ja36
Mała Wieś PL 130 Jb38
Malax FIN 81 Hd31
Malbekkvatnet N 65 Kc08
Malborghetto I 143 Ed56
Malbork PL 121 Hb31
Malborn D 133 Bd45
Malbouzon F 34 Hb50
Malbuisson F 31 Ka43
Mälby S 95 Ga41
Malča SRB 178 Bd69
Malcesine I 149 Db58
Mal'cevo RUS 113 Jc59
Malchin D 119 Ec32
Malching D 143 Ed50
Malchow D 119 Ec33
Malčice SK 139 Ka49
Malcoci MD 173 Fc58
Malcocinado E 51 Ca71
Malcontenta I 150 Ea60
Malcov SK 138 Jc46
Maldan TR 191 Ec84
Măldăreşti RO 175 Da63
Maldon GB 21 Ga27
Małdyty PL 122 Hd31
Måle DK 109 Dd26
Malé I 142 Dc56
Malechowo PL 121 Gb30
Male Drage HR 151 Fc60
Małe Gacno PL 121 Ha32
Máleme GR 200 Cb94
Malente D 119 Dd30
Malente D 119 Dd30
Male Pijace SRB 153 Jb57
Målerås S 103 Fd52
Máles GR 201 Db96
Malesco I 148 Cb57
Malesherbes F 29 Gd38
Malesina GR 189 Ca84
Malešov CZ 136 Fd45
Malestroit F 27 Ec40
Malesze PL 123 Kb34
Malevo BG 185 Dd74
Malexander S 103 Fd48
Malfa I 167 Fc82
Malga Ciapela I 143 Ea56
Malgaçmustafa TR 192 Fa87
Malgersdorf D 135 Ec49
Malgovik S 79 Ga26
Malgrat de Mar E 49 Hb60
Malhada Sorda P 45 Bc63
Malham GB 11 Ed19
Mālī LV 106 La50
Malia CY 206 Ja98
Mália GR 201 Db96
Malicorne-sur-Sarthe F 28 Fc40
Maliena LV 107 Lc48
Mali Idoš SRB 153 Ja59
Mali Izvor SRB 179 Ca68
Malijai F 42 Ka52
Mali Konjari MK 183 Bb75
Malilanniemi FIN 75 Lb24
Målilla S 103 Ga50
Mali Lošinj HR 151 Fb63
Malin IRL 9 Cc15
Malina BG 181 Fb69
Malin Beg IRL 8 Bd16
Málinec SK 138 Ja49
Malingsbo S 95 Fd41
Mălini RO 172 Eb56
Maliniec PL 129 Ha37
Malinniki PL 123 Kb35
Maļinovka LV 115 Lc53
Malinovka RUS 113 Jb58
Malinovka RUS 113 Jc58
Malinovo BG 180 Dc70
Malinovscoe MD 173 Fa55
Malinska HR 151 Fb61
Mali Ostros MNE 163 Ja71
Mali Požarevac SRB 174 Bb64
Maliq AL 182 Ad77
Malisensuo FIN 75 Kd22
Mališevo RUS 99 Ld45
Maliskylä FIN 82 Ka27
Mali Stapar SRB 153 Hd59
Mali Štupelj KSV 178 Ad70
Mali Štupelj SRB 159 Jc68
Maliuc RO 177 Fd64
Mali Vranjska SRB 153 Jb62
Malix CH 142 Cd55
Mali Zam SRB 174 Bd62
Maljala FIN 91 Lb34
Maljamäki FIN 97 Jc39
Maljasalmi FIN 83 Lb30
Maljasset F 35 Kb50
Maljiševo KSV 178 Ba71
Maljkovo HR 158 Gc65
Malkar TR 185 Ec78
Małkinia Górna PL 123 Jd35
Malki Văršec BG 180 Dc70
Malki Voden BG 185 Ea75
Malkkila FIN 91 Lb32
Malkoca TR 192 Fa85
Malkoçlar TR 185 Ec74
Malko gradište BG 185 Ea75
Malko Tărnovo BG 185 Ed74
Mal'kovo RUS 107 Mb51
Malko Vranovo BG 180 Eb68
Małkowice PL 139 Kb44
Mallaig GB 6 Db09
Mälläinen FIN 89 Jc37
Mallemort F 42 Jc53
Mallén E 47 Ed60
Mallersdorf-Pfaffenberg D 135 Eb49
Malles Venosta I 142 Db55
Mallıca TR 193 Gd84
Malling DK 108 Dc24
Malliß D 119 Ea34
Mallnitz A 143 Ec55
Mallow IRL 12 Bc25
Mallusjoki FIN 90 Kc38
Mallwyd GB 15 Ea24
Malm N 78 Eb28
Malmbäck S 103 Fb49
Malmberget S 67 Hb17
Malme N 77 Da31
Malmedy B 125 Bb42
Malmesbury GB 20 Ed28
Malmi FIN 98 Kb39
Malmivaara S 67 Hb17
Malmköping S 95 Gb44
Malmö S 110 Ed56
Malmön S 102 Eb47
Malmslätt S 103 Fd46
Mälmuiža LV 107 Lb49
Malmyž RUS 203 Fd08
Malnaş RO 176 Ea61
Malnate I 148 Cb58
Malnava LV 107 Ld50
Malnes N 77 Dc29
Malo I 150 Dd59
Maloarhangel'sk RUS 203 Fa12
Mal'oe Stremlenie RUS 99 Ld40
Małogoszcz PL 130 Ja41
Maloja CH 142 Cd56
Malojaroslavec RUS 202 Ed11
Malo Konare BG 179 Da73
Malo-les-Bains F 21 Gd29
Malo Malovo BG 179 Cb70
Małomice PL 128 Fd39
Malomir BG 180 Eb73
Malomirovo BG 185 Eb74
Malomožajskoe RUS 113 Jd58
Malónas GR 197 Fa93
Malonno I 149 Da57
Malonty CZ 136 Fb49
Malorad BG 179 Cd69
Malo Selo HR 151 Fc60
Malo Tičevo BIH 158 Gc64
Malounta CY 206 Jb97
Maløv DK 109 Ec25
Malovăt RO 174 Cb64
Malo Vukovje HR 152 Gc59
Małowidz PL 122 Jb33
Måløy N 84 Ca34
Malpaas GB 15 Eb23
Malpaga I 149 Cd59
Malpartida de Cáceres E 51 Bd67
Malpartida de Plasencia E 45 Ca65
Malpensado P 58 Ab72
Malpica de Arba E 39 Fa58
Malpica de Bergantiños E 36 Ad54
Malpica de Tajo E 52 Da66
Malpica do Tejo P 51 Bb66
Mālpils LV 106 Kd50
Malsătra S 96 Gd41
Malsch D 133 Cb48
Malschwitz D 128 Fb41
Målselv N 67 Gc11
Malsfeld D 126 Da41
Malšice CZ 136 Fb47
Mals im Vinschgau I 142 Db55
Malšín CZ 136 Fb49
Malsjö S 94 Ed43
Malsjöbodarna S 87 Fd33
Målsryd S 102 Ed49
Målsta S 79 Fc31
Malsta S 96 Ha42
Malta A 143 Ed55
Malta LV 107 Lc52
Maltarina BIH 158 Hb68
Maltat F 30 Hc44
Maltaverne F 29 Ha42
Maltby GB 16 Fa21
Maltby le Marsh GB 17 Fd22
Maltepe TR 185 Eb77
Maltepe TR 185 Ec80
Maltepe TR 191 Eb85
Malters CH 141 Ca54
Malton GB 16 Fb19
Maltträsk S 80 Ha26
Malu cu Flori RO 176 Dd63
Maluenda E 47 Ed62
Malujowice PL 129 Gd42
Malu Mare RO 175 Da66
Malung S 94 Fa39
Malungen N 94 Eb39
Malungen S 87 Gb34
Malungsfors S 94 Fa39
Malupe LV 107 Lc48
Măluréni RO 175 Dc64
Măluşteni RO 177 Fb60
Małuszów PL 128 Fd37
Małuszyn PL 130 Hd41
Malva E 45 Cc60
Malvaglia CH 142 Cc56
Malvaste EST 97 Jc44
Malveira P 50 Aa68
Malvinavas LT 115 Lb55
Malyj Sabsk RUS 99 Ma42
Malyn UA 202 Eb14
Mały Płock PL 123 Jd33
Malyševo RUS 203 Fb10
Mamadys RUS 203 Ga08
Mamaia RO 181 Fc67
Mamatlar TR 187 Hb78
Mambrilla de Castrejón E 46 Db60
Mambrillas de Lara E 46 Dd59
Mamer L 133 Bb45
Mamers F 28 Fd38
Mametz F 23 Ha33
Maminas AL 182 Ab74
Mamirolle F 31 Jd42
Mammendorf D 143 Dd50
Mamming D 135 Ec49
Mammola I 164 Gb83
Mamoiada I 169 Cb76
Mamone I 168 Cb75
Mamonovo RUS 113 Hd59
Mamuras AL 163 Jb72
Mamykovo RUS 203 Ga09
Måmyra N 78 Ea27
Maňa SK 145 Hb51
Manacor E 57 Hd67
Manamansalo FIN 82 Kc25
Manán E 36 Bc55
Mañaria E 39 Eb55
Manarola I 155 Cd64
Manasia RO 176 Ec65
Manasterz PL 139 Kb44
Manastir BG 181 Ed70
Manastir BG 184 Db75
Manastir BG 185 Dd74
Manastır TR 198 Fd90
Mănăstirea RO 181 Ec67
Mănăstirea Caşin RO 176 Ec60
Mănăstirea Humorului RO 172 Eb56
Mănăstirea Neamț RO 172 Eb57
Mănăstireni RO 171 Cd58
Manastirica SRB 174 Bd65
Mănăştiur RO 174 Ca60
Mănăştur RO 174 Bc60
Manavgat TR 199 Ha91
Mancera de Arriba E 45 Cc63
Mancha Real E 60 Db73
Manchecourt F 29 Gd39
Manchester GB 15 Ec21
Manching D 135 Dd49
Manchita E 51 Ca69
Manciano I 155 Dc69
Manciet F 40 Fd53
Mancılık TR 191 Ed81
Mandal N 92 Cc47
Mandanici I 167 Fd84
Mandas I 169 Ca78
Mandatoriccio I 165 Gd79
Mandayona E 47 Ea63
Mandelbachtal D 133 Bd46

Mandelieu-la Napoule – Massoult

Mandelieu-la Napoule F 43 Kc53
Mandello del Lario I 149 Cc58
Mandelsloh D 126 Da36
Mander NL 117 Bd36
Manderfeld B 125 Bc42
Manderscheid D 133 Bc43
Mandeure F 31 Ka41
Mandø DK 108 Cd26
Mándok H 139 Kb49
Mándra GR 184 Db77
Mándra GR 185 Ea76
Mándra GR 189 Cb86
Mândra RO 176 Dd61
Mandráki GR 197 Eb92
Mandre HR 151 Fc63
Mandria CY 206 Ja97
Mandrica BG 185 Ea76
Mandrikó GR 197 Ed93
Manduria I 162 Hb76
Mane F 40 Gb56
Mane F 42 Jd52
Manea GB 20 Fd25
Manebach D 126 Dc42
Măneciu RO 176 Ea63
Manent-Montaine F 40 Ga55
Manerba del Garda I 149 Db59
Manerbio I 149 Da60
Måneset N 78 Ec25
Mănești RO 176 Dd64
Mănești RO 176 Ea65
Manětín CZ 135 Ed45
Manevyči UA 202 Ea14
Mánfa H 152 Hb57
Manfredonia I 161 Ga72
Mangalia RO 181 Fc68
Manganeses de la Lampreana E 45 Cb60
Manganeses de la Polvorosa E 45 Cb59
Manganítis GR 196 Dd88
Mångbyn S 81 Hd26
Mangen N 94 Eb41
Manger N 84 Ca38
Mangskog S 94 Ed42
Mangualde P 44 Ba63
Manhay B 124 Ba42
Máni GR 185 Eb76
Maniago I 150 Eb57
Maniáki GR 183 Bc77
Manieczki PL 129 Gc38
Manikūnai LT 114 Kc53
Manilva E 59 Cb77
Maninghem F 23 Gc31
Manısa TR 191 Ed85
Manises E 54 Fb67
Manjärv S 73 Hb22
Manjärvträsk S 73 Hb23
Manjaur S 80 Ha25
Manjinac SRB 179 Ca68
Mank A 144 Fd51
Mankaičai LT 113 Jd56
Mankala FIN 90 Kd37
Mankarbo S 96 Gc40
Mańki PL 122 Ja32
Mankila FIN 82 Ka25
Mankūnai LT 114 Ka56
Manlleu E 49 Ha59
Manna DK 100 Dc20
Männamaa EST 97 Jc44
Mannersdorf Leithagebirge A 145 Gc51
Mannestad N 85 Ea40
Mannheim D 134 Cc46
Männikkö S 68 Hd17
Männiku EST 98 Kb42
Männiku EST 98 Kc44
Mannila FIN 89 Jb37
Manningtree GB 21 Ga26
Männistönpää FIN 68 Jb17
Mănoilești MD 173 Fb57
Manole BG 180 Db73
Manoleasa RO 172 Ed54
Manolovo BG 180 Dc72
Mañón E 36 Bb53
Manonville F 25 Jc36
Manoppello I 157 Fa70
Manorbier GB 18 Dc27
Manorhamilton IRL 8 Ca18
Manosque F 42 Jd53
Manowo PL 121 Gb31
Manresa E 49 Gd60
Månsåsen S 79 Fb31
Månsberg S 79 Ga27
Manschnow D 128 Fb36
Mansfeld D 127 Ea39
Mansfield GB 16 Fa22
Mansigné F 28 Fd40
Mansilla E 47 Ea59
Mansilla de las Mulas E 37 Cc57
Mansilla de las Mulas E 38 Dc58
Mansilla del Páramo E 37 Cb57
Manskivi FIN 90 Kb36
Mansle F 32 Fd47
Mansoniemi FIN 89 Jc34
Månsted S 102 Fa49
Månsträsk S 72 Gd23
Mansuè I 150 Eb58
Manta MD 177 Fb62
Mantamádos GR 191 Ea83
Mantasiá GR 189 Bd82
Manteigas P 44 Bb63
Mantel D 135 Eb46
Mantes-la-Jolie F 23 Gc36
Mantes-la-Ville F 23 Gc36
Mantet F 41 Ha58
Manthelan F 29 Ga42
Manthiréa GR 194 Bc88
Mantila FIN 89 Jb32
Mantiloperä FIN 89 Jd33
Mäntlahti FIN 91 Lb38
Mantorp S 79 Ga27
Mantorp S 103 Fd47
Mantoúdi GR 189 Cb84
Mantova I 149 Db60
Mäntsälä FIN 90 Kc38
Mänttä FIN 90 Ka33
Mantua = Mantova I 149 Db60
Manturovo RUS 203 Fb08
Mantviliškis LV 114 Kb55
Mäntyharju FIN 90 Kd35
Mäntyjärvi FIN 74 Jd18
Mäntyjärvi FIN 75 Kc20
Mäntyjärvi FIN 83 Lb29
Mäntylä FIN 82 Kc30
Mäntylahti FIN 82 Kd29
Mäntylänperä FIN 81 Jd25
Mäntyluoto FIN 89 Ja35
Mäntyvaara FIN 73 Jb19
Mäntyvaara FIN 83 Lc30
Mäntyvaara S 73 Hc18
Manuden GB 20 Fd27
Manuel E 54 Fb69
Manyas TR 192 Fa81
Mânzălești RO 176 Ec63
Manzanal del Puerto E 37 Ca57
Manzanares E 52 Dc69
Manzanares el Real E 46 Db63
Manzaneda E 36 Bc57
Manzaneda E 37 Ca58
Manzanedo E 38 Dc56
Manzaneque E 52 Db67
Manzanera E 54 Fa66
Manzano I 150 Ed58
Manzat F 34 Hb46
Manziana I 160 Ea71
Manziat F 34 Jb45
Mäo EST 98 Kd44
Maó E 57 Jb66
Maoča BIH 153 Hc62
Maothail IRL 9 Cb19
Maqellarë AL 182 Ad74
Maqueda E 46 Da65
Mar P 44 Ac59
Mara I 168 Bd76
Marac F 30 Jb39
Maracalagonis I 169 Ca79
Maracena E 60 Db75
Mărăcineni RO 175 Dc64
Mărăcineni RO 176 Ec64
Marainviller F 25 Ka37
Maramonovca MD 173 Fb54
Maranchón E 47 Eb62
Mărăndeni MD 173 Fb56
Maranello I 149 Db62
Maraneve I 167 Fc85
Maranhão P 50 Ad68
Marano di Napoli I 161 Fa75
Marano Lagunare I 150 Ec59
Marans F 32 Fa45
Maranville F 30 Ja39
Mărășești RO 176 Ed61
Marásia GR 185 Eb75
Mărașu RO 177 Fb65
Maratea I 164 Ga78
Marathiás GR 188 Bb85
Marathókambos GR 197 Eb88
Marathónas GR 189 Cc86
Marathópoli GR 194 Ba89
Marathoússa GR 184 Cc78
Marathovounos CY 206 Jc96
Marault F 30 Jb39
Maraye-en-Othe F 30 Hc39
Marazion GB 18 Da32
Marbach A 144 Fd51
Marbach A 144 Fd51
Marbach D 134 Cd48
Marbäck S 102 Fa49
Marbäck S 103 Fc48
Mårbacka S 94 Fa42
Mårbacken S 94 Ed41
Marbella E 60 Cc77
Marboué F 29 Gb39
Marboz F 34 Jb45
Marburg D 126 Cc41
Marburg = Maribor SLO 144 Ga56
Marby S 79 Fb31
Marca RO 171 Cc56
Marçà E 48 Ga62
Marcali H 145 Gd56
Marcaltő H 145 Gd53
Marčana HR 151 Fa61
Marcaria I 149 Db60
Mărcăuți MD 173 Fa53
Mărcăuți MD 173 Fd57
Marcé F 28 Fc41
Marceddì I 169 Bd78
Marcelová SK 145 Hb52
Marcena I 142 Dc56
Marcenat F 34 Hb48
Mărčevo BG 179 Cc68
March D 141 Ca50
March GB 17 Fd24
Marchagaz E 45 Ca64
Marchais F 24 Hc34
Marchamalo E 46 Dd64
Marche-en-Famenne B 132 Ba43
Marchegg A 145 Gc50
Marchenilla E 59 Cb77
Marchenoir F 29 Gb40
Marcheprime F 32 Fb50
Marchiennes F 24 Hb31
Marchin B 124 Ba42
Marchtrenk A 144 Fa51
Marchwiel GB 15 Eb23
Marciac F 40 Fd54
Marciana I 155 Cd68
Marciana Marina I 155 Cd68
Marcianise I 161 Fb74
Marciena LV 107 Lb50
Marcigny F 34 Hd45
Marcilla E 39 Ec58
Marcillac-la-Croisille F 33 Gd48
Marcillac-Vallon F 33 Ha51
Marcillat-en-Combraille F 33 Ha46
Marcilly-sur-Eure F 23 Gb37
Marcilloles F 34 Jb48
Marcilly-en-Gault F 29 Gc41
Marcilly-en-Villette F 29 Gd40
Marcilly-le-Hayer F 30 Hc38
Marcilly-sur-Seine F 24 Hc37
Marcinkonys LT 123 Kd30
Marcinkowice PL 129 Gd41
Marcinkowice PL 138 Jb45
Marcinowice PL 129 Gb42
Marciszów PL 128 Ga42
Marck F 21 Gc30
Marckolsheim F 31 Kc38
Marco E 36 Bb55
Marco de Canaveses P 44 Ba61
Marcoing F 24 Hb32
Mărculești MD 173 Fc55
Mărculești MD 173 Fc55
Mårdaklev S 102 Ed50
Mardal N 70 Ed23
Mardalen N 77 Db33
Mar de Cristal E 55 Fb74
Marden GB 20 Fd29
Mardilly F 22 Fd37
Mårdsel S 73 Hc20
Mårdsele S 80 Ha26
Mårdsjö S 79 Ga27
Mardsjö S 79 Fd30
Mårdsund S 79 Fb30
Mare DK 109 Dd27
Marebbe I 143 Ea56
Maredret B 124 Ad42
Mårem N 93 Db41
Marennes F 32 Fa47
Marentes E 37 Bd55
Maresfield GB 20 Fd30
Marettimo I 166 Dd84
Mareuil F 32 Fd48
Mareuil-en-Brie F 24 Hc36
Mareuil-sur-Arnon F 29 Gd43
Mareuil-sur-Lay F 28 Fa44
Mareuil-sur-Ourcq F 24 Hb36
Mar'evka RUS 203 Ga10
Marevo RUS 202 Eb10
Marezige SLO 151 Fa60
Marfa M 166 Eb87
Marga RO 174 Cb62
Margam GB 19 Dd27
Mărgăritești RO 176 Ec63
Margariti GR 188 Ac81
Margaritove RUS 205 Fc16
Margate GB 21 Gb28
Mărgău RO 171 Cc58
Margaux F 32 Fb49
Margecany SK 138 Jc48
Margès F 34 Jb49
Margetshöchheim D 134 Da45
Margherita di Savoia I 162 Gb73
Marghita RO 170 Cb56
Margina RO 174 Cb60
Marginea RO 172 Eb55
Mărgineni RO 172 Ec58
Mărgineni RO 172 Ed59
Margolles E 37 Cd54
Margon F 29 Ga38
Margone I 148 Bc60
Margonin PL 121 Gc35
Margraten NL 125 Bb41
Margretetorp S 110 Ed53
Marguerittes F 42 Ja53
Margueron F 32 Fd50
Margut F 24 Jb34
Marham GB 17 Fd24
Marhaň SK 139 Jd47
Marhanec' UA 205 Fa16
Marholm GB 17 Fc24
Mari CY 206 Jb98
Maria E 61 Eb73
Maria Alm A 143 Ec53
María de Huerva E 47 Fa61
Maria de la Salut E 57 Hc67
Maria Elend A 144 Fa56
Mariager DK 100 Dc22
Marialva P 45 Bc62
Mariana E 47 Eb65
Marianca de Jos MD 177 Ga60
Maria Neustift A 144 Fc51
Mariannelund S 103 Fd49
Marianopoli I 167 Fa85
Marianowo PL 120 Fd33
Mariánské Lázně CZ 135 Ec45
Maria Saal A 144 Fb56
Maria Schmolln A 143 Ed51
Maria Wörth A 144 Fb56
Mariazell A 144 Fd52
Maribáñez E 59 Ca74
Maribo DK 109 Ea29
Maribor SLO 144 Ga56
Marieberg S 95 Fd44
Marieby S 79 Fc31
Mariefred S 96 Gc44
Mariehamn FIN 96 Hc41
Marieholm S 102 Fa50
Marieholm S 110 Ed55
Marielund N 64 Ka06
Marielund S 72 Gc22
Marielund S 96 Gd42
Marielyst DK 109 Eb29
Marienbad = Mariánské Lázně CZ 135 Ec45
Mariënbad = Mariánské Lázně CZ 135 Ec45
Marienbaum D 125 Bc38
Marienberg D 127 Ed42
Mariënberg NL 117 Bd35
Marienfließ D 119 Eb33
Marienhafe D 117 Cb32
Marienhagen D 126 Da37
Marienheide D 125 Ca40
Marienmünster D 126 Da38
Mariental D 127 Dd37
Marienwerder D 120 Fa35
Mariés GR 184 Da78
Mariestad S 102 Fa46
Marifjora N 84 Cd36
Marigenta E 59 Bc73
Marigliano I 161 Fb75
Marignac F 32 Fb48
Marignane F 42 Jc54
Marigné F 28 Fb40
Marigny F 22 Fa36
Marigny-en-Orxois F 24 Hb36
Marigny-le Châtel F 30 Hc38
Marijampolė LV 114 Kb59
Marija na Muri HR 152 Gc57
Marijskoje RUS 113 Ja59
Marikostenovo BG 184 Cc75
Marín E 36 Ad57
Marina GR 183 Bc77
Marina HR 158 Gb66
Marina di Alberese I 155 Db69
Marina di Amendolara I 164 Gc78
Marina di Andora I 43 La52
Marina di Arbus I 169 Bd78
Marina di Ascea I 161 Fd77
Marina di Belmonte I 164 Gb80
Marina di Belvedere I 164 Ga79
Marina di Bibbona I 155 Da67
Marina di Camerota I 164 Fd78
Marina di Campo I 155 Da68
Marina di Caronia I 167 Fb84
Marina di Carrara I 155 Cd64
Marina di Castagneto-Donoratico I 155 Da67
Marina di Caulonia I 164 Gc83
Marina di Cecina I 155 Da66
Marina di Chieuti I 161 Fd71
Marina di Fuscaldo I 164 Gb79
Marina di Gairo I 169 Cc78
Marina di Ginosa I 162 Gd76
Marina di Gioia Tauro I 164 Ga83
Marina di Gioiosa Jonica I 164 Gc83
Marina di Grosseto I 155 Db68
Marina di Lago di Patria I 161 Fa75
Marina di Leuca I 165 Hc78
Marina di lu Impostu I 168 Cc74
Marina di Massa I 155 Da64
Marina di Minturno I 160 Ed74
Marina di Modica I 167 Fc88
Marina di Montemarciano I 156 Ed66
Marina di Montenero I 161 Fc71
Marina di Novaglie I 165 Hc78
Marina di Nova Siri I 162 Gc77
Marina di Orosei I 169 Cc76
Marina di Ostuni I 162 Ha75
Marina di Palma I 166 Ed87
Marina di Pescia Romana I 155 Dc70
Marina di Pietrasanta I 155 Da64
Marina di Pisa I 155 Da65
Marina di Pisciotta I 161 Fd77
Marina di Pulsano I 162 Ha76
Marina di Ragusa I 167 Fb88
Marina di Ravenna I 150 Ea63
Marina di San Vito I 157 Fb70
Marina di Sibari I 164 Gc78
Marina di Sorso I 168 Bd74
Marina di Strongoli I 165 Gd80
Marina di Torre Grande I 169 Bd77
Marina di Zambrone I 164 Gb82
Marinaleda E 60 Cc74
Marina Palmense I 157 Fa67
Marina Romea I 150 Ea63
Marina Schiavonea I 164 Gc79
Marina Serra I 165 Hc78
Marina Velca I 156 Dd70
Marinbrod HR 152 Gb60
Marine d'Albo F 154 Cc68
Marine de Sisco F 154 Cc68
Marinella I 166 Eb85
Marineo I 166 Ec84
Marines E 54 Fb67
Marines F 23 Gc36
Maringues F 34 Hc46
Marinha das Ondas P 44 Ac64
Marinha Grande P 44 Ab65
Marini I 165 Hc78
Marinka BG 181 Ed73
Marinkainen FIN 81 Jc27
Marino I 160 Eb72
Mar'insko RUS 99 Ld43
Mariotto I 162 Gc74
Maripérez E 53 Eb69
Mărișel RO 171 Cd58
Mărișelu RO 171 Dc57
Maritsá GR 197 Fa93
Mariupol' UA 205 Fb16
Marjaliza E 52 Db67
Märjamaa EST 98 Kb44
Marjan BG 180 Ea71
Marjanci HR 152 Hb59
Marjaniemi FIN 74 Jd24
Marjokylä FIN 75 Lc23
Marjoniemi FIN 90 Kc36
Marjoperä FIN 81 Jd30
Marjovaara FIN 83 Ma30
Marjusaari FIN 81 Jd29
Mark S 79 Ga26
Marka N 71 Fb18
Marka S 102 Fa47
Märkalne LV 107 Lc48
Markaryd S 110 Fa53
Markby FIN 81 Jb29
Mark Cross GB 20 Fd29
Markdorf D 142 Cd52
Markelo NL 117 Bd36
Market Bosworth GB 16 Fa24
Market Deeping GB 17 Fc24
Market Drayton GB 15 Ec23
Market Harborough GB 20 Fb25
Markethill GB 9 Cd18
Market Rasen GB 17 Fc22
Market Weighton GB 16 Fb20
Markfield GB 16 Fa24
Markgröningen D 134 Cd48
Markhausen D 117 Cb34
Marki PL 130 Jb36
Markina-Xemein E 39 Eb55
Märkisch-Buchholz D 128 Fa38
Markitta S 68 Hc17
Markivka UA 203 Fb14
Markkina FIN 68 Hd13
Markkleeberg D 127 Eb40
Markkula FIN 81 Jd27
Marklkofen D 135 Eb49
Marklohe D 118 Da35
Marklowice PL 137 Hb44
Marknesse NL 117 Bc34
Markneukirchen D 135 Eb43
Marko CY 206 Jc97
Markoldendorf D 126 Db38
Markop N 63 Ja06
Markópoulo GR 195 Cc87
Markovac SRB 174 Bb65
Markovac SRB 174 Bc65
Markovac SRB 174 Bb63
Markovo BG 180 Db73
Markovo BG 181 Ed70
Markovščina SLO 151 Fa59
Markov Sušica MK 178 Bb73
Markowa PL 139 Ka44
Markowice PL 121 Ha35
Markowo PL 122 Hd31
Markranstädt D 127 Eb40
Marksewo PL 122 Jb32
Marksuhl D 126 Db41
Markt Allhau A 145 Gb54
Marktbergel D 134 Db46
Markt Berolzheim D 134 Dc48
Markt Bibart D 134 Db45
Marktbreit D 134 Db45
Markt Einersheim D 134 Db45
Markt Erlbach D 134 Dc46
Marktgraitz D 135 Dd44
Marktheidenfeld D 134 Da45
Markt Indersdorf D 143 Dd50
Marktjärn S 87 Ga32
Marktl D 143 Ec50
Marktleugast D 135 Ea44
Marktleuthen D 135 Eb44
Markt Nordheim D 134 Db46
Marktoberdorf D 142 Db52
Marktoffingen D 134 Db48
Markt Piesting A 145 Gb52
Marktredwitz D 135 Eb45
Markt Rettenbach D 142 Db51
Marktrodach D 135 Dd44
Markt Sankt Florian A 144 Fb51
Markt Sankt Martin A 145 Gb53
Marktschorgast D 135 Ea44
Markt Schwaben D 143 Ea51
Marktsteft D 134 Db45
Marktzeuln D 135 Dd44
Markušica HR 153 Hc60
Markušovce SK 138 Jb48
Markutiškiai LT 114 Kc56
Markvarec CZ 136 Fd48
Marl D 125 Ca38
Marlborough GB 20 Ed28
Marle F 24 Hc34
Marlenheim F 25 Kb37
Marlishausen D 127 Dd42
Marloes GB 18 Db27
Marlow D 119 Ec31
Marlow GB 20 Fb28
Marly F 25 Jd35
Marly-Gomont F 24 Hc33
Marma S 96 Gc40
Marmagne F 30 Ja43
Marmande F 32 Fd51
Mármara GR 196 Db90
Marmara TR 185 Ed79
Marmaracık TR 186 Fa77
Marmaraereğlisi TR 186 Fa78
Marmári GR 190 Cd86
Marmári GR 197 Ec91
Marmaris TR 197 Fa91
Mármaro GR 191 Dd85
Marmav S 87 Gb37
Marmelete P 58 Ab73
Marmolejo E 52 Da72
Marmorbyn S 95 Ga44
Marmore I 156 Eb69
Marmoutier F 25 Kb36
Marnand CH 141 Bb54
Marnäs S 87 Fd38
Marnay F 31 Jc41
Marne D 118 Da31
Mårnes N 71 Fb18
Marnheim D 133 Cb45
Marnitz D 119 Eb33
Marnoch GB 7 Ec08
Maro E 60 Db76
Marœuil F 23 Ha32
Maroilles F 24 Hc32
Marola I 149 Da63
Maroldsweisach D 134 Dc44
Marolles-les-Braults F 28 Fd39
Maron F 25 Jd37
Maroñas E 36 Ac55
Marónia GR 184 Dc77
Maroslele H 153 Jc57
Marostica I 150 Dd59
Marotta I 156 Ec65
Maroufenha P 58 Ab72
Marovac KSV 178 Bc71
Marpingen D 133 Bd46
Marple GB 16 Ed21
Marpod RO 175 Db61
Marquartstein D 143 Eb52
Marquion F 23 Ha32
Marquise F 21 Gc30
Marradi I 156 Dd64
Marrasjärvi FIN 69 Jd17
Marraskoski FIN 74 Jd18
Marrault F 30 Hd41
Marrazes P 44 Ab65
Marrebæk DK 109 Eb29
Marroquin-Encina Hermosa E 60 Db73
Marroule F 33 Gd51
Marrubiu I 169 Bd78
Marrum NL 117 Bc32
Marrupe E 46 Cd65
Marsaglia I 149 Cc62
Marsais F 32 Fb46
Marsala I 166 Ea85
Maršal'skoe RUS 113 Ja58
Mărșani RO 179 Da67
Maršavicy RUS 107 Mb48
Marsberg D 126 Cd39
Marschacht D 118 Dc33
Marsciano I 156 Ea68
Marsden GB 16 Ed21
Marseillan F 41 Hc55
Marseillan-Plage F 41 Hc55
Marseille F 42 Jc55
Marseille-en-Beauvaisis F 23 Gc34
Marsh GB 19 Eb30
Marshfield GB 19 Ec28
Marsh Gibbon GB 20 Fb27
Marsia I 156 Ed68
Marsiconuovo I 161 Ga76
Marsicovetere I 161 Ga76
Marsiliana I 155 Dc69
Marsjärv S 73 Hd19
Marske-by-the-Sea GB 11 Fb18
Mars-la-Tour F 25 Jc35
Mårslet DK 108 Dc24
Marsliden S 71 Fd24
Mārsnēni LV 106 Kd48
Marson F 24 Hd36
Marssac-sur-Tarn F 41 Gd53
Marssum NL 117 Bc33
Märsta S 96 Gd42
Marstal DK 109 Dd28
Marston GB 16 Fb23
Marston Magna GB 19 Ec29
Marstrand S 102 Eb48
Marstrup DK 108 Db27
Marsvinsholm S 110 Fa56
Märsylä FIN 81 Jc27
Marszów PL 128 Fd39
Marta I 156 Dd69
Martainville F 23 Gb35
Martanesh AL 182 Ac74
Martano I 163 Hc77
Martebo S 104 Ha49
Martel F 33 Gc50
Martelange B 132 Ba44
Mártély H 146 Jb56
Mårtensboda S 80 Hc26
Martfeld D 118 Da35
Martfű H 146 Jb54
Mártha GR 201 Db96
Marthon F 32 Fd47
Martiago E 45 Bd64
Martignas-sur-Jalle F 32 Fb50
Martigné F 28 Fb39
Martigné-Briand F 28 Fc42
Martigné-Ferchaud F 28 Fa40
Martigny CH 148 Bc57
Martigny-le-Comte F 30 Ja44
Martigny-les-Bains F 31 Jc39
Martigny-lès-Gerbonvaux F 31 Jc38
Martigues F 42 Jc54
Martila FIN 97 Jc39
Martim Longo P 58 Ad73
Martin SK 138 Hc47
Martina CH 142 Db55
Martina Franca I 162 Ha75
Martiñán E 36 Bc54
Martin Brod BIH 152 Gb63
Martinci SRB 153 Ja61
Martinci Čepinski HR 153 Hc59
Martín de la Jara E 60 Cc75
Martín del Río E 47 Fa63
Martin de Yeltes E 45 Ca63
Martin Drove End GB 20 Ed30
Martinești RO 175 Cd61
Martinet E 40 Gc58
Martinganca P 44 Ab65
Mărtiniș RO 176 Dd60
Martín Muñoz de las Posadas E 46 Da62
Martinniemi FIN 74 Jd23
Martino GR 189 Ca84
Martinsberg A 144 Fd50
Martinšćica HR 151 Fb62
Martinsheim D 134 Db46
Martinsicuro I 157 Fa68
Martinskj HR 151 Fa61
Martinstown GB 9 Da16
Martizay F 29 Gb44
Martletwy GB 18 Db27
Martley GB 15 Ec25
Martna EST 98 Ka44
Martock GB 19 Eb30
Martofte DK 109 Dd26
Martonoš SRB 153 Jb57
Martonvaara FIN 83 Lc29
Martonvásár H 146 Hc53
Martorell E 49 Gd61
Martos E 60 Db73
Martragny F 22 Fb35
Martron F 32 Fc49
Mårtsbo S 96 Gc39
Mårtsviken S 86 Fa38
Martti FIN 69 Kc15
Marttila FIN 90 Kc37
Marttila FIN 98 Ka39
Martuzāni LV 107 Ld50
Maruflar TR 191 Ec84
Marugán E 46 Da63
Maruggio I 162 Ha76
Marum NL 117 Bd33
Marum S 102 Fa47
Marunowo PL 121 Gb35
Mărunței RO 175 Db66
Mārupe LV 106 Kb51
Maruševec HR 152 Gb57
Maruszów PL 131 Jd40
Marvão P 51 Bb67
Marvejols F 34 Hc51
Marvik N 92 Cb42
Marville F 24 Jb34
Marwałd PL 122 Hd33
Marwitz D 127 Ed36
Marxzell D 133 Cb48
Märy FIN 97 Jc39
Marybank GB 4 Dd07
Maryfield GB 5 Fa05
Marykirk GB 7 Ec10
Marynowy PL 121 Hb30
Marypark GB 7 Eb08
Maryport GB 10 Ea17
Mary Tavy GB 19 Dd31
Marzabotto I 149 Dc63
Marzahna D 127 Ec38
Marzamemi I 167 Fd88
Marzán E 37 Cb56
Marzęcice PL 122 Hc33
Marzell D 141 Bd51
Marzell D 141 Ca51
Marzewo PL 122 Hd31
Marzoa E 36 Ba55
Marzocca I 156 Ed66
Masa E 38 Dc57
Masahoca TR 191 Ed83
Masari CY 206 Ja96
Masarolis I 150 Ed57
Masboquera E 48 Ga63
Mascali I 167 Fd85
Mascalucia I 167 Fc85
Mascaraque E 52 Db66
Mas-Carbadès F 41 Ha55
Mas de Barberans E 48 Fd63
Mas de las Matas E 48 Fc63
Masegosa E 47 Ec64
Masegoso E 53 Eb70
Masegoso de Tajuña E 47 Ea63
Maselheim D 142 Da50
Måsenes N 64 Jc06
Maser I 150 Ea58
Masera I 148 Ca57
Masevaux F 31 Kb40
Masfjorden N 84 Ca38
Mas-Grenier F 40 Gb53
Masham GB 11 Fa19
Maside E 36 Ba57
Masi Måze N 63 Ja10
Maskaur S 72 Gc22
Maskjok N 64 Ka06
Masku FIN 97 Jb39
Maslacq F 39 Fb55
Maslarevo BG 180 Dd69
Masléon F 33 Gc47
Maslinica HR 158 Gb67
Mașloc RO 174 Bd60
Maslovare BIH 152 Ha63
Masłowice PL 130 Hd41
Masłowo PL 129 Gc38
Mas-Neuf-sur-Orb F 41 Hb53
Maso FIN 82 Kb31
Maso Corto I 142 Dc55
Masoúri GR 197 Eb90
Måsøy N 64 Jb04
Masquefa E 49 Gd61
Massa I 155 Da64
Massa d'Albe I 160 Ed71
Massa Finalese I 149 Dc61
Massa Fiscaglia I 150 Ea62
Massafra I 162 Gd76
Massagette F 33 Ha47
Massais F 28 Fc43
Massa Lombarda I 150 Dd63
Massa Lubrense I 161 Fb76
Massamagrell E 54 Fc67
Massa Marittima I 155 Db67
Massa Martana I 156 Eb68
Massarosa I 155 Da65
Massat F 40 Gb56
Massay F 29 Gd42
Maßbach D 134 Db44
Massenbachhausen D 134 Cd47
Masserano I 148 Ca59
Masserberg D 135 Dd43
Masseret F 33 Gc48
Masseria I 143 Dd55
Masseria Airili I 161 Fd73
Masseria Anzani I 162 Gb73
Masseria Candelaro I 161 Ga72
Masseria Cangiulli I 162 Gc75
Masseria Monaco Cappelli I 161 Ga72
Masseria Montanaro I 162 Gd75
Masseria Monte Panetteria I 161 Fd72
Masseria Petrulli I 161 Fd72
Masseria Stimpato I 167 Fc86
Masseube F 40 Ga55
Massford GB 9 Da18
Massiac F 34 Hb48
Massiaru EST 106 Kc47
Massignac F 33 Ga47
Massing D 143 Ec50
Massoult F 30 Ja40

Metamorfósi – Mo

Metamorfósi GR 195 Bd90
Metamórfossi GR 183 Ca76
Metamórfossi GR 184 Cc79
Metangítsi GR 184 Cc79
Meṭaparks LV 106 Kb50
Metaurilia I 156 Ec65
Metaxádes GR 185 Ea76
Metaxás GR 183 Bc79
Metelen D 125 Ca37
Meteliai LT 114 Kc59
Meteş RO 175 Cd60
Méthamis F 42 Jc52
Méthana GR 195 Ca88
Metheringham GB 17 Fc22
Methil GB 7 Eb12
Methlick GB 5 Ed08
Methóni GR 194 Ba89
Methven GB 7 Ea11
Methwold GB 20 Fd25
Metković HR 158 Ha68
Metlič SRB 153 Ja62
Metličina BG 181 Ed69
Metlika SLO 151 Fd59
Metnitz A 144 Fb55
Mętno PL 120 Fb35
Metodievo BG 181 Ec70
Metóhi GR 189 Cb84
Metóhi GR 189 Cc84
Metovnica SRB 179 Ca67
Mętów PL 131 Kb40
Metsäkansa FIN 89 Jd36
Metsäkantano FIN 83 Lb27
Metsäkylä FIN 75 Kd22
Metsäkylä FIN 90 La37
Metsälä FIN 75 Kc21
Metsälä FIN 89 Ja34
Metsämaa FIN 89 Jc37
Metsä-Muuronen FIN 91 Lb37
Metsküla EST 97 Jc45
Metslawier NL 117 Bc32
Métsovo GR 182 Ba80
Mettä Dokkas S 68 Hc17
Mettäjärvi S 74 Jb18
Mettälä FIN 90 Kd37
Metten D 135 Ec48
Mettenheim D 133 Cb45
Mettenheim D 143 Eb50
Mettersdorf am Saßbach A 144 Ga55
Mettevoll N 63 Hb08
Mettingen D 117 Cb36
Mettlach D 133 Bc45
Mettlen CH 141 Ca54
Mettmann D 125 Bd40
Mettmenstetten CH 141 Cb53
Metveit N 93 Da46
Metz F 25 Jd35
Metzeral F 31 Kb39
Metzervisse F 25 Jd35
Metzingen D 134 Cd49
Meucon F 27 Eb40
Meulan F 23 Gc36
Meung-sur-Loire F 29 Gc40
Meursault F 30 Ja43
Meuse F 31 Jc39
Meuselwitz D 127 Eb41
Meussia F 31 Jc44
Meuzac F 33 Gb48
Mevassvika N 78 Ed26
Meximieux F 34 Jb46
Mey GB 5 Eb04
Meydancik TR 205 Ga18
Meyenburg D 118 Cd33
Meyenburg D 119 Eb33
Meymac F 33 Gd48
Meyrargues F 42 Jd53
Meyrueis F 41 Hc52
Meysee F 34 Jb50
Meysey Hampton GB 20 Ed27
Meyssac F 33 Gc49
Meyzieu F 34 Jb47
Mézapos GR 194 Bb91
Mežāre LV 107 Lb51
Mežatites LV 107 Lb51
Mežda BG 180 Ea73
Mežden BG 181 Ed68
Mezdra BG 179 Cd70
Meždureč'e RUS 113 Jc59
Meždurečje RUS 113 Jd58
Meze F 41 Hc54
Mezek BG 185 Ea75
Mężenin PL 123 Ka34
Mézeray F 28 Fc40
Mézérial F 34 Jb45
Mežica SLO 144 Fc56
Mézidon-Canon F 22 Fc36
Mézières-en-Brenne F 29 Gb43
Mézières-sur-Issoire F 33 Ga46
Mézilhac F 34 Ja50
Mézilles F 30 Hb40
Mezimĕstí CZ 137 Gb43
Mézin F 40 Fd53
Mezit TR 192 Ga81
Mezitler TR 192 Fb82
Mezőberény H 147 Jd55
Mezőcsát H 146 Jc51
Mezőfalva H 146 Hc55
Mezőhegyes H 147 Jd56
Mezőhék H 146 Jb54
Mezőkeresztes H 146 Jc51
Mezőkomárom H 145 Hb55
Mezőkovácsháza H 147 Jd56
Mezőkövesd H 146 Jc51
Mezőladany H 147 Kb50
Mezőörs H 145 Ha53
Mézos F 39 Fa52
Mézos F 39 Fa53
Mezőszilas H 146 Hc55
Mežotne LV 106 Kb52
Mezőtúr H 146 Jc54
Mežvidi LV 107 Ld50
Mezzana I 149 Db57
Mezzano I 150 Ea63
Mezzojuso I 166 Ed85
Mezzoldo I 149 Cd57
Mezzolombardo I 149 Dc57
Mgarr M 166 Ea87
Miączyn PL 131 Kd41
Miajadas E 51 Ca68
Mialet F 33 Ga48
Mialet F 41 Hd52
Miały PL 120 Ga35
Mianowice PL 121 Gc30
Miasteczko Krajeńskie PL 121 Gc34
Miasteczko Śląskie PL 138 Hc43
Miastko PL 121 Gc31
Miastków Kościelny PL 131 Jd38
Miastkowo PL 123 Jd33
Miavaig GB 4 Cd05
Miazzina I 148 Cb57
Mica RO 171 Db57
Mica RO 171 Db59
Micaičiai LT 114 Ka54
Micăsasa RO 175 Db60
Micereces de Tera E 45 Cb59
Miceşti RO 175 Da60
Miceşti RO 175 Dc64
Miceştii de Câmpie RO 171 Db58
Michaelchurch Escley GB 15 Eb26
Michaelnbach A 144 Fa50
Michajlovskoe RUS 203 Fc09
Michal'any SK 139 Ka49
Michalin PL 121 Hb35
Michałkowo PL 122 Jb30
Michalová SK 138 Ja48
Michalovce SK 139 Ka48
Michałów PL 131 Kd42
Michałów PL 138 Jb43
Michałowice PL 129 Gd42
Michałowice PL 138 Ja44
Michałowo PL 123 Kc33
Michelau D 134 Db45
Michelbach A 144 Ga51
Michelbach D 134 Da47
Micheldorf in Oberösterreich A 144 Fb52
Michelfeld D 134 Da47
Michelsdorf D 127 Ec37
Michelsneukirchen D 135 Eb47
Michelstadt D 134 Cd45
Michendorf D 127 Ed37
Michery F 30 Hb38
Michnowce PL 123 Kb30
Michorzewo PL 129 Gb37
Michów PL 131 Ka39
Mičići SRB 153 Ja63
Mıcılar TR 192 Fb82
Mickai LT 113 Jb55
Mickelsträsk S 80 Hb27
Mickhausen D 142 Dc50
Mickleton GB 11 Ed17
Miclești MD 173 Fd57
Miclești RO 173 Fb58
Micula RO 171 Cd54
Mičurin BG 186 Fa74
Mičurinsk RUS 203 Fb12
Midbea GB 5 Ec02
Middelbeers NL 124 Ba38
Middelburg NL 124 Ab38
Middelfart DK 108 Db26
Middelharnis NL 124 Ac37
Middelkerke B 21 Ha29
Middels D 117 Cb32
Middelstum NL 117 Bd33
Middenbeemster NL 116 Ba35
Middenmeer NL 116 Ba34
Middleham GB 11 Ed19
Middlemarsh GB 19 Ec30
Middle Rasen GB 17 Fc22
Middlesbrough GB 11 Fa18
Middleton GB 21 Gb25
Middleton in Teesdale GB 11 Ed17
Middleton-on-Sea GB 20 Fb30
Middleton-on-the-Wolds GB 16 Fb20
Middletown GB 9 Cc18
Middletown GB 15 Eb24
Middle Wallop GB 20 Ed29
Middlewich GB 15 Ec22
Midgeholme GB 11 Ec16
Midhurst GB 20 Fb30
Midıklı TR 192 Fc85
Midleton IRL 12 Bd26
Midlum D 108 Cd28
Midlum D 118 Cd32
Midrevaux F 31 Jc38
Midskog S 79 Fd30
Midsomer Norton GB 19 Ec29
Midsund N 76 Cd32
Midtgård N 65 Kd07
Midtre Fingervatn N 64 Ka06
Midtskogberget N 86 Ec37
Mid Yell GB 5 Fa03
Miechów PL 128 Fd36
Miechów PL 138 Ja43
Miechów-Charsznica PL 138 Ja43
Miechucino PL 121 Ha30
Miecze PL 123 Ka32
Miedes E 47 Ed62
Miedes de Atienza E 47 Ea62
Miedzichowo PL 128 Ga37
Miedzna PL 131 Jd36
Miedźno PL 130 Hc41
Międzybórz PL 129 Gd40
Międzybrodzie Bialskie PL 138 Hc45
Międzychód PL 128 Ga36
Międzygórze PL 137 Gc44
Międzyleś PL 131 Kc37
Międzylesie PL 137 Gc44
Międzyrzec Podlaski PL 131 Kb37
Międzyrzecz PL 128 Fd36
Międzywodzie PL 120 Fc31
Międzyzdroje PL 120 Fb32
Miegėnai LT 114 Kc55
Miehikkälä FIN 91 Lb37
Miehlen D 133 Ca43
Miejsce Piastowe PL 139 Ka45
Miejska Górka PL 129 Gc39
Miekak S 72 Gb18
Miękinia PL 129 Gc41
Miekojärvi S 73 Ja20
Miękowo PL 120 Fc33
Mielagėnai LT 115 Lc55
Miélan F 40 Fd55
Mielec PL 139 Jd43
Mielęcin PL 121 Gb34
Mielęcin PL 130 Hc36
Mielenko Drawskie PL 120 Ga33
Mieleszyn PL 129 Gd36
Mielnik PL 131 Kb36
Mielno PL 120 Fd33
Mielno PL 120 Ga30
Mielno PL 128 Fc39
Mielno PL 129 Gd36
Mieluskylä FIN 82 Ka26
Mielżyn PL 129 Gd37
Mieming A 142 Dc53
Miemo I 155 Db66
Mień PL 123 Ka35
Miera E 37 Cc55
Mieraslompolo FIN 64 Ka08
Mierašluobbal FIN 64 Ka08
Miercurea-Ciuc RO 176 Ea60
Miercurea Nirajului RO 171 Dc59
Miercurea Sibiului RO 175 Da61
Mierczany PL 128 Fc37
Mieres E 37 Cc55
Mieres E 49 Hb59
Miereszyn PL 121 Ha30
Mierlo NL 125 Bb39
Mierojokka N 68 Hd11
Mieroszów PL 129 Gb42
Miersig RO 170 Ca57
Mieruniszki PL 123 Ka30
Mierzawa PL 130 Ja42
Mierzęcice PL 138 Hc43
Mierzyno PL 121 Gd29
Miesbach D 143 Ea52
Mieścisko PL 121 Gd35
Miesenbach A 144 Ga53
Miesenbach D 133 Ca46
Mieslahti FIN 82 Kd25
Mieste D 127 Dd36
Miesterhorst D 127 Dd36
Mieszków PL 129 Gd38
Mieszkowice PL 120 Fb35
Mietków PL 129 Gb41
Mietoinen FIN 97 Jb39
Miettinen FIN 89 Jc34
Mieza E 45 Bd61
Mieżaičiai LV 114 Kb55
Mieżiškiai LT 114 Kd55
Mifol AL 182 Aa77
Migennes F 30 Hc39
Migliarino I 150 Ea62
Migliarino I 155 Da65
Miglionico I 162 Gc76
Mignano Monte Lungo I 161 Fa73
Migné F 29 Gb44
Mignères F 29 Ha39
Miguel Esteban E 53 Dd67
Miguelturra E 52 Db69
Mihăești RO 175 Dc64
Mihăești RO 180 Dc67
Mihai Bravu RO 177 Fc65
Mihai Bravu RO 180 Ea67
Mihai Eminescu RO 172 Ec55
Mihăileni MD 173 Fa54
Mihăileni MD 173 Fa54
Mihăileni RO 172 Ea59
Mihăileni RO 172 Eb54
Mihăileni RO 175 Db61
Mihăileşti RO 176 Ea66
Mihăileşti RO 176 Ec65
Mihail Kogălniceanu RO 173 Fa57
Mihail Kogălniceanu RO 177 Fa65
Mihail Kogălniceanu RO 177 Fc64
Mihail Kogălniceanu RO 181 Fc67
Mihailovca MD 173 Fc56
Mihailovca MD 173 Fd55
Mihailovca MD 173 Fd56
Mihailovca MD 173 Fd59
Mihai Viteazu RO 171 Da59
Mihai Viteazu RO 177 Fc66
Mihajlov RUS 203 Fa11
Mihajlovac SRB 174 Bb64
Mihajlovac SRB 174 Cb65
Mihajlovka RUS 203 Fd13
Mihajlovo BG 179 Cd68
Mihajlovo BG 180 Dd73
Mihajlovo RUS 113 Jd58
Mihajlovo SRB 174 Bb61
Mihajlovskoe RUS 107 Mb49
Mihălăşeni MD 173 Fa53
Mihălăşeni RO 172 Ed55
Miháld H 145 Gd56
Mihalgazi TR 193 Gc81
Mihalıçcık TR 193 Ha81
Mihalkovo BG 184 Da74
Mihalț RO 175 Da60
Mihályfa H 145 Gd55
Mihas GR 188 Bb86
Miheşu de Câmpie RO 171 Db58
Mihkil EST 98 Kb45
Mihla D 126 Dc41
Mihnevo RUS 203 Fa10
Miholjska HR 158 Ha69
Mihovljan HR 151 Ga57
Miikkula FIN 91 Lc33
Miiluranta FIN 82 Kb27
Mijanès F 41 Gd57
Mijares E 46 Cd64
Mijas E 60 Cd76
Mijdrecht NL 116 Ba36
Mijoska SRB 159 Jb66
Mijoux F 31 Jd44
Mikaševičy BY 202 Eb13
Mikaszówka PL 123 Kb31
Mike H 152 Ha57
Mikeļtornis LV 105 Jc49
Miki GR 184 Db76
Mikicin PL 123 Kb32
Mikines GR 195 Bd87
Mikitamäe EST 107 Lc46
Mikkanen FIN 90 Kd35
Mikkelbostad N 67 Gb12
Mikkeli FIN 90 La34
Mikkelsnes N 65 Kc08
Mikkelvik N 62 Gd08
Mikkola FIN 69 Jd15
Mikkolanniemi FIN 91 Ld33
Miklavž na Dr. p. SLO 144 Ga56
Mikleuš HR 152 Ha59
Mikniūnai LT 114 Kb53
Mikołajki PL 122 Jc31
Mikołajki Pomorskie PL 122 Hc31
Mikolin PL 129 Gd42
Mikoliškiai LT 113 Jb55
Mikołów PL 138 Hc44
Míkonos GR 196 Db89
Mikorowo PL 121 Gd30
Mikorzyn PL 129 Ha40
Mikre BG 180 Db70
Mikrí Vólvi GR 184 Cc78
Mikró Dério GR 185 Ea76
Mikrókambos GR 183 Ca77
Mikrolímni GR 182 Ba77
Mikrolivado GR 182 Ba79
Mikromiliá GR 184 Db76
Mikró Monastíri GR 183 Bd77
Mikró Perivoláki GR 189 Bd81
Mikrópoli GR 184 Cd76
Mikstat PL 129 Ha39
Mikulov CZ 137 Gc49
Mikulovice CZ 137 Gd44
Mikytai LV 114 Kb57
Miladinovci MK 178 Bc73
Miłakowo PL 122 Hd31
Milano E 45 Bd62
Milano I 149 Cc59
Milano Marittima I 150 Eb63
Milanovo BG 179 Cc70
Milanovo BG 181 Ec70
Milanovo SRB 178 Bd70
Milanów PL 131 Kb38
Milanówek PL 130 Jb37
Milaş RO 171 Dc58
Milas TR 197 Ed89
Milašaičiai LV 114 Kb56
Milašiūnai LT 114 Kd56
Milatkoviće SRB 178 Ba68
Milatos GR 201 Db95
Milazzo I 167 Fd83
Milborne Saint Andrew GB 19 Ec30
Milcoiu RO 175 Db64
Milcov RO 175 Db66
Milcovul RO 176 Ed62
Mildenberg D 119 Ed35
Mildenhall GB 20 Fd25
Mıldı TR 192 Fd87
Mildstedt D 108 Da29
Miléa GR 182 Ba80
Miléa GR 183 Bc79
Mileanca RO 172 Ed54
Milehouse IRL 13 Cc24
Milejczyce PL 123 Kb35
Milejów-Wieś PL 131 Kb40
Milena I 166 Ed86
Miločevo SRB 153 Jb58
Milešov CZ 136 Fb46
Milešov CZ 136 Fa43
Mileşti MD 173 Fb57
Mileştii Mici MD 173 Fd58
Milestone IRL 13 Ca23
Mileszewy PL 122 Hc33
Miletićevo SRB 174 Bc62
Miletín CZ 136 Ga43
Miletkovo MK 183 Bd75
Mileto I 164 Gb82
Milevsko CZ 136 Fb46
Milewo Gałązki PL 123 Jd32
Milford GB 20 Fb29
Milford Haven GB 18 Db27
Milhars F 41 Gd52
Mili GR 195 Bd88
Miliá GR 185 Ea75
Miliá GR 194 Bc87
Miliá GR 194 Bc90
Milianni I 167 Fa84
Milice PL 137 Ha44
Milići BIH 159 Hd64
Milíčín CZ 136 Fc46
Miličinica SRB 153 Jb63
Milicz PL 129 Gd39
Miliés GR 189 Ca82
Milín CZ 136 Fa46
Milína GR 189 Cb82
Milino MK 183 Bc74
Miliotádes GR 182 Ad80
Milis I 169 Bd77
Milişăuţi RO 172 Eb55
Militello in Val di Catania I 167 Fc86
Milítsa GR 194 Ba89
Miljana HR 151 Ga58
Miljen BIH 159 Hd66
Miljević SRB 174 Bd64
Miljevina BIH 159 Hc66
Miljkovac SRB 178 Bd68
Miljutino RUS 99 Mb44
Milki PL 122 Jc31
Milkjovci BG 179 Cb71
Milkovica BG 180 Db68
Millancay F 29 Gc41
Millares E 54 Fb68
Millas F 41 Ha57
Millau F 41 Hb52
Millerovo RUS 203 Fc14
Millesimo I 148 Bd63
Millesvik S 94 Ed45
Millevaches F 33 Gd47
Millford IRL 9 Cb15
Mill Hill GB 20 Fc27
Millinge DK 108 Dc27
Millingen aan de Rijn NL 125 Bc37
Millisle GB 10 Db17
Millom GB 11 Eb19
Millport GB 6 Dc13
Mill-Sint Hubert NL 125 Bb38
Millstatt A 143 Ed55
Millstreet IRL 12 Bc25
Millstreet IRL 13 Ca25
Milltown GB 11 Eb16
Milltown GB 19 Dd29
Milltown IRL 8 Bd20
Milltown IRL 12 Bb24
Milltown Malbay IRL 12 Bb22
Milly-la-Forêt F 29 Gd38
Milly-le-Meugnon F 28 Fc42
Milmarcos E 47 Ec62
Milmersdorf D 120 Fa34
Milna HR 158 Gb68
Milnathort GB 7 Eb12
Milngavie GB 10 Dd13
Milnthorpe GB 11 Ec19
Milo I 167 Fd85
Milośaj SRB 178 Ba67
Miločer MNE 159 Hd70
Miłocice PL 121 Gc31
Miłogórze PL 122 Ja31
Miłomłyn PL 122 Hd32
Miłoradz PL 121 Hb31
Miloşeşti RO 176 Ed65
Miloševa Kula SRB 174 Ca66
Milošev Do SRB 159 Jb66
Miloševo SRB 174 Cb66
Miłosław PL 129 Gd37
Milos = Pláka GR 195 Cd91
Milot AL 163 Jb72
Milotice CZ 137 Gd48
Milovaig GB 4 Da07
Milow D 127 Eb36
Milówka PL 138 Hc46
Mils bei Imst A 142 Db54
Miltach D 135 Ec47
Milte D 125 Cb37
Miltenberg D 134 Cd45
Miltern D 127 Eb36
Milton GB 5 Ea07
Milton GB 7 Dd08
Milton Abbas GB 19 Ec30
Milton Abbot GB 18 Dc31
Milton Keynes GB 20 Fb26
Miltzow D 119 Ed31
Milutinovac SRB 174 Cb65
Milverton GB 19 Ea29
Milwich GB 16 Ed23
Milžavėnai LT 114 Ka56
Milżyn PL 129 Hb36
Mimizan F 39 Fa52
Mimizan-Plage F 39 Fa52
Mimoň CZ 136 Fc43
Mina GR 194 Bc91
Mina da Juliana P 50 Ad71
Mina de São Domingos P 58 Ba72
Miñagón E 37 Bd54
Minard GB 6 Dc12
Minare TR 198 Fd92
Minas de Riotinto E 59 Bc72
Minaya E 53 Eb68
Mincenii de Jos MD 173 Fd56
Minchinhampton GB 19 Ec27
Minde P 50 Ac66
Mindelheim D 142 Db51
Mindelo P 44 Ac60
Mindelstetten D 135 Ea48
Minden D 126 Cd36
Mindic MD 173 Fb54
Mindja BG 180 Ea71
Mindreşti MD 173 Fc56
Mindszent H 146 Jb56
Mindtangen N 70 Ed22
Minehead GB 19 Ea29
Mineo I 167 Fc86
Mineralni bani BG 184 Dc74
Mineral'nye Vody RUS 205 Ga16
Minerbe I 149 Dc60
Minerbio I 150 Dd62
Minerve F 41 Ha55
Minervino Murge I 162 Gb74
Minety GB 20 Ed27
Minfeld D 133 Cb47
Minfford GB 15 Dd24
Mingajny PL 122 Hd30
Mingajny PL 122 Ja30
Mingir MD 173 Fc59
Minglanilla E 54 Ed67
Mingorría E 46 Cd63
Minićevo SRB 179 Ca68
Minija LT 113 Jb56
Mining A 143 Ed50
Miniszków PL 130 Ja40
Minkiö FIN 89 Jd38
Minkowskie PL 129 Gd41
Minnetler TR 191 Ed82
Minnetler TR 192 Fc84
Miño de Medinaceli E 47 Eb62
Miño de San Esteban E 46 Dd61
Miñol E 36 Ba54
Minot F 30 Ja40
Miňovce SK 139 Jd47
Minsk BY 202 Ea12
Mińsk Mazowiecki PL 130 Jc37
Minster GB 21 Ga28
Minster GB 21 Gb28
Minster Lovell GB 20 Fa27
Mintia RO 175 Cc60
Mintiu Gherlii RO 171 Db57
Mintlaw GB 5 Ed08
Mintraching D 135 Eb48
Minturno I 160 Ed73
Mioarele RO 176 Dd63
Miočinovići HR 152 Gb60
Miodnica PL 128 Fd39
Miokovci SRB 159 Jc64
Miomo F 154 Cc68
Mionica SRB 153 Jb63
Mions F 34 Jb47
Mios F 32 Fa51
Mioska MNE 159 Ja68
Miotek PL 138 Hc43
Mioveni RO 175 Dc64
Mira E 54 Ed67
Míra GR 188 Bb85
Míra GR 189 Bd81
Mira I 150 Ea60
Mira P 44 Ac63
Mirabeau F 42 Jd53
Mirabel E 51 Ca66
Mirabel F 34 Ja50
Mirabel F 34 Jb50
Mirabel F 40 Gc52
Mirabel-aux-Baronnies F 42 Jc51
Mirabella Eclano I 161 Fc74
Mirabella Imbaccari I 167 Fb86
Mirachowo PL 121 Ha30
Miradoux F 40 Ga53
Miraflores de la Sierra E 46 Dc63
Miralrio E 47 Ea63
Miramar F 43 Kc54
Miramar P 44 Ac61
Miramare I 156 Eb64
Miramas F 42 Jb54
Mirambeau F 32 Fb48
Mirambel E 48 Fc64
Miramont-de-Guyenne F 32 Fd51
Miranda de Arga E 39 Ec58
Miranda de Ebro E 38 Ea57
Miranda del Castañar E 45 Ca64
Miranda do Corvo P 44 Ad64
Miranda do Douro P 45 Ca60
Mirande F 40 Fd54
Mirandela P 45 Bc60
Mirandilla E 51 Bd68
Mirandola I 149 Dc61
Mirandol-Bourgnounac F 41 Gd52
Miranje HR 157 Ga65
Mirano I 150 Ea59
Mirantes de Luna E 37 Cb56
Miraš KSV 178 Bb71
Mirăslău RO 171 Da59
Miraumont F 23 Ha32
Miravci MK 183 Bd75
Miravet E 48 Ga62
Miravete E 48 Fb64
Mircea Vodă RO 176 Ed64
Mircea Vodă RO 181 Fb67
Mirceşti RO 172 Ed57
Mircze PL 131 Kd41
Miré F 28 Fb40
Mirebeau F 28 Fd44
Mirebeau-sur-Bèze F 30 Jb41
Mirebel F 31 Jc43
Mirecourt F 31 Jd38
Miren SLO 150 Ed58
Mirepoix F 41 Gd56
Mires GR 200 Cd96
Mireşti MD 173 Fc58
Mireşu Mare RO 171 Da55
Mireval F 41 Hd54
Miribel F 34 Jb46
Miričina BIH 153 Hc62
Mirina GR 190 Db81
Miriokéfala GR 200 Cc95
Mirkovo BG 179 Cd71
Mirmande F 34 Jb50
Mirna SLO 151 Fc58
Mirocin PL 128 Fd39
Mirojedy RUS 107 Ma51
Mironeasa RO 173 Fa58
Mirones E 38 Dc55
Miroševce SRB 178 Bd70
Miroşi RO 175 Dc66
Miroslav CZ 137 Gb48
Miroslava RO 173 Fa57
Miroslavas LT 114 Kc59
Mirosławiec PL 120 Ga33
Miroslovești RO 172 Ec57
Mirošov CZ 136 Fa46
Mirostowice PL 128 Fc39
Mirotice CZ 136 Fa47
Mirovci BG 181 Ed69
Mirovec BG 181 Ec70
Mirovice CZ 136 Fa46
Mirović Zagora HR 158 Gb65
Mirovo BG 179 Ca72
Mirovo BG 180 Ea70
Mirow D 119 Ec34
Mirów PL 130 Hd42
Mirów PL 130 Jc40
Mirşid RO 171 Cd56
Mirsína GR 183 Bb79
Mirsíni GR 194 Bc90
Mirsk PL 128 Fd41
Mirto I 165 Gd79
Mírtos GR 201 Db96
Mirzec PL 130 Jc40
Misa LV 106 Kc52
Misano Adriatico I 156 Eb64
Mişca RO 170 Ca58
Mischii RO 175 Da66
Misefa H 145 Gc55
Mišelovo RUS 99 Ma39
Misi FIN 74 Kb18
Misilmeri I 166 Ec84
Mišinci BIH 152 Hb61
Mišiniai LV 123 Kb30
Miske H 146 Hd56
Miskolc H 146 Jc50
Miskolctapolca H 146 Jc51
Misliče SLO 151 Fa59
Mislina HR 158 Ha68
Mislinja SLO 144 Fd56
Mišnjak HR 151 Fc62
Missanello I 162 Gb77
Missen D 142 Da52
Missenträsk S 72 Ha24
Missery F 30 Hd42
Missillac F 27 Ec41
Misso EST 107 Lc47
Mistegná GR 191 Ea83
Mistelbach A 137 Gb49
Mistelbach D 135 Ea45
Mistelgau D 135 Dd45
Misten N 66 Fc17
Misterbianco I 167 Fc86
Misterdalsetra N 86 Eb35
Misterhult S 103 Gb50
Mistrás GR 194 Bc89
Mistretta I 167 Fb84
Mistrós GR 189 Cc85
Mišučiai LT 113 Jd56
Misurina I 143 Eb56
Misvær N 71 Fc18
Misvak TR 191 Eb82
Misy-sur-Yonne F 30 Hb38
Miszewo PL 121 Ha30
Miszewo Murowane PL 130 Hd36
Mitáto GR 201 Dd96
Mitcham GB 20 Fc28
Mitchell GB 18 Db31
Mitchelstown IRL 12 Bd24
Mithimna GR 191 Ea83
Mitikas GR 188 Ac82
Mitikas GR 188 Ad83
Mitilíni GR 191 Ea83
Mitilinií GR 197 Eb88
Mitkovcy RUS 107 Ld47
Mitlo HR 158 Gb66
Mitoc RO 172 Ed54
Mitocu Dragomirnei RO 172 Ec55
Mitragalys LT 114 La53
Mitrašinci MK 183 Ca74
Mitreni RO 181 Ec67
Mitrofanovka RUS 203 Fb14
Mitrópoli GR 188 Bb81
Mitrova Reka SRB 178 Ba68
Mitrovica SRB 153 Ja61
Mitrovići BIH 152 Hb63
Mitrovo SRB 178 Bb68
Mitry-Mory F 23 Ha36
Mitsero CY 206 Jb97
Mittådalen S 86 Ed32
Mittelbach D 127 Ec42
Mittelberg A 142 Da53
Mittelberg A 142 Dc55
Mittelbiberach D 142 Da51
Mitteldorf an der Raab A 144 Ga54
Mitteleschenbach D 134 Dc47
Mittelherwigsdorf D 128 Fc42
Mittelsinn D 134 Da44
Mittelurbach D 142 Da51
Mittenaar D 126 Cc42
Mittenwald D 143 Dd53
Mittenwalde D 120 Fa34
Mittenwalde D 128 Fa37
Mitterbach am Erlaufsee A 144 Fd52
Mitterfels D 135 Ec48
Mitterkirchen im Machland A 144 Fc51
Mittersheim F 25 Ka36
Mittersill A 143 Eb54
Mitterskirchen D 143 Ec50
Mitterteich D 135 Eb45
Mitterweissenbach A 144 Fa52
Mittet N 77 Da32
Mittewald an der Drau A 143 Eb55
Mittliden S 79 Fb25
Mittweida D 127 Ec41
Mittweide D 128 Fb38
Mitwitz D 135 Dd44
Mizija BG 179 Cd68
Mizil RO 176 Eb64
Mjadzel BY 202 Ea12
Mjakiševo RUS 107 Mb50
Mjaksa RUS 202 Ed08
Mjåland N 92 Cb44
Mjåland N 93 Da45
Mjäldrunga S 102 Ed48
Mjällby S 111 Fc54
Mjällom S 80 Gd31
Mjåvatn N 93 Db45
Mjåvatn N 93 Da46
Mjelde N 66 Fc15
Mjell N 84 Cc36
Mjels DK 108 Db27
Mjöbäck S 102 Ed50
Mjöhult S 110 Ec54
Mjölby S 103 Fd47
Mjölkberg S 72 Gc22
Mjölkvattnet S 78 Fa28
Mjølvik N 62 Gc08
Mjømna N 84 Ca37
Mjönäs S 94 Fa42
Mjøndalen N 93 Dd42
Mjønes N 77 Dd29
Mjørlund N 85 Ea39
Mjösjöby S 80 Gd28
Mjösund FIN 97 Jb40
Mladá Boleslav CZ 136 Fc43
Mladá Vožice CZ 136 Fc46
Mladé Buky CZ 136 Ga43
Mladen BG 180 Dc70
Mladenovac SRB 174 Bb65
Mladenovo SRB 153 Hd60
Mladikovina BIH 152 Hb63
Mladinovo BG 185 Ea74
Mlado MK 178 Bc73
Mladotice CZ 135 Ed45
Mladovo BG 180 Ea72
Mláka CZ 136 Fc48
Mlanča SRB 178 Ba68
Mława PL 122 Ja34
Mlebniko RUS 203 Fd08
Mlečevo BG 180 Dc71
Mlečino BG 184 Dc75
Mleczno PL 129 Gb40
Mlekarevo BG 180 Ea73
Mlik AL 182 Ab75
Mlini HR 159 Hc69
Mliništa BIH 158 Gb64
Mljetičak MNE 159 Ja68
Młock PL 122 Ja35
Młodasko PL 129 Gb36
Młodoszowice PL 129 Gd42
Młodzawy PL 138 Jb43
Młodzianów PL 129 Gd39
Młodzieszyn PL 130 Ja37
Młogoszyn PL 130 Hd37
Młynary PL 122 Hd30
Młynarze PL 122 Jc34
Mlyniv UA 204 Ea15
Mlýny CZ 136 Fc47
Mnich CZ 136 Fc47
Mnichov CZ 135 Ec44
Mnichovice CZ 136 Fc45
Mnichovo Hradiště CZ 136 Fc43
Mnichów PL 130 Jb42
Mniów PL 130 Jb41
Mników PL 130 Jb41
Mníšek nad Hnilcom SK 138 Jc48
Mniszew PL 130 Jc38
Mo N 70 Ed23
Mo N 76 Cd33
Mo N 77 Dc31
Mo N 84 Cb38

Mo – Montmelian

Mo N 92 Cd42
Mo N 93 Db45
Mo N 94 Eb40
Mo N 94 Eb42
Mo S 79 Gb30
Mo S 79 Gb29
Mo S 80 Gd30
Mo S 87 Gb37
Mo S 94 Ed44
Mo S 94 Eb45
Moacșa RO 176 Eb61
Moaña E 36 Ad57
Moara RO 172 Eb56
Moara de Piatră MD 173 Fb55
Moara Nouă MD 173 Fb57
Moara Vlăsiei RO 176 Eb65
Moate IRL 13 Cb21
Moçan AL 182 Ad76
Mocejón E 52 Db66
Močenok SK 145 Ha50
Mochau D 127 Ed41
Móchlos GR 201 Dc96
Mochowo PL 122 Hd35
Mochrum GB 10 Dd17
Mochy PL 129 Gb38
Močidlec CZ 135 Ed44
Mociu RO 171 Db58
Mockai LV 114 Kb59
Möckern D 127 Eb37
Mockfjärd S 95 Fc40
Möckmühl D 134 Cd46
Mockrehna D 127 Ec40
Mockträsk S 73 Hd22
Moclin E 60 Db74
Moclinejo E 60 Da76
Mocra MD 173 Fd56
Mocsa H 145 Hb52
Mőcsány H 153 Hc57
Moczydły-Kukiłki PL 123 Ka35
Modane F 35 Kb48
Modave B 124 Ba42
Modbury GB 19 Dd32
Modelu RO 181 Ed67
Modena I 149 Db62
Möderbrugg A 144 Fb54
Moderki PL 123 Ka35
Moderówka PL 139 Jd45
Módi GR 189 Bd84
Modica I 167 Fc88
Modigliana I 156 Dd64
Modliborzyce PL 131 Ka41
Mödling A 145 Gb51
Modliszewko PL 129 Gd36
Modlna PL 130 Hc38
Modolicy RUS 99 Mb44
Modolo I 169 Bd76
Modra SK 145 Gd50
Modran BIH 152 Hb61
Modrany SK 145 Hb52
Modrava CZ 135 Ed48
Modrej SLO 151 Fa57
Modriach A 144 Fc55
Modriča BIH 152 Hb61
Modrica SRB 178 Bc68
Mõdriku EST 98 La42
Modrovka SK 137 Ha49
Modruš HR 151 Fd61
Modrý Kameň SK 146 Hd50
Modrze PL 129 Gb37
Modrzejowice PL 130 Jc40
Modrzewie PL 120 Fc33
Modugno I 162 Gc74
Moeche E 36 Bb53
Moëlan-sur-Mer F 27 Dd40
Moelfre GB 15 Dd21
Moelv N 86 Ea38
Moen N 67 Gc11
Moen N 78 Eb29
Moena I 143 Dd56
Moerdijk NL 124 Ad37
Moergestel NL 124 Ba38
Moers D 125 Bd39
Mofalla S 103 Fb47
Moffat GB 11 Eb15
Mofreita P 45 Bd59
Moftinu Mic RO 171 Cc55
Mogadouro P 45 Bd61
Mogata S 103 Gb46
Møgeltønder DK 108 Da28
Mogenstrup DK 100 Da23
Mogenstrup DK 109 Eb27
Mogente E 55 Fb70
Moggio I 149 Cd58
Moggio Udinese I 143 Ed56
Mögglingen D 134 Da48
Mogielnica PL 130 Jb39
Mogila BG 181 Ed70
Mogila MK 183 Bb76
Mogilany PL 138 Ja45
Mogili RUS 107 Ma51
Mogilište BG 181 Fb69
Mogilno PL 129 Ha36
Moglia I 149 Db61
Mogliano I 156 Ed67
Mogliano Veneto I 150 Ea59
Möglingen D 134 Cd48
Mogón E 61 Dd72
Mogor E 36 Ad57
Mogorić HR 151 Ga63
Mogoro I 169 Bd78
Mogoșani RO 176 Dd65
Mogoșești RO 173 Fa58
Mogoșești-Siret RO 172 Ed57
Mogosoaia RO 176 Ea66
Mogro E 38 Dc54
Moguer E 59 Bb74
Mogutovo RUS 99 Ma45
Mohács H 153 Hc58
Moharras E 53 Eb68
Moheda S 103 Fc51
Mohedas E 45 Ca64
Mohedas de la Jara E 52 Cc67
Mohelnice CZ 137 Gc45
Mohelno CZ 137 Gb48
Mohil IRL 13 Cb23
Mohill IRL 9 Cb19
Möhkö FIN 83 Mb30
Möhlau D 127 Eb39
Möhnesee D 125 Cb39
Möhnesee D 126 Cc39
Moholm S 103 Fb46
Mohon F 27 Eb39
Mohora H 146 Hd51
Mohorn D 127 Ed41
Mohós GR 201 Db96
Mohrkirch D 108 Db29
Mohtola FIN 90 La32
Mohyliv-Podil's'kyj UA 204 Eb16
Moi N 92 Cb45
Moià E 49 Gd60
Moie I 156 Ec66
Moikipää FIN 81 Hd31
Moilala FIN 90 La33
Moimenta da Beira P 44 Bb62
Moinești RO 172 Ec59
Moinniemi FIN 91 Lc33
Moinsalmi FIN 91 Ld33
Móinteach Milic IRL 13 Cb22
Mo i Rana N 71 Fb20
Moirans F 35 Jc48
Moirans-en-Montagne F 31 Jc44
Moirax F 40 Ga52
Moircy B 132 Ba43
Mõisaküla EST 98 Ka45
Mõisaküla EST 106 Kc46
Moisburg D 118 Db33
Moisei RO 171 Dc55
Moisio FIN 90 La34
Moisiovaara FIN 75 Lb24
Moissac F 40 Gb52
Moissac-Bellevue F 42 Ka53
Moissey F 31 Jc42
Moisson F 23 Gc36
Moisund N 92 Cd46
Moisy F 29 Gb40
Moita F 154 Cc70
Moita P 50 Ab69
Moitaselkä FIN 69 Kc17
Moixent E 55 Fb70
Mõja S 96 Ha43
Mojácar E 61 Ec75
Mojados E 46 Da61
Moječice PL 129 Gb40
Mojeciu RO 176 Dd62
Mojkovac MNE 159 Jb68
Mojstrana SLO 144 Fa56
Møkland N 66 Fc12
Möklinta S 95 Gb41
Mokliště MK 183 Bd75
Mokobody PL 131 Jd36
Mokolai LV 114 Kb58
Mokra Gora SRB 159 Ja65
Mokre PL 121 Ha32
Mokre PL 129 Gb37
Mokren BG 180 Eb72
Mokreni MK 183 Bb74
Mokreš BG 179 Cc68
Mokrin SRB 153 Jc58
Mokrin SRB 174 Bb60
Mokro BIH 159 Hc65
Mokro MNE 159 Jb69
Mokronog SLO 151 Fd58
Mokronoge BIH 152 Gd65
Mokronoge BIH 158 Gd65
Mokro Polje HR 158 Gb64
Mokrous RUS 203 Ga11
Mokrzesz PL 130 Hd42
Mokrzyska PL 138 Jb44
Mokšan RUS 203 Fc11
Moksi FIN 90 Kb33
Møkster N 84 Bd40
Mol B 124 Ba39
Mol SRB 153 Jb58
Mola di Bari I 162 Gd74
Molai GR 195 Bd90
Molainiai LT 114 Kc54
Moland N 66 Fb14
Moland N 93 Da42
Molare I 148 Ca62
Molas F 40 Ga55
Molbergen D 117 Cb34
Mølby DK 108 Db26
Mold GB 15 Eb22
Moldava CZ 128 Fa42
Moldava nad Bodvou SK 138 Jc49
Mołdawin PL 120 Fd32
Molde N 76 Cd32
Moldova Nouă RO 174 Bd64
Moldova-Sulița RO 172 Dd55
Moldova Veche RO 174 Bd64
Moldovenești RO 171 Da59
Moldoveni RO 172 Ec58
Moldovița RO 172 Ea55
Møldrup DK 100 Db22
Moldusen N 94 Ed40
Moldvik N 66 Ga12
Moledo do Minho P 36 Ac58
Moleno CH 142 Cc56
Moléson CH 141 Bc55
Molești MD 173 Fd59
Molėtai LT 114 La56
Molezuelas de la Carballeda E 37 Ca58
Molfetta I 162 Gc74
Molfsee D 118 Dc30
Móli GR 183 Bd80
Moliden S 80 Gd30
Moliens-Dreuil F 23 Gc33
Molières F 40 Gb52
Moliets-et-Maa F 39 Ed53
Moliets-Plage F 39 Ed53
Molin SRB 153 Jc59
Molin SRB 174 Bb61
Molina I 150 Dd57
Molina Aterno I 160 Ed71
Molina de Aragon E 47 Ec63
Molina de Segura E 55 Fa72
Molinella I 150 Dd62
Molineuf F 29 Gb41
Molinges F 35 Jd45
Molinicos E 53 Eb71
Molinos E 36 Ac54
Molinos E 48 Fb63
Molinos de Duero E 47 Ea60
Molins del Rei E 49 Gd61
Moliterno I 161 Ga77
Molitg-les-Bains F 41 Ha57
Molkojärvi FIN 69 Jd16
Molkom S 94 Fa43
Molla S 102 Ed48
Mollafeneri TR 186 Ga78
Mollagjesh AL 182 Ac75
Molland N 93 Da46
Mollans-sur-Ouvèze F 42 Jc52
Mollaoğlu TR 193 Gc82
Mollas AL 182 Ac76
Mollasüleymanlı TR 192 Fc86
Möllbrücke A 143 Ed55
Mölle S 110 Ec54
Möllenhagen D 119 Ed33
Mollerussa E 48 Ga60
Mollet del Vallès E 49 Ha61
Mollia I 148 Ca58
Molliéres F 43 Kc51
Mollina E 60 Cd75
Mollis CH 142 Cc54
Molln A 144 Fb52
Mölln D 119 Dd32
Mölltorp S 103 Fb46
Mølna N 78 Eb29
Mölnbo S 96 Gc44
Mølnbukt N 77 Dd29
Mölndal S 102 Eb49
Mölnebo S 102 Eb48
Mölnlycke S 102 Ec49
Molochișul Mare MD 173 Fd55
Moločišče RUS 107 Mb47
Molodi RUS 99 Ld45
Molodi RUS 107 Ma46
Mołodycz PL 139 Kc43
Molompize F 34 Hb49
Mólos GR 189 Bd83
Moloskovicy RUS 99 Ma41
Molovata MD 173 Fd57
Molovata Nouă MD 173 Fd57
Moloy F 30 Jb41
Moložva RUS 107 Ld46
Molpe FIN 81 Hd31
Molsheim F 25 Kb37
Mołtajny PL 122 Jb30
Moltjorda N 71 Fc18
Mołtowo PL 120 Ga31
Moltrasio I 149 Cc58
Moltustranda N 76 Cb33
Molunat HR 159 Hc69
Molvero I 149 Dc57
Molvízar E 60 Db76
Mólyvos = Mithimna GR 191 Ea83
Molzbichl A 143 Ed55
Momán E 36 Bb54
Momarken N 94 Eb43
Mombaldone I 148 Ca62
Mombaroccio I 156 Ec65
Mombaruzzo I 148 Ca61
Mömbris D 134 Cd44
Mombuey E 45 Ca59
Momčilgrad BG 184 Dc75
Momino BG 180 Eb70
Momino Selo BG 180 Db73
Momin Sbor BG 180 Dd70
Mömlingen D 134 Cd45
Mommark DK 108 Dc28
Mommila FIN 90 Kb37
Momoty Górne PL 131 Kb42
Momrak N 93 Da44
Momuy F 39 Fb54
Mon CH 142 Cd55
Mon S 79 Fb26
Monå FIN 81 Ja29
Monachil E 60 Dc75
Monaghan IRL 9 Cc18
Monahiti GR 182 Ba79
Monar Lodge GB 6 Dc08
Monäs FIN 81 Ja29
Monasterace Marina I 164 Gc83
Monasterevin IRL 13 Cc22
Monasterio de la Sierra E 46 Dd59
Monasterio del Coto E 37 Bd55
Monasterio de Rodilla E 38 Dd58
Monastir I 169 Ca79
Monastiráki GR 184 Cd76
Monastiráki GR 188 Ad83
Monastyrek RUS 99 Ld42
Monastyrščina RUS 202 Ec12
Monastyryšče UA 204 Ec15
Monastyrys'ka UA 204 Ea16
Monbahus F 33 Ga51
Monbiel CH 142 Da55
Moncada E 54 Fc67
Moncalieri I 148 Bd60
Moncalvillo E 46 Dd59
Moncalvillo del Huete E 47 Ea65
Moncalvo I 148 Ca60
Monção P 36 Ad58
Moncarapacho P 58 Ad74
Moncel-sur-Seille F 25 Jd36
Mönchberg D 134 Cd45
Mönchdorf A 144 Fc50
Mönchengladbach D 125 Bc40
Mönchhof A 145 Gc52
Mönchholzhausen D 127 Dd41
Monchio delle Corti I 149 Da63
Monchique P 58 Ab73
Mönchkirchen A 144 Ga53
Mönchsdeggingen D 134 Dc48
Mönchsroth D 134 Db48
Monclar F 33 Ga51
Monclar-de-Quercy F 40 Gc53
Moncofa E 54 Fc66
Moncontour F 26 Eb38
Moncontour F 28 Fc43
Moncoutant F 28 Fb44
Monda E 60 Cc76
Mondaino I 156 Eb65
Mondariz E 36 Ad57
Mondavio I 156 Ec66
Mondéjar E 46 Dd65
Mondello, Partanna- I 166 Ec83
Mondim da Beira P 44 Ba61
Mondim de Basto P 44 Ba60
Mondolfo I 156 Ec65
Mondoñedo E 36 Bc54
Mondonville F 40 Gb54
Mondorf-les-Bains L 25 Jd34
Mondorf-les-Bains L 133 Bb45
Mondoubleau F 29 Ga40
Mondovì I 148 Bd62
Mondragon F 42 Jb52
Mondragone I 161 Fa74
Mondreganes E 37 Cd57
Mondriz E 36 Bc55
Mondsee A 143 Ed52
Möne S 102 Fa48
Moneasa RO 170 Cb58
Moneen IRL 8 Bd20
Moneglia I 149 Cc63
Monegrillo E 48 Fb61
Monein F 39 Fb55
Monemvassiá GR 195 Bd90
Moneo E 38 Dd56
Mones E 37 Ca54
Monesi I 148 Bc63
Monesiglio I 148 Bd62
Monesma y Cajigar E 48 Ga59
Monesterio E 51 Bd71
Monestier-de-Clermont F 35 Jd49
Monestiés F 41 Gd52
Moneteau F 30 Hc40
Moneva E 47 Fa62
Moneygall IRL 13 Ca22
Moneygold IRL 8 Ca17
Moneymore GB 9 Cd17
Moneyneany GB 9 Cd16
Moneyslane GB 9 Da18
Monfalcone I 150 Eb59
Monfarracinos E 45 Cb60
Monfero E 36 Bb54
Monflanquin F 33 Ga51
Monflorite E 48 Fc59
Monforte P 51 Bb68
Monforte d'Alba I 148 Bd62
Monforte del Cid E 55 Fb71
Monforte de Lemos E 36 Bb57
Monforte San Giorgio I 167 Fd84
Monghidoro I 155 Dc64
Mongiana I 164 Gc82
Mongiardino Ligure I 148 Cb62
Mongstad N 84 Ca37
Monguelfo I 143 Ea55
Monguilhem F 40 Fc53
Monheim D 134 Dc48
Monheim am Rhein D 125 Bd40
Monaive GB 10 Ea15
Moniatis CY 206 Ja97
Mon-Idée F 24 Hd33
Monifieth GB 7 Ec11
Moninmäki FIN 82 La31
Möniste EST 107 Lb48
Monistrol-d'Allier F 34 Hc49
Monistrol de Montserrat E 49 Gd61
Monistrol-sur-Loire F 34 Hd48
Mönkeberg D 118 Dc30
Monk Fryston GB 16 Fa20
Mońki PL 123 Ka32
Monleras E 45 Ca61
Monlezun-d'Armagnac F 40 Fc53
Monlong F 40 Ga55
Monmouth GB 19 Eb27
Monnai F 22 Fd37
Monnaie F 29 Ga41
Monnerville F 29 Gd38
Mönni FIN 83 Ld30
Monni FIN 90 Kb38
Monnickendam NL 116 Ba35
Monninkylä FIN 90 Kc38
Monnoinen FIN 97 Jb39
Monodéndri GR 182 Ad79
Monódrio GR 189 Cc85
Monolíthio GR 188 Ad81
Monólithos GR 196 Db92
Monólithos GR 197 Ed93
Monopoli I 162 Ha74
Monor H 146 Hd53
Monor RO 171 Dc57
Monoskylä FIN 89 Jd33
Monóspita GR 183 Bd77
Monostorapáti H 145 Ha55
Monóvar E 55 Fa71
Monpazier F 33 Ga51
Monreal D 133 Bd43
Monreal de Ariza E 47 Ec62
Monreal del Campo E 47 Ed63
Monreale I 166 Ec84
Monroy E 51 Ca66
Monroyo E 48 Fc63
Mons B 124 Ab41
Mons F 43 Kb53
Monsanto P 45 Bc65
Monsaraz P 50 Ba70
Monschau D 125 Bc42
Monsegur F 32 Fd51
Monselice I 150 Dd60
Monsheim D 133 Cb45
Mönsheim D 134 Cc48
Monsiega N 92 Cc44
Monsols F 34 Ja45
Mønsted DK 100 Db23
Monster NL 116 Ac36
Mönsterås S 103 Gb51
Monsummano Terme I 155 Db65
Montà I 148 Bd61
Montabaur D 125 Cb42
Montady F 41 Hb55
Montagna I 150 Dd60
Montagnac F 41 Hc54
Montagnac-d'Auberoche F 33 Gb49
Montagne F 35 Jc49
Montagnol F 41 Hb53
Montagny F 34 Hd46
Montaigu F 28 Fa43
Montaigu-de-Quercy F 40 Gb52
Montaiguët-en-Forez F 34 Hc45
Montaigu-les-Bois F 22 Fa37
Montaigut F 33 Ha45
Montaigut-le-Blanc F 33 Gc46
Montaigut-sur-Save F 40 Gb54
Montainville F 29 Gc39
Montaivo P 58 Ba72
Montalba-le-Château F 41 Ha57
Montalbán E 48 Fb63
Montalbán de Córdoba E 60 Cd73
Montalbanejo E 53 Ea67
Montalbano I 162 Ha75
Montalbano Elicona I 167 Fc84
Montalbano Jonico I 162 Gc77
Montalbo E 53 Ea66
Montalcino I 155 Dc67
Montaldo di Cosola I 149 Cc62
Montale I 155 Dc64
Montalegre P 44 Bb59
Montalieu-Vercieu F 35 Jc46
Montalivet-les-Bains F 32 Fa48
Montallegro I 166 Ec86
Montalto delle Marche I 156 Ed68
Montalto di Castro I 156 Dd70
Montalto Marina I 156 Dd70
Montalto Pavese I 149 Cc61
Montalto Uffugo I 164 Gb79
Montalvão P 50 Ba66
Montalvos E 53 Ec68
Montamarta E 45 Cb60
Montamy F 22 Fb36
Montán E 54 Fb66
Montana BG 179 Cc69
Montana CH 141 Bd56
Montañana E 48 Fb60
Montanaro I 148 Bd60
Montánchez E 51 Ca68
Montanejos E 54 Fb66
Montaner F 40 Fc55
Montano Antilia I 161 Fd77
Montans F 41 Gd53
Montargil P 50 Ad68
Montargis F 29 Ha39
Montargull E 48 Gb59
Montari FIN 90 Kc37
Montastruc-la-Coceillère F 40 Gc54
Montauban F 40 Gb53
Montauban-de-Bretagne F 27 Ec39
Montaud F 35 Jc48
Montazzoli I 161 Fb71
Montbard F 30 Hd41
Montbarrey F 31 Jc42
Montbazens F 33 Gd51
Montbazon F 29 Ga42
Montbéliard F 31 Ka40
Montbenidorm E 55 Fc71
Montbeugny F 30 Hc44
Montbizot F 28 Fd39
Montblanc E 48 Gb61
Montbovon CH 141 Bc55
Montbozon F 31 Jd41
Montbrand F 35 Jd50
Montbrió del Camp E 48 Gb62
Montbrison F 34 Hd47
Montbron F 33 Ga47
Montbrun-les-Bains F 42 Jc52
Montceau-les-Mines F 30 Ja44
Montceaux-les-Provins F 24 Hb37
Montcenis F 30 Ja43
Montchanin F 30 Ja43
Montchevrier F 33 Gc45
Montcornet F 24 Hc34
Montcresson F 29 Ha40
Montcuq F 40 Gb52
Montdardier F 41 Hc53
Mont-Dauphin F 35 Kb50
Mont-de-Marsan F 39 Fb53
Montdidier F 23 Gd34
Mont-Dol F 28 Ed38
Monteagudo E 47 Ed59
Monteagudo de las Salinas E 53 Ec66
Monteagudo de las Vicarías E 47 Eb61
Montealegre E 46 Cd59
Montealegre del Castillo E 55 Ed70
Montebello Vicentino I 150 Dd59
Montebelluna I 150 Ea59
Montebourg F 22 Fa35
Montebruno I 149 Cc62
Monte Buono I 156 Ea67
Montecalvo Irpino I 161 Fc74
Monte-Carlo MC 43 Kd53
Montecarotto I 156 Ec66
Montecastrilli I 156 Eb69
Montecatini Terme I 155 Db65
Montecchio I 156 Eb65
Montecchio Emilia I 149 Da62
Montecchio Maggiore I 150 Dd59
Monte Cerignone I 156 Eb65
Montech F 40 Gb53
Montechiarugolo I 149 Da62
Monteciccardo I 156 Eb65
Monte Claro P 50 Ba66
Montecorto E 59 Cb76
Montecorvino Rovella I 161 Fc75
Monte da Pedra P 50 Ba67
Monte das Flores P 50 Ad69
Monte de Baixo Grande P 58 Ba73
Monte de Goula P 44 Ba65
Montederramo E 36 Bb57
Montedor P 44 Ac59
Montedoro I 166 Ed86
Monte do Trigo P 50 Ba70
Monte Estremo F 154 Ca69
Montefalco I 156 Eb68
Montefalcone di Val Fortore I 161 Fc73
Montefalcone nel Sannio I 161 Fc71
Montefiascone I 156 Ea69
Monte Fidalgo P 50 Ba66
Montefiore Conca I 156 Eb65
Montefiore dell'Aso I 156 Ed68
Montefiorino I 149 Db63
Monteforte Cilento I 161 Fd76
Monteforte da Beira P 51 Bb66
Monteforte Irpino I 161 Fc75
Montefortino I 156 Ed68
Montefrío E 60 Da74
Montefurado E 36 Bc57
Montegil E 59 Cb75
Montegiordano Marina I 162 Gc77
Montegiorgio I 156 Ed67
Monte Gordo P 44 Ba65
Monte Gordo P 58 Ba74
Montegrotto Terme I 150 Dd60
Montehermoso E 45 Bd65
Montejaque E 59 Cb76
Montejícar E 60 Dc74
Montejo de Bricia E 38 Dc56
Montejo de la Sierra E 46 Dc62
Montejo de la Vega E 46 Dc61
Montejos del Camino E 37 Cc57
Montelanico I 160 Ec72
Montel-de-Gelat F 33 Ha46
Monteleone di Puglia I 161 Fd74
Monteleone di Spoleto I 156 Ec69
Monteleone d'Orvieto I 156 Ea68
Monteleone Rocca Doria I 168 Bd75
Montelepre I 166 Ec84
Montélimar F 42 Jb51
Montella I 161 Fc75
Montellano E 59 Cb75
Montellier F 34 Jb46
Monte Isola I 149 Da58
Montelungo I 149 Cd63
Montelupo Fiorentino I 155 Dc65
Montelupone I 156 Ed67
Montemaggiore Belsito I 166 Ed85
Montemagno I 148 Ca61
Montemarano I 161 Fc75
Montemarcello I 155 Cd64
Montemassi I 155 Db68
Montemayor E 60 Cd73
Montemayor del Río E 45 Cb64
Montemayor de Pililla E 46 Da61
Montemerano I 155 Dc69
Montemesola I 162 Ha76
Montemiletto I 161 Fc74
Montemilone I 162 Gb74
Montemolín E 51 Bd71
Montemor-o-Novo P 50 Ad69
Montemor-o-Velho P 44 Ac64
Montemurro I 162 Gb77
Montendre F 32 Fc49
Montenegro de Cameros E 47 Ea59
Montenero I 155 Da66
Montenero di Bisaccia I 161 Fc71
Montenerodomo I 161 Fb71
Monteneuf F 27 Ec40
Monte Novo P 50 Ab70
Montepaone Lido I 164 Gc82
Montepescali I 155 Dc68
Monte Petrosu I 168 Cc74
Montepiano I 155 Dc64
Montepulciano I 156 Dd67
Monterchi I 156 Ea66
Monterde de Albarracín E 47 Ed64
Monte Real P 44 Ab65
Montereale I 156 Ec69
Montereale Valcellina I 150 Eb57
Montereau F 29 Ha38
Montereau F 29 Ha40
Monte Redondo P 44 Ac65
Monterenzio I 149 Dc63
Monteriggioni I 155 Dc66
Monte Romano I 156 Dd70
Monteroni d'Arbia I 155 Dc67
Monterosi I 156 Ea70
Monterosso al Mare I 155 Cd64
Monterosso Almo I 167 Fc87
Monterosso Calabro I 164 Gb82
Monterotondo I 160 Eb71
Monterotondo Marittimo I 155 Db67
Monterroso E 36 Bb56
Monterrubio de la Serena E 51 Cb70
Monterrubio de la Sierra E 45 Cb63
Montesa E 54 Fb69
Montesalgueiro E 36 Ba54
Monte San Biagio I 160 Ed73
Monte San Giusto I 156 Ed67
Monte San Maria Tiberina I 156 Ea66
Montesano Salentino I 163 Hc77
Montesano sulla Marcellana I 161 Ga77
Monte San Savino I 156 Dd67
Monte Sant'Angelo I 162 Gb72
Monte San Vito I 156 Ec66
Montesarchio I 161 Fb74
Montescaglioso I 162 Gc76
Montesclaros E 46 Cd65
Montesilvano Marina I 157 Fa69
Montespertoli I 155 Dc65
Montespluga I 142 Cc56
Montesquieu-Volvestre F 40 Gb55
Montesquieux F 40 Gb52
Montesquiou F 40 Fd54
Montestruc-sur-Gers F 40 Ga54
Monteux F 42 Jb52
Montevago I 166 Eb85
Montevarchi I 156 Dd66
Montevecchio I 169 Bd78
Monteveglio I 149 Dc63
Monteverde I 161 Ga74
Montevil P 50 Ab70
Montezemolo I 148 Bd62
Montfalcó Murallat E 49 Gc60
Montfaucon CH 141 Bc53
Montfaucon F 28 Fa43
Montfaucon-d'Argonne F 24 Jb35
Montfaucon-en-Velay F 34 Ja49
Montferrand-du-Périgord F 33 Ga50
Montferrat F 43 Kb53
Montfleur F 35 Jc45
Montfoort NL 116 Ba36
Montfort F 40 Ga53
Montfort NL 125 Bb40
Montfort-en-Chalosse F 39 Fb54
Montfort-l'Amaury F 23 Gc37
Montfort-sur-Meu F 28 Ed39
Montfort-sur-Risle F 23 Ga35
Montfranc F 41 Ha53
Montfrin F 42 Jb53
Montfront-le-Gesnois F 28 Fd39
Montgarri E 40 Gb57
Montgeron F 23 Gd37
Montgerval F 28 Ed39
Montgomery GB 15 Eb24
Montgueux F 30 Hc38
Montguyon F 32 Fc49
Monthermé F 24 Ja33
Monthey CH 141 Bb56
Monthois F 24 Ja35
Monthureux-sur-Saône F 31 Jd39
Monti I 168 Cb74
Montiano E 38 Dd56
Montiano I 155 Dc69
Monticchio Bagni I 161 Ga74
Monticelli I 162 Ha75
Monticelli d'Ongina I 149 Cd61
Monticelli Terme I 149 Da62
Montichiari I 149 Da60
Monticiano I 155 Dc67
Montiel E 53 Dd70
Montier-en-Der F 30 Ja38
Montieri I 155 Db67
Montiers-sur-Saulx F 24 Jb37
Montiglio I 148 Bd60
Montignac F 33 Gb49
Montignac-le-Coq F 32 Fd48
Montignac-sur-Charente F 32 Fd47
Montigny F 25 Ka37
Montigny F 29 Ha42
Montigny-la-Resle F 30 Hc40
Montigny-le Chartif F 29 Gb39
Montigny-Lencoup F 30 Hb38
Montigny-le-Roi = Val-de-Meuse F 31 Jc39
Montigny-lès-Metz F 25 Jd35
Montigny-sur-Aube F 30 Ja39
Montigny-sur-Loing F 29 Ha38
Montijo E 51 Bc69
Montijo P 50 Ab69
Montilla E 60 Cd73
Montilly F 30 Hb44
Montivilliers F 22 Fd34
Montjay F 42 Jd51
Montjean F 28 Fb40
Montjean F 32 Fd46
Montjean-sur-Loire F 28 Fb42
Montlaur F 41 Ha56
Mont-lès-Lamarche F 31 Jc39
Montlieu-la-Garde F 32 Fc49
Montlivault F 29 Gb41
Mont-Louis F 41 Gd58
Montlouis-sur-Loire F 29 Ga42
Montluçon F 33 Ha45
Montluel F 34 Jb46
Montmajor E 49 Gc59
Montmarault F 34 Hb45
Montmaur F 35 Jd50
Montmaurin F 40 Ga55
Montmédy F 24 Jb34
Montmelian F 35 Jd47

259

N

Nekla – Niva

Nekla PL 129 Gd37
Nekrasovo RUS 113 Ja58
Nekrasovskoe RUS 203 Fa09
Nelas P 44 Ba63
Nelaug N 93 Da45
Nelidovo RUS 202 Ec10
Nellimö FIN 69 Kb11
Nellingen D 134 Da49
Nelson GB 16 Ed20
Nelson GB 19 Ea27
Nemajūnai LT 114 Kc58
Nemakščiai LT 114 Ka56
Neman RUS 113 Jc57
Nemanjica MK 178 Bd73
Nemanskoe RUS 113 Jd57
Nembro E 37 Cc54
Nembro I 149 Cd58
Němčice nad Hanou CZ 137 Gd47
Neméa GR 195 Bd87
Nemecká SK 138 Hd48
Nemenčinė LT 114 La57
Nemescsó H 145 Gc53
Nemesgulács H 145 Gd55
Nemesnádudvar H 153 Hd57
Nemesvámos H 145 Ha54
Németkér H 146 Hc55
Nemežis LT 114 La58
Nemi I 160 Eb72
Nemojevo RUS 107 Ma48
Nemours F 29 Ha39
Nemška Loka SLO 151 Fc59
Nemšová SK 137 Ha48
Nemțeni MD 173 Fb58
Nemti H 146 Ja51
Nemunaitis LT 114 Kc59
Nemunėlio Radviliškis LT 106 Kd52
Nemyriv UA 204 Dd15
Nemyriv UA 204 Eb15
Nenagh IRL 13 Ca22
Nendeln FL 142 Cd54
Nenince SK 146 Hd50
Nénita GR 191 Dd86
Nennhausen D 127 Ec36
Nennslingen D 135 Dd48
Nenovo BG 181 Ed70
Nenset N 93 Dc44
Nentershausen D 125 Cb42
Nentershausen D 126 Db41
Nenthead GB 11 Ec17
Nenzing A 142 Cd54
Nenzingen D 142 Cc51
Neo Chorio CY 206 Hd97
Neo Chorio CY 206 Jc96
Néo Erásmio GR 184 Db77
Neohoráki GR 189 Cb85
Neohóri GR 182 Ac80
Neohóri GR 184 Cc78
Neohóri GR 185 Eb76
Neohóri GR 188 Ab81
Neohóri GR 188 Ad82
Neohóri GR 188 Ba84
Neohóri GR 189 Cb82
Neohóri GR 189 Cc85
Neohóri GR 194 Bb89
Néo Horió GR 200 Cc95
Néo Monastíri GR 189 Bc82
Neoneli I 169 Ca77
Néo Petrítsi GR 183 Cb76
Neorić HR 158 Gc66
Néo Ríssio GR 183 Ca78
Néo Sidirohóri GR 184 Dc77
Néos Marmarás GR 184 Cc80
Néo Soúli GR 184 Cc76
Néos Pagóntas GR 189 Cb84
Néos Skopós GR 184 Cc77
Nepi I 156 Ea70
Nepolje KSV 178 Ba71
Nepomuk CZ 136 Fa46
Neppermin D 120 Fb32
Neptun RO 181 Fc68
Nérac F 40 Fd52
Neratovice CZ 136 Fb44
Nerchau D 127 Ec40
Nerdal N 66 Ga14
Nerdvika N 77 Db30
Néré F 32 Fc46
Nerehta RUS 203 Fa09
Nereju RO 176 Ec62
Neresheim D 134 Db48
Neresnica SRB 174 Bd65
Nereta LV 114 Kd53
Neretaslauki LV 114 Kd53
Nereto I 157 Fa68
Nerezine HR 151 Fb62
Nerežišće HR 158 Gc67
Nerimdaičiai LT 113 Jd54
Neringa-Juodkrantė LT 113 Jb56
Neringa-Nida LT 113 Jb56
Neringa-Pervalka LT 113 Jb56
Neringa-Preila LT 113 Jb56
Néris-les-Bains F 33 Ha45
Nerja E 60 Db76
Nerkoo FIN 82 Kd28
Nerkoo FIN 89 Jc33
Nerkoonniemi FIN 82 Kd28
Nerl' RUS 202 Ed09
Nerokoúros GR 200 Cb95
Nerola I 156 Eb70
Nérondes F 29 Ha43
Nerotriviá GR 189 Cb84
Nerpio E 61 Eb72
Nersac F 32 Fd47
Nersingen D 134 Db49
Nerskogen N 77 Dd32
Nerva E 59 Bc72
Nervei N 64 Ka05
Nervesa della Battaglia I 150 Ea58
Nervi I 148 Cb63
Nerviano I 148 Cb59
Nes N 66 Fd14
Nes N 78 Ed26
Nes N 78 Eb29
Nes N 84 Cb35
Nes N 84 Cd36
Nes N 85 Dd39
Nes N 92 Cb43
Nes N 92 Cb46
Nes N 93 Db43
Nes NL 117 Bc32
Nesan N 78 Fa25
Nesberg N 66 Fd15
Nesbø N 84 Ca34
Nesbyen N 85 Dc39
Neschwitz D 128 Fb40
Nesebăr BG 181 Fa72
Neset N 63 Hb07
Neset N 78 Fa26
Neset N 92 Cd45
Nesflaten N 92 Cc42
Nesheim N 65 Kc09
Nesheim N 84 Cb38
Nesheim N 93 Cb42
Nesjahverfi IS 3 Bb06
Nes Jernverk N 93 Db45
Neskaupstaður IS 3 Bc05
Neslandsvatn N 93 Db44
Nesle F 23 Ha34
Nesna N 70 Fa21
Nesodden N 93 Ea42
Nesoddtangen N 93 Ea41
Nesovice CZ 137 Gc47
Nesscliff GB 15 Eb24
Nesse D 117 Cb32
Nesselwang D 142 Db52
Nessental CH 141 Ca55
Neßmersiel D 117 Cb32
Nestáni GR 194 Bc87
Nestavoll N 77 Dd33
Nesteri LV 107 Ld50
Nesterov RUS 113 Jd58
Nesterov RUS 202 Dd12
Nestiary RUS 203 Fc09
Neštin SRB 153 Ja60
Neston GB 15 Eb22
Nestório GR 182 Ba78
Nesttun N 84 Ca39
Nesvady SK 145 Hb51
Nesvik N 92 Cb43
Nésza H 146 Hd52
Netherfield GB 20 Fd30
Nether Langwith GB 16 Fa22
Netherley GB 7 Ed09
Netherton GB 11 Ed15
Netherwitten GB 11 Ed15
Netičkampis LV 114 Kb59
Netlandsnes N 92 Cc45
Netolice CZ 136 Fb48
Netphen D 125 Cb41
Netretic HR 151 Fd60
Nettaa FIN 98 Kb39
Netta II PL 123 Ka31
Nettancourt F 24 Ja36
Nettersheim D 125 Bc42
Nettetal D 125 Bc39
Nettlebed GB 20 Fb28
Nettleton GB 17 Fc21
Nettuno I 160 Eb73
Netunice CZ 135 Ed46
Netvořice CZ 136 Fb45
Neualbenreuth D 135 Eb45
Neuanspach D 134 Cc43
Neuberg an der Mürz A 144 Fc52
Neubeuern D 143 Eb52
Neubörger D 117 Cb34
Neubrandenburg D 119 Ed33
Neubruck A 144 Fd51
Neubrunn D 134 Da45
Neubukow D 119 Ea31
Neuburg D 143 Ed50
Neuburg an der Donau D 135 Dd49
Neuburg-Steinhausen D 119 Ea31
Neuchâtel CH 141 Bc54
Neuchâtel-Hardelot F 23 Gc31
Neuching D 143 Ea50
Neu Darchau D 119 Dd34
Neudau A 145 Gb54
Neudenau D 134 Cd46
Neudietendorf D 127 Dd41
Neudorf A 142 Dc54
Neudorf D 135 Ec43
Neudorf, Graben- D 133 Cb47
Neudrossenfeld D 135 Ea44
Neu-Eichenberg D 126 Db40
Neuenbürg D 134 Cc48
Neuenburg D 141 Bd51
Neuendettelsau D 134 Dc47
Neuendorf D 118 Cc33
Neuendorf D 128 Fa36
Neuenhagen D 120 Fb35
Neuenhagen D 128 Fa36
Neuenhaus D 117 Ca35
Neuenkirch CH 141 Ca54
Neuenkirchen D 117 Ca36
Neuenkirchen D 117 Cb36
Neuenkirchen D 118 Cd32
Neuenkirchen D 118 Db34
Neuenkirchen D 119 Ed31
Neuenkirchen-Vöhrden D 117 Cc36
Neuenrade D 125 Cb40
Neuenstadt D 134 Cd47
Neuenstein D 126 Da41
Neuenstein D 134 Da47
Neuenweg D 141 Ca51
Neuerburg D 133 Bb43
Neufahrn D 135 Eb49
Neufahrn D 143 Ea50
Neuf-Brisach F 31 Kc39
Neufchâteau B 132 Ba44
Neufchâteau F 31 Jc38
Neufchâtel-en-Bray F 23 Gb34
Neufchâtel-en-Saosnois F 28 Fd38
Neufchâtel-sur-Aisne F 24 Hc35
Neuffen D 134 Cd49
Neuf-Marché F 23 Gc35
Neufra D 142 Cd50
Neugattersleben D 127 Ea38
Neugersdorf D 128 Fc41
Neuhardenberg D 128 Fb36
Neuharlingersiel D 117 Cb32
Neuhaus A 144 Fd52
Neuhaus D 118 Da32
Neuhaus D 119 Dd33
Neuhaus D 135 Ea46
Neuhaus D 143 Ed50
Neuhaus am Rennweg D 135 Dd43
Neuhausen CH 141 Cb52
Neuhausen D 127 Ed42
Neuhausen D 128 Fb39
Neuhausen D 134 Cc48
Neuhausen ob Eck D 142 Cc51
Neuhaus-Schierschnitz D 135 Dd43
Neuhof D 134 Da43
Neuhof D 134 Dc46
Neuhofen an der Krems A 144 Fb51
Neuillay-les-Bois F 29 Gc44
Neuillé-Pont-Pierre F 29 Ga41
Neuilly-en-Donjon F 34 Hd45
Neuilly-en-Thelle F 23 Gd35
Neuilly-le-Réal F 30 Hc44
Neuilly-Saint-Front F 24 Hb36
Neuilly-sur-Eure F 29 Ga38
Neu-Isenburg D 134 Cc44
Neukalen D 119 Ec32
Neu Kaliß D 119 Ea34
Neukamperfehn D 117 Cb33
Neukieritzsch D 127 Eb41
Neukirch CH 142 Cc55
Neukirch D 128 Fa40
Neukirch D 128 Fb41
Neukirch D 142 Da52
Neukirchen A 143 Eb54
Neukirchen A 143 Ec51
Neukirchen D 108 Cd28
Neukirchen D 119 Dd30
Neukirchen D 126 Da41
Neukirchen D 127 Ec42
Neukirchen D 135 Ea46
Neukirchen D 135 Ec47
Neukirchen D 135 Ec48
Neukirchen am Walde A 144 Fa50
Neukirchen-Balbini D 135 Eb47
Neukirchen-Vluyn D 125 Bc39
Neukirchen-Wyhra D 127 Ec41
Neukloster D 119 Ea32
Neu Kosenow D 120 Fa32
Neulengbach A 144 Ga51
Neuler D 134 Db48
Neulikko FIN 75 Kd23
Neulingen D 134 Cc47
Neulise F 34 Hd46
Neulliac F 27 Ea39
Neu Lübbenau D 128 Fa38
Neum BIH 158 Ha68
Neumagen-Dhron D 133 Bd44
Neumark D 127 Eb42
Neumarkt A 144 Fa50
Neumarkt D 135 Dd47
Neumarkt I 150 Dd57
Neumarkt I 150 Dd57
Neumarkt am Wallersee A 143 Ed51
Neumarkt an der Ybbs A 144 Fc51
Neumarkt im Mühlkreis A 144 Fb50
Neumarkt in Steiermark A 144 Fb54
Neumarkt-Sankt Veit D 143 Eb50
Neumünster D 118 Db31
Neunburg vorm Wald D 135 Eb47
Neundorf D 127 Ea38
Neung-sur-Beuvron F 29 Gc41
Neunkirch CH 141 Cb52
Neunkirchen A 145 Gb52
Neunkirchen D 125 Cb41
Neunkirchen D 133 Bd46
Neunkirchen D 135 Dd46
Neunkirchen-Seelscheid D 125 Ca41
Neuötting D 143 Ec50
Neupetershain D 128 Fb39
Neupölla A 136 Fd49
Neupré B 124 Ba42
Neuranft D 120 Fb35
Neurázy CZ 135 Ed47
Neureichenau D 136 Fa49
Neurenberg = Nürnberg D 135 Dd46
Neuried D 133 Ca49
Neuruppin D 119 Ec35
Neusach A 143 Ed55
Neusalza-Spremberg D 128 Fb41
Neu Sankt Johann CH 142 Cc53
Neusäß D 142 Dc50
Neuschönau D 135 Ed48
Neuschoo D 117 Cb32
Neusiedl am See A 145 Gc51
Neusitz D 134 Db46
Neusorg D 135 Ea45
Neuss D 125 Bd40
Neussargues-Moissac F 34 Hb49
Neustadt D 119 Dd31
Neustadt D 119 Ec35
Neustadt D 126 Da36
Neustadt D 126 Dc39
Neustadt D 127 Dd42
Neustadt D 128 Fb41
Neustadt, Titisee- D 141 Ca51
Neustadt/ Donau D 135 Ea48
Neustadt am Kulm D 135 Ea45
Neustadt am Main D 134 Da44
Neustadt an der Aisch D 134 Dc46
Neustadt an der Orla D 127 Ea42
Neustadt an der Waldnaab D 135 Eb45
Neustadt an der Weinstraße D 133 Cb46
Neustadt bei Coburg D 135 Dd43
Neustadt-Glewe D 119 Ea33
Neustadt (Hessen) D 126 Cd41
Neustadt (Wied) D 125 Ca42
Neustift A 144 Fa50
Neustift im Stubaital A 143 Dd54
Neustrelitz D 119 Ed33
Neutraubling D 135 Eb48
Neutrebbin D 128 Fb36
Neu-Ulm D 142 Da50
Neuves-Maisons F 25 Jd37
Neuvic F 32 Fd49
Neuvic F 33 Gd48
Neuvic-Entier F 33 Gc47
Neuville F 33 Gc49
Neuville-aux-Bois F 29 Gd39
Neuville-de-Poitou F 28 Fd44
Neuville-les-Dames F 34 Jb45
Neuville-les-Decize F 30 Hb43
Neuville-sur-Saône F 34 Jb46
Neuvilly-en-Argonne F 24 Ja35
Neuvola FIN 90 Kd32
Neuvosenniemi FIN 82 Kd25
Neuvy-Bouin F 28 Fb44
Neuvy-le-Roi F 29 Ga41
Neuvy-Pailloux F 29 Gc43
Neuvy-Saint-Sépulcre F 29 Gc44
Neuvy-Sautour F 30 Hc39
Neuvy-sur-Barangeon F 29 Gd42
Neuvy-sur-Loire F 29 Ha41
Neuwied D 125 Ca42
Neuwiller-lès-Saverne F 25 Kb36
Neu Wulmstorf D 118 Db33
Neuzelle D 128 Fc38
Neuzina SRB 174 Bb62
Neu Zittau, Gosen- D 128 Fa37
Neva S 95 Fb41
Névache F 35 Kb49
Nevalan vaara FIN 75 Lb19
Nevardenai LT 113 Jd55
Neveja LV 105 Jc49
Neveklov CZ 136 Fb45
Nevel' RUS 202 Eb11
Neverėnai LT 113 Jc54
Neverėnai LT 115 Lc55
Neverfjord N 63 Ja06
Nevernes N 70 Ed23
Nevernes N 71 Fc20
Nevers F 30 Hb43
Nevesinje BIH 158 Hb67
Nevest HR 158 Gb65
Nevestino BG 179 Cb72
Neviano I 163 Hc77
Nevinnomyssk RUS 205 Fd16
Nevlunghavn N 93 Dc44
Nevrin TR 187 Gc77
Nevša BG 181 Ed70
New Abbey GB 10 Ea16
New Aberdour GB 5 Ed07
New Alresford GB 20 Fa29
Newark-on-Trent GB 16 Fb23
Newbald GB 16 Fb20
Newbiggin GB 11 Ed17
Newbiggin-by-the-Sea GB 11 Fa16
Newbliss IRL 9 Cc18
Newborough GB 15 Dd22
Newbridge IRL 8 Cb21
Newbridge IRL 13 Cc22
Newbridge-on-Wye GB 15 Ea25
New Buckenham GB 21 Ga25
Newburgh GB 5 Ed08
Newburgh GB 7 Eb12
Newburn GB 11 Ed16
Newbury GB 20 Fa28
Newby Bridge GB 11 Eb19
Newcastle GB 9 Da18
Newcastle GB 15 Eb25
Newcastle IRL 13 Ca24
Newcastle IRL 13 Cd21
Newcastle IRL 13 Da22
Newcastle Emlyn GB 14 Dc26
New Castleton GB 11 Ec15
Newcastle-under-Lyme GB 15 Ec23
Newcastle upon Tyne GB 11 Fa16
Newcastle West IRL 12 Bc24
Newchurch GB 14 Dc26
New Cumnock GB 10 Dd15
New Deer GB 5 Ed08
Newent GB 15 Ec26
Newgale GB 14 Db26
New Galloway GB 10 Dd16
New Grimsby GB 18 Cc32
Newham GB 11 Fa14
Newhaven GB 20 Fd30
New Holland GB 17 Fc21
Newick GB 20 Fd30
New Inn IRL 9 Cc19
Newinn IRL 13 Ca24
New Luce GB 10 Dc16
Newmachar GB 7 Ed09
Newmains GB 10 Ea13
New Malden GB 20 Fc28
Newmarket GB 4 Da05
Newmarket GB 20 Fd25
Newmarket IRL 12 Bc24
Newmarket on Fergus IRL 12 Bc23
New Mills GB 15 Ea24
New Mills GB 16 Ed22
New Milton GB 20 Ed30
Newnham Bridge GB 15 Ec25
New Pitsligo GB 5 Ed07
Newport GB 14 Dc26
Newport GB 15 Ec24
Newport GB 19 Eb28
Newport GB 20 Fa31
Newport IRL 8 Bc19
Newport IRL 12 Bd23
Newport Pagnell GB 20 Fb26
Newport Trench GB 9 Cd17
New Quay GB 14 Dc25
Newquay GB 18 Db31
New Romney GB 21 Ga30
New Ross IRL 13 Cc24
New Rossington GB 16 Fb21
Newry GB 9 Cd18
Newton Abbot GB 19 Ea31
Newton-Aycliffe GB 11 Fa17
Newtonhill GB 7 Ed09
Newton-le-Willows GB 15 Ec21
Newtonmore GB 7 Ea09
Newton-on-Trent GB 16 Fb22
Newton Poppleford GB 19 Ea30
Newton Stewart GB 10 Dd16
Newtown GB 15 Ea24
Newtown GB 15 Ec26
Newtown IRL 12 Bc22
Newtown IRL 12 Bd24
Newtown IRL 12 Bd24
Newtown IRL 13 Ca21
Newtown IRL 13 Ca22
Newtown IRL 13 Cc23
Newtownabbey GB 9 Da17
Newtownards GB 10 Db17
Newtownbreda GB 9 Da17
Newtownbutler GB 9 Cc18
Newtown Cunningham IRL 9 Cc15
Newtown Forbes IRL 9 Cb19
Newtownhamilton GB 9 Cd18
Newtown Saint Boswells GB 11 Ec14
Newtown Sandes IRL 12 Bb23
Newtownshandrum IRL 12 Bc24
Newtownstewart GB 9 Cc16
New Tredegar GB 19 Eb27
New Twopothouse IRL 12 Bd25
Nexø DK 111 Fd58
Nexon F 33 Gb47
Nežilovo MK 183 Bb74
Nežnovo RUS 99 Ld40
Nezvěstice CZ 135 Ed46
Nianfors S 87 Gb36
Niáta GR 195 Bd90
Nibbiano I 149 Cc61
Nibe DK 100 Dc21
Nica LV 113 Ja53
Nicaj-Shalë AL 159 Jb70
Nicastro I 164 Gc81
Niccone I 156 Ea67
Nice F 43 Kd53
Nicey F 30 Hd40
Nickby FIN 98 Kc39
Nickelsdorf A 145 Gd51
Nicknoret S 72 Ha24
Nicolae Bălcescu RO 172 Ed59
Nicolae Bălcescu RO 176 Ec66
Nicolae Bălcescu RO 177 Fc66
Nicolinț RO 174 Bd63
Nicolosi I 167 Fc85
Nicoreni MD 173 Fb55
Nicorești RO 176 Ed61
Nicosia I 167 Fb85
Nicotera I 164 Gb82
Ničpur MK 178 Ba73
Nicșeni RO 172 Ec55
Niculițel RO 177 Fc64
Nida LT 113 Jb56
Nida LV 113 Ja54
Nidda D 134 Cd43
Niddatal D 134 Cc43
Nidderau D 134 Cc43
Nideggen D 125 Bc41
Nidri GR 188 Ac83
Nidzica PL 122 Ja33
Niebieszczany PL 139 Ka45
Niebla E 59 Bc73
Nieblum D 108 Cd28
Nieborów PL 130 Ja37
Niebüll D 108 Da28
Niechanowo PL 129 Gd36
Niechcice PL 130 Hd40
Niechłonin PL 122 Hd34
Niechlów PL 129 Gb39
Niechobórz PL 139 Ka44
Niechorze PL 120 Fc31
Niedalino PL 120 Ga31
Niederaichbach D 135 Eb49
Niederalp A 144 Fd52
Niederalteich D 135 Ec49
Niederau D 128 Fa41
Niederaula D 126 Da42
Niederbronn-les-Bains F 25 Kc35
Niederdorf I 143 Ea55
Niedereschach D 141 Cb50
Niederfischbach D 125 Cb41
Niederfüllbach D 135 Dd44
Niedergörsdorf D 127 Ed38
Niederkirchen D 133 Ca45
Niederkrüchten D 125 Bc40
Niederlangen D 117 Ca34
Niederleger A 143 Dd53
Niederlehme D 128 Fa37
Niedermurach D 135 Eb46
Niederndodeleben D 127 Ea37
Niedernhall D 134 Da47
Niedernwöhren D 126 Da36
Niederöblarn A 144 Fa53
Niederoderwitz D 128 Fc41
Nieder-Olm D 133 Cb44
Niederorschel D 126 Dc40
Niederrossbach D 125 Cb42
Niedersachswerfen D 126 Dc39
Nieder-Seifersdorf D 128 Fc41
Niederstetten D 134 Da46
Niederstotzingen D 134 Db49
Niedersulz A 145 Gc50
Niederurnen CH 142 Cc54
Niederviehbach D 135 Eb49
Nieder-Waroldern D 126 Cd40
Niederwerrn D 134 Db44
Niederwiesa D 127 Ed42
Niederwinkling D 135 Ec48
Niederwölz A 144 Fb54
Niederzier D 125 Bc41
Niedźwiednik PL 137 Gc43
Niedoradz PL 128 Ga38
Niedorp NL 116 Ba34
Niedrzew PL 130 Hc37
Niedrzwica Duża PL 131 Ka40
Niedzbórz PL 122 Ja34
Niedzica PL 138 Jb46
Niedźwiada PL 123 Jd32
Niedźwiada PL 131 Kb39
Niedźwiedź PL 122 Hc34
Niedźwiedź PL 128 Fd37
Niedźwiedź PL 138 Ja46
Niegosławice PL 128 Ga39
Niegosławice PL 130 Jb42
Niegowa PL 130 Hd42
Niegowonice PL 138 Hd43
Niegripp D 127 Ea37
Nieheim D 126 Cd38
Niekursko PL 121 Gb34
Nieledew PL 131 Kd41
Nielisz PL 131 Kc41
Nielstrup DK 101 Dd19
Niemberg D 127 Eb39
Niemce PL 131 Kb39
Niemcza PL 129 Gc42
Niemczyn PL 121 Gd35
Niemegk D 127 Ec38
Niemelä FIN 64 Ka07
Niemelä FIN 74 Kd18
Niemelänkylä FIN 81 Jd27
Niemenhylä FIN 90 Kc37
Niemenkylä FIN 82 Ka28
Niemenkylä FIN 89 Jb35
Niemenkylä FIN 89 Ja32
Niemenkylä FIN 89 Ja36
Niemenkylä FIN 90 La32
Niemetal D 126 Da39
Niemica PL 120 Fc32
Niemica PL 121 Gb30
Niemijärvi FIN 83 Mb29
Niemikylä FIN 83 Lb29
Nieminen FIN 82 Kd27
Niemirów PL 131 Kb36
Niemis S 73 Jb20
Niemisel S 73 Hd21
Niemisjärvi FIN 82 Kd30
Niemisjärvi FIN 90 Kc32
Niemiskylä FIN 82 Kc28
Niemiskylä FIN 89 Jd32
Niemodlin PL 129 Gd42
Niemojki PL 131 Ka36
Nienadowa PL 139 Kb44
Nienburg D 118 Da35
Nienburg D 127 Ea38
Nienhagen D 126 Db36
Nienstädt D 126 Da37
Niepars D 119 Ed30
Niepołomice PL 138 Ja44
Nieporęt PL 130 Jb36
Nierstein D 133 Cb44
Niesi FIN 69 Jd17
Niesky D 128 Fc40
Niestetal D 126 Da40
Niestronno PL 121 Ha35
Nieszawa PL 121 Hb35
Nietkowice PL 128 Fd38
Nieuil F 33 Gb46
Nieuil-l'Espoir F 32 Fd45
Nieul-le-Dolent F 28 Ed44
Nieuw-Amsterdam NL 117 Ca35
Nieuwegein NL 116 Ba36
Nieuwekerk aan de IJssel NL 124 Ad37
Nieuwendijk NL 124 Ba37
Nieuwe Pekela NL 117 Ca34
Nieuwerkerken B 124 Ba40
Nieuweschans NL 117 Ca33
Nieuwkerke B 21 Ha30
Nieuwkoop NL 116 Ba36
Nieuwleusen NL 117 Bc35
Nieuw Milligen NL 116 Bb36
Nieuwolda NL 117 Ca33
Nieuwpoort B 21 Ha29
Nieuwpoort-Bad B 21 Ha29
Nieves (Capela) E 36 Bb53
Niewęgłosz PL 131 Kb38
Niewierz PL 122 Hc34
Niewiesze PL 137 Hb43
Niezabyszewo PL 121 Gd31
Niezgoda PL 129 Gc40
Nigrán E 36 Ac58
Nigrande LV 105 Jc52
Nigrita GR 184 Cc77
Nigula EST 98 Ka44
Niharra E 46 Cd64
Nihattula FIN 90 Ka37
Niilivaara FIN 68 Jc15
Niinikumpu FIN 91 Ld32
Niinilahti FIN 82 Kb30
Niinilahti FIN 83 Lc28
Niinimaa FIN 89 Jc32
Niinimäki FIN 82 Kb28
Niinimäki FIN 83 Lb31
Niininkoski FIN 90 Kc37
Niinisalo FIN 89 Jb34
Niinivedenpää FIN 82 Kc30
Niinivesi FIN 82 Kc30
Niirala FIN 83 Ma31
Niittumaa FIN 89 Ja36
Níjar E 61 Eb76
Nij Beets NL 117 Bc33
Nijemci HR 153 Hd60
Nijkerk NL 116 Bb36
Nijmegen NL 125 Bb37
Nijverdal NL 117 Bd36
Nikaranperä FIN 90 Ka32
Nikea GR 189 Bd81
Nikea GR 189 Cb86
Niki GR 183 Bb76
Niki GR 189 Bd81
Nikifóros GR 184 Da76
Nikinci SRB 153 Jb61
Nikíssiani GR 184 Cd77
Nikitari CY 206 Ja97
Nikitas GR 184 Cc79
Nikitsch A 145 Gc53
Nikkala S 74 Jc21
Nikkaluokta S 67 Gd15
Nikkaroinen FIN 90 Kc35
Nikkeby N 63 Hb08
Nikodim MK 183 Bc75
Nikokleia CY 206 Hd98
Nikolaeskoe RUS 99 Ma43
Nikolaevka BG 181 Fa70
Nikolaevka RUS 203 Fd10
Nikolaevo BG 180 Db70
Nikolaevo BG 180 Dd72
Nikolaevo BG 180 Eb72
Nikolaevo RUS 99 Mb45
Nikolaevsk RUS 203 Fd13
Nikola Kozlevo BG 181 Ed69
Nikolinac SRB 179 Ca67
Nikolinci SRB 174 Bc63
Nikolovo BG 180 Ea68
Nikol'sk RUS 203 Fd10
Nikol'skoe RUS 99 Mb40
Nikopol BG 180 Dc68
Nikopol' UA 205 Fa16
Nikópoli GR 183 Cb77
Nikópoli GR 188 Ad82
Nikosia = Lefkosia CY 206 Jb96
Nikrace LV 105 Jc52
Niksar TR 205 Fc20
Nikšić MNE 159 Hd68
Nikulanperä FIN 69 Ka11
Nilivaara S 68 Hc17
Nilsebu N 92 Cb43
Nilsiä FIN 82 La29
Nilüfer TR 186 Fc80
Nim DK 108 Db25
Nimereuca MD 173 Fc54
Nîmes F 42 Ja53
Nimfasía GR 194 Bb87
Nimféo GR 183 Bb77
Nimfes GR 182 Ab79
Nimigea RO 171 Db56
Nimis I 150 Ed57
Nimisjärvi FIN 82 Kc25
Nimtofte DK 101 Dd23
Nin HR 157 Fd64
Nina EST 99 Lb44
Ninebanks GB 11 Ec17
Ninfield GB 20 Fd30
Ninivaara FIN 83 Lb29
Ninove B 124 Ab40
Niorcani MD 173 Fb53
Niort F 32 Fb45
Nipen N 66 Ga13
Nipuli FIN 90 Kd35
Nirza LV 107 Ma51
Niš SRB 178 Bb69
Nisa P 50 Ba66
Nișcani MD 173 Fc57
Niscemi I 167 Fb87
Niševac SRB 178 Bd68
Nisí GR 188 Ba86
Niška Banja SRB 178 Bd69
Niskala FIN 75 Kc20
Niskanperä FIN 74 Jd19
Niskanperä FIN 74 Jd20
Nisko PL 131 Ka42
Niskos FIN 89 Jc33
Nisou CY 206 Jb97
Nisovo BG 180 Ea69
Nispen NL 124 Ad38
Nisporeni MD 173 Fb58
Nissafors S 102 Fa50
Nissaki GR 182 Ab79
Nissan-lez-Enserune F 41 Hb55
Nissedal N 93 Da44
Nissi EST 98 Kb43
Nissí GR 183 Bc77
Nissí GR 183 Bd77
Nissilä FIN 82 Kc27
Nissumby DK 100 Cd22
Nissum Seminarieby DK 100 Cd22
Nistelrode NL 125 Bb38
Nisula FIN 90 Kc33
Nisus FIN 90 Kd34
Nitaure LV 106 Kd50
Nitchidorf RO 174 Bd61
Níthavris GR 200 Cd96
Niton GB 20 Fa31
Nitra SK 145 Hb50
Nitrianske Pravno SK 138 Hc48
Nitrianske Rudno SK 137 Hb48
Nitry F 30 Hc40
Nittedal N 93 Ea41
Nittel D 133 Bc45
Nittenau D 135 Eb47
Nittendorf D 135 Ea48
Nittorp S 102 Fa49
Niukkala FIN 91 Ld33
Niuraičiai LT 114 Kb53
Niūronys LT 114 Kd55
Nivå DK 109 Ec25
Niva FIN 83 Lb25

Nivala - Nufăru

Nivala FIN 82 Ka27
Nivankylä FIN 74 Jd18
Nivelles B 124 Ac41
Nivenskoe RUS 113 Ja59
Nivjanin BG 179 Cd69
Nivnice CZ 137 Ha48
Niwica PL 128 Fc39
Niwiska PL 128 Fd39
Niwiska PL 139 Jd43
Niyazcar TR 198 Ga89
Nižbor CZ 136 Fa45
Niziny PL 130 Jc42
Nižná SK 138 Hd47
Nižná Boca SK 138 Ja48
Nižna Polianka SK 139 Jd46
Nižná Slaná SK 138 Jb48
Nižnekamsk RUS 203 Ga08
Nižnij Novgorod RUS 203 Fb09
Nižný Hrabovec SK 139 Ka48
Nizovicy RUS 99 Ld45
Nizy-le-Comte F 24 Hc34
Nižyn UA 202 Ec14
Nizza Monferrato I 148 Ca61
Nizza = Nice F 43 Kd53
Njakaure S 73 Hb21
Njallavárri S 68 Hc17
Njallejaur S 72 Ha22
Njasviž BY 202 Ea13
Njavve S 72 Gc18
Njegoševo SRB 153 Ja58
Njegovuđa MNE 159 Ja67
Njellim FIN 69 Kb11
Njetsavare S 73 Hb19
Njivice HR 151 Fb61
Njuorggam FIN 64 Ka07
Njurunda S 88 Gc34
Njurundabommen S 88 Gc34
Njutånger S 87 Gb36
No DK 108 Cd24
Noailhac F 41 Ha54
Noailles F 23 Gd35
Noailly F 34 Hd45
Noale I 150 Ea59
Noalejo E 60 Db74
Noasca I 148 Bc59
Nöbbele S 103 Fc52
Nöbbele S 103 Fc52
Nöbbelöv S 111 Fb55
Nobber IRL 9 Cd20
Nöbdenitz D 127 Eb42
Nobitz D 127 Ec41
Noblejas E 52 Dc66
Nоćaj SRB 153 Ja61
Nocé F 29 Ga38
Noceda E 37 Ca56
Nocedo de Curueño E 37 Cc56
Nocedo do Val E 36 Bb58
Nocelleto I 161 Fa74
Nocera Inferiore I 161 Fb75
Nocera Terinese I 164 Gb81
Nocera Umbra I 156 Eb67
Noceto I 149 Da61
Nochowo PL 129 Gc38
Noci I 162 Gd75
Nociglia I 163 Hc77
Nociunai LT 114 Kb53
Nociūnai LT 114 Kc56
Nocrich RO 175 Db61
Nodanö S 95 Ga41
Nodar E 36 Bb55
Nødebo DK 109 Ec25
Nodeland N 92 Cd47
Nödinge-Nol S 102 Ec48
Nods F 31 Ka42
Noé F 40 Gb55
Noepoli I 162 Gb77
Nœux-les-Mines F 23 Ha31
Noevci BG 179 Cb71
Noez E 52 Da66
Nofuentes E 38 Dd56
Nogale LV 105 Jd49
Nogales E 51 Bc70
Nogara I 149 Dc60
Nogarejas E 37 Ca58
Nogaro F 40 Fc54
Nogawczyce PL 137 Hb43
Nogent F 30 Jb39
Nogent-le-Roi F 23 Gc37
Nogent-le-Rotrou F 29 Ga38
Nogent-sur-Aube F 30 Hd38
Nogent-sur-Marne F 23 Gd37
Nogent-sur-Seine F 30 Hb38
Nogent-sur-Vernisson F 29 Ha40
Nogersund S 111 Fc55
Nogheredo I 150 Eb58
Nõgiaru EST 98 La45
Noginsk RUS 203 Fa10
Nogna F 31 Jc44
Nógrádmegyer H 146 Ja51
Nogueira E 36 Ba57
Nogueira de Ramuín E 36 Bb57
Noguera E 47 Ed64
Nogueruelas E 54 Fb65
Nohant-en-Graçay F 29 Gc42
Nohant-Vic F 29 Gd44
Nohèdes F 41 Ha57
Nohfelden D 133 Bd45
Nohn D 133 Bc43
Nohra D 126 Dc40
Nohutalan TR 191 Ea86
Noia E 36 Ac55
Noicattaro I 162 Gd74
Noidanpola FIN 68 Ja14
Noidans-le-Ferroux F 31 Jd40
Noirefontaine F 31 Ka41
Noirétable F 34 Hc47
Noirlieu F 28 Fc43
Noirmoutier-en-l'Île F 27 Ec43
Nois E 36 Bc53
Noiseux B 124 Ba42
Noja E 38 Dd54
Nojewo PL 129 Gb36
Nojorid RO 170 Ca57
Nokia FIN 89 Jd36
Nokka FIN 90 Kc34
Nokkamäki FIN 82 La28
Nokkosmäenkulma FIN 89 Ja34
Nola I 161 Fb75
Nolay E 47 Eb61
Nolay F 30 Ja43
Noli I 148 Ca63
Nolimo FIN 74 Kc18
Nomansland GB 19 Ea30
Nõmba EST 97 Jc44
Nombela E 46 Da65
Nomeland N 92 Cd44
Nomeny F 25 Jd36
Nomexy F 31 Jd38
Nomí GR 189 Bc81
Nómia GR 195 Bd91
Nõmme EST 98 Kb42
Nõmmküla EST 97 Jd45
Nomparedes E 47 Eb61
Nonancourt F 23 Gb37
Nonant-le-Pin F 22 Fd37
Nonantola I 149 Dc62
Nonaspe E 48 Fd62
None I 148 Bc61
Nonnweiler D 133 Bd45
Nõnova EST 107 Lc47
Nontron F 33 Ga48
Nonvilliers F 29 Gb38
Nonza F 154 Cc68
Nõo EST 99 Lb45
Noordbeemster NL 116 Ba35
Noordwijk aan Zee NL 116 Ad36
Noordwijkerhout NL 116 Ad36
Noormarkku FIN 89 Ja35
Nopala FIN 91 Lb37
Nopankylä FIN 89 Ja32
Noposenaho FIN 81 Jd30
Noppikoski S 87 Fc36
Noppo FIN 90 Kb38
Nor N 84 Cc34
Nor N 94 Ec40
Nor S 87 Fd32
Nor S 94 Fa43
Nora S 87 Gb33
Nora S 88 Gd32
Nora S 95 Fc43
Nora S 95 Gb41
Norageliai LT 114 Kc59
Nørager DK 100 Db22
Noragugume I 169 Ca76
Norberg S 95 Ga41
Norbo S 95 Fd40
Norcia I 156 Ec68
Nordagutu N 93 Dc43
Nordanå S 110 Ed53
Nordanåker S 79 Ga30
Nordanås S 71 Ga23
Nordanås S 72 Gd22
Nordanås S 80 Gd27
Nordanholen S 95 Fc40
Nordankäl S 79 Ga29
Nordansjö S 79 Ga25
Nordarnøy N 66 Fb17
Nordausques F 21 Gc30
Nordbakk N 78 Fa26
Nordberg N 85 Db34
Nordbø N 93 Da47
Nordborg DK 108 Db27
Nordby DK 108 Cd26
Nordby DK 109 Dd25
Nordby N 86 Eb37
Nordby N 93 Ea41
Nordby N 93 Ea42
Norddal N 84 Cb35
Norddeich D 117 Ca32
Norddorf D 108 Cd28
Nordeidet N 64 Jb06
Nordelph GB 17 Fd24
Norden D 117 Ca32
Norden S 72 Ha21
Nordendorf D 134 Dc49
Nordenham D 118 Cd32
Nordenskov DK 108 Da25
Norderåsen S 79 Fc30
Norderhov N 93 Dd41
Norderney D 117 Ca31
Norderön S 79 Fb31
Norderstedt D 118 Db32
Nord-Etnedal N 85 Dc37
Nordfjord N 66 Fd17
Nordfjordbotn N 67 Gd11
Nordfjordeid N 84 Cc34
Nordfjorden N 70 Fa20
Nord-Flatanger N 78 Eb26
Nord-Fogn N 92 Ca43
Nordfold N 66 Fd16
Nord-Gutvika N 70 Ec24
Nordhalben D 135 Ea43
Nordhallen S 78 Ed30
Nordhamna N 63 Ja05
Nordhastedt D 118 Da30
Nordhausen D 126 Dc39
Nordheim D 134 Cd47
Nordheim vor der Rhön D 134 Db43
Nordhella N 62 Gd09
Nordholz D 118 Cd32
Nordhorn D 117 Ca36
Nordhorsfjord N 70 Ec24
Nordhus N 63 Hd08
Nordingrå S 80 Gd31
Nordkirchen D 125 Ca38
Nordkisa N 94 Eb40
Nordkjosbotn N 67 Gd11
Nordkroken S 102 Ec47
Nordland N 66 Fa16
Nordleda D 118 Cd32
Nord-Leirvåg N 65 Kc07
Nordli N 71 Fb23
Nördlingen D 134 Db48
Nordmaling S 80 Ha29
Nordmannset N 64 Jc04
Nordmannset N 64 Jb06
Nordmannvik N 62 Ha09
Nordmark S 95 Fb42
Nordmela N 66 Fd11
Nordnes N 71 Fd18
Nordnesøya N 70 Ed19
Nordomsjön S 86 Fa35
Nordøyvågen N 70 Ed21
Nordre Gavesluft N 64 Ka05
Nordre Osen N 86 Ec37
Nordrollnes N 67 Gb12
Nord-Sel N 85 Dc35
Nordseter N 85 Ea37
Nordsinni N 85 Dd38
Nordsjö S 79 Ga29
Nordsjö S 87 Ga36
Nordskjørin N 78 Ea27
Nordskov DK 109 Dd26
Nord-Statland N 78 Eb26
Nordstemmen D 126 Db37
Nordstrand D 108 Da29
Nordstrand N 62 Gc10
Nordstrand N 76 Cc32
Nord-Værnes N 70 Fa19
Nordvågen N 64 Jc04
Nordvik FIN 97 Jc40
Nordvik N 65 Kd08
Nordvik N 70 Ed21
Nordvik N 77 Dc31
Nordvika N 77 Db29
Nordwalde D 125 Ca37
Nore N 85 Db40
Nore S 87 Ga35
Norem N 78 Eb28
Noreña E 37 Cc54
Noresund N 85 Dc40
Noret S 81 Hd27
Norfjärden S 88 Gc34
Norg NL 117 Bd33
Norges-la-Ville F 30 Jb41
Norgravsjö S 80 Gd28
Nørhå DK 100 Da21
Norham GB 11 Ed14
Norheimsund N 84 Cb39
Norinkylä FIN 89 Ja32
Norje S 111 Fc54
Norma I 160 Ec72
Normandy GB 20 Fb29
Normanton GB 16 Fa21
Normée F 24 Hd37
Normlösa S 103 Fd47
Norn S 95 Fd40
Nornäs S 86 Fa36
Norola FIN 90 La34
Noroy-le-Bourg F 31 Jd40
Norra Åsum S 111 Fb55
Norra Avradsberg S 94 Fa40
Norra Björke S 102 Ec47
Norra Bredåker S 73 Hc21
Norra Fågelås S 103 Fb47
Norra Fårträsk S 72 Gd24
Norra Finnskoga S 86 Ed38
Norra Fjällnäs S 71 Fd22
Norrahammar S 103 Fb49
Norra Härene S 102 Ed46
Norra Hjulbäck S 95 Fc39
Norra Holmnäs S 72 Ha22
Norra Kedum S 102 Ed46
Norråker S 79 Gb25
Norråker S 79 Fd26
Norrala S 87 Gb37
Norra Latikberg S 79 Gb26
Norra Löten S 86 Ed38
Norra Lundby S 102 Fa47
Norra Mellby S 110 Fa54
Norra Möckleby S 103 Gb52
Norrånös S 79 Ga29
Norra Ny S 94 Fa40
Norra Örnäs S 72 Gb23
Norra Prästholm S 73 Hd21
Norra Rörum S 110 Fa55
Norra Sandby S 110 Fa54
Norra Sandsjö S 103 Fc50
Norra Skärvången S 79 Fb29
Norra Stensund S 72 Gb23
Norra Sunderbyn S 73 Hd22
Norra Ullerud S 94 Fa43
Norra Umstrand S 71 Ga24
Norra Unnaryd S 102 Fa49
Norra Vallgrund FIN 81 Hd30
Norra Vånga S 102 Fa47
Norra Vi S 103 Fd48
Norra Volgsjöfors S 79 Gb26
Norrback FIN 89 Ja32
Norrbäck S 80 Gc25
Norrberg S 72 Gb24
Norrbo S 87 Gb35
Norrboda FIN 96 Hc40
Norrboda S 87 Fd37
Norrboda S 96 Gd39
Norrby FIN 81 Jb28
Norrby S 80 Hb26
Norrby S 95 Gb41
Norrbyås S 95 Fd44
Norrbyberg S 80 Gd25
Norrbyn S 80 Hb29
Norrdal S 72 Gb24
Nørre Aaby DK 108 Dc26
Nørre Alslev DK 109 Eb28
Nørre Bork DK 108 Cd25
Nørre Broby DK 108 Dc27
Nørreby DK 109 Ea28
Nørre Halne DK 100 Dc20
Nørre Havrvig DK 108 Cd24
Nørre Herlev DK 109 Ec25
Nørre Jernløse DK 109 Eb26
Nørre Knudstrup DK 100 Db23
Nørre Kongerslev DK 100 Dc21
Nørre Lyndelse DK 108 Dc27
Nørre Lyngby DK 100 Dc20
Nørre Nebel DK 108 Cd25
Nørre Snede DK 108 Db24
Nørresundby DK 100 Dc21
Nørre Vejrup DK 108 Da26
Nørre Vilstrup DK 108 Db25
Nørre Vissing DK 108 Dc24
Nørre Vorupør DK 100 Cd21
Norrfjärden S 73 Hd23
Norrfjärden S 80 Hc28
Norrflärke S 80 Ha30
Norrfors S 80 Gd27
Norrfors S 80 Ha28
Norrgårdssälen S 86 Fa38
Norrhed S 73 Hc20
Norrhult S 103 Fd51
Norrian S 73 Hd20
Norrköping S 103 Ga46
Norrlanda S 104 Ha49
Norrlångträsk S 73 Hc24
Norrmjöle S 80 Hb29
Norrnäs FIN 89 Hd32
Norrnäs S 79 Ga28
Norrsjön S 79 Fd26
Norrskedika S 96 Gd40
Norrsundet S 87 Gb38
Norrtälje S 96 Ha42
Norrtannflo S 79 Gb30
Norrvik S 80 Gc26
Nors DK 100 Da21
Norsholm S 103 Ga46
Norsjö S 80 Ha25
Norsjövallen S 80 Ha25
Norskbukta N 65 Kc07
Norsminde DK 108 Dc24
Nörten-Hardenberg D 126 Db39
Northallerton GB 11 Fa18
Northam GB 18 Dc29
Northampton GB 20 Fb25
North Berwick GB 11 Ec13
Northchapel GB 20 Fb29
North Charlton GB 11 Fa15
North Dalton GB 16 Fb20
Northeim D 126 Db39
North Ferriby GB 17 Fc20
North Ferriby GB 17 Fc21
North Grimston GB 16 Fb19
Northiam GB 21 Ga30
North Kilworth GB 20 Fa25
Northleach GB 20 Ed27
North Molton GB 19 Dd29
North Petherton GB 19 Eb29
North Somercotes GB 17 Fd21
North Tawton GB 19 Dd30
North Thoresby GB 17 Fc21
North Tidworth GB 20 Ed29
Northton GB 4 Cd06
Northwall GB 5 Ed02
North Walsham GB 17 Gb23
North Weald Bassett GB 20 Fd27
Northwich GB 15 Ec22
Northwood GB 15 Eb23
North Wootton GB 17 Fd24
Nortmoor D 117 Cb33
Norton GB 16 Fb19
Nortorf D 118 Db30
Northh Creake GB 17 Ga23
Nortrup D 117 Cb35
Nort-sur-Erdre F 28 Ed41
Noruliai LT 123 Kd30
Norum N 84 Cd37
Norum S 102 Eb48
Norup DK 100 Dc22
Norup DK 108 Dc26
Norvaišiai LT 114 La54
Norvajärvi FIN 74 Jd18
Norvalahti FIN 74 Jd18
Nörvenich D 125 Bc41
Norwich GB 17 Gb24
Norwick GB 5 Fa03
Nosivka UA 202 Ec14
Noskovo RUS 107 Ma46
Nosków PL 129 Gd38
Noşlac RO 171 Da59
Nosovo RUS 107 Ld49
Nøss N 66 Fd11
Nossa Senhora da Graça do Divor P 50 Ad69
Nossa Senhora das Neves P 50 Ad71
Nossa Senhora da Torega P 50 Ad70
Nossa Senhora de Machede P 50 Ba69
Nossebro S 102 Ed47
Nössemark S 94 Eb44
Nossen D 127 Ed41
Nossendorf D 119 Ed31
Nösslinge S 102 Ec50
Noss Mayo GB 19 Dd32
Nösund S 102 Eb47
Noszolop H 145 Gd54
Notaresco I 157 Fa69
Notėnai LT 113 Jc54
Nótia GR 183 Bd76
Nötö FIN 97 Ja41
Noto I 167 Fc88
Notodden N 93 Dc42
Notre-Dame-de-Gravenchon F 23 Ga35
Notre-Dame-de-Monts F 27 Ec43
Notre Dame du Laus F 35 Ka50
Nötsch A 143 Ed56
Nottage GB 19 Dd28
Nottebäck S 103 Fd51
Nottingham GB 16 Fa23
Nöttja S 102 Fa52
Nottuln D 125 Ca37
Nouaillé-Maupertuis F 32 Fd45
Nouan-le-Fuzellier F 29 Gd41
Nouans-les-Fontaines F 29 Gb42
Nouart F 24 Ja34
Nousiainen FIN 97 Jb39
Nousionmäki FIN 82 La29
Nousu FIN 69 Kd16
Nouvelle F 29 Ha44
Nouvion F 23 Gc32
Nouzonville F 24 Ja33
Nõva EST 98 Ka43
Nova H 145 Gc56
Nová Baňa SK 146 Hc50
Nova Borova UA 202 Eb14
Nova Breznica MK 178 Bb73
Nová Bystrica SK 138 Hc47
Nová Bystřice CZ 136 Fd48
Novačane BG 180 Dc69
Novačene BG 179 Cd70
Nova Černa BG 180 Eb68
Novaci MK 183 Bb76
Novaci RO 175 Cd63
Nova Crnja SRB 153 Jc59
Nova Crnja SRB 174 Bb61
Nová Dubnica SK 137 Hb48
Novafeltria I 156 Ea65
Nova Gorica SLO 150 Ed58
Nova Gradiška HR 152 Gd60
Novaja Bur'a RUS 99 Ma40
Novaja Derevnja RUS 113 Jb58
Novaja Kališče RUS 99 Ma39
Novaja Ladoga RUS 202 Eb08
Novajidrány H 139 Jd49
Nova Kachovka UA 205 Fa16
Nova Kamena BG 181 Ed69
Nova Kapela HR 152 Ha60
Nova Kasaba BIH 159 Hd64
Nová Kelča SK 139 Ka47
Novakovo BG 184 Dc74
Nováky SK 137 Hb49
Novalaise F 35 Jd47
Novales E 48 Fc59
Novalesa I 148 Bb60
Nova Levante I 143 Dd56
Novalja HR 151 Fc63
Novallas E 47 Ed59
Novalukoml' BY 202 Eb12
Nova Mahala BG 184 Da74
Nova Nadežda BG 185 Dd74
Nova Odesa UA 204 Ed16
Nová Paka CZ 136 Fd43
Nová Pec CZ 136 Fa49
Novara I 148 Cb59
Nova-Rača HR 152 Gc59
Novara di Sicilia I 167 Fd84
Nová Říše CZ 136 Fd48
Nová Sedlica SK 139 Kb47
Nova Šipka BG 181 Ed71
Nova Siri I 162 Gc77
Novate Mezzola I 149 Cd57
Nova Topola BIH 152 Gd61
Nova Ušycja UA 204 Eb16
Nova Varoš SRB 159 Jb66
Nova vas SLO 151 Fb59
Nová Ves CZ 136 Fb44
Nová Ves nad Žitavou SK 145 Hb50
Nová Viska CZ 135 Ed43
Nova Vodolaha UA 203 Fa14
Nova Zagora BG 180 Ea72
Nove I 150 Dd59
Nové Heřminovy CZ 137 Gd44
Nové Hrady CZ 136 Fc49
Nové Hrady CZ 137 Gb45
Novelda E 55 Fb71
Novelda del Guadiana E 51 Bc68
Novellara I 149 Db61
Nové Město nad Metuji CZ 137 Gb43
Nové Mesto nad Vahom SK 137 Ha49
Nové Město na Moravě CZ 136 Ga46
Nové Město pod Smrkem CZ 128 Fd42
Nové Mitrovice CZ 136 Fa46
Noventa Vicentino I 150 Dd60
Noves F 42 Jb53
Novés E 46 Da65
Nove Sady SK 145 Ha50
Nové Strašecí CZ 136 Fa44
Nové Veselí CZ 136 Ga46
Nové Zámky SK 145 Hb51
Novgorod RUS 202 Eb09
Novgorodka RUS 107 Ma49
Novgorodskoje RUS 113 Ja58
Novgrad BG 180 Dd69
Novhorodka UA 204 Ed15
Novhorod-Sivers'kyj UA 202 Ed13
Novi Bečej SRB 153 Jb59
Novi Beograd SRB 153 Jc61
Novi Bilokorovyči UA 202 Eb14
Novi di Modena I 149 Db61
Novi Dojran MK 183 Ca76
Noviercas E 47 Ec60
Novi Glog SRB 178 Bd72
Novi Grad BIH 152 Gb61
Novi Grad BIH 152 Hb61
Novigrad HR 150 Ed60
Novigrad HR 157 Ga64
Novigrad-Podravski HR 152 Gc58
Novi Han BG 179 Cd71
Novi Iskăr BG 179 Cc71
Novik N 78 Eb28
Novi Karlovci SRB 153 Jc61
Novi Kneževac SRB 153 Jb57
Novi Korito SRB 179 Ca68
Novi Kozarci SRB 153 Jc58
Novi Kozarci SRB 174 Bb60
Novi Kozjak SRB 174 Bb62
Novi Ligure I 148 Cb61
Noville B 132 Ba43
Novi Marof HR 152 Gb57
Novion-Porcien F 24 Hd34
Novi Pazar BG 181 Ed70
Novi Pazar SRB 178 Ba69
Novi Sad SRB 153 Jb60
Novi Sanžary UA 204 Ed15
Novi Šeher BIH 152 Hb63
Novi Selo SRB 174 Bc65
Novi Slankamen SRB 153 Jc60
Novi Travnik BIH 158 Ha64
Novi Varoš HR 152 Gd61
Novi Vinodolski HR 151 Fc61
Novi Žednik SRB 153 Ja58
Novoaleksandrovsk RUS 205 Fd16
Novoanninskij RUS 203 Fc13
Novoarchanhel's'k UA 204 Ec15
Novoazovs'k UA 205 Fb16
Novo-Bobrujsk RUS 113 Jb59
Novo Brdo KSV 178 Bc71
Novočeboksarsk RUS 203 Fc09
Novočerkassk RUS 205 Fc15
Novocimljanskaja RUS 203 Fd14
Novofedorivka UA 204 Ed17
Novohrad-Volyns'kyj UA 202 Eb14
Novokašpirskij RUS 203 Ga10
Novokolhoznoe RUS 113 Jc57
Novokubansk RUS 205 Fd16
Novokujbyševsk RUS 203 Ga10
Novo Mesto SLO 151 Fd59
Novomičurinsk RUS 203 Fa11
Novomihajlovskij RUS 205 Fc17
Novo Miloševo SRB 153 Jc58
Novo Miloševo SRB 174 Bb60
Novomoskovsk RUS 203 Fa11
Novomoskovs'k UA 205 Fa15
Novomykolajivka UA 204 Ed17
Novomykolajivka UA 205 Fa15
Novomyrhorod UA 204 Ed15
Novonikolaevskij RUS Ma47
Novonikolskoe RUS 107 Ma47
Novooleksijivka UA 205 Fa17
Novo Orahovo SRB 153 Ja58
Novo Paničarovo BG 181 Ed73
Novopavlovsk RUS 205 Ga17
Novopokrovka UA 205 Fa15
Novopokrovskaja RUS 205 Fd16
Novopskov UA 203 Fb14
Novorossijsk RUS 205 Fc17
Novoržev RUS 202 Eb10
Novosad SK 139 Ka49
Novošahtinsk RUS 205 Fc15
Novo Sancti Petri E 59 Bd77
Novosedly nad Nežárkou CZ 136 Fc48
Novosel BG 181 Ec70
Novoselci BG 181 Ed73
Novosel'e RUS 99 Ld43
Novosel'e RUS 99 Ma45
Novosel'e RUS 99 Ma45
Novosel'e RUS 99 Mb44
Novosel'e RUS 99 Mb45
Novoselec BG 180 Ea73
Novoselija BIH 152 Gd62
Novoselivs'ke UA 205 Fa17
Novo Selo BG 174 Cb66
Novo Selo BG 179 Ca73
Novo Selo BG 179 Cd72
Novo Selo BG 180 Dd70
Novo Selo BG 180 Eb68
Novo selo BG 185 Ea75
Novo Selo BIH 152 Hb61
Novo Selo MK 183 Ca75
Novo Selo SRB 153 Jc62
Novo Selo SRB 178 Bb67
Novosokol'niki RUS 202 Eb10
Novostroevo RUS 113 Jc59
Novotroickoe RUS 203 Fc10
Novotrojic'ke UA 205 Fa17
Novotulka RUS 203 Ga12
Novoukrajinka UA 204 Ed16
Novouljanovsk RUS 203 Fd10
Novouzensk RUS 203 Ga12
Novovolyns'k UA 204 Dd15
Novo Zvečevo HR 152 Ha59
Novska HR 152 Gd60
Nový Bor CZ 128 Fb42
Nový Bydžov CZ 136 Fd44
Nový Dvůr CZ 137 Ha45
Novy Dwór PL 128 Ga40
Nowyj Oskol RUS 203 Fb13
Novyj Buh UA 204 Ed16
Nový Jičín CZ 137 Ha46
Novyj Izborsk RUS 107 Ld47
Novyj Usitva RUS 107 Ld48
Nový Knín CZ 136 Fb45
Nový Malín CZ 137 Gc45
Nový Rychnov CZ 136 Fd47
Nowa Brzeźnica PL 130 Hc41
Nowa Cerekwia PL 137 Ha44
Nowa Dęba PL 139 Jd43
Nowa Huta PL 138 Ja44
Nowa Karczma PL 121 Ha31
Nowa Rozedranka PL 123 Kb32
Nowa Ruda PL 137 Gb43
Nowa Sarzyna PL 139 Ka43
Nowa Słupia PL 130 Jc41
Nowa Sól PL 128 Ga39
Nowa Somianka PL 130 Jc36
Nowa Sucha PL 130 Ja37
Nowa Wieś PL 122 Jc34
Nowa Wieś Ełcka PL 123 Jd31
Nowa Wieś Lęborska PL 121 Gd29
Nowa Wieś Wielka PL 121 Ha35
Nowa Wola PL 123 Kc34
Nowe Berezowo PL 123 Kc34
Nowe Brzesko PL 138 Jb44
Nowe Dwór PL 122 Hd30
Nowe Kiejkuty PL 122 Jb32
Nowe Kościelnica PL 121 Hb30
Nowe Laski PL 120 Ga33
Nowe Ludzicko PL 120 Ga32
Nowe Miasteczko PL 128 Ga39
Nowe Miasto PL 122 Jb35
Nowe Miasto Lubawskie PL 122 Hd33
Nowe Miasto nad Pilicą PL 130 Jb39
Nowe Ostrowy PL 130 Hc37
Nowe Piekuty PL 123 Ka34
Nowe Skalmierzyce PL 129 Ha39
Nowe Warpno PL 120 Fb32
Nowe Witki PL 122 Jb30
Nowica PL 122 Hd30
Nowinka PL 123 Ka31
Nowiny Kasjerskie PL 123 Kb33
Nowiny Wielkie PL 128 Fc36
Nowodwór PL 131 Ka38
Nowogard PL 120 Fd32
Nowogród PL 123 Jd33
Nowogród Bobrzański PL 128 Fd39
Nowogrodziec PL 128 Fd41
Nowo Miasto nad Wartą PL 129 Gd38
Nowosady PL 123 Kc34
Nowosielce PL 139 Ka45
Nowosielec PL 131 Ka42
Nowosiółki PL 123 Kc33
Nowosiółki PL 131 Kc40
Nowosiółki PL 131 Kc42
Nowy Duninów PL 130 Hc36
Nowy Dwór PL 123 Kb31
Nowy Dwór Gdański PL 122 Hc30
Nowy Dwór Mazowiecki PL 130 Jb36
Nowy Gaj PL 130 Hc37
Nowy Jaromierz PL 128 Ga38
Nowy Kawęczyn PL 130 Ja38
Nowy Korczyn PL 138 Jb43
Nowy Kościoł PL 128 Ga41
Nowy Lubiel PL 122 Jc35
Nowy Orzechów PL 131 Kb39
Nowy Sącz PL 138 Jb45
Nowy Staw PL 121 Hb31
Nowy Targ PL 138 Ja46
Nowy Tomyśl PL 128 Ga37
Nowy Wiśnicz PL 138 Jb44
Nowy Wołkusz PL 123 Kb31
Nowy Żmigród PL 139 Jd45
Noyant F 28 Fd41
Noyant-de-Touraine F 29 Ga43
Noyant-la-Plaine F 28 Fc42
Noyelles-sur-Mer F 23 Gc32
Noyen-sur-Seine F 30 Hb38
Noyers F 30 Hd40
Noyers F 42 Jd52
Noyers-Saint-Martin F 23 Gd34
Noyon F 23 Ha34
Nozay F 28 Ed41
Nozdra MNE 159 Hd68
Nozdrzec PL 139 Ka45
Nozelos P 45 Bc61
Nozeroy F 31 Jd43
Nozières F 34 Ja49
N. Sedlo CZ 135 Ec44
Nuarbe E 39 Eb56
Nuars F 30 Hc41
Nuasjärvi FIN 74 Jc18
Nucăreni MD 173 Fc56
Nucet RO 171 Cc58
Nucet RO 176 Dd65
Nuci RO 176 Eb65
Nucşoara RO 175 Dc63
Nudersdorf D 127 Ec38
Nüdlingen D 134 Db44
Nudol' RUS 202 Ed10
Nueil-les Aubiers F 28 Fb43
Nuenen NL 125 Bb38
Nueno E 39 Fb58
Nueva E 37 Cd54
Nueva Andalucía E 60 Cc77
Nueva Carteya E 60 Cd73
Nueva Jarilla E 59 Bd76
Nuévalos E 47 Ec62
Nuevo Baztán E 46 Dd64
Nufăru RO 177 Fd64

Nuh – Ollikkala

Nuh TR 193 Gc85
Nuhören TR 193 Gb84
Nuiasodis LT 115 Lb54
Nuijamaa FIN 91 Lc36
Nuin E 39 Ed56
Nuisement-sur-Coole F 24 Hd36
Nuits F 30 Hd40
Nuits-Saint-Georges F 30 Jb42
Nukari FIN 90 Kb38
Nukkumajoki FIN 69 Ka11
Ņukši LV 107 Ld51
Nuksujärvi S 68 Hd16
Nuksujärvi S 73 Ja18
Nuland N 92 Cb46
Nule I 168 Cb75
Nules E 54 Fc66
Nulvi I 168 Ca74
Numana I 156 Ed66
Numanoluk TR 193 Gc83
Numansdorp NL 124 Ad37
Nümbrecht D 125 Ca41
Numerne LV 107 Ld50
Numijoki FIN 81 Jd30
Nummela FIN 89 Jd38
Nummela FIN 98 Ka39
Nummenkylä FIN 90 Ka37
Nummenpää FIN 98 Kb39
Nummi FIN 97 Jb39
Nummi FIN 98 Ka39
Nummijärvi FIN 89 Jb33
Nummikoski FIN 89 Jb33
Nummilahti FIN 89 Jb33
Numminen FIN 90 Kc38
Nünchritz D 127 Ed40
Nuneaton GB 16 Fa24
Nunnanen FIN 68 Jb13
Nunnanlahti FIN 83 Lc28
Nunney GB 19 Ec29
Nunspeet NL 116 Bb36
Nunton GB 20 Ed29
Nuojua FIN 82 Kc25
Nuolijärvi FIN 83 Lb27
Nuomininkai LT 113 Jd55
Nuoramoinen FIN 90 Kc35
Nuorgam FIN 64 Ka07
Nuoritta FIN 74 Kb23
Nuoro I 169 Cb76
Nuorpiniemi FIN 64 Jc08
Nuortikon S 73 Hb18
Nuorunka FIN 75 Kc21
Nuottikylä FIN 75 La24
Nuottiranta FIN 83 Lc29
Núpsstaður IS 2 Ba06
Nur PL 123 Ka35
Nurachi I 169 Bd77
Nuragus I 169 Ca78
Nurallao I 169 Ca78
Nuraminis I 169 Ca79
Nureci I 169 Ca78
Nuribey TR 193 Gc85
Nuriye TR 191 Ed85
Nurlat RUS 203 Ga09
Nurmaa FIN 90 Kd35
Nurme EST 98 Kb45
Nurmes FIN 83 Lb27
Nurmeslahti FIN 82 La28
Nurmesperä FIN 82 Kb27
Nurmi FIN 89 Jd36
Nurmi LV 106 Kd47
Nurmijärvi FIN 83 Lc27
Nurmijärvi FIN 98 Kb39
Nurmo FIN 81 Jb31
Nurmsi EST 98 Kd44
Nurmuiža LV 105 Jd50
Nürnberg D 135 Dd46
Nurney IRL 13 Cc22
Nurrasuanto S 68 Hd16
Nurri I 169 Cb78
Nürtingen D 134 Cd49
Nurzec PL 123 Kb35
Nurzec-Stacja PL 131 Kb36
Nus I 148 Bc58
Nusco I 161 Fd75
Nuşeni RO 171 Db57
Nuşfalau RO 171 Cc56
Nusfjord N 66 Fa15
Nüshetiye TR 186 Ga80
Nusnäs S 87 Fc38
Nusplingen D 142 Cc50
Nusratlı TR 185 Ed78
Nusret TR 192 Fa82
Nussdorf A 143 Ed52
Nußdorf D 143 Eb52
Nußloch D 134 Cc46
Nuthetal D 127 Ed37
Nutley GB 20 Fd29
Nuttuperä FIN 82 Kb27
Nuulanki S 68 Hd14
Nuupas FIN 74 Ka20
Nuutajärvi FIN 89 Jd37
Nuutila FIN 82 Kb25
Nuutilanmäki FIN 90 La33
Nuuttila FIN 89 Jd33
Nuvvos FIN 64 Jc08
Nuvvus FIN 64 Jc08
Ny S 94 Ec42
Nyåker S 80 Ha28
Nyåker S 80 Gc29
Nyárlőrinc H 146 Ja55
Nya Storbäcken S 80 Hc27
Nyberg S 80 Ha25
Nybergsund N 86 Ec37
Nyborg DK 109 Dd27
Nyborg N 65 Kb06
Nyborg N 79 Fb28
Nyborg S 73 Jb21
Nybro S 103 Ga52
Nybrostrand S 110 Fa57
Nybrott N 63 Hd08
Nyby FIN 81 Hd31
Nyby N 64 Jb07
Nyby S 79 Fd30
Nybyn S 73 Hc23
Nybyn S 73 Ja20
Nydala S 103 Fb50
Nyékládháza H 146 Jc51
Nyergesujfalu H 146 Hc52
Nygård N 67 Gc11
Nygård N 67 Gb13
Nygarden N 85 Ea35
Nyhammar S 95 Fc40
Nyhamnsläge S 110 Ec54
Nyheim N 65 Kd08
Nyhem S 87 Fd32
Ny Højen DK 108 Db25
Nyhyttan S 95 Fc42
Nýidalur IS 2 Ba05
Nyíkarász H 147 Kb50
Nyírábrány H 147 Kb52
Nyíracsád H 147 Kb52
Nyírád H 145 Gd54
Nyíradony H 147 Ka52
Nyírbátor H 147 Kb51
Nyírbéltek H 147 Kb52
Nyírbogát H 147 Kb51
Nyíregyháza H 147 Ka51
Nyírgyulaj H 147 Kb51
Nyírkáta H 147 Kb51
Nyírlugos H 147 Kb52
Nyírmada H 147 Kb50
Nyírmeggyes H 147 Kb51
Nyírtelek H 147 Ka51
Nyírtura H 147 Ka51
Nykälä FIN 90 Kd33
Nykarleby FIN 81 Ja29
Nyker DK 111 Fc57
Nykil S 103 Fd47
Nykirke N 85 Dd38
Nykirke N 93 Dd41
Nykirke N 93 Dd43
Nykøbing Falster DK 109 Eb29
Nykøbing M DK 100 Da21
Nykøbing S DK 109 Eb25
Nykøbing Strandhuse DK 109 Eb29
Nyköping S 95 Gb45
Nykroppa S 95 Fb42
Nyksund N 66 Fc12
Nykvarn S 96 Gc44
Nykyrka S 102 Fa48
Nyland S 79 Gb26
Nyland S 79 Fc30
Nyland S 80 Gc31
Nyland S 80 Ha29
Nyland S 80 Hb29
Nyland S 87 Gb33
Nylars DK 111 Fc58
Nyliden S 72 Gc22
Nyliden S 80 Gd29
Nyliden S 80 Ha27
Nyluspen S 79 Gb25
Nymburk CZ 136 Fc44
Nymindegab DK 108 Cd25
Nymo N 62 Ha08
Nymoen N 62 Gb10
Nynäshamn S 96 Gd45
Nyneset N 78 Ed26
Ny Nørup DK 108 Db25
Nyon CH 140 Ba55
Nyons F 42 Jc51
Nyord DK 109 Eb28
Nýřany CZ 135 Ed46
Nyröla FIN 90 Kb32
Nýrsko CZ 135 Ed47
Nyrud N 65 Kc09
Nysa PL 137 Gd43
Nysäter S 94 Ed44
Nysätern S 86 Fa33
Nysätra S 96 Gc42
Nysele S 80 Ha27
Nyseter N 85 Db34
Nyskoga S 94 Ed40
Nystadt = Uusikaupunki FIN 89 Ja38
Nysted DK 109 Eb29
Nystrand S 73 Hc22
Nystu Trønnes N 86 Eb36
Nysund S 95 Fb44
Nytjärn S 80 Gc28
Nytorp S 68 Hd17
Nyträsk S 73 Hb24
Nytrøa N 77 Ea33
Nyúl H 145 Ha53
Nyvall S 72 Ha23
Nyvoll N 63 Hd07
Nyvollen N 78 Ec29
Nyystölä FIN 90 Kb36
Nyžni Sirohozy UA 205 Fa16
Nyžni Torhaji UA 205 Fa16
Nyžn'ohirs'kyj UA 205 Fa17

O

Oaivos N 68 Hd11
Oakford GB 19 Ea30
Oakham GB 16 Fb24
Oakington GB 20 Fd25
Oakley GB 20 Fa29
Oakley GB 20 Fb27
Oalahti FIN 83 Lc31
Oancea RO 177 Fb61
Oanes N 92 Ca44
Oarda RO 175 Da60
Oarja RO 175 Dc65
Oarța de Jos RO 171 Cd55
Oassi GR 189 Bc86
Obalj BIH 159 Hc66
Oban GB 6 Db11
O Barco E 37 Bd57
Obârșia RO 179 Da67
Obârșia-Cloșani RO 174 Cb63
Obbekær DK 108 Da26
Obbnäs FIN 98 Ka40
Obbola S 80 Hb29
Obdach A 144 Fc54
Obecnice CZ 136 Fa46
Obedinenie BG 180 Dd69
Obejo E 60 Cd72
Obeliai LT 114 La53
Oberammergau D 142 Dc52
Oberasbach D 134 Dc46
Oberau A 143 Ea53
Oberau D 142 Dc53
Oberaudorf D 143 Eb52
Oberaula D 126 Da41
Oberaurach D 134 Dc45
Oberbeisheim D 126 Da41
Oberbergkirchen D 143 Eb50
Obercunnersdorf D 128 Fc41
Oberdachstetten D 134 Db46
Oberderdingen D 134 Cc47
Oberding D 143 Ea50
Oberdorla D 126 Dc40
Oberdrauburg A 143 Ec55
Oberei CH 141 Bd54
Obereisesheim D 134 Cd47
Oberelsbach D 134 Db43
Obergrafendorf A 144 Fd51
Obergünzburg D 142 Db51
Obergurgl A 142 Dc55
Oberhaching D 143 Dd51
Oberhaid D 134 Dc45
Oberharmersbach D 133 Cb49
Oberhausen D 125 Bd39
Oberheldrungen D 127 Dd40
Oberhof D 126 Dc42
Oberhofen CH 141 Bd55
Oberhoffen F 25 Kc36
Oberkail D 133 Bc43
Oberkappel A 136 Fa49
Oberkirch D 133 Ca49
Oberkirchen D 126 Cc40
Oberkochen D 134 Db48
Oberkotzau D 135 Ea44
Oberlödla D 127 Eb41
Oberlungwitz D 127 Ec42
Obermaßfeld-Grimmenthal D 134 Dc43
Obermehler D 126 Dc40
Ober-Mörlen D 134 Cc43
Obermoschel D 133 Ca45
Obernai F 25 Kb37
Obernberg A 143 Ed50
Obernberg am Brenner A 143 Dd54
Obernbreit D 134 Db45
Obernburg D 134 Cd45
Oberndorf D 118 Da32
Oberndorf am Neckar D 141 Cb50
Oberndorf an der Melk A 144 Fd51
Oberndorf bei Salzburg A 143 Ec51
Obernheim D 142 Cc50
Obernholz D 118 Dc35
Obernkirchen D 126 Da37
Obernzell D 136 Fa49
Obernzenn D 134 Db46
Oberostendorf D 142 Dc51
Oberpframmern D 143 Ea51
Oberpleis D 125 Ca41
Oberpullendorf A 145 Gb53
Ober-Ramstadt D 134 Cc45
Oberreute D 142 Da52
Oberrickenbach CH 141 Cb54
Oberried CH 141 Ca55
Oberried D 141 Ca51
Oberriet CH 142 Cd53
Oberröblingen D 127 Dd40
Oberrot D 134 Da47
Oberscheinfeld D 134 Db45
Oberschleißheim D 143 Dd50
Oberschöna D 127 Ed42
Oberschwarzach D 134 Db45
Obersiggenthal CH 141 Cb52
Obersontheim D 134 Da47
Oberstadion D 142 Da50
Oberstadtfeld D 133 Bc43
Oberstaufen D 142 Da52
Oberstdorf D 142 Db53
Obersteigen F 25 Kb37
Obersteinbach F 25 Kc35
Oberstenfeld D 134 Cd47
Oberstreu D 134 Db43
Obersulm D 134 Cd47
Obertauern A 143 Ed54
Obertaufkirchen D 143 Eb50
Oberthal D 133 Bd45
Oberthulba D 134 Db44
Obertiefenbach D 125 Cb42
Obertilliach A 143 Eb55
Obertraubling D 135 Eb48
Obertraun A 144 Fa53
Oberturm am See A 143 Ec51
Oberursel D 134 Cc43
Obervellach A 143 Ed55
Oberviechtach D 135 Eb46
Oberwald CH 141 Ca55
Oberwart A 145 Gb54
Oberweis D 133 Bc44
Oberweissbach A 143 Ec53
Oberweißbach D 127 Dd42
Oberwesel D 133 Ca43
Oberweser D 126 Da39
Oberwiesenthal D 135 Ec43
Oberwölz A 144 Fb54
Oberzeiring A 144 Fb54
Obhausen D 127 Ea40
Óbidos P 50 Ab67
Obiedzino PL 123 Jd33
Obileni MD 173 Fb58
Obilić KSV 178 Bb70
Obing D 143 Eb51
Obinitsa EST 107 Lc47
Obiža RUS 107 Ld46
Objat F 33 Gb49
Objazda PL 121 Gc29
Objezierze PL 129 Gc36
Öblarn A 144 Fa53
Obljaj HR 152 Gb60
Obninsk RUS 202 Ed11
Obnova BG 180 Dc69
Óbög H 146 Jb54
Oboga RO 175 Da66
Obojan' RUS 203 Fa13
Obolon' UA 204 Ed15
Obón E 48 Fb63
Oborci BIH 158 Ha64
Oborin SK 139 Ka49
Oborište BG 179 Da72
Oborište BG 181 Fa69
Oborniki PL 129 Gc36
Oborniki Śląskie PL 129 Gc40
Obornjača SRB 153 Jb58
Oborowo PL 121 Hb35
Obory CZ 136 Fb46
Oborzany PL 120 Fc35
Obra PL 128 Ga38
Obreja RO 174 Cb62
Obrenovac SRB 153 Jc62
Obretenik BG 180 Ea69
Obrež HR 151 Ga59
Obrež SRB 153 Jb62
Obrigheim D 134 Cd46
Obrnice CZ 136 Fa43
Obročište BG 181 Fb70
Obrov SLO 151 Fa59
Obrovac HR 157 Ga64
Obrovac SRB 153 Ja60
Obrovac Sinjski HR 158 Gc65
Obršani MK 183 Bb75
Obrtići BIH 159 Hd65
Obryte PL 122 Jc35
Obrytki PL 123 Jd33
Obrzycko PL 129 Gb36
Obšistvi CZ 136 Fb44
Obsza PL 139 Kc43
Obudovac BIH 153 Hc61
Øby DK 100 Cd23
Obzor BG 181 Fa72
Očakiv UA 204 Ed17
Ocaklar TR 186 Fa79
Ocaklı TR 185 Eb79
Ocaña E 52 Dc66
Ocana F 154 Ca71
O Canizo E 36 Bc58
Occhiobello I 150 Dd61
Occold GB 21 Gb25
Ocentejo E 47 Eb63
Očeretuvate UA 205 Fa16
Očevlja BIH 159 Hc64
Ocharán E 38 Dd55
Ochiltree GB 10 Dd14
Ochiul Alb MD 173 Fb54
Ochiul Roș MD 173 Fd59
Ochla PL 128 Fd38
Ochojec PL 137 Hb44
Ochsenfurt D 134 Db45
Ochsenhausen D 142 Da51
Ochtendung D 133 Ca43
Ochtrup D 117 Ca36
Ochtyrka UA 202 Ed14
Ocieka PL 139 Jd43
Ocieseki PL 130 Jc42
Ockelbo S 87 Gb38
Ockholm D 108 Da29
Ockle GB 6 Db10
Ockley GB 20 Fc29
Ocksjön S 87 Fc32
Ocland RO 176 Dd60
Ocna de Fier RO 174 Ca62
Ocna Dejului RO 171 Da57
Ocna Mureș RO 171 Da59
Ocna Sibiului RO 175 Db61
Ocna Șugatag RO 171 Db55
Ocnele Mari RO 175 Db64
Ocnița MD 173 Fa53
Ocnița MD 173 Fc54
Ocnița RO 176 Dd64
Ocoale RO 171 Cc58
Ocolina MD 173 Fc54
Ocoliș RO 171 Cd59
Ocón E 39 Eb58
Očová SK 138 Hd49
Ocrkavlje BIH 159 Hc66
Öcsa H 146 Hd53
Öcsárd H 152 Hb58
Öcsény H 153 Hc57
Öcsöd H 146 Jc54
Octeville, Cherbourg F 22 Ed34
Octeville-sur-Mer F 22 Fd34
Octon F 41 Hc54
Ocypel PL 121 Ha32
Öd S 79 Fc31
Od S 102 Ed48
Odăile RO 176 Ec63
Ödåkra S 110 Ed54
Odals verk N 94 Ec40
Ödängla S 103 Gb51
Odărne BG 180 Dc69
Odby DK 100 Da22
Odda N 84 Cc40
Odde DK 101 Dd22
Odden N 62 Ha09
Odden N 70 Ed23
Odden N 86 Eb36
Odden Færgehavn DK 109 Ea25
Oddense DK 100 Da22
Odder DK 108 Dc24
Oddernes N 92 Cd47
Oddesund Nord DK 100 Da22
Oddesund Syd DK 100 Da22
Ödeborg S 102 Ec46
Ödeby S 95 Fd43
Odeceixe P 58 Ab73
Odelzhausen D 143 Dd50
Odemira P 58 Ab72
Ödemiș TR 192 Fa86
Odèn E 49 Gc59
Ödena E 49 Gc61
Ödenäs S 102 Ec48
Odensåker S 103 Fb46
Odensala S 96 Gd42
Odensbacken S 95 Fd44
Odense DK 108 Dc26
Odensjö S 102 Fa52
Odensjö S 103 Fb49
Odensvi S 95 Ga43
Odensvi S 103 Ga48
Oderberg D 120 Fb35
Oderljunga S 110 Fa54
Oderwitz D 128 Fc42
Oderzo I 150 Eb59
Odesa UA 204 Ec17
Ödeshög S 103 Fc47
Ödestugu S 103 Fb49
Odiáxere P 58 Ab74
Odiham GB 20 Fb29
Odincovo RUS 202 Ed10
Ødis DK 108 Db26
Odivelas P 50 Ac71
Ödkarby FIN 96 Hc40
Odnes N 85 Dd38
Odobasca RO 176 Ed62
Odobești RO 176 Dd65
Odobești RO 176 Ed62
Odolanów PL 129 Gd39
Odolena Voda CZ 136 Fb44
Odón E 47 Ed63
Odoorn NL 117 Ca34
Odoreu RO 171 Cd54
Odorheiu Secuiesc RO 176 Dd60
Odos F 40 Fd55
Odou CY 206 Jb97
Odrinci BG 181 Fa69
Odrowąż PL 130 Jb40
Odry CZ 137 Ha46
Odry PL 121 Ha31
Odrzykoń PL 139 Jd45
Odrzywół PL 130 Jb39
Ödsköt S 94 Ec45
Ödsmål S 102 Eb46
Ödsmål S 102 Eb47
Ødsted DK 108 Db25
Ødum DK 100 Dc23
Odžaci SRB 153 Hd59
Odžak BIH 152 Hb61
Odžak BIH 158 Hb67
Odžak MNE 159 Ja67
Odziena LV 106 La51
Oebisfelde D 127 Dd36
Oed A 144 Fc51
Oederan D 127 Ed42
Oederquart D 118 Da32
Oeffelt NL 125 Bb38
Oegstgeest NL 116 Ad36
Oehna D 127 Ed38
Oeiras P 50 Aa69
Öekény H 146 Hd54
Oelde D 126 Cc38
Oelsig D 127 Ed39
Oelsnitz D 127 Ec42
Oelsnitz D 135 Eb43
Oencia E 37 Bd57
Oensingen CH 141 Bd53
Oerel D 118 Da33
Oerlenbach D 134 Db44
Oerlinghausen D 126 Cd38
Oestrich-Winkel D 133 Cb44
Oettingen D 134 Dc48
Oetz A 142 Dc54
Oetzen D 119 Dd34
Œuf-en-Ternois F 23 Gd32
Oeversee D 108 Db29
Ofatinți MD 173 Fd56
Ofena I 157 Fa70
Offenau D 134 Cd47
Offenbach D 134 Cc44
Offenbach an der Queich D 133 Cb47
Offenbach-Hundheim D 133 Ca45
Offenberg D 135 Ec48
Offenburg D 133 Ca49
Offenhausen D 135 Dd46
Offerdal S 79 Fb30
Offersøya N 66 Fd14
Offida I 156 Ed68
Offingen D 134 Db49
Offne S 79 Fb30
Offranville F 23 Ga33
Oftedal N 92 Cb45
Ofterdingen D 134 Cc49
Oftringen CH 141 Ca53
Ogardy PL 120 Fd35
Ogbourne Saint George GB 20 Ed28
Øgelund DK 108 Da25
Ogéviller F 25 Ka37
Öggestorp S 103 Fb49
Oggevatn N 92 Cd46
Oggiono I 149 Cc58
Ogļaine LV 106 Kb52
Oğlananasi TR 191 Ec86
Ogliastro Cilento I 161 Fc76
Ogliastro Marina I 161 Fc77
Öglunda S 102 Fa46
Ögmen TR 191 Ec81
Ogmore-by-Sea GB 19 Ea28
Ogna N 92 Ca45
Ognina I 167 Fd87
Ognjanovo BG 181 Fa68
Ognjanovo BG 184 Cd75
Ogoja BG 179 Cc70
Ogonki PL 122 Jc30
Ogonnelloe IRL 12 Bd22
Ogošte KSV 178 Bc71
Ogra CY 206 Ja96
Ogra RO 171 Db59
Ogre LV 106 Kc51
Ogreskalns LV 106 Kd50
Ogrezeni RO 176 Ea66
Ogródek PL 123 Jd31
Ogrodniczki PL 123 Kb33
Ogrodniki PL 123 Jd35
Ogrodniki PL 123 Kb30
Ogrodzieniec PL 138 Hd43
Ogrosen D 128 Fa39
O Grove E 36 Ac56
Ogulin HR 151 Fd60
Oğulpaşa TR 187 Gb79
Ohaba RO 175 Da60
Ohaba Lungă RO 174 Ca60
Ohanes E 61 Ea75
Ohenmäki FIN 82 Kd28
Ohey B 124 Ad42
Ohiró GR 184 Cd76
Ohkola FIN 90 Kb38
Ohlstadt D 143 Dd52
Öhningen D 142 Cc52
Ohotnoe RUS 113 Jc58
Ohrdruf D 126 Dc42
Ohrid MK 182 Ba75
Ohrikylä FIN 89 Ja33
Öhringen D 134 Cd47
Ohtaanniemi FIN 83 Lb30
Ohtanajärvi S 73 Ja18
Ohtinen FIN 89 Jd37
Ohtola FIN 89 Jd33
Ohtsejohka FIN 64 Jd07
Oiã P 44 Ac63
Oidrema EST 98 Ka45
Oijärvi FIN 74 Ka21
Oijusluoma FIN 75 La20
Oikarainen FIN 74 Ka19
Oileán Ciarraí IRL 12 Bb24
Oilgate IRL 13 Cc24
Oilgate IRL 13 Cd24
Oimbra E 44 Bb59
Oinaala FIN 90 Ka37
Oinacu RO 180 Ea68
Oinas FIN 69 Kb17
Oinasjärvi FIN 82 Kd27
Oinasjärvi FIN 97 Jd39
Oingt F 34 Ja46
Oinoskylä FIN 82 Ka30
Oinville F 23 Gc36
Oion E 39 Eb58
Oiron F 28 Fc43
Oirschot NL 124 Ba38
Ois E 36 Ba54
Øisang N 93 Db45
Oiselay-et-Grachaux F 31 Jd41
Oisemont F 23 Gc33
Oissel F 23 Gb35
Oisterwijk NL 124 Ba38
Oisu EST 98 Kd44
Õisu EST 106 Kd46
Oitti FIN 90 Kb37
Oittila FIN 90 Kc33
Oituz RO 176 Ec60
Oiu EST 98 La45
Oivu FIN 81 Jb28
Oix E 41 Ha58
Öja FIN 81 Jb28
Öja S 95 Ga44
Öja S 103 Fc52
Öja S 104 Gd51
Öjaby S 103 Fc52
Ojakkala FIN 98 Ka39
Ojakylä FIN 74 Jd24
Ojakylä FIN 74 Ka23
Ojakylä FIN 81 Jd27
Ojakylä FIN 82 Ka26
Ojakylä FIN 82 Ka27
Ojala FIN 81 Jc30
Ojalehto FIN 82 Ka27
Ojanperä FIN 82 Ka27
Ojanperä FIN 82 Kc26
Öjarn S 79 Fc28
Ojasoo EST 98 Kc43
Ojców PL 138 Ja44
Ojdula RO 176 Eb61
Öje S 88 Gc33
Öje S 95 Fb39
Öjebyn S 73 Hc23
Ojedo E 38 Da55
Ojén E 60 Cc77
Öjenäs S 94 Fa41
Ojinești MD 173 Fc57
Ojos Negros E 47 Ed63
Ojrzeń PL 122 Ja35
Ojuelos Altos E 51 Cb71
Öjvasseln S 86 Fa35
Okainiai LT 114 Kc56
Okalewko PL 122 Hd34
Okalewo PL 122 Hd34
Okány H 147 Jd54
Okartowo PL 122 Jc31
Okçu TR 193 Ha82
Okcyn PL 131 Kc37
Økdal N 78 Ea31
Okehampton GB 19 Dd30
Okeroinen FIN 90 Kc37
Okkelberg N 78 Eb29
Okkenhaug N 78 Ec29
Oklaj HR 158 Gb65
Okletac SRB 159 Ja64
Oključina HR 158 Gb68
Oklubalı TR 193 Gb82
Ökna S 103 Fd50
Okoč SK 145 Ha51
Okół PL 131 Jd41
Okoli HR 152 Gc59
Okome S 102 Ed51
Okonek PL 121 Gc33
Okonin PL 121 Hb33
Okop BG 180 Eb73
Okopy PL 131 Kd40
Okoråg H 152 Ha58
Okorš BG 181 Ec68
Okovcy RUS 202 Ec10
Okřišky CZ 136 Ga47
Okrouhlice CZ 136 Fd46
Okruglica HR 151 Fd60
Okrúhle SK 139 Jd47
Okrzeja PL 131 Ka38
Oksa PL 130 Ja42
Oksajärvi S 68 Hd15
Oksakoski FIN 81 Jd29
Oksava FIN 82 Ka27
Oksbøl DK 108 Cd25
Oksby DK 108 Cd25
Øksejdet N 68 Hd11
Øksendalen N 70 Fa22
Øksendalsøra N 77 Db32
Øksendalssetra N 85 Ea36
Øksfjord N 63 Hc07
Øksfjordbotn N 63 Hc08
Okskulma FIN 99 Kb34
Øksna N 86 Eb38
Øksnes N 78 Ec27
Øksneshavn N 66 Fd14
Øksninga N 78 Ec25
Okstad N 78 Eb30
Okstveit N 92 Cb41
Oksvoll N 77 Dd28
Okt'abr'skoje RUS 113 Jb59
Oktjabr'sk RUS 203 Ga10
Oktjabr'skij RUS 203 Fd14
Oktoniá GR 190 Cd85
Okučani HR 152 Gd60
Okuklje HR 158 Ha69
Okulice PL 138 Jb44
Okulovka RUS 202 Ec09
Okuniew PL 130 Jc36
Okuninka PL 131 Kc39
Okurçalar TR 199 Hb92
Öküzler TR 198 Fc90
Ólafsfjörður IS 2 Ba03
Ólafsvík IS 2 Ab03
Olagüe E 39 Ed56
Olaine LV 106 Kb51
Olalla E 47 Fa63
Oland N 93 Da45
Oland N 93 Da45
Olanes N 63 Hd07
Olang I 143 Ea55
Olanu RO 175 Db64
Olargues F 41 Hb54
Olari FIN 98 Kb40
Olari RO 170 Bd59
Oława PL 129 Gd41
Olazagutía E 39 Eb56
Olba E 54 Fb65
Olbernhau D 127 Ed42
Olbia I 168 Cb74
Olbięcin PL 131 Ka41
Olbramovice CZ 136 Fc46
Olbramovice CZ 137 Gb48
Olcea RO 170 Ca58
Olching D 143 Dd50
Ol'chovka RUS 113 Jb58
Old GB 20 Fb25
Oldcastle IRL 9 Cc20
Old Castleton GB 11 Ec15
Old Deer GB 5 Ed08
Olde DK 108 Dc28
Oldeberkoop NL 117 Bc34
Oldeboorn NL 117 Bc33
Oldebroek NL 117 Bc35
Oldeide N 84 Ca34
Oldekerk NL 117 Bd33
Oldemarkt NL 117 Bc34
Olden N 84 Cd34
Olden S 78 Fa29
Oldenburg D 117 Cc34
Oldenburg in Holstein D 119 Dd30
Oldendorf D 118 Da32
Oldenswort D 118 Da30
Oldenzaal NL 117 Bd36
Oldenzaal NL 117 Ca36
Olderdalen N 62 Ha09
Olderfjord N 64 Jb06
Oldernes N 63 Ja06
Olderneset N 64 Ka07
Oldervik N 62 Gd09
Oldervik N 64 Jd06
Oldervika N 70 Fa20
Oldham GB 16 Ed21
Oldhamstocks GB 11 Ec13
Old Head IRL 12 Bd26
Oldisleben D 127 Dd40
Old Lake GB 17 Fd23
Oldmeldrum GB 5 Ed08
Old Radnor GB 15 Eb25
Oldřichovice CZ 137 Hb46
Oldrões P 44 Ad61
Old Sodbury GB 19 Ec28
Old Somerby GB 16 Fb23
Old Warden GB 20 Fc26
Oldways End GB 19 Ea29
Olea E 38 Db56
Oleby S 94 Ed41
Olecko PL 123 Ka30
Olędy PL 123 Ka35
Oleggio I 148 Cb59
Oleiros E 36 Ac56
Oleiros P 44 Ba65
Oleksandrija UA 204 Ed15
Oleksandrivka UA 204 Ed15
Oleksandrivka UA 204 Ed15
Oleksandrivka UA 204 Ed17
Oleksandrivka UA 205 Fb15
Olelas E 36 Ba58
Olen B 124 Ad39
Ølen N 92 Ca42
Olenino RUS 202 Ec10
Olenivka UA 204 Ed17
Oleri LV 106 Kd47
Olesa de Montserrat E 49 Gd61
Olešná CZ 136 Fa45
Oleśnica PL 129 Gd40
Oleśnica PL 138 Jc43
Olešnice CZ 137 Gb46
Oleśniczka PL 129 Gd41
Olesno PL 129 Hb41
Olesno PL 138 Jc43
Oleszno PL 130 Ja41
Oleszyce PL 139 Kc43
Oletta F 154 Cc69
Olette F 41 Ha57
Olevs'k UA 202 Eb14
Olfen D 125 Ca38
Olgiate Comasco I 149 Cc58
Ol'gino RUS 99 Mb39
Ølgod DK 108 Da25
Olhalvo P 50 Ab67
Ølhammaren N 78 Ec26
Olhão P 58 Ad74
Olhava FIN 74 Jd22
Ol'hi RUS 203 Fb11
Ølholm DK 108 Db25
Ol'hovatka RUS 113 Jd59
Ol'hovatka RUS 203 Fb13
Ol'hovka RUS 203 Fd13
Oliana E 48 Gb59
Olib HR 151 Fc63
Oliena I 169 Cb76
Oliete E 48 Fb63
Olimbi GR 191 Dd86
Olimbía GR 194 Ba87
Ólimbos GR 197 Eb94
Olimp RO 181 Fc68
Olimpiáda GR 184 Cc78
Oliņas LV 106 La48
Olingdal S 87 Fb35
Olișcani MD 173 Fd55
Olite E 39 Ed58
Oliva E 54 Fc69
Oliva de la Frontera E 51 Bc71
Oliva de Mérida E 51 Ca69
Oliva de Plasencia E 45 Ca65
Olivadi I 164 Gc82
Olivares E 59 Bd73
Olivares de Júcar E 53 Eb67
Oliveira de Azeméis P 44 Ad62
Oliveira de Barreiros P 44 Ba63
Oliveira do Bairro P 44 Ad63
Oliveira do Douro P 44 Ba61
Oliveira do Hospital P 44 Ba64
Olivenza E 51 Bb69
Olivet F 29 Gc40
Olivione CH 142 Cc56
Öljehult S 111 Fc53
Ol'ka SK 139 Ka47
Olkamangi S 74 Jb18
Olkijoki FIN 81 Jd25
Olkiluoto FIN 89 Ja37
Olkkajärvi FIN 74 Ka18
Olkkala FIN 98 Ka39
Olkkola FIN 82 Ka27
Olkusz PL 138 Hd43
Ollaberry GB 5 Fa04
Ollala FIN 82 Ka26
Ollebacken S 79 Fc29
Ollerias E 38 Ea56
Olleros de Pisuerga E 38 Db57
Ollerton GB 16 Fb22
Ollerup DK 109 Dd27
Olleta E 39 Ed57
Olliergues F 34 Hc47
Ollikkala FIN 90 La35

Ollikkala FIN 91 Lb33
Ollila FIN 89 Jc38
Ollilanvaara FIN 74 Jd18
Ollioules F 42 Jd55
Öllölä FIN 83 Ma31
Ollomont I 148 Bc57
Ollon CH 141 Bc56
Olloniego E 37 Cc55
Ölmbratorp S 95 Fd43
Ölme S 95 Fb43
Olmeda de la Cuesta E 47 Eb65
Olmeda del Rey E 53 Ec66
Olmedilla de Alarcón E 53 Eb67
Olmedillo de Roa E 46 Db60
Olmedo E 46 Da61
Olmedo I 168 Bd75
Olmeto F 154 Ca71
Ölmevalla S 102 Ec50
Ölmhult S 95 Fb43
Olmi-Capella F 154 Cb69
Olmillos de Castro E 45 Cb60
Olmillos de Sasamón E 38 Db58
Olmo al Brembo I 149 Cd58
Olmos P 45 Bd60
Olmos de la Picaza E 38 Db58
Olmos de Ojeda E 38 Da57
Olmos de Pisuerga E 38 Db57
Ölmstad S 103 Fb48
Olmütz = Olomouc CZ 137 Gd46
Olney GB 20 Fb26
Ołobok PL 129 Ha39
Olocau E 54 Fb67
Olocau del Rey E 48 Fc64
Olofsfors S 80 Ha29
Olofstorp S 102 Ec48
Olofström S 111 Fc54
Olombrada E 46 Db61
Olomouc CZ 137 Gd46
Olonne-sur-Mer F 28 Ed44
Olonzac F 41 Ha55
Oloron-Sainte-Marie F 39 Fb55
Olosig RO 170 Cb56
Olost E 49 Gd59
Olot E 49 Ha59
Oloví CZ 135 Ec44
Olovo BIH 159 Hc64
Olpe D 125 Cb39
Olpe D 125 Cb40
Ol'ša RUS 202 Ec11
Olsberg D 126 Cc40
Olsbrücken D 133 Ca45
Olsbu N 93 Da45
Olseröd S 111 Fb55
Ölserud S 94 Ed44
Olsewo Werorzewskie PL 122 Jc30
Olshammar S 95 Fc45
Olši CZ 137 Gb46
Olsker DK 111 Fc57
Olsøy N 78 Ea29
Ölsremma S 102 Fa49
Olst NL 117 Bc36
Ølsted DK 108 Dc25
Ølsted DK 109 Eb25
Ølstrup DK 108 Cd24
Ølstykke DK 109 Eb25
Olsvika N 70 Ed24
Olszamy PL 130 Jb38
Olszanica PL 139 Kb46
Olszanka PL 123 Ka30
Olszanka PL 129 Gd42
Olszany PL 139 Kb45
Olszewka PL 123 Jb33
Olszewnica PL 131 Ka37
Olszewo-Borki PL 122 Jc34
Olsztyn PL 122 Ja32
Olsztyn PL 130 Hc42
Olsztynek PL 122 Ja33
Olszyn PL 131 Kc37
Olszyna PL 128 Fc35
Olszyna PL 128 Fd41
Olszyny PL 122 Jb32
Oltedal N 92 Ca44
Olteneşti RO 173 Fb59
Olteni RO 180 Dd67
Olteniţa RO 181 Ec67
Oltesvig N 92 Cb44
Oltina RO 181 Fa67
Oltre il Colle I 149 Cd58
Oltu TR 205 Ga19
Olukbaşı TR 198 Fb89
Olukbaşı TR 198 Fd90
Oluku TR 193 Gb81
Olula del Río E 61 Eb74
Olur TR 205 Ga19
Olustvere EST 98 Kd45
Olvan E 49 Gd59
Olvasjärvi FIN 75 Kc23
Ølve N 84 Ca40
Ólvega E 47 Ec60
Olveiroa E 36 Ac55
Olvera E 59 Cb75
Ólvio GR 184 Db77
Olynthos GR 183 Cb79
Olzai I 169 Ca76
Omagh GB 9 Cc17
Omalí GR 182 Ba78
Omaló GR 183 Bd77

Oman BG 181 Ec73
Omarčevo BG 180 Ea72
Omarska BIH 152 Gc62
Ómassa H 146 Jb50
Omblèze F 35 Jc49
Ömböly H 147 Kb51
Omeath IRL 9 Cd19
Omedu EST 99 Lb44
Omegna I 148 Ca58
Oparić SRB 178 Bd67
Ömen TR 186 Fc77
Omeñaca E 47 Eb60
Ömerköy TR 192 Fa81
Ömerler TR 192 Ga82
Ömerler TR 193 Hb82
Ömerler Bölüğü TR 197 Fa89
Ömeroba TR 185 Ec74
Omiš HR 158 Gc66
Omišalj HR 151 Fb61
Ommen NL 117 Bd35
Ommunddalen N 78 Ea28
Omø DK 109 Ea27
Omodos CY 206 Ja97
Omoljica SRB 174 Bb64
Omont F 24 Ja34
Omonville-la-Rogue F 22 Ed34
Omor RO 174 Bd62
Omorani MK 183 Bc74
Omorfohóri GR 189 Bd81
Ómossa FIN 89 Ja34
Omsjö S 79 Gb29
Omurlar TR 192 Fc84
Omvriaki GR 189 Bc82
øn N 84 Ca36
Ön S 73 Hc23
Ön S 79 Gb30
Ön S 79 Fd28
Oña E 38 Dd57
Ona N 76 Cd31
Onaç TR 199 Gc88
Onali FIN 90 Kc36
Onarheim N 84 Ca40
Oñati E 39 Eb56
Onceşti RO 172 Ed59
Onda E 54 Fc66
Ondara E 55 Fc70
Ondarroa E 39 Eb55
Ondić HR 151 Ga63
Ondres F 39 Ed53
Ondrovo RUS 99 Mb40
Önerler TR 186 Fa77
Onesse-et-Laharie F 39 Fa53
Oneşti MD 173 Fc57
Oneşti MD 173 Fc58
Oneşti RO 176 Ec60
Onet-le-Château F 33 Ha51
Oniceni RO 172 Ed58
Onich GB 6 Dc10
Onifai I 168 Cc76
Oniferi I 169 Cb76
Onil E 55 Fb70
Oniţcani MD 173 Fd57
Onkamaa FIN 91 Lb37
Onkamo FIN 69 Kd17
Onkamo FIN 74 Ka23
Onkamo FIN 83 La31
Onkemäki FIN 89 Jd36
Onkijoki FIN 89 Jc37
Onkiniemi FIN 90 Kc35
Onnaing F 24 Hb32
Önneköp S 110 Fa55
Önnestad S 111 Fb54
Önningeby FIN 96 Hc41
Onno I 149 Cc59
Onoz F 31 Jc44
Onsares E 53 Ea71
Onsbjerg DK 109 Dd25
Onsevig DK 109 Ea28
Onsey N 93 Ea44
Onslunda S 111 Fb56
Onstwedde NL 117 Ca34
Ontika EST 99 Lb41
Ontinar del Salz E 48 Fb59
Ontiñena E 48 Fd60
Ör S 103 Fc51
Ör H 147 Kb51
Ontojoki FIN 83 Lb26
Ontón E 38 Dd55
Onttola FIN 83 Ld30
Ontur E 55 Ed70
Onum S 102 Ed47
Onuškis LT 114 Kd58
Onuškis LT 114 La53
Onville F 25 Jc36
Onzain F 29 Gd41
Onzonilla E 37 Cc57
Oola IRL 12 Bd23
Oonga EST 98 Ka44
Orah BIH 159 Hc68
Oostburg NL 124 Ab38
Oosteeklo B 124 Ab38
Oostende = Oostende B 124 Ab38
Oosterend NL 116 Ba33
Oosterend NL 116 Bb32
Oosterhesselen NL 117 Bd35
Oosterhout NL 124 Ad38
Oosterwolde NL 117 Bd34
Oosterzee NL 117 Bc34
Oosthuizen NL 116 Ba35
Oostkapelle NL 124 Ab38
Oostmalle B 124 Ad39
Oost-Souburg NL 124 Ab38
Oostvleteren B 21 Ha31
Oostvoorne NL 124 Ac37
Ootmarsum NL 117 Bd36

Opaci MD 173 Ga59
Oräştie RO 175 Cd61
Opaka BG 180 Ea69
Opalenica PL 129 Gb37
Opalenie PL 121 Hb32
Opaleniec PL 122 Jb33
Opaljenik SRB 178 Bd67
Opan BG 180 Dd73
Oparany CZ 136 Fb47
Oparić SRB 178 Bd67
Opatinec HR 152 Gb59
Opatija HR 151 Fb60
Opatovac HR 153 Hd60
Opatovice nad Labem CZ 136 Ga44
Opatów PL 129 Ha40
Opatów PL 130 Hc41
Opatów PL 131 Jd41
Opatówek PL 129 Ha39
Opatowiec PL 138 Jb43
Opava CZ 137 Ha45
Opawica PL 137 Gd44
Opeinde NL 117 Bc33
O Pedrouzo (O Pino) E 36 Ba55
Opglabeek B 125 Bb40
Ophemert NL 125 Bb37
Opi I 161 Fb71
Opinan GB 4 Dc06
O Pindo E 36 Ac55
Opinogóra PL 122 Jb34
Opišnja UA 202 Ed14
Opitter B 125 Bb40
Oploo NL 125 Bb38
Oplotnica SLO 151 Fd57
Opocka RUS 107 Mb50
Opočka RUS 202 Ea10
Opočno CZ 137 Gb44
Opoczno PL 130 Ja40
Opole PL 129 Ha42
Opol'e RUS 99 Ld41
Opole Lubelskie PL 131 Jd40
Opolno-Zdrój PL 128 Fc42
Oporelu RO 175 Db65
Oporów PL 130 Hd37
Opovo SRB 153 Jc61
Opovo SRB 174 Bb63
Oppach D 128 Fb41
Oppala S 95 Gb39
Oppdal N 77 Dd32
Oppdal N 78 Ec26
Oppdalen N 85 Ea40
Oppdøl N 77 Db32
Oppeano I 149 Dc60
Oppeby S 103 Fd47
Oppède-le-Vieux F 42 Jc53
Oppegård N 93 Ea42
Oppegard N 94 Eb39
Oppenau D 133 Cb49
Oppenberg A 144 Fb53
Oppenheim D 133 Cb45
Oppenwehe D 117 Cc36
Oppenweiler D 134 Cd48
Oppidi Lucano I 162 Gb75
Oppido Mamertina I 164 Gb83
Oppmanna S 111 Fb54
Opponitz A 144 Fc52
Oppsal N 92 Ca44
Oppstryn N 84 Cc34
Oppurg D 127 Ea42
Oprişor RO 175 Cc66
Oqregcsertő H 146 Hd56
Öpregrund S 96 Gd40
Orehova RUS 107 Ma47
Orehova HR 152 Gb58
Orehovec MK 183 Bc75
Orehoved DK 109 Eb28
Orehovica BG 180 Db68
Orehovići RUS 107 Ma47
Orehovo RUS 99 Ma44
Orehovo BG 184 Cc76
Orehovo-Zuevo RUS 203 Fa10

Oreye B 124 Ba41
Öreyköy TR 185 Ec77
Orezu RO 176 Ec66
Orford GB 21 Gb26
Orgáni GR 185 Dd76
Organyà E 48 Gb59
Orgaz E 52 Db67
Orgelet F 31 Jc44
Orgères-en-Beauce F 29 Gc39
Órgiva E 60 Dc76
Orglandes F 22 Fa35
Orgnac-l'Aven F 34 Ja51
Orgnac-sur-Vézère F 33 Gc48
Orgon F 42 Jb53
Orgosolo I 169 Cb76
Orgovány H 146 Ja55
Orhaneli TR 192 Fc81
Orhangazi TR 186 Fd79
Orhaniye TR 185 Eb78
Orhaniye TR 186 Fd80
Orhaniye TR 186 Ga79
Orhaniye TR 187 Gb78
Orhaniye TR 193 Ha82
Orhanlar TR 191 Ed81
Orhanlı TR 186 Fd78
Orhanlı TR 198 Fd78
Orhanlı TR 198 Da89
Orhei MD 173 Fd57
Orhomenós GR 189 Ca85
Oria E 61 Ea74
Oria I 162 Hb76
Orichiv UA 205 Fa16
Origny-en-Thiérache F 24 Hc33
Origny-Sainte-Benoite F 24 Hb33
Orihuela E 55 Fa72
Orihuela del Tremedal E 47 Ed64
Orijahovo BG 179 Da68
Orikon AL 182 Aa77
Orillena E 48 Fc60
Orimattila FIN 90 Kc37
Oriniemi FIN 83 Lc29
Oriniemi FIN 89 Jc37
Orini Meligoú GR 195 Bd88
Oriñón E 38 Dd55
Orio E 39 Ec55
Ório GR 189 Cc85
Oriola P 50 Ad70
Oriolo I 162 Gc77
Oripää FIN 89 Jb31
Orisberg FIN 81 Jb31
Orismala FIN 81 Ja31
Orisoain E 39 Ed57
Orissaare EST 97 Jd45
Oristano I 169 Bd77
Orisuo FIN 89 Jc37
Öriszentpéter H 145 Gb55
Orivesi FIN 90 Ka35
Orizare BG 181 Fa72
Orizovo BG 180 Dc73
Orjaku EST 97 Jc45
Orjal E 36 Ba55
Orjanovo BG 185 Ea74
Ørje N 94 Eb43
Orkanger N 77 Dd30
Örkelljunga S 110 Ed54
Orkesta S 96 Gd42
Orkland N 77 Dd30
Orla PL 123 Kb35
Orlamünde D 127 Ea42
Orlane KSV 178 Bc70
Orlat RO 180 Db68
Orléans F 29 Gd40
Orlea RO 180 Db68
Orlovec BG 180 Ea69
Orlov dol BG 185 Ea74
Orlovec BG 180 Ea69
Orlov Gaj RUS 203 Ga12
Orlova Mogila BG 181 Fa69
Orlovat SRB 153 Jc60
Orlové CZ 137 Hb62
Orlov dol BG 185 Ea74
Orlov Gaj RUS 203 Ga12
Orlová CZ 137 Hd45
Orlovskij RUS 205 Fd15
Orłowo PL 123 Jd30
Orłowo PL 123 Jd32
Orly F 23 Gc37
Orly RUS 99 Lc41
Orma GR 183 Bd76
Ormaiztegi E 39 Eb56
Ormanköy TR 191 Ed86
Ormanlı TR 187 Hb77
Ormaryd S 103 Fc49
Ormea I 148 Bd63
Orménio GR 185 Eb76
Ormeni RO 176 Ea61
Ormeniş RO 176 Ea61
Ormesberga S 103 Fc51
Ormesby Saint Margaret GB 17 Gc24
Órmi GR 183 Bd80
Ormideia CY 206 Jd97
Orsdorf D 118 Dc30

Ortigueira E 36 Bb53
Ortiguera E 37 Bd53
Ortihovo RUS 107 Ld48
Orting DK 108 Dc25
Ortisei I 143 Dd56
Ortişoara RO 174 Bd60
Ortnevik N 84 Cb30
Orto F 154 Ca70
Örtomta S 103 Ga46
Orton GB 11 Ec18
Ortona I 157 Fb70
Ortrand S 128 Fa40
Orträsk S 80 Ha27
Örtschwaben CH 141 Bd54
Ortucchio I 160 Ed71
Ortueri I 169 Ca77
Örtülü TR 191 Ed84
Örtülü TR 198 Fb89
Örtülüce TR 185 Ec79
Ortved DK 108 Dd25
Ortwig D 128 Fb36
Oru EST 99 Lc41
Oru EST 106 La47
Orubica HR 152 Ha61
Öslejas LV 106 Ka51
Ortofta S 110 Fa56
Oru EST 99 Lc41
Oru EST 106 La47
Orubica HR 152 Ha61
Öslejas LV 106 Ka51
Öru EST 106 La47
Oruçoğlu TR 186 Ga77
Örüculer TR 192 Fb84
Ørum DK 100 Db23
Ørum DK 101 Dd23
Orune I 168 Cb76
Orusco E 46 Dd65
Orval F 29 Ha44
Orvault F 28 Ed42
Ørvella N 93 Db42
Orvelte NL 117 Bd34
Orvieto I 156 Ea69
Örviken S 80 Hc25
Orville F 30 Jb41
Orvilliers-Saint-Julien F 30 Hc38
Orvinio I 160 Ec71
Orwell GB 20 Fc26
Orzechowo PL 121 Hb34
Orzechowo PL 122 Ja31
Orzechowo PL 129 Gd37
Orzesze PL 138 Hc44
Orzinuovi I 149 Cd59
Orživ UA 202 Ea14
Oržycja UA 204 Ed15
Orzyny PL 122 Jb32
Orzysz PL 123 Jd31

Osinja BIH 152 Hb62
Osinki FIN 123 Ka30
Osinkino RUS 107 Mb48
Osinoviči RUS 107 Ma47
Osinovka RUS 113 Jb58
Osinów PL 120 Fb35
Osiny PL 130 Jc40
Osiny PL 131 Jd38
Osipaonica SRB 174 Bc64
Osišče RUS 99 Ld42
Osivica BIH 152 Ha62
Osječenica MNE 159 Hd69
Oskal N 68 Ja12
Oskar S 111 Ga53
Oskarshamn S 103 Gb50
Oskarström S 102 Ed52
Oškino RUS 203 Fb13
Oskola FIN 83 Ma31
Oskowo PL 121 Gd30
Öskü S 145 Hb54
Osłany E 137 Hb49
Öslejas LV 106 Ka51
Ošlje HR 158 Ha68
Oslo N 93 Ea41
Øsløs DK 100 Db23
Osłoß D 126 Dc36
Osma E 46 Dd61
Osma FIN 64 Jd07
Osma N 77 Db30
Osman TR 193 Gd81
Osmancalı TR 191 Ec85
Osmancık TR 185 Ed76
Osmancık TR 205 Fb20
Osmaneli TR 187 Gb80
Osmangazi TR 186 Fd80
Osmaniye TR 186 Ga80
Osmaniye TR 191 Ed86
Osmaniye TR 192 Fa82
Osmaniye TR 192 Fb86
Osmaniye TR 192 Fc83
Osmaniye TR 193 Gb82
Osmaniye TR 193 Gd81
Osmaniye TR 197 Fa91
Osmaniye TR 198 Fd91
Osmankalfalar TR 198 Ga90
Osmanlar TR 192 Fb83
Osmanlı TR 185 Ec75
Osmanville F 22 Fa35
Osmaslar TR 191 Ed82
Osmery F 29 Ha43
Osmington GB 19 Ec31
Os'mino RUS 99 Ma42
Os'mino RUS 202 Ea09
Osmo S 96 Gd44
Osmotherley GB 11 Fa18
Osnabrück D 117 Cc36
Osne-le-Val F 24 Jb37
Ošno PL 122 Hc32
Ošno Lubuskie PL 128 Fc36
Osny F 23 Gc37
Osoblaha CZ 137 Ha44
Osogna CH 142 Cc56
Osoppo I 150 Ec57
Osor E 49 Ha59
Osor HR 151 Fb62
Osorhei RO 170 Cb56
Osorno la Mayor E 38 Db58
Osowa PL 123 Ka30
Osøyro N 84 Ca40
Osoyvollen N 86 Ea32
Os Peares E 36 Bb57
Ospedaletti I 43 La52
Ospedaletto I 156 Ea68
Ospitale di Cadore I 150 Eb57
Ospitaletto I 149 Da59
Oss NL 125 Bb38
Ossa de Montiel E 53 Ea69
Össeby-Garn S 96 Gd43
Osses F 39 Fa55
Ossett GB 16 Fa21
Ossi I 168 Bd75
Ossiach A 144 Fa56
Össjö S 110 Ed54
Oßling D 128 Fb40
Oßmannstedt D 127 Ea41
Osso E 48 Fd60
Östa S 95 Gb41
Ostabat F 39 Fa55
Ostaná S 111 Fb54
Östanbäck S 80 Hc25
Östanbo S 87 Gb37
Östansjö S 72 Gb21
Østansjö S 87 Fb35
Östansjö S 95 Fc44
Östanskär S 87 Gb33
Ostaškov RUS 202 Ec10
Ostaszewo PL 121 Hb30
Ostatija SRB 178 Ba68
Östavall S 87 Fd37
Ostavik S 87 Fd37
Ostbevern D 125 Cb37
Østby DK 108 Dd24
Ostbjörka S 87 Fc38
Østby N 86 Ed37
Østby N 86 Ed37
Østed DK 109 Eb26
Osteel D 117 Cb32
Østellato I 150 Ea62
Osten D 118 Da32
Ostende = Oostende B 21 Ha29

Paljasmaa – Pembroke

Paljasmaa EST 98 Kb44
Paljevo SRB 178 Ba69
Pälkäene FIN 90 Ka36
Pålkem S 73 Hc20
Palkino RUS 107 Ld47
Palkisoja FIN 69 Kb12
Pallanza I 148 Cb58
Pallaruelo de Monegros E 48 Fc60
Pallasgreen (New) IRL 12 Bd23
Pallegney F 31 Jd38
Pallerols del Cantó E 40 Gb58
Palling D 143 Ec51
Pallosenvaara FIN 83 Ma28
Palma P 50 Ac69
Palma Campania I 161 Fb75
Pálmaces de Jadraque E 47 Ea62
Palma del Río E 59 Cb73
Palma de Mallorca E 57 Hb67
Palma di Montechiaro I 166 Ed87
Palmadula I 168 Bc74
Palmanova I 150 Ed58
Palmanyola E 57 Hb67
Palme P 44 Ac59
Palmeira E 36 Ac56
Palmeira P 44 Ad59
Palmela P 50 Ab69
Palmi I 164 Ga83
Palmiano I 156 Ed68
Palmiry PL 130 Jb36
Palmižana HR 158 Gb67
Palmones E 59 Cb78
Pálmonostora H 146 Jb55
Palmschoss I 143 Ea56
Palmse EST 98 Kd41
Palo FIN 68 Jb16
Palo FIN 83 Ma30
Palo I 148 Ca62
Palodeia CY 206 Ja98
Palo del Colle I 162 Gc74
Palohuornas S 73 Hc18
Palojärvi FIN 68 Ja12
Palojärvi FIN 74 Jd18
Palojärvi FIN 74 Kb18
Palojoensuu FIN 68 Ja13
Palojoki FIN 98 Kb39
Palokastër AL 182 Ac78
Palokki FIN 83 Lb31
Palomaa FIN 64 Ka09
Palomaa FIN 90 Kb37
Palomar de Arroyos E 48 Fb63
Palomares E 61 Ec75
Palomares del Campo E 53 Ea66
Palomas E 51 Ca69
Palombara Sabina I 160 Eb71
Palomenė LT 114 Kd57
Palomera E 53 Ec66
Palonai LV 114 Kb55
Palonen FIN 75 La19
Palonkylä FIN 81 Jd25
Palonurmi FIN 82 La28
Paloperä FIN 74 Kc18
Palopuro FIN 90 Kb38
Palos de la Frontera E 59 Bb74
Palosenjärvi FIN 82 Kd27
Paloskylä FIN 90 Kc33
Palota SK 139 Ka46
Palovaara FIN 74 Ka20
Palovaara FIN 75 Lb23
Palovaara FIN 83 Ma29
Palovitta FIN 82 Kc28
Pals E 49 Hc59
Palsankylä FIN 90 Kb32
Pålsboda S 95 Fd44
Palsina FIN 90 Ka34
Palsmane LV 106 La48
Pålsträsk S 73 Hc22
Paltamo FIN 82 Kd25
Paltanen FIN 90 Kd32
Paltaniemi FIN 82 Kd25
Paltin RO 176 Ec62
Păltiniș RO 172 Ec54
Păltiniș RO 174 Ca62
Păltiniș RO 175 Da62
Păltinoasa RO 172 Eb56
Pałubice PL 121 Gd30
Paludi I 164 Gc79
Pałuki PL 122 Jb35
Paluknys LT 114 La58
Palukūla EST 97 Jc44
Paluobiai LV 114 Kb57
Palupera EST 106 La46
Palupõhja EST 98 La45
Palus FIN 89 Ja36
Palūšė LT 115 Lb55
Paluzza I 143 Ec56
Palviainen FIN 90 La32
Palvis FIN 81 Ja30
Palzem D 133 Bc45
Pamati LV 107 Lb51
Pameče SLO 144 Fd56
Pámfilla GR 191 Ea83
Pamhagen A 145 Gc52
Pamiątkowo PL 129 Gb36
Pamiers F 40 Gc56
Pamiętowo PL 121 Gd33
Pamma EST 105 Jc46
Pammana EST 97 Jc45
Pampāļi LV 105 Jc52
Pamparato I 148 Bd63
Pampelone F 41 Gd52
Pampilhosa da Serra P 44 Ba65
Pampliega E 38 Db58
Pamplona E 39 Ed57
Pamporovo = V. Kolaro BG 184 Db75
Pampow D 120 Fb33
Pamucak TR 191 Ec87
Pamucak TR 192 Fb87
Pamukčii BG 181 Ed70
Pamukçu TR 192 Fa82
Pamukkale TR 198 Fd88
Pamukören TR 198 Fb88
Pamukova TR 187 Gb79
Pamukyazi TR 191 Ec87
Pamusiai LT 114 Kd59
Pamūšis LT 114 Kb53
Panaci RO 172 Ea57
Panagia CY 206 Jb97
Panagía GR 182 Ba80
Panagía GR 183 Bb79
Panagía GR 184 Db78
Panagía GR 195 Cd89
Panagía GR 201 Db96
Panagítsa GR 183 Bc77
Panagítsa GR 194 Bc87
Panagjurište BG 179 Da72
Panagra CY 206 Jb96
Panaja AL 182 Aa77
Pánakto GR 189 Cb86
Panamune LV 106 Kc52
Pănășești MD 173 Fc57
Panasqueira P 50 Ac71
Panassac F 40 Ga55
Pănătău RO 176 Eb63
Panazol F 33 Gb47
Pančarevo BG 179 Cc71
Pancarköy TR 191 Ec87
Pâncești RO 176 Ed60
Pančevo SRB 174 Bb63
Pancey F 30 Jb38
Panchia I 150 Dd57
Panciu RO 176 Ed61
Pancorbo E 38 Dd57
Pâncota RO 170 Ca59
Pancrudo E 47 Fa63
Pandánassa GR 195 Bd91
Pandeleimon AL 182 Ab79
Pandėlys LT 114 Kd53
Pandino I 149 Cd59
Pandivere EST 98 La43
Pándrossos GR 184 Dc77
Pandrup DK 100 Dc20
Pandy GB 15 Ea24
Panelia FIN 89 Ja37
Panemunė LT 113 Jc57
Panemunėlis LT 114 La54
Panes E 38 Da55
Panetólio GR 188 Ba84
Panevėžys LT 114 Kc54
Panfilovo RUS 113 Jc59
Panga EST 97 Jc45
Pângărați RO 172 Eb58
Pângărești RO 176 Ec60
Pangbourne GB 20 Fa28
Panicale I 156 Ea68
Panicarola I 156 Ea67
Paničište BG 179 Cc73
Paničkovo BG 184 Dc74
Panicovo BG 181 Fa71
Panike FIN 81 Hd30
Panikoviči RUS 107 Lc47
Panissières F 34 Ja47
Panix CH 142 Cc55
Paniza E 47 Fa62
Panjas F 40 Fc53
Panjevac SRB 174 Bc66
Panjik BIH 153 Hc62
Panka FIN 82 Kd29
Pankajärvi FIN 83 Ld28
Pankakoski FIN 83 Ld28
Pankasz H 145 Gb55
Panker D 119 Dd30
Panki PL 129 Hb41
Pannonhalma H 145 Ha53
Pano Archimandrita CY 206 Ja98
Pano Kivides CY 206 Ja98
Pano Lakatameia CY 206 Jb97
Pano Lefkara CY 206 Jb97
Pano Panagia CY 206 Hd97
Pano Platres CY 206 Ja97
Pano Pyrgos CY 206 Ja96
Panórama GR 183 Cb78
Panórama GR 184 Cd76
Panormitis GR 197 Ed92
Pánormos GR 196 Db88
Pánormos GR 197 Eb90
Pánormos GR 200 Cd95
Panoteriai LT 114 Kd56
Panoviai LT 114 Ka57
Panschwitz-Kuckau D 128 Fb41
Pantalowice PL 139 Kb44
Päntäne FIN 89 Ja33
Pantano del Chorro E 60 Cc75
Pantano del Guadelén E 52 Dc72
Pantano de Puentes E 61 Ec73
Pantelej MK 178 Bd73
Pantelimon RO 176 Eb66
Pantelimon RO 177 Fb66
Pantelleria I 166 Dd88
Panticeu RO 171 Da57
Panticosa E 40 Fc57
Pant Mawr GB 15 Ea25
Pantoja E 46 Db65
Panttila FIN 89 Jb32
Pantymenyn GB 14 Dc26
Panxón E 36 Ac57
Panyola H 147 Kb50
Paola I 164 Gb80
Pápa H 145 Gd53
Papadátes GR 188 Ba84
Papádes GR 189 Cb83
Papadiánika GR 195 Bd90
Pápakovácsi H 145 Gd54
Paparčiai LT 114 Kd57
Páparis GR 194 Bc88
Papartėliai LT 114 Kd57
Papasidero I 164 Gb78
Pápateszér H 145 Ha53
Papatrigo E 46 Cd63
Păpăuți MD 173 Fd55
Pape LV 113 Ja54
Papelkiai LT 114 Ka54
Papenburg D 117 Cb34
Pápigo GR 182 Ad79
Papilė LT 113 Jd53
Papilys LT 114 Kd53
Papin SK 139 Ka47
Papinniemi FIN 91 Ld32
Papiu Ilarian RO 171 Db59
Paplin PL 131 Jd36
Pápoc H 145 Gd53
Papowo Biskupie PL 121 Hb34
Pappenheim D 134 Dc48
Pappinen FIN 89 Jc33
Pappinen FIN 90 Kc34
Papradnik MK 182 Ad74
Papradno SK 137 Hb47
Papratna HR 158 Ha68
Paprotnia PL 130 Ja37
Paprotnia PL 131 Ka36
Paprūdžiai LT 114 Ka55
Papušynys LT 114 Ka55
Papworth Everard GB 20 Fc26
Papyvesiai LT 114 Kc53
Par GB 18 Db31
Parabiago I 148 Cb59
Parabita I 163 Hc77
Paraćin SRB 178 Bc67
Paracuellos E 53 Ec67
Paracuellos de Jiloca E 47 Ed62
Parád H 146 Jb51
Parada de Ester P 44 Ba62
Parada do Sil E 36 Bb57
Paradas E 59 Cb74
Paradavella E 36 Bc55
Paradela E 36 Bb55
Paradela E 36 Ba54
Paradela P 44 Ad62
Paradela P 44 Ba59
Paradinas de San Juan E 45 Cc62
Paradisgård S 95 Fb42
Paradisi GR 190 Cd86
Paradisi GR 197 Fa92
Paradísia GR 194 Bb88
Paradiso I 164 Ga83
Paradiso I 164 Gb83
Paradiso di Cevedale I 142 Db56
Parádissos GR 184 Db77
Paradyż PL 130 Ja40
Parage SRB 153 Ja60
Parainen FIN 97 Jb40
Parajes E 36 Bc54
Parakálamos GR 182 Ac79
Parakka S 68 Hc16
Paralı TR 187 Gd78
Paralía GR 183 Bd79
Paralía GR 188 Bb85
Paralía GR 189 Bd85
Paralia Agiou Andréa GR 195 Bd88
Paralía Akrátas GR 189 Bc85
Paralia Kimis GR 190 Cd84
Paralía Platánou GR 189 Bc85
Paralía Thermis GR 191 Ea83
Paralía Tiroú GR 195 Bd89
Paralimni CY 206 Jd97
Parálio Ástros GR 195 Bd88
Parálio Irion GR 195 Bd88
Paramithiá GR 188 Ac81
Páramo E 37 Cb55
Páramo del Sil E 37 Ca56
Paramos E 36 Ad55
Paranésti GR 184 Da76
Parapalu EST 99 Lc45
Parapótamos GR 182 Ac80
Pāras FIN 81 Jb28
Paras N 67 Ha11
Paraspuari AL 182 Ac77
Parasznya H 146 Jc50
Paratala FIN 82 Kb31
Parău RO 176 Dd61
Paray-le-Monial F 30 Hd44
Parbayón E 38 Dc55
Parcani MD 173 Fc54
Parcani SRB 153 Jc62
Parceiros de São João P 50 Ac66
Parcé-sur-Sarthe F 28 Fc40
Parcey F 31 Jc42
Parchen D 127 Eb37
Parcheș RO 177 Fc64
Parchim D 119 Eb33
Parchów PL 128 Ga40
Parchowo PL 121 Gd30
Parciaki PL 122 Jb33
Parcova MD 173 Fa54
Parczew PL 131 Kb38
Pardalítsa GR 182 Ac80
Pardavé E 37 Cc56
Pardesivil E 37 Cc56
Pardilla E 46 Dc61
Pardina RO 177 Fd63
Pardines E 41 Ha58
Pardoși RO 176 Ec63
Pardubice CZ 136 Ga45
Parečėnai LT 114 Kc59
Paredea de Buitrago E 46 Dc62
Paredes E 36 Ad57
Paredes P 44 Ad61
Paredes de Coura P 36 Ad58
Paredes de Nava E 38 Da58
Paredes de Sigüenza E 47 Ea62
Parekklisia CY 206 Jb98
Påreks sameviste S 72 Gc18
Parennes F 28 Fc39
Parentis-en-Born F 39 Fa52
Parets del Vallès E 49 Hb61
Parey D 127 Eb37
Parfondeval F 24 Hd33
Parga E 36 Bb55
Párga GR 188 Ac81
Pargas FIN 97 Jb40
Pargas FIN 97 Jd40
Pargny F 24 Ja37
Pargues F 30 Hd39
Parhalahti FIN 81 Jd25
Pári H 145 Hb56
Parigné-l'Evêque F 28 Fd40
Parikiá GR 196 Db90
Parikkala FIN 91 Ld34
Parincea RO 172 Ed59
Paris F 23 Gd37
Parisot F 41 Gd52
Pärispea EST 98 Kd41
Pärjänsou FIN 75 Kc21
Pârjoi RO 172 Ec59
Park GB 9 Cc16
Parkajoki S 68 Ja15
Parkalompolo S 68 Hd15
Parkano FIN 89 Jc34
Parka sameviste S 72 Gb19
Parkgate GB 10 Ea15
Parkham GB 18 Dc29
Parkkila FIN 75 Kd23
Parkkila FIN 82 Ka27
Parkkila FIN 90 La34
Parkkima FIN 82 Kb28
Parkstein D 135 Eb45
Parkstetten D 135 Ec48
Parkua FIN 82 Kd26
Parkumäki FIN 91 Lb33
Parkuu FIN 89 Jd34
Parla E 46 Dc65
Parlak TR 191 Ea85
Parlament D 108 Cd29
Parlavà E 49 Hb59
Parłówko PL 120 Fc32
Parma I 149 Da62
Parmakören TR 193 Gb83
Parmen D 120 Fa33
Pärnämäki FIN 90 Kd34
Pärnämäki FIN 90 Kd35
Parndorf A 145 Gc51
Párnica SK 138 Hd47
Pärnjõe EST 98 Kc45
Pärnu EST 106 Kb46
Pärnu-Jaagupi EST 98 Kb45
Parois F 24 Jb35
Parola FIN 90 La36
Parola FIN 90 Ka37
Parolise I 161 Fc75
Parona di Valpolicella I 149 Dc59
Parowa PL 128 Fd40
Parpan CH 142 Cd55
Parrillas E 45 Cc65
Parroy F 25 Ka37
Parsac F 33 Gd45
Parsau D 127 Dd36
Parsberg D 135 Ea47
Pârșcoveni RO 175 Da66
Parsęcko PL 121 Gb32
Pars-lès-Romilly F 30 Hc38
Parsów PL 120 Fc34
Pärsti EST 98 Kd45
Parszów PL 130 Jc41
Partaharju FIN 90 Kd32
Partakko FIN 65 Kb10
Partakoski FIN 91 Lb35
Partanna I 166 Eb85
Partanna-Mondello I 166 Ec83
Parteen IRL 12 Bd23
Partenkirchen, Garmisch- D 142 Dc53
Parteștii de Jos RO 172 Eb55
Parthenay F 28 Fc44
Parthéni GR 197 Eb90
Parthenónas GR 184 Cc80
Parthenstein D 127 Ec40
Partille S 102 Ec49
Partinico I 166 Ec84
Partizani BG 181 Ed71
Partizani SRB 153 Jc63
Partizanin BG 180 Dc73
Partizánske SK 137 Hb49
Partizanske Vode SRB 159 Jb65
Partizanskoe RUS 113 Ja59
Partney GB 17 Fd22
Parton GB 10 Ea16
Partoș RO 174 Bc62
Partry IRL 8 Bc19
Partsi EST 107 Lc46
Parudaminys LT 114 La58
Pårup DK 108 Db24
Parva RO 171 Dc56
Pârvenec BG 180 Db73
Pârvomaj BG 180 Dc73
Pârvomaj BG 183 Cb75
Parwich GB 16 Ed23
Paryčy BY 202 Eb13
Påryd S 111 Ga53
Parysów PL 131 Jd37
Parzán E 40 Fd57
Parzew PL 129 Gd38
Parznice PL 130 Jc40
Paša RUS 202 Eb08
Paşaçayır TR 185 Ec80
Paşaçiftliği TR 186 Fa80
Paşacık TR 193 Gb85
Pasai San Pedro E 39 Ec55
Paşaköy TR 185 Ea78
Paşaköy TR 191 Ea82
Paşaköy TR 191 Ed85
Paşaköy TR 192 Fa82
Paşaköy = Askeia CY 206 Jc96
Pasala FIN 82 Kb29
Pasalankylä FIN 82 La29
Paşalar TR 192 Fb81
Paşalimanı TR 185 Ed79
Pašaltuonys LT 113 Jd56
Pašaminė LT 115 Lb56
Pasarel BG 179 Cc72
Pasăreni RO 171 Dc59
Pasarón de la Vera E 45 Cb65
Paşayiğit TR 185 Eb77
Pașcani MD 173 Fc58
Pașcani MD 173 Fd57
Pașcani RO 172 Ec57
Paschero I 148 Bb62
Pășcoy RO 176 Ec63
Pas-de-Jeu F 28 Fc43
Pas-en-Artois F 23 Gd32
Paserninkai LT 123 Kc30
Pasewalk D 120 Fa33
Pashalitsa GR 189 Bc82
Pasi FIN 90 La36
Pasian di Prato I 150 Ec58
Pašiausė LT 114 Ka55
Pasiecznik PL 128 Fd41
Pasiene LV 107 Ma51
Pasikovci HR 152 Ha60
Pašilė LT 113 Jc53
Pašilė LT 113 Jd55
Pašiliai LT 114 Kc55
Pašina Voda MNE 159 Ja67
Pasinler TR 205 Ga19
Paskalevec BG 180 Dd70
Paskalevo BG 181 Fa69
Påskallavik S 103 Gb51
Paški RUS 107 Mb49
Paskov CZ 137 Hb45
Paškovskij RUS 205 Fc17
Pasłek PL 122 Hd31
Pasmajärvi FIN 68 Jc17
Pašman HR 157 Fd65
Påsmark FIN 89 Hd33
Passage East IRL 13 Cc25
Passail A 144 Fd54
Passais F 28 Fb38
Passariano I 150 Ec58
Passau D 135 Ed49
Passekårsa S 67 Ha15
Passignano sul Trasimeno I 156 Ea67
Passopisciaro I 167 Fc85
Passow D 119 Eb33
Passow D 120 Fb34
Pastavy BY 202 Ea12
Pastena I 161 Fb73
Pastende LV 105 Jd50
Pastetten D 143 Ea50
Paštiky CZ 136 Fa46
Pasto FIN 89 Jc32
Pastor E 36 Ba55
Pastorello I 149 Da62
Pastoriza E 36 Bc54
Pastovce SK 146 Hc51
Pastra BG 179 Cc73
Pástra GR 188 Ac85
Pastrana E 47 Ea64
Păstrăveni RO 172 Ec57
Păstren BG 180 Dd73
Pastrėvys LT 114 Kd58
Păstrovo BG 180 Dc72
Pastwa PL 121 Hb32
Pastwiska PL 130 Jc40
Pašuliene LV 115 Lb53
Pašušvys LT 114 Kb55
Pasvalys LT 114 Kc53
Pašvitinys LT 114 Kb53
Pasym PL 122 Jb32
Pasynki PL 123 Kb34
Pašyšiai LT 113 Jc56
Pásztó H 146 Ja51
Pat H 145 Gd56
Pataholm S 103 Gb52
Pataias P 50 Ab66
Patajoki FIN 90 Kb34
Patalenica BG 179 Da73
Patana FIN 81 Jc29
Pătârlagele RO 176 Eb63
Patašiai LV 114 Kb57
Patavesi FIN 90 Kb35
Patay F 29 Gc39
Patčino RUS 99 Mb44
Pateley Bridge GB 11 Ed19
Pateniemi FIN 74 Ka23
Paterek PL 121 Gd34
Paterna E 54 Fb67
Paterna del Campo E 59 Bd73
Paterna del Rio E 61 Dd75
Paterna de Madera E 53 Eb70
Paterna de Rivera E 59 Ca76
Paternieki LV 115 Ld53
Paternion A 143 Ed55
Paternò I 167 Fc85
Paternopoli I 161 Fc74
Patersdorf D 135 Ec48
Paterswolde NL 117 Bd33
Påterud S 94 Ec42
Pätiälä FIN 90 Kb36
Patika EST 98 Kc42
Patilčiai LT 114 Ka59
Patin AL 182 Ac74
Patiópoula GR 188 Ba82
Patiška MK 178 Bb73
Patitíri GR 189 Cc83
Patküla EST 106 La47
Patlangıç TR 198 Ga91
Pátmos GR 197 Ea89
Patna GB 10 Dd15
Pątnów PL 129 Hb41
Pato FIN 89 Ja37
Patokoski FIN 69 Jd17
Patolahti FIN 91 Lb37
Patolankylä FIN 89 Jb34
Patones E 46 Dc63
Patoniemi FIN 75 Kd19
Patoniva FIN 64 Jd08
Patosfa H 152 Ha57
Pátra GR 188 Bb85
Patras = Pátra GR 188 Bb85
Pătrăuți RO 172 Eb55
Patreksfjörður IS 2 Ac02
Patriarh-Evtimievo BG 184 Dc74
Patrickswell IRL 12 Bd23
Patriki CY 206 Jd96
Patrikka FIN 83 Mb30
Patrington GB 17 Fc21
Patsola FIN 83 Ma31
Pattada I 168 Cb75
Pattensen D 126 Db37
Patti I 167 Fc84
Pattijoki FIN 81 Jd25
Pattishall GB 20 Fb26
Patù I 165 Hc78
Pătulele RO 174 Cb66
Pau F 40 Fc55
Păuca RO 175 Da60
Pauillac F 32 Fb49
Paukarlahti FIN 82 La31
Paukkaja FIN 83 Ld29
Paularo I 143 Ec56
Păuleni-Ciuc RO 176 Ea60
Paulerspury GB 20 Fb26
Păulești RO 171 Cd54
Păulești RO 176 Ea64
Paulhac-en-Margeride F 34 Hc50
Paulhaguet F 34 Hc49
Paulhan F 41 Hc54
Pauliai LT 114 Ka57
Paúliani GR 189 Bc84
Paulilatino I 169 Ca77
Paulinenaue D 127 Ec36
Păuliș RO 170 Bd59
Paullo I 149 Cc59
Paüls E 48 Fd63
Paulx F 28 Ed43
Păunești RO 176 Ed61
Paunküla EST 98 Kc43
Paupys LT 114 Ka56
Pauri LV 107 Lb52
Pausa D 135 Eb43
Pausele S 80 Gc25
Păușești RO 175 Da64
Păușești-Măglași RO 175 Db63
Pauträsk S 80 Gc25
Pavabdenš LT 113 Jd55
Påvalsby FIN 97 Jc40
Pavasari LV 106 Ka51
Pavel BG 180 Dd69
Pavel Banja BG 180 Dc72
Pavezin F 34 Ja48
Pavia I 149 Cc60
Pavia P 50 Ad68
Pavias E 54 Fb66
Pavilly F 23 Ga34
Pāvilosta LV 105 Ja51
Pavino Polje MNE 159 Jb67
Pavištytis LT 114 Ka59
Pavlica SRB 178 Ba68
Pavlikeni BG 180 Dd70
Pavlohrad UA 205 Fa15
Pávlos GR 189 Ca84
Pavlov CZ 136 Fd47
Pavlovac HR 152 Gd59
Pavlovce SK 146 Jb50
Pavlovce nad Uhom SK 139 Ka48
Pavlovka RUS 203 Fd11
Pavlovo RUS 203 Fb09
Pavlovsk RUS 203 Fb13
Pavlovskaja RUS 205 Fc16
Pavlovskij Posad RUS 203 Fa10
Pavlovskoe RUS 203 Fb09
Pavlyš UA 204 Ed15
Pavoverė LT 115 Lb57
Pavullo nel Frignano I 149 Db63
Pavy RUS 99 Mb45
Pawełki PL 129 Hb42
Päwesein D 127 Ec36
Pawlett GB 19 Eb29
Pawlikowice PL 130 Hc39
Pawłosiów PL 139 Kb44
Pawłów PL 130 Jc41
Pawłów PL 131 Kc40
Pawłow PL 137 Ha44
Pawłówek PL 121 Gd34
Pawłowice PL 129 Gc39
Pawłowice PL 131 Jd39
Pawłowice PL 137 Hb45
Pawłowo PL 122 Jc30
Pawły PL 122 Ja30
Pawonków PL 129 Hb42
Pawłowiczki PL 137 Ha44
Payallar TR 199 Hb92
Payerne CH 141 Bc54
Paymogo E 58 Ba72
Payrac F 33 Gc50
Payzac F 33 Gb48
Paz HR 151 Fa60
Pazar TR 205 Ga19
Pazardžik BG 179 Da73
Pazarić BIH 158 Hb65
Pazarkaya TR 193 Hb86
Pazarköy TR 187 Gc79
Pazarköy TR 191 Ea81
Pazarköy TR 191 Ed81
Pazarköy TR 192 Fa85
Pazarlar TR 192 Fd84
Pazarlı TR 186 Fa75
Pazaryeri TR 193 Gb81
Pažėrai LV 114 Kb58
Pazin HR 151 Fa60
Paznauntal A 142 Da54
Pazos de Borbén E 36 Ad57
Pazuengos E 38 Ea58
Pčela BG 180 Eb73
Pčelarovo BG 181 Fa69
Pčelić HR 152 Ha59
Pčelin BG 179 Cd72
Pčelinovo BG 180 Dd72
Pčelnik BG 181 Fa71
Pchery CZ 136 Fb44
Pcim PL 138 Ja45
Pčinja MK 178 Bc73
Pčrvenec BG 181 Ec73
Peädsek FIN 64 Ka09
Peal de Becerro E 61 Dd72
Peanía GR 195 Cc87
Peasedown Saint John GB 19 Ec28
Peasemore GB 20 Fa28
Peasenhall GB 21 Gb25
Péaule F 27 Ec41
Pebworth GB 20 Ed26
Peć KSV 178 Ad70
Peć SRB 159 Jc68
Peccia CH 141 Cb56
Peccioli I 155 Db66
Pécel H 146 Hd53
Pećence SRB 178 Bc70
Peceneaga RO 177 Fb64
Pečenjevce SRB 178 Bd69
Pechea RO 177 Fa62
Pechina E 61 Ea76
Peći BIH 158 Gb64
Pecica RO 170 Bc59
Pećigrad BIH 151 Ga61
Pećinci SRB 153 Jb61
Pecineaga RO 181 Fc68
Peciu Nou RO 174 Bc61
Pecka SRB 153 Ja63
Peckelsheim D 126 Cd39
Pečki RUS 107 Ld46
Pecorini I 167 Fb82
Pečory RUS 107 Lc47
Pečory RUS 202 Ea10
Pec pod Sněžkou CZ 128 Ga42
Pécs H 152 Hb57
Pécsely H 145 Ha55
Pécsvárad H 153 Hc57
Pećurice MNE 163 Ja71
Pęczniew PL 129 Hb38
Pedagaggi I 167 Fc87
Pedaso I 157 Fa67
Pedaspea EST 98 Kc41
Peddenberg D 125 Bd38
Pedele LV 106 La47
Pederobba I 150 Ea58
Pedersker DK 111 Fc58
Pedersöre FIN 81 Jb29
Pedersören kunta FIN 81 Jb29
Pedescala I 150 Dd58
Pédi GR 197 Ed92
Pediní GR 182 Ad80
Pedinó GR 183 Ca77
Pedivigliano I 164 Gb80
Pedoulas CY 206 Ja97
Pedrafita Camporredondo E 36 Bc55
Pedrafita do Cebreiro E 37 Bd56
Pedrajas de San Esteban E 46 Da61
Pedralba E 54 Fb67
Pedras Salgadas P 44 Bb60
Pedraza E 36 Bb56
Pedraza E 46 Dc62
Pedre E 36 Ad56
Pedreguer E 55 Fc70
Pedreña E 38 Dc54
Pedrera E 60 Cc74
Pedro Abad E 52 Da72
Pedro Bernardo E 46 Cd65
Pedrógão P 44 Ab65
Pedrógão P 44 Bb65
Pedrógão Grande P 44 Ad65
Pedrógão Pequeno P 44 Ad65
Pedrola E 47 Fa60
Pedro Martínez E 60 Dc74
Pedro Muñoz E 53 Dd68
Pedrosa de Duero E 46 Db60
Pedrosa del Príncipe E 38 Db58
Pedrosa de Tobalina E 38 Dd56
Pėdžiai LT 114 Kc56
Peebles GB 11 Eb14
Peel GB 10 Dc19
Peenemünde D 120 Fa31
Peeni MD 173 Fc56
Peer B 124 Ba40
Peffingen D 133 Bc44
Péfka GR 197 Fa93
Pefkohóri GR 184 Cc80
Péfkos GR 182 Ba78
Péfkos GR 201 Db96
Pega P 45 Bc63
Pegalajar E 60 Db73
Pegau D 127 Eb41
Pegeia CY 206 Hd97
Peggau A 144 Fd54
Pegli I 148 Cb62
Pegnitz D 135 Ea45
Pego E 55 Fc70
Pegognaga I 149 Db61
Peguerinos E 46 Db63
Pehčevo MK 183 Cb74
Pehlivanköy TR 185 Ec76
Peille F 43 Kd53
Peillon F 43 Kd53
Peinchorran GB 4 Db08
Peine D 126 Dc37
Peipin F 42 Jd52
Peipohja FIN 89 Jb36
Peippu FIN 89 Ja35
Peisey-Nancroix F 35 Kb47
Peißen D 127 Ea39
Peißen D 127 Eb39
Peißenberg D 142 Dc52
Peiting D 142 Dc52
Peitz D 128 Fb38
Peize NL 117 Bd33
Pejkovac SRB 178 Bd69
Pejo Terme I 142 Db56
Pekankylä FIN 75 Lb24
Pekanpää FIN 73 Jb20
Pekisht AL 182 Ab75
Pekkala FIN 65 Kb09
Pekkala FIN 74 Kb19
Pekkaperä FIN 82 Ka28
Pektubaevo RUS 203 Fc08
Péla GR 183 Bd77
Pelacoy F 33 Gc51
Pelagićevo BIH 153 Hc61
Pelago I 156 Dd65
Pelahustán E 46 Da65
Pelaičiai LT 113 Jc55
Pelarne S 103 Fd49
Pelasgía GR 189 Ca83
Pelči LV 105 Jc51
Pełczyce PL 120 Fd34
Pełczyn PL 129 Gb40
Peleagonzalo E 45 Cc61
Pelėči LV 107 Lc52
Pelejaneta E 54 Fc65
Peleši RUS 99 Lc42
Peletá GR 195 Bd89
Pelev Prijeg MNE 159 Ja69
Pelhřimov CZ 136 Fd47
Pelinci MK 178 Bc72
Pelinei MD 177 Fc62
Pelinia MD 173 Fb55
Pelisalmi FIN 90 Ka35
Pelitköy TR 191 Eb82
Pelitözü TR 187 Gb80
Pelitözü TR 187 Ha79
Pelivan MD 173 Fd57
Pelkkikangos FIN 81 Jc30
Pelkoperä FIN 82 Ka25
Pelkosenniemi FIN 69 Kb16
Pellafol F 35 Jd50
Pellaro I 164 Ga84
Pellegrino Parmense I 149 Cd62
Pellegrue F 32 Fd50
Pellérd H 152 Hb58
Pellesmäki FIN 82 La30
Pellestrina I 150 Eb60
Pellevoisin F 29 Gb43
Pellinge FIN 98 Kd39
Pellingen D 133 Bc45
Pellini GR 189 Bc86
Pellinki FIN 98 Kd39
Pello FIN 74 Jb18
Pello S 74 Jb18
Pellonpää FIN 75 Kc23
Pellosniemi FIN 90 La35
Pellossalo FIN 91 Lc33
Pelnik PL 122 Hd32
Peloche E 52 Cc68
Pelovo BG 179 Da69
Pelplin PL 121 Hb31
Pelsin D 120 Fa32
Pelso FIN 82 Kb25
Peltokangas FIN 81 Jd30
Peltokorpi FIN 81 Jc28
Peltola FIN 97 Jd39
Peltomaa FIN 81 Ja31
Peltosalmi FIN 82 Kd28
Peltovuoma FIN 68 Jb13
Pełty PL 122 Hd30
Pełty PL 122 Ja30
Pelučiai LT 114 Kb57
Pélussin F 34 Ja48
Pély H 146 Jb53
Pembeli TR 199 Gc88
Pembroke GB 18 Db27

Pembroke Dock – Pilchów

Pembroke Dock GB 18 Db27
Pembury GB 20 Fd29
Pemfling D 135 Ec47
Pempelijärvi S 73 Hd18
Peñacerrada-Urizaharra E 38 Ea57
Penacova P 44 Ad64
Peña del Águila E 59 Bc76
Peñadiz E 36 Bb58
Peñafiel E 46 Db60
Penafiel P 44 Ad61
Peñaflor E 48 Fb60
Peñaflor E 59 Cb73
Peñafuente E 37 Bd55
Peñalba E 48 Fc61
Peñalba de Santiago E 37 Ca57
Peñalén E 47 Ec64
Peñalsordo E 52 Cc69
Penalva do Castelo P 44 Ba63
Peñalver E 47 Ea64
Penamacor P 45 Bc64
Penämö FIN 75 Kc20
Peñaranda de Bracamonte E 45 Cc62
Peñaranda de Duero E 46 Dc60
Peñarroya de Tastavins E 48 Fd63
Peñarroya-Pueblonuevo E 52 Cc71
Penarth GB 19 Eb28
Peñascosa E 53 Eb70
Peñas de San Pedro E 53 Ec70
Peñaullán E 37 Cb54
Peñausende E 45 Cb61
Penc H 146 Hd52
Pencaitland GB 11 Ec13
Pendálofos GR 185 Ea75
Penderyn GB 19 Ea27
Pendilla E 37 Cc55
Pendine GB 18 Dc27
Pendones E 37 Cd55
Pendueles E 38 Da54
Penedono P 44 Bb62
Penela P 44 Ad65
Pénestin F 27 Eb41
Penészlek H 147 Kb52
Penge GB 20 Fc28
Pengfors S 80 Hb28
Pengsjö S 80 Hb28
Penha Garcia P 45 Bc65
Penhas da Saúde P 44 Bb64
Penhas Juntas P 45 Bc59
Penhors F 27 Db39
Peniche P 50 Aa66
Penicuik GB 11 Eb13
Penig D 127 Ec41
Penikkajärvi FIN 75 Lb20
Penilhos P 58 Ad72
Peninki FIN 82 Kb29
Peñíscola E 54 Fd65
Penk A 143 Ed55
Penkridge GB 16 Ed24
Penkule LV 106 Ka52
Penkun D 120 Fb34
Penmachno GB 15 Ea23
Penmaenmawr GB 15 Dd22
Penmarc'h F 27 Dc40
Pennabilli I 156 Ea65
Pennainen FIN 97 Jc39
Pennala FIN 90 Kc37
Pennant GB 15 Ea24
Pennapiedimonte I 161 Fa71
Penne F 40 Gc53
Penne I 157 Fa70
Penne-d'Agenais F 40 Ga52
Pennerley GB 15 Eb24
Pennigsehl D 118 Cd35
Pennyghael GB 6 Da11
Peno RUS 202 Ec10
Penol F 34 Jb48
Penrhyn Bay GB 15 Ea22
Penrith GB 11 Ec17
Penruddock GB 11 Eb17
Penryn GB 18 Db32
Pensala FIN 81 Jb30
Pensilva GB 18 Dc31
Penta di Casinca F 154 Cc69
Pentageia CY 206 Ja96
Pentalia CY 206 Hd97
Pentálofos GR 182 Ba78
Pentápoli GR 184 Cc76
Pentávrisso GR 182 Ba78
Penteória GR 189 Bc85
Pentinkylä FIN 91 Lb37
Pentling D 135 Ea48
Pentraeth GB 15 Dd22
Pentrefoelas GB 15 Ea23
Penttäjä S 74 Jb18
Penttilänkylä FIN 89 Jd34
Pentyrch GB 19 Ea28
Penuja EST 106 Kd46
Penvins F 27 Eb41
Penybont GB 15 Ea25
Penygroes GB 15 Dd22
Penysarn GB 15 Dd21
Penza RUS 203 Fc11
Penzance GB 18 Da32
Penzberg D 143 Dd52
Penzing D 142 Dc51
Penzlin D 119 Ed33
Péone F 43 Kc52
Pepellash AL 182 Ad77
Pepinster B 125 Bb42
Péplos GR 185 Ea77
Peponiá GR 184 Cc77
Pępowo PL 129 Gc39
Peqin AL 182 Ab75
Peque E 37 Ca58
Pér H 145 Ha52
Pera CY 206 Jb97
Peraboa P 44 Bb64
Përa-Cava F 43 Kd52
Perach D 143 Ec50
Perafita P 44 Ac60
Perahóra GR 189 Ca86
Perahóri GR 188 Ac84
Perä-Hyyppä FIN 89 Jb34
Peräjävaara S 68 Ja17
Perakende TR 199 Ha91
Peräkylä FIN 81 Jb30
Peräkylä FIN 89 Ja32
Peräkylä FIN 91 Lb36
Perälä FIN 75 Kc19
Perälä FIN 89 Ja33
Peralada E 41 Hb58
Peraleda de la Mata E 51 Cb66
Peraleda del Zaucejo E 51 Cb70
Peralejos de las Truchas E 47 Ec64
Perales E 38 Da58
Perales del Alfambra E 47 Fa64
Perales de Tajuña E 46 Dc65
Peralta E 39 Ec58
Peralta E 53 Eb71
Peralta de Alcofea E 48 Fc60
Peralta de la Sal E 48 Fd59
Peraltilla E 48 Fc59
Peralveche E 47 Eb64
Pérama GR 182 Ad80
Pérama GR 189 Cb86
Pérama GR 191 Ea84
Pérama GR 200 Cd95
Péra Mélana GR 195 Bd89
Peranka FIN 75 La21
Peränkylä FIN 89 Ja36
Peränne FIN 89 Jd32
Peranzanes E 37 Ca56
Perä-Posio FIN 75 Kc19
Perarolo di Cadore I 150 Eb57
Perarrúa E 40 Fd58
Perasdorf D 135 Ec48
Peräseinäjoki FIN 89 Jc32
Perásma GR 183 Bb77
Perast MNE 159 Hd69
Perat AL 182 Ad79
Peratáta GR 188 Ac85
Perävaara S 73 Jb19
Perbal H 146 Hc52
Pērbone LV 105 Jc52
Perchtoldsdorf A 145 Gb51
Percosova RO 174 Bd62
Perdasdefogu I 169 Cb78
Perdaxius I 169 Bd80
Perdigão P 50 Ba66
Perdiguera E 48 Fb60
Pérdika GR 188 Ac81
Pérdika GR 188 Ad81
Pérdika GR 195 Cb87
Perdikáki GR 188 Ba82
Perdikas GR 183 Bb77
Perdiki GR 197 Ea88
Perdoche E 52 Cd71
Perduhovo Selo BIH 158 Gc64
Peréa GR 183 Bc77
Peréa GR 183 Ca78
Perečyn UA 204 Dd16
Pereda de Ancares E 37 Bd56
Peredkino RUS 99 Ma43
Peredo P 45 Bd60
Peregu Mare RO 170 Bc59
Perehins'ke UA 204 Ea16
Pereira E 36 Ad55
Pereiriña E 36 Ac55
Pereiro P 44 Ac65
Pereiro P 58 Ba73
Perejaslav-Chmel'nyc'kyj UA 202 Ec14
Perekopka RUS 203 Fd13
Pereles'e RUS 99 Ld40
Perelešinskij RUS 203 Fb12
Perelesnoje RUS 113 Jc58
Perelhal P 44 Ac59
Pereni MD 173 Fd56
Pererita MD 172 Ed54
Pereruela E 45 Cb61
Pereščepyne UA 205 Fa15
Peresecina MD 173 Fd57
Pereslavl'-Zalesskij RUS 203 Fa09
Pereslavskoje RUS 113 Hd58
Peressaare EST 98 La43
Peresznye H 145 Gc53
Péret F 41 Hc54
Peretu RO 180 Dc67
Perevalovo RUS 113 Jc59
Perevolok RUS 99 Lc42
Perevoz RUS 203 Fc09
Perfugas I 168 Ca74
Perg A 144 Fc50
Pergamos CY 206 Jc97
Pergine Valsugana I 149 Dc57
Pergola I 156 Ec66
Pergusa I 167 Fb86
Perheniemi FIN 90 Kd37
Perho FIN 81 Jd30
Peri I 149 Dc59
Periam RO 170 Bc59
Periana E 60 Da75
Perieni RO 177 Fa60
Périers F 22 Fa36
Perieţi RO 175 Db66
Perieţi RO 176 Ed66
Perigiáli GR 189 Bd86
Pérignac F 32 Fb47
Périgné F 32 Fc46
Périgueux F 33 Ga49
Perila EST 98 Kc42
Perino I 149 Cc61
Periprava RO 177 Ga63
Periş RO 176 Ea65
Perişani RO 175 Db63
Perişor RO 175 Cd66
Perişoru RO 177 Fa66
Périssa GR 196 Db92
Perísta GR 188 Bb84
Peristerá GR 183 Cb78
Peristéri GR 188 Ba86
Peristéri GR 189 Cb86
Peristerona CY 206 Jb97
Peristerónas GR 183 Cb78
Perithóri GR 188 Ba84
Perívlepto GR 189 Bd82
Perivóli GR 188 Ab81
Perivóli GR 189 Bc83
Perivolia CY 206 Jc97
Perivólia GR 194 Bc89
Perjasica HR 151 Fd60
Perkaliai LT 114 La55
Perkam D 135 Eb48
Perkáta H 146 Hc54
Pērkone LV 113 Ja53
Perković HR 158 Gb66
Perl A 144 Fc55
Perl D 133 Bb45
Perlé L 132 Ba44
Perleberg D 119 Eb34
Perlejewo PL 123 Ka35
Perlesreut D 135 Ed49
Perlez SRB 153 Jc60
Pērlis LV 106 La49
Perloja LT 114 Kd59
Perły PL 122 Jc30
Përmet AL 182 Ac78
Permisküla EST 99 Lc42
Pernå FIN 90 Kd38
Pernaa FIN 81 Jb30
Pernaja FIN 90 Kd38
Pernarava LV 114 Kb56
Pernarec CZ 135 Ed45
Pernat HR 151 Fb61
Pernay F 28 Fd41
Pernegg an der Mur A 144 Fd53
Pernek SK 145 Gd50
Pernera CY 206 Jd97
Pernes P 50 Ac67
Pernes-les-Fontaines F 42 Jc52
Pernica SLO 144 Ga56
Pernik BG 179 Cb71
Pernink CZ 135 Ec43
Perniö FIN 97 Jc40
Perniön asema FIN 97 Jc40
Pernitz A 144 Ga52
Perno FIN 90 La38
Pernu FIN 75 Kc19
Peroguarda P 50 Ad71
Péronnas F 34 Jb45
Péronne F 23 Ha33
Pêro Pinheiro P 50 Aa68
Perorribio E 46 Dc62
Perosa Argentina I 148 Bb60
Pérouges F 34 Jb46
Perpezac-le-Noir F 33 Gc48
Perpignan F 41 Hb57
Perranporth GB 18 Db31
Perrecy-les-Forges F 30 Hd44
Perrero I 148 Bb60
Perrone I 162 Gd76
Perros-Guirec F 26 Ea37
Persac F 33 Ga45
Persan F 23 Gd36
Persano I 161 Fc76
Persberg S 95 Fb42
Persbo S 95 Fd41
Perserud S 94 Ed42
Pershagen S 96 Gc44
Pershyttan S 95 Fc43
Perskogen N 67 Hb11
Persnäs S 103 Gb51
Persomajärvi S 73 Jb20
Persön S 73 Hd22
Perstorp S 110 Fa54
Pertala FIN 90 Kb34
Perth GB 7 Eb11
Perthes F 24 Hd34
Perthes F 29 Ha38
Pertisau A 143 Ea53
Pertoča SLO 145 Gb55
Pertoúli GR 188 Ba82
Pertrovskoe RUS 99 Ma39
Perttaus FIN 69 Jd17
Pertteli FIN 97 Jd39
Perttula FIN 98 Kb39
Pertuis F 42 Jd53
Pertunmaa FIN 90 Kd35
Pertusa E 48 Fc59
Peruc CZ 136 Fa43
Perućac SRB 159 Ja64
Perugia I 156 Ea67
Perukka FIN 81 Jd25
Perunika BG 185 Dd76
Perunkajärvi FIN 74 Ka18
Perušić HR 151 Fd62
Peruštica BG 180 Db73
Pervalka LT 113 Jb56
Pervijze B 21 Ha29
Pervomaisc MD 173 Fd59
Pervomajsk RUS 203 Fc10
Pervomajs'k UA 204 Ec16
Pervomajskaja RUS 99 Ld44
Pervomajskij RUS 203 Fb11
Pervomajskoe RUS 202 Ea08
Pervomajskoe RUS 203 Ga11
Pervomajs'kyj UA 203 Fa14
Perwez B 124 Ad41
Perzów PL 129 Ha40
Pesac RO 174 Bc60
Pesadas de Burgos E 38 Dc57
Pesaguero E 38 Da55
Pesaro I 156 Ec65
Pesčanokopskoe RUS 205 Fd16
Pescara I 157 Fb70
Pescasseroli I 161 Fa72
Pesceana RO 175 Da64
Peschici I 162 Gb71
Peschiera Borromeo I 149 Cc59
Peschiera del Garda I 149 Db59
Pescia I 155 Db65
Pescia Fiorentina I 155 Dc69
Pescina I 160 Ed71
Pescocostanzo I 161 Fa71
Pescolanciano I 161 Fb72
Pescopagano I 161 Fd75
Pesco Sannita I 161 Fc74
Pescueza E 45 Bd65
Peshkopi AL 178 Ad73
Pesinki FIN 91 Ld33
Pesiökylä FIN 75 La23
Pesiöranta FIN 75 La23
Peski RUS 107 Ld46
Pesmes F 31 Jc41
Pesnica SLO 144 Ga56
Peso P 45 Bd60
Peso P 50 Ba71
Pesočani MK 182 Ba75
Peso da Régua P 44 Ba61
Pesoz E 37 Bd54
Pesqueira E 36 Ac56
Pesquera de Duero E 46 Db60
Pessac F 32 Fb50
Pessáda GR 188 Ac85
Pessalompolo FIN 74 Jc19
Peštani MK 182 Ba76
Peštera BG 179 Cb72
Peštera BG 179 Da73
Peştera RO 181 Fb67
Pesterwitz D 128 Fa41
Peştişani RO 175 Cc63
Pestişu Mic RO 175 Cc61
Pestovo KSV 178 Bb70
Pestovo RUS 202 Ec09
Pestravka RUS 203 Ga10
Pešurići BIH 159 Hd65
Petääjärvi FIN 90 Ka34
Petacciato I 161 Fc71
Petacciato Marina I 161 Fc71
Petäiskylä FIN 83 Lb27
Petäjäjärvi FIN 74 Kb21
Petäjäkangas FIN 74 Kb22
Petäjäkylä FIN 82 Kb29
Petäjälahti FIN 82 Kc25
Petäjämäki FIN 82 Ka25
Petäjämäki FIN 82 La31
Petäjäniemi FIN 82 La25
Petäjäs koski FIN 74 Jd19
Petäjäskoski FIN 81 Jd26
Petäjävesi FIN 90 Kb33
Petalax FIN 81 Hd31
Petalidi GR 194 Bb89
Pétange L 132 Ba45
Petărč BG 179 Cc71
Pétas GR 188 Ad82
Petäys FIN 82 La28
Petäys FIN 89 Jb32
Petelea RO 171 Dc58
Petelevo BG 184 Dc74
Peteranec HR 152 Gc57
Peterborough GB 17 Fc24
Peterchurch GB 15 Eb26
Peterculter GB 7 Ed09
Petergof RUS 99 Mb39
Peterhead GB 5 Fa08
Peterlee GB 11 Fa17
Petersaurach D 134 Dc47
Petersberg D 126 Da42
Petersdorf D 134 Dc49
Petersfield GB 20 Fb30
Petershagen D 126 Cd36
Petershagen-Vogelsdorf D 128 Fa36
Petershausen D 143 Dd50
Peterstone Wentlooge GB 19 Eb28
Peterstow GB 15 Ec26
Peterswell IRL 12 Bd21
Pétervására H 146 Jb51
Pétfürdő H 145 Hb54
Pethelinos GR 184 Cc77
Peti RUS 107 Mb47
Petid RO 170 Cb58
Petiknäs S 80 Hb25
Petikträsk S 72 Ha24
Petilia Policastro I 165 Gd80
Petilla de Aragón E 39 Fa58
Petín E 36 Bc57
Pětipsy CZ 135 Ed44
Petisträsk S 80 Ha26
Petit-Palais-et-Cornemps F 32 Fc50
Petkovac BIH 152 Gc61
Petkovica SRB 153 Ja62
Petkula FIN 69 Ka15
Petkus D 127 Ed38
Petlovac HR 153 Hc58
Petlovača SRB 153 Ja62
Pet Mogili BG 180 Ea73
Petokladenci BG 180 Dc69
Petolahti FIN 81 Hd31
Petra CY 206 Ja97
Petra E 57 Hc67
Pétra GR 183 Bd79
Pétra GR 189 Ca85
Pétra GR 191 Ea83
Petrăchioaia RO 176 Eb66
Petrádes GR 185 Eb76
Petralia Soprana I 167 Fa85
Petralia Sottana I 167 Fa85
Petrálona GR 183 Cb79
Petran AL 182 Ac78
Petraná GR 183 Bc78
Petrašiūnai LT 114 Kb54
Petrčane HR 157 Fd64
Petrelë AL 182 Ab75
Petrella Tifernina I 161 Fc72
Petreni MD 173 Fb55
Petrer E 55 Fb71
Pétres GR 183 Bb77
Petreşti MD 173 Fb57
Petreşti RO 171 Cc55
Petreşti RO 175 Cd61
Petreşti RO 176 Dd65
Petreşti de Jos RO 171 Da58
Petreto-Bicchisano F 154 Ca71
Petrič BG 179 Cd72
Petrič BG 183 Cb75
Petricani RO 172 Ec57
Petričko selo HR 151 Fd59
Petrijanec HR 152 Gb57
Petrijevci HR 153 Hc59
Petrila RO 175 Cd62
Petrinja HR 152 Gb60
Petriş RO 174 Cb60
Petrítsi GR 194 Ba89
Petrivka UA 202 Ec14
Petrofani CY 206 Jc97
Pétrola E 55 Ed70
Petromäki FIN 82 La31
Petroman RO 174 Bc61
Petronell A 145 Gc51
Petropavlivka UA 205 Fa15
Petropavlovka RUS 203 Fc13
Petroşani RO 175 Cd62
Petrosino I 166 Ea85
Petrotá GR 185 Ea75
Petrova RO 171 Db54
Petrovaara FIN 83 Lb29
Petrovac MNE 159 Hd70
Petrovac SRB 174 Bc65
Petrovaradin SRB 153 Jb60
Petrova Ves SK 137 Gd49
Petrovce SK 146 Ja50
Petrovci HR 153 Hd60
Petrovec MK 178 Bc73
Petrovice CZ 128 Fa42
Petrovice CZ 136 Fb46
Petrovići BIH 159 Hd64
Petrovići MNE 159 Hc68
Petrovičky CZ 135 Ed47
Petrovo BG 184 Cc75
Petrovo RUS 113 Ja58
Petrovo RUS 202 Ec09
Petrovo Selo SRB 174 Cb65
Petrovsk RUS 203 Fd11
Petrovskoe RUS 203 Fa09
Petrovskoe RUS 203 Fb12
Petruma FIN 83 Lc31
Petrunea MD 173 Fa55
Petru Rareş RO 171 Db57
Petruşeni MD 173 Fa55
Petřvald CZ 137 Hb45
Petrykav BY 202 Eb13
Petrykozy PL 130 Ja40
Petsikko FIN 64 Ka09
Petsmo FIN 81 Ja30
Pettaugh GB 21 Gb26
Pettenbach A 144 Fa51
Pettendorf D 135 Ea48
Pettigoe GB 9 Cb17
Petting D 143 Ec52
Pettorano sul Gizio I 161 Fa71
Pettstadt D 134 Dc45
Petuški RUS 203 Fa10
Petworth GB 20 Fb30
Peuerbach A 144 Fa50
Peurajärvi FIN 74 Ka20
Peurajärvi FIN 83 Lb26
Peurajärvi FIN 83 Lb27
Peuralinna FIN 81 Jd30
Peurasuvanto FIN 69 Ka14
Peuravaara FIN 75 Kd24
Peure FIN 74 Jd20
Peuton F 28 Fa40
Pevensey GB 20 Fd30
Peveragno I 148 Bc63
Pewsey GB 20 Ed28
Peynirkuyusu TR 192 Fa81
Peypin F 42 Jd54
Peyrat-de-Bellac F 33 Gb46
Peyrat-la-Nonière F 33 Gd46
Peyrat-le-Château F 33 Gc47
Peyrefitte-du-Razès F 41 Gd56
Peyrehorade F 39 Fa54
Peyriac-Minervois F 41 Ha55
Peyrieu F 35 Jd47
Peyrolles-en-Provence F 42 Jd53
Peyruis F 42 Jd52
Peyrus F 34 Jb49
Peyrusse-le-Roc F 33 Gd51
Pėžaičiai LT 113 Jb55
Pézenas F 41 Hc54
Pezens F 41 Gd55
Pézilla-la-Rivière F 41 Hb57
Pezinok SK 145 Gd50
Pezou F 29 Gb40
Pezoúla GR 188 Bb82
Pezovo MK 178 Bd73
Pezuela de las Torres E 46 Dd64
Pézy F 29 Gc38
Pfaffenhausen D 142 Db51
Pfaffenhofen D 142 Db50
Pfaffenhofen an der Ilm D 135 Dd49
Pfaffenhoffen F 25 Kc36
Pfäffikon CH 142 Cc53
Pfäffikon CH 142 Cc53
Pfaffing D 143 Ea51
Pfaffroda D 127 Ed42
Pfakofen D 135 Eb48
Pfalzgrafenweiler D 133 Cb49
Pfarrkirchen D 143 Ec50
Pfarrweisach D 134 Dc44
Pfatter D 135 Eb48
Pfedelbach D 134 Cd47
Pfeffenhausen D 135 Ea49
Pfinztal D 134 Cc47
Pflach A 142 Dc53
Pflersch I 143 Dd55
Pfofeld D 134 Dc47
Pförring D 135 Ea48
Pforzen D 142 Db51
Pforzheim D 134 Cc48
Pfreimd D 135 Eb46
Pfronten D 142 Db52
Pfullendorf D 142 Cd51
Pfullingen D 134 Cd49
Pfunders I 143 Ea55
Pfunds A 142 Db54
Pfungstadt D 134 Cc45
Phalsbourg F 25 Kb36
Philippsburg D 133 Cb47
Philippsthal D 126 Db41
Piaam NL 116 Bb33
Piacenza I 149 Cd61
Piacenza d'Adige I 150 Dd61
Piadena I 149 Da60
Piaggio di Valmara I 148 Cb57
Piália GR 188 Bb81
Piamprato I 148 Bc58
Piana F 154 Ca70
Piána GR 194 Bc87
Piana Crixia I 148 Ca62
Piana degli Albanesi I 166 Ec84
Piancastagnaio I 156 Dd68
Piancavallo I 150 Eb57
Pianche I 148 Bb62
Piandelagotti I 149 Da63
Pianella I 155 Dc66
Pianella I 157 Fa70
Pianello Val Tidone I 149 Cc61
Piani Resinelli I 149 Cc58
Pian Munè I 148 Bb61
Pianoconte I 167 Fc83
Piano d'Arci I 167 Fc86
Pianoro I 149 Dc63
Pianosa I 155 Cd69
Pianottoli-Caldarello F 154 Cb72
Piansano I 156 Dd69
Pianu RO 175 Cd61
Pias P 50 Ba71
Pías E 36 Bc58
Piasecznik PL 120 Fd34
Piaseczno PL 120 Fc34
Piaseczno PL 120 Fc35
Piaseczno PL 120 Ga33
Piaseczno PL 121 Hb32
Piaseczno PL 130 Jb37
Piasek PL 120 Fb35
Piasek PL 122 Ja30
Piasek PL 130 Hc42
Piaski PL 121 Gb32
Piaski PL 122 Hc30
Piaski PL 128 Fd38
Piaski PL 129 Gc38
Piaski PL 131 Kb40
Piastów PL 130 Jb37
Piastowo PL 122 Hc30
Piastre I 155 Db64
Piaszczyna PL 121 Gc31
Piątek PL 130 Hd37
Piatra MD 173 Fd57
Piatra RO 177 Fc66
Piatra RO 180 Dc68
Piatra-Neamţ RO 172 Ec58
Piatra-Olt RO 175 Da66
Piatra Şoimului RO 172 Ec58
Piau-Engaly F 40 Fd57
Piazza al Serchio I 155 Da64
Piazza Armerina I 167 Fb86
Piazza Brembana I 149 Cd58
Piazzatore I 149 Cd57
Piazze I 156 Dd68
Piazzola sul Brenta I 150 Dd59
Pičaevo RUS 203 Fb11
Picamoixons E 48 Gb62
Pićan HR 151 Fa61
Picarreau F 31 Jc43
Picarrel P 50 Ba69
Picassent E 54 Fb68
Piccione I 156 Eb67
Piccovagia F 154 Cb72
Picerno I 161 Ga75
Pichl A 143 Ed53
Pickering GB 16 Fb19
Pickwillow GB 20 Fd25
Pico I 160 Ed73
Picón E 52 Db69
Picoto P 44 Ad61
Picquigny F 23 Gd33
Pidole LV 105 Jd50
Pidula EST 105 Jc46
Piece PL 121 Ha32
Piechcin PL 121 Ha35
Piechowice PL 128 Fd42
Piecki PL 122 Jc32
Piecki PL 123 Ka30
Piecnik PL 121 Gb33
Pieczonki PL 123 Jd30
Piedicavallo I 148 Bd58
Piediluco I 156 Eb69
Piedimonte Etnea I 167 Fd85
Piedimonte Matese I 161 Fb73
Piedimulera I 148 Ca57
Piedipaterno I 156 Ec68
Piedrabuena E 52 Da69
Piedrafita E 37 Cc55
Piedrafita de Babia E 37 Cb56
Piedrahita E 45 Cc64
Piedrahita de Castro E 45 Cb60
Piedralaves E 46 Cd64
Piedras Albas E 51 Bc66
Piedras Blancas E 37 Cb54
Piedrasluengas E 38 Da56
Piedratajada E 48 Fb59
Piedricroce F 154 Cb69
Piedroşani RO 175 Dc63
Piedruja LV 115 Ld53
Piehinki FIN 81 Jd25
Piekary Śląskie PL 138 Hc43
Piekielnik PL 138 Ja46
Piekoszów PL 130 Jb41
Pieksämäki FIN 90 Kd32
Pielavesi FIN 82 Kc29
Pielenhofen D 135 Ea48
Pieleşti RO 175 Da66
Pielgrzymka PL 128 Ga41
Pielrari RO 175 Da63
Pienava LV 106 Ka51
Pieneņi LV 107 Lc52
Pieniężno PL 122 Hd30
Pieńsk PL 128 Fc40
Pienza I 156 Dd67
Piera E 49 Gc61
Pieranie PL 121 Hb35
Pierkunowo PL 122 Jc30
Pierlas F 43 Kc52
Piérnigas E 38 Dd57
Pieros E 37 Bd57
Pierowall GB 5 Ec02
Pierre-Buffière F 33 Gb47
Pierre-de-Bresse F 30 Jb43
Pierrefeu-du-Var F 42 Ka55
Pierrefiche F 34 Hd50
Pierrefitte-Nestalès F 40 Fc56
Pierrefitte-sur-Aire F 24 Jb36
Pierrefitte-sur-Sauldre F 29 Gd41
Pierrefonds F 23 Ha35
Pierrefontaine-les-Blamont F 31 Kb41
Pierrefontaine-les-Varans F 31 Ka41
Pierrefontaines F 30 Jb40
Pierrefort F 34 Hb50
Pierrelatte F 42 Jb51
Pierremont F 23 Gd32
Pierremont-sur-Amance F 31 Jc40
Pierre-Perthuis F 30 Hc41
Pierrepont F 24 Hc34
Pierrepont F 25 Jc34
Pierrepont-sur-Avre F 23 Gd34
Pierroton F 32 Fb50
Piertinjaure S 72 Gd19
Pierzchnica PL 130 Jb42
Piesalankylä FIN 90 Kb33
Piesendorf A 143 Ec54
Piesjoki FIN 64 Jc09
Pieski PL 128 Fd37
Pieskowo PL 122 Ja30
Piesport D 133 Bd44
Piešťany SK 137 Ha49
Pieszyce PL 129 Gb42
Pietarsaari FIN 81 Jb28
Pieterburen NL 117 Bd32
Pietkowo PL 123 Kb34
Pietolansaari FIN 91 Lc34
Pietrabbondante I 161 Fb72
Pietracamela I 156 Ed69
Pietragalla I 161 Ga75
Pietraia I 156 Ea68
Pietralba F 154 Cb69
Pietra Ligure I 148 Ca63
Pietralunga I 156 Eb66
Pietramelara I 161 Fa73
Pietramontecorvino I 161 Fd73
Pietrapertosa I 162 Gb76
Pietraperzia I 167 Fa86
Pietraporzio I 148 Bb62
Pietraroja I 161 Fb73
Pietrasanta I 155 Da64
Pietrasecca I 160 Ec71
Pietraserena F 154 Cb70
Pietrastornina I 161 Fc74
Pietrelcina I 161 Fc74
Pietroasa RO 171 Cc58
Pietroasa RO 174 Cb61
Pietrosaele RO 176 Ec64
Pietroşani RO 180 Dd68
Pietroşiţa RO 176 Dd63
Pietrosu MD 173 Fb56
Pietrowice PL 137 Ha44
Pietrowice Wielkopolski PL 137 Ha44
Pietrzwałd PL 122 Hd32
Pietrzyk PL 122 Hd34
Pietrzykowo PL 121 Gc31
Pieve del Cairo I 148 Cb60
Pieve di Cadore I 143 Eb56
Pieve di Cento I 149 Dc62
Pieve di Ledro I 149 Db58
Pieve di Soligo I 150 Ea58
Pieve di Teco I 43 La52
Pieve d. Livinallongo I 143 Ea56
Pievepelago I 155 Db64
Pieve San Stefano I 156 Ea65
Pieve Torina I 156 Ec68
Piffonds F 30 Hb39
Pigádi GR 195 Bd89
Pigés GR 184 Da77
Pigés GR 188 Ba81
Pigi CY 206 Jc96
Pigi GR 188 Bb81
Pigi GR 201 Db96
Pigna I 43 Kd52
Pignataro Maggiore I 161 Fa74
Pigniu CH 142 Cc55
Pignola I 161 Ga76
Pihkainmäki FIN 82 Kd30
Pihkalanranta FIN 82 Kb26
Pihlaisto FIN 90 Ka34
Pihlajakoski FIN 90 Kb34
Pihlajalahti FIN 89 Jd34
Pihlajalahti FIN 91 Lb33
Pihlajamäki FIN 82 Kc27
Pihlajaniemi FIN 91 Ld32
Pihlajavaara FIN 75 La24
Pihlajavaara FIN 83 Ma28
Pihlajaveden asema FIN 90 Ka32
Pihlajavesi FIN 89 Jd33
Pihlava FIN 89 Jc38
Pihtipudas FIN 82 Kb29
Pihtisulku FIN 89 Jd32
Pihtla EST 105 Jd46
Piikiö FIN 97 Jc39
Piikkilänkylä FIN 89 Ja34
Piilijärvi S 68 Hc16
Piilijoki FIN 89 Jb36
Piilo FIN 83 Ma28
Piilonperä FIN 90 Kc32
Piippaharju FIN 90 Kc32
Piippola FIN 82 Kb26
Piipsjärvi FIN 81 Jd26
Piiri EST 99 Lc45
Piirsalu EST 98 Ka43
Piispajärvi FIN 75 La22
Piispala FIN 82 Ka30
Piittisjärvi FIN 74 Kb19
Pijnacker NL 116 Ad36
Pikalevo RUS 202 Ec08
Pikasilla EST 106 La46
Pikävere EST 98 Kd43
Pike IRL 13 Ca22
Pikeliai LT 113 Jc53
Pikeliškės LT 114 La57
Pike of Rush Hall IRL 13 Cb22
Pikkalanlahti FIN 98 Ka40
Pikkalaviken FIN 98 Ka40
Pikkarala FIN 74 Ka24
Pikknurme EST 98 La44
Pikku-Joensuu FIN 89 Jd38
Pikku-Kulus FIN 74 Ka19
Pikkukylä FIN 82 La26
Pikšari LV 106 Kd47
Piktupėnai LT 113 Jc57
Pikva EST 98 Kc42
Pila I 148 Bc58
Pila I 150 Eb61
Piła PL 121 Gb34
Pila SK 138 Hc49
Pilajamäki FIN 82 Kc28
Pilar de la Mola, el E 56 Gc70
Pilas E 59 Bd74
Pilaševo BG 184 Dc74
Pilastri I 149 Dc61
Pilat-Plage F 32 Fa51
Piława PL 130 Jc37
Piława Górna PL 129 Gc42
Pilawki PL 122 Hd32
Pilchów PL 131 Ka42

Pojo – Poyatos

Pojo FIN 97 Jd40
Pojorâta RO 172 Ea56
Pokāni LV 107 Lb48
Pokela FIN 81 Jc30
Pokka FIN 69 Jd13
Poklečani BIH 158 Ha66
Pokój PL 129 Ha41
Pokrota LV 107 Lc50
Pokrov RUS 203 Fa10
Pokrovsk RUS 107 Ma50
Pokrovskaja Arčada RUS 203 Fc11
Pokrovs'ke UA 203 Fb14
Pokrovs'ke UA 205 Fa15
Pokryváč SK 138 Hd47
Pokrzywnica PL 122 Jb35
Pokrzywnica Wielka PL 122 Ja33
Pokupska HR 151 Ga60
Polače HR 158 Ha68
Polack BY 202 Eb11
Pola de Allande E 37 Ca54
Pola de Laviana E 37 Cc55
Pola de Lena E 37 Cb55
Pola de Siero E 37 Cc54
Pola de Somiedo E 37 Ca55
Polaincourt-et-Clairfontaine F 31 Jd39
Połajewo PL 121 Gb35
Polán E 52 Da66
Polanco E 38 Dc55
Polanica-Zdrój PL 137 Gb43
Połaniec PL 138 Jc43
Polanów PL 121 Gb31
Polany PL 138 Jc46
Polbathic GB 18 Dc31
Polcenigo I 150 Eb58
Polch D 133 Ca43
Polcirkeln S 73 Hc19
Połczno PL 121 Gd31
Połczyn-Zdrój PL 120 Ga32
Polebrook GB 20 Fc25
Połęcko PL 128 Fc37
Polegate GB 20 Fd30
Polekėlė LT 114 Kb54
Polemi CY 206 Hd97
Polena BG 183 Cb74
Põlendmaa EST 106 Kc46
Poleny RUS 107 Ld47
Polesella I 150 Db61
Polešovice CZ 137 Gd48
Polessk RUS 113 Jb58
Polgár H 147 Jd51
Polgárdi H 145 Hb54
Polhov Gradec SLO 151 Fb58
Polia I 164 Gc82
Poliani GR 194 Bb89
Poliántho GR 184 Dc77
Polica MNE 159 Jb68
Poliçan AL 182 Ac78
Police PL 120 Fc33
Police nad Metují CZ 137 Gb43
Polichna PL 131 Ka41
Polichno PL 130 Hd41
Polička CZ 137 Gb46
Poličnik HR 157 Fd64
Polično RUS 99 Lc43
Policoro I 162 Gc77
Policzna PL 131 Jd39
Polidámio GR 189 Bd82
Polidéndri GR 189 Bd82
Polidendro GR 183 Bd78
Polidrosos GR 189 Bd84
Polídrosso GR 188 Ad82
Polientes E 38 Dc56
Polígiros GR 182 Ad80
Polígiros GR 183 Cb79
Polignac F 34 Hd49
Polignano a Mare I 162 Gd74
Poligny F 31 Jc43
Polihnitos GR 191 Ea83
Polihrono GR 184 Cc80
Polikárpi GR 183 Bc76
Polikástano GR 182 Ba78
Polikastro GR 183 Ca76
Polikraiste BG 180 Dd70
Polímilos GR 183 Bc78
Polinéri GR 182 Ba79
Polípetro GR 183 Bd77
Polipótamo GR 183 Bb77
Polirinía GR 200 Ca95
Polis AL 182 Ac75
Polis CY 206 Hd97
Polis'ke UA 202 Eb14
Polissito GR 184 Db77
Polistena I 164 Gb83
Polístilo GR 184 Da77
Polisy F 30 Hd39
Polítiká GR 189 Cb84
Polizzi Generosa I 167 Fa85
Pölja FIN 82 Kd29
Polja RUS 99 Mb42
Poljana BG 181 Ec73
Poljana BIH 158 Hb67
Poljana HR 152 Gb58
Poljanak HR 151 Ga61
Poljana Pakračka HR 152 Gd60
Poljance KSV 178 Ba70
Poljane RUS 107 Mb49
Poljane SLO 151 Fb57
Pöljänmylly FIN 82 La29
Poljanovo BG 185 Dd74
Poljčane SLO 151 Ga57
Polje BIH 152 Hb61
Polje SLO 151 Fc58
Poljica HR 157 Fd64
Poljice BIH 153 Hc63
Pölkki FIN 81 Jd30
Polkowice PL 128 Ga40
Pölla A 136 Fd49
Polla I 161 Fd76
Pollachar GB 6 Cc08
Pölläkkä FIN 90 Kd32
Pölläkkä FIN 91 Lc32
Pollari FIN 81 Jb31
Pollatomish IRL 8 Bb17
Pöllau A 144 Ga54
Pöllauberg A 144 Ga54
Polle D 126 Da38
Polleben D 127 Ea39
Pollen N 62 Ha10
Pollença E 57 Hc66
Pollenfeld D 135 Dd48
Pollhagen D 126 Da36
Pollica I 161 Fc77
Polling A 143 Ed51
Polling D 142 Dc52
Pollneset N 64 Jb04
Polloch GB 6 Db10
Pollone I 148 Bd59
Pollónia GR 195 Cd91
Pollos E 46 Cd61
Polná CZ 136 Ga46
Polna RUS 99 Ld44
Polná na Šumavě CZ 136 Fb49
Polne PL 121 Gb32
Polnica PL 121 Gd32
Polo FIN 75 La21
Pologoe Zajmišče RUS 203 Ga13
Polohy UA 205 Fb16
Połom PL 123 Jd31
Polom SRB 159 Jc64
Połomia PL 139 Ka44
Polomka SK 138 Ja48
Polonez TR 186 Fd77
Polonne UA 204 Eb15
Polope E 53 Ec70
Polopos E 61 Eb75
Pološko MK 183 Bc75
Polovragi RO 175 Da63
Polperro GB 18 Dc32
Polska Cerkiew PL 137 Ha44
Polski Gradec BG 180 Ea73
Polski Trămbeš BG 180 Dd69
Polso FIN 81 Jd29
Poltár SK 146 Ja50
Poltava UA 202 Ed14
Poltavskoe RUS 113 Jd58
Põltsamaa EST 98 Kd44
Polttila FIN 89 Ja37
Polumir SRB 178 Ba68
Põlva EST 107 Lb46
Polvela FIN 83 Lc29
Polvenkylä FIN 89 Ja32
Polverigi I 156 Ed66
Polvijärvi FIN 83 Lc30
Polvikoski FIN 83 Mb29
Półwieś PL 121 Hb32
Polythea GR 182 Ba80
Polzeath GB 18 Db31
Polzela SLO 151 Fc57
Pölzig D 127 Eb41
Pomarance I 155 Db67
Pomarão P 58 Ba73
Pomar de Cinca E 48 Fd60
Pomarez F 39 Fb54
Pomarico I 162 Gc76
Pomarkku FIN 89 Ja35
Pomârla RO 172 Ec54
Pombal P 44 Ac65
Pombalinho P 50 Ac67
Pómbia GR 200 Cd96
Pombriego E 37 Bd57
Pomeroy GB 9 Cc17
Pomezí CZ 137 Gb46
Pomezia I 160 Eb72
Pomi RO 171 Da55
Pomianowo PL 120 Ga31
Pomiechówek PL 130 Jb36
Pömiö FIN 74 Jd21
Pommelsbrunn D 135 Ea46
Pommeréval F 23 Gb34
Pommersfelden D 134 Dc45
Pomol BIH 159 Hd64
Pomonte I 155 Cd68
Pomorie BG 181 Fa72
Pomorska Wieś PL 122 Hc30
Pomorsko PL 128 Fd38
Pomos CY 206 Hd96
Pomoštnik BG 185 Ea74
Pomoy F 31 Jd40
Pompa MD 173 Fb56
Pompei I 161 Fb75
Pompeji = Pompei I 161 Fb75
Pompey F 25 Jd36
Pompierre F 31 Jc38
Pompignan F 41 Hd53
Pomysk Mł. PL 121 Gd30
Poncé-sur-le-Loir F 29 Ga40
Poncin F 35 Jc45
Pondorf D 135 Ea48
Ponferrada E 37 Ca57
Poniatowa PL 131 Ka40
Poniatowo PL 122 Hd34
Poniec PL 129 Gc39
Ponikiew Mała PL 122 Jc34
Ponikovica SRB 159 Jb64
Ponikva MK 179 Ca73
Poniky SK 138 Hd49
Pönitz D 119 Dd31
Ponjos E 37 Cb56
Pönniälä FIN 91 Lb35
Ponoarele RO 175 Cc64
Ponor RO 171 Cd59
Ponor SRB 179 Ca69
Ponoševac KSV 178 Ad71
Ponoševac SRB 159 Jc69
Ponova vas SLO 151 Fc58
Pons F 32 Fb48
Ponsa FIN 90 Ka35
Ponsacco I 155 Db65
Ponsworthy GB 19 Dd31
Pont I 148 Bc59
Pont-à-Bucy F 24 Hb34
Pontacq F 40 Fc56
Pontailler-sur-Saône F 31 Jc41
Pontaix F 35 Jc50
Pont-à-Marcq F 23 Ha31
Pont-à-Mousson F 25 Jc36
Pontão P 44 Ad65
Pontardawe GB 19 Dd27
Pontardulais GB 19 Dd27
Pontarion F 33 Gc46
Pontarlier F 31 Ka43
Pontarsais GB 15 Dd26
Pontassieve I 155 Dc65
Pontaubault F 22 Fa37
Pont-Audemer F 22 Fd35
Pontaumur F 33 Ha46
Pont-Authou F 23 Ga35
Pont-Aven F 27 Dd40
Pontavert F 24 Hc35
Pont Canavese I 148 Bc59
Pontcharra F 35 Jd47
Pontcharra-sur-Tudine F 34 Ja46
Pontcharraud F 33 Gd47
Pontchartrain F 23 Gc37
Pontchâteau F 27 Ec41
Pont-Croix F 27 Db39
Pont-d'Ain F 35 Jc46
Pont-d'Aspach F 31 Kb40
Pont-de-Chéruy F 34 Jb47
Pont-de-Dore F 34 Hc47
Pont-de-la-Chaux F 31 Jd44
Pont-de-l'Arche F 23 Gb35
Pont-de-l'Isère F 34 Jb49
Pont-de-Pany F 30 Ja42
Pont-de-Poitte F 31 Jc44
Pont-de Rhodes F 33 Gc51
Pont-de Roide F 31 Ka41
Pont-de-Salars F 41 Ha52
Pont-des-Plagnettes F 35 Ka45
Pont-de-Vaux F 30 Jb44
Pont-de-Veyle F 34 Jb45
Pont-d'Hèrault F 41 Hd53
Pont-d'Héry F 31 Jd43
Pont-d'Ouilly F 22 Fc37
Pont-du-Château F 34 Hb47
Pont-du-Navoy F 31 Jc43
Ponte I 161 Fa73
Ponte a Elsa I 155 Db65
Ponte Albar E 36 Ad55
Ponte alla Chiassa I 156 Dd66
Ponte Arche I 149 Dc58
Ponteareas E 36 Ad58
Ponte Barxas E 36 Ba58
Pontebba I 143 Ed56
Ponte Caffaro I 149 Db58
Pontecagnano I 161 Fc75
Ponte-Caldelas E 36 Ad57
Ponte Carreira E 36 Ba55
Ponte Castirla F 154 Cb69
Ponteceso E 36 Ad54
Pontechianale I 148 Bb61
Pontecorvo I 160 Ed73
Pontecurone I 148 Cb61
Ponte da Barca P 44 Ad59
Pontedecimo I 148 Cb62
Ponte de Lima P 44 Ad59
Ponte dell'Olio I 149 Cd61
Pontedera I 155 Db65
Ponte de Sor P 50 Ad67
Pontedeume E 36 Ba54
Ponte di Barbarano I 150 Dd60
Ponte di Ferro I 156 Eb68
Ponte di Legno I 149 Db57
Ponte di Nava I 148 Bd63
Ponte di Piave I 150 Eb59
Ponte do Porto E 36 Ac54
Pontefract GB 16 Fa21
Ponte in Valtellina I 149 Da57
Pontelagoscuro I 150 Dd61
Pontelandolfo I 161 Fc73
Ponte Leccia F 154 Cb69
Ponte Ledesma E 36 Ba56
Ponte nelle Alpi I 150 Eb57
Ponte Nossa I 149 Cd58
Pontenova Villaodriz E 36 Bc54
Pont-en-Royans F 35 Jc49
Ponte Nuovo F 154 Cb69
Pontenure I 149 Cd61
Pontenx-les-Forges F 39 Fa52
Pontepetri I 155 Db64
Ponterìccioli I 156 Eb66
Ponterwyd GB 15 Dd25
Ponte San Pietro I 149 Cd58
Pontesbury GB 15 Eb24
Pontestura I 148 Ca60
Ponte Tresa I 148 Cb57
Ponte Ulla E 36 Ba56
Ponte Valga E 36 Ad56
Pontevedra E 36 Ad57
Pont-Evêque F 34 Jb47
Pontevico I 149 Da60
Pont-Farcy F 22 Fa36
Pontgibaud F 33 Ha47
Pont-Hamon F 27 Eb39
Ponthibault F 28 Fd40
Ponthierry F 29 Ha38
Ponti I 169 Bd80
Pontigny F 22 Fc36
Pontigny F 30 Hc40
Pontijou F 29 Gb40
Pontinia I 160 Ec73
Pontinvrea I 148 Ca62
Pöntiö FIN 81 Jc27
Pontivy F 27 Ea39
Pont-l'Abbé F 22 Fa35
Pont-l'Abbé F 27 Dc40
Pont-l'Abbé-d'Arnoult F 32 Fb47
Pont-la-Ville F 30 Ja39
Pont-l'Evêque F 22 Fd35
Pontlevoy F 29 Gb42
Pont-Losquet F 26 Ea37
Pontmain F 28 Fa38
Pontoise F 23 Gd36
Pontokerasiá GR 183 Cb76
Pontokómi GR 183 Bb78
Pontones E 61 Ea72
Pontonx-sur-l'Adour F 39 Fa54
Pontoon IRL 8 Bc18
Pontorson F 28 Ed38
Pontremoli I 149 Cd63
Pont-Rémy F 23 Gc33
Pontresina CH 142 Da56
Pontrhydfendigaid GB 15 Dd25
Pontrhydygroes GB 15 Dd25
Pontrieux F 26 Ea37
Pontrilas GB 15 Eb26
Ponts E 48 Gb60
Pont-Sainte-Maxence F 23 Ha35
Pont-Saint-Esprit F 42 Jb52
Pont Saint-Mamet F 33 Ga50
Pont-Saint-Martin F 28 Ed42
Pont-Saint-Martin I 148 Bd58
Pont-Saint-Pierre F 23 Gb35
Pont-Saint-Vincent F 25 Jd37
Pont-Scorff F 27 Dd40
Pont-Scorff F 27 Ea40
Pont-sur-Yonne F 30 Hb38
Pontvallain F 28 Fd40
Pontyberem GB 19 Dd27
Pontyclun GB 19 Ea28
Pontypool GB 19 Eb27
Pontypridd GB 19 Ea27
Ponza I 160 Ec75
Ponzone I 148 Ca58
Ponzone I 148 Ca62
Poola FIN 81 Ja31
Poole GB 20 Ed31
Poolewe GB 4 Dc07
Pooley Bridge GB 11 Ec17
Pootsi EST 106 Kb46
Popčevo MK 183 Ca75
Pope LV 105 Jb49
Popeasca MD 173 Ga59
Popeni RO 177 Fb60
Popericu MD 173 Fd56
Poperinge B 21 Ha30
Popeşti RO 171 Cc56
Popeşti RO 172 Ed57
Popeşti RO 175 Da64
Popeşti RO 175 Dc66
Popeştii de Jos MD 173 Fb54
Popeştii de Sus MD 173 Fb54
Popeşti-Leordeni RO 176 Eb66
Popielów PL 129 Ha42
Popina BG 181 Ec67
Popinci BG 179 Da72
Popinci SRB 153 Jb61
Popioły PL 123 Jd30
Popkovo Gora RUS 99 Ld42
Poplaca RO 175 Da61
Popławy PL 122 Jb35
Popoli I 157 Fa70
Popovac HR 152 Gc59
Popovac HR 153 Hc58
Popovac SRB 178 Bc67
Popovača HR 152 Gc59
Popović BG 181 Fa71
Popovica BG 180 Dc73
Popovica SRB 174 Ca66
Popović-Brdo HR 151 Ga60
Popovo BG 180 Eb70
Popovo BG 181 Ec73
Popów PL 130 Hc41
Popów PL 130 Hd38
Popowo PL 121 Gd30
Popowo Kościelne PL 129 Gc36
Poppel B 124 Ba39
Poppenhausen D 134 Da43
Poppenhausen D 134 Db44
Poppenricht D 135 Ea46
Poppi I 156 Dd65
Poprad SK 138 Jb47
Popricani RO 173 Fa57
Poproč SK 138 Jc48
Popšica SRB 178 Bd68
Popsko BG 185 Dd75
Populonia I 155 Da67
Poraj PL 130 Hc42
Porajów PL 128 Fc42
Poranen FIN 81 Jd30
Porazava BY 202 Dd13
Pörböly H 153 Hc57
Porcari I 155 Db65
Porcsalma H 147 Kc51
Porcuna E 52 Da72
Pordenone I 150 Eb58
Pordim BG 180 Dc69
Poręba PL 138 Hd43
Porebeni MD 173 Fd56
Poreč HR 150 Ed60
Poreč'e RUS 99 Ld41
Poreč'e RUS 113 Jb59
Poredy PL 122 Jc33
Porhov RUS 202 Eb10
Porhovo RUS 99 Ld41
Pori EST 106 La46
Pori FIN 89 Ja36
Póri GR 183 Bd80
Porice BIH 158 Ha64
Porjus S 72 Ha18
Porkala FIN 98 Kb40
Porkanranta FIN 82 Ka25
Pörkenäs FIN 81 Ja29
Porkkakylät FIN 90 Ka33
Porkkala FIN 82 Kb27
Porkkala FIN 98 Kb40
Porkuni EST 98 Kd42
Porlákshöfn IS 2 Ac05
Porlammi FIN 90 Kd38
Porlezza I 149 Cc57
Porlock GB 19 Ea29
Porlom FIN 90 Kd38
Pornainen FIN 90 Kc38
Pornassio I 148 Bd63
Pörnbach D 135 Dd49
Pornello I 156 Ea68
Pornic F 27 Ec42
Pornichet F 27 Ec42
Pornópáti H 145 Gb54
Poroca i poshtëm AL 182 Ac76
Poroč'e RUS 99 Mb45
Porodin SRB 174 Bc65
Poroina Mare RO 175 Cc65
Porokylä FIN 83 Lb27
Pörölänmäki FIN 82 Kd31
Poromäki FIN 82 La25
Poronin PL 138 Ja46
Póros GR 188 Ac85
Póros GR 195 Cb88
Porosalmi FIN 91 Lb32
Porost PL 121 Gb31
Poroszló H 146 Jc52
Porovesi FIN 82 Kd28
Porozina HR 151 Fb61
Porpác H 145 Gc54
Pórpi GR 184 Dc77
Porquerolles F 42 Ka55
Porras FIN 89 Jd38
Porras FIN 90 Ka36
Porraskoski FIN 90 Kb36
Porrentruy CH 141 Bc52
Porreres E 57 Hc67
Porretta Terme I 155 Db64
Porriño E 36 Ad58
Porrogszentkirály H 152 Gd57
Porrosillo E 52 Dc71
Pörsänmäki FIN 82 Kd28
Porsgrunn N 93 Dc44
Þórshöfn IS 3 Bc04
Porsi S 73 Hb19
Pórszombat H 145 Gc55
Port IRL 8 Bd16
Port N 64 Jc08
Portacloy IRL 8 Bb17
Portadown GB 9 Cd18
Portaferry GB 10 Db18
Portagem P 51 Bb67
Portaje E 45 Bd65
Portalegre P 51 Bb67
Portalrubio E 47 Fa63
Portals Vells E 56 Ha67
Port Appin GB 6 Dc11
Portariá GR 183 Cb79
Portarlington IRL 13 Cc22
Port Askaig GB 6 Da13
Portavadie GB 6 Dc13
Porta Westfalica D 126 Cd37
Portbail F 22 Ed35
Port-Barcarès F 41 Hb57
Port-Blanc F 26 Ea37
Portbradden GB 9 Cd15
Portbron S 71 Fc22
Port-Camargue F 42 Ja54
Port Charlotte GB 6 Da13
Port-Cros F 43 Kb55
Port d'Addaia E 57 Ja65
Port-d'Agrès F 33 Gd51
Port d'Alcúdia E 57 Hc66
Port d'Andratx E 56 Ha67
Port d'Atelier-Amance F 31 Jd40
Port-de-Bouc F 42 Jb54
Port de Chiavari F 154 Ca71
Port-de-Miramar F 42 Ka55
Port de Pollença E 57 Hc66
Port-des-Barques F 32 Fa46
Port des Callonges F 32 Fb49
Port de Sóller E 57 Hb66
Port d'es Torrent E 56 Gb69
Port de Valldemossa E 57 Hb67
Port Durlainne IRL 8 Bc17
Porte-de-Lanne F 39 Fa54
Portegrandi I 150 Eb59
Portel P 50 Ba70
Portela P 58 Ad73
Portela de Santa Eulália P 44 Ba60
Portela de Vade P 44 Ad59
Portel-des-Corbières F 41 Hb56
Portell de Morella E 48 Fc64
Portelo E 37 Bd56
Portelo P 45 Bd59
Port-en-Bessin F 22 Fb35
Portencross GB 10 Dc14
Port Erin GB 10 Dc19
Pörtet S 94 Fa41
Port-Eynon GB 19 Dd28
Portezuelo E 51 Bd66
Port George GB 5 Ea07
Port Glasgow GB 10 Dd13
Portglenone GB 9 Cd16
Port Goulphar F 27 Ea42
Port Grimaud F 43 Kb54
Porth GB 19 Ea27
Porthcawl GB 19 Dd28
Porthleven GB 18 Da32
Porthmadog GB 15 Dd23
Porthoustock GB 18 Db32
Porticcio F 154 Ca71
Portichuelo E 55 Fa71
Portici I 161 Fb75
Portico di Romagna I 156 Dd64
Portiglione I 155 Db68
Portilla de la Reina E 38 Da56
Portillo E 46 Da61
Portimão P 58 Ab74
Portimo FIN 74 Ka20
Portimojärvi FIN 73 Jb19
Portinatx E 56 Gc69
Portinho da Arrábida P 50 Ab69
Portinniska FIN 74 Kc18
Port Isaac GB 18 Db31
Portishead GB 19 Eb28
Port-Joinville F 27 Ec44
Portknockie GB 5 Ec07
Port Láirge IRL 13 Cb25
Port Lamont GB 6 Dc13
Port-la-Nouvelle F 41 Hb56
Port Laoise IRL 13 Cb22
Portlaoise IRL 13 Cb22
Port-Leucate F 41 Hb56
Portloe GB 18 Db32
Port-Louis F 27 Ea40
Portmagee IRL 12 Ad25
Portmahomack GB 5 Ea07
Portman E 55 Fa74
Port-Manec'h F 27 Dd40
Portmarnock IRL 13 Cd21
Port Maubert F 32 Fb48
Port-Mort F 23 Gb36
Pörtmossen FIN 89 Hd32
Portmuck GB 10 Db16
Portnacroish GB 6 Dc11
Portnaguran GB 4 Db05
Portnahaven GB 6 Da13
Port Nan Long GB 6 Cd07
Port-Navalo F 27 Ea41
Portnoo IRL 8 Ca16
Porto E 37 Bd58
Porto F 154 Ca70
Pórto GR 196 Db88
Porto I 164 Ga78
Porto P 44 Ac61
Porto Alabe I 169 Bd76
Porto Alto P 50 Ab68
Porto Azzurro I 155 Da68
Portobello di Gallura I 168 Ca73
Porto Botte I 169 Bd80
Portobuffolè I 150 Eb58
Pórto Carrás GR 184 Cc80
Porto Cervo I 168 Cc73
Porto Cesareo I 162 Hb77
Porto Colom E 57 Hc68
Porto Covo P 50 Ab71
Porto Cristo E 57 Hc67
Porto da Balsa P 44 Ba64
Porto d'Ascoli I 157 Fa68
Porto de Bares E 36 Bc53
Porto de Espasante E 36 Bb53
Porto de Lagos P 58 Ab74
Porto de Mós P 50 Ab66
Porto do Barqueiro E 36 Bb53
Porto do Son E 36 Ac56
Porto Empedocle I 166 Ed86
Porto Ercole I 155 Dc70
Portoferraio I 155 Da68
Portofino I 149 Cc63
Port of Menteith GB 7 Dd12
Port of Ness GB 4 Db04
Porto Garibaldi I 150 Ea62
Porto Germenó GR 189 Ca86
Portogruaro I 150 Ec59
Portohéli GR 195 Ca88
Pórto Koufós GR 184 Cc80
Porto Levante I 150 Eb61
Pörtom FIN 89 Hd32
Portomaggiore I 150 Dd62
Portomarín E 36 Bb56
Porto Maurizio I 43 La52
Port Omna IRL 13 Ca22
Portomouro E 36 Ad55
Porton GB 20 Ed29
Portonovo E 36 Ac57
Portonovo I 156 Ed66
Porto Palermo AL 182 Ab78
Porto Palo I 166 Eb85
Portopalo di Capo Passero I 167 Fd88
Porto Pino I 169 Bd80
Porto Pollo F 154 Ca71
Porto Potenza Picena I 156 Ed67
Porto Pozzo I 168 Cb73
Porto Rafti GR 195 Cc87
Porto Recanati I 156 Ed66
Porto Rotondo I 168 Cc74
Portorož SLO 150 Ed60
Porto San Elpidio I 157 Fa67
Porto San Giorgio I 157 Fa67
Porto San Paolo I 168 Cc74
Porto Santo Stefano I 155 Db69
Portoscuso I 169 Bc79
Portosín E 36 Ac55
Porto Tolle I 150 Eb61
Porto Torres I 168 Bd74
Porto Valtravaglia I 148 Cb57
Porto-Vecchio F 154 Cb72
Portovenere I 155 Cd64
Portovesme I 169 Bc79
Portpatrick GB 10 Dc16
Port pétrolier du Havre-Antifer F 22 Fd34
Portreath GB 18 Da32
Portree GB 4 Da08
Portroe IRL 12 Bd22
Portrush GB 9 Cd15
Port-Sainte-Marie F 40 Fd52
Port-Saint-Louis-du-Rhône F 42 Jb54
Port-Saint-Père F 28 Ed42
Portsall F 26 Db37
Portsalon IRL 9 Cb15
Pörtschach am Wörthersee A 144 Fb56
Portslade-by-Sea GB 20 Fc30
Portsmouth GB 20 Fa30
Portsoy GB 5 Ec07
Portstewart GB 9 Cd15
Port-sur-Saône F 31 Jd40
Port Talbot GB 19 Dd27
Portugalete E 38 Ea55
Portumna IRL 13 Ca22
Porturlin IRL 8 Bc17
Port-Vendres F 41 Hb57
Port William GB 10 Dd17
Porúbka SK 139 Ka48
Porumbacu de Jos RO 175 Db61
Porvola FIN 90 Ka34
Porvoo FIN 98 Kc39
Porzádez E 46 Cd61
Porządzie PL 122 Jc35
Porzuna E 52 Da68
Posada E 38 Da54
Posada I 168 Cc75
Posada de Valdeón E 37 Cd55
Posada (Llanera) E 37 Cb54
Posadas E 38 Ea58
Posadas E 60 Cc72
Posadilla E 37 Cb57
Posadowice PL 129 Gd41
Poşaga RO 171 Cd59
Poşaga de Sus RO 171 Cd59
Poschiavo CH 142 Da56
Posedarje HR 157 Fd64
Pošehon'e RUS 202 Ed08
Posen = Poznań PL 129 Gc37
Poseritz D 119 Ed30
Posesse F 24 Ja36
Poseşti RO 176 Eb63
Poshnjë AL 182 Ab76
Posidóni GR 197 Eb88
Posidonía GR 196 Da89
Posina I 149 Dc58
Posio FIN 75 Kd19
Positano I 161 Fb75
Posjärv S 73 Ja19
Poškonys LT 115 Lb59
Poškos LT 113 Jb55
Posof TR 205 Ga18
Possagno I 150 Ea58
Posseck D 135 Eb43
Possendorf D 128 Fa41
Possens CH 141 Bb55
Pößneck D 127 Ea42
Posta I 156 Ec69
Poşta Cǎlnǎu RO 176 Ec63
Posta Demani I 161 Ga73
Posta Piana I 161 Ga74
Posta San Lucia I 161 Fd73
Postau D 135 Eb49
Postbauer-Heng D 135 Dd47
Postel B 124 Ba39
Posterholt NL 125 Bb40
Postiglione I 161 Fd76
Postojna SLO 151 Fb59
Postoloprty CZ 136 Fa43
Postomino PL 121 Gb30
Postranje HR 158 Gd66
Postřelmov CZ 137 Gc45
Postue N 63 Ja10
Postupice CZ 136 Fc46
Posušje BIH 158 Gd66
Poświętne PL 123 Ka34
Poświętne PL 130 Ja39
Poświętne PL 130 Jc36
Potamí GR 184 Cd76
Potamiá GR 184 Db78
Potamós GR 195 Bd92
Potamós GR 196 Dd90
Potamós GR 200 Ca93
Potamoúla GR 188 Ba83
Potcoava RO 175 Db66
Potęgowo PL 121 Gd30
Potenza I 161 Ga75
Potenza Picena I 156 Ed67
Potes E 38 Da55
Potidania GR 189 Bc84
Potka N 63 Hb09
Potkraj BIH 158 Gb65
Potku FIN 75 Kc24
Potlogi RO 176 Dd65
Potnjani HR 152 Hb60
Potočac SRB 178 Bc67
Potoci BIH 152 Gc63
Potoci BIH 158 Hb66
Potoci RO 172 Eb58
Potoczyzna PL 123 Ka32
Potok Górny Drugi PL 131 Kb42
Potok Złoty PL 130 Hd42
Pótor SK 146 Hd50
Potoskavaara FIN 91 Ma32
Potsdam D 127 Ed37
Potštát CZ 137 Gd46
Potštejn CZ 137 Gb44
Pottenstein D 135 Dd45
Potters Bar GB 20 Fc27
Pötting A 144 Fa50
Pöttmes D 134 Dc49
Potton GB 20 Fc26
Potworów PL 130 Jb39
Potzlow D 120 Fa34
Pouancé F 28 Fa40
Pouan-les-Vallées F 30 Hd38
Poudenas F 40 Fd53
Pougny F 30 Hb41
Pougues-les-Eaux F 30 Hb42
Pougy F 30 Hd38
Pouillenay F 30 Ja41
Pouillon F 39 Fa54
Pouilly-en-Auxois F 30 Ja42
Pouilly-sous-Charlieu F 34 Hd45
Pouilly-sur-Loire F 30 Hb42
Pouilly-sur-Saône F 30 Jb42
Poujols F 41 Hc53
Poulaines F 29 Gc42
Pouldreuzic F 27 Dc39
Poúlithra GR 195 Bd89
Poullaouen F 26 Dd38
Poulstrup DK 100 Dc20
Poulton-le-Fylde GB 15 Eb20
Poúnda GR 196 Db90
Pourí GR 189 Ca81
Pourlans F 30 Jb43
Pourrain F 30 Hb40
Pourrières F 42 Jd54
Pourunperä FIN 89 Jd33
Pousada E 36 Ba54
Poussu FIN 75 La20
Pouyastruc F 40 Fd55
Pouydesseaux F 40 Fc53
Pouy-de-Touges F 40 Gb55
Pouzac F 40 Fd56
Pouzauges F 28 Fb44
Pouzilhac F 42 Jb52
Pouzilli I 161 Fa73
Považská Bystrica SK 137 Hb47
Považská Teplá SK 137 Hb47
Povedilla E 53 Ea70
Poverišče RUS 107 Ma49
Poviglio I 149 Db61
Povja HR 158 Gc67
Povljana HR 151 Fd63
Póvoa das Quartas P 44 Ba64
Póvoa de Lanhoso P 44 Ad59
Póvoa de São Miguel P 50 Ba71
Póvoa de Varzim P 44 Ac60
Póvoa e Meadas P 50 Ba66
Powalice PL 120 Fd32
Powardennan Lodge GB 7 Dd12
Powburn GB 11 Ed15
Power's Cross IRL 12 Bd22
Powidz PL 129 Ha36
Powierz PL 122 Ja33
Powodów PL 130 Hc38
Powroźnik PL 138 Jc46
Poxdorf D 135 Dd45
Poyales del Hoyo E 45 Cc65
Poyatos E 47 Ec64

Poyaz – Putlitz

Poyaz TR 186 Fd77
Pöylä FIN 97 Jc39
Poynton GB 16 Ed22
Poyntz Pass GB 9 Cd18
Poyols F 35 Jc50
Poyra TR 193 Gb81
Poyralı TR 185 Ed75
Poyraz TR 192 Fa85
Poyrazcık TR 191 Ec84
Poyrazdamları TR 192 Fa85
Poyrazlı TR 185 Ed79
Pöyry FIN 90 Kd34
Poysdorf A 137 Gc49
Pöytiö FIN 97 Jd39
Pöytyä FIN 89 Jc38
Poza de la Sal E 38 Dd57
Pozal de Gallinas E 46 Cd61
Požarevac SRB 174 Bc64
Požarnica BIH 153 Hd63
Pozdeň CZ 136 Fa44
Pozdišovce SK 139 Ka48
Pozedrze PL 122 Jc30
Požega HR 152 Ha60
Požega SRB 159 Jb65
Požeranje KSV 178 Bb72
Požerė LT 113 Jd55
Pozières F 23 Ha33
Poznań PL 129 Gc37
Pozo Alcón E 61 Dd73
Pozoantiguo E 45 Cc60
Pozoblanco E 52 Cd71
Pozo-Cañada E 53 Ec70
Pozo de Guadalajara E 46 Dd64
Pozo de la Serna E 53 Dd70
Pozohondo E 53 Ec70
Pozo-Lorente E 54 Ed69
Pozondón E 47 Ed64
Pozořice CZ 137 Gc47
Pozorrubio E 53 Dd66
Poźrzadło Wielkie PL 120 Ga33
Pozuelo E 53 Eb70
Pozuelo de Alarcón E 46 Db64
Pozuelo de Aragón E 47 Ed60
Pozuelo de Calatrava E 52 Db69
Pozuelo del Páramo E 37 Cb58
Pozuelo de Zarzón E 45 Bd65
Pozza I 149 Db62
Pozza di Fassa I 143 Dd56
Pozzallo I 167 Fc88
Pozzillo I 167 Fd85
Pozzomaggiore I 168 Bd76
Pozzo San Nicola I 168 Bd74
Pozzuoli I 161 Fa75
Pozzuolo I 156 Dd67
Praag = Praha CZ 136 Fb44
Praaga EST 99 Lc45
Prabuty PL 122 Hc32
Prača BIH 159 Hd65
Prachatice CZ 136 Fa48
Prackenbach D 135 Ec48
Pračno HR 152 Gb60
Prada E 37 Bd57
Prádanos de Ojeda E 38 Db57
Pradelles F 34 Hd50
Pradelles-Cabardès F 41 Ha55
Prádena E 46 Dc62
Prades E 48 Gb62
Prades F 41 Ha57
Pradła PL 130 Hd42
Pradleves I 148 Bb62
Prado E 36 Ba56
Prado E 36 Ad57
Prado E 37 Cd54
Prado E 45 Cc59
Prado P 44 Ad59
Prado del Rey E 59 Ca76
Pradoluengo E 38 Dd58
Prads F 43 Kb51
Præstbro DK 101 Dd20
Præsteskov DK 109 Ec27
Præstø DK 109 Eb27
Prag = Praha CZ 136 Fb44
Pragelato I 148 Bb60
Prags I 143 Ea55
Praha CZ 136 Fb44
Prahecq F 32 Fc45
Prahovo SRB 174 Cb66
Praia a Mare I 164 Ga78
Praia da Areia Branca P 50 Aa67
Praia da Barra P 44 Ac62
Praia da Rocha P 58 Ab74
Praia das Maçãs P 50 Aa68
Praia da Tocha P 44 Ac63
Praia da Vagueira P 44 Ac63
Praia da Vieira P 44 Ab65
Praia de Esmoriz P 44 Ac61
Praia de Mira P 44 Ac63
Praia de Ofir P 44 Ac60
Praia de Quiaios P 44 Ab64
Praia de Santa Cruz P 50 Aa67
Praiano I 161 Fb76
Praid RO 172 Dd59
Prăjeni RO 172 Ed56
Prakovce SK 138 Jc48
Pralea RO 176 Ec61
Pralognan F 35 Kb47
Pralormo I 148 Bd61
Pra-Loup F 43 Kb51
Pram A 144 Fa50
Prámanda GR 188 Ba81
Prameny CZ 135 Ec44
Pramet A 143 Ed51
Pramort D 119 Ed30
Pramouton F 35 Kb50
Praniūnai LT 114 Kc59
Pranjani SRB 159 Jc64
Prapatnica HR 158 Gb66
Prapymas LT 113 Jc55
Prasés GR 200 Cb95
Prašice SK 137 Hb49
Prasiés GR 200 Cd95
Praslay F 30 Jb40
Praslovo RUS 122 Jc30
Prässebo S 102 Ec47
Prássino GR 194 Bb87
Prastavoniai LV 114 Kb55
Prastio CY 206 Ja98
Prastio CY 206 Jc96
Prästkulla FIN 97 Jd40
Prästö FIN 96 Hc40
Praszka PL 129 Hb41
Prat F 40 Gb56
Prata Sannita I 161 Fa73
Pratau D 127 Ec38
Prat-de-Chest F 41 Hb55
Prat de Comte E 48 Fd63
Pratella I 161 Fa73
Prati di Tivo I 156 Ed69
Prato CH 141 Cb56
Prato I 155 Dc65
Prato all'Isarco I 143 Dd56
Prato di Resia I 150 Ed57
Pratola Peligna I 161 Fa71
Pratola Serra I 161 Fc74
Prato Nevoso I 148 Bd63
Pratorotondo I 148 Bb62
Prats de Lluçanès E 49 Gd59
Prats-de-Mollo-la-Preste F 41 Ha58
Prats-du-Périgord F 33 Gb51
Pratteln CH 141 Bd52
Prauliena LV 107 Lb50
Pravda BG 181 Ec68
Pravdino RUS 113 Jd58
Pravdinsk RUS 113 Jb59
Pravec BG 179 Cd71
Praves E 38 Dc54
Pravia E 37 Cb54
Pravieniškės LT 114 Kc57
Praviņi LV 106 Ka51
Pravište BG 180 Db73
Prayssac F 33 Gb51
Prayssas F 40 Ga52
Praz I 148 Bc58
Praze-an-Beeble GB 18 Da32
Praznice HR 158 Gc67
Prazzo I 148 Bb62
Prčanj MNE 159 Hd69
Préaux F 23 Gb35
Prebitz D 135 Ea45
Prebold SLO 151 Fd57
Přebuz CZ 135 Ec43
Prečec HR 152 Gb59
Préchac F 40 Fc52
Preci I 156 Ec68
Précigné F 28 Fc40
Prečistoe RUS 202 Ec11
Prečistoe RUS 203 Fa08
Précy-sous-Thil F 30 Hd41
Précy-sur-Oise F 23 Gd35
Predajane SRB 178 Bd70
Predappio I 156 Ea64
Predazzo I 150 Dd57
Predeal RO 176 Ea62
Predeal-Sărari RO 176 Eb64
Predești RO 175 Cd66
Predești RO 175 Db64
Preding A 144 Fd55
Predjama SLO 151 Fa59
Predlitz A 144 Fa54
Predmeja SLO 151 Fa58
Predosa I 148 Cb61
Predošćica HR 151 Fb61
Pré-en-Pail F 28 Fc38
Prees GB 15 Ec23
Preetz D 118 Dc30
Préfailles F 27 Ec42
Prefontaines F 29 Ha39
Pregarten A 144 Fb50
Pregrada HR 151 Ga57
Preila LT 113 Jb56
Preiļi LV 107 Lc52
Preitenegg A 144 Fc55
Preiviiki FIN 89 Ja36
Préjano E 47 Eb59
Prejłowo PL 122 Ja32
Prejmer RO 176 Ea62
Prekaja BIH 158 Gc64
Preko HR 157 Fd64
Prekopčelica SRB 178 Bc70
Prélenfrey F 35 Jd49
Preljina SRB 159 Jc64
Prelog HR 152 Gc57
Prelošćica HR 152 Gb60
Přelouč CZ 136 Fd45
Prem SLO 151 Fb59
Premana I 149 Cd57
Premantura HR 151 Fa62
Premeno I 148 Cb57
Prémery F 30 Hb42
Premià de Mar E 49 Ha61
Premilcuore I 156 Dd64
Premnitz D 127 Eb36
Prémont F 24 Hb33
Premuda HR 151 Fb63
Prenčov SK 146 Hc50
Prendeignes F 33 Gd50
Prendwick GB 11 Ed15
Prenika MK 182 Ba74
Prénouvellon F 29 Gc40
Prenzlau D 120 Fa34
Prepelița MD 173 Fc56
Přerov CZ 137 Gd46
Prerow D 119 Ec30
Pré-Saint-Didier I 148 Bb58
Prescot GB 15 Eb21
Presedo E 36 Ba54
Preseľany SK 145 Hb50
Preselec BG 180 Eb70
Preselenci BG 181 Fb69
Presencio E 38 Dc58
Preševo KSV 178 Bc72
Preshkëp AL 182 Aa77
Presicce I 165 Hc78
Presjaka MNE 159 Hd68
Presly F 29 Gd42
Prešov SK 139 Jd47
Pressac F 33 Ga46
Pressath D 135 Ea45
Pressbaum A 144 Ga51
Preßburg = Bratislava SK 145 Gd51
Presseck D 135 Ea44
Pressgutz A 144 Ga54
Pressig D 135 Dd43
Prestatyn GB 15 Ea22
Prestbakken N 67 Gc12
Presteid N 66 Fd15
Presteigne GB 15 Eb25
Prestelvbakken N 64 Jd06
Prestesætra N 78 Ed27
Prestfoss N 93 Dc41
Přeštice CZ 135 Ed46
Preston GB 15 Ec20
Preston GB 19 Ec31
Preston GB 21 Gb29
Preston Capes GB 20 Fa26
Prestranek SLO 151 Fb59
Prestwick GB 10 Dd14
Prestwood GB 20 Fb27
Pretoro I 157 Fa70
Prettin D 127 Ec39
Pretzfeld D 135 Dd45
Pretzsch D 127 Ec39
Preuilly-sur-Claise F 29 Ga43
Preußisch Oldendorf D 117 Cc36
Preutești RO 172 Ec56
Prevala BG 179 Cb68
Prevalje SLO 144 Fc56
Prevediños E 36 Ba55
Prévenchères F 34 Hd51
Préveranges F 33 Gd45
Préveza GR 188 Ac82
Prey F 23 Gb36
Prezë AL 182 Ab74
Prezëe Madhe AL 182 Ab75
Prez-v.-N. CH 141 Bc54
Prhovo SRB 153 Jb61
Priaranza del Bierzo E 37 Bd57
Priatu I 168 Cb74
Pribelja BIH 158 Gd64
Pribeta SK 145 Hb51
Pribinić BIH 152 Ha62
Priboieni RO 175 Dc64
Priboj BIH 153 Hd62
Priboj SRB 178 Bd71
Pribojska Goleša SRB 159 Ja66
Příbor CZ 137 Ha46
Pribovce SK 138 Hc48
Příbram CZ 136 Fa46
Pribrežnoje RUS 113 Ja59
Pribude HR 158 Gb65
Pribylina SK 138 Ja47
Přibyslav CZ 136 Ga46
Pričaly RUS 113 Jb57
Priceaca RO 175 Db65
Pri Cerkvi Strugah SLO 151 Fc59
Pričević SRB 153 Jb63
Prichsenstadt D 134 Db45
Pridnieki LV 105 Jc50
Pridvorci BIH 158 Hb67
Pridvorica SRB 174 Bb65
Pridvorje HR 159 Hc69
Priedaine LV 106 Kb50
Priego E 47 Eb64
Priego de Córdoba E 60 Da74
Priekulė LT 113 Jb56
Priekule LV 113 Jb53
Priekuļi LV 106 Kd49
Prien D 143 Eb52
Prienai LT 114 Kc58
Priescas E 37 Cd55
Priesendorf D 134 Dd45
Prievidza SK 138 Hc48
Prignano Cilento I 161 Fd76
Prigor RO 174 Ca64
Prigoria RO 175 Da63
Prigorica SLO 151 Fc59
Prigradica HR 158 Gc68
Pripalu EST 106 La46
Prijeboj HR 151 Ga62
Prijedor BIH 152 Gc61
Prijepolje SRB 159 Jb66
Prijutnoe RUS 205 Ga15
Prikra SK 139 Ka46
Prikraj HR 152 Gb58
Prikula BIH 158 Gd65
Prikuļi LV 107 Lc52
Prilep BG 181 Ec71
Prilep MK 183 Bb75
Prilike SRB 178 Ad67
Prima Porta I 160 Eb71
Přimda CZ 135 Ec46
Primel-Trégastel F 26 Dd37
Primolano I 150 Dd58
Primorje RUS 113 Hd58
Primorsk RUS 113 Hd58
Primorsk RUS 202 Ea08
Primorsk RUS 203 Fd13
Primorsko BG 181 Fa73
Primorsko- Ahtarsk RUS 205 Fc16
Primorskoje Novoje RUS 113 Hd59
Primošten HR 157 Ga66
Primstal D 133 Bd45
Princetown GB 19 Dd31
Principina a Mare I 155 Db69
Prinos GR 184 Da78
Prinos GR 188 Bb81
Priodrožnoje RUS 113 Jc58
Prioiro E 36 Ba53
Priólithos GR 188 Bb86
Priolo I 167 Fb87
Priolo Gargallo I 167 Fd87
Prioro E 37 Cd56
Priozer'e RUS 113 Jc57
Pripiceni-Răzeși MD 173 Fd56
Priponești RO 177 Fa61
Prisad BG 181 Ed73
Prisad MK 183 Bc75
Prisches F 24 Hc32
Prisdorf D 118 Db32
Priselci BG 181 Fa71
Prisjan SRB 179 Ca70
Prisoja MNE 159 Jb68
Prisoje BIH 158 Gd65
Prissac F 29 Gb44
Pristeg HR 157 Ga65
Priština KSV 178 Bb71
Pristoe BG 181 Ed69
Prittitz D 127 Ea41
Prittriching D 142 Dc50
Pritzerbe D 127 Ec36
Pritzier D 119 Dd33
Pritzwalk D 119 Eb34
Privas F 34 Ja50
Priverno I 160 Ec73
Privlaka HR 153 Hd60
Privlaka HR 157 Fd64
Privol'noe RUS 113 Jc58
Privolžsk RUS 203 Fa09
Privuž RUS 99 Ld44
Prižba HR 158 Gc68
Priziac F 27 Ea39
Prizna HR 151 Fc63
Prizren KSV 178 Ba72
Prizzi I 166 Ec85
Prjamicyno RUS 203 Fa13
Prkosi BIH 152 Gb63
Prnjavor BIH 152 Ha62
Prnjavor SRB 153 Ja62
Proaza E 37 Cb55
Probota RO 172 Ec56
Probota RO 173 Fa57
Probsteierhagen D 118 Dc30
Probstzella D 135 Dd43
Probuda BG 181 Ec70
Probus GB 18 Db32
Procchio I 155 Da68
Próchnowo PL 121 Gc35
Prochod BG 181 Ec73
Prochowice PL 129 Gb40
Procida I 161 Fa75
Prodan AL 182 Ad78
Prodănești MD 173 Fc55
Prodo I 156 Ea68
Prodromi CY 206 Hd97
Prodromos CY 206 Ja97
Pródromos GR 188 Ad84
Pródromos GR 189 Ca85
Produlești RO 176 Dd65
Proença-a-Nova P 44 Ba65
Proença-a-Velha P 44 Bb65
Profesor Išírkovo BG 181 Ed68
Profitis GR 183 Cb78
Profítis Ilías GR 200 Da96
Progër AL 182 Ba77
Progresu RO 176 Eb66
Prohladnoe RUS 113 Jb57
Prohn D 119 Ed30
Próhoma GR 183 Ca77
Prohor Pčinski SRB 178 Bb72
Prokópi GR 189 Cb84
Prokuplje SRB 178 Bc69
Prolaz BG 180 Eb70
Proletarij RUS 202 Eb09
Proletarsk RUS 205 Fd15
Prolog HR 158 Ha67
Prolom SRB 178 Bc69
Prómahi GR 183 Bc76
Promahónas GR 184 Cc75
Promiri GR 189 Cb82
Promna PL 130 Jb38
Promnik PL 130 Jb41
Proniewicze PL 123 Kb34
Pronin RUS 203 Fc14
Pronsfeld D 133 Bc43
Pronstorf D 118 Dc31
Propriano F 154 Ca71
Proseč CZ 137 Ga45
Prosek AL 163 Jc71
Prösen D 128 Fa40
Prosenik BG 181 Ed72
Prosenjakovci SLO 145 Gb55
Prosienica PL 123 Jd34
Prosiměřice CZ 137 Gb48
Prosjek BIH 159 Ja65
Prosperous IRL 13 Cc21
Prossedi I 160 Ec73
Prosselsheim D 134 Db45
Prossotsáni GR 184 Cd76
Prostějov CZ 137 Gc46
Prostki PL 123 Ka32
Prostorno BG 180 Eb69
Prószków PL 137 Ha43
Proszowice PL 138 Jb44
Proszówki PL 138 Jb44
Próti GR 184 Cd77
Protići BIH 152 Gd63
Protivanov CZ 137 Gc46
Protivín CZ 136 Fb47
Protokklísi GR 185 Ea76
Prottes A 145 Gc50
Prötzel D 128 Fa36
Proussós GR 188 Bb83
Provadija BG 181 Ed70
Provadura E 36 Bb56
Provåker S 80 Ha28
Provatás GR 184 Cc76
Provató GR 185 Ea77
Provenchères F 31 Kb38
Provins F 30 Hb38
Provištip MK 178 Bd73
Provița de Sus RO 176 Ea64
Provo SRB 153 Jb62
Prozor HR 151 Fd62
Prozor = Rama BIH 158 Ha65
Prožura HR 158 Ha69
Prrenjas AL 182 Ad76
Pruchnik PL 139 Kb44
Prudentov RUS 203 Ga13
Prudhoe GB 11 Ed16
Prudnik PL 137 Gd43
Prudy RUS 113 Ja58
Prudziszki PL 123 Ka30
Prügy H 147 Jd50
Prüm D 133 Bc43
Pruna E 59 Cb75
Prundeni RO 175 Db65
Prundu RO 180 Eb67
Prundu Bârgăului RO 171 Dc57
Prunelli di Fiumorbo F 154 Cb70
Prunete F 154 Cc70
Prunetta I 155 Db64
Pruniers-en-Sologne F 29 Gc42
Prunișor RO 175 Cc65
Prunkila FIN 97 Jc39
Prusac BIH 158 Ha64
Prusak PL 129 Hb40
Pruśce PL 121 Gc35
Prūšeliai LT 114 Kd54
Prusice PL 129 Gc40
Prūšiši LV 107 Lb50
Pruské SK 137 Hb48
Pruszcz PL 121 Gd33
Pruszcz PL 121 Ha33
Pruszcz Gdański PL 121 Hb30
Pruszków PL 130 Jb37
Pruszyn PL 131 Ka37
Pruteni MD 173 Fa56
Pružany BY 202 Dd13
Pružicy RUS 99 Ma41
Pružina SK 137 Hb48
Pryazovs'ke UA 205 Fa16
Pryłęk PL 139 Jd43
Pryluky UA 202 Ed14
Prymors'k UA 205 Fb16
Przasnysz PL 122 Jb34
Przebród PL 123 Ka30
Przechlewo PL 121 Gc32
Przechów PL 137 Gd43
Przeciszów PL 138 Hd44
Przecław PL 120 Fb33
Przecław PL 139 Jd43
Przecławice PL 129 Gc41
Przeczów PL 129 Gd41
Przedbórz PL 130 Ja41
Przedbórz PL 139 Jd43
Przedecz PL 130 Hc37
Przedświt PL 122 Jc35
Przegędza PL 137 Hb44
Przekolno PL 120 Fd34
Przełęk PL 137 Gd43
Przelewice PL 120 Fc34
Przemęt PL 129 Gb38
Przemiarowo PL 122 Jb35
Przemków PL 128 Ga40
Przemocze PL 120 Fc33
Przemyśl PL 139 Kb44
Przerośl PL 123 Ka30
Przerzeczyn-Zdrój PL 129 Gc42
Przesmyki PL 131 Ka36
Przewłoka PL 121 Gc29
Przewłoka PL 131 Kb38
Przeworno PL 129 Gc42
Przeworsk PL 139 Kb44
Przewóz PL 128 Fc40
Przewóz PL 129 Hb36
Przewrotne PL 139 Ka43
Przezmark PL 122 Hc31
Przine Zdralovac BIH 158 Gc64
Przodkowo PL 121 Ha30
Przybiernów PL 120 Fc32
Przyborowice PL 130 Ja36
Przybychowo PL 121 Gb35
Przybysławice PL 131 Ka39
Przydonica PL 138 Jc45
Przygodzice PL 129 Ha39
Przyjezierze PL 129 Ha36
Przykona PL 129 Hb38
Przyłęg PL 120 Fd35
Przyłęki PL 121 Ha34
Przylep PL 128 Fd38
Przyłubie PL 121 Ha34
Przyrów PL 130 Hd42
Przystajń PL 129 Hb41
Przystawka PL 123 Kb32
Przystawy PL 121 Gb30
Przysucha PL 130 Jb40
Przyszów PL 131 Ka42
Przytoczna PL 128 Ga36
Przytoczno PL 131 Ka38
Przytyk PL 130 Jb39
Przywidz PL 121 Ha30
Przywory PL 137 Ha43
Przywóz PL 129 Hb41
Psača MK 178 Bd73
Psahná GR 189 Cb84
Psará GR 190 Dc85
Psarádes GR 182 Ba76
Psári GR 189 Bc86
Psary PL 130 Hc42
Psáthi GR 195 Cd90
Psáthi GR 196 Db91
Psebaj RUS 205 Fd17
Psérimos GR 197 Ec91
Psihikó GR 184 Cc77
Psínthos GR 197 Fa93
Pskov RUS 107 Ma46
Pskov RUS 202 Ea10
Pskovskoje RUS 113 Jd59
Pšovlky CZ 136 Fa44
Pstrągowa PL 139 Jd44
Pszczew PL 128 Ga36
Pszczółki PL 121 Hb31
Pszczyna PL 138 Hc44
Pszów PL 137 Hb44
Pteléa GR 184 Da76
Pteleós GR 189 Ca83
Pteriá GR 182 Ba77
Ptolemaïda GR 183 Bb78
Ptuj SLO 151 Ga57
Ptujska Gora SLO 151 Ga57
Pūces LV 105 Jd51
Pučež RUS 203 Fb09
Puchaczów PL 131 Kb39
Puchały Stare PL 123 Kb35
Püchau D 127 Ec40
Puchberg am Schneeberg A 144 Ga52
Pucheni RO 176 Dd63
Puchenii Mari RO 176 Eb65
Püchersreuth D 135 Eb45
Puchheim A 144 Fa51
Puchheim D 143 Dd51
Púchov SK 137 Hb47
Pucioasa RO 176 Dd64
Pučišća HR 158 Gc67
Puck PL 121 Ha29
Puckakaun IRL 13 Ca22
Puçol E 54 Fc67
Puczniew PL 130 Hc38
Pudas FIN 69 Ka14
Pudas S 73 Jb19
Pudasjärvi FIN 75 Kc22
Puddletown GB 19 Ec30
Puderbach D 125 Ca42
Pudinava LV 107 Lc50
Pudob SLO 151 Fb59
Pudost' RUS 99 Mb40
Puebla de Albortón E 47 Fa61
Puebla de Alcocer E 52 Cc69
Puebla de Alfindén E 48 Fb61
Puebla de Almenara E 53 Ea66
Puebla de Brollón E 36 Bc57
Puebla de Don Fadrique E 61 Ea72
Puebla de Don Rodrigo E 52 Cd68
Puebla de Guzmán E 59 Bb73
Puebla de la Calzada E 51 Bc69
Puebla de la Reina E 51 Ca69
Puebla de la Sierra E 46 Dc62
Puebla de Lillo E 37 Cd56
Puebla del Maestre E 51 Ca71
Puebla del Príncipe E 53 Dd70
Puebla del Prior E 51 Bd70
Puebla del Salvator E 53 Ec67
Puebla de Obando E 51 Bc68
Puebla de Sanabria E 37 Bd58
Puebla de Sancho Pérez E 51 Bd70
Puebla de San Julián (Láncara) E 36 Bc56
Puebla de San Miguel E 54 Fa66
Puebla de Trives E 36 Bc57
Puebla de Vallés E 46 Dd63
Puente Almuhey E 37 Cd56
Puente Arce E 38 Dc54
Puente de Domingo Flórez E 37 Bd57
Puente de Génave E 53 Ea71
Puente de los Fierros E 37 Cc55
Puente de Montañana E 48 Ga59
Puente de Sanabria E 37 Bd58
Puente de San Martín E 37 Cb54
Puente de Vadillos E 47 Eb64
Puentedey E 38 Dc56
Puentedura E 46 Dc59
Puente-Genil E 60 Cd74
Puente la Reina E 39 Ec57
Puente la Reina de Jaca E 39 Fb58
Puentelarrá E 38 Ea57
Puentenansa (Rionansa) E 38 Db55
Puente Pumar E 38 Db55
Puente Viesgo E 38 Dc55
Puertas E 45 Ca62
Puerto de Conil E 59 Bd77
Puerto de Mazarrón E 55 Ed74
Puerto de Santa Cruz E 51 Ca67
Puerto de San Vicente E 52 Cc67
Puerto de Vega E 37 Ca53
Puerto Hurraco E 51 Cb70
Puerto-Lápice E 52 Dc68
Puertollano E 52 Da70
Puerto Lumbreras E 61 Ec74
Puertomingalvo E 54 Fb65
Puerto Real E 59 Bd76
Puerto Rey E 52 Cc67
Puerto Seguro E 45 Bd62
Puerto Serrano E 59 Cb75
Pueyo de Fañanás E 48 Fc59
Pufești RO 176 Ed61
Pugačev RUS 203 Ga11
Pugačevo RUS 113 Jd59
Puget-Théniers F 43 Kc52
Puget-Ville F 42 Ka54
Pugieu F 35 Jc46
Pugnac F 32 Fb49
Pugnochiuso I 162 Gb72
Puhăceni MD 173 Ga58
Puhar-Onkimaa FIN 90 Kc38
Puhja EST 98 La45
Puhoi MD 173 Fd58
Puhos FIN 75 Kd22
Puhos FIN 91 Ld32
Puhovac BIH 158 Hb64
Puhtaleiva EST 99 Lb45
Pui RO 175 Cc62
Puianello I 149 Db62
Puiatu EST 98 Kd45
Puicheric F 41 Ha55
Puiești RO 176 Ed63
Puiești RO 177 Fa60
Puig E 54 Fc67
Puigcerdà E 41 Gd58
Puigpunyent E 57 Hb67
Puig-reig E 49 Gd59
Puijas LV 105 Jd52
Puikule LV 106 Kc48
Puise EST 98 Ka44
Puiseaux F 29 Gd39
Puissalicon F 41 Hc54
Puisserguier F 41 Hb55
Puivert F 41 Gd56
Puka EST 106 La46
Pukalaidun FIN 89 Jc37
Pukanec SK 146 Hc50
Pukara FIN 89 Jc34
Pukara FIN 89 Jc35
Pukaro FIN 90 Kd38
Pukavik S 111 Fc54
Pukë AL 163 Jb71
Pukiš BIH 153 Hd62
Pukkila FIN 90 Kc38
Pula HR 151 Fa62
Pula I 169 Ca80
Pulaj AL 163 Ja71
Puławy PL 131 Jd39
Pulborough GB 20 Fc30
Pulfero I 150 Ed57
Pulgar E 52 Da67
Pulham Market GB 21 Gb25
Pulheim D 125 Bd40
Puliciano I 156 Dd66
Pulju FIN 68 Jc13
Pulkarne LV 106 Kb51
Pulkau A 136 Ga49
Pulkkala FIN 97 Jb40
Pulkkaviita FIN 69 Kd16
Pulkkila FIN 82 Kb26
Pulkkila FIN 90 Kc36
Pulkkinen FIN 81 Jc29
Pulkonkoski FIN 82 Kd29
Pulkovo RUS 99 Mb39
Pullach D 143 Dd51
Pullar TR 192 Ga83
Pullenreuth D 135 Eb45
Pullenried D 135 Eb46
Pulpí E 61 Ec74
Pulsa FIN 91 Lb36
Pulsano I 162 Ha76
Pulsen D 127 Ed40
Pulsnitz D 128 Fa41
Pulsujärvi S 67 Hb13
Pułtusk PL 122 Jb35
Pülümür TR 205 Ga20
Pulversheim F 31 Kb39
Pumpėnai LT 114 Kc54
Pumpula FIN 91 Lb36
Pumsaint GB 15 Dd26
Puņas LV 105 Jc49
Punat HR 151 Fc61
Puncești RO 173 Fa59
Pundrovka RUS 107 Mb49
Pundsvika N 66 Ga13
Punduri RUS 107 Ld49
Punghina RO 175 Cc66
Pungsetrene N 85 Dd35
Punia LT 114 Kc59
Punkaharju FIN 91 Ld33
Punsk PL 123 Kb30
Punta Ala I 155 Db68
Punta di San Vigilio I 149 Db59
Punta Križa HR 151 Fb62
Punta Marina I 150 Ea63
Punta Prima E 57 Jb66
Puntari FIN 90 Ka35
Punta Sabbioni I 150 Eb60
Punta Secca I 167 Fb88
Punta skala HR 157 Fd64
Punta Umbria E 59 Bb74
Puoddopohki FIN 64 Jd08
Puokio FIN 75 Kc24
Puolakkavaara FIN 69 Ka15
Puolanka FIN 75 Kd23
Puoltikasvaara S 68 Hc16
Puoltsa S 67 Ha15
Puottaure S 73 Hb20
Pupāji LV 107 Lc52
Pupnat HR 158 Gd68
Puraći BIH 152 Ha61
Puračić BIH 153 Hc63
Puralankylä FIN 82 Ka30
Purani RO 180 Dd67
Puraperä FIN 82 Ka28
Puras FIN 75 Lb23
Purchena E 61 Eb74
Purda PL 122 Ja32
Purdoški RUS 203 Fc10
Pūre LV 105 Jd50
Purgatorio I 166 Eb84
Purila EST 98 Kb43
Purini LV 106 Kb52
Puriton GB 19 Eb29
Purkersdorf A 145 Gb51
Purkjaur S 72 Ha19
Pürksi EST 98 Ka44
Purmerend NL 116 Ba35
Purmo FIN 81 Jb29
Purmojärvi FIN 81 Jc30
Purmsati LV 113 Jb53
Purnu S 73 Hc18
Purnumukka FIN 69 Ka13
Purnuvaara FIN 75 Kd20
Purnuvaara S 68 Hc17
Purola Svartbäck FIN 90 La38
Puromäki FIN 83 Lc31
Puronkylä FIN 82 Kc30
Purontaka FIN 81 Jd28
Puroranta FIN 82 Kc25
Pürsünler TR 192 Fb83
Purtovaara FIN 83 Ma31
Purtse EST 99 Lb42
Purunpää FIN 97 Jb41
Purvėnai LT 114 La59
Purveniai LT 113 Jd53
Purviniškė LV 114 Kb58
Puryševo RUS 107 Mb50
Puša LV 107 Ld52
Pusaankylä FIN 89 Jd32
Pušalotas LT 114 Kc54
Puškarevo RUS 113 Jb59
Puski EST 97 Jc44
Puškino RUS 203 Ga12
Puškinskie Gory RUS 107 Mb49
Puškinskie Gory RUS 202 Ea10
Pušmucova LV 107 Ld50
Pusnė LT 114 La56
Püspökladány H 147 Jd53
Pussay F 29 Gc38
Püssi EST 99 Lb42
Pustec AL 182 Ba76
Pustelnik PL 130 Jc36
Pusterwald A 144 Fb54
Pustevny CZ 137 Hb46
Pustoe Voskresen'e RUS 107 Ma49
Pustoška RUS 99 Ma42
Pustoška RUS 202 Eb11
Pustoški RUS 107 Ma49
Pustritz A 144 Fc55
Pustynia PL 139 Jd44
Pustynki RUS 107 Mb47
Pusula FIN 98 Ka39
Puszcza Mariańska PL 130 Ja38
Puszczykowo PL 129 Gc37
Pusztacsalád H 145 Gc53
Pusztakovácsi H 145 Ha56
Pusztamiske H 145 Gd54
Pusztaszabolcs H 146 Hc54
Pusztaszentlászló H 145 Gc56
Pusztavám H 145 Hb53
Putaja FIN 89 Jb36
Putanges F 22 Fc37
Putbus D 120 Fa30
Putgarten D 120 Fa29
Putignano I 162 Gd75
Putikko FIN 91 Ld33
Putinci SRB 153 Jb61
Putineiu RO 180 Dc68
Putineiu RO 180 Ea68
Putkela FIN 83 Lb29
Putkilahti FIN 90 Kc34
Putkivaara FIN 74 Kb19
Putla EST 105 Jc46
Putlitz D 119 Eb34

Putna – Rathen

Putna RO 172 Ea55
Putnok H 146 Jb50
Putte NL 124 Ac38
Puttelange-aux-Lacs F 25 Ka35
Putten NL 116 Bb36
Puttenham GB 20 Fb29
Puttgarden D 119 Ea29
Püttlingen D 133 Bc46
Putula FIN 90 Kb36
Putyvl' UA 202 Ed13
Putzu'Idu I 169 Bd77
Puujaa FIN 90 Kb37
Puukari FIN 83 Lb27
Puukkoinen FIN 90 Kb34
Puukkokumpu FIN 74 Jd21
Puukonsaari FIN 90 Kd34
Puulansalmi FIN 90 Kd34
Puumala FIN 91 Lb34
Puuppola FIN 90 Kb32
Puurmani EST 98 La44
Puurtila FIN 90 La32
Puurtturinjärvi FIN 74 Kb24
Puutikkala FIN 90 Ka36
Puutossalmi FIN 82 La30
Puutteenperä FIN 74 Jd21
Puycasquier F 40 Ga54
Puydrouard F 32 Fb46
Puy-Guillaume F 34 Hc46
Puylagarde F 40 Gc52
Puylaroque F 40 Gc52
Puylaurens F 41 Gd54
Puy-l'Evêque F 33 Gb51
Puymiclan F 32 Fd51
Puymirol F 40 Ga52
Puyôo F 39 Fa54
Puy-Saint-Martin F 34 Jb50
Puy-Saint-Vincent F 35 Ka49
Puzači RUS 203 Fa13
Puzenieki LV 105 Jc50
Pwllheli GB 14 Dc23
Pyecombe GB 20 Fc30
Pyhäjärvi FIN 69 Jd11
Pyhäjärvi FIN 69 Kb16
Pyhäjärvi FIN 82 Kb28
Pyhäjoki FIN 81 Jc26
Pyhäjoki FIN 89 Jb37
Pyhäkoski FIN 90 Kd35
Pyhäkylä FIN 75 La22
Pyhälahti FIN 82 Kc31
Pyhältö FIN 90 La37
Pyhämaa FIN 89 Ja38
Pyhänkoski FIN 81 Jd26
Pyhänsivu FIN 74 Kb24
Pyhäntä FIN 82 Kb26
Pyhäntaka FIN 90 Kc36
Pyhäranta FIN 89 Ja38
Pyhäsalmi FIN 82 Kb28
Pyhäselkä FIN 83 Ld31
Pyhe FIN 97 Ja39
Pyhtää FIN 90 Kd38
Þykkvibær IS 2 Ac05
Pyla CY 206 Jc97
Pyla-sur-Mer F 32 Fa51
Pyle GB 19 Ea28
Pyli GR 188 Bb81
Pylkönmäki FIN 82 Ka31
Pylvänälä FIN 90 Kd33
Pylväsperä FIN 81 Jd27
Pyntäinen FIN 89 Ja34
Pyöli FIN 89 Jd38
Pyöree FIN 82 Kd27
Pyöreinen FIN 82 La29
Pyörni FIN 89 Ja32
Pyrbaum D 135 Dd47
Pyrénées 2000 F 41 Gd58
Pyrga CY 206 Jb97
Pyrga CY 206 Jc96
Þyrill IS 2 Ac04
Pyrjatyn UA 202 Ed14
Pyrzowice PL 138 Hc43
Pyrzyce PL 120 Fc34
Pyskowice PL 137 Hb43
Pyssykangas FIN 89 Ja36
Pyssyperä FIN 75 Kd23
Pystyoja FIN 64 Jc10
Pysznica PL 131 Ka42
Pytalovo RUS 107 Ld49
Pytalovo (Abrene) RUS 202 Ea10
Pytkynharju FIN 75 Kc21
Pytten N 92 Cc44
Pyttis FIN 90 Kd38
Pyydyskylä FIN 82 Kc31
Pyydysmäki FIN 89 Jd34
Pyykkölänvaara FIN 75 La24
Pyyli FIN 91 Lc32
Pyyrinlahti FIN 82 Kb31
Pyzdry PL 129 Gd37

Q

Qafë-Murrë AL 163 Jc72
Qafëzez AL 182 Ad77
Qarrishtë AL 182 Ad75
Qinam AL 182 Ab74
Qormi M 166 Eb88
Quafmollë AL 182 Ac74
Quaglietta I 161 Fd75
Quainton GB 20 Fb27
Quakenbrück D 117 Cc35
Qualiano I 161 Fa75
Quarff GB 5 Fa05
Quarnbek D 118 Dc30
Quarona I 148 Ca58
Quarré-les-Tombes F 30 Hd41
Quarteira P 58 Ac74
Quarto d'Altino I 150 Eb59
Quartu San Elena I 169 Ca79
Quasano I 162 Gc74
Quattro Venti, i I 161 Fb73
Quebradas P 50 Ab67
Quecedo E 38 Dd56
Quédillac F 27 Ec39
Quedlinburg D 127 Dd38
Queidersbach D 133 Ca46
Queiruga E 36 Ac56
Quelaines F 28 Fb40
Quellendorf D 127 Eb39
Quemada E 46 Dc60
Quemigny-Poisot F 30 Ja42
Quend F 23 Gc32
Quenstedt D 127 Ea39
Queralbs E 41 Gd58
Querceta I 155 Da64
Quercianella I 155 Da66
Querenhorst D 127 Dd37
Querfurt D 127 Ea40
Quero E 53 Dd67
Querol E 49 Gc61
Querrin IRL 12 Bb23
Quers F 31 Ka40
Quesada E 61 Dd73
Quessoy F 26 Eb38
Questembert F 27 Eb41
Quettehou F 22 Fa34
Quettetot F 22 Ed35
Queudes F 24 Hc37
Quevauvillers F 23 Gd33
Quevert F 26 Ec38
Quiaios P 44 Ac64
Quiberon F 27 Ea41
Quickborn D 118 Db32
Quiddelbach D 133 Bd43
Quigley's Point IRL 9 Cc15
Quillan F 41 Gd56
Quilly F 27 Ec41
Quilty IRL 12 Bb22
Quimper F 27 Dc39
Quimperlé F 27 Dd40
Quin IRL 12 Bc22
Quincoces de Yuso E 38 Dd56
Quindós E 37 Bd56
Quinéville F 22 Fa35
Quingey F 31 Jd42
Quiñonería E 47 Ec61
Quinsac F 32 Fb50
Quinson F 42 Ka53
Quinta do Lago P 58 Ac74
Quintana E 37 Ca55
Quintana E 37 Cc54
Quintana de Castillo E 37 Cb57
Quintana de la Serena E 51 Cb69
Quintana del Marco E 37 Cb58
Quintana del Puente E 46 Db59
Quintanadueñas E 38 Dc58
Quintanaélez E 38 Dd57
Quintana-Martín Galíndez E 38 Dd57
Quintanapalla E 38 Dc58
Quintanar de la Orden E 53 Dd67
Quintanar de la Sierra E 46 Dd59
Quintanar del Rey E 53 Ec68
Quintana Redonda E 47 Ea60
Quintanilla de Arriba E 46 Db60
Quintanilla de Flórez E 37 Cb58
Quintanilla del Agua E 46 Dc59
Quintanilla de la Mata E 46 Dc59
Quintanilla del Coco E 46 Dc59
Quintanilla del Molar E 45 Cc59
Quintanilla de Losada E 37 Ca58
Quintanilla de los Oteros E 37 Cc58
Quintanilla de Onésimo E 46 Da60
Quintanilla de Pienza E 38 Dd56
Quintanilla de Trigueros E 46 Da59
Quintanilla-Pedro Abarca E 38 Dc57
Quintanilla San García E 38 Dd57
Quintanilla-Sobresierra E 38 Dc57
Quintela E 37 Bd56
Quintela de Leirado E 36 Ba58
Quintes E 37 Cc54
Quint-Fonsegrives F 40 Gc54
Quintin F 26 Eb38
Quintinilla Rucandio E 38 Dc56
Quinto E 48 Fb61
Quintos P 50 Ad71
Quinto Vercellese I 148 Ca59
Quinzano d'Oglio I 149 Da60
Quiroga E 36 Bc57
Quirra I 169 Cb79
Quismondo E 46 Da65
Quissac F 41 Hd53
Quistello I 149 Dc61
Quistinic F 27 Ea40
Quittebeuf F 23 Ga36
Quitzdorf am See D 128 Fc40
Qukës AL 182 Ad75
Qundle GB 20 Fc25

R

Rå S 79 Gb30
Råå S 110 Ed55
Raab A 144 Fa50
Raabs an der Thaya A 136 Fd48
Raahe FIN 81 Jd25
Raajärvi FIN 74 Kb18
Raakku FIN 74 Kc18
Rääkkylä FIN 83 Ld31
Raalte NL 117 Bc36
Raanujärvi FIN 74 Jc18
Raappananmäki FIN 82 Kd25
Raappanansuo FIN 75 Kd21
Raasdorf A 145 Gb50
Raasiku EST 98 Kc42
Raasinkorpi FIN 89 Jb38
Raatala FIN 97 Jc39
Raate FIN 75 Lb23
Raatevaara FIN 83 Ma31
Raattama FIN 68 Jb14
Raatti FIN 82 La29
Rab HR 151 Fc62
Rabac HR 151 Fb61
Rabaçal P 44 Bb62
Rábade E 36 Bb55
Rábafüzes H 145 Gb55
Răbăgani RO 170 Cb58
Rabahidvég H 145 Gc54
Rabal E 36 Bc57
Rabanal de Camino E 37 Ca57
Rábano E 46 Db61
Rábano de Sanabria E 37 Bd58
Rábasömjen H 145 Gc54
Rabastens F 40 Gc53
Rabastens-de-Bigorre F 40 Fd55
Rabat M 166 Eb88
Rabatamasi H 145 Gd53
Raba Wyżna PL 138 Ja46
Rabenau D 126 Cd42
Rabenau D 128 Fa41
Rabensberg A 137 Gc49
Rabenstein A 144 Fd51
Råberg S 80 Gc26
Rabí CZ 136 Fa47
Rabino PL 120 Ga32
Rabiša BG 179 Cb68
Rabka-Zdrój PL 138 Ja46
Rabouillet F 41 Ha57
Rabrovo BG 179 Cb67
Rabrovo SRB 174 Bd64
Rabštejn nad St. CZ 135 Ed44
Rabsztyn PL 138 Hd43
Råby-Rekarne S 95 Ga43
Råby-Rönö S 95 Gb45
Rača SK 145 Gd51
Rača SRB 174 Bb65
Rača SRB 178 Bc70
Râcacaciuni RO 176 Ed60
Racale I 165 Hc78
Rácalmás H 146 Hc54
Racalmuto I 166 Ed86
Răcari RO 176 Ea65
Răcăria MD 173 Fa55
Răcășdia RO 174 Bd63
Racconigi I 148 Bc61
Raccuia I 167 Fc84
Rače SLO 144 Ga56
Rachanie PL 131 Kd42
Rachecourt-sur-Marne F 24 Jb37
Răchitoasa RO 177 Fa60
Răchitova RO 175 Cc61
Rachiv UA 204 Ea16
Raciąż PL 121 Gd32
Raciąż PL 122 Ja35
Raciążek PL 121 Hb35
Raciborsko PL 138 Ja44
Racibórz PL 137 Hb44
Raciechowice PL 138 Ja45
Račinovci HR 153 Hd61
Račišće HR 158 Gd68
Răciu RO 171 Db58
Răciula MD 173 Fd57
Račja Vas HR 151 Fa60
Rackeby S 102 Ed46
Ráckeve H 146 Hc54
Racków PL 129 Gb41
Racksund S 72 Gc21
Rackwitz D 127 Eb40
Racławice PL 138 Ja43
Racławice Śląskie PL 137 Ha43
Răcoasa RO 176 Ed61
Racoș RO 176 Dd61
Racot PL 129 Gb38
Racova RO 172 Ec59
Racovăț MD 173 Fc54
Racovița RO 175 Db62
Racovița RO 175 Db62
Racovițeni RO 176 Ec63
Răculești MD 173 Fd57
Rączki PL 122 Ja33
Råda S 94 Fa41
Råda S 102 Ed46
Radakowice PL 129 Gc41
Radalj SRB 153 Hd63
Rådanefors S 102 Ec46
Radanje MK 183 Bd74
Radanovo BG 180 Dd70
Radapole LV 107 Lc51
Rădășeni RO 172 Eb56
Radaškovičy BY 202 Ea12
Rădăuți RO 172 Eb55
Rădăuți-Prut RO 172 Ed54
Radawie PL 129 Hb42
Radawnica PL 121 Gc33
Radbruch D 118 Dc33
Radbyn S 102 Fa46
Radcliffe GB 15 Ec21
Radda in Chianti I 155 Dc66
Raddestorf D 126 Cd36
Raddon F 31 Ka39
Raddusa I 167 Fb86
Råde N 93 Ea43
Radeberg D 128 Fa41
Radebeul D 128 Fa41
Radeburg D 128 Fa40
Radeburg D 128 Fa41
Radeče SLO 151 Fd58
Radechiv UA 204 Ea15
Radęcin PL 120 Ga34
Radecki BG 180 Ea73
Radecznica PL 131 Kb41
Radefeld D 127 Eb40
Radegast D 119 Eb31
Radegast D 127 Eb39
Radenci SLO 145 Gb56
Rădeni MD 173 Fc57
Rădenii Vechi MD 173 Fb57
Radenthein A 144 Fa55
Rădești RO 171 Da59
Radevo BG 180 Ea73
Radevo KSV 178 Bb71
Radevormwald D 125 Ca40
Radgoszcz PL 138 Jc43
Radhimë AL 182 Aa77
Radibor D 128 Fb41
Radičevicevo SRB 153 Jb59
Radići BIH 152 Gd63
Radicofani I 156 Dd68
Radicondoli I 155 Db67
Radievo BG 185 Dd74
Radijovce MK 178 Ba73
Radilovo BG 179 Da73
Radis D 127 Ec39
Radizel SLO 144 Ga56
Radków PL 130 Ja42
Radków PL 137 Gb43
Radkowice PL 130 Jc41
Radlett GB 20 Fc27
Radlin PL 129 Gd38
Radlje ob Dravi SLO 144 Fd56
Radljevo SRB 153 Jc63
Radłow PL 129 Hb41
Radłow PL 138 Jc44
Radmansö S 96 Ha42
Radmer an der Hasel A 144 Fc53
Radmirje SLO 151 Fc57
Radnejaur S 72 Gc21
Radnevo BG 180 Ea73
Radnica PL 128 Fd38
Radnice CZ 136 Fa45
Rădoaia MD 173 Fb55
Radohova BIH 152 Ha63
Rădoiești RO 180 Dc67
Radojevo SRB 174 Bc60
Radojewice PL 121 Hb35
Radolfzell D 142 Cc52
Radom PL 130 Jc39
Rådom S 94 Ed41
Radomice PL 122 Hc35
Radomicko PL 128 Fc38
Radomicko PL 129 Gb38
Radomierzyce PL 128 Fc41
Radomin PL 122 Hc34
Radomir BG 179 Cb71
Radomirci BG 179 Da69
Radomirești RO 180 Db67
Radomno PL 122 Hc33
Radomsko PL 130 Hd41
Radomyšl CZ 136 Fa47
Radomyšl' UA 202 Eb14
Radomyśl n. Sanem PL 131 Ka42
Radomyśl Wielki PL 138 Jc43
Radonice CZ 135 Ed44
Radošice CZ 136 Fa46
Radošina SK 137 Ha49
Radošovce SK 137 Gd49
Radostowo PL 122 Ja31
Radoszewice PL 130 Hc40
Radoszki PL 122 Hd33
Radoszyce PL 130 Ja41
Radoszyn PL 128 Fd37
Radovac KSV 178 Ad70
Radovac SRB 159 Jc68
Radovan RO 175 Cd66
Radovanu RO 180 Ed67
Radovče MNE 159 Ja69
Radovec BG 185 Eb74
Radovel' RUS 99 Lc42
Radovesice CZ 136 Fb43
Radovići MNE 159 Hd70
Radoviš MK 183 Ca74
Radovljica SLO 151 Fb57
Radowo Wielkie PL 120 Fd32
Radozda MK 182 Ad75
Radstadt A 143 Ed53
Radsted DK 109 Eb29
Răducăneni RO 173 Fb58
Radučić HR 158 Gb64
Raduil BG 179 Cd72
Radujevac SRB 174 Cb66
Rădulenii Vechi MD 173 Fc55
Raduń PL 120 Fd34
Radunci BG 180 Dd72
Radu Negru RO 181 Ed67
Raduša MK 178 Bb72
Raduszec PL 128 Fd38
Radvaň nad Laborcom SK 139 Ka47
Radviliškis LT 114 Kb54
Radwanice PL 128 Ga39
Radwanów PL 128 Fd39
Radymno PL 139 Kb44
Radzanów PL 122 Ja34
Radzanów PL 130 Jb39
Radzanowo PL 130 Hd36
Radzewice PL 129 Gc37
Radzice Duże PL 130 Ja39
Radzieje PL 122 Jc30
Radziejów PL 129 Hb36
Radziejowice PL 130 Jb37
Radziemice PL 138 Ja43
Radziki Duże PL 122 Hc34
Radzików PL 128 Fc37
Radzików Wielki PL 131 Ka37
Radziłów PL 123 Ka33
Radzinciems LV 106 Ka50
Radzionków PL 138 Hc43
Radziszewo PL 120 Fb34
Radziwie PL 130 Hd36
Radziwiłłówka PL 131 Kb36
Radzymin PL 130 Jc36
Radzyń Chełmiński PL 121 Hb33
Radzyń Podlaski PL 131 Ka38
Raec MK 183 Bc75
Ræhr DK 100 Da20
Rækker Mølle DK 108 Da24
Raelingen N 93 Ea41
Rae na nDoirí IRL 12 Bb25
Raeren B 125 Bb41
Raesfeld D 125 Bd38
Rafelbuñol E 54 Fc67
Rafelbunyol E 54 Fc67
Raffadali I 166 Ed86
Rafina GR 189 Cc86
Rafov RO 176 Eb65
Rafsbotn N 63 Hd08
Raftópoulo GR 188 Ba82
Raftsjöhöjden S 79 Fc29
Ragaciems LV 106 Ka50
Ragály H 138 Jb49
Ragana LV 106 Kc49
Rågeleje DK 109 Ec24
Rägelin D 119 Ec35
Råggärd S 94 Ec45
Raghly IRL 8 Bd17
Råglanda S 94 Ed44
Ragnabo S 111 Ga53
Ragnitz A 144 Ga55
Ragösen D 127 Ec37
Ragow D 128 Fb37
Ragozino RUS 107 Ma48
Raguhn D 127 Eb39
Ragunda S 79 Ga31
Ragusa I 167 Fc87
Raguva LT 114 Kd55
Raguvėlė LT 114 Kd55
Raguviškiai LT 113 Jb55
Ragvaldsnäs S 88 Gc34
Rahačov BY 202 Eb13
Rahan IRL 13 Cb21
Raharney IRL 9 Cc20
Rahden D 126 Cd36
Ráhes GR 189 Bd83
Ráhes GR 194 Bb87
Raheste EST 106 Ka46
Rahikka FIN 89 Ja33
Rahja FIN 81 Jc27
Rahkee FIN 83 Ld29
Rahkio FIN 89 Jc38
Rahkla EST 98 La43
Rahkamala FIN 89 Ja38
Rahkonen FIN 81 Jd28
Rahman RO 177 Fb65
Rahmanca TR 185 Eb76
Rahmanlar TR 192 Fc85
Raholanvaara FIN 83 Lb29
Råholt N 94 Eb40
Rahoúla GR 188 Bb82
Rahoúla GR 189 Bc81
Rahula FIN 90 La34
Rahumäe EST 107 Lc46
Raiano I 161 Fa71
Raič HR 152 Gc58
Raijala FIN 89 Jb37
Raikküla EST 98 Kb44
Raikuu FIN 91 Ld32
Räimä FIN 82 La30
Raimonda P 44 Ad60
Rain D 134 Dc49
Rain D 135 Eb48
Rainbach im Mühlkreis A 136 Fb49
Rain in Taufers I 143 Ea55
Raipole LV 107 Ma51
Raippaluoto FIN 81 Hd30
Raippo FIN 91 Lb36
Raisälä FIN 74 Kc18
Raisälänmäki FIN 82 Ka28
Raisdorf D 118 Dc30
Raisio FIN 97 Jb39
Raiskio FIN 74 Ka20
Raiskio FIN 83 Lb26
Raiskums LV 106 Kd49
Raistakka FIN 75 Kc19
Raisting D 142 Dc51
Raitaperä FIN 81 Jd31
Raitenbuch D 135 Dd48
Raitenhaslach D 143 Ec51
Raitoo FIN 89 Jd37
Raivala FIN 89 Jb34
Rajac SRB 178 Ba67
Raja-Jooseppi FIN 69 Kb12
Rajala FIN 69 Jd15
Rajamäenkylä FIN 89 Ja33
Rajamäki FIN 90 Kb38
Rajaniemi FIN 90 Kd34
Rajanovci BG 179 Ca68
Rajastrand S 79 Fd26
Rajavaara FIN 91 Ld33
Rajcë AL 182 Ad75
Rajčinovica Banja SRB 178 Ba69
Rajcza PL 138 Hc46
Rajec SK 138 Hc47
Rájec-Jestřebí CZ 137 Gc47
Rajecké Teplice SK 138 Hc47
Rajec Poduchowny PL 130 Jc39
Rajgród PL 123 Ka31
Rajhrad CZ 137 Gc48
Rajince KSV 178 Bc72
Rajka H 145 Gd51
Rajkova moglia BG 185 Eb75
Rajković SRB 153 Jb63
Rajkovo BG 184 Db75
Rajkowy PL 121 Hb31
Rajnino BG 181 Ec68
Raka SLO 151 Fd58
Rakaca H 138 Jc49
Rakalj HR 151 Fa61
Rakamaz H 147 Jd50
Rakek SLO 151 Fb59
Rakeluft N 63 Hd07
Rakić BIH 153 Ja62
Rakita BG 179 Da69
Rakitna SLO 151 Fb58
Rakitnica BG 180 Dd73
Rakitnica BIH 159 Hc65
Rakitnica HR 152 Gc58
Rakitovica HR 152 Hb59
Rakitovo BG 184 Cd74
Rakke EST 98 La43
Rakkestad N 94 Eb43
Raklinovo BG 181 Ec72
Rákóczifalva H 146 Jb54
Rakoniewice PL 129 Gb37
Rákos H 146 Jc56
Rakoš KSV 178 Ba70
Rakoszyce PL 129 Gb41
Rakova Bara SRB 174 Bd65
Rakovica BG 179 Ca67
Rakovica HR 151 Ga61
Rakovník CZ 136 Fa44
Rakovo BG 180 Eb71
Rakovski BG 180 Dc73
Rakow D 119 Ed31
Raków PL 130 Jc42
Rakowo Piskie PL 123 Jd32
Rāksala LV 107 Lb51
Ráksi H 145 Ha56
Råkvågen N 78 Ea28
Rakvere EST 98 La42
Ralewice PL 129 Hb39
Ralingen D 133 Bc44
Ralja SRB 174 Bb64
Ralja SRB 174 Bb64
Raljin SRB 179 Ca70
Raljevo BG 180 Db69
Rälla S 103 Gb52
Ram SRB 174 Bc64
Rama BIH 158 Ha65
Ramacastañas E 46 Cd65
Ramacca I 167 Fc86
Rämälä FIN 89 Jd32
Rämälä FIN 90 La34
Ramales de la Victoria E 38 Dd55
Ramallosa (Teo) E 36 Ad55
Ramasaig GB 4 Da08
Ramatuelle F 43 Kb55
Rămăzan MD 173 Fa55
Ramberg N 66 Fa14
Rambervillers F 31 Ka38
Rambin D 119 Ed30
Rambjørgheia N 92 Cb45
Rambo S 80 Ha27
Rambouillet F 23 Gc37
Ramdala S 111 Ga54
Rameški RUS 202 Ed09
Râmeț RO 171 Da59
Ramfjordnes N 62 Gd10
Ramía GR 188 Ba81
Ramingstein A 144 Fa54
Ramirás E 36 Ba58
Ramji LV 106 Kd48
Ramkvilla S 103 Fc51
Ramljane HR 158 Gb65
Ramløse DK 109 Eb24
Ramma EST 98 Kd43
Ramme DK 100 Cd22
Rämmen S 95 Fb41
Ramna RO 174 Bd62
Ramnäs S 95 Ga42
Rämne S 94 Eb45
Ramnes N 93 Dd43
Râmnicelu RO 176 Ed63
Râmnicelu RO 177 Fa63
Râmnicu de Sus RO 177 Fc66
Râmnicu Sărăt RO 176 Ed63
Râmnicu Vâlcea RO 175 Db63
Ramonai LT 114 Kd54
Ramosch CH 142 Dd55
Ramså N 66 Ga11
Ramsau D 143 Ec53
Ramsau am Dachstein A 144 Fa53
Ramsbeck D 126 Cc40
Ramsbottom GB 15 Ec21
Ramsbury GB 20 Ed28
Ramsdorf D 125 Bd37
Ramsei CH 141 Bd54
Ramsele S 79 Ga29
Ramsele S 80 Ha28
Ramsey GB 10 Dd18
Ramsey GB 20 Fc25
Ramsey GB 21 Gb26
Ramsey Saint Mary's GB 20 Fc25
Ramsgate GB 21 Gb28
Rämshyttan S 95 Fd40
Ramsi EST 106 Kd46
Ramsjö S 87 Fd34
Ramsli N 92 Cb45
Rämsöö FIN 89 Jc36
Ramsta S 96 Gc42
Ramstad N 78 Eb25
Ramstein-Miesenbach D 133 Ca46
Ramsthal D 134 Db44
Ramsund N 66 Ga13
Ramsvika N 78 Ec26
Ramten DK 101 Dd23
Rāmuļi LV 106 Kd49
Ramundberget S 86 Ed32
Ramundeboda S 95 Fc45
Ramvik S 88 Gc32
Ramygala LT 114 Kc55
Raná CZ 136 Fa43
Ranalt A 142 Dc54
Rånäsudden S 73 Ja21
Rancon F 33 Gb46
Randaberg N 92 Ca43
Randalstown GB 9 Da16
Randan F 34 Hc46
Randanne F 34 Hb47
Randaträsk S 73 Hc20
Randazzo I 167 Fc84
Randbøldal DK 108 Db25
Rånddalen S 86 Fa34
Randebygd N 84 Cc34
Randegg A 144 Fc51
Randen N 85 Dc35
Randers DK 100 Dc23
Randersacker D 134 Db45
Randerup DK 108 Da27
Randesund N 92 Cd47
Randijaur S 72 Ha19
Randonnai F 23 Ga37
Randsverk N 85 Dc35
Randvere EST 98 Kb42
Rånea S 73 Hd21
Ranemsletta N 78 Ec26
Rânes F 22 Fc37
Rang-du-Fliers F 23 Gc32
Rångedala S 102 Ed49
Rangendingen D 134 Cc49
Rangersdorf A 143 Ec55
Rangsby FIN 89 Hd32
Rangsdorf D 127 Ed37
Rangstrup DK 108 Da27
Ranhados P 44 Bb62
Ranheim N 77 Ea30
Rani list BG 184 Dc75
Ranis D 127 Ea42
Ranizów PL 139 Ka43
Ranka LV 106 La49
Rankinen FIN 82 Ka25
Rankweil A 142 Cd53
Ranna EST 99 Lb44
Rannametsa EST 106 Kb46
Rannamõisa EST 98 Kb42
Rannankulma FIN 89 Jb37
Rannankylä FIN 81 Jd31
Rannankylä FIN 82 Kb27
Rannanmäki FIN 89 Jb38
Rannanpohjukka FIN 91 Ma32
Rännaväg S 102 Fa49
Rännelanda S 102 Ec46
Ränneslöv S 110 Ed53
Rännö S 87 Gb33
Rannoch Station GB 7 Dd10
Rannsundet S 86 Fa33
Rannu EST 106 La46
Rannungen D 134 Db44
Rånön S 73 Ja22
Ranovac SRB 174 Bc65
Ranrupt F 31 Kb38
Ransäter S 94 Fa42
Ransbach-Baumbach D 125 Ca42
Ransby S 94 Ed39
Ransbysätter S 94 Fa41
Ransjö S 87 Fb34
Rańsk PL 122 Jb32
Ranskill GB 16 Fb22
Ransta S 95 Gb42
Ranstadt D 134 Cd43
Rantajärvi S 74 Jb18
Rantakunta FIN 89 Jc33
Rantakylä FIN 82 Kc31
Rantakylä FIN 83 Lc29
Rantakylä FIN 90 La34
Rantala FIN 81 Jd31
Rantasalmen asema FIN 91 Lb33
Rantasalmi FIN 91 Lb32
Ranta-Töysä FIN 89 Jc32
Rante E 36 Bb57
Rantrum D 108 Da29
Rantsila FIN 82 Ka25
Ranttila FIN 64 Jc10
Rantum D 108 Cd28
Ranty PL 123 Jd31
Rantzausminde DK 109 Dd28
Ranua FIN 74 Kb20
Ranum DK 100 Db21
Ranzig D 128 Fb38
Rao E 37 Bd55
Raon-l'Etape F 31 Ka38
Raossi I 149 Dc58
Rapa PL 123 Jd30
Râpa RO 170 Cb57
Rapajin Dol HR 151 Fd61
Rapala FIN 90 Kb35
Rapallo I 149 Cc63
Rapattila FIN 91 Lc36
Rapëza AL 182 Ab76
Raphoe IRL 9 Cb16
Rąpice PL 128 Fc38
Räpina EST 107 Lc46
Rapla EST 98 Kb43
Rapness GB 5 Ec02
Rapolano Terme I 156 Dd67
Rapolla I 161 Ga74
Rapoltu Mare RO 175 Cc61
Raposa P 50 Ac68
Rapotín CZ 137 Gc45
Rapovce SK 146 Ja50
Rapperswil CH 142 Cc53
Rappin D 119 Ed30
Räpplinge S 103 Gb52
Rappottenstein A 144 Fc50
Rappvika N 63 Hb08
Rapsáni GR 183 Bd80
Rapuli FIN 83 Lb27
Rårup DK 109 Ea28
Ras SRB 178 Ad68
Raša HR 151 Fa61
Rasal E 39 Fb58
Räsälä FIN 82 La30
Räsälänlahti FIN 82 La30
Rasbokil S 96 Gd41
Râșca RO 172 Eb56
Rascafría E 46 Db63
Rașcov MD 173 Fd55
Rasdel BG 185 Eb74
Rasdorf D 126 Db42
Rašeljke BIH 158 Gd66
Raseiniai LT 114 Ka56
Rasharkin GB 9 Cd16
Rashedoge IRL 9 Cb16
Rasi FIN 90 La36
Rašica SLO 151 Fc58
Rasimäki FIN 82 La28
Rasimäki FIN 83 Lb29
Rasimbegov MK 183 Bc75
Rasina EST 99 Lc45
Rășinari RO 175 Da61
Rasines E 38 Dd55
Rasinkylä FIN 75 Kd24
Rasisalo FIN 83 Ld31
Rasivaara FIN 83 Ma30
Rasivaara FIN 83 Ld31
Rasivaara FIN 83 Ld31
Råsjö S 87 Fd33
Raška SRB 178 Ba68
Rask Mølle DK 108 Db25
Raškovo BG 179 Cd70
Raslavice SK 139 Jd47
Rășmirești RO 180 Dd67
Řasná CZ 136 Fd47
Rašnevo RUS 107 Ma47
Râșnov RO 176 Dd62
Rasova RO 181 Fb67
Rasovo BG 179 Cc68
Raspilla E 53 Eb71
Rășpopeni MD 173 Fc55
Rasquera E 48 Ga63
Rassach A 144 Fd55
Rassina I 156 Dd65
Rasskazovo RUS 203 Fc12
Rast RO 179 Cc67
Rastatt D 133 Cb48
Rasteau F 42 Jb52
Rasted DK 100 Dc23
Rastede D 118 Cc33
Rastenberg D 127 Ea41
Rastenfeld A 136 Fd49
Rastes MK 183 Bb74
Rasti FIN 68 Jc15
Rasti FIN 91 Ld32
Rastina SRB 153 Hd58
Rastinkylä FIN 83 Lc26
Rastolița RO 172 Dd57
Rastovac MNE 159 Hd68
Rastovica MK 183 Bb75
Rastow D 119 Ea33
Råstrand S 72 Gc24
Răsuceni RO 180 Ea67
Rasueros E 46 Cd62
Raszków PL 129 Gd39
Raszówka PL 129 Gb40
Raszujka PL 122 Jb33
Raszyn PL 130 Jb37
Ratan S 80 Hc28
Ratan S 87 Fc33
Ratasjärvi FIN 73 Jb19
Ratby GB 16 Fa24
Ratčino RUS 99 Ma40
Rateče SLO 144 Fa56
Ratekau D 119 Dd31
Ratevo MK 183 Cb74
Rathangan IRL 13 Cc21
Ráth Caola IRL 12 Bc23
Rathcoole IRL 13 Cd21
Rathcormack IRL 12 Bd25
Rathcroghan IRL 8 Ca19
Rathdangan IRL 13 Cd23
Rathdowney IRL 13 Cb23
Ráth Droma IRL 13 Cd23
Rathdrum IRL 13 Cd23
Rathen D 128 Fb41
Rathen GB 5 Ed07

Rijen – Rosoman

Rijen NL 124 Ad38
Rijnwarden NL 125 Bc37
Rijsbergen NL 124 Ad38
Rijsel = Lille F 23 Ha31
Rijssen NL 117 Bd36
Rijswijk NL 116 Ad36
Rikkaranta FIN 83 Lb30
Riksgränsen S 67 Gc13
Rikstad N 77 Dd31
Riksu EST 105 Jc47
Rila BG 179 Cb73
Rilax FIN 97 Jc41
Rilci BG 181 Fa69
Rilievo I 166 Ea84
Rillé F 28 Fd41
Rillo E 47 Fa63
Rilly-la-Montagne F 24 Hc35
Rima San Giuseppe I 148 Bd58
Rimasco I 148 Ca58
Rimaucourt F 30 Jb38
Rimavska Baňa SK 138 Ja49
Rimavska Seč SK 146 Jb50
Rimavská Sobota SK 146 Ja50
Rimbach D 134 Cc45
Rimbach D 135 Ec47
Rimbo S 96 Gd42
Rimella I 148 Ca57
Rimetea RO 171 Da59
Rimforsa S 103 Fd47
Rimicāni LV 107 Lb52
Rimini I 156 Eb64
Rimmi EST 107 Lb47
Rimmi FIN 81 Jb28
Rimmilä FIN 90 Ka37
Rimminjoki FIN 82 Kc30
Rimmu EST 106 Kd46
Rimnieki LV 105 Jc50
Rimnio GR 183 Bc79
Římov CZ 136 Fb48
Rimpar D 134 Da45
Rimpelä FIN 69 Jd15
Rimpilänniemi FIN 82 Kd26
Rimše LT 115 Lc54
Rimske Toplice SLO 151 Fd58
Rimsting D 143 Eb52
Rinchnach D 135 Ed48
Rincón de la Victoria E 60 Da76
Rinda LV 105 Jb49
Rindal N 77 Dc31
Rindbø N 66 Fd14
Rindby DK 108 Cd26
Rinde N 84 Cc37
Rindsholm DK 100 Db23
Rinella I 167 Fc82
Ringaliai LT 113 Jd56
Ringamåla S 111 Fc53
Ringarum S 103 Gb47
Ringaskiddy IRL 12 Bd26
Ringe D 117 Ca35
Ringe DK 109 Dd27
Ringebu N 85 Dd36
Ringelai D 135 Ed49
Ringgau D 126 Db41
Ringkøbing DK 108 Cd24
Ringleben D 127 Dd40
Ringnäs S 86 Fa37
Ringsend GB 9 Cd15
Ringsta S 79 Fc30
Ringsted DK 109 Eb26
Ringvattnet S 79 Fd27
Ringvoll N 93 Ea43
Ringwood GB 20 Ed30
Rinkaby S 95 Fd44
Rinkaby S 111 Fb55
Rinkabyholm S 103 Ga52
Rinkenæs DK 108 Db28
Rinkilä FIN 91 Lc33
Rinlo E 37 Bd53
Rinn A 143 Dd54
Rinna S 103 Fc47
Rinøya N 66 Fd14
Rinsumageest NL 117 Bc33
Rintala FIN 81 Jb30
Rintatalo FIN 81 Jb29
Rinteln D 126 Cd37
Rinyabesenyő H 152 Ha57
Rinyaszentkirály H 152 Gd57
Río GR 188 Bb85
Riocorvo E 38 Db55
Rio de Onor P 45 Bd59
Río de Trueba E 38 Dc55
Riodeva E 47 Fa65
Rio Frio P 45 Bd59
Rio Frio P 50 Ab69
Riofrío E 37 Cb57
Riofrío E 46 Cd64
Riofrío de Aliste E 45 Ca59
Riofrío del Llano E 47 Ea62
Riola I 149 Dc63
Riola Sardo I 169 Bd77
Riolobos E 45 Bd65
Riolo Terme I 150 Dd63
Riom F 34 Hb46
Riomaggiore I 155 Cd64
Rio Maior P 50 Ab67
Riomalo de Arriba E 45 Ca64
Rio Marina I 155 Da68
Rio Mau P 44 Ac60
Riom-ès-Montagnes F 33 Ha48
Rion-des-Landes F 39 Fa53
Rionegro del Puente E 45 Ca59
Rionero in Vulture I 161 Ga75
Rionero Sannitico I 161 Fa72
Riópar E 53 Eb71
Rioscuro E 37 Ca56
Rioseco E 47 Ea60
Rioseco de Tapia E 37 Cb56
Rioseco (Sobrescobio) E 37 Cc55
Riotord F 34 Ja48
Rioux F 32 Fb47
Rioveggio I 149 Dc63
Rioxuán E 36 Bc55
Rioz F 31 Jd41
Ripakluokta S 67 Gd17
Ripanj SRB 153 Jc62
Ripanj SRB 174 Bb64
Riparbella I 155 Da66
Ripatransone I 157 Fa68
Ripats S 73 Hb18
Ripatti FIN 90 Kd34
Ripiceni RO 172 Ed55
Ripky UA 202 Ec13
Ripley GB 16 Fa24
Ripoll E 49 Gd59
Ripollet E 49 Gd61
Ripon GB 11 Fa19
Riposto I 167 Fd85
Ripponden GB 16 Ed21
Rips NL 125 Bb38
Ripsa S 95 Gb45
Riquewihr F 31 Kb38
Riš BG 181 Ec71
Risan MNE 159 Hd69
Risåsen S 86 Ed33
Risbäck S 79 Fd26
Risbäck S 80 Gd29
Risberg S 80 Hb25
Risberg S 86 Fa38
Risberget N 94 Ec40
Risböle S 81 Hd26
Risby GB 21 Ga25
Risca GB 19 Eb27
Rișca RO 171 Cd58
Rișcani MD 173 Fa55
Riscle F 40 Fc54
Risco E 52 Cc69
Rișcova MD 173 Fd57
Risdal N 93 Da45
Risdal N 92 Cc46
Rise N 66 Fc12
Rise N 77 Dd33
Riseberga S 110 Ed54
Risede S 79 Fc27
Riseley GB 20 Fc25
Risholen S 95 Fd39
Risinge S 103 Ga46
Risipeni MD 173 Fa56
Risis FIN 97 Ja40
Riska N 92 Ca44
Risliden S 80 Hb25
Risliden S 80 Ha25
Risnabben S 73 Hb23
Risnes N 92 Cc45
Rišňovce SK 145 Ha50
Risögrund S 73 Jb21
Risør N 93 Db45
Risoul 1850 F 35 Kb50
Risøy N 62 Gc08
Risøyhamn N 66 Fd12
Rissa N 78 Ea29
Rissna S 79 Fd31
Riste FIN 89 Jb36
Ristee FIN 83 Ma31
Risteli FIN 83 Lb26
Risti EST 98 Ka44
Ristiina FIN 90 La35
Ristijärvi FIN 82 La25
Ristijärvi FIN 90 Ka34
Ristiküla EST 106 Kc46
Ristilä FIN 75 Kc19
Ristilä FIN 90 Kc32
Ristilampi FIN 69 Ka17
Ristimäki FIN 90 Kc32
Ristinen FIN 82 Kd29
Ristinge DK 109 Dd28
Ristinkylä FIN 83 Lc31
Ristonmännikkö FIN 69 Ka16
Ristovac KSV 178 Bc71
Risträsk S 79 Gb25
Risudden S 79 Ga28
Risulahti FIN 91 Lb34
Risum-Lindholm D 108 Da28
Risuperä FIN 75 Kd20
Risuperä FIN 82 Ka30
Risvolvollen N 78 Ec29
Ritabulli LV 106 Kb50
Ritamäki FIN 81 Jb31
Rite LV 114 La53
Rítíni GR 183 Bd79
Ritola FIN 81 Jd31
Ritoniemi FIN 82 La30
Ritopek SRB 174 Bb64
Ritsem S 67 Gb16
Ritten I 143 Dd56
Ritterhude D 118 Cd34
Ritupe RUS 107 Ma49
Ritvala FIN 90 Ka36
Ritzleben D 119 Ea35
Riudarenes E 49 Hb60
Riudoms E 48 Gb62
Riumar E 48 Ga63
Riutta FIN 81 Jd28
Riutta FIN 83 Ld29
Riutta FIN 89 Ja35
Riuttala FIN 82 Kd30
Riuttala FIN 89 Jb35
Riuttanen FIN 89 Jc34
Riutula FIN 69 Ka11
Riva E 38 Dd55
Riva LV 105 Jb51
Riva-Bella F 22 Fc35
Riva dei Tessali I 162 Gd76
Riva del Garda I 149 Db58
Riva di Solto I 149 Da58
Riva di Tures I 143 Ea55
Rivanazzano I 148 Cb61
Rivarbukt N 63 Hd08
Rivarolo Canavese I 148 Bd59
Rivarolo Mantovano I 149 Da61
Rivas E 47 Fa59
Riva SanVitale I 149 Cc58
Rivas de Tereso E 38 Ea57
Rive-de-Gier F 34 Ja47
Rivello I 161 Ga77
Rivergaro I 149 Cd61
Riverstick IRL 12 Bd26
Riverstown IRL 12 Bd25
Riverville IRL 12 Bb24
Rives F 35 Jc48
Rivesaltes F 41 Hb57
Rivignano I 150 Ec58
Rivinperä FIN 82 Kb26
Rivio GR 188 Ba83
Rivisondoli I 161 Fa71
Rivne UA 202 Ea14
Rivne UA 204 Ed16
Rivoli I 148 Bc60
Rivolta d'Adda I 149 Cd59
Rixö S 102 Eb47
Riza GR 188 Bb85
Rižana SLO 151 Fa59
Rizário GR 183 Bc77
Rize TR 205 Ga19
Rizenbach CH 141 Bc54
Rizes GR 194 Bc88
Rizia GR 185 Eb75
Rizokarpaso CY 206 Ka95
Rizoma GR 183 Bb80
Rizómilos GR 189 Ca81
Rjabinovka RUS 113 Ja59
Rjabovskij RUS 203 Fc13
Rjahovo BG 180 Eb68
Rjånes N 76 Cc33
Rjasino RUS 107 Mb50
Rjazan' RUS 203 Fa11
Rjazanka RUS 203 Fc12
Rjažsk RUS 203 Fb11
Rjukan N 93 Db41
Rø DK 111 Fc57
Rö S 88 Gc32
Rö S 96 Gd42
Roa E 46 Db60
Roa N 85 Ea40
Roade GB 20 Fb26
Roager DK 108 Da27
Roaillan F 32 Fc51
Roald N 76 Cc32
Roan N 78 Ea27
Roana I 150 Dd58
Roanne F 34 Hd46
Roaschia I 148 Bc63
Roasjö S 102 Ed49
Roata de Jos RO 176 Dd66
Roavvegiedde N 64 Jd07
Roavvesåvu FIN 64 Jc09
Röbäck S 80 Hb28
Robakowo PL 121 Hb33
Robănești RO 175 Da66
Robbio I 148 Cb60
Robeasca RO 176 Ed64
Robecco d'Oglio I 149 Da60
Röbel D 119 Ec33
Røberg N 78 Ea29
Roberton GB 11 Ec15
Robertsfors S 80 Hc27
Robertsholm S 95 Ga39
Robertville B 125 Bb42
Robeži LV 105 Jb50
Robežnieki LV 115 Ld53
Robič SLO 150 Ed57
Robilante I 148 Bc63
Robin Hood's Bay GB 17 Fc18
Robledillo de Trujillo E 51 Ca68
Robledo E 37 Bd57
Robledo E 53 Ea70
Robledo de Chavela E 46 Da64
Robledo del Buey E 52 Cd67
Robledo del Mazo E 52 Cd67
Robledollano E 51 Cb67
Robles de la Valcueva E 37 Cc56
Röblingen D 127 Ea40
Robliza de Cojos E 45 Cb62
Robregordo E 46 Dc62
Robres E 48 Fb60
Robres del Castillo E 39 Eb58
Robru N 85 Db38
Roc HR 151 Fa60
Rocafort de Queralt E 48 Gb61
Roca Llisa E 56 Gc69
Rocamadour F 33 Gc50
Roca Vecchia I 163 Hc76
Roccabianca I 149 Da61
Roccadaspide I 161 Fd76
Rocca di Cambio I 156 Ed70
Rocca di Mezzo I 156 Ed70
Rocca di Neto I 165 Gd80
Rocca di Papa I 160 Eb72
Roccaforte del Greco I 164 Gb84
Roccagorga I 160 Ec73
Rocca Imperiale I 162 Gc77
Roccalbegna I 155 Dc68
Roccalumera I 167 Fd84
Roccamandolfi I 161 Fb73
Roccamena I 166 Ec85
Roccamonfina I 161 Fa73
Roccanova I 162 Gb77
Roccapalumba I 166 Ed85
Rocca Pietore I 143 Ea56
Rocca Priora I 156 Ed66
Roccaraso I 161 Fa72
Rocca San Casciano I 156 Dd64
Roccasecca I 160 Ed72
Rocca Sinibalda I 156 Ec70
Roccastrada I 155 Dc67
Roccatederighi I 155 Db67
Roccaverano I 148 Ca62
Roccella Jonica I 164 Gc83
Rocchetta San Antonio I 161 Fd74
Rochdale GB 16 Ed21
Roche E 59 Bd77
Roche GB 18 Db31
Rochechouart F 33 Ga47
Rochecolombe F 34 Ja51
Rochefort B 132 Ad43
Rochefort F 32 Fa46
Rochefort-en-Terre F 27 Ec40
Rochefort-Montagne F 33 Ha47
Rochegude F 42 Jb52
Rochehaut B 132 Ad44
Rochemaure F 42 Jb51
Rocheservière F 28 Ed43
Rochester GB 11 Ed15
Rochester GB 20 Fd28
Rochetaillée F 35 Jd49
Rochetaillée-sur-Saône F 34 Jb46
Rochfortbridge IRL 13 Cb21
Rochlitz D 127 Ec41
Rochnia PL 122 Ja34
Rociana del Condado E 59 Bc74
Rociu RO 175 Dc65
Rock GB 18 Db31
Rockanje NL 124 Ac37
Rockchapel IRL 12 Bc24
Rockcorry IRL 9 Cc18
Rockenhausen D 133 Ca45
Rockhammar S 95 Fd43
Rockhill IRL 12 Bd24
Rockneby S 103 Gb52
Röcknitz-Böhlitz D 127 Ec40
Rockolding D 135 Ea49
Ročov CZ 136 Fa44
Rocroi F 24 Hd33
Rodach, Bad D 134 Dc43
Roda de Isábena E 40 Ga58
Roda de Ter E 49 Ha59
Rodaki PL 138 Hd43
Rodalben D 133 Ca46
Rodaljice HR 157 Ga64
Rodalquilar E 61 Eb76
Rödålund S 80 Hb27
Rödånäs S 80 Hb27
Rödåsel S 80 Hb26
Rodavgí GR 188 Ad81
Rødberg N 85 Db40
Rødbergshamn N 62 Gc10
Rödbo S 102 Eb48
Rødby DK 109 Ea29
Rødbyhavn DK 109 Ea29
Rødding DK 100 Da22
Rødding DK 100 Db23
Rødding DK 108 Da26
Rødding DK 109 Eb28
Rödinge DK 109 Eb28
Rödeberg D 126 Db40
Rödeby S 111 Fd54
Rode Heath GB 15 Ec22
Rodeiro E 36 Ba56
Rødekro DK 108 Db27
Rodel GB 4 Cd06
Roden NL 117 Bd33
Rodenbach D 134 Cd44
Rodenberg D 126 Da36
Rodenkirchen D 118 Cd33
Rödental D 135 Dd43
Rödermark D 134 Cc44
Rödermark D 134 Cd44
Rodersdorf D 135 Eb43
Rodewald D 118 Da35
Rodewisch D 135 Eb43
Rodewitz D 128 Fc41
Rodez F 33 Ha51
Rodgau D 134 Cc44
Rødhus Klit DK 100 Db20
Rodiá GR 182 Ba79
Rodiá GR 183 Bd80
Rodiá GR 189 Bc85
Rodiá GR 189 Bd83
Rodi-Fiesso CH 141 Cb56
Rodi Garganico I 161 Ga71
Roding D 135 Eb47
Rödingersdorf A 136 Ga49
Rödinghausen D 126 Cc37
Rödingträsk S 80 Gd26
Roditsa GR 189 Bd83
Rødkærsbro DK 100 Db23
Rodleben D 127 Eb38
Rodna RO 172 Dd56
Rodniki RUS 203 Fa09
Rodohóri GR 183 Bc77
Rodolivos GR 184 Cd77
Rödön S 79 Fb30
Rodonyà E 49 Gc62
Rodópoli GR 183 Cb76
Rodopós GR 200 Cb94
Ródos GR 197 Fa92
Rodováni GR 200 Cb95
Rødøy N 70 Fa19
Rodrażew PL 129 Gd39
Rodrigas (Riotorto) E 36 Bc54
Rødsand N 67 Gb11
Rødseidet N 78 Ec25
Rødsjøen N 78 Ea28
Rodskov DK 101 Dd23
Rødvig DK 109 Ec27
Rodzone PL 122 Hd33
Roela EST 98 La42
Røen N 77 Dc31
Roermond NL 125 Bb40
Roeselare B 21 Ha30
Roeselare B 124 Aa39
Roești RO 175 Da64
Roetgen D 125 Bb41
Roffiac F 34 Hb49
Röfors S 95 Fc45
Róg PL 122 Jb33
Rog S 95 Fd39
Rogač HR 158 Gb67
Rogačevka RUS 203 Fb13
Rogačica KSV 178 Bc71
Rogačica SRB 159 Jb64
Rogaieni MD 173 Fc55
Rogajny PL 122 Hd31
Rogale PL 123 Jd30
Rogalice PL 129 Gd41
Rogalin PL 129 Gc37
Rogant GB 5 Ea06
Rogäsen D 127 Eb37
Rogaška Slatina SLO 151 Ga57
Rogatec SLO 151 Ga57
Rogatica BIH 159 Hc65
Rogätz D 127 Ea37
Roggel NL 125 Bb39
Roggenburg D 142 Db50
Roggendorf D 119 Db32
Roggentin D 119 Ed33
Roggiano Gravina I 164 Gb79
Roghi MD 173 Fd57
Roghudi I 164 Gb84
Rogil P 58 Ab73
Rogliano F 154 Cc67
Rogliano I 164 Gc80
Rognan N 71 Fd18
Rogne N 85 Dc37
Rognes F 42 Jc53
Rognmo N 67 Gc11
Rognskog N 77 Db31
Rogny-les-Sept-Écluses F 29 Ha40
Rogoš BG 180 Db73
Rogovka LV 107 Ld50
Rogovo RUS 107 Ma47
Rogów PL 130 Hd38
Rogowo PL 121 Gd35
Rogowo PL 122 Hc34
Rogóż PL 122 Ja30
Rogoz RO 171 Db56
Rogozče BG 184 Dc76
Rogozina BG 181 Fb69
Rogoznica HR 157 Ga66
Rogoźnica PL 129 Gb41
Rogoźniczka PL 131 Kb37
Rogoźnik PL 129 Gb41
Rogoźno PL 121 Gc35
Rogóźno PL 121 Hb33
Rogóźno PL 130 Hd37
Rogslösa S 103 Fc47
Rogsta S 87 Gb35
Roguszyn PL 131 Jd36
Rohan F 27 Eb39
Rohia RO 171 Db56
Röhlingen D 134 Db48
Rohovládova Bělá CZ 136 Ga44
Rohozná CZ 137 Gb46
Rohožník SK 145 Gd50
Rohr D 126 Dc42
Rohr D 134 Dc47
Rohr D 135 Ea49
Rohrau A 145 Gc51
Rohrbach D 135 Dd49
Rohrbach an der Gölsen A 144 Ga51
Rohrbach an der Lafnitz A 144 Ga53
Rohrbach in Oberösterreich A 136 Fa49
Rohrbach-lès-Bitche F 25 Kb35
Rohrberg D 119 Dd35
Rohr im Gebirge A 144 Ga52
Röhrnbach D 135 Ed49
Röhrsdorf D 127 Ec42
Rohuküla EST 97 Jd44
Rohuneeme EST 98 Kb42
Rois E 36 Ad55
Roisel F 23 Ha33
Roismala FIN 89 Jc36
Roissy F 23 Ha37
Roitegi E 39 Eb57
Roitzsch D 127 Eb39
Roiu EST 99 Lb45
Roizy F 24 Hd34
Roja LV 105 Jd49
Rojales E 55 Fb72
Rojão P 44 Ad63
Röjdåfors S 94 Ed40
Rojewice PL 121 Ha35
Rojewo PL 121 Ha35
Rojiște RO 179 Da67
Röjnoret S 80 Hb25
Röka S 72 Gd24
Rokai LT 114 Kc57
Rokansalo FIN 91 Lb34
Röke S 110 Fa54
Røkenes N 66 Fd12
Røkenes N 67 Gb12
Rokiciny PL 130 Hd39
Rokietnica PL 129 Gc36
Rökiö FIN 81 Ja30
Rokiškis LT 114 La53
Rokitki PL 128 Ga40
Rokitnica PL 139 Kb44
Rokitno PL 131 Kc37
Rokity PL 121 Gd30
Rokkala FIN 91 Ma32
Rokkamäki FIN 90 Kc32
Rokke N 94 Eb44
Røkkum N 77 Db31
Roknäs S 73 Hc23
Rokua FIN 82 Kb25
Rokycany CZ 136 Fa46
Rokytne UA 202 Eb14
Rokytnice nad Jizerou CZ 128 Fd42
Rokytnice v. Orl. horźch CZ 137 Gb44
Rolampont F 30 Jb39
Rolanda S 94 Eb45
Rolandstorp S 79 Fb26
Rold DK 100 Dc22
Røldal N 92 Cc41
Roldán E 55 Fa73
Rolde NL 117 Bd34
Role PL 121 Gc31
Rolfs S 73 Ja21
Rolfstorp S 102 Ec51
Rollag N 93 Dc41
Rollamienta E 47 Eb59
Rollán E 45 Cb62
Röllbach D 134 Cd45
Rolle CH 140 Ba55
Rollshausen D 126 Db39
Rolsberga S 110 Fa55
Rolsted DK 109 Dd27
Rolvenden GB 21 Ga29
Rolvsnes N 92 Ca41
Rom F 32 Fd45
Roma I 160 Eb71
Roma RO 172 Ec55
Romagnano Sesia I 148 Ca58
Romakkajärvi FIN 74 Jc18
Romakloster S 104 Ha49
Roman BG 179 Cd70
Roman RO 172 Ed58
Românași RO 171 Cd57
Romancos E 47 Ea63
Românești RO 173 Fa55
Românești RO 173 Fa57
Români RO 172 Ec58
Români de Sus RO 175 Da63
Romanija BIH 159 Hc65
Romanillos de Medinaceli E 47 Ea62
Romankovka RUS 99 Mb40
Romano di Lombardia I 149 Cd59
Romanów PL 131 Kc38
Romanówka PL 123 Kb32
Romanowo Górne PL 121 Gb35
Romanshorn CH 142 Cd52
Romans-sur-Isère F 34 Jb49
Romanu RO 177 Fa63
Romanyà de la Selva E 49 Hb60
Rombak N 67 Gc13
Rombas F 25 Jd35
Rombiolo I 164 Gb82
Romeán E 36 Bc55
Romelanda S 102 Ec48
Romenay F 30 Jb44
Romeny-sur-Marne F 24 Hb36
Rome = Roma I 160 Eb71
Römerstein D 134 Cd49
Rometta I 167 Fd84
Romeu P 45 Bc60
Romfartuna S 95 Gb42
Romfo N 77 Dc32
Romford GB 20 Fd28
Romhány H 146 Hd51
Römhild D 134 Dc43
Romilly-sur-Seine F 30 Hc38
Romme S 95 Fd40
Rommele S 102 Ec47
Rommerskirchen D 125 Bd40
Romny UA 202 Ed14
Romodan UA 202 Ed14
Romont CH 141 Bb55
Romorantin-Lanthenay F 29 Gc42
Romos RO 175 Cd61
Romoșel RO 175 Cd61
Romppala FIN 83 Ld29
Romrod D 126 Cd42
Romsey GB 20 Fa30
Romsila FIN 97 Jd39
Rømskog N 94 Eb42
Romstad N 78 Ec27
Romuli RO 171 Dc55
Romund N 85 Dc35
Røn N 85 Dc37
Rona de Jos RO 171 Db54
Rona de Sus RO 171 Db54
Rönäs S 71 Fc22
Rønbjerg DK 100 Da22
Roncal E 39 Fa57
Roncegno I 150 Dd58
Ronce-les-Bains F 32 Fa47
Roncesvalles E 39 Ed56
Ronchamp F 31 Ka40
Ronchi di Legionari I 150 Ed58
Ronciglione I 156 Ea70
Roncobello I 149 Cd58
Ronco Canavese I 148 Bc59
Ronco Scrivia I 148 Cb62
Ronda E 59 Cb76
Rondablikk N 85 Db35
Rønde DK 101 Dd23
Rondissone I 148 Bd60
Rone S 104 Ha50
Ronehamn S 104 Ha50
Rones N 78 Eb28
Rong N 84 Cc39
Rongesund N 84 Bd38
Röngu EST 106 La46
Ronkaisperä FIN 82 Ka27
Ronkala FIN 91 Lb33
Rönkhausen D 125 Cb40
Rönkönlehto FIN 82 La26
Rönkönvaara FIN 83 Lc31
Rönnäs FIN 98 Kd39
Rönnäs S 79 Ga25
Rönnbäcken S 71 Fd23
Rønne DK 111 Fc58
Ronneburg D 127 Eb42
Ronneburg D 134 Cd43
Ronneby S 111 Fd54
Ronneby hamn S 111 Fd54
Rønnede DK 109 Eb27
Ronnenberg D 126 Da36
Rønnes N 93 Da46
Rønneshytta S 95 Fc45
Rönnfällan S 80 Ha25
Rönnholm FIN 81 Hd31
Rönnholm S 80 Ha29
Rönninge S 96 Gc44
Rønningen N 67 Gc12
Rönnliden S 72 Ha23
Rönnöfors S 79 Fb29
Rönnskär S 80 Hc25
Rönnynkylä FIN 82 Kb29
Rönnynranta FIN 75 Kd19
Rönö S 103 Gb46
Ronquières B 124 Ac41
Ronsberg D 142 Db51
Ronse B 124 Ab40
Ronshausen D 126 Db41
Ronzone I 142 Dc56
Roobaka EST 97 Jd45
Roobe EST 106 La47
Roodeschool NL 117 Ca32
Röölä FIN 97 Jb39
Roonah Quay IRL 8 Bb19
Roosendaal NL 124 Ad38
Roosinpohja FIN 90 Ka33
Roosky IRL 8 Bd19
Roosky IRL 8 Ca17
Roosky IRL 8 Ca19
Rooslepa EST 97 Jd43
Roosna-Alliku EST 98 Kd43
Ropa PL 138 Jc45
Ropaži LV 106 Kc50
Ropczyce PL 139 Jd44
Ropefield IRL 8 Bd18
Ropeid N 92 Cb42
Roperuelos del Páramo E 37 Cb58
Ropinsalmi FIN 68 Hc12
Ropley GB 20 Fa29
Ropotovo MK 183 Bb75
Roppe F 31 Kb40
Ropša RUS 99 Mb40
Ropsley GB 17 Fc23
Ropso RUS 99 Lc41
Roquebillière F 43 Kd52
Roquebrun F 41 Hb54
Roquebrune-sur-Argens F 43 Kb54
Roquecourbe F 41 Gd54
Roquefort F 40 Fc53
Roquefort-sur-Soulzon F 41 Hb53
Roquesteron F 43 Kc52
Roquetas de Mar E 61 Ea76
Roquetes E 48 Ga63
Røra N 78 Eb28
Röra S 102 Eb47
Rörbäck S 73 Ja21
Rörbäcksnäs S 86 Ed37
Rørbæk DK 100 Dc22
Rørby DK 109 Ea26
Rore BIH 158 Gc64
Rørholt DK 101 Dd21
Rørholt N 93 Dc44
Rørnes N 62 Ha09
Rörö S 102 Eb49
Rörön S 87 Fc32
Røros N 85 Eb32
Rørøya N 70 Ed22
Rorschach CH 142 Cd53
Rørstad N 66 Fd16
Rörum S 111 Fb56
Rörvattnet S 79 Fb28
Rørvig DK 109 Eb25
Rørvik N 78 Eb25
Rørvik N 78 Ea29
Rörvik S 103 Fc50
Rørvika N 66 Ga13
Rørvika N 66 Ga14
Ros' BY 202 Dd13
Ros E 38 Dc58
Rösa D 127 Ec39
Rosà I 150 Dd59
Rosal E 36 Ac58
Rošal' RUS 203 Fa10
Rosala FIN 97 Jc41
Rosal de la Frontera E 51 Bb71
Rosalejo E 45 Cc65
Rosans F 42 Jc51
Rosapenna IRL 9 Cb15
Rosapineta I 150 Eb61
Rosário P 51 Bb69
Rosarno I 164 Gb82
Rosbach vor der Höhe D 134 Cc43
Roscales E 38 Da56
Roșcani MD 173 Fc57
Roșcani RO 174 Cb61
Roscanvel F 26 Db38
Rosche D 119 Dd34
Rosciano I 156 Ec65
Roščino RUS 202 Ea08
Rościszewo PL 122 Hd35
Roscoff F 26 Dc37
Ros Comáin IRL 8 Ca20
Roscommon IRL 8 Ca20
Ros Cré IRL 13 Ca22
Roscrea IRL 13 Ca22
Roščyno RUS 113 Jb59
Rosdorf D 126 Db39
Rose I 164 Gb80
Rosebush GB 14 Dc26
Rosedale Abbey GB 11 Fb18
Rosegreen IRL 13 Ca24
Rosehearty GB 5 Ed07
Roseldorf A 136 Ga49
Rosell E 48 Fd64
Roselle I 155 Dc68
Rosen BG 181 Ed73
Rosenberg D 134 Cd46
Rosenberg D 134 Da47
Rosenbergergut D 136 Fa49
Rosendahl D 125 Ca37
Rosendal FIN 97 Jc40
Rosendal N 78 Ed25
Rosendal N 84 Cb40
Rosenfeld D 142 Cc50
Rosenfors S 103 Ga50
Rosengarten D 118 Db33
Rosengarten D 134 Da47
Rosenheim D 143 Eb52
Rosenow D 119 Ed32
Rosenthal D 126 Cd41
Rosenthal D 128 Fb40
Rosentorp S 87 Fc37
Roses E 41 Hc58
Roseți RO 181 Ed67
Roseto Capo Spulico I 164 Gc78
Roseto degli Abruzzi I 157 Fa69
Roseto Valfortore I 161 Fd73
Rosetti, C.A. RO 176 Ed64
Rosetti, C.A. RO 177 Ga64
Rosheim F 25 Kb37
Rosia I 155 Dc67
Roșia RO 170 Cb57
Roșia RO 175 Db61
Roșia de Amaradia RO 175 Da63
Roșia de Secaș RO 175 Da60
Roșia Montană RO 171 Cd59
Roșia Nouă RO 174 Cb60
Rosica BG 181 Fa68
Rosice CZ 137 Gb47
Rosières F 34 Ja51
Rosières-aux-Salines F 25 Jd37
Rosières-en-Blois F 25 Jc37
Rosieres-en-Santerre F 23 Ha33
Roșieșți RO 177 Fb60
Rosignano Marittima I 155 Da66
Rosignano Solvay I 155 Da66
Roșiile RO 175 Da64
Roșiori RO 170 Cb56
Roșiori RO 172 Ed59
Roșiori RO 176 Ed65
Roșiori de Vede RO 180 Dc67
Rositz D 127 Eb41
Roskhill GB 4 Da08
Roskilde DK 109 Eb26
Roskovec AL 182 Ab76
Roskow D 127 Ec36
Roslags-Bro S 96 Ha42
Roslags-Kulla S 96 Ha43
Ros Láir IRL 13 Cd25
Röslau D 135 Ea44
Roslavl' RUS 202 Ec12
Roslev DK 100 Da22
Rosli N 85 Dc35
Rosliston GB 16 Ed24
Rosmalen NL 124 Ba38
Rosmaninhal P 51 Bb66
Ros Mhic Thriúin IRL 13 Cc24
Rosmult IRL 13 Ca23
Rosnay F 29 Gb44
Rosnay-l'Hôpital F 30 Ja38
Rosnowo PL 121 Gb31
Rosochate Kościelne PL 123 Ka34
Rosolina I 150 Ea61
Rosolina Mare I 150 Eb61
Rosolini I 167 Fc88
Rosoman MK 183 Bc75

Sarliac-sur-l'Isle – Secuieni

Sarliac-sur-l'Isle F 33 Ga49
Šarlote LV 115 Lb53
Sărmaş RO 172 Ea58
Sărmăşag RO 171 Cc56
Sărmaşu RO 171 Db58
Sármellék H 145 Gd55
Sarmingstein A 144 Fc50
Sarmizegetusa RO 175 Cc62
Särna S 86 Fa36
Sarnadas de Ródão P 50 Ba66
Sarnaki PL 131 Kb36
Sarnano I 156 Ed68
Sārnate LV 105 Jb50
Sărnec BG 181 Ed68
Sărnegor BG 180 Db72
Sarnen CH 141 Ca54
Sărnevo BG 180 Dd73
Sărnevo BG 181 Ec73
Sarnıçköy TR 192 Fb82
Sarnıçköy TR 192 Ga81
Sarnıçköy TR 197 Fa88
Sarnıçköy TR 197 Fa90
Sarnico I 149 Da59
Sarn Meyllteyrn GB 14 Dc23
Sarno I 161 Fb75
Sarnowo PL 122 Hd34
Sarnowo PL 122 Ja33
Sarnowy PL 121 Ha31
Sarnthein I 143 Dd56
Sarnthein I 143 Dd56
Sarny PL 129 Hb39
Sarny UA 202 Ea14
Särö S 102 Eb49
Sarón E 38 Dc55
Saronida GR 195 Cb88
Saronida GR 195 Cc87
Saronno I 149 Cc59
Sárosd H 146 Hc54
Sárospatak H 147 Ka50
Šarovce SK 146 Hc51
Sarow D 119 Ed32
Sarpdere TR 185 Eb78
Sarpıncık TR 191 Ea85
Sarpsborg N 93 Ea43
Sarracín E 38 Dc58
Sarral E 48 Gb61
Sarralbe F 25 Ka35
Sarrance F 39 Fb56
Sarras F 34 Jb49
Sarreaus E 36 Bb58
Sarrebourg F 25 Kb36
Sarreguemines F 25 Ka35
Sárrétudvari H 147 Jd53
Sarre-Union F 25 Kb36
Sarrey F 30 Jb39
Sarria E 36 Bc56
Sarrià de Ter E 49 Hb59
Sarrians F 42 Jb52
Sarrikoski FIN 83 Lb25
Sarrión E 47 Fa65
Sarroca de Bellera E 40 Ga58
Sarroca de Lleida E 48 Ga61
Sarroch I 169 Ca80
Sarron F 40 Fc54
Sarry F 30 Hd40
Sarsina I 156 Ea65
Sarstedt D 126 Db37
Sárszentlőrinc H 146 Hc56
Sartaguda E 39 Ec58
Sarteano I 156 Dd68
Sartène F 154 Ca72
Sárti GR 184 Cd80
Sartilly F 22 Fa37
Sartininkai LT 113 Jc56
Sartmahmut TR 192 Fa86
Sarud H 146 Jc52
Şaru Dornei RO 172 Ea57
Saruhanlı TR 191 Ed85
Sarule I 169 Cb76
Sărulești RO 176 Ec63
Sărulești RO 176 Ec66
Sárvár H 145 Gc54
Sarvasåive S 72 Ha22
Sarvela FIN 89 Jb33
Sarves N 63 Hd08
Sarvi EST 106 Kb46
Sarvijoki FIN 81 Ja31
Sarvikas FIN 81 Jc31
Sarvikumpu FIN 83 Lc31
Sarvilahti FIN 90 Kd38
Sarviluoma FIN 89 Ja34
Sarvinki FIN 83 Ld30
Sarvisé E 40 Fc57
Sarvisvaara S 73 Hc18
Sarvivaara FIN 74 Kd18
Sarvlax FIN 90 Kd38
Särvsjön S 86 Fa32
Sarzana I 155 Cd64
Sarzeau F 27 Eb41
Sarzedas P 44 Ba65
Sarzyna PL 139 Ka43
Šaš HR 152 Gc60
Sasa MK 179 Ca73
Sasa del Abadiado E 48 Fc59
Sasamón E 38 Db58
sa Savina E 56 Gc70
Sasbach D 141 Bd50
Sasca Montană RO 174 Bd64
Saschiz RO 176 Dd60
Săsciori RO 175 Da61
Sascut RO 176 Ed60
Sásd H 152 Hb57
Sas de Penelas E 36 Bc57
Săseni MD 173 Fc57
Saševo BG 180 Dd70
Sasi FIN 89 Jc35
Sąsiadka PL 131 Kb41
Sasina BIH 152 Gc62
Sasino PL 121 Gd29
Sasiny PL 123 Kb35
Sasmalıpınar TR 187 Gd79
Sasnava LV 114 Kb58
Sason TR 205 Ga20
Sasovo RUS 203 Fb10
Sassali FIN 69 Jd16
Sassari I 168 Bd74
Sassello I 148 Ca62
Sassen D 119 Ed31
Sassenage F 35 Jd48
Sassenay F 30 Jb43
Sassenberg D 125 Cb37
Sassenburg D 126 Dc36
Sassenheim NL 116 Ad36
Sassetot-le Mauconduit F 22 Fd34
Sassetta I 155 Db67
Sassnitz D 120 Fa30
Sassocorvaro I 156 Eb65
Sassoferrato I 156 Ec66
Sasso Marconi I 149 Dc63
Sassonero I 150 Dd63
Sassuolo I 149 Db62
Sástago E 48 Fc61
Šaštín-Stráže SK 137 Gd49
Sas van Gent NL 124 Ab39
Såtåhaugen N 86 Eb32
Sátão P 44 Ba62
Sateikiai LT 113 Jc54
Såtenäs S 102 Ed46
Säter S 87 Fc33
Säter S 95 Fd40
Säter S 102 Fa46
Sätergården S 94 Fa41
Saterland D 117 Cb34
Sāti LV 105 Jd51
Satiķi LV 105 Jd51
Sätila S 102 Ec49
Satillieu F 34 Ja49
Sātiņi LV 105 Jc52
Sātiņi LV 105 Jd52
Satkūnai LT 114 Kd53
Sątoczno PL 122 Jb30
Såtofta S 110 Fa55
Satopäänkulma FIN 97 Jc39
Sątopy PL 122 Jb31
Sátoraljaújhely H 139 Ka49
Satosuo FIN 82 Kb31
Satov CZ 136 Ga49
Satovča BG 184 Cd75
Satow D 119 Eb31
Sätra brunn S 95 Ga42
Sátres GR 184 Db76
Satriano di Lucania I 161 Ga76
Satrup D 108 Db29
Sattajärvi FIN 74 Jc20
Sattajärvi S 68 Ja17
Sattanen FIN 69 Ka15
Satteins A 142 Cd53
Sattel CH 141 Cb54
Satteldorf D 134 Db47
Sattendorf A 144 Fa56
Satter S 73 Hd18
Sättersta S 96 Gc45
Sattledt A 144 Fa51
Satul Nou MD 173 Fd59
Satulung RO 171 Da55
Satu Mare RO 171 Cd54
Satu Mare RO 172 Eb55
Satu Nou RO 181 Fa67
Šatura RUS 203 Fa10
Saturn RO 181 Fc68
Saturnia I 155 Dc69
Saturo I 162 Ha76
Saubach D 127 Ea40
Sauca MD 173 Fb53
Saucats F 32 Fb51
Saucelle E 45 Bd62
Săucești RO 172 Ed59
Sauchen GB 7 Ec09
Sauclières F 41 Hc53
Sauda N 92 Cb42
Sauðárkrókur IS 2 Ba03
Saudasjøen N 92 Cb42
Saudersfoot GB 18 Dc27
Saudron F 30 Jb38
Saue EST 98 Kb42
Sauensiek D 118 Db33
Sauerlach D 143 Ea51
Sauga EST 98 Kb45
Saughtree GB 11 Ec15
Sauginiai LT 114 Ka54
Saugos LT 113 Jb56
Saugues F 34 Hc49
Sauherad N 93 Dc43
Saujon F 32 Fa47
Sauka LV 106 La52
Šaukėnai LT 114 Ka54
Saukko FIN 83 Lb26
Saukkojärvi FIN 74 Kb20
Saukkokangas FIN 69 Kd15
Saukkola FIN 90 Kb33
Saukkola FIN 98 Ka39
Saukkomaa FIN 74 Kb21
Saukkoriipi FIN 74 Jb18
Saukonkylä FIN 81 Jc31
Saukonperä FIN 89 Jc34
Saukonsaari FIN 91 Lc34
Šaukotas LV 114 Kb55
Sauland N 93 Db42
Săulești RO 175 Cd64
Saulgau, Bad D 142 Cd51
Saulgrub D 142 Dc52
Saulheim D 133 Cb44
Sauļi LV 106 Kd48
Şăulia RO 171 Db58
Saulieu F 30 Hd42
Saulīte LT 114 Kb53
Saulkrasti LV 106 Kc49
Saulnot F 31 Ka40
Sault F 42 Jc52
Sault-de-Navailles F 39 Fb54
Saulx F 31 Jd40
Saulxerotte F 25 Jc37
Saulxures-sur-Moselotte F 31 Ka39
Saulzais-le-Potier F 29 Ha44
Saulzoir F 24 Hb32
Saumeray F 29 Gb39
Saumos F 32 Fa50
Saumur F 28 Fc42
Saunajärvi FIN 83 Lc26
Saunakylä FIN 82 Ka30
Saunakylä FIN 89 Jb34
Saunalahti FIN 82 La31
Saunavaara FIN 69 Kb16
Saurat F 40 Gc56
Sauris I 143 Ec56
Saus N 70 Ed24
Sausgalviai LT 113 Jb57
Sausnēja LV 107 La50
Sausset-les-Pins F 42 Jc55
Saussy F 30 Jb41
Sausvatn N 70 Ed23
Sauvagnat F 33 Ha47
Sauve F 41 Hd53
Sauvere EST 105 Jc46
Sauveterre-de-Béarn F 39 Fa55
Sauveterre-de-Guyenne F 32 Fc51
Sauveterre-de-Rouergue F 41 Ha52
Sauveterre-la-Lémance F 33 Gb51
Sauveur-Lendelin F 22 Fa36
Sauvo FIN 97 Jc39
Sauvomäki FIN 90 Kd32
Sauxillanges F 34 Hc47
Sauze d'Oulx I 148 Bb60
Sauzet F 33 Gb51
Sauzet F 34 Jb50
Sauzet F 42 Ja53
Sauzé-Vaussais F 32 Fd46
Sauzon F 27 Ea42
Sava I 162 Ha76
Săvădisla RO 171 Cd58
Savalen N 77 Ea33
Savália GR 188 Ad86
Savaloja FIN 82 Ka25
Sävar S 80 Hc28
Săvârşin RO 174 Cb60
Sävast S 73 Hd22
Savaştepe TR 191 Ed83
Sävastnäs S 73 Hd22
Savci SLO 145 Gb56
Sávdijári S 68 Hc16
Säve S 102 Eb48
Sävedalen S 102 Ec49
Saveenkylä FIN 89 Jb32
Savelletri I 162 Ha75
Savelli I 165 Gd80
Savenaho FIN 90 Kc34
Savenay F 27 Ec42
Săveni RO 172 Ed54
Săveni RO 177 Fa66
Saverdun F 40 Gc55
Saverkeit FIN 97 Ja40
Saverna EST 107 Lb46
Saverne F 25 Kb36
Savero FIN 90 La37
Sävi FIN 89 Jb35
Säviä FIN 82 Kc29
Saviaho FIN 82 La26
Săviena LV 107 Lb51
Savigliano I 148 Bc62
Savignac F 41 Gd52
Savignac-les-Eglises F 33 Ga49
Savignano Irpino I 161 Fd74
Savignano sul Rubicone I 156 Eb64
Savigné F 32 Fd46
Savigné-l'Evêque F 28 Fd39
Savigny F 31 Jc40
Savigny-en-Revermont F 31 Jc44
Savigny-lès-Beaune F 30 Ja42
Savigny-sur-Braye F 29 Ga40
Savijärvi FIN 83 Lc27
Savijoki FIN 90 Kc38
Savikoski FIN 89 Jd36
Savikummunsalo FIN 91 Ld33
Savikylä FIN 83 Lb28
Savilahti FIN 91 Lc35
Savimäki FIN 82 Kc27
Saviñao E 36 Bb56
Savines-le-Lac F 35 Ka50
Săvinești RO 172 Ec58
Saviniemi FIN 89 Jd37
Savino Selo SRB 153 Ja59
Savio FIN 90 Kc32
Saviore d'Adamello I 149 Db57
Savipohja FIN 90 Kb33
Saviranta FIN 82 Kd25
Şavirii Vechi MD 173 Fb54
Saviselkä FIN 82 Kb27
Savitaipale FIN 91 Lb35
Sävja S 96 Gc42
Savköy TR 199 Gc88
Šavnik MNE 159 Hd68
Savoca I 167 Fd84
Savognin CH 142 Cd55
Savolanniemi FIN 82 Ka28
Savolanvaara FIN 83 Lc27
Sávoly H 145 Gd56
Savona I 148 Ca63
Savonkylä FIN 81 Jc30
Savonlinna FIN 91 Lc33
Savonranta FIN 91 Lc32
Savournon F 42 Jd51
Sävsjö S 103 Fc50
Sävsjön S 80 Ha26
Sävsjön S 95 Fc41
Sävsjöström S 103 Fd51
Savudrija HR 150 Ed60
Savukoski FIN 69 Kc15
Savulahti FIN 82 La30
Sawbridgeworth GB 20 Fd27
Sawin PL 131 Kc39
Sawley GB 15 Ec20
Sawrey GB 11 Eb18
Sawston GB 20 Fd26
Sax CH 142 Cd53
Sax E 55 Fa71
Saxdalen S 95 Fc41
Saxen A 144 Fc51
Saxhyttan S 95 Fb42
Saxilby GB 16 Fb22
Saxlingham Nethergate GB 17 Gb24
Saxnäs S 79 Fd25
Saxon CH 141 Bc56
Saxton GB 17 Fc19
Saxtorp S 110 Ed55
Saxtorpsskogen S 110 Ed55
Saxvallen S 78 Ed29
Sayatón E 47 Ea64
Sayda D 127 Ed42
Sayık TR 192 Fb84
Säynäjä FIN 75 La19
Säynätsalo FIN 90 Kc33
Säyneinen FIN 83 Lb29
Säynelahti FIN 91 Lb32
Sazak TR 191 Ec81
Sazak TR 198 Fd91
Sazak TR 198 Ga89
Sázava CZ 136 Fc45
Sazılar TR 193 Hb82
Sazköy TR 192 Fa85
Sazköy TR 198 Ga88
Sazlı TR 191 Ea82
Sazlı TR 197 Ed88
Sazlıbosna TR 186 Fc77
Sazoba TR 185 Ed80
Sazoba TR 191 Ed85
Scaër F 27 Dd39
Scăești RO 175 Cd65
Scafa I 157 Fa70
Scăieni MD 173 Fa54
Scalasaig GB 6 Da12
Scalea I 164 Ga78
Scaletta Zanclea I 167 Fd84
Scalloway GB 5 Fa05
Scamblesby GB 17 Fc22
Scandiano I 149 Db62
Scandicci I 155 Dc65
Scanno I 161 Fa71
Scansano I 155 Dc69
Scânteia RO 173 Fa58
Scânteia RO 177 Fa65
Scânteiești RO 177 Fb62
Scanzano Jonico I 162 Gc77
Scarborough GB 17 Fc19
Scardovari I 150 Eb61
Scardroy GB 4 Dc07
Scarinish GB 9 Da14
Scario I 161 Fd77
Scărișoara RO 171 Cc59
Scarnagh IRL 13 Cd23
Scarperia I 155 Dc64
Scarriff IRL 12 Bd22
Scartaglin IRL 12 Bb24
Scauri I 160 Ed73
Scauri I 166 Dd88
Sceaux F 23 Gd37
Sceaux-sur-Huisne F 29 Ga39
Ščegly RUS 113 Jd58
Ščekino RUS 203 Fa11
Šćenica- Bobani BIH 158 Hb68
Šćepan Polje BIH 159 Hd66
Scerni I 161 Fb71
Scey-sur-Saône-et-Saint-Albin F 31 Jd40
Schaafheim D 134 Cd44
Schaan FL 142 Cd54
Schabs I 143 Dd55
Schacht-Audorf D 118 Db30
Schaffhausen CH 141 Cb52
Schafflund D 108 Da28
Schafstädt D 127 Ea40
Schafstedt D 118 Da31
Schäftlarn D 143 Dd51
Schagen NL 116 Ba34
Schagenbrug NL 116 Ba34
Schaijk NL 125 Bb38
Schalchen A 143 Ed51
Schale D 117 Cb36
Schalkau D 135 Dd43
Schalkenmehren D 133 Bd43
Schalkham D 143 Eb50
Schalksmühle D 125 Ca40
Schangau CH 141 Bd54
Schangau CH 141 Ca54
Schänis CH 142 Cc54
Schapbach, Bad Rippoldsau- D 133 Cb49
Schapen D 117 Cb36
Scharans CH 142 Cd55
Scharbeutz D 119 Dd31
Schärding A 143 Ed50
Scharendijke NL 124 Ac37
Scharfenberg D 127 Ed41
Scharfenstein D 127 Ed42
Scharfling A 143 Ed52
S-charl CH 142 Db55
Scharnebeck D 118 Dc33
Scharnitz A 143 Dd53
Scharnstein A 144 Fa52
Scharrel D 117 Cb34
Schauenburg D 126 Da40
Schauenstein D 135 Ea44
Schaufling D 135 Ec48
Schechen D 143 Eb51
Schechingen D 134 Da48
Scheden D 126 Da39
Scheemda NL 117 Ca33
Scheer D 142 Cd51
Scheeßel D 118 Da34
Schefflenz D 134 Cd46
Scheggia I 156 Eb66
Şcheia RO 172 Eb55
Şcheia RO 173 Fa58
Scheibbs A 144 Fd51
Scheidegg D 142 Da52
Scheifling A 144 Fb54
Scheinfeld D 134 Db45
Schela RO 175 Cd63
Schela RO 177 Fa63
Schelklingen D 142 Da50
Schellerten D 126 Db37
Schellinghout NL 116 Ba35
Schemmerhofen D 142 Da50
Schenefeld D 118 Db31
Schenefeld D 118 Db32
Schengen L 133 Bb45
Schenkenzell D 141 Cb50
Schenklengsfeld D 126 Db42
Schermbeck D 125 Bd38
Schernberg D 126 Dc40
Schernfeld D 135 Dd48
Scherpenheuvel B 124 Ad40
Scherpenisse NL 124 Ac38
Scherpenzeel NL 116 Bb36
Scheßlitz D 135 Dd44
Scheveningen NL 116 Ad36
Scheyern D 135 Dd49
Schia I 149 Da63
Schiavi di Abruzzo I 161 Fb72
Schiedam NL 124 Ad37
Schieder-Schwalenberg D 126 Cd38
Schierke D 126 Dc38
Schierling D 135 Eb48
Schiermonnikoog NL 117 Bd32
Schiers CH 142 Cd54
Schiffdorf D 118 Cd32
Schifferstadt D 133 Cb46
Schiffweiler D 133 Bd46
Schijndel NL 124 Ba38
Schildau, Gneisenaustadt D 127 Ec40
Schillerslage D 126 Db36
Schillig D 117 Cc32
Schillingsfürst D 134 Db47
Schilpario I 149 Da58
Schiltach D 141 Cb50
Schiltberg D 135 Dd49
Schineni MD 173 Fb54
Schinoúsa GR 196 Db90
Schio I 150 Dd59
Schipkau D 128 Fa40
Schirgiswalde D 128 Fb41
Schirmeck F 25 Kb37
Schirmitz D 135 Eb46
Schirnding D 135 Eb44
Schisò I 167 Fd85
Schitu RO 175 Db66
Schitu RO 180 Ea67
Schitu Duca RO 173 Fb58
Schitu Golești RO 175 Dc63
Schkeuditz D 127 Eb40
Schkölen D 127 Ea41
Schkopau D 127 Eb40
Schlächtenhaus D 141 Bd52
Schladen D 126 Dc38
Schladming A 144 Fa53
Schlägl A 136 Fa49
Schlalach D 127 Ec37
Schlanders I 142 Dc56
Schlangen D 126 Cd38
Schlanstedt D 127 Dd38
Schlarigna CH 142 Da56
Schleching D 143 Eb52
Schlegel D 128 Fc41
Schlehdorf D 143 Dd52
Schleiden D 125 Bc42
Schleitheim D 141 Cb51
Schleiz D 135 Ea43
Schlema D 127 Ec42
Schleswig D 108 Db29
Schlettau D 135 Ec43
Schleusingen D 134 Dc43
Schlieben D 127 Ed39
Schlierbach A 144 Fb51
Schliersee D 143 Ea52
Schlitz D 126 Da42
Schlögen A 144 Fa50
Schloßberg A 144 Fd56
Schloß Holte-Stukenbrock D 126 Cc38
Schlotheim D 126 Dc40
Schluchsee D 141 Ca51
Schlüchtern D 134 Da43
Schluderbach I 143 Ea56
Schluderns I 142 Db55
Schlüsselfeld D 134 Dc45
Schmalfeld D 118 Db31
Schmalkalden D 126 Dc42
Schmallenberg D 126 Cc40
Schmelz D 133 Bc46
Schmerzke D 127 Ec37
Schmidgaden D 135 Eb46
Schmidmühlen D 135 Ea47
Schmidtheim D 125 Bc42
Schmiedeberg D 128 Fa42
Schmiedefeld D 135 Dd43
Schmiedefeld am Rennsteig D 126 Dc42
Schmitten D 134 Cc43
Schmölln D 120 Fb34
Schmölln D 127 Eb42
Schmölln-Putzkau D 128 Fb41
Schmon D 127 Ea40
Schnackenburg D 119 Ea34
Schnaitsee D 143 Eb51
Schnaittach D 135 Dd46
Schnaittenbach D 135 Ea46
Schnarup-Thumby D 108 Db29
Schneeberg D 134 Cd45
Schneeberg D 135 Ec43
Schnega D 119 Dd35
Schneidlingen D 127 Ea38
Schnelldorf D 134 Db47
Schneverdingen D 118 Db34
Schobüll D 108 Da29
Schöder A 144 Fa54
Schoenberg B 133 Bc43
Schöftland CH 141 Ca53
Schollene D 127 Eb36
Schöllkrippen D 134 Cd44
Schöllnach D 135 Ed49
Schömberg D 134 Cc48
Schömberg D 142 Cc50
Schonach D 141 Cb50
Schönau D 128 Fb40
Schönau D 141 Ca51
Schönau D 143 Ec50
Schönau a.Königssee D 143 Ec53
Schönau-Berzdorf D 128 Fc41
Schönau (Brend) D 134 Db43
Schönbach A 144 Fc50
Schönbeck D 120 Fa33
Schönberg D 119 Dd32
Schönberg D 135 Ed48
Schönbergerstrand D 118 Dc30
Schönberg (Holstein) D 118 Dc30
Schönborn D 127 Ed39
Schönbrunn D 134 Cc46
Schönbrunn D 134 Cc43
Schönbrunn D 134 Dc45
Schondorf D 142 Dc51
Schondra D 134 Da43
Schönebeck D 118 Cd34
Schönebeck D 127 Ea38
Schönecken D 133 Bc43
Schönefeld D 128 Fa37
Schönermark D 120 Fa33
Schönewalde D 127 Ed39
Schönewerda D 127 Dd40
Schönfeld D 128 Fa40
Schönfelde D 128 Fb36
Schönfeld-Weißig D 128 Fa41
Schongau D 142 Dc52
Schöngrabern A 136 Ga49
Schönhausen D 127 Eb36
Schönheide D 135 Ec43
Schöningen D 127 Dd37
Schönkirchen D 118 Dc30
Schönow D 128 Fa36
Schönsee D 135 Ec46
Schonstett D 143 Eb51
Schönthal D 135 Ec47
Schonungen D 134 Db44
Schönwald D 135 Eb44
Schönwald D 141 Cb50
Schönwalde D 119 Dd30
Schönwalde D 127 Ed36
Schoondijke NL 124 Ab38
Schoonebeek NL 117 Ca35
Schoonhoven NL 124 Ba37
Schoonloo NL 117 Bd34
Schoonoord NL 117 Bd34
Schoorl NL 116 Ba34
Schopfheim D 141 Ca52
Schopfloch D 133 Cb49
Schopfloch D 134 Db47
Schöppenstedt D 127 Dd37
Schoppernau A 142 Da53
Schöppingen D 125 Ca37
Schöpstal D 128 Fc41
Schorndorf D 134 Cd48
Schorstedt D 119 Ea35
Schortens D 117 Cc32
Schotten D 126 Cd42
Schotten D 134 Cd43
Schramberg D 141 Cb50
Schraplau D 127 Ea40
Schrecksbach D 126 Cd41
Schrems A 136 Fc49
Schriesheim D 134 Cc46
Schrobenhausen D 135 Dd49
Schröcken A 142 Da53
Schrozberg D 134 Da46
Schruns A 142 Da54
Schuddebeurs NL 124 Ac37
Schuld D 125 Bd42
Schull = Skull IRL 12 Bb27
Schuls CH 142 Db55
Schulzendorf D 128 Fa37
Schüpfheim CH 141 Ca54
Schussenried, Bad D 142 Cd51
Schuttertal D 141 Ca50
Schüttorf D 117 Ca36
Schwaan D 119 Eb31
Schwabach D 134 Dc47
Schwabhausen D 143 Dd50
Schwäbisch Gmünd D 134 Da48
Schwäbisch Hall D 134 Da47
Schwabmünchen D 142 Dc50
Schwabstedt D 118 Da30
Schwadorf A 145 Gb51
Schwaförden D 118 Cd35
Schwaigern D 134 Cd47
Schwaikheim D 134 Cd48
Schwalbach D 133 Bc46
Schwalenberg, Schieder- D 126 Da38
Schwalmstadt D 126 Cd41
Schwalmtal D 125 Bc39
Schwalmtal D 126 Cd42
Schwanau D 133 Ca49
Schwanbeck D 120 Fa32
Schwanberg A 144 Fd55
Schwanden CH 142 Cc54
Schwandorf D 135 Eb47
Schwanebeck D 127 Dd38
Schwanebeck D 128 Fa36
Schwanenstadt A 144 Fa51
Schwanewede D 118 Cd33
Schwangau D 142 Dc52
Schwanstetten D 135 Dd47
Schwante D 119 Ed35
Schwarme D 118 Cd34
Schwarmstedt D 118 Db35
Schwarz D 119 Ec34
Schwarzach D 134 Cc46
Schwarzach D 135 Ec48
Schwarzach am Main D 134 Db45
Schwarzach im Pongau A 143 Ec53
Schwarzbach D 128 Fa40
Schwarzbach bei Rochlitz D 127 Ec41
Schwarzenau A 136 Fd49
Schwarzenau im Gebirge A 144 Ga52
Schwarzenbach am Wald D 135 Ea43
Schwarzenbach an der Saale D 135 Ea44
Schwarzenbek D 118 Dc33
Schwarzenberg A 136 Fa49
Schwarzenberg D 135 Ec43
Schwarzenborn D 126 Da41
Schwarzenbruck D 135 Dd47
Schwarzenburg CH 141 Bc54
Schwarzenfeld D 135 Eb47
Schwarzenseealm A 144 Fa54
Schwarze Pumpe D 128 Fb40
Schwarzheide D 128 Fa40
Schwarzhofen D 135 Eb47
Schwarzwaldalp CH 141 Ca55
Schwaz A 143 Ea53
Schwechat A 145 Gb51
Schwedt D 120 Fb34
Schwefelbergbad CH 141 Bd55
Schwei D 118 Cc33
Schweich D 133 Bc44
Schweigen-Rechtenbach D 133 Ca47
Schweighausen D 141 Ca50
Schweighof A 143 Ed53
Schweinfurt D 134 Db44
Schweinitz D 127 Eb37
Schweinitz D 127 Ed39
Schweitenkirchen D 135 Ea49
Schwelm D 125 Ca40
Schwendi D 142 Da50
Schwenningen, Villingen- D 141 Cb50
Schwepnitz D 128 Fa40
Schwerfen D 125 Bc41
Schwerin D 119 Ea32
Schwerte D 125 Ca39
Schwetzingen D 134 Cc46
Schwichtenberg D 120 Fa32
Schwieberdingen D 134 Cc48
Schwielochsee D 128 Fb38
Schwiesau D 127 Dd36
Schwindegg D 143 Eb50
Schwörstadt D 141 Ca52
Schwülper D 126 Dc36
Schwyz CH 141 Cb54
Sciacca I 166 Ec86
Sciaves I 143 Dd55
Scicli I 167 Fc88
Sciez F 31 Ka44
Ščigry RUS 203 Fa13
Scilla I 164 Ga83
Scillato I 167 Fa85
Ścinawa PL 129 Gb40
Ścinawa PL 137 Gd43
Ścinawka Średnia PL 137 Gb43
Scioașetea RO 180 Dc67
Scionzier F 35 Ka45
Ščir RUS 99 Ma44
Šćit BIH 158 Ha65
Scampton GB 16 Fb22
Scoarța RO 175 Cd64
Scobinți RO 172 Ed56
Scoglitti I 167 Fb88
Sconser GB 4 Db08
Scopello I 148 Ca58
Scopello I 166 Eb84
Scopwick GB 17 Fc23
Scordia I 167 Fc86
Scoreni MD 173 Fc58
Scornicești RO 175 Db65
Ščors UA 202 Ec13
Scorțaru Nou RO 177 Fa63
Scorțeni MD 173 Fc56
Scorțoasa RO 176 Ec63
Scorzè I 150 Ea59
Scorzo I 161 Fd76
Scotch Corner GB 11 Fa18
Scotch Town GB 9 Cc16
Scoțeni RO 172 Ec59
Scotter GB 16 Fb21
Scottow GB 17 Gb24
Scourie GB 4 Dc05
Scoury F 29 Gb44
Scousburgh GB 5 Fa06
Scrabster GB 5 Eb04
Scramoge IRL 8 Ca19
Scraptoft GB 16 Fb24
Scredington GB 17 Fc23
Scribbagh GB 8 Ca17
Ščuča Gora RUS 107 Mb46
Ščučyn BY 202 Dd13
Sculeni MD 173 Fa57
Scumpia MD 173 Fb56
Scunthorpe GB 16 Fb21
Scuol CH 142 Db55
Scurcola Marsicana I 160 Ed71
Scurtu Mare RO 176 Dd66
Scutaru RO 176 Ec61
Scutelnici RO 176 Ec65
Sczeglino PL 121 Gb31
Seaca RO 180 Dc67
Seaca RO 180 Dc68
Seaca de Câmp RO 179 Cc67
Seaca de Pădure RO 175 Cc66
Seaford GB 20 Fd30
Seahouses GB 11 Fa14
Seamer GB 17 Fc19
Sea Palling GB 17 Gb24
Seascale GB 10 Ea18
Seaton GB 19 Eb30
Seaton Delaval GB 11 Fa16
Seave Green GB 11 Fb18
Sébazac-Concurès F 33 Ha51
Sebbersund DK 100 Db21
Sebečevo SRB 178 Ba69
Šebekino RUS 203 Fa14
Seben TR 187 Hb80
Sebenardı TR 187 Ha79
Sebepti TR 191 Ed81
Sebersdorf A 144 Ga54
Sebeș RO 175 Cd60
Šebetov CZ 137 Gc46
Sebež RUS 107 Mb51
Sebež RUS 202 Ea11
Sebiller TR 193 Hb87
Şebinkarahisar TR 205 Fd20
Sebiș RO 170 Cb59
Sebnitz D 128 Fb41
Seboncourt F 24 Hb33
Sebuzín CZ 136 Fb43
Seč CZ 136 Ga45
Sečan SRB 174 Bb62
Secăria RO 176 Ea63
Secaș RO 174 Ca60
Seccagrande I 166 Ec86
Sece LV 106 Kd51
Secemin PL 130 Ja42
Sečenovo RUS 203 Fc09
Séchault F 24 Ja35
Séchilienne F 35 Jd49
Seckach D 134 Cd46
Seçköy TR 186 Fd80
Seclin F 23 Ha31
Secondigny F 28 Fb44
Sečovce SK 139 Ka48
Sečovská Polianka SK 139 Ka48
Secu RO 172 Ea57
Secu RO 175 Cc65
Secuieni RO 172 Ed58
Secuieni RO 172 Ed59

Siemczyno – Skødstrup

Siemczyno PL 120 Ga33
Siemianowice Śląskie PL 138 Hc43
Siemianówka PL 123 Kc34
Siemiany PL 122 Hc32
Siemiatycze PL 131 Kb36
Siemień PL 131 Kb38
Siemkowice PL 130 Hc40
Siemyśl PL 120 Fd31
Sien D 133 Ca45
Siena I 155 Dc67
Siene S 102 Ed48
Sieniawa PL 139 Kb43
Sienica PL 120 Ga33
Sienlaukis LT 114 Ka56
Siennica PL 131 Jd37
Siennica Różana PL 131 Kc40
Sienno PL 131 Jd40
Sieppijärvi FIN 68 Jb17
Sieradz PL 129 Hb39
Sieraków PL 128 Ga36
Sieraków PL 129 Hb42
Sierakowice PL 121 Gd30
Sierakowice PL 137 Hb44
Sierck-les-Bains F 25 Jd34
Siercz PL 128 Ga37
Sierentz F 31 Kc40
Sierksdorf D 119 Dd31
Sierndorf A 145 Gb50
Sierniki PL 121 Gc35
Sierning A 144 Fb51
Siero de la Reina E 37 Cd56
Sieroszewice PL 129 Ha39
Sierpc PL 122 Hd35
Sierra de Luna E 47 Fa59
Sierra de Yeguas E 60 Cc75
Sierre CH 141 Bd56
Sierre S 73 Hb19
Sierro E 61 Ea74
Siershahn D 125 Ca42
Siersleben D 127 Ea39
Siesikai LT 114 Kd56
Siestrzeń PL 130 Jb37
Siete Aguas E 54 Fa68
Siete Iglesias E 45 Cc61
Şieu RO 171 Dc57
Şieu-Măgheruş RO 171 Dc57
Şieu-Odorhei RO 171 Db57
Şieuţ RO 171 Dc57
Sieverstedt D 108 Db29
Sievi FIN 81 Jd27
Siewierz PL 138 Hc43
Sifferbo S 95 Fd39
Sig DK 108 Cd25
Sığacık TR 191 Eb86
Sigdal N 93 Dc41
Sigean F 41 Hb56
Sigerfjord N 66 Fd13
Sigetec HR 152 Gc57
Siggavuono FIN 64 Ka10
Siggelkow D 119 Eb33
Siggerud N 93 Ea42
Sighetu Marmaţiei RO 171 Db54
Sighişoara RO 175 Dc60
Sığırcık TR 193 Ha84
Sığırlık TR 199 Gd89
Sigloy F 29 Gd40
Siglufjörður IS 2 Ba03
Sigmaringen D 142 Cd50
Sigmaringendorf D 142 Cd51
Sigmarszell D 142 Da52
Sigmen BG 181 Ec72
Sigmir RO 171 Dc57
Sigmundsherberg A 136 Ga49
Signa I 155 Dc65
Signalnes N 67 Ha11
Signes F 42 Jd55
Signy-l'Abbaye F 24 Hd34
Signy-le-Petit F 24 Hd33
Sigogne F 32 Fc47
Sigonce F 42 Jd52
Šigony RUS 203 Ga10
Sigrás E 36 Ba54
Sigrí GR 191 Dd83
Sigtuna S 96 Gc42
Sigüeiro E 36 Ba55
Sigüenza E 47 Ea62
Sigüés E 39 Fa57
Sigüeya E 37 Bd57
Sigulda LV 106 Kc50
Šihany RUS 203 Fd11
Sihlea RO 176 Ed63
Sihtuuna FIN 74 Jc20
Sihva EST 106 La46
Siikainen FIN 89 Ja34
Siikajärvi FIN 98 Ka39
Siikajoki FIN 74 Jd24
Siika-Kämä FIN 74 Kb19
Siikakoski FIN 90 La34
Siikakoski FIN 91 Lb34
Siikala FIN 90 Ka38
Siikamäki FIN 82 La28
Siikamäki FIN 90 La32
Siikaselkä FIN 90 Kc33
Siikava FIN 90 Kd36
Siikavaara FIN 91 Ld32
Siiksaare EST 105 Jd46
Siilinjärvi FIN 82 La29
Siimika EST 98 Ka43
Siimusti EST 98 La44
Siipyy FIN 89 Hd34
Siironen FIN 81 Jc26
Siitama FIN 90 Ka35
Siivikko FIN 75 Kc22
Sijarinska Banja SRB 178 Bc70
Sijekovac BIH 152 Hb61
Sikakylä FIN 89 Jb32
Sikaminiá GR 183 Bd80
Sikaminiá GR 191 Ea83
Sikås S 79 Fd29
Sikéa GR 195 Bd90
Sikeå S 80 Hc27
Sikeå hamn S 80 Hc27
Sikés GR 194 Bb87
Sikfőkút H 146 Jb51
Sikfors S 73 Hc22
Sikiá GR 183 Bc80
Sikiá GR 184 Cd80
Sikiés GR 189 Bc81
Síkinos GR 196 Da91
Sikióna GR 189 Bd86
Siklesciems LV 113 Ja53
Siklós H 152 Hb58
Siknäs S 73 Ja21
Sikorráhi GR 185 Dd77
Sikórz PL 130 Hd36
Sikourió GR 183 Bd80
Sikovaara FIN 83 Ld28
Sikovicy RUS 99 Ma44
Sikovuono FIN 64 Ka10
Sikrags LV 105 Jc48
Siksele S 80 Ha25
Siksjö S 79 Gb26
Siksjö S 80 Gc27
Siksjönäs S 79 Ga25
Sikšņi LV 113 Jb53
Šikšniai LT 114 Ka58
Sikvaland N 92 Ca45
Sil S 79 Ga29
Sila N 70 Fa20
Šilagaliai LT 114 La54
Silagals LV 107 Lb51
Šilagalys LT 114 Kc55
Šilai LT 114 Kd55
Šilainiai LV 114 Kb56
Silajāņi LV 107 Lc52
Šilalė LT 113 Jd56
Silandro I 142 Dc56
Silanus I 169 Ca76
Šilavoas LT 114 Kc58
Silba HR 151 Fc63
Silbaš SRB 153 Ja60
Silbertal A 142 Da54
Silbodal S 94 Ec43
Silchester GB 20 Fa28
Sildhopen N 66 Fd16
Şile TR 186 Ga77
Sileby GB 16 Fa24
Silec PL 122 Jc30
Silen BG 185 Dd75
Šilėnai LT 114 Kb54
Šilėnai LT 114 La58
Silene LV 115 Lc54
Silenieki LV 106 Kb51
Siles E 53 Ea71
Silfiac F 27 Ea39
Siligo I 168 Ca75
Şilindia RO 170 Ca59
Siliqua I 169 Bd79
Siliştea RO 176 Dd66
Siliştea RO 177 Fa63
Siliştea RO 177 Fb66
Siliştea Crucii RO 179 Cd67
Siliştea Guimeşti RO 175 Dc66
Silistra BG 181 Ed67
Silius I 169 Cb79
Silivaşu de Câmpie RO 171 Db58
Silivri TR 186 Fb77
Silixen D 126 Cd37
Siljan N 93 Dc43
Siljansnäs S 95 Fc39
Siljeåsen S 79 Fd27
Silkeborg DK 108 Db24
Silla E 54 Fb68
Silla EST 98 Ka44
Silla I 155 Db64
Sillamäe EST 99 Lc41
Sillano I 149 Da63
Sillanpää FIN 81 Jc29
Sillans-la-Cascade F 42 Ka54
Silleda E 36 Ba56
Sillé-le-Guillaume F 28 Fc39
Sillenstede D 117 Cc32
Sillerud S 94 Ec43
Sillery F 24 Hd35
Silli GR 184 Da76
Sillian A 143 Eb55
Sillingebyn S 94 Ed44
s'Illot E 57 Hd67
Sillre S 87 Ga33
Sillre S 87 Gb32
Silmala LV 107 Lc51
Silnica PL 130 Hd41
Silno PL 121 Gd32
Silo HR 151 Fc61
Šilovo RUS 203 Fa12
Silovo RUS 203 Fb11
Sils CH 142 Cd56
Sils E 49 Hb60
Silsand N 67 Gc11
Silsden GB 16 Ed20
Silsjönäs S 79 Ga29
Silstrup DK 100 Da21
Siltaharju FIN 69 Ka14
Siltakylä Broby FIN 90 La38
Siltala FIN 82 Kc25
Siltala FIN 89 Jc32
Siltalanperä FIN 82 Kd26
Siltavaara FIN 83 Lc27
Silte S 104 Gd50
Siltene LV 107 Lc50
Šilukains LV 107 Lc51
Šilutė LT 113 Jb56
Šiluva LT 114 Ka55
Silva E 36 Ad54
Silván E 37 Bd57
Silvana Mansio I 164 Gc80
Silvaplana CH 142 Cd56
Silvares P 44 Ba64
Silvberg S 95 Fd40
Silveiros P 44 Ad60
Šilvėnai LT 114 Ka57
Silver Bridge GB 9 Cd19
Silverdalen S 103 Fd49
Silverdalen S 103 Ga49
Silvergruvan S 95 Fb42
Silverstone GB 20 Fb26
Silves P 58 Ab74
Silvi Marina I 157 Fa69
Silvola FIN 91 Lc33
Šima RUS 99 Ld43
Simakivka UA 202 Eb14
Simala I 169 Ca78
Simalan Metsäkulm FIN 97 Jc39
Simanala FIN 91 Lc32
Simancas E 46 Cd60
Şimand RO 170 Bd58
Simanda GR 183 Cb79
Simandre F 30 Jb44
Simanes N 63 Hd08
Šimanovci SRB 153 Jb61
Simat de la Valldigna E 54 Fc69
Simav TR 192 Fc84
Simaxis I 169 Bd77
Simbach D 135 Ec49
Simbach am Inn D 143 Ec50
Simbario I 164 Gc82
Simbirsk RUS 203 Fd09
Simeonovograd BG 185 Dd74
Simeria RO 175 Cc61
Simested DK 100 Db22
Simferopol' UA 205 Fa17
Simi GR 197 Ed92
Şimian RO 170 Cb55
Simian RO 174 Cb65
Simiane-la-Rotonde F 42 Jd52
Simići BIH 153 Hd63
Siminicea RO 172 Ec55
Simiö FIN 90 Ka33
Simitli BG 183 Cb74
Šimkai LT 113 Jb55
Šimkaičiai LT 114 Ka56
Simlångsdalen S 102 Ed52
Simleu Silvaniei RO 171 Cc56
Simmelkær DK 100 Da23
Simmerath D 125 Bc42
Simmerberg D 142 Da52
Simmern D 133 Ca44
Simmersfeld D 133 Cb49
Simmershofen D 134 Db46
Simmertal D 133 Ca44
Simnas LV 114 Kb59
Simniča MK 182 Ba74
Simo FIN 74 Jd21
Simola FIN 91 Lc36
Simonburn GB 11 Ed16
Simonby FIN 97 Jb40
Şimoneşti RO 176 Dd60
Simoniemi FIN 74 Jd22
Simonkylä FIN 74 Jd22
Simonsbath GB 19 Dd29
Simonsberg D 108 Da29
Simonstad N 93 Da45
Simonstorp S 95 Ga45
Simonswald D 141 Ca50
Simontornya H 146 Hc55
Šimonys LT 114 Kd54
Simorre F 40 Ga55
Simos GR 188 Bb84
Simou CY 206 Hd97
Simpelveld NL 125 Bb41
Simpiänniemi FIN 90 Kd34
Simplon CH 148 Ca57
Simpnäs S 96 Ha41
Simremarken S 110 Ed57
Simrishamn S 111 Fb56
Simsk RUS 202 Eb09
Simskälä FIN 96 Hc40
Simskardet N 70 Fa24
Simuna EST 98 La43
Simuna FIN 90 Kc32
Sinac HR 151 Fd62
Sinaia RO 176 Ea63
Sinalunga I 156 Dd67
Sinanaj AL 182 Ab77
Sinandele TR 192 Fa83
Sinanlı TR 186 Fa76
Sinanlıballi TR 187 Gb78
Sinanoğlu TR 187 Gc78
Sinarádes GR 182 Ab80
Sinarcas E 54 Ed67
Sin'avino RUS 113 Jd59
Şinca RO 176 Dd61
Şincai RO 171 Db58
Sincan TR 205 Fd20
Sincanlı TR 193 Gb85
Şinca Nouă RO 176 Dd62
Sincansarnıç TR 192 Fc81
Sindal DK 101 Dd19
Sindel BG 181 Fa71
Sindelfingen D 134 Cc48
Sindendro GR 182 Ba79
Sindi EST 98 Kb45
Sindia I 169 Bd76
Sındırgı TR 192 Fa83
Sindos GR 183 Ca78
Sinekçi TR 185 Ed80
Sinekli TR 186 Fb77
Sinemorec BG 186 Fa74
Sinersig RO 174 Ca61
Sines P 50 Ab71
Sineşti RO 172 Ed57
Sineşti RO 175 Da64
Sineşti RO 176 Eb66
Sinettä FIN 74 Jd18
Sineu E 57 Hc67
Singen D 142 Cc51
Singera MD 173 Fd58
Singerei MD 173 Fb56
Singereii Noi MD 173 Fb55
Singilej RUS 203 Fd10
Singleton GB 20 Fb30
Singö S 96 Ha40
Singsby FIN 81 Hd30
Singsjön S 79 Fc31
Singureni MD 173 Fb55
Singureni RO 180 Ea67
Singusdal N 93 Db43
Sinie Lipjagi RUS 203 Fb13
Sinij Nikola RUS 107 Ma49
Sinirli TR 191 Ed85
Siniscola I 168 Cc75
Siniselkä FIN 82 Ka25
Sini Vir BG 181 Ec69
Sinj HR 158 Gc65
Sinjac MNE 159 Hd67
Sinjavka BY 202 Ea13
Sinjo Bărdo BG 179 Cd70
Sinksundet S 73 Hd22
Sin-le-Noble F 23 Ha32
Sinn D 126 Cc42
Sinnai I 169 Ca79
Sinnes N 92 Cc44
Sinntal D 134 Da43
Sinodskoe RUS 203 Fd11
Sinogóra PL 122 Hd34
Sinoie RO 177 Fc66
Sinole LV 107 Lb49
Sinop TR 205 Fb19
Sinopoli I 164 Ga83
Sins CH 141 Cb53
Sinsheim D 134 Cc47
Sinspelt D 133 Bb44
Sint Annaparochie NL 117 Bc33
Sintautai LT 114 Ka58
Sintea Mare RO 170 Ca58
Şintereag RO 171 Db57
Şinteu RO 171 Cc56
Sint Jacobiparochie NL 117 Bc33
Sint Martensbrug NL 116 Ba34
Sint Michielsgestel NL 124 Ba38
Sint Nicolaasga NL 117 Bc34
Sint-Niklaas B 124 Ac39
Sint Oedenrode NL 125 Bb38
Sint Philipsland NL 124 Ac38
Sintra P 50 Aa68
Sintsi FIN 83 Ld31
Sint-Truiden B 124 Ba41
Sinués E 39 Fb57
Sinzheim D 133 Cb48
Sinzig D 125 Bd42
Sinzing D 135 Ea48
Siófok H 145 Hb55
Sion CH 141 Bc56
Sion F 31 Jd38
Sion-les-Mines F 28 Ed40
Sion Mills GB 9 Cc16
Siorac-en-Périgord F 33 Gb50
Sipa EST 98 Kb44
Sipahi TR 185 Ec77
Sipahiler TR 199 Gd88
Šipanska Luka HR 158 Hb69
Şipca MD 173 Ga57
Sipilä FIN 82 Kb30
Sipilä FIN 90 Ka32
Sipinen FIN 82 La25
Šipka BG 180 Dc71
Šipkovica MK 183 Ca74
Šipkovo BG 180 Db71
Sipola FIN 74 Ka24
Sipola FIN 82 Kb25
Siponys LT 114 Kc58
Sipoo FIN 98 Kc39
Şipote RO 172 Ed56
Şipotele RO 181 Fb68
Şipoteni MD 173 Fc58
Šipovo BIH 158 Gd64
Sippola FIN 90 La37
Sira N 92 Cb46
Sirač HR 152 Gd59
Siracusa I 167 Fd87
Sir'ajevo RUS 107 Mb48
Siráko GR 182 Ba80
Sirakovo BG 184 Dc74
Şiran TR 205 Fd20
Şirăuţi MD 172 Ed54
Sircova MD 173 Fd55
Siret RO 172 Eb54
Siretel RO 172 Ec56
Sireţi MD 173 Fd57
Sirevåg N 92 Ca45
Sirgala EST 99 Lc42
Şiria RO 170 Ca59
Sirig SRB 153 Jb59
Şirince TR 191 Ec87
Sirinçsvuş TR 185 Ed80
Sirineasa RO 175 Db64
Şirinköy TR 198 Fc88
Siritovci HR 158 Gb65
Siriu RO 176 Eb63
Sirk SK 138 Jb49
Sirkka FIN 68 Jc15
Sirkkakoski FIN 74 Jc18
Sirkkamäki FIN 82 Kc31
Sirkön S 111 Fc53
Sirma MD 173 Fb59
Sirma N 64 Ka07
Sirmione I 149 Db59
Şirna RO 176 Ea65
Sirnach CH 142 Cc53
Sirniö FIN 75 Kd20
Sirogojno SRB 178 Ad67
Sirok H 146 Jb51
Široka lăka BG 184 Da75
Široká Niva CZ 137 Gd44
Široké SK 138 Jc47
Široki Brijeg BIH 158 Ha66
Široko Polje HR 153 Hc60
Širokovo BG 180 Ea69
Sirolo I 156 Ed66
Sırpsındığı TR 185 Eb75
Siruela E 52 Cc69
Sirvaste EST 107 Lb46
Širvintos LT 114 Kd57
Sisak HR 152 Gb60
Šišan HR 151 Fa62
Sisante E 53 Eb68
Sisättö FIN 89 Jc34
Sisbacka FIN 81 Jb29
Şişcani MD 173 Fb58
Sisco F 154 Cc68
Şişeler TR 199 Ha91
Šišenci BG 179 Ca67
Sises GR 200 Da95
Şişeşti RO 171 Da55
Şişeşti RO 175 Cc64
Sislioba TR 186 Fa74
Šišljavic HR 151 Ga59
Šišmanci BG 180 Dc73
Sissach CH 141 Ca52
Sissinghurst GB 21 Ga29
Sissonne F 24 Hc34
Sista Palkino RUS 99 Ld40
Şiştăroval RO 174 Ca60
Sistelo P 36 Ad58
Sisteron F 42 Jd52
Sistiana I 150 Ed59
Sistín E 36 Bb57
Sisto E 36 Bb53
Sistranda N 77 Dc28
Sita Buzăului RO 176 Eb62
Sitagrí GR 184 Cd76
Šit'ane RUS 107 Ma48
Sitaniec PL 131 Kc41
Sitariá GR 183 Bb77
Sitarla FIN 98 Ka39
Sitasjaurestugorna S 67 Gb15
Šitbořice CZ 137 Gc48
Sitena GR 194 Bc88
Sitges E 49 Gd62
Sitia GR 201 Dd96
Sitikala FIN 90 Kd37
Sitkowo PL 123 Kb32
Sitkunai LV 114 Kb57
Sitnica BIH 152 Gd63
Sitno PL 121 Gb32
Sitno PL 122 Hc34
Sitohóri GR 184 Cc77
Sitómena GR 188 Ba83
Sitovo BG 181 Ec68
Sitovo BG 184 Db74
Sittard NL 125 Bb40
Sittensen D 118 Da33
Sitter N 78 Eb26
Sittersdorf A 144 Fc56
Sittingbourne GB 21 Ga28
Sitzendorf an der Schmida A 136 Ga49
Siuntio FIN 98 Ka40
Siuntion kirkonkylä FIN 98 Ka40
Šiupyliai LT 114 Ka53
Siuro FIN 89 Jc36
Siurua FIN 74 Kb22
Siurunmaa FIN 69 Ka15
Siusi I 143 Dd56
Sivac SRB 153 Ja59
Šivačevo BG 180 Ea72
Sivakka FIN 83 Lb27
Sivakka FIN 83 Lc26
Sivakkajoki FIN 83 Lb27
Sivakkavaara FIN 83 Lb29
Siva reka BG 185 Ea75
Sivas TR 205 Fc20
Sivaslı TR 192 Ga86
Siverić HR 158 Gb65
Sivers LV 115 Ld53
Siverskij RUS 99 Mb41
Siverskij RUS 202 Eb09
Sivertbukt N 65 Kb07
Siviken S 102 Ec46
Sivle N 84 Cc38
Sivota GR 188 Ac81
Sivrihisar TR 193 Hb83
Sivriler TR 186 Fa75
Sivros GR 188 Ac83
Six Crosses IRL 12 Bb24
Six-Fours-les-Plages F 42 Jd55
Sixmilebrige IRL 12 Bd23
Sixmilecross GB 9 Cc17
Six Road Ends GB 10 Dc17
Sixt F 35 Kb45
Sixt-sur-Aff F 27 Ec40
Siziano I 149 Cc60
Sizun F 26 Dc38
Sjabero RUS 99 Ma43
Själlarim S 73 Hb19
Sjanno BY 202 Eb12
Sjanovo BG 180 Eb68
Sjas'stroj RUS 202 Eb08
Sjåstad N 93 Dd41
Sjava RUS 203 Fc08
Sjelle DK 108 Dc24
Sjenica SRB 178 Ad68
Sjeničak Lasinjski HR 151 Ga60
Sjerogošte MNE 159 Jb68
Sjetlina BIH 159 Hc65
Sjetnemarka N 77 Ea30
Sjeverodonec'k UA 203 Fb14
Sjisjka S 67 Ha16
Sjoåsen N 78 Eb27
Sjöberg S 71 Ga23
Sjöberg S 79 Ga25
Sjöbo S 110 Fa56
Sjöbotten S 80 Hc26
Sjöbrånet S 80 Hb26
Sjödiken S 110 Ed56
Sjogerstad S 102 Fa47
Sjögestad S 103 Fd47
Sjøholt N 76 Cd32
Sjøli N 86 Eb36
Sjöliden S 80 Gc25
Sjølund DK 108 Db26
Sjömarken S 102 Ed49
Sjona N 70 Fa20
Sjonbotn N 71 Fb20
Sjonhem S 104 Ha49
Sjørring DK 100 Da21
Sjörröd S 110 Fa54
Sjørslev DK 100 Db23
Sjørup DK 100 Da23
Sjösa S 96 Gc45
Sjötofta S 102 Ed50
Sjötorp S 95 Fb45
Sjøtun N 62 Gc10
Sjoutnäset S 79 Fc26
Sjøvegan N 67 Gc12
Sjövik S 102 Ec48
Sjugare S 95 Fc39
Sjulnäs S 73 Hc23
Sjulsmark S 73 Hd22
Sjunberget S 68 Hc17
Sjundeå FIN 98 Ka40
Sjundeå kby FIN 98 Ka40
Sjuntorp S 102 Ec47
Sjursvik N 66 Ga11
Sjusjøen N 85 Ea37
Skabland N 85 Ea40
Skaborai LT 113 Jc55
Skadovs'k UA 204 Ed17
Skælskør DK 109 Ea27
Skærbæk DK 108 Da27
Skærbæk DK 108 Db26
Skærum DK 101 Dd20
Skærup DK 108 Db25
Skævinge DK 109 Ec25
Skafidiá GR 194 Ad87
Skafså N 93 Da43
Skäfthammar S 96 Gd41
Skaftung FIN 89 Hd34
Skagaströnd IS 2 Ad03
Skage N 78 Ec26
Skagen DK 101 Dd19
Skagen N 70 Fa19
Skaiå N 92 Cd46
Skáidi N 63 Ja06
Skaill GB 5 Ec03
Skaistgiriai LT 114 Kc54
Skaistgirys LT 114 Ka53
Skaistkalne LV 106 Kc52
Skaitekojan S 73 Hb19
Skakdupiai LT 114 Ka59
Skála GR 182 Ab80
Skála GR 184 Db77
Skála GR 188 Ac85
Skála GR 189 Ca84
Skála GR 191 Ea83
Skála GR 194 Bc90
Skála GR 197 Ea89
Skała PL 138 Ja44
Skála Eressú GR 191 Dd83
Skála Foúrka GR 183 Cb80
Skałągi PL 129 Ha41
Skála Marión GR 184 Da78
Skaland N 62 Gb10
Skåland N 92 Cb46
Skála Oropoú GR 189 Cc85
Skala-Podil's'ka UA 204 Ea16
Skála Sikaminiás GR 191 Ea83
Skála Sotíros GR 184 Da78
Skålavík DK 3 Ca07
Skalbmierz PL 138 Jb43
Skålbygget S 87 Fc37
Skålderviken S 110 Ed54
Skåldö FIN 97 Jd41
Skålen S 87 Fb32
Skålevik N 84 Ca39
Skalhamn S 102 Eb47
Skalica BG 180 Ea73
Skalica SK 137 Gd48
Skalité SK 138 Hc46
Skallebølle DK 108 Dc26
Skallelv N 65 Kd06
Skällernd S 94 Ea45
Skällersud S 94 Ec45
Skallerup Klit DK 100 Dc19
Skällinge S 102 Ec51
Skallmeja S 102 Ed47
Skallttivaara FIN 64 Jd08
Skällvik S 103 Gb46
Skalmodal S 71 Fc23
Skalmsjö S 80 Gc29
Skalná CZ 135 Eb44
Skålö S 95 Fb39
Skalohóri GR 182 Ba78
Skalohóri GR 191 Dd83
Skalotí GR 184 Da76
Skalotí GR 200 Cc96
Skals DK 100 Db22
Skalsko BG 180 Dd71
Skalsvika N 71 Fc18
Skalunda S 102 Ed46
Skälvum S 102 Fa46
Skam'ja RUS 99 Lc43
Skamsdalssetra N 77 Dc33
Skandáli GR 190 Dc81
Skandawa PL 122 Jb30
Skanderborg DK 108 Dc24
Skånela S 96 Gd43
Skånes-Fagerhult S 110 Fa53
Skåne-Tranås S 111 Fb56
Skånevik N 92 Cb41
Skangali RUS 107 Ld50
Skåningbukt N 62 Ha08
Skånings-Åsaka S 102 Fa46
Skänknäsberget S 79 Ga27
Skänninge S 103 Fc47
Skanör S 110 Ed57
Skansbacken S 95 Fb40
Skansholm S 79 Ga26
Skansnäs S 71 Ga24
Skansnäs S 72 Gb22
Skansnäset S 79 Fd27
Skåpafors S 94 Ec44
Skąpe PL 128 Fd37
Skapiškis LT 114 Kd54
Skara S 102 Fa47
Skarberget N 66 Ga14
Skärblacka S 103 Ga46
Skard N 71 Fd18
Skarda S 80 Gd27
Skardet N 71 Fc20
Skardsgard N 85 Db38
Skare N 92 Cc41
Skåre S 94 Fa43
Skares GB 10 Dd15
Skares LV 105 Jd52
Skåret N 86 Ed36
Skärgårdsstad S 96 Gd43
Skärhamn S 102 Eb48
Skärkind S 103 Ga46
Skärlöv S 111 Gb53
Skarmunken N 62 Gd09
Skarness N 94 Eb40
Skarø By DK 109 Dd28
Skarpengland N 92 Cd46
Skärplinge S 96 Gc40
Skarpnåtö FIN 96 Hb40
Skarp Salling DK 100 Db21
Skarrild DK 108 Da24
Skärså S 87 Gb37
Skarset N 76 Cd31
Skarsfjord N 62 Gc08
Skärsjövålen S 86 Fa34
Skarstad N 66 Ga14
Skarstad S 102 Ed47
Skårstad S 103 Fb48
Skarstein N 66 Ga11
Skarsvåg N 64 Jb04
Skarszewy PL 121 Ha31
Skarszyn PL 129 Gc40
Skårup DK 109 Dd27
Skärv S 102 Fa47
Skarvången S 79 Fb29
Skarvfjordhamn N 63 Hd05
Skårvik N 67 Gc12
Skarvsjöby S 79 Gb25
Skaryszew PL 130 Jc40
Skarżyn PL 123 Jd32
Skarżysko-Kamienna PL 130 Jb40
Skasenden N 94 Ec40
Skästra S 87 Ga35
Skatelöv S 103 Fc52
Skåtøy N 93 Dc45
Skattkärr S 94 Fa43
Skattungbyn S 87 Fc37
Skatval N 78 Eb29
Skatvik N 67 Gb11
Skaudvilė LT 113 Jd56
Skaulo S 68 Hc16
Škaune LV 107 Ma52
Skauvoll N 71 Fb18
Skavaricy RUS 99 Mb40
Skave DK 100 Da23
Skavik N 63 Ja05
Skavnakk N 63 Hb07
Skawina PL 138 Ja44
Skeagh IRL 9 Cb20
Skebobruk S 96 Ha41
Skebokvarn S 95 Gb44
Skeby S 102 Fa46
Skeda S 103 Fd47
Šķēde LV 105 Jc51
Skede S 103 Fd50
Skedevi S 95 Ga45
Skedshult S 103 Gb48
Skedsmokorset N 93 Ea41
Skee S 94 Eb45
Skegness GB 17 Fd22
Skegrie S 110 Ed57
Skehanagh IRL 8 Bd20
Skehanagh IRL 12 Bd21
Skei N 70 Ec24
Skei N 77 Dc31
Skei N 78 Ec28
Skei N 84 Cc35
Skejby DK 108 Dc24
Skela SRB 153 Jb62
Skelby DK 109 Eb27
Skelby DK 109 Eb29
Skelde DK 108 Db28
Skelhøje DK 100 Db23
Skellefteå S 80 Hc25
Skelleftehamn S 80 Hc25
Skellingsted DK 109 Ea26
Skelmanthorpe GB 16 Fa21
Skelmersdale GB 15 Ec21
Skelmorlie GB 6 Dc13
Šķelteni LV 115 Lc53
Skelton GB 11 Fb18
Skėmiai LT 114 Kb55
Skender Vakuf BIH 152 Gd63
Skene S 102 Ec50
Skenfrith GB 19 Eb27
Skenshyttan S 95 Fd40
Skepastí GR 200 Cd95
Skepastó GR 184 Cc77
Skepastó GR 188 Ac81
Skępe PL 122 Hc35
Skephult S 102 Ed49
Skepperstad S 103 Fc50
Skepplanda S 102 Ec48
Skeppshult S 102 Fa51
Skeppsvik S 80 Hc28
Skepptuna S 96 Gd42
Skerike S 95 Gb42
Skerping DK 100 Db21
Skerries IRL 9 Da20
Ski N 93 Ea42
Skiadás GR 188 Ba86
Skíathos GR 189 Cb83
Skibbereen IRL 12 Bb26
Skibbild DK 108 Da24
Skibby DK 109 Eb25
Šķibe LV 106 Ka52
Skibet DK 108 Db25
Skibice PL 128 Fd39
Skibotn N 62 Ha10
Skidal' BY 202 Dd13
Skidby GB 17 Fc20
Skidby GB 17 Fc21
Skídra GR 183 Bd77
Skieblewo PL 123 Kb31
Skiemonys LT 114 La55
Skien N 93 Dc44
Skierbieszów PL 131 Kc41
Skierniewice PL 130 Ja38
Skiftenes N 93 Da46
Skiippagurra N 64 Ka06
Šķilbēni LV 107 Ld49
Skilingmark S 94 Ec42
Skille N 70 Ed23
Skillefjord N 63 Hd07
Skillerhult S 103 Ga52
Skillingaryd S 103 Fb50
Skillinge S 111 Fb56
Skimtleflaten N 85 Ea40
Skinburness GB 11 Eb16
Skiniás GR 201 Db96
Skinnerup DK 100 Da21
Skinnskatteberg S 95 Fd42
Skipavig N 92 Cb43
Skipnes N 77 Dc30
Skipsea GB 17 Fc20
Skipton GB 16 Ed20
Skipton-on-Swale GB 11 Fa19
Skiptvet N 93 Ea43
Skirmantiškė LV 114 Kb56
Skirö S 103 Fd50
Skíros GR 190 Da84
Skirsnemunė LT 114 Ka57
Skirva N 93 Db41
Skiti GR 189 Ca81
Skitte N 67 Gb12
Skittenelv N 62 Gd09
Skivarp S 110 Fa57
Skive DK 100 Da22
Skivika N 70 Fa20
Skivjane KSV 178 Ad71
Skivsjön S 80 Ha27
Skjæragenta N 63 Hd08
Skjærholla N 86 Ed37
Skjærli N 84 Ca35
Skjærnes N 64 Ka06
Skjåmoen N 70 Fa22
Skjånes N 64 Jd05
Skjånes N 64 Ka04
Skjåvika N 71 Fb22
Skjeberg N 93 Ea44
Skjee N 93 Dd44
Skjeggedal N 84 Cc40
Skjeggedal N 93 Da45
Skjeggestad N 92 Cb45
Skjelbreid N 78 Fa26
Skjellelv N 67 Gb12
Skjelmoen N 71 Fc22
Skjelnes N 62 Ha10
Skjelstad N 78 Eb28
Skjelstad N 78 Ec28
Skjelten N 76 Cc32
Skjelvareid N 66 Fd15
Skjelvika N 71 Fb18
Skjern DK 108 Cd24
Skjerstad N 66 Fc17
Skjervøy N 63 Hb08
Skjevlo N 78 Ec27
Skjød DK 100 Dc23
Skjold N 92 Ca42
Skjoldastraumen N 92 Ca42
Skjoldehamn N 66 Fd12
Skjolden N 85 Da36
Skjombotn N 67 Gb14
Skjønhaug N 94 Eb42
Skjønne N 85 Db40
Skleně SK 138 Hc48
Sklithro GR 189 Ca81
Šklov BY 202 Eb12
Skoby S 96 Gd41
Škočivir MK 183 Bb76
Škocjan SLO 151 Fd58
Skocze PL 123 Jd30
Skoczów PL 138 Hc45
Skodborg DK 108 Da26
Skodje N 76 Cd32
Skødstrup DK 108 Dc24

Somberek – Stănița

Somberek H 153 Hc57
Sombernon F 30 Ja42
Sombor SRB 153 Hd58
Şomcuta Mare RO 171 Da55
Someo CH 141 Cb56
Sõmera EST 105 Jc46
Somere FIN 75 Kd24
Someren NL 125 Bb39
Somerniemi FIN 89 Jd38
Somero FIN 89 Jd38
Someronkylä FIN 81 Jd26
Somerovaara FIN 74 Ka23
Sõmerpalu EST 107 Lb47
Somersham GB 20 Fd25
Somersham GB 21 Ga26
Somerton GB 19 Eb29
Someş-Oderhei RO 171 Cd56
Sominy PL 121 Gd31
Somlóvásárhely H 145 Gd54
Sommacampagna I 149 Db60
Somma Lombardo I 148 Cb58
Sommanelm N 92 Cd45
Sommariva del Bosco I 148 Bd61
Sommarøy N 62 Gc09
Sommarset N 66 Fd16
Sommatino I 167 Fa86
Sommauthe F 24 Ja34
Sommecaise F 30 Hb40
Somme-Leuze B 124 Ba42
Sommen S 103 Fc47
Sommepy-Tahure F 24 Hd35
Sömmerda D 127 Dd41
Sommerfeld D 119 Ed35
Sommerhausen D 134 Db45
Sommersete N 65 Kc05
Sommersted DK 108 Db26
Sommery F 23 Gb34
Sommesous F 24 Hd37
Somme-Tourbe F 24 Ja35
Sommevoire F 30 Ja38
Sommières F 41 Hd53
Sommières-du-Clain F 32 Fd45
Somo E 38 Dc54
Somogyapáti H 152 Ha57
Somogyaszalo H 145 Ha56
Somogycsicsó H 152 Gd57
Somogyfajsz H 145 Ha56
Somogyhárságy H 152 Ha57
Somogyjád H 145 Ha56
Somogysárd H 145 Ha56
Somogysimony H 145 Gd56
Somogytúr H 145 Ha55
Somogyudvarhely H 152 Gd57
Somogyvár H 145 Ha56
Somogyzsitfa H 145 Gd56
Somolinos E 46 Dd62
Somonino PL 121 Ha30
Somoskőújfalu H 146 Ja50
Somotor SK 139 Ka49
Somova RO 177 Fc64
Somovit BG 180 Db68
Sompa EST 99 Lb42
Sompolno PL 129 Hb36
Sompuis F 24 Hd37
Sompujärvi FIN 74 Jd21
Somsois F 24 Hd37
Somvix CH 142 Cc55
Son N 93 Ea43
Şona RO 175 Db60
Son Bou E 57 Ja66
Sonceboz CH 141 Bc53
Sonchamp F 29 Gc38
Soncillo E 38 Dc56
Soncino I 149 Cd60
Sonda EST 98 La42
Sondalo I 142 Da56
Sondby FIN 98 Kc39
Søndeled N 93 Db45
Sønder Bindslev DK 101 Dd19
Sønder Bjert DK 108 Db26
Sønderborg DK 108 Db28
Sønder Bork DK 108 Cd25
Sønderby DK 100 Da22
Sønderby DK 108 Db28
Sønder Dråby DK 100 Da21
Sønder Felding DK 108 Da24
Sønderho DK 108 Cd26
Sønderholm DK 100 Dc21
Sønder Hostrup DK 108 Db28
Sønder Hygum DK 108 Da26
Sønder Kirkeby DK 109 Eb29
Sønder Nissum DK 100 Cd23
Sønder Omme DK 108 Da25
Sønder Onsild DK 100 Dc22
Sønder Ørslev DK 109 Eb29
Sønder Rind DK 100 Db23
Sønder Rubjerg DK 100 Dc20
Sondershausen D 127 Dd40
Søndersø DK 108 Dc26
Sønder Solbjerg DK 100 Da21
Sønder Stenderup DK 108 Db26
Sønderup DK 100 Dc22
Søndervig DK 108 Cd24
Sønder Vilstrup DK 108 Db27
Sønder Vissing DK 108 Db24
Sondheim D 134 Db43
Søndre Osen N 86 Ec37
Sondrio I 149 Cd57
Söndrum S 102 Ed52
Söne S 102 Ed46
Soneja E 54 Fb66
Son en Breugel NL 125 Bb38
Songe N 93 Db45
Songeons F 23 Gc34
Songesand N 92 Cb44
Songy F 24 Hd37
Sonico I 149 Db57
Sonka FIN 74 Jd18
Sonkaja FIN 83 Ma30
Sonkajärvi FIN 82 Kd27
Sonkakoski FIN 82 Kd27
Sonkamuotka FIN 68 Ja14
Sonkari FIN 82 Kc30
Sonkovo RUS 202 Ed09
Son Macià E 57 Hc67
Son Marroig E 57 Hb67
Sonnboda FIN 97 Kd44
Sonneberg D 135 Dd43
Sonnefeld D 135 Dd44
Sonnewalde D 128 Fa39
Sonnino I 160 Ec73
Sonntag A 142 Da53
Sonogno CH 141 Cb56
Sonsbeck D 125 Bc38
Sons-de-Bretagne F 28 Ed38
Sonseca E 52 Db67
Son Servera E 57 Hc67
Sońsk PL 122 Jb35
Sonstorp S 95 Fd45
Sonta SRB 153 Hd59
Sontheim D 142 Db51
Sontheim a.d. Brenz D 134 Db49
Sonthofen D 142 Db53
Sontra D 126 Db41
Soodla EST 98 Kc42
Soomevere EST 98 Kd44
Söörmarkku FIN 89 Ja35
Sööru EST 99 Lb44
Sopeke FIN 91 Ma32
Sopelana E 38 Ea55
Sopište MK 178 Bb73
Sopje HR 152 Ha58
Sopkino RUS 122 Jb30
Soponya H 145 Hb54
Sopot AL 182 Ac75
Sopot BG 179 Da70
Sopot BG 180 Db72
Sopot PL 121 Hb30
Sopot RO 175 Cd66
Sopot SRB 153 Jc62
Sopot SRB 174 Bb64
Sopotnica MK 182 Ba75
Şopotu Nou RO 174 Bd64
Sopparjok N 64 Jc08
Soppela FIN 74 Kc18
Sopron H 145 Gc52
Sopronhorpács H 145 Gc53
Sopronkövesd H 145 Gc53
Sopsko Rudare MK 178 Bb73
Šor SRB 153 Ja62
Sora I 160 Ed72
Soragna I 149 Da61
Soråker S 88 Gc33
Sorano I 156 Dd69
Sørarnøy N 71 Fb18
Sør-Åvika N 70 Ed21
Sorbara I 149 Dc62
Sorbas E 61 Eb75
Sorbiers F 42 Jd51
Sørbø N 92 Ca43
Sörbo S 102 Eb46
Sorbolo I 149 Da61
Sörby S 94 Fa41
Sörby S 102 Fa47
Sörbygden S 87 Ga32
Sørbymagle DK 109 Ea27
Sörbyn S 73 Hd21
Sörbyn S 80 Hb26
Sord IRL 13 Cd21
Sordal N 92 Cd44
Sore F 39 Fb52
Söred H 145 Hb53
Sorede F 41 Hb57
Søreidet N 62 Gd08
Søre Moen N 78 Ed29
Sørenget N 78 Ec26
Soresina I 149 Cd60
Sørfinnset N 71 Fb18
Sörfjärden S 88 Gc34
Sørfjord N 63 Hc09
Sørfjord N 67 Gb12
Sørfjorden N 66 Fd13
Sörflärke S 80 Gc30
Sörfors S 80 Hb28
Sörforsa S 87 Gb35
Sørfossbogen N 67 Gc11
Sørgård N 71 Fb23
Sorges F 33 Ga48
Sorgono I 169 Ca77
Sør-Grunnfjord N 62 Gd08
Sorgues-l'Ouvèze F 42 Jb52
Sør-Gutvika N 70 Ec24
Sørheim N 84 Cd36
Sørhorsfjord N 70 Ec24
Sori I 148 Cb63
Soria E 47 Eb60
Soriano nel Cimino I 156 Ea70
Sorica SLO 151 Fa57
Sorico I 149 Cc57
Sorigny F 29 Ga42
Sorihuela E 45 Cb64
Sorihuela del Guadalimar E 53 Dd71
Sorila FIN 89 Jd35
Sorisdale GB 6 Da10
Sorita E 48 Fc63
Sörjön S 86 Fa36
Sørkedalen N 93 Ea41
Sorken N 86 Ec35
Sørkjos N 63 Hc08
Sørkjosen N 63 Hb09
Sørkjosen N 63 Ja05
Sorkkala FIN 89 Jd36
Sorknes N 86 Eb37
Sorkun TR 193 Gb86
Sorkuncak TR 199 Gd88
Sorkwity PL 122 Jb31
Sørland N 66 Fa16
Sør-Lenangen N 62 Ha09
Sørli N 79 Fb27
Sørlia N 78 Ec28
Sörmark S 94 Ed40
Sörmjöle S 80 Hb29
Sørmo N 67 Gc13
Sormula FIN 82 Kd26
Sorn GB 10 Dd14
Sornac F 33 Gd47
Sørnesøya N 70 Ed19
Sorno D 128 Fa39
Sörnoret S 79 Gb27
Sorø DK 109 Ea26
Soroca MD 173 Fc54
Soroč'i Gory RUS 203 Fd09
Soročkino RUS 99 Mb42
Sorokpolány H 145 Gc54
Soroní GR 197 Fa93
Sorpe E 40 Gb57
Sørreisa N 67 Gc11
Sörrenberg CH 141 Ca54
Sorrento I 161 Fb76
Sorribes E 49 Gc59
Sorring DK 108 Dc24
Sørrollnes N 66 Ga12
Sorsa FIN 82 Kc26
Sorsakoski FIN 82 La31
Sorsele S 72 Gc23
Sörskog S 87 Fd38
Sorso I 168 Bd74
Sörstafors S 95 Ga43
Sørstrand N 77 Da31
Sørstraumen N 63 Hc08
Sort E 40 Gb58
Sortino I 167 Fc87
Sortland N 66 Fd13
Sør-Tverrfjord N 63 Hb07
Sõru EST 97 Jc45
Sørum N 85 Dd39
Sørumsand N 94 Eb41
Sorunda S 96 Gd44
Sörup D 108 Db29
Sørup DK 100 Dc21
Sørvad DK 100 Da23
Sørvær N 63 Hc06
Sørvågen N 66 Fa15
Sørvágur DK 3 Ca06
Sørvik N 67 Gb12
Sørvik N 77 Dd28
Sörvik S 95 Fc41
Sørvika N 66 Ga13
Sørvika N 86 Ec33
Sörviken S 79 Ga29
Sörviken S 86 Fa33
Sørvollen N 86 Eb34
Sos F 40 Fd53
Sosa D 135 Ec43
Sösdala S 110 Fa54
Sos del Rey Católico E 39 Fa58
Sosedka RUS 203 Fc11
Sosedno RUS 99 Ma45
Soses E 48 Ga61
Sošichino RUS 107 Mb48
Sosnenskij RUS 202 Ed11
Sośnica PL 120 Ga33
Sośnica PL 139 Kc44
Sośnicowice PL 137 Hb44
Sosnicy RUS 99 Mb41
Sośnie PL 129 Gd40
Sosno PL 121 Gd33
Sosno RUS 99 Lc44
Sosnova RUS 107 Mb47
Sosnove UA 202 Ea14
Sosnovka RUS 113 Ja58
Sosnovka RUS 113 Jb58
Sosnovka RUS 203 Fb11
Sosnovka RUS 203 Fd08
Sosnovo RUS 99 Mb41
Sosnovo RUS 107 Ma46
Sosnovyj Bor RUS 99 Ld39
Sosnovyj Bor RUS 202 Ea08
Sosnowica PL 131 Kb39
Sosnowiec PL 138 Hc43
Sosnówka PL 131 Kc38
Soso FIN 74 Ka24
Sospel F 43 Kd52
Sossano I 150 Dd60
Šossejnoe RUS 113 Ja59
Sossonniemi FIN 75 La20
Sost F 40 Ga56
Šoštanj SLO 151 Fc57
Sóstis GR 184 Dc77
Šostka UA 202 Ed13
Sostógyogyfürdo H 147 Ka51
Sosynje RUS 107 Mb46
Sot SRB 153 Ja60
Şotânga RO 176 Dd64
Sotaseter N 85 Da35
Soteska SLO 151 Fa57
Soteska SLO 151 Fc59
Sotiel Coronada E 59 Bb73
Sotiello E 37 Cc54
Sotillo E 52 Db68
Sotillo de la Adrada E 46 Da65
Sotillo de la Ribera E 46 Dc60
Sotillo de las Palomas E 46 Cd65
Sotillo del Rincón E 47 Ea59
Sotillos E 37 Cd56
Sotin HR 153 Hd60
Sotira CY 206 Jd97
Sotíra GR 183 Bc77
Sotkamo FIN 82 La26
Sotkaniemi FIN 69 Jd11
Sotkanniemi FIN 82 La31
Sotkuma FIN 83 Lc30
Sotobañado y Priorato E 38 Da57
Soto de Campóo E 38 Db56
Soto de Dueñas E 37 Cd54
Soto de la Marina E 38 Dc54
Soto de la Vega E 37 Cb58
Soto del Barco E 37 Cb54
Soto de los Infantes E 37 Ca54
Soto del Real E 46 Dc63
Soto de Ribera E 37 Cb54
Soto en Cameros E 39 Eb58
Sotogrande E 59 Cb77
Sótony H 145 Gc54
Sotosalbos E 46 Db62
Sotoserrano E 45 Ca64
Sotres E 38 Da55
Sotresgudo E 38 Db57
Sotrondio E 37 Cc55
Sotta F 154 Cb72
Sotteville-lès-Rouen F 23 Gb35
Sottomarina I 150 Eb60
Sottrum D 118 Da34
Sottrupskov DK 108 Db28
Sottunga FIN 97 Hd40
Sotuélamos E 53 Ea69
Soual F 41 Gd54
Souancé-au-Perche F 29 Ga39
Soubise F 32 Fa46
Soucy F 30 Hb39
Soúda GR 200 Cc95
Soudan F 28 Fa40
Soudan F 32 Fc45
Soudé F 24 Hd37
Soudes P 58 Ba73
Soues F 40 Fd55
Souesmes F 29 Gd41
Soufflenheim F 25 Kc36
Souflí GR 185 Ea77
Soúgia GR 200 Cb95
Sougy F 29 Gc39
Souillac F 33 Gc50
Souilly F 24 Jb36
Soukainen FIN 89 Ja38
Soukka FIN 98 Kb40
Soukkio FIN 90 Kb38
Soukolojärvi S 73 Jb19
Soulac-sur-Mer F 32 Fa48
Soulaines-Dhuys F 30 Ja38
Soulgé-sur-Ouette F 28 Fb39
Soúli GR 189 Bd86
Soulignonne F 32 Fb47
Soullans F 27 Ec43
Soulle F 32 Fa46
Soulópoulo GR 182 Ad80
Soultz-Haut-Rhin F 31 Kb39
Soultz-sous-Forêts F 25 Kc36
Soumoulou F 40 Fc55
Souni CY 206 Ja98
Soúnio GR 184 Db77
Souppes-sur-Loing F 29 Ha39
Souprosse F 39 Fb54
Sourdeval F 22 Fb37
Sourdon F 23 Gd34
Soure P 44 Ac64
Sourhope GB 11 Ed15
Souria F 41 Ha57
Sourpi GR 189 Ca83
Sours F 29 Gc38
Soursac F 33 Gd48
Souru FIN 82 Kd30
Souru FIN 91 Lb33
Sousceyrac F 33 Gd50
Sousel P 50 Ba68
Sous-Parsat F 33 Gd46
Soussac F 32 Fc50
Soustons F 39 Ed54
Soutelo P 45 Bd61
Southall GB 20 Fc28
Southam GB 20 Ed26
Southampton GB 20 Fa30
South Benfleet GB 21 Ga28
Southborough GB 20 Fd29
South Cave GB 16 Fb20
South Cave GB 16 Fb21
Southend GB 10 Db15
Southend-on-Sea GB 21 Ga28
Southery GB 17 Fd24
South Ferriby GB 17 Fc21
Southgate GB 20 Fc27
South Harting GB 20 Fb30
South Hayling GB 20 Fb30
South Hole GB 18 Dc29
South Kyme GB 17 Fc23
Southminster GB 21 Ga27
South Molton GB 19 Dd29
South Moreton GB 20 Fa28
South Ockendon GB 20 Fd28
South Perrott GB 19 Eb30
South Petherton GB 19 Eb30
Southport GB 15 Eb21
Southrope GB 20 Fb29
Southsea GB 20 Fa30
South Shields GB 11 Fa16
South Skirlaugh GB 17 Fc20
Southwater GB 20 Fc29
Southwell GB 16 Fb23
South Witham GB 16 Fb24
Southwold GB 21 Gc25
Soutochao E 45 Bc59
Souvála GR 195 Cb87
Souvigné F 28 Fd41
Souvigny F 30 Hb44
Sovana I 156 Dd69
Søvang DK 108 Da28
Søvang DK 109 Ec26
Søvassli N 77 Dd30
Sovata RO 172 Dd59
Söve TR 192 Fa81
Soveja RO 176 Ec61
Sover I 150 Dd57
Soverato I 164 Gc82
Sovereto I 162 Gc74
Soveria F 154 Cb69
Soveria Mannelli I 164 Gc81
Søvestad S 110 Fa56
Sovetsk RUS 113 Jc57
Sovetskaja RUS 203 Fc14
Sovetskaja RUS 205 Fd17
Sovetskij RUS 113 Ja59
Sovetskij RUS 203 Fd08
Sovetskoe RUS 205 Ga17
Sovietscoe MD 173 Fd55
Søvik N 76 Cc32
Søvika N 70 Ed22
Søvind DK 108 Dc25
Sovlje HR 157 Ga65
Sovoljano BG 179 Ca72
Sowczyce PL 129 Hb42
Sowia Góra PL 128 Ga36
Sowno PL 120 Fc33
Soye F 31 Ka41
Soyen D 143 Eb51
Soyhières CH 141 Bd52
Søyland N 92 Ca44
Søyland N 92 Ca45
Soylu TR 185 Ec77
Sozopol BG 181 Fa73
Spa B 125 Bb42
Spabrücken D 133 Ca44
Spadafora I 167 Fd83
Spahievo BG 184 Dc74
Spahnharrenstätte D 117 Cb34
Spaichingen D 142 Cc50
Spała PL 130 Ja39
Spalding GB 17 Fc24
Spálené Poříčí CZ 136 Fa46
Spálov CZ 137 Ha45
Spalt D 134 Dc47
Spalviškiai LT 106 Kd52
Spanbroek NL 116 Ba34
Spančevci BG 179 Cc69
Spandowerhagen D 120 Fa31
Spangenberg D 126 Da40
Spangereid N 92 Cc47
Spannarp S 102 Ec51
Spantekow D 120 Fa32
Spanțov RO 181 Ec67
Sparagoviči HR 158 Ha68
Sparanise I 161 Fa74
Sparbu N 78 Ec28
Spåre LV 105 Jc50
Spāre LV 106 Kd49
Sparkær DK 100 Db23
Sparkford GB 19 Ec29
Sparlösa S 102 Ed47
Sparneck D 135 Ea44
Sparreholm S 95 Gb44
Sparrsätra S 95 Gb42
Sparsås N 93 Da45
Sparta I 164 Ga83
Spárti GR 194 Bc89
Spartiás GR 188 Ba84
Spárto GR 188 Ad83
Spartohóri GR 188 Ac83
Spas-Klepiki RUS 203 Fa10
Spas-Kotorsk RUS 99 Ma43
Spasovo BG 180 Dc73
Spasovo BG 181 Fb69
Spassk- Rjazanskij RUS 203 Fb11
Spáta GR 195 Cc87
Spatharéi GR 197 Eb88
Spathovúni GR 195 Bd87
Spavča HR 153 Hd61
Spean Bridge GB 6 Dc10
Specchia I 165 Hc78
Specchiarica I 162 Hb76
Specke S 94 Ed42
Speia MD 173 Ga58
Speia MD 173 Ga58
Speicher D 133 Bc44
Speichersdorf D 135 Ea45
Spekedalssetra N 86 Eb34
Spekeröd S 102 Eb48
Spelle D 117 Cb36
Spello I 156 Eb68
Spenge D 126 Cc37
Spennymoor GB 11 Fa17
Spentrup DK 100 Dc23
Sperenberg D 127 Ed37
Spergau D 127 Eb40
Sperhiáda GR 189 Bc83
Sperlinga I 167 Fb85
Sperlonga I 160 Ed73
Spermezeu RO 171 Db56
Sperone I 166 Eb84
Spessa I 150 Ed58
Spetisbury GB 19 Ec30
Spétses GR 195 Ca89
Spey Bay GB 5 Ec07
Speyer D 133 Cb46
Spezzano Albanese I 164 Gb79
Spezzano della Sila I 164 Gc80
Spiazzi I 149 Da58
Spicino RUS 99 Lc44
Spiddal IRL 12 Bc21
Spiegelau D 135 Ed48
Spiegelberg D 134 Cd47
Spiekeroog D 117 Cb31
Spielfeld A 144 Ga56
Spiez CH 141 Bd55
Spigno Monferrato I 148 Ca62
Spijkenisse NL 124 Ac37
Spilamberto I 149 Dc63
Spildra N 62 Gc10
Spíli GR 200 Cd96
Spiliá GR 183 Bd80
Spiliá GR 200 Cb94
Spilimbergo I 150 Ec57
Spiljani SRB 159 Jc68
Spiljani SRB 178 Ad69
Spille AL 182 Ab75
Spillum N 78 Ec26
Spilsby GB 17 Fd22
Spinazzola I 162 Gb74
Spincourt F 25 Jc35
Spind N 92 Cb47
Špindlerův Mlýn CZ 128 Fd42
Spineni RO 175 Db65
Spineta Nuova I 161 Fc76
Spinetta I 148 Cb61
Spink IRL 13 Cb22
Spiņņi LV 105 Jb49
Spino d'Adda I 149 Cd59
Spinoso I 162 Gb77
Spinuş RO 170 Cb56
Špionica BIH 153 Hc62
Spirgus LV 106 Ka51
Spiringen CH 141 Cb54
Spirovo RUS 202 Ec09
Špišić-Bukovica HR 152 Gd58
Spiss A 142 Db54
Spišská Belá SK 138 Jb47
Spišská Nová Ves SK 138 Jb48
Spišská Stará Ves SK 138 Jb46
Spišské Bystré SK 138 Jb48
Spišské Podhradie SK 138 Jc47
Spišské Vlachy SK 138 Jc48
Spišský Štvrtok SK 138 Jb47
Spital am Phyrn A 144 Fb52
Spital am Semmering A 144 Ga53
Spithami EST 97 Jd43
Spittal an der Drau A 143 Ed55
Spitz A 144 Fd50
Spjærøy N 93 Ea44
Spjald DK 108 Cd24
Spjelkavik N 76 Cc32
Spjutsbygd S 111 Fd54
Spjutsund FIN 98 Kc39
Spliding N 92 Cc47
Split HR 158 Gb66
Splügen CH 142 Cc56
Spóa GR 201 Eb95
Spodnja Kokra SLO 151 Fb57
Spodnja Pohanca SLO 151 Ga58
Spodnje Fužine SLO 151 Fb57
Spodnje Hoče SLO 144 Ga56
Spodnje Škofije SLO 151 Fa59
Spodnji Ivanjci SLO 144 Ga56
Spodnji Log SLO 151 Fc58
Spodsbjerg DK 109 Dd28
Spofforth GB 16 Fa20
Špogi LV 115 Lc53
Spohle D 118 Cc33
Špola UA 204 Ec15
Spoleto I 156 Eb69
Spondigna I 142 Db55
Spondinig I 142 Db55
Spontin B 124 Ad42
Spontour F 33 Gd49
Spora D 127 Eb41
Spore PL 121 Gb32
Spornitz D 119 Ea33
Sportgastein A 143 Ec54
Sporysz PL 121 Gc32
Spotorno I 148 Ca63
Spott GB 11 Ec13
Spraitbach D 134 Da48
Sprakensehl D 118 Dc35
Sprâncenata RO 180 Db67
Sprang-Capelle NL 124 Ba38
Sprängsviken S 88 Gc32
Spraudis LT 113 Jc55
Spreenhagen D 128 Fa37
Spremberg D 128 Fb39
Spresiano I 150 Ea59
Spridlington GB 17 Fc22
Sprimont B 132 Ba43
Şpring RO 175 Da60
Springe D 126 Da37
Springfield GB 9 Cb18
Sproatley GB 17 Fc20
Sprockhövel D 125 Ca39
Sproge S 104 Gd50
Sprogi LV 107 Lb49
Sproughton GB 21 Ga26
Spuž MNE 159 Ja69
Spychowo PL 122 Jc32
Spydeberg N 93 Ea42
Spytkowice PL 138 Hd44
Spytkowice PL 138 Ja46
Spytkowo PL 122 Jc30
Squillace I 164 Gc81
Squinzano I 162 Hb76
Sračinec HR 152 Gb57
Sraghmore IRL 13 Cd22
Srahmore IRL 8 Bc18
Sráid na Cathrach IRL 12 Bb22
Sraith Salach IRL 8 Bb20
Sramora Română RO 174 Bd61
Srbac BIH 152 Ha61
Srbica KSV 178 Ba70
Srbica MK 182 Ba74
Srbinovo MK 182 Ba74
Srbobran SRB 153 Jb59
Srbovac KSV 178 Ba69
Srđevići BIH 158 Gd65
Srdiečko SK 138 Hd48
Srebărna BG 181 Ed67
Srebrenica BIH 159 Ja64
Srebrna PL 123 Jd34
Srebrna Góra PL 137 Gb43
Sredec BG 180 Dd73
Sredec BG 181 Ed73
Središče ob Dravi SLO 152 Gb57
Središte BG 181 Ed68
Sredni Kolibi BG 180 Dd71
Srednja Besnica SLO 151 Fc58
Srednje BIH 159 Hc64
Srednjevo SRB 174 Bd64
Srednogorci BG 184 Db75
Srednogorovo BG 180 Dc72
Sredno Gradište BG 180 Dc73
Sredno Selo BG 180 Ea71
Srel'na RUS 99 Mb39
Śrem PL 129 Gc38
Sremska Kamenica SRB 153 Jb60
Sremska Mitrovica SRB 153 Ja61
Sremski Karlovci SRB 153 Jb60
Srezojevci SRB 159 Jc64
Sribne UA 202 Ed14
Srmska Rača SRB 153 Ja61
Srnetica BIH 152 Gc63
Srní CZ 135 Ed48
Srnice BIH 153 Hc62
Środa Śląska PL 129 Gb41
Środa Wielkopolska PL 129 Gd37
Srokowo PL 122 Jc30
Srpci MK 183 Bb75
Srpska Crnja SRB 174 Bb60
Srpski Hebej SRB 174 Bb61
Srpski Miletic SRB 153 Hd59
Stå S 78 Ed30
Staatz A 137 Gb49
Stabbfors S 71 Fc22
Stabbursnes N 64 Jb07
Stabulnieki LV 107 Lc51
Staburnäs S 79 Ga25
Staby DK 100 Cd23
Stachanov UA 205 Fb15
Stachy CZ 136 Fa48
Stachy PL 122 Jb33
Stačiūnai LT 114 Kb54
Staðarskáli IS 2 Ad04
Stade D 118 Da32
Stadecken-Elsheim D 133 Cb44
Stadel CH 141 Cb52
Stadelhofen D 135 Dd44
Staden B 21 Ha30
Stadensen D 118 Dc35
Stadhampton GB 20 Fa27
Stadil Kirkeby DK 100 Cd23
Stádio GR 194 Bc88
Stadland D 118 Cc33
Stadl an der Mur A 144 Fa54
Stadl Paura A 144 Fa51
Stadra S 95 Fc43
Stadskanaal NL 117 Ca34
Stadtallendorf D 126 Cd41
Stadtbergen D 142 Dc50
Stadthagen D 126 Da36
Stadtilm D 127 Dd42
Stadtkyll D 125 Bc42
Stadtlauringen D 134 Db44
Stadtlengsfeld D 126 Db42
Stadtlohn D 125 Bd37
Stadtoldendorf D 126 Da38
Stadtprozelten D 134 Cd45
Stadtroda D 127 Ea42
Stadtsteinach D 135 Ea44
Stadum D 108 Da28
Stae DK 100 Dc21
Stăeşti RO 180 Ea68
Stäfa CH 141 Cb53
Staffans S 73 Jb21
Staffanstorp S 110 Ed56
Staffarda I 148 Bc61
Staffolo I 156 Ec66
Stafford GB 16 Ed23
Staggia I 155 Dc66
Staggträsk S 72 Gc23
Stágira GR 184 Cc78
Stahnsdorf D 127 Ed37
Stahovica SLO 151 Fc57
Staicele LV 106 Kc47
Stainach A 144 Fa53
Stainforth GB 11 Ec19
Stainville F 24 Jb37
Stainz A 144 Fd55
Staithes GB 11 Fb18
Staiti I 164 Gb84
Stajčovci BG 179 Ca71
Stajićevo SRB 174 Bb62
Stajnica HR 151 Fd61
Stakčín SK 139 Kb47
Stake Pool GB 15 Eb20
Stakevci BG 179 Cb68
Staķi LV 107 Lb49
Stakiai LT 114 Ka57
Stakkvik N 62 Gd08
Stakliškės LT 114 Kd58
Stakroge DK 108 Da25
Stalać SRB 178 Bc67
Stalbe LV 106 Kd49
Stalbridge GB 19 Ec30
Stalden CH 141 Bd56
Staldzene LV 105 Jb49
Stale PL 131 Jd42
Stalgėnai LT 113 Jc55
Staļģene LV 106 Kb52
Stalijska Mahala BG 179 Cc68
Stall A 143 Ec55
Stallarholmen S 96 Gc43
Stållberg S 95 Fc41
Ställdalen S 95 Fc41
Stalling Busk GB 11 Ed19
Stallwang D 135 Ec48
Staloluokta sameviste S 66 Ga17
Stalon S 79 Fd25
Stalowa Wola PL 131 Ka42
Stâlpeni RO 175 Dc64
Stâlpu RO 176 Ec64
Stalti LV 115 Ld53
Stalybridge GB 16 Ed21
Stambolijski BG 179 Da73
Stambulčić BIH 159 Hc65
Stamford GB 17 Fc24
Stamford Bridge GB 16 Fb20
Stamfordham GB 11 Ed16
Stammbach D 135 Ea44
Stammham D 135 Dd48
Stamnes N 66 Fd12
Stamnes N 84 Cb38
Stamora Germană RO 174 Bc62
Stams A 142 Dc54
Stamsele S 79 Fd29
Stamsried D 135 Eb47
Stamsund N 66 Fb14
Stamullin IRL 9 Cd20
Stânceni RO 172 Dd58
Stâncuța RO 177 Fa65
Standlake GB 20 Fa27
Stănești RO 175 Cd63
Stănești RO 175 Da64
Stanevo BG 179 Cd67
Stanford-le-Hope GB 20 Fd28
Stånga S 104 Ha50
Stangaland N 92 Bd42
Stange N 94 Eb39
Stangerum DK 100 Dc22
Stanghede DK 100 Db23
Stanghella I 150 Dd61
Stanghelle N 84 Cb38
Stangnes N 67 Gb11
Stangnes N 94 Ec41
Stangvik N 77 Db31
Stanhope GB 11 Ed17
Stanica Bagaevskaja RUS 205 Fc15
Staniewice PL 121 Gb30
Stănileşti RO 173 Fb59
Stanin PL 131 Ka38
Staninci BG 179 Cb70
Stănișești RO 176 Ed60
Stanišić SRB 153 Hd58
Stanisławów PL 130 Jc36
Stanišovi HR 151 Fa61
Stănița RO 172 Ed58

Štanjel - Strandža

Štanjel SLO 151 Fa59
Stanjevci MK 178 Bc73
Staňkov CZ 135 Ed46
Stankovci HR 157 Ga65
Stanley GB 7 Eb11
Stanley GB 11 Fa17
Stanomino PL 120 Ga31
Stanovoe RUS 203 Fa12
Stans CH 141 Cb54
Stanton GB 21 Ga25
Stany PL 131 Ka42
Stanyčno-Luhans'ke UA 203 Fc14
Stanz A 144 Fd53
Stanzach A 142 Db53
Stapar SRB 153 Hd59
Stapari SRB 159 Jb65
Stapelburg D 126 Dc38
Staphorst NL 117 Bc35
Stapleford GB 16 Fa23
Stapleford GB 20 Ed29
Staplehurst GB 21 Ga29
Stąporków PL 130 Jb40
Stara PL 130 Ja40
Stara Baška HR 151 Fc61
Stara Błotnica PL 130 Jc39
Stará Bystrica SK 138 Hc47
Starachowice PL 130 Jc41
Stara Fužina SLO 151 Fa57
Stara Gradina HR 152 Ha58
Stará Huta SK 138 Hd49
Staraja Russa RUS 202 Eb09
Stara Jastrząbka PL 138 Jc44
Stara Kamionka PL 123 Kc32
Stara Kiszewa PL 121 Ha31
Stara Kornica PL 131 Kb36
Stara Łubianka PL 121 Gb34
Stará L'ubovňa SK 138 Jc46
Stara Moravica SRB 153 Ja58
Stara Novalja HR 151 Fc63
Stara Pazova SRB 153 Jb61
Stara Ploščica HR 152 Gc59
Stara Rečka BG 180 Ea70
Stara Reka BG 180 Ea71
Stara Rózanka PL 122 Jc30
Stará Ves nad Ondřejnicí CZ 137 Hb45
Stara Wieś PL 122 Jb33
Stara Wieś PL 131 Jd36
Stara Wiśniewka PL 121 Gc33
Stara Zagora BG 180 Dd72
Stara Žednik SRB 153 Ja58
Starchiojd RO 176 Eb63
Starcross GB 19 Ea31
Starcza PL 130 Hc42
Stare Czarnowo PL 120 Fc34
Stare Dębno PL 120 Ga32
Stare Dobrzyca PL 120 Fd32
Stare Dolistowo PL 123 Ka32
Stare Drawsko PL 120 Ga33
Stare Dyniska PL 131 Kd42
Stare Gronowo PL 121 Gd33
Staré Hamry CZ 137 Hb46
Staré Hrady CZ 136 Fd43
Stare Jabłonki PL 122 Hd32
Stare Jarosław PL 121 Gb30
Stare Jeżewo PL 123 Ka33
Stare Juchy PL 123 Jd31
Stare Kiejkuty PL 122 Jb32
Stare Kiełbonki PL 122 Jc32
Stare Komorowo PL 123 Jd34
Staré Město CZ 137 Gc44
Staré Město CZ 137 Gc45
Staré Město CZ 137 Gd48
Staré Město pod Landštejnem CZ 136 Fd48
Stare Miastko PL 129 Ha37
Stare Pole PL 122 Hc31
Staré Sedlo CZ 135 Ec46
Stare Sioło PL 139 Kc43
Stare Sobótka PL 130 Hc37
Stare Strącze PL 128 Ga38
Stare Waliszew PL 130 Hd38
Stare Wierzchowo PL 121 Gb32
Stargard Szczeciński PL 120 Fc33
Stårheim N 84 Cb34
Stari Bar MNE 159 Ja70
Starica RUS 202 Ec10
Starica RUS 202 Ed12
Starice Lisičkovo BG 179 Cb73
Staricy RUS 99 Mb42
Stari Dojran MK 183 Ca76
Stari Dulići BIH 159 Hc67
Starigrad HR 151 Fc62
Starigrad HR 158 Gc67
Stari Grad MK 183 Bc74
Stari Gradac HR 152 Gd58
Starigrad-Paklenica HR 157 Fd64
Stari Jankovci HR 153 Hd60
Stari Lec SRB 174 Bc62
Stari Log SLO 151 Fc59
Stari Majdan BIH 152 Gc62
Stari Mikanovci HR 153 Hc60
Stari Raušić KSV 178 Ad70
Stari Raušić SRB 159 Jc69
Stari trg SLO 151 Fd60
Stari Trogir HR 158 Gb66
Starkenbach A 142 Db54
Starkenbach CH 142 Cc54
Starkenberg D 127 Eb41
Starnberg D 143 Dd51
Starobil's'k UA 203 Fb14
Starobin BY 202 Ea13
Starodub RUS 202 Ec13
Staroec MK 182 Ba74
Starogard PL 120 Fd32
Starogard Gdański PL 121 Hb31
Staroglavice BIH 159 Ja64
Starojur'evo RUS 203 Fb11
Starokostjantyniv UA 204 Eb15
Starokrzepice PL 129 Hb41
Starominskaja RUS 205 Fc16
Staro Nagoričane MK 178 Bc72
Staronja RUS 107 Ma47
Staro Orjahovo BG 181 Fa71
Staropatica BG 179 Ca67
Staro Petrovo Selo HR 152 Ha60
Staropol'e RUS 99 Ld42
Starosel BG 180 Db72
Staroselci BG 179 Da69
Staroselec BG 180 Ea73
Staro Selo BG 180 Eb68
Staro Selo BIH 158 Gd64
Staro Selo Topusko HR 151 Ga60
Starosiverskaja RUS 99 Mb41
Staro Stefanje HR 152 Gc58
Starotitarovskaja RUS 205 Fb17
Starowice PL 121 Gb33
Starozagorski Bani BG 180 Dd72
Staro Železare BG 180 Db72
Starožilovo RUS 203 Fa11
Starożreby PL 130 Hd36
Starrkärr S 102 Ec48
Starše SLO 144 Ga56
Starti LV 106 Kd49
Starup DK 108 Db27
Stary Borek PL 139 Ka44
Stary Brus PL 131 Kc39
Stary Brzozów PL 130 Ja37
Stary Chwalim PL 121 Gb32
Stary Ciotusza PL 131 Kc42
Stary Dzierzgoń PL 122 Hc32
Stary Dzikowiec PL 139 Ka43
Stary Folwark PL 123 Kb30
Starý Hrozenkov CZ 137 Ha48
Staryi Oskol RUS 203 Fa13
Staryja Darohi BY 202 Eb13
Starý Jičín CZ 137 Ha46
Staryj Nizkovicy RUS 99 Mb40
Staryj Prud RUS 107 Mb52
Stary Nieskurzów PL 130 Jc41
Starý Plzenec CZ 135 Ed46
Stary Sącz PL 138 Jb46
Starý Smokovec SK 138 Jb47
Stary Szelków PL 122 Jc35
Stary Targ PL 122 Hc31
Stary Tychów PL 130 Jc40
Stary Wieś PL 131 Kb41
Starzyno PL 121 Ha29
Staševica HR 158 Ha67
Stasiówka PL 139 Jd44
Staškov SK 138 Hc46
Staßfurt D 127 Ea38
Staszów PL 130 Jc42
Stathelle N 93 Dc44
Stathos Agios Fotios CY 206 Hd97
Statsås S 79 Ga26
Stăuceni MD 173 Fd58
Stăuceni RO 172 Ed55
Stauchlitz D 127 Ed40
Staufen D 141 Ca51
Staufenberg D 126 Cc42
Staughton Highway GB 20 Fc25
Staume N 84 Cb35
Staupitz D 128 Fa39
Stava S 103 Fc47
Štava SRB 178 Bb69
Štavalj SRB 178 Ad68
Stavang N 84 Ca35
Stavanger N 92 Ca44
Stavarygala LT 114 Kd57
Stavaträsk S 73 Hb24
Stavby S 96 Gd41
Stave N 66 Fd11
Stave N 92 Cb47
Stave SRB 153 Jb63
Stavelot B 125 Bb42
Stavely GB 16 Fa22
Stavenisse NL 124 Ac38
Stavern D 117 Cb35
Stavern N 93 Dd44
Stavnäs S 94 Ed43
Stavning DK 108 Cd24
Stavoren NL 116 Bb34
Stavós GR 184 Cc78
Stavre S 79 Fb30
Stavre S 87 Fd32
Stavreviken S 88 Gc33
Stavrodrómi GR 182 Ba78
Stavrodrómi GR 188 Ba86
Stavrodrómi GR 194 Bb87
Stavroménos GR 200 Cd95
Stavropol' RUS 205 Fd16
Stavros CY 206 Hd97
Stavrós GR 183 Bd78
Stavrós GR 184 Cc78
Stavrós GR 188 Ac84
Stavrós GR 189 Cb84
Stavrós GR 200 Cc94
Stavroskiádi GR 182 Ac79
Stavroúpoli GR 184 Db76
Stavsätra S 87 Fd36
Stavsjø N 86 Ea38
Stavsjöholm S 80 Ha29
Stavsnäs S 96 Ha43
Stavträsk S 80 Hb26
Stavtrup DK 108 Dc24
Staw PL 120 Fc35
Staw PL 129 Hb39
Stawiguda PL 122 Ja32
Stawiszyn PL 129 Ha38
Stawnica PL 121 Gc33
Staylittle GB 15 Ea24
Stazione di Mandatoriccio-Campana I 165 Gd79
Stazione di Motta Sant'Anastasia I 167 Fc86
Steane N 93 Da43
Steart GB 19 Eb29
Stębark PL 122 Hd33
Stebuliai LV 114 Kb59
Steccato I 165 Gd81
Stechelberg CH 141 Bd55
Štěchovice CZ 136 Fb45
Stechow D 127 Ec36
Steckborn CH 142 Cc52
Stede Broec NL 116 Bb34
Stedesdorf D 117 Cb32
Štědrá CZ 135 Ed44
Steeg A 142 Db54
Steenbergen NL 124 Ac38
Steenderen NL 125 Bc37
Steenvoorde F 21 Gd30
Steenwijk NL 117 Bc34
Steeple GB 21 Ga27
Steeple Aston GB 20 Fa26
Steeple Bumpstead GB 20 Fd26
Steeple Claydon GB 20 Fb26
Ştefan cel Mare RO 172 Ec58
Ştefan cel Mare RO 173 Fa59
Ştefan cel Mare RO 176 Dd66
Ştefan cel Mare RO 176 Ec60
Ştefan cel Mare RO 177 Fa66
Ştefan cel Mare RO 179 Da68
Ştefăneşti MD 173 Fc55
Ştefăneşti MD 177 Ga60
Ştefăneşti RO 172 Ed55
Ştefăneşti RO 175 Db65
Ştefăneşti RO 175 Dc64
Ştefăneşti de Jos RO 176 Eb66
Stefaniá GR 194 Bc90
Stefaniná GR 184 Cc77
Stefan Karadža BG 181 Ec68
Stefan Karadžovo BG 181 Ec73
Stefanovo BG 181 Fa69
Stefanóvouno GR 183 Bc80
Ştefan-Vodă MD 177 Ga60
Ştefan Vodă RO 176 Ed66
Steffeln D 133 Bc43
Steffenberg D 126 Cc41
Steffisburg CH 141 Bd54
Stefjordbotn N 66 Ga14
Stegaurach D 134 Dc45
Stege DK 109 Ec28
Stegelitz D 127 Eb37
Stegersbach A 145 Gb54
Stegna PL 122 Hc30
Stegny PL 122 Hd31
Stehnovo RUS 107 Mb48
Ştei RO 170 Cb58
Steikvasselva N 71 Fc22
Steimbke D 118 Da35
Stein D 134 Dc46
Stein N 78 Ea27
Stein N 93 Dd41
Steinaberg bru N 92 Cc41
Steinach A 143 Dd54
Steinach D 135 Dd43
Steinach D 135 Ec48
Steinach D 141 Ca50
Steinakirchen am Forst A 144 Fc51
Steinamanger = Szombathely H 145 Gc54
Stein am Rhein CH 142 Cc52
Stein an der Ens A 144 Fa53
Steinau D 118 Cd32
Steinau D 134 Da43
Steinbach A 143 Ed52
Steinbach am Wald D 135 Dd43
Steinbach-Hallenberg D 126 Dc42
Steinbeck D 128 Fa36
Steinberg A 143 Ea53
Steinberg D 135 Eb47
Steinberg N 92 Cb45
Steinbergkirche D 108 Db28
Steinburg D 118 Dc32
Steine N 78 Ec29
Steine N 78 Ec25
Steine N 92 Cb45
Steineien N 94 Ec41
Steinen D 141 Bd52
Steinen D 141 Ca52
Steinfeld A 143 Ed55
Steinfeld D 125 Bc42
Steinfeld D 134 Da44
Steinfeld (Oldenburg) D 117 Cc35
Steinfort L 133 Bb45
Steinfurt D 125 Ca37
Steingaden D 142 Dc52
Steinhagen D 119 Ed30
Steinhagen D 126 Cc37
Steinhaus I 143 Ea54
Steinheid D 135 Dd43
Steinheim D 126 Cd38
Steinheim D 134 Cd48
Steinheim D 134 Da49
Steinhöfel D 128 Fb37
Steinhöring D 143 Ea51
Steinibach CH 142 Cc54
Steinigtwolmsdorf D 128 Fb41
Steinkirchen D 118 Db32
Steinkirchen D 143 Eb50
Steinkirchen an der Traun A 144 Fa51
Steinkjer N 78 Ec28
Steinkjer N 78 Ed27
Steinkjernes N 65 Kc07
Steinløysa N 77 Da31
Steinnes N 62 Gd08
Steinsdal N 77 Dd29
Steinsfeld D 134 Db46
Steinshamn N 76 Cd31
Steinsholt N 93 Dc43
Steinsland N 70 Fa20
Steinsland N 93 Db44
Steinsøynes N 77 Da30
Steinsstaðabyggð IS 2 Ba04
Steinvik N 64 Ka06
Steinwiesen D 135 Dd43
Steinwiesen D 135 Ea43
Steira N 66 Fb14
Steiro N 70 Fa20
Stejari RO 175 Cd64
Stejaru RO 177 Fc65
Stejaru RO 180 Dc67
Steje MK 182 Ba76
Stekenjokk S 71 Fc24
Steki LV 107 Lb52
Stellata I 150 Dd61
Stelle D 118 Dc33
Stellendam NL 124 Ac37
Stelmužė LT 115 Lb54
Stelnica RO 177 Fa66
Stelpe LV 106 Kc52
Stemnitsa GR 194 Bb87
Stemplės LT 113 Jc56
Stemwede D 117 Cc36
Stenalees GB 18 Db31
Stenåsa S 111 Gb53
Stenay F 24 Jb34
Stenbacken S 67 Ha14
Stenbäcken S 80 Ha26
Stenbjerg DK 100 Cd21
Stenbrohult S 111 Fb53
Stende LV 105 Jd50
Stenderup DK 108 Da25
Steneby S 94 Ec45
Stengårdshult S 102 Fa49
Stengelsen N 63 Hd08
Stengelsrud N 93 Dc42
Stenhamra S 96 Gc43
Stenhøj DK 101 Dd20
Stenico I 149 Dc57
Steni Dirfios GR 189 Cc85
Steniés GR 190 Da87
Stenimahos GR 183 Bc78
Steninge S 102 Ec52
Steningestrand S 102 Ec52
Stenkullen S 102 Ec49
Stenkumla S 104 Gd49
Stenkvista S 95 Gb44
Stenkyrka S 104 Ha48
Stenlille DK 109 Eb26
Stenløse DK 109 Ec25
Stennäs S 80 Gd28
Stenness GB 5 Ed04
Stenó GR 189 Bc86
Stenó GR 194 Bc88
Sténoma GR 188 Bb83
Stěnovice CZ 135 Ed46
Stensele S 72 Gb24
Stensjön S 103 Fc49
Stensryr S 102 Eb46
Stenstorp S 102 Fa47
Stensträsk S 72 Ha24
Stenstrup DK 109 Dd27
Stensund S 72 Gb23
Stensund S 72 Gc21
Stensund S 72 Gd24
Stensved DK 109 Eb28
Stenton GB 11 Ec13
Stentorp S 102 Ed48
Stenträsk S 72 Ha20
Stenudden S 72 Gc19
Stenum DK 100 Dc20
Stenungsund S 102 Eb48
Stepanci MK 183 Bc74
Štěpánov CZ 137 Gd46
Stepaside IRL 13 Cd22
Stepen BIH 159 Hc67
Stephanskirchen D 143 Eb52
Stephansposching D 135 Ec49
Stępień PL 122 Hd30
Štepivka UA 202 Ed14
Stepnica PL 120 Fc32
Stepnoe Matjunico RUS 203 Fd10
Stepnoje RUS 113 Jc58
Stepojevac SRB 153 Jc62
Stepping DK 108 Db26
Step-Soci MD 173 Fd56
Sterdyń-Osada PL 123 Ka35
Sterławki Wielkie PL 122 Jc31
Stern I 143 Ea56
Stérna GR 184 Da76
Stérna GR 185 Eb75
Sternberg D 119 Eb32
Šternberk CZ 137 Gd45
Sternenfels D 134 Cc47
Stérnes GR 200 Cc94
Sterringi N 85 Db34
Sterro I 167 Fc86
Sterup D 108 Db29
Sterup DK 100 Dc20
Sterzing I 143 Dd55
Stęszew PL 129 Gb37
Štětí CZ 136 Fb43
Stette N 76 Cd32
Stetten D 142 Cc50
Stettin = Szczecin PL 120 Fc33
Steuden D 127 Ea40
Steutz D 127 Eb38
Stevenage GB 20 Fc27
Stevenston GB 10 Dc14
Stevning DK 108 Db28
Stevnstrup DK 100 Dc23
Stevrek BG 180 Ea71
Stewarton GB 10 Db14
Stewarton GB 10 Dd14
Stewartstown GB 9 Cd17
Steyerberg D 126 Cd36
Steyning GB 20 Fc30
Steyr A 144 Fb51
Steyrbrücke A 144 Fb52
Steyregg A 144 Fb50
Stężyca PL 121 Ha31
Stężyca PL 131 Jd39
Stia I 156 Dd65
Štiavnik SK 137 Hb47
Stibanken DK 109 Ea28
Stibb Cross GB 18 Dc30
Stichill GB 11 Ec14
Stickney GB 17 Fc23
Stična SLO 151 Fc58
Stiege D 127 Dd39
Stige DK 109 Dd26
Stigen N 86 Ec36
Stigen S 102 Ec46
Stigersand N 94 Eb39
Stiglava LV 107 Lc49
Stigliano I 162 Gb76
Stigsjö S 88 Gc32
Stigsnæs DK 109 Ea27
Stigtomta S 95 Gb45
Stiklestad N 78 Ec28
Stikli LV 105 Jc49
Stilia GR 189 Bc86
Stilida GR 189 Bd83
Stilling DK 108 Dc24
Stilo I 164 Gc82
Stilton GB 20 Fc25
Stimfalía GR 189 Bc86
Štimlje KSV 178 Bb71
Stimpfach D 134 Db47
Stinăpari RO 174 Bd64
Stinik MK 183 Cb75
Stinsford GB 19 Ec30
Stintino I 168 Bd74
Stio I 161 Fd77
Štip MK 183 Bd74
Stipsi GR 191 Ea83
Stira GR 190 Cd86
Stirfaka GR 189 Bc83
Stiri GR 189 Bd85
Stiring-Wendel F 25 Ka35
Stirling GB 7 Ea12
Stirniene LV 107 Lc51
Štit BG 185 Eb75
Štitar SRB 153 Ja62
Štítary CZ 136 Ga48
Štítnik SK 138 Jb49
Štíty CZ 137 Gc45
Ştiubieni RO 172 Ed54
Stiuca RO 174 Ca61
Stival F 27 Ea39
Štivan HR 151 Fb62
Stivica HR 152 Ha61
Stivos GR 183 Cb78
Stjärnfors S 95 Fc42
Stjärnhov S 95 Gb44
Stjärnorp S 103 Fd46
Stjärnsund S 95 Ga40
Stjärnvik S 95 Ga42
Stjern N 78 Ea28
Stjørdal N 78 Eb29
Støa N 78 Ec28
Stoļerova LV 107 Ld51
Stobierna PL 139 Ka43
Stobnica PL 130 Hd40
Stobno PL 121 Gb34
Stobrawa PL 129 Gd42
Stobs Castle GB 11 Ec15
Stochov CZ 136 Fa44
Stocka S 88 Gc35
Stockach D 142 Cc51
Stockamöllan S 110 Fa55
Stockaryd S 103 Fc50
Stockbridge GB 20 Fa29
Stöcke S 80 Hb28
Stockelsdorf D 119 Dd31
Stocken S 102 Eb47
Stockenboi A 143 Ed55
Stockerau A 145 Gb50
Stockheim D 134 Db43
Stockheim D 135 Dd43
Stockholm S 96 Gd43
Stockland Bristol GB 19 Eb29
Stockleigh Pomeroy GB 19 Ea30
Stocklen-Alm A 142 Dc54
Stockport GB 16 Ed22
Stocksbo S 87 Fd35
Stocksbridge GB 16 Fa21
Stöckse D 118 Da35
Stöcksjö S 80 Hb28
Stockstadt am Main D 134 Cd44
Stockton-on-Tees GB 11 Fa18
Stoczek Lukowski PL 131 Jd37
Stoczek-Osada PL 123 Jd35
Stod CZ 135 Ed46
Stöde S 87 Ga33
Stødle N 92 Cb41
Stödtlen D 134 Db48
Stöðvarfjörður IS 3 Bc06
Stoeneşti RO 176 Dd63
Stoeneşti RO 180 Db67
Stoeneşti RO 180 Ea67
Stoholm DK 100 Db23
Stoianovca MD 177 Fb60
Stoicăneşti RO 180 Db67
Stoiceni RO 171 Db55
Stoidraga HR 151 Ga58
Stoileşti RO 175 Db64
Stoina RO 175 Cd65
Stojakovo MK 183 Ca76
Stojan Mihajlovski BG 181 Ed70
Stojanovo BG 180 Db70
Stojanovo BG 184 Dc75
Stojkite BG 184 Db75
Stojkovo BG 185 Dd74
Stoke GB 18 Dc29
Stoke-by-Nayland GB 21 Ga26
Stoke Ferry GB 17 Fd24
Stoke Goldington GB 20 Fb26
Stoke-on-Trent GB 16 Ed23
Stokesley GB 11 Fa18
Stoke upon Tern GB 15 Ec23
Stokite BG 180 Dc71
Stokka N 70 Ed22
Stokke N 93 Dd44
Stokkeland N 92 Cd47
Stokkemarke DK 109 Ea28
Stokkseyri IS 2 Ac05
Stokksund N 78 Ea28
Stokkvågen N 70 Fa20
Stokmarknes N 66 Fc13
Stolac BIH 158 Hb67
Stolăt BG 180 Dc71
Stolberg D 125 Bc41
Stolberg D 127 Dd39
Stolbovo RUS 99 Ld43
Stolec PL 120 Fb33
Stołeczna PL 120 Fc35
Stolice SRB 153 Ja63
Stolin BY 202 Ea14
Stollberg D 127 Ec42
Stöllet S 94 Fa40
Stollhamm D 117 Cc32
Stolniceni MD 173 Fa54
Stolnici RO 175 Dc65
Stolnik BG 179 Cd71
Stolno PL 121 Hb33
Stoloiceni MD 173 Fc58
Stólos GR 194 Bc88
Stolpe D 118 Dc31
Stolpe D 119 Ed33
Stolpe D 120 Fb35
Stolpen D 128 Fb41
Stolzenau D 126 Cd36
Stolzenhain D 127 Ed38
Stómio GR 183 Ca80
Stommen S 94 Eb43
Stömne S 94 Ed43
Stomorska HR 158 Gb67
Stompetoren NL 116 Ba35
Ston HR 158 Ha68
Stone GB 16 Ed23
Stone GB 20 Fb27
Stonehaven GB 7 Ed10
Stongfjorden N 84 Ca35
Stonglandet N 67 Gb11
Stoniškiai LT 113 Jc57
Stonne F 24 Ja34
Stønnesbotn N 62 Gb10
Stonyford IRL 13 Cb24
Stopanja SRB 178 Bb68
Stopki PL 122 Jb30
Stopnica PL 138 Jc43
Stopnik SLO 151 Fa58
Storå S 95 Fc42
Stora Blåsjön S 79 Fb25
Stora Dyrön S 102 Eb48
Stora Höga S 102 Eb48
Stora Kil S 94 Fa43
Stora Levene S 102 Ed47
Stora Malm S 95 Ga45
Stora Mellby S 102 Ec47
Stora Mellösa S 95 Fd44
Stora rör S 103 Gb52
Storås N 77 Dd31
Störåsen S 79 Fc29
Stora Skedvi S 95 Fd40
Stora Stensjön S 79 Fb28
Stora Tuna S 95 Fd40
Stora Vika S 96 Gd45
Storbäck S 79 Fd26
Storbäcken S 73 Ja19
Storbacken S 73 Hb20
Storbekken N 86 Ed37
Storberg S 72 Gd23
Storberget S 73 Hd18
Storberget S 79 Gb26
Storboda S 87 Ga33
Storborgarn S 80 Gd29
Storbørja N 70 Ed23
Storbränna S 79 Fc29
Storbrännan S 80 Hb26
Storbukt N 64 Jc04
Storby FIN 96 Hb40
Stord N 92 Ca41
Stordal N 76 Cd33
Stordalen N 63 Hc07
Stordalen N 84 Cb37
Stordalen S 67 Gd14
Stordalselv N 62 Gd10
Štore SLO 151 Fd57
Store Andst DK 108 Db26
Storebro S 103 Ga49
Store Darum DK 108 Cd26
Storegarden N 86 Eb38
Storehaug N 84 Cb36
Store Heddinge DK 109 Ec27
Storekorsnes N 63 Hd07
Storelv N 63 Hd06
Storelvavoll N 86 Ec32
Stor-Elvdal N 86 Eb36
Store Lyndevad DK 108 Da28
Store Merløse DK 109 Eb26
Støren N 78 Ea31
Storeng N 63 Hb08
Storeng N 71 Fd18
Store Rise DK 108 Dc28
Store Rørbæk DK 109 Eb25
Store-Strandal N 76 Cc33
Storfall S 80 Ha29
Storfjäten S 86 Fa35
Storfjellseter N 85 Ea35
Storfjord N 62 Ha10
Storfors S 95 Fb43
Storforshei N 71 Fc20
Storfossen N 64 Jc10
Storgård FIN 97 Jc41
Storgranliden S 73 Hb23
Storhågna S 87 Fb33
Storhallaren N 77 Dc29
Storhögen S 79 Fd30
Storhöjden S 79 Fd29
Stor-Holmträsk S 80 Gd25
Štorje SLO 151 Fa59
Storjola S 79 Fc25
Storjord N 71 Fd19
Storjord N 71 Fc18
Storjorda N 71 Fb19
Storkågeträsk S 73 Hc24
Storkow D 128 Fa37
Storkowo PL 120 Fd33
Storli N 67 Gc11
Storliden S 80 Hb26
Storlien S 78 Ec30
Stormark S 73 Hc24
Stormi FIN 89 Jc36
Stormo N 62 Gd09
Stormoen N 71 Fb23
Stormoen N 71 Fb20
Stornara I 161 Ga73
Stornarella I 161 Ga73
Stornäs S 71 Fd24
Stornäset S 79 Ga28
Stornes N 63 Hb08
Stornes N 66 Ga12
Stornoway GB 4 Da05
Störnstein D 135 Eb45
Storo I 149 Db58
Ştorobăneasa RO 180 Dd68
Storoddan N 77 Dc30
Storön S 73 Ja22
Storožinec RUS 99 Lc44
Storožynec' UA 204 Ea16
Storrington GB 20 Fc30
Storsaivis S 73 Hd19
Storsand N 93 Ea42
Storsand S 73 Hb20
Storsandsjö S 80 Hb27
Storsätern S 86 Ec34
Storsävarträsk S 80 Hb26
Storseleby S 79 Gb25
Storselet S 80 Hb25
Storsjö S 86 Fa32
Storskog N 65 Kc06
Storskog S 71 Ga23
Storslett N 63 Hb09
Storstein N 63 Hb08
Storsteinnes N 67 Gd11
Storsund S 73 Hb22
Stortinden N 63 Hd06
Storträsk S 73 Hb24
Storulvåns fjällstation S 78 Ed30
Storuman S 72 Gb24
Storvallen S 78 Ec30
Storvatnet N 66 Ga13
Storvik N 63 Hb09
Storvik S 95 Gb39
Storvika N 71 Fb18
Storvika N 78 Ea27
Storvoll N 62 Ha09
Storvollen N 62 Ha08
Storvollen N 71 Fc20
Storvollen N 71 Fb23
Storvollen N 77 Dd33
Storvorde DK 100 Dc21
Storvreta S 96 Gc41
Štós SK 138 Jc48
Stößen D 127 Ea41
Stoszowice PL 137 Gc43
Stöten S 86 Ed37
Stotfold GB 20 Fc26
Støtt N 70 Fa18
Stötten D 142 Dc52
Stotternheim D 127 Dd41
Stottesdon GB 15 Ec25
Stouby DK 108 Db25
Stoulton GB 20 Ed26
Stoumont B 125 Bb42
Stoúpa GR 194 Bb90
Stourport-on-Severn GB 15 Ec25
Stovbcy BY 202 Ea13
Støvring DK 100 Dc21
Støvset N 66 Fc17
Stow GB 11 Ec14
Stowięcino PL 121 Gd29
Stowmarket GB 21 Ga26
Stow-on-the-Wold GB 20 Ed26
Stowupland GB 21 Ga26
Stožer BG 181 Fa70
Stożne PL 123 Jd30
Stra I 150 Ea60
Straach D 127 Ec38
Straasdorf an der Nordbahn A 145 Gc50
Straatsburg = Strasbourg F 25 Kc37
Strabane GB 9 Cc16
Strabla PL 123 Kb34
Strachan GB 7 Ec09
Strachomino PL 120 Ga31
Strachówka PL 130 Jc36
Strachus GB 6 Dc12
Strączno PL 121 Gb34
Strada in Chianti I 155 Dc65
Strådalen S 86 Fa34
Stradalovo BG 179 Ca73
Strada San Zeno I 156 Dd64
Stradbally IRL 13 Cb25
Stradella I 149 Cc60
Stradishall GB 20 Fd26
Stradola I 161 Fd74
Stradone IRL 9 Cc19
Stradsett GB 17 Fd24
Straduny PL 123 Jd31
Stradzde LV 105 Jd50
Straelen D 125 Bc39
Stræte N 67 Gb12
Stragan SRB 174 Bb66
Stragavallen S 86 Fa34
Strahilovo BG 180 Dd69
Strahwalde D 128 Fc41
Straimont B 132 Ba44
Straiton GB 10 Dd15
Straja RO 172 Ea54
Straja RO 181 Fc67
Stråkan S 73 Ja19
Štråklevo BG 180 Ea68
Strakonice CZ 136 Fa47
Straldža BG 180 Eb72
Straloch GB 7 Eb10
Strålsnäs S 103 Fc47
Stralsund D 119 Ed30
Štramberk CZ 137 Ha46
Strambino I 148 Bd59
Strămeriena LV 107 Lc49
Stramproy NL 125 Bb39
Strâmtura RO 171 Db55
Strand N 65 Kd08
Strand N 66 Fd13
Strand N 77 Db30
Strand N 86 Eb37
Strand N 92 Ca43
Strand S 72 Gd20
Strand S 79 Fd28
Strand S 95 Fd40
Stranda N 64 Jb05
Stranda N 76 Cd33
Strandbaden S 110 Ec54
Strandby DK 100 Db22
Strandby DK 101 Dd19
Strande D 118 Dc30
Strandebarm N 84 Cb39
Strandhill IRL 8 Bd18
Strandlykkja N 94 Eb39
Strandvalen N 78 Ec25
Strandvallen S 86 Ed36
Strandvik N 84 Ca40
Strandža BG 185 Ec74

Svartlå S 73 Hc21
Svartnäs S 80 Hb25
Svartnäs S 87 Ga38
Svartnes N 71 Fc18
Svartö S 103 Gb51
Svartöstaden S 73 Hd22
Svartrå S 102 Ec51
Svarttjärn S 72 Gb22
Svarttorp S 103 Fb49
Svartträsk S 72 Gb24
Svartvik S 88 Gc33
Švary RUS 107 Mb52
Svatá Kateřina CZ 135 Ed47
Svatobořice-Mistřín CZ 137 Gc48
Svatove UA 203 Fb14
Svatsum N 85 Dd37
Svätý Jur SK 145 Gd50
Švebdruoė LT 123 Kc30
Svebølle DK 109 Ea26
Svedala S 110 Ed56
Svėdasai LT 114 La54
Svedja S 87 Gb35
Svedjan S 80 Gc28
Svedje S 79 Fd27
Svedje S 80 Gd29
Sveg S 87 Fb34
Sveggesundet N 77 Da30
Sveindal N 92 Cd46
Sveio N 92 Ca42
Švėkšna LT 113 Jc56
Svelgen N 84 Cb34
Svelvik N 93 Dd42
Svenarum S 103 Fb50
Švenčionėliai LT 115 Lb56
Švenčionys LT 115 Lb56
Svendborg DK 109 Dd27
Svene N 93 Dc42
Sveneby S 103 Fb46
Svenes N 85 Dc38
Svenes N 93 Da45
Svengestøl N 92 Cd46
Svenkerud N 85 Dc39
Svenljunga S 102 Ed50
Sveneby S 102 Eb46
Svennevad S 95 Fd44
Svenningsneset N 78 Ea27
Svensby N 62 Ha09
Svensbyn S 73 Hc23
Svenshögen S 102 Eb47
Svenskby FIN 97 Jd40
Svensköp S 110 Fa55
Svenstavik S 87 Fb32
Svenstrup DK 100 Dc21
Svenstrup DK 100 Dc23
Svenstrup DK 108 Db28
Svenstrup DK 109 Ea27
Švente LV 115 Lb53
Šventežeris LV 123 Kb30
Šventininkai LT 114 La58
Šventoj LT 113 Jb54
Šventragis LV 114 Kb59
Sveom N 85 Dc35
Sverdlove UA 204 Ed17
Sverdlovs'k UA 205 Fc15
Svetajevka RUS 113 Jb59
Sveta Petka BG 179 Cd73
Svetciems LV 106 Kb48
Svēte LV 106 Kb52
Sveti Ana Tenja HR 153 Hc59
Sveti Filip i Jakov HR 157 Fd65
Sveti Ivan HR 150 Ed60
Sveti Ivan Žabno HR 152 Gc58
Sveti Ivan Zelina HR 152 Gb58
Sveti Juraj HR 151 Fc61
Sveti Marina HR 151 Fb61
Sveti Nedelja HR 151 Ga59
Sveti Nikola BG 181 Fc70
Sveti Nikola MNE 163 Ja71
Sveti Nikole MK 178 Bd73
Sveti Petar na moru HR 157 Fd64
Sveti rok HR 151 Ga63
Sveti Stefan MNE 159 Hd70
Sveti Sveti Konstantin i Elena BG 181 Fb70
Sveti Vlas BG 181 Fa72
Světlá Hora CZ 137 Gd44
Svetlahorsk BY 202 Eb13
Světlá nad Sázavou CZ 136 Fd46
Svetlen BG 180 Eb70
Svetlice SK 139 Ka47
Svetlii MD 177 Fc61
Světlík CZ 136 Fb49
Svetlina BG 180 Ea73
Svetloe RUS 113 Ja59
Svetlogorsk RUS 113 Hd58
Svetlograd RUS 205 Ga16
Svetlyj Jar RUS 203 Ga14
Svetlyj RUS 113 Hd59
Svetozar Miletić SRB 153 Hd58
Svetvinčenat HR 151 Fa61
Svežen BG 180 Dc72
Sviby EST 97 Jd44
Švica HR 151 Fd62
Svidník SK 139 Jd46
Švihov CZ 135 Ed46
Svilajnac SRB 174 Bc65
Sviland N 92 Ca44
Svilengrad BG 185 Ea75
Sviliai LT 114 Kd53
Svindalen N 66 Fd12
Svineng N 64 Jc09
Svinesund N 94 Eb44
Svinhult S 103 Fd49
Svinia SK 138 Jc47
Svinița RO 174 Ca65
Svinná SK 137 Hb49
Svinndal N 93 Ea43
Svinnegarn S 95 Gb43
Svinninge DK 109 Ea25
Svinninge S 96 Gd43
Svinvik N 77 Db30
Svirači BG 185 Ea76
Svirkos LT 115 Lc56
Svirkovo BG 185 Ea74
Sviščaki SLO 151 Fb59
Svislač BY 202 Dd13
Svislač BY 202 Eb12
Svištov BG 180 Dd69
Svit SK 138 Jb47
Svitava BIH 158 Hb68
Svitávka CZ 137 Gb46
Svitavy CZ 137 Gb45
Svitlovods'k UA 204 Ed15
Svoboda BG 181 Fa69
Svoboda RUS 113 Jc59
Svoboda nad Úpou CZ 136 Ga43
Svobodinovo BG 184 Dc75
Svobody RUS 205 Ga17
Svode BG 179 Cd70
Svodín SK 145 Hb51
Svodje SRB 179 Ca70
Svoge BG 179 Cc70
Svojetin CZ 136 Fa44
Svojšín CZ 135 Ec45
Svolvær N 66 Fc14
Svorkmo N 77 Dd30
Svratka CZ 136 Ga46
Svrčinovec SK 138 Hc46
Svrljig SRB 178 Bd68
Svržno CZ 135 Ec46
Svullrya N 94 Ec40
Svylionys LT 115 Lc56
Swadlincote GB 16 Fa24
Swaffham GB 17 Ga24
Swallowcliffe GB 20 Ed29
Swalmen NL 125 Bb39
Swanage GB 20 Ed31
Swanbridge GB 19 Ea28
Swanley GB 20 Fd28
Swanlinbar IRL 9 Cb18
Swansea GB 19 Dd27
Swarland GB 11 Fa15
Swarożyn PL 121 Hb31
Swarzędz PL 129 Gc37
Swatragh GB 9 Cd16
Świadki Iławeckie PL 122 Ja30
Świątki PL 122 Ja31
Świątkowa PL 139 Jd46
Świątniki PL 131 Jd42
Świątniki Górne PL 138 Ja44
Świba PL 129 Ha40
Świbno PL 121 Hb30
Świdnica PL 128 Fd38
Świdnica PL 129 Gb42
Świdnik PL 131 Kb40
Świdnik PL 138 Jb45
Świdry PL 123 Jd32
Świdwin PL 120 Ga32
Świebodzice PL 129 Gb42
Świebodzin PL 128 Fd37
Święcany PL 139 Jd45
Świecie PL 121 Hb33
Świeciechowa PL 129 Gb38
Świeciechów Duży PL 131 Jd41
Świecie nad Osą PL 122 Hc33
Świecko PL 128 Fc37
Świedziebnia PL 122 Hd34
Świekatowo PL 121 Ha33
Świeradów-Zdrój PL 128 Fd42
Świercze PL 122 Jb35
Świerczów PL 129 Ha41
Świerczyna PL 121 Gb33
Świerczyna PL 138 Jb43
Świerklany Górne PL 137 Hb44
Świerkowo PL 122 Jb35
Świerzawa PL 128 Ga41
Świerzenko PL 121 Gc31
Świerzno PL 120 Fc31
Świeszyno PL 120 Ga31
Święta PL 120 Fc33
Święta Anna PL 130 Hd42
Świętajno PL 122 Jb32
Święta Katarzyna PL 130 Jb41
Święta Lipka PL 122 Jb31
Świętno PL 128 Ga38
Świętochłowice PL 138 Hc43
Świętoszów PL 128 Fd40
Swifterbant NL 116 Bb35
Swilcza PL 139 Ka44
Swindon GB 20 Ed28
Swinefleet GB 16 Fb21
Swinemünde = Świnoujście PL 120 Fb32
Swinford IRL 8 Bd19
Świniary PL 122 Jb34
Świnna PL 138 Hd45
Świnoujście PL 120 Fb32
Swinton GB 11 Ed14
Świny PL 128 Ga41
Swisttal D 125 Bd41
Swobnica PL 120 Fc34
Swords IRL 13 Cd21
Swornegacie PL 121 Gd32
Swory PL 131 Kb37
Swyre GB 19 Eb30
Sya S 103 Fd47
Syam F 31 Jd43
Syčevka RUS 202 Ec10
Sycewice PL 121 Gc30
Syców PL 129 Gd40
Sycowice PL 128 Fd38
Sydänmaa FIN 89 Jb34
Sydänmaa FIN 89 Ja37
Sydänmaankylä FIN 82 Kb27
Sydmo FIN 97 Jb40
Sygkrasi CY 206 Jd96
Sykäräinen FIN 81 Jd28
Syke D 118 Cd34
Sykkylven N 76 Cc33
Sykoúnda GR 191 Ea83
Sylda D 127 Ea39
Šyliai LT 113 Jc56
Sylling N 93 Dd41
Syltanovo RUS 107 Ma51
Sylte N 77 Da31
Syltevikmyra N 65 Kc05
Sylt-Ost D 108 Cd28
Sylväjä FIN 83 Lb25
Sylvänä FIN 89 Jd38
Sylvanès F 41 Hb53
Sylvéréal F 42 Ja54
Symbister GB 5 Fa04
Symonds Yat GB 19 Ec27
Synanohori CY 206 Ja96
Synel'nykove UA 205 Fa15
Synnerby S 102 Fa47
Synnes N 78 Ec25
Synod Inn GB 14 Dc25
Synsiö FIN 90 Kd33
Syötekylä FIN 75 Kc21
Sypniewo PL 121 Gb33
Sypniewo PL 121 Gc33
Sypniewo PL 122 Jc34
Syrau D 135 Eb43
Syre GB 5 Ea05
Syre N 92 Bd43
Syri FIN 81 Jd28
Syrjä FIN 83 Lb31
Syrjajeve UA 204 Ec16
Syrjäkoski FIN 90 Kc35
Syrjäntaka FIN 90 Kb36
Syrkesnes N 66 Fd16
Syrkovicy RUS 99 Ma41
Syroke UA 204 Ed16
Syrokoje RUS 122 Jb30
Syrynia PL 137 Hb44
Syščycy BY 202 Ea13
Šyškrantė LT 113 Jb56
Sysmä FIN 90 Kc35
Sysslebäck S 94 Ed39
Syväjärvi FIN 69 Jd16
Syväjoki FIN 82 Kd26
Syvänniemi FIN 82 Kd30
Syvänojankylä FIN 89 Jb32
Syvärinpää FIN 82 La28
Syvävaara FIN 83 Lc27
Syvde N 76 Cb33
Syvdsnes N 76 Cb33
Syvsten DK 101 Dd20
Sywell GB 20 Fb25
Syyspohja FIN 91 Lc35
Syzran' RUS 203 Ga10
Szabadbattyán H 145 Hb54
Szabadegyháza H 146 Hc54
Szabadszállás H 146 Hd55
Sząbruk PL 122 Ja32
Szadek PL 130 Hc39
Szadłowice PL 121 Ha35
Szaflary PL 138 Ja46
Szajol H 146 Jb54
Szakály H 145 Hb56
Szakcs H 145 Hb56
Szakmár H 146 Hd56
Szalánta H 152 Hb58
Szalapa H 145 Gd55
Szalejów PL 137 Gb43
Szalkszentmárton H 146 Hd54
Szalonna H 138 Jc49
Szamocin PL 121 Gc34
Szamotuły PL 129 Gb36
Szandaszőlős H 146 Jb54
Szank H 146 Ja56
Szany H 145 Gd53
Szarvas H 146 Jc55
Szarvaskő H 146 Jb51
Szászvár H 152 Hb57
Szatarpy PL 121 Ha31
Szatmárcseke H 147 Kc50
Szatymaz H 146 Jb56
Százhalombatta H 146 Hc53
Szczaniek PL 128 Ga37
Szczawa PL 138 Jb46
Szczawin Borowy PL 130 Hd36
Szczawin Kościelny PL 130 Hd36
Szczawne PL 139 Ka46
Szczawnica PL 138 Jb46
Szczawno-Zdrój PL 129 Gb42
Szczebrzeszyn PL 131 Kc41
Szczecin PL 120 Fc33
Szczecinek PL 121 Gb32
Szczeinki PL 123 Ka30
Szczejkowice PL 137 Hb44
Szczekociny PL 130 Ja42
Szczepańcowa PL 139 Jd45
Szczepankowo PL 123 Jd34
Szczepanów PL 129 Gb41
Szczepkowo Borow PL 122 Ja33
Szczerców PL 130 Hc40
Szczpiorno PL 129 Ha39
Szczucin PL 138 Jc43
Szczuczarz PL 120 Ga34
Szczuczyn PL 123 Jd32
Szczuka PL 122 Hc34
Szczurowa PL 138 Jb44
Szczyrk PL 138 Hc45
Szczyrzyc PL 138 Ja45
Szczytna PL 137 Gb43
Szczytniki PL 120 Fc32
Szczytniki PL 129 Ha39
Szczytno PL 122 Jb32
Szczyty PL 137 Ha44
Szécsény H 146 Hd51
Szederkény H 153 Hc58
Szedres H 146 Hc56
Szeged H 153 Jb57
Szeghalom H 147 Jd54
Szegvár H 146 Jb56
Székely H 147 Ka50
Székesfehérvár H 145 Hb54
Székkutas H 146 Jc56
Szekszárd H 153 Hc57
Szeleste H 145 Gc54
Szelevény H 146 Jb55
Szellő H 153 Hc57
Szembruk PL 122 Hc32
Szemere H 139 Jd49
Szemud PL 121 Ha30
Szendrő H 138 Jc49
Szenenyecsörnye H 145 Gc56
Szenna H 152 Ha57
Szentbalázs H 152 Ha57
Szentendre H 146 Hd52
Szentes H 146 Jb55
Szentgál H 145 Ha54
Szentgotthárd H 145 Gb55
Szentlászló H 152 Ha57
Szentliszló H 145 Gc56
Szentlőrinc H 152 Hb58
Szentmártonkáta H 146 Ja53
Szenttamáspuszta H 152 Ha57
Szenyér H 145 Gd56
Széphalom H 139 Ka49
Szepietowo PL 123 Ka34
Szerencs H 147 Jd50
Szerokopas PL 121 Hb34
Szerzyny PL 138 Jc45
Szestno PL 122 Jb31
Szewna PL 130 Jc41
Szigethalom H 146 Hd53
Szigetszentmiklós H 146 Hd53
Szigetvár H 152 Ha58
Szigliget H 145 Gd55
Szikáncs H 146 Jc56
Szikszó H 146 Jc50
Szilvásvárad H 146 Jb51
Szin H 138 Jc49
Szirak H 146 Ja52
Szklarska Poręba PL 128 Fd42
Szklary Górne PL 128 Ga40
Szkody PL 123 Jd32
Szkotowo PL 122 Ja33
Szlichtyngowa PL 129 Gb39
Szob H 146 Hc52
Szokolya H 146 Hc51
Szolnok H 146 Jb54
Szombathely H 145 Gc54
Szomor H 146 Hc52
Szőny H 145 Hb52
Szorce PL 123 Ka33
Szóstka PL 131 Kb37
Szówsko PL 139 Kb44
Szozurkowo PL 122 Jb30
Szprotowa PL 128 Fd39
Szreńsk PL 122 Ja34
Sztabin PL 123 Kb31
Sztum PL 121 Hb31
Sztumska Wieś PL 121 Hb31
Sztutowo PL 122 Hc30
Sztynort PL 122 Jc30
Szubin PL 121 Gd34
Szúcs H 146 Jb51
Szűcsi H 146 Ja52
Szudziałowo PL 123 Kc33
Szulborze Wielkie PL 123 Jd35
Szulmierz PL 122 Ja34
Szulok H 152 Ha58
Szumowo PL 123 Jd34
Szurkowo PL 129 Gc39
Szwecja PL 121 Gb33
Szydlak PL 122 Hd32
Szydłów PL 130 Jc42
Szydłowiec PL 130 Jb40
Szydłowo PL 121 Gb34
Szydłowo PL 122 Ja34
Szymany PL 122 Jb33
Szymbark PL 122 Hc32
Szymbark PL 138 Jc45
Szymki PL 123 Kc34
Szymonka PL 122 Jc31
Szyndziel PL 123 Kb32
Szynwałd PL 138 Jc44
Szynych PL 121 Hb33
Szypliszki PL 123 Kb30
Szyszki Włościańskie PL 122 Jb35

T

Taagepera EST 106 Kd47
Tääksi EST 98 Kd45
Taaliku EST 97 Jd45
Taalintehdas FIN 97 Jc41
Taapajärvi FIN 68 Jc17
Taasia FIN 90 Kd37
Taastrup DK 109 Ec26
Taattola FIN 82 La26
Tab H 145 Hb55
Tabágon E 36 Ac58
Tabajd H 146 Hc53
Tabanera de Cerrato E 46 Db59
Tabanera la Luenga E 46 Db62
Tabani MD 172 Ed53
Tabanköy TR 185 Ed80
Tabanlar TR 191 Ed83
Tabanovce MK 178 Bc72
Tabaqueros E 54 Ed68
Tábara E 45 Cb59
Tabariškės LT 115 Lb58
Tabarz D 126 Dc41
Tabasalu EST 98 Kb42
Tabaza E 37 Cc54
Tabeirós E 36 Ad56
Taberg S 103 Fb49
Tabernas E 61 Ea75
Taberna Seca P 44 Ba65
Taberno E 61 Eb74
Tabiano Bagni I 149 Da61
Tabina EST 107 Lc47
Tabivere EST 98 La44
Tablate E 60 Dc76
Taboada E 36 Bb56
Taboada E 36 Ba54
Tabód H 146 Hc56
Tábor CZ 136 Fc47
Tabórz PL 122 Hd32
Tábua P 44 Ba63
Tabuaço P 44 Bb61
Tabuenca E 47 Ed60
Tabuyo de Monte E 37 Ca58
Täby S 95 Fc44
Täby S 96 Gd43
Täby S 103 Ga46
Tăcău RO 177 Fb65
Taceno I 149 Cc57
Tacettin TR 193 Hb81
Tacherting D 143 Eb51
Taching D 143 Ec51
Tachov CZ 135 Ec45
Tacinskij RUS 203 Fc14
Tacir TR 186 Ga79
Tackåsen S 87 Fc36
Tăcuta RO 173 Fa58
Tadaiķi LV 105 Jb52
Tadcaster GB 16 Fa20
Tadmarton GB 20 Fa26
Taebla EST 98 Ka44
Taevaskoja EST 107 Lb46
Tafalla E 39 Ed58
Tafjord N 77 Da33
Taft A 144 Ga52
Täftea S 80 Hc28
Täfteå S 80 Ha30
Țaga RO 171 Db57
Tagaj RUS 203 Fd10
Taganrog RUS 205 Fc15
Tagaranna EST 97 Jc45
Tågarp S 110 Ed55
Tagelvdal N 67 Gd11
Tägerwilen CH 142 Cc52
Taggia I 43 La52
Taghmon IRL 13 Cc25
Tagliacozzo I 160 Ec71
Taglio di Po I 150 Ea61
Tagmersheim D 134 Dc48
Tagnon F 24 Hd34
Tagoat IRL 13 Cd25
Tagsdorf F 31 Kb40
Tagula EST 106 La47
Tahal E 61 Eb75
Tahal TR 185 Ec76
Tähemaa EST 99 Lb45
Taheva EST 106 La48
Tahilla IRL 12 Ba25
Tahivilla E 59 Ca78
Tahkolanranta FIN 75 La19
Tahkuna EST 97 Jc44
Tahta RUS 205 Fd16
Tahtacı TR 191 Ec83
Tahtacı TR 192 Fc85
Tahtacı TR 198 Fc88
Tahtaköprü TR 192 Ga81
Tahtakuşlar TR 191 Eb82
Tähtelä FIN 69 Ka16
Tähtelä FIN 98 Ka40
Taian RO 180 Dc68
Taicy RUS 99 Mb40
Taillebois F 22 Fc37
Tailovo RUS 107 Lc47
Taimoniemi FIN 82 Kb30
Tain GB 5 Ea07
Taingy F 30 Hb41
Tainiemi FIN 74 Ka21
Tainijoki FIN 74 Ka20
Tain-l'Hermitage F 34 Jb49
Tainuskylä FIN 89 Ja32
Taipale FIN 74 Jd22
Taipale FIN 82 Kc29
Taipale FIN 82 Ka31
Taipale FIN 82 Kd28
Taipale FIN 89 Jb35
Taipale FIN 89 Jd37
Taipale FIN 90 Kd33
Taipale FIN 90 Kc35
Taipaleenharju FIN 74 Kb22
Taipalsaari FIN 91 Lb35
Taipalus FIN 89 Jc32
Taiskirchen im Innkreis A 143 Ed50
Taivalkoski FIN 75 Kd21
Taivalkunta FIN 89 Jc36
Taivalmaa FIN 89 Jb32
Taivassalo FIN 97 Ja39
Taizé F 28 Fc43
Taizé F 30 Ja44
Taizon F 28 Fc43
Taja E 37 Cb55
Tajmište MK 182 Ba74
Tajno Podjeziorne PL 123 Ka31
Tăkač BG 181 Ec69
Takamaa FIN 89 Jd35
Takamaa FIN 90 Kd37
Takeley GB 20 Fd27
Takene S 94 Fa44
Takhuranna EST 106 Kb46
Takkula FIN 82 La26
Takkulankulma FIN 89 Jb38
Taklax FIN 89 Hd32
Takniškiai LT 114 Kc59
Takovo SRB 153 Jb62
Takovo SRB 159 Jc64
Takserås N 93 Db45
Taktaharkány H 147 Jd50
Täkter FIN 98 Ka40
Taktikoúpoli GR 195 Ca88
Taktkom FIN 97 Jd41
Tal E 36 Ac55
Talačyn BY 202 Eb12
Talairan F 41 Ha56
Talais F 32 Fa48
Talamanca E 49 Gd60
Talamantes E 47 Ed60
Talamillo del Tozo E 38 Db57
Talamone I 155 Dc69
Talana I 169 Cb77
Talarn E 48 Ga59
Talarrubias E 52 Cc68
Talasani F 154 Cc69
Talasjoki FIN 82 Kd27
Talaván E 51 Bd66
Talavera de la Reina E 52 Cd66
Talavera la Real E 51 Bc69
Talayuela E 45 Cb65
Talayuelas E 54 Ed66
Talcy F 29 Gb40
Taldom RUS 202 Ed10
Talea RO 176 Ea63
Talefe P 50 Aa67
Taleggio I 149 Cd58
Tales E 54 Fc66
Talgarreg GB 15 Dd26
Talgarth GB 15 Ea26
Talgje N 92 Ca43
Tali EST 106 Kc47
Táliga E 51 Bb70
Talinen S 68 Hd17
Talisker GB 4 Da08
Talkowszczyzna PL 123 Kc33
Talladale GB 4 Dc07
Tallaght IRL 13 Cd21
Tállara E 36 Ac56
Tallard F 42 Ka51
Tallåsen S 87 Ga35
Tallberg S 73 Hd20
Tallberg S 80 Ha28
Tallberg S 80 Hb28
Tällberg S 87 Fc38
Talley GB 15 Dd26
Tallhed S 87 Fc37
Tallinn EST 98 Kb42
Talljärv S 73 Hd20
Talloires F 35 Ka46
Tallowbridge IRL 13 Ca25
Tallsjö S 80 Gc27
Tällträsk S 73 Hc23
Tallträsk S 80 Gc26
Tallträsk S 80 Hb26
Talluskylä FIN 82 Kd30
Tallvik S 73 Ja20
Tállya H 147 Jd50
Tălmaciu RO 175 Db62
Talmas F 23 Gd33
Talmay F 31 Jc41
Talmaz MD 173 Ga59
Talmine GB 5 Ea04
Talmontiers F 23 Gc35
Talmont-Saint-Hilaire F 32 Ed45
Talmont-sur-Gironde F 32 Fb48
Tal'ne UA 204 Ec15
Talovaja RUS 203 Fb13
Talpa RO 176 Dd66
Talpaki RUS 113 Jb59
Talsano I 162 Ha76
Talsarnau GB 15 Dd23
Talsi LV 105 Jd50
Taluskylä FIN 81 Jd26
Talviainen FIN 90 Ka34
Talvik N 63 Hd08
Talvisilta FIN 89 Jd38
Tal-y-bont GB 15 Dd24
Tal-y-cafn GB 15 Ea22
Tamădău Mare RO 176 Ec66
Tamajón E 46 Dd62
Tamala RUS 203 Fc11
Tamallancos E 36 Bb57
Tamame E 45 Cb61
Tamames E 45 Ca63
Tamanhos P 44 Bb62
Tamarë AL 159 Jb69
Tamarino BG 181 Ec73
Tamarit E 49 Gc62
Tamarite de Litera E 48 Fd60
Tamariz de Campos E 46 Cd59
Tămășeni RO 172 Ed58
Tamási H 145 Hb56
Tamași RO 172 Ed59
Tambach-Dietharz D 126 Dc42
Tâmboești RO 176 Ed63
Tambohuse DK 100 Da22
Tambov RUS 203 Fb12
Ţambula MD 173 Fb55
Tåme S 73 Hc24
Tamengont RUS 99 Ma39
Tåmeträsk S 73 Hc24
Tamins CH 142 Cd55
Tamış TR 191 Ea82
Tamlaght GB 9 Cb18
Tammela FIN 75 Lb20
Tammela FIN 89 Jd38
Tammenlahti FIN 91 Lc33
Tammeråsen S 87 Fc38
Tammijärvi FIN 90 Kc34
Tammikkoski FIN 90 Kc34
Tammiku EST 98 La43
Tammiku EST 98 La44
Tammilahti FIN 90 Ka33
Tammilahti FIN 90 Kc34
Tammisaari FIN 97 Jd40
Tammispää EST 99 Lb43
Tammistu EST 99 Lb45
Tammneeme EST 98 Kb42
Tammuna EST 105 Jb47
Tâmna RO 175 Cc65
Tamnay-en-Bazois F 30 Hc42
Tamnes N 86 Ec32
Tamnić SRB 174 Cb66
Tamniès F 33 Gb50
Tamoga E 36 Bb54
Tampere FIN 89 Jd35
Tamsalu EST 98 Kd43
Tamsweg A 144 Fa54
Tämta S 102 Ed48
Tamurejo E 52 Cc69
Tamworth GB 16 Ed24
Tån S 102 Ec46
Tana bru N 64 Ka06
Tanacu RO 173 Fb59
Tanágra GR 189 Cb85
Tanakajd H 145 Gc54
Tananger N 92 Ca44
Tănăsoaia RO 177 Fa61
Tănătari MD 173 Ga59
Tănătarii Noi MD 173 Ga59
Tanaunella I 168 Cc75
Tanda SRB 174 Ca66
Țăndărei RO 177 Fa66
Tandern D 143 Dd50
Tandır TR 193 Gd81
Tandö S 86 Fa38
Tandragee GB 9 Cd18
Tandsbyn S 79 Fc31
Tandsjöborg S 87 Fc36
Tanem N 77 Ea30
Tang IRL 9 Cb20
Tångaberg S 102 Ec51
Tanganheira P 50 Ab71
Tangaveane IRL 8 Ca16
Tångböle S 78 Ed30
Tangen N 76 Cd31
Tangen N 79 Fb27
Tangen N 93 Ea44
Tangen N 94 Eb39
Tångeråsa S 95 Fc44
Tangerhütte D 127 Ea36
Tangermünde D 127 Eb36
Tangnesland N 63 Hc09
Tångsta S 79 Gb30
Tangstedt D 118 Db32
Tangstedt D 118 Dc32
Tångvattnet S 71 Fc22
Tanhua FIN 69 Kb15
Tani FIN 91 Lb36
Taninges F 35 Ka45
Tankavaara FIN 69 Ka13
Tankolampi FIN 82 Kc31
Tănkovo BG 181 Fb72
Tănkovo BG 185 Dd75
Tanlay F 30 Hd40
Tann D 143 Ec50
Tanna D 135 Ea43
Tanna D 135 Ea43
Tannadice GB 7 Ec10
Tannåker S 102 Fa51
Tännäs S 86 Ed33
Tannay F 24 Ja34
Tannay F 30 Hc41
Tänndalen S 86 Ed33
Tanne D 126 Dc39
Tännesberg D 135 Eb46
Tannhausen D 134 Db48
Tannheim A 142 Db53
Tannheim D 142 Da51
Tannila FIN 74 Ka22
Tannisby DK 101 Dd19
Tännö S 103 Fb51
Tann (Rhön) D 126 Db42
Tannroda D 127 Dd42
Tannsjön S 79 Fd29
Tanoiro E 36 Ad57
Tanowo PL 120 Fb33
Tansa RO 172 Ed58
Tânțareni RO 175 Cd65
Tantonville F 25 Jd37
Tantow D 120 Fb34
Tanttala FIN 90 Kb37
Tanttila FIN 90 Kb37
Tånum DK 100 Dc23
Tanum N 93 Dd41
Tanum N 93 Dc44
Tanum S 94 Eb45
Tanumshede S 94 Eb45
Tanus F 41 Ha52
Tanvald CZ 128 Fd42
Tan-y-llyn GB 15 Dd24
Tan-y-pistyll GB 15 Ea23
Taormina I 167 Fd85
Táp H 145 Ha53
Tapa EST 98 Kd42
Tapala FIN 89 Jc38
Tapani vaara FIN 75 Lb24
Tapdrup DK 100 Db23
Tapfheim D 134 Dc49
Tapia de Casariego E 37 Bd53
Tapiku EST 98 La44
Tápióbicske H 146 Ja53
Tápiógyörgye H 146 Ja53
Tapiola FIN 98 Kb39
Tapionkylä FIN 74 Jd18
Tapionniemi FIN 69 Kb17
Tápiószele H 146 Ja53
Tápiószentmárton H 146 Ja53
Tápiószőlős H 146 Ja53
Tapizë AL 182 Ab74
Tapojärvi FIN 68 Ja16
Tapolca H 145 Gd55
Tappeluft N 63 Hc08
Tappen N 63 Ja06
Tappernøje DK 109 Eb27
Taps DK 108 Db26
Tapsony H 145 Gd56
Tar HR 150 Ed60
Tarabo S 102 Ed48
Taraclia MD 173 Fd59
Taraclia MD 177 Fd61
Taraclica de Salcie MD 177 Fc61
Tarácsi H 145 Gd53
Taradell E 49 Ha60
Taragona E 36 Ad56
Taraguilla E 59 Cb78
Taraklı TR 187 Gc80
Tărân BG 184 Db75
Tarancón E 53 Dd66
Taranto I 162 Ha76
Tárány H 145 Ha53
Tarany H 152 Gd57
Tarare F 34 Ja46
Taraš SRB 153 Jb59
Tarašča UA 204 Ec15
Taraşçı TR 199 Hb89
Tarascon F 42 Jb53
Tarascon-sur-Ariège F 40 Gc57
Tarasova MD 173 Fd55
Tarasovka RUS 113 Jb58
Tarasp Fontana CH 142 Da55
Tarassac F 41 Hb54
Taravilla E 47 Ec64
Tarazona E 47 Ec60
Tarazona de Guareña E 45 Cc62
Tarazona de la Mancha E 53 Ec68
Tårbæk DK 109 Ec25
Tarbert GB 4 Da06
Tarbert GB 6 Db13
Tarbert IRL 12 Bb23
Tarbes F 40 Fd55
Tarbolton GB 10 Dd14
Tärby S 102 Ed48
Tărcaia RO 170 Cb58
Tarcal H 147 Jd50
Tarcău RO 172 Eb58
Tarcea RO 170 Cb55
Tarcenay F 31 Jd42
Tarcento I 150 Ed57
Tarčin BIH 158 Hb65
Tarczyn PL 130 Jb38
Tard H 146 Jc51
Tardajos E 38 Dc58
Tardelcuende E 47 Ea61
Tardets-Sorholus F 39 Fa56
Tardienta E 48 Fb59
Tärendö S 68 Hd17
Tarente = Taranto I 162 Ha76
Tarent = Taranto I 162 Ha76
Țareuca MD 173 Fd55
Targale LV 105 Jb50
Targon F 32 Fb50
Tărgovište BG 180 Eb70
Târgoviște RO 176 Dd64
Targowo PL 122 Jb32
Târgșoru Vechi RO 176 Ea64
Târgu Bujor RO 177 Fb62
Târgu Cărbunești RO 175 Cd64
Târgu Frumos RO 172 Ed57
Târgu Gângulești RO 175 Da64
Târgu Jiu RO 175 Cd63
Târgu Lăpuș RO 171 Db56
Târgu Mureș RO 171 Dc59
Târgu-Neamț RO 172 Ec57
Târgu Ocna RO 176 Ec60
Târgu Secuiesc RO 176 Eb61
Târgușor RO 177 Fc66
Târgu Trotuș RO 176 Ec60
Tarhapää FIN 90 Ka32
Tarhos H 147 Jd55
Tarian RO 170 Ca56
Tarifa E 59 Ca78
Țarigrad MD 173 Fb54
Tarinmaa FIN 90 Ka37
Tariquejo E 59 Bb73
Tarján H 145 Hb52

Tarland – Tigveni

Tarland GB 7 Ec09
Tarleton GB 15 Eb21
Târlişua RO 171 Db56
Tarlo PL 131 Kb39
Tarłów PL 131 Jd41
Tărlungeni RO 176 Ea62
Tarm DK 108 Cd24
Tarmaankylä FIN 89 Ja34
Tarmon IRL 8 Ca18
Tarmstedt D 118 Da33
Tarna E 37 Cd55
Tärna S 95 Gb42
Tärnaby S 71 Fd22
Tarnac F 33 Gd47
Tărnak BG 179 Da69
Tarnala FIN 91 Ld33
Tarnalelesz H 146 Jb51
Tarna Mare RO 171 Cd53
Tarnaméra H 146 Jb52
Tärnamo S 71 Fc22
Tarnaörs H 146 Jb52
Tărnava BG 179 Cd69
Târnava RO 175 Db60
Târnăveni RO 171 Db59
Tarnawa PL 139 Kb46
Tarnawatka PL 131 Kc42
Tårnby DK 109 Ec26
Tårnes N 78 Ea28
Tårnet N 65 Kd07
Tårnev N 62 Gc10
Tarnobrzeg PL 131 Jd42
Tarnogóra PL 131 Kc41
Tarnogród PL 139 Kb43
Tárnok H 146 Hc53
Tarnov SK 138 Jc46
Târnova RO 170 Ca59
Târnova RO 174 Ca62
Tarnów PL 120 Fc35
Tarnów PL 130 Jc38
Tarnów PL 138 Jc44
Tarnówek PL 128 Ga40
Tarnowiec PL 139 Jd45
Tarnówka PL 121 Gc33
Tarnówko PL 120 Fc33
Tarnowo-Podgórne PL 129 Gb36
Tarnów Opolski PL 137 Ha43
Tarnowska Wola PL 131 Jd42
Tarnowskie Góry PL 138 Hc43
Tärnsjö S 95 Gb41
Tårnvik N 64 Jd06
Tårnvika N 66 Fc16
Tarouca P 44 Ba61
Tarp D 108 Db29
Tarp DK 108 Cd26
Tarpa H 147 Kc50
Tarporley GB 15 Ec22
Tarprubežiai LV 114 Kb59
Tarquinia I 156 Dd70
Tarquinia Lido I 156 Dd70
Tarragona E 48 Gb62
Tårrajaur S 72 Ha20
Tàrrega E 48 Gb60
Tårs DK 100 Dc20
Tårs DK 109 Dd28
Tarsdorf A 143 Ec51
Tarsia I 164 Gb79
Tarsogno I 149 Cd63
Târşolţ RO 171 Da54
Tartaki LV 115 Lc53
Tartanedo E 47 Ec63
Tartano I 149 Cd57
Tartas F 39 Fb53
Tărtăşeşti RO 176 Ea65
Tartaul MD 177 Fc60
Tartaul de Salcie MD 177 Fc61
Tartigny F 23 Gd34
Tartonne F 42 Ka52
Tarttila FIN 89 Jd36
Tartu EST 99 Lb45
Tarumaa EST 99 Lb42
Tårup DK 109 Dd27
Tarusa RUS 202 Ed11
Tarvaala FIN 82 Kb31
Tarvaala FIN 90 Kc32
Tarvaanperä FIN 74 Jd20
Tarvainen FIN 89 Jb38
Tarvasjoki FIN 97 Jc39
Tarvin GB 15 Eb22
Tarvisio I 143 Ed56
Tarvola FIN 81 Jc30
Taşağıl TR 199 Ha91
Taşağıl TR 199 Hb89
Tasapää FIN 91 Ld32
Taşarasi TR 191 Ec82
Taşbükü TR 197 Fa90
Taşca RO 172 Eb58
Täsch CH 148 Bd57
Taşdibi TR 198 Fc91
Taşdibi TR 199 Gd90
Taşevi TR 193 Gd87
Taši LV 105 Jb52
Tåsjö S 79 Ga27
Táska H 145 Ha56
Taşkapı TR 199 Gc89
Taşkesiği TR 199 Gb90
Taşkesiği TR 199 Hb91
Taşkesti TR 187 Gd79
Taşkısığı TR 187 Gc78
Taşköprü TR 185 Ec76
Taşköprü TR 192 Fb81
Taşköprü TR 205 Fb20
Taşköy TR 192 Fa82
Taşköy TR 192 Fb83
Taşköy TR 192 Fc86
Taslı TR 197 Ed89
Taşlic MD 173 Ga58
Taşlıca TR 197 Fa92
Taşlık TR 187 Hb80
Tăşnad RO 171 Cc55
Taşoluk TR 193 Gc85
Tasov CZ 136 Ga47
Taşova TR 205 Fc20
Taşpınar TR 186 Fc80
Tass H 146 Hd54
Tassenières F 31 Jc43
Tåssjö S 110 Ed54
Tast FIN 81 Jc28
Tåstarp S 110 Ed54
Tastula FIN 81 Jc28
Taşumurca TR 185 Ec77
Tata H 145 Hb52
Tatabánya H 145 Hb52
Tătădrăştii de Jos RO 176 Dd66
Tataháza H 153 Hd57
Tatanovo RUS 203 Fb11
Tatar TR 192 Ga86
Tătărăni RO 173 Fb59
Tătărani RO 176 Dd64
Tătăranu RO 176 Ed63
Tătărăşti RO 176 Ed60
Tătărăştii de Sus RO 175 Dc66
Tatarbunary UA 204 Ec17
Tatarcık TR 192 Ga87
Tătăreşti MD 177 Fc61
Tatarköy TR 185 Ed76
Tatarlar TR 185 Ec75
Tatarlı TR 185 Ec78
Tatarlı TR 193 Gc87
Tatarocağı TR 192 Fa85
Tatárszentgyörgy H 146 Hd54
Tătaru RO 176 Eb64
Tătăruşi RO 172 Ec56
Taterma EST 97 Jc45
Tatiščevo RUS 203 Fd12
Tatköy TR 199 Gb91
Tatlısu TR 186 Fa79
Tatlısu TR 191 Eb83
Tatranská Lomnica SK 138 Jb47
Tatranská Štrba SK 138 Ja47
Tattershall GB 17 Fc23
Tătuleşti RO 175 Db65
Tătuleşti RO 176 Ed65
Tau N 92 Ca43
Taubenheim D 127 Ed41
Tauberbischofsheim D 134 Da45
Taucha D 127 Ec40
Täuffelen CH 141 Bc53
Taufkirchen A 143 Ed50
Taufkirchen D 143 Eb51
Taufkirchen (Vils) D 143 Eb50
Taujėnai LT 114 Kd55
Ţaul MD 173 Fb54
Taulakylä FIN 89 Jd35
Taulé F 26 Dd37
Taulignan F 42 Jb51
Taulov DK 108 Db26
Taunton GB 19 Eb29
Taunusstein D 133 Cb43
Tauplitz A 144 Fa53
Tauragė LT 113 Jd56
Tauragnai LT 115 Lb55
Ţaura Veche MD 173 Fb56
Taurene LV 106 La49
Tăureni RO 171 Db59
Taurianova I 164 Gb83
Taurisano I 165 Hc78
Taurkalne LV 106 Kd51
Taurupe LV 106 Kd50
Taús E 40 Gb58
Tauscha D 128 Fa40
Taussat F 32 Fa50
Tauste E 47 Fa60
Tauţ RO 170 Ca59
Tautavel F 41 Hb57
Tăuteu RO 170 Cb56
Tăuţii-Măgherăuş RO 171 Da55
Tautkaičiai LV 114 Kb58
Tautušiai LV 114 Kb55
Tauves F 33 Ha47
Tauvo FIN 74 Jd24
Tauvola FIN 98 Ka39
Tavaklı TR 191 Ea82
Tavankut SRB 153 Ja57
Tavannes CH 141 Bc53
Tavarnelle Val di Pesa I 155 Dc66
Tavas TR 198 Fc89
Tavastila FIN 90 La38
Tavastkenkä FIN 82 Kb26
Tavaux F 31 Jb44
Tavaux-et-Pontséricourt F 24 Hc34
Tavel F 42 Jb52
Tävelsås S 103 Fc52
Tavelsjö S 80 Hb28
Taverna I 164 Gc81
Tavernelle I 149 Da63
Tavernelle I 156 Ea68
Tavernes F 42 Ka54
Tavernes de la Valldigna E 54 Fc69
Tavernola I 161 Ga73
Tavernola Bergamasca I 149 Da58
Taverny F 23 Gd36
Taviano I 163 Hc77
Tavíkovice CZ 136 Ga48
Tavira P 58 Ad74
Tavistock GB 19 Dd31
Tavnik SRB 178 Ba67
Tavoleto I 156 Eb65
Tavrou CY 206 Jd96
Tavşancık TR 191 Ed83
Tavşanlı TR 186 Ga78
Tavşanlı TR 192 Ga82
Tavuklar TR 187 Gc79
Täxan S 79 Fd29
Taxenbach A 143 Ec54
Taxiárhes GR 189 Bc81
Taxiárhes GR 189 Cc85
Taxiárhis GR 184 Cc79
Taxinge S 96 Gc44
Taxobeni MD 173 Fa56
Tayakadın TR 186 Fc77
Taycılar TR 193 Gd81
Tayfurköy TR 185 Eb79
Taylıeli TR 191 Eb82
Taynloan GB 10 Db14
Tayport GB 7 Ec11
Tăža BG 180 Dc72
Tazlar TR 193 Gb85
Tazlău RO 172 Ec59
Tazona E 53 Ec71
Tazones E 37 Cc54
Tczew PL 121 Hb31
Tczów PL 130 Jc40
Tczyca PL 138 Ja43
Teaca RO 171 Dc58
Teano I 161 Fa74
Teasc RO 175 Da66
Teba E 60 Cc75
Tébar E 53 Eb67
Tebay GB 11 Ec18
Teberda RUS 205 Ga17
Tebongo E 37 Ca55
Tebra E 36 Ac58
Tebstrup DK 108 Dc24
Techendorf A 143 Ed55
Techirghiol RO 181 Fc68
Těchlovice CZ 128 Fb42
Tecklenburg D 125 Cb37
Teckomatorp S 110 Ed55
Tecuci RO 177 Fa62
Teda S 95 Gb43
Tedburn Saint Mary GB 19 Dd30
Teddington GB 20 Ed26
Teenuse EST 98 Kb44
Teeranea IRL 12 Bb21
Teerijärvi FIN 81 Jc29
Teeriranta FIN 75 Lb21
Teerisalo FIN 97 Ja39
Teerivaara FIN 74 Kb19
Teerivaara FIN 83 Lc29
Teernakil IRL 8 Bb20
Teféli GR 200 Da96
Tefenni TR 198 Ga90
Tegau D 127 Ea42
Tegelen NL 125 Bc39
Tegelsmora S 96 Gc40
Tegelträsk S 80 Gc28
Tegernau D 141 Ca51
Tegernsee D 143 Ea52
Teggiano I 161 Ga76
Téglás H 147 Ka52
Teglio I 149 Da57
Tegneby S 102 Eb47
Tęgoborze PL 138 Jb45
Tegnsäset S 80 Ha27
Tehi FIN 90 Kb35
Teicha D 127 Eb39
Teichel D 127 Dd42
Teichwolframsdorf D 127 Eb42
Teigen N 62 Ha08
Teignmouth GB 19 Ea31
Teijo FIN 97 Jc40
Teillay F 28 Ed40
Teillet F 41 Ha53
Teillet-Argently F 33 Ha45
Teisendorf D 143 Ec52
Teising D 143 Eb50
Teisko FIN 89 Jd35
Teisnach D 135 Ec48
Teistungen D 126 Db39
Teiu MD 173 Ga58
Teiu RO 175 Dc65
Teiuş RO 175 Da60
Teixeira P 44 Ba64
Teixeiro (Curtis) E 36 Bb55
Tejadillos E 47 Ed65
Tejado E 47 Eb61
Tejeda y Segoyuela E 45 Ca63
Tejerina E 37 Cd56
Tejkovo RUS 203 Fa09
Tejn DK 111 Fc57
Teke TR 186 Ga77
Teke TR 198 Ga92
Tekeler TR 193 Hb86
Tekeriš SRB 153 Ja62
Tekija BIH 153 Hd63
Tekija SRB 174 Cb64
Tekin TR 193 Gb87
Tekirdağ TR 185 Ed78
Tekirler TR 187 Gd80
Tekirova TR 199 Gc92
Tekkeköy TR 191 Ec83
Tekkeköy TR 198 Fd88
Tekman TR 205 Ga20
Tekovské Lužany SK 145 Hb51
Teksdalen N 77 Dd28
Ţela RO 174 Ca60
Telašćica (Mir) HR 157 Fd65
Telataipale FIN 91 Lc34
Telatyn PL 131 Kd42
Telavåg N 84 Bd39
Telążna Leśna PL 130 Hc36
Telč CZ 136 Fd47
Telciu RO 171 Dc56
Tel'cy RUS 99 Mb42
Teldau D 119 Dd33
Telečka SRB 153 Ja58
Telega RO 176 Ea64
Teleneşti MD 173 Fc56
Telerig BG 181 Fa68
Telese Terme I 161 Fb74
Teleşeu MD 173 Fc57
Teleşti RO 175 Cc63
Telfes A 143 Dd54
Telford GB 15 Ec24
Telfs A 142 Dc53
Telgárt SK 138 Jb48
Telgte D 125 Cb37
Telheiro P 58 Ab72
Telicino RUS 99 Ld44
Teliţa RO 177 Fc64
Teliu RO 176 Ea62
Teliucu Inferior RO 175 Cc61
Teljo FIN 83 Lc27
Telkibánya H 139 Jd49
Telkkälä FIN 74 Kb21
Tellancourt F 24 Jb34
Tellaro I 155 Cd64
Tellejåkk S 72 Ha21
Tellingstedt D 118 Da30
Tel'manove UA 205 Fb15
Telnice CZ 128 Fa42
Telšiai LT 113 Jc54
Telti I 168 Cb74
Teltow D 127 Ed37
Telžiai LT 114 Kc53
Tembleque E 52 Dc67
Temeleuţi MD 173 Fb57
Temeleuţi MD 173 Fc55
Temelín CZ 136 Fb47
Téméni GR 189 Bc85
Temenica SLO 151 Fc58
Temerin SRB 153 Jb60
Temiño E 38 Dc58
Temletouhy IRL 13 Ca23
Temmes FIN 82 Ka25
Temnica SLO 151 Fa58
Tempakka FIN 89 Jd32
Tempio Pausania I 168 Cb74
Templederry IRL 13 Ca23
Templeglentan IRL 12 Bc24
Templemore IRL 13 Ca23
Templenoe IRL 12 Ba25
Templepatrick GB 9 Da17
Temple Sowerby GB 11 Ec17
Templetown IRL 13 Cc25
Templewo PL 128 Fd36
Templin D 120 Fa34
Tempo GB 9 Cb18
Temrek TR 191 Eb85
Temrjuk RUS 205 Fb17
Temska SRB 179 Ca69
Temu I 149 Db57
Tenala FIN 97 Jd40
Tenay F 35 Jc46
Ten Boer NL 117 Bd33
Tenbury Wells GB 15 Ec25
Tenby GB 18 Dc27
Tence F 34 Ja49
Tencin F 35 Jd48
Tendais P 44 Ba61
Tende F 43 Kc52
Tendilla E 46 Dd64
Tenec RUS 107 Mb47
Teneniai LT 113 Jc56
Tenevo BG 180 Eb73
Tengen D 141 Cb51
Tengene S 102 Ed47
Tenhola FIN 97 Jd40
Tenhult S 103 Fb49
Teningen D 141 Ca50
Tenk H 146 Jb52
Tenna CH 142 Cc55
Tennänget S 86 Fa38
Tennenbronn D 141 Cb50
Tenneville B 132 Ba43
Tennevoll N 67 Gc12
Tennie F 28 Fc39
Tennilä FIN 74 Ka19
Tennilä FIN 90 Kb37
Tennilä FIN 90 Kc37
Tenno I 149 Db58
Tennskjer N 62 Gc10
Tennstrand N 66 Fc14
Tensjö S 79 Gb27
Tensta S 96 Gc41
Tentellatge E 49 Gc59
Tenterden GB 21 Ga29
Teofipol' UA 204 Ea15
Teolo I 150 Dd60
Teora I 161 Fd75
Teovo MK 183 Bc74
Tepasto FIN 68 Jc14
Tepebaşı TR 187 Gd80
Tepeboz TR 191 Ea85
Tepecik TR 186 Fb80
Tepecik TR 186 Ga78
Tepecik TR 187 Gb79
Tepecik TR 192 Fc81
Tepeeynihan TR 192 Fc84
Tepeköy TR 185 Dd80
Tepeköy TR 192 Fb86
Tepeköy TR 192 Fc82
Tepelenë AL 182 Ab78
Tepepanayır TR 186 Ga78
Teplá CZ 135 Ec45
Teplice CZ 128 Fa42
Teplice nad Metují CZ 137 Gb43
Teplička nad Váhom SK 138 Hc47
Teploe RUS 203 Fa11
Teplý Vrch SK 138 Jb49
Tepsa FIN 69 Jd15
Ţepu RO 177 Fa61
Terälahti FIN 89 Jd35
Teramo I 156 Ed69
Tērande LV 105 Jb50
Ter Apel NL 117 Ca34
Teratyn PL 131 Kd41
Terbačeno RUS 99 Ld44
Terbuny RUS 203 Fa12
Tercan TR 205 Ga20
Terchová SK 138 Hc47
Terebeşti RO 171 Cc55
Terebišče RUS 99 Ld45
Terebišče RUS 107 Ld46
Terebna MD 173 Fa54
Terebovlja UA 204 Ea15
Terechovo RUS 107 Mb48
Teregova RO 174 Cb63
Terehova LV 107 Ma51
Teremia Mare RO 174 Bb60
Terena P 50 Ba69
Teren'ga RUS 203 Fd10
Teresa E 54 Fb66
Teresa de Cofrentes E 54 Fa69
Teresin PL 130 Ja37
Terešov CZ 136 Fa45
Terespol PL 121 Ha33
Terespol PL 131 Kc37
Tereszpol-Zaorenda PL 131 Kb42
Terezín CZ 136 Fb43
Terezino Polje HR 152 Ha58
Tergnier F 24 Hb34
Tergu I 168 Ca74
Ter Hole NL 124 Ac39
Terikeste EST 99 Lb45
Terjärv FIN 81 Jc29
Terka PL 139 Kb46
Terlan I 142 Dc56
Terland N 92 Cb45
Terlano I 142 Dc56
Terlizzi I 162 Gc74
Termachivka UA 202 Eb14
Termal TR 186 Fd79
Termas de Monfortinho P 45 Bc65
Terme TR 205 Fc19
Terme Aurora I 168 Cb76
Terme di Antonimina I 164 Gb83
Terme di Bagnolo I 155 Db67
Terme di Caldana I 155 Da67
Terme di Casteldoria I 168 Ca74
Terme di Comano I 149 Dc58
Terme di Lurisia I 148 Bc63
Terme di Miradolo I 149 Cc60
Terme di Salvarola I 149 Db63
Terme di Suio I 161 Fa73
Terme di Valdieri I 148 Bb63
Terme Luigiane I 164 Gb79
Térmens E 48 Ga60
Termes-d'Armagnac F 40 Fc54
Termignon F 35 Kb48
Termini I 161 Fb76
Terminiers F 29 Gc39
Termini Imerese I 166 Ed84
Terminillo I 156 Ec70
Termoli I 161 Fc71
Termonbarry IRL 8 Ca20
Termonfeckin IRL 9 Cd20
Termunten NL 117 Ca33
Ternberg A 144 Fb51
Terndrup DK 100 Dc22
Terneuzen NL 124 Ab38
Terni I 156 Eb69
Ternitz A 144 Ga52
Ternopil' UA 204 Ea15
Ternovë AL 182 Ad74
Térovo GR 188 Ad81
Terpeziţa RO 175 Cd66
Terpilicy RUS 99 Ma41
Terpillos GR 183 Cb76
Terpnás GR 188 Ba81
Terpní GR 184 Cc77
Terrachán (Entrimo) E 36 Ba58
Terracina I 160 Ec73
Terrades E 41 Hb58
Terradillos de los Templarios E 37 Cd58
Terråk N 70 Ed24
Terralba I 169 Bd78
Terranova da Sibari I 164 Gc79
Terranova di Pollino I 164 Gb78
Terranuova Bracciolini I 156 Dd66
Terras de Bouro P 44 Ad59
Terrasini I 166 Ec84
Terrassa E 49 Gd61
Terrasson-Lavilledieu F 33 Gb49
Terrati I 164 Gb80
Terravecchia I 165 Gd79
Terrazos E 38 Dd57
Terreiro das Bruxas P 45 Bc64
Terrer E 47 Ec61
Terriente E 47 Ed65
Terrinches E 53 Dd70
Terrugem P 50 Aa68
Terrugem P 51 Bb69
Terskanperä FIN 82 Kb26
Terslev DK 109 Eb27
Tersløse DK 109 Ea26
Tertenia I 169 Cb78
Tertiveri I 161 Fd73
Teruel E 47 Fa65
Tervahauta FIN 89 Jb36
Tervajoki FIN 81 Ja31
Tervakoski FIN 90 Ka37
Tervala FIN 90 Kb34
Tervaoja FIN 68 Jb17
Tervasalmi FIN 83 Lb26
Tervavaara FIN 75 La23
Tervel BG 181 Ed68
Tērvete LV 106 Ka52
Tervo FIN 82 Kc30
Tervola FIN 74 Jc20
Terwolde NL 117 Bc36
Terzaga E 47 Ec64
Terzialan TR 191 Ec81
Terzidere TR 185 Ec74
Terzijsko BG 181 Ec72
Terzili TR 185 Ec76
Tešanj BIH 152 Hb62
Teşcureni MD 173 Fb56
Tešel BG 184 Da75
Tesero I 150 Dd57
Tešetice CZ 135 Ed44
Tešica SRB 178 Bd68
Tesjoki FIN 90 Kd38
Teskánd H 145 Gc55
Teslić BIH 152 Ha62
Teslui RO 175 Da66
Teslui RO 175 Db65
Tespe D 118 Dc33
Tessenderlo B 124 Ba40
Tesseosen N 85 Dc35
Tesserete CH 149 Cc57
Tessin D 119 Ec31
Tessjö FIN 90 Kd38
Tesson F 32 Fb47
Tessy-sur-Vire F 22 Fa36
Testa dell'Acqua I 167 Fc87
Teşvikiye TR 186 Fd79
Tét H 145 Ha53
Tetbury GB 19 Ec27
Ţeţcani MD 172 Ed54
Teţchea RO 170 Cb57
Tetėnai LT 114 La59
Teterow D 119 Ec32
Teteven BG 179 Da71
Tetford GB 17 Fc22
Teti I 169 Ca77
Tetijiv UA 204 Ec15
Tetirvina LT 114 Kc53
Tetovo BG 180 Eb68
Tetovo MK 178 Ba73
Tetrákomo GR 188 Ba81
Tetrálofo GR 183 Bc78
Tettau D 128 Fa40
Tettau D 135 Dd43
Tettenhausen D 143 Ec51
Tettenweis D 143 Ed50
Tettnang D 142 Cd52
Teublitz D 135 Eb47
Teuchern D 127 Eb41
Teufen CH 142 Cd53
Teufenbach A 144 Fb54
Teugerträsk S 73 Hc22
Teugn D 135 Ea48
Teulada E 55 Fd70
Teulada I 169 Bd80
Teunz D 135 Eb46
Teupitz D 128 Fa37
Teurajärvi S 73 Ja18
Teuro FIN 89 Jd37
Teuschnitz D 135 Dd43
Teutschenthal D 127 Ea40
Teuva FIN 89 Ja32
Teuvaniemi FIN 89 Jc34
Tevel H 146 Hc56
Teverga = La Plaza E 37 Cb55
Tevrin IRL 9 Cc20
Tewkesbury GB 15 Ec26
Tezköy TR 193 Ha84
Tezze I 150 Eb58
Tgilevo RUS 107 Mb47
Thale D 127 Dd39
Thaleischweiler-Fröschen D 133 Ca46
Thalfang D 133 Bd44
Thalheim D 127 Ec42
Thalkirch CH 142 Cc55
Thallwitz D 127 Ec40
Thalmässing D 135 Dd47
Thalmassing D 135 Eb48
Thalwil CH 141 Cb53
Thame GB 20 Fb27
Thamsbrück D 126 Dc41
Thann F 31 Kb39
Thannenkirch F 31 Kb38
Thannhausen D 142 Db50
Thaon F 22 Fc35
Thaon-les-Vosges F 31 Jd38
Tharandt D 128 Fa41
t Harde NL 117 Bc35
Tharon-Plage F 27 Ec42
Tharsis E 59 Bb73
Thássos GR 184 Db78
Thatcham GB 20 Fa28
Thaumiers F 29 Ha43
Thavmakó GR 189 Bc82
Thaxted GB 20 Fd26
Thaya A 136 Fd48
Thayngen CH 142 Cc52
Theberton GB 21 Gb25
The Butts IRL 13 Cc23
Thedinghausen D 118 Da34
Theeßen D 127 Eb37
The Five Roads IRL 13 Cd21
The Hand Cross Roads IRL 12 Bc22
The Harrow IRL 13 Cd24
Theillay F 29 Gd42
Theißen D 127 Eb41
Theix F 27 Eb41
Thelbridge GB 19 Dd30
The Leap IRL 13 Cc24
Thelkow D 119 Ec31
The Loup GB 9 Cd17
Them DK 108 Db24
Themar D 134 Dc43
The Mumbles GB 19 Dd27
Thénezay F 28 Fc44
Thénissey F 30 Ja41
Thenon F 33 Gb49
Theodoráki GR 183 Bd76
Theodório GR 183 Cb76
Theodósia GR 183 Cb77
Theológos GR 184 Da78
Theológos GR 189 Ca84
Theológos GR 189 Cc85
Theópetra GR 183 Bb80
The Pike IRL 13 Ca25
The Pole of Law GB 5 Ec07
Theres D 134 Db44
Theresienstadt = Terezín CZ 136 Fb43
Thermá GR 184 Cc77
Thérma GR 185 Dd79
Thérma GR 197 Ea88
Thermisía GR 195 Ca88
Thermo GR 188 Bb84
Thérouanne F 23 Gd31
The Rower IRL 13 Cc24
The Sheddings GB 9 Da16
The Six Towns GB 9 Cd16
Thespiés GR 189 Ca85
Thesprotikó GR 188 Ad81
Thessaloníki GR 183 Ca78
The Stocks GB 21 Ga30
The Temple GB 9 Da17
Thetford GB 21 Ga25
Theth AL 159 Jb69
Theux B 125 Bb42
Thevet-Saint-Julien F 29 Gd44
Theys F 35 Jd48
Thèze F 40 Fc55
Thèze F 42 Jd51
Thiaucourt-Regniéville F 25 Jc36
Thiberville F 22 Fd36
Thibie F 24 Hd36
Thiéblemont-Farémont F 24 Ja37
Thiel-sur-Acolin F 30 Hc44
Thiendorf D 128 Fa40
Thiene I 150 Dd59
Thierhaupten D 134 Dc49
Thierrens CH 141 Bb55
Thiers F 34 Hc46
Thiersheim D 135 Eb44
Thiery F 43 Kc52
Thiesi I 168 Ca75
Thiessow D 120 Fa30
Thímena GR 197 Ea88
Thimianá GR 191 Dd86
Thines F 34 Hd51
Thionville F 25 Jd34
Thíra GR 196 Db92
Thirasía GR 196 Db92
Thiréa GR 185 Eb76
Thiron F 29 Ga38
Thirsk GB 11 Fa19
Thísbi GR 189 Ca85
Thisted DK 100 Da21
Thíva GR 189 Ca85
Thivars F 29 Gb38
Thiviers F 33 Ga48
Thixendale GB 16 Fb19
Thizay F 29 Gc43
Thizy F 34 Ja46
Thoard F 42 Ka52
Thoirette F 35 Jc45
Thoissey F 34 Jb45
Tholária GR 196 Dd90
Tholey D 133 Bd45
Thollon-les-Mémises F 31 Kb44
Thomas Street IRL 8 Ca20
Thomastown IRL 13 Cb24
Thomm D 133 Bc44
Thommen B 133 Bb43
Thompson GB 17 Ga24
Thonelle F 24 Jb34
Thônes F 35 Ka46
Thonon-les-Bains F 31 Ka44
Thorame-Basse F 43 Kb52
Thorame-Haute F 43 Kb52
Thorembais-les-Béguines B 124 Ad41
Thorenc F 43 Kb53
Thorens-Glières F 35 Ka46
Thorigné-sur-Dué F 29 Ga39
Thorikó GR 195 Cc87
Thorigny-sur-Oreuse F 30 Hb38
Thörl A 143 Ed56
Thörl A 144 Fd53
Thorn NL 125 Bb40
Thorn = Toruń PL 121 Hb34
Thornbury GB 19 Ec27
Thornby GB 20 Fb25
Thorne GB 16 Fb21
Thorney GB 17 Fc24
Thornfalcon GB 19 Eb29
Thornham GB 17 Ga23
Thornhill GB 10 Ea15
Thornhill GB 19 Ea28
Thorning DK 100 Db23
't Horntje NL 116 Ba33
Thornton GB 15 Eb20
Thornton Curtis GB 17 Fc21
Thorpe-le-Soken GB 21 Gb27
Thorpe Market GB 17 Gb23
Thorpeness GB 21 Gb26
Thors F 30 Ja38
Thors F 32 Fc47
Thorsager DK 101 Dd23
Thorshøj DK 101 Dd20
Thorsminde DK 100 Cd23
Thorstrup DK 108 Cd25
Thorum DK 100 Db22
Thouarcé F 28 Fb42
Thouars F 28 Fc43
Thourie F 28 Ed40
Thourotte F 23 Ha34
Thourotte F 23 Ha35
Thrapsanó GR 200 Da96
Thrapston GB 20 Fc25
Three Cocks GB 15 Eb26
Threlkeld GB 11 Eb17
Thresfield GB 11 Ed19
Thropton GB 11 Ed15
Thrumster GB 5 Ec05
Thueyts F 34 Ja50
Thuilley-aux-Groseilles F 25 Jc37
Thuin B 124 Ac42
Thuine D 117 Cb36
Thuir F 41 Hb57
Thüle D 126 Cc38
Thum D 127 Ec42
Thumby D 108 Db29
Thumeries F 23 Ha31
Thumersbach A 143 Ec53
Thun CH 141 Bd55
Thüngen D 134 Da44
Thurcroft GB 16 Fa22
Thuré F 28 Fd43
Thuret F 34 Hb46
Thurey F 30 Jb43
Thüringen A 142 Da54
Thürkow D 119 Ec32
Thurles IRL 13 Ca23
Thurlow GB 20 Fd26
Thurmaston GB 16 Fb24
Thurnau D 135 Dd44
Thurø By DK 109 Dd28
Thursby GB 11 Eb17
Thurso GB 5 Eb04
Thurstonfield GB 11 Eb16
Thury F 30 Ja42
Thury-Harcourt F 22 Fc36
Thusis CH 142 Cd55
Thyborøn DK 100 Cd22
Thyon-2000 CH 141 Bc56
Thyregod DK 108 Db25
Thyrnau D 135 Ed49
Tia Mare RO 180 Db68
Tiarp S 102 Fa47
Ţibana RO 173 Fa58
Ţibăneşti RO 173 Fa58
Tibarrié F 41 Ha53
Tibava SK 139 Kb48
Tibberton GB 15 Ec24
Tibi E 55 Fb71
Ţibirica MD 173 Fc57
Tibro S 103 Fb46
Ţibucani RO 172 Ec57
Ţibuleuca MD 173 Fd57
Tiča BG 180 Eb71
Tice BIH 158 Gc64
Tichileşti RO 177 Fb64
Ticleni RO 175 Cd64
Ticuşu RO 176 Dd61
Ticvaniu Mare RO 174 Bd63
Tidaholm S 103 Fb47
Tidan S 103 Fb46
Tidavad S 102 Fa46
Tidersrum S 103 Fd48
Tideswell GB 16 Ed22
Tidilov Bor RUS 107 Ld46
Tiduff IRL 12 Ba24
Tiedra E 45 Cc60
Tiefenbach D 127 Ed41
Tiefenbach D 135 Ec46
Tiefenbach D 135 Ed49
Tiefenbronn D 134 Cc48
Tiefencastel CH 142 Cd55
Tiefenort D 126 Db41
Tiefensee D 128 Fa36
Tiel NL 125 Bb37
Tielmes E 46 Dd65
Tielt B 124 Aa39
Tielt B 124 Ad40
Tiemassaari FIN 91 Lb32
Tienen B 124 Ad40
Tienen B 124 Ad41
Tiercé F 28 Fc41
Tierga E 47 Ed61
Tiermas E 39 Fa57
Tierp S 96 Gc40
Tierrantona E 40 Fd58
Tierzo E 47 Ec63
Tiétar del Caudillo E 45 Cb65
Tieva FIN 69 Jd14
Tievaperä FIN 68 Jb16
Tievemore IRL 9 Cb17
Ţifeşti RO 176 Ed61
Tiffauges F 28 Fa43
Tiganca MD 177 Fb60
Ţigănaşi MD 173 Fc57
Ţigăneşti RO 180 Dd68
Tigare BIH 159 Ja64
Tigerton GB 7 Ec10
Tigharry GB 6 Cc07
Tigheci MD 177 Fc60
Tighina MD 173 Ga59
Ţighira MD 173 Fb56
Tığlı TR 192 Ga82
Tignale I 149 Db58
Tignécourt F 31 Jc39
Tignes F 35 Kb47
Tigveni RO 175 Db63

Torvsjö – Turany

Torvsjö S 79 Gb27
Torysa SK 138 Jc47
Torysky SK 138 Jc47
Toržok RUS 202 Ec10
Torzym PL 128 Fc37
Tosåsen S 87 Fb32
Tosaunet N 70 Ed24
Tosbotn N 70 Fa23
Toscaig GB 4 Db08
Toscolano-Maderno I 149 Db59
Tösens A 142 Db54
Tosno RUS 202 Eb08
Tossa S 73 Jb20
Tossa de Mar E 49 Hb60
Tossåsen S 87 Fb32
Tossavanlahti FIN 82 Kc29
Tosse F 39 Ed54
Tösse S 94 Ed45
Tosseberg S 94 Ed41
Tossene S 102 Eb46
Töstamaa EST 106 Ka46
Tostared S 102 Ec50
Tostedt D 118 Db33
Tosunlar TR 192 Fc87
Tosya TR 205 Fb20
Tószeg H 146 Jb54
Toszek PL 137 Hb43
Totana E 55 Ed73
Totebo S 103 Ga49
Totenviken N 85 Ea39
Tôtes F 23 Gb34
Totești RO 175 Cc62
Tótkomlós H 146 Jc56
Totland GB 20 Fa31
Tøtlandsvik N 92 Cb43
Totleben BG 180 Dc69
Totnes GB 19 Dd31
Totsås N 78 Fa26
Tótszerdahely H 152 Gc57
Tøttdal N 78 Eb26
Tottenham GB 20 Fc28
Tottijärvi FIN 89 Jc36
Totton GB 20 Fa30
Tótvázsony H 145 Ha54
Touça P 45 Bc62
Toucy F 30 Hb40
Toudon F 43 Kc52
Touët-sur-Var F 43 Kc52
Touillon F 30 Ja40
Toul F 25 Jc37
Toulat FIN 82 Kc30
Toulon F 42 Ka55
Toulon-sur-Arroux F 30 Hd44
Toulouse F 40 Gc54
Toulx Sainte-Croix F 33 Gd45
Toúmba GR 183 Ca77
Tourcoing F 21 Ha30
Tourigo P 44 Ad63
Touriñán E 36 Ac54
Tourlaville F 22 Ed34
Tourlída GR 188 Ba85
Tourmakeady IRL 8 Bc19
Tournai B 124 Aa41
Tournan-en-Brie F 23 Ha37
Tournay F 40 Fd56
Tournecoupe F 40 Ga53
Tournefeuille F 40 Gb54
Tournefort F 43 Kc52
Tournehem-sur-la-Hem F 21 Gc30
Tournon-d'Agenais F 33 Gb51
Tournon-Saint-Martin F 29 Ga44
Tournon-sur-Rhône F 34 Jb49
Tournus F 30 Jb44
Tourny F 23 Gc36
Tourouvre F 29 Ga38
Tours F 29 Ga42
Tours-en-Vimeu F 23 Gc33
Tourteron F 24 Ja34
Tourtoirac F 33 Gb49
Tourtour F 42 Ka53
Tourula FIN 89 Jb37
Tourves F 42 Ka54
Tourville-sur-Sienne F 22 Ed36
Toury F 29 Gc39
Toutencourt F 23 Gd33
Touvois F 28 Ed43
Touzac F 33 Gb51
Toužim CZ 135 Ec44
Tovačov CZ 137 Gd46
Tovariševo SRB 153 Ja60
Tovarkovskij RUS 203 Fa11
Tovarnik HR 153 Hd60
Tovdal N 93 Da45
Tøvelde DK 109 Ec28
Toven N 70 Fa21
Tovrljane SRB 178 Bc69
Tovsli N 92 Cd44
Towcester GB 20 Fb26
Tow Law GB 11 Ed17
Town Yetholm GB 11 Ed14
Toxotes GR 184 Db77
Toya E 61 Dd73
Toybelen TR 192 Fa81
Tøymskardlia N 70 Fa23
Töysä FIN 89 Jd32
Töysänperä FIN 90 Ka32
Tozaklı TR 185 Ed76
Tozalmoro E 47 Eb60
Trabada E 36 Bc54
Trabadelo E 37 Bd56
Trabanca E 45 Ca61
Trabazos E 45 Ca59
Traben-Trarbach D 133 Bd44
Trabia I 166 Ed84
Trabitz D 135 Ea45
Traboch A 144 Fc53
Trabotivište MK 183 Ca74
Trabzon TR 205 Fd19
Trachslau CH 141 Cb54
Tracino I 166 Dd88
Tradate I 148 Cb58
Træna N 70 Ed20
Trættlia N 78 Eb29
Trafask IRL 12 Ba26
Trafoi I 142 Db56
Tragacete E 47 Ec65
Traganó GR 188 Ad86
Traghetto I 150 Dd62
Tragöss-Oberort A 144 Fc53
Tragwein A 144 Fc50
Trahiá GR 195 Ca88
Trahila GR 194 Bb90
Trahíli GR 189 Cc85
Trahütten A 144 Fd55
Traian RO 172 Ed59
Traian RO 177 Fa64
Traian RO 177 Fb64
Traian RO 177 Fc66
Traian RO 180 Db67
Traian Vuia RO 174 Ca61
Traiguera E 48 Fd64
Traînel F 30 Hb38
Trainou F 29 Gd40
Traisen A 144 Ga51
Traiskirchen A 145 Gb51
Traismauer A 144 Ga50
Trăisteni RO 176 Ea63
Traitsching D 135 Ec47
Trakai LT 114 Kd58
Trakai LT 114 La58
Trakija BG 180 Dd73
Trakiszki PL 123 Kb30
Trakošćan HR 151 Ga57
Trakšėdžiai LT 113 Jb56
Träkumla S 104 Gd49
Tralee IRL 12 Bb24
Trá Lí IRL 12 Bb24
Tramacastilla E 47 Ed64
Tramariglio I 168 Bc75
Tramatza I 169 Bd77
Tramayes F 34 Ja45
Tramelan CH 141 Bc53
Trá Mhór IRL 13 Cb25
Tramm D 119 Ea33
Tramonti di Sopra I 150 Ec57
Tramore IRL 13 Cb25
Trampot F 30 Jb38
Tramutola I 161 Ga77
Trăn BG 179 Ca70
Trana I 148 Bc60
Tranås S 103 Fc48
Tranbjerg DK 108 Dc24
Tranby N 93 Dd42
Trancault F 30 Hc38
Tranco E 61 Ea72
Trancoso P 44 Bb62
Trandal N 76 Cc33
Tranebjerg DK 109 Dd25
Tranekær DK 109 Dd28
Tranemo S 102 Fa50
Tranent GB 11 Ec13
Tranestederne DK 101 Dd19
Trångmon S 79 Fc26
Trängslet S 86 Fa37
Trångsviken S 79 Fb30
Trani I 162 Gc73
Trânica BG 181 Ed69
Traniș RO 171 Cd56
Trankil S 94 Ec44
Trănkovo BG 180 Dd73
Trannes F 30 Ja38
Tranóvalto GR 183 Bc79
Tranøya N 66 Fd14
Trans F 28 Ed38
Transinne B 132 Ad43
Transtrand S 86 Fa38
Tranum DK 100 Db20
Tranum S 102 Ed46
Tranum Enge DK 100 Db20
Tranvik S 96 Ha43
Tranvikan N 77 Dc29
Trapani I 166 Ea84
Trapene LV 107 Lb48
Trapoklovo BG 180 Eb72
Trapp GB 19 Dd27
Trappenkamp D 118 Dc31
Trappes F 23 Gc37
Trappeto I 166 Eb84
Trappstadt D 134 Dc43
Trapyd S 110 Fa53
Trasacco I 160 Ed71
Trasadingen CH 141 Cb52
Trasanquelos E 36 Ba54
Trascastro E 36 Ba56
Trasdorf A 144 Ga50
Trashan AL 163 Jb71
Trasierra E 51 Ca71
Träskholm S 73 Hb24
Träskvik FIN 89 Ja33
Träslövsläge S 102 Ec51
Trasmonte E 36 Bb55
Traspinedo E 46 Da60
Trässberg S 102 Ed46
Trassem D 133 Bc45
Trästena S 103 Fb46
Trästenik BG 180 Db69
Trăstenik BG 180 Ea69
Trăstikovo BG 181 Ed73
Tratnach A 144 Fa51
Traun A 144 Fb51
Traunkirchen A 144 Fa52
Traunreut D 143 Eb51
Traunstein D 143 Ec52
Traupis LT 114 Kd55
Trausnitz D 135 Eb46
Trauten N 94 Eb40
Trautskirchen D 134 Dc46
Tråvad S 102 Ed47
Travassós P 44 Ba60
Trävattna S 102 Fa47
Travemünde D 119 Dd31
Travers CH 141 Bb54
Traversella I 148 Bd59
Traversetolo I 149 Da62
Traves F 31 Jd40
Traviesas E 36 Ba54
Travnik BIH 158 Ha64
Travnik SLO 151 Fb59
Travo F 154 Cb71
Trawniki PL 131 Kb40
Trawsfynydd GB 15 Dd23
Trazo E 36 Ad55
Trbovlje SLO 151 Fc57
Trbuk BIH 152 Hb62
Trbušani SRB 159 Jc64
Trbušnica SRB 153 Jc63
Trdevac KSV 178 Ba71
Trean IRL 8 Bc20
Trearddur Bay GB 14 Dc22
Trébago E 47 Ec60
Tréban F 34 Hb45
Třebařov CZ 137 Gc45
Trebbin D 127 Ed37
Trebbus D 128 Fa39
Třebechovice pod Orebem CZ 136 Ga44
Trebel D 119 Ea34
Třeben CZ 135 Eb44
Treben D 127 Eb41
Trebenište MK 182 Ba75
Trebenow D 120 Fa33
Trèbes F 41 Ha55
Trébeurden F 26 Dd37
Trebgast D 135 Ea44
Třebíč CZ 136 Ga47
Trebinjë AL 182 Ad76
Trebinje BIH 159 Hc69
Trebisacce I 164 Gc78
Trebisăuți MD 173 Fa53
Trebisht AL 182 Ad74
Trebisov SK 139 Ka48
Trebitz D 127 Ec39
Treblinka PL 123 Jd35
Trebnje SLO 151 Fc58
Třebohostice CZ 136 Fa47
Třeboň CZ 136 Fc48
Tréboul F 27 Dc39
Třebovice CZ 137 Gb45
Trebsen D 127 Ec40
Trebujena E 59 Bd75
Trebujeni MD 173 Fd57
Trebur D 134 Cc44
Treburley GB 18 Dc31
Trecastagni I 167 Fd85
Trecastle GB 15 Ea26
Trecate I 148 Cb59
Trecchina I 161 Ga77
Trecenta I 150 Dd61
Trechtlingshausen D 133 Ca44
Trecwn GB 14 Db26
Tredegar GB 19 Ea27
Trédion F 27 Eb40
Tredòs E 40 Ga57
Tredozio I 156 Dd64
Treehoo IRL 9 Cc19
Treen GB 18 Da32
Trefeglwys GB 15 Ea24
Tréfeuntec F 27 Dc39
Treffelstein D 135 Ec46
Treffen A 144 Fa56
Treffieux F 28 Ed41
Treffort-Cuisat F 35 Jc45
Treffurt D 126 Db41
Trefnant GB 15 Ea22
Tre Fontane I 166 Eb85
Trefor GB 15 Dd22
Trefriw GB 15 Ea22
Tregaron GB 15 Dd25
Trégastel-Plage F 26 Dd37
Treglio I 157 Fb70
Tregnago I 149 Dc59
Trégomeur F 26 Eb38
Tregony GB 18 Db32
Trégourez F 27 Dd39
Tréguier F 26 Ea37
Trégunc F 27 Dd40
Trehörna S 103 Fc47
Trehörningsjö S 80 Ha29
Treia D 108 Da29
Treia I 156 Ed67
Treignac F 33 Gc48
Treignat F 33 Gd45
Treignes B 132 Ac43
Treigny F 30 Hb41
Treillières F 28 Ed42
Treimani EST 106 Kb47
Treis-Karden D 133 Bd43
Trekanten S 103 Ga52
Trekilen S 79 Fc30
Trekljano BG 179 Ca71
Trelawnyd GB 15 Ea22
Trélazé F 28 Fc41
Trélaze F 28 Fc41
Trelde DK 108 Db26
Trelech GB 14 Dc26
Treleth GB 11 Eb19
Trélissac F 33 Ga49
Trelkowo PL 122 Jb32
Trelleborg S 110 Ed57
Trelleck GB 19 Eb27
Trélon F 24 Hc32
Treluminjt AL 182 Ad77
Tremblay F 28 Ed38
Tremblois-lès-Rocroi F 24 Hd33
Tremedal E 45 Cb64
Tremedal de Tormes E 45 Ca62
Tremelo B 124 Ad40
Trémentines F 28 Fb42
Tremês P 50 Ab67
Třemešná CZ 137 Gd44
Tremezzo I 149 Cc57
Tréminis F 35 Jd50
Tremoli I 164 Ga78
Tremor de Arriba E 37 Ca56
Tremosine I 149 Db58
Třemošná CZ 135 Ed45
Třemošnice CZ 136 Fd45
Tremp E 48 Ga59
Trenance GB 18 Db31
Trenči LV 106 Kb51
Trenčianska Turná SK 137 Ha48
Trenčianske Stankovce SK 137 Ha48
Trenčianske Teplice SK 137 Hb48
Trenčín SK 137 Ha48
Trend DK 100 Db21
Trendelburg D 126 Da39
Trengereiddal N 84 Ca39
Trensacq F 39 Fb52
Trent D 119 Ed30
Trenta SLO 151 Fa57
Trento I 149 Dc58
Trentola I 161 Fa74
Tréogan F 27 Dd39
Tréon F 23 Gb37
Treorchy GB 19 Ea27
Trepča HR 151 Ga60
Trepča KSV 178 Bb70
Trepča Atomska SRB 159 Jc64
Treppeln D 128 Fb38
Trept F 35 Jc47
Trepuzzi I 163 Hc76
Terrulefoot GB 18 Dc31
Třešť CZ 136 Fd47
Trescares E 38 Da55
Trescore Balneario I 149 Cd59
Trescore Cremasco I 149 Cd59
Tresfjord N 76 Cd32
Tresigallo I 150 Ea62
Tresjuncos E 53 Ea67
Treskë AL 182 Ad77
Treski EST 107 Lc46
Treskog S 94 Ed42
Tresnja SRB 153 Jc62
Tresnja SRB 174 Bb64
Trešnjevica SRB 178 Ad67
Trešnjevo MNE 159 Hd69
Tresnuraghes I 169 Bd76
Tresonče MK 182 Ba74
Trespaderne E 38 Dd56
Tressait GB 7 Ea10
Tresson F 29 Ga40
Treteau F 34 Hc45
Tretjakovo RUS 114 Ka58
Trets F 42 Jd54
Tretten N 63 Hb09
Tretten N 85 Dd37
Treuchtlingen D 134 Dc48
Treuen D 135 Eb43
Treuenbrietzen D 127 Ec38
Treungen N 93 Da44
Trevalampi FIN 98 Ka39
Trevélez E 60 Dc75
Tréveray F 24 Jb37
Trevi I 156 Eb68
Treviana E 38 Ea57
Trévières F 22 Fb35
Treviglio I 149 Cd59
Trevignano Romano I 156 Ea70
Trévignon F 27 Dd40
Treviño E 38 Ea57
Treviso I 150 Ea59
Trevor GB 14 Dc23
Trewithian GB 18 Db32
Trézelles F 34 Hc45
Trezzano sul Naviglio I 149 Cc59
Trezzo sull' Adda I 149 Cd59
Trgovište SRB 178 Bd72
Trhanov CZ 135 Ec47
Trhová Kamenice CZ 136 Ga45
Trhovište SK 139 Ka48
Triacastela E 36 Bc56
Triaize F 32 Fa45
Triana I 156 Dd68
Triánda GR 197 Fa92
Triangelen N 65 Kc09
Triantafiliá GR 183 Bb77
Triaucourt-en-Argonne F 24 Ja36
Triberg D 141 Cb50
Tribsees D 119 Ec31
Tribunj HR 157 Ga65
Tricarico I 162 Gb76
Tricase I 165 Hc78
Tricase Porto I 165 Hc78
Tricesimo I 150 Ed57
Tricot F 23 Ha34
Triebel D 135 Eb43
Trieben A 144 Fb53
Triebes D 127 Eb42
Trie-Château F 23 Gc35
Triefenstein D 134 Da45
Triei I 169 Cc77
Triengen CH 141 Ca53
Trier D 133 Bc44
Trierweiler D 133 Bc44
Trieste I 151 Fa59
Triest = Trieste I 151 Fa59
Trie-sur-Baïse F 40 Fd55
Trifăneşti MD 173 Fb55
Trifeşti MD 173 Fd56
Trifeşti RO 172 Ed58
Trifeşti RO 173 Fa56
Triftern D 143 Ec50
Trigance F 43 Kb53
Triglitz D 119 Eb34
Trignac F 27 Ec42
Trigóna GR 182 Ba80
Trígono GR 182 Ba77
Trigrad BG 184 Da75
Triguères F 30 Hb40
Trigueros E 59 Bb73
Trigueros del Valle E 46 Da60
Trijebine SRB 159 Jb67
Trijebine SRB 178 Ad68
Trijueque E 46 Dd63
Tríkala GR 183 Bd78
Tríkala GR 188 Bb81
Trikāta LV 106 La48
Trikéri GR 189 Ca83
Tri Kladenci BG 179 Cd69
Trikokiá GR 183 Bb80
Trikomo CY 206 Jd96
Tríkorfo GR 182 Ba79
Trilj HR 158 Gc66
Trillevallen S 78 Fa30
Trillo E 47 Ea63
Trílofos GR 183 Bd78
Trim IRL 9 Cc20
Trimbach CH 141 Ca53
Trimiklini CY 206 Ja97
Trimsaran GB 19 Dd27
Trin CH 142 Cd55
Trinay F 29 Gc39
Trinca MD 172 Ed54
Trindade P 45 Bc60
Trindade P 58 Ad72
Třinec CZ 137 Hb45
Tring GB 20 Fb27
Trinità I 148 Bc63
Trinità I 148 Bd62
Trinità d'Agultu I 168 Ca74
Trinitapoli I 162 Gb73
Trinity GBJ 26 Ec35
Trino I 148 Ca60
Trinta P 44 Bb63
Triodos GR 194 Bb89
Triogo E 37 Cd54
Triollo E 38 Da56
Triora I 43 Kd52
Trípes GR 194 Bb87
Trípiti GR 184 Cd79
Trípiti GR 194 Ba87
Trípoli GR 194 Bc88
Triponzo I 156 Ec68
Tripótama GR 188 Bb86
Tripótamo GR 188 Ba83
Tripótamos GR 183 Bd78
Triptis D 127 Ea42
Trispen GB 18 Db31
Tři Studně CZ 136 Ga46
Tritenii de Jos RO 171 Db58
Trittau D 118 Dc32
Trittenheim D 133 Bd44
Trivalea-Moșteni RO 176 Dd66
Trivento I 161 Fb72
Trivero I 148 Ca58
Trivignano Udinese I 150 Ed58
Trivigno I 162 Gb76
Trizac F 33 Ha48
Trizeļnieki LV 107 Lb51
Trizina GR 195 Ca88
Trjavna BG 180 Dd71
Trnakovac HR 152 Gd60
Trnava SK 145 Ha50
Trnava SRB 159 Jb64
Trnavce KSV 178 Ba70
Trnjane SRB 178 Bc68
Trnjani BIH 152 Gc61
Trnjani HR 152 Hb60
Trnovac SRB 179 Ca68
Trnovec HR 152 Gb57
Trnovec nad Váhom SK 145 Ha51
Trnovica BIH 159 Hc66
Trnovica HR 158 Hb68
Trnovo BIH 159 Hc65
Trnovska vas SLO 144 Ga56
Troarn F 22 Fc36
Tröbitz D 127 Ed39
Trobo E 36 Bb54
Tročany SK 139 Jd47
Trochry GB 7 Ea11
Trochtelfingen D 142 Cd50
Trödje S 88 Gc38
Troedyrhiw GB 19 Ea27
Troekurovo RUS 203 Fb11
Troense DK 109 Dd28
Trofa P 44 Ad60
Trofa P 44 Ad60
Trofaiach A 144 Fc53
Trofors N 70 Fa23
Trogen CH 142 Cd53
Trogir HR 158 Gb66
Troglan Bara SRB 178 Bd67
Tröglitz D 127 Eb41
Troia I 161 Fd73
Tróia P 50 Ab69
Troianul RO 180 Dc67
Troickaja RUS 205 Fc17
Troina I 167 Fb85
Troisdorf D 125 Bd41
Trois Ponts B 125 Bb42
Troistorrents CH 141 Bb56
Troisvierges L 133 Bb43
Troița Nouă MD 173 Ga59
Troițcoe MD 173 Fd59
Trojaci MK 183 Bc75
Trojan BG 180 Db71
Trojane SLO 151 Fc57
Trojanovo BG 181 Ec72
Trojanów PL 131 Jd38
Trójca PL 128 Fc41
Trökörna S 102 Ed47
Troldhede DK 108 Da24
Trolla N 78 Ea29
Trollfjord N 63 Ja04
Trollhättan S 102 Ec47
Trollknuten N 93 Db43
Trollshovda FIN 97 Jc40
Trollvik N 63 Hb10
Trømborg N 94 Eb43
Tromello I 148 Cb60
Tromøy N 93 Db46
Tromsdal N 78 Ec29
Tromsdalen N 62 Gd09
Tromsø N 62 Gd09
Tromvik N 62 Gc09
Trönbyn S 87 Gb37
Troncedo E 40 Fd58
Tronco P 45 Bc59
Trondheim N 77 Ea30
Trondstad N 92 Cd47
Trones N 71 Fc18
Trones N 78 Fa25
Trönninge S 102 Ec51
Trönninge S 102 Ed52
Trönö S 87 Gb36
Trontveit N 93 Da44
Tronvik N 78 Eb29
Tronvik N 84 Cb36
Trõo F 29 Ga40
Troodos CY 206 Ja97
Troon GB 10 Dd14
Troøyen N 78 Ea31
Trooz B 124 Ba41
Trópea GR 194 Bb87
Tropea I 164 Ga82
Tropojë AL 159 Jc69
Tropojë AL 178 Ad71
Tröpolach A 143 Ed56
Tropy Sztumskie PL 122 Hc31
Trory GB 9 Cb17
Trosa S 96 Gc45
Trosby N 93 Dc44
Troškas LV 107 Lb51
Troškūnai LT 114 Kd55
Trošmarija HR 151 Fd60
Trosna RUS 202 Ed12
Trossin D 127 Ec39
Trossingen D 141 Cb50
Trostan' RUS 202 Ec13
Tröstau D 135 Ea44
Trostberg D 143 Eb51
Trostjanec' UA 202 Ed14
Trostjanskij RUS 203 Fc13
Troszczyno PL 120 Fd32
Troszyn PL 122 Jc34
Trotby FIN 97 Jc40
Trouans F 24 Hd37
Troubelice CZ 137 Gc45
Troubky CZ 137 Gd46
Troulloi CY 206 Jc97
Troutbeck GB 11 Eb18
Trouville-sur-Mer F 22 Fd35
Troviscal P 44 Ad65
Trowbridge GB 19 Ec28
Troyes F 30 Hd38
Trpanj HR 158 Gd68
Trpezi MNE 159 Jc68
Trpezi MNE 178 Ad69
Trpezjca MK 182 Ad76
Trpinja HR 153 Hd60
Trsa MNE 159 Hd67
Tršće HR 151 Fc59
Tršic SRB 153 Ja63
Trstená SK 138 Hd46
Trstenik HR 158 Ha68
Trstenik SRB 178 Bb67
Trsteno HR 158 Hb69
Trstice SK 145 Ha51
Trübbach CH 142 Cd54
Trubčevsk RUS 202 Ed13
Trubetčino RUS 203 Fb12
Trubia E 37 Cb54
Trubjela MNE 159 Hd68
Trubschachen CH 141 Bd54
Trucco I 43 Kd52
Truchas E 37 Ca58
Trud BG 180 Db73
Trudovec BG 179 Cd70
Trujillanos E 51 Bd69
Trujillo E 51 Ca67
Trulben D 133 Ca47
Trumieje PL 122 Hc32
Trumiejki PL 122 Hc32
Trumpji LV 105 Jc49
Trun CH 142 Cc55
Trun F 22 Fd37
Trundön S 73 Hd23
Trupel PL 122 Hc32
Truro GB 18 Db32
Trușeni MD 173 Fc58
Trușești RO 172 Ed55
Trusetal D 126 Dc42
Truskava LT 114 Kc55
Truskolasy PL 130 Hc42
Truskolasy-Lachy PL 123 Ka34
Trustrup DK 101 Dd23
Trutnov CZ 136 Ga43
Trutnowy PL 121 Hb30
Try N 92 Cd47
Tryczówka PL 123 Kb34
Trydal N 92 Cd43
Tryde S 111 Fb56
Tryggelev DK 109 Dd28
Tryggestad N 84 Cd34
Trygort PL 122 Jc30
Tryland N 92 Cc46
Tryńcza PL 139 Kb43
Trypimeni CY 206 Jc96
Tryserum S 103 Gb47
Trysil N 86 Ec37
Tryškiai LT 113 Jd54
Trysnes N 92 Cd47
Tryszczyn PL 121 Ha34
Tržac BIH 151 Ga61
Trzciana PL 139 Ka44
Trzcianka PL 121 Gb34
Trzcianka PL 122 Jc35
Trzcianka PL 123 Kb32
Trzcianne PL 123 Ka33
Trzciel PL 128 Ga37
Trzcinica PL 129 Ha41
Trzcinna PL 120 Fc35
Trzcinno PL 121 Gc31
Trzcińsk PL 121 Hb31
Trzcińsko-Zdrój PL 120 Fc35
Trzebce PL 130 Hd41
Trzebiatów PL 120 Fd31
Trzebicz PL 120 Ga35
Trzebiel PL 128 Fc39
Trzebielino PL 121 Gc31
Trzebień PL 128 Fd40
Trzebieszów PL 131 Ka37
Trzebieszowice PL 137 Gc43
Trzebież PL 120 Fb32
Trzebin PL 120 Ga34
Trzebinia PL 138 Hd44
Trzebnica PL 129 Gc40
Trzebnice PL 128 Ga40
Trzebów PL 128 Fc36
Trzeciewiec PL 121 Ha34
Trzemeszno PL 129 Gd36
Trzemżal PL 129 Ha36
Trzepnica PL 130 Hd40
Trześcianka PL 123 Kc34
Trześń PL 131 Jd42
Trześniów PL 139 Ka45
Trzęsów PL 129 Gb39
Trzeszczany PL 131 Kd41
Tržič SLO 151 Fb57
Trzin SLO 151 Fb57
Tržišče SLO 151 Fd58
Trzydnik Duży PL 131 Ka41
Tsada CY 206 Hd97
Tsangaráda GR 189 Cb82
Tsaritsáni GR 183 Bc80
Tschenstochau = Częstochowa PL 130 Hc42
Tschernitz D 128 Fc39
Tschiertschen CH 142 Cd55
Tschierv CH 142 Db56
Tschlin I 142 Db55
Tsepélovo GR 182 Ad79
Tseri CY 206 Jb97
Tséria GR 194 Bb89
Tševetjärvi FIN 65 Kb08
Tsikalariá GR 200 Cb95
Tsilivi GR 188 Ac86
Tsirguliina EST 106 La47
Tsirgumäe EST 107 Lb48
Tsitália GR 195 Bd89
Tsjernobyl UA 202 Ec14
Tsooru EST 107 Lb47
Tsotili GR 182 Ba78
Tsoúka GR 189 Bc83
Tsoukaládes GR 188 Ac83
Tsoútsouros GR 200 Da96
Tsz-lakótelep H 146 Hd55
Tua N 78 Eb28
Tua P 44 Bb61
Tuaim IRL 8 Bd20
Tuam IRL 8 Bd20
Tuapse RUS 205 Fc17
Tuar Mhic Éadaigh IRL 8 Bc19
Tubausiai LT 113 Jb54
Tubbergen NL 117 Bd36
Tubilla de Agua E 38 Dc57
Tubilleja E 38 Dc56
Tūbinės LT 113 Jd56
Tübingen D 134 Cc49
Tučapy CZ 136 Fc47
Tučepi HR 158 Gd67
Tuchan F 41 Ha56
Tüchen D 119 Eb34
Tuchheim D 127 Eb37
Tuchlino PL 121 Gd30
Tuchola PL 121 Gd33
Tuchomie PL 121 Gc31
Tuchów PL 138 Jc44
Tuckur FIN 81 Ja30
Tučovo RUS 202 Ed10
Tuczki PL 122 Hd33
Tuczna PL 131 Kc37
Tuczno PL 120 Fd35
Tuczno PL 120 Ga34
Tudanca E 38 Db55
Tuddal N 93 Db41
Tuddenham GB 20 Fd25
Tudeils F 33 Gc49
Tudela E 47 Ed59
Tudela de Duero E 46 Da60
Tudela Veguín E 37 Cc54
Tudora RO 172 Ec56
Tudor Vladimirescu RO 172 Ed57
Tudor Vladimirescu RO 177 Fa62
Tudu EST 98 La42
Tudulinna EST 99 Lb43
Tudweiliog GB 14 Dc23
Tuéjar E 54 Fa67
Tuen DK 101 Dd19
Tuenno I 149 Dc57
Tufeni RO 175 Dc66
Tufești RO 177 Fa64
Tuffé F 29 Ga39
Tufjord N 63 Ja05
Tufjord N 64 Jb04
Tugford GB 15 Ec25
Tuggensele S 80 Gd26
Ţuglui RO 175 Cd66
Tugotino RUS 107 Mb46
Tuhala EST 98 Kc43
Tuhalaane EST 106 Kd46
Tuhań CZ 136 Fb43
Tuhkakylä FIN 82 La26
Tui E 36 Ad58
Tuin MK 182 Ba74
Tuiskula FIN 89 Jb32
Tuixén E 49 Gc59
Tuiza E 37 Cb55
Tūja LV 106 Kb49
Tuk Mrkopaljski HR 151 Fc60
Ţukovicy RUS 99 Ma45
Ţukovo RUS 107 Ld48
Tukums LV 106 Ka51
Tula I 168 Ca75
Tula RUS 203 Fa11
Tulach Mhór IRL 13 Cb21
Tulare SRB 178 Bc70
Tülau D 127 Dd36
Tuławki PL 122 Ja31
Tulca RO 170 Ca57
Tulcea RO 177 Fc64
Tul'cevo RUS 107 Ld48
Tulčik SK 139 Jd47
Tul'čyn UA 204 Eb16
Tulette F 42 Jb51
Tulgheș RO 172 Ea58
Tuliharju FIN 82 Kd25
Tuliszków PL 129 Hb38
Tulje BIH 158 Hb68
Tulla IRL 12 Bc22
Tullaghanstown IRL 9 Cc20
Tullamore IRL 13 Cb21
Tulle F 33 Gc49
Tullebølle DK 109 Dd28
Tulleråsen S 79 Fb30
Tullins F 35 Jc48
Tulln A 144 Ga50
Tullow IRL 13 Cc23
Tully GB 9 Cb17
Tullyamalra IRL 9 Cc19
Tulnici RO 176 Ec61
Tulovo BG 180 Dd72
Tułowice PL 130 Ja36
Tułowice PL 137 Gd43
Tulppio FIN 69 Kd14
Tulsk IRL 8 Ca19
Tulstrup DK 108 Db24
Tulstrup DK 109 Dc25
Tulucești RO 177 Fb63
Tum PL 130 Hc38
Tuma RUS 203 Fb10
Tumba S 96 Gd44
Tumbo E 36 Bc54
Tumbo S 95 Ga43
Tume LV 106 Ka51
Tumleberg S 102 Ed47
Tummel Bridge GB 7 Ea10
Tun S 102 Ed46
Tuna S 87 Gb33
Tuna S 96 Gd41
Tuna S 103 Ga49
Tunaberg S 103 Gb46
Tunadal S 88 Gc33
Tuna-Hästberg S 95 Fd40
Tunari RO 176 Eb66
Tunby S 87 Gb36
Tunçbilek TR 192 Ga82
Tunceli TR 205 Fd20
Tune DK 109 Eb26
Tune N 93 Ea43
Tungaseter N 77 Da33
Tunge S 102 Ec48
Tungelsta S 96 Gd44
Tunhovd N 85 Db39
Tuningen D 141 Cb51
Tunjë AL 182 Ac76
Tunkkari FIN 81 Jc29
Tunneberga S 110 Ec54
Tunnerstad S 103 Fb48
Tunnsjørvika N 78 Fa25
Tunnstad N 66 Fc12
Tunø By DK 109 Dd25
Tunstall GB 11 Ec19
Tunstall GB 17 Fc21
Tunstall GB 21 Gb26
Tuntenhausen D 143 Ea51
Tunturikeskus Kiilopää FIN 69 Kb12
Tunvågen S 87 Fc32
Tuohikotti FIN 90 La36
Tuohikylä FIN 69 Kd16
Tuohisaari FIN 91 Lc33
Tuohittu FIN 97 Jd40
Tuolluvaara S 67 Hb15
Tuolpukka S 68 Hc15
Tuomela FIN 74 Ka18
Tuomikylä FIN 81 Jb31
Tuomioja FIN 81 Jd25
Tuomiperä FIN 81 Jd27
Tuomiperä FIN 82 Ka28
Tuopanjoki FIN 83 Lc29
Tuorila FIN 89 Ja35
Tuoro sul Trasimeno I 156 Ea67
Tuovila FIN 81 Ja31
Tuovilanlahti FIN 82 Kd29
Tupicino RUS 99 Ld44
Tupilați RO 172 Ec57
Tupilați RO 177 Fb60
Tuplice PL 128 Fc39
Tupos FIN 74 Ka24
Tuppu FIN 74 Ka22
Tuppurinmäki FIN 82 La31
Tur PL 121 Gd34
Tur PL 130 Hc38
Tura H 146 Ja52
Turaida LV 106 Kc49
Turajärvi FIN 89 Ja37
Turanj HR 157 Fd65
Turanköy TR 186 Fd80
Turanlar TR 197 Ed88
Turany SK 138 Hc47

Usson-les-Bains – Vangsvik

Usson-les-Bains F 41 Gd57
Ussy F 22 Fc36
Ustaritz F 39 Ed55
Ust'Džeguta RUS 205 Fd17
Ust'e RUS 99 Ma41
Úštěk CZ 136 Fb43
Uster CH 141 Cb53
Ustia MD 173 Fa56
Uștia MD 173 Fd57
Ustibar BIH 159 Ja66
Ustikolina BIH 159 Hd66
Ústí nad Labem CZ 128 Fa42
Ústí nad Orlicí CZ 137 Gb45
Ustiprača BIH 159 Hd65
Ustjužna RUS 202 Ec08
Ustka PL 121 Gc29
Ust'-Labinsk RUS 205 Fc17
Ust'-Luga RUS 99 Lc40
Ust'Luga RUS 202 Ea08
Ustovo BG 184 Db75
Ustrem BG 185 Eb74
Ustroń PL 138 Hc45
Ustronie Morskie PL 120 Ga31
Ust'-Rudicy RUS 99 Ma39
Ustrzyki Dolne PL 139 Kb46
Ustrzyki Górne PL 106 Kb47
Üstünler TR 199 Hb89
Ustyluh UA 202 Dd14
Usvjaty RUS 202 Eb11
Uszyce PL 129 Hb41
Utajärvi FIN 74 Kb24
Utåker N 92 Cb41
Utakleiv N 66 Fb14
Utanen FIN 74 Kb24
Utäng S 94 Eb45
Utansjö S 88 Gc32
Utbjoa N 92 Ca41
Utby S 102 Ec47
Utby S 103 Fb46
Utebo E 47 Fa60
Utekáč SK 138 Ja49
Utena LT 114 La55
Útery CZ 135 Ec45
Uthaug N 77 Dd29
Uthmöden D 127 Ea37
Utiel E 54 Fa67
Utne N 84 Cc39
Utnes N 65 Kd08
Utö S 96 Gd45
Utoslahti FIN 74 Kb24
Utrasniemi FIN 91 Ld33
Utrecht NL 116 Ba36
Utrera E 59 Ca74
Utriala FIN 90 La32
Utrillas E 47 Fa63
Utrine SRB 153 Jb58
Utset N 77 Dc29
Utsiktstårn N 65 Kd08
Utsjö S 94 Fa39
Utsjoki FIN 64 Jd07
Utskarpen N 71 Fb20
Uttendorf A 143 Eb54
Uttenweiler D 142 Cd50
Utterbyn S 94 Ed41
Utterliden S 72 Ha23
Uttermossa FIN 89 Ja34
Uttersberg S 95 Fd42
Uttersjöbäcken S 81 Hd26
Utterslev DK 109 Ea28
Utti FIN 90 La37
Utting D 142 Dc51
Uttoxeter GB 16 Ed23
Utula FIN 91 Lc35
Utvängstorp S 102 Fa48
Utvik N 84 Cc34
Utvin RO 174 Bc61
Utvina CZ 135 Ec44
Utvorda N 78 Eb26
Uue-Kariste EST 106 Kd46
Uukuniemen kirkonkylä FIN 91 Ma33
Uukuniemi FIN 91 Ld33
Uulu EST 106 Kb46
Uura FIN 82 Kd25
Uurainen FIN 90 Kb32
Uuro FIN 83 Lc27
Uuro FIN 89 Ja33
Uusijoki FIN 69 Kb12
Uusikaarlepyy FIN 81 Ja29
Uusikartano FIN 89 Jb38
Uusikaupunki FIN 89 Ja38
Uusikylä FIN 81 Jc27
Uusikylä FIN 81 Jd30
Uusikylä FIN 90 Kc37
Uusi-Värtsilä FIN 83 Ma31
Uusküla EST 99 Lb43
Uutela FIN 69 Ka14
Uva FIN 75 Kd24
Uvac SRB 159 Ja65
Úvaly CZ 136 Fc44
Uvanå S 94 Fa40
Uvarovo RUS 203 Fc12
Uvdal N 85 Db40
Üvecik TR 191 Ea81
Uxbridge GB 20 Fc28
Uyanık TR 193 Hb85
Üyük TR 187 Gb80
Üyüklü Tatar TR 185 Eb76
Užava LV 105 Jb50
Užbičiai LT 113 Jc57
Uzdin SRB 174 Bb62
Uzdowo PL 122 Hd33
Uzel F 27 Eb39
Uzemain F 31 Jd39
Uzerche F 33 Gc48
Uzès F 42 Ja52
Uzeste F 32 Fc51
Užhorod UA 204 Dd16
Užice SRB 159 Jb65
Užlieknė LT 113 Jd53
Užlieknis LT 113 Jc54
Uzlovaja RUS 203 Fa11
Uzlovoe RUS 113 Ja58
Uzlovoe RUS 113 Jd58
Užovka RUS 203 Fc10
Užpaliai LT 114 La54
Uzsa H 145 Gd55
Uztarroz E 39 Fa56
Užtiltė LT 115 Lb54
Užuguostis LT 114 Kd58
Üzümdere TR 199 Hb90
Üzümler TR 191 Ed87
Üzümlü TR 192 Fa86
Üzümlü TR 198 Fd91
Üzümlü TR 199 Hb89
Üzümlü TR 205 Fd20
Üzümlüpınar TR 199 Gc89
Uzunbey TR 187 Gb78
Uzundere TR 191 Ec86
Uzundžovo BG 185 Dd74
Uzunköprü TR 185 Eb76
Uzunkoyu TR 191 Ea86
Uzunpınar TR 192 Fd87
Uzunpınar TR 193 Gc86
Uzuntarla TR 187 Gb79
Uzunyurt TR 198 Fc92
Uzupis LT 115 Lc54
Užusaliai LT 114 Kc57
Užusienis LT 114 La58
Užventis LT 113 Jd55
Uzyn UA 204 Ec15

V

Vå N 92 Cd41
Vä S 111 Fb55
Vaabina EST 107 Lb47
Vaadinselkä FIN 69 Kd17
Vaahersalo FIN 91 Ld33
Vaajakoski FIN 90 Kc32
Vaajasalmi FIN 82 Kd31
Vääkiö FIN 75 La22
Vaala FIN 82 Kc25
Vaalajärvi FIN 69 Ka16
Vaale D 118 Da31
Vaalimaa FIN 91 Lb37
Vaaljoki FIN 89 Jb38
Vaals NL 125 Bb41
Väänä EST 98 Kb42
Väänälänranta FIN 82 Kd30
Vaania FIN 90 Kc36
Vääräkoski FIN 89 Jd32
Vaarakylä FIN 83 Lb27
Väärämäki FIN 81 Jd30
Vaaraniva FIN 75 Kd22
Vaarankylä FIN 82 Kd25
Vaaranperä FIN 74 Jb18
Vaaraperä FIN 75 La21
Vaaraslahti FIN 82 Kc29
Väärinmaja FIN 89 Jd34
Vaartsi EST 107 Lc46
Vaas F 28 Fd41
Vaasa FIN 81 Hd30
Vaassen NL 117 Bc36
Väästa EST 98 Kd44
Väätäiskylä FIN 90 Ka32
Vaattojärvi FIN 68 Jb17
Vabaliai LT 113 Jc53
Vabalninkas LT 114 Kd53
Văbel BG 180 Dc68
Vabole LV 115 Lb53
Vabre F 41 Ha54
Vabres-l'Abbaye F 41 Hb53
Vác H 146 Hd52
Vácduka H 146 Hd52
Vače SLO 151 Fc58
Vacha D 126 Db42
Vachdorf D 134 Dc43
Vachendorf D 143 Eb52
Vacherauville F 24 Jb35
Väckelsång S 103 Fc52
Väcklax FIN 97 Jb40
Václavov u Bruntálu CZ 137 Gd45
Vacov CZ 136 Fa48
Vacqueyras F 42 Jb52
Vacquiers F 40 Gc53
Văculești RO 172 Ec55
Vad RO 171 Da56
Vad S 95 Fd41
Vada I 155 Da66
Vadakste LV 113 Jd53
Vădastra RO 180 Db68
Vădăstrița RO 180 Db68
Väddö S 96 Ha41
Vădeni MD 173 Fc54
Vădeni RO 177 Fb63
Vadeolivas E 47 Eb64
Väderstad S 103 Fc47
Vadheim N 84 Cb36
Vadla N 92 Cb43
Vadna H 146 Jb50
Vado I 149 Dc63
Vadocondes E 46 Dc60
Vadokliai LT 114 Kc55
Vado Ligure I 148 Ca63
Vadsbro S 95 Gb45
Vadsø N 65 Kc06
Vadstena S 103 Fc46
Vadu RO 177 Fc66
Vadu Crișului RO 171 Cc57
Vadu Dobrii RO 174 Cb61
Vadu Izei RO 171 Db54
Vadul lui Isac MD 177 Fb62
Vadul lui Vodă MD 173 Fd58
Vadul-Rașcov MD 173 Fd55
Vadul Turcului MD 173 Fd55
Vadum DK 100 Dc21
Vadu-Moldovei RO 172 Ec56
Vadu Moților RO 171 Cc59
Vaduz FL 142 Cd54
Vadžgirys LT 114 Ka56
Væggerløse DK 109 Eb29
Vaeküla EST 98 La42
Værebro DK 109 Ec25
Værløse DK 109 Ec25
Vafiohóri GR 183 Ca76
Vafoss N 93 Dc45
Våg N 70 Ed24
Vågaholmen N 70 Fa19
Vågåmo N 85 Dc35
Vagan BIH 158 Gc64
Vågan N 67 Gc11
Vågan N 77 Dd29
Vågane N 84 Ca35
Vagani RO 172 Dd58
Vágáshuta H 139 Jd49
Vågbø N 77 Db31
Vågdalen S 79 Fd29
Våge N 77 Da32
Vågen N 77 Dc29
Vågersjön S 79 Ga30
Vägeva EST 98 La43
Väggarp S 110 Ed55
Vaggatem N 65 Kc09
Vagge N 65 Kc07
Väggeryd S 103 Fb50
Vaggevaratj sameviste S 67 Gc17
Vágia GR 189 Ca85
Văgiulești RO 175 Cc64
Vaglia I 155 Dc65
Vaglio Basilicata I 161 Ga75
Vagli Sotto I 155 Da64
Vagney F 31 Ka39
Vagnhärad S 96 Gc45
Vägnön S 88 Gc32
Vagos P 44 Ac63
Vagøy N 76 Cd31
Vågsbygd N 92 Cd47
Vägsele S 80 Gd26
Vägsjöfors S 94 Ed40
Vågsodden N 70 Ed22
Vágur DK 3 Ca07
Vähä-Äiniö FIN 90 Kb36
Vähä-Joutsa FIN 90 Kc34
Vähäkangas FIN 81 Jd27
Vähäkyrö FIN 81 Ja31
Vähä-Leppijärvi FIN 89 Ja34
Vähäniva FIN 68 Hd13
Vahanka FIN 81 Jd31
Vahastu EST 98 Kc43
Vahderpää FIN 90 Ka35
Vaheri FIN 90 Kb34
Vähikkälä FIN 90 Ka38
Vähimaa FIN 90 Kb36
Vahl-Ebersing F 25 Ka35
Váhlia GR 188 Bb86
Vahojärvi FIN 89 Jc34
Vahterpää FIN 98 Kd39
Vähtjer S 67 Hb17
Vahto FIN 97 Jb39
Vahtseliina EST 107 Lc47
Vai GR 201 Dd96
Vaiamonte P 50 Ba68
Vaiano I 155 Dc64
Vaickūniškės LT 114 Kd58
Vaida EST 98 Kc42
Vaideeni RO 175 Da63
Vaiges F 28 Fb39
Vaiguva LT 113 Jd55
Vaihingen (Enz) D 134 Cc48
Vaikantonys LT 114 Kd59
Väike-Maarja EST 98 La43
Väike Rakke EST 98 La45
Vaikko FIN 83 Lb28
Vaillant F 30 Jb40
Vailly F 35 Ka45
Vailly-sur-Aisne F 24 Hb35
Vailly-sur-Sauldre F 29 Ha41
Vaimaro FIN 89 Ja38
Vaimastvere EST 98 La44
Vaimela EST 107 Lb47
Vaimõisa EST 98 Kb44
Vaimosuo FIN 75 La19
Vainikkala FIN 91 Lc36
Vainiūai LT 123 Kc30
Vainiži LV 106 Kc49
Vainode LV 113 Jc53
Vainova LV 107 Lc52
Vainupea EST 98 Kd41
Vainutas LT 113 Jc56
Väisälä FIN 75 La24
Väisälä FIN 90 La33
Väisälänmäki FIN 82 Kd29
Vaisaluokta sameviste S 67 Gb16
Vaisi EST 98 Ka43
Vaisodžiai LT 114 Kc59
Vaison-la-Romaine F 42 Jc52
Vaiste EST 106 Ka46
Vaišvydava LT 114 Kc57
Vaite F 31 Jc40
Vaiteliai LT 113 Jb55
Vaitkūnai LT 114 La54
Vaivadiškiai LT 114 Kc56
Vaivara EST 99 Lc41
Vaivio FIN 83 Lc30
Vajangu EST 98 Kd43
Vaje N 93 Db46
Väjern S 102 Ea46
Vajkijaur S 72 Ha19
Vajmat S 72 Ha19
Vajska SRB 153 Hd60
Vajszló H 152 Hb58
Vajta H 146 Hc55
Vajzë AL 182 Ab77
Vakern S 95 Fb40
Vakıfkebir TR 205 Fd19
Vakıf TR 185 Ea79
Vakıf TR 187 Gc79
Vakıflaro TR 186 Fa77
Vakıftaş TR 187 Ha80
Vakkola FIN 90 Kc38
Vakkotovare S 67 Gc16
Vaklino BG 181 Fc69
Vaksala S 96 Gc42
Vaksdal N 84 Cb39
Vākšēni LV 106 Kd48
Vaksevo BG 179 Cb73
Vaksvik N 76 Cd32
Val E 36 Ba53
Vál H 146 Hc53
Valada P 50 Ab68
Vålådalen S 78 Ed31
Valadares E 36 Ad57
Valady F 33 Ha51
Valainiai LT 114 Kb54
Valajanaapa FIN 74 Ka21
Valajärvi FIN 89 Jc37
Valajaskoski FIN 74 Jd19
Valakbūdis LT 114 Ka57
Valalta HR 150 Ed61
Valand N 92 Cd47
Valandovo MK 183 Ca75
Valanhamn N 63 Hb08
Valanída GR 183 Bc80
Vălani de Pomezeu RO 170 Cb57
Valareña E 47 Ed59
Valaská SK 138 Hd48
Valaská Belá SK 137 Hb48
Vålåskaret N 77 Dd31
Valašská Polanka CZ 137 Ha47
Valašské Klobouky CZ 137 Ha47
Valašské Meziříčí CZ 137 Ha46
Valasti EST 98 Kd43
Valatkoniai LT 114 Kb55
Vålax FIN 98 Kc39
Valay F 31 Jc41
Valbella CH 142 Cc56
Valberg F 43 Kc52
Valberg N 66 Fb14
Vålberg S 94 Fa43
Valbiska HR 151 Fb61
Valbo S 95 Gb39
Valboa E 36 Ba56
Valbona E 47 Fa65
Valbonë AL 159 Jb69
Valbondione I 149 Da57
Valbonilla E 38 Db58
Valbonne F 43 Kc53
Valbo-Ryr S 102 Eb46
Valbruna I 143 Ed56
Valbuena de Duero E 46 Db60
Valbukta N 65 Kc07
Valby DK 109 Ec26
Valcabadillo E 38 Da57
Vălcănești RO 176 Ea64
Vălcani RO 170 Bb59
Valcau de Jos RO 171 Cc56
Valcavado E 37 Cb58
Vălčedrăm BG 179 Cd68
Vâlcele RO 175 Db66
Vâlcele RO 176 Ea61
Vâlcelele RO 176 Ed63
Vâlcelele RO 176 Ed66
Vălčevo BG 180 Db71
Vălčidol BG 181 Fa70
Valcineț MD 173 Fb57
Valcivières F 34 Hd47
Valdagno I 149 Dc59
Valdahon F 31 Ka42
Valdaj RUS 202 Ec09
Valdanzo E 46 Dd61
Valdaora I 143 Ea55
Valdaracete E 46 Dd65
Valdeajos E 38 Dc57
Valdealgorfa E 48 Fc63
Valdearcos E 37 Cc57
Valdearcos de la Vega E 46 Db60
Val de Asón E 38 Dc55
Valdeazores E 52 Cd67
Valdebeix F 34 Hb48
Valdebótoa E 51 Bc68
Valdecaballeros E 52 Cc68
Valdecabras E 47 Ec65
Valdecañas de Cerrato E 46 Db59
Valdecarros E 45 Cc63
Valdecastillo E 37 Cd56
Valdecuenca E 47 Ed65
Valdeflores E 59 Bd72
Valdefuentes E 51 Ca67
Valdefuentes del Páramo E 37 Cb58
Valdeganga E 53 Ec69
Valdeganga de Cuenca E 53 Eb66
Valdehierro E 52 Db68
Valdeķi LV 105 Jd51
Valdelacasa de Tajo E 52 Cc66
Valdelagrana E 59 Bd76
Valdelagua E 52 Dc66
Valdelamusa E 59 Bb72
Valdelinares E 54 Fb65
Val della Torre I 148 Bc60
Valdelosa E 45 Cb61
Valdeltormo E 48 Fd63
Valdemaluque E 46 Dd60
Valdemārpils LV 105 Jd49
Valdemarsvik S 103 Gb47
Valdemeca E 47 Ec65
Val-de-Meuse F 31 Jc39
Valdemorales E 51 Ca68
Valdemorillo E 46 Db64
Valdemoro E 46 Dc65
Valdemoro-Sierra E 47 Ec65
Valdenebro de los Valles E 46 Cd59
Valdenoceda E 38 Dc56
Valdenoguera E 45 Bd62
Valdeobispo E 45 Ca65
Valdepeñas E 52 Dc70
Valdepeñas de Jaén E 60 Db73
Valdepeñas de la Sierra E 46 Dd63
Valdepolo E 37 Cd57
Valderas E 45 Cc59
Val-de-Reuil F 23 Gb35
Valderice I 166 Ea84
Valderiès F 41 Gd53
Valderrama E 38 Dd57
Valderrobres E 48 Fd63
Valderrodilla E 47 Ea61
Val-de-Saâne F 23 Ga34
Valdesalor E 51 Bd67
Valdesamario E 37 Cb56
Val de San Román E 37 Ca57
Valdestillas E 46 Cd61
Valdetorres E 51 Ca69
Valdetorres de Jarama E 46 Dc63
Valdeverdeja E 52 Cc66
Valdevimbre E 37 Cc57
Valdgale LV 105 Jd50
Valdieri I 148 Bc63
Valdilecha E 46 Dd65
Valdín E 37 Bd58
Val d'Isère F 35 Kb47
Valdivia E 51 Cb68
Valdivienne F 29 Ga44
Val-d'Izé F 28 Fa39
Valdobbiadene I 150 Ea58
Valdongo dos Azeites P 44 Bb61
Valdrôme F 42 Jd51
Valdshult S 102 Fa50
Valdunquillo E 45 Cc59
Valdurna I 143 Dd55
Våle N 93 Dd43
Valea Adîncă MD 173 Fd55
Valea Argovei RO 176 Ec66
Valea Călugărească RO 176 Eb64
Valea Chioarului RO 171 Da56
Valea Ciorii RO 177 Fa65
Valea Crișului RO 176 Ea61
Valea Dacilor RO 181 Fb67
Valea Danului RO 175 Dc63
Valea de Brazi RO 175 Cc62
Valea Doftanei RO 176 Ea63
Valea Iașului RO 175 Dc63
Valea Ierii RO 171 Cd58
Valea Largă RO 171 Db58
Valea lui Mihai RO 170 Cb55
Valea Lungă RO 175 Db60
Valea Lungă RO 176 Ea64
Valea Măcrișului RO 176 Ec65
Valea Mare MD 173 Fb57
Valea Mare RO 175 Da65
Valea Mare RO 175 Db66
Valea Mare RO 176 Dd65
Valea Mare-Pravăț RO 176 Dd63
Valea Mărului RO 177 Fa62
Valea Mică RO 175 Cd60
Valea Moldovei RO 172 Eb56
Valea Neagră RO 171 Da55
Valea Nucarilor RO 177 Fd64
Valea Perjei MD 173 Fc59
Valea Perjei MD 177 Fd61
Valea Râmnicului RO 176 Ed63
Valea Sării RO 176 Ec61
Valea Seacă RO 172 Ec57
Valea Seacă RO 176 Ed60
Valea Stanciului RO 179 Da67
Valea-Trestieni MD 173 Fb58
Valea Ursului RO 172 Ed58
Valea Uzului RO 176 Eb60
Valea Viilor RO 175 Db60
Valea Vinului RO 171 Cd55
Valea Vinului RO 172 Dd56
Valebjørg N 93 Da44
Valebø N 93 Dc43
Valeč CZ 135 Ed44
Vale da Telha P 58 Aa73
Vale da Vinha P 50 Ba67
Vale de Açor P 58 Ad72
Vale de Cambra P 44 Ad62
Vale de Moura P 50 Ad70
Vale de Nogueira P 45 Bd60
Vale de Salgueiro P 45 Bc60
Vale de Vargo P 50 Ba71
Vale do Lobo P 58 Ac74
Valeggio sul Mincio I 149 Db60
Valeia CY 206 Jd96
Valen N 63 Ja05
Valen N 65 Kc07
Valença do Minho P 36 Ad58
Valençay F 29 Gc42
Valence F 32 Fd47
Valence F 34 Jb49
Valence F 40 Ga52
Valence-d'Albigeois F 41 Ha53
Valence-en-Brie F 29 Ha38
Valence-sur-Baïse F 40 Fd53
València E 54 Fc68
Valencia de Alcántara E 51 Bb67
Valencia de Don Juan E 37 Cc58
Valencia de las Torres E 51 Ca70
Valencia del Mombuey E 51 Bb71
Valencia del Ventoso E 51 Bd71
Valenciennes F 24 Hb32
Văleni MD 177 Fb62
Văleni RO 173 Fa59
Văleni RO 175 Dc66
Văleni-Dâmbovita RO 176 Dd63
Vălenii de Munte RO 176 Eb63
Văleni-Stânișoara RO 172 Eb56
Valensole F 42 Ka53
Valentano I 156 Dd69
Valentín E 61 Ec72
Valentinovo HR 151 Ga57
Valenzuela E 60 Da73
Valenzuela de Calatrava E 52 Db69
Våler N 93 Ea43
Våler N 94 Ec39
Valera de Abajo E 53 Eb67
Valera Fratta I 149 Cc60
Valeria E 53 Eb66
Valero E 45 Ca63
Vales Mortos P 58 Ba72
Valestrand N 92 Ca41
Valestrandsfossen N 84 Ca39
Valevac SRB 179 Ca68
Valevåg N 92 Ca41
Valeyrac F 32 Fb48
Valfabbrica I 156 Eb67
Valfarta E 48 Fc61
Valflaunès F 41 Hd53
Valfréjus F 35 Kb48
Valga EST 106 La47
Valgale LV 105 Jd50
Valgejõgi EST 98 Kd42
Välgi EST 99 Lb44
Valgorge F 34 Hd51
Valgu EST 97 Jc45
Valgu EST 98 Kb44
Valguarnera Caropepe I 167 Fb86
Valgunde LV 106 Kb51
Valguta EST 106 La46
Valhelhas P 44 Bb64
Valhosszúfalu H 145 Gd54
Valhuon F 23 Gd31
Valie S 111 Fc54
Välijoki FIN 74 Ka19
Välijoki FIN 91 Lb36
Välikangas FIN 74 Ka19
Väli-Kannus FIN 81 Jc27
Välikylä FIN 81 Jc28
Valin F 32 Fc49
Valinge S 102 Ec51
Väli-Olhava FIN 74 Ka22
Valíra GR 194 Bb89
Välișoara RO 175 Cc60
Välitalo FIN 69 Ka15
Välittula FIN 90 Kc35
Väliug RO 174 Ca62
Välivaara FIN 83 Ld28
Välivaara FIN 91 Ma32
Väli-Viirre FIN 81 Jc27
Valjala EST 105 Jd46
Valjevo SRB 153 Jb63
Valjok N 64 Jc08
Valjunquera E 48 Fd63
Valka LV 106 La47
Valkeajärvi FIN 89 Jd32
Valkeakoski FIN 89 Jd36
Valkeala FIN 90 La37
Valkealuomi FIN 90 Kb33
Valkeavaara FIN 91 Ma32
Valkeiskylä FIN 82 Kc28
Valkeiskylä FIN 82 La29
Valkenburg aan de Geul NL 125 Bb41
Valkenswaard NL 124 Ba39
Valkiamäki FIN 91 Lc34
Valkininkai LT 114 La59
Valkla EST 98 Kc42
Valko FIN 90 Kd38
Valkó H 146 Ja52
Valkola FIN 90 Kb32
Valkom FIN 90 Kd38
Valkosel BG 184 Cd75
Valky UA 203 Fa14
Vall S 104 Gd49
Valla S 79 Fb29
Valla S 79 Ga31
Valla S 95 Ga44
Vallada E 54 Fb69
Valladolid E 46 Da60
Vallåkra S 110 Ed55
Vallargärdet S 94 Fa43
Vallarta de Bureba E 38 Dd57
Vallata I 161 Fd74
Vallauris-Golfe-Juan F 43 Kc53
Vallberga S 110 Ed53
Vallbona de les Monges E 48 Gb61
Vallby S 95 Gb43
Vallda S 102 Eb50
Valldal N 76 Cd33
Valldemossa E 57 Hb67
Valldossera E 49 Gc61
Valle LV 106 Kc52
Valle N 76 Cd32
Valle N 92 Cd43
Valleberga S 111 Fb57
Valle Castellana I 156 Ed69
Vallecillo E 37 Cd58
Vallecorsa I 160 Ed73
Valle Dame I 156 Ea67
Valle de Abdalajís E 60 Cd75
Valle de Cabuérniga E 38 Db55
Valle de Cerrato E 46 Da59
Valle de Finolledo E 37 Bd56
Valle de la Serena E 51 Ca69
Valle de Santa Ana E 51 Bc70
Valledolmo I 166 Ed85
Valleiry F 35 Jd45
Vallelado E 46 Da61
Valle Lomellina I 148 Cb60
Vallelunga Pratameno I 166 Ed85
Valle Mosso I 148 Ca58
Vallen S 79 Ga29
Vallen S 79 Gb29
Vallen S 80 Hc26
Vallentuna S 96 Gd43
Vallepietra I 160 Ec71
Vallerås S 94 Fa39
Valleraugue F 41 Hc52
Vallerheim N 92 Cd43
Vallermosa I 169 Bd79
Vallerstad S 103 Fd46
Vallersund N 77 Dd28
Vallery F 30 Hb39
Vallespinoso de Aguilar E 38 Db56
Vallestad N 84 Ca35
Vallet F 28 Fa42
Valletta M 166 Eb88
Valleviken S 104 Ha48
Valley D 143 Ea51
Valley GB 14 Dc22
Vallfogona de Ripollès E 49 Ha59
Vallibona E 48 Fd64
Valli del Pasubio I 149 Dc59
Vallières F 33 Gd46
Vallières F 35 Jd46
Vallinfreda I 160 Ec71
Vallmoll E 48 Gb62
Vallø N 93 Dd43
Vallobal E 37 Cd54
Valløby DK 109 Ec27
Vallo della Lucania I 161 Fd77
Vallo di Nera I 156 Ec69
Valloire F 35 Ka48
Vallombrosa I 156 Dd65
Vallon-Pont-d'Arc F 34 Ja51
Vallon-sur-Gée F 28 Fc40
Vallorbe CH 140 Ba54
Vallouise F 35 Ka49
Vallrun S 79 Fb29
Valls E 48 Gb62
Vallsbo S 87 Gb38
Vallset N 94 Eb39
Vallsjärv S 73 Ja19
Vallsta S 87 Ga36
Vallstena S 104 Ha49
Vallus H 145 Gd55
Vallvik S 87 Gb37
Valmadrera I 149 Cc58
Valmadrid E 47 Fa61
Valmanya F 41 Ha57
Valmiera LV 106 Kd48
Valmigère F 41 Ha56
Valmo EST 98 La45
Valmojado E 46 Db65
Valmont F 22 Fd34
Valmontone I 160 Ec72
Valmorel F 35 Ka47
Valnari BG 181 Ed69
Valnontey I 148 Bc58
Valö S 96 Gd40
Valognes F 22 Fa35
Valongo P 44 Ad61
Válor E 61 Dd75
Valoria la Buena E 46 Da60
Valøya N 78 Eb25
Valøya N 78 Ec27
Valožyn BY 202 Ea12
Valpaços P 45 Bc60
Valpalmas E 48 Fb59
Valpelline I 148 Bc58
Valperga I 148 Bd59
Valpiana I 155 Db67
Valpovo HR 153 Hc59
Valpperi FIN 89 Jb38
Valprato Soana I 148 Bc59
Valras-Plage F 41 Hc55
Valréas F 42 Jb51
Vals CH 142 Cc55
Valsaín E 46 Db63
Valsavarenche I 148 Bc58
Valse DK 109 Eb28
Valsebo S 94 Ec44
Valseca E 46 Db62
Valsecca I 149 Cd58
Valseco E 37 Ca56
Valsemé F 22 Fd36
Valsenestre F 35 Ka49
Valsequillo E 51 Cb70
Valserres F 42 Ka51
Valset N 77 Dd29
Valsgård DK 100 Dc22
Valsinni I 162 Gc77
Valsjöbyn S 79 Fb28
Valsjön S 87 Ga34
Valskog S 95 Ga43
Vals-les-Bains F 34 Ja50
Valsølille DK 109 Eb26
Valsonne F 34 Ja46
Valsøybotn N 77 Dc31
Valsøyfjord N 77 Db30
Välsta S 87 Gb35
Valstad S 102 Fa47
Valstagna I 150 Dd58
Valsted DK 100 Db21
Valtaiķi LV 105 Jc52
Valtessiniko GR 194 Bb87
Valtétsi GR 194 Bc88
Val-Thorens F 35 Kb48
Valtice CZ 137 Gc49
Valtierra E 47 Ed59
Valtimo FIN 83 Lb27
Valtola FIN 90 La36
Valtola FIN 91 Lc34
Valtopina I 156 Eb68
Valtorp S 102 Fa47
Valtorta I 149 Cd58
Váltos GR 185 Eb76
Valtournenche I 148 Bd57
Valtura HR 151 Fa62
Valujki RUS 203 Fb14
Valu lui Traian RO 181 Fc67
Valun HR 151 Fb62
Väluste EST 106 Kd46
Valvåg N 77 Db29
Valverde E 47 Ec59
Valverde de Burguillos E 51 Bc71
Valverde de Júcar E 53 Eb67
Valverde de la Vera E 45 Cb65
Valverde de la Virgen E 37 Cc57
Valverde del Camino E 59 Bc73
Valverde de Leganés E 51 Bb69
Valverde del Fresno E 45 Bc64
Valverde de Llerena E 51 Ca71
Valverde del Majano E 46 Db62
Valverde de Mérida E 51 Bd69
Valverdón E 45 Cb62
Valvträsk S 73 Hd20
Vama RO 171 Da54
Vama RO 172 Ea56
Vama Buzăului RO 176 Eb62
Vama Veche BG 181 Fc69
Vamberk CZ 137 Gb44
Vamdrup DK 108 Db26
Våmhus S 87 Fb37
Vamlingbo S 104 Gd51
Vamma N 93 Ea43
Vammala FIN 89 Jc36
Vammen DK 100 Db22
Vámos GR 200 Cc95
Vámosgyörk H 146 Ja52
Vámospércs H 147 Ka52
Vampula FIN 89 Jc37
Vanagi LV 107 Lb52
Vanaja FIN 90 Kd32
Vanaja FIN 90 Ka37
Vana-Kojola EST 107 Lb46
Vana-Kuuste EST 99 Lb45
Vana-Roosa EST 107 Lb47
Vânători RO 170 Ca58
Vânători RO 172 Ed56
Vânători RO 175 Cc66
Vânători RO 175 Dc60
Vânători RO 176 Ed62
Vânători RO 177 Fb63
Vânătorii Mici RO 176 Dd66
Vânători-Neamț RO 172 Ec57
Vanattara FIN 89 Jd36
Vanault-les-Dames F 24 Ja36
Vana-Vigala EST 98 Kb44
Vancé F 29 Ga40
Vanda FIN 98 Kb39
Vandāni LV 107 Lb52
Vandans A 142 Da54
Vandel DK 108 Db25
Vandenesse F 30 Hc43
Vandoies I 143 Dd55
Vändra EST 98 Kc45
Vändträsk S 73 Hc22
Vandzene LV 105 Jd49
Vandžiogala LT 114 Kc57
Vāne LV 105 Jd51
Väne-Åsaka S 102 Ec47
Vänersborg S 102 Ec47
Vänersnäs S 102 Ec47
Väne-Ryr S 102 Ec47
Vaneze I 149 Dc58
Vang DK 100 Da21
Vang N 85 Db37
Väng S 94 Eb43
Vånga S 103 Fd46
Vånga S 111 Fb54
Vangaži LV 106 Kc50
Vänge S 96 Gc42
Vänge S 104 Ha50
Vängel S 79 Ga29
Vangså DK 100 Da21
Vangshamn N 62 Gc10
Vangshylla N 78 Eb28
Vangsnes N 84 Cc37
Vangsvik N 67 Gb11

Vanha-Kihlanki - Vendinha

Vanha-Kihlanki FIN 68 Ja16
Vanhakylä FIN 81 Jd31
Vanhakylä FIN 89 Ja33
Vanhakylä FIN 89 Ja36
Vanhamäki FIN 90 Kd34
Vanjärvi FIN 98 Ka39
Vänjaurbäck S 80 Gd27
Vänjaurträsk S 80 Gd27
Vânju Mare RO 174 Cb65
Vankiva S 110 Fa54
Vanlay F 30 Hd39
Vannareid N 62 Gd08
Vannäs FIN 81 Jb29
Vännäs S 80 Hb28
Vännäs S 80 Ha28
Vännäsberget S 73 Ja20
Vännäsby S 80 Hb28
Vannavalen N 62 Ha08
Vanneberga S 111 Fb55
Vannes F 27 Eb41
Vannes-sur-Cosson F 29 Gd40
Vannholman N 64 Jb04
Vannsätter S 87 Gb37
Vannvåg N 62 Ha08
Våno FIN 97 Jb40
Vänö FIN 97 Jb41
Vanonen FIN 90 La35
Vansbro S 95 Fb39
Vanse N 92 Cb47
Vänsjö S 87 Fc35
Vansjö S 95 Gb41
Vansö S 95 Gb43
Vantaa FIN 98 Kb39
Vantilla FIN 89 Jc37
Vanttausjärvi FIN 74 Ka19
Vanttaus koski FIN 74 Kb19
Vanvikan N 78 Ea29
Vanyarc H 146 Hd52
Vanyola H 145 Ha53
Vanzay F 32 Fd45
Vanzone I 148 Ca57
Vaour F 40 Gc53
Vapavaara FIN 75 La19
Vápenná CZ 137 Gc44
Vaplan S 79 Fb30
Vaprio d'Adda I 149 Cd59
Vaqueira E 40 Gb57
Vaqueiros P 58 Ad73
Var RO 174 Cb62
Vara EST 99 Lb44
Vara S 102 Ed47
Varacieux F 35 Jc48
Varades F 28 Fa42
Varădia RO 174 Bd63
Varages F 42 Ka54
Varaire F 40 Gc52
Varaize F 32 Fc46
Varajärvi FIN 74 Jc20
Varakļāni LV 107 Lc51
Varäla FIN 90 Kd37
Varaldsøy N 84 Cb40
Varallo I 148 Ca58
Varanauskas LT 114 Kc59
Varăncău MD 173 Fd56
Varangerbotn N 65 Kb06
Varano de'Melegari I 149 Cd62
Varanpää FIN 89 Ja38
Varăşti RO 180 Eb67
Varászió H 145 Gd56
Vărătec RO 172 Eb57
Văratic MD 173 Fa55
Văratic MD 173 Fd59
Varaždin HR 152 Gb57
Varaždinske Toplice HR 152 Gb57
Varazze I 148 Ca63
Varbalog H 145 Gd52
Varberg S 102 Ec51
Vărbešnica BG 179 Cd70
Varbevere EST 98 La44
Vărbica BG 179 Cd69
Vărbica BG 180 Db69
Vărbica BG 180 Ea70
Vărbica BG 180 Eb71
Vărbilău RO 176 Ea64
Vărbjane BG 181 Ec70
Varbola EST 98 Kb43
Vărbovka BG 180 Dc70
Vărbovo BG 179 Cb68
Vărbovo BG 185 Dd75
Vârciorog RO 170 Cb57
Várda GR 188 Ba86
Vardal N 86 Ea38
Varde DK 108 Cd25
Varden N 77 Db30
Vardim BG 180 Dd69
Vårdinge S 96 Gc44
Vardište BIH 159 Ja65
Vårdnäs S 103 Fd47
Vårdö FIN 96 Hc40
Vardø N 65 Kd05
Vardofjäll S 71 Fc24
Várdomb H 153 Hc57
Vardun BG 180 Eb70
Varejoki FIN 74 Jc20
Varekil S 102 Eb47
Varel D 118 Cc33
Varelas E 36 Ba55
Varen F 41 Gd52
Varena I 150 Dd57
Varėna LT 114 Kd59
Varena I LT 114 Kd59
Varengeville-sur-Mer F 23 Ga33
Varenna I 149 Cc57
Varennes-Changy F 29 Ha40
Varennes-en-Argonne F 24 Ja35
Varennes-le-Grand F 30 Jb43
Varennes-Saint-Sauveur F 30 Jb44
Varennes-sur-Allier F 34 Hc45
Varennes-sur-Usson F 34 Hc48
Vareš BIH 159 Hc64
Varese I 148 Cb58
Varese Ligure I 149 Cc63
Varetz F 33 Gc49
Vârfu Câmpului RO 172 Ec55
Vârfuri RO 176 Dd64
Vârfurile RO 170 Cb59
Vårgårda S 102 Ed48
Vargas E 38 Dc55
Vargeneset N 66 Ga13
Várgesztes H 145 Hb53
Varghiet N 78 Ea28
Vârghiş RO 176 Ea60
Vargön S 102 Ec47
Vargträsk S 80 Gd27
Varhaug N 92 Ca45
Varhela FIN 89 Ja38
Vårhus N 86 Eb32
Vári GR 196 Da89
Variaş RO 174 Bc60
Varieba LV 105 Jd51
Variešas LV 106 La51
Varigotti I 148 Ca63
Variku EST 98 Ka43
Varilhes F 40 Gc56
Varin SK 138 Hc47
Väring S 103 Fb46
Variņi LV 106 La49
Váris GR 183 Bb79
Variskylä FIN 82 Kd25
Varislahti FIN 83 Lb31
Varistaipale FIN 83 Lb31
Varisvaara FIN 82 La26
Varize F 29 Gc39
Varjakka FIN 74 Jd24
Varjisträsk S 72 Ha21
Varkaus FIN 90 La32
Várkiza GR 195 Cc87
Vårkumla S 102 Fa48
Varland N 93 Da41
Varlaukis LT 113 Jd56
Vârlezi RO 177 Fb61
Varmahlíð IS 2 Ba03
Varmdal N 77 Ea30
Värme LV 105 Jc51
Värminmäki FIN 89 Jd35
Varmo FIN 91 Ld32
Varmsätra S 95 Gb42
Värmskog S 94 Ed43
Varmvattnet S 80 Hb27
Varna BG 181 Fa70
Värna S 103 Ga47
Varna SRB 153 Ja62
Varnæs DK 108 Db28
Värnamo S 103 Fb51
Värnäs S 94 Fa40
Vārnava LV 106 La52
Varnenci BG 181 Ec68
Varnhem S 102 Fa47
Varniai LT 113 Jd55
Varniţal MD 173 Ga58
Varnja EST 99 Lb44
Varnsdorf CZ 128 Fc42
Varntresk N 71 Fb22
Varnum S 102 Ed48
Varnupiai LV 114 Kb59
Väröbacka S 102 Ec50
Varola S 103 Fb47
Város GR 190 Dc81
Varoška Rijeka BIH 151 Ga61
Városlőd H 145 Ha54
Varp S 94 Eb45
Varpaisjärvi FIN 82 La28
Várpalota H 145 Hb54
Varpanen FIN 83 Lc28
Varpanen FIN 90 Kd35
Varparanta FIN 83 Ld30
Varparanta FIN 91 Lc33
Varpasalo FIN 83 Lc31
Varpkuselkä FIN 69 Kd16
Varpsjö S 79 Gb27
Varpuperä FIN 75 Kc21
Varputėnai LT 114 Ka54
Varpuvaara FIN 69 Kc17
Varrains F 28 Fc42
Varreddes F 23 Ha36
Varriö FIN 69 Kc15
Varrio FIN 69 Kb17
Vars F 35 Kb50
Vârşag RO 172 Dd59
Vârşand RO 170 Bd58
Värsås S 103 Fb47
Varšec BG 179 Cc69
Varsedžiai LT 113 Jd56
Varsi I 149 Cd62
Văršilo BG 181 Ed73
Värska EST 107 Lc46
Varşolţ RO 171 Cd56
Varsseveld NL 125 Bd37
Värst DK 100 Dc21
Varstu EST 107 Lb47
Vartai LT 114 Ka59
Vartdal N 76 Cc33
Varteig N 93 Ea43
Vârteşcoiu RO 176 Ed62
Vartholomió GR 188 Ad86
Vartiala FIN 82 La30
Vartius FIN 75 Lc24
Vartiusniemi FIN 75 Lc24
Varto TR 205 Ga20
Vârtoapele RO 180 Dc67
Vartofta S 102 Fa48
Vartofta-Åsaka S 102 Fa48
Vârtop RO 175 Cc66
Vartsala FIN 97 Jc39
Värtsilä FIN 83 Ma31
Varuntee FIN 90 Kb37
Varuträsk S 80 Hc25
Varv S 102 Fa47
Varv S 103 Fc46
Vārva LV 105 Jb52
Varva S 95 Gb39
Varva UA 202 Ed14
Varvara BG 179 Da73
Varvara BG 186 Fa74
Varvára GR 184 Cc78
Vărvăreuca MD 173 Fc55
Varvarin SRB 178 Bc67
Vārve LV 105 Jb50
Varvikko FIN 69 Kc16
Varvitsa GR 194 Bc88
Vărvoru de Jos RO 175 Cd66
Vărzăreşti MD 173 Fb57
Vărzăreştii Noi MD 173 Fc57
Várzea Cova P 44 Ba60
Varzi I 149 Cc61
Varziela P 44 Ac63
Varzo I 148 Ca57
Varzy F 30 Hb42
Vasa FIN 81 Hd30
Vasalemma EST 98 Kb43
Vasankari FIN 81 Jc26
Vasaraperä FIN 75 Kd19
Vásárosnamény H 147 Kb50
Vasbotna N 78 Ed26
Vaşcău RO 170 Cb58
Văscăuţi MD 173 Fc55
Vascœuil F 23 Gb35
Väse S 94 Fa43
Vashtëmi AL 182 Ad77
Vašica SRB 153 Hd61
Văsieni MD 173 Fc56
Văsieni MD 173 Fc58
Vasilaţi RO 180 Eb67
Vasilátika GR 182 Ab80
Vasilcău MD 173 Fc54
Vasileuţi MD 173 Fa54
Vasilevo BG 181 Fb69
Vasil'evo RUS 107 Ld47
Vasil'evo RUS 203 Fd09
Vasilevskoje RUS 107 Mb49
Vasiliká GR 189 Cb83
Vasiliká GR 191 Ea83
Vasilikí GR 188 Ac83
Vasiliko GR 182 Ad79
Vasilitsi GR 194 Ba90
Vasil Levski BG 180 Db72
Vasilovci BG 179 Cc68
Vaškai LT 114 Kc53
Vaski FIN 74 Jd23
Vaski LV 106 Ka51
Väskinde S 104 Ha49
Vaskio FIN 97 Jc39
Vaskivesi FIN 89 Jd33
Vasknarva EST 99 Lc43
Vaskovo RUS 107 Mb50
Vaskrääma EST 106 Kc46
Vaskuu FIN 89 Jc33
Vasles F 28 Fc44
Vaslui RO 173 Fa59
Vass- FIN 98 Ka40
Vassa CY 206 Jb98
Vassarás GR 194 Bc89
Vassås N 93 Dd43
Vassbø N 92 Cb45
Vassbotn N 92 Cc45
Vassbotnfjell N 71 Fd18
Vassbygdi N 84 Cd38
Vassdal N 93 Dc43
Vassdalen N 67 Gb13
Vassdalsvik N 71 Fb19
Vasselbodarna S 86 Fa37
Vasselhyttan S 95 Fd42
Vassenden N 84 Cc35
Vassenden N 85 Dd36
Vassenden N 93 Da46
Vassieux-en-Vercors F 35 Jc49
Vassijaure S 67 Gc13
Vassiláki GR 194 Ba87
Vassilika GR 183 Cb78
Vassilikí GR 189 Cb85
Vassilikós GR 188 Ac86
Vassilís GR 189 Bd82
Vassilópoulo GR 182 Ac80
Vassilópoulos GR 188 Ad84
Vasskogen N 63 Hd08
Vassli N 77 Dc30
Vassmolösa S 111 Ga53
Vassnäs S 78 Fa29
Vassor FIN 81 Ja30
Vasstrand N 62 Gc09
Vasstudal N 85 Db40
Vassy F 22 Fb37
Vassy F 30 Hd41
Vasszent mihály H 145 Gb55
Västan S 87 Gb34
Västanån S 79 Fc28
Västanbäck S 79 Ga29
Västanfjärd FIN 97 Jc40
Västannäs S 73 Ja20
Västansjö S 71 Fc22
Västansjö S 71 Fd24
Västansjö S 79 Ga26
Västansjö S 80 Gc26
Västansjö S 80 Gc31
Västansjö S 87 Ga37
Västansjön S 87 Gb34
Västanvik S 95 Fc39
Västbacka S 87 Fc36
Västbacken S 79 Fb30
Vastemõisa EST 98 Kd45
Västenjaure sameviste S 67 Gb16
Västeråker S 96 Gc42
Västeränga FIN 96 Hc41
Väster-Arådalen S 78 Fa31
Västerås S 80 Ha28
Västerås S 95 Gb43
Västerbäcken S 86 Ec34
Västerberg S 95 Gb39
Västerby S 95 Ga40
Västerby S 96 Gd44
Västerfärnebo S 95 Ga41
Västerfjäll S 72 Gb19
Västergarn S 104 Gd50
Västerhaninge S 96 Gd44
Västerhankmo FIN 81 Ja30
Västerhejde S 104 Gd49
Västerhus S 80 Gd30
Västerlanda S 102 Ec47
Västerlandsjö S 80 Gd30
Västerljung S 96 Gc45
Västermo S 95 Ga44
Västermyckeläng S 87 Fb37
Västerplana S 102 Fa46
Västerrottna S 94 Ed42
Västerrud S 95 Fb42
Västersel S 80 Gd30
Västerstråsjö S 87 Ga35
Västervåla S 95 Ga41
Västervik FIN 81 Hd30
Västervik S 103 Gb49
Vastila FIN 90 Kd38
Västilä FIN 90 Ka35
Vastinki FIN 82 Ka30
Västland S 96 Gc40
Vasto I 161 Fc71
Västpånäset S 72 Gb24
Västra S 96 Gd44
Västra Ämtervik S 94 Ed42
Västra Ansvar S 73 Ja19
Västra Eneby S 103 Fd48
Västra Fägelvik S 94 Eb43
Västra Fors S 94 Fa39
Västra Gafsele S 79 Gb28
Västra Gerum S 102 Fa47
Västra Harg S 103 Fd47
Västra Hjäggböle S 80 Hc26
Västra Husby S 103 Ga46
Västra Karup S 110 Ed53
Västra Merasjärvi S 68 Ja14
Västra Ny S 103 Fc46
Västra Ormsjö S 79 Ga26
Västra Örträsk S 80 Ha27
Västra Sjulsmark S 80 Hc27
Västra Skedvi S 95 Fd43
Västra Stenby S 103 Fc46
Västra Tåsjö S 79 Fd27
Västra Torup S 110 Fa54
Västra Tunhem S 102 Ec47
Västra Yttermark FIN 89 Hd32
Västrum S 103 Gb49
Vastse-Kuuste EST 107 Lb46
Vastseliina EST 107 Lc47
Vastse-Roosa EST 107 Lb48
Västsjö S 79 Fd26
Västsjön S 78 Fa29
Västvallen S 86 Fa33
Vasvár H 145 Gc54
Vasylivka UA 205 Fa16
Vasyl'kiv UA 204 Ec15
Vasyl'kivka UA 205 Fa15
Vasyščeve UA 203 Fa14
Vaţa de Jos RO 171 Cc59
Vatajankylä FIN 89 Jb34
Vatajankylä FIN 89 Jc33
Vatala FIN 83 Ma31
Vatan F 29 Gc43
Vătava RO 171 Dc57
Väte S 104 Gd50
Váthi GR 183 Cb76
Vathí GR 188 Ac83
Vathí GR 188 Ac84
Vathí GR 197 Ea91
Vathí GR 197 Eb88
Váthia GR 194 Bc91
Vathilakkos GR 184 Cd76
Vathilakos GR 183 Bc79
Vathis GR 197 Eb90
Våthult S 102 Fa50
Vathy GR 189 Cb85
Vatici MD 173 Fc57
Vatin SRB 174 Bc62
Vatjusjärvi FIN 82 Ka27
Vätkölssätern S 86 Ed36
Vatku EST 98 Kd42
Vatla EST 98 Ka45
Vatland N 92 Ca46
Vatland N 92 Cc46
Vatland N 92 Cc47
Vatnås N 93 Dc41
Vatne N 76 Cd32
Vatne N 76 Cc33
Vatne N 92 Cb44
Vatne N 92 Cd45
Vatne N 92 Cd46
Vatneli N 92 Cd46
Vatnøyra N 66 Fd15
Vatnstrøm N 92 Cd46
Vätö S 96 Ha42
Vatohóri GR 182 Ba77
Vatoússa GR 191 Dd83
Vatra MD 173 Fd58
Vatra Dornei RO 172 Ea56
Vatra Moldoviţei RO 172 Ea55
Vatry F 24 Hd37
Vats N 92 Ca42
Vätta EST 105 Jd46
Vatta H 146 Jc51
Vättak S 102 Fa48
Vattholma S 96 Gc41
Vattjom S 87 Gb33
Vattland S 87 Gb35
Vättlax FIN 97 Jc41
Vattukylä FIN 82 Ka26
Vatula FIN 89 Jc35
Vatutine UA 204 Ec15
Vatutino RUS 122 Jc30
Vatvet N 94 Eb43
Vauchamps F 24 Hc36
Vauchassis F 30 Hc39
Vauclaix F 30 Hc42
Vauconcourt-Nervezain F 31 Jc40
Vaucouleurs F 25 Jc37
Vaudeurs F 30 Hc39
Vaudoy-en-Brie F 24 Hb37
Vaudrey F 31 Jc42
Vau i Dejës AL 163 Jb71
Vaujany F 35 Ka48
Vauldalen N 86 Ec32
Vaulruz CH 141 Bc55
Vaulx-Vraucourt F 23 Ha32
Vaupoisson F 30 Hd38
Vau-Spas AL 159 Jc70
Vau-Spas AL 178 Ad72
Vausseroux F 28 Fc44
Vautorte F 28 Fb39
Vauvenargues F 42 Jd54
Vauvert F 42 Ja54
Vauvillers F 31 Jd39
Vaux-s-Sûre B 132 Ba44
Vaux-sur-Aubigny F 30 Jb40
Vavd S 96 Gd39
Vávdos GR 183 Cb78
Väversunda S 103 Fc47
Vavincourt F 24 Jb36
Vavkavysk BY 202 Dd13
Vavla CY 206 Jb97
Vavylas CY 206 Jb96
Växbö S 87 Gb36
Vaxholm S 96 Gd43
Växjö S 103 Fc52
Växtorp S 110 Ed53
Vay F 28 Ed41
Väylä FIN 64 Ka10
Väylänpää FIN 68 Jb17
Vayrac F 33 Gc50
Väyrylä FIN 75 Kd24
Vaysal TR 185 Ec74
Väystäjä FIN 74 Jc20
Vazáš S 68 Hc15
Važec SK 138 Ja47
V'azka RUS 99 Ma44
Veähtšaknjarga FIN 64 Ka07
Veaikevárri S 67 Hb16
Vean N 77 Dc30
Veaugues F 29 Ha42
Vebbestrup DK 100 Dc22
Veberöd S 110 Fa56
Veblungsnes N 77 Da32
Vebomark S 80 Hc26
Vecate LV 106 Kc47
Vecbāta LV 113 Jc53
Vecbebri LV 106 La51
Vecborne LV 115 Lc53
Vecgaiķi LV 105 Jd51
Vechelde D 126 Dc37
Vechno RUS 107 Mb49
Vechta D 117 Cc35
Vecinos E 45 Cb63
Vecpiebalga LV 106 La50
Veckalsnava LV 106 La51
Veckebo S 87 Fd35
Veckenstedt D 126 Dc38
Veckholm S 96 Gc43
Veclaicene LV 107 Lc48
Vecmilgravis LV 106 Kb50
Vecsaule LV 106 Kc52
Vecses H 146 Hd53
Vectilža LV 107 Ld49
Vecumi LV 107 Ld49
Vecumnieki LV 106 Kc51
Veczvärde LV 105 Jd52
Vėdariai LT 115 Lb54
Vedavågen N 92 Bd42
Vedbæk DK 109 Ec25
Vedby S 110 Ed54
Veddelev DK 109 Eb26
Veddige S 102 Ec50
Veddum DK 100 Dc22
Vedea RO 175 Db65
Vedea RO 180 Dc67
Vedea RO 180 Ea68
Vederslöv S 103 Fc52
Vedersø DK 100 Cd23
Vedevåg S 95 Fd43
Vedhall S 102 Eb48
Vedjeön S 79 Fd28
Vědlice CZ 136 Fb43
Vedrare BG 180 Db72
Vedrina BG 181 Fa69
Vedrines-Saint-Loup F 34 Hb49
Vedro Polje BIH 152 Gb63
Vedrovo RUS 203 Fb08
Vedum S 102 Ed47
Veelikse EST 106 Kc47
Veendam NL 117 Ca33
Veenendaal NL 125 Bb37
Veenwouden NL 117 Bc33
Veere EST 105 Jb46
Veere NL 124 Ab38
Vefall N 93 Db44
Vega E 38 Dc55
Vegacerneja E 37 Cd56
Vegacervera E 37 Cc56
Vega de Anzo E 37 Cb54
Vega de Espinareda E 37 Bd56
Vegadeo E 37 Bd54
Vega de Pas E 38 Dc55
Vega de Terrón E 45 Bc62
Vega de Valcarce E 37 Bd56
Vega de Valdetronco E 46 Cd60
Vegafriosa E 37 Cb54
Vegaquemada E 37 Cc56
Vegarienza E 37 Cb56
Vegårshei N 93 Db45
Vegas de Coria E 45 Ca64
Vegas del Condado E 37 Cc57
Vegaviana E 45 Bc65
Vegby S 102 Fa49
Vegeriai LT 106 Ka52
Veggen N 67 Gb13
Vegger DK 100 Db21
Veggli N 93 Db41
Veghel NL 125 Bb38
Vegi LV 105 Jd50
Veglie I 162 Hb76
Vegset N 78 Ed27
Veguilla E 38 Dd55
Veguillas de la Sierra E 47 Ed65
Vegusdal N 93 Da45
Vehendi EST 106 La46
Vehkajärvi FIN 90 Ka35
Vehkakorpi FIN 89 Jb36
Vehkalah FIN 90 Kc35
Vehkalahti FIN 90 La38
Vehkaperä FIN 81 Jd30
Vehkataipale FIN 91 Lb35
Vehmaa FIN 89 Ja38
Vehmaa FIN 90 La33
Vehmasjärvi FIN 82 La27
Vehmaskylä FIN 90 La32
Vehmaskylä FIN 90 La34
Vehmasmäki FIN 82 La30
Vehmersalmi FIN 82 La30
Vehniä FIN 90 Kb32
Vehtovo BG 181 Ec70
Vehu FIN 81 Jd31
Vehus N 92 Cd47
Vehuvarpee FIN 89 Jc35
Vehvilä FIN 82 Kd31
Veidholmen N 77 Db29
Veidnes N 64 Jc05
Veierland N 93 Dd44
Veiesund N 84 Ca35
Veikåker N 85 Dc40
Veikkola FIN 74 Kc18
Veikkola FIN 98 Ka39
Veillac F 33 Ha48
Veilsdorf D 134 Dc43
Veines N 65 Kb04
Veinge S 110 Ed53
Veiprty CZ 135 Ed43
Veiros P 50 Ba68
Veisiejai LT 123 Kc30
Veitsbronn D 134 Dc46
Veitsch A 144 Fd53
Veitservasa FIN 68 Jc14
Veitshöchheim D 134 Dd45
Veitsiluoto FIN 74 Jc21
Veiveriai LT 114 Kb58
Veivirženai LT 113 Jc55
Vejano I 156 Ea70
Vejby DK 109 Ec24
Vejbystrand S 110 Ed53
Vejdelevka RUS 203 Fb14
Vejen DK 108 Da26
Vejer de la Frontera E 59 Bd77
Vejers Strand DK 108 Cd25
Vejlby DK 108 Db26
Vejle DK 108 Db25
Vejlen DK 100 Dc21
Vejno RUS 99 Ld43
Vejprnice CZ 135 Ed45
Vejrumbro DK 100 Db23
Vejrumstad DK 100 Da23
Vejruplund DK 109 Dd26
Vekarajärvi FIN 90 La36
Vekilski BG 181 Ed69
Vekkula FIN 90 Kb33
Vektarlia N 78 Fa25
Vela RO 175 Cd66
Velaatta FIN 89 Jd35
Velada E 46 Cd65
Velada P 59 Ba66
Velagići BIH 152 Gc63
Velaines F 24 Jb37
Vela Luka HR 158 Gc68
Velanda S 102 Ec47
Velanidiá GR 182 Ba78
Velanidia GR 195 Bd91
Velaóra GR 188 Ba82
Vel'aty SK 139 Ka49
Velayos E 46 Da63
Velbert D 125 Bd39
Velburg D 135 Ea47
Velda LV 105 Jc52
Velden D 135 Dd46
Velden D 143 Eb50
Velden am Wörthersee A 144 Fa56
Veldhoek NL 125 Bc37
Veldhoven NL 124 Ba39
Veldre N 86 Ea38
Vel'e RUS 107 Ld47
Vel'e RUS 107 Ma49
Velea Tailor RO 177 Fc64
Velebit SRB 153 Jb58
Velefique E 61 Ea75
Velehrad CZ 137 Gd48
Velemin CZ 136 Fa43
Vele Mun HR 151 Fb60
Velen D 125 Bd37
Velēna LV 107 Lb49
Veleni RUS 99 Mb45
Velenje SLO 151 Fd57
Velentzikó GR 188 Ba82
Velereč SRB 159 Jc64
Veles MK 183 Bc73
Veleševec HR 152 Gb59
Veleso I 149 Cc58
Velešta MK 182 Ad75
Velestino GR 189 Bd82
Velestovo MK 182 Ba76
Velestovo MNE 159 Hd69
Vélez Blanco E 61 Eb73
Vélez de Benaudalla E 60 Dc76
Vélez-Málaga E 60 Da76
Vélez Rubio E 61 Eb73
Velgast D 119 Ec30
Velhartice CZ 135 Ed47
Velholan FIN 75 Kc24
Veliés GR 195 Bd90
Veligonty RUS 99 Mb39
Veli Iž HR 157 Fd64
Velika GR 183 Ca80
Velika GR 194 Bb89
Velika HR 152 Ha60
Velika SRB 159 Jc68
Velika Bršljanica HR 152 Gc59
Velika Cista HR 158 Gc66
Velika Drenova SRB 178 Bb67
Velika Gorica HR 152 Gb59
Velika Jablonica KSV 178 Ad70
Velika Jablonica SRB 159 Jc68
Velika Kladuša BIH 151 Ga61
Velika Krsna SRB 174 Bb64
Velika Kruša KSV 178 Ba71
Velika Lukanja SRB 179 Cb69
Velika Moštanica SRB 153 Jc62
Velika Peratovica HR 152 Gd59
Velika Pisanica HR 152 Gd58
Velika Plana SRB 178 Bc69
Velika Preska SLO 151 Fc58
Velika Slatina KSV 178 Bb71
Velike Krčmare SRB 174 Bb66
Velike Lašče SLO 151 Fc58
Velike Račna SLO 151 Fc58
Velikie Luki RUS 202 Eb10
Veliki Gaj SRB 174 Bc62
Veliki Gradište SRB 174 Bd64
Veliki Greda SRB 174 Bc62
Veliki Grotevac HR 152 Gd59
Veliki Izvor SRB 179 Ca67
Veliki Kupci SRB 178 Bc68
Velikino RUS 99 Ld40
Veliki Plana SRB 174 Bb65
Veliki Poganac HR 152 Gc57
Veliki Popović SRB 174 Bc66
Veliki Preslav BG 181 Ec70
Veliki Radinci SRB 153 Ja61
Veliki Raven HR 152 Gb58
Veliki Šiljegovac SRB 178 Bc68
Veliki Srediste SRB 174 Bd62
Veliki Trnovac KSV 178 Bc71
Veliki Zdenci HR 152 Gd59
Veliko Orašje SRB 174 Bc65
Veliko Selo SRB 174 Bc65
Veliko Tărnovo BG 180 Dd70
Veliko Tirgovišće HR 151 Ga58
Veliko Trebeljevo SLO 151 Fc58
Velilla de Cinca E 48 Fd61
Velilla de Ebro E 48 Fb61
Velilla del Río Carrión E 38 Da56
Veli Lošinj HR 151 Fb63
Velimáhi GR 188 Bb86
Velimese TR 186 Fa77
Velimlje MNE 159 Hc68
Vélines F 32 Fd50
Velinga S 103 Fb48
Velingrad BG 179 Cd73
Velise EST 98 Kb44
Veliuona LV 114 Kb57
Veliž RUS 202 Eb11
Velje Duboko MNE 159 Ja68
Velji Breg KSV 178 Ba69
Veljun HR 151 Ga60
Veljusa MK 183 Ca75
Velká Bíteš CZ 137 Gb47
Velká Bystřice CZ 137 Gd46
Velká Černoc CZ 136 Fa44
Velká Hleďsebe CZ 135 Ec45
Vel'ká Ida SK 139 Jd49
Vel'ká Lomnica SK 138 Jb47
Vel'ka Mača SK 145 Ha50
Vel'ká nad Ipl'om SK 146 Ja50
Velká nad Veličkou CZ 137 Gd48
Velké Bílovice CZ 137 Gc48
Velké Heraltice CZ 137 Ha45
Vel'ké Kapušany SK 139 Ka49
Velké Karlovice CZ 137 Hb47
Vel'ké Kostol'any SK 137 Ha49
Velké Kunětice CZ 137 Gd43
Vel'ke-Levàre SK 145 Gc50
Velké Losiny CZ 137 Gc44
Vel'ke Lovce SK 145 Hb51
Vel'ke Ludince SK 145 Hb51
Velké Meziříčí CZ 136 Ga47
Velké Němčice CZ 137 Gc48
Velké Opatovice CZ 137 Gc46
Velké Pavlovice CZ 137 Gc48
Vel'ké Ripňany SK 137 Ha49
Vel'ké Rovné SK 137 Hb47
Vel'ke Turovce SK 146 Hc51
Vel'ke Ul'any SK 145 Ha51
Vel'ké Zálužie SK 145 Ha50
Velkmossen FIN 89 Hd32
Velkua FIN 97 Ja39
Velkuankaupunki FIN 97 Ja39
Vel'ký Blh SK 138 Jb49
Velký Bor CZ 136 Fa47
Vel'ký Ďur SK 145 Hb50
Vel'ký Krtiš SK 146 Hd50
Vel'ký Meder SK 145 Ha52
Vel'ký Šariš SK 139 Jd47
Vel'ký Slavkov SK 138 Jb47
Velký Újezd CZ 137 Gd46
Vellahn D 119 Dd33
Vellamelen N 78 Ec27
Vellberg D 134 Da47
Velle N 76 Cd33
Vellechevreux F 31 Ka40
Vellefaux F 31 Jd41
Velle-le-Châtel F 31 Jd40
Velles F 29 Gc44
Vellescot F 31 Kb40
Velletri I 160 Eb72
Vellev DK 100 Dc23
Vellevans F 31 Ka41
Vellila de Tarilonte E 38 Da56
Vellinge S 110 Ed56
Vellisca E 47 Ea65
Velliza E 46 Cd60
Vellmar D 126 Da40
Vellua FIN 89 Ja38
Vélo GR 189 Bd86
Velovo HR 152 Ha60
Velpke D 127 Dd36
Velsen NL 116 Ad35
Velta N 94 Ec39
Velten D 127 Ed36
Věltrní CZ 136 Fb49
Veltrusy CZ 136 Fb44
Velušina MK 183 Bb76
Velvang N 78 Eb29
Velventós GR 183 Bc79
Velvina GR 188 Bb84
Velyka Lepetycha UA 205 Fa16
Velyka Pysarivka UA 203 Fa14
Velyki Dederkaly UA 204 Ea15
Velykyj Burluk UA 203 Fa14
Velżys LT 114 Kc55
Vemb DK 100 Cd23
Vemdalen S 87 Fb33
Vemdalsskalet S 87 Fb33
Véménd H 153 Hc57
Vemhån S 87 Fb34
Vemmedrup DK 109 Eb26
Vemmenæs DK 109 Dd28
Vemmetofte Strand DK 109 Ec27
Ven N 92 Cb44
Vena S 103 Ga49
Venabu N 85 Dd35
Venabygd N 85 Dd36
Venaco F 154 Cb70
Venafro I 161 Fa73
Venäjä FIN 89 Jc37
Venarey-les-Laumes F 30 Ja41
Venarsal F 33 Gc49
Venasca I 148 Bc62
Venas di Cadore I 143 Eb56
Venåsen N 85 Dd35
Venasque F 42 Jc52
Venčan BG 181 Ed70
Venčane SRB 153 Jc63
Vence F 43 Kc53
Venckai LT 113 Jb56
Venclovìškiai LT 114 Ka57
Venda P 50 Ba70
Venda Nova P 44 Ba59
Vendas Novas P 50 Ac69
Vendays-Montalivet F 32 Fa48
Vendegies-sur-Ecaillon F 24 Hb32
Vendel S 96 Gc41
Vendelä FIN 98 Ka39
Vendenheim F 25 Kc36
Vendeuil F 24 Hb33
Vendeuvre F 22 Fc36
Vendeuvre-sur-Barse F 30 Hd38
Vendine F 40 Gc54
Vendinha P 50 Ba70

Villafranca in Lunigiana I 149 Cd63
Villafranca-Montes de Oca E 38 Dd58
Villafranca Piemonte I 148 Bc61
Villafranca Sicula I 166 Ec85
Villafranca Tirrena I 167 Fd83
Villafranco del Guadalquivir E 59 Bd74
Villafrati I 166 Ed84
Villafrechos E 45 Cc59
Villafruela E 46 Db59
Villafuerte E 46 Db60
Villagarcía de Campos E 46 Cd60
Villagarcía de la Torre E 51 Ca71
Villagarcía del Llano E 53 Ec68
Villagatón E 37 Cb57
Villaggio Coppola Pinetamare I 161 Fa74
Villaggio Moschella I 161 Ga74
Villaggio Racise I 164 Gc80
Villagonzalo E 51 Bd69
Villagrains F 32 Fb51
Villagrande I 156 Ec70
Villagrande Strisaili I 169 Cb77
Villagrazia I 166 Ec84
Villaharta E 52 Cc71
Villähde FIN 90 Kc37
Villahermosa E 53 Dd70
Villahermosa del Río E 54 Fb65
Villaherreros E 38 Da58
Villahizán E 46 Dc59
Villáhizan de Treviño E 38 Db58
Villahoz E 46 Dc59
Villaines-en-Duesmois F 30 Ja40
Villaines-la-Juhel F 28 Fc38
Villajimena E 46 Da59
Villajoyosa E 55 Fc71
Villala FIN 91 Ld32
Villalambrús E 38 Dd56
Villalangua E 39 Fd48
Villalba E 36 Bb54
Villalba I 166 Ed85
Villalba Calatrava E 52 Dc70
Villalba de la Sierra E 47 Eb65
Villalba de los Alcores E 46 Cd59
Villalba de los Barros E 51 Bd70
Villalba de los Morales E 47 Ed63
Villalba del Rey E 47 Ea65
Villalba de Rioja E 38 Ea57
Villalcampo E 45 Ca60
Villalcázar de Sirga E 38 Da58
Villaldemiro E 38 Db58
Villalebrín E 37 Cd58
Villalengua E 47 Ec61
Villalgordo del Júcar E 53 Eb68
Villalgordo del Marquesado E 53 Ea67
Villa Literno I 161 Fa74
Villalobar de Rioja E 38 Ea58
Villalobos E 45 Cc59
Villalón de Campos E 46 Cd59
Villalonga E 54 Fc69
Villalpando E 45 Cc59
Villalpardo E 54 Ed68
Villalquite E 37 Cc57
Villalube E 45 Cc60
Villaluenga de la Sagra E 46 Db65
Villaluenga del Rosario E 59 Cb76
Villalumbroso (Valle Retortillo) E 38 Da58
Villalvernia I 148 Cb61
Villamalea E 54 Ed68
Villamañán E 37 Cc58
Villamanín E 37 Cc56
Villamanrique E 53 Dd70
Villamanrique de la Condesa E 59 Bd74
Villamanta E 46 Db65
Villamantilla E 46 Db65
Villamanzo E 46 Dc59
Villamar E 36 Bc54
Villamar I 169 Ca78
Villamarco E 37 Cd57
Villamartín de Campos E 46 Da59
Villamartín de Don Sancho E 37 Cd57
Villamarzana I 150 Dd61
Villamassargia I 169 Bd79
Villamayor E 37 Cd54
Villamayor E 45 Cb62
Villamayor E 48 Fb60
Villamayor de Calatrava E 52 Da69
Villamayor de Campos E 45 Cc59
Villamayor del Río E 38 Dd58
Villamayor de Santiago E 53 Dd67

Villamblard F 33 Ga49
Villambrán de Cea E 37 Cd57
Villambroz E 37 Cd58
Villameca E 37 Cb57
Villamediana E 46 Da59
Villamejil E 37 Cb57
Villamesías E 51 Ca68
Villaminaya E 52 Db67
Villa Minozzo I 149 Da63
Villamizar E 37 Cd57
Villamo FIN 89 Ja34
Villamontán de la Valduerna E 37 Cb58
Villamor de los Escuderos E 45 Cb61
Villamuelas E 52 Dc66
Villamuera de la Cueza E 38 Da58
Villamuriel de Campos E 46 Cd59
Villamuriel de Cerrato E 46 Da59
Villanasur E 38 Dd58
Villandraut F 32 Fc51
Villandry F 29 Ga42
Villanueva de Duero E 46 Cd60
Villanova I 148 Bb61
Villanova d'Albenga I 43 La52
Villanova d'Asti I 148 Bd61
Villanova del Battista I 161 Fd74
Villanovaforru I 169 Ca78
Villanovafranca I 169 Ca78
Villanova Mondoví I 148 Bc62
Villanova Monteleone I 168 Bd73
Villanova Strisaili I 169 Cb77
Villanova Truschedu I 169 Ca77
Villanovatulo I 169 Cb78
Villanovilla E 39 Fb57
Villanubla E 46 Cd60
Villanueva E 37 Bd56
Villanueva E 37 Cd54
Villanueva de Alcardete E 53 Dd67
Villanueva de Alcorón E 47 Eb64
Villanueva de Algaidas E 60 Cd75
Villanueva de Argaño E 38 Db58
Villanueva de Bogas E 52 Dc67
Villanueva de Cameros E 47 Ea59
Villanueva de Cauche E 60 Cd75
Villanueva de Córdoba E 52 Cd71
Villanueva de Gállego E 48 Fb60
Villanueva de Gumiel E 46 Dc60
Villanueva del Aceral E 46 Cd62
Villanueva de la Concepción E 60 Cd75
Villanueva de la Condesa E 37 Cd58
Villanueva de la Fuente E 53 Ea70
Villanueva de la Jara E 53 Ec68
Villanueva de la Nia E 38 Db56
Villanueva de la Peña E 38 Db55
Villanueva del Árbol E 37 Cc57
Villanueva de la Reina E 60 Db72
Villanueva del Arzobispo E 61 Dd72
Villanueva de las Cruzes E 59 Bb73
Villanueva de la Serena E 51 Ca69
Villanueva de la Sierra E 45 Bd64
Villanueva de las Manzanas E 37 Cc57
Villanueva de las Torres E 61 Dd74
Villanueva de la Vera E 45 Cb65
Villanueva del Campo E 45 Cc59
Villanueva del Duque E 52 Cc71
Villanueva del Fresno E 51 Bb70
Villanueva del Huerva E 47 Fa61
Villanueva de los Castillejos E 58 Ba73
Villanueva de los Infantes E 53 Dd70
Villanueva de los Nabos E 38 Da58
Villanueva del Rey E 52 Cc71
Villanueva del Río y Minas E 59 Ca73
Villanueva del Trabuco E 60 Da75
Villanueva de Oscos E 37 Bd54
Villanueva de San Carlos E 52 Db70

Villanueva de San Juan E 59 Cb75
Villanueva de Sigena E 48 Fc60
Villanueva de Tapia E 60 Da75
Villanuño de Valdavia E 38 Da57
Villány H 153 Hc58
Villapaderna E 37 Cd57
Villapalacios E 53 Ea70
Villapeceñil E 37 Cd58
Villapedre E 37 Ca54
Villapiana Lido I 164 Gc78
Villapiana Scalo I 164 Gc78
Villa Potenza I 156 Ed67
Villaputzu I 169 Cb79
Villaquejida E 37 Cc58
Villaquilambre E 37 Cc57
Villaquirán de los Infantes E 38 Db58
Villar E 60 Cc73
Villaralbo E 45 Cb60
Villaralto E 52 Cc70
Villarcayo E 38 Dc56
Villard-de-Lans F 35 Jc49
Villar de Cañas E 53 Ea66
Villar de Chinchilla E 54 Ed69
Villar de Ciervo E 45 Bd63
Villardeciervos E 45 Ca59
Villar de Corneja E 45 Cc64
Villar de Domingo García E 47 Eb65
Villardefrades E 45 Cc60
Villar de la Encina E 53 Ea67
Villar del Arzobispo E 54 Fa67
Villar del Buey E 45 Ca61
Villar del Cobo E 47 Ec65
Villar del Horno E 47 Eb65
Villar del Humo E 54 Ed66
Villar de los Navarros E 47 Fa62
Villar del Pedroso E 52 Cc66
Villar del Rey E 51 Bc68
Villar del Río E 47 Eb59
Villar del Salz E 47 Ed65
Villar del Saz de Navalón E 47 Eb65
Villar de Olmos E 54 Fa67
Villar de Peralonso E 45 Ca62
Villardíaz E 37 Bd54
Villardiegua de la Ribera E 45 Ca60
Villardompardo E 60 Db73
Villard Saint-Christophe F 35 Jd49
Villareal de los Infantes E 54 Fc66
Villarejo de Fuentes E 53 Ea66
Villarejo de Montalbán E 52 Da66
Villarejo de Salvanés E 46 Dd65
Villarejo-Peristeban E 53 Eb66
Villarente E 37 Cc57
Villargordo E 60 Db72
Villargordo del Cabriel E 54 Ed67
Villaricos E 61 Ec75
Villarino E 45 Bd61
Villarluengo E 48 Fb64
Villarmayor E 45 Cb62
Villarmid E 36 Ac54
Villarosa I 167 Fa85
Villaroya de los Pinares E 48 Fb64
Villarquemado E 47 Ed64
Villarramiel E 46 Cd59
Villarrasa E 59 Bc73
Villarreal E 51 Bb69
Villarrín de Campos E 45 Cc59
Villarrobledo E 53 Ea68
Villarrodrigo E 38 Da57
Villarrodrigo E 53 Ea71
Villarroquel E 37 Cb57
Villarroya de la Sierra E 47 Ec61
Villarrubia E 60 Cc72
Villarrubia de los Ojos E 52 Dc68
Villarrubia de Santiago E 52 Dc66
Villars CH 141 Bc56
Villars F 29 Gc39
Villars F 33 Ga48
Villars-en-Azois F 30 Ja39
Villars-les-Dombes F 34 Jb46
Villars-Santenoge F 30 Jb40
Villarta E 53 Ec68
Villarta de los Montes E 52 Cd68
Villarta de San Juan E 52 Dc68
Villasalto I 169 Cb79
Villasana de Mena E 38 Dd56
Villasandino E 38 Db58
Villa San Giovanni I 164 Ga83
Villa Santa Maria I 161 Fb71

Villasante de Montija E 38 Dd56
Villa Santina I 143 Ec56
Villasarracino E 38 Da58
Villasayas E 47 Ea61
Villaseca E 38 Ea57
Villasecino E 37 Cb56
Villaseco E 45 Cb60
Villaseco de los Gamitos E 45 Ca62
Villaseco de los Reyes E 45 Ca61
Villasequilla de Yepes E 52 Dc66
Villasimius I 169 Cb80
Villasmundo I 167 Fd86
Villasor I 169 Ca79
Villastar E 47 Fa65
Villastellone I 148 Bd61
Villasur de Herreros E 38 Dd58
Villatalla I 43 La52
Villatobas E 53 Dd66
Villatoro E 45 Cc64
Villatoya E 54 Ed68
Villaturiel E 37 Cc57
Villaurbana I 169 Ca78
Villaute E 38 Db57
Villa Vela I 167 Fd87
Villaverde de Guadalimar E 53 Ea71
Villaverde del Río E 59 Ca73
Villaverde de Medina E 46 Cd61
Villaverde de Monte E 46 Dc59
Villaverde de Pontones E 38 Dc54
Villaverde de Trucios E 38 Dd55
Villaverde y Pasaconsol E 53 Eb67
Villaviciosa E 37 Cc54
Villaviciosa de Córdoba E 60 Cc72
Villaviciosa de Odón E 46 Db64
Villavieja de Yeltes E 45 Bd62
Villaviudas E 46 Db59
Villa Vomano I 157 Fa69
Villayón E 37 Ca54
Villazanzo de Valderaduey E 37 Cd57
Villberga S 96 Gc42
Villé F 31 Kb38
Ville RO 181 Fa67
Villebaudon F 22 Fa36
Villebois-Lavalette F 32 Fd48
Villebrumier F 40 Gc53
Villecerf F 29 Ha38
Villecomtal F 33 Ha51
Villeconin F 29 Gd38
Villecroze F 42 Ka54
Villedaigne F 41 Hb55
Villedieu F 30 Hd40
Villedieu-les-Poêles F 22 Fa37
Villedieu-sur-Indre F 29 Gc43
Villedômain F 29 Gb43
Villefagnan F 32 Fd46
Villefloure F 41 Ha56
Villefontaine F 34 Jb47
Villefort F 34 Hd45
Villefranche-d'Albigeois F 41 Ha53
Villefranche-d'Allier F 33 Ha45
Villefranche-de-Conflent F 41 Ha57
Villefranche-de-Lauragais F 40 Gc55
Villefranche-de-Lonchat F 32 Fd50
Villefranche-de-Panat F 41 Ha52
Villefranche-de-Rouergue F 41 Gd52
Villefranche-du-Périgord F 33 Gb51
Villefranche-sur-Cher F 29 Gc43
Villefranche-sur-Mer F 43 Kd53
Villefranche-sur-Saône F 34 Ja46
Villegailhenc F 41 Ha55
Villegenon F 29 Ha41
Villel E 47 Fa65
Villela E 38 Dd58
Ville-la-Grand F 35 Ka45
Villel de Mesa E 47 Ec62
Villemaur-sur-Vanne F 30 Hc38
Villemer F 29 Ha38
Villemeux-sur-Eure F 23 Gb37
Villemorien F 30 Hd39
Villemur-sur-Tarn F 40 Gc53
Villena E 55 Fa70
Villenauxe-la-Grande F 24 Hc37
Villeneuve CH 141 Bb56
Villeneuve F 33 Gd51
Villeneuve F 34 Jb46
Villeneuve F 42 Jb54

Villeneuve-au-Chemin F 30 Hc39
Villeneuve-d'Ascq F 24 Hb31
Villeneuve-de-Berg F 34 Ja51
Villeneuve-de-Marsan F 40 Fc53
Villeneuve-en-Montagne F 30 Ja43
Villeneuve-la-Comtesse F 32 Fb46
Villeneuve-la-Guyard F 30 Hb38
Villeneuve-l'Archevêque F 30 Hc39
Villeneuve-lès-Avignon F 42 Jb53
Villeneuve-les-Bordes F 30 Hb38
Villeneuve-sur-Allier F 30 Hd44
Villeneuve-sur-Lot F 33 Ga51
Villeneuve-sur-Yonne F 30 Hb39
Villentrois F 29 Gb42
Villeréal F 33 Ga51
Villerest F 34 Hd46
Villerías de Campos E 46 Cd59
Villeromain F 29 Gb40
Villerouge-Termenès F 41 Ha56
Villers-Bocage F 22 Fb36
Villers-Bocage F 23 Gd33
Villers Bretonneux F 23 Gd33
Villers-Carbonnel F 23 Ha33
Villers-Cotterêts F 24 Hb35
Villers-en-Argonne F 24 Ja36
Villersexel F 31 Ka40
Villers-Farlay F 31 Jc42
Villers-le-Lac F 31 Ka42
Villers-sur-Mer F 22 Fc35
Villerupt F 25 Jc34
Villeséneux F 24 Hd36
Villesèque F 33 Gb51
Villes-sur-Auzon F 42 Jc52
Ville-sur-Illon F 31 Jd38
Ville-sur-Tourbe F 24 Ja35
Villeta Barrea I 161 Fa72
Villetrun F 29 Gb41
Villeurbanne F 34 Jb47
Villevallier F 30 Hb39
Villeveyrac F 41 Hb55
Villiers-Charlemagne F 28 Fb40
Villiers-en-Plaine F 32 Fb45
Villiers-Saint-Benoît F 30 Hb40
Villiers-Saint-Georges F 24 Hb37
Villiers-sur-Beuvron F 30 Hc42
Villikkala FIN 90 Kc37
Villikkala FIN 90 Kd37
Villingebæk DK 109 Ec24
Villingen-Schwenningen D 141 Cb50
Villmergen CH 141 Ca53
Villodrigo E 46 Db59
Villoldo E 38 Da58
Villon F 30 Hd40
Villora E 54 Ed67
Villoria E 45 Cc62
Villoruela E 45 Cc62
Villotta I 150 Ec58
Villotte-sur-Aire F 24 Jb36
Villstad S 102 Fa51
Villuis F 30 Hb38
Villvattnet S 80 Hb26
Villy-en-Auxois F 30 Ja41
Vilnes N 84 Ca36
Vilnius LT 114 La58
Vil'njans'k UA 205 Fa15
Vil'nohirs'k UA 204 Ed15
Vilobacka FIN 81 Jb29
Vilor RO 175 Dc60
Viloria E 39 Ea57
Vilovo SRB 153 Jb60
Vilppula FIN 90 Ka34
Vilpulka LV 106 Kd47
Vils D 142 Db52
Vils DK 100 Da22
Vilsandi EST 105 Jb46
Vil'šany UA 203 Fa14
Vilsbiburg D 135 Eb50
Vilseck D 135 Ea46
Vilshofen D 135 Ed49
Vilske-Kleva S 102 Fa47
Vilslev DK 108 Da26
Vilsted DK 100 Db21
Vilsund Vest DK 100 Da21
Viluče EST 107 Lc46
Vilūnai LT 114 Kc58
Vilusi BIH 152 Gd61
Vilusi BIH 152 Gd62
Vilusi MNE 159 Hc68
Vilviestre del Pinar E 46 Dd59
Vilzēni LV 106 Kc48
Vilzēnmuiža LV 106 Kc48
Vima Mică RO 171 Da56
Vimbodí E 48 Gb61
Vimeiro P 50 Aa67
Vimercate I 149 Cc59
Vimianzo E 36 Ac54
Vimieiro P 50 Ad68
Vimioso P 45 Bd60

Vimmerby S 103 Ga49
Vimont F 22 Fc36
Vimoutiers F 22 Fd36
Vimpeli FIN 81 Jc30
Vimperk CZ 136 Fa48
Vimy F 23 Ha32
Vinac BIH 158 Gd64
Vinaceite E 48 Fb62
Vinadi CH 142 Db55
Vinadio I 148 Bb62
Vinaixa E 48 Ga61
Viñales E 37 Ca57
Vinarós E 48 Ga64
Vinarsko BG 181 Ed72
Vinäs S 87 Fc38
Vinatori MD 173 Fb57
Vinay F 35 Jc48
Vinberg S 102 Ec51
Vinça F 41 Ha57
Vinchiaturo I 161 Fb73
Vinci I 155 Db65
Vinci MK 178 Bc73
Vinciarello I 164 Gc82
Vind DK 100 Da23
Vindblæs DK 100 Db21
Vindbyholt DK 109 Eb27
Vindeballe DK 108 Dc28
Vindel-Ånäset S 80 Hb27
Vindelgransele S 72 Gd24
Vindeln S 80 Hb27
Vindinge DK 109 Dd27
Vindornyaszőlős H 145 Gd55
Vindrej RUS 203 Fc10
Vinebre E 48 Ga62
Vinga RO 174 Bd60
Vingåker S 95 Ga44
Vingelen N 77 Dc30
Vingnes N 85 Ea37
Vingrau F 41 Hb56
Vingrom N 85 Ea37
Vingsand N 78 Ea27
Vingstad N 67 Ha11
Vinhais P 45 Bc59
Vinica HR 152 Gb57
Vinica SK 146 Hd51
Vinica SLO 151 Fc59
Viničani MK 183 Bc74
Viniegra de Abajo E 47 Ea59
Vinišče HR 158 Gb66
Vinište BG 179 Cc68
Vinjak AL 182 Ac78
Vinje F 29 Ha42
Vinje N 84 Cc38
Vinjen N 66 Fc15
Vinjeøra N 77 Dc30
Vinkeveen NL 116 Ba36
Vinköl S 102 Fa47
Vinkovci HR 153 Hc60
Vinksniniai LT 114 Kd53
Vinliden S 80 Gc26
Vinnari FIN 89 Jb36
Vinne N 78 Ea27
Vinné SK 139 Jd46
Vinnelys N 63 Hb09
Vinnersjö S 95 Gb40
Vinni FIN 81 Jc30
Vinninga S 102 Fa46
Vinnycja UA 204 Eb15
Vinodol HR 151 Fc60
Vinograd BG 180 Dd70
Vinogradnoe MD 173 Ga58
Vinon F 29 Ha42
Vinon S 95 Fd44
Viñón E 38 Dd55
Vinon-sur-Verdon F 42 Jd53
Vinslöv S 110 Fa54
Vinsnes N 93 Da44
Vinsternes N 77 Db30
Vinstra N 85 Dd36
Vintala FIN 97 Jd39
Vintervollen N 65 Kd07
Vintilă Vodă RO 176 Ec63
Vintileasca RO 176 Ec62
Vintjärn S 87 Ga38
Vintl I 143 Dd55
Vintrosa S 95 Fd44
Vintu de Jos RO 175 Cd60
Vintzelberg D 127 Ea36
Viñuela E 60 Da76
Viñuela de Sayago E 45 Cb61
Viñuelas E 46 Dd63
Visoca MD 173 Fd56
Viso del Marqués E 52 Dc70

Virane LV 107 Lb50
Vimont F 22 Fc36 →
Virbalis LT 114 Ka58
Virböle FIN 90 Kd38
Vircava LV 106 Kb52
Vire F 22 Fb37
Viré F 30 Jb44
Vireda S 103 Fc48
Vireši LV 107 Lb48
Virestad S 111 Fb53
Vireux-Wallerand F 24 Ja32
Virga LV 113 Jb53
Virgen A 143 Eb54
Virgen de la Cabeza E 52 Da71
Virgilio I 149 Db61
Virginia IRL 9 Cc19
Virieu F 35 Jc47
Virignin F 35 Jd47
Virisen S 71 Fd23
Viriville F 35 Jc48
Virje HR 152 Gc57
Virkby FIN 98 Ka40
Virkkala FIN 98 Ka40
Virkkula FIN 75 Kd21
Virkkunen FIN 75 Kd21
Virklund DK 108 Db24
Virla S 80 Hb27
Virmaanpää FIN 82 Kd30
Virmutjoki FIN 91 Lc35
Virneburg D 133 Bd43
Virojoki FIN 91 Lb37
Virolahden FIN 91 Lb38
Virollet F 32 Fc46
Vironchaux F 23 Gc32
Virovia GR 183 Cb76
Virovitica HR 152 Gd58
Virovsko BG 179 Cc68
Virpazar MNE 159 Ja70
Virpe LV 105 Jc49
Virrankylä FIN 75 La19
Virrat FIN 89 Jd33
Virsbo S 95 Ga42
Virserum S 103 Fd50
Virtaa FIN 90 Kc35
Virtala FIN 81 Jc31
Virtaniemi FIN 65 Kb10
Virtasalmi FIN 90 La32
Virton B 132 Ba45
Virtsu EST 98 Ka45
Virttaa FIN 89 Jc37
Viru-Jaagupi EST 98 La42
Viru-Kabale EST 98 La42
Viru-Nigula EST 98 La41
Viry F 35 Jd45
Vis HR 158 Gb68
Visag RO 174 Ca61
Visaginas LT 115 Lc54
Višakio Rūda LV 114 Kb58
Visalaukė LT 114 La57
Vişani RO 176 Ed64
Visbek D 117 Cc35
Visborg DK 100 Dc22
Visby DK 108 Da27
Visby S 104 Gd49
Višćauți MD 173 Fd56
Visčhegrad BIH 159 Ja65
Višegrád H 146 Hc52
Viseu P 44 Ba63
Vişeu de Jos RO 171 Dc55
Vişeu de Sus RO 171 Dc55
Višević SRB 174 Bb65
Viševoje RUS 113 Ja59
Višgorodok RUS 107 Ld49
Visiedo E 47 Fa64
Vişina RO 176 Dd65
Vişina RO 180 Db68
Vişineşti RO 176 Dd64
Visingsö S 103 Fb48
Viskafors S 102 Ed49
Viskāļi LV 106 Kd51
Viškeri LV 107 Ld52
Viški LV 115 Lc53
Visking DK 109 Ea26
Visky RUS 107 Ld47
Visland N 92 Cb45
Vislanda S 103 Fb52
Vislevo RUS 107 Mb48
Višļi LV 105 Jd51
Visnes N 92 Bd42
Visnevo RUS 113 Jd28
Visniovca MD 177 Fc60
Višnja Gora SLO 151 Fc58
Višňova CZ 128 Fc41
Višňové CZ 137 Gb48
Visnum S 95 Fb44
Visnums-Kil S 95 Fb44
Viso del Marqués E 52 Dc70

Vissec F 41 Hc53
Visseljärda S 111 Fd53
Visseiche F 28 Fa40
Visselhövede D 118 Db34
Visseltofta S 110 Fa53
Vissenberg DK 108 Dc26
Vissinéa GR 183 Bb77
Visso I 156 Ec68
Vissoie CH 141 Bd56
Vist N 78 Ec28
Vista Alegre E 36 Ba53
Vistabella E 47 Fa62
Vistabella del Maestrat E 54 Fc65
Vistbäcken S 73 Hb22
Vistdal N 77 Db32
Vistheden S 73 Hb22
Visthus N 70 Ed22
Vistino RUS 99 Ld40
Vistnes N 92 Ca43
Vistorp S 102 Fa48
Vistträsk S 73 Hb22
Vištytis LT 114 Ka59
Visukums LV 107 Lc48
Visuvesi FIN 89 Jd33
Vita I 166 Eb84
Vitaby S 111 Fb56
Vitåfors S 73 Ja21
Vitănești RO 180 Dd67
Vitanje SLO 151 Fd57
Vitanovac SRB 178 Bb67
Vitanovac SRB 179 Ca69
Vitanvaara FIN 75 Kc20
Vitberget S 73 Hb21
Vitebsk BY 202 Eb11
Vitemölla S 111 Fb56
Viterbo I 156 Ea70
Vitez BIH 158 Ha64
Vithkuq AL 182 Ad77
Viti EST 98 Kb42
Vitigudino E 45 Bd62
Vitikkala FIN 90 Kb33
Vitina BIH 158 Ha67
Vitina BIH 158 Ha67
Vitina GR 194 Bb87
Vitina KSV 178 Bb72
Vitiņi LV 105 Jd52
Vitino RUS 99 Mb40
Vitis A 136 Fd49
Vitkov CZ 137 Ha45
Vitkovac SRB 178 Bb67
Vitkovci BIH 159 Hd66
Vitkovo SRB 178 Bb67
Vitolište MK 183 Bc76
Vitomirești RO 175 Db64
Vitoria E 38 Ea56
Vitoševac SRB 178 Bc67
Vitovlje BIH 152 Ha63
Vitré F 28 Fa39
Vitrolles F 42 Jc54
Vitrupe LV 106 Kc48
Vitry-en-Artois F 23 Ha32
Vitry-la-Ville F 24 Hd36
Vitry-le-François F 24 Ja37
Vitry-sur-Seine F 23 Gd37
Vitsa GR 182 Ad79
Vitsand S 94 Ed40
Vitsaniemi S 73 Jb20
Vittangi S 68 Hc22
Vittaryd S 103 Fb51
Vitteaux F 30 Ja41
Vittel F 31 Jc38
Vittikko FIN 69 Kc17
Vittikkovuoma FIN 68 Jb17
Vittinge S 95 Gb41
Vittjärn S 94 Ed40
Vittjärv S 73 Hd21
Vittoria I 167 Fb87
Vittorio Veneto I 150 Eb58
Vittsjö S 110 Fa53
Vittskövle S 111 Fb55
Vittuone I 148 Cb59
Vitulano I 161 Fb74
Vitvatnet S 73 Jb20
Vitvatnet S 80 Ha28
Vitvatnet S 87 Fc33
Viù I 148 Bc59
Viuf DK 108 Db26
Vium DK 100 Da22
Viuruniemi FIN 83 Lc30
Vivar del Cid E 38 Dc58
Vivares E 51 Ca68
Vivario F 154 Cb70
Viveiro E 36 Bc53
Viveiro P 44 Ba63
Vivel del Río Martín E 47 Fa63
Viver E 54 Fb66
Viverols F 34 Hd48
Viverone I 148 Bd59
Vivestad N 93 Dd43
Viviers F 42 Jb51
Viviez F 33 Gd51
Vivonne F 32 Fd45
Vivungi S 68 Hd15
Vix F 32 Fb45
Vizancăi LT 113 Jc53
Vizantea-Livezi RO 176 Ec61
Vizcaínos E 46 Dd59
Vize TR 186 Fa76
Vizille F 35 Jd49
Vižina CZ 136 Fb45
Vižinada HR 151 Fa60
Ziziru RO 177 Fa64
Vizovice CZ 137 Ha47
Vizsoly H 139 Jd49
Vizzavona F 154 Cb70

Vizzini – Wąsosz

Vizzini I 167 Fc87
Vjatskie Poljany RUS 203 Ga08
Vjatskoe RUS 203 Fa08
Vjaz'ma RUS 202 Ec11
Vjazniki RUS 203 Fb09
V. Kolaro (Pamporovo) BG 184 Db75
Vlaardingen NL 124 Ac37
Vlachovo SK 138 Jb48
Vlachovo Březí CZ 136 Fa48
Vlad AL 159 Jc70
Vlad AL 178 Ad71
Vlădaia RO 175 Cc66
Vladaja BG 179 Cc71
Vlădeni RO 172 Ec55
Vlădeni RO 173 Fa56
Vlădeni RO 177 Fa66
Vlădeşti RO 175 Db63
Vlădeşti RO 175 Dc63
Vlădeşti RO 177 Fb62
Vladičin-Han SRB 178 Bd71
Vlădila RO 180 Db67
Vladilovce MK 183 Bc74
Vladimir MNE 163 Ja71
Vladimir RO 175 Cd64
Vladimir RUS 203 Fa10
Vladimirci SRB 153 Jb62
Vladimirescu RO 170 Bd59
Vladimirovac SRB 174 Bb63
Vladimirovci BG 181 Ec69
Vladimirovo BG 179 Cc68
Vladimirovo BG 181 Fa69
Vladimirovo MK 183 Ca74
Vladimirovo RUS 113 Ja59
Vladinja BG 180 Db70
Vladinos MNE 163 Ja71
Vladislav CZ 136 Ga47
Vlad Ţepeş RO 176 Ed66
Vladyčkino RUS 99 Mb42
Vlagtwedde NL 117 Ca34
Vlaháta GR 188 Ac85
Vlaháva GR 183 Bb80
Vlahi BG 183 Cb74
Vlahiá GR 189 Cb84
Vlahióti GR 194 Bc90
Vlăhiţa RO 176 Ea60
Vlahokerassiá GR 194 Bc88
Vlahović HR 152 Gb60
Vlahovići BIH 158 Hb68
Vlăiculeşti RO 176 Ec66
Vlaina Okruglica SRB 179 Ca71
Vlajkovac SRB 174 Bc63
Vlajkovci SRB 178 Bb68
Vlas BG 181 Fa72
Vlasenica BIH 159 Hd64
Vlashuk AL 182 Ab76
Vlasi SRB 179 Ca70
Vlašici HR 157 Fd64
Vlašim CZ 136 Fc46
Vlaşin RO 180 Ea67
Vlasina Rid SRB 179 Ca71
Vlăsineşti RO 172 Ed55
Vlaški Drenovac KSV 178 Ba71
Vlasotince SRB 178 Bd70
Vlastiboř CZ 136 Fc47
Vlatten D 125 Bc41
Vledder NL 117 Bc34
Vlesno RUS 107 Ma49
Vleuten NL 116 Ba36
Vlijmen NL 124 Ba38
Vlissingen NL 124 Ab38
Vlorë AL 182 Aa77
Vlotho D 126 Cd37
V. Nedelja SLO 152 Gb57
Vnorovy CZ 137 Gd48
Vobbia I 148 Cb62
Vocance F 34 Ja49
Voćin HR 152 Ha59
Vockerode D 127 Eb38
Vöcklabruck A 144 Fa51
Vöcklamarkt A 143 Ed51
Vodable F 34 Hb48
Vodanj SRB 174 Bb64
Voden BG 185 Dd74
Voden BG 185 Ec74
Vođenica BIH 152 Gb62
Vodeničane BG 180 Eb72
Vodica BG 180 Ea70
Vodica BIH 158 Gd64
Vodicë AL 182 Ad78
Vodice HR 151 Fa60
Vodice HR 157 Ga65
Vodice SLO 151 Fb57
Vodňany CZ 136 Fb47
Vodnjan HR 151 Fa61
Vodnjanci BG 179 Cb68
Vodno BG 180 Ea70
Vodovrar MK 183 Bc74
Vodskov DK 100 Dc21
Vodstrup DK 100 Da21
Voe GB 5 Fa04
Voel DK 108 Db24
Voerde D 125 Bd38
Voerladegård DK 108 Db24
Voerså DK 101 Dd20
Vœu F 29 Gc43
Voganj SRB 153 Jb61
Vogatsikó GR 183 Bb78
Vogelsdorf, Petershagen- D 128 Fa36
Vögelsen D 118 Dc33
Voggenau A 144 Fc52
Voghera I 148 Cb61
Voghiera I 150 Dd62
Vognill N 77 Dd32
Vognsild DK 100 Db22
Vogogna I 148 Ca57
Vogorno CH 148 Cb57
Vogt D 142 Da52
Vogtareuth D 143 Eb51
Vogtsburg D 141 Bd50
Vogüe F 34 Ja51
Vohburg D 135 Dd49
Vohburg D 135 Ea49
Vohenstrauß D 135 Eb46
Vöhl D 126 Cd40
Võhma EST 97 Jc45
Võhma EST 98 Ka45
Võhma EST 98 Kd41
Võhma EST 98 Kd44
Vohonjoki FIN 74 Kb20
Vohonovo RUS 99 Mb40
Vöhrden, Neuenkirchen- D 117 Cc36
Vöhrenbach D 141 Cb50
Vöhringen D 142 Cc50
Vöhringen D 142 Da50
Voiceşti RO 175 Db65
Void-Vacon F 25 Jc37
Voievoda RO 180 Dc68
Voigtsdorf D 120 Fa33
Voigtstedt D 127 Dd40
Voikoski FIN 90 Kd35
Voila RO 175 Dc61
Voiluoto FIN 89 Ja37
Voineasa RO 175 Da62
Voineasa RO 175 Da66
Voinescu MD 173 Fc59
Voineşti RO 173 Fa57
Voineşti RO 173 Fa59
Voineşti RO 176 Dd64
Voiron F 35 Jc48
Voise F 29 Gc38
Võisiku EST 98 Kd44
Voisines F 30 Jb40
Võiste EST 106 Kb46
Voiteg RO 174 Bc61
Voiteur F 31 Jc43
Voitoinen FIN 89 Jb37
Voitsberg A 144 Fd54
Voivodeni RO 171 Dc58
Vojakkala FIN 74 Jc21
Vojakkala FIN 90 Ka38
Vojčice SK 139 Ka48
Vojens DK 108 Db27
Vojinka UA 205 Fa17
Vojka SRB 153 Jb61
Vojkovice CZ 135 Ec44
Vojkovici BIH 159 Hc65
Vojmån S 79 Gb25
Vojnić HR 151 Ga60
Vojnik SLO 151 Fd57
Vojnika BG 181 Ec73
Vojnjagovo BG 180 Db72
Vojno-Selo MNE 159 Jb69
Vojnovo BG 181 Ed68
Vojšanci MK 183 Bd75
Vojsil BG 180 Db73
Vojska SRB 174 Bc66
Vojtjajaure S 71 Fd23
Vojvoda BG 181 Ed69
Vojvoda Stepa SRB 174 Bb61
Vojvodino BG 181 Fa70
Vojvodinovo BG 180 Db73
Voka EST 99 Lc41
Voladilla Alta E 60 Cc77
Vólakas GR 184 Cd76
Volargne I 149 Db59
Volary CZ 136 Fa48
Vólax GR 196 Db89
Volda N 85 Dc37
Volče SLO 151 Fa57
Volciano I 149 Db59
Volčki RUS 203 Fb12
Voldby DK 101 Dd23
Volden N 73 Ea31
Volders A 143 Dd54
Voldi EST 98 La44
Voldum DK 100 Dc23
Volendam NL 116 Ba35
Volga RUS 202 Ed09
Volgelsheim F 31 Kc39
Volgodonsk RUS 205 Fd15
Volgograd RUS 203 Fd14
Volgorečensk RUS 203 Fa09
Volgovo RUS 99 Ma40
Volgsele S 79 Gb25
Volhov RUS 202 Eb08
Volimes GR 188 Ac86
Volintiri MD 177 Ga60
Volissós GR 191 Dd85
Voljice BIH 158 Ha65
Volkach D 134 Db45
Volkenschwand D 135 Ea49
Völkermarkt A 144 Fc56
Völklingen D 133 Bc46
Volkmarsen D 126 Cd39
Volkovija MK 178 Ba73
Volkovo RUS 107 Ld48
Volkstedt D 127 Ea39
Voll N 86 Ea38
Vollen N 62 Gc10
Vollen N 78 Ec28
Vollenhove NL 117 Bc35
Vollersode D 118 Cd33
Vollerup DK 108 Db28
Vollheim N 79 Fb26
Vollore-Montagne F 34 Hc47
Vollore-Ville F 34 Hc47
Vollsjö S 110 Fa56
Volmsjö S 80 Gc27
Volna RUS 99 Ma42
Volnay F 28 Fd40
Volnovacha UA 205 Fb15
Voloave MD 173 Fc54
Voločaevskij RUS 205 Fd15
Voločajevskoje RUS 113 Hd59
Voločys'k UA 204 Ea15
Volodarka UA 204 Ec15
Volodarovka RUS 113 Jc59
Volodarsk RUS 203 Fb09
Volodarskij Toriki RUS 99 Mb39
Volodymyrec' UA 202 Ea14
Volodymyr-Volyns'kyj UA 202 Dd14
Vologda RUS 202 Ed08
Voloiac RO 175 Cc65
Volokolamsk RUS 202 Ed10
Volokonovka RUS 203 Fb13
Volonne F 42 Ka52
Vólos GR 189 Ca82
Volosovo RUS 99 Ld43
Volosovo RUS 99 Ma41
Vološovo RUS 99 Mb43
Volosovo RUS 202 Ea08
Volotovo RUS 203 Fb13
Volovăţ RO 172 Eb55
Volovec' UA 204 Dd16
Voloviţa MD 173 Fc54
Volovo BG 180 Ea69
Volpiano I 148 Bd60
Völpke D 127 Dd37
Völschow D 119 Ed32
Vol'sk RUS 203 Ga11
Voltaggio I 148 Cb62
Volta Mantovana I 149 Db60
Volterra I 155 Db66
Voltlage D 117 Cb36
Voltri I 148 Cb62
Voltti FIN 81 Jb30
Volturara Appula I 161 Fc73
Volturara Irpina I 161 Fc75
Volvic F 34 Hb46
Volyně CZ 136 Fa47
Volžsk RUS 203 Fd09
Volžskij RUS 203 Fd13
Vömmorski EST 107 Lc47
Vomp A 143 Dd53
Vonêche B 132 Ad43
Vonešta Voda BG 180 Dd71
Vóni GR 200 Da96
Vónitsa GR 188 Ad82
Vonnas F 34 Jb45
Võnnu EST 99 Lb45
Vonsild DK 108 Db26
Vööpste EST 99 Lb45
Vööpsu EST 107 Lc46
Voorburg NL 116 Ad36
Voore EST 99 Lb44
Voorschoten NL 116 Ad36
Voorthuizen NL 116 Bb36
Vopnafjörður IS 3 Bc04
Vörå FIN 81 Ja30
Vorau A 144 Ga53
Voray-sur-l'Ognon F 31 Jd41
Vorbasse DK 108 Da25
Vorchdorf A 144 Fa51
Vorden NL 125 Bc37
Vordernberg A 144 Fc53
Vorderriß D 143 Dd53
Vorderstoder A 144 Fb52
Vorderweissenburg A 136 Fb49
Vordingborg DK 109 Eb28
Vordónia GR 194 Bc89
Vordorf D 126 Dc37
Vorë AL 182 Ab76
Voreppe F 35 Jd48
Vorey F 34 Hd49
Vóri GR 200 Cd96
Vorinó GR 183 Bc76
Vorly F 29 Hd43
Vormsele S 80 Gd25
Vormsund N 94 Eb41
Vormträsk S 80 Gd25
Vorna FIN 82 Kb26
Vorniceni RO 172 Ec54
Vorning DK 100 Dc22
Vorona RO 172 Ec56
Voroncovo RUS 107 Mb48
Voroneţ RO 172 Eb56
Voronež RUS 203 Fb13
Voronkina RUS 107 Lc47
Voronovo RUS 99 Ld42
Vorožba UA 202 Ed13
Vorpbukta N 78 Ea28
Vorra D 135 Dd46
Vorsma RUS 203 Fb09
Vorţa RO 175 Cc60
Vorterøyskagen N 62 Ha08
Võru EST 107 Lb47
Vorzova LV 115 Ma53
Vosbutai LV 114 Kb56
Voshod RUS 203 Ga14
Vosiliškis LV 114 Kb55
Voskop AL 182 Ad77
Voskopojë AL 182 Ad77
Voskresensk RUS 203 Fa10
Voskresenskoe RUS 202 Ed09
Voskresenskoe RUS 203 Fc08
Voşlăbeni RO 172 Ea59
Voss N 84 Cc38
Võsu EST 98 Kd41
Vothylakas CY 206 Jd95
Votice CZ 136 Fc46
Võtikvere EST 99 Lb43
Voudenay-l'Église F 30 Ja42
Voúdia GR 195 Cd91
Voue F 30 Hd38
Vougécourt F 31 Jd39
Vougeot F 30 Jb42
Vouguinha P 44 Ba62
Vouhé F 32 Fb46
Vouillé F 28 Fd44
Vouillé F 32 Fc45
Voukoliés GR 200 Cb95
Voúla GR 195 Cb87
Vouliagméni GR 195 Cb87
Vouliásta GR 188 Ad81
Voúlpi GR 188 Ba82
Voulx F 29 Ha38
Voumajärvi S 73 Jb20
Voúnargo GR 188 Ba86
Vounihóra GR 189 Bc85
Vourgareli GR 188 Ba81
Vourijärvi FIN 89 Jc34
Vourkári GR 195 Cd88
Vourvouroú GR 184 Cc79
Vousnainen FIN 97 Ja39
Voussac F 34 Hb45
Voutás GR 200 Ca95
Voutenay-sur-Cure F 30 Hc41
Voutiáni GR 194 Bc89
Voutsarás GR 182 Ac80
Voútsis GR 194 Bb87
Vouvant F 28 Fb44
Vouvray F 29 Ga41
Vouzailles F 28 Fd44
Vouzela P 44 Ba62
Vouzeron F 29 Gd42
Voúzi GR 189 Bd82
Vouziers F 24 Ja35
Vouzon F 29 Gd41
Vovčans'k UA 203 Fa14
Voves F 29 Gc39
Voxna S 87 Fd37
Voxtorp S 103 Fb51
Voxtorp S 111 Ga53
Vöyri FIN 81 Ja30
Vozneseni MD 173 Fc59
Voznesens'k UA 204 Ed16
Voznesenskoe RUS 203 Fb10
Voznice CZ 136 Fb45
Vrå DK 100 Dc20
Vrå S 102 Fa52
Vrabča BG 179 Cb70
Vrabevo BG 180 Db70
Vráble SK 145 Hb50
Vraca BG 179 Cd69
Vračeš BG 179 Cd71
Vračev Gaj SRB 174 Bc63
Vračević SRB 153 Jc63
Vracov CZ 137 Gd48
Vrådal N 93 Da43
Vradijivka UA 204 Ec16
Vrads DK 108 Db24
Vragočanica SRB 153 Jb63
Vrahneika GR 188 Ba85
Vráhos GR 188 Ac82
Vråliosen N 93 Da43
Vrana HR 151 Fb62
Vrana HR 157 Ga65
Vranče MK 183 Bb75
Vrâncioaia RO 176 Ec61
Vranduk BIH 152 Hb63
Vranes MD 173 Fa56
Vrangiana GR 188 Ba82
Vrångö S 102 Eb49
Vrani RO 174 Bd63
Vranić SRB 153 Jc62
Vrani Kon BG 180 Eb71
Vranilovci BG 180 Dc71
Vranino BG 181 Fb69
Vranja HR 151 Fa60
Vranjak BG 179 Cd69
Vranje SRB 178 Bd71
Vranjska Banja SRB 178 Bd71
Vranov nad Dyjí CZ 136 Ga48
Vranov nad Topľou SK 139 Ka48
Vranovo SRB 174 Bc64
Vranovská ves CZ 136 Ga48
Vransko SLO 151 Fc57
Vrap AL 182 Ab75
Vrapce Polje MNE 159 Jb67
Vrapčište MK 178 Ba73
Vrassná GR 184 Cc78
Vrástama GR 184 Cc79
Vrata SLO 144 Fd56
Vratarnica SRB 179 Ca67
Vratěnín CZ 136 Ga48
Vratimov CZ 137 Hb45
Vratlo MNE 159 Ja68
Vrátna SK 138 Hc47
Vratnica MK 178 Bb72
Vravróna GR 195 Cc87
Vrba MNE 159 Ja66
Vrbanj HR 158 Gc67
Vrbanja BIH 152 Gd62
Vrbanja HR 153 Hd61
Vrbanjci BIH 152 Ha62
Vrbanje MNE 159 Hc69
Vrbas SRB 153 Ja59
Vrbaška BIH 152 Gd61
Vrbeštica KSV 178 Ba72
Vrbnica KSV 178 Ad72
Vrbnik HR 151 Fc61
Vrbno pod Pradědem CZ 137 Gd44
Vrboska HR 158 Gc67
Vrbov SK 138 Jb47
Vrbovce SK 137 Gd48
Vrbové SK 137 Ha49
Vrbovec HR 152 Gb58
Vrbovski SRB 153 Jc61
Vrbovsko HR 151 Fd60
Vrchlabí CZ 136 Fd43
Vrčice SLO 151 Fd59
Vrcin SRB 174 Bb64
Vrdy CZ 136 Fd45
Vrebac HR 151 Fd63
Vrécourt F 31 Jc38
Vreden D 125 Bd37
Vrees D 117 Cb34
Vrela KSV 178 Ad70
Vrela SRB 159 Jc68
Vrelo SRB 178 Bd68
Vremski Britof SLO 151 Fa59
Vrena S 95 Gb45
Vrensted DK 100 Dc20
Vreoci SRB 153 Jc62
Vresovo BG 181 Ed71
Vresse-s.-Semois B 132 Ad44
Vrésthena GR 194 Bc88
Vreta FIN 97 Jc40
Vreta kloster S 103 Fd46
Vreten S 95 Gb39
Vretstorp S 95 Fc44
Vrgada HR 157 Fd65
Vrgorac HR 158 Ha67
Vrhnika SLO 151 Fb58
Vrhopolje BIH 152 Gc62
Vrhovine HR 151 Fd62
Vrhovo SLO 151 Fd58
Vries NL 117 Bd33
Vriezenveen NL 117 Bd36
Vrigne-au-Bois F 24 Ja33
Vrigstad S 103 Fb50
Vrin CH 142 Cc55
Vrinners DK 109 Dd24
Vrisári GR 188 Bb86
Vríses GR 200 Cc95
Vríssa GR 191 Ea84
Vrissiá GR 189 Bc82
Vrissohóri GR 182 Ad79
Vrissoúla GR 188 Ad81
Vrizy F 24 Ja34
Vrlika HR 158 Gb65
Vrnjačka Banja SRB 178 Bb67
Vrnograč BIH 151 Ga61
Vrodoú GR 183 Bd79
Vron F 23 Gc32
Vrondádos GR 191 Dd86
Vronderó GR 182 Ba77
Vrontamás GR 194 Bc89
Vroomshoop NL 117 Bd35
Vrossina GR 182 Ac80
Vroutek CZ 135 Ed44
Vrpolje HR 153 Hc60
Vrpolje HR 158 Gb66
Vršac SRB 174 Bc63
Vršani BIH 153 Hd62
Vrsar HR 150 Ed61
Vrsi HR 157 Fd64
Vrtoče BIH 152 Gb62
Vruda RUS 99 Ma41
Vrujci SRB 153 Jc63
Vrulja MNE 159 Ja67
Vrulje HR 157 Fd65
Vrútky SK 138 Hc47
Vrutok MK 178 Ba73
Všeruby CZ 135 Ec47
Všestary CZ 136 Ga44
Všetaty CZ 136 Fc44
Vsetín CZ 137 Ha47
Vsevoložsk RUS 202 Eb08
Vtroja RUS 99 Lc43
Vuarrens CH 141 Bb55
Vučedo HR 153 Hd60
Vučić SRB 174 Bb65
Vućijak BIH 152 Ha62
Vučinice SRB 178 Ba69
Vučinići HR 151 Fc60
Vučitrn KSV 178 Bb70
Vučja Lokva KSV 178 Ba69
Vučja Luka BIH 159 Hc65
Vučje SRB 178 Bd70
Vučkovica SRB 178 Ad67
Vught NL 124 Ba38
Vuillafons F 31 Jd42
Vukan BG 179 Ca71
Vukosanka FIN 83 Lb25
Vukovar HR 153 Hd60
Vukovina HR 152 Gb59
Vuku N 78 Ec29
Vulaines-sur-Seine F 29 Ha38
Vulcan RO 175 Cd62
Vulcan RO 176 Dd62
Vulcana-Băi RO 176 Dd64
Vulcăneşti MD 177 Fc62
Vulcăneşti UA 204 Ec18
Vulcano Piano I 167 Fc83
Vulcano Porto I 167 Fc83
Vulpeni RO 175 Da65
Vultureni RO 171 Da57
Vultureni RO 176 Ed60
Vultureşti RO 172 Ec56
Vultureşti RO 173 Fa58
Vultureşti RO 175 Db65
Vulturu RO 177 Fa62
Vulturu RO 177 Fb60
Vuobmaved FIN 64 Jc10
Vuoggatjålme S 71 Ga19
Vuohijärvi FIN 69 Ka13
Vuohijärvi FIN 90 Kd36
Vuohiniemi FIN 90 Ka37
Vuohtomäki FIN 82 Kb28
Vuojalahti FIN 90 Kd33
Vuojärvi FIN 69 Ka17
Vuokatti FIN 82 La26
Vuoksenniska FIN 91 Lc35
Vuolenkoski FIN 90 Kd36
Vuolijoki FIN 82 Kc26
Vuolinko FIN 90 La34
Vuolle FIN 81 Jc28
Vuolledalen N 63 Ja09
Vuollerim S 73 Hb20
Vuonamo FIN 82 Kc29
Vuonisjärvi FIN 83 Ld28
Vuonislahti FIN 83 Ld28
Vuono S 74 Jc21
Vuonos FIN 83 Lc30
Vuontee FIN 90 Kc32
Vuontisjärvi FIN 68 Jb13
Vuorenkylä FIN 90 Kc34
Vuorenmaa FIN 89 Jb37
Vuorenmaa FIN 90 La33
Vuoreslahti FIN 82 Kd26
Vuorilahti FIN 82 Kb30
Vuorimäki FIN 89 Jd32
Vuoriniemi FIN 91 Ld34
Vuosaari FIN 98 Kb39
Vuoskojaure sameviste S 67 Ha13
Vuostimo FIN 69 Kb17
Vuostimojärvi FIN 69 Kb17
Vuotinainen FIN 90 Ka38
Vuotjärvi FIN 82 La29
Vuotner S 72 Ha22
Vuotsa FIN 83 Ma29
Vuotso FIN 69 Ka13
Vuottas S 73 Hd20
Vuottolahti FIN 82 Kc26
Vuotunki FIN 75 La19
Vuovdakuoihka FIN 64 Jc09
Vurnary RUS 203 Fc09
Vurpăr RO 175 Db61
Vust DK 100 Db20
Vutcani RO 177 Fb60
Vybor RUS 107 Mb48
Vybor RUS 202 Ea10
Vyborg RUS 202 Ea08
Výčapy CZ 136 Ga47
Výčapy Opatovce SK 145 Hb50
Východná SK 138 Ja47
Vydeniai LT 114 Kd59
Vydmantai LT 113 Jb54
Vygoniči RUS 202 Ed12
Vygréliai LT 114 Ka59
Vyksa RUS 203 Fb10
Vy-lès-Lure F 31 Ka40
Vylkove UA 204 Ec18
Vynnyky UA 204 Dd15
Vypolzovo RUS 202 Ec09
Vyra RUS 99 Mb41
Vyrica RUS 202 Eb08
Vyšgorodok RUS 107 Ld49
Vyshorod UA 202 Ec14
Vyskatka RUS 99 Ld42
Vyškov CZ 137 Gc47
Vyskytná CZ 136 Fd46
Vyšné Nemecké SK 139 Kb48
Vyšné Ružbachy SK 138 Jb46
Vyšnij Voloček RUS 202 Ec09
Vysockoe RUS 107 Mb49
Vysoká SK 137 Hb46
Vysoké Mýto CZ 137 Gb45
Vysokij Most RUS 107 Ld47
Vysokoe RUS 113 Jc58
Vysokoje RUS 113 Jd58
Vysokovsk RUS 202 Ed10
Vysoký Chlumec CZ 136 Fb46
Vyšší Brod CZ 136 Fb49
Vystavka RUS 107 Mb46
Vyžiai LT 113 Jc56
Vyžnycja UA 204 Ea16
Vyžuonos LT 114 La55
Vzmor'e RUS 113 Hd59

W

Waabs D 108 Dc29
Waake D 126 Db39
Waakirchen D 143 Ea52
Waal D 142 Dc51
Waalre NL 124 Ba39
Waalwijk NL 124 Ba38
Waase D 119 Ed30
Wabcz PL 121 Hb33
Waben F 23 Gc32
Wabern D 126 Da40
Wabienice PL 129 Gd41
Wąbrzeźno PL 121 Hb33
Wach PL 122 Jc33
Wachenheim D 133 Cb46
Wachenroth D 134 Dc45
Wąchock PL 130 Jc41
Wachow D 127 Ec36
Wachów PL 129 Hb42
Wachtberg D 125 Bd42
Wachtendonk D 125 Bc39
Wächtersbach D 134 Cd43
Wacken D 118 Da31
Wackersdorf D 135 Eb47
Wackersleben D 127 Dd37
Waddesdon GB 20 Fb27
Waddewarden D 117 Cc32
Waddington GB 17 Fc22
Waddingtown IRL 13 Cc25
Waddinxveen NL 116 Ad36
Wadebridge GB 18 Db31
Wädenswil CH 141 Cb53
Wadern D 133 Bc45
Wadersloh D 126 Cc38
Wadhurst GB 20 Fd29
Wadlew PL 130 Hd39
Wadowice PL 138 Hd45
Waffenbrunn D 135 Ec47
Wagenfeld D 126 Cd36
Wageningen NL 125 Bb37
Waghäusel D 134 Cc47
Waging am See D 143 Ec51
Wagna A 144 Fd55
Wagrain A 143 Ed53
Wągrowiec PL 121 Gc35
Wahlstedt D 118 Dc31
Wahrenberg D 119 Ea35
Wahrenholz D 126 Dc36
Waiblingen D 134 Cd48
Waibstadt D 134 Cc46
Waidhaus D 135 Eb46
Waidhofen an der Thaya A 136 Fd49
Waidhofen an der Ybbs A 144 Fc51
Waidring A 143 Eb53
Waimes B 125 Bb42
Wainfleet All Saints GB 17 Fd23
Wainhouse Corner GB 18 Dc30
Waischenfeld D 135 Dd45
Waizenkirchen A 144 Fa50
Wakefield GB 16 Fa21
Walbeck D 125 Bc39
Walbeck D 127 Dd37
Walberswick GB 21 Gc25
Wałbrzych PL 129 Gb42
Walchen A 143 Dd54
Walchum D 117 Ca34
Walchwil CH 141 Cb54
Wałcz PL 121 Gb34
Wald A 143 Ed54
Wald A 144 Fc53
Wald CH 142 Cc53
Wald D 142 Cd51
Waldaschaff D 134 Cd44
Waldbach A 144 Ga53
Waldböckelheim D 133 Ca44
Waldbreitbach D 125 Ca42
Waldbröl D 125 Ca41
Waldbronn D 133 Cb48
Waldbrunn D 134 Cd46
Waldbrunn (Westerwald) D 125 Cb42
Waldburg D 142 Da52
Walddrehna D 128 Fa39
Wälde, Betzweiler- D 133 Cb49
Waldeck D 126 Cd40
Waldems D 133 Cb43
Waldenbuch D 134 Cd49
Waldenburg D 127 Ec42
Waldenburg D 134 Da47
Waldenstein-Twimberg A 144 Fc55
Walderbach D 135 Eb47
Walderton GB 20 Fb30
Waldfeucht D 125 Bb40
Waldfischbach-Burgalben D 133 Ca46
Waldhausen im Strudengau A 144 Fc50
Waldheim D 127 Ed41
Waldkappel D 126 Db40
Waldkirch CH 142 Cd53
Waldkirch D 141 Ca50
Waldkirchen D 127 Ed42
Waldkirchen D 136 Fa49
Waldkraiburg D 143 Eb50
Wald-Michelbach D 134 Cc46
Waldmohr D 133 Bd46
Waldmünchen D 135 Ec47
Waldneukirchen A 144 Fb51
Wałdowo PL 121 Gd33
Waldringfield GB 21 Gb26
Waldsassen D 135 Eb45
Waldsee D 133 Cb46
Waldsee, Bad D 142 Da51
Waldshut-Tiengen D 141 Ca52
Waldsieversdorf D 128 Fb36
Waldsolms D 134 Cc43
Waldstetten D 134 Cd46
Wałdyki PL 122 Hd32
Waldzell A 143 Ed51
Walenstadt CH 142 Cd54
Wales GB 16 Fa22
Walewice PL 130 Hd37
Walferdange L 133 Bb45
Walgherton GB 15 Ec23
Walichnowy PL 129 Hb40
Walim PL 129 Gb42
Walincourt-Selvigny F 24 Hb33
Walkenried D 126 Dc39
Walkerburn GB 11 Eb14
Walkern GB 20 Fc27
Walkowice PL 121 Gb34
Wallasey GB 15 Eb21
Walldorf D 126 Dc42
Walldorf D 134 Cc46
Walldürn D 134 Cd46
Wallendorf D 133 Bb44
Wallenfels D 135 Dd44
Wallenhorst D 117 Cb36
Wallerfing D 135 Ec49
Wallern A 144 Fa50
Wallern im Burgenland A 145 Gc52
Wallers F 24 Hb32
Wallersdorf D 135 Ec49
Wallerstein D 134 Db48
Wallgau D 143 Dd53
Wallhalben D 133 Ca46
Wallhausen D 127 Dd40
Wallhausen D 134 Db47
Wallingford GB 20 Fa28
Wallisellen CH 141 Cb53
Wallmoden D 126 Dc38
Walls GB 5 Ed05
Wallsee A 144 Fc51
Wallstawe D 119 Dd35
Walluf D 133 Cb44
Wallwitz D 127 Eb39
Walmerod D 125 Cb42
Wałowice PL 128 Fc38
Walpertskirchen D 143 Ea50
Walpole Saint Andrew GB 17 Fd24
Walsall GB 16 Ed24
Walschleben D 127 Dd41
Walsdorf D 134 Dc45
Walsrode D 118 Db35
Waltenhofen D 142 Db52
Waltersdorf D 128 Fc42
Waltershausen D 126 Dc41
Waltham GB 17 Fc21
Waltham-on-the-Wolds GB 16 Fb24
Walton East GB 14 Db26
Walton-on-the-Naze GB 21 Gb27
Waltrop D 125 Ca38
Waly F 24 Jb36
Wamba E 46 Cd60
Wambierzyce PL 137 Gb43
Wanborough GB 20 Ed28
Wanderup D 108 Da29
Wandlitz D 119 Ed35
Wanfried D 126 Db40
Wangen CH 141 Bd53
Wangenbourg F 25 Kb37
Wangen im Allgäu D 142 Da52
Wangerland D 117 Cc32
Wangerooge D 117 Cc31
Wängi CH 142 Cc52
Wanlockhead GB 10 Ea15
Wanna D 118 Cd32
Wansleben D 127 Ea40
Wanssum NL 125 Bc38
Wantage GB 20 Fa28
Wanzleben D 127 Ea38
Wapenveld NL 117 Bc35
Wąpielsk PL 122 Hc34
Wapienne PL 139 Jd45
Waplewo PL 122 Ja33
Wapnica PL 120 Fd34
Wapno PL 121 Gd35
Warberg D 127 Dd37
Warbomont B 124 Ba42
Warboys GB 20 Fc25
Warburg D 126 Cd39
Warchlino PL 120 Fc33
Warcino PL 121 Gb31
Warcq F 25 Jc35
Ward IRL 13 Cd21
Wardenburg D 117 Cc34
Wardin B 133 Bb43
Wardington GB 20 Fa26
Ware GB 20 Fc27
Waregem B 124 Aa40
Wareham GB 19 Ec31
Waremme B 124 Ba41
Waren D 119 Ec33
Warendorf D 125 Cb37
Warffum NL 117 Bd32
Warga NL 117 Bc33
Warin D 119 Ea32
Warka PL 130 Jc38
Warkworth GB 11 Fa15
Warley GB 20 Ed25
Warlingham GB 20 Fc29
Warlubie PL 121 Hb32
Warluis F 23 Gd35
Warmenhuizen NL 116 Ba34
Warmensteinach D 135 Ea44
Warminster GB 19 Ec29
Warmsen D 126 Cd36
Warmwell GB 19 Ec31
Warnemünde D 119 Eb31
Warnford GB 20 Fa30
Warngau D 143 Ea52
Warnice PL 120 Fc35
Warnikajmy PL 122 Jb30
Warnino PL 120 Ga31
Warnołęka PL 120 Fb32
Warnowo PL 120 Fb32
Warrenpoint IRL 9 Cd19
Warrington GB 15 Ec21
Warschau = Warszawa PL 130 Jb37
Warslow GB 16 Ed22
Warsop GB 16 Fa22
Warsow D 119 Ea33
Warstein D 126 Cc39
Warszawa PL 130 Jb37
Warszkowo PL 121 Gb30
Wart, Altensteig- D 134 Cc49
Warta PL 129 Hb39
Warta Bolesławiecka PL 128 Ga41
Wartenberg D 126 Da42
Wartenberg D 143 Ea50
Wartenburg D 127 Ec39
Warth A 142 Da53
Warthausen D 142 Da50
Warthe D 120 Fa31
Wartin D 120 Fb34
Wartkowice PL 130 Hc38
Wartmannsroth D 134 Da44
Warton GB 11 Ed15
Warwick GB 20 Fa25
Wasbek D 118 Db31
Wasbister GB 5 Ec02
Wasbüttel D 126 Dc36
Washaway GB 18 Db31
Washington GB 11 Fa17
Wasigny F 24 Hd34
Wasilków PL 123 Kb33
Waskemeer NL 117 Bd33
Waśniów PL 130 Jc41
Wąsosz PL 121 Gd35

Wólka Pełkińska – Zalegošč

Wólka Pełkińska PL 139 Kb43
Wolkenstein D 127 Ed42
Wolkenstein I 143 Dd56
Wolkersdorf A 145 Gb50
Wolkowe PL 122 Jc33
Wołkowyja PL 139 Kb46
Wolkramshausen D 126 Dc40
Wollbach D 134 Db43
Wollersheim D 125 Bc41
Wöllstadt D 134 Cc43
Wöllstein D 133 Cb45
Wolmirstedt D 127 Ea37
Wolnica PL 122 Ja31
Wolnzach D 135 Ea49
Wołomin PL 130 Jc36
Wołosate PL 139 Kc47
Wołów PL 129 Gb40
Wołowe Lasy PL 121 Gb34
Wolpertshausen D 134 Da47
Wolpertswende D 142 Cd51
Wolphaartsdijk NL 124 Ab38
Wolsingham GB 11 Ed17
Wolsztyn PL 128 Ga38
Woltersdorf D 119 Dd35
Wolvega NL 117 Bc34
Wolverhampton GB 16 Ed24
Wolverley GB 15 Ec25
Wombourn GB 15 Ec24
Wommels NL 116 Bb33
Wonersh GB 20 Fb29
Wonfurt D 134 Dc44
Woodborough GB 16 Fb23
Woodbridge GB 21 Gb26
Woodchurch GB 21 Ga29
Woodcuts GB 20 Ed30
Wood Dalling GB 17 Ga24
Woodenbridge IRL 13 Cd23
Woodford GB 20 Fd28
Woodford IRL 12 Bd22
Woodhall Spa GB 17 Fc22
Woodhouse GB 16 Fa22
Woodhouse Eaves GB 16 Fa24
Wooding-Dean GB 20 Fc30
Woodseaves GB 15 Ec23
Woodstock GB 20 Fa27
Woodton GB 21 Gb25
Wool GB 19 Ec31
Woolacombe GB 18 Dc29
Wooler GB 11 Ed14
Woolpit GB 21 Ga26
Woolverstone GB 21 Gb26
Woolwich GB 20 Fd28
Wooperton GB 11 Ed15
Wootton GB 20 Fb26
Wootton Bassett GB 20 Ed28
Wootton-Wawen GB 20 Ed25
Worb CH 141 Bd54
Worbis, Leinefelde- D 126 Dc40
Worcester GB 15 Ec26
Wördern A 145 Gb50
Wörgl A 143 Ea53
Woringen D 142 Db51
Wörishofen, Bad D 142 Db51
Workington GB 10 Ea17
Worksop GB 16 Fa22
Workum NL 116 Bb33
Wörlitz D 127 Ec38
Wormeldange L 25 Jd34
Wormeldange L 133 Bc45
Wormerveer NL 116 Ba35
Wormhout F 21 Gd30
Worms D 133 Cb45
Wörnharts A 136 Fc49
Wörnitz D 134 Db47
Worpswede D 118 Cd33
Wörrstadt D 133 Cb44
Wört D 134 Db47
Wörth A 143 Ec54
Wörth D 133 Cb47
Wörth D 135 Eb49
Wörth D 143 Ea50
Wörth am Main D 134 Cd45
Wörth an der Donau D 135 Eb48
Worthen GB 15 Eb24
Worthing GB 20 Fc30
Worton GB 20 Ed28
Woskowice Górne PL 129 Ha41
Woszczyce PL 138 Hc44
Woudenberg NL 116 Bb36
Woudsend NL 116 Bb34
Woumen B 21 Ha29
Woziwoda PL 121 Gd32
Woźławki PL 122 Jb30
Woźnawieś PL 123 Ka32
Woźnice PL 122 Jc31
Woźniki PL 130 Hc42
Wożuczyn PL 131 Kd42
Wragby GB 17 Fc22
Wrangle GB 17 Fd23
Wręczyca Wielka PL 130 Hc42
Wredenhagen D 119 Ec34
Wrelton GB 16 Fb19
Wremen D 118 Cd32
Wrentham GB 21 Gc25
Wrestedt D 118 Dc35
Wrexham GB 15 Eb23
Wriedel D 118 Dc34
Wriezen D 128 Fb36
Wrist D 118 Db31
Wróblew PL 129 Hb39
Wróblewo PL 129 Gb36
Wróblewo PL 130 Ja36
Wróbliniec PL 129 Gd39
Wroceń PL 123 Ka32
Wrocki PL 122 Hc34
Wrocław PL 129 Gc41
Wroczyny PL 130 Hc37
Wroniawy PL 128 Ga38
Wronki PL 129 Gb36
Wronki Wielkie PL 123 Jd30
Wronowy PL 129 Ha36
Wrotnów PL 131 Jd36
Wroughton GB 20 Ed28
Wroxham GB 17 Gb24
Wrząca PL 121 Gb34
Wrzesina PL 122 Ja32
Września PL 122 Hd34
Września PL 129 Gd37
Wrzoski PL 121 Ha35
Wrzosowo PL 120 Ga31
Wschowa PL 129 Gb39
Wulfen D 127 Eb38
Wülfershausen D 134 Db43
Wülfrath D 125 Bd39
Wulfsen D 118 Dc33
Wulften D 126 Db39
Wulkau D 119 Eb35
Wülknitz D 127 Ed40
Wulsbüttel D 118 Cd33
Wunderstetten A 144 Fc56
Wünnenberg D 126 Cd39
Wünschendorf D 127 Eb42
Wünsdorf D 127 Ed37
Wunsiedel D 135 Eb44
Wunstorf D 126 Da36
Wuppertal D 125 Ca40
Würenlos CH 141 Cb53
Wurmannsquick D 143 Ec50
Wurmsham D 143 Eb50
Würnsdorf A 144 Fd50
Würselen D 125 Bb41
Wurzach, Bad D 142 Da51
Würzburg D 134 Da45
Wurzen D 127 Ec40
Wüstenrot D 134 Cd47
Wusterhausen D 119 Ec35
Wusterhusen D 120 Fa31
Wustermark D 127 Ed36
Wusterwitz D 127 Eb37
Wüstimg D 117 Cc34
Wustrow D 119 Dd35
Wustrow D 119 Ec30
Wustrow D 119 Ed31
Wuustwezel B 124 Ad38
Wybcz PL 121 Hb34
Wyborów PL 130 Jc38
Wyczechy PL 121 Gc32
Wycześniak PL 130 Ja38
Wydmusy PL 122 Jc33
Wydrza PL 131 Jd42
Wye GB 21 Ga29
Wygoda PL 123 Jd34
Wygoda PL 129 Hb38
Wygoda PL 130 Hc42
Wygoda PL 131 Jd39
Wyk auf Föhr D 108 Cd29
Wykrot PL 122 Jc33
Wylatowo PL 129 Ha36
Wymondham GB 17 Ga24
Wyningen CH 141 Bd53
Wyryki-Połód PL 131 Kc38
Wyrzysk PL 121 Gc34
Wysall GB 16 Fa23
Wyśmierzyce PL 130 Jb39
Wysocice PL 138 Ja43
Wysoka PL 120 Fc35
Wysoka PL 121 Gc34
Wysoka PL 128 Ga40
Wysoka PL 138 Hd43
Wysoka PL 139 Jd44
Wysoka Cerkiew PL 129 Gb39
Wysoka Lelowska PL 130 Hd42
Wysokie PL 123 Ka31
Wysokie PL 131 Kb41
Wysokie Mazowieckie PL 123 Ka34
Wysoki Most PL 123 Kb30
Wysowa PL 138 Jc46
Występ PL 122 Jc32
Wystok PL 128 Fc37
Wyszanów PL 129 Ha40
Wyszki PL 123 Kb34
Wyszków PL 122 Jc35
Wyszków PL 131 Jd36
Wyszogród PL 130 Ja36
Wyszomierz Wielki PL 123 Jd34
Wyszonki-Kościelny PL 123 Ka35
Wyszyna PL 129 Hb37
Wyszyny PL 121 Gc35
Wyszyny PL 122 Ja34
Wythall GB 20 Ed25
Wyvis Lodge GB 4 Dd07
Wziąchowo PL 129 Gd39

X

Xàbia E 55 Fd70
Xanten D 125 Bc38
Xánthi GR 184 Db77
Xàtiva E 54 Fb69
Xendive E 36 Ba58
Xeraco E 54 Fc69
Xermaménil F 25 Jd37
Xert E 48 Fd64
Xerta E 48 Ga63
Xertigny F 31 Jd39
Xesta E 36 Ba56
Xestoso E 36 Bb54
Xhyrë AL 182 Ad75
Xibrrakë AL 182 Ac75
Xifianí GR 183 Bc76
Xilagani GR 184 Dc77
Xilókastro GR 189 Bd86
Xilokeratiá GR 195 Cc91
Xiloúpoli GR 183 Cb77
Xilxes E 54 Fc67
Xinó Neró GR 183 Bb77
Xinorlet E 55 Fa71
Xinóvrisi GR 189 Cb82
Xinzo de Limia E 36 Bb58
Xirokámbi GR 194 Bc89
Xirókambo GR 197 Eb90
Xirolímni GR 183 Bb78
Xirólofos GR 188 Ac81
Xironda E 44 Bb59
Xiropígado GR 188 Bb85
Xiropótamos GR 184 Cd76
Xitta I 166 Ea84
Xixona E 55 Fb71
Xove E 36 Bc53
Xuño E 36 Ac56
Xunqueira de Ambia E 36 Bb58
Xylofagou CY 206 Jd97
Xylóskalo GR 200 Cb95
Xylotymvou CY 206 Jc97

Y

Yabacı TR 192 Fb85
Yağca TR 199 Gc90
Yağcı TR 191 Ed83
Yağcıdereköy TR 197 Ed88
Yağcılar TR 186 Ga78
Yağcılar TR 191 Eb86
Yağcılar TR 192 Fa81
Yağcılar TR 192 Fb83
Yağdiran TR 191 Ed82
Yağhane TR 197 Ec89
Yağılar TR 198 Fc88
Yağmurlar TR 192 Ga84
Yağmurlu TR 191 Ed83
Yahşieli TR 191 Ea81
Yaka TR 199 Ha88
Yakaafşar TR 199 Ha88
Yakacık TR 198 Fd92
Yakaköy TR 191 Ec85
Yakaköy TR 197 Ec91
Yakaköy TR 197 Ed90
Yakaören TR 199 Gc88
Yakasinek TR 193 Ha86
Yakuplar TR 192 Fd84
Yalakdere TR 186 Ga79
Yalding GB 20 Fd29
Yalıçiftlik TR 197 Ed90
Yalıkavak TR 197 Ec90
Yalıköy TR 186 Fb76
Yalımkaya TR 193 Ha81
Yalnız TR 199 Gb92
Yalnızdam TR 191 Ed83
Yalova TR 185 Ea80
Yalova TR 186 Fd79
Yalvaç TR 193 Ha86
Yamaç TR 197 Ec88
Yamadı TR 198 Ga90
Yamanlar TR 191 Ec85
Yancıklar TR 185 Ed76
Yanguas E 47 Eb59
Yanıkağıl TR 186 Fa77
Yaniköy TR 193 Gd83
Yanişehir TR 192 Fc85
Yanuslar TR 191 Ec83
Yapıldak TR 185 Eb80
Yapıldak TR 193 Gc84
Yarbasan TR 192 Fc84
Yarbasan TR 193 Gc83
Yarbaşı TR 199 Gc91
Yarcombe GB 19 Eb30
Yarıkkaya TR 193 Gd86
Yarıkkaya TR 193 Ha84
Yarımca TR 193 Gc81
Yariş TR 192 Fd83
Yarışlı TR 193 Gc86
Yarpuz TR 199 Hb90
Yassıbel TR 193 Ha87
Yassıgeçit TR 187 Gc78
Yassıören TR 186 Fc77
Yassıören TR 192 Fc83
Yassıören TR 193 Gc87
Yaşyer TR 191 Ec82
Yatağan TR 197 Fa89
Yátova E 54 Fa68
Yattendon GB 20 Fa28
Yavaşça TR 185 Ed77
Yavaşlar TR 193 Gb86
Yavaşlı TR 193 Hb85
Yaveröreń TR 193 Ha83
Yaxham GB 17 Ga24
Yayaağaç TR 185 Ec78
Yayakent TR 191 Ec84
Yayakent TR 191 Ed84
Yayakırıldık TR 192 Fa84
Yayalar TR 192 Ga86
Yayıklı TR 193 Gd82
Yaykın TR 192 Fa84
Yayla TR 191 Ed82
Yaylaalan TR 199 Ha91
Yaylabaşı TR 192 Fb82
Yaylabayır TR 192 Fa81
Yaylaçayırı TR 192 Fb81
Yaylacık TR 191 Ea82
Yaylaköy TR 185 Ea78
Yaylaköy TR 191 Ea85
Yaylaköy TR 192 Ga84
Yaylaköy TR 198 Ga88
Yaylaköy TR 199 Gb90
Yaylalı TR 186 Ga77
Yaylapınar TR 198 Fd90
Yaylasöğüt TR 198 Fb90
Yaylatepe TR 187 Hb78
Yazıbaşı TR 192 Fd82
Yazıca TR 187 Hb80
Yazıcık TR 187 Hb78
Yazıdere TR 193 Gd83
Yazıkent TR 198 Fb88
Yazıköy TR 197 Ec91
Yazıköy TR 199 Gb89
Yazılıkaya TR 193 Gc84
Yazıpınar TR 199 Gc89
Yazır TR 198 Ga89
Yazır TR 199 Gb91
Yazır TR 199 Gb92
Yazırköy TR 198 Fb88
Yazıtepe TR 193 Gb85
Yazla TR 193 Hb86
Yazlık TR 186 Fc77
Ybbs an der Donau A 144 Fc51
Ybbsitz A 144 Fc51
Ychoux F 39 Fa52
Ydby DK 100 Cd22
Yderby DK 109 Dd28
Yeadon GB 16 Ed20
Yealmpton GB 19 Dd31
Yebra E 46 Dd65
Yebra de Basa E 40 Fc58
Yéchar E 55 Ed72
Yecla E 55 Fa70
Yediburun TR 198 Fd93
Yedisu TR 205 Ga20
Yekli TR 192 Fd84
Yeleğen TR 192 Fc86
Yeles E 46 Db65
Yelken TR 198 Fd92
Yelland GB 19 Dd29
Yelten TR 199 Gb90
Yelvertoft GB 20 Fa25
Yelverton GB 19 Dd31
Yemişendere TR 198 Fb90
Yenibağarası TR 191 Eb85
Yenibosna TR 186 Fc78
Yeniçam TR 192 Fc87
Yenice TR 185 Ea78
Yenice TR 185 Ec78
Yenice TR 186 Fa75
Yenice TR 186 Fa80
Yenice TR 191 Ec81
Yenice TR 192 Fa82
Yenice TR 192 Fa84
Yenice TR 192 Fb81
Yenice TR 192 Fd83
Yenice TR 192 Ga85
Yenice TR 193 Gc84
Yenice TR 193 Gd81
Yenice TR 198 Fb88
Yenicekent TR 192 Fc87
Yeniceköy TR 186 Fa77
Yeniceşehler TR 187 Gd79
Yeniçiftlik TR 185 Ec80
Yeniçiftlik TR 186 Fa77
Yeni Çiftlik TR 191 Ed87
Yenidibek TR 185 Eb78
Yenidoğan TR 197 Ec88
Yenidoğan TR 199 Hb88
Yenierenköy = Aigialousa CY 206 Jd95
Yenifoça TR 191 Eb85
Yenigürle TR 186 Fd80
Yenikarabağ TR 193 Ha85
Yeni Karpuzlu TR 185 Ea78
Yenikavak TR 192 Fa81
Yenikent TR 193 Gd82
Yenikızılelma TR 192 Fc81
Yeniköy TR 185 Eb76
Yeniköy TR 185 Ec79
Yeniköy TR 185 Ed78
Yeniköy TR 186 Fb80
Yeniköy TR 186 Fc77
Yeniköy TR 186 Fd79
Yeniköy TR 187 Gb79
Yeniköy TR 187 Gc78
Yeniköy TR 191 Ea81
Yeniköy TR 191 Ec84
Yeniköy TR 191 Ec86
Yeniköy TR 191 Ec86
Yeniköy TR 191 Ec87
Yeniköy TR 191 Ec87
Yeniköy TR 191 Ed85
Yeniköy TR 191 Ed85
Yeniköy TR 192 Fa81
Yeniköy TR 192 Fa82
Yeniköy TR 192 Fa85
Yeniköy TR 192 Fa85
Yeniköy TR 192 Fd82
Yeniköy TR 192 Fd85
Yeniköy TR 193 Gb81
Yeniköy TR 193 Ha84
Yeniköy TR 193 Ha87
Yeniköy TR 198 Ga93
Yenimahalle TR 185 Ec75
Yenimahalle TR 187 Gc77
Yenimuhacir TR 185 Eb78
Yenioba TR 191 Ed87
Yenipazar TR 187 Gc80
Yenipazar TR 197 Fa88
Yenişakran TR 191 Ec84
Yenişarbademli TR 199 Ha88
Yenişehir TR 186 Ga80
Yenişehir TR 192 Fa87
Yeniyurt TR 193 Ha82
Yenizıraatlı TR 186 Fa80
Yenne F 35 Jd47
Yeovil GB 19 Eb30
Yepes E 52 Dc66
Yera E 38 Dc55
Yerkesik TR 197 Fa90
Yerlisu TR 185 Eb78
Yeroluk TR 192 Fa81
Yerseke NL 124 Ac38
Yerville F 23 Ga34
Yesa E 39 Fa57
Yeşilbağ TR 199 Ha89
Yeşilbağcılar TR 197 Fa89
Yesilçay = Ağva TR 187 Gb77
Yeşilce TR 186 Fa75
Yeşilçukurca TR 192 Ga82
Yeşildağ TR 199 Gb89
Yeşildağ TR 199 Ha89
Yeşildon TR 193 Gd82
Yeşilhisar TR 191 Ed83
Yeşilhüyük TR 193 Gb87
Yeşilkaraman TR 199 Gd90
Yeşilkavak TR 192 Fc86
Yeşilköy TR 191 Ed85
Yeşilköy TR 192 Fc84
Yeşilköy TR 192 Ga82
Yeşilköy TR 193 Gd87
Yeşilköy TR 197 Ec89
Yeşilköy TR 198 Fc88
Yeşilköy TR 198 Fd93
Yeşilköy TR 198 Ga90
Yeşiller TR 192 Fc81
Yeşilova TR 185 Ec76
Yeşilova TR 192 Fa81
Yeşilova TR 192 Fd87
Yeşilova TR 198 Ga89
Yeşiltepe TR 193 Gc83
Yeşilvadi TR 186 Fd77
Yeşilyayla TR 199 Gb90
Yeşilyurt TR 185 Ed77
Yeşilyurt TR 191 Eb82
Yeşilyurt TR 192 Fc86
Yeşilyurt TR 192 Ga85
Yeşilyurt TR 197 Fa90
Yeşilyuva TR 198 Fd89
Yesnaby GB 5 Eb03
Yeste E 53 Eb71
Yetre Brenna N 64 Jc06
Yetre Kjæs N 64 Jc05
Yetterlännäs S 80 Gc31
Yetts o'Muckhart GB 7 Ea12
Yg S 87 Ga35
Ygos-Saint-Saturnin F 39 Fb53
Ygrande F 30 Hb44
Yığılca TR 187 Ha78
Yiğitler TR 185 Ed79
Yiğitler TR 191 Eb81
Yliрää FIN 81 Jd26
Yıldızeli TR 205 Fc20
Yıldızköy TR 192 Fb81
Yıldızören TR 193 Ha83
Yılmazlı TR 198 Ga91
Yırcaköy TR 191 Ed83
Yitäkylä FIN 97 Jd39
Ykspihlaja FIN 81 Jb28
Ylakiai LT 113 Jc53
Ylä-Kintaus FIN 90 Kb32
Ylä-Kolkki FIN 89 Jd33
Ylä-Kuona FIN 91 Lc32
Ylä-Luosta FIN 83 Lb28
Ylämaa FIN 91 Lb37
Ylämylly FIN 83 Lc30
Yläne FIN 89 Jb38
Ylä-Valtimo FIN 83 Lb27
Ylemmäinen FIN 90 Kc35
Ylhäisi FIN 97 Jc39
Ylihärmä FIN 81 Jb30
Yli-Ii FIN 74 Ka22
Ylijärvi FIN 91 Lb37
Ylijoki FIN 89 Jc32
Yli-Kannus FIN 81 Jc28
Yli-Kärppä FIN 74 Ka21
Ylikiiminki FIN 74 Kb23
Yli-Körkkö FIN 74 Ka19
Ylikulma FIN 97 Jd40
Yli-Kurki FIN 75 Kd22
Ylikylä FIN 69 Kb17
Ylikylä FIN 81 Jd29
Ylikylä FIN 81 Jc31
Ylikylä FIN 81 Jb30
Ylikylä FIN 83 Lb27
Ylikylä FIN 89 Jb32
Ylikylä FIN 89 Ja33
Yli-Kyrö FIN 68 Jb14
Yli-Lesti FIN 82 Ka29
Yli-Livo FIN 75 Kc21
Ylimarkku FIN 89 Hd32
Yli-Muonio FIN 68 Ja14
Yli-Nampa FIN 74 Ka18
Yli-Olhava FIN 74 Ka22
Ylipää FIN 74 Jd24
Ylipää FIN 74 Jd24
Ylipää FIN 74 Ka24
Ylipää FIN 81 Jd25
Ylipää FIN 81 Jc30
Ylipää FIN 81 Jd25
Ylipää FIN 82 Kb25
Ylipää FIN 82 Ka28
Yli-Paakkola FIN 74 Jc20
Yli-Siurua FIN 74 Kb21
Yliskulma FIN 97 Jc39
Yliskylä FIN 89 Jc34
Yliskylä FIN 90 Ka35
Ylistaro FIN 81 Jb31
Yli-Tannila FIN 74 Ka22
Ylitornio FIN 73 Jb20
Yli-Tynkä FIN 81 Jc27
Yli-Utos FIN 75 Kc24
Yli-Valli FIN 89 Jb33
Ylivesi FIN 90 La34
Ylivieska FIN 81 Jd27
Yli-Vuotto FIN 74 Kb23
Yläsjärvi FIN 68 Jb16
Ylläsjokisuu FIN 68 Jb16
Yllasmaja FIN 68 Jb15
Yllestad S 102 Fa48
Ylöjärvi FIN 89 Jd35
Ylönkylä FIN 97 Jc40
Ylvingen N 70 Ed22
Ymonville F 29 Gc39
Yngsjö S 111 Fb55
Ynyslas GB 15 Dd24
Yoğunpelit TR 187 Hb78
Yoğuntaş TR 185 Ec75
Yolağazı TR 185 Ea79
Yolağzı TR 186 Fb80
Yolçatı TR 186 Fc80
Yolören TR 186 Ga80
Yolüstü TR 192 Fa87
Yolüstü TR 198 Fb89
Yorazlar TR 193 Hb86
Yörgüç TR 185 Ec78
York GB 16 Fb20
Yortanlı TR 191 Ec83
Youghal IRL 13 Ca26
Youlgreave GB 16 Ed22
Yoxford GB 21 Gb25
Ypäjä FIN 89 Jc38
Ypäjankyla FIN 89 Jc38
Yppäri FIN 81 Jc26
Ypsonas CY 206 Ja98
Ypyä FIN 81 Jd27
Ypykänvaara FIN 75 La22
Yrittäperä FIN 75 Kd23
Yrkje N 92 Ca42
Yrouerre F 30 Hc40
Yrttivaara S 73 Hc18
Ysane S 111 Fc54
Yset N 86 Ea32
Ysjö S 79 Gb29
Ysselsteyn NL 125 Bb39
Yssingeaux F 34 Hd49
Ystad S 110 Fa57
Ystebrød N 92 Ca45
Ystrad-Aeron GB 15 Dd25
Ystradfellte GB 19 Ea27
Ystradowen GB 19 Ea28
Yterturingen S 87 Fc33
Ytre Andersdal N 62 Gd10
Ytre Arna N 84 Ca39
Ytre Dåsvatn N 92 Cd45
Ytre Enebakk N 93 Ea42
Ytre Kårvik N 62 Gc09
Ytre Leirpollen N 64 Jc06
Ytre Ølydna N 92 Cc46
Ytre Oppedal N 84 Ca37
Ytre Ramse N 93 Da45
Ytre Sandvik N 64 Jb06
Ytre Snillfjord N 77 Dd30
Ytre Søndeled N 93 Db45
Ytre Veines N 64 Jb06
Ytterån S 79 Fb30
Ytteräng S 78 Fa29
Ytterås N 78 Eb30
Ytteråträsk S 80 Hb27
Ytterberg S 87 Fc34
Ytterboda S 80 Hc28
Ytterboda S 95 Fc39
Ytterbrätö FIN 81 Jb28
Ytter-Busjö S 80 Ha26
Ytterby S 102 Eb48
Yttergran S 96 Gc42
Ytterhogdal S 87 Fc34
Ytterjärna S 96 Gc44
Ytterjeppo FIN 81 Jb29
Yttermalung S 95 Fb39
Ytterrissjö S 80 Gc28
Yttersby S 96 Ha40
Ytterselö S 96 Gc43
Yttersjön S 80 Ha26
Yttersta S 73 Hc23
Ytterstad N 66 Fd14
Yttertällmo S 80 Gc29
Yttertavle S 80 Hc28
Ytter-Torga N 70 Ed23
Yttervik S 71 Fd23
Yttervik S 80 Hc25
Yttilä FIN 89 Jb37
Yttre Lansjärv S 73 Hd19
Yücebağ TR 205 Ga20
Yukarıdudullu TR 186 Fd78
Yukarıalıçomak TR 193 Hb84
Yukarıballı TR 192 Fc81
Yukarıbey TR 191 Ec83
Yukarıçamozü TR 205 Fd20
Yukarıdereköy TR 198 Fd91
Yukarıdinek TR 193 Ha87
Yukarıdolaylar TR 192 Fc83
Yukarı Dumanlı TR 185 Ec80
Yukarıfındıklı TR 187 Gc78
Yukarıgökdere TR 199 Gd88
Yukarıgüllüce TR 192 Fc85
Yukarıgüney TR 187 Ha79
Yukarıığdeağacı TR 193 Ha82
Yukarıkadıköy TR 185 Ed75
Yukarıkalabak TR 193 Gc82
Yukarıkaraçay TR 198 Fd88
Yukarıkaraman TR 199 Gc91
Yukarıkılıçlı TR 185 Ed78
Yukarıkızılca TR 191 Ed86
Yukarı Kocayatak TR 199 Gd91
Yukarımusalar TR 192 Fb82
Yukarıotluk TR 193 Gb86
Yukarıpiribeyli TR 193 Hb84
Yukarısapçı TR 191 Eb81
Yukarısoku TR 187 Hb78
Yumaklar TR 199 Gd90
Yumaklı TR 193 Gc83
Yumaklı TR 198 Fb89
Yumrutaı TR 198 Fd89
Yunak TR 193 Hb85
Yuncos E 46 Db65
Yunquera E 60 Cc76
Yunquera de Henares E 46 Dd63
Yunuseli TR 186 Fd80
Yunusemre TR 193 Ha82
Yunuslar TR 192 Ga84
Yunuslar TR 199 Hb88
Yüreğil TR 192 Fb84
Yüreğil TR 198 Fd89
Yüreğil TR 198 Ga88
Yüreklı TR 191 Ec82
Yürücekler TR 192 Fc81
Yürük TR 185 Ec78
Yürükkaracaören TR 193 Gd85
Yürükler TR 185 Ed77
Yürükler TR 186 Ga79
Yürükmezarı TR 193 Gb85
Yürüköğlu TR 198 Fc90
Yusufca TR 197 Ed89
Yusufça TR 198 Ga90
Yusufeli TR 205 Ga19
Yuva TR 185 Ec78
Yuva TR 187 Hb78
Yuva TR 198 Ga91
Yuvacık TR 187 Gb79
Yuvacık TR 197 Fa91
Yuvalı TR 186 Fa76
Yuvalı TR 199 Gd88
Yuvalıdere TR 187 Gc78
Yüylük TR 193 Gb84
Yverdon CH 141 Bb54
Yvetot F 23 Ga34
Yvignac F 26 Ec38
Yvoire F 31 Ka44
Yvré-le-Pôlin F 28 Fd40
Yxnerum S 103 Ga47
Yxpila FIN 81 Jb28
Yxsjö S 80 Gc27
Yxskaftkälen S 79 Fd29
Yzeron F 34 Ja47

Z

Zaamslag NL 124 Ab39
Zaanstad NL 116 Ba35
Zabala RO 176 Eb61
Žabalj SRB 153 Jb60
Zabalocce BY 202 Ec13
Zabar H 146 Jb50
Zabărdo BG 184 Db74
Žabari SRB 174 Bc65
Zabartowo PL 121 Gd34
Zabeltitz D 127 Ed40
Zaberfeld D 134 Cc47
Żabia Wola PL 130 Jb37
Zabica BIH 159 Hc68
Zabierzów PL 138 Ja44
Żabin PL 122 Jc34
Żabin PL 129 Gb39
Żabinka BY 202 Dd14
Żabiny PL 122 Hd33
Ząbki PL 130 Jc36
Ząbkowice Śląskie PL 137 Gc43
Zablaće BIH 152 Gc63
Záblatí CZ 136 Fa48
Zāblava LV 107 Lc48
Žabljak MNE 159 Ja67
Zabłocie PL 128 Fc39
Zabłocie PL 139 Kb46
Zabłudów PL 123 Kb34
Żabno PL 129 Gc37
Żabno PL 131 Kb41
Żabno PL 138 Jc44
Zabok HR 151 Ga58
Zabolotje LV 107 Lc51
Zabór PL 128 Ga38
Zaboreni MD 173 Fd56
Zaborov'e RUS 99 Lc44
Zaborovka RUS 99 Ld45
Zaborów PL 129 Gb40
Zaborowice PL 129 Gb39
Zaborowo PL 122 Ja33
Żabów PL 120 Fc34
Zăbrani RO 174 Bd60
Zabrđe SRB 159 Ja66
Zábřeh CZ 137 Gc45
Zabrežje SRB 153 Jc62
Zăbriceni MD 173 Fa54
Zabrodzie PL 122 Jb31
Zabrodzie PL 130 Jc36
Zabrodzie PL 139 Kb46
Zabrost Wielki PL 122 Jc30
Ząbrowo PL 120 Fd32
Zabrze PL 138 Hc43
Zabrzeź PL 138 Jb46
Zaburalan TR 198 Fd91
Zabzuni AL 182 Ad75
Zacharzyn PL 121 Gc34
Zachenberg D 135 Ec48
Zacláu RO 177 Fb63
Žaclér CZ 128 Ga42
Zadar HR 157 Fd64
Zădăreni RO 170 Bd59
Zaddžje RUS 107 Mb49
Žadeikiai LT 113 Jc55
Žadeikiai LT 113 Jc55
Žadeikiai LT 114 Kd53
Zadonsk RUS 203 Fb12
Zadruga BG 180 Eb68
Zadworzany PL 123 Kc32
Zadzim PL 130 Hc39
Zafarraya E 60 Da75
Zafferana Etnea I 167 Fd85
Zafirovo BG 181 Ec68
Zafra E 51 Bd70
Zafra de Záncara E 53 Ea66
Zafrilla E 47 Ed65
Žaga SLO 150 Ed57
Żagań PL 128 Fd39
Zagăr RO 172 Dc59
Zagarancea MD 173 Fb57
Žagarė LT 114 Ka53
Žagariai LT 114 Kc59
Zagarise I 164 Gc81
Zaglavak SRB 159 Jb64
Zaglav HR 157 Fd65
Zagnańsk PL 130 Jb41
Zagon RO 176 Eb62
Zagorá GR 189 Ca82
Zagorci BG 180 Ea72
Zagorci BG 181 Ec73
Zagor'e RUS 99 Ld42
Zagorje RUS 107 Mb46
Zagorje ob Savi SLO 151 Fc57
Zagórów PL 129 Ha37
Zagorskoe RUS 113 Jc58
Zagórz PL 139 Kb45
Zagórze Śląskie PL 129 Gb42
Zagość PL 138 Jb43
Zagra E 60 Da74
Zagra RO 171 Db56
Zagražden BG 180 Db68
Zagreb HR 151 Ga58
Zagrilla E 60 Da74
Zagrodno PL 128 Ga41
Žagubica SRB 174 Bd66
Zagvozd HR 158 Gd66
Zahara de la Sierra E 59 Cb76
Zahara de los Atunes E 59 Ca78
Zaháro GR 194 Ba87
Zahinos E 51 Bb70
Zahman TR 192 Fd85
Zahna D 127 Ec38
Zahody RUS 99 Ld45
Zahody RUS 107 Ld49
Záhony H 139 Kb49
Zahora E 59 Bd77
Záhoří CZ 136 Fb47
Záhorská Bystrica SK 145 Gc50
Záhorská Ves SK 145 Gc50
Zahrádky CZ 136 Fb43
Zăicana MD 173 Fd57
Zăicani MD 173 Fa55
Zaiceva LV 107 Lc48
Zaidín E 48 Fd61
Žaiginys LV 114 Kb55
Zaim MD 173 Ga59
Zaimčevo BG 181 Ed71
Zaimovo KSV 178 Ba71
Zainsk RUS 203 Ga08
Zaisenhausen D 134 Cc47
Zaistovec HR 152 Gb58
Zajača SRB 153 Ja63
Zajač'e RUS 203 Fa13
Zajączek PL 128 Fc39
Zajan'e RUS 99 Lc43
Zajas MK 182 Ba74
Zajcevo RUS 107 Ma47
Zaječar SRB 179 Ca67
Zaječov CZ 136 Fa45
Zajeczniki PL 131 Ka36
Zajezierze PL 120 Ga33
Zajezierze PL 131 Jd39
Zajk H 145 Gb56
Zakaki CY 206 Ja98
Žákamenné SK 138 Hd46
Zákány H 152 Gb57
Zákányszék H 153 Jb57
Žakarovce SK 138 Jc48
Zákas GR 182 Ba79
Zaķi LV 106 La48
Zákinthos GR 188 Ac86
Zakl SLO 151 Ga57
Zakliczyn PL 138 Jc45
Zaklików PL 131 Ka41
Zaklopača BIH 159 Hd64
Zakobjakino RUS 203 Fa08
Zakomo BIH 159 Hd65
Zakopane PL 138 Ja47
Zakroczym PL 130 Jb36
Zákros GR 201 Dd96
Zakrzew PL 130 Jc39
Zakrzew PL 131 Kb41
Zakrzewo PL 121 Gc33
Zakrzewo PL 121 Hb35
Zakrzewo PL 129 Gc37
Zakrzówek Osada PL 131 Ka41
Zákupy CZ 128 Fc42
Zalaapáti H 145 Gd55
Zalabaska H 145 Gc56
Zalaegerszeg H 145 Gc55
Zaļenieki LV 106 Ka52
Zalaháláp H 145 Gd55
Zalahtov'e RUS 99 Lc44
Zalaistvánd H 145 Gc55
Zalakaros H 145 Gd56
Zalakomár H 145 Gd56
Zalakoppány H 145 Gd55
Zalalövő H 145 Gc55
Zalamea de la Serena E 51 Cb70
Zalamea la Real E 59 Bc73
Zalamillas E 37 Cc58
Zalas PL 122 Jc33
Zalasowa PL 138 Jc44
Zalaszabar H 145 Gd56
Zalaszántó H 145 Gd55
Zalaszentbalázs H 145 Gc56
Zalaszentgrót H 145 Gd55
Zalaszentgyörgy H 145 Gc55
Zalatárnok H 145 Gc56
Zalău RO 171 Cd56
Zalavár H 145 Gd56
Zalavas LT 115 Lb56
Załazy PL 131 Jd39
Zalec PL 122 Jc31
Žalec SLO 151 Fd57
Załęcze PL 129 Gc39
Zalegošč' RUS 203 Fa12

Żalesa – Żywocice

Żalesa LT 114 La57
Zales'e RUS 107 Lc47
Zales'e RUS 113 Jc58
Zalesie PL 121 Gc33
Zalesie PL 121 Gd35
Zalesie PL 130 Jb37
Zalesie PL 131 Kc37
Zalesie PL 139 Kc43
Zalesina HR 151 Fc60
Zaļesje LV 107 Ma51
Zaleskie PL 121 Gb30
Zaleszany PL 131 Ka42
Zalewo PL 122 Hc31
Załęże PL 122 Ja33
Žalgiriai LT 113 Jb56
Zalha RO 171 Da56
Žalioji LT 114 Ka58
Zališčyky UA 204 Ea16
Zaliszewo PL 120 Fd34
Zalivino RUS 113 Jb57
Zalivino RUS 113 Jb58
Zalivnoe RUS 113 Ja58
Zalizci UA 204 Ea15
Zall-Dardhë AL 178 Ad73
Zaļmežnieki LV 107 Lb50
Žalno PL 121 Gd32
Zalogovac SRB 178 Bc67
Załom PL 128 Ga36
Žalpiai LT 114 Ka56
Zaltbommel NL 124 Ba37
Záltsa GR 189 Bd85
Zaluč'e RUS 202 Eb09
Załuski PL 130 Ja36
Zalusteż'e RUS 99 Ma42
Zalužje BIH 159 Ja64
Zalužnica HR 151 Fd62
Zalve LV 106 Kd52
Zam RO 174 Cb60
Zamárdi H 145 Ha55
Zamarte PL 121 Gd33
Žamberk CZ 137 Gb44
Zambra E 60 Da74
Zambrana E 38 Ea57
Zâmbreasca RO 175 Dc66
Zambrów PL 123 Jd34
Zambski-Kościelne PL 122 Jc35
Zambujeira do Mar P 58 Ab72
Zamch PL 139 Kc43
Zamęcin PL 120 Fd34
Zamfirovo BG 179 Cc69
Zamłynie PL 130 Hc42
Zamogil'e RUS 99 Lc44
Zámoly H 145 Hb53
Zamora E 45 Cb60
Zamość PL 121 Gd34
Zamość PL 122 Jc34
Zamość PL 131 Kc41
Zamoš'e RUS 99 Lc43
Zamostea RO 172 Eb55
Zámutov SK 139 Jd48
Zaņa LV 105 Jc52
Zanat H 145 Gc54
Žandov CZ 128 Fb42
Zandvoort NL 116 Ad35
Zănești RO 172 Ec58
Zanglivéri GR 183 Cb78
Zangora E 39 Fa57
Zaniemyśl PL 129 Gc37
Zánka H 145 Ha55
Zante LV 105 Jd51
Zaokskij RUS 203 Fa11
Zaorejas E 47 Eb63
Zaozer'e RUS 99 Ma45
Zaozer'e RUS 99 Mb42
Zaoz'ernoje RUS 113 Jc59
Zapadnaja Dvina RUS 202 Ec10
Zapałów PL 139 Kc43
Zapesen'e RUS 99 Mb44
Zapfendorf D 134 Dc44
Zapljus'e RUS 99 Mb44
Zăpodeni RO 173 Fa59
Zapole PL 129 Hb39
Zapol'e RUS 99 Ld41
Zapol'e RUS 99 Ma41
Zapol'e RUS 99 Mb44
Zaporižžja UA 205 Fa15
Zaporožskoe RUS 202 Ea08
Zapovednoe RUS 113 Jb57
Zappendorf D 127 Ea39
Zapponeta I 162 Gb73
Zaprešić HR 151 Ga58
Zaprudnja RUS 202 Ed10
Zapyškis LV 114 Kb57
Zár CZ 136 Fc49
Zara TR 205 Fd20
Zaraevo BG 180 Eb69
Zaragoza E 47 Fa61
Zarajsk RUS 203 Fa11
Zărand RO 170 Ca58
Zarańsko PL 120 Ga33
Zarasai LT 115 Lb54
Zaratán E 46 Cd60
Zarautz E 39 Ec55
Zarbince KSV 178 Bc71
Zar'binka RUS 99 Ma44
Zarcilla de Ramos E 61 Ec73
Żarczyn PL 120 Fb34
Zaręby PL 122 Jb33
Zaręby Kościelne PL 123 Jd35
Zaręby-Warchoły PL 123 Ka34
Zareč'e RUS 113 Jb58
Zareč'e RUS 113 Jb59
Zarečnoe RUS 113 Jd57
Žarėnai LT 113 Jc54
Žarėnai LT 114 Ka53
Zarga de Alange E 51 Bd69
Żarki PL 128 Fc39
Żarki PL 130 Hd42
Zárko GR 189 Bc81
Žarkovo RUS 107 Mb51
Zărnești RO 176 Dd62
Zărnești RO 176 Ec63
Zărnevo BG 181 Ed69
Žarnovica SK 138 Hc49
Żarnów PL 130 Ja40
Żarnowiec PL 112 Ha58
Żarnowiec PL 138 Ja43
Żarnowo PL 120 Fc32
Zarojeni MD 173 Fb55
Zarós GR 200 Da96
Žarošice CZ 137 Gc48
Zaroúhla GR 189 Bc86
Žarovnica HR 152 Gb57
Żarów PL 129 Gb41
Zarrentin D 119 Dd33
Zarskoe Selo RUS 202 Eb08
Zarszyn PL 139 Ka45
Zaruč'e RUS 99 Ld43
Zaručenoe RUS 113 Jb58
Żary PL 128 Fd39
Zarza Capilla (Nueva) E 52 Cc69
Zarza de Granadilla E 45 Ca64
Zarza de Tajo E 53 Dd66
Zarzadilla de Totana E 61 Ec73
Zarza la Mayor E 45 Bc65
Zarzecze PL 131 Jd40
Zarzecze PL 131 Ka42
Zarzecze PL 139 Kb44
Zarzosa E 47 Eb59
Zarzuela E 47 Eb65
Zarzuela del Monte E 46 Da63
Żarzyn PL 128 Fd37
Zás E 36 Ad54
Zasa LV 107 Lb52
Zasavica SRB 153 Ja61
Zaseki RUS 107 Ma46
Zasieki PL 128 Fc39
Zasip SLO 151 Fa57
Zasitino RUS 107 Ma51
Zaškiv UA 204 Ec15
Žasliai LT 114 Kd57
Zásmuky CZ 136 Fc45
Zasos'e RUS 99 Ld42
Zasów PL 139 Jd44
Zaspy Małe PL 120 Ga31
Zastávka CZ 137 Gb47
Zastînca MD 173 Fc54
Zastražišće HR 158 Gc67
Zaszków PL 123 Ka35
Žatec CZ 136 Fa44
Zatom PL 120 Ga34
Zaton HR 157 Ga65
Zaton MNE 159 Jb67
Zatonie PL 128 Fd38
Zator PL 138 Hd44
Zatory PL 122 Jc35
Zătreni RO 175 Da64
Zatwarnica PL 139 Kb46
Zaube LV 106 Kd50
Zauchwitz D 127 Ed37
Zau de Câmpie RO 171 Db58
Zavala BIH 158 Hb68
Zavala HR 158 Gc67
Zavalatica HR 158 Gd68
Zavalinë AL 182 Ac76
Zavalje BIH 151 Ga62
Zavattarello I 149 Cc61
Zavelstein, Bad Teinach- D 134 Cc48
Zavet BG 181 Ec68
Zavetnoe RUS 205 Ga15
Zavidov CZ 136 Fa44
Zavidoviči BIH 152 Hb63
Zavitne UA 205 Fb17
Zavlaka SRB 153 Ja63
Zăvoaia RO 177 Fa64
Zăvoi RO 174 Cb62
Zavoj MK 182 Ba75
Zavoj SRB 179 Cb69
Zavolž'e RUS 203 Fb09
Zawada PL 121 Gb34
Zawada PL 128 Fd38
Zawada PL 129 Gd40
Zawada PL 130 Hd41
Zawada PL 131 Kc41
Zawady PL 123 Ka33
Zawady PL 123 Kb33
Zawady PL 130 Ja38
Zawady PL 131 Kd42
Zawadzkie PL 129 Hb42
Zawda PL 122 Hc32
Zawichost PL 131 Jd41
Zawidów PL 128 Fc41
Zawidz Kościelny PL 122 Hd35
Zawiercie PL 138 Hd43
Zawierki PL 123 Kb33
Zawoja PL 138 Hd45
Zawonia PL 129 Gc40
Zazid SLO 151 Fa59
Zázrivá SK 138 Hd47
Zazuela del Pinar E 46 Db61
Zbaraž UA 204 Ea15
Zbarzewo PL 129 Gb38
Zbąszyń PL 128 Ga37
Zbąszynek PL 128 Ga37
Zbečno CZ 136 Fa44
Zbelovo SLO 151 Fd57
Zberki PL 129 Gd37
Zbiczno PL 122 Hc33
Zbiersk PL 129 Ha38
Zbiroh CZ 136 Fa45
Zblewo PL 121 Ha31
Zboj SK 139 Kb47
Zbójno PL 122 Hc34
Zbojštica SRB 159 Jb65
Zboriv UA 204 Ea15
Zborov SK 139 Jd46
Zborowice PL 138 Jc45
Zborowskie PL 129 Hb42
Zbože PL 121 Gd33
Zbraslavice CZ 136 Fd45
Zbrosławice PL 138 Hc43
Zbrudzewo PL 129 Gc37
Zbůch CZ 135 Ed46
Zbuczyn PL 131 Ka37
Zbýšov CZ 136 Fd45
Zbýšov CZ 137 Gb47
Žďár CZ 136 Fc43
Ždala HR 152 Gd57
Ždaňa SK 139 Jd49
Ždánice CZ 137 Gc48
Žďár CZ 135 Ed44
Žďár CZ 135 Ed47
Žďárec CZ 137 Gb47
Žďár nad Sázavou CZ 136 Ga46
Zdbice PL 121 Gb33
Zdenci HR 152 Hb59
Zdenska vas SLO 151 Fc58
Ždiar SK 138 Jb47
Zdice CZ 136 Fa45
Zdíkov CZ 136 Fa48
Ždírec nad Doubravou CZ 136 Ga46
Zdobnice CZ 137 Gb44
Zdolbuniv UA 204 Ea15
Zdounky CZ 137 Gd47
Zdrajsh AL 182 Ac75
Ždralovac BIH 158 Gc65
Zdravec BG 180 Eb70
Zdravec BG 181 Fa71
Zdrelo SRB 174 Bc65
Zdroisko PL 120 Fd35
Zdunje MK 178 Bb73
Zduńska Wola PL 130 Hc39
Zduny PL 129 Gd39
Zduny PL 130 Hd37
Zdżary PL 129 Ha37
Zdżary PL 130 Jb39
Zdziebórz PL 122 Jc35
Zdzieszowice PL 137 Ha43
Zdziłowice PL 131 Kb41
Zębowice PL 129 Hb42
Żebrak PL 131 Jd37
Zebreira P 45 Bc65
Zebrene LV 105 Jd52
Žebrokai LT 113 Jb53
Żebry-Wierzchlas PL 122 Jc34
Zebrzydowa PL 128 Fd40
Zebrzydowice PL 137 Hb45
Zechlin D 119 Ec34
Zechlinerhütte D 119 Ed34
Zeddam NL 125 Bc37
Zedelgem B 21 Ha29
Zedenac HR 151 Fd58
Zederhaus A 143 Ed54
Žedricy RUS 107 Mb49
Zeebrugge B 124 Aa38
Zeeland NL 125 Bb38
Zeesen D 128 Fa37
Zeewolde NL 116 Bb36
Zegama E 39 Eb56
Žegar SLO 151 Fd57
Żegary PL 123 Kb30
Zegerscappel F 21 Gd30
Żegiestów PL 138 Jc46
Žeglarci BG 181 Ed69
Żegocina PL 138 Jb45
Żegoty PL 122 Ja31
Žegra KSV 178 Bc72
Zegrze PL 130 Jb36
Zegrze Pomorskie PL 120 Ga31
Zegrzynek PL 130 Jb36
Zehdenick D 119 Ed35
Zehlendorf D 119 Ed35
Zehren, Diera- D 127 Ed41
Zeil D 134 Dc44
Zeilarn D 143 Ec50
Žeimelis LT 114 Kb53
Žeimiai LT 114 Ka54
Žeimiai LT 114 Kc56
Zeist NL 116 Ba36
Zeithain D 127 Ed40
Zeitlarn D 135 Eb48
Zeitlofs D 134 Da43
Zeitz D 127 Eb41
Žejane HR 151 Fb60
Zekeriyaköy TR 186 Fd77
Zekeriyaköy TR 187 Gd78
Żelazków PL 129 Ha38
Żelazna PL 121 Gd29
Żelazna Góra PL 122 Hd30
Żelazna PL 137 Gc43
Żelazowa Wola PL 130 Ja37
Żelechlinek PL 130 Ja39
Żelechów PL 131 Jd38
Zelencovo RUS 113 Jc59
Zelenčukskaja RUS 205 Fd16
Zeleni Jadar BIH 159 Ja64
Zelenik SRB 174 Bd65
Zelenika MNE 159 Hd69
Zelenikovo BG 180 Dc72
Zelenivka UA 205 Fb16
Zelenodol'sk RUS 203 Fd09
Zelenodol's'k UA 204 Ed16
Zelenograd RUS 202 Ed10
Zelenogradsk RUS 113 Ja58
Zelenokumsk RUS 205 Ga16
Zelenov CZ 136 Fa47
Zelenovo RUS 113 Jb58
Želetava CZ 136 Ga47
Železan BG 185 Ea76
Železino BG 185 Ea76
Železná Ruda CZ 135 Ed47
Železné SK 138 Hd48
Železnica BG 179 Cc72
Železnik BG 181 Ec72
Železnik SRB 153 Jc62
Železniki SLO 151 Fb57
Železnodorožnyj RUS 122 Jb30
Železnogorsk RUS 202 Ed13
Železný Brod CZ 128 Fd42
Zelgauska LV 107 Lb50
Zelhem NL 125 Bc37
Żelichów PL 138 Jc43
Želiezovce SK 146 Hc51
Zelinja BIH 152 Hb62
Zélio GR 189 Ca84
Żelisławice PL 130 Ja42
Żeliszew PL 131 Jd37
Żelizna PL 131 Kb38
Zeljazkovo BG 185 Ec74
Željuša BIH 158 Hb66
Želju Vojoda BG 180 Eb72
Zelki PL 123 Jd31
Żelkowo PL 121 Gc29
Zell A 144 Fa50
Zell D 133 Ca49
Zell D 134 Da45
Zell D 135 Eb47
Zell D 141 Ca51
Zella-Mehlis D 126 Dc42
Zell am Moos A 143 Ed52
Zell am See A 143 Ec53
Zell am Ziller A 143 Ea54
Zellerfeld, Clausthal- D 126 Dc38
Zellingen D 134 Da45
Zell (Mosel) D 133 Bd44
Zell-Pfarre A 144 Fb56
Želnava CZ 136 Fa49
Želovce SK 146 Hd51
Zelovo HR 158 Gc65
Żelów PL 130 Hc39
Želsva LV 114 Kb59
Zeltiņi LV 107 Lb48
Zeltweg A 144 Fc54
Želva LT 114 La56
Žemaičių Kalvarija LT 113 Jc54
Žemaičių Naumiestis LT 113 Jc56
Žemaitkiemis LT 114 Kd56
Žemaitkiemis LV 123 Kb30
Žemalė LT 113 Jc53
Žemberovce SK 146 Hc50
Zemblak AL 182 Ba77
Zembry PL 131 Ka37
Zembrze PL 122 Hd33
Zembrzyce PL 138 Hd45
Zemen BG 179 Cb72
Zemeș RO 172 Ec59
Zemgale LV 115 Lc54
Zemianska Oľča SK 145 Ha52
Zemite LV 105 Jd51
Zemitz D 120 Fa31
Zemmer D 133 Bc44
Zemné SK 145 Ha51
Zemplénagárd H 139 Kb49
Zemplínska Teplica SK 139 Jd48
Zemsko PL 128 Fd36
Zemun SRB 153 Jc61
Zenica BIH 158 Hb64
Zennor GB 18 Da32
Zentene LV 105 Jd50
Zenting D 135 Ed49
Zepa BIH 159 Hd64
Žepče BIH 152 Hb63
Zepernick D 128 Fa36
Žeravna BG 180 Eb71
Zerbísia GR 194 Bb88
Zerbst D 127 Eb38
Żerczyce PL 123 Kb35
Žerdevka RUS 203 Fc12
Zerenikovo MK 178 Bc73
Zerf D 133 Bc45
Zeri I 149 Cd63
Zerind RO 170 Bd58
Żerków PL 129 Gd38
Żerkowice PL 128 Fd41
Zermatt CH 148 Bd57
Zernez CH 142 Da55
Zernien D 119 Dd34
Żerniki PL 129 Gd38
Zernograd RUS 205 Fc15
Zernsdorf D 128 Fa37
Žeronys LT 114 Kd58
Zerpenschleuse D 120 Fa35
Zerqan AL 182 Ad74
Zervynos LT 123 Kd30
Zestoa E 39 Eb55
Zetea RO 172 Dd59
Zetel D 118 Cc33
Zetjovo BG 180 Dc73
Zeulenroda D 127 Eb42
Zeuthen D 128 Fa37
Zeven D 118 Da33
Zevenaar NL 125 Bc37
Zevenbergen NL 124 Ad38
Zevgolatió GR 189 Bd86
Zevio I 149 Dc60
Ževloki RUS 107 Mb50
Zeybekçayırı TR 191 Ec81
Zeyköyü TR 193 Ha82
Zeytin TR 197 Fa89
Zeytinbağı TR 186 Fc80
Zeytindağ TR 191 Ec84
Zeytineli TR 191 Ea86
Zeytinköy TR 191 Ec87
Zeytinli TR 185 Dd80
Zeytinli TR 191 Ea81
Zeytinli TR 191 Ec82
Zeževo HR 157 Ga66
Zgalevo BG 180 Db69
Zgărdești MD 173 Fb56
Zgierz PL 130 Hc38
Zgłobień PL 139 Ka44
Zgniłoche PL 122 Ja32
Zgon PL 122 Jc32
Zgornja Kungota SLO 144 Ga56
Zgornje Jezersko SLO 151 Fb57
Zgórsko PL 138 Jc43
Zgorzelec PL 128 Fc41
Zgozhd AL 182 Ad75
Zgurița MD 173 Fb54
Zhukë AL 182 Aa77
Žiar nad Hronom SK 138 Hc49
Zibello I 149 Da61
Žibikai LT 113 Jd53
Žiča SRB 178 Ba67
Zicavo F 154 Cb71
Zichow D 120 Fb34
Ziçisht AL 182 Ba77
Zidani Most SLO 151 Fd58
Zidarovo BG 181 Ed73
Ziddorf D 119 Ec32
Židikai LT 113 Jc53
Židina LV 115 Lc53
Židlochovice CZ 137 Gc48
Ziduri RO 176 Ed63
Ziębice PL 137 Gc43
Zięby PL 122 Ja30
Ziegenhagen D 126 Da40
Ziegenrück D 127 Ea42
Ziegra-Knobelsdorf D 127 Ed41
Ziēkas LV 105 Jb50
Zielenice PL 129 Gc42
Zieleniec PL 137 Gb43
Zieleniewo PL 120 Fd34
Zieleniewo PL 120 Fd31
Zielin PL 121 Gc30
Zielitz D 127 Ea37
Zielona PL 122 Hd34
Zielona Góra PL 128 Fd38
Zielonka PL 130 Jc36
Zieluń PL 122 Hd34
Ziemeris LV 107 Lc48
Ziemetshausen D 142 Db50
Ziemiełowice PL 129 Ha41
Ziemupe LV 105 Ja52
Ziérbena E 38 Ea55
Zierenberg D 126 Da40
Zierikzee NL 124 Ac37
Ziersdorf A 136 Ga49
Zierzow D 119 Ea34
Ziesar D 127 Eb37
Ziethen D 120 Fa32
Zieuwent NL 125 Bd37
Žiežmariai LT 114 Kd57
Zigós GR 184 Da77
Žīguri LV 107 Ld48
Žihle CZ 135 Ed44
Zilaiskalns LV 106 Kd48
Zilāni LV 106 La51
Zile LV 106 La47
Zile TR 205 Fc20
Žiliai LT 113 Jd54
Žilina SK 138 Hc47
Žilinai LT 114 Kd59
Žilino RUS 113 Jc58
Zillis CH 142 Cd55
Zilly D 127 Dd38
Zilshausen D 133 Ca43
Ziltendorf D 128 Fc37
Zilupe LV 107 Ma51
Zimandu-Nou RO 170 Bd59
Zimány H 145 Ha56
Zimari RUS 107 Mb49
Zimbor RO 171 Cd57
Zimbreni MD 173 Fd58
Zimlje = Rujišta BIH 158 Hb66
Zimmern D 141 Cb50
Zimna Brzeźnica PL 128 Ga39
Zimna Woda PL 122 Ja33
Zimnica BG 180 Eb72
Zimnicea RO 180 Dd68
Zimnice Wielkie PL 137 Ha43
Zimovniki RUS 205 Fd15
Zinal CH 148 Bd57
Zinasco Vecchio I 148 Cb60
Žindaičiai LT 114 Ka57
Zingst D 119 Ec30
Zinkgruvan S 95 Fc45
Zin'kiv UA 202 Ed14
Žinkovy CZ 135 Ed46
Zinnowitz D 120 Fa31
Žiopeliai LT 113 Jd53
Zipári GR 197 Ec91
Ziras LV 105 Jb50
Zirc H 145 Ha54
Zirchow D 120 Fb32
Zirgi LV 107 Ma52
Žiri SLO 151 Fa58
Žirje HR 157 Ga66
Zirl A 143 Dd53
Zirndorf D 134 Dc46
Žirņi LV 105 Jc52
Žirnovsk RUS 203 Fd12
Zíros GR 201 Dd96
Žirovica MK 182 Ad74
Žirovnica SLO 151 Fb57
Žirovnice CZ 136 Fd47
Zistersdorf A 137 Gc49
Žitište SRB 153 Jc59
Žitište SRB 174 Bb61
Žitkovac SRB 178 Bd68
Žitnica BG 180 Db72
Žitnica BG 181 Ed71
Žitni Potok SRB 178 Bc69
Žitomislići BIH 158 Hb67
Žitoradja SRB 178 Bd69
Žitosvjat BG 181 Ec73
Zitsa GR 182 Ad80
Zittau D 128 Fc42
Žiūronys LT 114 Kc59
Živaja HR 152 Gc60
Živinice BIH 153 Hc63
Živkovo BG 179 Cd72
Živojno MK 183 Bb76
Ziyamet TR 187 Gc77
Złaków Kościelny PL 130 Hd37
Zlarin HR 157 Ga66
Zlata SRB 178 Bc69
Zlatá Baňa SK 139 Jd47
Zlatá Idka SK 138 Jc48
Zlatar BG 181 Ec70
Zlatar HR 152 Gb58
Zlatar Bistrica HR 152 Gb58
Zlatarevo BG 183 Cb75
Zlatari SRB 178 Bb68
Zlatarica BG 180 Ea71
Zlaté Hory CZ 137 Gd44
Zlaté Klasy SK 145 Gd51
Zlaté Moravce SK 145 Hb50
Zlatica BG 179 Da71
Zlatinica BG 185 Eb74
Zlati Vojvoda BG 180 Ea72
Zlatna RO 175 Cd60
Zlatna Greda HR 153 Hd59
Zlatna Ostrove SK 145 Ha52
Zlatna Panega BG 179 Da70
Zlatni Pjasăci BG 181 Fb70
Zlatograd BG 184 Dc76
Zlatoklas BG 181 Ed68
Zlatokop SRB 178 Bd71
Zlatoličje SLO 144 Ga56
Zlatopole BG 185 Dd74
Zlatovo SRB 174 Bc66
Žlebič SLO 151 Fc59
Žlibinai LT 113 Jc54
Zliechov SK 137 Hb48
Zlín CZ 137 Ha47
Zliv CZ 136 Fb48
Žljebovi BIH 159 Hd64
Żłobek PL 139 Kb46
Žlobin BY 202 Eb13
Zlobin HR 151 Fc60
Złochowice PL 130 Hc41
Złocieniec PL 120 Ga33
Złoczew PL 129 Hb40
Zlogonje HR 152 Gb57
Zlogoš BG 179 Ca72
Zlosela BIH 158 Gd64
Zlostup MNE 159 Hd68
Zlot SRB 174 Bd66
Złotniki Kujawskie PL 121 Ha35
Złotoria PL 121 Hb34
Złotoryja PL 128 Ga41
Złotów PL 121 Gc33
Złotowo PL 122 Hd33
Złotowo PL 129 Hb36
Złoty Stok PL 137 Gc43
Žlunice CZ 136 Fd44
Žlutice CZ 135 Ed44
Zmajevac BIH 152 Gb61
Zmajevac HR 153 Hc58
Zmajevo SRB 153 Ja59
Žman HR 157 Fd65
Žmerynka UA 204 Eb15
Zmievka RUS 203 Fa12
Żmigród PL 129 Gc40
Żmigródek PL 129 Gc40
Zmijiv UA 203 Fa14
Zminica MNE 159 Ja67
Žminj HR 151 Fa61
Znamenka RUS 99 Ld45
Znamenosec BG 180 Ea73
Znamensk RUS 113 Jb59
Znamenskoe RUS 202 Ed12
Znam'janka UA 204 Ed15
Żnin PL 121 Gd35
Znojmo CZ 136 Ga48
Zoagli I 149 Cc63
Zocca I 149 Dc63
Zocene LV 105 Jd49
Žodzina BY 202 Eb12
Zoetermeer NL 116 Ad36
Zofingen CH 141 Ca53
Zogaj AL 163 Ja71
Žogi LV 107 Lc50
Zogno I 149 Cd58
Žogotas LV 107 Lc51
Žogotas LV 107 Ld50
Zohor SK 145 Gc50
Zoio P 45 Bd59
Zoldo Alto I 143 Ea56
Zoljan HR 152 Hb60
Żółkiewka PL 131 Kb41
Zollhaus CH 141 Bc55
Zolling D 143 Ea50
Zollino I 163 Hc77
Zoločiv UA 204 Ea15
Zolote UA 203 Fb14
Zolotievca MD 173 Fd59
Zolotonoša UA 204 Ed15
Żółtwino PL 120 Ga34
Żołynia PL 139 Ka43
Zomba H 146 Hc56
Zonguldak TR 187 Hb76
Zonhoven B 124 Ba40
Zoni GR 185 Ea76
Zóni GR 194 Bb88
Zonianá GR 200 Cd95
Zonza F 154 Cb71
Żórawina PL 129 Gc41
Zörbig D 127 Eb39
Zorge D 126 Dc39
Zorile MD 173 Fd56
Zorita E 51 Cb68
Zorita de la Loma E 37 Cd58
Zorita de los Canes E 47 Ea65
Zorlar TR 198 Fd92
Zorleni RO 177 Fa60
Zorlențu Mare RO 174 Ca62
Zorneding D 143 Ea51
Zornica BG 181 Ec73
Żory PL 137 Hb44
Zosna LV 107 Ld52
Zossen D 127 Ed37
Zoutkamp NL 117 Bd33
Zoutleeuw B 124 Ba41
Zoúzouli GR 182 Ba78
Zovka RUS 99 Ma44
Žovkva UA 204 Dd15
Žovti Vody UA 204 Ed15
Žovtneve UA 202 Ed14
Zreče SLO 151 Fd57
Zrenjanin SRB 153 Jc60
Zrenjanin SRB 174 Bb61
Zrin HR 152 Gb61
Zrinski Topolovac HR 152 Gc58
Zrmanja-Vrelo HR 158 Gb64
Zrnovci MK 183 Ca74
Žrnovnica HR 158 Gc66
Zruč nad Sázavou CZ 136 Fd45
Zruč-Senec CZ 135 Ed45
Zrze KSV 178 Ba71
Zrze MK 183 Bb74
Zsadány H 147 Ka54
Zsámbék H 146 Hc53
Zsámbok H 146 Ja52
Zsana H 146 Ja56
Zschadraß D 127 Ec41
Zscherben D 127 Ea40
Zschocken D 127 Ec42
Zschopau D 127 Ed42
Zschoppach D 127 Ec41
Zschornewitz D 127 Eb39
Zschortau D 127 Eb40
Zsedeny H 145 Gc53
Zsurk H 139 Kb49
Zuazo de Cuartango E 38 Ea56
Zubcov RUS 202 Ec10
Zuberec SK 138 Hd47
Zubia E 60 Db75
Zubialde E 38 Ea55
Zubići BIH 158 Ha64
Zubieta E 39 Ec56
Zubiškes LT 114 Kd57
Zubova Poljana RUS 203 Fb11
Zubowo PL 123 Kb34
Zubrești MD 173 Fc57
Żubrówka PL 123 Kb30
Zubrzyca Górna PL 138 Hd46
Žuč SRB 178 Bb69
Zucaina E 54 Fb65
Zudaire E 39 Ec57
Zudar D 119 Ed30
Zudibiarte E 38 Ea55
Zuera E 48 Fb60
Zufia E 39 Ec57
Zufre E 59 Bd72
Zug CH 141 Cb53
Zuheros E 60 Da73
Zuid-Beijerland NL 124 Ac37
Zuidhorn NL 117 Bd33
Zuidlaren NL 117 Bd33
Zuidwolde NL 117 Bd35
Zújar E 51 Cb70
Zújar E 61 Dd74
Zuji LV 107 Lc51
Zujkovo RUS 107 Mb50
Žukai LT 113 Jd57
Žukovka RUS 202 Ed12
Żuków PL 131 Kc38
Żukowice PL 128 Ga39
Żukowo PL 121 Ha30
Žuljana HR 158 Ha68
Žulová CZ 137 Gc44
Zülpich D 125 Bc41
Zumaia E 39 Eb55
Zumarraga E 39 Eb56
Zundert NL 124 Ad38
Zundi LV 107 Ld52
Zuoz CH 142 Da56
Zupa HR 158 Gd67
Županja HR 153 Hc61
Župelevec SLO 151 Ga58
Žur KSV 178 Ba72
Zūras LV 105 Jb50
Żurawica PL 139 Kb44
Zurbarán E 51 Cb68
Zurgena E 61 Eb74
Zürich CH 141 Cb53
Zurich NL 116 Bb33
Zuriza E 39 Fb57
Zurndorf A 145 Gc51
Żurobice PL 123 Kb35
Żuromin PL 122 Hd34
Żurominek PL 122 Ja34
Zurrieq M 166 Eb88
Zürs A 142 Da54
Zurzach CH 141 Cb52
Zusmarshausen D 142 Db50
Züssow D 120 Fa31
Žuta Lokva HR 151 Fd61
Zutphen NL 117 Bc36
Zuydcoote F 21 Gd29
Zuzela PL 123 Jd35
Žužemberk SLO 151 Fc58
Zvăničevo BG 179 Da73
Zvārtava LV 107 Lb48
Zvečan KSV 178 Ba70
Zvegor MK 179 Cb73
Zvejniekciems LV 106 Kc49
Zvenigorod RUS 202 Ed10
Zvenigovo RUS 203 Fd09
Zvenimir BG 181 Ec68
Zvenyhorodka UA 204 Ec15
Zverino BG 179 Cd70
Zvezd SRB 153 Jb62
Zvezdec BG 185 Ed74
Zvezdel BG 185 Dd75
Zvidziena LV 107 Lc50
Žvingiai LT 113 Jc56
Žvirče SLO 151 Fc59
Žvirgždaičiai LT 114 Ka58
Zvirgzde LV 106 Kc51
Žvirgždėnai LT 114 Kd59
Zvirinë AL 182 Ad76
Zvole CZ 137 Gb46
Zvole CZ 137 Gc45
Zvolen SK 138 Hd49
Zvolenská Slatina SK 138 Hd49
Zvonce SRB 179 Ca70
Zvony RUS 107 Mb50
Zvoriștea RO 172 Ec55
Zvornik BIH 153 Hd63
Zwaagwesteinde NL 117 Bc33
Zwanenburg NL 116 Ba35
Zwardoń PL 138 Hc46
Zwaring A 144 Fd55
Zwartemeer NL 117 Ca35
Zwartsluis NL 117 Bc35
Zweeloo NL 117 Bd34
Zweibrücken D 133 Bd46
Zweiflingen D 134 Cd47
Zweisimmen CH 141 Bc55
Zwenkau D 127 Eb40
Zwethau D 127 Ed39
Zwettl A 136 Fd49
Zwettl an der Rodl A 144 Fb50
Zwiastowice PL 137 Ha43
Zwickau D 127 Ec42
Zwiefalten D 142 Cd50
Zwiemik PL 138 Jc44
Zwierzno PL 122 Hc31
Zwierzyn PL 120 Fd35
Zwierzyniec PL 131 Kc42
Zwiesel D 135 Ed48
Zwieselstein A 142 Dc55
Zwillbrock D 125 Bd37
Zwingenberg D 134 Cc45
Zwischenwasser I 143 Ea55
Zwochau D 127 Eb40
Zwoleń PL 131 Jd39
Zwolle NL 117 Bc35
Zwönitz D 127 Ec42
Żychlin PL 130 Hd37
Žydačiv UA 204 Ea15
Żydów PL 129 Ha39
Żydowo PL 121 Gb31
Żydowo PL 129 Gd36
Žygaičiai LT 113 Jc56
Zygi CY 206 Jb98
Zygmantiškė LV 114 Kb57
Zypliai LT 114 Ka57
Żyraków PL 139 Jd44
Żyrardów PL 130 Ja37
Żyrowa PL 137 Ha43
Żyrzyn PL 131 Ka39
Žytkavičy BY 202 Eb13
Żytkiejmy PL 123 Ka29
Żytniów PL 129 Hb41
Żytno PL 130 Hd41
Žytomyr UA 204 Eb15
Żywiec PL 138 Hd45
Żywocice PL 137 Ha43

				1:15.000			
(GB)	**(D)**	**(F)**	**(DK)**		**(GB)**	**(D)**	**(F)**	**(DK)**
City map	**Stadtplan**	**Plan de ville**	**Bykort**		**City map**	**Stadtplan**	**Plan de ville**	**Bykort**
Motorway	Autobahn	Autoroute	Motorvej	Central station, bus station	Hauptbahnhof, Busbahnhof	Gare centrale, gare routière	Hovedbanegård, busterminal
Major road	Wichtige Hauptstraße	Route principale importante	Vigtig hovedvej	Hospital	Krankenhaus	Hôpital	Sygehus
Main road	Hauptstraße	Route régionale	Hovedvej	Information, post office	Information, Post	Information, bureau de poste	Information, posthus
Pedestrian zone	Fußgängerzone	Zone piétonne	Gågade	Church, mosque	Kirche, Moschee	Église, mosquèe	Kirke, moske
Railway	Bahnlinie	Ligne de tramway	Jernbane	Synagogue	Synagoge	Synagogue	Synagoge
Stadium	Stadion	Stade	Stadion	Theatre	Theater	Théâtre	Teater
Parking, garage parking	Parkplatz, Parkhaus	Parking	Parkeringsplads, parkeringshus	Museum	Museum	Musée	Museum
Exhibition Hall	Messe	Palais des expositions	Messe	Library	Bibliothek	Bibliothèque	Bibliotek

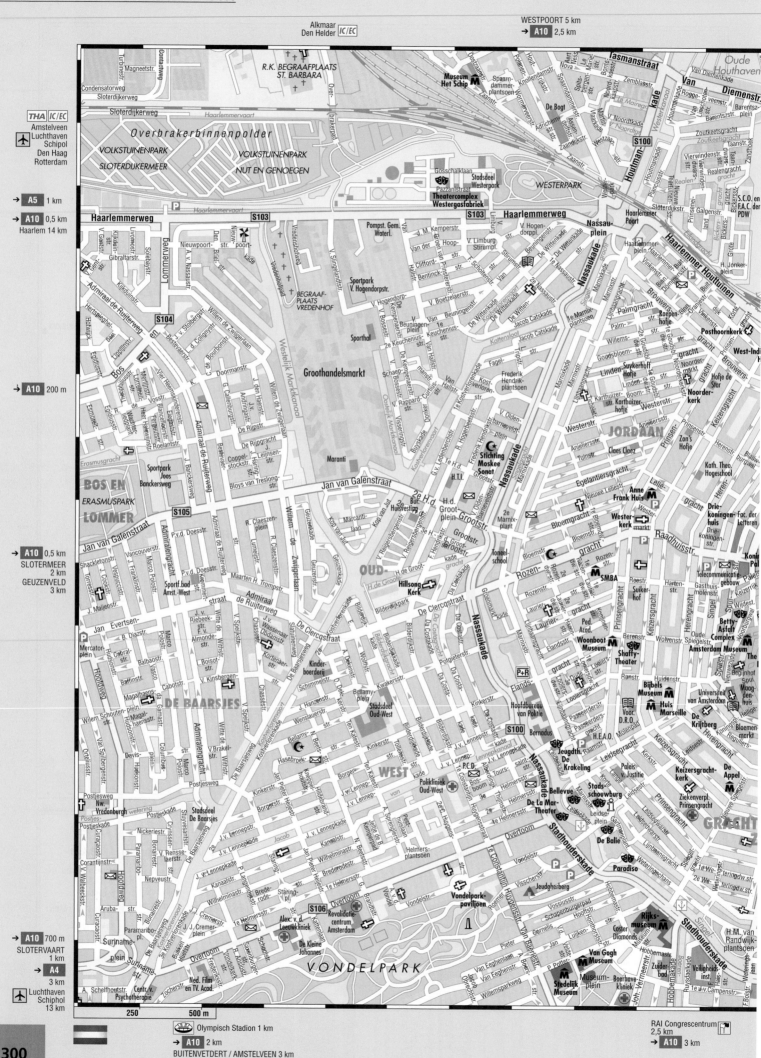

Monnickendam 9 km
→ N 247 1,5 km
→ A10 1,5 km   ⇄ Noord   NIEUWENDAM 0,5 km
BUIKSLOOT 1 km

FLORA PARK
VOLE-PARK
NOORD 8

NOORD
NOORDERPARK

Het IJ

STENEN HOOFD

NOORD 5

Centraal Station-NDSM

Caffij-boornstr.
Lelie-daalse-str.
Westerdok
Westerdoks-dijk
Winthont-str.
Westerdoks-plein

IJdock
City Marina IJdock

EYE, Film Instituut Nederland

S 116

NOORD 6

Westerdokskade
Raiverkeer-sleiding Regio Nordwest
K.v.K.
Haven-gebouw

S100

De Ruijterkade

Nieuwe Westerdokstr.
Nieuwe of Ronde Lutherse Kerk
Dominicus-kerk

Prins Hendrikkade

Centraal Station
CENTRAAL STATION
THA ICE IC/EC
St. Nicolaaskerk
Schreierstoren

Oosterdokseiland
De Ruijterkade
De Chocoladefabriek
IHLIA Homodok
Reve Museum
Conservatorium

Muziekgebouw aan 't IJ
Bimhuis
Passenger Terminal Amsterdam
Piet Heinkade

Java-eiland
Javakade
Sumatrakade
Taman Sapitului
IJhaven

Oostelijk Havengebied
Veemkade
Piet Heinkade

HAVENS OOST 0,5 km

Museum Ons' Lieve Heer op Solder
Beurs van Berlage (Koopmansbeurs)
Oude Kerk
Koffie- en Theemuseum
't Kolkje ('t Sluisje)
Effecten-beurs

Nieuwe Kerk
Dam
Nationaal Mon.
Madame Tussauds
De Brakke Grond
De Waag
NIEUWMARKT

Oosterdok

NEMO Science & Technology Museum

Marine Etablissement

Het Scheepvaart-museum
ARCAM Architectuur Centrum Amsterdam
Kattenburg-plein
Oosterkerk

Wittenburgervaart
Windroos-plein

Hash Marih. & Hemp Mus.
Vm. Stadhuis Oost-Indisch Huis
Vm. Zuiderkerk
Montelbaans-toren
Brandweer
Swift

Prins Hendrikkade

Amsterdam Dungeon
Allard Pierson Museum
Museum Het Rembrandthuis
Amsterdamse Hoogeschool voor de Kunsten
Stadhuis
WATERLOOPLEIN
Stopera
Muziek-theater
Joods Portugese Synagoge
Historisch Mus.
Hortus Botanicus
Universiteit
Hollandsche Schouwburg
Herv. Ped. Acad.
Verzetsmus.
Planetarium
NATURA
Artisbibliotheek
ARTIS
Museumwerf 't Kromhout
De Molen De Gooyer
EnergetiCA
Zeeburgerpad
A10 5 km
Zeeburgerdijk

Universiteits-theater
De Kleine Komedie
Muntplein
Singel
Amstel
Rembrandt-plein
Museum Willet-Holthuysen
Hermitage
Amstelhof

Zoo Artis
MAGISTRA
Aquarium
Middenlaan
St. Jacob

FOAM
ENGORDEL
Museum Van Loon
Amstelkerk
De Duif
Theater Carré

Dr.Sarphatihuis
Fac. Scheik.
Org. Chem.
Fac. Nat. en Sterrenk.
Natuurk. Lab. Valckenierstr.
Fac. Wisk./Inf.

Tropenmuseum
Soeterijn theater
Linnaeus-kerk

Mauritskade

A10 5 km
ICE IC/EC
Utrecht Arnhem

Heineken Experience
Stadhouderskade
Rijksacad.
P.D.I.S.
Den Texstr.
Nicolaas Witsen-gracht
2e Wetering-Plantsoen
Nederlandse Bank
Rijksbel.-kantoor
Frederiks-plein
Rhijn-spoorpl.

OOSTERPARK
O.L.V. Gasthuis
Muiderpoort
S113

De IJsbreker Muziekcentrum en TV-Studio
Stadsdeel Oost

→ A2 / A10 3,5 km
Utrecht 24 km
→ A10 3 km
DUIVENDRECHT 3,5 km
ArenA 5 km
⇄ Gaasperplas Gein
WATERGRAAFSMEER 200 m
→ A10 2,5 km

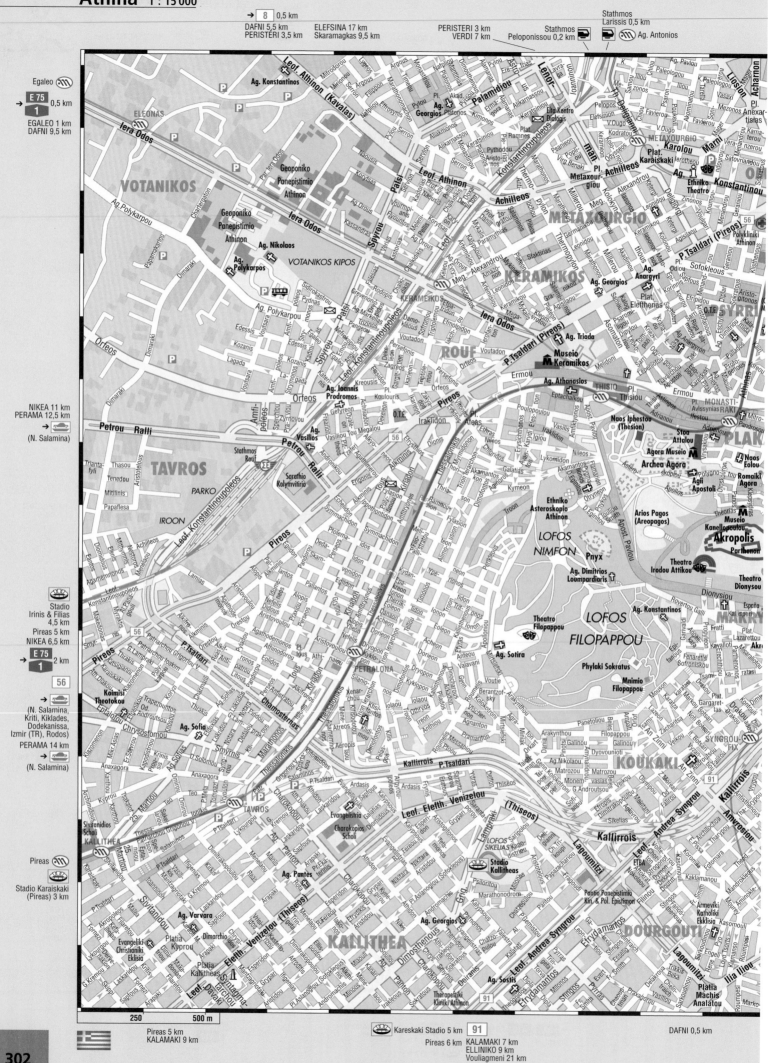

NEA FILADELFIA 9,5 km
PATISSIA 5,5 km
GALATSI 4 km

Kifisia → E 75 4 km
1

Doukissis
Plakentias

E 94 12 km
6

Pallini 13 km
Rafina 28 km
Athens Int. Airport
(Eleftherios
Venizelos)
29 km

83
CHOLARGOS 3 km

Athens Int. Airport
(Eleftherios
Venizelos) 20 km
Rafina 23 km

(Marmari, Karistos,
Kiklades)

Marathonas 34 km

ZOGRAFOU 0,5 km

KESARIANI 0,5 km

Ag. Dimitrios
(Alex. Panagoulis)   Vouliagmeni 15 km

IMITOS 0,5 km
AG. DIMITRIOS 3,5 km

Flughafen Tegel 3,5 km
→ 100 0,5 km

Osloer Straße (U9) U B-REINICKENDORF 7 km
B-WEDDING 3 km

B-WEDDING 3 km

Hamburg 1h 33'
B-Gesundbrunnen 4'
IC/EC ICE

Oranienburg 28 km
B-WAIDMANNSLUST 10 km
B-WEDDING 2 km
96

Left margin directions:

Schloss Charlottenburg 3,5 km
B-CHARLOTTENBURG 4 km

Schloss Charlottenburg 3 km
B-CHARLOTTENBURG 3,5 km

2 / 5 1,5 km
B-CHARLOTTENBURG 2 km
Schloss Charlottenburg 2,5 km

2 / 5
B-CHARLOTTENBURG 1,5 km
Schloss Charlottenburg 2 km
→ 100 3 km
Messe Berlin 4 km
B-WESTEND 5 km
Flughafen Tegel 6,5 km
Olympiastadion 6,5 km
B-SPANDAU 10 km

U Ruhleben (U2)

Messe Berlin 3 km
→ 2 / 5 3,5 km

S5 Westkreuz 7'
S75 Spandau 21'
S7 Potsdam 34'
IC/EC ICE
B-Spandau 8'
Wolfsburg 1h 4'
Hannover 1h 39'
IC/EC Potsdam 26'

→ 100 3 km
B-SCHMARGENDORF 4 km

→ 100 2,5 km
B-SCHMARGENDORF 3,5 km

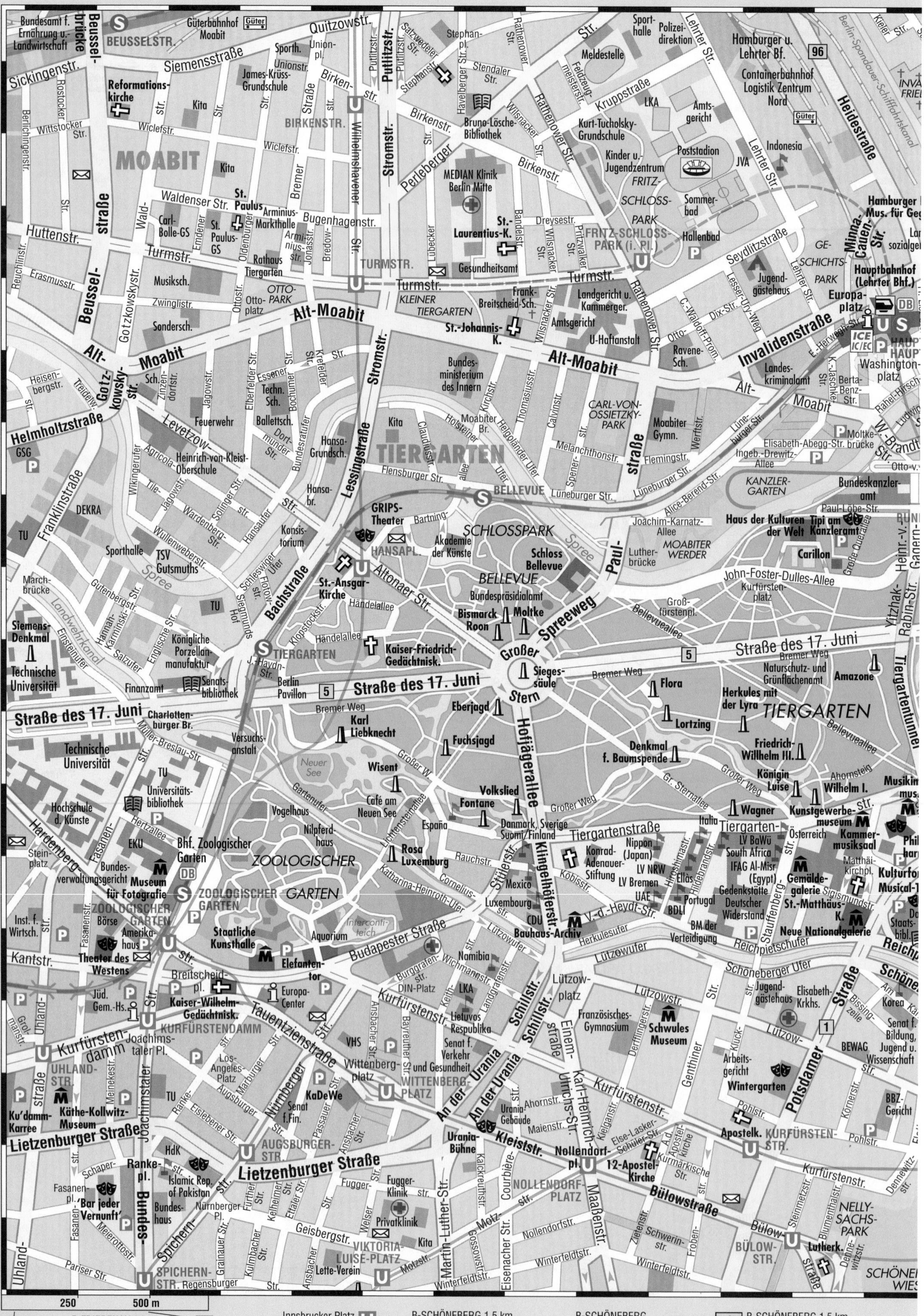

Bottom margin directions:

B-FRIEDENAU 3 km
→ 103 3,5 km
B-STEGLITZ 5 km
B-ZEHLENDORF 9 km
Potsdam 27 km

U Innsbrucker Platz (U4)
Rathaus Steglitz (U9)
Krumme Lanke (U3)

B-SCHÖNEBERG 1,5 km
B-STEGLITZ 5 km
B-ZEHLENDORF 9 km

B-SCHÖNEBERG 1,5 km

1 B-SCHÖNEBERG 1,5 km
→ 100 3,5 km
B-STEGLITZ 6 km
B-ZEHLENDORF 10 km
→ 103 4 km

Major area labels:

MOABIT
TIERGARTEN
ZOOLOGISCHER GARTEN
WITTENBERGPLATZ
NOLLENDORFPLATZ
KURFÜRSTENSTR.
NELLY-SACHS-PARK
SCHÖNEBERGER WIESE

Straße des 17. Juni
Kurfürstendamm
Lietzenburger Straße
Alt-Moabit
Turmstr.

250   500 m

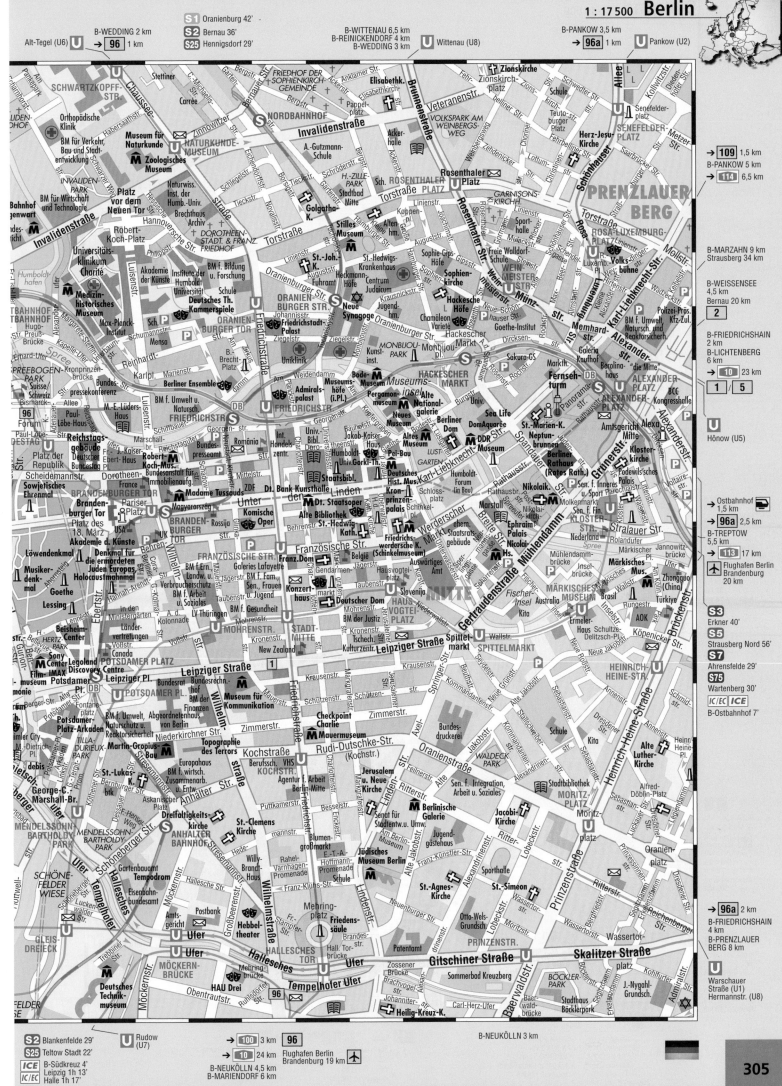

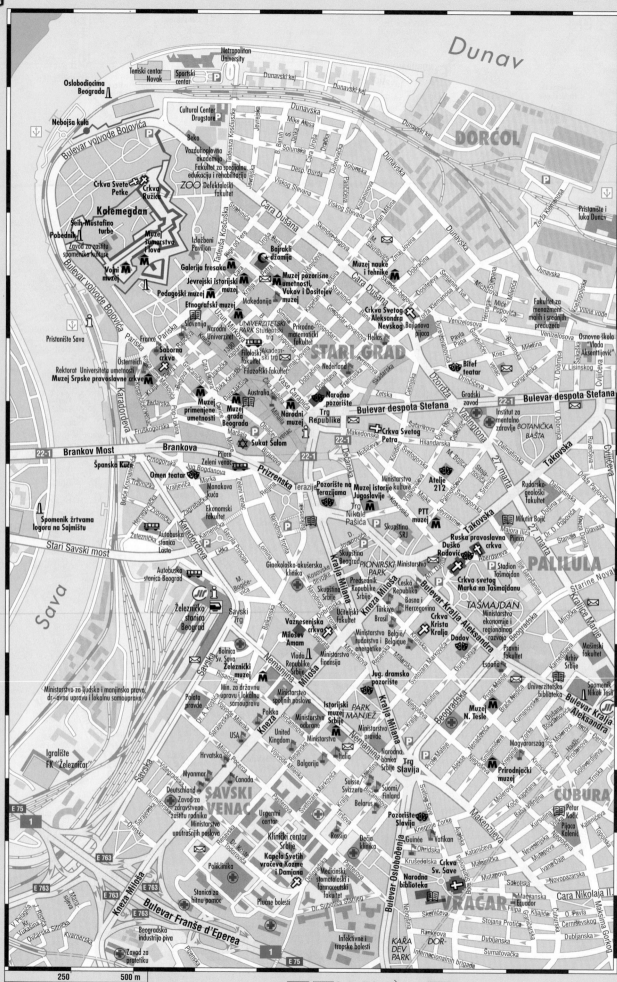

Dunav

DORĆOL

Metropolitan University

Oslobodiocima Beograda

Nebojša kula

Cultural Center Drugstore

Beko

Vazduhoplovna akademija
Fakultet za specijalnu edukaciju i rehabilitaciju

ZOO Defektološki fakultet

Crkva Svete Petke
Crkva Ružica

Kalemegdan

Šeih-Mustafino turbe
Pobednik
Zavod za zaštitu spomenika kulture
Vojni muzej

Izložbeni Paviljon

Galerija fresaka

Jevrejski istorijski muzej

Pedagoški muzej

Etnografski muzej

Bajrakli džamija

Muzej nauke i tehnike

Muzej pozorišne umetnosti, Vukov i Dositejev muzej

Makedonija

Crkva Svetog Aleksandra Nevskog

Bajlonova pijaca

STARI GRAD

KRNJAČA 3 km
BORČA 8 km
ZRENJANIN 70 km
24-1 2 km
KARABURMA 2,5 km
ZVEZDARA 3 km
VIŠNJIČKA BANJA 4 km
Višnjica 6,5 km
1-9 200m
E 70
Pančevo 17 km
Kovin 53 km
Vršac 80 km
Timişoara (RO) 156 km

Slovenija

Narodni Univerzitet

UNIVERZITETSKI PARK Studentski trg

Prirodno-matematički fakultet

Hellas

Osnovna škola "Vlada Aksentijević"

Rektorat Universiteta
Österreich
Muzej Srpske pravoslavne crkve

Saborna crkva

France

Filološki fakultet
Akademski trg
Filozofski fakultet

Nederland

Vase Čarapica

Bifet teatar

Muzej primenjene umetnosti
Muzej grada Beograda
Trg Republike

Narodno pozorište

Narodni muzej

Bulevar despota Stefana

Crkva Svetog Petra

Gradski zavod

Bulevar despota Stefana

Institut za mentalno zdravlje
BOTANIČKA BAŠTA

Rudarsko-geološki fakultet

Sukat Salom

Australia

Maršala

Obilićev venac

Makedonska

Hilandarska

22-1

22-1

22-1
ZEMUN 3,5 km
GORNJI GRAD 4 km
NOVA GALENIKA 5,5 km
Batajnica 15,5 km
Stara Pazova 31 km
Novi Sad 74 km

Brankov Most
Brankova

Španska Kuća

Zeleni venac
Pijaca

Omen teatar

Spomenik žrtvama logora na Sajmištu

Stari Savski most

Autobuska stanica Lasta

Autobuska stanica Beograd

Ekonomski fakultet

Manakova kuća

Prizrenska
Terazija

Pozorište na Terazijama

Muzej istorije Jugoslavije

Atelje 212

Trg Nikole Pašića

PTT muzej

Takovska

Milutin Bojić

Ruska pravoslavna crkva
Duško Radović

PALILULA

Stadion Tašmajdan

Skupština SRJ

Crkva svetog Marka na Tašmajdanu

TAŠMAJDAN

Ministarstvo ekonomije i regionalnog razvoja

Sava

Ginekološko-akušerska klinika

Skupština Beograd

PIONIRSKI PARK

Predsednik Republike Srbije

Ministarstvo

Ceská Republika
Türkiye
Bosna i Hercegovina
Brasil

Crkva Krista Kralja

Dadov

Pravni fakultet

Espana

Mašinski fakultet

Železnička stanica Beograd

Savski Trg

Vaznesenjska crkva

Učiteljski fakultet

Ministarstvo belgië/Belgique

Ministarstvo rudarstva i energetike

Jug. dramsko pozorište

Milošev Amam

Bolnica Sv. Sava
Železnički muzej

Risanska

Vlada Republike Srbije

Ministarstvo finansija

Spomenik Nikoli Tesli

Univerzitetska biblioteka

Muzej N. Tesle

Min. za državnu upravu i lokalnu samoupravu

Ministarstvo spoljnih poslova

Istorijski muzej Srbije

PARK MANJEŽ

Ministarstvo odbrane

Ministarstvo pravde

Arhiv Srbije

Ministarstvo za ljudska i manjinska prava, dr-avnu upravu i lokalnu samoupravu

Polata pravde

Polska

Kneza

United Kingdom

Ministarstva

Narodna banka Srbije

Trg Slavija

Prirodnjački muzej

3,5 km
1-9 E 70
100 4 km
ZVEZDARA 3,5 km
MALI MOKRI LUG 5,5 km
Grocka 30 km
Smederevo 49 km

Igralište FK "Železničar"

Myanmar

Hrvatska

USA

Italia

Bulgaria

SAVSKI VENAC

Deutschland

Zavod za zdravstvenu zaštitu radnika

Ministarstvo unutrašnjih poslova

Canada

Suisse/Svizzera

Suomi/Finland

Belarus

Pozorište Slavija

ČUBURA

1
BEŽANIJA 4 km
ZEMUN 5,5 km
Aerodrom Beograd-Surčin 15 km
Sremska Mitrovica 73 km
Slavonski Brod 207 km

E 75

1

Urgentni centar

Klinički centar Srbije

Rossija

Dečja klinika

Guinée

Ohridska

Crkva Sv. Save

Petar Kočić

Pijaca Kalenić

E 763

E 763
Beogradski sajam 0,5 km
ČUKARICA 3,5 km
RAKOVICA 7 km
Železnik 10,5 km
Obrenovac 23 km

E 75

E 763

E 763

Kneza Miloša

Kapela Svetih vračeva Kozme i Damjana

Medicinski stomatološki i farmaceutski fakultet

Narodna biblioteka

VRAČAR

Cara Nikolaja II

Ecuador

Bulevar Franše d'Eperea

Beogradska industrija piva

Zavod za protetiku

Infektivne i tropske bolesti

Plućne bolesti

KARA ĐEV PARK

Stanica za hitnu pomoć

250   500 m

Stadion FK Partizan 1 km
Stadion FK Crvena Zvezda 1,5 km

SENJAK 200 m
BANJICA 3 km
VOŽDOVAC 5 km
Mladenovac Varos 58 km
Kragujevac 124 km

1 Stadion FK Crvena Zvezda 1,5 km
ZVEZDARA 5 km
Vrčin 18 km
Velika Plana 85 km
Kragujevac 138 km

1 Stadion FK Crvena Zvezda 1,5 km
VOŽDOVAC 2 km
BANJICA 2,5 km

1 300 m

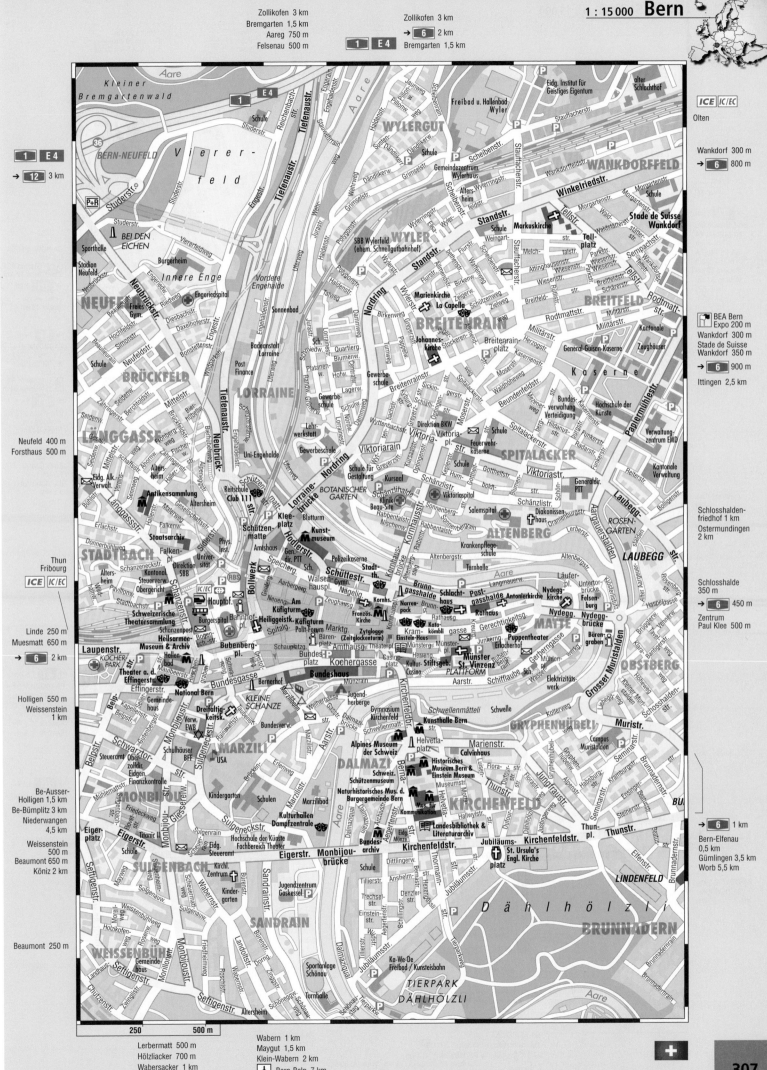

Bratislava 1 : 15 000

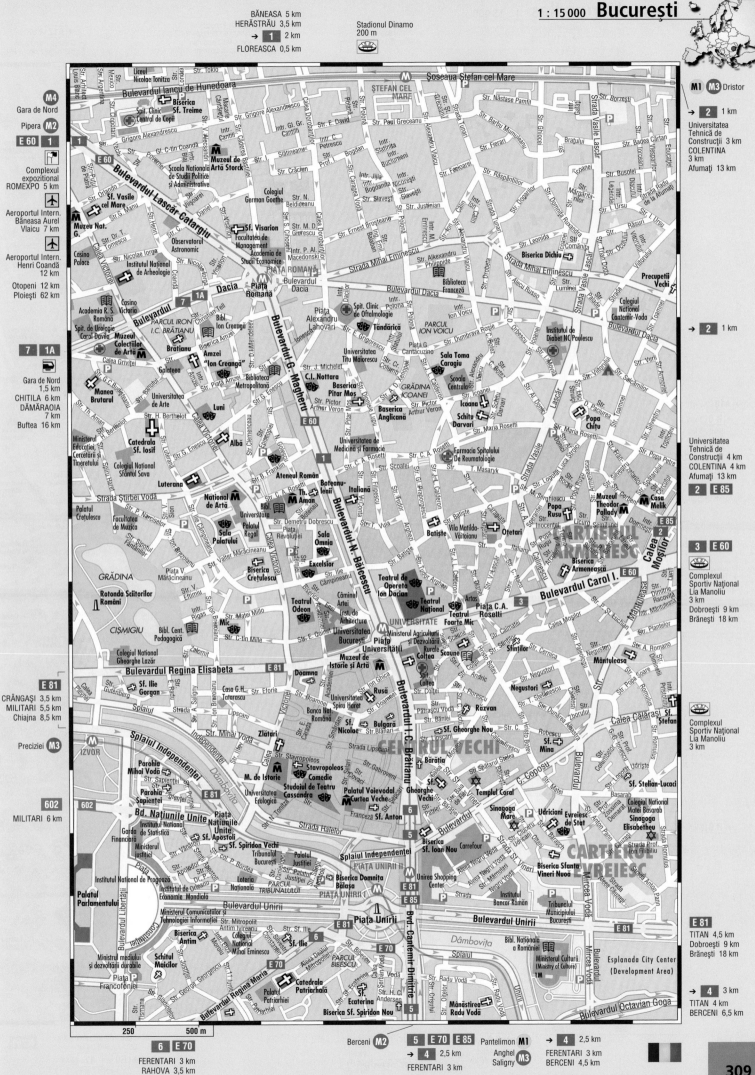

Brussel/Bruxelles 1 : 15 000

WEMMEL 4 km
A10 3 km
JETTE 2 km
Parc de Expositions / Tentoonstellingspark 4,2 km
Stade Roi Baudouin / Koning Boudewijn Stadion 4 km
A12 4 km
Château Royal 2 km / Koninklijk Paleis 2 km
Roi Baudouin / Koning Boudewijn (6)

A10 2 km — Gent 56 km / Gand 56 km

A10 2,5 km — R0 3 km — Gent 56 km / Gand 56 km

R0 2,5 km — Dilbeek 4,5 km

Érasme / Erasmus (5)

R0 3 km

N 6

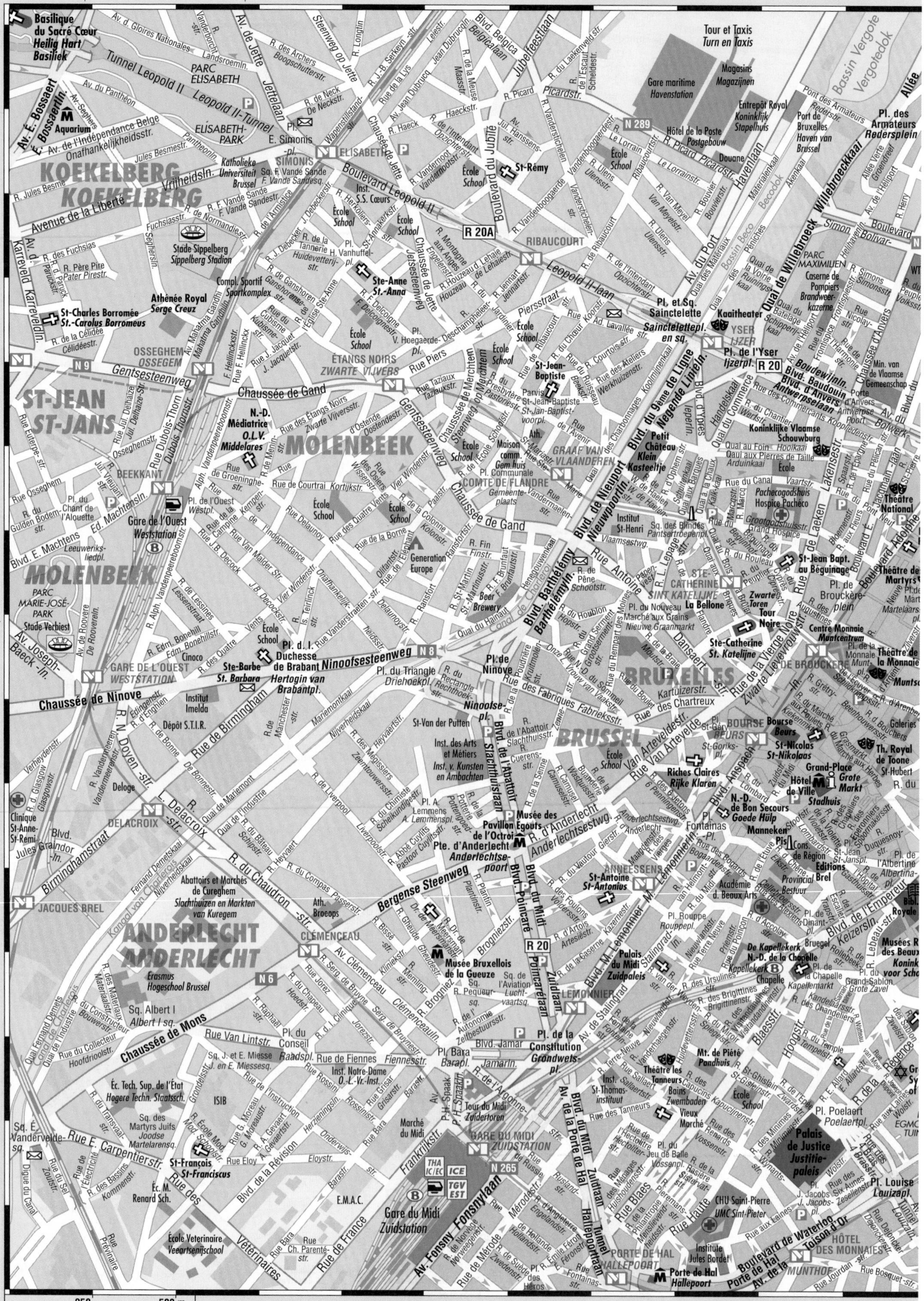

KOEKELBERG

ST-JEAN / ST-JANS

MOLENBEEK

ANDERLECHT

BRUXELLES / BRUSSEL

Basilique du Sacré Cœur / Heilig Hart Basiliek

Aquarium

PARC ELISABETH

ELISABETH-PARK

Katholieke Universiteit Brussel

Stade Sippelberg / Sippelberg Stadion

St-Charles Borromée / St-Carolus Borromeus

OSSEGHEM / OSSEGEM

Athénée Royal Serge Creuz

Gentsesteenweg

N.-D. Médiatrice / O.L.V. Middelares

ÉTANGS NOIRS / ZWARTE VIJVERS

Chaussée de Gand

St-Jean-Baptiste

PARC MARIE-JOSÉ PARK

Stade Verbiest

GARE DE L'OUEST / WESTSTATION

BEEKKANT

Chaussée de Ninove

Ste-Barbe / St. Barbara

Duchesse de Brabant / Hertogin van Brabantpl.

Ninoofsesteenweg

Dépôt S.T.I.B.

DELACROIX

Clinique St-Anne-St-Remi

JACQUES BREL

Abattoirs et Marchés de Cureghem / Slachthuizen en Markten van Kuregem

Erasmus Hogeschool Brussel

Sq. Albert I / Albert I sq.

Chaussée de Mons

ISIB

Éc. Tech. Sup. de l'État / Hogere Techn. Staatssch.

Sq. des Martyrs Juifs / Joodse Martelarensq.

St-François / St-Franciscus

École Vétérinaire / Veeartsenijschool

Gare du Midi / Zuidstation

THA IC/EC ICE TGV EST TVA

Av. Fonsny / Fonsnylaan

N 265

GARE DU MIDI / ZUIDSTATION

Tour et Taxis / Turn en Taxis

Gare maritime / Havenstation

Magasins / Magazijnen

Entrepôt Royal / Koninklijk Stapelhuis

Port de Bruxelles / Haven van Brussel

Douane

PARC MAXIMILIEN

Caserne de Pompiers / Brandweerkazerne

Pl. des Armateurs / Redersplein

Bossin Vergote / Vergotedok

YSER / IJZER

Pl. de l'Yser / IJzerpl. R 20

Blvd. Baudouin / Blvd. d'Anvers / Antwerpselaan

Koninklijke Vlaamse Schouwburg

GRAAF VAN / VLAANDEREN

COMTE DE FLANDRE

Ste-Catherine / Sint Katelijne

Tour Noire / Zwarte Toren

Théâtre de la Monnaie

DE BROUCKÈRE

Bourse / Beurs

St-Nicolas / St-Nikolaas

Grand-Place / Grote Markt

Hôtel de Ville / Stadhuis

N.-D. de Bon Secours / Goede Hulp

Manneken Pis

Théâtre Royal de Toone

ANNEESSENS

St-Antoine / St-Antonius

Académie d. Beaux Arts

Musée Bruxellois de la Gueuze

Palais du Midi / Zuidpaleis

LEMONNIER

Pl. de la Constitution / Grondwetspl.

Théâtre les Tanneurs

Mt. de Piété / Pandhuis

Porte de Hal / Hallepoort

Palais de Justice / Justitiepaleis

Pl. Louise / Louizapl.

Hôtel des Monnaies

250 — 500 m

R0 4 km — Mons 68 km / Bergen 68 km
Mons / Braine-l'Alleud / Charleroi / Lille (F) / London (GB)
IC/EC — TGV — EST — THA
Lille (F) / Paris (F) / Lyon (F)

ST-GILLES / ST-GILLES 0,5 km
UCCLE / UKKEL 4 km
R0 / A7 5 km
Drogenbos 7 km / Halle 15 km / Braine-l'Aleud 16 km

N261

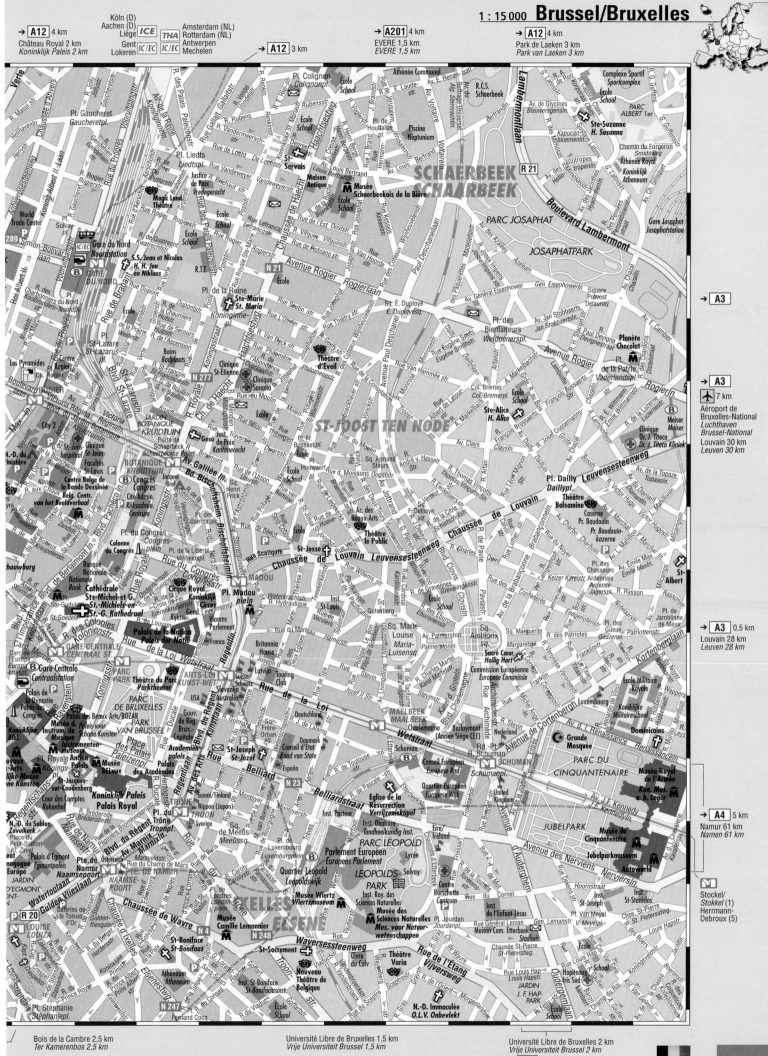

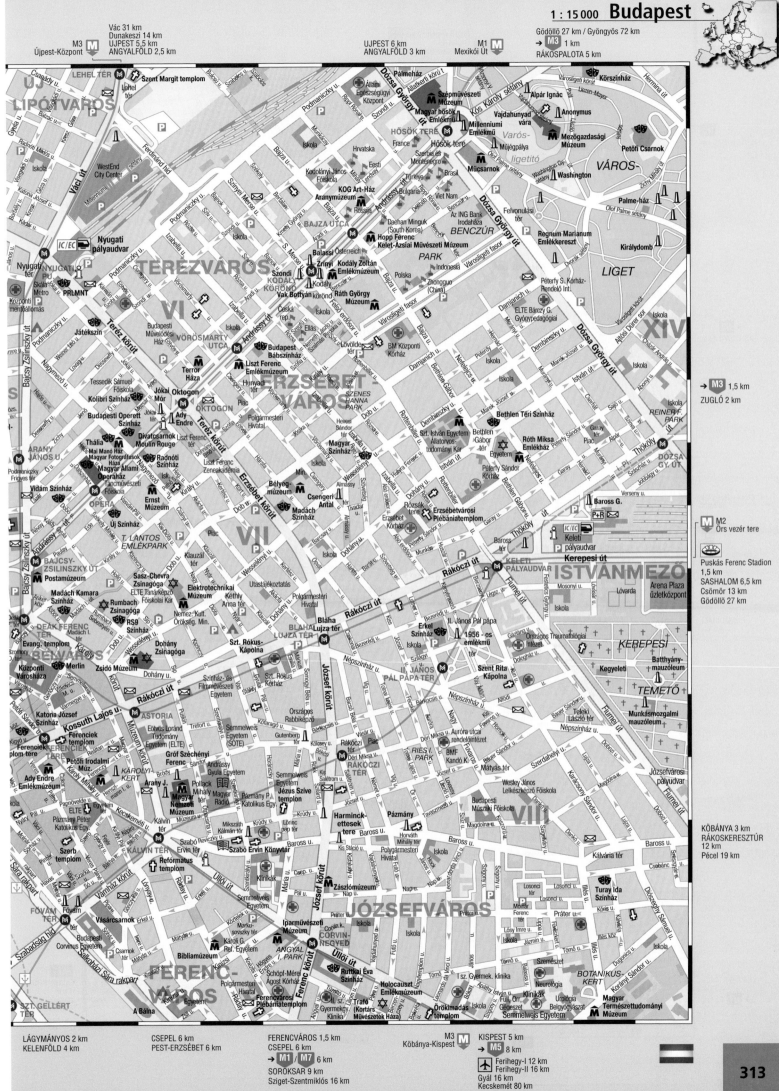

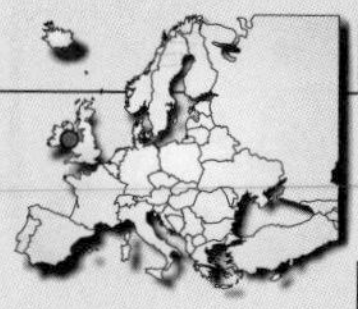

Dublin Airport 12 km
Finglas 4 km
N2 Botanic Gardens 1,5 km
→ M20 3 km

PHIBSBOROUGH
BALLYBOUGH

EAST WALL 1,5 km
MARINO 1 km
MARINO 1,5 km
CLONTARF 4 km
Howth 12 km
DART Malahide Howth

N3 ASHTOWN 3,5 km
Cabra Road N3
→ N3 1 km
ASHTOWN 4 km

STONEYBATTER
Grangegorman Campus (under development)
Dublin Institute of Technology (future site)

Croke Park Stadium
GAA Museum

NORTH WALL 1 km
→ 4 km
Holyhead (GB)
Douglas (GB)

RINGSEND 1,5 km
IRISHTOWN 2 km
DART Greystones

LUAS – Red Line Tallaght
N4 Heuston Station 0,5 km
Phoenix Park 1 km

KILMAINHAM 4,5 km

River Liffey

Temple Bar

Trinity College Dublin

BALLSBRIDGE 2 km
Dun Laoghaire 10 km

CRUMLIN 2,5 km

MARYLAND

Guinness Brewery

St. Patrick's Cathedral

SAINT STEPHEN'S GREEN

IVEAGH GARDENS
National Concert Hall

IRISHTOWN 2 km

DOLPHIN'S BARN 0,5 km
→ N7 4,5 km

City Centre Mosque
National Stadium
Griffith College

Irish Jewish Museum

RANELAGH

N11 DONNY BROOK 1 km
University College 3 km
→ M20 12 km

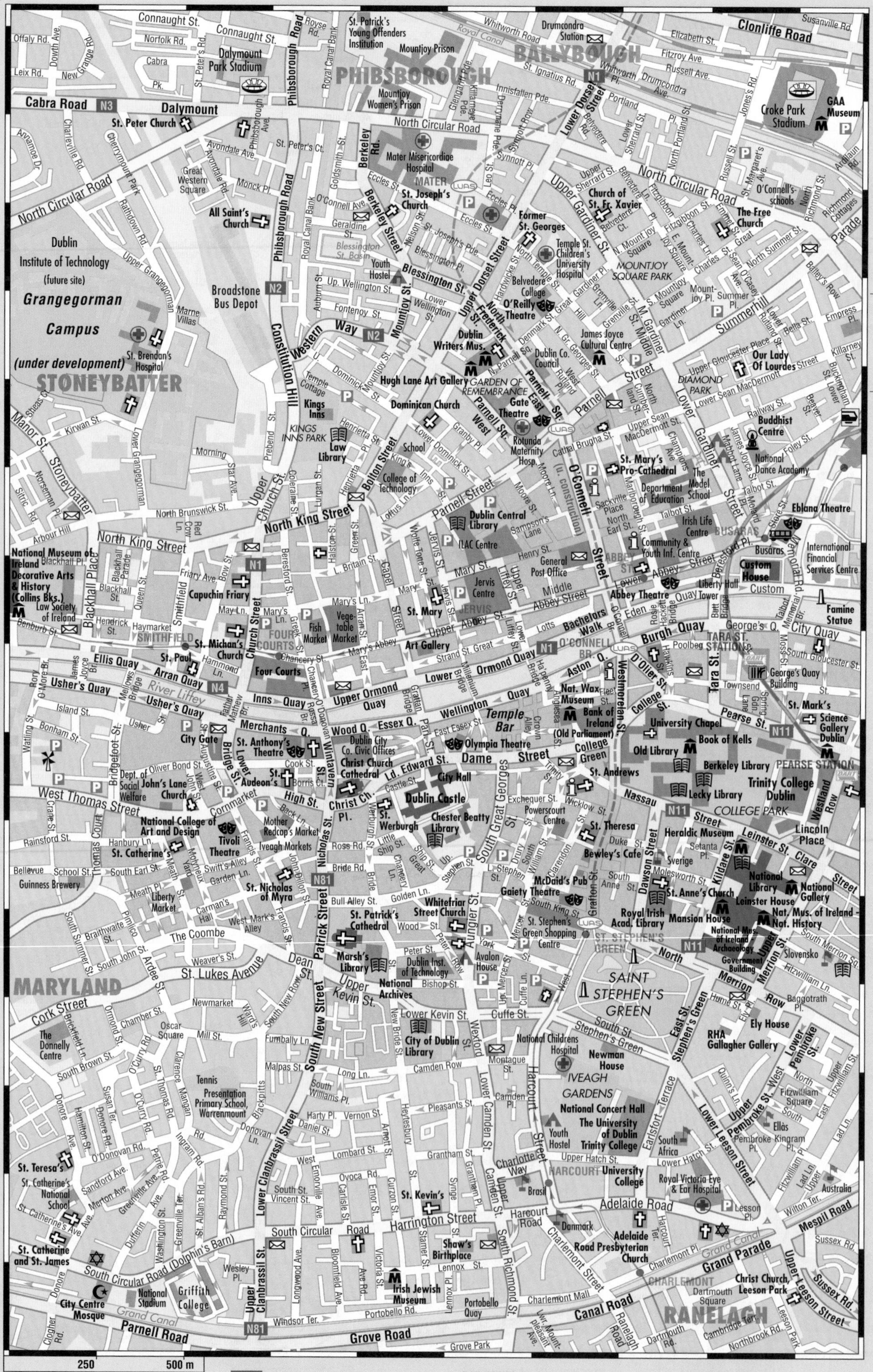

250   500 m

RATHMINES 1 km
N81 TERENURE 2,5 km
Dundrum 5 km

LUAS – Green Line Sandyford

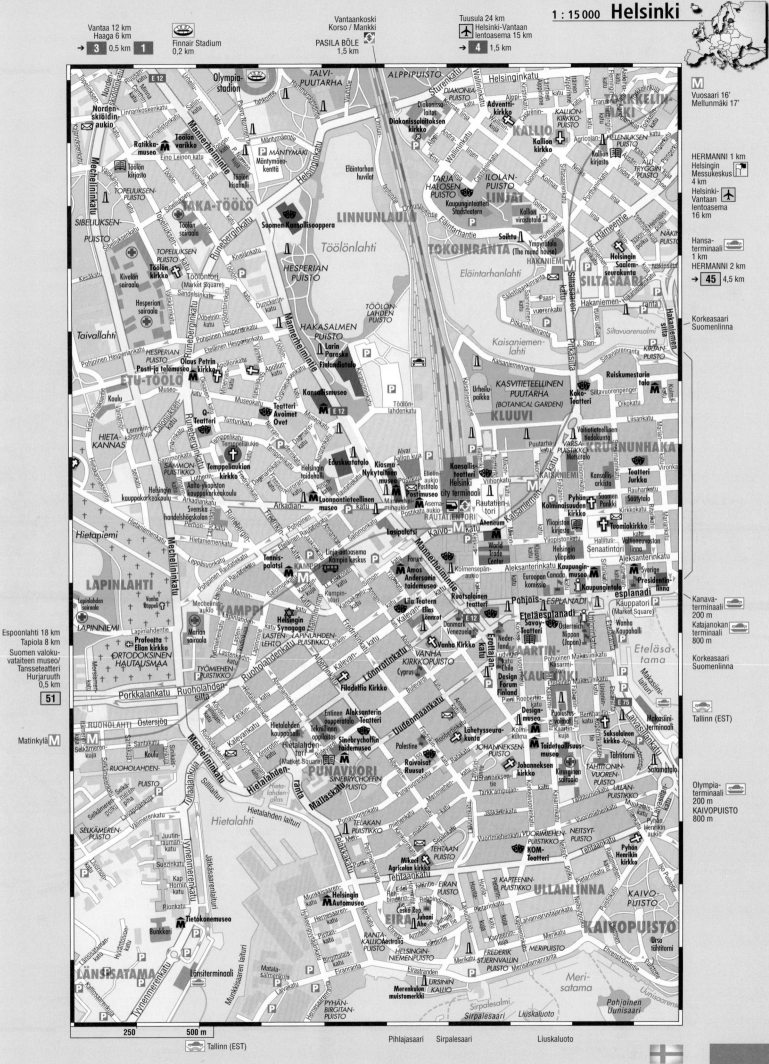

Istanbul 1 : 15 000

EYÜP 2 km
0-1 0,5 km
EYÜP 1,5 km
EYÜP 2 km
AYVANSARAY 1 km
Balat Vapur iskelesi

BAYRAMPAŞA
200 m

Otogar
Bağcılar
Hava Limanı

0-1 1 km
BAYRAMPAŞA
0,5 km

0-1 1 km

Atatürk Hava
Limanı 12 km

SAMATYA 200 m

Halkalı

250   500 m

Atatürk Hava Limanı
10 km

Bandırma 4h 30'
Kuşadası 17h
İzmir 19h 30'
Pireas (GR) 19h 30'
Venézia (I) 57h 30'

Bakırköy

FATİH

Haliç (Golden Horn)

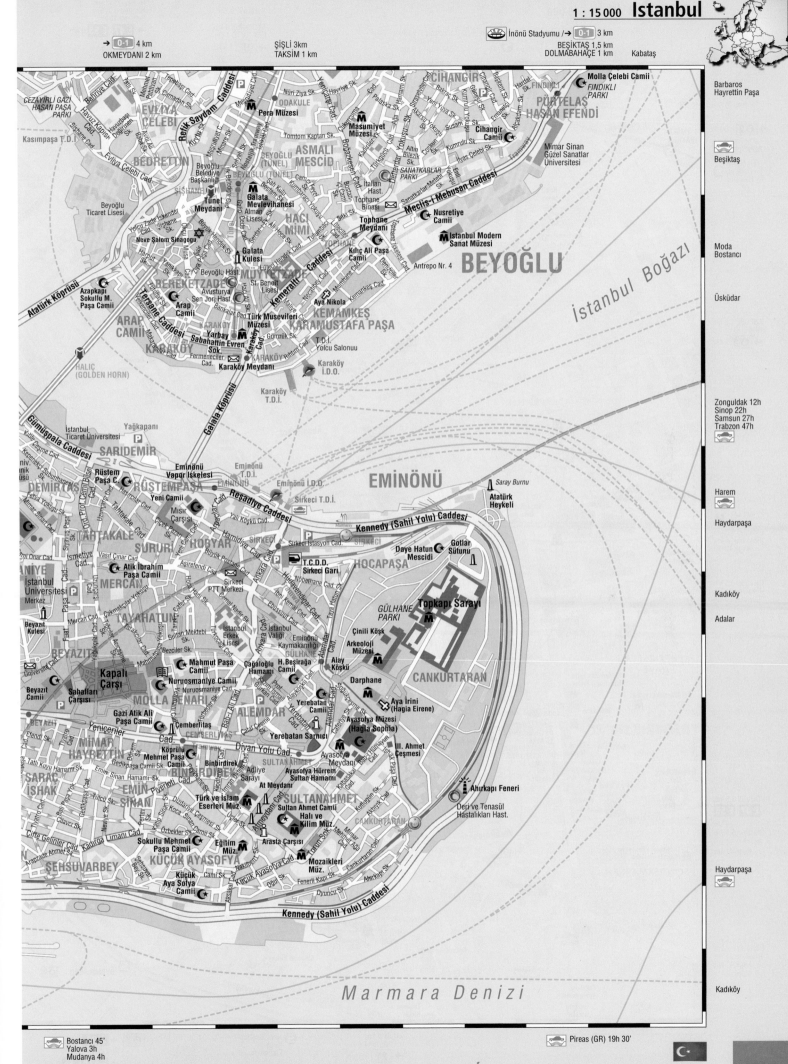

İnönü Stadyumu / → 0-1 3 km

→ 0-1 4 km
OKMEYDANI 2 km
ŞİŞLİ 3km
TAKSİM 1 km
BEŞİKTAŞ 1,5 km
DOLMABAHÇE 1 km
Kabataş

Barbaros
Hayrettin Paşa

Beşiktaş

Moda
Bostancı

Üsküdar

Zonguldak 12h
Sinop 22h
Samsun 27h
Trabzon 47h

Harem

Haydarpaşa

Kadıköy

Adalar

Haydarpaşa

Kadıköy

CEZAYİRLİ GAZİ
HASAN PAŞA
PARKI

Kasımpaşa T.D.İ.

EVLİYA
ÇELEBİ

BEDRETTİN

Beyoğlu
Ticaret Lisesi

Azapkapı
Sokullu M.
Paşa Camii

ARAP
CAMİİ

KÖPRÜ

HALİÇ
(GOLDEN HORN)

Pera Müzesi

ODAKULE

Masumiyet
Müzesi

ASMALI
MESCİD

BEYOĞLU
(TÜNEL)

Tünel
Meydanı

Galata
Mevlevihanesi

HACI
MİMİ

Neve Şalom Sinagogu

Galata
Kulesi

MÜEYYEDZADE

BEREKETZADE

Arap
Camii

Türk Musevileri
Müzesi

Yarbay
Sabahattin Evren
Sok.

Karaköy Meydanı

KEMERALTI

KEMAMKEŞ
KARAMUSTAFA PAŞA

Aya Nikola

Kılıç Ali Paşa
Camii

Tophane
Meydanı

Nusretiye
Camii

İstanbul Modern
Sanat Müzesi

Antrepo Nr. 4

BEYOĞLU

CİHANGİR

Molla Çelebi Camii
FINDIKLI
PARKI

PÜRTELAŞ
HASAN EFENDİ

Cihangir
Camii

Mimar Sinan
Güzel Sanatlar
Üniversitesi

SANATKARLAR
PARKI

Meclis-i Mebusan Caddesi

İstanbul Boğazı

Karaköy
T.D.İ.

Karaköy
İ.D.O.

T.D.İ.
Yolcu Salonuu

Gümüşpala Caddesi

İstanbul
Ticaret Üniversitesi

Yağkapanı

SARIDEMİR

Rüstem
Paşa C.

RÜSTEMPAŞA

DEMİRTAŞ

Yeni Camii

Mısır
Çarşısı

Eminönü
Vapur İskelesi

EMİNÖNÜ

Eminönü
T.D.İ.

Reşadiye Caddesi

Eminönü İ.D.O.

Sirkeci T.D.İ.

EMİNÖNÜ

Saray Burnu

Atatürk
Heykeli

Kennedy (Sahil Yolu) Caddesi

TAHTAKALE

SURURİ

HOBYAR

SİRKECİ

Sirkeci İstasyon Cad.

SİRKECİ

T.C.D.D.
Sirkeci Garı

HOCAPAŞA

Daye Hatun
Mescidi

Gotlar
Sütunu

İstanbul
Üniversitesi
Merkez

Atik İbrahim
Paşa Camii

MERCAN

PTT Merkezi

TAYAHATUN

İstanbul
Erkek Lisesi

İstanbul
Valiliği

Eminönü
Kaymakamlığı

GÜLHANE

GÜLHANE
PARKI

Çinili Köşk

Arkeoloji
Müzesi

Alay
Köşkü

Topkapı Sarayı

CANKURTARAN

Beyazıt
Kulesi

BEYAZIT

Mahmut Paşa
Camii

Kapalı
Çarşı

Nuruosmaniye Camii

Nuruosmaniye Cad.

Çağaloğlu
Hamamı

H. Beşirağa
Camii

Darphane

Beyazıt
Camii

Sahaflar
Çarşısı

Gazi Atik Ali
Paşa Camii

Çemberlitaş

ÇEMBERLİTAŞ

Yerebatan
Camii

Yerebatan Sarnıcı

Aya İrini
(Hagia Eirene)

Ayasofya
Müzesi
(Hagia Sophia)

III. Ahmet
Çeşmesi

MOLLA FENARİ

ALEMDAR

Divan Yolu Cad.

SULTANAHMET

Ayasofya
Meydanı

MİMAR
HAYRETTİN

Köprülü
Mehmet Paşa
Camii

BİNBİRDİREK

Binbirdirek

Adliye
Sarayı

Ayasofya Hürrem
Sultan Hamamı

At Meydanı

Ahırkapı Feneri

Deri ve Tenasül
Hastalıkları Hast.

SARAÇ
İSHAK

EMİN
SİNAN

Türk ve İslam
Eserleri Müz.

Sultan Ahmet Camii

Halı ve
Kilim Müz.

SULTANAHMET

CANKURTARAN

Arasta Çarşısı

Sokullu Mehmet
Paşa Camii

Eğitim
Müz.

Mozaikleri
Müz.

ŞEHSUVARBEY

KÜÇÜK AYASOFYA

Küçük
Aya Sofya
Camii

Marmara Denizi

Kennedy (Sahil Yolu) Caddesi

Top margin directions:

Helsingør 43 km
Hørsholm 21 km
Søllerød 10 km

Søllerød 10 km
Lyngby 6 km
BUDDINGE 6 km
GENTOFTE 4 km

→ E 47 / E 55 6 km

Gladsaxe 7,5 km
BUDDINGE 6 km
EMDRUP 3,5 km

→ 19 1,5 km

→ 19 1,5 km

Klampenborg
Hellerup

Left margin directions:

BRØNSHØJ 1,5 km
HULSUM 3,5 km
Gladsaxe 7 km
Herlev 6 km
Farum 15 km
Hillerød 31 km

→ O2 0,5 km

VANLØSE 2 km
RØDOVRE 5 km

Flintholm
Danshøj
Ny Ellebjerg

VANLØSE 1,5 km
BRØNSHØJ 2 km

→ O2 2 km

(M1/M2)
Vanløse

Glostrup 6,5 km
Roskilde 34 km
Køge 42 km

Glostrup 6,5 km
Roskilde 34 km
Taastrup 10 km
Køge 42 km

RØDOVRE 3,5 km

→ E 47 / E 55

4 km
Glostrup 6,5 km
Roskilde 34 km
Køge 41 km

VALBY 1,5 km
Glostrup 6,5 km
Roskilde 34 km
Køge 41 km

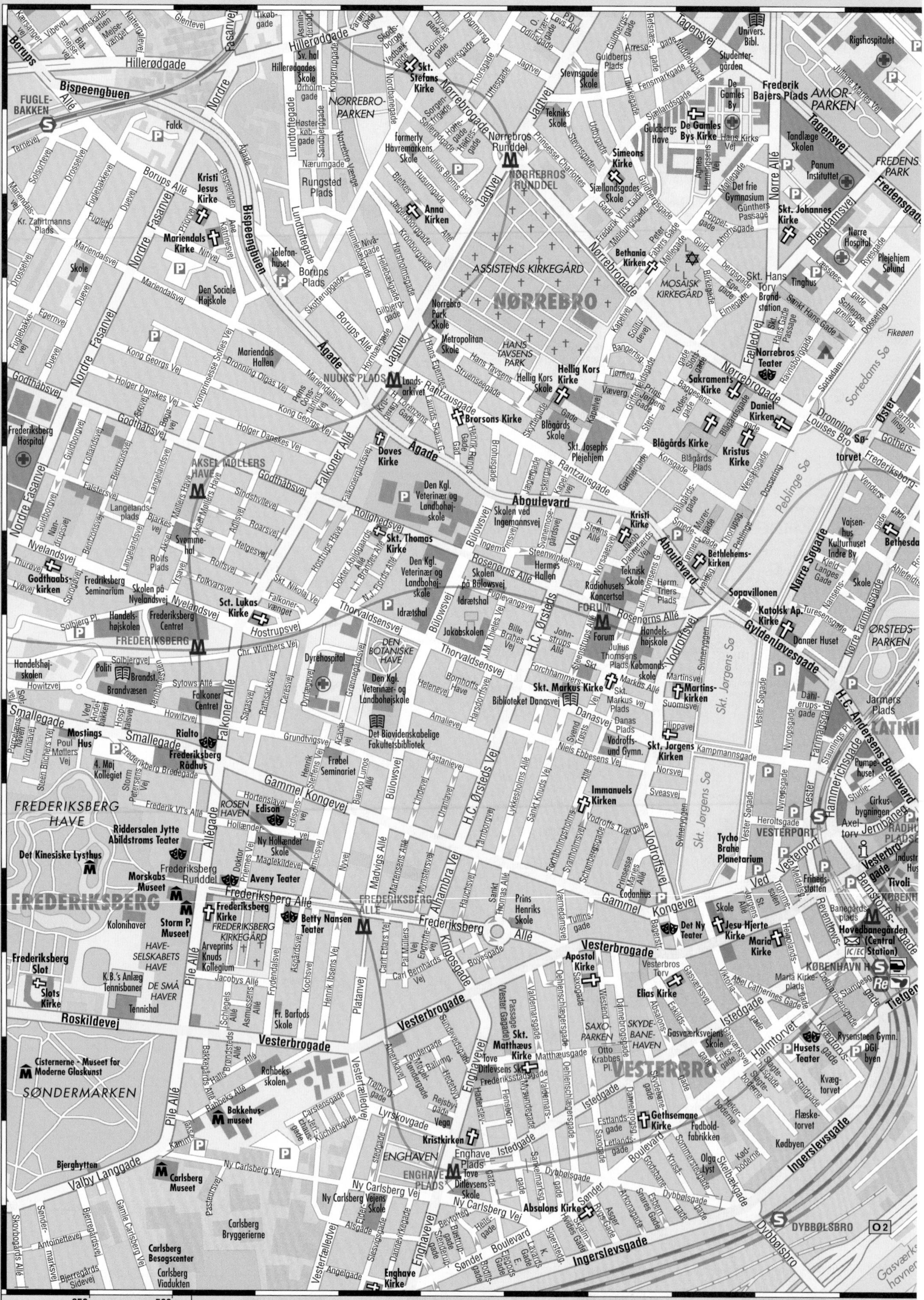

Bottom margin directions:

VALBY 2 km
HVIDOVRE 4,5 km
Høje Taastrup
Køge
Frederikssund

→ 21 3,5 km

→ E 47 / E 55 6 km

O2 → E 20 3,5 km
HVIDOVRE 5 km
→ E 47 / E 55 7 km
Roskilde 35 km
Køge 42 km

Major area labels:

NØRREBRO
FREDERIKSBERG
VESTERBRO
FREDERIKSBERG HAVE
SØNDERMARKEN
AMORPARKEN
FREDENS PARK
ØRSTEDSPARKEN
ASSISTENS KIRKEGÅRD
MOSAISK KIRKEGÅRD
HANS TAVSENS PARK
DEN BOTANISKE HAVE

Scale bar: 250 — 500 m

Selected labels:

Skt. Stefans Kirke, Anna Kirken, Kristi Jesus Kirke, Mariendals Kirke, Brorsons Kirke, Doves Kirke, Skt. Thomas Kirke, Sct. Lukas Kirke, Godthaabs kirken, Hellig Kors Kirke, Sakraments Kirke, Daniel Kirken, Blågårds Kirke, Kristus Kirke, Simeons Kirke, Skt. Johannes Kirke, Bethania Kirken, Kristi Kirke, Bethlehems-kirken, Skt. Markus Kirke, Martins-kirken, Skt. Jørgens Kirken, Immanuels Kirken, Bethesda, Jesu Hjerte Kirke, Maria Kirke, Apostel Kirke, Elias Kirke, Skt. Matthæus Kirke, Gethsemane Kirke, Kristkirken, Absalons Kirke, Enghave Kirke, Slots Kirke

Frederiksberg Rådhus, Frederiksberg Slot, Frederiksberg Kirke, Storm P. Museet, Morskabs Museet, Det Kinesiske Lysthus, Cisternerne – Museet for Moderne Glaskunst, Bakkehus-museet, Carlsberg Museet, Carlsberg Bryggerierne, Carlsberg Besøgscenter

Nørrebros Teater, Aveny Teater, Betty Nansen Teater, Riddersalen Jytte Abildstroms Teater, Det Ny Teater, Husets Teater

Tycho Brahe Planetarium, Tivoli, Hovedbanegården (Central Station), KØBENHAVN H, Vesterport

Rigshospitalet, Panum Instituttet, Frederiksberg Hospital, Nørre Hospital

NØRREBROS RUNDDEL, NUUKS PLADS, Frederik Bajers Plads, Jarmers Plads, ENGHAVE PLADS

Vesterbrogade, Gammel Kongevej, Ny Carlsberg Vej, Valby Langgade, Roskildevej, Ingerslevsgade, Nørrebrogade, Jagtvej, Falkoner Allé, Nordre Fasanvej, Godthåbsvej, Bispeengbuen, Borups Allé, Hillerødgade, Frederiksberg Allé, H.C. Andersens Boulevard, Åboulevard, Agade, H.C. Ørsteds Vej, Gyldenløvesgade, Vodroffsvej

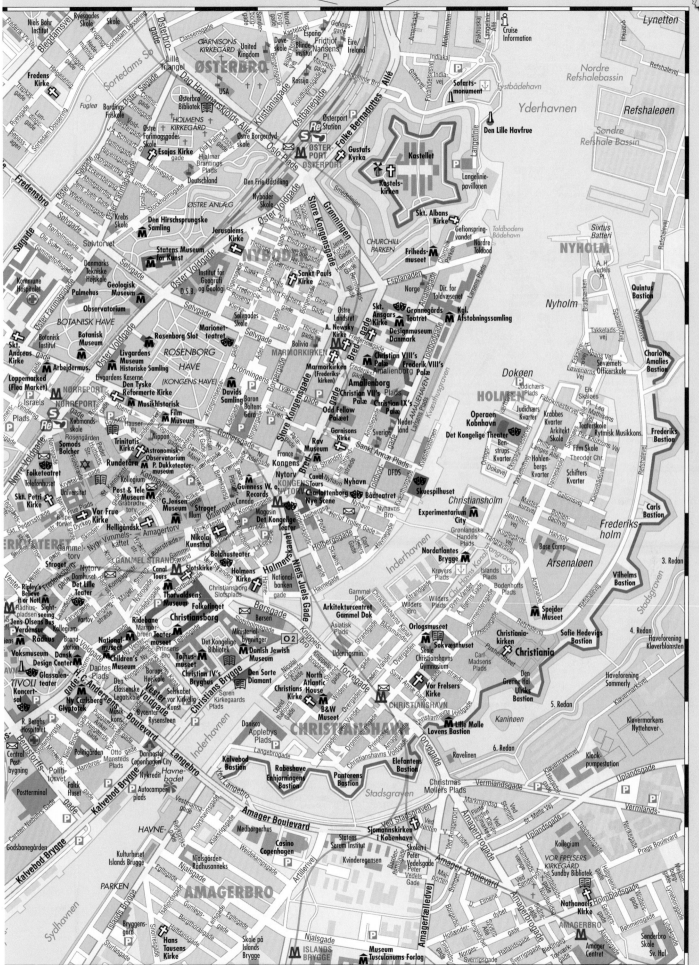

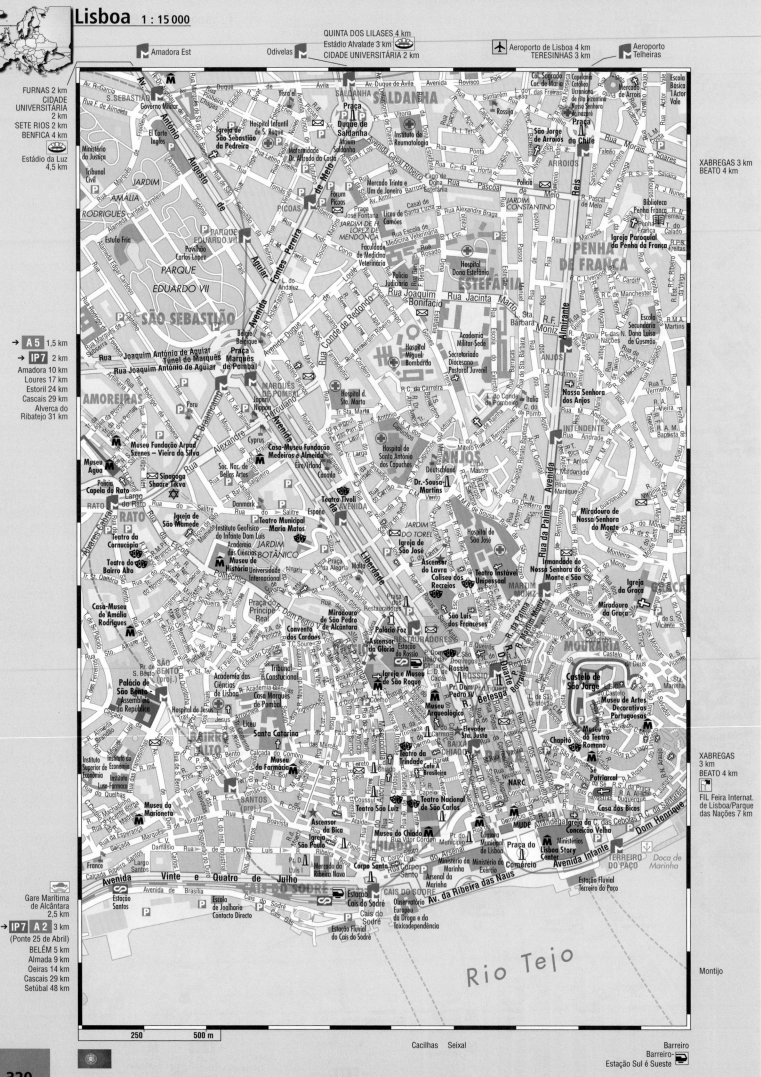

Lisboa 1 : 15 000

LJ-STOŽICE 1,5 km
ŠRC Stožice 1,5 km
→ 104 1,5 km
→ H3 1,5 km

IC/EC Villach (A) Jesenice

→ H3
8 1,5 km
→ A 2 4 km
ŠENTVID 4 km
Medno 7 km
Medvode 11 km
Vodice 15 km
Letališče Jožefa Pučnika Ljubljana 19 km

→ H3 3 km
LJ-ŠMARTNO 4 km
→ A 1 E 57 5 km
LJ-ŠENTJAKOB 6 km
Litija 31 km

IC/EC Zidani Most Maribor Zagreb (HR)

LJ-NOVE FUŽINE 2,5 km
→ A 1 4 km
ZALOG 8 km

IC/EC Pivka Trieste (I)

LJ-ZGORNJA HRUŠICA 2 km
→ A 1 4 km
ZADVOR 6 km

→ 409 2,5 km
→ A 1 2,5 km
Brezovica pri Ljubljani 7 km
Dragomer 9 km
Vrhnika 18 km

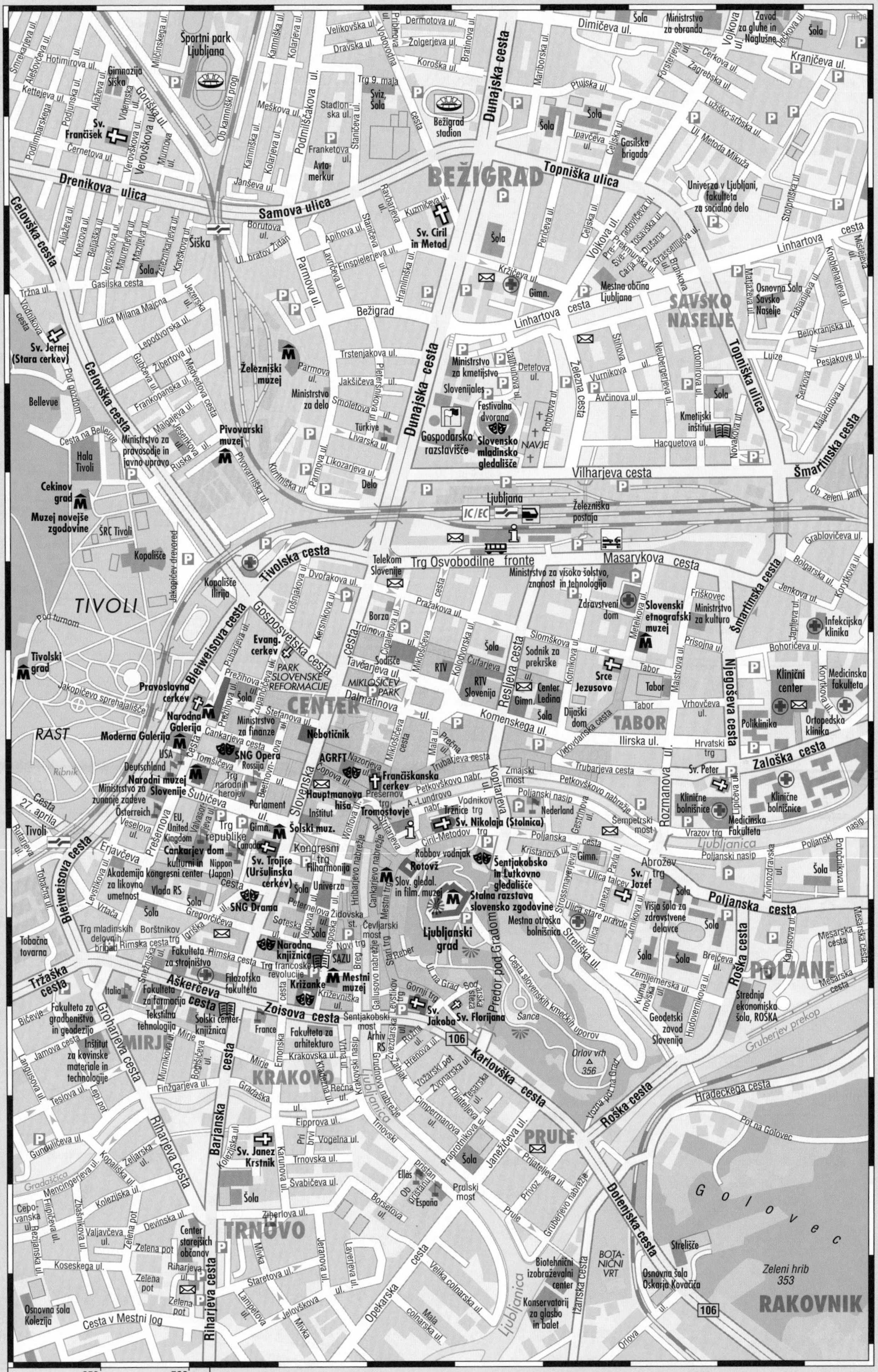

250 500 m

→ A 1 1,5 km

LJ-ILOVICA 1 km
Ig 11 km
Borovnica 30 km

106
Lavrica 6 km
Škofica 10 km
→ A 1 A 2 3,5 km

HARROW 11 km
→ M1 7 km
WILLESDEN 6 km
Elephant & Castle
Edgware Road

Harrow 11 km
Regent's Park 2,5 km
→ A40 300 m
Harrow Weddelstone

Harrow & Wealdstone
Stanmore

→ A40
WEMBLEY 9 km

Kensington
Wimbledon
Richmond
Ealing Broadway

→ M41 3 km
WILLESDEN 7 km

West Ruislip
Ealing Broadway

Congestion Charging Zone

HAMMERSMITH 3 km
HOUNSLOW 6 km

Circle line

Earls Court
Exhibition Centre 1 km

HAMMERSMITH 2,5 km

→ M4 6,5 km

✈ Heathrow Airport 21 km

Ealing Broadway
Kensington
Richmond
Uxbridge
Wimbledon
✈ Heathrow Airport

BAYSWATER
PADDINGTON (Hamm. & City)
Paddington Station
PADDINGTON
South Wharf Rd.
Praed

KENSINGTON GARDENS
The Round Pond
Speke's Monument
Peter Pan Statue
Physical Energy Statue
Queens Temple
The Long Water

HYDE PARK
New Lodge
The old Police House
Ranger Lodge
Reservoir
Reformer's Tree
Underground Car Park
The Four Winds Fountain
Nursery
Magazine
Sackler Serpentine Gallery
Rima Statue
Norwegian / British Monument
Bandstand
War Memorial
Achilles Statue
Holocaust Memorial
The Serpentine
Boating Lake
Boat Houses
The Diana, Princess of Wales Memorial Fountain
The Lido
Serpentine Gallery
Bandstand

Wellington Museum, Apsley House
Hyde Park Corner
Wellington Mon.
Wellington Arch
HYDE PARK CORNER

MAYFAIR
Roosevelt Memorial
Marble Arch
Speaker's Corner
Cumberland Gate
Bayswater Road
Park Lane

PALACE GARDENS

FOOTBALL PITCHES
Rotten Row
New Ride
KNIGHTSBRIDGE

Albert Memorial
Kensington Gore
Royal College of Art
Royal Albert Hall
KNIGHTSBRIDGE
Westminster Synagogue
Hyde Park Barracks
Russian Orthodox Cath.
Goethe Institut
College

Royal College of Music
Imperial College
Science Museum
Victoria and Albert Museum
Brompton Oratory
Natural History Museum
Cromwell Road
Lycée Français Charles de Gaulle (French Univ. Coll.)
SOUTH KENSINGTON

Harrods
BELGRAVIA
Belgrave Square
Sloane Street
Sloane Square
Holy Trinity
Royal Ct. Theatre
Saatchi Gallery
Duke of York's Headquarters
Victoria Coach Sta.
The Colonnades Shopping Centre
St. Barnabas

BROMPTON
Royal Marsden Hospital
St. Luke's Gardens
St. Luke
Royal Brompton Hospital
Police
King's Road

CHELSEA
Welsh United Reformed Chapel
Chelsea Square
Carlyle Square
National Army Museum
Chilianwalla Memorial
Royal Hospital Chelsea
RANELAGH GARDENS
BURTON'S COURT
Chelsea Barracks
Grosvenor Canal
Lister Hospital
CHELSEA PHYSIC GARDEN
Chelsea Embankment
Chelsea Bridge
Grosvenor Road
Battersea Park 200 m
CLAPHAM 2,5 km
✈ Gatwick Airport 43 km

250   500 m

FULHAM 2 km
WANDSWORTH 4,5 km
PUTNEY 5,5 km
RICHMOND 8 km
Hampton Court Pier

Stamford Bridge (Chelsea F.C.) 0,5 km
FULHAM 1,5 km
WANDSWORTH 4 km

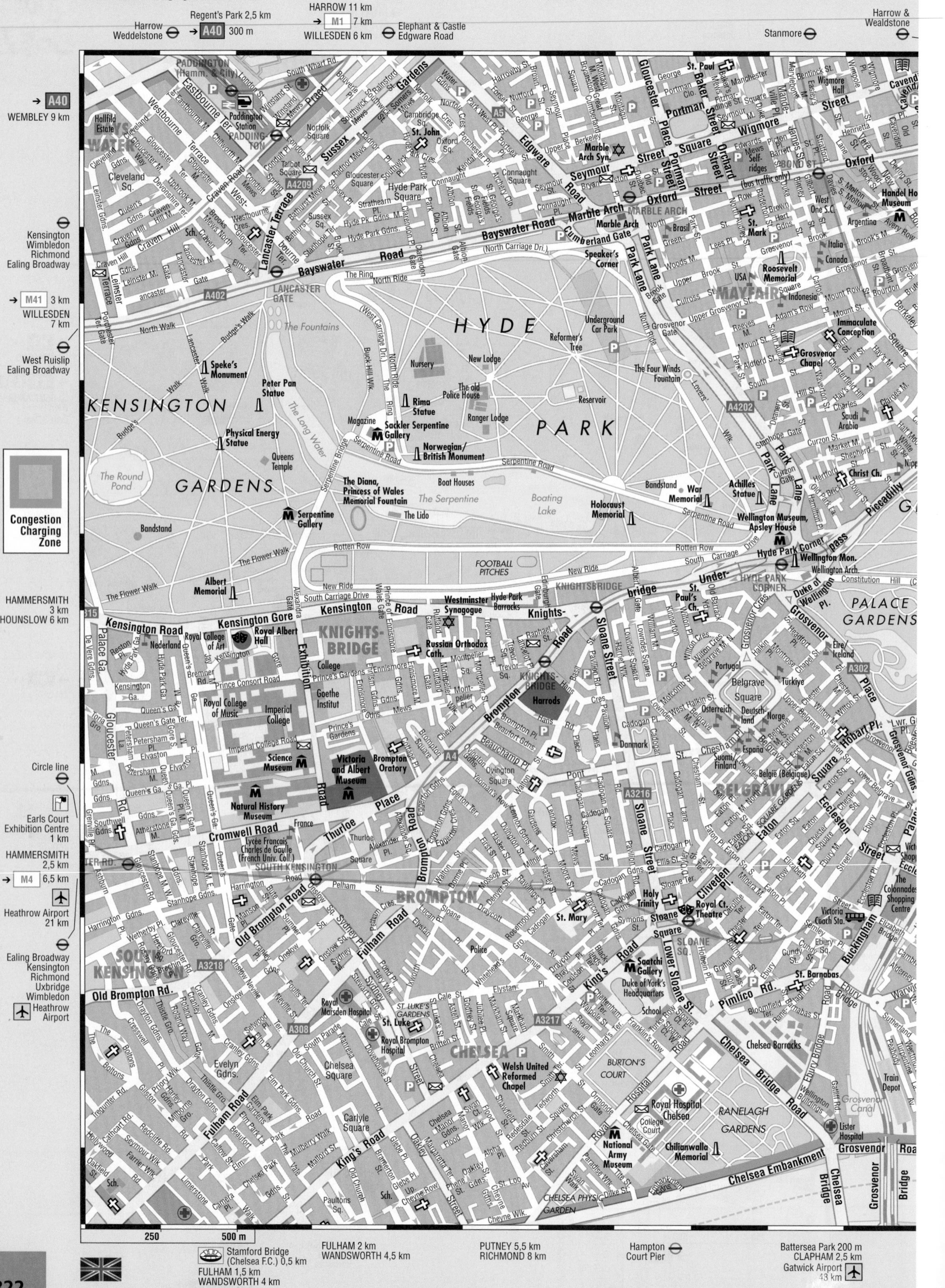

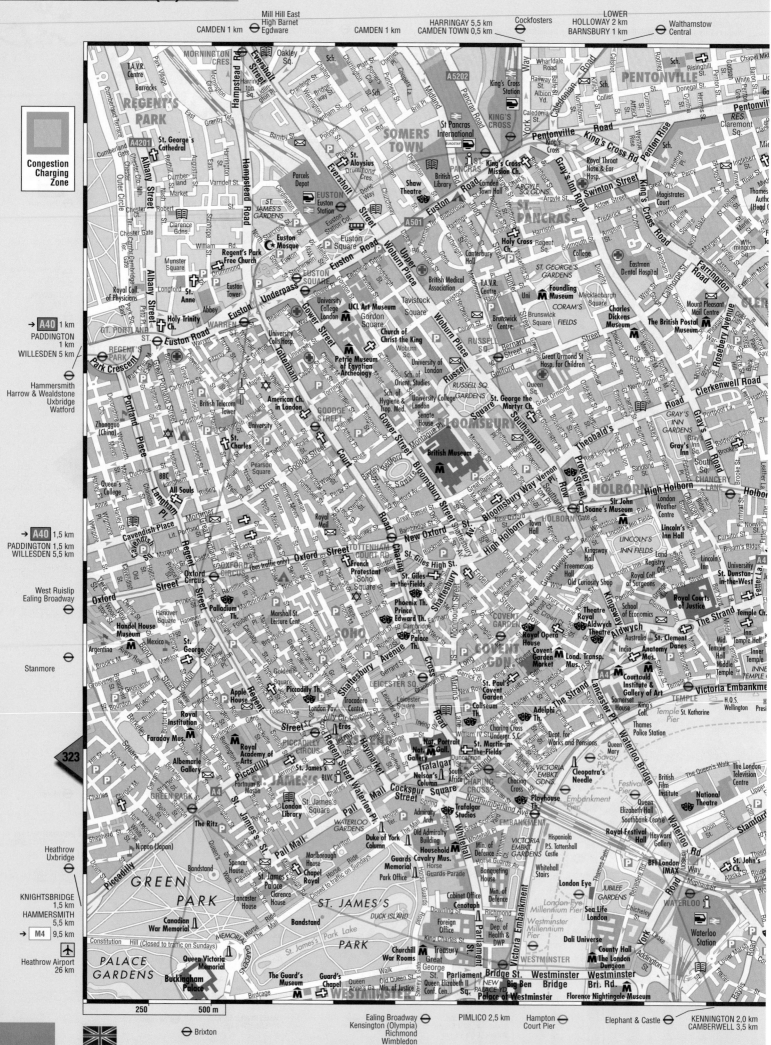

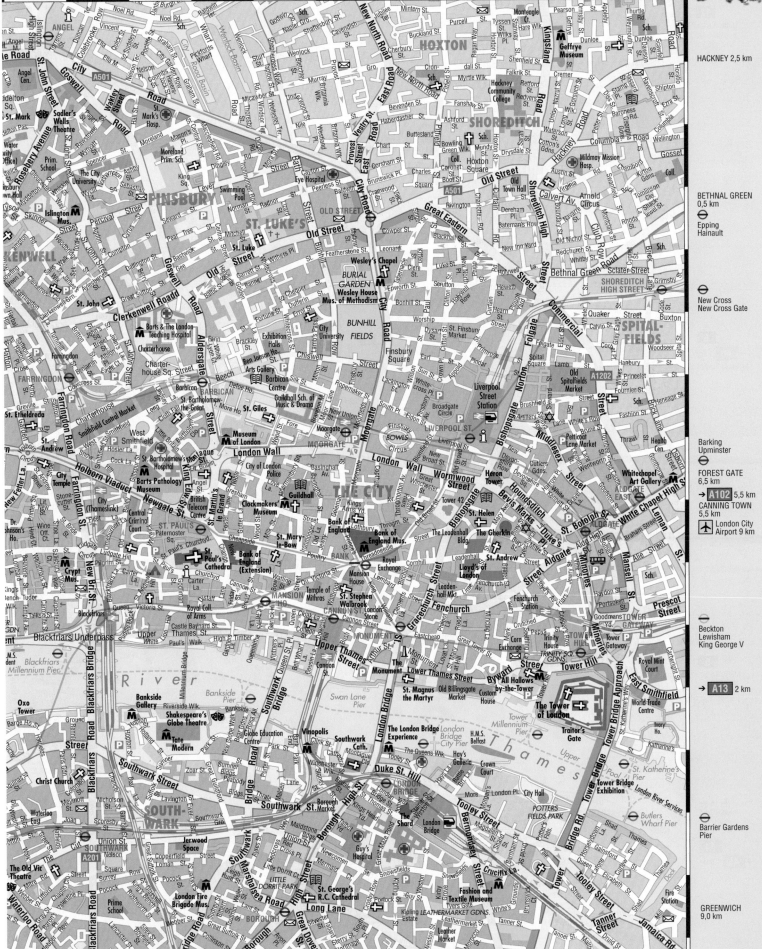

Steinsel 6 km
Walferdange 3,5 km **7**

12
Bridel 3,5 km
Kopstal 5 km
Saeul 25 km

11
7

EICH

Rue de Muehlenbach

Rue de Rollingergrund

Rue Albert Unden

MUHLENBACH

215
55

PARC
LAVAL

Bellevue

Château de
Septfontaines

Villeroy
et Boch

Faïencerie

ROLLINGER-
GRUND

Reckendallerkopp

Château de
Limpertsberg

Rue de Kopstal

Rue des Sept-Fontaines

Avenue Pasteur

Rue de l'Avenir

Ecole

230
Rue du Reckenthal

Centre Universitaire de
Luxembourg

Intern. Don Bosco

Ecole

Lycée Technique
Michel Lucius

Centres
d'enseignements
professionnels

Couvent

Côte d'Eich

CIMETIÈRE
ISRAÉLITE

52

Lycée techn.
des Arts
et Metiers

215

Saint Jog

Pl.
Auguste
Laurent

Lycée
Garçons

Rue de Gibraltar

Centre
de Logopédie

Ecole

Ecole

PARC
TONNY
NEUMANN

Pl. LIMPERTSBERG

Maurice
Pescatore

Rue Thomas Edison

Val Saint André

R. Nicolas
Braunshausen

R. A. Fleming

Ecole

Centre Hospitalier
de Luxembourg

Maternité Grande
Duchesse Charlotte

Rue Edmund Duné

Rue Michel Engels

Château
d'eau

Stade Josy Barthel

Boulevard Napoléon 1er

Blvd.
Napoléon 1er

Rue de François Boch

CIMETIÈRE

NOTRE DAME

Rue de Rollingergrund

Eire/Ireland

12

Grand Théâtre
de la ville

España

Pont Grande-Duchesse

Fondation
J. P. Pescatore

Tours
Vauban

PFAFFEN-
THAL

57

6
→ A6 1 km
Strassen 1,5 km

Route d'Arlon

6

P+R

Route d'Arlon

Pl.
de l'Etoile

Deutschland

Villa Vauban

Boulevard Royal

STATEC

Österreich

Schweiz

Théâtre
des Capucins

Cercle

Val Sainte-Croix

Val Sainte-Croix

Pl. des
Pays-Bas

Allée Leopold Goebel

Blvd. Grande-Duchesse Joséphine-Charlotte

CIMETIÈRE
DE MERL

BÉLAIR

Rue Schroblgen

Clinique
Sacré Cœur

Couvent de
Franciscaines

Belair
Diderich
Ecole

Av. Gaston Diderich

Avenue Gaston Diderich

Chap. du
Christ-Roi

51

PARC
DE
VILLE

Grande
Synagogue de
Luxembourg

Nippon
(Japan)

Av. Emile Reuter

Gare
des autobus

Sainte
Elisabeth

Pl.
Winston
Churchill

USA

Pl. de
Bruxelles

Casino **50**

Blvd. F.D.

Notre-
Dame

CENTRE

5

X Septembre

Pont et
Chaussées
Admin

France

United
Kingdom

Avenue Marie-Thérèse

PARC
ED. KLEIN

4

Palais
Episcopal
(Conv. Centre)

Monument
Constitution du
Souvenir

Pl. de
Metz

2

3

Avenue Guillaume

5A

Théâtre
National du
Luxembourg

Portugal

5
MERL 0,5 km
→ A6 1 km

Route de Longwy

PARC
DE
MERL

VALLÉE

Villa Pauly

DE

Nederland

Italia

Eglise du
Sacré-Cœur

ARBED

Avenue de la Gare

50

Athénée
de Luxembourg

Clinique
Sainte Thérèse

Place
de Paris

Ecole Privée
Fieldgen

GARE

PÉTRUSSE

LA

Conservatoire
de Musique

Ecole
de Commerce
et de Gestion

Terrain
de Sport

Lycée
Michel Rodange

230

Abattoirs
Communaux

Salzhof

Pl. Saints
Pierre
et Paul

Eglise Saints-Pierre
et Paul

Direction

Musée des
Tramways
et des Bus

Dépôt Autobus

Gazomètre

Usine à Gaz

HOLLERICH

56

CIMETIÈRE
HOLLERICH

Rue de Bouillon

Rue de Hollerich

56

A4

Autoroute d'Esch

Merlebach

230

P+R

Namur (B) 1h 39'
Arlon (B) 17'
IC/EC

A4
→ A6 1,5 km

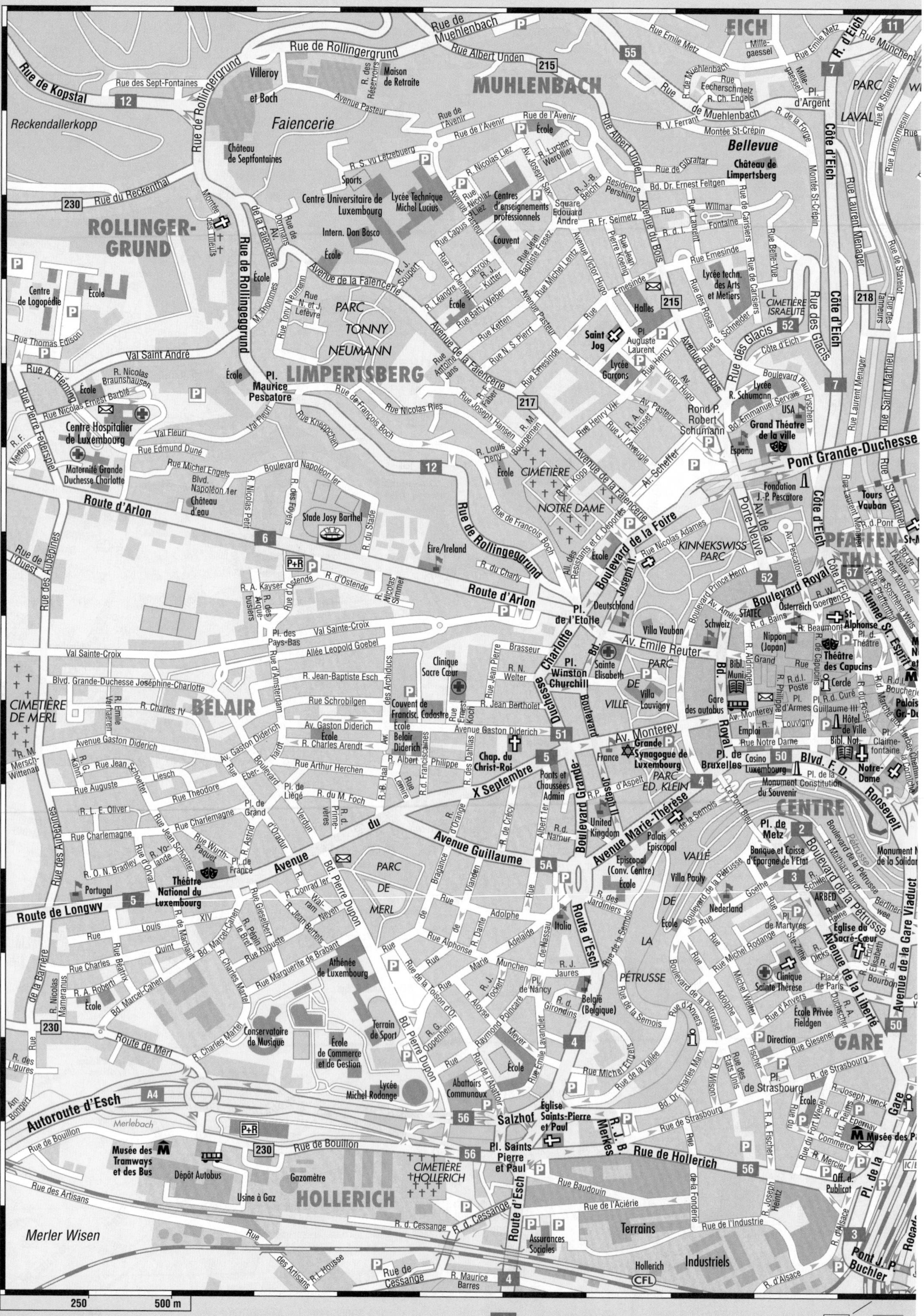

Merler Wisen

Rue des Artisans

Assurances
Sociales

Terrains
Industriels

Hollerich

Pont J.P.
Buchler

3

250   500 m

4 GASPERICH 1 km
→ A6 2 km
Leudelange 5,5 km

Metz (F) 39' IC/EC **→ A3**
→ A1
2,3 km

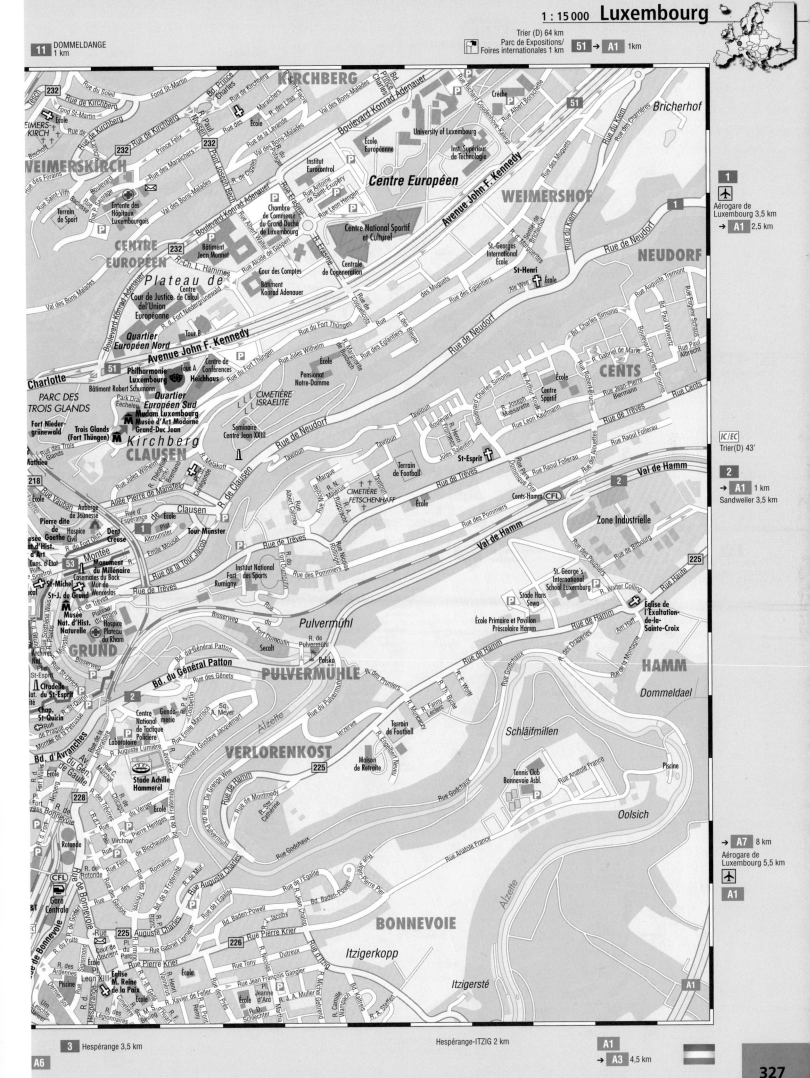

Trier (D) 64 km
Parc de Expositions/
Foires internationales 1 km

51 → **A1** 1km

11 DOMMELDANGE
1 km

232

KIRCHBERG

WEIMERSKIRCH

Bd. Prince Charles

Boulevard Konrad Adenauer

232

232

University of Luxembourg

École Européenne

Inst. Supérieur de Technologie

Institut Eurocontrol

Centre Européen

WEIMERSHOF

1
Aérogare de
Luxembourg 3,5 km
→ **A1** 2,5 km

CENTRE EUROPÉEN

Chambre de Commerce du Grand Duché de Luxembourg

Bâtiment Jean Monnet

Plateau de

Centre Cour de Justice de Calcul del'Union Européenne

Cour des Comptes

Centrale de Cogeneration

Bâtiment Konrad Adenauer

Centre National Sportif et Culturel

St-Georges International École

St-Henri

NEUDORF

Quartier Européen Nord

Tour B

Avenue John F. Kennedy

51

Philharmonie Luxembourg

Heichhaus

Centre de Conférences

Tour A

Quartier Européen Sud

Bâtiment Robert Schumann

Park Drai Eechelen

Pensionat Notre-Damme

CENTS

Charlotte

PARC DES TROIS GLANDS

Mudam Luxembourg Musée d'Art Moderne Grand-Duc Jean

Fort Nieder-grünewald

Trois Glands (Fort Thüngen)

CIMETIÈRE ISRAÉLITE

Seminaire Centre Jean XXIII

Centre Sportif

IC/EC
Trier (D) 43'

Kirchberg

2
→ **A1** 1 km
Sandweiler 3,5 km

CLAUSEN

218

Cents-Hamm **CFL**

Zone Industrielle

Auberge de Jeunesse

Pierre dite de Goethe

Hospice Civil

Tour Münster

Altmünster

St-George's International School Luxemburg

225

Musée Goethe d'Hist. d'Art

Cons. d'État

Monument du Millénaire

53

Casemates du Bock Mur de Wenceslas

Institut National des Sports

Fort Rumigny

Stade Hans Sowa

École Primaire et Pavillon Préscolaire Hamm

Église de l'Exaltation-de-la-Sainte-Croix

St-Michel

St-J. du Grund

Musée Nat. d'Hist. Naturelle

Hospice Plateau du Rhom

Rue de Trèves

Pulvermühl

HAMM

Dommeldael

GRUND

Bisserweg

Secalt

Polska

Citadelle du St-Esprit

Chap. St-Quirin

2

Centre National de Tactique Policière

Laboratoire

PULVERMÜHLE

Maison de Retraite

225

Schläifmillen

Bd. d'Avranches

Stade Achille Hammerel

VERLORENKOST

Terrain de Football

Tennis Club Bonnevoie Asbl.

Piscine

228

Oolsich

→ **A7** 8 km
Aérogare de
Luxembourg 5,5 km

A1

Rotonde

CFL

Garé Centrale

225

226

BONNEVOIE

Itzigerkopp

Eglise M. Reine de la Paix

Itzigersté

A1

Madrid 1 : 15 000

El Escorial 49 km
→ A-6 3 km
→ A-6 CIUDAD DE UNIVERSITARIA 3 km
MONCLOA 2 km
TETUÁN 2 km   TETUÁN 2 km

M-30 → A-6
El Escorial 49 km

A-5
LATINA 2 km
Alcorcon 11 km

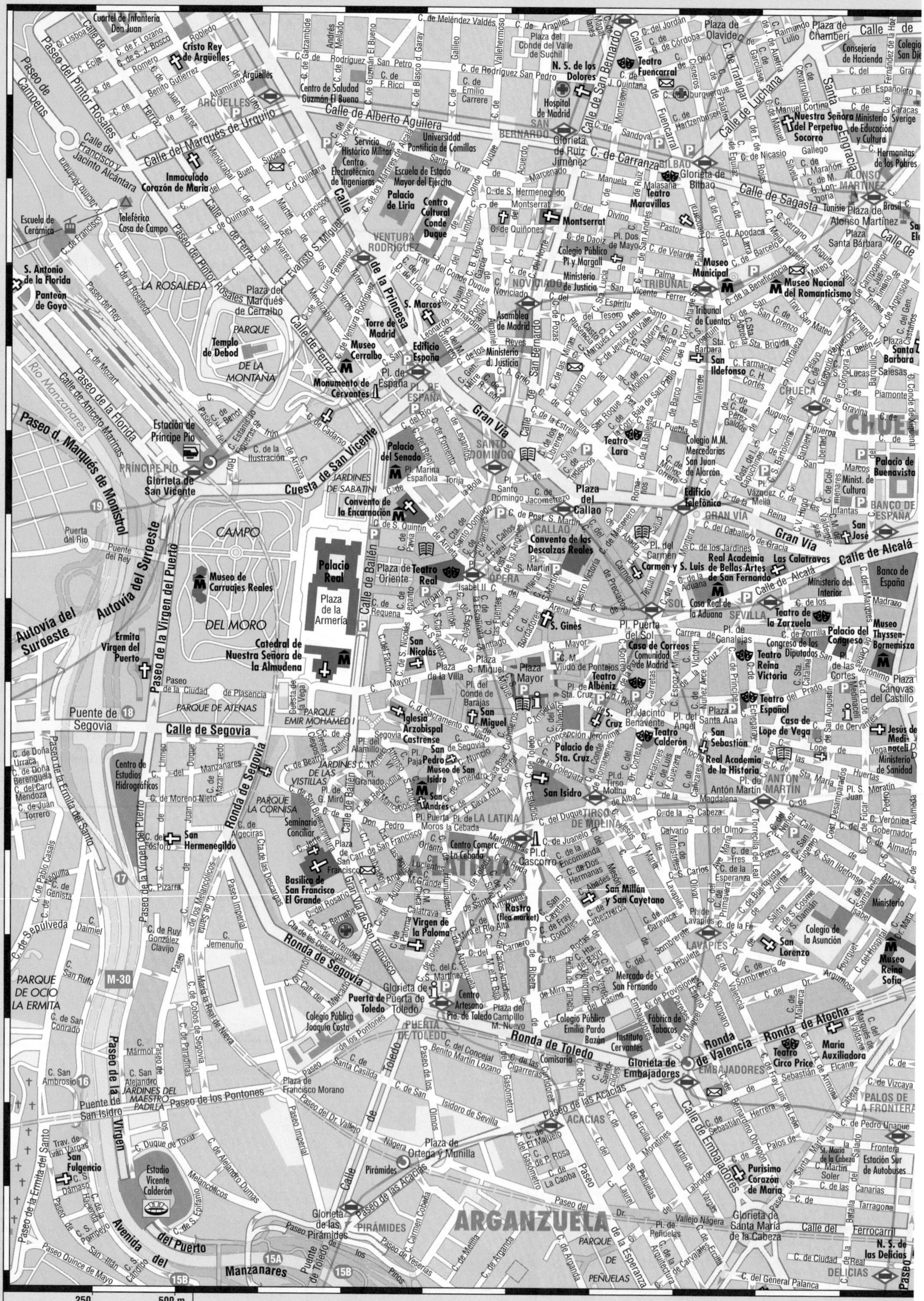

M-30 VILLAVERDE 5 km
Aranjuez 47 km
→ M-30 VILLAVERDE 3 km
→ A-4

250   500 m

Aranda de Duero 157 km
CHAMARTIN 2 km
Estadio Santiago Bernabéu 2 km

Aeropuerto
Madrid-Barajas 12 km
CHAMARTIN 2 km
A-2 1,5 km

M-30 50 m
CIUDAD LINEAL 1 km
A-2 1,5 km
SAN BLAS 3 km
Parque Ferial Juan Carlos I (IFEMA) 7 km
Aeropuerto Madrid-Barajas 12 km

CIUDAD LINEAL 1 km

M-23 → R-3
MORTALAZ 3 km
Arganda del Rey 34 km

M-30
Aeropuerto Madrid-Barajas 10 km

MORTALAZ 2 km

A-3
VALLECAS 4 km
Tarancón 85 km

MEDIODIA 4 km   VALLECAS 4 km   M-30 VILLAVERDE 7 km
Aranjuez 47 km

Moskva 1 : 15 000

Sheremetevo 25 km ✈
KHOVRINO 10 km
→ M10 2,5 km Ⓜ Rechnoy Vokzal

Dmitrov 67 km
Dolgoprudny 16 km
BESKUDNIKOVO 9 km
→ A104 3 km

Marina Roshcha Ⓜ

PRESNESKY 1,5 km
DOROGOMILOVO 3 km

Planernaya Ⓜ

SHELEPIKHA 3 km
KHOROSHEVSKY 3 km
KUNTSEVO 8 km
STROGINO 10 km

DOROGOMILOVO 2 km
KUNTSEVO 8 km
MOZHAYSKY 9 km
→ M1 10 km
Nemchinovka 11 km
Odintsovo 12 km

Kuntsevskaya Ⓜ

Pyatnitskoe Shosse Ⓜ

Novodevichy monastyr 2 km

250   500 m

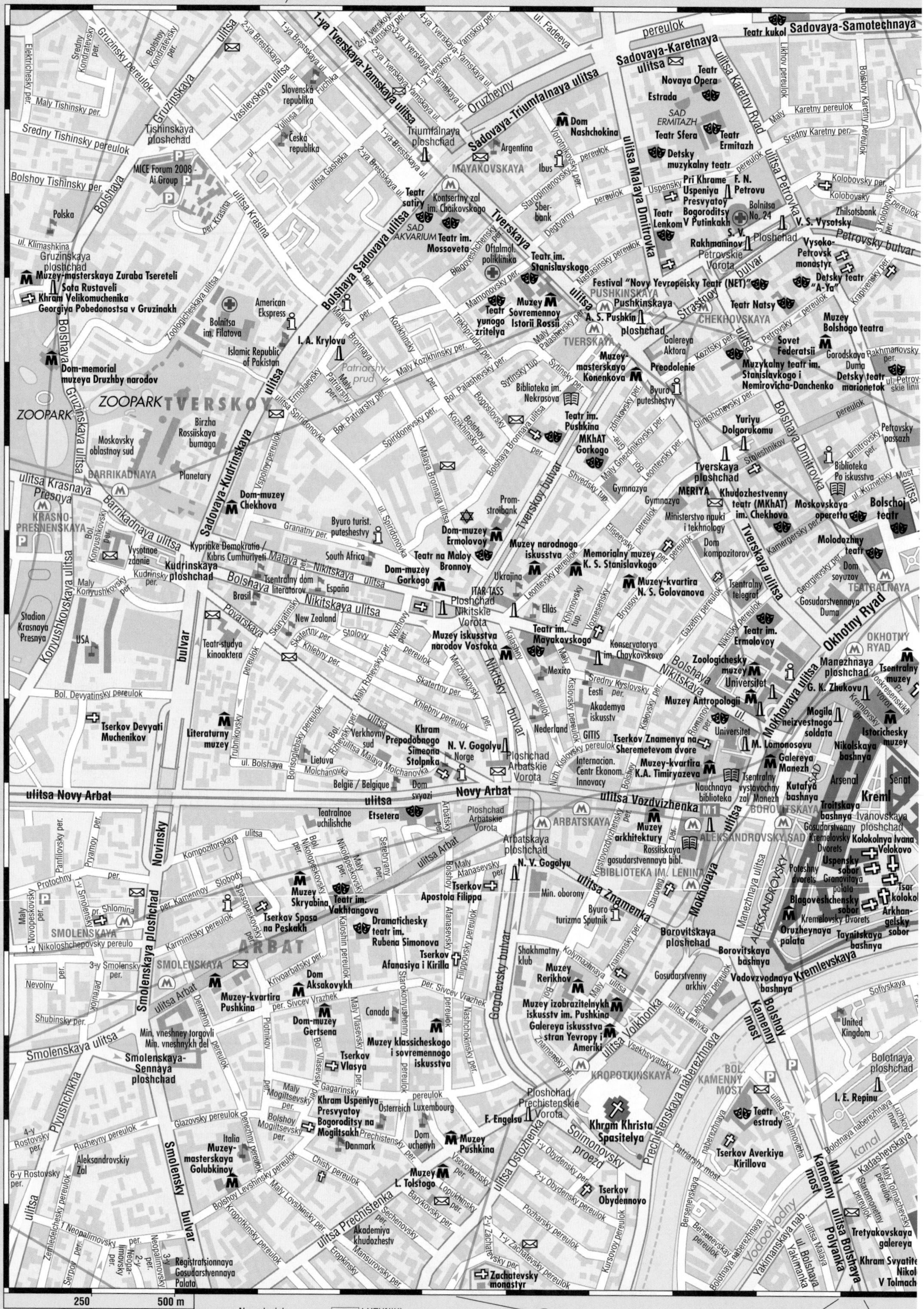

Vnukovo 22 km ✈
Domodedovo 37 km ✈

Novodevichy monastyr 2 km

LUZHNIKI-
Tsentralny stadion 3 km
LENINSKIE GORY -
MGU im. Lomonosova 5 km
OLYMPYSKAYA DEREVNYA 10 km

Ⓜ Troparyovo

CHEREMUSHKI 7,5 km
TEPLY STAN 10 km
Rumyantsevo 15 km
→ M3 15 km

Bul. Dmitriya
Donskogo Ⓜ

Sadovaya-Samotechnaya
Teatr kukol
Sadovaya-Karetnaya ulitsa
Teatr Novaya Opera
Estrada
SAD ERMITAZH
Teatr Sfera
Teatr Ermitazh
Detsky muzykalny teatr
Pri Khrame Uspeniya Presvyatoy Bogoroditsy v Putinkakh
F. N. Petrovu
Bolnitsa No. 24
V. S. Vysotsky
S. V. Rakhmaninov
Petrovskie Vorota
Vysoko-Petrovsk monastyr
Kammerny teatr "A-Ya"
Teatr Natsy
Muzey Bolshogo teatra
Sovet Federatsii
Muzykalny teatr im. Stanislavskogo i Nemirovicha-Danchenko
Detsky teatr marionetok

MAYAKOVSKAYA Ⓜ
Dom Nashchokina
Argentina
Ibus

Teatr satiry
Konsertny zal im. Chaikovskogo
Teatr im. Mossoveta
SAD AKVARIUM
Oftalmol. poliklinika
Teatr im. Stanislavskogo
PUSHKINSKAYA Ⓜ
Festival "Novy Yevropeysky Teatr (NET)"
A. S. Pushkin ploshchad
Galereya Aktora
Muzey-masterskaya Konenkova
Preodolenie

CHEKHOVSKAYA Ⓜ
TVERSKAYA Ⓜ

Sberbank

Teatr yunogo zritelya
Muzey Sovremennoy Istorii Rossii
I. A. Krylovu
Biblioteka im. Nekrasova
Teatr im. Pushkina
MKhAT Gorkogo
Yuriyu Dolgorukomu
Tverskaya ploshchad
MERIYA
Khudozhestvenny teatr (MKhAT) im. Chekhova
Ministerstvo nauki i teknology
Moskovskaya operetta
Bolshoj teatr
Biblioteka Po iskusstvu
Molodozhny teatr

ZOOPARK
TVERSKOY
ZOOPARK
Moskovsky oblastnoy sud
Planetary
Birzha Rossiiskaya bumaga
BARRIKADNAYA Ⓜ
Dom-muzey Chekhova

KRASNO-PRESNENSKAYA Ⓜ
Vysotnoe zdanie
Kudrinskaya ploshchad
Stadion Krasnaya Presnya

Muzey-masterskaya Zuraba Tsereteli
Sota Rustaveli
Khram Velikomuchenika Georgiya Pobedonostsa v Gruzinakh
Dom-memorial muzeya Druzhby narodov
American Ekspress
Bolnitsa im. Filatova
Islamic Republic of Pakistan

Patriarshy prud

Dom-muzey Ermolovoy
Muzey narodnogo iskusstva
Memorialny muzey K. S. Stanislavskogo
Dom kompozitorov
Muzey-kvartira N. S. Golovanova
TEATRALNAYA

Teatr-studiya kinoaktera
Dom-muzey Gorkogo
Teatr na Maloy Bronnoy
ITAR-TASS
Ploshchad Nikitskie Vorota
Muzey iskusstva narodov Vostoka
Teatr im. Mayakovskogo
Konservatoriya im. Chaykovskogo
Zoologichesky muzey
Universitet
Muzey Antropologii
Universitet
Tserkov Znameniya na Sheremetyevo dvore
Muzey-kvartira K.A. Timiryazeva
Tsentralny vystavochny zal Manezh
OKHOTNY RYAD Ⓜ
Tsentralny muzey
G. K. Zhukovu
Manezhnaya ploshchad
Istorichesky muzey
Nikolskaya bashnya
Mogila neizvestnogo soldata
Galereya Manezh
Arsenal
Senat

Tserkov Devyati Muchenikov
Literaturny muzey
Khram Prepodobnogo Simeona Stolpnka
N. V. Gogolyu
Ploshchad Arbatskie Vorota
Dom svyazi

ulitsa Novy Arbat
Novy Arbat

ARBATSKAYA Ⓜ
Muzey arkhitektury
Rossiiskaya gosudarstvennaya biblioteka
N. V. Gogolyu
BIBLIOTEKA IM. LENINA Ⓜ
ulitsa Znamenka
Min. oborony
Byuro turizma Sputnik

Kreml
Troitskaya bashnya
Kutafya bashnya
Kolokolnya Ivana Velokovo
Uspensky sobor
Granovitaya palata
Tsar pushka
Blagoveshchensky sobor
Arkhan-gelsky sobor
Kremlevsky Dvorets
Oruzheynaya palata
Taynitskaya bashnya
Vodovzvodnaya bashnya
Kremlevskaya

Teatralnoe uchilishche
Etsetera
Arbatskaya ploshchad
Shakhmatny klub
Muzey Rerikhov
Borovitskaya bashnya
Borovitskaya ploshchad
Gosudarstvenny arkhiv
Gosudarstvenny ploshchad

Muzey Skryabina
Teatr im. Vakhtangova
Tserkov Apostola Filippa
Dramatichesky teatr im. Rubena Simonova
Tserkov Afanasiya i Kirilla
Dom Aksakovykh
Muzey-kvartira Pushkina
Dom-muzey Gertsena
Muzey klassicheskogo i sovremennogo iskusstva
Muzey izobrazitelnykh iskusstv im. Pushkina
Galereya iskusstv stran Yevropy i Ameriki
Tserkov Vlasya
United Kingdom

ARBAT
SMOLENSKAYA
Smolenskaya-Sennaya ploshchad
Min. vneshney torgovli
Min. vneshnikh del

KROPOTKINSKAYA Ⓜ
Ploshchad Prechistenskie Vorota
Khram Khrista Spasitelya
Solomonovsky proezd
BOL KAMENNY MOST
Bolotnaya ploshchad
I. E. Repinu
Teatr estrady

Khram Uspeniya Presvyatoy Bogoroditsy na Mogiltsakh
Dom uchenykh
Muzey Pushkina
Muzey-masterskaya Golubkinoy
Aleksandrovsky Zal
Muzey L. Tolstogo
Tserkov Obydennoyo
Tserkov Averkiya Kirillova

Registratsionnaya Gosudarstvennaya Palata
Akademiya khudozhestv
Zachatevsky monastyr
Tretyakovskaya galereya
Khram Svyatitelya Nikol V Tolmach

kanal

Vodootvodny
Vodootvodny kanal

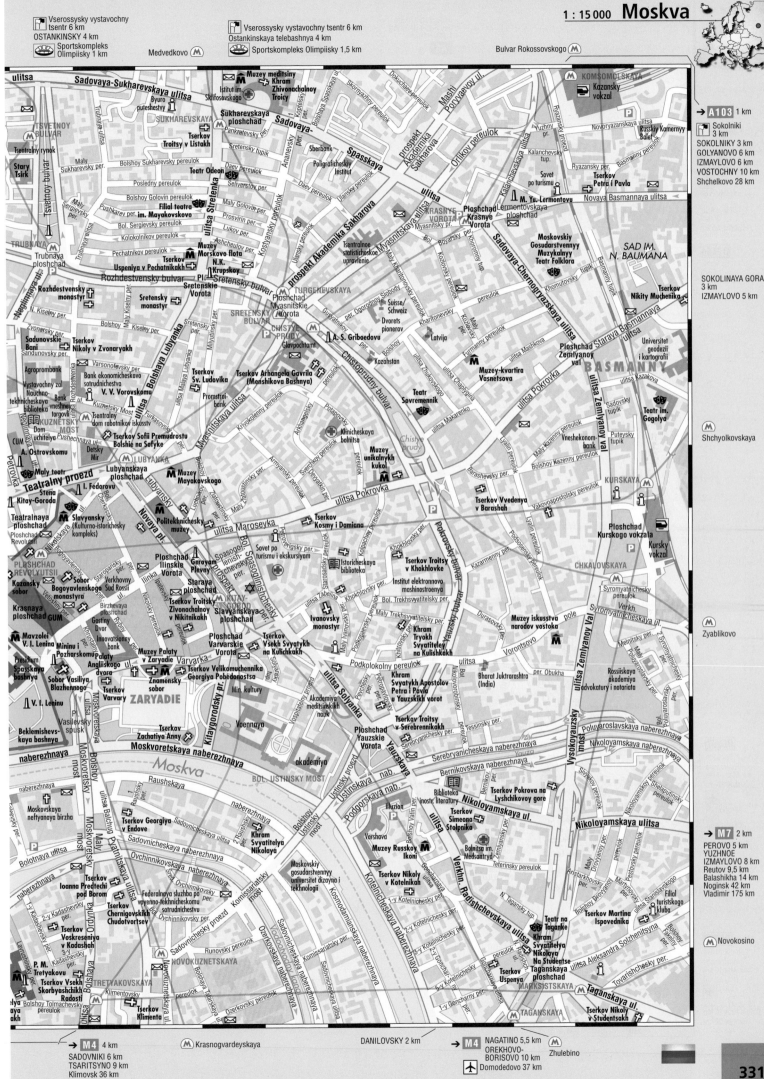

Vserossysky vystavochny tsentr 6 km
OSTANKINSKY 4 km
Sportskompleks Olimpiisky 1 km

Vserossysky vystavochny tsentr 6 km
Ostankinskaya telebashnya 4 km
Sportskompleks Olimpiisky 1,5 km

Medvedkovo Ⓜ

Bulvar Rokossovskogo Ⓜ

KOMSOMOLSKAYA
Kazansky vokzal

→ **A103** 1 km
🏨 Sokolniki 3 km
SOKOLNIKI 3 km
GOLYANOVO 6 km
IZMAYLOVO 6 km
VOSTOCHNY 10 km
Shchelkovo 28 km

Tsvetnoy bulvar
TSVETNOY BULVAR
Tsentralny rynok
Stary Tsirk

Sadovaya-Sukharevskaya ulitsa

Muzey meditsiny
Khram Zhivonachalnoy Troicy
Istitut im. Skifosovskogo

SUKHAREVSKAYA
Sukharevskaya ploshchad
Tserkov Troitsy v Listakh
Teatr Odeon
Filial teatra im. Mayakovskovo

Byuro puteshestvy

Sadovaya-Spasskaya

Sberbank
Poligraficheskiy Institut

prospekt Akademika Sakharova

Mashi Porryaevoy ul.

Novoryazanskaya ulitsa
Russkiy Kamerny Balet

Tserkov Petra i Pavla
Novaya Basmannaya ulitsa

M. Yu. Lermontovu
Ploshchad Lermontovskaya
KRASNYE VOROTA
Krasnye Vorota
ploshchad

SAD IM. N. BAUMANA

Moskovskiy Gosudarstvennyy Muzykalnyy Teatr Folklora

Sadovaya-Chernogryazskaya ulitsa

Staraya Basmannaya ulitsa

BASMANNY

Universitet geodezii i kartografii

SOKOLINAYA GORA 3 km
IZMAYLOVO 5 km

Tserkov Nikity Muchenika

TRUBNAYA
Trubnaya ploshchad

Rozhdestvensky bulvar
Rozhdestvensky monastyr

ulitsa Strelenka

Tserkov Uspeniya v Pechatnikakh
Muzey Morskovo flota
N.K. Krupskoy

Sretensky bulvar
Sretensky monastyr
Sretensky Vorota

TURGENEVSKAYA
Ploshchad Myasnitskie Vorota
SRETENSKY BULVAR

Ploshchad Zemlyanoy val

Ploshchad Staraya Zemlyanoy val

Teatr im. Gogolya

Shchyolkovskaya Ⓜ

Sadunovskie Bani

Tserkov Nikoly v Zvonaryakh

Agroprombank
Vystavochnyi zal Nauchno-tekhnicheskaya biblioteka
Dom uchitelya
CUM
A. Ostrovskomu

Bank ekonomicheskovo sotrudnichestva
V. V. Vorovskomu
Bank vneshney torgovli
Tsentralny dom rabotnikov iskusstv
Tserkov Sofii Premudrosti Bolshie na Sofyke

Kuznetsky Most ulitsa
Promstroi-bank

Tserkov Sv. Ludovika
Tserkov Arhangela Gavrila (Menshikova Bashnya)

CHISTYE PRUDY
Glavpochtamt

A. S. Griboedovu

Kazakhstan
Latvija

Muzey-kvartira Vasnetsova

KUZNETSKY MOST
Pushechnaya ul.
Maly teatr
I. Fedorovu

Detsky Mir
LUBYANKA
Lubyanskaya ploshchad
Muzey Mayakovskogo

Teatr Sovremennik

ulitsa Pokrovka

KURSKAYA

Teatralny proezd
Stena Kitay-Goroda
Teatralnaya ploshchad
Ploshchad Revolutsii

Slavyansky (Kulturno-istorichesky kompleks)
Politekhnichesky muzey

ulitsa Maroseyka

Klinicheskaya bolnitsa

Muzey unikalnykh kukol

Tserkov Vvedenya v Barashah

Ploshchad Kurskogo vokzala
Kursky vokzal

CHKALOVSKAYA

PLOSHCHAD REVOLUTSII
Kazansky sobor
Sobor Bogoyavlenskogo monastyra
Krasnaya ploshchad
GUM

Ploshchad Ilinskie Vorota
Geroyam Plevny
Staraya ploshchad
Verkhovny Sud Rossii

ulitsa Pokrovka

Tserkov Kosmy i Damiani

Tserkov Troitsy v Khokhlovke
Institut elektronnovo mashinostroenya
Bol. Trekhsvyatitelsky per.
Maly Trekhsvyatitelsky per.

Muzey iskusstva narodov vostoka

Zyablikovo Ⓜ

Mavzolei
V. I. Lenina
Minini i Pozharskomu
Presidium
Spasskaya bashnya
Sobor Vasiliya Blazhennogo
V. I. Leninu
Beklemishevskaya bashnya

Innovatsionny bank
Birzhevaya ploshchad
Gostiny Dvor
Tserkov Troitsky Zivonachalnoy v Nikitinkakh
Ploshchad Varvarskie Vorota
Muzey Palaty v Zaryade

KITAY-GOROD
Slavyanskaya ploshchad
Ivanovsky monastyr
Tserkov Vsekh Svyatykh na Kulichkakh

Istoricheskaya biblioteka

Khram Tryokh Svyatiteley na Kulishkakh

Khram Svyatykh Apostolov Petra i Pavla u Yauzskikh vorot

Bharat Juktrarashtra (India)

Rossiiskaya akademiya advokatury i notariata

Tserkov Velikomuchennika Georgiya Pobedonostsa

Varvarka

Znamensky sobor
Tserkov Varvary

ZARYADIE
Tserkov Zachatiya Anny

Moskvoretskaya naberezhnaya

Pl. Vasilevsky spusk
Moskvoretsky most

Podkolokolny pereulok
ulitsa Solyanka
Akademiya meditsinskikh nauk

Podkopaevsky per.

Tserkov Troitsy v Serebrennikakh

Muzey iskusstva narodov vostoka

Voennaya

Ploshchad Yauzskie Vorota
Yauzskaya ulitsa

Serebryanicheskaya naberezhnaya

Vysokoyauzsky most

Poluyaroslavskaya naberezhnaya
ulitsa Zemlyanoy Val
Nikoloyamskaya naberezhnaya

Moskva

BOL. USTINSKY MOST
akademiya

Moskvoretskaya naberezhnaya
Raushskaya

Ustinsky proezd
Ustinskaya nab.

Biblioteka inostr. literatury

Tserkov Pokrova na Lyshchikovoy gore

Nikoloyamskaya ulitsa

Moskovskaya neftyanaya birzha

Tserkov Georgiya v Endove

naberezhnaya

Bolshoy Ustinsky most

Illuzion

Tserkov Simeona Stolpnika

Nikoloyamskaya ulitsa

→ **M7** 2 km
PEROVO 5 km
YUZHNOE IZMAYLOVO 8 km
Reutov 9,5 km
Balashikha 14 km
Noginsk 42 km
Vladimir 175 km

Khram Svyatitelya Nikolaya

Sadovnicheskaya naberezhnaya
ulitsa Balchug
Maly Moskvoretsky most

Varshava

Muzey Russkoy Ikoni

Tserkov Nikoly v Kotelnikah

Verkhn. Radishchevskaya ulitsa
Bolnitsa im. Medsantryd

Teatr na Taganke

Tserkov Martina Ispovednika

Bolotnaya ulitsa
Ovchinnikovskaya naberezhnaya

Tserkov Ioanna Predtechi pod Borom
Tserkov Chernigovskikh Chudotvortsev

Moskovskiy gosudarstvennyy universitet dizayna i tekhnologii

Federalnaya sluzhba po voyenno-tekhnicheskomu sotrudnichestvu

Kosmodamianskaya naberezhnaya

Taganskaya ploshchad

Khram Svyatitelya Nikolaya Na Studentse

Novokosino Ⓜ

Tserkov Voskreseniya v Kadashah

P. M. Tretyakovu

Tserkov Vsekh Skorbyashchikh Radosti

Tserkov Klimenta

NOVOKUZNETSKAYA
TRETYAKOVSKAYA

ulitsa Aleksandra Solzhenitsyna

Tserkov Nikoly v Studentsakh

MARKSISTSKAYA

Taganskaya ul.
Taganskaya ploshchad
Tserkov Uspenya
TAGANSKAYA Ⓜ

→ **M4** 4 km
SADOVNIKI 6 km
TSARITSYNO 9 km
Klimovsk 36 km

Krasnogvardeyskaya Ⓜ

DANILOVSKY 2 km

→ **M4** NAGATINO 5,5 km
OREKHOVO-BORISOVO 10 km
✈ Domodedovo 37 km

Zhulebino Ⓜ

331

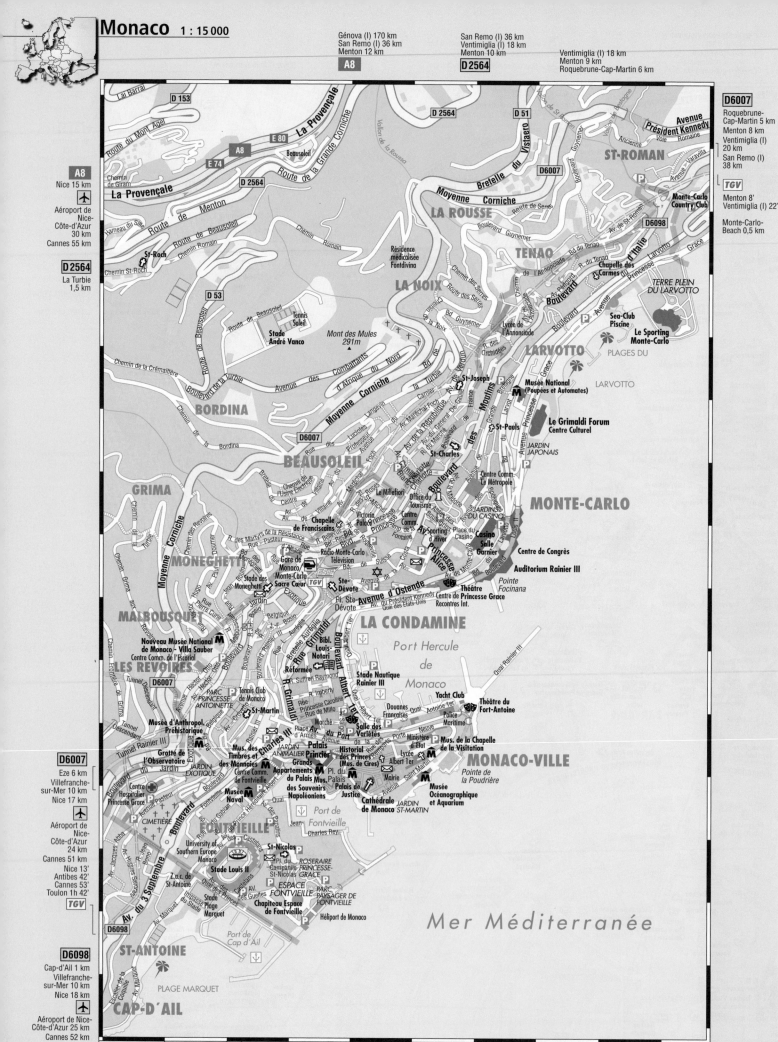

Génova (I) 170 km
San Remo (I) 36 km
Menton 12 km

A8

San Remo (I) 36 km
Ventimiglia (I) 18 km
Menton 10 km

D 2564

Ventimiglia (I) 18 km
Menton 9 km
Roquebrune-Cap-Martin 6 km

D6007
Roquebrune-Cap-Martin 5 km
Menton 8 km
Ventimiglia (I) 20 km
San Remo (I) 38 km

TGV
Menton 8'
Ventimiglia (I) 22'

Monte-Carlo-Beach 0,5 km

A8
Nice 15 km
Aéroport de Nice-Côte-d'Azur 30 km
Cannes 55 km

D 2564
La Turbie 1,5 km

D6007
Eze 6 km
Villefranche-sur-Mer 10 km
Nice 17 km
Aéroport de Nice-Côte-d'Azur 24 km
Cannes 51 km
Nice 13'
Antibes 42'
Cannes 53'
Toulon 1h 42'

TGV

D6098

D6098
Cap-d'Ail 1 km
Villefranche-sur-Mer 10 km
Nice 18 km
Aéroport de Nice-Côte-d'Azur 25 km
Cannes 52 km

Mer Méditerranée

250   500 m

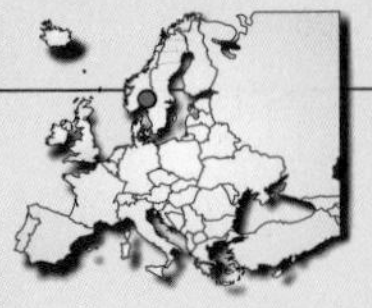

SOGNSVANN 2 km
→ Ring 3 800 m

Frognerseteren 1
Avløs 2
Storo 3
Ring 4
Østerås 5
Sognsvann 6

168
→ Ring 3
800 m
RØA 2 km

Ring 2
SKØYEN 1,2 km
→ E 18 1,3 km
SJØLYST 1,5 km

E 18
BYGDØY 1,5 km
→ Ring 2
2 km
→ Ring 3
3,5 km
✈ 5 km

Bygdøy

Stockholm (S)
Helsinki (FIN)
Fredrikshavn (DK)
Helsingborg (DK)
København (DK)

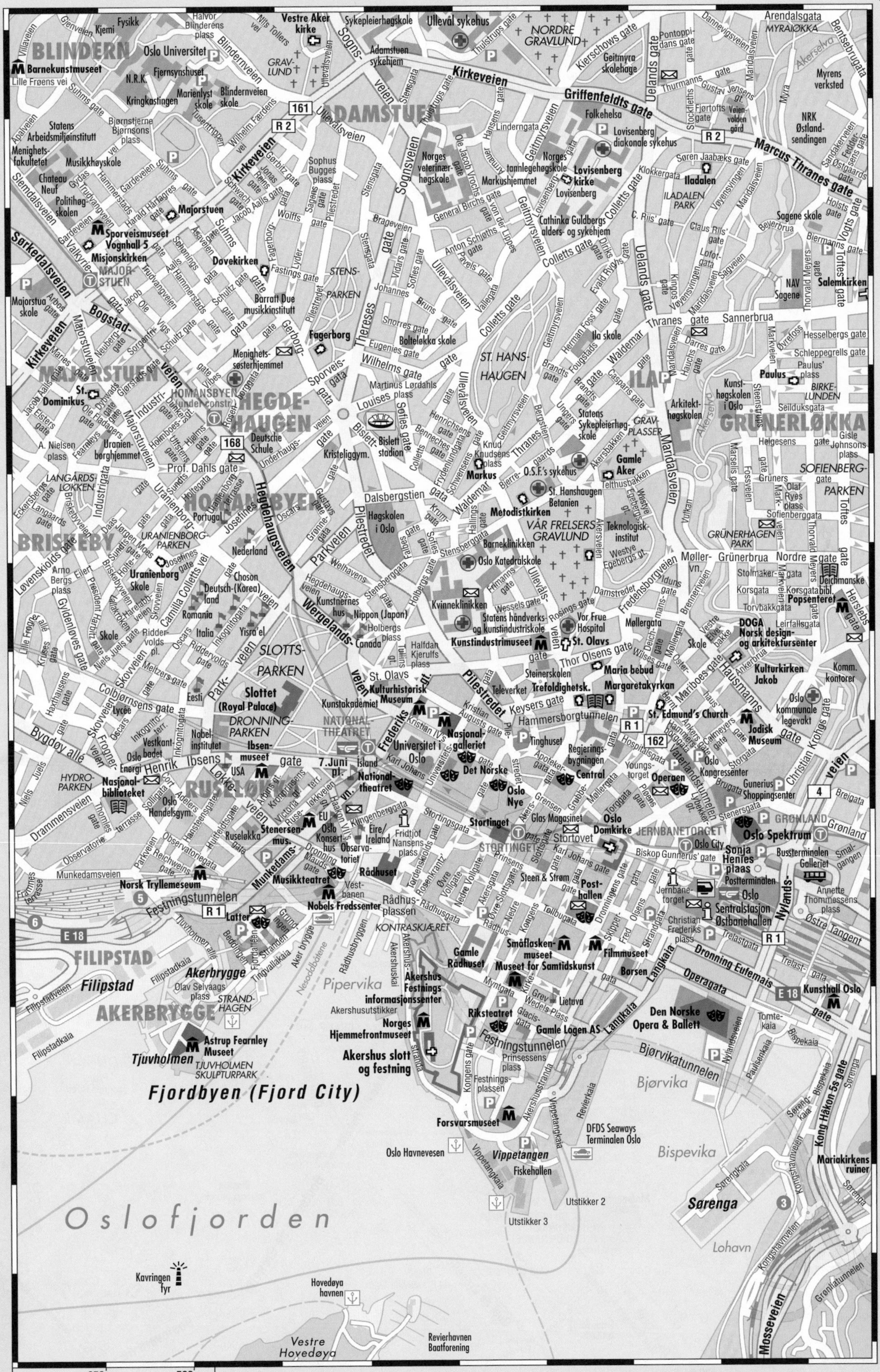

Ring 2
ROSENHOFF
700 m
→ Ring 3
→ 4 2 km
Romsås 5,5 km

→ 4
TOYEN 300 m

1/2 Ellingsrudåsen
3 Mortensrud
4 Bergkrystallen
5 Vestli
6 Ring

Oslo Lufthaven
✈ Gardermoen
50 km
190
→ E 6 2 km

BLINDERN
DAMSTUEN
MAJORSTUEN
BRISKEBY
HOMANSBYEN
HEGDEHAUGEN
RUSELØKKA
FILIPSTAD
AKERBRYGGE
ILAG
GRÜNERLØKKA
SOFIENBERG PARKEN
Fjordbyen (Fjord City)
Filipstad
Tjuvholmen

SLOTTS-PARKEN
DRONNING-PARKEN
Slottet (Royal Palace)

NATIONAL THEATRET

Oslo Universitet
Kirkeveien
Griffenfeldts gate
Marcus Thranes gate

Ullevål sykehus
NORDRE GRAVLUND

O s l o f j o r d e n

Pipervika
Bjørvika
Bispevika
Lohavn
Sørenga

NORDSTRAND 2 km E 18
LJAN 3km

Bleikøy

333

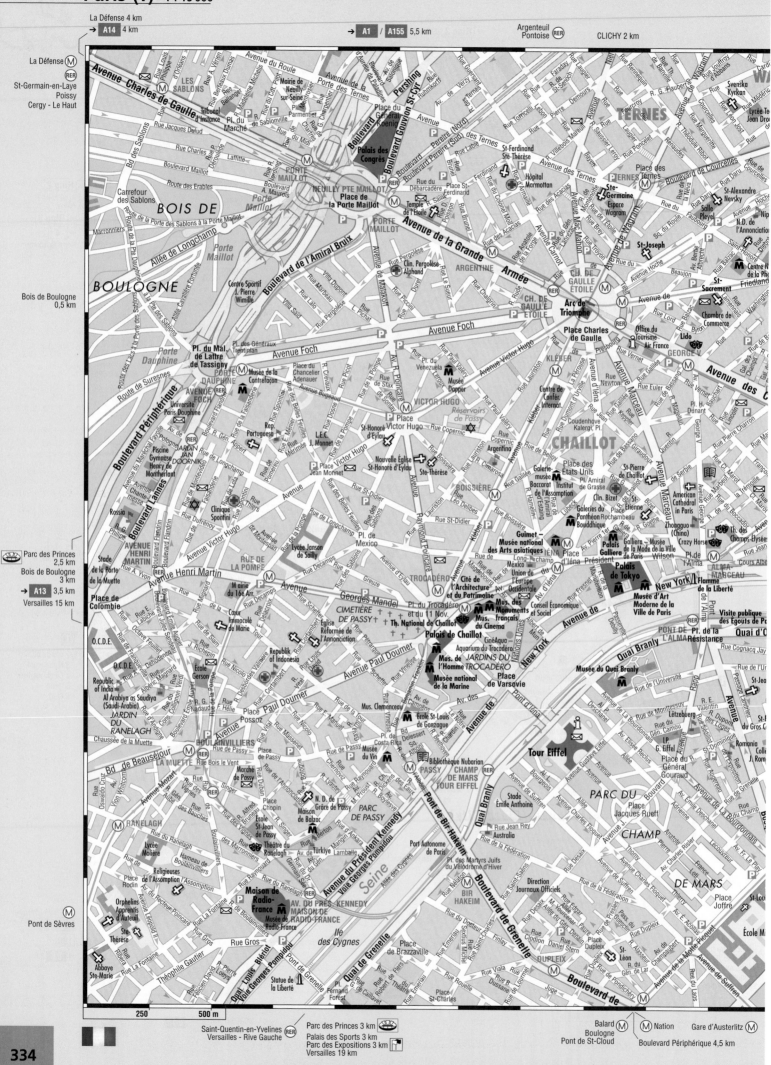

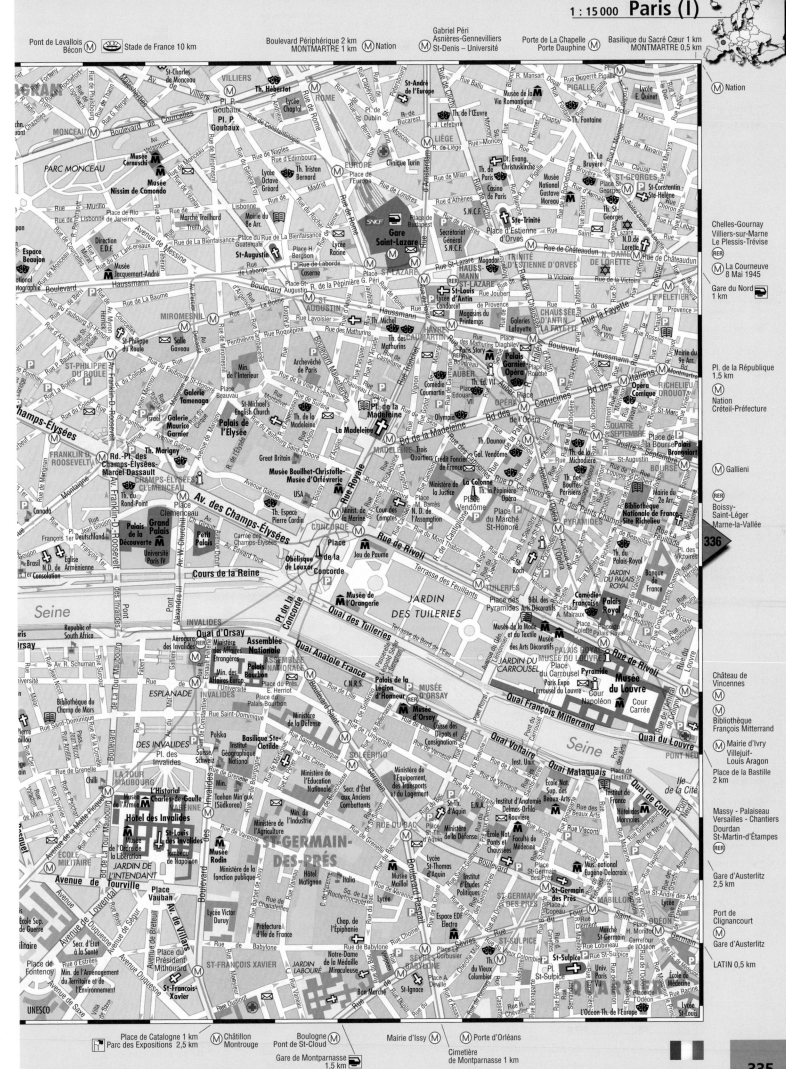

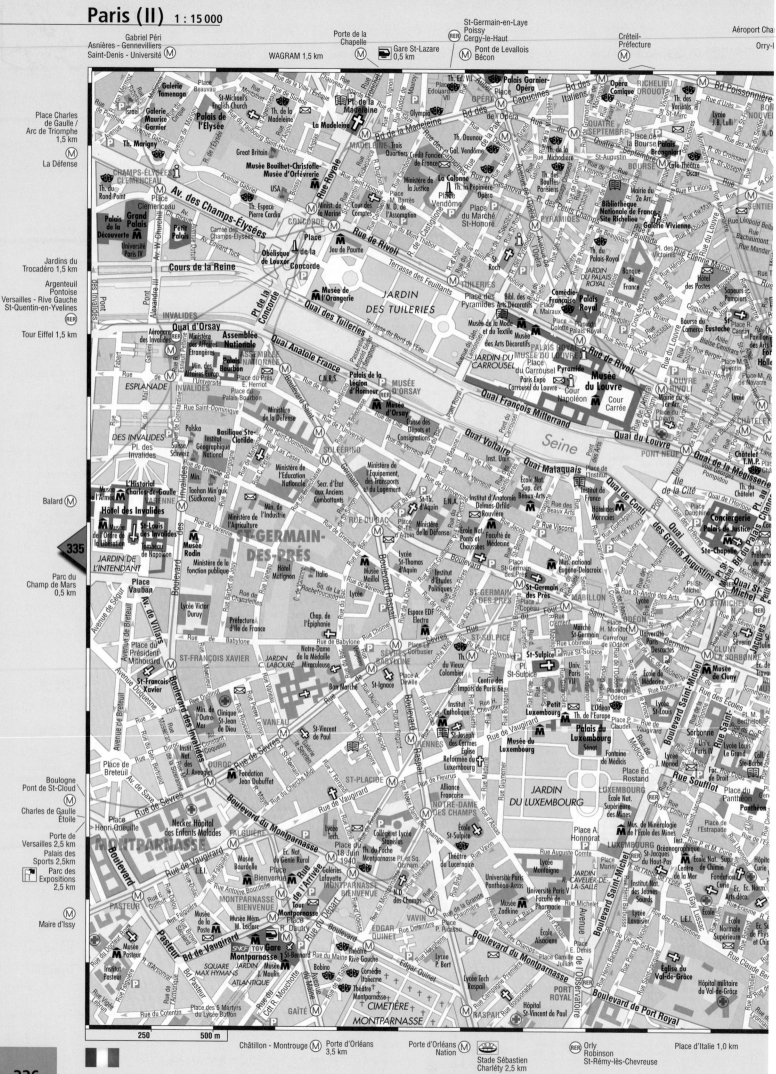

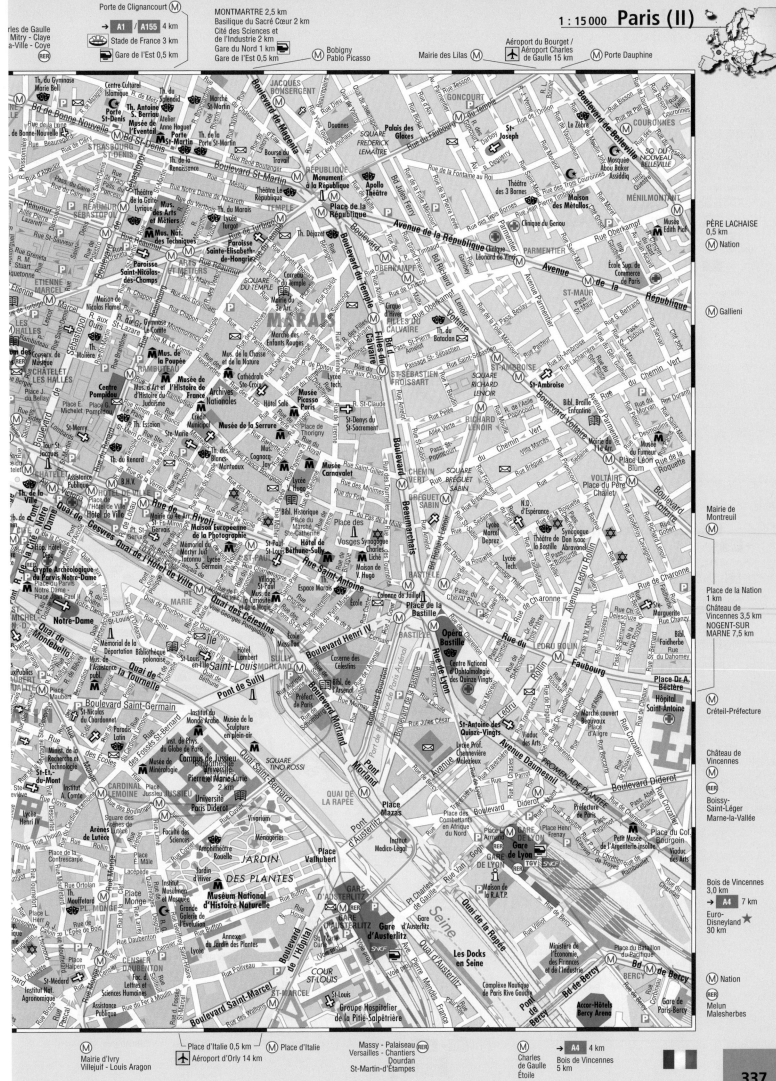

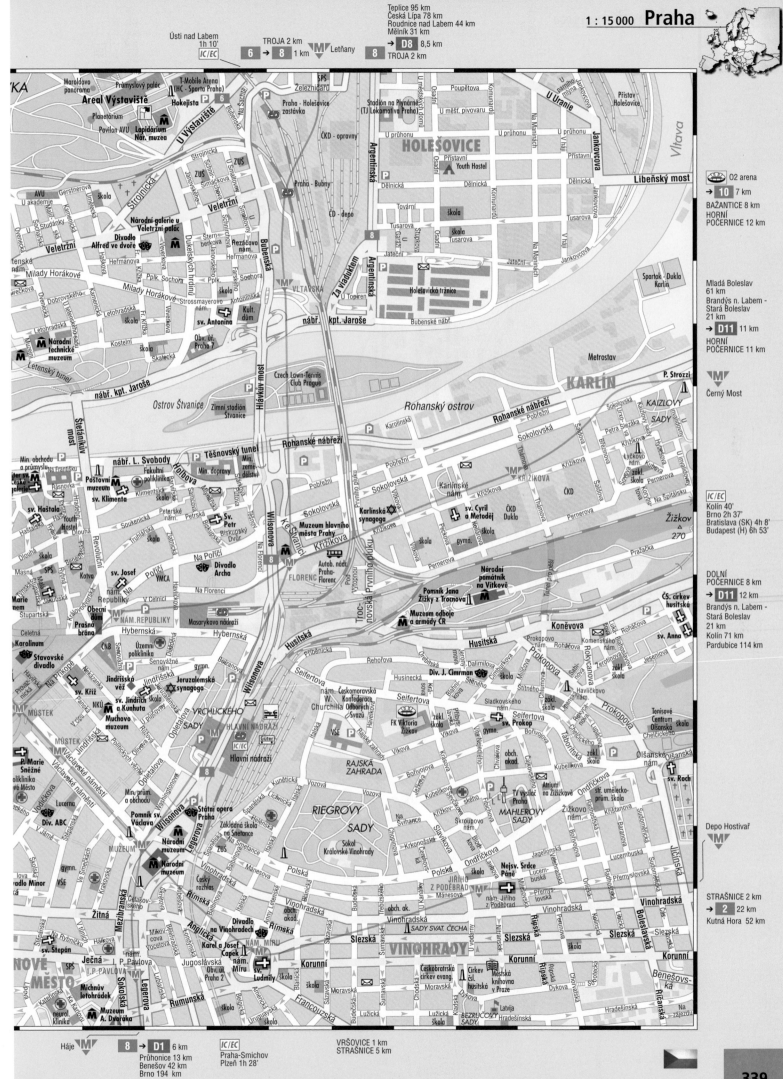

Faxaflói

Skerjafjörður

Lübeck (D)
Stockholm (S)

Mangaļsala 19 km
Mangaļi 15 km
SARKANDAUGAVA 2,5 km

PĒTERSALA 1 km

GANĪBAS 0,5 km
SKANSTE 100 m
RĪGA ARENA 100 m

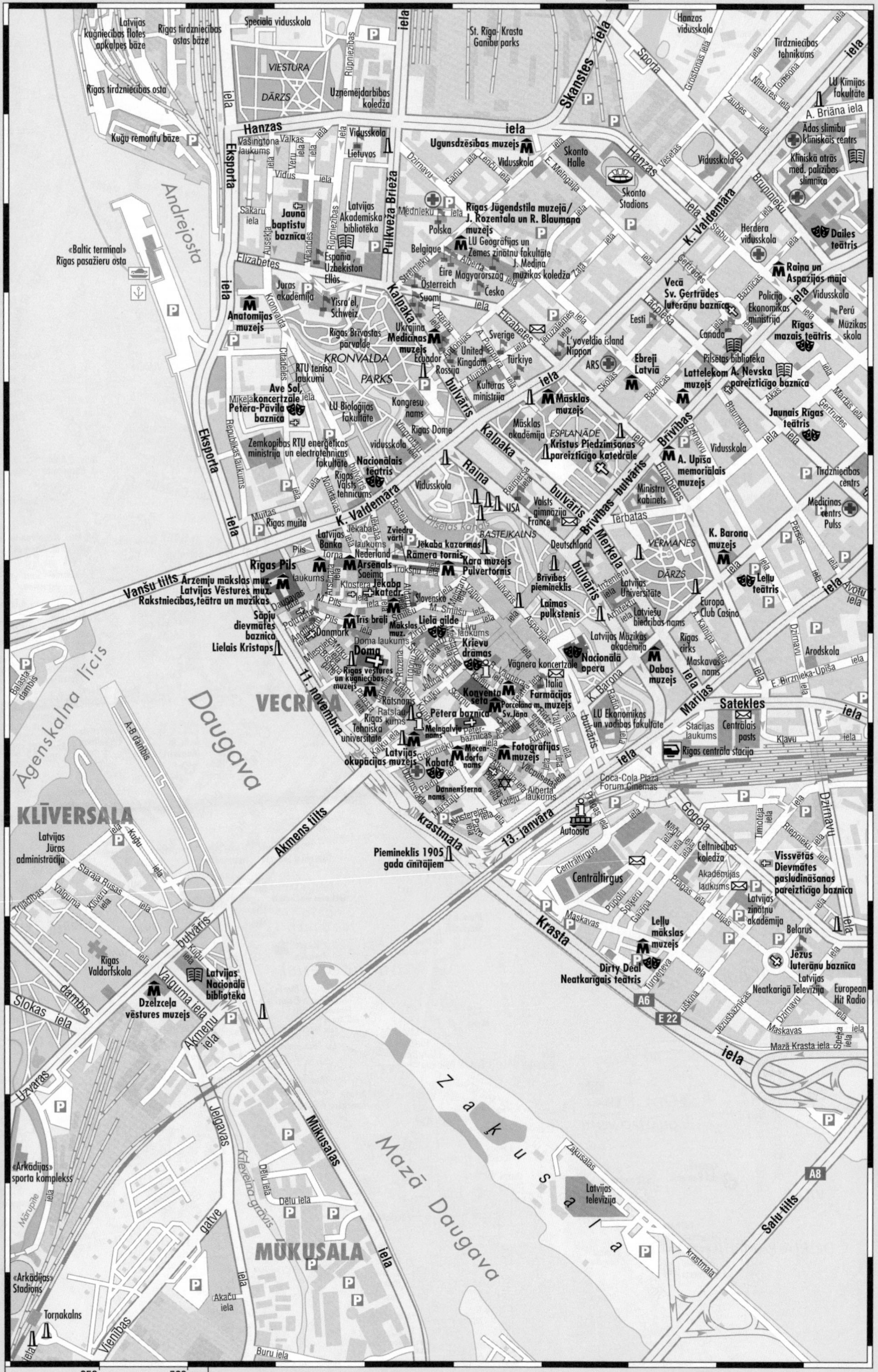

SARKANDAUGAVA
1,5 km
Mangaļi 14 km
Mangaļsala 18 km

A2 3 km
GRĪZINKALNS 1 km
PURVCIEMS 3 km
Jugla 9 km
Bergi 12 km
Sigulda 43 km

Daugavas stadions
2 km

A6
KEHGARAGS
3,5 km
Ogre 27 km

Riga

341

Andrejosta

«Baltic terminal»
Rīgas pasažieru osta

Latvijas kuģniecības flotes apkalpes bāze
Rīgas tirdzniecības ostas bāze

Kuģu remonta bāze

Rīgas tirdzniecības osta

VIESTURA DĀRZS

Speciālā vidusskola

Uzņēmējdarbības koledža

Eksporta iela

Hanzas

Vidusskola
Lietuvos

St. Riga-Krasta
Ganību parks

Ugunsdzēsības muzejs

Skonto Halle
Skonto Stadions

Hanzas iela

Tirdzniecības tehnikums

LU Ķīmijas fakultāte

A. Briāna iela

Ādas slimību
Klīniskais centrs

Klīniskā ātrās med. palīdzības slimnīca

Jauna baptistu baznīca

Latvijas Akadēmiskā bibliotēka

España Uzbekistan
Ellás
Österreich
Suomi

Rīgas Jūgendstila muzejs/
J. Rozentāla un R. Blaumaņa muzejs

LU Ģeogrāfijas un Zemes zinātņu fakultāte
J. Mediņa mūzikas koledža

Polska
Belgique
Éire Magyarország
Cesko

Vidusskola

Herdera vidusskola

Dailes teātris

Raiņa un Aspazijas māja

Jūras akadēmija

Anatomijas muzejs

KRONVALDA PARKS

RTU tenisa laukumi

Medicīnas muzejs
Ecuador

Rīgas Brīvostas pārvalde

Ukraina
Eesti
Sverige
United Kingdom
Türkiye
Rossija

L'yoveldio island
Nippon
ARS

Ebreji Latvijā
Canada

Vecā Sv. Ģertrūdes luterāņu baznīca

Policija
Ekonomikas ministrija

Perú
Rīgas mazais teātris
Mūzikas skola

Ave Sol koncertzāle
Petera-Pāvila baznīca

LU Bioloģijas fakultāte

Kongresu nams

Rīgas Dome

Kultūras ministrija

Pilsētas bibliotēka

Lattelekom
A. Ņevska pareizticīgo baznīca
muzejs

Jaunais Rīgas teātris

Zemkopības ministrija un elektrotehnicas fakultāte

Nacionālais teātris

Mākslas akadēmija

ESPLANĀDE

Kristus Piedzimšanas pareizticīgo katedrāle

Mākslas muzejs

Brīvības

A. Upīša memoriālais muzejs

Tirdzniecības centrs

Raina

Vidusskola

Valsts gimnāzija
France

Deutschland

VĒRMANES DĀRZS

K. Barona muzejs

Medicīnas centrs Pulss

K. Valdemāra

Rīgas Valsts tehnikums

Zviedru vārti
Jēkaba kazarmas
Rāmera tornis

Kara muzejs
Pulvertornis

Brīvības piemineklis

Latvijas Universitāte

Lelļu teātris

Muitas

Rīgas muita

Rīgas Pils
Arzēmju mākslas muz.
Latvijas Vēstures muz.

Vanšu tilts

Rakstniecības, teātra un mūzikas

Sāpju dievmātes baznīca

Lielais Kristaps

Arsenāls
Saeima
Klostera
Jēkaba katedr.

Trīs brāļi

Doma laukums

Doma

Mākslas muz.

Laimas pulkstenis

Krievu drāmas

Latvijas biedrības nams
Rīgas biedrības nams

Europa Club Casino

Nacionālā opera

Vāgnera koncertzāle

Italia

Dabas muzejs

Maskavas nams

Arodskola

Danmark

VECRĪGA

Latvijas okupācijas muzejs

Mencendorfa nams

Pētera baznīca

Melngalvju nams

Konventa sēta

Porcelāna m. muzejs
Sv. Jāņa

Farmācijas muzejs

Fotogrāfijas muzejs

LU Ekonomikas un vadības fakultāte

Satekles

Stacijas laukums
Centrālais pasts

Rīgas centrālā stacija

Daugava

Ģertrūde

Dannenšterna nams

Kabata

Coca-Cola Plaza Forum Cinemas

Autoosta

Gogoļa

 KLĪVERSALA

Latvijas Jūras administrācija

Rīgas Valdorfskola

Latvijas Nacionālā bibliotēka

Dzelzceļa vēstures muzejs

Akmens tilts

krastmala

13. janvāra

Piemineklis 1905 gada cīnītājiem

Centrāltirgus

Celtniecības koledža

Akadēmijas laukums

Latvijas zinātņu akadēmija

Lelļu mākslas muzejs

Vissvētās Dievmātes pasludināšanas pareizticīgo baznīca

Belarus

Ägenskalna līcis

Dirty Deal Neatkarīgais teātris

Jēzus luterāņu baznīca

Neatkarīgā Televīzija

European Hit Radio

E 22

A6

Mazā Krasta iela

Mūkusalas

ZAKUSALA

Mazā Daugava

Latvijas televīzija

MŪKUSALA

«Arkādijas» sporta komplekss

«Arkādijas» Stadions

Tornakalns

Vienības

Salu tilts

A8

250   500 m

Baloži 8 km

A8 SALAS 0,5 lm
LUCAVSALA 0,5 km
Jelgava 39 km
Lidosta 5 km

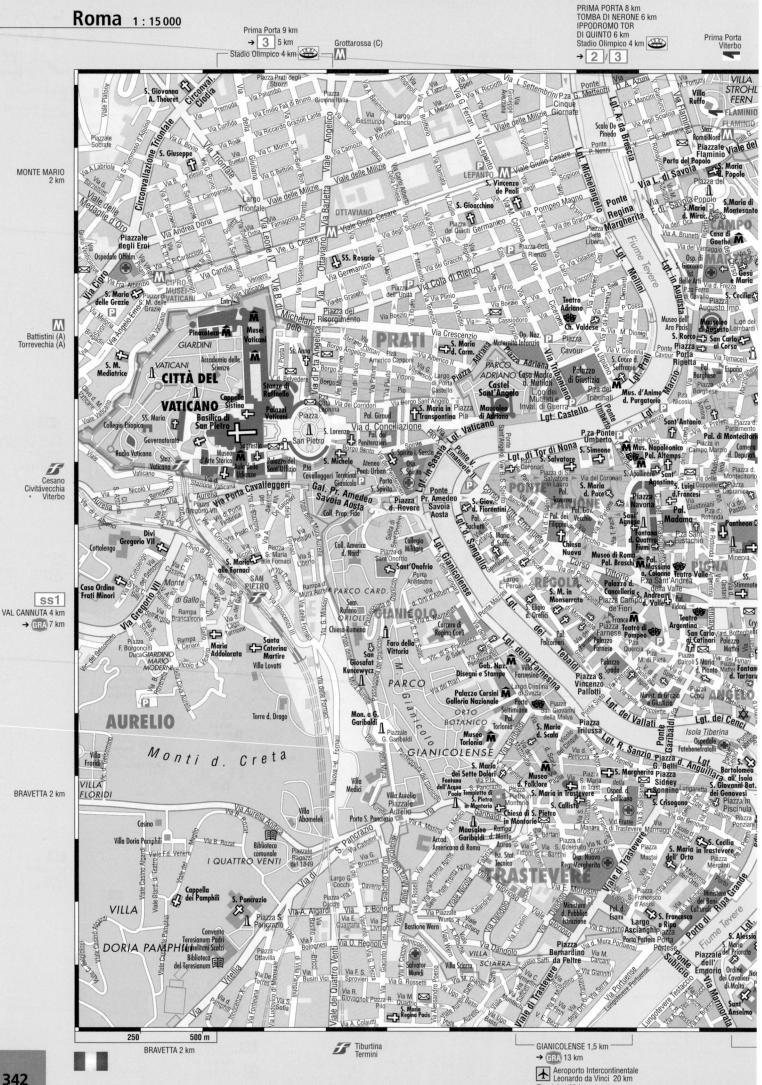

PRIMA PORTA 8 km
TOMBA DI NERONE 6 km
IPPODROMO TOR
DI QUINTO 6 km
Stadio Olimpico 4 km

Prima Porta 9 km
→ 3 5 km
Stadio Olimpico 4 km
Grottarossa (C)

Prima Porta
Viterbo

MONTE MARIO
2 km

Battistini (A)
Torrevecchia (A)

Cesano
Civitàvecchia
Viterbo

VAL CANNUTA 4 km
→ GRA 7 km

BRAVETTA 2 km

AURELIO

Monti d. Creta

VILLA
FLORIDI

I QUATTRO VENTI

VILLA

DORIA PAMPHILI

CIPRO
MUSEI
VATICANI

CITTÀ DEL
VATICANO

PRATI

GIANICOLO

GIANICOLENSE

TRASTEVERE

REGOLA

PIGNA

CAMPO

250 500 m

BRAVETTA 2 km

Tiburtina
Termini

GIANICOLENSE 1,5 km
→ GRA 13 km

Aeroporto Intercontinentale
Leonardo da Vinci 20 km
Fiumicino 25 km

MONTE SACRO 3 km
NOMENTANO 0,5 km   → GRA 9 km

ss5
PORTONACCIO
2,5 km
→ 24   2,5 km
→ GRA 9 km
Carsóli 31 km
L'Aquila 73 km
M Casal Monastero (B)
Cimitero di Campo
Verano 0,5 km
TIBURTINO 1,5 km

TIBURTINO 1,5 km

ES
IC/EC
Firenze
Pescara
Nápoli

Pantano

→ **ss6**
PRENESTINO
LABICANO 2 km

Monte Compatri/
Pantano (C)

M Anagnina (A)

ss6
PRENESTINO
LABICANO 1,5 km

ss7
TUSCULANO 2 km
→ GRA 11 km
Albano 18 km

8 OSTIENSE 2 km
E.U.R. 5 km
→ GRA 10 km
Lido di Ostia 25 km

M Laurentina (B)

GARBATELLA 3 km
Fiera Campionaria 3 km
E.U.R. 6 km
→ GRA 10 km

148

343

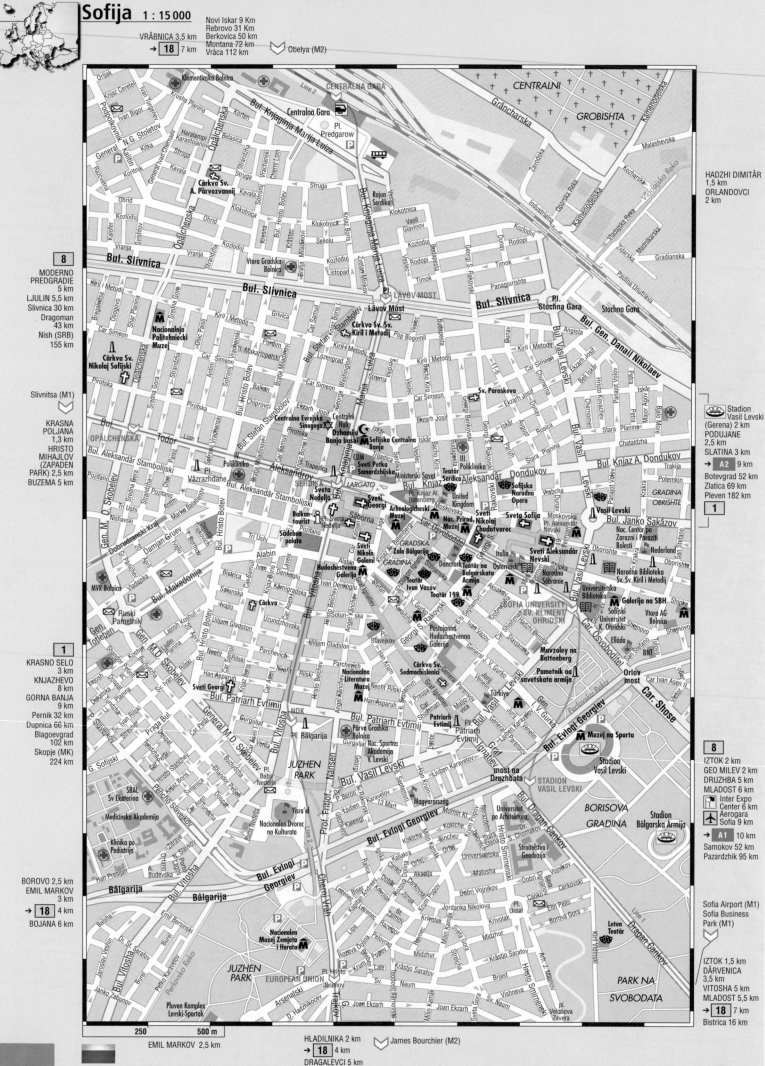

Sofija 1 : 15 000

Novi Iskar 9 Km
Rebrovo 31 Km
Berkovica 50 km
Montana 72 km
Vrâca 112 km

VRÂBNICA 3,5 km
→ 18 7 km

∨ Obelya (M2)

CENTRALNA GARA

CENTRALNI GROBISHTA

HADZHI DIMITÂR
1,5 km
ORLANDOVCI
2 km

Centralna Gara
Pl. Predgarow

Bul. Knjaginja Marija Luiza

Cârkva Sv. A. Pârvozvannij

8
MODERNO
PREDGRADIE
5 km
LJULIN 5,5 km
Slivnica 30 km
Dragoman
43 km
Nish (SRB)
155 km

Slivnitsa (M1)
∨

KRASNA
POLJANA
1,3 km
HRISTO
MIHAJLOV
(ZAPADEN
PARK) 2,5 km
BUZEMA 5 km

Bul. Slivnica

Vtora Gradska Bolnica

Bul. Slivnica

Lâvov Most
Pl. Lâvov Most

Bul. Slivnica
Pl. Stochna Gara
Stochna Gara

Bul. Gen. Danail Nikolaev

Cârkva Sv. Sv. Kiril i Metodij

Nacionalnja Politehniecki Muzej

Cârkva Sv. Nikolaj Sofijski

Sv. Paraskeva

Stadion
Vasil Levski
(Gerena) 2 km
PODUJANE
2,5 km
SLATINA 3 km
→ A2 9 km
Botevgrad 52 km
Zlatica 69 km
Pleven 182 km

1

GRADINA OBRISHTE

Centralna Evrejska Sinagoga
Dzhamija
Banja bashi
Centralni Hali
Sofijska Centralna Banja

CUM
Sveti Petka Samardzhijska

Sofijska Narodna Opera

Poliklinika

Aleksandrov
SERDIKA
Aleksandâr
Bul. Aleksandâr Stambolijski

Bul. Aleksandâr Stambolijski
LARGATO

Bul. Knjaz
Pl. Knjaz Al. Batenberg
United Kingdom
Moskovska

Sveti Aleksandâr Nevski

Vasil Levski

Sveta Nedelja
Sveti Georgi

Arheologicheski Muzej

Sveti Nikolaj Chudotvorec
Sveta Sofija
Pl. Alexandâr Nevski

Narodna Biblioteka Sv. Sv. Kiril i Metodij

Balkan-tourist
Sveta Nedelja

Sâdebna palata

Sveti Nikola Golemi
Zala Bâlgarija
GRADINA
Danmark
Italia
Österreich

Dondukov
Bul. Knjaz A. Dondukov

Nac. Centâr po Zarazni i Paraziti Bolesti
Nederland

Hudoshestvena Galerija
Teatâr na Bâlgarskata Armija

Universitetska Biblioteka

Galerija na SBH

Cârkva
Teatâr Ivan Vazov
Teatâr 199

SOFIA UNIVERSITY SV. KLIMENT OHRIDSKI
Sofijski Universitet K. Ohridski

Vtora AG Bolnica

Ellâda
BNT

Postojanna Hudozhestvenna Galerija

Mavzoley na Battenberg

Orlov most

1
KRASNO SELO
3 km
KNJAZHEVO
8 km
GORNA BANJA
9 km
Pernik 32 km
Dupnica 66 km
Blagoevgrad
102 km
Skopje (MK)
224 km

Nacionalna Literatura Muzej

Cârkva Sv. Sedmochislenici

Pametnik na savetskata armija

Sveti Georgi

Bul. Patriarh Evtimij

Türkije

Parva Gradska Bolnica
Bul. Patriarh Evtimij
Pl. Bul. Patriarh Evtimij

NDK
Pl. Bâlgarija

Muzej na Sporta

Bul. Evlogi Georgiev
Stadion Vasil Levski

JUZHEN PARK

STADION VASIL LEVSKI

BORISOVA GRADINA
Stadion Bâlgarska Armija

8
IZTOK 2 km
GEO MILEV 2 km
DRUZHBA 5 km
MLADOST 6 km
Inter Expo
Center 6 km
Aerogara
Sofia 9 km
→ A1 10 km
Samokov 52 km
Pazardzhik 95 km

SBAL Sv Ekaterina
Medicinska Akademija

Klinika po Pediatrija

most na Druzhbata

Universitet po Arhitektura, Dr. S. Chomakov
Stroitelstvo i Geodezija

Yisra'el

Nacionalen Dvorec na Kulturata

Magyarország

BOROVO 2,5 km
EMIL MARKOV
3 km
→ 18 4 km
BOJANA 6 km

Bul. Vitosha
Bâlgarija

Bul. Evlogi Georgiev

Leten Teatâr

Sofia Airport (M1)
Sofia Business
Park (M1)

Nacionalen Muzej Zemjata i Horata

JUZHEN PARK
EUROPEAN UNION

PARK NA SVOBODATA

IZTOK 1,5 km
DÂRVENICA
3,5 km
VITOSHA 5 km
MLADOST 5,5 km
→ 18 7 km
Bistrica 16 km

Pluven Kompleks Levski-Spartak

250   500 m

EMIL MARKOV 2,5 km

HLADILNIKA 2 km
→ 18 4 km
DRAGALEVCI 5 km

∨ James Bourchier (M2)

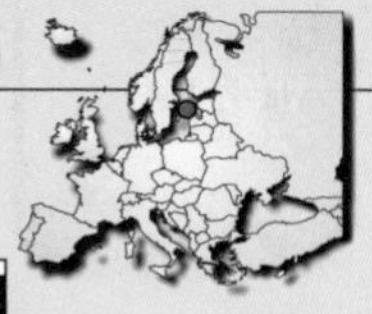

Solna 3,5 km
NORBACKA 1,5 km
→ E4 1,5 km

Mörby centrum

Solna 4 km
NORBACKA 2 km
→ E4 2 km

HJORTHAGEN 1,5 km
Lidingö 3,5 km

Hässelby strand

Fotbollsstadion 3,7 km
Sundbyberg 4 km

KRISTINEBERG 2,8 km
→ E4
Solna 3,5 km

Arlanda Flygplats 37 km

Akalla
Hjulsta

→ E4 1,5 km

Bromma Flygplats 5,5 km
Sundbyberg 7,5 km

Drottningholm
Mariefred

Fruängen
Norsborg

→ E4 / E20 2,5 km
LISEBERG 4 km
HAGSÄTRA 6 km

LADUGÅRDS-GÄRDET 1,5 km

Ropsten

DJURGÅRDEN 1,5 km
LADUGÅRDS-GÄRDET 2 km

Djurgården
Fjäderholmarna

Djurgården

Fjäderholmarna

Mariehamnn (FIN),
Visby (Gotland),
Klaipeda (LT)

→ 74 Nacka 3,5 km

→ 74 Nacka 3,5 km

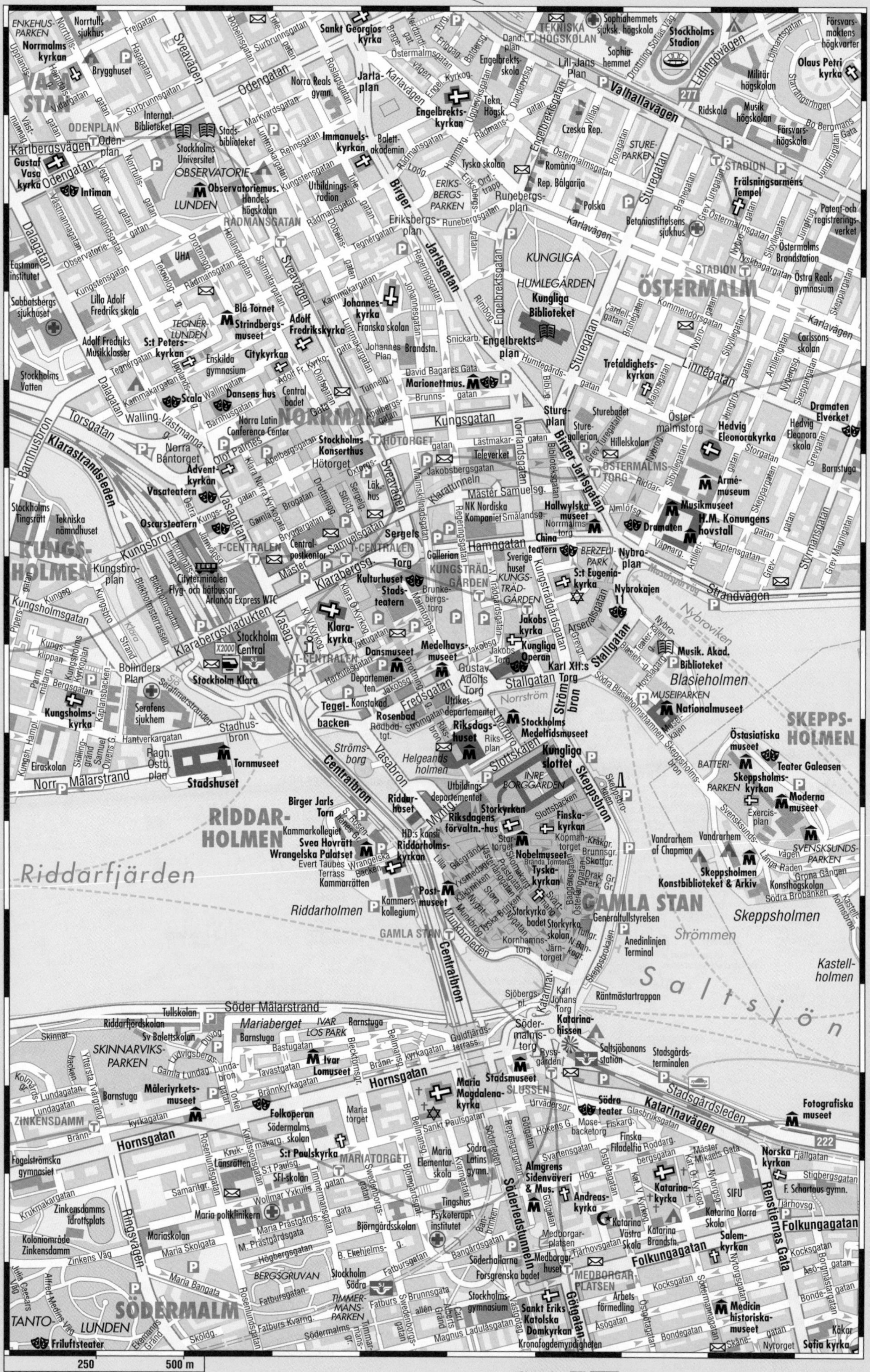

VASASTAN

ODENPLAN

NORRMALM

KUNGSHOLMEN

ÖSTERMALM

RIDDARHOLMEN

Riddarfjärden

GAMLA STAN

Skeppsholmen

SKEPPSHOLMEN

Strömmen

Saltsjön

Kastellholmen

SÖDERMALM

Söder Mälarstrand

Mariaberget

Hornsgatan

Folkungagatan

Skarpnäck
Hagsätra
Farsta strand

JOHANNESHOF 2,2 km
HÖKARÄNGEN 5 km
→ 229 5,5 km

345

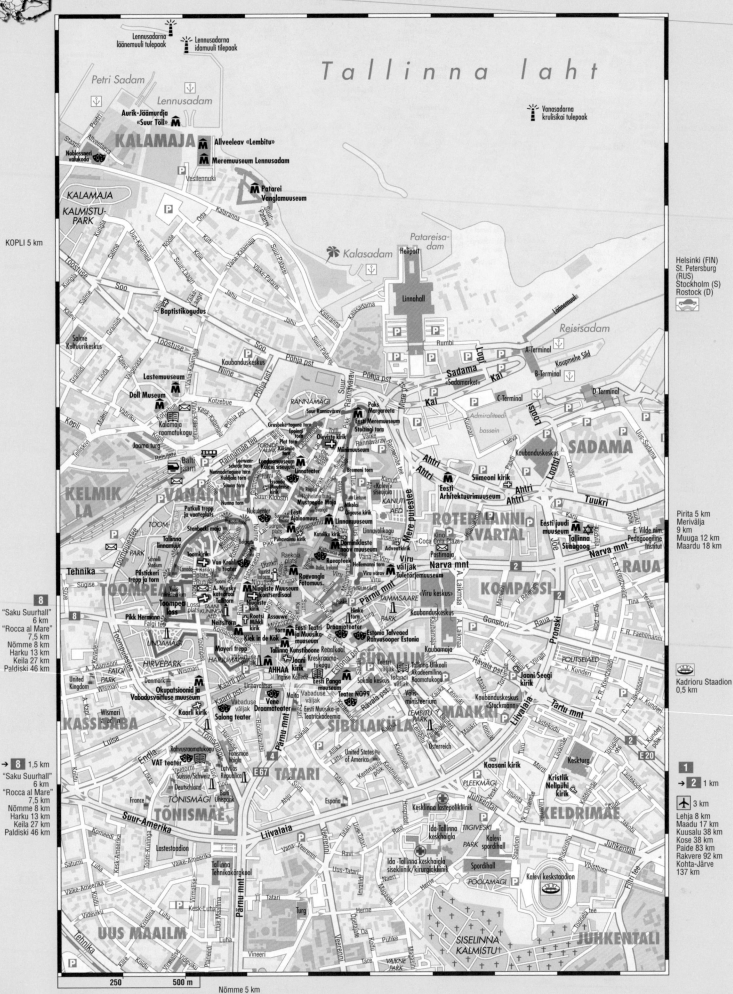

Petri Sadam

Lennusadarna läänemuuli tulepaak
Lennusadarna idamuuli tilepaak

Lennusadam

T a l l i n n a   l a h t

Vanasadarna krulisikai tulepaak

Aurik-Jäämurdja «Suur Töll»

KALAMAJA

Noblessneri valukoda

Allveeleav «Lembitu»
Meremuuseum Lennusadam

Vesilennuki

Patarei Vanglamuuseum

KALAMAJA
KALMISTU-PARK

KOPLI 5 km

Kalasadam Heliport

Patareisa-dam

Linnahall

Reisisadam

Helsinki (FIN)
St. Petersburg (RUS)
Stockholm (S)
Rostock (D)

Baptistikogudus

Rumbi

Sadama «Sadamarket»

A-Terminal
Kaupmehe Sild
B-Terminal
C-Terminal
D-Terminal

Admiraliteedi bassein

Salone Kultuurikeskus

Kaubanduskeskus

Lastemuuseum
Doll Museum

Niine
Põhja pst

Suur Rannavärav

RANNAMÄGI

Paks Margareeta
Eesti Meremuuseum
Stolfingi torn

Laevapassa

SADAMA

Kalamaja raamatukogu

Jaama turg
Balti jaam

Grusbeke-togune torn
Epping torn
Plat torn
Loewenschede torn
Nunnadetagune torn
Kuldjala torn
Sauna torn

Olevist kirik
Miiamuuseum

Bremeni torn

Kaubanduskeskus

KELMIK LA

VANALINN

Patkuli trepp ja vaateplats

Nukuteater

Suurgildi plats

Eesti Ajaloomuus.

Mustpeade Maja

Rohelise turg

Nunna torn

Stenbocki maja

Tallinna linnamüür

Toomkirik

Schnelli Stadion

Pilstickeri trepp ja torn

Rootsi Mihkli kirik

TOOMPEA

Von Krahli teater

A. Nevsky katedraal Tallitorn

Niguliste Museum

Niguliste kirik

Toompea loss

Pikk Hermann

Neitsitorn

Mayeri frepp

HIRVEPARK

Kiek in de Kök

AHHAA

Inglise Kolledz

Okupatsioonid ja Vabadusvõitluse muuseum

United Kingdom

Danmark

Kaarli kirik

KASSIBABA

Vene Drammteater

Salong teater

TÕNISMÄE

VAT teater

Rahvusraamatukogu

Veetorn
Suisse/Schweiz
Latvija/Republica

TATARI

Deutschland

France

España

UUS MAAILM

Lastestaadion

Tallinna Tehnikakõrgkool

SISELINNA KALMISTU

Ahtri

Siimeoni kirik

Eesti Arhitektuurimuuseum

ROTERMANNI KVARTAL

Eesti juudi muuseum

Tallinna Sünagoog

Narva mnt

RAUA

KOMPASSI

Tammsaare PARK

Viru väljak
Viru värav
Viru keskus

Kaubanduskeskus

Pärnu mnt

SÜDALINN

Dramaateater
Estonia Talveaed Rahvusooper Estonia

Kaubamaja

Tallinna Ülikooli Akadeemiline Raamatukogu

MAAKRI

Jaani Seegi kirik

Kadrioru Staadion 0,5 km

Pirita 5 km
Merivälja 9 km
Muuga 12 km
Maardu 18 km

Jaani kirik

Eesti Panga muuseum

Teater NO99

Vabaduse väljak

Eesti Muusika- ja Teatriakadeemia

SIBULAKÜLA

Tartu mnt

KELDRIMÄE

Kaasani kirik

Kristlik Nelipühi kirik

Kesklinna lastepolikliinik

Ida-Tallinna keskhaigla

Ida-Tallinna keskhaigla siseklinik/kirurgiakliinik

Kalevi spordihall

Spordihall

Kalevi keskstadion

JUHKENTALI

8
"Saku Suurhall" 6 km
"Rocca al Mare" 7,5 km
Nõmme 8 km
Harku 13 km
Keila 27 km
Paldiski 46 km

8 1,5 km
"Saku Suurhall" 6 km
"Rocca al Mare" 7,5 km
Nõmme 8 km
Harku 13 km
Keila 27 km
Paldiski 46 km

1
2 1 km

3 km
Lehja 8 km
Maadu 17 km
Kuusalu 38 km
Kose 38 km
Paide 83 km
Rakvere 92 km
Kohta-Järve 137 km

250   500 m

Nõmme 5 km

346

Ukmergė 73 km
Maišagala 25 km
→ A2 8 km
ŠEŠKINE 1 km

Molėtai 70 km
Purnušklės 23 km
VERKIAI 3 km

LAZDYNAI 5 km
→ A1 8 km
Kaunas 98 km

LAZDYNAI 3 km
→ A1 6 km
Kaunas 96 km

→ A1 / A4
6 km
Elektrėnai
41 km

102
Pabradė 50 km
Nemenlčine 22 km

103
NAUJOJI
VILNIA 6 km
Šumskas 34 km

KIRTINAI 4 km
✈ 5 km
Šalčininkai 42 km

→ A15 1,5 km
→ A3 6 km
Medininkai 28 km

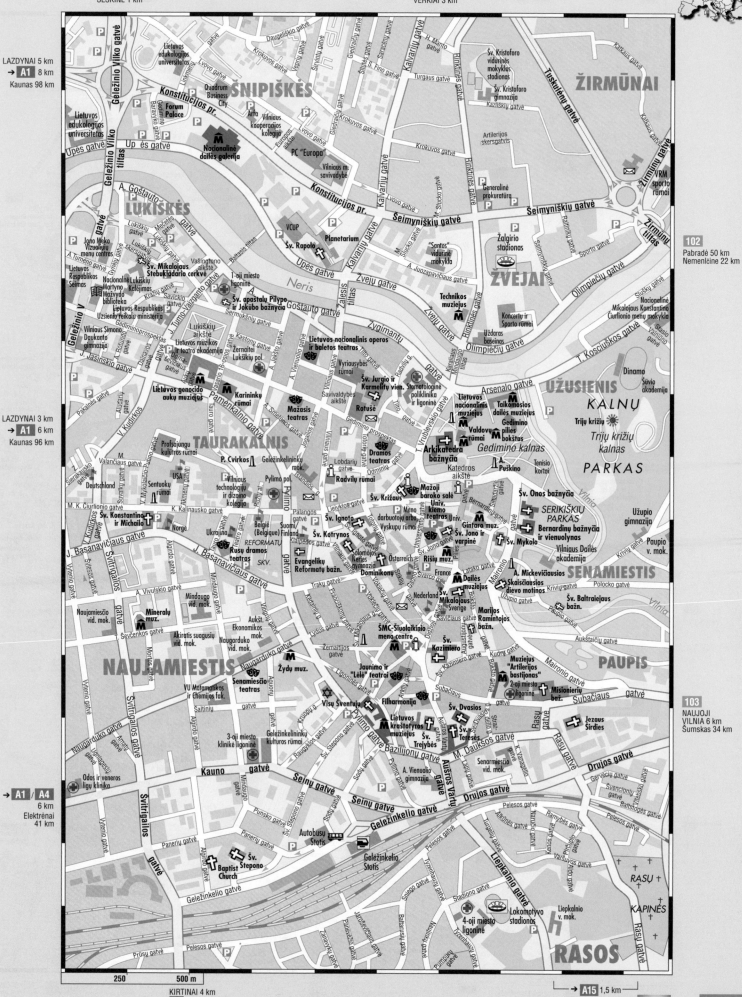

ŽIRMŪNAI

ŠNIPIŠKĖS

LUKIŠKĖS

ŽVEJAI

UŽUSIENIS

KALNŲ PARKAS

TAURAKALNIS

SENAMIESTIS

PAUPIS

NAUJAMIESTIS

RASOS

RASŲ KAPINĖS

250　500 m

Warszawa 1 : 15 000

TARCHOMIN 9 km
801

ZACISZE 3,5 km
TARGÓWEK 2 km
629 Ⓜ Szwedzka

Ⓜ Mińska

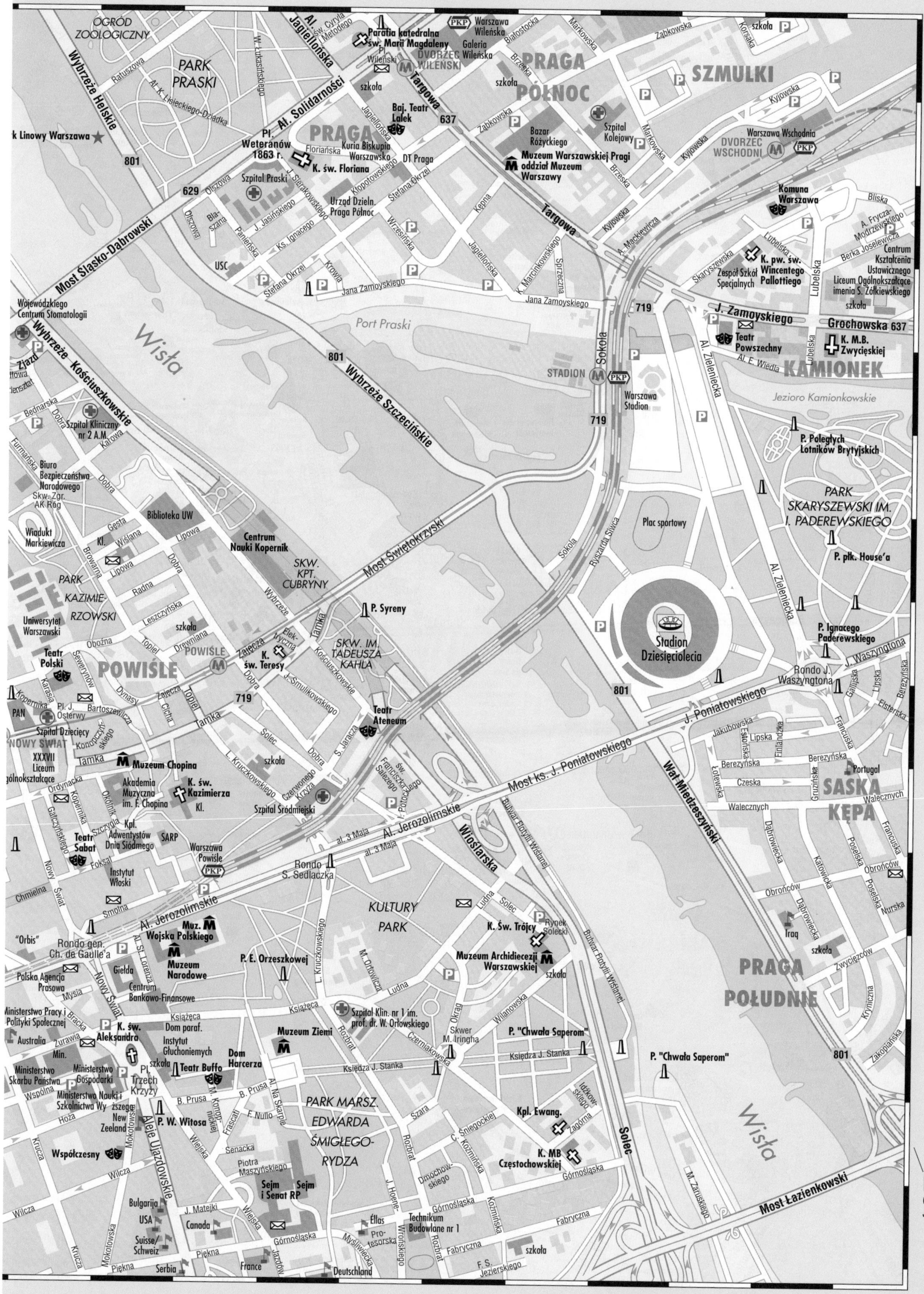

OGRÓD ZOOLOGICZNY

PARK PRASKI

k Linowy Warszawa

801

Most Śląsko-Dąbrowski

629

Al. Solidarności

Al. Jagiellońska

Pl. Weteranów 1863 r.

PRAGA

Parafia katedralna św. Marii Magdaleny

Warszawa Wileńska PKP
DWORZEC WILEŃSKI
Galeria Wileńska

Baj. Teatr Lalek

637

szkoła

PRAGA PÓŁNOC

SZMULKI

Bazar Różyckiego

Szpital Kolejowy

Muzeum Warszawskiej Pragi oddział Muzeum Warszawy

Warszawa Wschodnia
DWORZEC WSCHODNI PKP

Komuna Warszawa

Florianska
K. św. Floriana
Kuria Biskupia
DT Praga
Urząd Dzieln. Praga Północ

Szpital Praski

USC

K. pw. św. Wincentego Pallottiego

Zespół Szkół Specjalnych

Centrum Kształcenia Ustawicznego
Liceum Ogólnokształcące imienia S. Żółkiewskiego
szkoła

Wojewódzkiego Centrum Stomatologii

Wybrzeże Kościuszkowskie

Zjazd

Port Praski

801

Wybrzeże Szczecińskie

J. Zamoyskiego

Teatr Powszechny

Grochowska **637**

637
GROCHÓW 1,5 km

K. M.B. Zwycięskiej

KAMIONEK

Jezioro Kamionkowskie

Szpital Kliniczny nr 2 A.M.

Biuro Bezpieczeństwa Narodowego
Skw. Zgr. AK Róg

Wiadukt Markiewicza

PARK KAZIMIERZOWSKI

Uniwersytet Warszawski

Biblioteka UW

Centrum Nauki Kopernik

SKW. KPT. CUBRYNY

Most Świętokrzyski

P. Syreny

SKW. IM. TADEUSZA KAHLA

STADION
Warszawa Stadion

719

Plac sportowy

P. Poległych Lotników Brytyjskich

PARK SKARYSZEWSKI IM. I. PADEREWSKIEGO

P. płk. House'a

Stadion Dziesięciolecia

P. Ignacego Paderewskiego

Rondo J. Waszyngtona

GROCHÓW 2 km
GOCŁAWEK 5 km

POWIŚLE

Teatr Polski

K. św. Teresy

Warszawa Powiśle

719

Teatr Ateneum

J. Poniatowskiego

Most ks. J. Poniatowskiego

Wał Miedzeszyński

SASKA KĘPA

PAN
Szpital Dziecięcy
NOWY ŚWIAT

XXXVII Liceum Ogólnokształcące

Muzeum Chopina

Akademia Muzyczna im. F. Chopina

K. św. Kazimierza

Szpital Śródmiejski

Al. 3 Maja

Al. Jerozolimskie

Włoślańska

Portugal

Teatr Sabat

Adwentystów Dnia Siódmego

SARP

Instytut Włoski

Rondo S. Sedlaczka

KULTURY PARK

K. św. Trójcy
Rynek Solecki

Muzeum Archidiecezji Warszawskiej
szkoła

Iraq

PRAGA POŁUDNIE

"Orbis"
Rondo gen. Ch. de Gaulle'a

Muz. Wojska Polskiego

P. E. Orzeszkowej

Polska Agencja Prasowa

Giełda

Muzeum Narodowe

Centrum Bankowo-Finansowe

Ministerstwo Pracy i Polityki Społecznej

K. św. Aleksandra

Dom paraf.
Instytut Głuchoniemych

Szpital Klin. nr 1 im. prof. dr. W. Orłowskiego

Muzeum Ziemi

Skwer M. Iringha

P. "Chwała Saperom"

P. "Chwała Saperom"

Australia
Min.

Ministerstwo Skarbu Państwa

Ministerstwo Gospodarki

Teatr Buffo

Dom Harcerza

Kpl. Ewang.

Ministerstwo Nauki i Szkolnictwa Wy ższego

Pl. Trzech Krzyży

P. W. Witosa

Aleje Ujazdowskie

PARK MARSZ. EDWARDA ŚMIGŁEGO-RYDZA

K. MB Częstochowskiej

Współczesny

New Zeeland

Sejm i Senat RP
Sejm i Senat RP

Bulgarija
USA
Suisse/ Schweiz
Serbia

Canada

Éllas

France

Deutschland

Technikum Budowlane nr 1

F. S. Jezierski

801
GOCŁAW 1,5 km
Jozefów 15 km

Most Łazienkowski

Wisła

Stadion "Legia" 0,5 km
Stadion BKS "Skra" 3,5 km

Floridsdorf U 221 | W-DÖBLING (XIX.) 2 km | W-WÄHRING (XVIII.) 0,5 km
W-GROSSJEDLERSDORF (XXI.) 7 km | W-FLORIDSDORF (XXI.) 5 km | W-HEILIGENSTADT (XIX.) 3 km 227 U Heiligenstadt

W-HERNALS (XVII.) 2 km
W-DORNBACH (XVII.) 3,5 km

W-OTTAKRING (XIV.) 3 km

223
W-HÜTTELDORF (XIV.) 5,5 km

W-PENZING (XIV.) 3 km
W-HÜTTELDORF (XIV.) 5,5 km
W-HADERSDORF (XIV.) 8,5 km

Rekawinkel
Ottakring

Schloss Schönbrunn 1,5 km
Tivoli 2 km
W-HIETZING (XIII.) 3 km

ALSERGRUND 9.

Allgemeines Krankenhaus der
Stadt Wien - Medizinischer Universitätscampus
Krankenanst. Goldenes Kreuz
Martin-Luther-Kirche
A.-CARLSSON-PARK
Narrenturm
Universitätscampus
Josephinum-Museum f. Geschichte der Medizin
Schauspielhaus
Sigmund-Freud-Museum
Pathologisch-Anatomisches-Bundesmuseum
Votivkirche
SIGMUND FREUD-PARK
Roosevelt-platz
Schottentor Maria
Börse
Dreifaltigkeits-kirche
Minoriten-kloster
Universitätsstraße
Schottenstift
Schottenkirche
Freyung
MOYA

JOSEFSTADT 8.

Museum für Volkskunde
SCHÖNBORN-PARK
Piaristen-kirche
Maria-Treu-Kloster
Bezirksamt
RATHAUS
Rat-haus
Rathausplatz
Burgtheater
Theater in der Josefstadt
Finanzamt
English Theatre
Kabarett Niedermair
Heilige Zuflucht
JOSEPH-STRAUSS-PARK
KARL-FARKAS-PARK
Parlament
Volks-garten
VOLKSGARTEN
BURGGARTEN

NEUBAU 7.

Burggasse
St. Ulrich
St. Ulrichs-Platz
Notre Dame de Sion
Renaissance Theater
Pfarrkirche Westbahn-St. Laurenz
Theater Spielraum
Zum Göttlichen Heiland
Auferstehungs-kirche
Mariahilfi-Kloster
Hofmobilien-depot
Stiftskirche
St. Joseph
Volkstheater
Naturhistorisches Museum
Neue Hofburg
Burgtor (Heldentor)
Maria-Theresien-Platz
Maria-Theresien-Denkmal
MUMOK
Kunsthalle
Museumsquartier
Leopold Museum
Kunsthistorisches Museum
MUSEUMSQUARTIER
Akad. d. bild. Künste
Secession
Karlsplatz
RESSELPARK
Karlskirche
Technische Universität
Staatsoper
Kärntner Ring

MARIAHILF 6.

Haydn-Museum
Raimundtheater
Krankenhaus der Barmherzigen Schwestern
Gustav-Adolf-Kirche
St. Aegid
Theater an der Wien
Haus des Meeres
Foltermus.
ESTERHAZY-PARK
ALFRED-GRÜNWALD-PARK
Naschmarkt
Dritte Mann
Schuberts Sterbewohnung
Brahms-platz

MARGARETEN 5.

Bezirksmuseum Margareten
St. Joseph
Klarissinenkirche "Zur ewigen Anbetung"
St. Thekla

WIEDEN 4.

Palais Schönburg
ALOIS-DRASCHE-PARK
HAUPTBAHNHOF

W-MARGARETEN (V.) 0,5 km
W-FAVORITEN (X.) 3 km
Erholungsgebiet Wienerberg 2 km
W-ALTMANNSDORF (XII.) 3 km
W-HIETZING (XIII.) 5,5 km
Reumannplatz U
W-FAVORITEN (X.) 2 km
W-INZERSDORF (XXIII.) 4 km

250   500 m